MW01042518

GARDNER'S

ART

THROUGH THE

AGES

GARDNER'S
ART
THROUGH THE
AGES

A CONCISE WESTERN HISTORY

....

FOURTH EDITION

FRED S. KLEINER

CENGAGE
Learning·

Australia · Brazil · Mexico · Singapore · United Kingdom · United States

CENGAGE
Learning®

Gardner's Art through the Ages:
A Concise Western History, Fourth Edition
Fred S. Kleiner

Product Director: Monica Eckman

Product Manager: Sharon Adams Poore

Content Developer: Rachel Harbour

Associate Content Developer: Erika Hayden

Product Assistant: Rachael Bailey

Media Developer: Chad Kirchner

Marketing Manager: Jillian Borden

Senior Content Project Manager: Lianne Ames

Senior Art Director: Cate Rickard Barr

Manufacturing Planner: Julio Esperas

IP Analyst: Jessica Elias

IP Project Manager: Farah J. Fard

Production Service and Layout:
    Joan Keyes, Dovetail Publishing Services

Compositor: Cenveo® Publisher Services

Text Designer: tani hasegawa

Cover Designer: Cate Rickard Barr

Cover Image: *Nocturne in Black and Gold, the*
    Falling Rocket, 1875 (oil on panel), Whistler,
    James Abbott McNeill (1834–1903) / Detroit
    Institute of Arts, USA / Gift of Dexter M.
    Ferry Jr. / The Bridgeman Art Library

© 2017, 2013, 2009 Cengage Learning

WCN: 01-100-101

ALL RIGHTS RESERVED. No part of this work covered by the copyright herein may be reproduced, transmitted, stored, or used in any form or by any means graphic, electronic, or mechanical, including but not limited to photocopying, recording, scanning, digitizing, taping, web distribution, information networks, or information storage and retrieval systems, except as permitted under Section 107 or 108 of the 1976 United States Copyright Act, without the prior written permission of the publisher.

For product information and technology assistance, contact us at
Cengage Learning Customer & Sales Support, 1-800-354-9706

For permission to use material from this text or product,
submit all requests online at **www.cengage.com/permissions**.
Further permissions questions can be emailed to
permissionrequest@cengage.com.

Library of Congress Control Number: 2015940836

Student Edition:
ISBN: 978-1-305-58106-7

Loose-leaf Edition:
ISBN: 978-1-305-87253-0

Cengage Learning
20 Channel Center Street
Boston, MA 02210
USA

Cengage Learning is a leading provider of customized learning solutions with employees residing in nearly 40 different countries and sales in more than 125 countries around the world. Find your local representative at **www.cengage.com**.

Cengage Learning products are represented in Canada by Nelson Education, Ltd.

To learn more about Cengage Learning Solutions, visit **www.cengage.com**. Purchase any of our products at your local college store or at our preferred online store **www.cengagebrain.com**.

Printed in the United States of America
Print Number: 01   Print Year: 2015

COVER ART

JAMES ABBOTT MCNEILL WHISTLER, *Nocturne in Black and Gold* (*The Falling Rocket*), ca. 1875. Oil on panel, 1' 11$\frac{5}{8}$" × 1' 6$\frac{1}{2}$". Detroit Institute of the Arts, Detroit (gift of Dexter M. Ferry Jr.).

American painter James Abbott McNeill Whistler (1834–1903) spent most of his career in London, but also resided briefly in Paris. There, he met many of the Impressionists, with whom he shared a fondness for recording contemporary life and the sensations that color produces on the eye. To these interests Whistler added a desire to create harmonies paralleling those achieved in music, and thus began calling some of his works "nocturnes." *Nocturne in Black and Gold,* or *The Falling Rocket,* is a daring painting with gold flecks and splatters representing an exploded firework in the night sky. More interested in conveying the atmospheric effects than in providing details of the scene, Whistler emphasized creating a harmonious arrangement of shapes and colors, an approach that many 20th-century painters would adopt. Whistler's works angered many 19th-century viewers, however. The British critic John Ruskin (1819–1900) responded to this painting by accusing Whistler of "flinging a pot of paint in the public's face."

Whistler's distinctive personal approach to painting characterizes the art of the modern era in general, but it is not typical of many periods of the history of art when artists toiled in anonymity to fulfill the wishes of their patrons, whether Egyptian pharaohs, Roman emperors, or medieval monks. *Art through the Ages: A Concise Western History* surveys the art of all periods from prehistory to the present and examines how Western artworks of all kinds have always reflected the historical contexts in which they were created.

Brief Contents

Contents

13 Impressionism, Post-Impressionism, and Symbolism, 1870 to 1900 356

14 Modernism in Europe and America, 1900 to 1945 376

15 Modernism and Postmodernism in Europe and America, 1945 to 1980 410

16 Contemporary Art Worldwide 438

Preface

I take great pleasure in introducing the extensively revised and expanded 4th edition of *Gardner's Art through the Ages: A Concise Western History*, which for the first time is, like the unabridged 15th edition published last year, a hybrid textbook—the only introductory survey of the history of art and architecture of its kind. This innovative new type of "Gardner" retains all of the best features of traditional books on paper while harnessing 21st-century technology to increase the number of works and themes discussed without enlarging the size of the printed book—and at negligible additional cost to the reader.

When Helen Gardner published the first edition of *Art through the Ages* in 1926, she could not have imagined that nearly a century later instructors all over the world would still be using her textbook in their classrooms. (The book has even been translated into Mandarin Chinese.) Nor could Professor Gardner have foreseen that a new publisher would make her text available in special editions corresponding to a wide variety of introductory art history courses ranging from yearlong global surveys to Western- and non-Western-only surveys to the one-semester course for which this concise edition was designed. Indeed, if Helen Gardner were alive today, she would not recognize the book that long ago became—and remains—the world's most widely read introduction to the history of art and architecture. I hope that instructors and students alike will agree that this new edition lives up to that venerable tradition and, in fact, exceeds their high expectations.

KEY FEATURES OF THE 4TH EDITION

For the 4th concise edition of *Art through the Ages*, in addition to updating the text of every chapter to incorporate the latest research, I have added several important new features while retaining the basic format and scope of the previous edition. The new edition boasts more photographs, plans, and drawings than the previous three versions of the book, nearly all in color and reproduced according to the highest standards of clarity and color fidelity. The illustrations include a new set of maps and scores of new images, among them a series of superb photographs taken by Jonathan Poore exclusively for *Art through the Ages* in Germany and Italy (following similar forays into France and Italy in 2009–2011). The online MindTap® component also includes custom videos made by Sharon Adams Poore during those five photo campaigns. This extraordinary new archive of visual material ranges from ancient temples in Rome; to medieval, Renaissance, and Baroque churches in France, Germany, and Italy; to such modern masterpieces as Notre-Dame-du-Haut in Ronchamp, France, and the Bauhaus in Dessau, Germany. The 4th edition also features an expanded number of the highly acclaimed architectural drawings of John Burge. Together, these exclusive photographs, videos, maps, and drawings provide readers with a visual feast unavailable anywhere else.

Once again, scales accompany the photograph of every painting, statue, or other artwork discussed—another distinctive feature of the Gardner text. The scales provide students with a quick and effective way to visualize how big or small a given artwork is and its relative size compared with other objects in the same chapter and throughout the book—especially important given that the illustrated works vary in size from tiny to colossal.

Also retained in this edition are the Quick-Review Captions (brief synopses of the most significant aspects of each artwork or building illustrated) that students have found invaluable when preparing for examinations. These extended captions accompany not only every image in the printed book but also all the digital images in the MindTap version of the text. Each chapter also again ends with the highly popular full-page feature called *The Big Picture*, which sets forth in bullet-point format the most important characteristics of each period or artistic movement discussed in the chapter. Also retained from the third edition are the timelines summarizing the major artistic and architectural developments during the era treated (again in bullet-point format for easy review) and the chapter-opening essays called *Framing the Era* discussing a characteristic painting, sculpture, or building and illustrated by four photographs.

Boxed essays on special topics again appear throughout the book as well. These essays fall under eight broad categories, three of which are new to the 4th edition:

Architectural Basics boxes provide students with a sound foundation for the understanding of architecture. These discussions are concise explanations, with drawings and diagrams, of the major aspects of design and construction. The information included is essential to an understanding of architectural technology and terminology.

Materials and Techniques essays explain the various media that artists have employed from prehistoric to modern times. Since materials and techniques often influence the character of artworks, these discussions contain important information on why many monuments appear as they do.

Religion and Mythology boxes introduce students to the principal elements of the world's great religions, past and present, and to the representation of religious and mythological themes in painting and sculpture of all periods and places. These discussions of belief systems and iconography give readers a richer understanding of some of the greatest artworks ever created.

Art and Society essays treat the historical, social, political, cultural, and religious context of art and architecture. In some instances, specific monuments are the basis for a discussion of broader themes.

In the *Artists on Art* boxes, artists and architects throughout history discuss both their theories and individual works.

New to the 4th edition are three new categories of boxed essays: *Written Sources*, *The Patron's Voice*, and *Problems and Solutions*. The first category presents and discusses key historical documents illuminating major monuments of art and architecture throughout the world. The passages quoted permit voices from the past to speak directly to the reader, providing vivid insights into the creation of artworks in all media. *The Patron's Voice* essays underscore the important roles that individuals and groups played in determining the character of the artworks and buildings that they commissioned and paid for. The new *Problems and Solutions* boxes are designed to make students think critically about the decisions that went into the making of every painting, sculpture, and building from the Old Stone Age to the present. These essays address questions of how and why various forms developed, the problems that painters, sculptors, and architects confronted, and the solutions that they devised to resolve them.

Other noteworthy features retained from the 3rd edition are the (updated) bibliography of books in English; a glossary containing definitions of all italicized terms introduced in both the printed text and MindTap essays; and a complete museum index, now housed online only, listing all illustrated artworks by their present location. The host of state-of-the-art MindTap online resources are enumerated on page xxi.

ACKNOWLEDGMENTS

A work as extensive as a global history of art could not be undertaken or completed without the counsel of experts in all areas of world art. As with previous editions, Cengage Learning has enlisted more than a hundred art historians to review every chapter of *Art through the Ages* in order to ensure that the text lives up to the Gardner reputation for accuracy as well as readability. I take great pleasure in acknowledging here those individuals who made important contributions to the 4th concise edition and to the unabridged 15th edition on which the shorter version is based: Patricia Albers, San Jose State University; Kirk Ambrose, University of Colorado Boulder; Jenny Kirsten Ataoguz, Indiana University–Purdue University Fort Wayne; Paul Bahn, Hull; Denise Amy Baxter, University of North Texas; Nicole Bensoussan, University of Michigan–Dearborn; Amy R. Bloch, University at Albany, State University of New York; Susan H. Caldwell, The University of Oklahoma; David C. Cateforis, The University of Kansas; Gina Cestaro, University of West Florida; Thomas B. F. Cummins, Harvard University; Joyce De Vries, Auburn University; Scott Douglass, Chattanooga State Community College; Verena Drake, Hotchkiss School; Jerome Feldman, Hawai'i Pacific University; Maria Gindhart, Georgia State University; Tracie Glazer, Nazareth College of Rochester; Annabeth Headrick, University of Denver; Shannen Hill, University of Maryland; Angela K. Ho, George Mason University; Julie Hochstrasser, The University of Iowa; Hiroko Johnson, San Diego State University; Julie Johnson, The University of Texas at San Antonio; Molly Johnson, Ocean County College; Paul H. D. Kaplan, Purchase College, State University of New York; Nancy Lee-Jones, Endicott College; Rob Leith, Buckingham Browne & Nichols School; Brenda Longfellow, The University of Iowa; Susan McCombs, Michigan State University; Jennifer Ann McLerran, Northern Arizona University; Patrick R. McNaughton, Indiana University Bloomington; Mary Miller, Yale University; Erin Morris, Estrella Mountain Community College; Nicolas Morrissey, The University of Georgia; Basil Moutsatsos, St. Petersburg College–Seminole; Johanna D. Movassat, San Jose State University; Micheline Nilsen, Indiana University South Bend; Catherine Pagani, The University of Alabama; Anna Pagnucci, Ashford University; Allison Lee Palmer, The University of Oklahoma; William H. Peck, University of Michigan–Dearborn; Lauren Peterson, University of Delaware; Holly Pittman, University of Pennsylvania; Romita Ray, Syracuse University; Wendy Wassyng Roworth, The University of Rhode Island; Andrea Rusnock, Indiana University South Bend; Bridget Sandhoff, University of Nebraska at Omaha; James M. Saslow, Queens College, City University of New York;

James Slauson, Carroll University; Anne Rudolph Stanton, University of Missouri; Suzanne Thomas, Rose State College; Achim Timmermann, University of Michigan; David Turley, Weber State University; Lee Ann Turner, Boise State University; Marjorie S. Venit, University of Maryland; Shirley Tokash Verrico, Genesee Community College; Louis A. Waldman, The University of Texas at Austin; Ying Wang, University of Wisconsin–Milwaukee; Lindsey Waugh, University of Tennessee; Gregory H. Williams, Boston University; and Benjamin C. Withers, University of Kentucky.

I am especially indebted to the following for creating the instructor and student materials for the 4th edition: Ivy Cooper, Southern Illinois University Edwardsville; Patricia D. Cosper (retired), The University of Alabama at Birmingham; Anne McClanan, Portland State University; Amy M. Morris, The University of Nebraska Omaha; Erika Schneider, Framingham State University; and Camille Serchuk, Southern Connecticut State University. I also thank the more than 150 instructors and students who participated in surveys, focus groups, design sprints, and advisory boards to help us better understand your needs in our print and digital products.

I am also happy to have this opportunity to express my gratitude to the extraordinary group of people at Cengage Learning involved with the editing, production, and distribution of *Art through the Ages*. Some of them I have now worked with on various projects for nearly two decades and feel privileged to count among my friends. The success of the Gardner series in all of its various permutations depends in no small part on the expertise and unflagging commitment of these dedicated professionals, especially Sharon Adams Poore, product manager (as well as videographer extraordinaire); Lianne Ames, senior content project manager; Rachael Bailey, senior product assistant; Cate Barr, senior art director and cover designer of this edition; Jillian Borden, marketing manager; Rachel Harbour, content developer; Erika Hayden, associate content developer; Chad Kirchner, content developer; and the entire team of professionals, too numerous to list fully here, who had a hand in the design, creation, and implementation of the new e-reader featured in this edition's MindTap. Finally, I owe my gratitude to the incomparable group of learning consultants nationwide who have passed on to me the welcome advice offered by the hundreds of instructors they speak to daily.

I am also deeply grateful to the following out-of-house contributors to the 4th concise edition: the incomparable quarterback of the entire production process, Joan Keyes, Dovetail Publishing Services; Michele Jones, copy editor; Susan Gall, proofreader; Pat Rimmer, Indexer; PreMediaGlobal, photo researchers; Cenveo® Publisher Services; Jay and John Crowley, Jay's Publishing Services; Mary Ann Lidrbauch, art log preparer; and, of course, Jonathan Poore and John Burge, for their superb photos and architectural drawings.

I also owe thanks to two individuals not currently associated with this book but who loomed large in my life for many years: Clark Baxter, who retired from Cengage in 2013 at the end of a long and distinguished career, from whom I learned much about textbook publishing and whose continuing friendship I value highly, and my former co-author and longtime friend and colleague, Christin J. Mamiya of the University of Nebraska–Lincoln, with whom I have had innumerable conversations not only about *Art through the Ages* but the history of art in general. Her thinking continues to influence my own, especially with regard to the later chapters on the history of Western art. I conclude this long (but no doubt incomplete) list of acknowledgments with an expression of gratitude to my colleagues at Boston University and to the thousands of students and the scores of teaching fellows in my art history courses since I began teaching in 1975, especially my research assistant, Angelica Bradley. From them I have learned much that has helped determine the form and content of *Art through the Ages* and made it a much better book than it otherwise might have been.

Fred S. Kleiner

CHAPTER-BY-CHAPTER CHANGES IN THE 4TH EDITION

All chapters include changes in the text reflecting new research and discoveries, new maps, revised timelines and The Big Picture, and online bonus images, essays, videos, and other features included within the MindTap version of the text, an integral part of the complete learning package for this 4th edition of *Art through the Ages: A Concise Western History*.

A chapter-by-chapter enumeration of the most important revisions follows.

Introduction: What Is Art History?: New chapter-opening illustration of Claude Lorrain's *Embarkation of the Queen of Sheba* with new details. Added 18th-century Benin altar to the hand.

1: Prehistory and the First Civilizations: New Framing the Era essay "Pictorial Narration in Ancient Sumer." New Problems and Solutions boxes "How to Represent an Animal" and "How Many Legs Does a Lamassu Have?" Added the Apollo 11 Cave in Namibia, the head of Inanna from Uruk, the seated scribe from Saqqara, and the *Judgment of Hunefer*. New photographs of the *Warka Vase*, Stonehenge, the lamassu from the citadel of Sargon II, a model of the Gizeh pyramids, the Great Sphinx and pyramid of Khafre, and the temple of Amen-Re at Karnak.

2: Ancient Greece: New Art and Society box "Archaeology, Art History, and the Art Market." New Problems and Solutions box "Polykleitos's Prescription for the Perfect Statue." New Materials and Techniques box "White-Ground Painting." New Architectural Basics box "The Corinthian Capital." Added the calf bearer from the Athenian Acropolis, the *Charioteer of Delphi*, the *Massacre of the Niobids* by the Niobid Painter, the tholos at Delphi, and the Hellenistic bronze boxer. New photographs of the Parthenon (general view, Doric columns, and the cavalcade and seated gods of the frieze), the Lion Gate and exterior and interior of the Treasury of Atreus at Mycenae, the Erechtheion and Temple of Athena Nike on the Athenian Acropolis, the theater at Epidauros, and the *Barberini Faun*. New reconstruction drawing of the palace at Knossos.

3: The Roman Empire: New Framing the Era essay "Roman Art as Historical Fiction." New Art and Society boxes "The 'Audacity' of Etruscan Women" and "Spectacles in the Colosseum." New Written Sources box "Vitruvius's *Ten Books on Architecture*." New Problems and Solutions boxes "The Spiral Frieze of the Column of Trajan," "The Ancient World's Largest Dome," and "Tetrarchic Portraiture." Added Apotheosis of Antoninus Pius, Banditaccia necropolis tumuli, the Maison Carrée at Nîmes, and third-century sarcophagus of a philosopher. New photographs of the Tomb of the Leopards at Tarquinia, the Tomb of the Reliefs at Cerveteri, the brawl in the Pompeii amphitheater, the Third Style cubiculum from Boscotrecase, and, in Rome, the Ara Pacis Augustae, the facade of the Colosseum, the Arch of Titus (general view and two reliefs), the Column of Trajan (general view and three details), the interior of the Markets of Trajan, the exterior of the Pantheon, the colossal portrait head of Constantine, the Basilica Nova, and the Arch of Constantine (general view and Constantinian frieze).

4: Early Christianity and Byzantium: New Religion and Mythology box "Jewish Subjects in Christian Art." New Art and Society box "Medieval Books." New Problems and Solutions boxes "Picturing the Spiritual World" and "Placing a Dome over a Square." Added an Early Christian statuette of the Good Shepherd, and images of Santa Sabina in Rome and of the *Rabbula Gospels*. New photographs of Santa Costanza in Rome, of Hagia Sophia in Constantinople, and of the Katholikon at Hosios Loukas.

5: The Islamic World: New Art and Society box "Major Muslim Dynasties." Added the ivory pyxis of al-Mughira, the *Baptistère de Saint Louis*, and Sultan-Muhammad's *Court of Gayumars*. New photographs of the exterior and interior of the Dome of the Rock in Jerusalem and the Great Mosque at Kairouan.

6: Early Medieval and Romanesque Europe: New Framing the Era essay "The Door to Salvation." New Problems and Solutions box "Beautifying God's Words." New The Patron's Voice box "Terrifying the Faithful at Autun." New Written Sources boxes "The Burning of Canterbury Cathedral" and "Bernard of Clairvaux on Cloister Sculpture." New Religion and Mythology box "The Crusades." Added two Merovingian looped fibulae, the abbey church at Corvey, the *Gospel Book of Otto III*, and the *Morgan Madonna*. New photographs of the Palatine Chapel at Aachen and the south portal and cloister of Saint-Pierre at Moissac, and a new restored cutaway view of the Aachen chapel.

7: Gothic and Late Medieval Europe: New Framing the Era essay "'Modern Architecture' in the Gothic Age." New Art and Society boxes "Paris, the New Center of Medieval Learning" and "Gothic Book Production." New The Patron's Voice boxes "Abbot Suger and the Rebuilding of Saint-Denis" and "Artists' Guilds, Artistic Commissions, and Artists' Contracts." Added Nicholas of Verdun's *Shrine of the Three Kings*, Pietro Cavallini's *Last Jugdment*, and the Doge's Palace, Venice. New photographs or drawings of Gothic rib vaults, the facade and rose window of Reims Cathedral, plan and elevation of Chartres Cathedral, elevation of Amiens Cathedral, aerial view and interior of Salisbury Cathedral, *Death of the Virgin* tympanum of Strasbourg Cathedral, the Naumburg Master's *Ekkehard and Uta*, and the Pisa baptistery pulpit by Nicola Pisano.

8: The Early Renaissance in Europe: New Framing the Era essay "Rogier van der Weyden and Saint Luke." New Art and Society box "The Artist's Profession during the Renaissance." New Written Sources box "The *Commentarii* of Lorenzo Ghiberti." New Artists on Art box "Leon Battista Alberti's *On the Art of Building*." Added Memling's diptych of Martin van Nieuwenhove, the *Buxheim Saint Christopher*, Brunelleschi's San Lorenzo and Pazzi Chapel, and Alberti's Palazzo Rucellai. New photographs of Riemenschneider's *Creglingen Altarpiece* and Donatello's *Gattamelata*.

9: High Renaissance and Mannerism in Europe: New Framing the Era essay "Michelangelo in the Service of Julius II." New Artists on Art box "Leonardo and Michelangelo on Painting versus Sculpture." New Written Sources box "Giorgio Vasari's *Lives*." New The Patron's Voice box "The Council of Trent." New Problems and Solutions box "Rethinking the Basilican Church." New Religion and Mythology box "Catholic versus Protestant Views of Salvation." Added Michelangelo's *Fall of Man*, the facade and plan of Il Gesú in Rome, Giulio Romano's *Fall of the Giants from Mount Olympus*, and Lucas Cranach the Elder's *Law and Gospel*. New photographs of the Sistine Chapel and Bramante's Tempietto in Rome.

10: Baroque Europe: New Problems and Solutions boxes "Completing Saint Peter's," "Rethinking the Church Facade," "How to

Make a Ceiling Disappear," and "Frans Hals's Group Portraits." Added Bernini's *Apollo and Daphne*, Gentileschi's *Judith Slaying Holofernes*, Gaulli's *Triumph of the Name of Jesus*, Vermeer's *Woman Holding a Balance*, and Girardon and Regnaudin's *Apollo Attended by the Nymphs of Thetis*. New photographs of Saint Peter's, Bernini's *Ecstasy of Saint Teresa*, Borromini's San Carlo alle Quattro Fontane (exterior and dome), and Rembrandt's *Night Watch*.

11: Rococo to Neoclassicism in Europe and America: New Framing the Era essay "The Enlightenment, Angelica Kauffman, and Neoclassicism." New Written Sources box "Femmes Savantes and Rococo Salon Culture." New Art and Society boxes "Joseph Wright of Derby and the Industrial Revolution" and "Vigée-Lebrun, Labille-Guiard, and the French Royal Academy." New Problems and Solutions box "Grand Manner Portraiture." New The Patron's Voice box "Thomas Jefferson, Patron and Practitioner." Added Labille-Guiard's *Self-Portrait with Two Pupils*, Batoni's *Charles John Crowle*, Boyle and Kent's Chiswick House, and Jefferson's Monticello.

12: Romanticism, Realism, and Photography, 1800 to 1870: New Framing the Era essay "The Horror—and Romance—of Death at Sea." New Problems and Solutions boxes "Unleashing the Emotive Power of Color" and "Prefabricated Architecture." New Artists on Art box "Thomas Cole on the American Landscape." New Art and Society box "Edmonia Lewis, an African American Sculptor in Rome." Added Vignon's La Madeleine in Paris, Daumier's *Nadar Raising Photography to the Height of Art*, and Muybridge's *Horse Galloping*. New photographs of Daumier's *Rue Transnonain* and the Houses of Parliament, London.

13: Impressionism, Post-Impressionism, and Symbolism, 1870 to 1900: New Framing the Era essay "Modernism at the Folies-Bergère." New Problems and Solutions boxes "Painting Impressions of Light and Color" and "Making Impressionism Solid and Enduring." New Art and Society box "Women Impressionists." Added Manet's *A Bar at the Folies-Bergère* and *Claude Monet in His Studio Boat*, Monet's *Saint-Lazare Train Station*, Morisot's *Summer's Day*,

Rodin's *Burghers of Calais*, Gaudi's Casa Milà in Barcelona, and Sullivan's Carson, Pirie, Scott Building in Chicago. New photographs of the Eiffel Tower and a detail of Seurat's *A Sunday on La Grande Jatte*.

14: Modernism in Europe and America, 1900 to 1945: New Framing the Era essay "Picasso Disrupts the Western Pictorial Tradition." New Art and Society boxes "The Armory Show" and "Jacob Lawrence's *Migration of the Negro*." New Written Sources box "André Breton's *First Surrealist Manifesto*." Added Derain's *The Dance*, Léger's *The City*, Dove's *Nature Symbolized No. 2*, Lam's *The Jungle*, Moore's *Reclining Figure*, and Orozco's *Hispano-America 16*. New photograph of the Bauhaus, Dessau.

15: Modernism and Postmodernism in Europe and America, 1945 to 1980: New Framing the Era essay "After Modernism: Postmodernist Architecture." New Artists on Art boxes "David Smith on Outdoor Sculpture," "Roy Lichtenstein on Pop Art and Comic Books," and "Chuck Close on Photorealist Portrait Painting." Added Moore's Piazza d'Italia, Krasner's *The Seasons*, Noguchi's *Shodo Shima Stone Study*, Warhol's *Marilyn Diptych*, Freud's *Naked Portrait*, and White's *Moencopi Strata*. New photographs of the interior of Le Corbusier's Notre-Dame-du-Haut and of Graves's Portland Building.

16: Contemporary Art Worldwide: Major reorganization and expansion of the text with the addition of many new artists, architects, artworks, and buildings: Burtynsky's *Densified Scrap Metal #3A*, Rosler's *Gladiators*, Botero's *Abu Ghraib 46*, Zhang's *Big Family No. 2*, Schnabel's *The Walk Home*, Song's *Summer Trees*, Murray's *Can You Hear Me?*, Anatsui's *Bleeding Takari II*, Behnisch's Hysolar Institute in Stuttgart, Hadid's Signature Towers project in Dubai, Serra's *Tilted Arc*, Kapoor's *Cloud Gate*, and Suh's *Bridging Home*. New Artists on Art box "Shirin Neshat on Iran after the Revolution." New Problems and Solutions box "Rethinking the Shape of Painting." New Art and Society box "Richard Serra's *Tilted Arc*." New photographs of Christo and Jeanne-Claude's *Surrounded Islands* and Gehry's Guggenheim Museo in Bilbao.

ABOUT THE AUTHOR
Fred S. Kleiner

FRED S. KLEINER (Ph.D., Columbia University) has been the author or coauthor of *Gardner's Art through the Ages* beginning with the 10th edition in 1995. He has also published more than a hundred books, articles, and reviews on Greek and Roman art and architecture, including *A History of Roman Art*, also published by Cengage Learning. Both *Art through the Ages* and the book on Roman art have been awarded Texty prizes as the outstanding college textbook of the year in the humanities and social sciences, in 2001 and 2007, respectively. Professor Kleiner has taught the art history survey course since 1975, first at the University of Virginia and, since 1978, at Boston University, where he is currently professor of the history of art and architecture and classical archaeology and has served as department chair for five terms, most recently from 2005 to 2014. From 1985 to 1998, he was editor-in-chief of the *American Journal of Archaeology*.

Long acclaimed for his inspiring lectures and devotion to students, Professor Kleiner won Boston University's Metcalf Award for Excellence in Teaching as well as the College Prize for Undergraduate Advising in the Humanities in 2002, and he is a two-time winner of the Distinguished Teaching Prize in the College of Arts & Sciences Honors Program. In 2007, he was elected a Fellow of the Society of Antiquaries of London, and, in 2009, in recognition of lifetime achievement in publication and teaching, a Fellow of the Text and Academic Authors Association.

Also by Fred Kleiner: *A History of Roman Art, Enhanced Edition* (Wadsworth/Cengage Learning 2010; ISBN 9780495909873), winner of the 2007 Texty Prize for a new college textbook in the humanities and social sciences. In this authoritative and lavishly illustrated volume, Professor Kleiner traces the development of Roman art and architecture from Romulus's foundation of Rome in the eighth century bce to the death of Constantine in the fourth century ce, with special chapters devoted to Pompeii and Herculaneum, Ostia, funerary and provincial art and architecture, and the earliest Christian art. The enhanced edition also includes a new introductory chapter on the art and architecture of the Etruscans and of the Greeks of South Italy and Sicily.

Resources

FOR FACULTY

MindTap® for Instructors

Leverage the tools in MindTap for *Gardner's Art through the Ages: A Concise Western History*, 4th edition, to enhance and personalize your course. Add your own images, videos, web links, readings, projects, and more either in the course Learning Path or right in the chapter reading. Set project due dates, specify whether assignments are for practice or a grade, and control when your students see these activities in their Learning Path. MindTap can be purchased as a stand-alone product or bundled with the print text. Connect with your Learning Consultant for more details via www.cengage.com/repfinder/.

Instructor Companion Site

Access the Instructor Companion Website to find resources to help you teach your course and engage your students. Here you will find the Instructor's Manual; Cengage Learning Testing, powered by Cognero; and Microsoft PowerPoint slides with lecture outlines and images that can be used as offered or customized by importing personal lecture slides or other material.

Digital Image library

Display digital images in the classroom with this powerful tool. This one-stop lecture and class presentation resource makes it easy to assemble, edit, and present customized lectures for your course. Available on flash drive, the Digital Image Library provides high-resolution images (maps, diagrams, and the fine art images from the text) for lecture presentations and allows you to easily add your own images to supplement those provided. A zoom feature allows you to magnify selected portions of an image for more detailed display in class, or you can display images side-by-side for comparison.

Google Earth™

Take your students on a virtual tour of art through the ages! Resources for the 4th edition include Google Earth coordinates for all works, monuments, and sites featured in the text, enabling students to make geographical connections between places and sites. Use these coordinates to start your lectures with a virtual journey to locations all over the globe, or take aerial screenshots of important sites to incorporate in your lecture materials.

FOR STUDENTS

MindTap for *Art through the Ages*

MindTap for *Gardner's Art through the Ages: A Concise Western History*, 4th edition, helps you engage with your course content and achieve greater comprehension. Highly personalized and fully online, the MindTap learning platform presents authoritative Cengage Learning content, assignments, and services offering you a tailored presentation of course curriculum created by your instructor.

MindTap guides you through the course curriculum via an innovative Learning Path Navigator where you will complete reading assignments, annotate your readings, complete homework, and engage with quizzes and assessments. This new edition features a two-pane e-reader, designed to make your online reading experience easier. Images discussed in the text appear in the left pane, while the accompanying text scrolls on the right. Highly accessible and interactive, this new e-reader pairs videos, Google Map links, and 360-degree panoramas with the matching figure in the text. Artworks are further brought to life through zoom capability right in the e-reader. Numerous study tools are included, such as image flashcards; glossary complete with an audio pronunciation guide; downloadable Image Guide (a note taking template with all chapter images); and the ability to synchronize your eBook notes with your personal EverNote account.

New Flashcard App

The new and improved Flashcard App in MindTap gives you more flexibility and features than ever before. Study from the preexisting card decks with all the images from the text, or create your own cards with new images from your collection or those shared by your instructor. Create your own custom study deck by combining cards from separate chapters or those you've created. Once you've compiled your flashcard deck, you can save it for later use or print it for on-the-go studying.

GARDNER'S

ART

THROUGH THE

AGES

I-1a Among the questions art historians ask is why artists chose the subjects they represented. Why would a 17th-century French painter set a biblical story in a contemporary harbor with a Roman ruin?

▲ I-1b Why is the small boat in the foreground much larger than the sailing ship in the distance? What devices did Western artists develop to produce the illusion of deep space in a two-dimensional painting?

1 ft.

I-1 CLAUDE LORRAIN, *Embarkation of the Queen of Sheba*, 1648. Oil on canvas, 4' 10" × 6' 4". National Gallery, London.

▶ I-1c Why does the large port building at the right edge of this painting seem normal to the eye when the top and bottom of the structure are not parallel horizontal lines, as they are in a real building?

What Is Art History?

What is art history? Except when referring to the modern academic discipline, people do not often juxtapose the words *art* and *history.* They tend to think of history as the record and interpretation of past human actions, particularly social and political events. In contrast, most think of art, quite correctly, as part of the present—as something that people can see and touch. Of course, people cannot see or touch history's vanished human events, but a visible, tangible artwork is a kind of persisting event. One or more artists made it at a certain time and in a specific place, even if no one now knows who, when, where, or why. Although created in the past, an artwork continues to exist in the present, long surviving its times. The first painters and sculptors died at least 30,000 years ago, but their works remain, some of them exhibited in glass cases in museums built only during the past few years.

Modern museum visitors can admire these objects from the remote past and countless others produced over the millennia—whether a large painting on canvas by a 17th-century French artist (FIG. I-1), a wood portrait from an ancient Egyptian tomb (FIG. I-12), or an 18th-century bronze altar glorifying an African king (FIG. I-13)—without any knowledge of the circumstances leading to the creation of those works. The beauty or sheer size of an object can impress people, the artist's virtuosity in the handling of ordinary or costly materials can dazzle them, or the subject depicted can move them emotionally. Viewers can react to what they see, interpret the work in the light of their own experience, and judge it a success or a failure. These are all valid responses to a work of art. But the enjoyment and appreciation of artworks in museum settings are relatively recent phenomena, as is the creation of artworks solely for museum-going audiences to view.

Today, it is common for artists to work in private studios and to create paintings, sculptures, and other objects for sale by commercial art galleries. This is what American artist CLYFFORD STILL (1904–1980) did when he produced his series of paintings (FIG. I-2) of pure color titled simply with the year of their creation. Usually, someone the artist has never met will purchase the artwork and display it in a setting the artist has never seen. This practice is not a new phenomenon in the history of art—an ancient potter decorating a vase for sale at a village market stall probably did not know who would buy the pot or where it would be housed—but it is not at all typical. In fact, it is exceptional. Throughout history, most artists created paintings, sculptures, and other objects for specific patrons and settings and to fulfill a specific purpose, even if today no one knows the original contexts of those artworks. Museum visitors can appreciate the visual and tactile qualities of these objects, but they cannot understand why they were made or why they appear as they do without knowing the circumstances of their creation. Art *appreciation* does not require knowledge of the historical context of an artwork (or a building). Art *history* does.

1 ft.

I-2 CLYFFORD STILL, *1948-C*, 1948. Oil on canvas, 6' 8⅞" × 5' 8¾". Hirshhorn Museum and Sculpture Garden, Smithsonian Institution, Washington, D.C. (purchased with funds of Joseph H. Hirshhorn, 1992).

Clyfford Still painted this abstract composition without knowing who would purchase it or where it would be displayed, but throughout history, most artists created works for specific patrons and settings.

Thus a central aim of art history is to determine the original context of artworks. Art historians seek to achieve a full understanding not only of why these "persisting events" of human history look the way they do but also of why the artistic events happened at all. What unique set of circumstances gave rise to the construction of a particular building or led an individual patron to commission a certain artist to fashion a singular artwork for a specific place? The study of history is therefore vital to art history. And art history is often indispensable for a thorough understanding of history. In ways that other historical documents may not, art objects and buildings can shed light on the peoples who made them and on the times of their creation. Furthermore, artists and architects can affect history by reinforcing or challenging cultural values and practices through the objects they create and the structures they build. Although the two disciplines are not the same, the history of art and architecture is inseparable from the study of history.

The following pages introduce some of the distinctive subjects that art historians address and the kinds of questions they ask, and explain some of the basic terminology they use when answering these questions. Readers armed with this arsenal of questions and terms will be ready to explore the multifaceted world of art through the ages.

ART HISTORY IN THE 21ST CENTURY

Art historians study the visual and tangible objects that humans make and the structures that they build. Beginning with the earliest Greco-Roman art critics, scholars have studied objects that their makers consciously manufactured as "art" and to which the artists assigned formal titles. But today's art historians also study a multitude of objects that their creators and owners almost certainly did not consider to be "works of art." Few ancient Romans, for example, would have regarded a coin bearing their emperor's portrait as anything but money. Today, an art museum may exhibit that coin in a locked case in a climate-controlled room, and scholars may subject it to the same kind of art historical analysis as a portrait by an acclaimed Renaissance or modern sculptor or painter.

The range of objects that art historians study is constantly expanding and now includes, for example, computer-generated images, whereas in the past almost anything produced using a machine would not have been regarded as art. Most people still consider the performing arts—music, drama, and dance—as outside art history's realm because these arts are fleeting, impermanent media. But during the past few decades even this distinction between "fine art" and "performance art" has become blurred. Art historians, however, generally ask the same kinds of questions about what they study, whether they employ a restrictive or expansive definition of art.

The Questions Art Historians Ask

HOW OLD IS IT? Before art historians can write a history of art, they must be sure they know the date of each work they study. Thus an indispensable subject of art historical inquiry is *chronology*, the dating of art objects and buildings. If researchers cannot determine a monument's age, they cannot place the work in its historical context. Art historians have developed many ways to establish, or at least approximate, the date of an artwork.

Physical evidence often reliably indicates an object's age. The material used for a statue or painting—bronze, plastic, or oil-based pigment, to name only a few—may not have been invented before a certain time, indicating the earliest possible date (the *terminus post quem*: Latin, "point after which") someone could have fashioned the work. Or artists may have ceased using certain materials—such as specific kinds of inks and papers for drawings—at a known time, providing the latest possible date (the *terminus ante quem*: Latin, "point before which") for objects made of those materials. Sometimes the material (or the manufacturing technique) of an object or a building can establish a very precise date of production or construction. The study of tree rings, for instance, usually can determine within a narrow range the date of a wood statue or a timber roof beam.

Documentary evidence can help pinpoint the date of an object or building when a dated written document mentions the work. For example, archival records may note when church officials commissioned a new altarpiece—and how much they paid to which artist.

Internal evidence can play a significant role in dating an artwork. A painter or sculptor might have depicted an identifiable person or a kind of hairstyle or clothing fashionable only at a certain time. If so, the art historian can assign a more accurate date to that painting or sculpture.

Stylistic evidence is also very important. The analysis of *style*—an artist's distinctive manner of producing an object—is the art historian's special sphere. Unfortunately, because it is a subjective assessment, stylistic evidence is by far the most unreliable chronological criterion. Still, art historians sometimes find style a very useful tool for establishing chronology.

WHAT IS ITS STYLE? Defining artistic style is one of the key elements of art historical inquiry, although the analysis of artworks solely in terms of style no longer dominates the field the way it once did. Art historians speak of several different kinds of artistic styles.

Period style refers to the characteristic artistic manner of a specific time, usually within a distinct culture, such as "Archaic Greek." But many periods do not display any stylistic unity at all. How would someone define the artistic style of the second decade of the third millennium in North America? Far too many crosscurrents exist in contemporary art for anyone to describe a period style of the early 21st century—even in a single city such as New York.

Regional style is the term that art historians use to describe variations in style tied to geography. Like an object's date, its *provenance,* or place of origin, can significantly determine its character.

Very often two artworks from the same place made centuries apart are more similar than contemporaneous works from two different regions. To cite one example, usually only an expert can distinguish between an Egyptian statue carved in 2500 BCE and one made in 500 BCE. But no one would mistake an Egyptian statue of 500 BCE for one of the same date made in Greece or Mexico.

Considerable variations in a given area's style are possible, however, even during a single historical period. In late medieval Europe, French architecture differed significantly from Italian architecture. The interiors of Beauvais Cathedral (FIG. I-3) and the church of Santa Croce (Holy Cross, FIG. I-4) in Florence typify the architectural styles of France and Italy, respectively, at the end of the 13th century. The rebuilding of the east end of Beauvais Cathedral began in 1284. Construction commenced on Santa Croce only 10 years later. Both structures employ the *pointed arch* characteristic of this era, yet the two churches differ strikingly. The French church has towering stone ceilings and large expanses of colored-glass windows, whereas the Italian building has a low timber roof and small, widely separated windows. Because the two contemporaneous churches served similar purposes, regional style mainly explains their differing appearance.

Personal style, the distinctive manner of individual artists or architects, often decisively explains stylistic discrepancies among artworks and buildings of the same time and place. For example, in

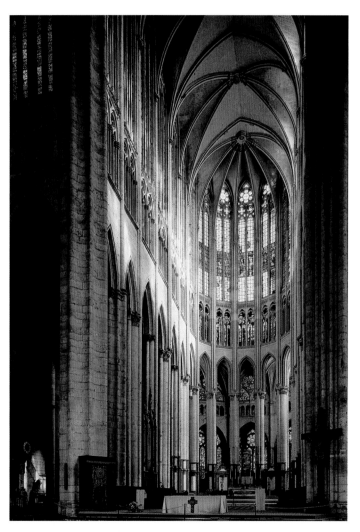

I-3 Choir of Beauvais Cathedral (looking east), Beauvais, France, rebuilt after 1284.

The style of an object or building often varies from region to region. This cathedral has towering stone vaults and large stained-glass windows typical of 13th-century French architecture.

I-4 Interior of Santa Croce (looking east), Florence, Italy, begun 1294.

In contrast to Beauvais Cathedral (FIG. I-3), this contemporaneous Florentine church conforms to the quite different regional style of Italy. The building has a low timber roof and small windows.

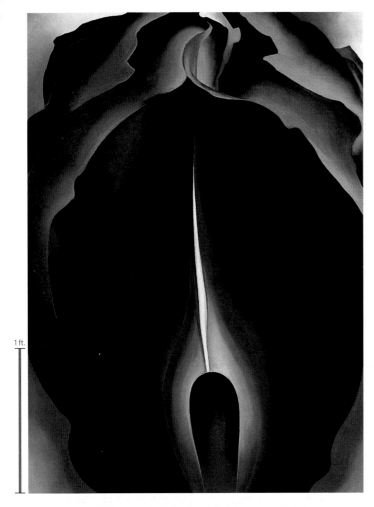

1 ft.

I-5 GEORGIA O'KEEFFE, *Jack-in-the-Pulpit No. 4,* 1930. Oil on canvas, 3' 4" × 2' 6". National Gallery of Art, Washington, D.C. (Alfred Stieglitz Collection, bequest of Georgia O'Keeffe).

O'Keeffe's paintings feature close-up views of petals and leaves in which the organic forms become powerful abstract compositions. This approach to painting typifies the artist's distinctive personal style.

1 ft.

I-6 BEN SHAHN, *The Passion of Sacco and Vanzetti,* 1931–1932. Tempera on canvas, 7' $\frac{1}{2}$" × 4'. Whitney Museum of American Art, New York (gift of Edith and Milton Lowenthal in memory of Juliana Force).

O'Keeffe's contemporary, Shahn developed a style markedly different from hers. His paintings are often social commentaries on recent events and incorporate readily identifiable people.

1930, GEORGIA O'KEEFFE (1887–1986) painted *Jack-in-the-Pulpit No. 4* (FIG. I-5), a sharply focused close-up view of petals and leaves. O'Keeffe captured the growing plant's slow, controlled motion while converting the plant into a powerful abstract composition of lines, shapes, and colors (see the discussion of art historical vocabulary in the next section). Only a year later, another American artist, BEN SHAHN (1898–1969), painted *The Passion of Sacco and Vanzetti* (FIG. I-6), a stinging commentary on social injustice inspired by the trial and execution of two Italian anarchists, Nicola Sacco and Bartolomeo Vanzetti. Many people believed that Sacco and Vanzetti had been unjustly convicted of killing two men in a robbery in 1920. Shahn's painting compresses time in a symbolic representation of the trial and its aftermath. The two executed men lie in their coffins. Presiding over them are the three members of the commission (headed by a college president wearing academic cap and gown) who declared the original trial fair and cleared the way for the executions. Behind, on the wall of a stately government building, hangs the framed portrait of the judge who pronounced the initial sentence. Personal style, not period or regional style, sets Shahn's canvas apart from O'Keeffe's. The contrast is extreme here because of the very different subjects the artists chose. But even when two artists depict the same subject, the results can vary widely. The *way* O'Keeffe painted flowers and the *way* Shahn painted faces are distinctive and unlike the styles of their contemporaries. (See the "Who Made It?" discussion on page 5.)

The different kinds of artistic styles are not mutually exclusive. For example, an artist's personal style may change dramatically during a long career. Art historians then must distinguish among the different period styles of a particular artist, such as the "Blue Period" and the "Cubist Period" of the prolific 20th-century artist Pablo Picasso.

1 in.

I-7 ALBRECHT DÜRER, *The Four Horsemen of the Apocalypse*, ca. 1498. Woodcut, 1' 3$\frac{1}{4}$" × 11". Metropolitan Museum of Art, New York (gift of Junius S. Morgan, 1919).

Personifications are abstract ideas codified in human form. Here, Albrecht Dürer represented Death, Famine, War, and Pestilence as four men on charging horses, each man carrying an identifying attribute.

Artists may depict figures with unique *attributes* identifying them. In Christian art, for example, each of the authors of the biblical gospel books, the four evangelists, has a distinctive attribute. People can recognize Saint Matthew by the winged man associated with him, John by his eagle, Mark by his lion, and Luke by his ox.

Throughout the history of art, artists have also used *personifications*—abstract ideas codified in human form. Because of the fame of the colossal statue set up in New York City's harbor in 1886, people everywhere visualize Liberty as a robed woman wearing a rayed crown and holding a torch. Four different personifications appear in *The Four Horsemen of the Apocalypse* (FIG. I-7) by German artist ALBRECHT DÜRER (1471–1528). The print is a terrifying depiction of the fateful day at the end of time when, according to the Bible's last book, Death, Famine, War, and Pestilence will annihilate the human race. Dürer personified Death as an emaciated old man with a pitchfork. Famine swings the scales for weighing human souls, War wields a sword, and Pestilence draws a bow.

Even without considering style and without knowing a work's maker, informed viewers can determine much about the work's period and provenance by iconographical and subject analysis alone. In *The Passion of Sacco and Vanzetti* (FIG. I-6), for example, the two coffins, the trio headed by an academic, and the robed judge in the background are all pictorial clues revealing the painting's subject. The work's date must be after the trial and execution, probably while the event was still newsworthy. And because the two men's deaths caused the greatest outrage in the United States, the painter–social critic was probably American.

WHAT IS ITS SUBJECT? Another major concern of art historians is, of course, subject matter. Some artworks, such as modern *abstract* paintings (FIG. I-2), have no subject, not even a setting. But when artists represent people, places, or actions, viewers must identify these features to achieve complete understanding of the work. Art historians traditionally separate pictorial subjects into various categories, such as religious, historical, mythological, *genre* (daily life), portraiture, *landscape* (a depiction of a place), *still life* (an arrangement of inanimate objects), and their numerous subdivisions and combinations.

Iconography—literally, the "writing of images"—refers both to the content, or subject, of an artwork, and to the study of content in art. By extension, it also includes the study of *symbols,* images that stand for other images or encapsulate ideas. In Christian art, two intersecting lines of unequal length or a simple geometric cross can serve as an emblem of the religion as a whole, symbolizing the cross of Jesus Christ's crucifixion. A symbol also can be a familiar object that an artist has imbued with greater meaning. A balance or scale, for example, may symbolize justice or the weighing of souls on judgment day.

WHO MADE IT? If Ben Shahn had not signed his painting of Sacco and Vanzetti, an art historian could still assign, or *attribute,* the work to him based on knowledge of the artist's personal style. Although signing (and dating) works is quite common (but by no means universal) today, in the history of art countless works exist whose artists remain unknown. Because personal style can play a major role in determining the character of an artwork, art historians often try to attribute anonymous works to known artists. Sometimes they assemble a group of works all thought to be by the same person, even though none of the objects in the group is the known work of an artist with a recorded name. Art historians thus reconstruct the careers of artists such as "the Achilles Painter," the anonymous ancient Greek artist whose masterwork is a depiction of the hero Achilles. Scholars base their *attributions* on internal

1 in.

I-8 Bust of Augustus wearing the *corona civica* (civic wreath), early first century CE. Marble, 1' 5" high. Glyptothek, Munich.

Patrons frequently dictate the form their portraits will take. The Roman emperor Augustus demanded that he always be portrayed as a young, godlike head of state even though he lived to age 76.

personal style is of paramount importance. But in many times and places, artists had little to say about what form their work would take. They toiled in obscurity, doing the bidding of their *patrons,* those who paid them to make individual works or employed them on a continuing basis. The role of patrons in dictating the content and shaping the form of artworks is also an important subject of art historical inquiry.

In the art of portraiture, to name only one category of painting and sculpture, the patron has often played a dominant role in deciding how the artist represented the subject, whether that patron or another individual, such as a spouse, son, or mother. Many Egyptian pharaohs and some Roman emperors, for example, insisted that artists depict them with unlined faces and perfect youthful bodies no matter how old they were when portrayed. In these cases, the state employed the sculptors and painters, and the artists had no choice but to portray their patrons in the officially approved manner. This is why Augustus, who lived to age 76, looks so young in his portraits (FIG. I-8). Although Roman emperor for more than 40 years, Augustus demanded that artists always represent him as a young, godlike head of state.

All modes of artistic production reveal the impact of patronage. Learned monks provided the themes for the sculptural decoration of medieval church portals. Renaissance princes and popes dictated the subject, size, and materials of artworks destined for display in buildings also constructed according to their specifications. An art historian could make a very long list of commissioned works, and it would indicate that patrons have had diverse tastes and needs throughout history and consequently demanded different kinds of art. Whenever a patron contracts an artist or architect to paint, sculpt, or build in a prescribed manner, personal style often becomes a very minor factor in the ultimate appearance of the painting, statue, or building. In these cases, the identity of the patron reveals more to art historians than does the identity of the artist or school.

The Words Art Historians Use

As in all fields of study, art history has its own specialized vocabulary consisting of hundreds of words, but certain basic terms are indispensable for describing artworks and buildings of any time and place. They make up the essential vocabulary of *formal analysis,* the visual analysis of artistic form. Definitions and discussions of the most important art historical terms follow.

FORM AND COMPOSITION *Form* refers to an object's shape and structure, either in two dimensions (for example, a figure painted on a wall) or in three dimensions (such as a statue carved from a stone block). Two forms may take the same shape but differ in their color, texture, and other qualities. *Composition* refers to how an artist organizes (*composes*) forms in an artwork, either by placing shapes on a flat surface or by arranging forms in space.

MATERIAL AND TECHNIQUE To create art forms, artists shape materials (pigment, clay, marble, gold, and many more) with tools (pens, brushes, chisels, and so forth). Each of the materials and tools available has its own potentialities and limitations. Part of all artists' creative activity is to select the *medium* and instrument most suitable to the purpose—or to develop new media and tools, such as bronze and concrete in antiquity and cameras and computers in modern times. The processes that artists employ, such as applying paint to canvas with a brush, and the distinctive, personal ways they

evidence, such as the distinctive way an artist draws or carves drapery folds, earlobes, or flowers. It requires a keen, highly trained eye and long experience to become a *connoisseur,* an expert in assigning artworks to "the hand" of one artist rather than another.

Sometimes a group of artists works in the same style at the same time and place. Art historians designate such a group as a *school.* "School" does not mean an educational institution. The term connotes only shared chronology, style, and geography. Art historians speak, for example, of the Dutch school of the 17th century and, within it, of subschools such as those of the cities of Haarlem, Utrecht, and Leyden.

WHO PAID FOR IT? The interest that many art historians show in attribution reflects their conviction that the identity of an artwork's maker is the major reason the object looks the way it does. For them, handle materials constitute their *technique.* Form, material, and technique interrelate and are central to analyzing any work of art.

LINE Among the most important elements defining an artwork's shape or form is *line.* A line can be understood as the path of a point moving in space, an invisible line of sight. More commonly, however, artists and architects make a line visible by drawing (or chiseling) it on a *plane,* a flat surface. A line may be very thin, wirelike, and delicate. It may be thick and heavy. Or it may alternate quickly from broad to narrow, the strokes jagged or the outline broken. When a continuous line defines an object's outer shape, art historians call it a *contour line.* All of these line qualities are present in Dürer's *Four Horsemen of the Apocalypse* (FIG. I-7). Contour lines define the basic shapes of clouds, human and animal limbs, and weapons. Within the forms, series of short broken lines create shadows and textures. An overall pattern of long parallel strokes suggests the dark sky on the frightening day when the world is about to end.

COLOR Light reveals all colors. Light in the world of the painter and other artists differs from natural light. Natural light, or sunlight, is whole or *additive light.* As the sum of all the wavelengths composing the visible *spectrum,* it may be disassembled or fragmented into the individual colors of the spectral band. The painter's light in art—the light reflected from pigments and objects—is *subtractive light.* Paint pigments produce their individual colors by reflecting a segment of the spectrum while absorbing all the rest. Green pigment, for example, subtracts or absorbs all the light in the spectrum except that seen as green.

Artists call the three basic colors or *hues*—red, yellow, and blue—the *primary colors.* The *secondary colors* result from mixing pairs of primaries: orange (red and yellow), purple (red and blue), and green (yellow and blue). *Complementary colors*—red and green, yellow and purple, and blue and orange—complete, or "complement," each other, one absorbing colors the other reflects.

Painters can manipulate the appearance of colors, however. One artist who made a systematic investigation of the formal aspects of art, especially color, was JOSEPH ALBERS (1888–1976), a German-born artist who emigrated to the United States in 1933. In *Homage to the Square: "Ascending"* (FIG. I-9)—one of hundreds of color variations on the same composition of concentric squares—Albers demonstrated "the discrepancy between physical fact and psychic effect."[1] Because the composition remains constant, the *Homage* series succeeds in revealing the relativity and instability of color perception. Albers varied the *saturation* (a color's brightness or dullness) and *tonality* (lightness or darkness) of each square in each painting. As a result, the sizes of the squares from painting to painting appear to vary (although they remain the same), and the sensations emanating from the paintings range from clashing dissonance to delicate serenity. In this way, Albers proved that "we see colors almost never unrelated to each other."[2]

TEXTURE The term *texture* refers to the quality of a surface, such as rough or shiny. Art historians distinguish between true texture—that is, the tactile quality of the surface—and represented texture, as when painters depict an object as having a certain texture, even though the pigment is the true texture. Texture is, of course, a key determinant of any sculpture's character. People's first impulse is usually to handle a work of sculpture—even though museum signs often warn "Do not touch!" Sculptors plan for this natural human response, using surfaces varying in texture from rugged coarseness to polished smoothness. Textures are often intrinsic to a material, influencing the type of stone, wood, plastic, clay, or metal that a sculptor selects.

SPACE AND PERSPECTIVE *Space* is the bounded or boundless "container" of objects. For art historians, space can be the real three-dimensional space occupied by a statue or a vase or contained within a room or courtyard. Or space can be *illusionistic,* as when painters depict an image (or illusion) of the three-dimensional spatial world on a two-dimensional surface.

Perspective is one of the most important pictorial devices for organizing forms in space. Throughout history, artists have used various types of perspective to create an illusion of depth or space on a two-dimensional surface. The French painter CLAUDE LORRAIN (1600–1682) employed several perspective devices in *Embarkation of the Queen of Sheba* (FIG. I-1), a painting of a biblical episode set in a 17th-century European harbor with an ancient Roman ruin in the left foreground, an irrationally anachronistic combination that can be

1 ft.

I-9 JOSEF ALBERS, *Homage to the Square: "Ascending,"* 1953. Oil on composition board, 3' 7½" × 3' 7½". Whitney Museum of American Art, New York.

Albers painted hundreds of canvases using the same composition but employing variations in color saturation and tonality in order to reveal the relativity and instability of color perception.

I-10 Ogata Korin, *Waves at Matsushima*, Edo period, ca. 1700–1716. Six-panel folding screen, ink, colors, and gold leaf on paper, 4' 11⅛" × 12' ⅞". Museum of Fine Arts, Boston (Fenollosa-Weld Collection).

Asian artists rarely employed Western perspective (FIG. I-1). Korin was more concerned with creating an intriguing composition of shapes on a surface than with locating boulders, waves, and clouds in space.

I-11 Peter Paul Rubens, *Lion Hunt*, 1617–1618. Oil on canvas, 8' 2" × 12' 5". Alte Pinakothek, Munich.

Foreshortening—the representation of a figure or object at an angle to the picture plane—is a common device in Western art for creating the illusion of depth. Foreshortening is a kind of perspective.

explained only in the context of the cultural values of the artist's time and place. In the painting, the figures and boats on the shoreline are much larger than those in the distance, because decreasing an object's size makes it appear farther away. The top and bottom of the port building are not parallel horizontal lines, as they are in a real building. Instead, the lines converge beyond the structure, leading the viewer's eye toward the hazy, indistinct sun on the horizon. These perspective devices—the reduction of figure size, the convergence of diagonal lines, and the blurring of distant forms—have been familiar features of Western art since they were first employed by the ancient Greeks. It is important to state, however, that all kinds of perspective are only pictorial conventions, even when one or more types of perspective may be so common in a given culture that people accept them as "natural" or as "true" means of representing the natural world.

In *Waves at Matsushima* (FIG. I-10), a Japanese seascape painting on a six-part folding screen, OGATA KORIN (1658–1716) ignored these Western perspective conventions. A Western viewer might interpret the left half of Korin's composition as depicting the distant horizon, as in the French painting, but the sky is an unnatural gold, and the clouds which fill that sky are almost indistinguishable from the waves below. The rocky outcroppings decrease in size with distance, but all are in sharp focus, and there are no shadows. The Japanese artist was less concerned with locating the boulders, waves, and clouds in space than with composing shapes on a surface, playing the swelling curves of waves and clouds against the jagged contours of the rocks. Neither the French nor the Japanese painting can be said to project "correctly" what viewers "in fact" see. One painting is not a "better" picture of the world than the other. The European and Asian artists simply approached the problem of picture making differently.

FORESHORTENING Artists also represent single figures in space in varying ways. When Flemish artist PETER PAUL RUBENS (1577–1640) painted *Lion Hunt* (FIG. I-11), he used *foreshortening* for all the hunters and animals—that is, he represented their bodies at angles to the picture plane. When in life someone views a figure at an angle, the body appears to contract as it extends back in space. Foreshortening is a kind of perspective. It produces the illusion that one part of the body is farther away than another, even though all the painted forms are on the same surface. Especially noteworthy in *Lion Hunt* are the gray horse at the left, seen from behind with the bottom of its left rear hoof facing the viewer and most of its head hidden by its rider's shield, and the fallen hunter at the painting's lower right corner, whose barely visible legs and feet recede into the distance.

The artist who carved the portrait of the ancient Egyptian official Hesire (FIG. I-12) did not employ foreshortening. That artist's purpose was to present the various human body parts as clearly as possible, without overlapping. The lower part of Hesire's body is in profile to give the most complete view of the legs, with both the heels and toes of each foot visible. The frontal torso, although unnaturally twisted 90 degrees, presents its full shape, including both shoulders, equal in size, as in nature. (Compare the shoulders of the hunter on the gray horse or those of the fallen hunter in *Lion Hunt*'s left foreground.) Rubens and the Egyptian sculptor used very different means of depicting forms in space. Once again, neither is the "correct" manner.

PROPORTION AND SCALE *Proportion* concerns the relationships (in terms of size) of the parts of persons, buildings, or objects. People

I-12 Hesire, relief from his tomb at Saqqara, Egypt, Third Dynasty, ca. 2650 BCE. Wood, 3' 9" high. Egyptian Museum, Cairo.

Egyptian artists combined frontal and profile views to give a precise picture of the parts of the human body, as opposed to depicting how an individual body appears from a specific viewpoint.

can judge "correct proportions" intuitively ("that statue's head seems the right size for the body"). Or proportion can be a mathematical relationship between the size of one part of an artwork or building and the other parts within the work. Proportion in art implies using a *module,* or basic unit of measure. When an artist or architect

I-13 **Altar to the Hand (ikegobo), from Benin, Nigeria, ca. 1735–1750. Bronze, 1' 5½" high. British Museum, London (gift of Sir William Ingram).**

One of the Benin king's praise names is Great Head, and on this cast-bronze royal altar, the artist represented him larger than all other figures and with a disproportionately large head.

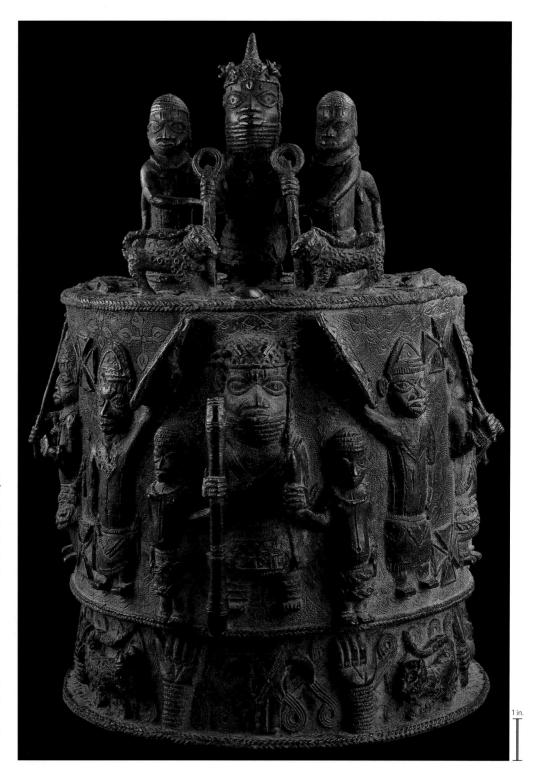

1 in.

uses a formal system of proportions, all parts of a building, body, or other entity will be fractions or multiples of the module. A module might be the diameter of a *column,* the height of a human head, or any other component whose dimensions can be multiplied or divided to determine the size of the work's other parts.

In certain times and places, artists have devised *canons,* or systems, of "correct" or "ideal" proportions for representing human figures, constituent parts of buildings, and so forth. In ancient Greece, many sculptors formulated canons of proportions so strict and all-encompassing that they calculated the size of every body part in advance, even the fingers and toes, according to mathematical ratios.

Proportional systems can differ sharply from period to period, culture to culture, and artist to artist. Part of the task that art history students face is to perceive and adjust to these differences. In fact, many artists have used disproportion and distortion deliberately for expressive effect. Dürer's Death (FIG. I-7) has hardly any flesh on his bones, and his limbs are distorted and stretched. Disproportion and distortion distinguish him from all the other figures in the work, precisely as the artist intended.

In other cases, artists have used disproportion to focus attention on one body part (often the head) or to single out a group member (usually the leader). These intentional "unnatural" discrepancies in proportion constitute what art historians call *hierarchy of scale,* the enlarging of elements considered the most important.

On the bronze altar from Benin, Nigeria, illustrated here (FIG. I-13), the sculptor varied the size of each figure according to the person's social status. Largest, and therefore most important, is the Benin king, depicted twice, each time flanked by two smaller attendants. The king's head is also disproportionately large compared to his body, consistent with one of the Benin ruler's praise names: Great Head.

One problem that students of art history—and professional art historians too—confront when studying illustrations in art history books is that although the relative sizes of figures and objects in a painting or sculpture are easy to discern, it is impossible to determine the absolute size of the work reproduced because they

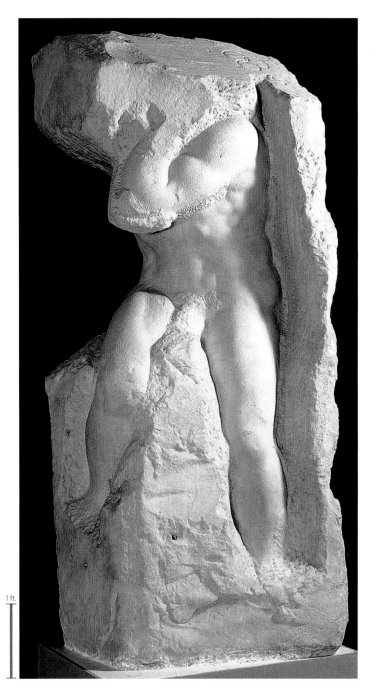

I-14 MICHELANGELO BUONARROTI, unfinished captive, 1527–1528. Marble, 8' 7½" high. Galleria dell'Accademia, Florence.

Carving a freestanding figure from stone or wood is a subtractive process. Italian master sculptor Michelangelo thought of sculpture as a process of "liberating" the statue within the block of marble.

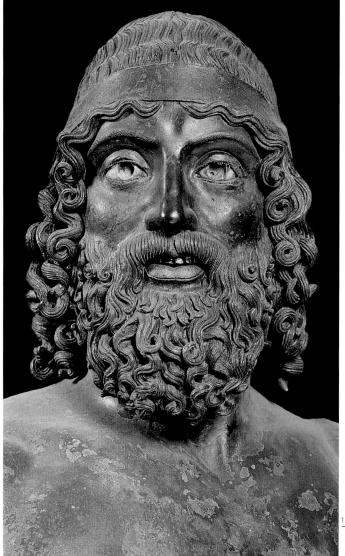

I-15 Head of a warrior, detail of a statue (FIG. 2-34A) from the sea off Riace, Italy, ca. 460–450 BCE. Bronze, full statue 6' 6" high. Museo Archeologico Nazionale, Reggio Calabria.

The sculptor of this life-size statue of a bearded Greek warrior cast the head, limbs, torso, hands, and feet in separate molds, then welded the pieces together and added the eyes in a different material.

all are printed at approximately the same size on the page. Readers of *Art through the Ages* can learn the exact size of all artworks from the dimensions given in the captions and, more intuitively, from the scales positioned at the lower left or right corner of each illustration.

CARVING AND CASTING Sculptural technique falls into two basic categories, *subtractive* and *additive*. *Carving* is a subtractive technique. The final form is a reduction of the original mass of a block of stone, a piece of wood, or another material. Wood statues were once tree trunks, and stone statues began as blocks pried from mountains. The unfinished marble statue illustrated here (FIG. I-14) by

renowned Italian artist MICHELANGELO BUONARROTI (1475–1564) clearly reveals the original shape of the stone block. Michelangelo thought of sculpture as a process of "liberating" the statue within the block. All sculptors of stone or wood cut away (subtract) "excess material." When they finish, they "leave behind" the statue—in this example, a twisting nude male form whose head Michelangelo never freed from the stone block.

In additive sculpture, the artist builds up the forms, usually in clay around a framework, or *armature*. Or a sculptor may fashion a *mold*, a hollow form for shaping, or *casting*, a fluid substance such as bronze. The ancient Greek sculptor who made the bronze statue of a warrior found in the sea near Riace, Italy, cast the head (FIG. I-15) as well as the limbs, torso, hands, and feet (FIG. 2-34A ⟋) in separate molds and then *welded* them together (joined them by heating). Finally, the artist added features, such as the pupils of the eyes (now missing), in other materials. The warrior's teeth are silver, and his lower lip is copper.

RELIEF SCULPTURE *Statues* and *busts* (head, shoulders, and chest) that exist independent of any architectural frame or setting and that viewers can walk around are *freestanding sculptures,* or *sculptures in the round.* In *relief sculpture,* the subjects project from the background but remain part of it. In *high reliefs* (FIG. I-13), the images project boldly and may even cast shadows. In *low reliefs* (FIG. I-12), the projection is slight.

ARCHITECTURAL DRAWINGS People experience buildings both visually and by moving through and around them, so they perceive architectural space and *mass* together. Architects can represent these spaces and masses graphically in several ways, including as plans, sections, elevations, and cutaway drawings.

A *plan,* essentially a map of a floor, shows the placement of a structure's masses and, therefore, the spaces they circumscribe and enclose. A *section,* a kind of vertical plan, depicts the placement of the masses as if someone cut through the building along a plane. Drawings showing a theoretical slice across a structure's width are *lateral sections.* Those cutting through a building's length are *longitudinal sections.* Illustrated here are the plan and lateral section (FIG. I-16) of Beauvais Cathedral, which readers can compare with the photograph of the church's *choir* (FIG. I-3). The plan shows the choir's shape and the location of the *piers* dividing the *aisles* and supporting the *vaults* above, as well as the pattern of the crisscrossing vault *ribs.* The lateral section shows not only the interior of the choir with its vaults and *stained-glass* windows but also the structure of the roof and the form of the exterior *flying buttresses* holding the vaults in place.

Other types of architectural drawings appear throughout this book. An *elevation* drawing is a head-on view of an external or internal wall. A *cutaway* combines in a single drawing an exterior view with an interior view of part of a building.

This overview of the art historian's vocabulary is not exhaustive, nor have artists used only painting, drawing, sculpture, and architecture as media over the millennia. Ceramics, jewelry, textiles, photography, and computer graphics are just some of the numerous other arts. All of them involve highly specialized techniques described in distinct vocabularies. As in this introductory chapter, new terms appear in *italics* when they first appear. The comprehensive glossary at the end of the book contains definitions of all italicized terms.

Art History and Other Disciplines

By its very nature, the work of art historians intersects with the work of others in many fields of knowledge, not only in the humanities but also in the social and natural sciences. Today, art historians must go beyond the boundaries of what the public and even professional art historians of previous generations considered the specialized discipline of art history. Art historical research in the 21st century is typically interdisciplinary in nature. To cite one example, in an effort to unlock the secrets of a particular statue, an art historian might conduct archival research hoping to uncover new documents shedding light on who paid for the work and why, who made it and when, where it originally stood, how people of the time reacted to it, and a host of other questions. Realizing, however, that the authors of the written documents often were not objective recorders of fact but observers with their own biases and agendas, the art historian may also use methodologies developed in fields such as literary criticism, philosophy, sociology, and gender studies to weigh the evidence that the documents provide.

At other times, rather than attempting to master many disciplines at once, art historians band together with other specialists in multidisciplinary inquiries. Art historians might call in chemists to date an artwork based on the composition of the materials used, or might ask geologists to determine which quarry furnished the stone for a particular statue. X-ray technicians might be enlisted in an attempt to establish whether a painting is a forgery. Of course, art historians often reciprocate by contributing their expertise to the solution of problems in other disciplines. A historian, for example,

I-16 Plan (*left*) and lateral section (*right*) of Beauvais Cathedral, Beauvais, France, rebuilt after 1284.

Architectural drawings are indispensable aids for the analysis of buildings. Plans are maps of floors, recording the structure's masses. Sections are vertical "slices," across either a building's width or length.

might ask an art historian to determine—based on style, material, iconography, and other criteria—if any of the portraits of a certain king date after his death. Such information would help establish the ruler's continuing prestige during the reigns of his successors. For example, some portraits of Augustus (FIG. I-8), the founder of the Roman Empire, postdate his death by decades, even centuries.

DIFFERENT WAYS OF SEEING

The history of art can be a history of artists and their works, of styles and stylistic change, of materials and techniques, of images and themes and their meanings, and of contexts and cultures and patrons. The best art historians analyze artworks from many viewpoints. But no art historian (or scholar in any other field), no matter how broad-minded in approach and no matter how experienced, can be truly objective. Like the artists who made the works illustrated and discussed in this book, art historians are members of a society, participants in its culture. How can scholars (and museum visitors and travelers to foreign locales) comprehend cultures unlike their own? They can try to reconstruct the original cultural contexts of artworks, but they are limited by their distance from the thought patterns of the cultures they study and by the obstructions to understanding—the assumptions, presuppositions, and prejudices peculiar to their own culture—that their own thought patterns raise. Art historians may reconstruct a distorted picture of the past because of culture-bound blindness.

A single instance underscores how differently people of diverse cultures view the world and how various ways of seeing can result in sharp differences in how artists depict the world. Illustrated here are two contemporaneous portraits of a 19th-century Maori chieftain (FIG. I-17)—one by an Englishman, JOHN SYLVESTER (active early 19th century), and the other by the New Zealand chieftain himself, TE PEHI KUPE (d. 1829). Both reproduce the chieftain's facial *tattoo*. The European artist (FIG. I-17, *left*) included the head and shoulders and downplayed the tattooing. The tattoo pattern is one aspect of the likeness among many, no more or less important than the chieftain's European attire. Sylvester also recorded his subject's momentary glance toward the right and the play of light on his hair, fleeting aspects having nothing to do with the figure's identity.

In contrast, Te Pehi Kupe's self-portrait (FIG. I-17, *right*)—made during a trip to Liverpool, England, to obtain European arms to take back to New Zealand—is not a picture of a man situated in space and bathed in light. Rather, it is the chieftain's statement of the supreme importance of the tattoo design announcing his rank among his people. Remarkably, Te Pehi Kupe created the tattoo patterns from memory, without the aid of a mirror. The splendidly composed insignia, presented as a flat design separated from the body and even from the head, is the Maori chieftain's image of himself. Only by understanding the cultural context of each portrait can art historians hope to understand why either representation appears as it does.

As noted at the outset, the study of the context of artworks and buildings is one of the central concerns of art historians. *Art through the Ages* seeks to present a history of art and architecture that will help readers understand not only the subjects, styles, and techniques of paintings, sculptures, buildings, and other art forms created in all parts of the world during 30 millennia but also their cultural and historical contexts. That story now begins.

I-17 *Left:* JOHN HENRY SYLVESTER, *Portrait of Te Pehi Kupe,* 1826. Watercolor, $8\frac{1}{4}" \times 6\frac{1}{4}"$. National Library of Australia, Canberra (Rex Nan Kivell Collection). *Right:* TE PEHI KUPE, *Self-Portrait,* 1826. From Leo Frobenius, *The Childhood of Man: A Popular Account of the Lives, Customs and Thoughts of the Primitive Races* (Philadelphia: J. B. Lippincott, 1909), 35, fig. 28.

These strikingly different portraits of the same Maori chief reveal the different ways of seeing of a European artist and an Oceanic one. Understanding the cultural context of artworks is vital to art history.

◀ **1-1a** The *Warka Vase* is the first great work of narrative relief sculpture known. It represents a ceremony in honor of the goddess Inanna in which a priest-king brings votive offerings to deposit in her shrine.

▲ **1-1b** The Sumerians were the first to use pictures to tell coherent stories. This sculptor placed the figures in three registers. In each band, all the humans and animals stand on a common ground line.

1 ft.

1-1 Presentation of offerings to Inanna (*Warka Vase*), from the Inanna temple complex, Uruk (modern Warka), Iraq, ca. 3200–3000 BCE. Alabaster, 3' ¼" high. National Museum of Iraq, Baghdad.

▲ **1-1c** The two lowest registers show ewes, rams, and crops above a wavy line representing water. The animals and food are Inanna's blessings to the inhabitants of the city-state.

Prehistory and the First Civilizations

PICTORIAL NARRATION IN ANCIENT SUMER

Mesopotamia—a Greek word meaning "the land between the [Tigris and Euphrates] rivers"—is the core of the region often called the Fertile Crescent, where humans first learned how to use the wheel and plow and how to control floods and construct irrigation canals. In the fourth millennium BCE, the inhabitants of ancient Sumer, "the cradle of civilization," established the earliest complex urban societies, called *city-states*. The Sumerians also invented writing and were the first to use pictures to tell coherent stories, far surpassing all earlier artists' tentative efforts at pictorial narration.

The *Warka Vase* (FIG. 1-1) from Uruk (modern Warka) is the first great work of narrative *relief sculpture* known. Its depiction of a religious ceremony honoring the Sumerian goddess Inanna (FIG. 1-1A ⬈) incorporates all of the pictorial conventions that would dominate narrative art for the next 2,000 years. The artist divided the pictorial field into three bands (called *registers* or *friezes*) and placed all the figures on a common *ground line,* a format that marks a significant break with the haphazard figure placement of Stone Age art (FIGS. 1-4 to 1-6). The lowest band shows crops above a wavy line representing water. Then comes a register with alternating ewes and rams. Agriculture and animal husbandry were the staples of the Sumerian economy, but the produce and the female and male animals are also fertility symbols. They underscore that Inanna blessed Uruk's inhabitants with good crops and increased herds.

A procession of naked men moving in the opposite direction of the animals fills the band at the center of the vase. The men carry baskets and jars overflowing with the earth's abundance. They will present their bounty to the goddess as a *votive offering* (gift of gratitude to a deity usually made in fulfillment of a vow). In the uppermost band of the *Warka Vase* is Inanna wearing a tall horned headdress. Facing her is a nude male figure bringing a large vessel brimming with offerings to be deposited in the goddess's shrine, and behind her (not visible in FIG. 1-1), a man wearing a tasseled skirt and an attendant carrying his long train. Near the man is the *pictograph* for the Sumerian official that scholars ambiguously refer to as a "priest-king"—that is, both a religious and secular leader. Some art historians interpret the scene as a symbolic marriage between the priest-king and the goddess, ensuring her continued goodwill—and reaffirming the leader's exalted position in society. The greater height of the priest-king and Inanna compared with the offering bearers indicates their greater importance, a convention called *hierarchy of scale,* which the Sumerians also pioneered.

PREHISTORY

Humankind originated in Africa in the very remote past. Yet it was not until millions of years later that ancient hunters began to represent (literally, "to present again"—in different and substitute form) the world around them and to fashion the first examples of what people generally call "art." The immensity of this intellectual achievement cannot be exaggerated.

Paleolithic Age

The earliest preserved art objects date to around 40,000 to 30,000 BCE, during the Old Stone Age or *Paleolithic* period (from the Greek *paleo*, "old," and *lithos*, "stone"). Paleolithic artworks are astonishingly varied. They range from simple shell necklaces to human and animal forms in ivory, clay, and stone to life-size paintings, *engravings*, and relief sculptures covering the walls and ceilings of caves.

VENUS OF WILLENDORF One of the oldest sculptures discovered to date, carved using simple stone tools, is the tiny limestone figurine (FIG. 1-2) of a woman nicknamed the *Venus of Willendorf* after its *findspot* in Austria (MAP 1-1). Art historians can only speculate on the function and meaning of this and similar objects because they date to a time before writing, before (or pre-) history. Yet the preponderance of female over male figures in the art of the Old Stone Age seems to indicate a preoccupation with women, whose childbearing capabilities ensured the survival of the species. The

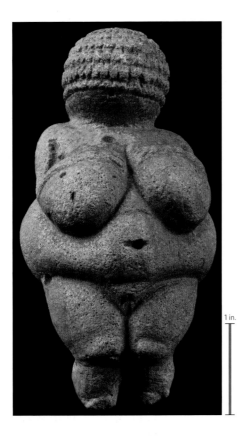

1-2 Nude woman (*Venus of Willendorf*), from Willendorf, Austria, ca. 28,000–25,000 BCE. Limestone, $4\frac{1}{4}$" high. Naturhistorisches Museum, Vienna.

The anatomical exaggerations in this tiny figurine—one of the oldest sculptures known—are typical of Paleolithic representations of women, whose child-bearing capabilities ensured the survival of the species.

1 in.

MAP 1-1 Stone Age sites in western Europe.

PREHISTORY AND THE FIRST CIVILIZATIONS

40,000–3500 BCE
Stone Age

- Paleolithic (40,000–9000 BCE) humans create the first sculptures and paintings. The works range in scale from tiny figurines to life-size paintings on cave walls.
- In the Neolithic (8000–3500 BCE) age, the first settled communities appear in Anatolia and Mesopotamia. Artists produce the first large-scale sculptures and earliest paintings with coherent narratives.

3500–2150 BCE
Sumer, Akkad, Old Kingdom

- Sumerians (3500–2332 BCE)—establish the first city-states, construct temples on lofty mud-brick platforms, and adopt the register format for narrative art.
- Akkadians (2332–2150 BCE) produce the earliest known life-size hollow-cast metal sculptures.
- Old Kingdom (2575–2134 BCE) Egyptian sculptors create statuary types expressing the eternal nature of divine kingship. The Fourth Dynasty kings build three colossal pyramids at Gizeh.

2150–1070 BCE
Babylonia, New Kingdom

- Hammurabi, the greatest Babylonian king (r. 1792–1750 BCE), sets up a stele recording his comprehensive laws.
- Egyptian New Kingdom (1550–1070 BCE) architects construct grandiose pylon temples. Akhenaton introduces a new religion and new art forms.

1070–900 BCE

900–330 BCE
Assyria, Achaemenid Persia

- Assyrians (900–612 BCE) construct fortified citadels guarded by lamassu, and carve large-scale reliefs celebrating their prowess in warfare and hunting.
- Achaemenid Persians (559–330 BCE) build an immense palace complex at Persepolis featuring an audience hall that could accommodate 10,000 guests.

PROBLEMS AND SOLUTIONS
How to Represent an Animal

Like every artist in every age in every medium, the sculptor of the pair of bison (FIG. 1-3) in the cave at Le Tuc d'Audoubert had to answer two questions before beginning work: *What* shall be my subject? *How* shall I represent it? In Paleolithic art, in Africa (FIG. **1-3A** ↗) as well as in Europe, the almost universal answer to the first question was an animal. In fact, Paleolithic painters and sculptors depicted humans infrequently, and men almost never. In equally stark contrast to today's world, there was also agreement on the best answer to the second question. During the Old Stone Age and for thousands of years thereafter, artists represented virtually every animal in every painting in the same manner: in strict profile. Why?

The profile is the only view of an animal in which the head, body, tail, and all four legs are visible. The frontal view conceals most of the body, and a three-quarter view shows

neither the front nor side fully. Only the profile view is completely informative about the animal's shape, and that is why Paleolithic painters and relief sculptors universally chose it.

A very long time passed before artists placed any premium on "variety" or "originality" either in subject choice or in representational manner. These are quite modern notions in the history of art. The aim of the earliest artists was to create a convincing image of their subject, a kind of pictorial definition of the animal capturing its very essence, and only the profile view met their needs.

1-3 Two bison, reliefs in the cave at Le Tuc d'Audoubert, France, ca. 15,000–10,000 BCE. Clay, right bison 2' $\frac{7}{8}$" long.

Animals are far more common subjects in Paleolithic art than are humans. In both relief sculpture and painting, animals always appear in profile, the only view completely informative about their shape.

1 ft.

anatomical exaggeration of the Willendorf figurine has suggested to many scholars that this and other prehistoric statuettes of women served as fertility images. The breasts of the Willendorf woman are enormous, far larger in proportion than the tiny forearms and hands resting on them. In addition to using a stone *chisel*, the sculptor also used a *burin* to *incise* (scratch) into the stone the outline of the pubic triangle. Sculptors often omitted this detail in other Paleolithic female figurines, however, and many of the women also have far more slender proportions than the Willendorf woman, leading some scholars to question the nature of these figures as fertility images. In any case, it seems clear that the makers' intent was not to represent a specific woman but the female form.

LE TUC D'AUDOUBERT Far more common than Paleolithic representations of humans are sculptures and paintings of animals (see "How to Represent an Animal," above). An early example of animal sculpture is the pair of clay bison reliefs (FIG. 1-3) in the cave at Le Tuc d'Audoubert, France. The sculptor modeled the forms by pressing the clay against the surface of a large boulder at the back of the cave. After using both hands to form the overall shape of the animals, the artist smoothed the surfaces with a spatula-like tool and used fingers to shape the eyes, nostrils, mouths, and manes.

CAVE PAINTING The bison of Le Tuc d'Audoubert are among the largest sculptures of the Paleolithic period, but they are dwarfed by the "herds" of painted animals that roam the cave walls of southern France and northern Spain. Examples of Paleolithic painting now have been found at more than 200 European sites. Nonetheless, archaeologists still regard painted caves as rare occurrences, because even though the cave images number in the hundreds, prehistoric artists created them over a period of some 10,000 to 20,000 years.

Paleolithic painters drew their subjects using chunks of red and yellow ocher. For painting, they ground these same ochers into powders that they mixed with water before applying. Large flat stones served as *palettes* to hold the pigment. The painters made brushes from reeds, bristles, or twigs, and may have used a blowpipe of reed or hollow bone to spray pigments on out-of-reach surfaces. Some caves have natural ledges on the rock walls, on which the painters could have stood in order to reach the upper surfaces of the naturally formed chambers and corridors. To illuminate their work, the painters used stone lamps filled with marrow or fat, perhaps with a wick of moss. Despite the difficulty of making the tools and pigments, modern attempts at replicating the techniques of Paleolithic painting have demonstrated that skilled workers could cover large surfaces with images in less than a day.

ART AND SOCIETY
Why Is There Art in Paleolithic Caves?

Ever since the discovery of the first cave paintings at Altamira in north-western Spain in 1879, scholars have wondered why the hunters of the Old Stone Age decided to cover the walls of dark caverns with animal images (FIGS. 1-3 to 1-6). Researchers have proposed various theories, including that the animals were mere decoration, but this explanation cannot account for the narrow range of subjects or the inaccessibility of many of the representations. In fact, the remote locations of many of the images, and indications that the caves were in use for centuries, are precisely why many experts have suggested that prehistoric peoples attributed magical properties to the images they painted and sculpted. According to this argument, by confining animals to the surfaces of their cave walls, Paleolithic communities believed they were bringing the beasts under their control. Some scholars have even hypothesized that rituals or dances were performed in front of the images and that these rites served to improve hunters' luck in tracking and killing the animals. Others have speculated that the animal representations may have served as teaching tools to instruct new hunters about the character of the various species they would encounter or even that the images served as targets for spears.

In contrast, some prehistorians have argued that the magical purpose of the paintings and reliefs was not to facilitate the *destruction* of animal species. Instead, they believe that the first painters and sculptors created animal images to assure the *survival* of the herds on which Paleolithic peoples depended for their food supply and for their clothing. A central problem for both the hunting-magic and food-creation theories is that the animals that were the staple foods of Old Stone Age diets did not include the species most frequently portrayed.

Other researchers have sought to reconstruct an elaborate mythology based on the cave paintings and sculptures, suggesting that Paleolithic humans believed they had animal ancestors. Still others have equated certain species with men and others with women and postulated various meanings for the abstract signs that sometimes accompany the images.

Almost all of these theories have been discredited over time, and most prehistorians admit that the intent of these representations is unknown. In fact, a single explanation for all Paleolithic animal images, even ones similar in subject, style, and *composition* (how the motifs are arranged on the surface), is unlikely to apply universally. The meaning of these works remains an unsolved mystery—and always will, because before the invention of writing, no contemporaneous explanations could be recorded.

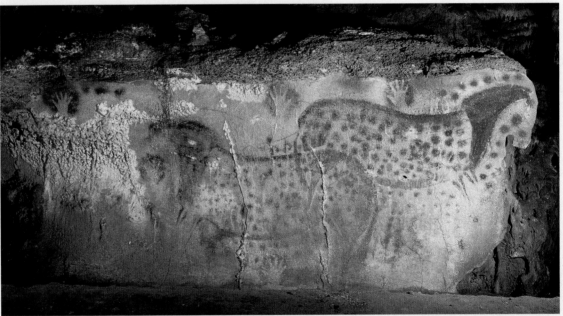

1-4 Spotted horses and negative hand imprints, wall painting in the cave at Pech-Merle, France, ca. 23,000–22,000 BCE. 11' 2" long.

Many Paleolithic paintings include abstract signs and handprints. Some scholars think that the Pech-Merle painted hands are "signatures" of cult or community members or, less likely, of individual painters.

PECH-MERLE A *mural* (wall) painting (FIG. 1-4) in a cave at Pech-Merle, France, provides some insight into the reason Stone Age artists chose certain subjects for specific locations. The horse at the right may have been inspired by the rock formation in the wall surface resembling a horse's head and neck. Like the clay bison at Le Tuc d'Audoubert, the Pech-Merle horses are in strict profile. Here, however, painted hands accompany them. These and the majority of painted hands at other sites are "negative"—that is, the painter placed one hand against the wall and then brushed or blew or spat pigment around it. Occasionally, the painter dipped a hand in the pigment and then pressed it against the wall, leaving a "positive" imprint. These handprints must have had a purpose. Some scholars

have considered them "signatures" of cult or community members or, less likely, of individual painters. Checks, dots, squares, and other abstract signs appear near the painted animals in other Paleolithic caves. In fact, the "spotted horses" of Pech-Merle may not have spots. The "spots" also surround the horses and may be stones or signs. Several observers think that these various signs are a primitive form of writing, but like the hands—and everything else in Paleolithic art—their meaning is unknown (see "Why Is There Art in Paleolithic Caves?" above).

LASCAUX The best-known Paleolithic cave is that at Lascaux, near Montignac, France, which features a large circular gallery called

1 ft.

1-5 Left wall of the Hall of the Bulls in the cave at Lascaux, France, ca. 16,000–14,000 BCE. Largest bull 11' 6" long.

The purpose and meaning of Paleolithic cave paintings are unknown, but it is clear that the painters' sole concern was representing the animals, not locating them in a specific place or on a common ground line.

the Hall of the Bulls (FIG. 1-5). Not all of the painted animals are bulls, despite the modern nickname. Some of the animals, such as the great bull at the right in FIG. 1-5, were represented using outline alone, but others are colored silhouettes. These are the two basic approaches to drawing and painting in the history of art. Here, they appear side by side, suggesting that different artists painted the animals at various times. The impression that a modern viewer gets of a rapidly moving herd is therefore almost certainly false. The "herd" consists of several different species of animals of disparate sizes moving in different directions. Although most share a common ground line, some—for example, those in the upper right corner of FIG. 1-5—seem to float above the viewer's head, like clouds in the sky. The painting has no setting, no background, no indication of place. The Paleolithic painter's sole concern was representing the animals, not locating them in a specific place.

Another feature of the Lascaux paintings deserves attention. The bulls show a convention of representing horns that art historians call *twisted perspective*, or *composite view*, because viewers see the heads in profile but the horns from the front. Thus the painter's approach is not consistently optical (seen from a fixed viewpoint). Rather, the approach is descriptive of the fact that cattle have two horns. Two horns are part of the concept "bull." In strict profile, only one horn would be visible, but painting the animal in that way would be an incomplete picture of it.

Perhaps the most perplexing painting in any Paleolithic cave is the mural (FIG. 1-6) deep in the well shaft at Lascaux, where man (as opposed to woman) makes one of his earliest appearances in the history of art. At the left, and moving to the left, is a rhinoceros. Beneath its tail are two rows of three dots of uncertain significance. At the right is a bison, with less realistic proportions, probably the work of someone else. The second painter nonetheless successfully suggested the bristling rage of the animal, whose bowels hang from its belly in a heavy coil. Between the two beasts is a bird-faced (masked?) man with outstretched arms and hands having only four fingers. The painter depicted the man with far less care and detail than either animal, but made the hunter's gender explicit by the prominent penis. The position of the man is ambiguous. Is he wounded or dead or merely tilted back and unharmed? Do the staff(?) with

1 ft.

1-6 Rhinoceros, wounded man, and disemboweled bison, painting in the well of the cave at Lascaux, France, ca. 16,000–14,000 BCE. Bison 3' 4½" long.

If these paintings of two animals and a bird-faced (masked?) man, deep in a well shaft in the Lascaux cave, depict a hunting scene, they constitute the earliest example of narrative art ever discovered.

the bird on top and the spear belong to him? Is it he or the rhinoceros that gravely wounded the bison—or neither? Which animal, if either, has knocked the man down, if indeed he is on the ground? Are these three images related at all? Modern viewers can be sure of nothing, but if the painter(s) placed the figures beside each other to tell a story, this is evidence for the creation of narrative compositions involving humans and animals at a much earlier date than anyone had imagined only a few generations ago. Yet it is important to remember that even if the painter(s) intended to tell a story, very few people would have been able to "read" it. The mural, in a deep shaft, is very difficult to reach and could have been viewed only in flickering lamplight. Like all Paleolithic art, the scene in the Lascaux well shaft is a puzzle.

Neolithic Age

Around 9000 BCE, the ice covering much of northern Europe during the Paleolithic period melted as the climate warmed. The sea level rose more than 300 feet, separating England from continental Europe, and Spain from Africa. The Paleolithic gave way to a transitional period, the *Mesolithic* (Middle Stone Age). Then, for several thousand years at different times in different parts of the globe, a great new age, the *Neolithic* (New Stone Age), dawned. Humans began to domesticate plants and animals and settle in fixed abodes. Their food supply assured, many groups changed from hunters to herders to farmers and finally to townspeople. Wandering hunters settled down to organized community living in villages surrounded by cultivated fields. In addition to agriculture, these Neolithic societies originated weaving, metalworking, pottery, and counting and recording with tokens, and constructed religious shrines as well as homes.

This traditional sequence may recently have been overturned, however, by excavations at Göbekli Tepe in southeastern Turkey. There, German archaeologists discovered that prehistoric hunter-gatherers had built stone temples with animal reliefs on T-shaped *pillars* around 9000 BCE, long before sedentary farmers established permanent village communities at sites such as Çatal Höyük.

timber frames, varied in size but repeated the same basic plan. The rooms have plastered and painted floors and walls, with platforms along the walls that served as sites for sleeping, working, and eating. The living buried the dead beneath the floors.

The excavators have found many rooms decorated with mural paintings and plaster reliefs. These "shrines" had an uncertain function, but their number indicates that the rooms played an important role in the life of the Neolithic settlement. On the wall of one room, archaeologists discovered a painted representation of a deer hunt (FIG. 1-7). The mural is worlds apart from the cave paintings that the hunters of the Paleolithic period produced. Perhaps what is most strikingly new about the Çatal Höyük painting and similar Neolithic examples is the regular appearance of the human figure—not only singly but also in large, coherent groups with a wide variety of poses, subjects, and settings. As noted earlier, humans rarely figured in Paleolithic paintings, and pictorial narratives are almost unknown. Even the Lascaux "hunting scene" (FIG. 1-6) is doubtful as a narrative. In Neolithic art, scenes with humans dominating animals are central subjects.

In the Çatal Höyük hunt, the group of hunters—and no one doubts that it is, indeed, an organized hunting party, not a series of individual figures—is a rhythmic repetition of basic shapes, but the painter took care to distinguish important descriptive details (bows, arrows, and garments), and the heads have clearly defined noses, mouths, chins, and hair. The Neolithic painter placed all the heads in profile for the same reason Paleolithic painters universally chose the profile view for representations of animals. Only the side view of the human head shows all its shapes clearly. However, at Çatal Höyük the painter presented the torsos from the front—again, the most informative viewpoint—whereas the profile view was the choice for the legs and arms. This composite view of the human body is as artificial as the twisted horns of the Lascaux bulls (FIG. 1-5) because the human body cannot make an abrupt 90-degree shift at the hips. But it well describes the parts of a human body, as opposed to how a body appears from a particular viewpoint.

The technique of painting also changed dramatically from the Paleolithic to the Neolithic Age. The Çatal Höyük painters used

ÇATAL HÖYÜK The Neolithic settlement at Çatal Höyük on the central Anatolian plateau flourished between 6500 and 5700 BCE and was one of the world's first experiments in urban living. The regularity of the town's plan suggests that the inhabitants built the settlement to some predetermined scheme. The houses, constructed of mud brick strengthened by sturdy

1-7 Deer hunt, detail of a wall painting from level III, Çatal Höyük, Turkey, ca. 5750 BCE. Museum of Anatolian Civilization, Ankara.

This Neolithic painter depicted human figures as composites of frontal and profile views, the most descriptive picture of the shape of the human body. This format would become the rule for millennia.

1-8 Human figure, from Ain Ghazal, Jordan, ca. 6500 BCE. Plaster, painted and inlaid with cowrie shell and bitumen, 3' 5$\frac{3}{8}$" high. Musée du Louvre, Paris.

At Ain Ghazal, archaeologists have uncovered dozens of large white plaster Neolithic statuettes with details added in paint and shell. They mark the beginning of large-scale sculpture in the history of art.

1 ft.

brushes to apply their pigments to a background of dry white plaster. The careful preparation of the wall surface is in striking contrast to the direct application of pigment to the irregularly shaped walls and ceilings of Old Stone Age caves.

AIN GHAZAL A second well-excavated Neolithic settlement is Ain Ghazal, near Amman, Jordan. Occupied from around 7200 to 5000 BCE, Ain Ghazal has produced striking finds, including two caches containing three dozen plaster statuettes (FIG. 1-8) datable to around

6500 BCE. The sculptures, which appear to have been ritually buried, are white plaster built up over a core of reeds and twine, with black bitumen, a tarlike substance, for the pupils of the eyes. Some of the figures have painted clothing. Only rarely did the sculptors indicate the gender of the figures. Whatever their purpose, the size (as much as 3 feet tall) and sophisticated technique of the Ain Ghazal statuettes sharply differentiate the Neolithic figurines from tiny, faceless Paleolithic sculptures such as the *Venus of Willendorf* (FIG. 1-2). The Ain Ghazal statues mark the beginning of large-scale sculpture in the ancient world.

STONEHENGE In western Europe, where Paleolithic paintings and sculptures abound, no comparably developed towns of the time of Çatal Höyük or Ain Ghazal have been found. However, in succeeding millennia, perhaps as early as 4000 BCE, the local Neolithic populations in several areas developed a monumental architecture employing massive rough-cut stones. The very dimensions of the stones, some as tall as 24 feet and weighing as much as 50 tons, have prompted historians to call them *megaliths* ("great stones") and to designate the culture that produced them *megalithic*.

Although megalithic monuments are plentiful throughout Europe, the arrangement of huge stones in a circle (called a *henge*), often surrounded by a ditch, is almost entirely limited to Britain. The most imposing example is Stonehenge (FIG. 1-9) near Salisbury, a complex of rough-cut sarsen (a form of sandstone) stones and smaller "bluestones" (various volcanic rocks) built in several stages over hundreds of years. In its final form, Stonehenge consists of an outermost ring, 97 feet in diameter, of 24-foot-tall sarsen *monoliths* (one-piece pillars) supporting *lintels* (horizontal stone blocks used to span an opening). This simple *post-and-lintel system* of construction is still in use today. Inside is a ring of bluestones, which in turn encircles a horseshoe (open end facing east) of *trilithons* (three-stone constructions)—five lintel-topped pairs of the largest sarsens, each weighing 45 to 50 tons. Standing apart and to the east (outside the aerial view) is the "heel-stone," which, for a person looking outward from the center of the complex, would have marked the

1-9 Aerial view of Stonehenge (looking northwest), Salisbury Plain, Wiltshire, England, ca. 2550–1600 BCE.

One of the earliest examples of monumental stone architecture in Neolithic Europe, the circles of 24-foot-tall trilithons at Stonehenge probably functioned as an astronomical observatory and solar calendar.

point where the sun rose at the summer solstice. Perhaps originally a burial site, Stonehenge in its latest phase seems to have been a kind of astronomical observatory and a remarkably accurate solar calendar that may also have served as a center of healing, attracting the sick and dying from throughout the region. Whatever function Stonehenge served in Neolithic Britain, it is an enduring testament to the rapidly developing intellectual powers of humans as well as to their capacity for heroic physical effort.

ANCIENT MESOPOTAMIA AND PERSIA

The fundamental change in human society from the dangerous and uncertain life of the hunter and gatherer to the more predictable and stable life of the farmer and herder first occurred in Mesopotamia, the land mass that forms a huge "fertile crescent" from the mountainous border between Turkey and Syria through Iraq to Iran's Zagros Mountain range (MAP 1-2). There, in present-day southern Iraq, the world's first great civilization—Sumer (FIG. 1-1)—arose in the valley between the Tigris and Euphrates Rivers.

Sumer

Ancient Sumer was not a unified nation. Rather, it comprised a dozen or so independent city-states under the protection of different Mesopotamian deities. The Sumerian rulers were the gods' representatives on earth and the stewards of their earthly treasure. The rulers and priests directed all communal activities, including canal construction, crop collection, and food distribution. Because the Sumerians developed agriculture to such an extent that only a portion of the population had to produce food, some members of the community were free to specialize in other activities, including manufacturing, trade, and administration. Specialization of labor is the hallmark of the first complex urban societies. In the Sumerian city-states of the fourth millennium BCE, activities that once had been individually initiated became institutionalized for the first time. The community, whether ruled by a single person or a council chosen from among the leading families, assumed functions such as protection from enemy attack and the whims of nature. The city-state was one of the many Sumerian inventions.

MAP 1-2 **Ancient Mesopotamia and Persia.**

WHITE TEMPLE, URUK The layout of Sumerian cities reflected the central role of the gods in daily life. The main temple to each state's chief god formed the city's nucleus. In fact, the temple complex was a kind of city within a city, where priests and scribes carried on official administrative and commercial business as well as oversaw all religious functions. The outstanding preserved example of early Sumerian temple architecture is the 5,000-year-old White Temple (FIG. 1-10) at Uruk, a city with a population of about 40,000 that was the home of the legendary Gilgamesh. Sumerian builders did not have access to stone quarries and instead formed mud bricks for the superstructures of their temples and other buildings. Mud brick is a durable building material, but unlike stone, it deteriorates with exposure to water. The Sumerians nonetheless erected towering works, such as the Uruk temple, several centuries before the Egyptians built their stone pyramids (FIGS. 1-25 to 1-27). This says a

1-10 **White Temple, Uruk (modern Warka), Iraq, ca. 3200–3000 BCE.**

Using only mud bricks, the Sumerians erected temples on lofty platforms several centuries before the Egyptians built stone pyramids. This temple was probably dedicated to Anu, the sky god.

1-11 Ziggurat (looking southwest), Ur (modern Tell Muqayyar), Iraq, ca. 2100 BCE.

The 50-foot-tall Ur ziggurat is one of the largest in Mesopotamia. It has three (restored) ramplike stairways of 100 steps each that originally ended at a gateway to a brick temple, which does not survive.

great deal about the Sumerians' desire to provide grandiose settings for the worship of their deities.

The Uruk temple (whose whitewashed walls suggested its modern nickname) stands atop a platform 40 feet above street level. A stairway leads to the temple at the top. As in other Sumerian temples, the corners of the White Temple are oriented to the cardinal points of the compass. The building, probably dedicated to Anu, the sky god, is of modest proportions (61 by 16 feet). By design, Sumerian temples did not accommodate large throngs of worshipers but only a select few, the priests and perhaps the leading community members. The White Temple had several chambers. The central hall, or *cella,* was the divinity's room and housed a stepped altar. The Sumerians referred to their temples as "waiting rooms," a reflection of their belief that the deity would descend from the heavens to appear before the priests in the cella. It is unclear whether the Uruk temple had a roof.

ZIGGURAT, UR Eroded temples on mud-brick platforms still dominate most of the ruined cities of Sumer. The best preserved is the *ziggurat* (tiered Mesopotamian temple platform) at Ur (FIG. 1-11), the home of the biblical Abraham. Built about a millennium after Uruk's White Temple and much grander, the Ur ziggurat is a solid mass of mud brick 50 feet high, faced with baked bricks laid in bitumen. Three (restored) ramplike stairways of a hundred steps each converge on a tower-flanked gateway. From there another flight of steps (which has not been rebuilt) probably led to the temple that once crowned the ziggurat.

The loftiness of the Sumerian temple platforms made a profound impression on the peoples of ancient Mesopotamia. The tallest, at Babylon, was about 270 feet high. Known to the Hebrews as the Tower of Babel, it became the centerpiece of a cautionary biblical tale (Gen. 11:1–9) about arrogance. Humankind's desire to build a tower to Heaven angered God. The Lord caused the workers to speak different languages, preventing them from communicating with one another and bringing construction of the ziggurat to a halt.

ESHNUNNA STATUETTES The *Warka Vase* (FIG. 1-1), discussed in the introduction to this chapter, provides priceless information about the rituals that took place in Sumerian temples. Further insight into Sumerian religion comes from a cache of gypsum statuettes inlaid with shell and black limestone found in a temple at Eshnunna (modern Tell Asmar). The two largest figures (FIG. 1-12), like all the others, represent mortals rather than deities. They hold the small beakers

1-12 Statuettes of two worshipers, from the Square Temple at Eshnunna (modern Tell Asmar), Iraq, ca. 2700 BCE. Gypsum, shell, and black limestone. Man 2' $4\frac{1}{4}$" high, woman 1' $11\frac{1}{4}$" high. National Museum of Iraq, Baghdad.

The oversized eyes probably symbolize the perpetual wakefulness of these substitute worshipers offering prayers to the deity. The beakers that the figures hold were used to pour libations in honor of the gods.

that the Sumerians used for *libations* (ritual pouring of liquid) in honor of the gods. The men wear belts and fringed skirts. Most have beards and shoulder-length hair. The women wear long robes, with the right shoulder bare. Similar figurines from other sites bear inscriptions with the name of the donor and the god or even specific prayers to the deity on the owner's behalf. With their heads tilted upward, the figures wait in the Sumerian "waiting room" for the divinity to appear. Most striking is the disproportionate relationship between the inlaid oversized eyes and the tiny hands. Scholars have explained the exaggeration of the eye size in various ways. Because the purpose of these votive figures was to offer constant prayers to the gods on their donors' behalf, the open-eyed stares most likely symbolize the eternal wakefulness necessary to fulfill their duty.

STANDARD OF UR Agriculture, trade, and the spoils of war brought considerable wealth to some of the city-states of ancient Sumer. Nowhere is this clearer than in the so-called Royal Cemetery at Ur. Archaeologists debate whether those buried in this cemetery were true kings and queens or simply aristocrats, priests, and priestesses, but their tombs were regal in character. They contained gold helmets and daggers with handles of lapis lazuli (a rich azure-blue stone imported from Afghanistan), gold beakers and bowls, jewelry

1-13 War side of the *Standard of Ur,* from tomb 779, Royal Cemetery, Ur (modern Tell Muqayyar), Iraq, ca. 2600–2400 BCE. Wood, lapis lazuli, shell, and red limestone, 8" × 1' 7". British Museum, London.

In this early example of historical narrative, a Sumerian artist depicted a battlefield victory in three registers, reading from bottom to top. The size of the figures varies with their importance in society.

1-14 Peace side of the *Standard of Ur,* from tomb 779, Royal Cemetery, Ur (modern Tell Muqayyar), Iraq, ca. 2600–2400 BCE. Wood, lapis lazuli, shell, and red limestone, 8" × 1' 7". British Museum, London.

Entertaining the Sumerian nobility at this banquet are a harp player and a singer. The artist represented all of the standing and seated humans in composite views and all the animals in strict profile.

of gold and lapis, musical instruments, chariots, and other luxurious items. Not the costliest object found in the "royal" graves, but the most significant for the history of art, is the so-called *Standard of Ur* (FIGS. 1-13 and 1-14), the sloping sides of which are inlaid with shell, lapis lazuli, and red limestone. The excavator who discovered this box-shaped object thought the Sumerians mounted it on a pole as a kind of military standard, hence its nickname. The "standard" may have been the sound box of a musical instrument.

Art historians usually refer to the two long sides of the box as the "war side" (FIG. 1-13) and "peace side" (FIG. 1-14). On the war side, four ass-drawn four-wheeled war chariots crush enemies, whose bodies appear on the ground in front of and beneath the animals. Above, foot soldiers gather up and lead away captured foes. In the uppermost register, soldiers present bound captives (whom the victors have stripped naked to degrade them) to a kinglike figure, who has stepped out of his chariot. His central place in the composition and his greater stature (his head breaks through the border at the top) set him apart from all the other figures.

In the lowest band on the peace side, men carry provisions, possibly war booty, on their backs. Above, attendants transport animals, perhaps also spoils of war, and fish for the great banquet depicted in the uppermost register. There, seated dignitaries and a larger-than-life personage (third from the left; probably a king, whose head interrupts the upper border) attend a feast. A harp player and a long-haired bare-chested singer (a court *eunuch*) entertain the group. Some art historians have interpreted the scene as a celebration after the victory in warfare represented on the other side of the box. But the two sides may be independent narratives illustrating the two principal roles of a Sumerian ruler—the mighty warrior who defeats enemies of his city-state and the chief administrator who, with the blessing of the gods, assures the bountifulness of the land in peacetime (compare FIG. 1-1). The absence of an inscription prevents connecting the scenes with a specific event or person, but, like the *Warka Vase,* the *Standard of Ur* undoubtedly is another early example of historical narrative, even if only of a generic kind.

Akkad

In 2334 BCE, the loosely linked group of cities known as Sumer came under the domination of a great ruler, Sargon of Akkad (r. 2332–2279 BCE). Archaeologists have yet to locate Akkad, but the city was in the vicinity of Babylon. Under Sargon (whose name means "true king") and his successors, the Akkadians introduced a new concept of royal power based on unswerving loyalty to the king rather than to the city-state. Naram-Sin (r. 2254–2218 BCE), Sargon's grandson, regarded the governors of his cities as mere royal servants, and called himself King of the Four Quarters—in effect, ruler of the earth, akin to a god.

AKKADIAN PORTRAITURE A magnificent copper head (FIG. 1-15) portraying an Akkadian king embodies this new concept of absolute monarchy. The head is all that survives of a statue knocked over in antiquity, perhaps during the sack of Nineveh in 612 BCE. To make a political statement, the enemy forces not only toppled the Akkadian royal portrait but gouged out the eyes (once inlaid with precious or semiprecious stones), broke off the lower part of the beard, and slashed the ears. Nonetheless, the king's majestic serenity, dignity, and authority are evident. So, too, is the masterful way the sculptor balanced *naturalism* and *abstract* patterning. The artist carefully observed and recorded the distinctive profile of the king's nose and

long, curly beard, and brilliantly communicated the differing textures of flesh and hair, even the contrasting textures of the mustache, beard, and braided hair on the top of the head. The coiffure's triangles, lozenges, and overlapping disks of hair and the great arching eyebrows that give such character to the portrait reveal that the artist was also sensitive to formal pattern. No less remarkable is the fact that this is the oldest extant life-size, hollow-cast metal sculpture (see "Hollow-Casting Life-Size Bronze Statues," page 64). The head demonstrates the sculptor's skill in casting and polishing copper and in engraving the details.

NARAM-SIN The godlike sovereignty the kings of Akkad claimed is also evident in the victory stele that Naram-Sin set up at Sippar. A *stele* is a carved stone slab erected to commemorate a historical event or, in some other cultures, to mark a grave (FIG. 2-45). Naram-Sin's

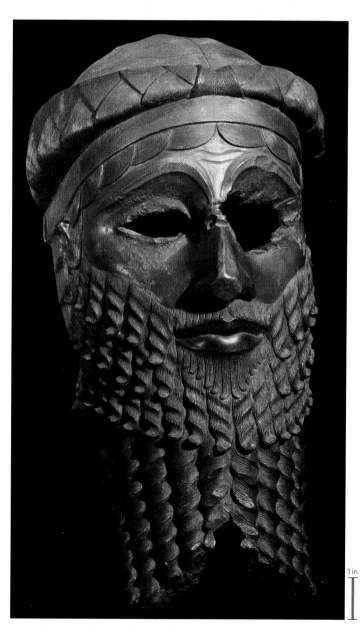

1 in.

1-15 Head of an Akkadian ruler, from Nineveh (modern Kuyunjik), Iraq, ca. 2250–2200 BCE. Copper, 1' 2$\frac{3}{8}$" high. National Museum of Iraq, Baghdad.

The sculptor of this oldest known life-size hollow-cast head captured the distinctive features of the ruler while also displaying a keen sense of abstract pattern. Vandals defaced the head in antiquity.

1 ft.

1-16 Victory stele of Naram-Sin, set up at Sippar, Iraq, found at Susa, Iran, ca. 2254–2218 BCE. Pink sandstone, 6′ 7″ high. Musée du Louvre, Paris.

To commemorate his conquest of the Lullubi, Naram-Sin set up this stele showing him leading his army up a mountain. The sculptor staggered the figures, abandoning the traditional register format.

stele (FIG. 1-16) commemorates his defeat of the Lullubi, a people of the Iranian mountains to the east. The sculptor depicted the grandson of Sargon leading his army up the slopes of a wooded mountain. His routed enemies fall, flee, die, or beg for mercy. The king stands alone, far taller than his men, treading on the bodies of two of the fallen Lullubi. He wears the horned helmet signifying divinity—the first time a king appears as a god in Mesopotamian art. At least three favorable stars (the stele is damaged at the top) shine on his triumph.

By storming the mountain, Naram-Sin seems also to be scaling the ladder to the heavens, the same idea that lies behind Mesopotamian ziggurats. His troops march up the slope behind him in orderly files, suggesting the discipline and organization of the king's forces. In contrast, the Lullubi are in disarray, depicted in a great variety of postures. One falls headlong down the mountainside. The Akkadian artist adhered to older conventions in many details, especially by portraying the king and his soldiers in composite views and by placing a frontal two-horned helmet on Naram-Sin's profile

1 ft.

1-17 Hammurabi and Shamash, detail of the law stele of Hammurabi, set up at Babylon, Iraq, found at Susa, Iran, ca. 1780 BCE. Basalt, stele 7′ 4″ high, detail 2′ high. Musée du Louvre, Paris.

Crowning Hammurabi's law stele is a relief of the king and the flame-shouldered sun god Shamash, one of the first examples of an artist representing a figure or object from an angle (foreshortening).

head. But the sculptor showed daring innovation in creating a *landscape* setting for the story and placing the figures on staggered levels. This was a bold rejection of the millennium-old compositional formula of telling a story in a series of horizontal registers.

Babylon

Around 2150 BCE, a mountain people, the Gutians, brought an end to Akkadian power. The cities of Sumer, however, soon united in response to the alien presence, drove the Gutians out of Mesopotamia, and established a Neo-Sumerian state ruled by the kings of Ur. Historians call this period the Third Dynasty of Ur. It was then that the Ur ziggurat (FIG. 1-11) was constructed, but Sumer's resurgence was short lived. The last of the Ur kings fell at the hands of the Elamites, who ruled the territory east of the Tigris River. In the following two centuries, the traditional Mesopotamian political pattern of several independent city-states existing side by side reemerged and persisted until one of those cities, Babylon, succeeded in establishing a centralized government that ruled southern Mesopotamia in the 18th and 17th centuries BCE.

HAMMURABI Babylon's most powerful king was Hammurabi (r. 1792–1750 BCE). Famous in his own time for his conquests, he is best known today for his comprehensive laws, which prescribed penalties for everything from adultery and murder to the cutting down of a neighbor's trees. Hammurabi's laws are inscribed on a tall black-basalt stele (FIG. 1-16A ⬈) discovered at Susa in Iran. At the top (FIG. 1-17), Hammurabi stands before Shamash, the flame-shouldered sun god. The king raises his hand in respect. The god extends to Hammurabi the rod and ring that symbolize authority. The symbols are builders' tools—measuring rods and coiled rope.

How Many Legs Does a Lamassu Have?

Guarding the gate to Sargon II's palace at Dur Sharrukin and many of the other Assyrian royal complexes were colossal limestone monsters (FIG. 1-18), which the Assyrians probably called *lamassu*. These winged, man-headed bulls (or lions in some instances) served to ward off the king's enemies.

The task of moving and installing these immense stone sculptures was so difficult that several reliefs in the palace of Sargon's successor, Sennacherib (r. 705–681 BCE), celebrate the feat, showing scores of men dragging lamassu figures with the aid of ropes and sledges.

The two lamassu guarding the gateway of Sargon's Dur Sharrukin palace are nearly 14 feet tall. But transporting these mammoth blocks from the quarry to the building site was not the only problem the Assyrian sculptors had to confront. The artists also had to find a satisfactory way to represent a composite beast no one had ever seen, and they had to make the monster's unfamiliar form intelligible from every angle. They came up with a solution that may seem strange to modern eyes, but one consistent with the pictorial conventions of the age and perfectly suited to the problem.

The Assyrian lamassu sculptures are partly in the round, but the sculptors nonetheless conceived them as high reliefs on adjacent sides of a corner. They combine the front view of the animal at rest with the side view of it in motion. Seeking to present a complete picture of the lamassu from both the front and the side, the sculptors of all the extant Assyrian guardian statues gave each of the monsters five legs—two seen from the front, four seen from the side.

The Assyrian lamassu sculptures, therefore, are yet another case of early artists providing a *conceptual representation* of an animal or person and all its important parts, as opposed to an *optical representation* of the composite monster as it would stand in the real, versus the pictorial, world.

1-18 Lamassu (man-headed winged bull), from the citadel of Sargon II, Dur Sharrukin (modern Khorsabad), Iraq, ca. 720–705 BCE. Limestone, 13' 10" high. Musée du Louvre, Paris.

Ancient sculptors insisted on showing complete views of animals. This four-legged composite monster that guarded an Assyrian palace has five legs—two when seen from the front and four in profile view.

They connote Hammurabi's capacity to build the social order and to measure people's lives—that is, to render judgments and enforce laws. The sculptor depicted Shamash in the familiar convention of combined front and side views, but with two important exceptions. The god's great headdress with its four pairs of horns is in true profile so that only four, not all eight, of the horns are visible. Also, the artist seems to have tentatively explored the notion of *foreshortening*—a means of suggesting depth by representing a figure or object at an angle, instead of frontally or in profile. Shamash's beard is a series of diagonal rather than horizontal lines, suggesting its recession from the picture plane. The sculptor also depicted the god's throne at an angle, further enhancing the illusion of spatial recession. Innovations such as these and the bold abandonment of the register format in favor of a tiered landscape on the Naram-Sin stele were exceptional in early eras of the history of art. These occasional departures from conventional representational modes testify to the creativity of Mesopotamian artists, but they did not displace the age-old formulas.

Assyria

The Babylonian Empire toppled in the face of an onslaught by the Hittites, an Anatolian people who conquered and sacked Babylon around 1595 BCE. They then retired to their homeland, leaving Babylon in the hands of the Kassites. By around 900 BCE, however, the Assyrians had overtaken Mesopotamia. The new conquerors took their name from Assur, the city in northern Iraq dedicated to the god Ashur. At the height of their power, the Assyrians ruled an empire that extended from the Tigris to the Nile and from the Persian Gulf to Asia Minor.

DUR SHARRUKIN The royal citadel of Sargon II (r. 721–705 BCE) at Dur Sharrukin is the most completely excavated of the many Assyrian palaces. The citadel measured about a square mile in area and included a great ziggurat and six sanctuaries for six different gods. The palace, elevated on a mound 50 feet high, covered some 25 acres and had more than 200 courtyards and timber-roofed rooms. The ambitious layout reveals the confidence of the Assyrian kings in their all-conquering might, but its strong defensive walls and gateway guarded by monstrous beasts (see "How Many Legs Does a Lamassu Have?" above, and FIG. 1-18) also reflect a society ever fearful of attack during a period of almost constant warfare.

KALHU Sheathing the mud-brick walls of the Assyrian palaces were extensive series of painted gypsum reliefs exalting royal power and piety. The sculptures record official ceremonies, religious rituals, battlefield victories, and the slaying of wild animals. (The Assyrians,

1-19 Assyrian archers pursuing enemies, relief from the northwest palace of Ashurnasirpal II, Kalhu (modern Nimrud), Iraq, ca. 875–860 BCE. Gypsum, 2' 10$\frac{5}{8}$" high. British Museum, London.

Extensive reliefs exalting the king and recounting his great deeds adorned the walls of Assyrian palaces. This one depicts Ashurnasirpal II's archers driving the enemy into the Euphrates River.

like many other societies before and after, regarded prowess in hunting as a manly virtue on a par with success in warfare.) One of the most extensive cycles of Assyrian narrative reliefs comes from the northwest palace of Ashurnasirpal II (r. 883–859 BCE) at Kalhu.

The relief illustrated here (FIG. 1-19) depicts an episode in an 878 BCE battle during which the Assyrians drove the enemy's forces into the Euphrates River. Two Assyrian archers shoot arrows at three fleeing foes. One swims with an arrow in his back. The other two attempt to float to safety by inflating animal skins. Their destination is a fort where their compatriots await them. The artist showed the fort as if it were in the middle of the river, but it was, of course, on land, perhaps at some distance from the battle. Ancient artists often compressed distances and enlarged the human actors so that they would stand out from their environment (compare FIG. 1-16). The Assyrian sculptor also combined different viewpoints in the same composition. The spectator views the river from above, and the men, trees, and fort from the side. The artist also made other adjustments for clarity. The archers' bowstrings are in front of their bodies but behind their heads in order not to hide their faces. (The men will snare their heads in their bows when they launch their arrows.) All these liberties with optical reality, however, result in a vivid and easily legible narrative, which was the sculptor's primary goal.

Neo-Babylonia

The Assyrian Empire was never very secure, and in the mid-seventh century BCE it began to disintegrate, eventually collapsing from the simultaneous onslaught of the Medes from the east and the resurgent Babylonians from the south. For almost a century beginning in 612 BCE, Neo-Babylonian kings held sway over the former Assyrian Empire.

ISHTAR GATE The most renowned Neo-Babylonian king was Nebuchadnezzar II (r. 604–562 BCE), who restored Babylon to its rank as one of the great cities of antiquity. The centerpiece of Nebuchadnezzar's vast mud-brick city was an enormous ziggurat—the

Tower of Babel—dedicated to Marduk, the chief god of the Babylonians. Throughout the city, the most important monuments were faced with dazzling blue *glazed* bricks. Some of the buildings, such as the Ishtar Gate (FIG. 1-20), with its imposing *arcuated* (arch-shaped) opening flanked by towers, featured glazed bricks with molded reliefs of animals, real and imaginary. The Babylonian artists molded and glazed each brick separately, then set them in proper sequence on the wall. On the Ishtar Gate, profile figures of Marduk's dragon and Adad's bull alternate. (Ishtar was the Babylonian equivalent of Inanna; Adad was the Babylonian god of storms.) Lining the processional way leading up to the gate were reliefs of Ishtar's sacred lion, glazed in yellow, brown, and red against a blue background.

Achaemenid Persia

Although Nebuchadnezzar—the "king of kings" in the book of Daniel (2:37)—had boasted that he "caused a mighty wall to circumscribe Babylon . . . so that the enemy who would do evil would not threaten," Cyrus of Persia (r. 559–529 BCE) captured the city in 539 BCE. Cyrus was the founder of the Achaemenid dynasty and traced his ancestry back to a mythical King Achaemenes. Babylon was but one of the Persians' conquests. Egypt fell to them in 525 BCE, and by 480 BCE the Persian Empire was the largest the world had yet known, extending from the Indus River in South Asia to the Danube River in northeastern Europe. If the Greeks had not turned back the Persians in 479 BCE, the Achaemenids would have taken control of southeastern Europe as well (see page 63). The Achaemenid line ended with the death of Darius III in 330 BCE, after his defeat at the hands of Alexander the Great (FIG. 2-50).

PERSEPOLIS The most important source of knowledge about Persian art and architecture is the ceremonial and administrative complex within the citadel at Persepolis (FIG. 1-21), which the successors of Cyrus, Darius I (r. 522–486 BCE) and Xerxes (r. 486–465 BCE), built between 521 and 465 BCE. Situated on a high plateau, the

Babylon under King Nebuchadnezzar II was one of the greatest cities of the ancient world. Its gigantic arcuated Ishtar Gate featured glazed-brick reliefs of Marduk's dragon and Adad's bull.

heavily fortified complex of royal buildings stood on a wide platform overlooking the plain. Alexander the Great razed the site in a gesture symbolizing the destruction of Persian imperial power. Even in ruins, the Persepolis citadel is impressive. The approach to the citadel led through a monumental gateway called the Gate of All Lands, a reference to the harmony among the peoples of the vast Persian Empire. Assyrian-inspired colossal man-headed winged bulls flanked the great entrance. Broad ceremonial stairways provided access to the platform and the huge royal audience hall, or

apadana, in which 10,000 guests could stand at one time amid 36 colossal *columns* with 57-foot *shafts* topped by sculpted animals.

The reliefs decorating the walls of the terrace and staircases leading to the apadana represent processions of royal guards, Persian nobles and dignitaries, and representatives from 23 subject nations bringing tribute to the king. Every emissary wears a characteristic costume and carries a typical regional gift for the conqueror. Traces of paint prove that the reliefs were brightly colored. Although Assyrian palace reliefs may have inspired those at Persepolis, the

1-21 Aerial view of Persepolis (looking west with the apadana in the background), Iran, ca. 521–465 BCE.

The Persian capital at Persepolis boasted a grandiose column-filled royal audience hall capable of housing 10,000 guests. The terraces featured reliefs of subject nations bringing tribute to the king.

Ancient Mesopotamia and Persia **29**

Persian sculptures differ in style. The forms are more rounded, and they project more from the background. Some of the details, notably the treatment of drapery folds, echo forms characteristic of contemporaneous Greek sculpture. Achaemenid art testifies to the active exchange of ideas and artists among Mediterranean, Mesopotamian, and Persian civilizations at this date. A building inscription at Susa, for example, names Ionian Greeks, Medes (who occupied the land north of Persia), Egyptians, and Babylonians among those who built and decorated the palace.

THE SASANIANS Alexander the Great's conquest of Persia in 330 BCE marked the beginning of a long period of first Greek and then Roman rule in western Asia. In the third century CE, however, a new power rose up in Persia that challenged the Romans and sought to force them out of the region. The new rulers called themselves Sasanians. They traced their lineage to a legendary figure named Sasan, said to be a direct descendant of the Achaemenid kings. The first Sasanian king, Artaxerxes I (r. 211–241), founded the New Persian Empire in 224 CE after he defeated the Parthians (another of Rome's eastern enemies). The son and successor of Artaxerxes, Shapur I (r. 241–272), succeeded in further extending Sasanian territory. So powerful was the Sasanian army that in 260 CE, Shapur I was able to capture the Roman emperor Valerian near Edessa (in modern Turkey). The New Persian Empire endured more than 400 years, until the Arabs drove the Sasanians out of Mesopotamia in 636, just four years after the death of Muhammad. Thereafter, the greatest artists and architects of Mesopotamia worked in the service of Islam (see Chapter 5).

ANCIENT EGYPT

Blessed with ample sources of stone of different hues suitable for carving statues and fashioning building blocks, the ancient Egyptians left to posterity a profusion of spectacular monuments spanning three millennia. Many of them, as in Mesopotamia, glorify gods and were set up by kings, whom the Egyptians believed were also divine. Indeed, the Egyptians devoted enormous resources to erecting countless monuments and statues to honor their god-kings during their lifetimes and to constructing and furnishing magnificent tombs to serve as the divine kings' eternal homes in the afterlife.

The backbone of Egypt was, and still is, the Nile River, which, through its annual floods, supported all life in that ancient land (MAP 1-3). Even more so than the Tigris and the Euphrates Rivers of Mesopotamia, the Nile defined the cultures that developed along its banks. Originating deep in Africa, the world's longest river flows through regions that may not receive a single drop of rainfall in a decade. Yet crops thrive from the rich soil that the Nile brings thousands of miles from the African hills. In antiquity, the land bordering the Nile consisted of marshes dotted with island ridges. Amphibious animals swarmed in the marshes, where the Egyptians hunted them through tall forests of *papyrus* and rushes (FIG. 1-30). Egypt's fertility was famous. When the Kingdom of the Nile became a province of the Roman Empire after the death of Queen Cleopatra (r. 51–30 BCE), it served as the granary of the Mediterranean world.

Predynastic and Early Dynastic Periods

The Predynastic, or prehistoric, beginnings of Egyptian civilization are obscure. Nevertheless, tantalizing remains of tombs, paintings, pottery, and other artifacts attest to the existence of a sophisticated

culture on the banks of the Nile around 3500 BCE. In Predynastic times, Egypt was divided geographically and politically into Upper Egypt (the southern, upstream part of the Nile Valley) and Lower (northern) Egypt. The ancient Egyptians began the history of their kingdom with the unification of the two lands, which until recently historians thought occurred during the First Dynasty kingship of Menes.

PALETTE OF KING NARMER Many Egyptologists have identified Menes with King Narmer, whose image and name appear on both sides of a ceremonial *palette* (stone slab with a circular depression) found at Hierakonpolis. The palette (FIGS. 1-22 and 1-23) is an elaborate, formalized version of a utilitarian object commonly used in the Predynastic period to prepare eye makeup, which Egyptians used to protect their eyes against the glare of the sun. Narmer's palette is the earliest extant labeled work of historical art. Although Egyptologists no longer believe that it commemorates the founding of the first of Egypt's 31 dynasties around 2920 BCE (the last ended in 332 BCE),[1] it does record the unification of Upper and Lower Egypt at the end of the Predynastic period. Historians now think that this unification occurred over several centuries, but the palette presents the creation of the "Kingdom of the Two Lands" as a single great event.

King Narmer's palette is important not only as a document marking the transition from the prehistorical to the historical period in ancient Egypt but also as a kind of early blueprint of the formula for figure representation that characterized most Egyptian art for 3,000 years. At the top of each side of the palette are two heads of a cow with a woman's face, whom scholars usually identify as Hathor,

MAP 1-3 **Ancient Egypt.**

1-22 Back of the palette of King Narmer, from Hierakonpolis, Egypt, Predynastic, ca. 3000–2920 BCE. Slate, 2' 1" high. Egyptian Museum, Cairo.

Narmer's palette is the earliest surviving labeled work of historical art. The king, the largest figure in the composition, wears the crown of Upper Egypt and slays a captured enemy as his attendant looks on.

1-23 Front of the palette of King Narmer, from Hierakonpolis, Egypt, Predynastic, ca. 3000–2920 BCE. Slate, 2' 1" high. Egyptian Museum, Cairo.

Narmer, now wearing the crown of Lower Egypt, reviews the beheaded enemy bodies. At the center of the palette, the intertwined animal necks may symbolize the unification of the two kingdoms.

the divine mother of all Egyptian kings, but who may instead be the sky goddess Bat. Between the goddess heads is a *hieroglyph* giving Narmer's name (catfish = *nar*; chisel = *mer*) within a frame representing the royal palace. Below, the story of the unification of Egypt unfolds in registers.

On the back of the palette (FIG. 1-22), the king, wearing the high, white, conical crown of Upper Egypt and accompanied by a much smaller attendant carrying his sandals, slays a captured enemy. Above and to the right, the king appears again in his role as the "Living Horus"—here as a falcon with one human arm. The falcon-king takes captive a man-headed pictograph with a papyrus plant growing from it that stands for the land of Lower Egypt. Below the king are two fallen enemies. On the front (FIG. 1-23), the elongated necks of two felines form the circular depression that would have held eye makeup in an ordinary palette not made for display. The intertwined necks of the animals may be a pictorial reference to Egypt's unification. In the uppermost register, Narmer, now wearing Lower Egypt's distinctive crown, reviews the beheaded bodies of the enemy. The artist depicted each body with its severed head neatly placed between its legs. In the lowest band, a great bull symbolizing

the king's superhuman strength knocks down the fortress walls of a rebellious city.

On both sides of the palette, the god-king performs his ritual task alone and, by virtue of his superior rank, towers over his own men and the enemy. Specific historical narrative was not the artist's goal in this work. What was important was the characterization of the king as supreme, isolated from and larger than all ordinary men and solely responsible for the triumph over the enemy. These pictorial and ideological conventions endured in Egyptian art for millennia.

TOMBS AND THE AFTERLIFE Narmer's palette is exceptional among surviving Egyptian artworks because it is commemorative rather than funerary in nature. The majority of monuments the Egyptians left behind were dedicated to ensuring safety and happiness in the next life (see "Mummification and Immortality," page 32). In fact, the contents of tombs provide the principal evidence for the historical reconstruction of Egyptian civilization.

The standard tomb type in early Egypt was the *mastaba* (Arabic, "bench"), a rectangular brick or stone structure with sloping sides

Mummification and Immortality

The Egyptians did not make the sharp distinction between body and soul that is basic to many religions. Rather, they believed that from birth a person had a kind of other self—the *ka*—which, on the death of the body, could inhabit the corpse and live on. For the ka to live securely, however, the body had to remain as nearly intact as possible. To ensure that it did, the Egyptians developed the technique of embalming (*mummification*) to a high art.

Embalming generally lasted 70 days. The first step was the surgical removal of the lungs, liver, stomach, and intestines through an incision in the left flank. The Egyptians thought that these organs were most subject to decay, and wrapped them individually and placed them in four jars for eventual deposit in the burial chamber with the corpse. Egyptian surgeons extracted the brain through the nostrils and then discarded it because they did not attach any special significance to that organ. But they left in place the heart, necessary for life and also regarded as the seat of intelligence.

Next, the body was treated for 40 days with natron, a naturally occurring salt compound that dehydrated the body. Then the embalmers filled the corpse with resin-soaked linens, and closed and covered the incision with a representation of Horus's eye, a powerful *amulet* (a device to ward off evil and promote rebirth). Finally, they treated the body with lotions and resins and wrapped it tightly with hundreds of yards of linen bandages to maintain its shape. The Egyptians often placed other amulets within or on the resulting *mummy*. Masks (FIG. 1-38) covered the linen-wrapped faces of the wealthy.

Preserving the deceased's body by mummification was only the first requirement for immortality. Food and drink also had to be provided, as did clothing, utensils, and furniture. Often, Egyptian tombs contained papyrus scrolls with collections of spells and prayers needed to secure a happy afterlife (FIG. 1-23A ◩). Nothing that had been enjoyed on earth was to be lacking in the tomb (FIG. 1-24). Statuettes called *ushabtis* ("answerers") performed any labor the deceased required in the afterlife, answering whenever his or her name was called. The Egyptians also set up portrait statues of the dead in their tombs. The statues guaranteed the permanence of the person's identity

by providing substitute dwelling places for the ka in case the mummy disintegrated. Wall paintings and reliefs recorded the recurring round of human activities. The Egyptians hoped and expected that the images and inventory of life, collected and set up within the protective stone walls of the tomb, would ensure immortality.

1. Chapel
2. False door
3. Shaft into burial chamber
4. Serdab (chamber for statue of deceased)
5. Burial chamber

1-24 Section (*top*), plan (*center*), and restored view (*bottom*) of typical Egyptian mastaba tombs.

Egyptian mastabas had underground chambers, which housed the mummified body, portrait statues, and offerings to the deceased. Scenes of daily life often decorated the interior walls.

erected over an underground burial chamber (FIG. 1-24). The form probably developed from earthen mounds that had covered even earlier tombs. Although mastabas originally housed single burials, as in FIG. 1-24, they later became increasingly complex in order to accommodate many members of the same or several families. The main feature of these tombs, other than the burial chamber itself, was the chapel, which had a false door through which the ka could join the world of the living and partake in the meals placed on an offering table. Some mastabas also had a *serdab*, a small room housing a statue of the deceased. Adorning the chapel's interior walls and the ancillary rooms were paintings and reliefs depicting scenes from daily life with symbolic overtones (FIG. 1-30).

IMHOTEP AND DJOSER One of the most renowned figures in Egyptian history was IMHOTEP, master builder for King Djoser (r. 2630–2611 BCE) of the Third Dynasty. Imhotep's is the first recorded name of an artist. A man of legendary talent, he also served as Djoser's official seal bearer and as high priest of the sun

god Re. After his death, the Egyptians deified Imhotep and in time probably inflated the list of his achievements, but he undoubtedly designed Djoser's stepped pyramid (FIG. 1-25) at Saqqara, near Memphis, Egypt's capital at the time. The pyramid was the centerpiece of an immense (37-acre) rectangular enclosure surrounded by a wall of white limestone 34 feet high and 5,400 feet long. The huge precinct also enclosed a funerary temple, where priests performed daily rituals in celebration of the divine king, and several structures connected with the Jubilee Festival, the event that perpetually reaffirmed the royal existence in the hereafter.

Built before 2600 BCE, Djoser's pyramid is one of the oldest stone structures in Egypt and, in its final form, the first truly grandiose royal tomb. Begun as a large mastaba with each of its faces oriented toward one of the cardinal points of the compass, the tomb was enlarged at least twice before assuming its ultimate shape. About 200 feet high, the stepped pyramid seems to be composed of a series of mastabas of diminishing size, stacked one atop another. The tomb's dual function was to protect the mummified

Djoser's tomb, the first pyramid, resembles a series of stacked mastabas. It was the centerpiece of an immense funerary complex glorifying the god-king and his eternal existence in the hereafter.

king and his possessions and to symbolize, by its gigantic presence, his absolute and godlike power. Beneath the pyramid was a network of several hundred underground rooms and galleries, resembling a palace. It was to be Djoser's new home in the afterlife.

Old Kingdom

The Old Kingdom is the first of the three great periods of Egyptian history, called the Old, Middle, and New Kingdoms, respectively. Many Egyptologists now begin the Old Kingdom with Sneferu

(r. 2575–2551 BCE), the first king of the Fourth Dynasty, although the traditional division of kingdoms places Djoser and the Third Dynasty in the Old Kingdom. It ended with the breakup of the Eighth Dynasty around 2134 BCE.

GIZEH PYRAMIDS At Gizeh stand the three Fourth Dynasty pyramids (FIG. 1-26) that are the oldest of the Seven Wonders of the ancient world. The prerequisites for membership in this elite club were colossal size and enormous cost. The Gizeh pyramids testify to the wealth and pretensions of three kings: Khufu (r. 2551–2528 BCE),

1-26 Model of the Fourth Dynasty pyramid complex, Gizeh, Egypt. Harvard University Semitic Museum, Cambridge.
(1) pyramid of Menkaure, ca. 2490–2472 BCE; (2) pyramid of Khafre, ca. 2520–2494 BCE; (3) mortuary temple of Khafre;
(4) causeway; (5) Great Sphinx, ca. 2520–2494 BCE; (6) valley temple of Khafre; (7) Great Pyramid of Khufu, ca. 2551–2528 BCE;
(8) pyramids of the royal family and mastabas of nobles.

The three pyramids of Gizeh took the shape of the ben-ben, the emblem of the sun god, Re. The sun's rays were the ladder that the Egyptian kings used to ascend to the heavens after their death and rebirth.

PROBLEMS AND SOLUTIONS
Building the Pyramids of Gizeh

The Fourth Dynasty pyramids (FIG. 1-26) across the Nile from modern Cairo are on every list of the Wonders of the ancient world. How did the Egyptians solve the myriad problems they encountered in constructing these colossal tombs?

Like all building projects of this type, the process of erecting the pyramids began with leveling the building site and quarrying the stone, in this case primarily the limestone of the Gizeh plateau itself. Teams of workers had to cut into the rock and remove large blocks of roughly equal size using stone or copper chisels and wood mallets and wedges. Often, the artisans had to cut deep tunnels to find high-quality stone free of cracks and other flaws. To remove a block, the stonemasons cut channels on all sides and partly underneath. Then they pried the stones free from the bedrock with wood levers.

After workers liberated the stones, the rough blocks had to be transported to the building site on wood sleds. There, the stonemasons shaped the blocks to the exact dimensions required, with smooth faces (*dressed masonry*) for a perfect fit. The Egyptians dressed the blocks by chiseling and pounding the surfaces and, in the last stage, by rubbing and grinding the surfaces with fine polishing stones. Architectural his-

torians call this kind of construction *ashlar masonry*—carefully cut and regularly shaped blocks of stone piled in successive rows, or *courses*.

To set the ashlar blocks in place, workers erected great rubble ramps against the core of the pyramid. They adjusted the ramps' size and slope as work progressed and the tomb grew in height. Scholars debate whether the Egyptians used simple linear ramps inclined at a right angle to one face of the pyramid, or zigzag or spiral ramps akin to staircases. Linear ramps would have had the advantage of simplicity and would have left three sides of the pyramid unobstructed. But zigzag ramps placed against one side of the structure or spiral ramps winding around the pyramid would have greatly reduced the slope of the incline and would have made dragging the blocks easier. Some scholars also have suggested a combination of straight and spiral ramps, and one recent theory posits a system of spiral ramps within, instead of outside, the pyramid.

The Egyptians used ropes and levers both to lift and to lower the stones, guiding each block into its designated place. Finally, the pyramid received a casing of white limestone cut so precisely that the eye could scarcely detect the joints. Some casing stones are still in place at the peak of the pyramid of Khafre (FIG. 1-27).

The Gizeh pyramids attest not only to Egyptian builders' mastery of masonry construction but also their ability to mobilize, direct, house, and feed a huge workforce engaged in one of the most labor-intensive enterprises ever undertaken.

1-27 Great Sphinx (with pyramid of Khafre in the background), Gizeh, Egypt, Fourth Dynasty, ca. 2520–2494 BCE. Sandstone, 65' high.

Carved out of the Gizeh quarry, the Great Sphinx is of colossal size. Sphinxes have the body of a lion and the head of a man, in this case a king (probably Khafre) wearing the royal headdress and false beard.

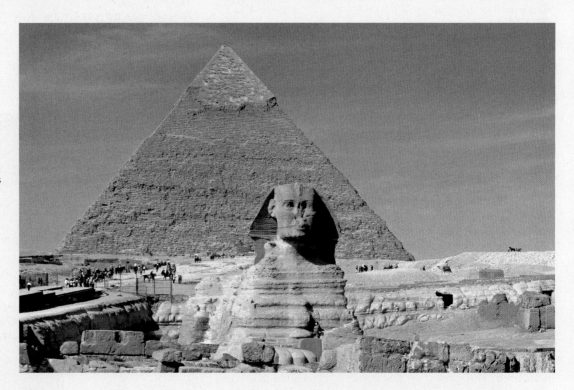

Khafre (r. 2520–2494 BCE), and Menkaure (r. 2490–2472 BCE). Built in the course of about 75 years, these colossal tombs represent the culmination of an architectural evolution that began with the mastaba. The classic pyramid form, however, is not simply a refinement of the stepped pyramid (FIG. 1-25). The new tomb shape probably reflects the influence of Heliopolis, the seat of the powerful cult of Re, whose emblem was a pyramidal stone, the *ben-ben*. The pyramids are symbols of the sun. The Pyramid Texts, inscribed on the burial chamber walls of many royal tombs, refer to the sun's rays as the ladder that the god-king uses to ascend to the heavens. (Djoser's

stepped pyramid may also have been conceived as a giant stairway.) The pyramids were where Egyptian kings were reborn in the afterlife, just as the sun is reborn each day at dawn. As with Djoser's tomb, the four sides of each of the Gizeh pyramids are oriented to the cardinal points of the compass. But the funerary temples associated with the Gizeh pyramids are not on the north side, facing the stars of the northern sky, as was Djoser's temple. The temples are on the east side, facing the rising sun and underscoring their connection with Re.

The tomb of Khufu, known as the Great Pyramid, is the oldest and largest. At the base, the pyramid covers some 13 acres, and the length of each side is approximately 775 feet. Its present height is about 450 feet (originally 480 feet). Except for the galleries and burial chamber, the Great Pyramid is an almost solid mass of limestone masonry comprising roughly 2.3 million blocks of stone, each weighing an average of 2.5 tons (see "Building the Pyramids of Gizeh," page 34).

From the remains surrounding the pyramid of Khafre, archaeologists have been able to reconstruct an entire funerary complex consisting of the pyramid itself with the burial chamber; the *mortuary temple* (FIG. 1-26, no. 3) adjoining the pyramid on the east side, where priests made offerings to the god-king; the roofed *causeway* (raised road; no. 4) leading to the mortuary temple; and the *valley temple* (no. 6) at the edge of the floodplain. Many Egyptologists believe that the complex served not only as the king's tomb and temple but also as his palace in the afterlife.

GREAT SPHINX Beside the causeway and dominating the valley temple of Khafre rises the Great Sphinx (FIGS. 1-26, no. 5, and 1-27). Carved from a spur of rock in the Gizeh quarry, the colossal statue is probably an image of Khafre (originally complete with the royal ceremonial beard and *uraeus* cobra headdress), although some scholars believe that it portrays Khufu and antedates Khafre's complex. Whomever it portrays, the *sphinx*—a lion with a human head—was an appropriate royal image. The composite form suggests that the king combines human intelligence with the fearsome strength and authority of the king of beasts.

KHAFRE ENTHRONED Although the Egyptians used wood, clay, and other materials, mostly for images of those not of the royal or noble classes, the primary material for funerary statuary was stone to ensure a permanent substitute home for the ka if the deceased's mummy was destroyed (see "Mummification and Immortality," page 32). The seated statue of Khafre illustrated here (FIG. 1-28) comes from the pharaoh's valley temple (FIG. 1-26, no. 6) near the Great Sphinx. The stone is diorite, an exceptionally hard dark stone brought some 400 miles down the Nile from royal quarries in the south. Khafre wears a simple kilt and sits rigidly upright on a throne formed of two stylized lions' bodies. Between the legs of the throne are intertwined lotus and papyrus plants—symbolic of the united Egypt. Khafre has the royal false beard fastened to his chin and wears the royal linen *nemes* headdress with uraeus cobra. The headdress covers his forehead and falls in pleated folds over his shoulders. Behind Khafre's head is the falcon that identifies the king as the "Living Horus." As befitting a divine ruler, the sculptor portrayed Khafre with a well-developed, flawless body and a perfect face, regardless of his real age and appearance. Because Egyptians considered ideal proportions appropriate for representing their god-kings, the statue of Khafre is not a true likeness and was not intended to be. The purpose of Egyptian royal portraiture (in vivid contrast to nonroyal portraiture; FIG. 1-28A ⬈) was not to record individual features or the distinctive shapes of bodies, but rather to proclaim the divine nature of Egyptian kingship.

The enthroned Khafre radiates serenity. The sculptor created this effect in part by giving the figure great compactness and solidity, with few projecting, breakable parts. The form of the statue expresses its purpose: to last for eternity. Khafre's body is one with the simple slab that forms the back of the king's throne. His arms follow the bend of his body and rest on his thighs, and his legs are close together. Part of the original stone block still connects the king's legs to his chair. Khafre's pose is frontal and, except for the

1-28 Khafre enthroned, from Gizeh, Egypt, Fourth Dynasty, ca. 2520–2494 BCE. Diorite, 5' 6" high. Egyptian Museum, Cairo.

This portrait from his pyramid complex depicts Khafre as an enthroned divine ruler with a perfect body. The formality of the pose creates an aura of eternal stillness, appropriate for the timeless afterlife.

hands, *bilaterally symmetrical* (the same on either side of an axis, in this case the vertical axis). The sculptor suppressed all movement and with it the notion of time, creating an aura of eternal stillness.

To produce Khafre's statue, the Egyptian artist first drew the front, back, and two profile views of the enthroned king on the four vertical faces of the stone block. Next, apprentices chiseled away the excess stone on each side. Finally, the workshop head sculpted the parts of Khafre's body, the falcon, and so forth. The polished surface was achieved by *abrasion* (rubbing or grinding). This subtractive method accounts in large part for the blocklike look of the standard Egyptian statue. Nevertheless, other sculptors, both ancient and modern, with different aims, have transformed stone blocks into dynamic, twisting human forms (for example, FIGS. I-14 and 2-57).

1-29 Menkaure and Khamerernebty(?), from Gizeh, Egypt, Fourth Dynasty, ca. 2490–2472 BCE. Graywacke, 4' 6½" high. Museum of Fine Arts, Boston.

The statue of Menkaure and his wife (or Hathor?) displays the conventional postures used for Egyptian statues designed as substitute homes for the ka. The embrace denotes the close association of the two figures.

MENKAURE The seated statue is one of only a small number of basic formulaic types that Old Kingdom sculptors employed to represent the human figure. Another is the image of a person or deity standing, either alone or in a group—for example, the pair (FIG. 1-29) of Menkaure and either one of his wives, probably Khamerernebty, or the goddess Hathor. The statue once stood in Menkaure's valley temple at Gizeh. Here, too, the figures remain wedded to the stone block. Menkaure's pose—duplicated in countless other Egyptian statues—is rigidly frontal with the arms hanging straight down and close to his well-built body. He clenches his hands into fists with the thumbs forward and advances his left leg slightly, but no shift occurs in the angle of the hips to correspond to the uneven distribution of weight. Khamerernebty(?) stands in a similar position. Her right arm, however, circles around the king's waist, and her left hand gently rests on his left arm. This frozen stereotypical gesture indicates their marital status or, if king and goddess, their shared divinity. The two figures show no other sign of affection or emotion and look not at each other but out into space.

TOMB OF TI In Old Kingdom tombs, images of the deceased also frequently appear in relief sculpture and in mural painting, sometimes singly (FIG. I-12), sometimes in a narrative context. The painted limestone relief scenes decorating the walls of the Saqqara mastaba of a Fifth Dynasty official named Ti typify the subjects that Old Kingdom patrons favored for the adornment of their final resting places. Depictions of agriculture and hunting fill Ti's tomb. The

Egyptians associated these activities with providing nourishment for the ka in the hereafter, but the subjects also had powerful symbolic overtones. In ancient Egypt, success in the hunt, for example, was a metaphor for triumph over the forces of evil.

In the relief illustrated here (FIG. 1-30), Ti, his men, and his boats move slowly through the Nile marshes, hunting hippopotami and birds in a dense growth of towering papyrus. The sculptor delineated the reedy stems of the plants with repeated fine grooves that fan out gracefully at the top into a commotion of frightened birds and stalking foxes. The water beneath the boats, signified by a pattern of wavy lines, is crowded with hippopotami and fish. Ti's men are frantically busy with their spears, whereas Ti, depicted twice their size, stands aloof. The basic conventions of Egyptian figure representation—used a half millennium earlier for King Narmer's palette (FIG. 1-22)—appear again here. As in the Predynastic work, the artist exaggerated the size of Ti to announce his rank, and combined frontal and profile views of Ti's body to show its characteristic parts clearly. This conceptual (as opposed to optical) approach to representation was well suited for Egyptian funerary art because it emphasizes the essential nature of the deceased, not his accidental appearance. Ti's conventional pose contrasts with the realistically rendered activities of his tiny servants and with the naturalistically carved and painted birds and animals among the papyrus buds. Ti's immobility implies that he is not an actor in the hunt. He does not *do* anything. He simply *is*—a figure apart from time and an impassive observer of life, like his ka. Scenes such as this one demonstrate that Egyptian artists could be close observers of daily life. The suppression of the anecdotal (that is, of the time-bound) from their representations of the deceased both in relief and in the round was a deliberate choice. Egyptian artists' primary purpose was to suggest the deceased's eternal existence in the afterlife, not to portray his activities while alive.

The idealized image of Ti is typical of Egyptian relief sculpture. Egyptian artists regularly ignored the endless variations in body types of real human beings. Painters and sculptors did not sketch their subjects from life but applied a strict *canon,* or system of proportions, to the human figure. They first drew a grid on the wall. Then they placed various human body parts at specific points on the network of squares. The height of a figure, for example, was a fixed number of squares, and the head, shoulders, waist, knees, and other parts of the body also had a predetermined size and place within the scheme. This approach to design lasted for more than 2,500 years. Specific proportions might vary from workshop to workshop and change over time, but the principle of the canon persisted.

New Kingdom

About 2150 BCE, the Egyptians challenged the weak kings of the Sixth Dynasty, and for more than a century the land was in a state of civil unrest and near anarchy. But in 2040 BCE, the king of Upper Egypt, Mentuhotep II (r. 2050–1998 BCE), managed to unite Egypt again under the rule of a single king and established the Middle Kingdom (11th to 14th Dynasties), which brought stability to Egypt for four centuries. In the 17th century BCE, it too disintegrated. Power passed to the Hyksos (Shepherd Kings) who descended on Egypt from the Syrian and Mesopotamian uplands. But in the 16th century, native Egyptian kings of the 17th Dynasty rose up in revolt. Ahmose I (r. 1550–1525 BCE), final conqueror of the Hyksos and first king of the 18th Dynasty, ushered in the New Kingdom, the most glorious period in Egypt's long history. At this time, Egypt

1 ft.

In Egypt, a successful hunt was a metaphor for triumph over evil. In this painted tomb relief, the deceased stands aloof from the hunters busily spearing hippopotami. Ti's size reflects his high rank.

HATSHEPSUT One of the most intriguing figures in ancient history was the New Kingdom pharaoh Hatshepsut (r. 1473–1458 BCE). In 1479 BCE, Thutmose II (r. 1492–1479 BCE), the fourth pharaoh of the 18th Dynasty, died. Hatshepsut, his principal wife (and half sister), had not given birth to any sons who survived, so the title of king went to the 12-year-old Thutmose III, son of Thutmose II by a minor wife. Hatshepsut became regent for the boy-king. Within a few years, however, the queen proclaimed herself pharaoh and insisted that her father, Thutmose I, had chosen her as his successor during his lifetime. Hatshepsut is the first great female monarch whose name has been recorded. For two decades, she ruled what was then the most powerful and prosperous empire in the world. As always, Egyptian sculptors produced statues of their pharaoh in great numbers for display throughout the kingdom. Hatshepsut uniformly wears the costume of the male pharaohs, with royal headdress and kilt, and in some cases even a false ceremonial beard. Many inscriptions refer to Hatshepsut as "*His* Majesty."

One of the most impressive of the many grandiose monuments that the New Kingdom pharaohs built is Hatshepsut's mortuary temple (FIG. 1-31) on the Nile at Deir el-Bahri. The temple rises from the valley floor in three terraces connected by ramps on the central axis. It is striking how visually well suited the structure is to its natural setting. The long horizontals and verticals of the *colonnades* of the terraces repeat the pattern of the limestone cliffs above. In Hatshepsut's day, the terraces were not the barren places they are now but gardens with frankincense trees and rare plants that the pharaoh brought from the

extended its borders by conquest from the Euphrates River in the east deep into Nubia to the south (MAP 1-3). A new capital—Thebes, in Upper Egypt—became a great metropolis with magnificent palaces, tombs, and temples along both banks of the Nile. The Egyptian kings began to call themselves *pharaohs*.

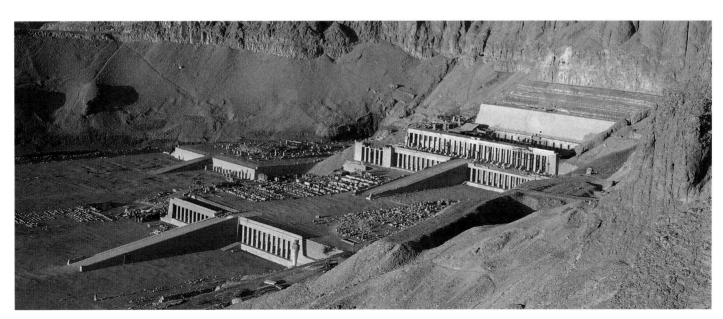

1-31 Mortuary temple of Hatshepsut (looking southwest), Deir el-Bahri, Egypt, 18th Dynasty, ca. 1473–1458 BCE.

Hatshepsut was the first great female monarch in history. Her immense terraced funerary temple featured an extensive series of painted reliefs recounting her divine birth, coronation, and great deeds.

10 ft.

1-32 Facade of the temple of Ramses II, Abu Simbel, Egypt, 19th Dynasty, ca. 1290–1224 BCE. Sandstone, seated portraits 65' high.

Four rock-cut colossal images of Ramses II dominate the facade of his mortuary temple. Inside, more gigantic figures of the long-reigning king depict him as Osiris, god of the dead and giver of eternal life.

faraway "land of Punt" on the Red Sea. Her expedition to Punt figures prominently in the once brightly painted low reliefs that cover many walls of the complex. In addition to representing great deeds, the reliefs also show Hatshepsut's divine birth and coronation. She was said to be the daughter of the sun god Amen, whose sanctuary was on the temple's uppermost level. The reliefs of Hatshepsut's mortuary temple, unfortunately defaced after her death, constitute the first great tribute to a woman's achievements in the history of art.

RAMSES II Perhaps the greatest pharaoh of the New Kingdom was Ramses II (r. 1290–1224 BCE), who ruled Egypt for two-thirds of a century, an extraordinary accomplishment in an era when life expectancy was far less than it is today. Four colossal images of Ramses never fail to impress visitors to the pharaoh's mortuary temple (FIG. 1-32) at Abu Simbel. The 65-foot-tall portraits, carved directly into the cliff face, are almost a dozen times an ancient Egyptian's height, even though the pharaoh is seated. The grand scale of the *facade* statues extends inside the temple also, where gigantic (32-foot-tall) figures of the king, carved as one with the pillars, face each other across the narrow corridor. Ramses appears in his *atlantids* (statue-columns) in the guise of Osiris, god of the dead and king of the underworld, as well as giver of eternal life.

KARNAK Colossal scale also characterizes the temples that the New Kingdom pharaohs built to honor one or more of the gods. Successive kings often added to them until they reached enormous size. The temple of Amen-Re (FIG. 1-33) at Karnak, for example,

begun during the Middle Kingdom, was largely the work of the 18th Dynasty pharaohs, including Hatshepsut, but Ramses II (19th Dynasty) and others also contributed sections. Parts of the complex date as late as the 26th Dynasty.

The Karnak temple has an artificial sacred lake within its precinct, a reference to the primeval waters before creation. The temple rises from the earth as the original sacred mound rose from the waters at the beginning of time. In other respects, however, the temple is a typical, if especially large, New Kingdom *pylon temple*. The name derives from the simple and massive *pylons* (gateways with sloping walls) that are characteristic features of New Kingdom temple design. A typical pylon temple is bilaterally symmetrical along a single axis that runs from an approaching avenue through a colonnaded court and hall into a dimly lit sanctuary. Only the pharaohs and the priests could enter the sanctuary. A chosen few were admitted to the great columnar hall. The majority of the people could proceed only as far as the open court. The central feature of the New Kingdom pylon temple plan—a narrow axial passageway through the complex—characterizes much of Egyptian architecture. The approaches to the Old Kingdom pyramids (FIG. 1-26) of Gizeh and to the multilevel mortuary temple of Hatshepsut (FIG. 1-31) at Deir el-Bahri also conform to the Egyptian preference for *axial plans*.

In the Karnak plan, the hall (FIG. 1-34) between the court and sanctuary has its long axis placed at right angles to the corridor of the entire building complex. Inside this 58,000-square-foot *hypostyle hall* (one in which columns support the roof) are 134 massive sandstone columns, which support a roof of stone slabs carried on

1-33 Aerial view of the temple of Amen-Re (looking east), Karnak, Egypt, major construction 15th to 13th centuries BCE.

The vast Karnak temple complex contains a pylon temple with a bilaterally symmetrical axial plan and an artificial lake associated with the primeval waters of the Egyptian creation myth.

stone lintels. The columns have bud-cluster or bell-shaped *capitals* (heads) resembling lotus or papyrus (the plants symbolizing Upper and Lower Egypt). The 12 central columns are 75 feet tall, and their capitals are 22 feet in diameter at the top, large enough for a hundred people to stand on them. The Egyptians, who used no cement,

depended on precise cutting of the joints and the weight of the huge stone blocks to hold the columns in place.

In the Amen-Re temple at Karnak and in many other Egyptian hypostyle halls, the two central rows of columns are taller than those at the sides. Raising the roof's central section created a

1-34 Model of the hypostyle hall, temple of Amen-Re, Karnak, Egypt, 19th Dynasty, ca. 1290–1224 BCE. Metropolitan Museum of Art, New York.

The two central rows of columns of Karnak's hypostyle hall are 75 feet high, with capitals 22 feet in diameter. The columns support a clerestory that admitted sunlight to illuminate the hall's interior.

Ancient Egypt **39**

clerestory. Openings in the clerestory enabled sunlight to filter into the interior, although the stone grilles would have blocked much of the light. This method of construction appeared in primitive form in the Old Kingdom valley temple of Khafre at Gizeh. The clerestory is evidently an Egyptian innovation, and its significance cannot be overstated. Before the invention of the electric light bulb, illuminating a building's interior was always a challenge for architects. The clerestory played a key role in the history of architecture until very recently.

AKHENATON The Karnak sanctuary also provides evidence for a period of religious upheaval during the New Kingdom and for a corresponding revolution in Egyptian art. In the mid-14th century BCE, Amenhotep IV, later known as Akhenaton (r. 1353–1335 BCE), abandoned the worship of most of the Egyptian gods in favor of Aton, identified with the sun disk, whom the pharaoh declared to be the universal and only god. Akhenaton deleted the name of Amen from all inscriptions and even from his own name and that of his father, Amenhotep III (r. 1390–1353 BCE). He emptied the great temples, enraged the priests, and moved his capital downriver from Thebes to present-day Amarna, a site he named Akhetaton (Horizon of Aton). The pharaoh claimed to be both the son and sole prophet of Aton. Moreover, in stark contrast to earlier practice, artists represented Akhenaton's god neither in animal nor in human form but simply as the sun disk emitting life-giving rays. The pharaohs who followed Akhenaton reestablished the cult and priesthood of Amen and restored the temples and the inscriptions. Akhenaton's religious revolution was soon undone, and his new city largely abandoned.

During the brief heretical episode of Akhenaton, profound changes also occurred in Egyptian art. A colossal statue (FIG. 1-35) of Akhenaton from Karnak, toppled and buried after his death, retains the standard frontal pose of Egyptian royal portraits. But the effeminate body, with its curving contours, and the long face with full lips and heavy-lidded eyes are a far cry indeed from the idealized faces and heroically proportioned bodies (FIG. 1-29) of the pharaoh's predecessors. Akhenaton's body is curiously misshapen, with weak arms, a narrow waist, protruding belly, wide hips, and fatty thighs. Modern physicians have tried to explain his physique by attributing a variety of illnesses to the pharaoh. They cannot agree on a diagnosis, and their premise—that the statue is an accurate depiction of a physical deformity—is probably faulty. Some art historians think that Akhenaton's portrait is a deliberate artistic reaction against the established style, paralleling the suppression of traditional religion. They argue that Akhenaton's artists tried to formulate a new androgynous image of the pharaoh as the manifestation of Aton, the sexless sun disk. But no consensus exists other than that the style was revolutionary and short-lived.

NEFERTITI A painted limestone bust (FIG. 1-36) of Akhenaton's queen, Nefertiti (her name means "the beautiful one has come"), also breaks with the past. The portrait exhibits an expression of entranced musing and an almost mannered sensitivity and delicacy of curving contour. Nefertiti was an influential woman during her husband's kingship. She frequently appears in the decoration of the Aton temple at Karnak, and not only equals her husband in size but also sometimes wears pharaonic headgear. Excavators discovered the portrait illustrated here in the workshop of the sculptor THUTMOSE. It is a deliberately unfinished model very likely by the

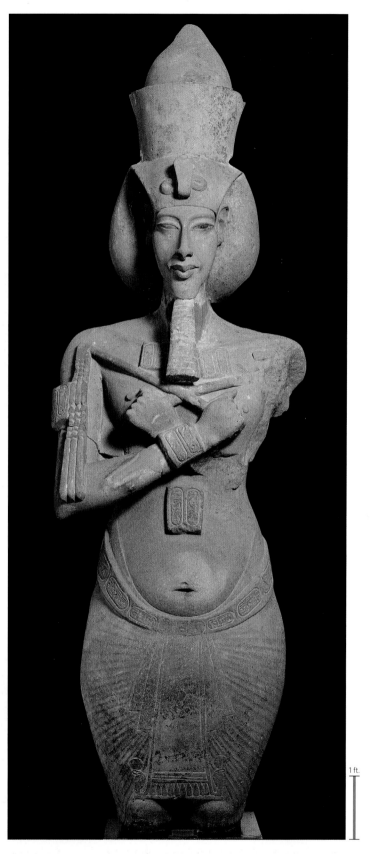

1-35 Akhenaton, colossal statue from the temple of Aton, Karnak, Egypt, 18th Dynasty, ca. 1353–1335 BCE. Sandstone, 13' high. Egyptian Museum, Cairo.

Akhenaton initiated both religious and artistic revolutions. This androgynous figure is a deliberate reaction against tradition. It may be an attempt to portray the pharaoh as Aton, the sexless sun disk.

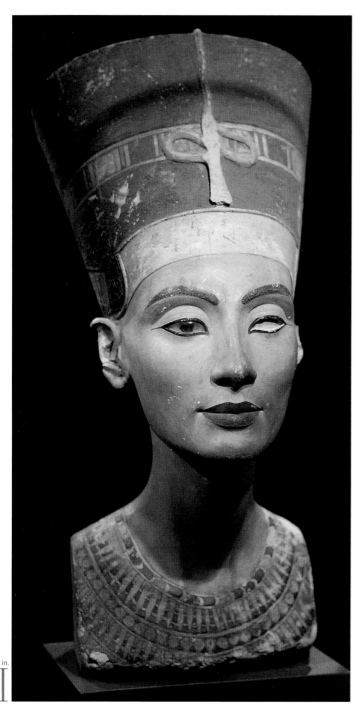

1-36 THUTMOSE, bust of Nefertiti, from Amarna, Egypt, 18th Dynasty, ca. 1353–1335 BCE. Painted limestone, 1' 8" high. Ägyptisches Museum, Staatliche Museen zu Berlin, Berlin.

Found in the workshop of the master sculptor Thutmose, this unfinished bust portrait of Nefertiti depicts Akhenaton's influential wife with a thoughtful expression and a long, delicately curved neck.

1-37 Innermost coffin of Tutankhamen, from his tomb at Thebes, Egypt, 18th Dynasty, ca. 1323 BCE. Gold with inlay of enamel and semiprecious stones, 6' 1" long. Egyptian Museum, Cairo.

The boy-king Tutankhamen owes his fame to the discovery of his treasure-filled tomb. His mummy was encased in three nested coffins. The innermost one, made of gold, portrays the pharaoh as Osiris.

master's own hand. The left eye socket still lacks the inlaid eyeball, making the portrait a kind of before-and-after demonstration piece. With this elegant bust, Thutmose may have been alluding to a heavy flower on its slender stalk by exaggerating the weight of the crowned head and the length of the almost serpentine neck. The sculptor seems to have adjusted the likeness of his subject to meet the era's standard of spiritual beauty.

TUTANKHAMEN Probably Akhenaton's son by a minor wife, Tutankhamen (r. 1333–1323 BCE) ruled Egypt for a decade and died at age 18. Although a minor figure in Egyptian history, Tutankhamen is famous today because of the fabulously rich treasure of sculpture, furniture, and jewelry discovered in 1922 in his tomb at Thebes. The principal find was the enshrined body of the pharaoh himself (FIG. 1-37). The royal mummy reposed in the innermost of three

1-38 Death mask of Tutankhamen, from the innermost coffin (FIG. 1-37) in his tomb at Thebes, Egypt, 18th Dynasty, ca. 1323 BCE. Gold with inlay of semiprecious stones, 1' 9$\frac{1}{4}$" high. Egyptian Museum, Cairo.

The gold mask that covered the head of Tutankhamen's mummy radiates grandeur and richness. It is a sensitive portrayal of the teenaged pharaoh featuring the traditional false beard and uraeus cobra headdress.

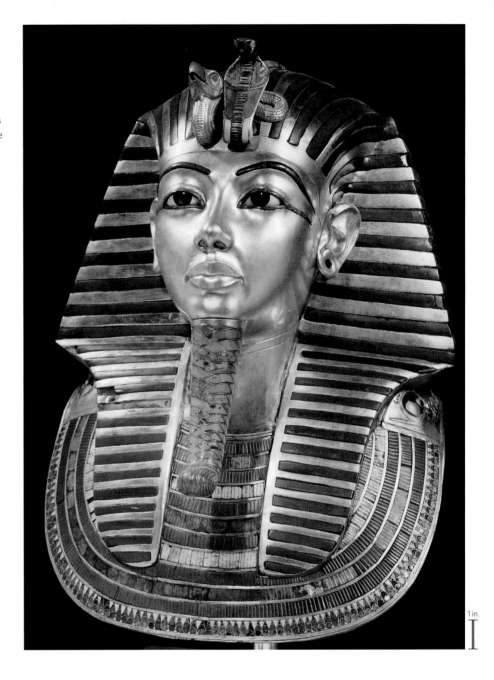

1 in.

coffins, nested one within the other. The innermost coffin shows Tutankhamen in the guise of Osiris and is the most luxurious of the three. Made of beaten gold (about a quarter ton of it) and inlaid with semiprecious stones such as lapis lazuli, turquoise, and carnelian, it is a supreme monument to the sculptor's and goldsmith's crafts. The portrait mask (FIG. 1-38), which covered the king's face, is also made of gold with inlaid semiprecious stones. It is a sensitive portrayal of the serene adolescent king dressed in his official regalia, including the nemes headdress and false beard. The general effect of the mask and of the tomb treasures as a whole is one of grandeur and richness expressive of Egyptian power, pride, and limitless wealth.

EGYPT IN DECLINE During the first millennium BCE, Egypt lost the commanding role it once had played in the ancient world. The empire dwindled away, and foreign powers invaded, occupied, and ruled the land, until Alexander the Great of Macedon and his Greek successors and, eventually, the emperors of Rome took control of the land of the Nile. Many of the formal traditions of Egyptian art endured, however. Indeed, the exceptional longevity of the Egyptian artistic style is one of the marvels of the history of art. It attests to a way of making pictures and statues so satisfactory that it was maintained for millennia, whereas everywhere else in the ancient Mediterranean, artistic change was the only common denominator.

🖆 Explore the era further in MindTap with videos of major artworks and buildings, Google Earth™ coordinates, and essays by the author on the following additional subjects:

- Head of Inanna(?), from Uruk (FIG. 1-1A)
- Apollo 11 Cave, Namibia (FIG. 1-3A)
- Law stele of Hammurabi (FIG. 1-16A)
- *Judgment of Hunefer,* from Thebes (FIG. 1-23A)
- Seated scribe, from Saqqara (FIG. 1-28A)

PREHISTORY AND THE FIRST CIVILIZATIONS

Prehistory

- The first sculptures and paintings antedate the invention of writing by tens of thousands of years. No one knows why humans began to paint and carve images or what role those images played in the lives of Paleolithic hunters. Women were far more common subjects than men, but animals, not humans, dominate Paleolithic art (ca. 40,000–9000 BCE). Surviving works range in size from tiny figurines to painted walls and ceilings covered with over-life-size animals. Animals always appear in profile in order to show clearly the head, body, tail, and all four legs.

- The Neolithic Age (ca. 8000–3500 BCE) revolutionized human life with the beginning of agriculture and the formation of the first settled communities. The earliest known large-scale sculptures date to the seventh millennium BCE. In painting, coherent narratives became common, and artists began to represent human figures as composites of frontal and profile views.

Hall of the Bulls, Lascaux,
ca. 16,000–14,000 BCE

Ancient Mesopotamia and Persia

- The Sumerians (ca. 3500–2332 BCE) founded the world's first city-states and invented writing in the fourth millennium BCE. They were also the first to build towering mud-brick temple platforms and to tell coherent stories in pictures by placing figures in superposed registers.

- The Akkadians (ca. 2332–2150 BCE) were the first Mesopotamian rulers to call themselves kings of the world and to assume divine attributes. Akkadian artists may have been the first to cast hollow life-size metal sculptures and to place relief figures at different levels in a landscape setting.

- During the Third Dynasty of Ur (ca. 2150–1800 BCE) and under the kings of Babylon (ca. 1800–1600 BCE), the Neo-Sumerians constructed one of the largest Mesopotamian ziggurats at Ur. Babylonian artists were among the first to experiment with foreshortening.

- At the height of their power, the Assyrians (ca. 900–612 BCE) ruled an empire extending from the Persian Gulf to the Nile and Asia Minor. Assyrian palaces were fortified citadels with gates guarded by monstrous lamassu. Painted reliefs glorifying the king decorated the ceremonial halls.

- The Neo-Babylonian kings (612–559 BCE) erected the biblical Tower of Babel and the Ishtar Gate.

- The capital of the Achaemenid Empire (559–330 BCE) was Persepolis, where the Persians built a huge palace complex with an audience hall that could accommodate 10,000 people.

Warka Vase, Uruk, ca. 3200–3000 BCE

Persepolis, ca. 521–465 BCE

Ancient Egypt

- The palette of King Narmer, which commemorates the unification of Upper and Lower Egypt around 3000–2920 BCE, established the basic principles of Egyptian representational art for 3,000 years.

- Imhotep, architect of the funerary complex of King Djoser (r. 2630–2611 BCE) at Saqqara, is the first artist in history whose name was recorded.

- During the Old Kingdom (ca. 2575–2134 BCE), the Egyptians built three colossal pyramids at Gizeh, emblems of the sun on whose rays the pharaohs ascended to the heavens after their death. Old Kingdom artists established the statuary types that would dominate Egyptian art for 2,000 years. Egyptian artists suppressed all movement in their statues to express the eternal nature of divine kingship.

- During the New Kingdom (ca. 1550–1070 BCE), the most significant architectural innovation was the axially planned pylon temple incorporating an immense gateway, columnar courtyards, and a hypostyle hall with clerestory windows. Powerful pharaohs such as Hatshepsut (r. 1473–1458 BCE) and Ramses II (r. 1290–1224 BCE) constructed gigantic temples in honor of their patron gods and, after their deaths, for their own worship. Akhenaton (r. 1353–1335 BCE) abandoned the traditional Egyptian religion in favor of Aton, the sun disk, and initiated a short-lived artistic revolution in which physical deformities and undulating curves replaced the idealized physiques and cubic forms of earlier Egyptian art.

Khafre enthroned,
ca. 2520–2494 BCE

Mortuary temple of Hatshepsut,
Deir el-Bahri, ca. 1473–1458 BCE

2-1a Iktinos, the architect of the Parthenon, calculated the dimensions of every part of the building using harmonic numerical ratios, which determined, for example, the height and diameter of each column.

▲ **2-1b** The reliefs depicting Greeks battling semi-human centaurs are allegories of the triumph of civilization and rational order over barbarism and chaos—and of the Greek defeat of the Persians in 479 BCE.

2-1 **IKTINOS, Parthenon (looking southeast), Acropolis, Athens, Greece, 447–438 BCE.**

▶ **2-1c** The costliest part of the Parthenon's lavish sculptural program was inside the temple—Phidias's colossal gold-and-ivory statue depicting Athena presenting the personification of Victory to Athens.

Ancient Greece

THE PERFECT TEMPLE

Although the Greeks borrowed many ideas from the artists and architects of Mesopotamia and Egypt, they quickly developed an independent artistic identity. Their many innovations in painting, sculpture, and architecture became the foundation of the Western tradition in the history of art. Indeed, no building type has ever had a longer and more profound impact on the later history of architecture than the Greek temple, which was itself a multimedia monument, richly adorned with painted statues and reliefs.

The greatest Greek temple was the Parthenon (FIG. 2-1), the shrine dedicated to the patron goddess of Athens—Athena, the *parthenos* ("the virgin"). Erected on the Athenian Acropolis in the mid-fifth century BCE, it represents the culmination of a century-long effort by Greek architects to design a building having perfect proportions. The architect IKTINOS calculated the dimensions of every part of the Parthenon in terms of a fixed proportional scheme, consistent with the thinking of the philosopher and mathematician Pythagoras of Samos, who believed that beauty resides in harmonic numerical ratios. (An important geometric theorem still bears Pythagoras's name.) Consequently, in the Parthenon, the ratio of the length to the width of the building, the number of columns on the long versus the short sides, and even the relationship between the diameter of a column and the space between neighboring columns conformed to the all-encompassing mathematical formula used by Iktinos. The result was a "perfect temple."

The Athenians did not, however, construct the Parthenon to solve a purely formal problem of architectural design. Nor did this shrine honor Athena alone. The Parthenon also celebrated the Athenian people, who a generation earlier had led the Greeks to victory over the Persians after they had sacked the Acropolis in 480 BCE. Under the direction of PHIDIAS, a team of gifted sculptors lavishly decorated the building with statues and reliefs that in many cases alluded to the Persian defeat. For example, the sculptural program included reliefs depicting nude Greek warriors battling with the part-horse, part-human *centaurs*—an allegory of the triumph of civilization (that is, Greek civilization) over barbarism (in this case, the Persians). The statues on the front of the building told the story of the birth of Athena, who emerged from the head of her father, Zeus, king of the gods, fully armed and ready to protect her people. The costliest sculpture, and most prestigious of all, however, Phidias reserved for himself: the colossal gold-and-ivory statue of Athena inside, which depicted the warrior goddess presenting the Athenians with the winged personification of Victory—an unmistakable reference to the Greek victory over the Persians.

THE GREEKS AND THEIR GODS

Ancient Greek art occupies a special place in the history of art through the ages. Many of the cultural values of the Greeks, especially the exaltation of humanity as "the measure of all things," remain fundamental principles of Western civilization today. In fact, these ideas are so completely part of modern Western habits of mind that most people are scarcely aware that the concepts originated in Greece 2,500 years ago.

The Greeks, or *Hellenes,* as they called themselves, never formed a single nation but instead established independent city-states on the Greek mainland, on the islands of the Aegean Sea, and on the western coast of Asia Minor (MAP 2-1). In 776 BCE, the separate Greek states held their first athletic games in common at Olympia. From then on, despite their differences and rivalries, the Greeks regarded themselves as citizens of *Hellas,* distinct from the surrounding "barbarians" who did not speak Greek.

Even the gods of the Greeks (see "The Gods and Goddesses of Mount Olympus," page 47) were distinct from those of neighboring civilizations. Unlike Mesopotamian and Egyptian deities, the Greek gods and goddesses differed from humans only in being immortal. The Greeks made their gods into humans and their humans into gods. This humanistic worldview led the Greeks to create the concept of democracy (rule by the *demos,* the people) and to make seminal contributions in the fields of art, literature, and science.

The distinctiveness and originality of Greek civilization should not, however, obscure the enormous debt the Greeks owed to the

MAP 2-1 The Greek world.

ANCIENT GREECE

3000–2000 BCE **Early Cycladic**	2000–1200 BCE **Minoan and Mycenaean**	1200–900 BCE	900–480 BCE **Geometric and Archaic**	480–323 BCE **Classical**	323–30 BCE **Hellenistic**
■ Early Cycladic sculptors create marble figurines for graves to accompany the dead into the afterlife.	■ Minoans construct major palaces on Crete with frescoed walls. ■ Volcanic eruption destroys Thera, ca. 1628 BCE. ■ Mycenaeans bury their dead in deep shaft graves with gold masks. ■ Mycenaeans construct fortified citadels and build tombs featuring corbeled domes.		■ Greek artists revive figure painting during the Geometric period. ■ Greek architects erect the first peripteral Doric and Ionic temples. ■ Greek sculptors carve life-size stone statues with "Archaic smiles." ■ Greek ceramists perfect black- and, later, red-figure vase painting.	■ Sculptors introduce contrapposto in Greek statuary. ■ Polykleitos formulates his canon of proportions. ■ Pericles rebuilds the Athenian Acropolis after the Persian sack. ■ Praxiteles humanizes the Greek gods and goddesses.	■ Hellenistic kingdoms replace Athens as leading cultural centers. ■ Artists explore new subjects in sculpture and painting.

RELIGION AND MYTHOLOGY
The Gods and Goddesses of Mount Olympus

The Greek deities most often represented in art—not only in antiquity but also in the Middle Ages, the Renaissance, and up to the present—are the 12 gods and goddesses of Mount Olympus. Listed here are those Olympian gods (and their Roman equivalents).

- **Zeus (Jupiter)** was king of the gods and ruled the sky. His weapon was the thunderbolt, and with it he led the other gods to victory over the giants, who had challenged the Olympians for control of the world.
- **Hera (Juno)**, the wife and sister of Zeus, was the goddess of marriage.
- **Poseidon (Neptune)**, Zeus's brother, was lord of the sea. He controlled waves, storms, and earthquakes with his three-pronged pitchfork (*trident*).
- **Hestia (Vesta)**, sister of Zeus, Poseidon, and Hera, was goddess of the hearth.
- **Demeter (Ceres)**, Zeus's third sister, was the goddess of grain and agriculture.
- **Ares (Mars)**, the god of war, was the son of Zeus and Hera and the lover of Aphrodite. His Roman counterpart, Mars, was the father of the twin founders of Rome.
- **Athena (Minerva)**, the goddess of wisdom and warfare, was a virgin (parthenos), born not from a woman's womb but from the head of her father, Zeus.
- **Hephaistos (Vulcan)**, the son of Zeus and Hera, was the god of fire and of metalworking. He provided Zeus his scepter and Poseidon his trident, and fashioned the armor that Achilles wore in battle against Troy. He was also the "surgeon" who split open Zeus's head to facilitate the birth of Athena. Hephaistos was lame and, uncharacteristically for a god, ugly. His wife, Aphrodite, was unfaithful to him.
- **Apollo (Apollo)** was the god of light and music, and a great archer. He was the son of Zeus with **Leto (Latona)**, daughter of one of the Titans who preceded the Olympians. His epithet, *phoibos,* means "radiant," and the young, beautiful Apollo was sometimes identified with the sun, **Helios (Sol)**.
- **Artemis (Diana)**, the sister of Apollo, was the goddess of the hunt and of wild animals. As Apollo's twin, she was occasionally regarded as the moon, **Selene (Luna)**.
- **Aphrodite (Venus)**, the daughter of Zeus and Dione (one of the *nymphs*—the goddesses of springs, caves, and woods), was the goddess of love and beauty. She was the mother of the Trojan hero Aeneas by a mortal named Anchises.
- **Hermes (Mercury)**, the son of Zeus and another nymph, was the fleet-footed messenger of the gods and possessed winged sandals. He was also the guide of travelers and carried the *caduceus,* a magical herald's rod.

Several non-Olympian deities also appear frequently in ancient and later art.

- **Hades (Pluto)**, Zeus's other brother, was equal in stature to the Olympian deities but never resided on Mount Olympus. He was the god of the dead and lord of the Underworld (also called Hades).
- **Dionysos (Bacchus)** was the god of wine and the son of Zeus and a mortal woman.
- **Eros (Amor or Cupid)** was the winged child-god of love and the son of Aphrodite and Ares.
- **Asklepios (Aesculapius)**, the son of Apollo and a mortal woman, was the healing god whose serpent-entwined staff is the emblem of modern medicine.

---

cultures of Mesopotamia and Egypt. The ancient Greeks themselves readily acknowledged borrowing ideas, motifs, conventions, and skills from those older civilizations. Nor should a high estimation of Greek art and culture blind anyone to the realities of Hellenic life and society. Even "democracy" was a political reality for only one segment of the demos. Slavery was a universal institution among the Greeks, and Greek women were in no way the equals of Greek men. Well-born women normally remained secluded in their homes, emerging usually only for weddings, funerals, and religious festivals, in which they had a prominent role. Otherwise, they played little part in public or political life.

The story of art in Greece does not begin with the Greeks, however, but with their prehistoric predecessors in the Aegean world—the people who would later become the heroes of Greek mythology.

PREHISTORIC AEGEAN

Historians, art historians, and archaeologists alike divide the prehistoric Aegean into three geographic areas. Each has a distinctive artistic identity. *Cycladic* art is the art of the Cycladic Islands (so named because they "circle" around Delos), as well as of the adjacent islands in the Aegean, excluding Crete. *Minoan* art, named for the legendary King Minos, encompasses the art of Crete. *Mycenaean* art, which takes its name from the great citadel of Mycenae celebrated in Homer's *Iliad,* the epic tale of the Trojan War, is the art of the Greek mainland.

Cycladic Art

Archaeologists have uncovered evidence that humans inhabited Greece as far back as the Paleolithic period and that village life was firmly established in Neolithic times. However, the earliest distinctive Aegean artworks date to the third millennium BCE and come from the Cyclades.

STATUETTES Marble was abundantly available in the Aegean Islands, and many Cycladic marble sculptures survive. Most of these, like many of their Stone Age predecessors (FIG. 1-2), represent nude women with their arms folded across their abdomens. One example, about a foot-and-a-half tall—but only about a half-inch

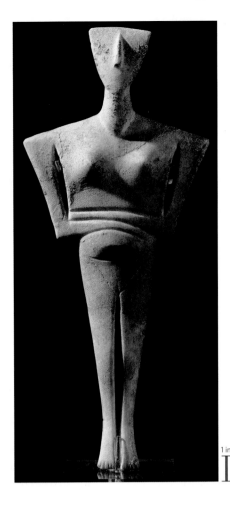

2-2 Figurine of a woman, from Syros (Cyclades), Greece, ca. 2600–2300 BCE. Marble, 1' 6" high. National Archaeological Museum, Athens.

Most Cycladic statuettes depict nude women. This one comes from a grave, but whether it represents the deceased is uncertain. The sculptor rendered the female body schematically as a series of triangles.

feet have the toes pointed downward, so the figurine cannot stand upright and must have been placed on its back in the grave—lying down, like the deceased. Archaeologists debate whether the Syros and similar Cycladic statuettes represent dead women or fertility figures or goddesses. In any case, the artist took pains to emphasize the breasts as well as the pubic area. The slight swelling of the belly of the Syros woman may suggest pregnancy.

Traces of paint found on some of the Cycladic figurines indicate that at least parts of these sculptures were colored. The now almost featureless faces would have had painted eyes and mouths in addition to the sculpted noses. Red and blue necklaces and bracelets, as well as painted dots on the cheeks and necks, characterize a number of the surviving figurines.

Minoan Art

During the third millennium BCE, both on the Aegean Islands and the Greek mainland, most settlements were small and consisted only of simple buildings. Rarely did graves contain costly offerings such as the Syros statuette. In contrast, the hallmark of the opening centuries of the second millennium BCE is the construction of major architectural complexes on Crete. This was the golden age of the prehistoric Aegean, the era when the first great Western civilization emerged. The Cretan buildings, conventionally called palaces, may not have served as royal residences. They were administrative, commercial, and religious centers with a central courtyard for ceremonies and games, and dozens of offices, shrines, and storerooms. The size and number of the "palaces," as well as the rich finds they have yielded, attest to the power and prosperity of the Minoans.

thick—comes from a grave on Syros (FIG. 2-2). The sculptor rendered the human body in a highly schematic manner, not unlike many modern abstract sculptures, which accounts for the popularity of Cycladic statuettes among collectors (see "Archaeology, Art History, and the Art Market"). Large simple triangles dominate the form—the head, the body itself (which tapers from exceptionally broad shoulders to tiny feet), and the incised triangular pubis. The

KNOSSOS The largest Cretan palace—at Knossos (FIG. 2-3)—was the legendary home of King Minos and of the *minotaur*, a creature half man and half bull. According to the myth, the minotaur inhabited a vast *labyrinth*, and when the Athenian king Theseus defeated the monster, he was able to find his way out of the maze only with the aid of Minos's daughter, Ariadne. She had given Theseus a spindle of thread to mark his path through the labyrinth and safely retrace his steps. The Knossos palace was indeed mazelike in plan. The central

2-3 Restored view (looking northwest) of the palace, Knossos (Crete), Greece, ca. 1700–1370 BCE (John Burge).

The Knossos palace, the largest on Crete, was the legendary home of King Minos. Scores of rooms surrounded a large court. The palace's mazelike plan gave rise to the myth of the minotaur in the labyrinth.

2-4 Stairwell in the residential quarter of the palace, Knossos (Crete), Greece, ca. 1700–1370 BCE.

The Knossos palace was complex in elevation as well as plan. It had at least three stories on all sides of the court. Minoan columns taper from top to bottom, the opposite of Egyptian and Greek columns.

feature of the rambling complex was its large rectangular court. The builders arranged the other palace units around this primary space. The palace was complex in *elevation* as well as plan. Around the central court, there were as many as three stories, and on the south and east sides, where the terrain sloped off sharply, up to five stories. Interior light and air wells (FIG. 2-4), some with staircases,

provided necessary illumination and ventilation. The Minoans fashioned their columns of wood and usually painted the shafts red. The columns had black, bulbous, cushionlike capitals resembling those of the later Greek Doric order (FIG. 2-20, *left*), but the shafts taper from a wide top to a narrower base, the opposite of both Egyptian and later Greek columns.

Mural paintings liberally adorned the Knossos palace, constituting one of its most striking features. The paintings depict many aspects of Minoan life (bull-leaping, processions) and of nature (birds, animals, flowers, marine life). Unlike the Egyptians, who painted in *fresco secco* (dry fresco), the Minoans coated the rough fabric of their rubble walls with a fine white lime plaster and applied the pigments while the plaster was still wet (see "Fresco Painting," page 208). The Minoan frescoes required rapid execution and great skill.

The most famous fresco (FIG. 2-5) from the palace at Knossos depicts Minoan bull-leaping, in which young men grasped the horns of a bull and vaulted onto its back—a perilous and extremely difficult acrobatic maneuver. The young women have fair skin and the leaping youth has dark skin in accord with the widely accepted ancient convention for distinguishing male and female. The painter brilliantly suggested the powerful charge of the bull (which has all four legs off the ground) by elongating the animal's shape and using sweeping lines to form a funnel of energy, beginning at the very narrow hindquarters of the bull and culminating in its large, sharp horns. The human figures also have stylized shapes, with typically Minoan pinched waists. The elegant, elastic, highly animated Cretan figures, with their long curly hair and proud and self-confident bearing, are easy to distinguish from Mesopotamian and Egyptian figures.

THERA Much better preserved than the Knossos frescoes are the mural paintings discovered in the excavations of Akrotiri on the island of Thera in the Cyclades, some 60 miles north of Crete. The excellent condition of the Akrotiri paintings is due to an enormous volcanic eruption on the island that buried the site in pumice

1 ft.

2-5 Bull-leaping, from the palace, Knossos (Crete), Greece, ca. 1500 BCE. Fresco, 2' 8" high, including border. Archaeological Museum, Iraklion.

Frescoes decorated the Knossos palace walls. The Minoan men and women have stylized bodies with narrow waists. The skin color varies with gender, a common convention in ancient paintings.

2-6 Landscape with swallows (*Spring Fresco*), south and west walls of room Delta 2, Akrotiri, Thera (Cyclades), Greece, ca. 1650–1625 BCE. Fresco, 7' 6" high. Reconstructed in National Archaeological Museum, Athens.

Aegean muralists painted in wet fresco, which required rapid execution. In this wraparound landscape, the painter used vivid colors and undulating lines to capture the essence of nature.

and ash around 1628 BCE. One almost perfectly preserved mural painting, known as the *Spring Fresco* (FIG. 2-6), is the largest prehistoric example of a pure *landscape*—a picture of a place without humans or animals. The artist's aim, however, was not to render the rocky island terrain realistically but to capture its essence. The irrationally undulating and vividly colored rocks, the graceful lilies swaying in the cool island breezes, and the darting swallows express the vigor of growth, the delicacy of flowering, and the lightness of birdsong and flight. In the lyrical language of curving line, the Theran muralist celebrated the rhythms of nature. The *Spring Fresco* represents the polar opposite of the first efforts at painting in the caves of Paleolithic Europe, where animals (and occasionally humans) appeared as isolated figures with no indication of setting.

MINOAN POTTERY Minoan painters also decorated small objects, especially ceramic pots, usually employing dark silhouettes against a cream-colored background. On a flask (FIG. 2-7) found at Palaikastro on Crete, the tentacles of an octopus reach out over the curving surface of the vessel, embracing the piece and emphasizing its volume. The flask is a masterful realization of the relationship between the vessel's decoration and its shape, always an issue for the vase painter.

SNAKE GODDESS In contrast to Mesopotamia and Egypt, Minoan Crete has yielded no trace of temples or life-size statues of gods, kings, or monsters, although large wood images may once have existed. What remains of Minoan sculpture is uniformly small in scale, such as the *faience* (low-fired opaque glasslike silicate) statuette found in the palace at Knossos and popularly known as the *Snake Goddess* (FIG. 2-8). Reconstructed from many fragments and in large part modern in its present form, it is one of several similar

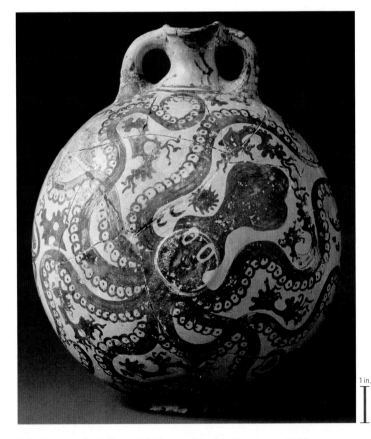

2-7 Octopus flask, from Palaikastro (Crete), Greece, ca. 1500 BCE. 11" high. Archaeological Museum, Iraklion.

The sea figures prominently in Minoan art. Here, the painter perfectly matched the octopus motif to the shape of the flask by spreading the sea creature's tentacles over the curving surface of the vessel.

2-8 *Snake Goddess,* from the palace, Knossos (Crete), Greece, ca. 1600 BCE. Faience, 1' 1½" high. Archaeological Museum, Iraklion.

This Minoan figurine may represent a priestess, but she is more likely a bare-breasted goddess. The snakes in her hands and the feline on her head imply that she wields power over the animal world.

figurines that some scholars believe may represent mortal priestesses rather than a deity. The prominently exposed breasts suggest, however, that these figurines stand in the long line of prehistoric fertility images usually considered divinities. The Knossos woman holds snakes in her hands and, as reconstructed, supports a tamed leopardlike feline on her head. If the feline was part of the statuette, the implied power over the animal world would be appropriate for

a deity. The frontality of the figure is reminiscent of Mesopotamian and Egyptian statuary, but the costume, with its open bodice and flounced skirt, is distinctly Minoan.

MINOAN DECLINE Scholars dispute the circumstances ending the Minoan civilization, although most now believe that Mycenaeans had already moved onto Crete and established themselves at Knossos in the 15th century BCE. Parts of the palace continued to be occupied until its final destruction around 1200 BCE, but its importance as a cultural center faded soon after 1400 BCE, as the focus of Aegean civilization shifted to the Greek mainland.

Mycenaean Art

The origin of the Mycenaeans is also a subject of continuing debate. The only certainty is the presence of these forerunners of the Greeks on the mainland at the beginning of the second millennium BCE. Some scholars believe that the mainland was a Minoan economic dependency for a long time, but by 1500 BCE a distinctive Mycenaean culture was flourishing in Greece.

TIRYNS The destruction of the Cretan palaces left the mainland culture supreme. Although historians refer to this civilization as Mycenaean, Mycenae was but one of several large sites. The best-preserved and most impressive Mycenaean remains are those of the citadels at Tiryns and Mycenae. Construction of both complexes began about 1400 BCE. Homer, writing in the mid-eighth century BCE, called the citadel of Tiryns (FIG. 2-9), located about 10 miles from Mycenae, "Tiryns of the Great Walls." In the second century CE, when Pausanias, author of an invaluable guidebook to Greece, visited the long-abandoned site, he marveled at the imposing fortifications and considered the walls of Tiryns to be as spectacular as the pyramids of Egypt. Indeed, the Greeks of the historical age did not believe that mere humans could have built such a fortress. They attributed the construction of the great Mycenaean citadels to the mythical *Cyclopes,* a race of one-eyed giants. Architectural historians still employ the term *Cyclopean masonry* to refer to the huge, roughly cut stone blocks forming the massive fortification walls of Tiryns and other Mycenaean sites. The Tiryns walls average about 20 feet in thickness and incorporate blocks often weighing several tons each. The heavily fortified Mycenaean palaces contrast sharply with the open Cretan palaces (FIG. 2-3) and clearly reveal their defensive character.

2-9 Aerial view of the citadel (looking east), Tiryns, Greece, ca. 1400–1200 BCE.

In the *Iliad,* Homer called the fortified citadel of Tiryns the city "of the great walls." Its huge, roughly cut stone blocks are examples of Cyclopean masonry, named after the mythical one-eyed giants.

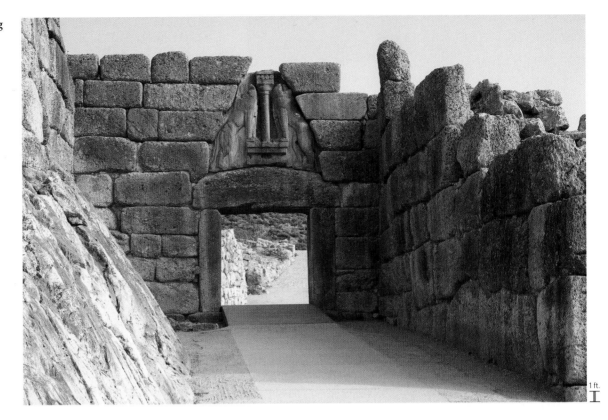

2-10 Lion Gate (looking east), Mycenae, Greece, ca. 1300–1250 BCE. Limestone, relief panel 9' 6" high.

The largest sculpture in the prehistoric Aegean is the relief of confronting lions that fills the relieving triangle of Mycenae's main gate. The gate itself consists of two great monolithic posts and a huge lintel.

LION GATE, MYCENAE The gateway to the citadel at Mycenae is the so-called Lion Gate (FIG. 2-10), protected on the left by a wall built on a natural rock outcropping and on the right by a projecting bastion of large blocks. Any approaching enemies would have had to enter this 20-foot-wide channel and face Mycenaean defenders above them on both sides. The gate itself consists of two great monolithic posts capped with a huge lintel (compare Stonehenge, FIG. 1-9). Above the lintel, the masonry courses form a *corbeled arch,* constructed by placing the blocks in horizontal courses and then cantilevering them inward until they meet, leaving an opening that lightens the weight the lintel carries. Filling this *relieving triangle* is a great limestone slab with two lions in high relief facing a central Minoan-type column. The whole design admirably matches its triangular shape, harmonizing in dignity, strength, and scale with the massive stones forming the walls and gate. Similar groups appear in miniature on Cretan seals, but the concept of placing monstrous guardian figures at the entrances to palaces,

tombs, and sacred places has its origin in Mesopotamia and Egypt (FIGS. 1-18 and 1-27). At Mycenae, the sculptors fashioned the animals' heads separately. Because those heads are lost, some scholars have speculated that the "lions" may have been composite beasts, possibly sphinxes.

TREASURY OF ATREUS The Mycenaeans erected the Lion Gate and the adjoining fortification wall circuit a few generations before the presumed date of the Trojan War. At that time, elite families buried their dead outside the citadel walls in beehive-shaped *tholos tombs* covered by enormous earthen mounds. The best preserved is the so-called Treasury of Atreus (FIG. 2-11), which the later Greeks mistakenly believed was the repository of the treasure of Atreus, father of King Agamemnon, who waged war against Troy. A long passageway leads to a doorway surmounted by a relieving triangle similar to that in the roughly contemporaneous Lion Gate. Composed of a series of stone courses laid on a circular base, the *tholos*

2-11 Exterior of the Treasury of Atreus (looking west), Mycenae, Greece, ca. 1300–1250 BCE.

The best-preserved Mycenaean tholos tomb is named after Homer's King Atreus. An earthen mound covers the burial chamber, reached through a doorway at the end of a long passageway.

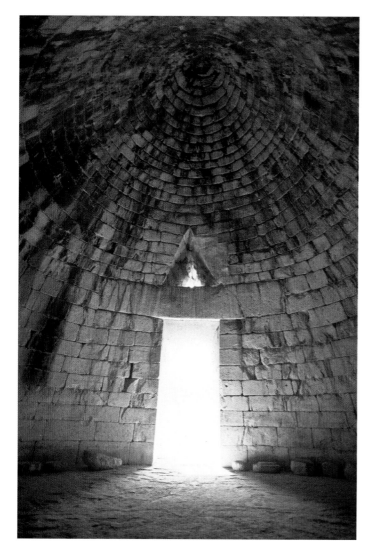

2-12 Interior of the Treasury of Atreus (looking east toward the entrance), Mycenae, Greece, ca. 1300–1250 BCE.

The beehive-shaped tholos of the Treasury of Atreus consists of corbeled courses of stone blocks laid on a circular base. The 43-foot-high dome was the largest in the ancient world for almost 1,500 years.

2-13 Funerary mask, from Grave Circle A, Mycenae, Greece, ca. 1600–1500 BCE. Beaten gold, 1' high. National Archaeological Museum, Athens.

Homer described the Mycenaeans as "rich in gold." This beaten-gold (repoussé) mask of a bearded man comes from a royal shaft grave. It is one of the first attempts at life-size sculpture in Greece.

has a lofty pointed *corbeled dome* (FIG. 2-12). The principle involved is no different from a corbeled arch. The builders probably constructed the dome using cantilevered rough-hewn blocks. After the masons set the stones in place, they had to finish the surfaces with great precision to make them conform to both the horizontal and vertical curvature of the wall. About 43 feet high, this Mycenaean domed chamber was the largest *vault*-covered space without interior supports ever built before the Roman Empire.

ROYAL SHAFT GRAVES The Treasury of Atreus was thoroughly looted long before its modern rediscovery, but archaeologists have unearthed spectacular grave goods elsewhere at Mycenae. Just inside the Lion Gate, but predating it by some three centuries, is the burial area designated as Grave Circle A. Here, at a site protected within the circuit of the later walls, six deep shafts served as tombs for kings and their families. The excavation of the royal shaft graves yielded many gold artifacts, including beaten (*repoussé*) gold masks. (Homer described the Mycenaeans as "rich in gold.") Art historians have often compared the Mycenaean mask illustrated here (FIG. 2-13) to Tutankhamen's gold mummy mask (FIG. 1-38).

The treatment of the human face is, of course, more primitive in the Mycenaean mask. But this is one of the first known attempts in Greece to render the human face at life-size, whereas the Egyptian mask stands in a long line of large-scale sculptures going back more than a millennium. No one knows whether the Mycenaean masks were intended as portraits, but the goldsmiths took care to record different physical types. The illustrated mask, with its full beard, must depict a mature man, perhaps a king—although not Agamemnon, as its 19th-century discoverer wished. If Agamemnon was a real king, he lived some 300 years after the death of the man buried in Grave Circle A.

THE END OF MYCENAE Despite their mighty walls, the citadels of Mycenae and Tiryns were burned between 1250 and 1200 BCE, when the Mycenaeans seem to have been overrun by northern invaders or to have fallen victim to internal warfare. By Homer's time, the greatest days of Aegean civilization were but a distant memory, and the men and women of Crete and Mycenae had assumed the stature of heroes from a lost golden age.

GREECE

The destruction of the Mycenaean palaces had a profound impact on both Aegean society and art. The disappearance of powerful kings and their retinues led to the loss of the knowledge of how to construct fortified citadels and vaulted tombs, to paint frescoes, and to sculpt in stone. Depopulation, poverty, and an almost total loss of contact with the outside world characterized the succeeding centuries, sometimes called the Dark Age of Greece.

Geometric and Archaic Art

Only in the eighth century BCE did economic conditions improve and the population begin to grow again. This era was in its own way a heroic age, a time when the Greeks established the Olympic Games, wrote down Homer's epic poems (formerly passed orally from bard to bard), and began to trade with their neighbors to both the east and the west.

GEOMETRIC KRATER This formative period, which art historians call the *Geometric* age, because Greek vase painting of the time consisted primarily of abstract motifs, also marked the return of the human figure to Greek art. One of the earliest examples of Greek figure painting is the huge *krater* (FIG. 2-14), or bowl for mixing wine and water, that stood atop the grave of a man buried around 740 BCE in the Dipylon Cemetery in Athens. At well over 3 feet tall, this vase is a considerable technical achievement. The artist covered much of the krater's surface with precisely painted abstract angular motifs in horizontal bands. Especially prominent is the *meander,* or key, pattern around the rim. But the Geometric painter reserved the widest part of the krater for two bands of human figures and horse-drawn chariots. Befitting the vase's funerary function, the scenes depict the mourning for a man laid out on his bier and a chariot procession in his honor. The painter filled every empty space around the figures with circles and M-shaped ornaments, negating any sense that the mourners or soldiers inhabit open space. The human figures, animals, chariots, and furniture are as two-dimensional as the geometric shapes elsewhere on the vessel.

In the upper band, the shroud, raised to reveal the corpse, is an abstract checkerboard-like backdrop. The figures are silhouettes constructed of triangular (that is, frontal) torsos with attached profile arms, legs, and heads (with a single large frontal eye in the center), following the age-old convention. To distinguish male from female, the painter added a penis growing out of the deceased's right thigh. The mourning women, who tear their hair out in grief, have breasts rendered as simple lines beneath their armpits. In both cases the artist's concern was specifying gender, not anatomical accuracy. Below, the warriors look like walking shields, and the two wheels of the chariots appear side by side. The horses have the correct number of heads and legs but seem to share a common body, so that there is no sense of depth. Despite the highly stylized and conventional manner of representation, this krater marks a significant turning point in the history of Greek art. Not only did the human figure reenter the painter's repertoire, but Geometric artists also revived the art of storytelling in pictures.

LADY OF AUXERRE During the seventh century BCE, the first stone sculptures since the Mycenaean Lion Gate (FIG. 2-10) began to appear in Greece. One of the earliest, probably originally from Crete, is a limestone statuette of a goddess or maiden (*kore*; plural, *korai*) popularly

2-15 *Lady of Auxerre,* from Crete, probably Eleutherna, Greece, ca. 650–625 BCE. Limestone, 2' 1½" high. Musée du Louvre, Paris.

One of the earliest Greek stone sculptures, this kore (maiden) typifies the Daedalic style of the seventh century BCE with its triangular face and hair and lingering Geometric fondness for abstract pattern.

1 ft.

2-14 Geometric krater, from the Dipylon cemetery, Athens, Greece, ca. 740 BCE. 3' 4½" high. Metropolitan Museum of Art, New York.

Figure painting returned to Greek art in the Geometric period, named for the abstract motifs on vessels such as this funerary krater featuring a mourning scene and procession in honor of the deceased.

known as the *Lady of Auxerre* (FIG. 2-15) after the French town that is her oldest recorded location. Because she does not wear a head-dress, as early Greek goddesses frequently do, and the placement of her right hand across the chest is probably a gesture of prayer, the *Lady of Auxerre* is most likely a kore. The style is characteristic of the early *Archaic* period (ca. 700–480 BCE). The flat-topped head takes the form of a triangle framed by complementary triangles of four long strands of hair each. Also typical are the small belted waist and a fondness for pattern, seen, for example, in the almost Geometric treatment of the long skirt with its incised concentric squares, once brightly painted.

Art historians refer to this early Greek style as *Daedalic,* after the legendary artist Daedalus, whose name means "the skillful one." In addition to his stature as a great sculptor, Daedalus reputedly built the labyrinth of Knossos (FIG. 2-3) and designed a temple at Memphis in Egypt. The historical Greeks attributed to him almost all the great achievements in early sculpture and architecture. The story that Daedalus worked in Egypt reflects the enormous influence of Egyptian art and architecture on the Greeks.

NEW YORK KOUROS One of the earliest Greek examples of life-size statuary (FIG. 2-16) is the marble *kouros* ("youth"; plural, *kouroi*) now in New York, which emulates the stance of Egyptian statues (FIG. 1-29). In both Egypt and Greece, the figure is rigidly frontal with the left foot advanced slightly. The arms are held beside the body, and the fists are clenched with the thumbs forward. Nevertheless, Greek kouros statues differ from their Egyptian models in two important ways. First, the Greek sculptors liberated the figures from the stone block. The Egyptian obsession with permanence was alien to the Greeks, who

were preoccupied with finding ways to represent motion rather than stability in their sculpted figures. Second, the kouroi are nude, just as Greek athletes competed nude in the Olympic Games. In the absence of identifying attributes, Greek youths as well as maidens are formally indistinguishable from Greek statues of deities.

The New York kouros shares many traits with the *Lady of Auxerre* (FIG. 2-15), especially the triangular shape of head and hair and the flatness of the face—the hallmarks of the Daedalic style. The eyes, nose, and mouth all sit on the front of the head, and the ears on the sides. The long hair forms a flat backdrop behind the head. This is the result of the sculptor's having drawn these features on the four vertical sides of the marble block, following the same workshop procedure used in Egypt for millennia. The kouros also has the slim waist of earlier Greek statues and exhibits the same love of pattern. The pointed arch of the rib cage, for example, echoes the V-shaped ridge of the hips, which suggests but does not accurately reproduce the rounded flesh and muscle of the human body.

KROISOS Sometime around 530 BCE, a young man named Kroisos died a hero's death in battle, and his family erected a kouros statue (FIG. 2-17) over his grave at Anavysos, not far from Athens. Although the Egyptian-inspired stance is the same as in the earlier New York kouros, this sculptor rendered the human body in a far more naturalistic manner. The head is no longer too large for the body, and the face is more rounded, with swelling cheeks replacing the flat planes of the earlier work. The long hair does not form a stiff backdrop to the head but falls naturally over the back. The V-shaped ridges of the New York kouros have become rounded, fleshy hips. Also new is that Kroisos smiles—or seems

2-16 Kouros, from Attica, possibly Anavysos, Greece, ca. 600 BCE. Marble, 6' $\frac{1}{2}$" high. Metropolitan Museum of Art, New York.

The sculptors of the earliest life-size statues of kouroi (young men) adopted the Egyptian pose for standing figures (FIG. 1-29), but the kouroi are nude and freestanding, liberated from the stone block.

2-17 Kroisos, from Anavysos, Greece, ca. 530 BCE. Marble, 6' 4" high. National Archaeological Museum, Athens.

This later kouros displays increased naturalism in its proportions and more rounded modeling of face, torso, and limbs. Kroisos also smiles—the Archaic sculptor's way of indicating that a person is alive.

2-18 *Peplos Kore,* from the Acropolis, Athens, Greece, ca. 530 BCE. Marble, 4' high. Acropolis Museum, Athens.

Unlike men, women are always clothed in Archaic statuary. This smiling kore is a votive statue of a goddess wearing four garments. She held her identifying attribute in her missing left hand.

1 ft.

and polished. Artists painted the eyes, lips, hair, and drapery in *encaustic,* a technique in which the pigment is mixed with hot wax before applying it to the statue.

PEPLOS KORE A stylistic "sister" to Kroisos, also with preserved paint, is the smiling *Peplos Kore* (FIG. 2-18), so called because until recently scholars thought she wore a *peplos,* a simple, long, wool belted garment. She wears four different garments, however, one of which only goddesses wore. The attribute the goddess held in her missing left hand would have identified her. Whichever goddess she is, the contrast with the *Lady of Auxerre* (FIG. 2-15) is striking. Although in both cases the drapery conceals the entire body save for head, arms, and feet, the sixth-century BCE sculptor rendered the soft female form much more naturally. This softer treatment of the flesh also sharply differentiates later korai from kouroi, which have hard, muscular bodies.

GREEK TEMPLES In addition to providing models for the earliest Greek stone statues, Egypt also influenced the development of Archaic Greek architecture. Around 650–630 BCE, the Greeks established a trading colony at Naukratis (MAP 1-3). Soon after, Greek builders began to erect the first stone edifices since the fall of the Mycenaean kingdoms. Although Greek temples cannot be confused with Egyptian temples (for example, FIG. 1-33), New Kingdom columnar halls clearly inspired Greek architects.

The basic plan of all Greek temples (see "Doric and Ionic Temples," page 57, and FIGS. 2-19 and 2-20) reveals an order, compactness, and symmetry that reflect the Greeks' sense of proportion and their effort to achieve ideal forms in terms of numerical relationships and geometric rules. The earliest temples tended to be long and narrow, with the proportion of the ends to the sides roughly expressible as 1:3. From the sixth century BCE on, temples tended to be a little longer than twice their width. To the Greek mind, proportion in architecture and sculpture was comparable to harmony in music. Both were reflections and embodiments of the cosmic order. A primary goal of sixth- and fifth-century BCE Greek architects was to find the most perfect proportions for each part of the building and for the structure as a whole (see "The Perfect Temple," page 45).

The Greeks gathered to worship outside, not inside, their temples. The altar stood outside the temple—at the east end, facing the rising sun. The temple proper housed a life-size or larger image of the deity—the *cult statue* (FIG. 2-1c), the grandest of all votive offerings. Both in its early and mature manifestations, the Greek temple was the house of the god or goddess, not of his or her followers.

Figural sculpture played a major role in the exterior program of the Greek temple from early times. The Greeks painted their architectural sculptures and usually placed statues and reliefs only in the building parts that had no structural function. This is true particularly of the Doric order, in which decorative sculpture appears only in the "voids" of the metopes and pediment. Ionic builders, less severe in this respect as well, were willing to decorate the entire frieze. Occasionally, they replaced their columns with female figures (*caryatids;* FIG. 2-42). The Greeks also often painted the capitals, decorative moldings, and other architectural elements (FIG. 2-28). The original appearance of Greek temples was therefore quite different than their gleaming white, if ruined, state today.

PAESTUM The premier example of early Greek efforts at Doric temple design is not in Greece but in Italy, at Paestum. The huge

to. Beginning around 560 BCE with the statue of a calf bearer (FIG. 2-17A 🔗), Archaic Greek statues always smile—even in the most inappropriate contexts (FIG. 2-29). Art historians have interpreted this so-called *Archaic smile* in various ways, but the happy face should not be taken literally. Rather, the smile is the way Archaic sculptors indicated that the person portrayed is alive. By adopting this convention, Greek artists signaled that their intentions were very different from those of their Egyptian counterparts.

Traces of paint remain on the Kroisos statue, enhancing the sense of life. Greek artists painted all their stone statues. The modern notion that Greek statuary was pure white is mistaken. The Greeks did not color their statues garishly, however. They left the flesh in the natural color of the stone, which they waxed

ARCHITECTURAL BASICS
Doric and Ionic Temples

The plan and elevation of Greek temples varied with date, geography, and the requirements of individual projects, but all Greek temples share defining elements that set them apart from both the religious shrines of other civilizations and other kinds of Greek buildings.

- **Plan** (FIG. 2-19) The core of a Greek temple was the *naos*, or *cella*, a windowless room that housed a statue of the deity. In front was a *pronaos*, or porch, often with two columns between the *antae*, or extended walls (columns *in antis*—that is, between the antae). A smaller second room might be placed behind the cella, but more frequently the Greek temple had a porch at the rear (*opisthodomos*) set against the blank back wall of the cella. The second porch served only a decorative purpose, satisfying the Greek passion for balance and symmetry. Around this core, Greek builders might erect a colonnade across the front of the temple (*prostyle*; FIG. 2-42), across both front and back (*amphiprostyle*; FIG. 2-43), or, more commonly, all around the cella and its porch(es) to form the *peristyle* of a *peripteral* temple (FIGS. 2-1, 2-19, 2-21, and 2-37).

- **Elevation** (FIG. 2-20) The elevation of a Greek temple consists of the platform, the colonnade, and the superstructure (*entablature*). In the Archaic period, two basic systems, or *orders*, evolved for articulating the three units. The Greek architectural orders differ both in the nature of the details and in the relative proportions of the parts. The names of the orders derive from the Greek regions where they were most commonly employed. The *Doric*, formulated on the mainland (FIG. 2-1), remained the preferred manner there and in the Greeks' western colonies (FIG. 2-21). The *Ionic* was the order of choice in the Aegean Islands and on the western coast of Asia Minor. The geographical distinctions are by no means absolute. The Ionic order, for example, was often used in Athens (FIGS. 2-42 and 2-43).

In both orders, the columns rest on the *stylobate*, the uppermost course of the platform. The columns have two or three parts, depending on the order: the *shaft*, usually marked with vertical channels (*flutes*); the *capital*; and, in the Ionic order, the *base*. Greek column shafts, in contrast to their Minoan and Mycenaean forebears, taper gradually from bottom to top. Greek capitals have two elements. The lower part (the *echinus*) varies with the order. In the Doric, it is convex and cushionlike, similar to the echinus of Minoan (FIG. 2-4) and Mycenaean (FIG. 2-10) capitals. In the Ionic, it is small and supports a bolster ending in scroll-like spirals (the *volutes*). The upper element, present in both orders, is a flat square block (the *abacus*), which provides the immediate support for the entablature.

The entablature has three parts: the *architrave*, the main weight-bearing and weight-distributing element; the *frieze*; and the *cornice*, a molded horizontal projection that together with two *raking* (sloping) *cornices* forms a triangle framing the *pediment*. In the Ionic order, the architrave is usually subdivided into three horizontal bands. Doric architects subdivided the frieze into *triglyphs* and *metopes*, whereas Ionic builders left the frieze open to provide a continuous field for relief sculpture.

The Doric order is massive in appearance, its sturdy columns firmly planted on the stylobate. Compared with the weighty and severe Doric, the Ionic order seems light, airy, and much more decorative. Its columns are more slender and rise from molded bases. The most obvious differences between the two orders are, of course, in the capitals—the Doric, severely plain, and the Ionic, highly ornamental.

2-19 Plan of a typical Greek peripteral temple.
Greek temples had peripteral colonnades and housed cult statues of the gods in the central room, or cella. Worshipers gathered outside the temples, where priests made offerings at open-air altars.

2-20 Elevations of the Doric and Ionic orders (John Burge).

The major orders of Greek architecture were the Doric and Ionic. They differ primarily in the form of the capitals and the treatment of the frieze. The Doric frieze is subdivided into triglyphs and metopes.

2-21 Temple of Hera (looking northeast), Paestum, Italy, ca. 550 BCE.

The peristyle of this huge early Doric temple consists of heavy, closely spaced cigar-shaped columns with bulky, pancakelike capitals, characteristic features of Archaic Greek architecture.

(80-by-170-foot) Temple of Hera (FIG. 2-21) erected there around 550 BCE retains its entire peripteral colonnade, but most of the entablature, including the frieze, pediment, and all of the roof, has vanished. The building's plan (FIG. 2-22)—with a central row of columns dividing the cella into two aisles—is unusual and characteristic only of Archaic temples. Placing columns underneath the *ridgepole* (the timber beam running the length of the building below the peak of the gabled roof) might seem the logical way to provide internal support for the roof structure, but it had several disadvantages. The row of columns on the cella's axis allowed no place for a central cult statue. Further, in order to correspond with the interior, the temple's facade required an odd number of columns (nine in this case). At Paestum, there are also three columns in antis instead of the standard two, which in turn ruled out a central doorway for viewing the statue. However, the architect still achieved a simple 1:2 ratio of facade and flank columns by erecting 18 columns on each side of the temple.

Another early aspect of the Paestum temple is the shape of its heavy, closely spaced columns (FIG. 2-21) with their large, bulky, pancakelike Doric capitals, which seem compressed by the overbearing weight of what probably was a high, massive entablature. The columns have a pronounced swelling (*entasis*) at the middle of the shafts, giving them a profile akin to that of a cigar. The columns and capitals thus express in a vivid manner their weight-bearing function. One reason for the heaviness of the design and the narrowness of the spans between the columns might be that the Archaic builders feared that thinner and more widely spaced columns would result in the superstructure's collapse. In later Doric temples (FIG. 2-1), the builders placed the columns farther apart, and the shafts became more slender, the entasis subtler, the capitals smaller, and the entablature lighter.

CORFU Even older than the Paestum temple is the Doric temple of Artemis at Corfu, one of the first stone peripteral temples built in Greece. The building is unfortunately in ruins, but most of the sculpture that embellished its pediments (FIG. 2-23) survives. Designing figural decoration for a pediment was never an easy task for the Greek sculptor because of the pediment's awkward triangular shape. The central figures had to be of great size (more than

N

| 0 | 10 | 20 | 30 | 40 | 50 feet |
| 0 | | 5 | | 10 | 15 meters |

1. Cella with central row of columns
2. Pronaos with three columns in antis

2-22 Plan of the Temple of Hera, Paestum, Italy, ca. 550 BCE.

The Hera temple's plan also reveals its early date. The building has an odd number of columns on the facade and a single row of columns in the cella, leaving no place for a central cult statue.

9 feet tall at Corfu), but as the pediment tapered toward the corners, the available area became increasingly cramped.

At the center of the Corfu pediment is the *gorgon* Medusa, a demon with a woman's body and a bird's wings. Medusa also had a hideous face and snake hair, and anyone who gazed at her turned into stone. The sculptor depicted her in the conventional Archaic bent-leg, bent-arm, pinwheel-like posture that signifies running or, for a winged creature, flying. To Medusa's left and right are two great felines. Together they serve as temple guardians, repulsing all enemies from the sanctuary of the goddess. Between Medusa and the great beasts are two smaller figures—the human Chrysaor at her left and the winged horse Pegasus at her right (only the rear legs remain). Chrysaor and Pegasus were Medusa's children. They sprang from her head when the Greek hero Perseus decapitated her with his sword. Their presence here with the living Medusa is therefore a chronological impossibility. The Archaic artist's interest was not in telling a coherent story but in identifying the central figure by depicting her offspring. Narration was, however, the purpose

2-23 West pediment, Temple of Artemis, Corfu, Greece, ca. 600–580 BCE. Limestone, greatest height 9' 4". Archaeological Museum, Corfu.

The hideous Medusa and two panthers at the center of this early pediment served as temple guardians. To either side, and much smaller, are scenes from the Trojan War and the battle of gods and giants.

of the much smaller groups situated in the pediment corners. To the viewer's right is Zeus, brandishing his thunderbolt and slaying a kneeling giant. In the extreme corner was a dead giant. The *gigantomachy* (battle of gods and giants) was a popular Greek theme that was a metaphor for the triumph of reason and order over chaos. In the pediment's left corner is one of the Trojan War's climactic events: Achilles's son Neoptolemos kills the enthroned King Priam. The fallen figure to the left of this group may be a dead Trojan.

The master responsible for the Corfu pediments was a pioneer, and the composition shows all the signs of experimentation. The lack of narrative unity in the Corfu pediment and the figures' extraordinary diversity of scale eventually gave way to pediment designs in which all the figures are the same size and act out a single event. But the Corfu designer already had shown the way by realizing, for example, that the area beneath the raking cornice could be filled with gods and heroes of similar size by employing a combination of standing, leaning, kneeling, seated, and lying figures. The Corfu master also discovered that animals could be very useful space fillers because, unlike humans, they have one end taller than the other.

BLACK-FIGURE PAINTING During the Archaic period, Greek vase painters replaced the simple silhouettes of the Geometric style with much more detailed representations using a new ceramic painting technique that art historians call *black-figure painting*. Black-figure painters still applied black silhouettes to the clay surface, but then used a sharp, pointed instrument to incise linear details in the black *glaze* forms, usually adding highlights in purplish red or white before firing the vessel. The combination of the weighty black silhouettes with the delicate detailing and the bright polychrome overlay proved to be irresistible, and painters throughout Greece quickly adopted the new technique.

EXEKIAS The acknowledged master of the black-figure technique was an Athenian named EXEKIAS. An *amphora,* or two-handled storage jar (FIG. 2-24), bears his signature as both painter and potter. Such signatures,

2-24 EXEKIAS, Achilles and Ajax playing a dice game (detail of an Athenian black-figure amphora), from Vulci, Italy, ca. 540–530 BCE. Amphora 2' high; detail $8\frac{1}{2}$" high. Musei Vaticani, Rome.

The dramatic tension, coordination of figural poses with vase shape, and intricacy of the engraved patterns of the cloaks are hallmarks of Exekias, the greatest master of black-figure painting.

common on Greek vases, reveal the artists' pride in their work but also served as "brand names," ensuring a higher price for the products of the most famous ceramists. Unlike his Geometric predecessors, Exekias did not divide the surface of his vases with bands filled with small figures and abstract ornament. Instead, he placed large figures in a single framed panel. In the illustrated example, Achilles, fully armed, is at the left. He plays a dice game with his comrade Ajax during a lull in the Trojan War. Ajax has taken off his helmet, but both men hold their spears. Their shields are nearby, and each man is ready for action at a moment's notice. The gravity and tension that characterize this composition are rare in Archaic art.

Exekias had no equal as a black-figure painter. This is evident in such details as the extraordinarily intricate engraving of the patterns on the heroes' cloaks (highlighted with delicate touches of white) and in the masterful composition. The arch formed by the backs of the two warriors echoes the shape of the rounded shoulders of the amphora. The shape of the vessel (compare FIG. 2-26) is echoed again in the void between the heads and spears of Achilles and Ajax. Exekias also used the spears to lead the viewer's eye toward the thrown dice, where the heroes' gazes are fixed. Of course, their eyes do not really look down at the table but stare out from the profile heads. For all his brilliance, Exekias was still wedded to many of the old conventions. Real innovation in figure drawing would have to await the invention of a new ceramic painting technique of greater versatility than black-figure.

RED-FIGURE PAINTING The birth of this new technique, called *red-figure painting*, occurred around 530 BCE. Red-figure is the opposite of black-figure. What was previously black became red, and vice versa. The artist used the same black glaze for the figures, but instead of creating silhouettes, the painter outlined the figures and then colored the background black, reserving the red clay for the figures themselves. For the interior details, the artist used a soft brush in place of a metal *graver*. The painter could now vary the thickness of the lines and even build up the glaze to give relief to curly hair or dilute it to create brown shades, thereby expanding the color range of the Greek vase painter's craft.

EUPHRONIOS One of the most admired red-figure painters was EUPHRONIOS, whose krater depicting the struggle between Herakles (Roman Hercules), the greatest Greek hero, and the giant Antaios (FIG. 2-25) reveals the exciting possibilities of the new technique. Antaios was a son of Earth, and he derived his power from contact with the ground. To defeat him, Herakles had to lift him into the air and strangle him while no part of the giant's body touched the earth. Here, the two wrestle on the ground, and Antaios still possesses enormous strength. Nonetheless, Herakles has the upper hand. The giant's face is a mask of pain. His eyes roll, and he bares his teeth. His right arm is paralyzed, with the fingers limp.

Euphronios used diluted glaze to delineate the muscles of both figures and to produce a golden brown hue for Antaios's hair—intentionally contrasting the giant's unkempt hair with the neat coiffure and carefully trimmed beard of the emotionless Herakles. But rendering human anatomy and hair convincingly was not his only interest. Euphronios also wished to show that his figures occupy space. He deliberately rejected the conventional composite posture for the human figure and attempted instead to reproduce how a particular human body is *seen*. He presented, for example, not only Antaios's torso but also his right thigh from the front. The lower leg disappears behind the giant, and only part of the right foot is visible. The viewer must mentally make the connection between the upper leg and the foot. Euphronios's panel is a window onto a mythological world with protagonists moving in three-dimensional space—a revolutionary new conception of what a picture is supposed to be.

EUTHYMIDES A preoccupation with the art of drawing per se is evident in a remarkable amphora (FIG. 2-26) painted by EUTHYMIDES, a rival of Euphronios's. The subject is appropriate for a wine storage jar—three tipsy revelers. But the theme was little more than an excuse for the artist to experiment with the representation of unusual positions of the human form. It is no coincidence that the bodies do not overlap, for each is an independent figure study. Euthymides cast aside the conventional frontal and profile composite views. Instead, he painted torsos that are not two-dimensional

2-25 EUPHRONIOS, Herakles wrestling Antaios (detail of an Athenian red-figure calyx krater), from Cerveteri, Italy, ca. 510 BCE. Krater 1' 7" high; detail 7¾" high. Musée du Louvre, Paris.

The early red-figure master Euphronios rejected the age-old composite view for painted figures and instead attempted to reproduce the way the human body appears from a specific viewpoint.

1 in.

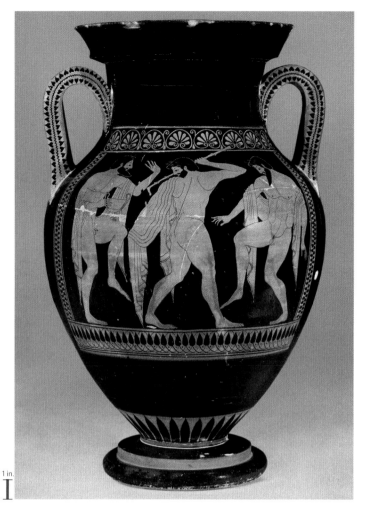

2-26 EUTHYMIDES, three revelers (Athenian red-figure amphora), from Vulci, Italy, ca. 510 BCE. 2' high. Staatliche Antikensammlungen, Munich.

Euthymides chose this theme as an excuse to represent bodies in unusual positions, including a foreshortened three-quarter rear view. He claimed to have surpassed Euphronios as a draftsman.

2-27 Model showing internal elevation (*top*) and plan (*bottom*) of the Temple of Aphaia, Aegina, Greece, ca. 500–490 BCE. Model: Glyptothek, Munich.

In this refined Doric design, the columns are more slender and widely spaced, there are only six columns on the facade, and the cella has two colonnades of two stories each framing the cult statue.

surface patterns but are *foreshortened*—that is, drawn in a three-quarter view. Most noteworthy is the central figure, shown from the rear with a twisting spinal column and buttocks in three-quarter view. Earlier artists had no interest in attempting to depict figures seen from behind or at an angle because those postures not only are incomplete but also do not show the "main" side of the human body. For Euthymides, however, the challenge of drawing a figure from this unusual viewpoint was a reward in itself. With understandable pride he proclaimed his achievement by adding to the formulaic signature "Euthymides painted me" the phrase "as never Euphronios [could do!]"

AEGINA The years just before and after 500 BCE were also a time of dynamic transition in architecture and architectural sculpture. The key monument is the temple (FIGS. 2-27 and 2-28) dedicated to Aphaia, a local nymph, at Aegina. The colonnade consists of 6 Doric columns on the facade and 12 on the flanks. This is a much more compact structure than Paestum's impressive but ungainly Hera temple (FIGS. 2-21 and 2-22), even though the ratio of width to length is similar. Doric architects had learned a great deal in the half-century that elapsed between construction of the two temples.

2-28 GUILLAUME-ABEL BLOUET, restored view (1828) of the facade of the Temple of Aphaia, Aegina, Greece, ca. 500–490 BCE.

The Aegina designer solved the problem of composing figures in a pediment by using the whole range of body postures from standing to lying. The restored view suggests how colorful Greek temples were.

2-29 Dying warrior, from the west pediment of the Temple of Aphaia, Aegina, Greece, ca. 490 BCE. Marble, 5' 2½" long. Glyptothek, Munich.

The two sets of Aegina pediment statues date about a decade apart. The earlier statues exhibit Archaic features. This fallen warrior still has a rigidly frontal torso and an Archaic smile on his face.

1 ft.

2-30 Dying warrior, from the east pediment of the Temple of Aphaia, Aegina, Greece, ca. 480 BCE. Marble, 6' 1" long. Glyptothek, Munich.

This later dying warrior already belongs to the Classical era. His posture is more natural, and he exhibits a new self-consciousness. Concerned with his own pain, he does not face the viewer.

1 ft.

The columns of the Aegina temple are more widely spaced and more slender. The capitals create a smooth transition from the vertical shafts below to the horizontal architrave above. Gone are the Archaic flattened echinuses and bulging shafts of the Paestum columns. The Aegina architect also refined the internal elevation and plan. In place of a single row of columns down the center of the cella is a double colonnade of two stories each. This arrangement enabled a statue to be placed on the central axis and also gave those gathered in front of the building an unobstructed view through the pair of columns in the pronaos.

Painted life-size statuary filled the Aegina temple's pediments. The theme of both statuary groups was the war between the Greeks and Trojans, and the compositions differed only slightly. In both pediments, Athena stands at the center. She is larger than all the other figures because she is superhuman, but all the mortal heroes are the same size, regardless of their position in the pediment. Unlike the experimental design at Corfu (FIG. 2-23), the Aegina pediments feature a unified theme and consistent scale. The designer achieved the latter by using the whole range of body postures from upright (Athena) to leaning, falling, kneeling, and lying (Greeks and Trojans).

The sculptures of the west pediment were set in place upon completion of the building around 490 BCE. The eastern statues are a decade later. It is instructive to compare the earlier and later figures. The sculptor of the west pediment's dying warrior (FIG. 2-29) still conceived the statue in the Archaic mode. The warrior's torso is rigidly frontal, and he looks out directly at the spectator—with his face set in an Archaic smile despite the bronze arrow puncturing his

chest. He is like a mannequin in a store window whose arms and legs have been arranged by someone else for effective display.

The comparable figure (FIG. 2-30) in the east pediment is fundamentally different. This warrior's posture is more natural and more complex, with the torso placed at an angle to the viewer (compare FIG. 2-25). Moreover, he reacts to his wound. He knows that death is inevitable, but still struggles to rise once again, using his shield for support. He does not look out at the viewer. This dying warrior is concerned with his plight, not with the viewer.

The two statues belong to different eras. The eastern warrior is not a creation of the Archaic world, when sculptors imposed anatomical patterns (and smiles) on statues. This statue belongs to the Classical world, where statues move as humans move and possess the self-consciousness of real men and women. This constitutes a radical change in the conception of the nature of statuary. In sculpture, as in painting, the Classical revolution had occurred.

Early and High Classical Art

Art historians mark the beginning of the *Classical** age from a historical event: the defeat of the Persian invaders of Greece by the allied Hellenic city-states. Shortly after the sack of Athens in 480 BCE, the Greeks won a decisive naval victory over the Persians at Salamis.

*In *Art through the Ages*, the adjective "Classical," with uppercase C, refers specifically to the Classical period of ancient Greece, 480–323 BCE. Lowercase "classical" refers to Greco-Roman antiquity in general—that is, the period treated in Chapters 2 and 3.

It had been a difficult war, and at times it appeared that Asia would swallow up Greece and that the Persian king Xerxes (see page 28) would rule over all. The narrow escape of the Greeks from domination by Asian "barbarians" nurtured a sense of Hellenic identity so strong that from then on, European civilization would be distinct from Asian civilization. Historians universally consider the decades following the removal of the Persian threat the high point of Greek civilization. This is the era of the dramatists Aeschylus, Sophocles, and Euripides; the historian Herodotus; the statesman Pericles; the philosopher Socrates; and many of the most famous Greek architects, sculptors, and painters.

KRITIOS BOY The sculptures of the Early Classical period (ca. 480–450 BCE) display a seriousness that contrasts sharply with the smiling figures of the Archaic period. But a more fundamental and significant break from the Archaic style was the abandonment of the rigid and unnatural Egyptian-inspired pose of Archaic statuary. The earliest example of the new approach is the marble statue known as the *Kritios Boy* (FIG. 2-31)—because art historians once thought it was the work of the sculptor Kritios. Never before had a sculptor been concerned with portraying how a human being (as opposed to a stone image) truly stands. Real people do not stand in the stiff-legged pose of the kouroi and korai or their Egyptian predecessors. Humans shift their weight and the position of the torso around the vertical (but flexible) axis of the spine. The sculptor of the *Kritios Boy* was among the first to grasp this anatomical fact and to represent it in statuary. The youth dips his right hip slightly, indicating the shifting of weight onto his left leg. His right leg is bent, at ease. The head, which no longer exhibits an Archaic smile, also

2-31 *Kritios Boy,* from the Acropolis, Athens, Greece, ca. 480 BCE. Marble, 2' 10" high. Acropolis Museum, Athens.

This is the first statue to show how a person naturally stands. The sculptor depicted the weight shift from one leg to the other (contrapposto). The head also turns slightly, and the youth no longer smiles.

turns slightly to the right and tilts, breaking the unwritten rule of frontality that dictated the form of virtually all earlier statues. This weight shift, called *contrapposto* ("counterbalance"), separates Classical from Archaic Greek statuary.

MYRON Early Classical Greek sculptors also explored the problem of representing figures engaged in vigorous action. The famous *Diskobolos* (*Discus Thrower*; FIG. 2-32) by MYRON, with its arms boldly extended, body twisted, and right heel raised off the ground, is such a statue. Nothing comparable survives from the Archaic period. The pose suggests the motion of a pendulum clock. The athlete's right arm has reached the apex of its arc but has not yet begun to swing down again. Myron froze the action and arranged the body and limbs to form two intersecting arcs, creating the impression of a tightly stretched bow a moment before the archer releases the string.

2-32 MYRON, *Diskobolos* (*Discus Thrower*). Roman copy from the Esquiline hill, Rome, Italy, of a bronze statue of ca. 450 BCE. Marble, 5' 1" high. Palazzo Massimo alle Terme, Museo Nazionale Romano, Rome.

This marble copy of Myron's lost bronze statue captures how the sculptor froze the action of discus throwing and arranged the nude athlete's body and limbs so that they form two intersecting arcs.

MATERIALS AND TECHNIQUES
Hollow-Casting Life-Size Bronze Statues

Large-scale bronze statues such as Myron's *Diskobolos* (known only through marble copies; FIG. 2-32) could not be manufactured using a single mold, as could simpler small-scale figures. Weight, cost, and the tendency of large masses of bronze to distort when cooling made life-size castings in solid bronze impractical. Instead, the Greeks hollow-cast large statues using the *cire perdue* (*lost-wax*) method (FIG. 2-33). The process entailed several steps and had to be repeated many times, because sculptors typically cast life-size statues such as the *Charioteer of Delphi* (FIG. 2-34) in parts—head, arms, hands, feet, and so forth.

First, the sculptor fashioned a full-size clay model of the intended statue. Then an assistant formed a clay master mold around the model and removed the mold in sections. When dry, the various pieces of the master mold were reassembled for each separate body part. Next, assistants applied a layer of beeswax to the inside of each mold. When the wax cooled, the sculptor removed the mold, revealing a hollow wax model in the shape of the original clay model. The artist could then correct or refine details—for example, engrave fingernails on the wax hands or individual locks of hair in a beard.

2-34 Charioteer (*Charioteer of Delphi*), from a group dedicated by Polyzalos of Gela in the Sanctuary of Apollo, Delphi, Greece, ca. 470 BCE. Bronze, 5' 11" high. Archaeological Museum, Delphi.

The *Charioteer of Delphi* was part of a large bronze group that also included a chariot, a team of horses, and a groom. The assemblage required hundreds of individually cast pieces soldered together.

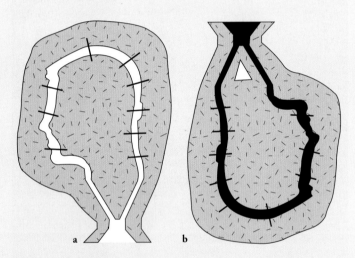

1 ft.

2-33 Two stages of the lost-wax method of bronze-casting (after Sean A. Hemingway).

Drawing *a* shows a clay mold (investment), wax model, and clay core connected by chaplets. Drawing *b* shows the wax melted out and the molten bronze poured into the mold to form the cast bronze head.

In the next stage, an assistant applied a final clay mold (*investment*) to the exterior of the wax model and poured liquid clay inside the model. Apprentices then hammered metal pins (*chaplets*) through the new mold to connect the investment with the clay core (FIG. 2-33*a*). Next, the wax was melted out ("lost") and molten bronze poured into the mold in its place (FIG. 2-33*b*). When the bronze hardened and assumed the shape of the wax model, the sculptor removed the investment and as much of the core as possible. The last step was to fit together and solder the individually cast pieces, smooth the joins and any surface imperfections, inlay the eyes, and add teeth, eyelashes, and accessories such as swords and wreaths.

The illustrated marble statue, however, is not Myron's, which was bronze (see "Hollow-Casting Life-Size Bronze Statues," above). It is a copy made in Roman times, when demand so far exceeded the supply of Greek statues that a veritable industry was born to meet the call for replicas of famous works to display in public places and private villas alike. Usually, the copies were of less costly painted marble, which presented a very different appearance from shiny bronze. In most cases, the copyist also had to add an intrusive tree trunk to support the great weight of the stone statue, and to place struts between arms and body to strengthen weak points. The replicas rarely approach the quality of the originals, but the Roman statues

are indispensable today. Without them it would be impossible to reconstruct the history of Greek sculpture after the Archaic period.

CHARIOTEER OF DELPHI Two rare extant Early Classical bronze statues are the *Charioteer of Delphi* (FIG. 2-34) and a warrior from Riace, Italy (FIG. 2-34A ⊿). The former was the centerpiece of a chariot group set up by the tyrant Polyzalos of Gela (Sicily) to commemorate his brother Hieron's victory in the Delphic Pythian Games. The group originally comprised the Sicilian driver, the chariot, the team of horses, and a young groom. The charioteer stands in an almost Archaic pose, but the turn of the head and feet in opposite

PROBLEMS AND SOLUTIONS
Polykleitos's Prescription for the Perfect Statue

In his treatise simply called the *Canon*, Polykleitos of Argos sought to define what constituted a perfect statue, one that could serve as the standard by which all other statues might be judged. How does one make a "perfect statue"? What principles guided the Greek master in formulating his canon?

One of the most influential philosophers and mathematicians of the ancient world was Pythagoras of Samos, who lived during the latter part of the sixth century BCE (see page 45). Pythagoras discovered that harmonic chords in music are produced on the strings of a lyre at regular intervals that may be expressed as ratios of whole numbers—for example, 2:1, 3:2, 4:3. He believed more generally that underlying harmonic proportions could be found in all of nature, determining the form of the cosmos as well as of things on earth, and that beauty resided in harmonious numerical ratios.

Following this reasoning, Polykleitos concluded that the way to create a perfect statue would be to design it according to an all-encompassing mathematical formula. That is what Polykleitos achieved in his *Doryphoros*. Galen, a physician who lived during the second century CE, summarized the sculptor's philosophy as follows:

> [Beauty arises from] the commensurability of the parts, such as that of finger to finger, and of all the fingers to the palm and the wrist, and of these to the forearm, and of the forearm to the upper arm, and, in fact, of everything to everything else, just as it is written in the *Canon* of Polykleitos. . . . Polykleitos supported his treatise [by making] a statue according to the tenets of his treatise, and called the statue, like the work, the *Canon*.*

This is why Pliny the Elder, writing in the first century CE, maintained that Polykleitos "alone of men is deemed to have rendered art itself [that is, the theoretical basis of art] in a work of art."†

* Galen, *De placitis Hippocratis et Platonis*, 5. Translated by J. J. Pollitt, *The Art of Ancient Greece: Sources and Documents* (New York: Cambridge University Press, 1990), 76.

† Pliny the Elder, *Natural History*, 34.55. Translated by Pollitt, 75.

2-35

POLYKLEITOS, *Doryphoros* (*Spear Bearer*). Roman copy from the palaestra, Pompeii, Italy, of a bronze statue of ca. 450–440 BCE. Marble, 6' 11" high. Museo Archeologico Nazionale, Naples.

Polykleitos sought to portray the perfect man and to impose order on human movement. He achieved his goals through harmonic proportions and a system of cross balancing for all parts of the body.

1 ft.

directions as well as a slight twist at the waist are in keeping with the Early Classical manner. The moment the sculptor chose for depiction was not during the frenetic race but after, when the charioteer modestly held his horses quietly in the winner's circle. He grasps the reins in his outstretched right hand (the lower left arm, cast separately, is missing), and he wears the standard charioteer's garment, girdled high and held in at the shoulders and the back to keep it from flapping. The folds emphasize both the verticality and calm of the figure and recall the flutes of a Greek column. The fillet that holds the charioteer's hair in place is inlaid with silver. The eyes are glass paste, shaded by delicate lashes individually cut from a sheet of bronze and soldered to the head.

POLYKLEITOS One of the most frequently copied Greek statues was the *Doryphoros* (FIG. 2-35), or *Spear Bearer*, by POLYKLEITOS, the sculptor whose work exemplifies the intellectual rigor of High Classical (ca. 450–400 BCE) statuary design. Polykleitos created the *Doryphoros* as a demonstration piece to accompany a treatise on

the ideal statue of a nude male warrior or athlete. *Spear Bearer* is a modern descriptive title for the statue. The name that the artist assigned to it was *Canon* (see "Polykleitos's Prescription for the Perfect Statue," above).

The *Doryphoros* is the culmination of the evolution in Greek statuary from the Archaic kouros (FIGS. 2-16 and 2-17) to the *Kritios Boy* (FIG. 2-31) to the Riace warrior (FIG. 2-34A ⏎). The contrapposto is more pronounced than ever before in a standing statue, but Polykleitos was not content with simply rendering a figure that stands naturally. His aim was to impose order on human movement, to make it "beautiful," to "perfect" it. He achieved this through a system of cross balance of the figure's various parts. Note, for instance, how the straight-hanging arm echoes the rigid supporting leg, providing the figure's right side with the columnar stability needed to anchor the left side's dynamically flexed limbs. The tensed and relaxed limbs oppose each other diagonally. The right arm and the left leg are relaxed, and the tensed supporting leg opposes the flexed arm, which held a spear. In like manner, the head turns to the right while the hips twist slightly to the left. And although the *Doryphoros* seems to take a step forward, he does not move. This dynamic asymmetrical balance, this motion while at rest, and the resulting harmony of opposites are the essence of the Polykleitan style.

ATHENIAN ACROPOLIS While Polykleitos was formulating his *Canon* in Argos, the Athenians, under the leadership of Pericles (ca. 495–429 BCE), initiated one of the most ambitious building projects ever undertaken—the reconstruction of the Acropolis (*acropolis* means "high city") after the Persian sack. In 478 BCE, in the aftermath of the Persian defeat, the Greeks formed an alliance for mutual protection against any renewed threat from the East. The new confederacy came to be known as the Delian League, because its headquarters were on the Cycladic island of Delos. Although at the outset each league member had an equal vote, Athens was "first among equals," providing the allied fleet commander and determining which cities were to furnish ships and which were instead to pay an annual tribute to the treasury at Delos. Continued fighting against the Persians kept the alliance intact, but Athens gradually assumed a dominant role. In 454 BCE, the league transferred the Delian treasury to Athens, ostensibly for security reasons. Tribute continued to be paid, but Pericles did not spend the surplus reserves for the common good of the allied Greek states. Instead, he expropriated the money to resurrect the Acropolis (FIG. 2-36). The Periclean building program was therefore not the glorious fruit of Athenian democracy, as commonly thought, but the by-product of tyranny and the abuse of power. Too often art and architectural historians do not ask how an art or building project was financed. The answer can be very revealing.

The centerpiece of the Periclean Acropolis was the Parthenon (FIGS. 2-1 and 2-36, no. 1), erected in the remarkably short period between 447 and 438 BCE. (Work on the temple's ambitious sculptural ornamentation continued until 432 BCE.) In 437 BCE, construction commenced on a grand new gateway to the Acropolis, the Propylaia (FIG. 2-36, no. 2). Two later temples, the Erechtheion (FIGS. 2-36, no. 3, and 2-42) and the Temple of Athena Nike (FIGS. 2-36, no. 4, and 2-43), built after Pericles died, were probably also part of the original project.

PARTHENON: ARCHITECTURE Most of the peripteral colonnade of the Parthenon (FIG. 2-1) still stands (or has been reerected), and art historians know a great deal about the building and its sculptural program. The architect was Iktinos, assisted, according to some

2-36 Restored view of the Acropolis, Athens, Greece (John Burge). (1) Parthenon, (2) Propylaia, (3) Erechtheion, (4) Temple of Athena Nike.

Under Pericles, the Athenians undertook one of history's most ambitious building projects—the reconstruction of the Acropolis after the Persian sack. The funds came from the Delian League treasury.

sources, by KALLIKRATES. The statue of Athena (FIG. 2-1c) in the cella was the work of Phidias, who was also the overseer of the temple's sculptural decoration. In fact, Plutarch stated in his biography of Pericles that Phidias was in charge of the entire Acropolis project. Just as the contemporaneous *Doryphoros* may be seen as the culmination of nearly two centuries of searching for the ideal proportions of the human body, so, too, the Parthenon may be viewed as the ideal solution to the Greek architect's quest for perfect proportions in Doric temple design (see "The Perfect Temple," page 45). The Parthenon architects and Polykleitos were kindred spirits in their belief that strict adherence to harmonious numerical ratios resulted in beautiful proportions. For the Parthenon, the controlling ratio may be expressed algebraically as $x = 2y + 1$. Thus, for example, the temple's plan (FIG. 2-37) called for 8 columns on the short ends and 17 on the long sides, because $17 = (2 \times 8) + 1$. The stylobate's ratio of length to width is 9:4, because $9 = (2 \times 4) + 1$.

2-37 Plan of the Parthenon, Acropolis, Athens, Greece, with diagram of the sculptural program (after Andrew Stewart), 447–432 BCE.

The Parthenon was lavishly decorated. Statues filled both pediments, and reliefs adorned all 92 Doric metopes as well as the 524-foot Ionic frieze. In the cella was Phidias's colossal gold-and-ivory Athena.

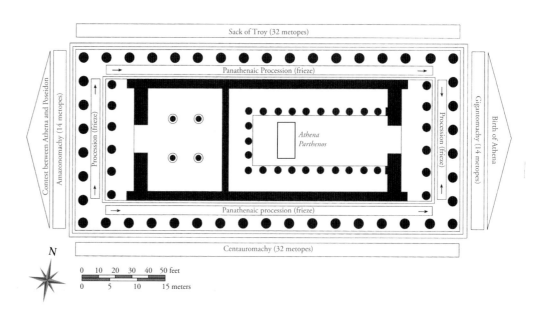

The Parthenon's harmonious design and the mathematical precision of the sizes of its constituent elements obscure the fact that throughout the building are pronounced deviations from the strictly horizontal and vertical lines assumed to be the basis of all Greek temples. The stylobate, for example, curves upward at the center on all four sides, forming a kind of shallow dome, and this curvature carries up into the entablature. Moreover, the peristyle columns (FIG. 2-1a) lean inward slightly. Those at the corners have a diagonal inclination and are also about 2 inches thicker than the rest. If their lines continued, they would meet about 1.5 miles above the temple. These deviations from the norm meant that virtually every Parthenon block had to be carved according to the special set of specifications dictated by its unique place in the structure. Vitruvius, a Roman architect of the late first century BCE, explained these adjustments as compensations for optical illusions. Vitruvius noted, for example, that if a stylobate is laid out on a level surface, it will appear to sag at the center. He also recommended that the corner columns of a building should be thicker because they are surrounded by light and would otherwise appear thinner than their neighbors (see "Vitruvius's *Ten Books on Architecture*" ⬈).

One of the ironies of the Parthenon, the world's most famous Doric temple, is that it incorporates major Ionic elements. Although the cella (FIG. 2-37) had a two-story Doric colonnade, the back room (which housed the goddess's treasury and the tribute collected from the Delian League) had four tall and slender Ionic columns as sole supports for the superstructure. And whereas the temple's exterior had a standard Doric frieze, the inner frieze (FIG. 2-41) running around the top of the cella wall was Ionic. Perhaps this fusion of Doric and Ionic elements reflects the Athenians' belief that the Ionians of the Aegean Islands and Asia Minor were descendants of Athenian settlers and were therefore their kin. Or it may be Pericles and Iktinos's way of suggesting that Athens was the leader of *all* the Greeks. In any case, a mix of Doric and Ionic features characterizes the fifth-century BCE buildings of the Acropolis as a whole.

ATHENA PARTHENOS The Parthenon was more lavishly decorated than any Greek temple before it, Doric or Ionic. A mythological scene appears in every one of the 92 Doric metopes (FIGS. 2-37 and 2-38), and a cavalcade and procession unfold along the 524-foot-long Ionic frieze (FIG. 2-41). Dozens of larger-than-life-size statues filled both pediments (FIGS. 2-39 and 2-40). And inside was the most expensive item of all—Phidias's gold-and-ivory 38-foot-tall *chryselephantine* (gold-and-ivory) *Athena Parthenos* (FIG. 2-1c). Fully armed, the goddess held Nike (the winged female personification of victory) in her extended right hand. No one doubts that this Nike referred to the victory of 479 BCE. The memory of the Persian sack of the Acropolis was still vivid, and the Athenians were intensely conscious that by driving back the Persians, they were saving their civilization from the "barbarians" who had committed atrocities against the Greeks of Asia Minor. In fact, Phidias incorporated multiple allusions to the Persian defeat in his colossal statue. On the thick soles of Athena's sandals was a representation of a *centauromachy*. Emblazoned on the exterior of her shield were high reliefs depicting the battle of Greeks and Amazons (*Amazonomachy*), in which Theseus drove the Amazons (female warriors) out of Athens. On the shield's interior, Phidias painted a gigantomachy. Each of these mythological contests was a metaphor for the triumph of order over chaos, of civilization over barbarism, and of Athens over Persia.

PARTHENON: METOPES Phidias took up these same themes again in the Parthenon's metopes (FIG. 2-37). The south metopes, for example, depicted the battle of Lapiths (a northern Greek people) and centaurs, a combat in which Theseus of Athens played a major role. On one extraordinary slab (FIG. 2-38), a triumphant centaur rises up on its hind legs, exulting over the crumpled body of the Greek whom the horse-man has defeated. The relief is so high that parts are fully in the round. Some have broken off. The sculptor brilliantly distinguished the vibrant, powerful form of the living beast from the lifeless corpse on the ground. In other metopes, the Greeks have the upper hand, but the full set suggests that the battle was a difficult one against a dangerous enemy and that losses as well as victories occurred. The same was true of the war against the Persians.

2-38 *Centauromachy,* metope from the south frieze of the Parthenon, Acropolis, Athens, Greece, ca. 447–438 BCE. Marble, 4' 8" high. British Museum, London.

The Parthenon's centauromachy metopes allude to the Greek defeat of the Persians. Here the High Classical sculptor brilliantly distinguished the vibrant living centaur from the lifeless Greek corpse.

1 ft.

PARTHENON: PEDIMENTS The subjects of the two pediments were especially appropriate for a temple celebrating Athena—and the Athenians. The east pediment depicted the birth of the goddess. At the west was the contest between Athena and Poseidon to determine which one would become the city's patron deity. Athena won, giving her name to the city and its people. It is significant that in the story and in the pediment, the Athenians are the judges of the relative merits of the two gods. The selection of this theme reflects the same arrogance that led to the use of Delian League funds to rebuild the Acropolis.

All that remains of the east pediment's statues are the spectators to the left and right who witnessed Athena's birth on Mount Olympus. At the far left (FIG. 2-39) are the head and arms of Helios (Sun) and his chariot horses rising from the pediment floor. Next to them is a powerful male figure usually identified as Dionysos or possibly Herakles, who entered the realm of the gods after he completed 12 impossible labors. At the right (FIG. 2-40) are three goddesses, probably Hestia, Dione, and Aphrodite, and either Selene (Moon) or Nyx (Night) and more horses, this time sinking below the pediment's floor. Here, Phidias discovered an entirely new way to deal with the awkward triangular frame of the pediment. Its floor is the horizon line, and charioteers and their horses move through it effortlessly.

Phidias and his assistants were master sculptors. They fully understood not only the surface appearance of human and animal anatomy but also the mechanics of how muscles and bones make bodies move. The Athenian sculptors mastered the rendition of clothed forms as well. In the Dione-Aphrodite group (FIG. 2-40), the thin and heavy folds of the garments alternately reveal and conceal the main and lesser body masses while swirling in a compositional tide that subtly unifies the figures. The articulation and integration of the bodies produce a wonderful variation of surface and play of light and shade. Moreover, all the figures, even the animals, are brilliantly characterized. The horses of the Sun, at the beginning of the day, are energetic. Those of the Moon or Night, having labored until dawn, are weary.

PARTHENON: IONIC FRIEZE In many ways, the most remarkable part of the Parthenon's sculptural decoration is the inner Ionic frieze (FIG. 2-41), which represents the Panathenaic Festival procession that took place every four years in Athens. The procession began at the Dipylon Gate to the city and ended on the Acropolis, where the Athenians placed a new peplos on an ancient wood statue of Athena. That statue (probably similar in general appearance to the *Lady of Auxerre,* FIG. 2-15) had been housed in the Archaic temple that the Persians razed, but the Athenians removed it on the eve of the Persian attack. On the Parthenon frieze, the procession begins on the west side—that is, at the temple's rear, facing the gateway to the Acropolis. It then moves in parallel lines down the long north and south sides of the building and ends at the center of the east frieze, over the doorway to the cella housing Phidias's statue (FIG. 2-37). The upper part of the frieze is in higher relief than the lower part so that the more distant and more shaded upper zone is as legible from the ground as the lower part of the frieze. This is another instance of how the builders took optical effects into consideration.

The frieze vividly communicates the procession's acceleration and deceleration. At the outset, on the west side, marshals gather and youths mount their horses. In the north and south friezes (FIG. 2-41, *top*), the momentum of the cavalcade picks up. On the

2-39 Helios and his horses, and Dionysos (Herakles?), from the east pediment of the Parthenon, Acropolis, Athens, Greece, ca. 438–432 BCE. Marble, greatest height 4' 3". British Museum, London.

The east pediment of the Parthenon depicts the birth of Athena. At the left, Helios and his horses energetically emerge from the pediment's floor, suggesting the sun rising above the horizon at dawn.

1 ft.

2-40 Three goddesses (Hestia, Dione, and Aphrodite?), from the east pediment of the Parthenon, Acropolis, Athens, Greece, ca. 438–432 BCE. Marble, greatest height 4' 5". British Museum, London.

These statues representing three goddesses conform perfectly to the sloping right side of the Parthenon's east pediment. The thin and heavy folds of the garments alternately reveal and conceal the body forms.

1 ft.

east side, seated gods and goddesses (FIG. 2-41, *center*), the invited guests, watch the procession slow to a halt (FIG. 2-41, *bottom*). The role assigned to the Olympian deities is extraordinary. They do not take part in the festival or determine its outcome. They are merely spectators, admiring the Athenian people, the new masters of a new Aegean empire who considered themselves worthy of depiction on a temple. The Parthenon celebrated the greatness of Athens and the Athenians as much as it honored Athena.

2-41 Three details of the Panathenaic Festival procession frieze, from the Parthenon, Acropolis, Athens, Greece, ca. 447–438 BCE. Marble, 3' 6" high. *Top:* horsemen (south frieze), British Museum, London. *Center:* Poseidon, Apollo, Artemis, Aphrodite, and Eros (east frieze), Acropolis Museum, Athens. *Bottom:* elders and maidens (east frieze), Musée du Louvre, Paris.

The Parthenon's Ionic frieze represents the Panathenaic procession of citizens on horseback and on foot under the gods' watchful eyes. The Parthenon celebrated the Athenians as much as the goddess Athena.

2-42 Erechtheion (looking northeast), Acropolis, Athens, Greece, ca. 421–405 BCE.

The asymmetrical form of the Erechtheion is unique for a Greek temple. It reflects the need to incorporate preexisting shrines into the plan. The decorative details are perhaps the finest in Greek architecture.

ERECHTHEION In 421 BCE, work finally began on the temple that was to replace the Archaic Athena temple that the Persians had destroyed. The new structure, the Erechtheion (FIG. 2-42), built to the north of the old temple's remains, was to be a multiple shrine, however. It honored Athena and became the new home of the ancient wood image of the goddess that was the goal of the Panathenaic Festival procession. But it also incorporated shrines to a host of other gods and demigods who loomed large in the city's legendary past. Among these were Erechtheus, an early king of Athens, during whose reign the Athena idol fell from the heavens, and Kekrops, another king of Athens, who served as judge of the contest between Athena and Poseidon. In fact, the site chosen for the new temple was the very spot where that contest occurred. Poseidon had staked his claim to Athens by striking the Acropolis rock with his trident and producing a salt-water spring. Athena had miraculously caused an olive tree to grow.

The asymmetrical plan of the Ionic Erechtheion is unique for a Greek temple and the antithesis of the simple and harmoniously balanced plan of the Doric Parthenon across the way. Its irregular form reflected the need to incorporate the tomb of Kekrops and other preexisting shrines, the trident mark, and the olive tree into a single complex. The unknown architect responsible for the building also had to struggle with the problem of uneven terrain. The area could not be leveled by terracing because that would disturb the sacred sites. As a result, the Erechtheion has four sides of very different character, and each side rests on a different ground level.

Perhaps to compensate for the awkward character of the building as a whole, the architect took great care with the Erechtheion's decorative details. The Ionic capitals were inlaid with gold, rock crystal, and colored glass, and the frieze received special treatment. The stone chosen was grey-blue limestone to contrast with the white marble relief figures attached to the dark frieze and the white walls and columns. The temple's most striking and famous feature is its south porch, where caryatids replaced Ionic columns. Although the caryatids exhibit the weight shift that was standard for the era, the flutelike drapery folds concealing their stiff, weight-bearing legs underscore their role as architectural supports. The figures have enough rigidity to suggest the structural column and just the degree of flexibility needed to suggest the living body.

TEMPLE OF ATHENA NIKE Another Ionic building on the Athenian Acropolis is the small Temple of Athena Nike (FIG. 2-43), designed by Kallikrates, who may have been responsible for the Parthenon's Ionic elements. The temple stands on what was once a Mycenaean bastion and greets all visitors entering Athena's great sanctuary. Like the Parthenon, the Athena Nike temple commemorated the victory over the Persians—and not just in its name. Part of the frieze represented the battle of Marathon in 490 BCE, a turning point in the war against the Persians—a human event, as in the Parthenon's Panathenaic Festival procession frieze. But on the later temple, the sculptors chronicled a specific occasion, not a recurring event involving anonymous citizens.

Around the building, at the bastion's edge, was a *parapet* decorated with exquisite reliefs. The theme matched that of the

2-43 KALLIKRATES, Temple of Athena Nike (after restoration, 2012; looking southwest), Acropolis, Athens, Greece, ca. 427–424 BCE.

The small Ionic temple at the entrance to the Acropolis celebrates Athena as bringer of victory. One of its friezes depicts the Greek defeat of the Persian forces at Marathon in 490 BCE.

temple proper—victory. Dozens of images of Nike adorned the parapet, always in different attitudes. Sometimes she erects trophies bedecked with Persian spoils. Other times she brings forward sacrificial bulls for Athena. One relief (FIG. 2-44) shows Nike adjusting her sandal—an awkward posture rendered elegant and graceful by a sculptor who carried the style of the Parthenon pediments (FIG. 2-40) even further and created a figure whose garments cling so tightly to the body that they seem almost transparent, as if drenched with water. The drapery folds form intricate linear patterns unrelated to the body's anatomical structure and have a life of their own as abstract designs.

HEGESO STELE Decorating temples was not the only job available to sculptors in fifth-century BCE Athens. Around 400 BCE, the family of a young woman named Hegeso, daughter of Proxenos, set up a grave stele (FIG. 2-45) in her memory in the Dipylon cemetery, where, centuries earlier, Athenians had marked graves with enormous vases (FIG. 2-14). Hegeso is the well-dressed woman seated on an elegant chair (with footstool). She examines a piece of jewelry (once rendered in paint, not now visible) selected from a box a servant girl brings to her. The maid's simple unbelted *chiton* contrasts sharply with the more elaborate attire of her mistress. The garments of both women reveal the body forms beneath them, as on the parapet reliefs of the Athena Nike temple. The faces are serene, without a trace of sadness. Indeed, the sculptor depicted both mistress and maid during a characteristic shared moment out of daily life. Only the epitaph reveals that Hegeso is the one who has departed.

The simplicity of the scene on the Hegeso stele is deceptive, however. This is not merely a bittersweet scene of tranquil domestic life before an untimely death. The setting itself is significant—the secluded women's quarters of a Greek house, from which Hegeso rarely would have emerged. Contemporaneous grave stelae of men regularly show them in the public domain, often as warriors. The servant girl is not so much the faithful companion of the deceased in life

2-44 Nike adjusting her sandal, from the south side of the parapet of the Temple of Athena Nike, Acropolis, Athens, Greece, ca. 410 BCE. Marble, 3' 6" high. Acropolis Museum, Athens.

Dozens of images of winged Victory adorned the parapet on three sides of the Acropolis's Athena Nike temple. The sculptor carved this Nike with garments that appear almost transparent.

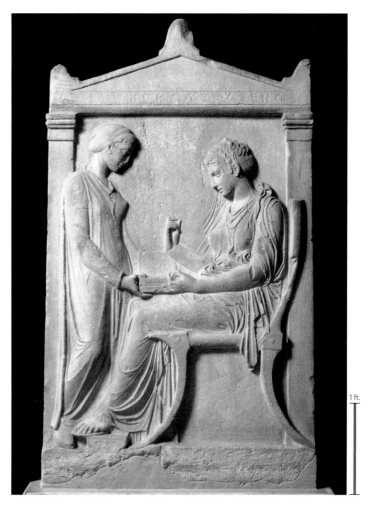

2-45 Grave stele of Hegeso, from the Dipylon cemetery, Athens, Greece, ca. 400 BCE. Marble, 5' 2" high. National Archaeological Museum, Athens.

On her tombstone, Hegeso examines jewelry from a box that her servant girl holds. Mistress and maid share a serene moment out of daily life. Only the epitaph reveals that Hegeso is the one who died.

MATERIALS AND TECHNIQUES
White-Ground Painting

White-ground painting takes its name from the chalky white *slip* (lique-fied clay) used to provide a background for the painted figures. One of the best examples is the *lekythos* (FIG. 2-46)—a flask to hold perfumed oil—painted around 440 BCE by the Achilles Painter. White-ground is essentially a variation of the red-figure technique. First the painter covered the pot with a slip of very fine white clay, then applied black glaze to outline the figures, and diluted brown, purple, red, and white to color them. The artist could use other colors—for example, the yellow the Achilles Painter chose for the garments of both figures on this lekythos—but these had to be applied after firing because the Greeks did not know how to make them withstand the intense heat of the kiln.

Despite the obvious attractions of the technique, the imperma-nence of the expanded range of colors discouraged white-ground paint-ing on everyday vessels, such as amphoras and kraters. In fact, Greek artists explored the full polychrome possibilities of the white-ground technique almost exclusively on lekythoi, which families commonly placed in graves as offerings to the deceased. For vessels designed for short-term use, the fragile nature of white-ground painting was of little concern.

The subject of the illustrated lekythos is appropriate for the vase's funerary purpose. A youthful warrior takes leave of his wife. The red scarf, mirror, and jug hanging on the wall behind the woman indicate that the setting is the interior of their home. The motif of the seated woman is strikingly similar to that of Hegeso on her grave stele (FIG. 2-45), but here the woman is the survivor. It is her husband, preparing to go to war, who will depart, never to return. On his shield is a large painted eye, roughly life-size. Greek shields often bore decorative devices such as the horrific face of Medusa, intended to ward off evil spirits and frighten the enemy. This eye recalls that tradition, but for the Achilles Painter it was little more than an excuse to display his superior drawing skills. Since the late sixth century BCE, Greek painters had abandoned the Archaic habit of placing frontal eyes on profile faces and attempted to render the eyes in profile. The Achilles Painter's mastery of this dif-ficult problem in foreshortening is on exhibit here.

2-46 ACHILLES PAINTER, warrior taking leave of his wife (Athenian white-ground lekythos), from Eretria, Greece, ca. 440 BCE. 1' 5" high. National Archaeologi-cal Museum, Athens.

White-ground painters applied the colors after firing because most colored glazes could not withstand the kiln's heat. The Achilles Painter here displayed his mastery at drawing an eye in profile.

as she is Hegeso's possession, like the jewelry box. The slave girl may look at her mistress, awaiting her next command, but Hegeso has eyes only for her ornaments. Both slave and jewelry attest to the wealth of Hegeso's father, unseen but prominently cited in the epitaph. (It is noteworthy that there is no mention of the mother's name.) Indeed, even the jewelry box carries a deeper significance, for it probably rep-resents the dowry Proxenos would have provided to his daughter's husband when she left her father's home to enter her husband's home. In the patriarchal society of ancient Greece, the dominant position of men is manifest even when only women are depicted.

WHITE-GROUND PAINTING All the masterpieces of Classical painting have vanished because they were on wood panels, but Greek vases of this period—for example, a red-figure krater by the so-called NIOBID PAINTER (FIG. 2-45A ⏩) and especially those painted using the *white-ground painting* technique (see "White-Ground Painting," above)—give some idea of the lost panel paint-ings. One of the masters of white-ground painting was the ACHILLES PAINTER (FIG. 2-46).

Late Classical Art

The Peloponnesian War, which began in 431 BCE, ended in 404 BCE with the defeat of a plague-weakened Athens. The victor, Sparta, and then Thebes undertook the leadership of Greece, both unsuccess-fully. In the middle of the fourth century BCE, a threat from without caused the rival Greek states to put aside their animosities and unite for their common defense, as they had earlier against the Persians. But at the battle of Chaeronea in 338 BCE, the Greek cities suffered a devastating loss and had to relinquish their independence to the Macedonian king, Philip II (r. 359–336 BCE). After Philip's assassi-nation, his son Alexander III, better known as Alexander the Great (r. 336–323 BCE), succeeded him. Alexander led a powerful army on an extraordinary campaign that overthrew the Persian Empire (the ultimate revenge for the Persian invasion of Greece), wrested control of Egypt, and even reached India.

The fourth century BCE was thus a time of political upheaval, which had a profound impact on the psyche of the Greeks and on the art they produced. In the fifth century BCE, Greeks had generally believed that rational human beings could impose order on their environment, create "perfect" statues such as Polykleitos's *Canon* (FIG. 2-35), and discover the "correct" mathematical formulas for constructing temples such as the Parthenon (FIG. 2-1). The Parthenon frieze (FIG. 2-41) celebrated the Athenians as a community of citizens with shared values. The Peloponnesian War and the unceasing strife of the fourth century BCE brought an end to the serene idealism of the previous century. Disillusionment and alienation followed. Greek thought and Greek art began to focus more on the individual and on the real world of appearances instead of on the community and the ideal world of perfect beings and perfect temples.

PRAXITELES The new approach to art is immediately apparent in the work of PRAXITELES, one of the great masters of the Late Classical period (ca. 400–323 BCE). Praxiteles did not reject the favored statuary themes of the High Classical period, and his Olympian gods and goddesses retained their superhuman beauty. But in his hands, those deities lost some of their solemn grandeur and took on a worldly sensuousness. Nowhere is this new humanizing spirit plainer than in the statue of Aphrodite (FIG. 2-47) that Praxiteles sold to the Knidians after another city had rejected it. The lost marble original is known only through copies of Roman date, but Pliny considered it "superior to all the works, not only of Praxiteles, but indeed in the whole world."[1] The statue made Knidos famous, and Pliny reported that many people sailed there just to

see it. The *Aphrodite of Knidos* caused such a sensation in its time because Praxiteles took the unprecedented step of representing the goddess of love completely nude. Female nudity was rare in earlier Greek art and had been confined almost exclusively to paintings on vases designed for household use. The women so depicted also were usually not noblewomen or goddesses but courtesans or slave girls, and no one had ever dared fashion a life-size statue of an undressed goddess. Moreover, Praxiteles's Aphrodite is not a cold and remote image. In fact, the goddess engages in a trivial act out of everyday life. She has removed her garment and draped it over a large *hydria* (water pitcher), and is about to step into the bath.

Although shocking in its day, the *Aphrodite of Knidos* is not openly erotic (the goddess modestly shields her pelvis with her right hand), but she is quite sensuous. Lucian, writing in the second century CE, noted that she had a "welcoming look," a "slight smile," and "dewy eyes,"[2] and that Praxiteles was renowned for his ability to transform marble into soft and radiant flesh.

Unfortunately, the rather mechanical Roman copies do not capture the quality of Praxiteles's modeling of the stone, but the statue of Hermes and the infant Dionysos (FIG. 2-48) found in the Temple of Hera at Olympia provides a good idea of the Praxitelean "touch." The statue was once thought to be by the master himself, but is now generally considered a copy of the highest quality or an original work by a son or grandson with the same name. The statue depicts Hermes resting in a forest during his journey to deliver Dionysos to

2-47

PRAXITELES, *Aphrodite of Knidos.* Roman copy of a marble statue of ca. 350–340 BCE. Marble, 6' 8" high. Musei Vaticani, Rome.

This first nude statue of a Greek goddess caused a sensation. But Praxiteles was also famous for his ability to transform marble into soft and radiant flesh. His Aphrodite had "dewy eyes."

2-48

PRAXITELES(?), Hermes and the infant Dionysos, from the Temple of Hera, Olympia, Greece. Copy of a marble statue of ca. 340 BCE or an original work of ca. 330–270 BCE by a son or grandson. Marble, 7' 1" high. Archaeological Museum, Olympia.

Praxiteles humanized the Olympian deities. This Hermes is as sensuous as the sculptor's Aphrodite. The god gazes dreamily into space while he dangles grapes to tempt the infant wine god.

the *satyr* Papposilenos and the nymphs, who assumed responsibility for raising the child. Hermes leans on a tree trunk (here it is an integral part of the composition and not the copyist's addition), and his slender body forms a sinuous, shallow S-curve that is the hallmark of many of Praxiteles's statues. Hermes gazes dreamily into space while he dangles a bunch of grapes (now missing) to tempt the infant who is to become the Greek god of the vine. This is the kind of tender human interaction between an adult and a child that one encounters frequently in real life but that had been absent from Greek statuary before the fourth century BCE.

The quality of the carving is superb. The modeling is deliberately smooth and subtle, producing soft shadows that follow the planes as they flow almost imperceptibly one into another. The delicacy of the marble facial features stands in sharp contrast to the metallic precision of Polykleitos's bronze *Doryphoros* (FIG. 2-35). The High Classical sculptor even subjected the *Spear Bearer*'s locks of hair to the laws of symmetry, and the hair does not violate the skull's perfect curve. The comparison of these two statues reveals the sweeping changes in artistic attitude and intent that took place from the fifth to the fourth century BCE. In the statues of Praxiteles, the Olympian deities still possess a beauty mortals can aspire to, although not achieve, but they are no longer aloof. Praxiteles's gods have stepped off their pedestals and entered the world of human experience.

LYSIPPOS Equal in stature to Praxiteles was LYSIPPOS, whom Alexander the Great selected to create his official portrait. (Alexander could afford to employ the best. His father, Philip II, hired the leading thinker of his age, Aristotle, as the young Alexander's tutor.) Lysippos introduced a new canon of proportions in which the bodies were more slender than those of Polykleitos and the heads roughly one-eighth the height of the body rather than one-seventh, as in the previous century. One of Lysippos's most famous works, a bronze statue of an *apoxyomenos* (an athlete scraping oil from his body after exercising)—known, as usual, only from Roman copies in marble (FIG. 2-49)—exhibits the new proportions. A comparison with Polykleitos's *Doryphoros* (FIG. 2-35) reveals more than a change in physique, however. A nervous energy, lacking in the balanced form of the *Doryphoros,* runs through Lysippos's *Apoxyomenos.* The *strigil* (scraping tool) is about to reach the end of the right arm, and at any moment the athlete will switch it to the other hand so that he can scrape his left arm. At the same time, he will shift his weight and reverse the positions of his legs. Lysippos also began to break down the dominance of the frontal view in statuary and encouraged the observer to view his athlete from multiple angles. Because Lysippos represented the apoxyomenos with his right arm boldly thrust forward, the figure breaks out of the shallow rectangular box that defined the boundaries of earlier statues. To comprehend the action, the observer must move to the side and view Lysippos's work at a three-quarter angle or in full profile.

BATTLE OF ISSUS The life of Alexander the Great very much resembled an epic saga, full of heroic battles, exotic locales, and unceasing drama. Alexander was a man of singular character, an inspired leader with boundless energy and an almost foolhardy courage, who always personally led his army into battle. A Roman *mosaic* captures the extraordinary character of the Macedonian king. It also provides a welcome glimpse at the lost art of Greek panel painting during Alexander's time. In the so-called *Alexander Mosaic* (FIG. 2-50) the mosaicist employed *tesserae* (cubical pieces of glass or tiny stones cut to the desired size and shape) to "paint" what art historians believe is a reasonably faithful copy of *Battle of Issus,* a famous painting of

2-49 LYSIPPOS, *Apoxyomenos* (*Scraper*). Roman copy from Trastevere, Rome, Italy, of a bronze statue of ca. 330 BCE. Marble, 6' 9" high. Musei Vaticani, Rome.

Lysippos introduced a new canon of proportions and a nervous energy to his statues. He also broke down the dominance of the frontal view and encouraged looking at his statues from multiple angles.

1 ft.

around 310 BCE by PHILOXENOS OF ERETRIA. The subject is the great battle in southeastern Turkey between the armies of Alexander the Great and the Achaemenid Persian king Darius III (r. 336–330 BCE), who fled from the Macedonian forces in humiliating defeat.

Battle of Issus is notable for the artist's technical mastery of problems that had long fascinated Greek painters. Even Euthymides (FIG. 2-26) would have marveled at Philoxenos's depiction of the rearing horse seen in a three-quarter rear view below Darius. The subtle modulation of the horse's rump through shading in browns and yellows goes far beyond anything even a white-ground vase painter (FIG. 2-46) ever attempted. Other details are even more impressive. The Persian to the right of the rearing horse has fallen to the ground and raises, backward, a dropped Macedonian shield to protect himself from being trampled. Philoxenos recorded the reflection of the man's terrified face on the polished surface of the shield. Everywhere in the scene, men, animals, and weapons cast shadows on the ground. This interest in the reflection of insubstantial light on a shiny surface, and in the absence of light (shadows), stands in sharp contrast to earlier painters' preoccupation with the clear presentation of weighty figures seen against a blank background. Philoxenos here truly opened a window into a world filled not only with figures, trees, and sky but also with light.

Perhaps most impressive, however, about *Battle of Issus* is the psychological intensity of the drama unfolding before the viewer's eyes. Alexander leads his army into battle without even a helmet to

2-50 PHILOXENOS OF ERETRIA, *Battle of Issus*. Roman copy (*Alexander Mosaic*) from the House of the Faun, Pompeii, Italy, late second or early first century BCE, of a panel painting of ca. 310 BCE. Tessera mosaic, 8' 10" × 16' 9". Museo Archeologico Nazionale, Naples.

Battle of Issus reveals Philoxenos's mastery of foreshortening, of modeling figures in color, and of depicting reflections and shadows, as well as his ability to capture the psychological intensity of warfare.

protect him. He drives his spear through one of Darius's bodyguards while the Persian's horse collapses beneath him. The Macedonian king is only a few yards away from Darius, and Alexander directs his gaze at the king, not at the man impaled on his now-useless spear. Darius has called for retreat. In fact, his charioteer is already whipping the horses and speeding the king to safety. Before he escapes, Darius looks back at Alexander and in a pathetic gesture reaches out toward his brash foe. But the victory has slipped from his hands. In Pliny's opinion, Philoxenos's painting of the battle between Alexander and Darius was "inferior to none."[3]

EPIDAUROS In ancient Greece, actors did not perform plays repeatedly over months or years as they do today, but only during sacred festivals. Greek drama was closely associated with religious rites and was not pure entertainment. In the fifth century BCE, for example, the Athenians staged performances of the great tragedies of Aeschylus, Sophocles, and Euripides during the Dionysos festival in the theater dedicated to the god on the southern slope of the Acropolis. Yet it is Epidauros that boasts the finest theater (FIG. 2-51) in Greece. The architect was POLYKLEITOS THE YOUNGER.

2-51 POLYKLEITOS THE YOUNGER, aerial view of the theater (looking southwest), Epidauros, Greece, ca. 350 BCE.

The Greeks always situated theaters on hillsides to support the cavea of stone seats overlooking the circular orchestra. The Epidauros theater is the finest in Greece. It accommodated 12,000 spectators.

The precursor of the formal Greek theater was a circular piece of earth where actors performed sacred rites, songs, and dances. This area later became the *orchestra* ("dancing place") of the theater. The actors and chorus performed there, and at Epidauros, an altar to Dionysos stood at the center of the circle. The spectators sat on a slope overlooking the orchestra—the *theatron,* or "place for seeing," and watched the actors and chorus in the orchestra. When the Greek theater took architectural shape, the builders always situated the auditorium (*cavea,* Latin for "hollow place, cavity") on a hillside. The cavea at Epidauros, composed of wedge-shaped sections of stone benches separated by stairs, is somewhat greater than a semicircle in plan. The auditorium is 387 feet in diameter, and its 55 rows of seats accommodated about 12,000 spectators. They entered the theater via a passageway between the seating area and the scene building (*skene*), which housed dressing rooms for the actors and also formed a backdrop for the plays. The design is simple but perfectly suited to its function. Even in antiquity, the Epidauros theater was famous for the harmony of its proportions. Although spectators sitting in some of the seats would have had a poor view of the skene, all had unobstructed views of the orchestra. Because of the excellent acoustics of the open-air cavea, everyone could hear the actors and chorus.

The theater at Epidauros is about 500 yards southeast of the sanctuary of Asklepios, and Polykleitos the Younger worked there as well. He was the architect of the *tholos,* the circular shrine that probably housed the sacred snakes of the healing god. That building lies in ruins today, but the Greek archaeological service is in the process of reconstructing it. One can get an approximate idea of the Epidauros tholos's original appearance from the somewhat earlier and already partially rebuilt tholos (FIG. 2-51A ⬈) at Delphi, designed by THEODOROS OF PHOKAIA. Both tholoi had an exterior colonnade of Doric columns, but the interior columns had molded bases and *Corinthian capitals* (see "The Corinthian Capital" and FIG. 2-51B ⬈), an invention of the second half of the fifth century BCE.

Hellenistic Art

Alexander the Great's conquest of Mesopotamia and Egypt ushered in a new cultural age that historians and art historians alike call *Hellenistic.* The Hellenistic period opened with the death of Alexander in 323 BCE and lasted nearly three centuries, until the double suicide of Queen Cleopatra of Egypt and her Roman consort, Mark Antony, in 30 BCE, after their decisive defeat at the battle of Actium by Antony's rival, Augustus (see page 97). That year, Augustus made Egypt a province of the Roman Empire.

The cultural centers of the Hellenistic period were the court cities of the Greek kings who succeeded Alexander and divided his far-flung empire among themselves. Chief among them were Antioch in Syria, Alexandria in Egypt (named after Alexander), and Pergamon in Asia Minor. An international culture united the Hellenistic world, and its language was Greek. Hellenistic kings became enormously rich, and prided themselves on their libraries, art collections, and scientific enterprises, as well as on the learned men they could assemble at their courts. The world of the small, austere, and heroic city-state passed away, as did the power and prestige of its center, Athens. A cosmopolitan ("citizen of the world," in Greek) civilization, much like today's, replaced it.

PERGAMON The kingdom of Pergamon, founded in the early third century BCE after the breakup of Alexander's empire, embraced almost all of western and southern Asia Minor. The Pergamene kings enjoyed immense wealth and expended much of it on embellishing their capital. The Altar of Zeus, erected about 175 BCE, is the most famous Hellenistic sculptural ensemble. The monument's west front (FIG. 2-52) has been reconstructed in Berlin. The altar proper was on an elevated platform, framed by an Ionic colonnade with projecting wings on either side of a broad central staircase.

All around the altar platform was a sculpted frieze almost 400 feet long, populated by about a hundred larger-than-life-size figures. The subject is the battle of Zeus and the gods against the giants. The Pergamene frieze is the most extensive representation Greek artists ever attempted of that epic conflict for control of the world. The gigantomachy also appeared on the shield of Phidias's *Athena Parthenos* and on some of the Parthenon metopes, because the Athenians wished to draw a parallel between the defeat of the giants and the defeat of the Persians. The Pergamene king Attalos I (r. 241–197 BCE) had successfully turned back an invasion of the Gauls in Asia Minor. The gigantomachy of the Altar of Zeus alluded to his victory over those barbarians. It also established a connection

2-52 Reconstructed west front of the Altar of Zeus, Pergamon, Turkey, ca. 175 BCE. Pergamonmuseum, Staatliche Museen zu Berlin, Berlin.

The gigantomachy frieze of Pergamon's monumental Altar of Zeus is almost 400 feet long. The battle of gods and giants alluded to the victory of King Attalos I over the Gauls of Asia Minor.

2-53 Athena battling Alkyoneos, detail of the gigantomachy frieze of the Altar of Zeus, Pergamon, Turkey, ca. 175 BCE. Marble, 7' 6" high. Pergamonmuseum, Staatliche Museen zu Berlin, Berlin.

The tumultuous battle scenes of the Pergamon altar have an emotional power unparalleled in earlier Greek art. Violent movement, swirling draperies, and vivid depictions of suffering fill the frieze.

with Athens, whose earlier defeat of the Persians was by then legendary, and with the Parthenon, which the Hellenistic Greeks already recognized as a Classical monument—in both senses of the word. The figure of Athena (FIG. 2-53), for example, who grabs the hair of the giant Alkyoneos as Nike flies in to crown her, resembles Athena in the Parthenon's east pediment.

The Pergamene frieze is not a dry series of borrowed motifs, however. On the contrary, its tumultuous narrative has an emotional intensity that has no parallel in earlier sculpture. The battle rages everywhere, even up and down the steps leading to Zeus's altar (FIG. 2-52). Violent movement, swirling draperies, and vivid depictions of death and suffering fill the frieze. Wounded figures writhe in pain, and their faces reveal their anguish. Deep carving creates dark shadows. The figures project from the background like bursts of light.

DYING GAUL The Altar of Zeus was not the only Pergamene monument to celebrate the victory of Attalos I over the Gauls. An earlier Pergamene statuary group had explicitly represented the defeat of the barbarians, instead of cloaking it in mythological disguise. The Pergamene victors were apparently not part of this group, however. The viewer saw only their Gallic foes and their noble and moving response to defeat. Roman copies of some of these figures survive, including a trumpeter (FIG. 2-54) who collapses on his large oval shield as blood pours out of the gash in his chest. If this figure is the *tubicen* ("trumpeter") that Pliny mentions in his *Natural History,* then the sculptor's name was EPIGONOS. In any case, the sculptor carefully studied and reproduced the distinctive features of the foreign Gauls, most notably their long, bushy hair and mustaches and the *torques* (neck bands) they frequently wore. The artist also closely observed male

2-54 EPIGONOS(?), dying Gaul. Roman copy of a bronze statue of ca. 230–220 BCE. Marble, 3' $\frac{1}{2}$" high. Museo Capitolino, Rome.

The defeat of the Gauls was also the subject of Pergamene statuary groups. The barbaric Gauls have bushy hair, mustaches, and neck bands, but the sculptor portrayed them as powerful and noble foes.

anatomy. Note the tautness of the fallen Gaul's chest and the bulging veins of his left leg—implying that the unseen Greek hero who struck down this noble and savage foe must have been an extraordinarily powerful man. The Hellenistic figure is reminiscent of the dying warrior from the east pediment of the Temple of Aphaia at Aegina (FIG. 2-30), but the pathos and drama of the suffering Gaul are far more pronounced.

NIKE OF SAMOTHRACE Another masterpiece of Hellenistic sculpture is the statue of winged Victory set up in the Sanctuary of the Great Gods on the island of Samothrace. The *Nike of Samothrace* (FIG. 2-55) has just alighted on the prow of a Greek warship. She raises her (missing) right arm to crown the naval victor, just as Nike places a wreath on Athena's head on the Altar of Zeus (FIG. 2-53). But the Pergamene relief figure seems calm by comparison. The Samothracian Nike's wings still beat, and the wind sweeps her drapery. Her *himation* (wool mantle) bunches in thick folds around her right leg, and her linen chiton is pulled tightly across her abdomen and left leg.

The statue's setting amplified this theatrical effect. The sculptor set the war galley in the upper basin of a two-tiered fountain. In the lower basin were large boulders. The fountain's flowing water created the illusion of rushing waves hitting the prow of the ship. The statue's reflection in the shimmering water below accentuated the sense of lightness and movement. The sound of splashing water added another dimension to the visual drama. Here, the Hellenistic sculptor combined art and nature, and resoundingly rejected the Polykleitan conception of a statue as an ideally proportioned, self-contained entity on a bare pedestal. The Hellenistic statue interacts with its environment and appears as a living, breathing, and intensely emotive presence.

VENUS DE MILO In the Hellenistic period, sculptors regularly followed Praxiteles's lead in undressing Aphrodite, but they also openly explored the eroticism of the nude female form. The *Venus de Milo* (FIG. 2-56) is a larger-than-life-size marble statue of Aphrodite found on Melos together with its inscribed base (now lost) signed by the sculptor ALEXANDROS OF ANTIOCH-ON-THE-MEANDER. In

2-55 Nike alighting on a warship (*Nike of Samothrace*), from Samothrace, Greece, ca. 190 BCE. Marble, Nike 8' 1" high. Musée du Louvre, Paris.

Victory lands on a ship's prow to crown a naval victor. Her wings still beat, and the wind sweeps her drapery. The statue's placement in a fountain of splashing water heightened the dramatic visual effect.

2-56 ALEXANDROS OF ANTIOCH-ON-THE-MEANDER, Aphrodite (*Venus de Milo*), from Melos, Greece, ca. 150–125 BCE. Marble, 6' 7" high. Musée du Louvre, Paris.

Displaying the eroticism of many Hellenistic statues, this Aphrodite is more overtly sexual than the Knidian Aphrodite (FIG. 2-47). The goddess's slipping garment teases the spectator.

this statue, the goddess of love is more modestly draped than the *Aphrodite of Knidos* (FIG. 2-47), but is more overtly sexual. Her left hand (separately preserved) holds the apple that the Trojan hero Paris awarded her when he judged her the most beautiful goddess. Her right hand may have lightly grasped the edge of her drapery near the left hip in a halfhearted attempt to keep it from slipping farther down her body. The sculptor intentionally designed the work to tease the spectator, instilling this partially draped Aphrodite with a sexuality absent from Praxiteles's entirely nude image of the goddess.

BARBERINI FAUN Archaic statues smile at the viewer, and even when Classical statues look away, they are always awake and alert. Hellenistic sculptors often portrayed sleep. The suspension of consciousness and the entrance into the fantasy world of dreams—the antithesis of the Classical ideals of rationality and discipline—had great appeal for them. This newfound interest is evident in a marble statue (FIG. 2-57) of a drunken, restlessly sleeping satyr known as the *Barberini Faun* after the Italian cardinal who once owned it. The satyr has consumed too much wine and has thrown down his panther skin on a convenient rock, then fallen into a disturbed, intoxicated sleep. His brows are furrowed, and one can almost hear him snore.

Eroticism also comes to the fore in this statue. Although men had been represented naked in Greek art for hundreds of years,

Archaic kouroi and Classical athletes and gods do not exude sexuality. Sensuality surfaced in the works of Praxiteles and his followers in the fourth century BCE. But the dreamy and supremely beautiful Hermes playfully dangling grapes before the infant Dionysos (FIG. 2-48) has nothing of the blatant sexuality of the *Barberini Faun,* whose wantonly spread legs focus attention on his genitals. Homosexuality was common in the man's world of ancient Greece. It is not surprising that when Hellenistic sculptors began to explore the sexuality of the human body, they turned their attention to both men and women.

OLD MARKET WOMAN Hellenistic sculpture stands in contrast to Classical sculpture in other ways too. Many Hellenistic sculptors had a deep interest in exploring realism—the very opposite of the Classical period's idealism. This realistic mode is evident in a Hellenistic bronze statue of a defeated boxer (FIG. 2-57A ↗) and above all in Hellenistic statues of old men and women from the lowest rungs of the social order. Shepherds, fishermen, and drunken beggars are common—the kinds of people pictured earlier on red-figure vases but never before thought worthy of life-size statuary. One statue of this type depicts a haggard old woman (FIG. 2-58) bringing chickens and a basket of fruits and vegetables to sell in the market or, according to a recent interpretation suggested by the ivy wreath in her hair, bringing gifts to Dionysos at one of the god's festivals. In either case, the woman's face is wrinkled and her body bent with

2-57 Sleeping satyr (*Barberini Faun*), from Rome, Italy, ca. 230–200 BCE. Marble, 7' 1" high. Glyptothek, Munich.

Here, a Hellenistic sculptor represented a restlessly sleeping, drunken satyr, a semihuman in a suspended state of consciousness—the antithesis of the Classical ideals of rationality and discipline.

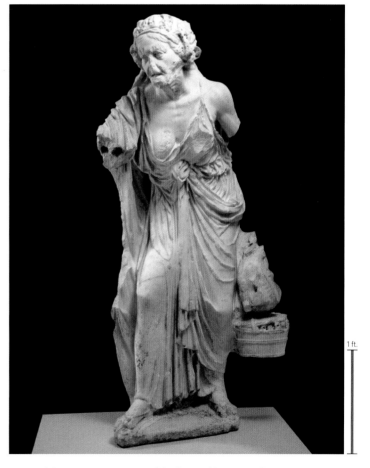

2-58 Old woman. Roman copy(?) of a marble statue of ca. 150–100 BCE. Marble, 4' 1⅝" high. Metropolitan Museum of Art, New York.

Consistent with the realism of much Hellenistic art, many statues portray the elderly of the lowest rungs of society. Earlier Greek artists did not consider them suitable subjects for statuary.

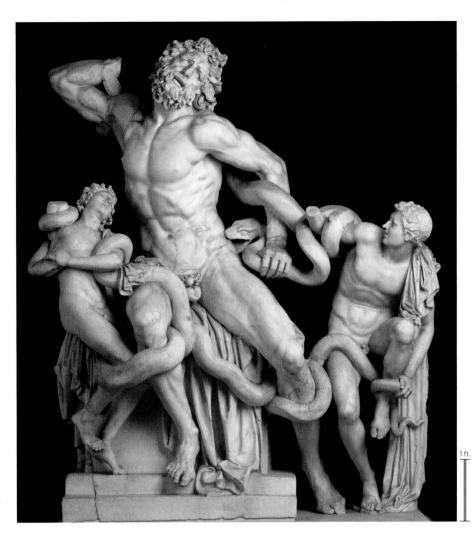

2-59 ATHANADOROS, HAGESANDROS, and POLYDOROS OF RHODES, *Laocoön and his sons*, from Rome, Italy, early first century CE. Marble, 7' 10½" high. Musei Vaticani, Rome.

Hellenistic style lived on in Rome. Although stylistically akin to Pergamene sculpture (FIG. 2-53), this statue of sea serpents attacking Laocoön and his two sons matches the account given only in the *Aeneid*.

1 ft.

age. Whatever the purpose of this and similar statues, they attest to an interest in social realism absent in earlier Greek statuary.

LAOCOÖN In the opening years of the second century BCE, the Roman general Flamininus defeated the Macedonian army and declared the old city-states of Classical Greece free once again. The Greek cities never regained their former glory, however. Greece became a Roman province in 146 BCE. When Athens 60 years later sided with King Mithridates VI of Pontus (r. 120–63 BCE) in his war against Rome, the general Sulla crushed the Athenians. Thereafter, although Athens retained some of its earlier prestige as a center of culture and learning, politically it was merely another city in the ever-expanding Roman Empire. Nonetheless, Greek artists continued to be in great demand, both to furnish the Romans with an endless stream of copies of Classical and Hellenistic masterpieces and to create new statues in Greek style for Roman patrons.

The most famous work of this type is the statue of the Trojan priest Laocoön and his sons (FIG. 2-59). The marble group, long believed to be an original of the second century BCE, was found in the palace of the emperor Titus (r. 79–81 CE) in Rome. Pliny attributed the statue to three sculptors—ATHANADOROS, HAGESANDROS, and POLYDOROS OF RHODES—who most art historians now think worked in the early first century CE. These artists probably based their group on a Hellenistic masterpiece depicting Laocoön and only one son. Their variation on the original added the son at Laocoön's left (note the greater compositional integration of the other two figures) to conform with the Roman poet Vergil's account in the *Aeneid*. Vergil vividly described the strangling of Laocoön and his *two* sons by sea serpents while sacrificing at an altar. The gods who favored the Greeks in the war against Troy had sent the serpents to punish Laocoön, who had tried to warn his compatriots about the danger of bringing the Greeks' wood horse within the walls of their city. In Vergil's graphic account, Laocoön suffered in terrible agony. The Rhodian sculptors communicated the torment of the priest and his sons in a spectacular fashion in this marble group. The three Trojans writhe in pain as they struggle to free themselves from the death grip of the serpents. One bites into Laocoön's left hip as the priest lets out a ferocious cry. The serpent-entwined figures recall the suffering giants of the frieze of the Altar of Zeus at Pergamon, and Laocoön himself is strikingly similar to Alkyoneos (FIG. 2-53), Athena's opponent. In fact, many scholars believe that a Pergamene statuary group of the second century BCE was the inspiration for the three Rhodian sculptors.

That the work seen by Pliny and displayed in the Vatican Museums today was made for Romans rather than Greeks was confirmed in 1957 by the discovery of fragments of several Hellenistic-style groups illustrating scenes from Homer's *Odyssey* in a grotto that served as the picturesque summer banquet hall of the seaside villa of the Roman emperor Tiberius (r. 14–37 CE) at Sperlonga, some 60 miles south of Rome. The same three sculptors Pliny cited as the creators of the Laocoön group signed one of the Sperlonga groups. At Tiberius's villa and in Titus's palace, Hellenistic sculpture lived on long after Greece ceased to be a political force. When Rome inherited the Pergamene kingdom in 133 BCE, it also became heir to the Greek artistic legacy. What Rome adopted from Greece it passed on to the medieval and modern worlds. If Greece was the inventor of the European spirit, Rome was its propagator and amplifier.

⊞ Explore the era further in MindTap with videos of major artworks and buildings, Google Earth™ coordinates, and essays by the author on the following additional subjects:

▮ ART AND SOCIETY: Archaeology, Art History, and the Art Market
▪ Calf bearer, from the Athenian Acropolis (FIG. 2-17A)
▪ Warrior, from Riace (FIG. 2-34A)
▮ WRITTEN SOURCES: Vitruvius's Ten Books on Architecture
▪ Niobid Painter: *Massacre of the Niobids* (FIG. 2-45A)
▮ ARCHITECTURAL BASICS: The Corinthian Capital
▪ Theodoros of Phokaia: Tholos, Delphi (FIG. 2-51A)
▪ Polykleitos the Younger: Corinthian capital, Epidauros (FIG. 2-51B)
▪ Seated boxer, from Rome (FIG. 2-57A)

ANCIENT GREECE

Prehistoric Aegean

- The major surviving artworks of the third millennium BCE in Greece are Cycladic marble statuettes. Most come from graves and may represent the deceased.

- The golden age of Crete was the Late Minoan period (ca. 1600–1200 BCE). The palace at Knossos was a vast multistory structure so complex in plan that it gave rise to the myth of the minotaur in the labyrinth of King Minos. Large fresco paintings adorned the walls, but all surviving Minoan sculptures are of small scale.

- The Mycenaeans (ca. 1600–1200 BCE) constructed great citadels at Mycenae, Tiryns, and elsewhere with "Cyclopean" walls of huge irregularly shaped stone blocks. Masters of corbel vaulting, the Mycenaeans also built beehive-shaped tholos tombs such as the Treasury of Atreus, which boasted the largest dome before the Roman Empire. The graves of the kings of Mycenae have yielded gold masks and other luxury items.

Palace, Knossos, ca. 1700–1370 BCE

Gold funerary mask, Mycenae, ca. 1600–1500 BCE

Geometric and Archaic Art

- The human figure returned to Greek art during the Geometric period (ca. 900–700 BCE) in the form of simple silhouettes amid other abstract motifs on vases.

- Around 600 BCE, during the Archaic period (ca. 700–480 BCE), the first life-size stone statues appeared in Greece. The earliest kouroi emulated the frontal poses of Egyptian statues, but artists depicted the young men nude, the way Greek athletes competed in the Olympic Games. During the course of the sixth century BCE, Greek sculptors refined the proportions and added "Archaic smiles" to the faces of their statues to make them seem more lifelike. The Archaic age also saw the construction of the first stone temples with peripteral colonnades and the codification of the Doric and Ionic orders. Vase painters developed in turn the black- and red-figure techniques. Euphronios and Euthymides rejected the age-old composite view for the human figure and experimented with foreshortening.

Euthymides, three revelers, ca. 510 BCE

Classical Art

- The fifth century BCE was the golden age of Greece, when Aeschylus, Sophocles, and Euripides wrote their plays, and Herodotus, the "father of history," lived. During the Early Classical period (480–450 BCE), which opened with the Greek victory over the Persians, sculptors revolutionized statuary by introducing contrapposto (weight shift) to their figures.

- In the High Classical period (450–400 BCE), under the patronage of Pericles and the artistic directorship of Phidias, the Athenians rebuilt the Acropolis after 447 BCE. Polykleitos developed a canon of proportions for the perfect statue, and Iktinos applied mathematical formulas to temple design in the belief that beauty resulted from the use of harmonic numbers.

- In the aftermath of the Peloponnesian War, which ended in 404 BCE, Greek artists began to focus more on the real world of appearances than on the ideal world of perfect beings. During the Late Classical period (400–323 BCE), sculptors humanized the remote deities and athletes of the fifth century BCE. Praxiteles, for example, caused a sensation when he portrayed Aphrodite undressed.

Praxiteles, *Aphrodite of Knidos*, ca. 350–340 BCE

Hellenistic Art

- The Hellenistic age (323–30 BCE) extended from the death of Alexander the Great until the death of Cleopatra, when Egypt became a province of the Roman Empire. The great cultural centers of the era were no longer the city-states of Archaic and Classical Greece, but royal capitals such as Pergamon in Asia Minor. Hellenistic sculptors explored new subjects—for example, Gauls with mustaches and necklaces, and impoverished old women—and treated traditional subjects in new ways. Hellenistic artists delighted in depicting violent movement and unbridled emotion.

Epigonos(?), dying Gaul, ca. 230–220 BCE

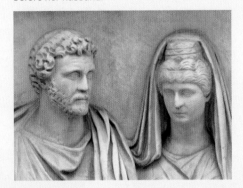

▼ 3-1a On the pedestal of the memorial column erected in his honor, Antoninus Pius ascends to the realm of the gods with his wife, Faustina. The empress, however, died 20 years before her husband.

◄ 3-1b The setting of Antoninus's apotheosis is the Campus Martius, here personified by a reclining long-haired, seminude young man holding the Egyptian obelisk that was an important local landmark.

3-1 **Apotheosis of Antoninus Pius and Faustina the Elder, relief on the pedestal of the Column of Antoninus Pius, Rome, Italy, ca. 161 CE. Marble, 8' 1½" high. Musei Vaticani, Rome.**

► 3-1c Bidding farewell to the emperor and empress is the seated goddess Roma (Rome personified), leaning on a shield decorated with the she-wolf suckling Rome's two founders, Romulus and Remus.

The Roman Empire

ROMAN ART AS HISTORICAL FICTION

The name "Rome" almost invariably conjures images of power and grandeur, of mighty armies and fearsome gladiators, of marble cities and far-flung roads. Indeed, at the death of Emperor Trajan in 117 CE, the "eternal city" was the capital of the greatest empire the world had ever known. For the first time in history, a single government ruled territories extending from the Strait of Gibraltar to the Nile, from the Tigris and Euphrates to the Rhine, Danube, Thames, and beyond (MAP 3-1). The Romans presided over prosperous cities and frontier outposts on three continents, ruling virtually all of Europe, North Africa, and West Asia.

No government, before or after, ever used art more effectively as a political tool. Indeed, the Romans were masters at creating pictorial fictions to glorify their emperors and advance their political agendas. For example, after the death of Antoninus Pius (r. 138–161 CE) in 161, the emperor's two adopted sons, Marcus Aurelius (r. 161–180 CE) and Lucius Verus (r. 161–169 CE), erected a memorial column in his honor. Atop the column was a gilded-bronze portrait statue of Antoninus. On the pedestal were a dedicatory inscription and three narrative reliefs. The subject of one of them was a central theme of Roman imperial ideology—the *apotheosis* (FIG. 3-1), or ascent to Heaven, of the emperor after his death, when he takes his place among the other gods. Empresses could also become goddesses.

The setting of Antoninus's apotheosis is the Campus Martius (Field of Mars) in Rome, here personified by a reclining long-haired, seminude young man holding the Egyptian obelisk that was an important local landmark. Opposite him is the seated goddess Roma (Rome personified), leaning on a shield decorated with the she-wolf suckling Rome's founder, Romulus, and his brother, Remus. Roma waves farewell to Antoninus and his wife, Faustina the Elder (ca. 100–141 CE), whom a winged youthful male personification of uncertain identity lifts into the realm of the gods.

The representation of the apotheosis of Antoninus and Faustina is an example of what art historians generally call "Roman historical reliefs," but there is nothing historical about this scene. Not only is the very notion of apotheosis historical fiction, but this joint apotheosis is doubly so. Faustina died 20 years before Antoninus. By depicting the emperor and empress ascending to Heaven together, the Roman artist wished to suggest not only the divinity of the deceased rulers but also that Antoninus, who by all accounts had been devoted to his wife, would now be reunited with her in the afterlife.

ROME, *CAPUT MUNDI*

The Roman Empire spanned three continents, and Roman monuments of art and architecture are the most conspicuous and numerous of any ancient civilization. In Europe, the Middle East, and North Africa today, Roman temples and basilicas have an afterlife as churches. The powerful concrete vaults of ancient Roman buildings form the cores of modern houses, stores, restaurants, factories, and museums. Bullfights, sports events, operas, and rock concerts are staged in Roman amphitheaters. Ships dock in what were once Roman ports, and Western Europe's highway system still closely follows the routes of Roman roads. Ancient Rome also lives on in the Western world in concepts of law and government, in languages, in the calendar—even in the coins used daily.

The art of the ancient Romans speaks a language almost every Western viewer today can readily understand. Indeed, the diversity and eclecticism of Roman art foreshadowed the art of the modern world. The Roman use of art, especially portraits and narrative reliefs, to manipulate public opinion is similar to the carefully crafted imagery of contemporary political campaigns (see "Roman Art as Historical Fiction," page 83). And the Roman invention of concrete construction began an architectural revolution still felt today. But in 753 BCE, when according to legend, Romulus founded

MAP 3-1 The Roman Empire at the death of Trajan in 117 CE.

THE ROMAN EMPIRE

700–27 BCE
Etruscan and Republican

- The Etruscans build wood and mud-brick temples with columns and stairs only on the front and with statues on the roof.
- At Cerveteri, the Etruscans bury their dead beneath earthen tumuli in tombs resembling houses. Tarquinian tombs feature fresco paintings.
- Republican builders Hellenize Etruscan architecture and decorate walls in the First and Second Styles.
- Republican sculptors produce veristic (superrealistic) portraits.

27 BCE–96 CE
Early Empire

- Augustan artists revive the Classical style in art and architecture.
- Architects realize the full potential of concrete construction in buildings such as the Colosseum, the ancient world's largest amphitheater.
- Roman painters introduce the Third and Fourth Styles of mural decoration.

96–192 CE
High Empire

- Trajan extends the Empire and builds a new forum in Rome from the spoils of two wars against the Dacians.
- Hadrian builds the Pantheon (the temple of all gods), a triumph of concrete technology.
- The domination of the Classical style begins to erode under the Antonines.

193–337 CE
Late Empire

- A new non-Classical Late Antique style takes root under the Severans.
- Portraits of the soldier emperors reveal the insecurity of the age.
- Diocletian establishes the tetrarchy.
- Constantine reestablishes one-man rule and founds a New Rome at Constantinople.

what would become the *caput mundi*—the "head [capital] of the world"—Rome was neither the most powerful nor the most sophisticated city even in central Italy. In fact, in the sixth century BCE, the rulers of Rome were Etruscan kings.

ETRUSCAN ART

The heartland of the Etruscans was the territory between the Arno and Tiber rivers of central Italy. During the eighth and seventh centuries BCE, the Etruscans, as highly skilled seafarers, enriched themselves through trade abroad. By the sixth century BCE, they controlled most of northern and central Italy. Their most powerful cities included Tarquinia, Cerveteri, Vulci, and Veii. The Etruscan cities never united to form a state, however. Any semblance of unity among the independent cities was based primarily on common linguistic ties and religious beliefs and practices. This lack of political cohesion eventually made the Etruscans relatively easy prey for the Romans.

ETRUSCAN TEMPLES In the sixth century BCE, the most innovative artists and architects in the Mediterranean were the Greeks. Still, however eager Etruscan artists may have been to emulate Greek works, their distinctive Etruscan temperament always manifested itself. In religious architecture, for example, the differences between Etruscan temples and their Greek prototypes outweigh the similarities. Because of the materials that Etruscan builders employed, usually only the foundations of their temples have survived. Supplementing the archaeological record is the Roman architect Vitruvius's treatise on architecture written near the end of the first century BCE (see *"Vitruvius's Ten Books on Architecture"* ⟨↗⟩). In it, Vitruvius provided an invaluable chapter on Etruscan temple design.

The typical Archaic Etruscan temple (FIG. **3-2**) resembled Greek stone gable-roofed temples (FIG. 2-1), but it had wood columns, a tile-covered timber roof, and walls of sun-dried mud brick. Entrance was via a narrow staircase at the center of the front of the temple, which sat on a high podium, the only part of the building made of stone. Columns were placed only at the front of the building, creating a deep porch occupying roughly half the podium and setting off one side of the structure as the main side. In contrast, the front and rear of Greek temples were indistinguishable, and their builders placed steps and columns on all sides (FIG. 2-19). Furthermore, although the columns of Etruscan temples resembled Greek Doric columns (FIG. 2-20, *left*), *Tuscan columns* were made of wood, were unfluted, and had bases. Also, because of the lightness of the superstructure, fewer, more widely spaced columns were the rule in Etruscan temples. Unlike their Greek counterparts, Etruscan temples also frequently had three cellas—one for each of their chief gods: Tinia (Greek Zeus/Roman Jupiter), Uni (Hera/Juno), and Menrva (Athena/Minerva). Pediment statuary was also rare in Etruria. The Etruscans normally placed statues—made of *terracotta* instead of stone—on the roofs of their temples.

APOLLO OF VEII The finest surviving Etruscan rooftop statue is the life-size image of Apulu (FIG. **3-3**)—the Greco-Roman Apollo—from the Portonaccio sanctuary at Veii. The *Apollo of Veii* was one of a group of at least four painted terracotta figures that stood atop the ridgepole of the Portonaccio temple. Apulu confronted Hercle (Hercules/Herakles) for possession of the Ceryneian hind, a wondrous gold-horned beast sacred to the god's sister Artumes (Diana/Artemis). The bright paint and the rippling folds of the god's garment immediately distinguish the statue from the nude images of the Greek gods. Apulu's vigorous striding motion, gesticulating arms, fanlike calf muscles, and animated face are also distinctly Etruscan.

3-2 Model of a typical Etruscan temple of the sixth century BCE, as described by Vitruvius. Istituto di Etruscologia e di Antichità Italiche, Università di Roma, Rome.

Etruscan temples resembled Greek temples but had widely spaced, unfluted wood columns placed only at the front, walls of sun-dried mud brick, and a narrow staircase at the center of the facade.

3-3 Apulu (*Apollo of Veii*), from the roof of the Portonaccio temple, Veii, Italy, ca. 510–500 BCE. Painted terracotta, 5' 11" high. Museo Nazionale di Villa Giulia, Rome.

This statue of Apulu was part of a group depicting a Greek myth. Distinctly Etruscan, however, are the god's vigorous motion and gesticulating arms and the placement of the statue on a temple roof.

1 ft.

3-4 Sarcophagus with reclining couple, from the Banditaccia necropolis, Cerveteri, Italy, ca. 520 BCE. Painted terracotta, 3' 9½" × 6' 7". Museo Nazionale di Villa Giulia, Rome.

Sarcophagi in the form of a husband and wife on a dining couch have no parallels in Greece. The artist's focus on the upper half of the figures and the emphatic gestures are Etruscan hallmarks.

CERVETERI SARCOPHAGUS Also made of terracotta, the favored medium for life-size statuary in Etruria, is a sarcophagus (FIG. 3-4) that comes from a tomb at Cerveteri. *Sarcophagus* literally means "flesh-eater," and most ancient sarcophagi contained the bodies of the deceased, but this one, which takes the form of a husband and wife reclining on a banqueting couch, contained only ashes. Cremation was the most common means of disposing of the dead in Etruscan Italy. This kind of funerary monument had no parallel at this date in Greece, where there were no tombs big enough to house large sarcophagi. The Greeks buried their dead in simple graves marked by a large vase (FIG. 2-14), a statue (FIG. 2-17), or a stele (FIG. 2-45). Moreover, only men dined at Greek banquets. Their wives remained at home, excluded from most aspects of public life. The image of a husband and wife sharing the same banqueting couch is uniquely Etruscan (see "The 'Audacity' of Etruscan Women" ⬀).

The man and woman on the Cerveteri sarcophagus are as animated as the *Apollo of Veii* (FIG. 3-3), even though they are at rest. The woman may have held a perfume flask and a pomegranate in her hands, the man an egg, a symbol of regeneration (compare FIG. 3-7). They are the antithesis of the stiff and formal figures encountered in Egyptian funerary sculpture (FIG. 1-29). Also typically Etruscan, and in sharp contrast to contemporaneous Greek statues with their emphasis on proportion and balance, is the manner in which the Cerveteri sculptor rendered the upper and lower parts of each body. The artist shaped the legs only summarily, and the transition to the torso at the waist is unnatural. The sculptor's interest focused on the upper half of the figures, especially on the vibrant faces and gesticulating arms. The Cerveteri banqueters and the Veii Apulu speak to the viewer in a way that Greek statues of similar date never do.

BANDITACCIA NECROPOLIS The exact findspot of the Cerveteri sarcophagus is not known, but the kind of tomb that housed Etruscan sarcophagi is well documented. The typical tomb in Cerveteri's Banditaccia *necropolis* took the form of a mound, or *tumulus* (FIG. 3-5), not unlike the Mycenaean Treasury of Atreus (FIG. 2-11). But whereas the Mycenaeans constructed their tholos tombs with masonry blocks and then encased them in earthen mounds, each Etruscan tumulus covered one or more underground multichambered tombs cut out of the dark local limestone called tufa. The largest Banditaccia mounds are truly of colossal size, exceeding 130 feet in diameter and reaching nearly 50 feet in height. Arranged in an orderly manner along a network of streets, the Cerveteri cemetery was a veritable city of the dead (the literal meaning of the Greek word *necropolis*). The Cerveteri tumuli highlight the very different values of the Etruscans and the Greeks. The Greeks employed stone for the shrines of their gods, but only rarely built monumental tombs

3-5 Tumuli in the Banditaccia necropolis, Cerveteri, Italy, seventh to second centuries BCE.

In the Banditaccia necropolis at Cerveteri, the Etruscans buried several generations of families in multichambered rock-cut underground tombs covered by great earthen mounds (tumuli).

3-6 Interior of the Tomb of the Reliefs, Banditaccia necropolis, Cerveteri, Italy, late fourth or early third century BCE.

The Tomb of the Reliefs takes its name from the painted stucco reliefs of domestic items that cover its walls and piers. The interior was intended to mimic the appearance of an Etruscan house.

TOMB OF THE LEOPARDS The Etruscans also decorated their underground burial chambers with mural paintings. Painted tombs are statistically rare, the privilege of only the wealthiest Etruscan families. Most have been found in the Monterozzi necropolis at Tarquinia. A well-preserved example is the Tomb

for their dead. The Etruscans' temples no longer stand because they were constructed of wood and mud brick, but Etruscan tombs are as permanent as the bedrock itself.

The most elaborately decorated Cerveteri tomb is the so-called Tomb of the Reliefs (FIG. 3-6), which accommodated the remains of several generations of a single family. The walls, ceiling beams, piers, and funerary couches of this tomb were, as in other Cerveteri tombs, gouged out of the tufa bedrock, but in this instance brightly painted stucco reliefs cover the stone. The stools, mirrors, drinking cups, pitchers, and knives effectively suggest a domestic context, underscoring the visual and conceptual connection between Etruscan houses of the dead and those of the living.

of the Leopards (FIG. 3-7), named for the beasts guarding the tomb from their perch within the pediment of the rear wall. The leopards recall the panthers on each side of Medusa in the pediment (FIG. 2-23) of the Artemis temple at Corfu. But mythological figures, whether Greek or Etruscan, are uncommon in Tarquinian murals. Instead, the Tomb of the Leopards features banqueting couples (the men with dark skin, the women with light skin, in conformity with the age-old convention; compare FIG. 2-5). They are the painted counterparts of the husband and wife on the terracotta sarcophagus (FIG. 3-4) from Cerveteri. Pitcher- and cup-bearers serve the guests, and musicians entertain them. The banquet takes place in the open air or perhaps in a tent set up for the occasion. In characteristic Etruscan fashion, the banqueters, servants, and entertainers all make exaggerated gestures with unnaturally enlarged hands. The man on the couch at the far right on the rear wall holds up an egg. The tone is joyful—a celebration of the good life of the Etruscan elite, rather than a somber contemplation of death.

3-7 Interior of the Tomb of the Leopards, Monterozzi necropolis, Tarquinia, Italy, ca. 480 BCE.

Mural paintings adorn many Tarquinian tombs. Here, beneath two guardian leopards, banqueting couples celebrate the good life, attended by servants and musicians. The men have dark skin, the women fair skin.

1 ft.

3-8 Aule Metele (*Arringatore*), from Cortona, Italy, early first century BCE. Bronze, 5' 7" high. Museo Archeologico Nazionale, Florence.

Inscribed in Etruscan, this bronze statue of an orator is Etruscan in name only. Aule Metele wears the short toga and high boots of a Roman magistrate, and the portrait style is Roman as well.

ETRUSCAN DECLINE The fifth century BCE was a golden age in Greece, but not in Etruria. In 509 BCE, the Romans expelled the last of their Etruscan kings and replaced the monarchy with a republican form of government. In 474 BCE, the allied Greek forces of Cumae and Syracuse defeated the Etruscan fleet off Cumae, effectively ending Etruscan dominance of the seas. Veii fell to the Romans in 396 BCE, after a terrible 10-year siege. Rome concluded peace with Tarquinia in 351 BCE, but by the beginning of the next century, the Romans had annexed Tarquinia too, and they conquered Cerveteri in 273 BCE. By the first century BCE, Roman control of central Italy became total.

AULE METELE A life-size bronze portrait statue (FIG. 3-8) dating to the early first century BCE is an eloquent symbol of the Roman absorption of the Etruscans. Known as the *Arringatore* (*Orator*), the statue portrays Aule Metele raising his arm to address an assembly.

Although the sculptor inscribed the man's Etruscan name and the names of both of his Etruscan parents on the hem of his garment, the orator wears the short *toga* and high, laced boots of a Roman magistrate. His head also resembles contemporaneous Roman portraits. Aule Metele is Etruscan in name only. If the origin of the Etruscans remains the subject of debate, the question of their demise has a ready answer. Aule Metele and his compatriots became Romans, and Etruscan art became Roman art.

ROMAN ART

Imperial Rome (FIG. 3-9) was a densely populated metropolis crowded with temples, *fora* (singular, *forum*), theaters, bathing complexes, and triumphal arches. But the Rome of King Romulus in the eighth century BCE consisted only of small huts clustered together on the Palatine Hill overlooking what was then uninhabited marshland. In the Archaic period, Rome was essentially an Etruscan city, both politically and culturally. Its greatest shrine, the late-sixth-century BCE Temple of Jupiter on the Capitoline Hill, was built by an Etruscan king, designed by an Etruscan architect, made of wood and mud brick in the Etruscan manner, and decorated with terracotta statuary fashioned by an Etruscan sculptor. When, in 509 BCE, the Romans overthrew Tarquinius Superbus, the last of Rome's Etruscan kings (see "Who's Who in the Roman World," page 90), they established a constitutional government, or republic.

Republic

The new Roman Republic vested power mainly in a *senate* (literally, "a council of elders," *senior* citizens) and in two elected *consuls*. Under extraordinary circumstances, a *dictator* could be appointed for a limited term and a specific purpose, such as commanding the army during a crisis. Before long, the Republican descendants of Romulus conquered Rome's neighbors one by one: the Etruscans to the north, the Samnites and the Greek colonists to the south. Even the Carthaginians of North Africa, who under Hannibal's dynamic leadership had destroyed some of Rome's legions and almost brought down the Republic, fell before the mighty Roman armies.

The year 211 BCE was a turning point both for Rome and for Roman art. Breaking with precedent, Marcellus, conqueror of the fabulously wealthy Sicilian Greek city of Syracuse, brought back to Rome not only the usual spoils of war—captured arms and armor, gold and silver coins, and the like—but also the city's artistic patrimony. Thus began, in the words of the historian Livy, "the craze for works of Greek art."[1] Exposure to Greek sculpture and painting and to the splendid marble temples of the Greek gods increased as the Romans expanded their conquests beyond Italy. Greece became a Roman province in 146 BCE, and in 133 BCE the last king of Pergamon willed his kingdom in Asia Minor to Rome. Nevertheless, although the Romans developed a virtually insatiable taste for Greek "antiques," the influence of Etruscan art and architecture persisted. The artists and architects of the Roman Republic drew on both Greek and Etruscan traditions.

TEMPLE OF PORTUNUS The mixing of Greek and Etruscan forms is the primary characteristic of the temple dedicated to Portunus (FIGS. 3-9, no. 1, and 3-10), the Roman god of harbors. Its plan

3-9 **Model of the city of Rome during the early fourth century CE. Museo della Civiltà Romana, Rome.** (1) Temple of Portunus, (2) Palatine Hill, (3) Capitoline Hill, (4) Pantheon, (5) Forum of Trajan, (6) Markets of Trajan, (7) Forum Romanum, (8) Basilica Nova, (9) Arch of Titus, (10) Arch of Constantine, (11) Colossus of Nero, (12) Colosseum.

At the height of its power, Rome was the capital of the greatest empire in the ancient world. The Romans ruled from the Tigris and Euphrates to the Thames and beyond, from the Nile to the Rhine and Danube.

3-10 **Temple of Portunus (looking south, after restoration, 2013), Rome, Italy, ca. 75 BCE.**

Republican temples combined Etruscan plans and Greek elevations. This pseudoperipteral stone temple employs the Ionic order, but it has a staircase and freestanding columns only at the front.

follows the Etruscan pattern with a high podium, a flight of steps at the front, and freestanding columns only in the deep porch. But the builders constructed the temple of stone (local tufa and travertine), overlaid originally with *stucco* in imitation of Greek marble. The columns are not Tuscan but Ionic, complete with flutes and bases, and there is a matching Ionic frieze. Moreover, in an effort to approximate a peripteral Greek temple yet maintain the basic Etruscan plan, the architect added a series of Ionic *engaged columns* (attached half-columns) to the sides and back of the cella. Although the design combines Etruscan and Greek elements, the resultant mix—a *pseudoperipteral* temple—is distinctively Roman.

VERISM The patrons of Republican religious and civic buildings were in almost all cases men from old and distinguished families, often generals who used the spoils of war to finance public works. These aristocratic *patricians* were fiercely proud of their lineage. They kept likenesses (*imagines*) of their ancestors in wood cupboards in their homes and paraded them at the funerals of prominent relatives. Ancestral portraiture was one way that the patrician class celebrated its elevated position in society. The subjects of these portraits were almost exclusively men of advanced age, for generally only elders held power in the Republic. These patricians did not ask sculptors to idealize them. Instead, they requested brutally realistic images immortalizing their distinctive features, in the tradition of the treasured household imagines.

MONARCHY (753–509 BCE)

Latin and Etruscan kings ruled Rome from the city's founding by Romulus on April 21, 753 BCE, until the revolt in 509 BCE against Rome's last king, Tarquinius Superbus (exact dates of rule unreliable).

REPUBLIC (509–27 BCE)

The Republic lasted almost 500 years, until the Senate bestowed the title of Augustus on Octavian, the grandnephew of Julius Caesar and victor over Mark Antony in the civil war that ended the Republic. Some major figures were

- Marcellus, b. 268(?), d. 208 BCE, consul
- Sulla, b. 138, d. 79 BCE, consul and dictator
- Julius Caesar, b. 100, d. 44 BCE, consul and dictator
- Mark Antony, b. 83, d. 30 BCE, consul

EARLY EMPIRE (27 BCE–96 CE)

The Early Empire began with the rule of Augustus and his Julio-Claudian successors and continued until the end of the Flavian dynasty. The emperors discussed in this chapter were

- Augustus, r. 27 BCE–14 CE (FIGS. I-8 and 3-25)
- Nero, r. 54–68

- Vespasian, r. 69–79
- Titus, r. 79–81 (FIG. 3-34)
- Domitian, r. 81–96

HIGH EMPIRE (96–192 CE)

The High Empire began with the death of Domitian and the rule of the Spanish emperors, Trajan and Hadrian, and ended with the last emperor of the Antonine dynasty. The emperors of this period were

- Trajan, r. 98–117 (FIG. 3-36B ⬚)
- Hadrian, r. 117–138
- Antoninus Pius, r. 138–161 (FIG. 3-1)
- Marcus Aurelius, r. 161–180 (FIG. 3-41)
- Lucius Verus (r. 161–169)
- Commodus (r. 180–192)

LATE EMPIRE (192–337 CE)

The Late Empire began with the Severan dynasty and included the so-called soldier emperors of the third century, the tetrarchs, and Constantine, the first Christian emperor. Among these emperors were

- Septimius Severus, r. 193–211 (FIG. 3-43)
- Caracalla, r. 211–217 (FIGS. 3-43 and 3-44)
- Trajan Decius, r. 249–251 (FIG. 3-47)
- Diocletian, r. 284–305 (FIG. 3-50)
- Constantine I, r. 306–337 (FIGS. 3-51 and 3-54)

One of the most striking of these so-called *veristic* (superrealistic) portraits is the head (FIG. 3-11) of an unidentified patrician from Osimo. The sculptor painstakingly recorded each rise and fall, each bulge and fold, of the facial surface, like a mapmaker who did not want to miss the slightest detail of surface change. Scholars debate whether Republican veristic portraits are truly blunt records of individual features or exaggerated types designed to make a statement about personality: serious, experienced, determined, loyal to family and state—the most admired virtues during the Republic.

Pompeii and the Cities of Vesuvius

On August 24, 79 CE, Mount Vesuvius, a long-dormant volcano, suddenly erupted, burying many prosperous towns around the Bay of Naples, among them Pompeii. The eruption was a catastrophe for the region's inhabitants but a boon for archaeologists, enabling a reconstruction of the art and life of Roman towns of the Late Republic and Early Empire to a degree impossible anywhere else.

The Oscans, one of the many Italian population groups during the peak of Etruscan power, were the first to settle at Pompeii, but toward the end of the fifth century BCE, the Samnites took over the town. Under the influence of their Greek neighbors, the Samnites greatly expanded the original settlement and gave monumental shape to the city center (FIG. 3-12). Pompeii fought with other Italian cities on the losing side against Rome in the so-called Social War that ended in 89 BCE, and in 80 BCE, the Roman consul Sulla founded a new Roman colony on the site, with Latin as its official language. The colony's population had grown to between 10,000 and 15,000 when Mount Vesuvius buried Pompeii in volcanic ash.

FORUM The center of civic life in any Roman town was its forum, or public square. Pompeii's forum (FIG. 3-12, no. 1) lies in the southwest corner of the expanded Roman city but at the heart of the original town. In the second century BCE, the Samnites constructed two-story *porticos* (colonnades) on three sides of the long and narrow plaza. At

3-11 Head of an elderly patrician, from Osimo, mid-first century BCE. Marble, life-size. Palazzo del Municipio, Osimo.

Veristic (superrealistic) portraits of old men from distinguished families were the norm during the Republic. The sculptor of this head painstakingly recorded every detail of the elderly man's face.

1 in.

3-12 Aerial view of the forum (looking northeast), Pompeii, Italy, second century BCE and later. (1) forum, (2) Temple of Jupiter (Capitolium), (3) basilica.

The center of Roman civic life was the forum. At Pompeii, colonnades frame a rectangular plaza with the city's main temple at the north end and the basilica (law court) at the southwest corner.

All around the square, behind the colonnades, were secular and religious structures, including the town's administrative offices. Most important was the *basilica* at the southwest corner (FIG. 3-12, no. 3). It is the earliest well-preserved building of its kind. Constructed during the late second century BCE, the basilica was Pompeii's law court and chief administrative center. In plan it resembled the forum itself: long and narrow, with colonnades dividing the central *nave* from the flanking *aisles*.

AMPHITHEATER Shortly after the Romans took control of Pompeii, two of the town's wealthiest officials used their own funds to erect a large amphitheater (FIGS. 3-13 and 3-14)

the north end, they built a temple of Jupiter (FIG. 3-12, no. 2). When Pompeii became a Roman colony, the Romans converted the temple into a *Capitolium*—a triple shrine to Jupiter, Juno, and Minerva. The temple is of standard Republican type, constructed of tufa covered with fine white stucco and combining an Etruscan plan with Corinthian columns. It faces into the civic square, dominating the area. This contrasts with the siting of Greek temples (FIG. 2-36), which stood in isolation and could be approached and viewed from all sides, like colossal statues on giant stepped pedestals. The Roman forum, like the Etrusco-Roman temple, had a chief side, a focus of attention.

at the southeastern end of town. The earliest amphitheater known, it could seat some 20,000 spectators—more than the entire population of the town even a century and a half after its construction. The word *amphitheater* means "double theater," and Roman amphitheaters resemble two Greek theaters put together. Amphitheaters nonetheless stand in sharp contrast, both architecturally and functionally, to Greco-Roman theaters, where actors performed comedies

3-13 Aerial view of the amphitheater (looking northeast), Pompeii, Italy, ca. 70 BCE.

Pompeii's amphitheater is the oldest known and an early example of Roman concrete technology. In the arena, bloody gladiatorial combats and wild animal hunts took place before 20,000 spectators.

3-14 Brawl in the Pompeii amphitheater, wall painting from House I,3,23, Pompeii, Italy, ca. 60–79 CE. Fresco, 5' 7" × 6' 1". Museo Archeologico Nazionale, Naples.

This wall painting records a brawl that broke out in the Pompeii amphitheater in 59 CE. The painter included the awning (velarium) that could be rolled down to shield the spectators from sun and rain.

ARCHITECTURAL BASICS
Roman Concrete Construction

The history of Roman architecture would be very different had the Romans been content to use the same building materials that the Greeks, Etruscans, and other ancient peoples did. Instead, the Romans developed *concrete* construction, which revolutionized architectural design. Roman builders mixed concrete according to a changing recipe of lime mortar, volcanic sand, water, and small stones (*caementa,* from which the English word "cement" derives). Workers poured the mixture into wood frames and left it to dry. When the concrete hardened, they removed the wood molds, revealing a solid mass of great strength, though rough in appearance. The Romans often covered the coarse concrete with stucco or with marble *revetment* (facing). Despite this lengthy procedure, concrete walls were much less costly to construct than walls of imported Greek marble or even local tufa and travertine.

The advantages of concrete went well beyond cost, however. It is possible to fashion concrete shapes unachievable in masonry construction, especially huge vaulted and domed rooms without internal supports. The new medium became a vehicle for shaping architectural space and enabled Roman architects to design buildings in unprecedented ways.

The most common types of Roman concrete vaults and domes are

- **Barrel Vaults** Also called the *tunnel vault,* the *barrel vault* (FIG. 3-15a) is an extension of a simple arch, creating a semicylindrical ceiling over parallel walls. Pre-Roman builders constructed barrel vaults using traditional ashlar masonry (FIG. 1-20), but those earlier vaults were less stable than concrete barrel vaults. If even a single block of a cut-stone vault comes loose, the whole vault may collapse. Also, masonry barrel vaults can be illuminated only by light entering at either end of the tunnel. Using concrete, Roman builders could place windows at any point in a barrel vault, because once the concrete hardens, it forms a seamless sheet of

"artificial stone" in which the openings do not lessen the vault's structural integrity. Whether made of stone or concrete, barrel vaults require *buttressing* (lateral support) of the walls below the vaults to counteract their downward and outward *thrust.*

- **Groin Vaults** A *groin* (or *cross*) *vault* (FIG. 3-15b) is formed by the intersection at right angles of two barrel vaults of equal size. Besides appearing lighter than the barrel vault, the groin vault needs less buttressing. Whereas the barrel vault's thrust is continuous along the entire length of the supporting walls, the groin vault's thrust is concentrated along the groins, the lines at the juncture of the two barrel vaults. Buttressing is needed only at the points where the groins meet the vault's vertical supports, usually *piers.* The system leaves the area between the piers open, enabling light to enter. Builders can construct groin vaults as well as barrel vaults using stone blocks, but stone groin vaults have the same structural limitations as stone barrel vaults do compared to their concrete counterparts.

When a series of groin vaults covers an interior hall (FIG. 3-15c; compare FIG. 3-37), the open lateral arches of the vaults form the equivalent of a *clerestory* of a traditional timber-roofed structure (FIG. 4-3). A *fenestrated* (with openings or windows) sequence of groin vaults has a major advantage over a timber clerestory: concrete vaults are relatively fireproof.

- **Hemispherical Domes** If a barrel vault is a round arch extended in a line, then a hemispherical *dome* (FIG. 3-15d) is a round arch rotated around the full circumference of a circle. Masonry domes (FIG. 2-12), like masonry vaults, cannot accommodate windows without threat to their stability. Concrete domes can be opened up even at their apex with a circular *oculus* ("eye"), enabling light to reach the sometimes vast spaces beneath (FIGS. 3-39 and 3-40). Hemispherical domes usually rest on concrete cylindrical *drums.*

3-15 Roman concrete construction. (*a*) barrel vault, (*b*) groin vault, (*c*) fenestrated sequence of groin vaults, (*d*) hemispherical dome with oculus (John Burge).

Concrete domes and vaults of varying designs enabled Roman builders to revolutionize the history of architecture by shaping interior spaces in novel ways.

a b c d

ARCHITECTURAL BASICS
The Roman House

The entrance to a typical Roman *domus* ("private house") was through a narrow foyer (*fauces,* the "jaws" of the house), which led to a large central reception area, the *atrium.* The rooms flanking the fauces could open onto the atrium, as in FIG. 3-16, or onto the street, in which case the owner could operate or rent them as shops. The roof over the atrium (FIG. 3-17) was partially open to the sky, not only to admit light but also to channel rainwater into a basin (*impluvium*) to be stored in cisterns for household use. Opening onto the atrium were small bedrooms called *cubicula* ("cubicles"). At the back were two recessed areas (*alae,* "wings") and the owner's *tablinum,* or home office; one or more *triclinia* ("dining rooms"); a kitchen; and sometimes a small garden. Extant houses display endless variations of the same basic plan, dictated by the owners' personal tastes and means, the size and shape of the lot, and so forth, but all Roman houses of this type were inward-looking in nature. The design shut off the street's noise and dust, and all internal activity focused on the brightly illuminated atrium at the center of the residence (where patricians displayed their family imagines).

During the second century BCE, the Roman house took on Greek airs. Builders added a *peristyle* (colonnaded) garden at the rear, as in FIG. 3-16, providing a second internal source of illumination as well as a pleasant setting for meals served in a summer triclinium. The axial symmetry of the plan meant that on entering the fauces of the house, a visitor had a view through the atrium directly into the colonnaded garden (as in FIG. 3-17), which often boasted a fountain or pool, marble statuary, mural paintings, and mosaic floors.

3-16 Restored view and plan of a typical Roman house of the Late Republic and Early Empire (John Burge). (1) fauces, (2) atrium, (3) impluvium, (4) cubiculum, (5) ala, (6) tablinum, (7) triclinium, (8) peristyle.

Roman houses were inward-looking, with a central atrium open to the sky and an impluvium to collect rainwater. A visitor standing in the fauces had an axial view through to the peristyle garden.

3-17 Atrium of the House of the Vettii, Pompeii, Italy, second century BCE, rebuilt 62–79 CE.

Older Roman houses had a small garden behind the atrium, but beginning in the second century BCE, builders added peristyles with Greek columns at the rear, as in the House of the Vettii.

and tragedies. Amphitheaters were where the Romans staged violent games (see "Spectacles in the Colosseum" 🔊). Greek theaters (FIG. 2-51) were always on natural hillsides, but supporting an amphitheater's continuous elliptical *cavea* (seating area) required building an artificial mountain. Only concrete, unknown to the Greeks, could easily meet that challenge (see "Roman Concrete Construction," page 92, and FIG. 3-15). In the Pompeii amphitheater, shallow concrete *barrel vaults* form a giant retaining wall holding up the earthen mound and stone seats. Barrel vaults running all the way through the elliptical mountain of earth form the tunnels leading to the *arena,* the central area where the violent contests took place. (*Arena* is Latin for "sand," which soaked up the blood of the wounded and killed.)

A painting (FIG. 3-14) found in one of Pompeii's houses records a brawl that occurred in the amphitheater during a gladiatorial contest in 59 CE. The fighting—between the Pompeians and their neighbors, the Nucerians—left many seriously wounded and led to the banning of games in the amphitheater for a decade. The painting holds further interest because it shows the awning (*velarium*) destroyed in the Vesuvian eruption. The velarium could be rolled down from the top of the cavea to shield spectators from sun and rain.

HOUSE OF THE VETTII The evidence from Pompeii regarding Roman domestic architecture (see "The Roman House," above, and FIG. 3-16) is unparalleled anywhere else. One of the best-preserved houses at Pompeii is the House of the Vettii. A photograph (FIG. 3-17) taken in the *fauces* shows the *impluvium* in the center of the *atrium,* the opening in the roof above, and, in the background, the *peristyle* garden. Of course, only the wealthy—whether patricians or former slaves like the Vettius brothers, who made their fortune as merchants—could own large private houses. The masses, especially in expensive cities like Rome, lived in multistory apartment houses.

SAMNITE HOUSE The houses and villas around Mount Vesuvius have also yielded the most complete record of the changing fashions in mural painting anywhere in the ancient world. Art historians divide the various Roman mural types into four "Pompeian Styles." In the *First Style,* the decorator's aim was to imitate costly marble panels (compare FIG. 3-40) using painted stucco relief. The fauces (FIG. 3-18) of the Samnite House at Herculaneum greets visitors with a stunning illusion of walls faced with marbles imported from quarries all over the Mediterranean. This approach to wall decoration is comparable to the modern practice of using inexpensive manufactured materials to approximate the look and shape of genuine wood paneling. The practice is not, however, uniquely Roman. First Style walls are well documented in Greece from the late fourth century BCE on. The use of the First Style in Italian houses is yet another example of the Hellenization of Republican architecture.

VILLA OF THE MYSTERIES In contrast, the *Second Style,* introduced around 80 BCE, seems to be a Roman innovation and is in most respects the antithesis of the First Style. Second Style painters aimed to dissolve a room's confining walls and replace them with the illusion of an imaginary three-dimensional world. An early example of the new style is the room (FIG. 3-19) that gives its name to the Villa of the Mysteries at Pompeii. Many archaeologists believe that this chamber was used to celebrate, in private, the rites of the Greek god Dionysos (Roman Bacchus). Dionysos was the focus of an unofficial mystery religion popular among women in Italy at this time. The precise nature of the Dionysiac rites is unknown, but the figural cycle in the Villa of the Mysteries, illustrating mortals (all female save for one boy) interacting with mythological figures, probably provides evidence of the cult's initiation rites. In these rites, young women symbolically united in marriage with Dionysos.

The Second Style painter created the illusion of a shallow ledge on which the human and divine actors move around the room. Especially striking is the way some of the figures interact across the corners of the room. For example, a seminude winged woman at the far right of the rear wall lashes out with her whip across the space

3-18 First Style wall painting in the fauces of the Samnite House, Herculaneum, Italy, late second century BCE.

In First Style murals, the aim was to imitate costly marble panels using painted stucco relief. The style is Greek in origin and another example of the Hellenization of Republican architecture.

3-19 Dionysiac mystery frieze, Second Style wall paintings in room 5 of the Villa of the Mysteries, Pompeii, Italy, ca. 60–50 BCE. Frieze, 5' 4" high.

Second Style painters created the illusion of an imaginary three-dimensional world on the walls of Roman houses. The figures in this room are acting out the initiation rites of the Dionysiac mysteries.

1 ft.

3-20 Second Style wall paintings (general view, *left,* and detail of tholos, *right*) from cubiculum M of the Villa of Publius Fannius Synistor, Boscoreale, Italy, ca. 50–40 BCE. Fresco, 8' 9" high. Metropolitan Museum of Art, New York.

In this Second Style bedroom, the painter opened up the walls with vistas of towns, temples, and colonnaded courtyards. The convincing illusionism is due in part to the artist's use of linear perspective.

of the room at a kneeling woman with a bare back (the initiate and bride-to-be of Dionysos) on the left end of the right wall.

BOSCOREALE In later Second Style designs, painters created a three-dimensional setting that also extends beyond the wall, as in cubiculum M (FIG. 3-20) of the Villa of Publius Fannius Synistor at Boscoreale. All around the room, the painter opened up the walls with vistas of Italian towns, marble tholos temples, and colonnaded courtyards. Painted doors and gates invite the viewer to walk through the wall into the magnificent world the painter created. Familiarity with *linear perspective* (see "Linear and Atmospheric Perspective," page 232) explains in large part the Boscoreale muralist's success in suggesting depth. In this kind of perspective, all the

receding lines in a composition converge on a single point along the painting's central axis. Ancient writers state that Greek painters of the fifth century BCE first used linear perspective for the design of Athenian stage sets (hence its Greek name, *skenographia,* "scene painting"). In the Boscoreale cubiculum, the painter most successfully used linear perspective in the far corners, where a low gate leads to a peristyle framing a round temple (FIG. 3-20, *right*).

PRIMAPORTA The ultimate example of a Second Style picture-window mural is the gardenscape (FIG. 3-21) in the Villa of Livia, wife of the emperor Augustus, at Primaporta, just north of Rome. To suggest recession, the painter employed another kind of perspective—*atmospheric perspective*—in which the illusion of depth

3-21 Gardenscape, Second Style wall paintings, from the Villa of Livia, Primaporta, Italy, ca. 30–20 BCE. Fresco, 6' 7" high. Palazzo Massimo alle Terme, Museo Nazionale Romano, Rome.

The ultimate example of a Second Style "picture window" wall is this gardenscape in Livia's villa. To suggest recession, the painter used atmospheric perspective, intentionally blurring the distant forms.

3-22 Third Style wall painting, from cubiculum 15 of the Villa of Agrippa Postumus, Boscotrecase, Italy, ca. 10 BCE. Fresco, 7' 8" high. Metropolitan Museum of Art, New York.

In the Third Style, Roman painters decorated walls with delicate linear fantasies sketched on monochromatic backgrounds. Here, a tiny floating landscape on a black ground is the central motif.

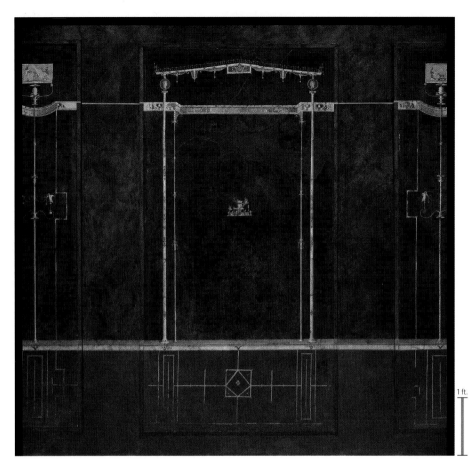

is achieved by the increasingly blurred appearance of objects in the distance. At Primaporta, the Second Style muralist precisely painted the fence, trees, and birds in the foreground, whereas the details of the dense foliage in the background are indistinct.

BOSCOTRECASE The Primaporta gardenscape is the polar opposite of First Style designs, which reinforce, rather than deny, the heavy presence of confining walls. But tastes changed rapidly in the Roman world, as in society today. Not long after Livia had her villa decorated, Roman patrons began to favor mural designs that reasserted the primacy of the wall surface. In the *Third Style* of Pompeian painting, popular from about 15 BCE to 60 CE, artists no longer attempted to replace the walls with three-dimensional worlds of their own creation. Nor did they seek to imitate the appearance of the marble walls of Hellenistic palaces. Instead they adorned walls with delicate linear fantasies sketched on predominantly *monochromatic* (one-color) backgrounds.

One of the earliest and also the finest examples of the new style is cubiculum 15 (FIG. 3-22) in the Villa of Agrippa Postumus at Boscotrecase. Nowhere did the artist use illusionistic painting to penetrate the wall. In place of the stately columns of the Second Style are insubstantial and impossibly thin *colonnettes* supporting featherweight canopies barely reminiscent of pediments. In the center of this delicate and elegant architectural frame is a tiny floating landscape painted directly on the jet-black ground. It is hard to imagine a sharper contrast with the panoramic gardenscape at Livia's villa. Third Style walls can never be mistaken for windows opening onto a world beyond the room. Not everyone approved of the new Roman mural fashion, however. One of those who disliked the Third Style was the Augustan architect Vitruvius, author of the most important extant ancient treatise on architecture (see "Vitruvius's *Ten Books on Architecture*" [↗]).

IXION ROOM A taste for illusionism returned once again in the *Fourth Style*, which was the most popular way to decorate walls during the last two decades of the life of Pompeii. The style is characterized by crowded and confused compositions mixing fragmentary architectural vistas, framed panel paintings, and motifs favored in the First and Third Styles. The Ixion Room (FIG. 3-23), a triclinium opening onto the peristyle of the House of the Vettii (FIG. 3-17), features a Fourth Style design that dates just before 79 CE. The mural scheme is a kind of summation of all the previous Pompeian styles. The lowest zone, for example, is one of the most successful imitations anywhere of costly multicolored imported marbles. The large white panels in the corners of the room, with their delicate floral frames and floating central motifs, would fit naturally into the most elegant Third Style design. Unmistakably Fourth Style, however, are the fragmentary architectural vistas of the central and upper zones of the walls. They are unrelated to one another and do not constitute a unified cityscape beyond the wall. Moreover, the figures depicted would tumble into the room if they took a single step forward.

The Ixion Room takes its name from the mythological painting at the center of the rear wall. Ixion had attempted to seduce Hera, and Zeus punished him by binding him to a perpetually spinning wheel. The panels on the two adjacent walls also have Greek myths as subjects. The Ixion Room is a kind of private art gallery. Many art historians believe that lost Greek panel paintings were the models for the many mythological paintings on Third and Fourth Style walls. Although few, if any, of the Pompeiian paintings can be described as true copies of famous Greek works, they attest to the Romans' continuing admiration for Greek art.

STILL LIFE Another important genre of Roman mural painting was the *still life* (a painting of inanimate objects, artfully arranged). A still life with peaches and a carafe (FIG. 3-24), a detail of a Fourth Style wall from Herculaneum, is one of the finest extant examples. The painter was a master of illusionism who devoted as much attention to the shadows and highlights on the fruit, the stem and leaves, and the glass jar as to the objects themselves.

Early Empire

The murder of Julius Caesar on the Ides of March, 44 BCE, plunged the Roman world into a bloody civil war. The fighting lasted until 31 BCE, when Octavian, Caesar's grandnephew and adopted son, crushed the naval forces of Mark Antony and Queen Cleopatra

3-23 Fourth Style wall paintings in the Ixion Room (triclinium P) of the House of the Vettii (FIG. 3-17), Pompeii, Italy, ca. 70–79 CE.

Fourth Style murals are often multicolored, crowded, and confused compositions with a mixture of fragmentary architectural views, mythological paintings, and First and Third Style motifs.

of Egypt at Actium in northwestern Greece. Antony and Cleopatra committed suicide, and in 30 BCE, Egypt, once the wealthiest and most powerful kingdom of the ancient world, became another province in the ever-expanding Roman Empire.

AUGUSTUS Historians mark the passage from the Roman Republic to the Roman Empire from the day in 27 BCE when the Senate conferred the title of *Augustus* (the Majestic, or Exalted, One; r. 27 BCE–14 CE) on Octavian. The Empire was ostensibly a continuation of the Republic, with the same constitutional offices, but in fact Augustus, as *princeps* ("first citizen"), occupied all the key positions. He was consul and *imperator* (commander in chief; root of the word "emperor") and even, after 12 BCE, *pontifex maximus* ("chief priest" of the state religion). These offices gave Augustus control of all aspects of Roman public life.

With powerful armies keeping order on the Empire's frontiers and no opposition at home, Augustus brought peace and prosperity to a war-weary Mediterranean world. Known in his day as the *Pax Augusta* (Augustan Peace), the peace Augustus established prevailed for two centuries. It came to be called simply the *Pax Romana*. During this time, the emperors commissioned a huge number of public works throughout the Empire, all on an unprecedented scale. Imperial portraits and monuments covered with reliefs recounting the emperors' great deeds reminded people everywhere that the emperors were the source of peace and prosperity. These portraits and reliefs, however, often presented a picture of the emperors and their achievements bearing little resemblance to historical fact (see "Roman Art as Historical Fiction," page 83). Their purpose was not to provide an objective record but to mold public opinion.

When Augustus vanquished Antony and Cleopatra and became undisputed master of the Mediterranean world, he was not yet 32 years old. The rule by elders that had characterized the Roman Republic for nearly 500 years came to an abrupt end. Suddenly,

1 in.

3-24 Still life with peaches, detail of a Fourth Style wall painting, from the House of the Stags, Herculaneum, Italy, ca. 62–79 CE. Fresco, 1' 2" × 1' 1½". Museo Archeologico Nazionale, Naples.

The Roman interest in illusionism explains the popularity of still-life paintings. This painter paid scrupulous attention to the play of light and shadow on different shapes and textures.

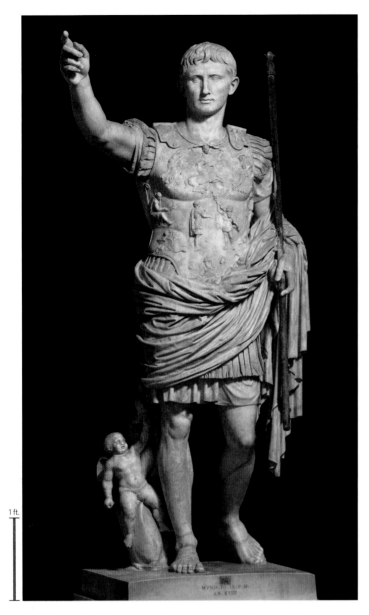

3-25 Portrait of Augustus as imperator (general), from Primaporta, Italy, early-first-century CE copy of a bronze original of ca. 20 BCE. Marble, 6′ 8″ high. Musei Vaticani, Rome.

The models for Augustus's idealized portraits, which depict him as a never-aging youth, were Classical Greek statues (FIG. 2-35). This statue portrays the armor-clad emperor as commander in chief.

Roman portraitists had to produce images of a youthful head of state. But Augustus was not merely young. The Senate had declared Caesar a god after his death, and Augustus, though never claiming to be a god himself, widely advertised himself as the son of a god. His portraits (FIG. I-8) were designed to present the image of a god-like leader who miraculously never aged.

The models for Augustus's idealized portraits were Classical Greek statues. In the portrait of Augustus as imperator (FIG. 3-25), the emperor's pose recalls Polykleitos's *Doryphoros* (FIG. 2-35), but Augustus raises his right arm to address his troops in the manner of the orator Aule Metele (FIG. 3-8). Augustus's head, although depicting a recognizable individual, also emulates the Polykleitan youth's head in its overall shape, the sharp ridges of the brows, and the tight cap of layered hair. Augustus is not nude, however, and the details of

3-26 Portrait bust of Livia, from Arsinoe, Egypt, early first century CE. Marble, 1′ 1½″ high. Ny Carlsberg Glyptotek, Copenhagen.

Although Livia sports the latest Roman coiffure, her youthful appearance and sharply defined features derive from images of Greek goddesses. She died at 87, but, like Augustus, never aged in her portraits.

the statue carry political messages. The reliefs on his *cuirass* (breast-plate) celebrate a victory over the Parthians, Rome's enemies to the east. The Cupid at Augustus's feet refers to his divine descent from Venus through Julius Caesar.

LIVIA A marble portrait (FIG. 3-26) of Livia shows that the imperial women of the Augustan age shared the emperor's perpetual youthfulness. Although the empress sports the latest Roman coiffure, with the hair rolled over the forehead and knotted at the nape of the neck, her blemish-free skin and sharply defined features derive from images of Classical Greek goddesses. Livia outlived Augustus by 15 years, dying at age 87. In her portraits, the coiffure changed with the introduction of each new fashion, but her face remained ever young, befitting her exalted position in the Roman state.

ARA PACIS AUGUSTAE On Livia's birthday in 9 BCE, Augustus dedicated the Ara Pacis Augustae (Altar of Augustan Peace; FIG. 3-27), the monument celebrating his most important achievement, the establishment of peace. Acanthus tendrils adorn the lower zone of the altar's marble precinct walls. The rich botanical ornament of the altar's exterior alludes to the prosperity that peace brings. Four panels on the east and west ends of the Ara Pacis depict carefully selected mythological subjects, including (at the right in FIG. 3-27) a relief of Aeneas making a sacrifice. Aeneas was the son of Venus and one of Augustus's forefathers. The connection between the emperor

3-27 West facade of the
Ara Pacis Augustae (Altar
of Augustan Peace), Rome,
Italy, 13–9 BCE.

Augustus sought to present
his new order as a Golden
Age equaling that of Athens
under Pericles. The Ara Pacis
celebrates the emperor's most
important achievement, the
establishment of peace.

and Aeneas was a key element of Augustus's political ideology. It is no coincidence that Vergil wrote the *Aeneid* during the rule of Augustus. The epic poem glorified the young emperor by celebrating the founder of the Julian line.

Processions of the imperial family (FIG. 3-28) and other important dignitaries appear on the long north and south sides of the Ara Pacis. The inspiration for these parallel friezes was very likely the Panathenaic procession frieze (FIG. 2-41, *bottom*) of the Parthenon. Augustus sought to present his new order as a Golden Age equaling that of Athens under Pericles, and he consciously revived the Classical style in both architecture (see *"Vitruvius's Ten Books on Architecture"* and FIG. 3-28A ☑) and sculpture. The emulation of Classical models thus made a political as well as an artistic statement. Even so, the Roman and Greek processions are very different in character. On the Parthenon, anonymous figures act out an event that recurred every four years. The frieze stands for all Panathenaic Festival processions. The Ara Pacis depicts a specific event—probably the inaugural ceremony of 13 BCE—and recognizable historical figures. Among those portrayed are children, who restlessly tug on their elders' garments and talk to one another when they should be quiet on a solemn occasion. Augustus was concerned about a decline in the birthrate among the Roman nobility, and he enacted a series of laws designed to promote marriage, marital fidelity, and raising children. The portrayal of men with their families on the Altar of Peace served as a moral exemplar.

1 ft.

3-28 Procession of the
imperial family, detail of
the south frieze of the Ara
Pacis Augustae, Rome,
Italy, 13–9 BCE. Marble,
5' 3" high.

Although inspired by the Ionic
frieze (FIG. 2-41, *bottom*) of the
Parthenon, the Ara Pacis procession depicts recognizable
individuals, including children.
Augustus promoted marriage
and childbearing.

3-29 Pont-du-Gard (looking northeast), Nîmes, France, ca. 16 BCE.

Roman engineers constructed roads and bridges throughout the empire. This aqueduct-bridge brought water from a distant mountain spring to Nîmes—about 100 gallons a day for each inhabitant.

PONT-DU-GARD During the Pax Romana, Rome sent engineers to construct roads, bridges, and *aqueducts* throughout its far-flung empire. In southern France, outside Nîmes, the aqueduct-bridge known as the Pont-du-Gard (FIG. 3-29) still stands. The aqueduct provided about 100 gallons of water a day for each inhabitant of Nîmes from a mountain spring some 30 miles away. The water flowed over the considerable distance by gravity alone, which required channels built with a continuous gradual decline over the entire route from source to city. The three-story Pont-du-Gard maintained the height of the water channel where the water crossed the Gard River. Each large arch spans some 82 feet and consists of blocks weighing up to two tons each. The bridge's uppermost level is a row of smaller arches, three above each of the large openings below. They carry the water channel itself. The harmonious proportional relationship between the larger and smaller arches reveals that the Roman hydraulic engineer who designed the aqueduct also had a keen aesthetic sense.

THE FLAVIANS For a half century after Augustus's death, Rome's emperors all came from his family, the Julians, or his wife Livia's, the Claudians. But the outrageous behavior of Nero (r. 54–68 CE) produced a powerful backlash. Facing assassination, Nero committed suicide in 68 CE, bringing the Julio-Claudian dynasty to an end. A year of renewed civil strife followed. The man who emerged triumphant in this brief but bloody conflict was Vespasian (r. 69–79 CE), a general who had served under Nero. Vespasian, whose family name was Flavius, had two sons, Titus (r. 79–81 CE) and Domitian (r. 81–96 CE). The Flavian dynasty ruled Rome for more than a quarter century.

COLOSSEUM The Flavian Amphitheater, or Colosseum (FIGS. 3-9, no. 12, and 3-30), was one of Vespasian's first undertakings after becoming emperor. The decision to build the Colosseum was politically shrewd. The site chosen was on the property that Nero had confiscated from the Roman people after a great fire in 64 CE in order to build a private villa for himself. By constructing the new amphitheater there, Vespasian reclaimed the land for the public and also provided Romans with the largest arena for gladiatorial combats and other lavish spectacles ever constructed (see "Spectacles in

3-30 Facade of the Colosseum (Flavian Amphitheater; looking south), Rome, Italy, ca. 70–80 CE.

Vespasian began construction of the Flavian Amphitheater on land that Nero had confiscated from the public. The Colosseum's facade mixes Roman arches and Tuscan, Ionic, and Corinthian engaged columns.

the Colosseum" and FIG. **3-30A** 🔗). To mark the opening of the Colosseum, the Flavians staged games for 100 days. Some later writers reported that the highlight was the flooding of the arena to stage a complete naval battle with more than 3,000 participants.

The Colosseum, like the much earlier Pompeian amphitheater (FIGS. 3-13 and 3-14), could not have been built without concrete. A complex system of barrel-vaulted corridors holds up the enormous oval seating area. This concrete "skeleton" is exposed today because the amphitheater's marble seats were hauled away during the Middle Ages and Renaissance. Originally, there were seats for more than 50,000 spectators. (The Colosseum takes its name, however, not from its enormous size but from its location beside the Colossus of Nero [FIG. 3-9, no. 11], a 120-foot-tall statue of the emperor in the guise of the sun god.) Also visible now are the arena substructures, which housed waiting rooms for the gladiators, animal cages, and machinery for raising and lowering stage sets as well as animals and humans.

The exterior travertine shell (FIG. 3-30) is approximately 160 feet high, the height of a modern 16-story building. The architect divided the facade into four bands, with large arched openings piercing the lower three. Ornamental Greek orders frame the arches in the standard Roman sequence for multistory buildings: from the ground up, Tuscan, Ionic, and then Corinthian. The use of engaged columns and a lintel to frame the openings in the Colosseum's facade is a common motif on Roman buildings. Like the pseudoperipteral temple (FIGS. 3-10 and 3-28A 🔗), which combines Greek orders and Etruscan plan, this way of decorating a building's facade mixed Greek orders with an architectural form foreign to Greek post-and-lintel architecture—the arch. The Roman practice of framing an arch with Greek engaged columns had no structural purpose, but it added variety to the surface and unified the towering facade by casting a net of verticals and horizontals over it.

FLAVIAN PORTRAITURE Flavian portraits survive in large numbers, but a marble bust (FIG. **3-31**) of a young woman, probably a Flavian princess, is of special interest. The portrait is notable for its elegance and delicacy and for the virtuoso way the sculptor rendered the differing textures of hair and flesh. The elaborate Flavian coiffure, with its corkscrew curls picked out using a drill instead of a chisel, is a dense mass of light and shadow set off boldly from the softly modeled and highly polished skin of the face and swanlike neck.

ARCH OF TITUS When Titus died in 81 CE, his younger brother, Domitian, succeeded him. The new emperor set up a *triumphal arch* (FIGS. 3-9, no. 9, and **3-32**) in Titus's honor on the road leading into the Forum Romanum (FIG. 3-9, no. 7). The Arch of Titus is a typical

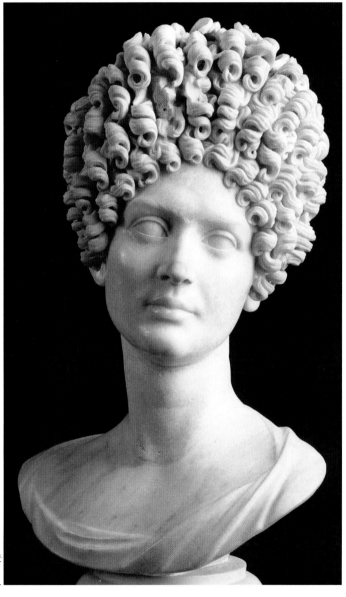

3-31 Portrait bust of a Flavian woman, from Rome, Italy, ca. 90 CE. Marble, 2' 1" high. Museo Capitolino, Musei Capitolini, Rome.

The Flavian sculptor reproduced the elaborate coiffure of this elegant woman by drilling deep holes for the corkscrew curls. The rest of the hair and the face were carved with a hammer and chisel.

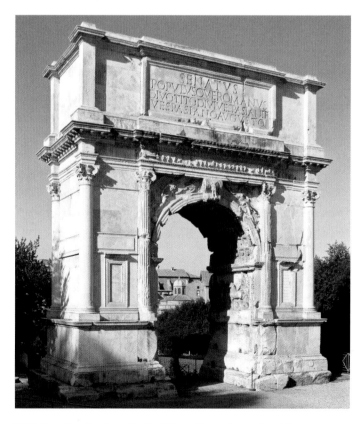

3-32 East facade of the Arch of Titus, Rome, Italy, after 81 CE.

Domitian built this arch on the road leading into the Forum Romanum to honor his brother, the emperor Titus, who became a god after his death. Victories fill the spandrels of the arcuated passageway.

early triumphal arch in having only one passageway. As on the Colosseum, engaged columns frame the *arcuated* (curved or arched) opening. Reliefs depicting personified Victories fill the *spandrels* (the area between the arch's curve and the framing columns and entablature). The dedicatory inscription on the *attic* states that the Senate erected the arch to honor the god Titus, son of the god Vespasian. The Senate normally proclaimed Roman emperors gods after they died (see "Roman Art as Historical Fiction," page 83), unless they ran afoul of the senators and were damned. The statues of those who suffered *damnatio memoriae* were toppled, and their names were erased from public inscriptions. This was Nero's fate.

Inside the passageway of the Arch of Titus are two great relief panels. They represent the triumphal parade of Titus after his return from the conquest of Judaea at the end of the Jewish War in 70 CE. One of the reliefs (FIG. 3-33) depicts Roman soldiers carrying the spoils from the Jewish temple in Jerusalem. Despite considerable damage to the relief, the illusion of movement is convincing. The parade emerges from the left background into the center foreground and disappears through the obliquely placed arch in the right background. The energy and swing of the column of soldiers suggest a rapid march. The sculptor rejected the Classical low-relief style of the Ara Pacis (FIG. 3-28) in favor of extremely deep carving, which produces strong shadows. The heads of the foreground figures have broken off because they stood free from the block. Their high relief emphasized their different placement in space compared with the heads in low relief, which are intact. The play of light and shade

3-33 Spoils of Jerusalem, relief panel on the south wall of the passageway of the Arch of Titus, Rome, Italy, after 81 CE. Marble, 7' 10" high.

The relief panels inside the bay of the Arch of Titus commemorate the emperor's conquest of Judaea. Here, Roman soldiers carry in triumph the spoils taken from the Jewish temple in Jerusalem.

3-34 Triumph of Titus, relief panel on the north wall of the passageway of the Arch of Titus, Rome, Italy, after 81 CE. Marble, 7' 10" high.

Victory crowns Titus in his triumphal chariot. Also present are personifications of Honor and Valor in this first known instance of the intermingling of human and divine figures in a Roman historical relief.

across the protruding foreground and receding background figures enhances the sense of movement.

On the other side of the passageway, the panel (FIG. 3-34) shows Titus in his triumphal chariot. Victory rides with the emperor and places a wreath on his head. Below her is a bare-chested youth who is probably a personification of Honor (*Honos*). A female personification of Valor (*Virtus*) leads the horses. These allegorical figures transform the relief from a record of Titus's battlefield success into a celebration of imperial virtues. A comparable intermingling of divine and human figures characterized the Dionysiac mysteries frieze (FIG. 3-19) at Pompeii, but the Arch of Titus panel is the first known instance of divine beings interacting with humans on an official Roman historical relief. (On the Ara Pacis, FIG. 3-27, the gods, heroes, and personifications appear in separate framed panels, carefully segregated from the procession of living Romans.) The Arch of Titus, however, does not honor the living emperor but the deified Titus, who has entered the realm of the Roman gods. But soon afterward, this kind of interaction between mortals and immortals became a staple of Roman narrative relief sculpture, even on monuments erected in honor of living emperors.

High Empire

Domitian's extravagant lifestyle and ego resembled Nero's. He so angered the senators that he was assassinated in 96 CE. The first emperor of the second century, chosen with the consent of the Senate, was Trajan (r. 98–117 CE), a popular general. Born in Spain, Trajan was the first non-Italian to rule Rome. During his reign, the Roman Empire reached its greatest extent (MAP 3-1), and the imperial government took on ever greater responsibility for its people's welfare by instituting a number of farsighted social programs.

FORUM OF TRAJAN Trajan's major building project in Rome was a huge new forum (FIGS. 3-9, no. 5, and 3-35), which glorified his victories in two wars against Dacia, in present-day Romania. The architect was APOLLODORUS OF DAMASCUS, Trajan's chief military engineer, who during the first Dacian campaign had constructed a world-famous bridge across the Danube River. Apollodorus's plan incorporated the main features of most early fora (FIG. 3-12), except that a huge basilica, not a temple, dominated the colonnaded open square. The temple (completed after the emperor's death and dedicated to the newest god in the Roman pantheon, Trajan himself) stood instead behind the basilica facing two libraries and a giant commemorative column (FIG. 3-36). Entry to Trajan's forum was through an impressive gateway resembling a triumphal arch. Inside the forum were other reminders of Trajan's military prowess. A larger-than-life-size gilded-bronze statue of the emperor on horseback, trampling a terrified Dacian, stood at the center of the great court in front of the basilica. Statues of captive Dacians stood above the columns of the forum porticos.

The Basilica Ulpia (Trajan's family name was Ulpius) was a much larger and far more ornate version of the basilica adjoining the forum of Pompeii (FIG. 3-12, no. 3). As shown in FIG. 3-35, no. 4, it had *apses*, or semicircular recesses, on each short end. Two aisles flanked the nave on each side. The building was vast: about 400 feet long (without the apses) and 200 feet wide. Light entered through clerestory windows, made possible by elevating the timber-roofed nave above the colonnaded aisles. In the Republican basilica at Pompeii, light reached the nave only indirectly through aisle windows. The clerestory (used already at Karnak in Egypt; FIG. 1-34) was a much better solution.

3-35 APOLLODORUS OF DAMASCUS, Forum of Trajan (restored view), Rome, Italy, dedicated 112 CE (James E. Packer and John Burge). (1) Temple of Trajan, (2) Column of Trajan, (3) libraries, (4) Basilica Ulpia, (5) forum, (6) equestrian statue of Trajan.

Funded by Dacian spoils, Rome's largest forum featured statues of bound Dacian captives and of Trajan on horseback, a basilica with clerestory lighting, and a commemorative column (FIG. 3-36).

The Spiral Frieze of the Column of Trajan

The 128-foot-tall Column of Trajan (FIG. 3-36), which celebrates Trajan's successes in Dacia and once had a heroically nude statue of the emperor at the top, was probably the brainchild of Apollodorus of Damascus, Trajan's official architect and designer of the emperor's forum (FIG. 3-35) and markets (FIG. 3-37). The problem that Apollodorus faced was how to incorporate a pictorial record of the emperor's military campaigns in a monument—a freestanding column—ill-suited for narrative relief sculpture except on its pedestal. Apollodorus's solution was to invent a new artistic mode: a 625-foot frieze winding 23 times around the shaft of Trajan's Column from bottom to top. A measure of his success is that the column was widely imitated, not only in antiquity but in the Middle Ages and as late as the 19th century (by Napoleon in Paris).

Carving the frieze was a complex process. First, the stonemasons had to fashion enormous marble column drums, hollowed out to accommodate an internal spiral staircase running the entire length of the column shaft. The sculptors carved the relief scenes after the drums were in place to ensure that the figures and buildings lined up perfectly. The sculptors carved the last scenes in the narrative first, working from the top to the bottom of the shaft so that falling marble chips or a dropped hammer or chisel would not damage the reliefs below.

Art historians have likened the sculptured frieze winding around the column to an illustrated scroll of the type housed in the neighboring libraries (FIG. 3-35, no. 3) of the Forum of Trajan. The reliefs (FIGS. 3-36A, 3-36B, and 3-36C ⬀) recount Trajan's two successful campaigns against the Dacians in more than 150 episodes, in which some 2,500 figures appear. The band increases in width as it winds to the top of the column in order to make the upper portions easier to see. Throughout, the relief is very low so as not to distort the contours of the shaft. Paint enhanced the legibility of the figures, but it still would have been very difficult for anyone to follow the narrative from beginning to end.

Easily recognizable compositions such as those found on coin reverses and on historical relief panels—Trajan addressing his troops, sacrificing to the gods, and so on—fill most of the frieze. The narrative is not a reliable chronological account of the Dacian wars, as once thought. The sculptors nonetheless accurately recorded the general character of the campaigns. Notably, battle scenes (FIG. 3-36A ⬀) take up only about a quarter of the frieze. As is true of modern military operations, the Romans spent more time constructing forts (FIG. 3-36C ⬀), transporting men and equipment, and preparing for battle than fighting. The focus is always on the emperor, who appears repeatedly in the frieze (FIG. 3-36B ⬀). From every vantage point, Trajan can be seen directing the military operation. His involvement in all aspects of the Dacian campaigns—and in expanding Rome's empire on all fronts—is one of the central messages of the Column of Trajan.

3-36 Column of Trajan (looking west), Forum of Trajan, Rome, Italy, dedicated 112 CE.

The spiral frieze of Trajan's Column tells the story of the Dacian wars in 150 episodes. The reliefs depict all aspects of the campaigns, from battles to sacrifices to road and fort construction.

COLUMN OF TRAJAN Behind the ruins of the Basilica Ulpia still stands the almost perfectly preserved Column of Trajan (FIG. **3-36**). The column's large pedestal, decorated with captured Dacian arms and armor, encloses a chamber that originally served as Trajan's tomb. The Column of Trajan is most noteworthy, however, for its frieze recounting the defeat of the Dacians (see "The Spiral Frieze of the Column of Trajan," above, and FIGS. **3-36A**, **3-36B**, and **3-36C** ⬀).

MARKETS OF TRAJAN On the Quirinal Hill overlooking the forum, Apollodorus built the Markets of Trajan (FIG. 3-9, no. 6) to house both shops and administrative offices. Concrete made possible the transformation of the hill into a multilevel complex. The basic unit was the *taberna*, a single-room shop covered by a barrel vault. The tabernae were on several levels. They opened either onto a concave semicircular facade winding around one of the large *exedras* (semicircular recessed areas) of Trajan's forum, onto a paved

3-37 APOLLODORUS OF
DAMASCUS, interior of the
great hall (looking southwest), Markets of Trajan,
Rome, Italy, ca. 100–112 CE.

The great hall of Trajan's
markets resembles a modern
shopping mall. It housed two
floors of shops, with the upper
ones set back and lit by skylights. Concrete groin vaults
cover the central space.

street higher up the hill, or onto a great indoor market hall (FIG.
3-37) resembling a modern shopping mall. The hall housed two
floors of tabernae, with the upper shops set back on each side and lit
by skylights. Light from the same sources reached the ground-floor
shops through arches beneath the great umbrella-like groin vaults
(FIG. 3-15*c*) covering the hall.

PANTHEON Upon Trajan's death, Hadrian (r. 117–138 CE), also
a Spaniard and a relative of Trajan's, succeeded him as emperor.
Almost immediately, Hadrian began work on the Pantheon (FIGS.
3-9, no. 4, and 3-38), the temple of all the gods. The Pantheon reveals
the full potential of concrete, both as a building material and as a
means for shaping architectural space. The approach to the temple

3-38 Pantheon (look-
ing south), Rome, Italy,
118–125 CE.

The Pantheon's traditional
facade masked its revolutionary cylindrical drum and its
huge hemispherical dome. The
interior symbolized both the
orb of the earth and the vault
of the heavens.

3-39 Restored cutaway view (*left*) and lateral section (*right*) of the Pantheon, Rome, Italy, 118–125 CE (John Burge).

Originally, the approach to Hadrian's "temple of all gods" was from a columnar courtyard. Like a temple in a Roman forum (FIG. 3-12), the Pantheon stood at one narrow end of the enclosure.

PROBLEMS AND SOLUTIONS
The Ancient World's Largest Dome

If the design of the dome of Hadrian's Pantheon (FIGS. 3-38, 3-39, and 3-40) is simplicity itself (a dome whose diameter and height from the floor are equal), executing that design took all the ingenuity of Hadrian's engineers. The builders were faced with the problem of constructing the largest dome in the world up to that time—a feat not surpassed until the 16th century. Their solution was to build up the cylindrical drum level by level using concrete of varied composition. Extremely hard and durable basalt went into the mix for the foundations, and the recipe gradually changed until, at the top of the dome, featherweight pumice replaced stones to lighten the load. The dome's thickness also decreases as it nears the oculus, the circular opening 30 feet in diameter that is the only light source for the interior. The use of *coffers* (sunken decorative panels) lessened the dome's weight without weakening its structure, further reduced its mass, and even provided a handsome pattern of squares within the vast circle. Renaissance drawings suggest that each coffer once had a glistening gilded-bronze rosette at its center, enhancing the symbolism of the dome as the starry heavens.

Below the dome, much of the original marble veneer of the walls, niches, and floor has survived. In the Pantheon, visitors can appreciate, as almost nowhere else (compare FIG. 3-46), how magnificent the interiors of Roman concrete buildings could be. But despite the luxurious skin of the Pantheon's interior, on first entering the structure, visitors do not sense the weight of the walls but the vastness of the space they enclose. In pre-Roman architecture, the form of the enclosed space was determined by the placement of the solids, which did not so much shape space as interrupt it. Roman architects were the first to conceive of architecture in terms of units of space that could be shaped by the enclosures. The Pantheon's interior is a single unified, self-sufficient whole, uninterrupted by supporting solids. It encloses people without imprisoning them, opening through the oculus to the drifting clouds, the blue sky, the sun, and the gods.

3-40 Interior of the Pantheon (looking south), Rome, Italy, 118–125 CE.

The coffered dome of the Pantheon is 142 feet in diameter and 142 feet high. The light entering through its oculus forms a circular beam that moves across the dome as the sun moves across the sky.

was from a columnar courtyard, and, like a temple in a Roman forum, the Pantheon stood at one narrow end of the enclosure (FIG. 3-39, *left*). Its facade of eight Corinthian columns was a bow to tradition. Everything else about the Pantheon was revolutionary. Behind the columnar porch is an immense concrete cylinder covered by a huge hemispherical dome (FIG. 3-40) 142 feet in diameter (see "The Ancient World's Largest Dome," page 106). The dome's top is also 142 feet from the floor (FIG. 3-39, *right*). The design is thus based on the intersection of two circles (one horizontal, the other vertical). The interior space can be imagined as the orb of the earth, and the dome as the vault of the heavens. The unknown architect enhanced this impression by using light not merely to illuminate the darkness but to create drama and underscore the symbolism of the building's shape. On a sunny day, the light passing through the oculus forms a circular beam, a disk of light that moves across the coffered dome in the course of the day as the sun moves across the sky itself. Escaping from the noise and heat of a Roman summer day into the Pantheon's cool, calm, and mystical immensity is an experience not to be missed.

MARCUS AURELIUS Early in 138 CE, Hadrian adopted the 51-year-old Antoninus Pius. At the same time, he required Antoninus to adopt Marcus Aurelius and Lucius Verus (see page 83), thereby assuring a peaceful succession for at least another generation. Perhaps the most majestic surviving portrait of a Roman emperor is the larger-than-life-size gilded-bronze equestrian statue (FIG. 3-41) of Marcus Aurelius. The emperor possesses a superhuman grandeur and is much larger than any normal human would be in relation to his horse. Marcus stretches out his right arm in a gesture that is both a greeting and an offer of clemency. Beneath the horse's raised right foreleg, an enemy once cowered, begging the emperor for mercy, underscoring the Roman emperor's role as ruler of the whole world. This message of supreme confidence is not, however, conveyed by the emperor's head, with its long, curly hair and full beard, consistent with the latest fashion. Marcus's forehead is lined, and he seems weary, saddened, and even worried. For the first time, the strain of constant warfare on the frontiers and the burden of ruling a worldwide empire show in the emperor's face. The Antonine sculptor ventured beyond Republican verism, exposing the ruler's character, his thoughts, and his soul for all to see, as Marcus revealed them himself in his *Meditations,* a deeply moving philosophical treatise setting forth the emperor's personal worldview. This kind of introspective portraiture was a profound change from classical idealism. It marks a major turning point in the history of ancient art.

MUMMY PORTRAITS Painted portraits were common in the Roman Empire, but most have perished. In Roman Egypt, however, large numbers have been found because the Egyptians continued to bury their dead in mummy cases (see "Mummification," page 32), with painted wood panels depicting the deceased replacing the traditional stylized portrait masks (FIG. 1-37). One example (FIG. 3-42)

3-42 Mummy portrait of a priest of Serapis, from Hawara (Faiyum), Egypt, ca. 140–160 CE. Encaustic on wood, 1' 4¾" × 8¾". British Museum, London.

In Roman times, the Egyptians continued to bury their dead in mummy cases, but painted portraits replaced the traditional masks. The painting medium is encaustic—colors mixed with hot wax.

1 ft.

3-41 Equestrian statue of Marcus Aurelius, from Rome, Italy, ca. 175 CE. Bronze, 11' 6" high. Palazzo dei Conservatori, Musei Capitolini, Rome.

In this majestic portrait of Marcus Aurelius on horseback, the emperor stretches out his arm in a gesture of clemency. An enemy once cowered beneath the horse's raised foreleg.

1 in.

depicts a priest of the Egyptian god Serapis. The technique is *encaustic,* in which the painter mixes colors with hot wax and then uses a spatula to apply the wax pigment. The priest's portrait exhibits the painter's masterful use of the brush and spatula to depict different textures and the play of light over the soft and delicately modeled face. Artists also applied encaustic to stone, and the mummy portraits give some idea of the original appearance of Roman marble portraits. According to Pliny, when Praxiteles (FIGS. 2-47 and 2-48), perhaps the greatest marble sculptor of the ancient world, was asked which of his statues he preferred, the master replied, "Those that Nikias painted."[2] This anecdote underscores the importance of coloration in ancient statuary.

Late Empire

By the time of Marcus Aurelius, two centuries after Augustus established the Pax Romana, Roman power was beginning to erode. It was increasingly difficult to keep order on the frontiers, and even within the Empire, many challenged the authority of Rome. The assassination of Marcus's son Commodus (r. 180–192 CE) brought the Antonine dynasty to an end. The economy was in decline, and the efficient imperial bureaucracy was disintegrating. Even the official state religion was losing ground to Eastern cults, Christianity among them. The Late Empire was a pivotal era in world history during which the polytheistic ancient world gradually gave way to the Christian Middle Ages.

THE SEVERANS Civil conflict followed Commodus's death. When it ended, an African-born general named Septimius Severus (r. 193–211 CE) was master of the Roman world. The only preserved painted

portrait of an emperor (FIG. 3-43) depicts Severus and his family—his wife, Julia Domna, and their two sons, Caracalla and Geta. The *tondo* (circular) portrait is of special interest for two reasons beyond its survival. Severus's hair is tinged with gray, suggesting that his marble portraits also may have revealed his advancing age in this way. Also noteworthy is the erasure of Geta's face. When Caracalla (r. 211–217 CE) succeeded his father as emperor, he had his younger brother murdered, and ordered the Senate to damn Geta's memory. The Severan family portrait is an eloquent testimony to the long arm of Roman authority, which reached all the way to Egypt in this case. This kind of defacement of a rival's image is not unique to ancient Rome, but the Roman government employed damnatio memoriae as a political tool more often and more systematically than any other civilization.

CARACALLA In the Severan family portrait, the artist portrayed Caracalla as a boy with long, curly Antonine hair. The portraits of Caracalla as emperor are very different. In a bust (FIG. 3-44) in Berlin, Caracalla appears in heroic nudity save for a mantle over one shoulder and a *baldric* across his chest. His hair and beard are much shorter than his father's—initiating a new fashion in male coiffure during the third century CE. More remarkable, however, is the moving characterization of Caracalla's personality, a further development from the groundbreaking introspection of Marcus Aurelius's likenesses. Caracalla's brow is knotted, and he abruptly turns his head over his left shoulder. The sculptor probably intended the facial expression and the dramatic movement to suggest energy and strength, but it appears to modern viewers as if the emperor suspects danger from behind. Caracalla had reason to be fearful. An assassin's dagger felled him in the sixth year of his rule.

3-43 Painted portrait of Septimius Severus and his family, from Egypt, ca. 200 CE. Tempera on wood, 1' 2" diameter. Altesmuseum, Staatliche Museen zu Berlin, Berlin.

This only known painted portrait of an emperor shows Septimius Severus with gray hair. With him are his wife, Julia Domna, and their two sons, but Geta's head was removed after his damnatio memoriae.

3-44 Portrait bust of Caracalla, ca. 211–217 CE. Marble, 1' 10¾" high. Altesmuseum, Staatliche Museen zu Berlin, Berlin.

Caracalla's portraits introduced a new fashion in male coiffure, but are more remarkable for the dramatic turn of the emperor's head and the moving characterization of his personality.

3-45 Plan of the Baths of Caracalla, Rome, Italy, 212–216 CE. (1) natatio, (2) frigidarium, (3) tepidarium, (4) caldarium, (5) palaestra.

Caracalla's baths could accommodate 1,600 bathers. They resembled a modern health spa and included libraries, lecture halls, and exercise courts in addition to bathing rooms and a swimming pool.

BATHS OF CARACALLA The Severans were active builders in the capital, and even during his short reign, Caracalla built the greatest in a long line of imperial bathing and recreational complexes intended to win the public's favor. The Baths of Caracalla (FIG. 3-45) covered an area of almost 50 acres. All the rooms had thick brick-faced concrete walls up to 140 feet high, covered by enormous concrete vaults. The design was symmetrical along a central axis, facilitating the Roman custom of taking sequential plunges in warm-, hot-, and cold-water baths in, respectively, the *tepidarium, caldarium,* and *frigidarium.* There were stucco-covered vaults, mosaic floors, marble-faced walls, and colossal statuary throughout the complex, which also had landscaped gardens, lecture halls, libraries, colonnaded exercise courts (*palaestras*), and a giant swimming pool (*natatio*). Archaeologists estimate that up to 1,600 bathers at a time could enjoy this Roman equivalent of a modern health spa. A branch of one of the city's major aqueducts supplied water, and furnaces circulated hot air through hollow floors and walls throughout the bathing rooms.

The concrete vaults of the Baths of Caracalla collapsed long ago, but a good idea of the original appearance of the central bathing hall can be gleaned from the nave (FIG. 3-46) of Santa Maria degli Angeli in Rome, which was once the frigidarium of the later Baths of Diocletian. Although the interior of that Renaissance church has many new features foreign to a Roman bath, its rich wall treatment, colossal columns, immense groin vaults, and clerestory lighting provide a better sense of what it was like to be in a Roman imperial bathing complex than does any other building in the world.

3-46 Frigidarium, Baths of Diocletian, Rome, ca. 298–306 CE (remodeled by MICHELANGELO BUONARROTI as the nave of Santa Maria degli Angeli, 1563).

The groin-vaulted nave of the church of Santa Maria degli Angeli in Rome was once the frigidarium of the Baths of Diocletian. It gives an idea of the lavish adornment of imperial Roman baths.

TRAJAN DECIUS The assassination of Caracalla opened a half century of almost continuous civil war. The Roman legions declared as emperor one general after another, only to have each murdered in turn by another general a few years or even a few months later. The unstable times of the so-called soldier emperors nonetheless produced some of the most moving portraits in the history of art. Following the lead of the sculptors of the Marcus Aurelius and Caracalla portraits, artists fashioned likenesses of the soldier emperors that are as notable for their emotional content as they are for their technical virtuosity. Portraits (FIG. 3-47) of Trajan Decius (r. 249–251), for example, show the emperor best known for persecuting Christians as an old man with bags under his eyes and a sad expression. The eyes glance away nervously rather than engage the viewer directly, revealing the anxiety of a man who knows he can do little to restore order to an out-of-control world. The sculptor modeled the marble as if it were pliant clay, compressing the sides of the head at the level of the eyes, incising the hair and beard into the stone, and chiseling deep lines in the forehead and around the mouth. The portrait reveals the anguished soul of the man—and of the times.

LUDOVISI BATTLE SARCOPHAGUS Under Trajan and Hadrian and especially during the rule of the Antonines, Romans began to favor burial over cremation. This reversal of funerary practices may reflect the influence of Christianity and other Eastern religions, whose adherents believed in an afterlife for the human body. Whatever the explanation, the shift to burial led to a sudden demand for sarcophagi. By the third century CE, burial of the dead had become so widespread that even the imperial family practiced it in place of cremation. An unusually large sarcophagus—the *Ludovisi Battle Sarcophagus* (FIG. 3-48)—dating to the mid-third century is decorated on the front with a chaotic scene of Romans battling one of their northern foes, probably the Goths. The sculptor spread the writhing and highly emotive figures evenly across the entire relief, with no illusion of space behind them. This piling of figures is an emphatic rejection of perspective, and underscores the increasing dissatisfaction that third-century CE artists felt with the Classical style.

Within the dense mass of intertwined bodies, the central horseman stands out vividly. He wears no helmet and thrusts out his open right hand to demonstrate that he holds no weapon. Several scholars have identified him as one of the sons of Trajan Decius. In an age when the Roman army was far from invincible and emperors were constantly assassinated by other Romans, this young general boasts that he is a fearless commander assured of victory. His self-assurance may stem from his having embraced one of the increasingly popular Eastern mystery religions. On the youth's forehead is the emblem of Mithras, the Persian god of light, truth, and victory over death.

PHILOSOPHER SARCOPHAGUS The insecurity of the times led some Romans to seek solace in philosophy. On the sarcophagus illustrated here (FIG. 3-49), the deceased assumed the role of the learned intellectual, posing as a seated Roman philosopher holding a scroll. Two standing women (also with portrait features) gaze at him from left and right, confirming his importance. In the background are other philosophers, students or colleagues of the central deceased teacher. The two women may be the deceased's wife and daughter, two sisters, or some other combination of family members. The composition, with a frontal central figure and two subordinate flanking figures, is typical of what art historians call the *Late Antique* style (compare FIG. 3-54). This type of sarcophagus became popular for Christian burials. Sculptors used the wise-man motif to portray not only the deceased but also Christ flanked by saints (FIG. 4-1b).

3-47 Portrait bust of Trajan Decius, 249–251 CE. Marble, full bust 2' 7" high; detail 1' 7" high. Museo Capitolino, Musei Capitolini, Rome.

This portrait of a short-lived soldier emperor depicts an older man with bags under his eyes and a sad expression. The eyes glance away nervously, reflecting the anxiety of an insecure ruler.

1 in.

3-48 Sarcophagus with battle of Romans and barbarians (*Ludovisi Battle Sarcophagus*), from Rome, Italy, ca. 250–260 CE. Marble, 5' high. Palazzo Altemps, Museo Nazionale Romano, Rome.

A chaotic scene of battle between Romans and barbarians decorates the front of this sarcophagus. The sculptor piled up the writhing, emotive figures in an emphatic rejection of classical perspective.

3-49 Sarcophagus of a philosopher, ca. 270–280 CE. Marble, 4' 11" high. Musei Vaticani, Rome.

On many third-century CE sarcophagi, the deceased appears as a learned intellectual. Here, the seated philosopher is the central frontal figure. His two female muses also have portrait features.

PROBLEMS AND SOLUTIONS
Tetrarchic Portraiture

With the establishment of the tetrarchy in 293 CE, the sculptors in the emperors' employ suddenly had to grapple with a new problem—namely, how to represent four individuals who oversaw different regions of a vast empire but were equal partners in power. Although in life the four tetrarchs were rarely in the same place, in art they usually appeared together, both on coins and in statues. Artists did not try to capture their individual appearances and personalities—the norm in portraiture of the preceding soldier emperors (FIG. 3-47)—but sought instead to represent the power-sharing nature of the tetrarchy itself.

The finest extant tetrarchic portraits are the two pairs of porphyry (purple marble) statues (FIG. 3-50) that have since medieval times adorned the southwestern corner of the great church dedicated to Saint Mark in Venice. In this and similar tetrarchic group portraits, it is impossible to name the rulers. Each of the four emperors has lost his identity as an individual and been absorbed into the larger entity of the tetrarchy. All the tetrarchs are identically clad in cuirass and cloak. Each grasps a sheathed sword in his left hand. With their right arms, the corulers embrace one another in an overt display of concord. The figures have large cubical heads and squat bodies. The drapery is schematic, the bodies are shapeless, and the faces are emotionless masks, distinguished only by the beards of two of the tetrarchs (probably the older Augusti, differentiating them from the younger Caesars). Other than the presence or absence of facial hair, each pair is as alike as freehand carving can achieve.

In this group portrait, carved eight centuries after Greek sculptors first freed the human form from the rigidity of the Egyptian-inspired kouros stance, an artist or artists once again conceived the human figure in iconic terms. Idealism, naturalism, individuality, and personality have disappeared, replaced by a new approach to representing the human figure that was perfectly suited to the portrayal of four corulers.

1 ft.

3-50 Portraits of the four tetrarchs, from Constantinople, ca. 305 CE. Porphyry, 4' 3" high. Saint Mark's, Venice.

Diocletian established the tetrarchy to bring order to the Roman world. In group portraits, artists always depicted the four rulers as nearly identical partners in power, not as distinct individuals.

TETRARCHY In an attempt to restore order to the Roman Empire, Diocletian (r. 284–305 CE), whose troops proclaimed him emperor, decided to share power with his potential rivals. In 293, he established the *tetrarchy* (rule by four) and adopted the title of Augustus of the East. The other three *tetrarchs* were a corresponding Augustus of the West, and Eastern and Western Caesars (whose allegiance to the two Augusti was cemented by marriage to their daughters). The four coemperors often appeared together in group portraits (FIG. 3-50) to underscore their harmonious partnership (see "Tetrarchic Portraiture," above).

CONSTANTINE AND CHRISTIANITY The short-lived concord among the tetrarchs ended with Diocletian's retirement in 305 CE. An all-too-familiar period of conflict among rival Roman armies followed. The eventual victor was Constantine (r. 306–337 CE), son of Constantius Chlorus, Diocletian's Caesar of the West. After the death of his father, Constantine invaded Italy in 312 and took control of Rome. Constantine attributed his decisive victory at the Milvian Bridge, the gateway to the capital, to the aid of the Christian god. The next year, he and Licinius, Constantine's coemperor in the East, issued the Edict of Milan, ending persecution of Christians. In time, Constantine and Licinius became foes, and in 324 Constantine defeated and executed Licinius near Byzantium (modern Istanbul, Turkey). Constantine, now unchallenged ruler of the whole Roman Empire, founded a "New Rome" at the site of Byzantium and named it Constantinople (City of Constantine). In 325, at the Council of Nicaea, Christianity became the de facto official religion of the Roman Empire. From this point on, the ancient cults declined rapidly. Constantine dedicated Constantinople on May 11, 330, "by the commandment of God," and in 337 the emperor was baptized on his deathbed.

For many scholars, the transfer of the seat of power from Rome to Constantinople and the recognition of Christianity mark the beginning of the Middle Ages. Constantinian art is a mirror of this transition from the classical to the medieval world. In Rome, for example, Constantine was a builder in the grand tradition of the emperors of the first, second, and early third centuries, constructing public baths, a basilica in the Forum Romanum, and a triumphal arch. But he was also the patron of the city's first churches (see page 120).

COLOSSUS OF CONSTANTINE The most impressive of Constantine's preserved portraits is an eight-and-one-half-foot-tall head (FIG. 3-51), one of several fragments of a colossal enthroned statue of the emperor composed of a brick core, a wood torso covered with bronze, and a head and limbs of marble. Constantine's artist modeled the seminude seated portrait on Roman images of Jupiter, but also resuscitated the Augustan image of a perpetually youthful head of state. The emperor held an orb (possibly surmounted by the cross of Christ), the symbol of global power, in his extended left hand. The colossal size, the likening of the emperor to Jupiter, the eyes directed at no person or thing of this world—all combine to produce a formula of overwhelming authority appropriate to Constantine's exalted position as absolute ruler.

BASILICA NOVA Constantine's gigantic portrait sat in the western apse of the Basilica Nova (New Basilica; FIGS. 3-9, no. 8, and 3-52) in Rome. From its position in the apse, the emperor's image dominated the interior of the basilica in much the same way that enthroned statues of Greco-Roman divinities loomed over awestruck mortals in temple cellas. The Basilica Nova ruins never fail to impress tourists with their size and mass. The original structure was 300 feet long and 215 feet wide. Brick-faced concrete walls 20 feet thick supported coffered barrel vaults in the aisles. These vaults also buttressed the groin vaults of the nave, which was 115 feet high. Marble slabs and stuccoes covered the walls and floors. The restored view (FIG. 3-52) effectively suggests the immensity of the interior, where the great vaults dwarf even the emperor's colossal portrait. The drawing also clearly reveals the fenestrated groin vaults, a lighting system akin to the clerestory of a traditional stone-and-timber basilica (FIG. 3-35, no. 4). The architect here applied to basilica design the lessons learned in the construction of buildings such as Trajan's great market hall (FIG. 3-37) and the Baths of Caracalla and Diocletian (FIG. 3-46).

1 ft.

3-51 Portrait of Constantine, from the Basilica Nova (FIG. 3-52), Rome, Italy, ca. 315–330 CE. Marble, 8' 6" high. Palazzo dei Conservatori, Musei Capitolini, Rome.

Constantine's portraits revive the Augustan image of a perpetually youthful ruler. This colossal head is one fragment of an enthroned Jupiter-like statue of the emperor holding the orb of world power.

3-52 Restored cutaway view of the Basilica Nova, Rome, Italy, ca. 306–312 CE (John Burge).

Roman builders applied the lessons learned constructing baths and market halls to the Basilica Nova, in which fenestrated concrete groin vaults replaced the clerestory of a stone-and-timber basilica.

3-53 Arch of Constantine (looking southwest), Rome, Italy, 312–315 CE.

Much of the sculptural decoration of Constantine's arch came from monuments of Trajan, Hadrian, and Marcus Aurelius. Sculptors recut the heads of the earlier emperors to substitute Constantine's features.

ARCH OF CONSTANTINE Also grandiose is the triple-passageway arch (FIGS. 3-9, no. 10, and 3-53) that Constantine erected next to the Colosseum. The arch was the largest set up in Rome since the end of the Severan dynasty. The builders, however, took much of the sculptural decoration from earlier monuments of Trajan, Hadrian, and Marcus Aurelius. Constantine's sculptors refashioned the second-century reliefs to honor him by recutting the heads of the earlier emperors with his features. Some art historians have cited the Arch of Constantine as evidence of a decline in creativity and technical skill in the Late Roman Empire. Although such a judgment is in part deserved, it ignores the fact that the reused sculptures were carefully selected to associate Constantine with famous emperors of the second century. One of the arch's few Constantinian reliefs (not illustrated) underscores that message. It shows Constantine on the speaker's platform in the Forum Romanum between statues of Hadrian and Marcus Aurelius.

In another Constantinian relief (FIG. 3-54), the emperor distributes largesse to grateful citizens, who approach him from right and left. Constantine is a frontal and majestic presence, elevated on a throne above the recipients of his generosity. The figures are squat in proportion, like the tetrarchs (FIG. 3-50). They move, not according to any Classical principle of naturalistic motion, but rather with the mechanical and repeated stances and gestures of puppets. The relief is very shallow, the forms are not fully modeled, and the details are incised. The frieze is less a narrative of action than a picture of actors frozen in time so that the viewer can distinguish the all-important imperial donor (the largest figure, enthroned at the center) from his attendants (to the left and right above) and the recipients of the largesse (below), both of smaller stature than the emperor.

An eminent art historian once characterized this approach to pictorial narrative as a "decline of form,"[3] and when judged by the standards of Classical art, it was. But the composition's rigid formality, determined by the rank of those portrayed, was consistent with a new set of values. It soon became the preferred mode, supplanting the Classical notion that a picture is a window onto a world of anecdotal action. Comparing this Constantinian relief with a Byzantine icon (FIG. 4-20) reveals that the compositional principles of the Late Antique style are those of early medieval art. They were very different from, but not "better" or "worse" than, those of Greco-Roman art. The Arch of Constantine is the quintessential monument of its era, exhibiting a respect for the past in its reuse of second-century sculptures while rejecting the norms of Classical design in its frieze and thereby paving the way for the iconic art of the Middle Ages.

1 ft.

3-54 Distribution of largesse, detail of the north frieze of the Arch of Constantine, Rome, Italy, 312–315 CE. Marble, 3' 4" high.

This Constantinian frieze is less a narrative of action than a picture of actors frozen in time. The composition's rigid formality reflects the new values that would come to dominate medieval art.

Explore the era further in MindTap with videos of major artworks and buildings, Google Earth™ coordinates, and essays by the author on the following additional subjects:

▐ ART AND SOCIETY: The "Audacity" of Etruscan Women
▐ WRITTEN SOURCES: Vitruvius's *Ten Books on Architecture*
• Maison Carrée, Nîmes (FIG. 3-28A)
▐ ART AND SOCIETY: Spectacles in the Colosseum
• Aerial view of the Colosseum, Rome (FIG. 3-30A)
• Three details of the Column of Trajan, Rome (FIGS. 3-36A, 3-36B, and 3-36C)

THE ROMAN EMPIRE

Etruscan Art

- The Etruscans admired Greek art and architecture but did not copy Greek works. They constructed their temples of wood and mud brick instead of stone and placed the columns and stairs only at the front. Terracotta statuary decorated the roof. Most surviving Etruscan artworks come from underground tomb chambers. At Cerveteri, earthen mounds (tumuli) covered tombs with interiors sculptured to imitate the houses of the living. At Tarquinia, painters adorned tomb walls with frescoes, usually depicting funerary banquets.

Model of a typical Etruscan temple, sixth century BCE

Republican Art

- In the centuries following the establishment of the Republic (509–27 BCE), Rome conquered its neighbors in Italy and then moved into Greece, bringing exposure to Greek art and architecture. Republican temples combined Etruscan plans with the Greek orders, and houses boasted peristyles with Greek columns. The Romans, however, pioneered the use of concrete as a building material. The First Style of mural painting derived from Greece, but the illusionism of the Second Style is distinctly Roman. Republican portraits were usually superrealistic likenesses of elderly patricians.

Head of a patrician, mid-first century BCE

Early Imperial Art

- Augustus (r. 27 BCE–14 CE) established the Roman Empire after defeating Antony and Cleopatra. The Early Empire (27 BCE–96 CE) extends from Augustus to the Flavian emperors (r. 68–96 CE).
- Augustan art celebrated the emperor's establishment of peace and revived the Classical style with frequent references to Periclean Athens. Augustus's portraits always depict him as an idealized youth. Under the Flavians, architects exploited the full potential of concrete in buildings such as the Colosseum, the largest amphitheater in the Roman world. The eruption of Mount Vesuvius in 79 CE buried Pompeii and Herculaneum, preserving Early Imperial murals of the Third and Fourth Styles.

Ara Pacis Augustae, Rome, 13–9 BCE

High Imperial Art

- During the High Empire (96–192 CE), beginning with Trajan (r. 98–117 CE), the Roman Empire reached its greatest extent.
- Trajan's new forum and markets transformed the center of Rome. The Column of Trajan commemorated his Dacian campaigns in a spiral frieze with some 2,500 figures. Hadrian (r. 117–138 CE) built the Pantheon, the temple to all the gods, incorporating in its design the forms of the orb of the earth and the dome of the heavens. Under the Antonines (r. 138–192 CE), imperial artists introduced a psychological element in portraiture.

Pantheon, Rome, 118–125 CE

Late Imperial Art

- The Late Empire (193–337 CE) opened with the Severans (r. 193–235 CE) and closed with Constantine (r. 306–336 CE), who ended persecution of the Christians and transferred the imperial capital from Rome to Constantinople in 330.
- During the chaotic era of the soldier emperors (r. 235–284 CE), artists revealed the anxiety and insecurity of the emperors in moving portraits. Diocletian (r. 284–305 CE) reestablished order by sharing power. Statues of the tetrarchs portray the four emperors as identical and equal rulers, not as individuals. Constantine restored one-man rule. The abstract formality of Constantinian art paved the way for the iconic art of the Middle Ages.

Arch of Constantine, Rome, 312–315 CE

4-1a Episodes from the Hebrew scriptures, including Abraham's sacrifice of Isaac, appear beside scenes from the life of Jesus on the sarcophagus of Junius Bassus, a recent convert to Christianity.

4-1b The enthroned Christ is long-haired and youthful in the Early Christian tradition. Below him is the personified Roman sky god. Flanking the new ruler of the universe are Saints Peter and Paul.

1 ft.

4-1   **Sarcophagus of Junius Bassus, from Rome, Italy, ca. 359. Marble, 3' 10½" × 8'. Museo Storico del Tesoro della Basilica di San Pietro, Rome.**

4-1c The Jewish scenes on this mid-fourth-century sarcophagus had special significance for Christians. Adam and Eve's original sin of eating the apple in the Garden of Eden necessitated Christ's sacrifice.

Early Christianity and Byzantium

ROMANS, JEWS, AND CHRISTIANS

During the third and fourth centuries, a rapidly growing number of Romans rejected *polytheism* (belief in multiple gods) in favor of *monotheism* (the worship of a single all-powerful god)—but they did not stop commissioning works of art picturing the divine. A prominent example is Junius Bassus, the mid-fourth-century city prefect of Rome who converted to Christianity and, according to the inscription on his sarcophagus (FIG. 4-1), was baptized just before his death in 359. He grew up immersed in traditional Roman culture and initially paid homage to the old Roman gods, but when he died, he chose to be buried in a sarcophagus decorated with episodes from the Hebrew scriptures and the life of Jesus.

The sculptor of Junius Bassus's sarcophagus decorated the front with 10 figural scenes in two rows of five compartments, each framed by columns, a well-established format for Roman sarcophagi. However, the deceased does not appear in any of those compartments. Instead, Jewish and Christian biblical stories fill the niches. Jesus has pride of place and appears in the central compartment of each row: enthroned between Saints Peter and Paul (FIG. 4-1b), and entering Jerusalem on a donkey. Both compositions derive from official Roman art. In the upper zone, Jesus, like an enthroned Roman emperor, sits above the sky god, who holds a billowing mantle over his head, indicating that Christ is ruler of the cosmos. The scene below is based on portrayals of Roman emperors entering conquered cities on horseback, but Jesus's steed and the absence of imperial attributes break sharply with the imperial models that the sculptor used as compositional sources.

The Jewish scenes on the Junius Bassus sarcophagus include the stories of Adam and Eve (FIG. 4-1c) and Abraham and Isaac (FIG. 4-1a), which took on added significance for Christians as foretelling events in the life of their savior (see "Jewish Subjects in Christian Art," page 119). Christians believe that Adam and Eve's original sin of eating the apple in the Garden of Eden ultimately necessitated Christ's sacrifice for the salvation of humankind. Christians view the Genesis story of Abraham's willingness to sacrifice his son as a parallel to God's sacrifice of his son, Jesus.

The crucifixion, however, does not appear on this sarcophagus and was rarely depicted in Early Christian art. Artists emphasized Jesus's exemplary life as teacher and miracle worker, not his suffering and death at the hands of the Romans (see "The Life of Jesus in Art," pages 120–121). Nonetheless, this sculptor alluded to the crucifixion in the scenes in the two compartments at the upper right depicting Jesus being led before Pontius Pilate for judgment. The Romans condemned and executed Jesus, but he triumphantly overcame death. Junius Bassus hoped for a similar salvation.

EARLY CHRISTIANITY

Very little is known about the art of the first Christians. When art historians speak about "Early Christian art," they are referring to the earliest preserved artworks having Christian subjects, not the art of Christians at the time of Jesus. Few Christian artworks can be dated before the late third and early fourth centuries*—that is, to the time when Christians were a persecuted minority in the Roman Empire. For example, the emperor Diocletian (r. 284–305; FIG. 3-50) became so concerned by the growing popularity of Christianity in the Roman army ranks that he ordered a fresh round of persecutions in 303 to 305, a half century after the last great persecutions under Trajan Decius (r. 249–251; FIG. 3-47). As Christianity's appeal grew, so too did the Roman state's fear of weakening imperial authority, because the Christians refused to pay even token homage to the Roman state's official gods (which included deified emperors as well as the traditional pantheon of gods and goddesses). Persecution ended only when Constantine (r. 306–337; FIG. 3-51) embraced the Christian god as the source of his power rather than a threat to it (see page 112). In 313, he issued the Edict of Milan, which established Christianity as a legal religion with equal or superior standing to the traditional Roman cults.

Catacombs

Most of the Early Christian art in Rome is found in the *catacombs*—vast underground networks of galleries and chambers that served as cemeteries. The name derives from the Latin *ad catacumbas*, which means "in the hollows." The Christian community tunneled the catacombs out of the tufa bedrock, much as the Etruscans excavated their tomb chambers beneath earthen tumuli (FIGS. 3-5 and 3-6).

*From this point on, all dates are CE unless otherwise indicated.

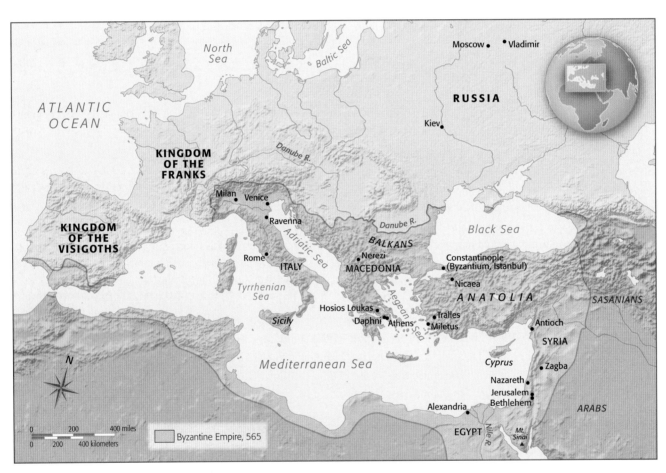

MAP 4-1 The Byzantine Empire at the death of Justinian in 565.

EARLY CHRISTIANITY AND BYZANTIUM

1–527	527–726	726–843	843–1453
Early Christian	**Justinian to Iconoclasm**	**Iconoclasm**	**Middle and Late Byzantine**
▪ Earliest Christian catacomb paintings and sarcophagi appear in the third century.	▪ Justinian (r. 527–565) builds Hagia Sophia with a 180-foot-high dome resting on pendentives.		▪ Theodora repeals iconoclasm in 843.
▪ Constantine (r. 306–337) constructs the first churches in Rome and founds Constantinople as the New Rome.	▪ Bishop Maximianus dedicates San Vitale at Ravenna with its rich mosaic program in 547.		▪ Churches feature exterior walls with decorative patterning, Greek-cross plans, and domes on drums.
▪ Mosaics become the primary medium for church decoration.	▪ Icon painting flourishes at Mount Sinai until Leo III bans picturing the divine in 726.		▪ Ivory triptychs for personal prayer become popular.
			▪ Michael VIII recaptures Constantinople after the Crusader sack of 1204.
			▪ Constantinople falls to the Ottoman Turks in 1453.

RELIGION AND MYTHOLOGY
Jewish Subjects in Christian Art

When the Christians codified the Bible in its familiar form, they incorporated the Hebrew *Torah* and other writings, and designated the Jewish books as the "Old Testament" in contrast to the Christian books of the "New Testament." From the beginning, the Hebrew scriptures played an important role in Christian life and Christian art, in part because Jesus was a Jew and so many of the first Christians were converted Jews, but also because Christians came to view many of the persons and events of the Old Testament as *prefigurations* of New Testament persons and events. Christ himself established the pattern for this kind of biblical interpretation when he compared Jonah's spending three days in the belly of the sea dragon (usually translated as "whale" in English) to the comparable time he would be entombed in the earth before his resurrection (Matt. 12:40). In the fourth century, Saint Augustine (354–430) confirmed the validity of this reading of the Old Testament when he stated that "the New Testament is hidden in the Old; the Old is clarified by the New."*

The following are three of the most popular Jewish biblical stories depicted in Early Christian art:

- **Adam and Eve** (FIG. 4-1c) Eve, the first woman, tempted by a serpent, ate the forbidden fruit of the tree of knowledge and fed some to Adam, the first man. As punishment, God expelled Adam and Eve from Paradise. This "original sin" ultimately led to Christ's sacrifice on the cross so that all humankind could be saved. Christian theologians often consider Christ the new Adam and his mother, Mary, the new Eve.
- **Sacrifice of Isaac** (FIG. 4-1a) God instructed Abraham, the father of the Hebrew nation, to sacrifice his son Isaac as proof of his faith. When it became clear that Abraham would obey, the Lord sent an angel to restrain him and provided a ram for sacrifice in Isaac's place. Christians view this episode as a prefiguration of the sacrifice of God's son, Jesus.
- **Jonah** (FIGS. 4-2) The Old Testament prophet Jonah had disobeyed God's command. In his wrath, the Lord caused a storm

4-2 The Good Shepherd, the story of Jonah, and orants, frescoed ceiling of a cubiculum in the Catacomb of Saints Peter and Marcellinus, Rome, Italy, early fourth century.

Christian catacomb paintings often mixed Old and New Testament themes. Jonah was a popular subject because he emerged safely from a sea monster after three days, prefiguring Christ's resurrection.

while Jonah was at sea. Jonah asked the sailors to throw him overboard, and the storm subsided. A sea dragon then swallowed Jonah, but God answered his prayers, and the monster spat Jonah out after three days, foretelling Christ's resurrection (see "The Life of Jesus in Art," pages 120–121).

*Augustine, *City of God*, 16.26.

The catacombs are less elaborate than the Etruscan tombs, but much more extensive. The known catacombs on the outskirts of Rome run for 60 to 90 miles and housed as many as four million bodies.

PETER AND MARCELLINUS Often, the Christians carved out small rooms, called *cubicula* (as in Roman houses), to serve as mortuary chapels opening off the catacomb galleries. The painted ceiling (FIG. 4-2) of a cubiculum in the Catacomb of Saints Peter and Marcellinus in Rome features a large circle enclosing the symbol of the Christian faith, the cross. The arms of the cross end in four *lunettes* (semicircular frames) illustrating the key episodes from the biblical story of Jonah. Sailors throw Jonah from his ship on the left. He emerges on the right from the sea dragon that swallowed him. At the bottom, safe on land, Jonah contemplates the miracle of his salvation and the mercy of God. Jonah was a popular figure in Early Christian painting and sculpture because Christians regard him as a

prefiguration (prophetic forerunner) of Christ (see "Jewish Subjects in Christian Art," above).

A man, a woman, and at least one child occupy the compartments between the Jonah lunettes. They are *orants* (praying figures), raising their arms in the ancient attitude of prayer. Together they make up a cross-section of the Christian family seeking a heavenly afterlife. The central medallion shows Christ as the Good Shepherd (compare FIG. 4-2A ⬈), whose powers of salvation the painter underscored by placing the four episodes of the Jonah story around him. In Early Christian art, Jesus often appears as the youthful and loyal protector of the Christian flock who said to his disciples, "I am the good shepherd; the good shepherd gives his life for the sheep" (John 10:11). Only after Christianity became the Roman Empire's official religion in 380 did Christ take on in art such imperial *attributes* as the *halo*, the purple robe, and the throne, which denoted rulership (see "The Life of Jesus in Art," pages 120–121).

RELIGION AND MYTHOLOGY
The Life of Jesus in Art

Christians believe that Jesus of Nazareth is the son of God, the prophesied *Messiah* (Savior, *Christ*) of the Jews. His life—his miraculous birth from the womb of a virgin mother, his preaching and miracle working, his execution by the Romans and subsequent ascent to Heaven—has been the subject of countless artworks from Roman times through the present day. Although during certain periods artists rarely, if ever, depicted many of the events of Jesus's life, it is useful to summarize at the outset the entire cycle of events as they usually appear in artworks.

INCARNATION AND CHILDHOOD

The first "cycle" of the life of Jesus consists of the events of his conception (incarnation), birth, infancy, and childhood.

- **Annunciation to Mary** (FIGS. 7-35 and 8-23) The archangel Gabriel announces to the Virgin Mary that she will miraculously conceive and give birth to God's son, Jesus. Artists sometimes indicated God's presence at the incarnation by a dove, the symbol of the Holy Spirit, the third "person" of the *Trinity* with God the Father and Jesus.
- **Visitation** (FIG. 7-15) The pregnant Mary visits Elizabeth, her older cousin, who is pregnant with the future John the Baptist. Elizabeth is the first to recognize that the baby in Mary's womb is the son of God.
- **Nativity** (FIG. 7-28), **Annunciation to the Shepherds,** and **Adoration of the Shepherds** (FIG. 8-8) Jesus is born at night in Bethlehem and placed in a basket. Mary and her husband, Joseph, marvel at the newborn, while an angel announces the birth of the Savior to shepherds in the field.
- **Adoration of the Magi** (FIG. 8-20) A bright star alerts three wise men (*magi*) in the East that the King of the Jews has been born. They travel 12 days to find the holy family and present precious gifts to the infant Jesus.
- **Presentation in the Temple** Mary and Joseph bring their son to the temple in Jerusalem, where the aged Simeon, who God said

would not die until he had seen the Messiah, recognizes Jesus as the prophesied savior of humankind.

- **Massacre of the Innocents** and **Flight into Egypt** King Herod, fearful that a rival king has been born, orders the massacre of all infants in Bethlehem, but an angel warns the holy family, and they escape to Egypt.
- **Dispute in the Temple** Joseph and Mary travel to Jerusalem for the feast of *Passover* (the celebration of the release of the Jews from bondage to the pharaohs of Egypt). Jesus, only 12 years old at the time, engages in learned debate with astonished Jewish scholars in the temple, foretelling his ministry.

PUBLIC MINISTRY

The public-ministry cycle comprises the teachings of Jesus and the miracles he performed.

- **Baptism** Jesus's public ministry begins with his *baptism* at age 30 by John the Baptist in the Jordan River. The Holy Spirit appears, and God's voice proclaims Jesus as his son.
- **Apostles and Miracles** In the course of his teaching and travels, Jesus enlists 12 disciples, or *apostles,* including the fisherman Peter and the tax collector Matthew (FIG. 10-9). Jesus performs many miracles, revealing his divine nature. These include acts of healing and raising the dead, turning water into wine, and walking on water. In the miracle of loaves and fishes (FIG. 4-8), for example, Jesus transforms a few loaves of bread and a handful of fish into enough food to feed several thousand people.
- **Delivery of the Keys to Peter** (FIG. 8-34) Jesus chooses the apostle Peter (whose name means "rock") as his successor. He declares that Peter is the rock on which his church will be built, and symbolically delivers to Peter the keys to the kingdom of Heaven.
- **Transfiguration** Jesus scales a high mountain and, in the presence of Peter and two other disciples, James and John the Evangelist, transforms into radiant light. God, speaking from a cloud, discloses that Jesus is his son.
- **Cleansing of the Temple** Jesus returns to Jerusalem, where he finds moneychangers and merchants conducting business in the temple. He rebukes them and drives them out of the sacred precinct.

Architecture and Mosaics

Constantine believed that the Christian god had guided him to victory, and in lifelong gratitude he protected and advanced Christianity throughout the Empire. As emperor, he was, of course, obliged to safeguard the ancient Roman religion, traditions, and monuments, and he was (for his time) a builder on a grand scale in the heart of the city (FIGS. 3-52 and 3-53). But Constantine also was the first major patron of Christian architecture. He constructed elaborate Christian shrines not only in Rome but also in Constantinople, his "New Rome" in the East, and at sites sacred to Christianity, most notably Bethlehem, the birthplace of Jesus, and Jerusalem, the site of his crucifixion (MAP 4-1). And he also built Rome's first *churches,* buildings designed specifically to meet the requirements of Christian *liturgy* (the ritual of public worship) to house a rapidly growing number of worshipers. Prior to Constantine, Christian places of worship were usually remodeled private houses that could accommodate only a small community.

OLD SAINT PETER'S The greatest of Constantine's churches in Rome was Old Saint Peter's (FIGS. 4-3 and 4-4), probably begun as early as 319. The present-day church (FIGS. 10-2 and 10-3) is a replacement for the Constantinian structure. Old Saint Peter's stood on the spot where the emperor and Pope Sylvester (r. 314–335) believed that Peter—the founder of the Christian community in Rome, its first pope, and one of the first Christian *saints*—had been buried. Excavations in the Roman cemetery beneath the church have in fact revealed a second-century memorial erected in honor of the Christian *martyr* at his reputed grave. Old Saint Peter's therefore fulfilled Jesus's prophecy when he said, "Thou art Peter, and upon this rock [in Greek, *petra*] I will build my church" (Matt. 16:18).

The plan and elevation of the immense church, capable of housing 3,000 to 4,000 worshipers at one time, resemble those of Roman *basilicas,* such as Trajan's Basilica Ulpia (FIG. 3-35, no. 4), rather than the design of any Greco-Roman temple. The Christians, understandably, did not want their houses of worship to mimic the form of polytheistic shrines, but practical considerations also contributed

PASSION

The passion (from Latin *passio,* "suffering") cycle includes the episodes leading to Jesus's death, resurrection, and ascent to Heaven.

- **Entry into Jerusalem** (FIG. 4-1, *bottom center*) On the Sunday before his crucifixion (Palm Sunday), Jesus rides triumphantly into Jerusalem on a donkey, accompanied by disciples. People place palm fronds in his path.

- **Last Supper** (FIGS. 8-24 and 9-3) In Jerusalem, Jesus celebrates Passover with his disciples. During this last supper, Jesus foretells his imminent betrayal, arrest, and death and invites the disciples to remember him when they eat bread (symbol of his body) and drink wine (his blood). This ritual became the celebration of *Mass* (*Eucharist*).

- **Agony in the Garden** Jesus goes to the Mount of Olives in the Garden of Gethsemane, where he struggles to overcome his human fear of death by praying for divine strength.

- **Betrayal** and **Arrest** One of the disciples, Judas Iscariot, agrees to betray Jesus to the Jewish authorities in return for 30 pieces of silver. Judas identifies Jesus to the soldiers by kissing him, whereupon the soldiers arrest Jesus.

- **Trials of Jesus** (FIG. 4-1, *top right*) The soldiers bring Jesus before Caiaphas, the Jewish high priest, who interrogates Jesus about his claim to be the Messiah. Jesus is then brought before the Roman governor of Judaea, Pontius Pilate, on the charge of treason because he had proclaimed himself as the Jews' king. Pilate asks the crowd to choose between freeing Jesus or Barabbas, a murderer. The people select Barabbas, and the judge condemns Jesus to death. Pilate washes his hands, symbolically relieving himself of responsibility for the mob's decision.

- **Flagellation** and **Mocking** The Roman soldiers who hold Jesus captive whip (*flagellate*) him and mock him by dressing him as king of the Jews and placing a crown of thorns on his head.

- **Carrying of the Cross, Raising of the Cross** (FIG. 10-15), and **Crucifixion** (FIGS. 4-23 and 6-15) The Romans force Jesus to carry the cross on which he will be crucified from Jerusalem to Mount Calvary (Golgotha, the Place of the Skull, Adam's burial place). Jesus falls three times, and his robe is stripped along the way. Soldiers erect the cross and nail his hands and feet to it. Jesus's mother, John the Evangelist, and Mary Magdalene mourn at the foot of the cross, while the Roman soldiers torment Jesus. One of them (Longinus) stabs Jesus in the side with a spear. After suffering great pain, Jesus dies. The crucifixion occurred on a Friday, and Christians celebrate the day each year as Good Friday.

- **Deposition** (FIG. 8-7), **Lamentation** (FIG. 7-32), and **Entombment** Joseph of Arimathea and Nicodemus remove Jesus's body from the cross (the deposition) and take him to the tomb that Joseph had purchased for himself. Joseph, Nicodemus, the Virgin Mary, John the Evangelist, and Mary Magdalene mourn over the dead Jesus (the lamentation). (When in art the isolated figure of the Virgin Mary cradles her dead son in her lap, it is called a *Pietà* (FIGS. 7-27 and 9-7)—Italian for "pity.") In portrayals of the entombment, Jesus's followers lower his body into a sarcophagus in the tomb.

- **Descent into Limbo** During the three days he spends in the tomb, Jesus descends into Hell, or Limbo, and triumphantly frees the souls of the righteous, including Adam, Eve, Moses, David, Solomon, and John the Baptist.

- **Resurrection** (FIG. 8-34A ▨) and **Three Marys at the Tomb** On the third day (Easter Sunday), Jesus rises from the dead and leaves the tomb while the Roman guards sleep. The Virgin Mary, Mary Magdalene, and Mary, the mother of James, visit the tomb but find it empty. An angel informs them of Jesus's resurrection.

- **Noli Me Tangere** and **Doubting of Thomas** During the 40 days between Jesus's resurrection and his ascent to Heaven, he appears on several occasions to his followers. Christ warns Mary Magdalene, weeping at his tomb, with the words "Don't touch me" (*Noli me tangere* in Latin), but he tells her to inform the apostles of his return. Later, he invites Thomas, who cannot believe that Jesus has risen, to touch the wound in his side received at his crucifixion.

- **Ascension** (FIG. 4-18A ▨) On the 40th day, on the Mount of Olives, with his mother and some followers as witnesses, Christ gloriously ascends to Heaven in a cloud.

to their rejection of the classical temple type. Greco-Roman temples housed only the cult statue of the deity. All rituals took place outside at open-air altars. Therefore, architects would have found it difficult to adapt the classical temple to accommodate large numbers of people within it. The Roman basilica, in contrast, was ideally suited as a place for congregation, and Early Christian builders readily selected the basilica as the standard format for the first churches.

Like Roman basilicas, Old Saint Peter's had a wide central *nave* with flanking *aisles* and an *apse* at the end (FIG. 4-4). Worshipers entered the 300-foot-long nave through a *narthex,* or vestibule, whereupon they had an uninterrupted view of the altar and the officiating priest in the apse. In front of the building proper was an open colonnaded courtyard, very much like the forum proper in the Forum of Trajan (FIG. 3-35, no. 5) but called an *atrium,* like the central room in a private house. A special feature of the Constantinian basilica was the *transept,* or transverse aisle, an area perpendicular to the nave between the nave and apse. It housed Saint Peter's *relics* (the body parts, clothing, or any object associated with a saint or Christ; see "Pilgrimages and the Veneration of Relics," page 170), which hordes of pilgrims came to see. The transept became a standard element of church design in the West only much later, when it also took on, with the nave and apse, the symbolism of the Christian cross.

Compared with Roman temples, which usually displayed statuary in pediments on their facades, most Early Christian basilicas were quite austere on the exterior. Inside, however, were frescoes and mosaics, marble columns, grandiose chandeliers, and gold and silver vessels on jeweled altar cloths for use in the Mass. In Saint Peter's, a huge marble *baldacchino* (domical canopy over an altar), supported by four spiral porphyry columns, stood at the *crossing* of the nave and transept, marking the location of Saint Peter's tomb. Some idea of the character of the interior and exterior of Old Saint Peter's can be gleaned from the restored view (FIG. 4-3) of the church and from the century-later basilica of Santa Sabina (FIGS. 4-4A and 4-4B ▨) in Rome. The columns of both *nave arcades* produce a steady rhythm that focuses all attention on the apse, which frames the altar. In Santa Sabina, as in Old Saint Peter's, the

4-3 Restored cutaway view of Old Saint Peter's (looking northwest, with later mosaics decorating the east facade), Rome, Italy, begun ca. 319 (John Burge).

Built by Constantine, the first imperial patron of Christianity, this huge church stood over Saint Peter's grave. The building's plan and elevation resemble those of Roman basilicas, not temples.

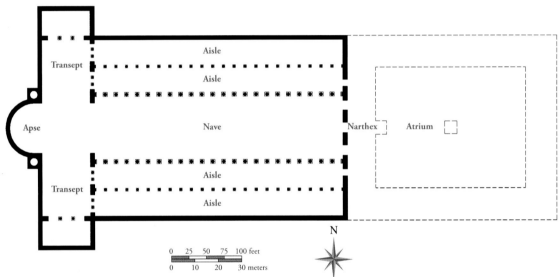

4-4 Restored plan of Old Saint Peter's, Rome, Italy, begun ca. 319.

Old Saint Peter's closely followed the plan of a Roman basilica and had a 300-foot-long nave with flanking aisles leading to an apse, but unlike other early churches, it also had a transept and an atrium.

nave is drenched with light from the *clerestory* windows piercing the thin upper wall beneath the timber roof. Clerestory lighting was essential for illuminating the mosaics and frescoes that commonly adorned the nave and apse of Early Christian churches.

SANTA COSTANZA The rectangular basilican church design featuring a *longitudinal plan* was long the favorite of the Western Christian world. But Early Christian architects also adopted another classical architectural type: the *central-plan* building, a structure in which the parts are of equal or almost equal dimensions around the center. Roman central-plan buildings were usually round or polygonal domed structures. Byzantine architects developed this form in numerous ingenious variations (FIGS. 4-12, 4-22, and 4-24). In the West, builders generally used the central plan for structures adjacent to the main basilicas, such as *mausoleums, baptisteries,* and private chapels, rather than for churches, as in the East.

A highly refined example of the central-plan design is Santa Costanza (FIGS. 4-5 and 4-6) in Rome, built in the mid-fourth century, possibly as the mausoleum for Constantina, Constantine's daughter. Recent excavations have called the traditional identification into question, but the building housed Constantina's monumental porphyry sarcophagus, even if the structure was not originally her tomb. The mausoleum, later converted into a church, stood next to the basilica of Saint Agnes, erected over the catacomb in which she was buried.

Santa Costanza's design derives from the domed structures of the Romans, such as the Pantheon (FIGS. 3-38 to 3-40), but the architect introduced an *ambulatory,* a ringlike barrel-vaulted corridor separated from the central domed cylinder by 12 pairs of columns. Like most Early Christian basilicas, Santa Costanza has a severe brick exterior, but its interior was very richly adorned with mosaics, although most are lost.

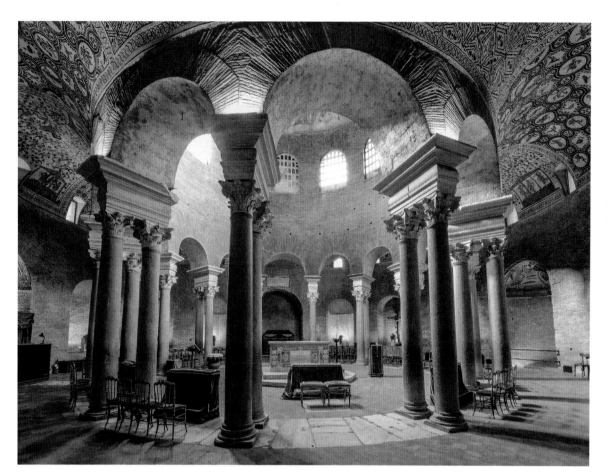

4-5 **Interior of Santa Costanza (looking southwest), Rome, Italy, ca. 337–351.**

Possibly built as the mausoleum of Constantine's daughter, Santa Costanza later became a church. Its central plan, featuring a domed interior, would become the preferred form for Byzantine churches.

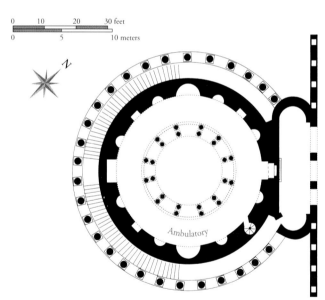

4-6 **Plan of Santa Costanza, Rome, Italy, ca. 337–351.**

Santa Costanza has antecedents in the domed temples (FIG. 3-40) and mausoleums of the Romans, but its plan, which features a circle of 12 pairs of columns and a vaulted ambulatory, is new.

MAUSOLEUM OF GALLA PLACIDIA Mosaic decoration (see "Mosaics," page 124) played an important role in the interiors of Early Christian buildings of all types. Mosaics not only provided a beautiful setting for Christian rituals but also were vehicles for instructing

the congregation about biblical stories and Christian dogma, especially in an age of widespread illiteracy. The so-called Mausoleum of Galla Placidia in Ravenna is a rare example of a virtually intact Early Christian mosaic program. Galla Placidia was the half sister of the emperor Honorius (r. 395–423), who had moved the capital of his crumbling Western Roman Empire from Milan to Ravenna in 404. Built shortly after 425, almost a quarter century before Galla Placidia's death in 450, the "mausoleum" was probably originally a chapel honoring the martyred Saint Lawrence. The building has a characteristically unadorned brick exterior. Inside, however, mosaics cover every square inch above the marble-faced walls.

Christ in his role as Good Shepherd is the subject of the lunette (FIG. 4-7) above the entrance. No earlier version of the Good Shepherd is as regal as this one. Instead of carrying a lamb on his shoulders (FIGS. 4-2 and 4-2A 🔼), Jesus sits among his flock, haloed and robed in gold and purple. To his left and right, the sheep are distributed evenly in groups of three. But their arrangement is rather loose and informal, and they occupy a carefully described landscape extending from foreground to background beneath a blue sky. All the forms have three-dimensional bulk, and the shadows they cast reveal that this representation is still deeply rooted in the classical tradition.

SANT'APOLLINARE NUOVO In 476, Ravenna fell to Odoacer, the first Germanic king of Italy, whom Theodoric, king of the Ostrogoths, overthrew in turn. Theodoric established his capital at Ravenna in 493. The mosaics in his palace church, Sant'Apollinare Nuovo, date from different periods, but those that Theodoric commissioned reveal a new, much more abstract and formal, style (see "Picturing the Spiritual World," page 125).

MATERIALS AND TECHNIQUES
Mosaics

As an art form, *mosaic* had a rather simple and utilitarian beginning, seemingly invented primarily to provide inexpensive and durable flooring. Originally, mosaicists set small beach pebbles, unaltered from their natural form and color, into a thick coat of cement. Artisans soon discovered, however, that the stones could be arranged in decorative patterns. At first, these *pebble mosaics* were uncomplicated and confined to geometric shapes. Generally, the artists used only black and white stones. The earliest examples of this type date to the eighth century BCE. Eventually, mosaicists arranged the stones to form more complex pictorial designs, and by the fourth century BCE, artists depicted elaborate figural scenes using a broad range of colors—red, yellow, and brown, in addition to black, white, and gray—and shaded the figures, clothing, and setting to suggest volume.

By the middle of the third century BCE, Greek artists had invented a new kind of mosaic employing *tesserae* (Latin, "cubes" or "dice"). These tiny cut stones gave mosaicists much greater flexibility because their size and shape could be adjusted. More gradual gradations of color also became possible (FIG. 2-50), and mosaicists finally could aspire to rival the achievements of painters. In Early Christian mosaics (FIGS. 4-7 and 4-8), the tesserae are usually made of glass, which reflects light and makes the surfaces sparkle. Ancient mosaicists occasionally used glass tesserae, but the Romans preferred opaque marble pieces.

Mosaics quickly became a popular, if expensive, means of decorating walls and vaults in Early Christian buildings, although less costly mural paintings were more common. The mosaics caught the light flooding through the windows in vibrant reflection, producing sharp contrasts and concentrations of color that could focus attention on a composition's central, most relevant features. Early Christian mosaics were not meant to incorporate the subtle tonal changes that a naturalistic painter's approach would require. Artists "placed," rather than blended, colors. Bright, hard, glittering texture, set within a rigorously simplified pattern, became the rule. For mosaics situated high in an apse or ambulatory vault or over the nave colonnade, far above the observer's head, the painstaking use of tiny tesserae seen in Roman floor mosaics would be pointless. Early Christian mosaics, designed to be seen from a distance, usually consisted of larger tesserae. The mosaicists also set the cubes unevenly so that their surfaces could catch and reflect the light.

4-7 *Christ as Good Shepherd,* **mosaic on the interior entrance wall of the Mausoleum of Galla Placidia, Ravenna, Italy, ca. 425.**

Jesus sits among his flock, haloed and robed in gold and purple. The landscape and the figures, with their cast shadows, are the work of a mosaicist still deeply rooted in the naturalistic classical tradition.

BYZANTIUM

In the decades following the foundation in 324 of Constantinople—the New Rome in the East, on the site of the Greek city of Byzantium—the pace of Christianization of the Roman Empire quickened. In 380, Theodosius I (r. 379–395) issued an edict finally establishing Christianity as the state religion. In 391, he enacted a ban against worshiping the old gods, and in 394, the emperor abolished the Olympic Games, the enduring symbol of the classical world and its values.

Theodosius died in 395, and imperial power passed to his two sons, Arcadius, who became emperor of the East, and Honorius, emperor of the West. Though not formally codified, this division of the Roman Empire became permanent. In the western half, the Visigoths, under their king Alaric, sacked Rome in 410. The Western Roman Empire soon collapsed, replaced by warring kingdoms that, during the Middle Ages, formed the foundations of the modern nations of Europe (see page 158). The Eastern Roman Empire, only loosely connected by religion to the West and with only minor territorial holdings there,

PROBLEMS AND SOLUTIONS
Picturing the Spiritual World

The early-sixth-century mosaics of Sant'Apollinare Nuovo in Ravenna depict scenes from Jesus's life (see "The Life of Jesus in Art," pages 120–121)—for example, *Miracle of the Loaves and Fishes* (FIG. 4-8). The mosaic stands in sharp contrast to the 80-year-earlier *Christ as Good Shepherd* mosaic (FIG. 4-7) in the Mausoleum of Galla Placidia. Jesus, again beardless but now wearing the imperial dress of gold and purple and distinguished by the cross-inscribed *nimbus* (halo) that signifies his divinity, faces directly toward the viewer. With extended arms, he directs his disciples to distribute to the great crowd the miraculously increased supply of bread and fish he has produced. The mosaicist told the story with the least number of figures necessary to make its meaning explicit, aligning the figures laterally, moving them close to the foreground, and placing them in a shallow picture box. The

landscape setting, which the artist who worked for Galla Placidia so explicitly described, is here merely a few rocks and bushes enclosing the figure group like parentheses. The blue sky of the physical world has given way to the otherworldly splendor of heavenly gold. This represents a major stylistic shift away from classical illusionism toward a more abstract style.

Why did Early Christian artists begin to depict the sky as golden instead of blue? The answer is clear. These artists were seeking a means to conjure a spiritual world before the eyes of the faithful, not to represent the everyday world outside the sacred space of the church. A new aesthetic is on exhibit in the Sant'Apollinare Nuovo mosaic, one quite foreign to classical art, with its worldly themes, naturalism, perspective illusionism, and modeling in light and shade. Indeed, the ethereal golden background suggests that the holy figures exist not on earth but in the palatial kingdom of Heaven far above the heads of the Christian worshipers below. This is precisely the impression the Christian mosaicist wished to create.

4-8 *Miracle of the Loaves and Fishes,* **mosaic in the top register of the nave wall above the clerestory windows of Sant'Apollinare Nuovo, Ravenna, Italy, ca. 504.**

In contrast to FIG. 4-7, Jesus here faces directly toward the viewer. Blue sky has given way to the otherworldly splendor of heavenly gold, the standard background color for medieval mosaics.

had a long and complex history of its own. Centered at New Rome, the Eastern Roman Empire remained a cultural and political entity for a millennium, until the last of a long line of emperors, ironically named Constantine XI, died at Constantinople in 1453, in a futile attempt to defend the city against the Muslim Ottoman Turks (see page 140).

Historians refer to that eastern empire as Byzantium, employing Constantinople's original name, and use the term *Byzantine* to identify whatever pertains to Byzantium—its territory, its history,

and its culture. The Byzantine emperors, however, did not use that term to define themselves. They called their empire Rome and themselves Romans. Though they spoke Greek and not Latin, the Eastern Roman emperors never relinquished their claim as the legitimate successors to the ancient Roman emperors.

The Byzantine emperors considered themselves the earthly vicars of Jesus Christ. Their will was God's will, and they exercised the ultimate spiritual as well as temporal authority. As sole executives for Church and State, the emperors shared power with neither senate nor

4-9 ANTHEMIUS OF TRALLES and ISIDORUS OF MILETUS, aerial view of Hagia Sophia (looking north), Constantinople (Istanbul), Turkey, 532–537.

Justinian's reign was the first golden age of Byzantine art and architecture. Hagia Sophia was the most magnificent of the more than 30 churches Justinian built or restored in Constantinople alone.

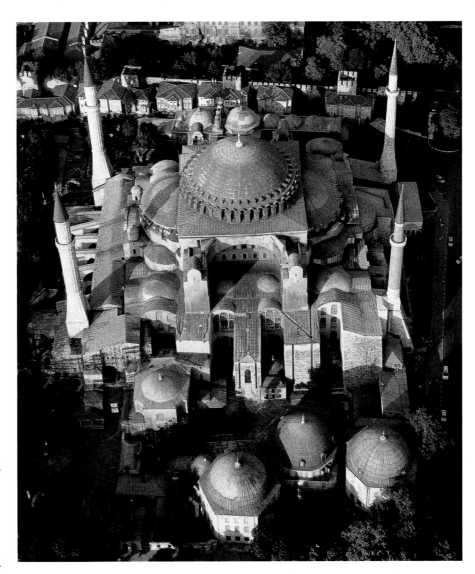

Church council. They reigned supreme, combining the functions of both pope and Caesar, which the Christian West would keep strictly separate. The Byzantine emperors' exalted position made them quasi-divine. The imperial court was an image of the kingdom of Heaven.

Art historians divide the history of Byzantine art into three periods. The first, Early Byzantine, extends from the founding of Constantinople in 324 to the onset of *iconoclasm* (the destruction of images used in religious worship) in 726 under Emperor Leo III. The Middle Byzantine period begins with the renunciation of iconoclasm in 843 and ends with Western Crusaders' occupation of Constantinople in 1204. Late Byzantine corresponds to the two centuries after the Byzantines recaptured Constantinople in 1261 until its final loss in 1453 to the Ottoman Turks.

Early Byzantine Art

The first golden age of Byzantine art is the reign of Justinian (r. 527–565), during which the Eastern Roman Empire briefly rivaled the old united Roman Empire in power and extent (MAP 4-1). At this time, Byzantine art emerged as a recognizable style distinct from Early Christian art. In Constantinople alone, Justinian built or restored more than 30 churches, and his activities as builder extended throughout his empire. Procopius of Caesarea (ca. 500–565), the official chronicler of Justinian's reign, admitted that the emperor's extravagant building program was an obsession that cost his subjects dearly in taxation. But Justinian's monuments defined the Byzantine style in architecture forever after.

HAGIA SOPHIA The emperor's most important project was the construction of Hagia Sophia (FIGS. 4-9 to 4-12), the Church of Holy Wisdom, in Constantinople. ANTHEMIUS OF TRALLES and ISIDORUS OF MILETUS designed and built the church for Justinian between 532 and 537. It is Byzantium's grandest building and one of the supreme accomplishments of world architecture. Hagia Sophia's dimensions are formidable: about 270 feet long and 240 feet wide.

4-10 ANTHEMIUS OF TRALLES and ISIDORUS OF MILETUS, plan of Hagia Sophia, Constantinople (Istanbul), Turkey, 532–537.

In Hagia Sophia, Justinian's architects succeeded in fusing two previously independent architectural traditions: the vertically oriented central-plan building and the longitudinally oriented basilica.

4-11 ANTHEMIUS OF TRALLES and ISIDORUS OF MILETUS, restored cutaway view of Hagia Sophia (looking northwest), Constantinople (Istanbul), Turkey, 532–537 (John Burge).

Hagia Sophia is a domed basilica. Buttressing the great dome are eastern and western half-domes whose thrusts descend, in turn, into smaller half-domes surmounting columned exedrae.

The church's dome is 108 feet in diameter, and its crown rises some 180 feet above the pavement. In exterior view (FIG. 4-9), the great dome dominates the structure, but the building's external aspects today are much changed from their original appearance. The huge buttresses are later additions to the Justinianic design, as are the four towering *minarets* that the Turks constructed after their conquest of 1453 and conversion of Hagia Sophia into a *mosque* (see page 147).

The characteristic Byzantine plainness and unpretentiousness of the exterior (FIG. 4-9) scarcely prepare visitors for the building's interior (FIG. 4-12), which was once richly appointed. Colored stones from throughout the known world covered the walls and floors. But the feature that distinguishes Hagia Sophia from equally lavishly revetted Roman buildings such as the Pantheon (FIG. 3-40) is the special mystical quality of the light flooding the interior. The soaring canopy-like dome that dominates the inside as well as the outside of the church rides on a halo of light from 40 windows in the dome's base, which creates the illusion that the dome rests on light, not masonry. Procopius observed that the dome looked as if it were suspended by "a golden chain from Heaven" and that "the space is not illuminated by the sun from the outside, but the radiance is generated within, so great an abundance of light bathes this shrine all around."[1]

A Justinianic poet and *silentiary* (an usher responsible for maintaining silence), Paulus Silentiarius, compared the dome to "the firmament which rests on air" and described the vaulting as covered with "gilded tesserae from which a glittering stream of golden rays pours abundantly and strikes men's eyes with irresistible force. It is as if one were gazing at the midday sun in spring."[2] Thus Hagia Sophia has a vastness of space shot through with light, and a central dome that appears to be supported by the light it admits. Light is the mystic element—light that glitters in the mosaics, shines forth from the marbles, and pervades and defines spaces that escape definition. Light seems to dissolve material substance and transform it into an abstract spiritual vision.

4-12 ANTHEMIUS OF TRALLES and ISIDORUS OF MILETUS, interior of Hagia Sophia (looking southwest), Constantinople (Istanbul), Turkey, 532–537.

Pendentive construction made possible Hagia Sophia's lofty dome, which seems to ride on a halo of light. A contemporary said that the dome seemed to be suspended by "a golden chain from Heaven."

PROBLEMS AND SOLUTIONS
Placing a Dome over a Square

Perhaps the most characteristic feature of Byzantine architecture is the use of a dome, which is circular at its base, over an interior space that is square in plan, as in the Justinianic church of Hagia Sophia (FIGS. 4-10 to 4-12) and countless later structures (for example, FIGS. 4-22 and 4-24). Unlike other engineering marvels that the Byzantine Empire inherited from imperial Rome, the placement of a dome over a square was a problem that Byzantine builders had to solve themselves. Two innovative structural devices that became hallmarks of Byzantine engineering made this feat possible: *pendentives* and *squinches.*

In pendentive construction (from the Latin *pendere,* "to hang"), a dome rests on what is, in effect, a second, larger dome (FIG. 4-13, *left*). The builders omit the top portion and four segments around the rim of the larger dome, producing four curved triangles, or pendentives. The pendentives join to form a ring and four arches whose planes bound a square. The pendentives and arches transfer the weight of the dome not to the walls but to the four piers from which the arches spring. The first use of pendentives on a monumental scale was in Hagia Sophia in the mid-sixth century, although Mesopotamian architects had experimented with pendentives earlier. In Roman and Early Christian central-plan buildings, such as the Pantheon (FIGS. 3-39 and 3-40) and Santa Costanza (FIG. 4-5), the domes spring directly from the circular top of a cylinder (FIG. 3-15d).

The pendentive system is a dynamic solution to the problem of setting a round dome over a square, making possible a union of centralized and longitudinal (basilican) structures. A similar effect can be achieved using squinches (FIG. 4-13, *right*)—arches, corbels, or lintels—that bridge the corners of the supporting walls and form an octagon inscribed within a square. To achieve even greater height, a builder can rest a dome on a cylindrical *drum* that in turn rests on either pendentives or squinches, as in the 11th-century Church of the Dormition (FIG. 4-22) at Daphni, but the principle of supporting a dome over a square is the same.

4-13 Dome on pendentives (*left*); dome on squinches (*right*) (John Burge).

Pendentives (triangular sections of a sphere) make it possible to place a dome on a ring over a square. Squinches achieve the same goal by bridging the corners of the square to form an octagonal base.

PENDENTIVES To achieve this illusion of a floating "dome of Heaven," Anthemius and Isidorus used *pendentives* (see "Placing a Dome over a Square," above, and FIG. 4-13) to transfer the weight from the great dome to the piers beneath rather than to the walls. With pendentives, not only could the space beneath the dome be unobstructed, but scores of windows could puncture the walls. The pendentives created the impression of a dome suspended above, not held up by, walls. Experts today can explain the technical virtuosity of Justinian's builders, but it remained a mystery to their contemporaries. Procopius communicated the sense of wonderment experienced by those who entered Hagia Sophia: "No matter how much they concentrate . . . they are unable to understand the craftsmanship and always depart from there amazed by the perplexing spectacle."[3]

By placing a hemispherical dome on a square base instead of on a circular base, Anthemius and Isidorus succeeded in fusing two previously independent and seemingly mutually exclusive architectural traditions: the vertically oriented central-plan building and the longitudinally oriented basilica. Hagia Sophia is, in essence, a domed basilica (FIG. 4-11)—a uniquely successful conclusion to several centuries of experimentation in Christian church architecture. However, the thrusts of the pendentive construction at Hagia Sophia made external buttresses necessary, as well as huge internal northern and southern wall piers and eastern and western half-domes (FIG. 4-9). The semidomes' thrusts descend, in turn, into still smaller half-domes surmounting columned *exedrae* that give a curving flow to the design (FIG. 4-12).

The diverse vistas and screenlike ornamented surfaces mask the structural lines. The columnar arcades of the nave and second-story galleries have no real structural function. Like the walls they pierce, they are only part of a fragile "fill" between the huge piers. Structurally, although Hagia Sophia may seem Roman in its great scale and majesty, the organization of its masses is not Roman. The very fact that the "walls" in Hagia Sophia are concealed (and barely adequate) piers indicates that the architects sought Roman monumentality as an effect and did not design the building according to Roman principles. Hagia Sophia's eight great supporting piers are ashlar masonry, but the screen walls are brick, as are the vaults of the aisles and galleries and the dome and semicircular half-domes. Using brick in place of concrete was a further departure from Roman practice and marks Byzantine architecture as a distinctive structural style.

The ingenious design of Hagia Sophia provided the illumination and the setting for the solemn liturgy of the Eastern Christian Orthodox faith (as opposed to the Catholicism of the Roman Church). The large windows along the rim of the great dome poured light down upon the interior's jeweled splendor, where priests staged the sacred spectacle. Sung by clerical choirs, the Orthodox equivalent of the Latin Mass celebrated the sacrament of the Eucharist at the altar in the *apsidal* sanctuary, in spiritual reenactment of Jesus's crucifixion. Processions of chanting priests, accompanying the *patriarch* (archbishop) of Constantinople, moved slowly to and from the sanctuary and the vast nave. The gorgeous array of their vestments rivaled the interior's polychrome marbles and mosaics

Justinian's general Belisarius captured Ravenna from the Ostrogoths. The city became the seat of Byzantine dominion in Italy. San Vitale honored Saint Vitalis, a second-century Ravenna martyr.

and the gold and silver candlesticks and candelabras, all glowing in shafts of light from the dome.

The nave of Hagia Sophia was reserved for the clergy, not the congregation. The laity, segregated by sex, had only partial views of the brilliant ceremony, the men from the shadows of the aisles and galleries, the women from the galleries. The emperor was the only layperson privileged to enter the sanctuary. When he participated with the patriarch in the liturgical drama, standing at the pulpit beneath the great dome, his rule was sanctified and his person exalted. Church and State were symbolically made one. Hagia Sophia was the earthly image of the court of Heaven, its light the image of God and God's holy wisdom. At Hagia Sophia, the ambitious scale of imperial Rome and the religious mysticism of the Orthodox Christian faith combined to create a monument that is at once a summation of antiquity and a positive assertion of the triumph of Christianity.

SAN VITALE In 539, Justinian's general Belisarius captured Ravenna from the Ostrogoths. As the Eastern Roman Empire's foothold in Italy, Ravenna enjoyed great prosperity, and its culture became an extension of Constantinople's. Its art, even more than that of the Byzantine capital (where relatively little outside of architecture has survived), clearly reveals the transition from the Early Christian to the Byzantine style.

Dedicated by Bishop Maximianus (r. 546–556) in 547 in honor of Saint Vitalis, a second-century martyr, San Vitale (FIGS. 4-14 and 4-15) is the most spectacular building in Ravenna. Work on the church began under Bishop Ecclesius (r. 522–532) shortly after Theodoric's death in 526 and was made possible by Julianus Argentarius (Julian the Banker), who provided the enormous sum of 26,000 *solidi* (gold coins), weighing in excess of 350 pounds, required to proceed with the work. San Vitale is unlike any of the Early Christian churches of Ravenna. It is not a basilica. Rather, it is centrally planned, like Justinian's churches in Constantinople.

0 10 20 30 40 50 feet
0 5 10 15 20 meters

1. Narthex
2. Domed octagon
3. Apse

N

4-15 Plan of San Vitale, Ravenna, Italy, 526–547.

Centrally planned like Justinian's churches in Constantinople, San Vitale is unlike any other church in Italy. The design features two concentric octagons. A dome crowns the taller, inner octagon.

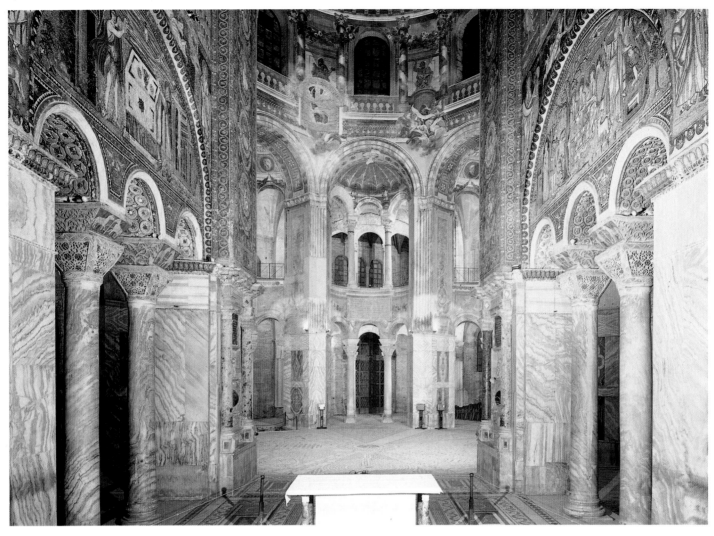

4-16 **Interior of San Vitale (looking west from the apse), Ravenna, Italy, 526–547.**

Natural light, filtered through alabaster-paned windows, plays over the glittering mosaics and glowing marbles sheathing San Vitale's complex wall and vault shapes, producing a splendid effect.

The design features two concentric octagons. The dome-covered inner octagon rises above the surrounding octagon to provide the interior (FIG. 4-16) with clerestory lighting. Eight large rectilinear piers alternate with curved, columned exedrae, pushing outward into the surrounding two-story ambulatory and creating an intricate eight-leafed plan (FIG. 4-15). The exedrae closely integrate the inner and outer spaces that otherwise would have existed simply side by side as independent units. A cross-vaulted *choir* preceding the apse interrupts the ambulatory and gives the plan some axial stability. Weakening this effect, however, is the off-axis placement of the narthex, whose odd angle never has been explained. (The atrium, which no longer exists, may have paralleled a street running in the same direction as the angle of the narthex.)

San Vitale's intricate plan and elevation combine to produce an effect of great complexity. The exterior's octagonal regularity is not readily apparent inside. A rich diversity of ever-changing perspectives greets visitors walking through the building. Arches looping over arches, curving and flattened spaces, and wall and vault shapes seem to change constantly with the viewer's position. Natural light, filtered through alabaster-paned windows, plays over the glittering mosaics and glowing marbles that cover the building's complex surfaces, producing a splendid effect.

The mosaics in San Vitale's choir and apse, like the building itself, must be regarded as one of the greatest achievements of Byzantine art. Completed less than a decade after the Ostrogoths surrendered Ravenna, the apse and choir decorations form a unified composition, whose theme is the holy ratification of Justinian's right to rule. In the apse vault is Christ, who extends the golden martyr's wreath to Saint Vitalis. Beside him is Bishop Ecclesius, who offers a model of San Vitale to Christ. On the choir wall to the left of the apse mosaic appears Justinian (FIG. 4-17). Uniting the Savior and the emperor visually and symbolically are the imperial purple they wear and their halos. A dozen attendants accompany Justinian, paralleling Christ's 12 apostles. Thus the mosaic program underscores the dual political and religious role of the Byzantine emperor.

In the mosaic panel representing Justinian and his retinue, the emperor is at the center. At his left is Bishop Maximianus. The mosaicist stressed the bishop's importance by labeling his figure with the only identifying inscription in the composition. The artist divided the figures into three groups: the emperor and his staff;

4-17 **Justinian, Bishop Maximianus, and attendants, mosaic on the north wall of the apse, San Vitale, Ravenna, Italy, ca. 547.**

San Vitale's mosaics reveal the new Byzantine aesthetic. Justinian is foremost among the weightless and speechless frontal figures hovering before the viewer, their positions in space uncertain.

the clergy; and the imperial guard, bearing a shield with the *Christogram,* the monogram made up of *chi* (X), *rho* (P), and *iota* (I), the initial letters of Christ's name in Greek. Each group has a leader whose feet precede (by one foot overlapping) the feet of those who follow. The positions of Justinian and Maximianus are curiously ambiguous. Although the emperor appears to be slightly behind the bishop, the golden *paten* (large shallow bowl for the Eucharist bread) he carries overlaps the bishop's arm. Thus, symbolized by place and gesture, the imperial and churchly powers are in balance. The emperor's paten, the bishop's cross, and the attendant clerics' book and censer produce a slow forward movement that strikingly modifies the scene's rigid formality. The artist placed nothing in the background, wishing the observer to understand the procession as taking place in this very sanctuary. Thus the emperor appears forever as a participant in the sacred rites and as the proprietor of this royal church and the ruler of the western territories of the Eastern Roman Empire.

The procession at San Vitale recalls but contrasts with that of Augustus and his entourage on the Ara Pacis (FIG. 3-28), carved more than a half millennium earlier in Rome. There, the fully modeled marble figures have their feet planted firmly on the ground. The Romans talk among themselves, unaware of the viewer's presence.

All is anecdote, all very human and of this world, even if the figures themselves conform to a classical ideal of beauty that cannot be achieved in reality. The frontal figures of the Byzantine mosaic hover before viewers, weightless and speechless, their positions in space uncertain. Tall, spare, angular, and elegant, the figures have lost the rather squat proportions characteristic of much Early Christian figural art. The garments fall straight, stiff, and thin from the narrow shoulders. The organic body has dematerialized, and, except for the heads, some of which seem to be true portraits, viewers see a procession of solemn spirits gliding silently in the presence of the sacrament. Indeed, the theological basis for this approach to representation was the idea that the divine was invisible and that the purpose of religious art was to stimulate spiritual seeing (see "Picturing the Spiritual World," page 125). Theodulf of Orleans summed up this idea around 790: "God is beheld not with the eyes of the flesh but only with the eye of the mind."[4] The mosaics of San Vitale reveal this new Byzantine aesthetic, one very different from that of the classical world but equally compelling. Byzantine art disparages matter and material values. It is an art in which blue sky has given way to heavenly gold, an art without solid bodies or cast shadows, and with the perspective of Paradise, which is nowhere and everywhere.

4-18 Theodora and attendants, mosaic on the south wall of the apse, San Vitale, Ravenna, Italy, ca. 547.

Justinian's counterpart on the opposite wall is the Empress Theodora, Justinian's influential consort. Neither of them ever visited Ravenna. San Vitale's mosaics are proxies for the absent sovereigns.

Justinian's counterpart on the opposite wall of the apse is his empress, Theodora (FIG. 4-18), with her corresponding retinue. Both processions move into the apse, Justinian proceeding from left to right and Theodora from right to left, in order to take part in the Eucharist. Justinian carries the paten containing the bread, Theodora the golden cup with the wine. The portraits in the Theodora mosaic exhibit the same stylistic traits as those in the Justinian mosaic, but the artist represented the women within a definite architecture, perhaps the atrium of San Vitale. The empress stands in state beneath an imperial canopy, waiting to follow the emperor's procession. An attendant beckons her to pass through the curtained doorway. That she is outside the sanctuary in a courtyard with a fountain and only about to enter attests that, in the ceremonial protocol, her rank was not quite equal to her consort's. But the very presence of Theodora at San Vitale is significant. Neither she nor Justinian ever visited Ravenna. Their participation in the liturgy at San Vitale is pictorial fiction. The mosaics are proxies for the absent sovereigns. Justinian is present because he was the head of the Byzantine state, and his inclusion in the decoration of the church underscores that his authority extends over his territories in Italy. But Theodora's portrayal is more surprising and testifies to her unique position in Justinian's court. She was the emperor's most trusted adviser as well as his spouse. Theodora's prominent role in the mosaic program of San Vitale is proof of the power she wielded at Constantinople and, by extension, at Ravenna. In fact, the representation of the three

magi on the border of her robe suggests that the empress belongs in the elevated company of the three monarchs bearing gifts who approached the newborn Jesus.

MANUSCRIPTS Of much smaller scale than mosaics but of no less importance for the history of medieval art are painted *manuscripts* (handwritten books, from the Latin *manu scriptus*). The long tradition of placing pictures in manuscripts began in Egypt (FIG. 1-23A [⌐]). Illustrated ancient books are rare, however. An important invention during the Early Roman Empire was the *codex* (plural, *codices*), which greatly aided the dissemination of manuscripts as well as their preservation. Codices are much like modern books, composed of separate leaves (*folios*) enclosed within a cover and bound together at one side. The new format, with pages with a front (*recto*) and back (*verso*), superseded the long manuscript scroll (*rotulus*) of the Egyptians, Greeks, Etruscans, and Romans. (Jesus holds a rotulus in his left hand in FIG. 4-1b; compare FIG. 3-49.) Much more durable *vellum* (calfskin) and *parchment* (lambskin), which provided better surfaces for painting, also replaced the comparatively brittle papyrus used for ancient scrolls. As a result, luxuriousness of ornament became increasingly typical. Art historians refer to the painted books produced before the invention of the printing press as *illuminated manuscripts,* from the Latin *illuminare,* meaning "to adorn, ornament, or brighten." Because of the time and expense involved in producing handwritten and hand-painted books, complete Bibles and other very lengthy texts are exceptional. Usually, medieval codices consist of sections of the Bible, such as a single book (for example, Genesis) or the set of four Gospel books (see "Medieval Books" and FIG. 4-18A ⬈).

VIENNA GENESIS The oldest well-preserved painted manuscript containing biblical scenes is the early-sixth-century *Vienna Genesis,* so called because of its present location. The book was probably produced in Constantinople. The pages are fine vellum dyed with rich purple, the same dye used to give imperial cloth its distinctive color. The Greek text is in silver ink. The front of folio 7 (FIG. 4-19) combines the biblical text with the corresponding illustration of the story of Rebecca and Eliezer at the well (Gen. 24:15–61). When Isaac, Abraham's son, was 40 years old, his parents sent their servant Eliezer to find a wife for him. Eliezer chose Rebecca, because when he stopped at a well, she was the first woman to draw water for him and his camels. The *Vienna Genesis* illustration presents two episodes of the story within a single frame. In the first episode, at the left, Rebecca leaves the city of Nahor to fetch water from the well. In the second episode, she offers water to Eliezer and his camels, while one of them already laps water from the well. The artist painted Nahor as a walled city seen from above, like the cityscapes of the Column of Trajan frieze (FIG. 3-36C ⬈). Rebecca walks to the well along the colonnaded avenue of a Roman city. A seminude female personification of a spring is the source of the well water. These are further reminders of the persistence of classical motifs and stylistic modes in Early Christian and Byzantine art even while other artists (FIG. 4-8) were rejecting classical norms in favor of a style better suited for a focus on the spiritual instead of the natural world.

MOUNT SINAI During Justinian's reign, almost continuous building activity took place, not only in Constantinople and Ravenna but throughout the Byzantine Empire. Between 548 and 565, Justinian rebuilt an important early *monastery* (monks' compound) at Mount Sinai in Egypt where Moses received the Ten Commandments from God. Now called Saint Catherine's, the monastery marked the spot at the foot of the mountain where the Bible says that God first spoke to the Hebrew prophet from a burning bush.

Monasticism began in Egypt in the third century and spread rapidly to Palestine and Syria in the East and as far as Ireland in the West (see page 159). It began as a migration to the wilderness by those who sought a more spiritual way of life, far from the burdens, distractions, and temptations of town and city. In desert places, these refuge seekers lived austerely as hermits, in contemplative isolation, cultivating the soul's perfection. So many thousands fled the cities that the authorities became alarmed—noting the effect on the tax base, military recruitment, and business in general. The origins of the monastic movement are associated with Saints Anthony and Pachomius in Egypt in the fourth century. By the fifth century, many of the formerly isolated monks had begun to live together within a common enclosure and formulate regulations governing communal life under the direction of an *abbot* (see "Medieval Monasteries and Benedictine Rule," page 165). The monks typically lived in a walled monastery, an architectural complex that included the monks' residence (an alignment of single sleeping cells), an *oratory* (monastic church), a *refectory* (dining hall), a kitchen, storage and service quarters, and a guesthouse for pilgrims (FIG. 6-10). Mount Sinai had been an important pilgrimage destination since the fourth century, and Justinian's fortress protected not only the monks but also the lay pilgrims during their visits. The Mount Sinai church was dedicated to the Virgin Mary, whom the Orthodox Church had officially recognized in the mid-fifth century as the Mother of God (*Theotokos,* "she who bore God" in Greek).

1 in.

4-19 *Rebecca and Eliezer at the Well,* **folio 7 recto of the *Vienna Genesis,* early sixth century. Tempera, gold, and silver on purple vellum, $1' \frac{1}{4}" \times 9\frac{1}{4}"$. Österreichische Nationalbibliothek, Vienna.**

This luxuriously dyed vellum book is the oldest well-preserved manuscript containing biblical scenes. Two episodes of the Rebecca story appear in a single setting filled with classical motifs.

ART AND SOCIETY
Icons and Iconoclasm

Icons (Greek, "images") are small portable paintings depicting Christ, the Virgin, or saints (or a combination of all three, as in FIG. 4-20). Icons survive from as early as the fourth century. From the sixth century on, they became enormously popular in Byzantine worship, both public and private. Eastern Christians considered icons a personal, intimate, and indispensable medium for spiritual transaction with holy figures. Some icons (for example, FIG. 4-27) came to be regarded as wonder-working, and believers ascribed miracles and healing powers to them.

Icons were by no means universally accepted, however. From the beginning, many Christians were deeply suspicious of the practice of imaging the divine, whether on portable panels, on the walls of churches, or especially as statues that reminded them of ancient idols. The opponents of Christian figural art had in mind the prohibition of images that the Lord dictated to Moses in the Second Commandment: "Thou shalt not make unto thee any graven image or any likeness of anything that is in heaven above, or that is in the earth beneath, or that is in the water under the earth. Thou shalt not bow down thyself to them, nor serve them" (Exod. 20:4, 5).

Opposition to icons became especially strong in the eighth century, when the faithful often burned incense and knelt before the icons in prayer to seek protection or a cure for illness. Although their purpose was only to evoke the presence of the holy figures addressed in prayer, for many, the icons became identified with the personages represented. Icon veneration became confused with idol worship, and this brought about an imperial ban on all sacred images, as well as edicts ordering the destruction of existing images (*iconoclasm*).

The consequences of iconoclasm for the study of Early Byzantine art are difficult to overstate. For more than a century, not only did the portrayal of Christ, the Virgin, and the saints cease, but the *iconoclasts* ("breakers of images") also destroyed countless works from the first several centuries of Christendom.

4-20 Virgin (Theotokos) and Child between Saints Theodore and George, icon, sixth or early seventh century. Encaustic on wood, 2' 3" × 1' 7 3/8". Monastery of Saint Catherine, Mount Sinai, Egypt.

Byzantine icons are the heirs to the Roman tradition of portrait painting on small wood panels (FIG. 3-42), but their Christian subjects and function as devotional objects broke sharply from classical models.

ICONS As important as books in the daily lives of monks were *icons* (see "Icons and Iconoclasm," above). Unfortunately, few early icons survive because of the wholesale destruction of images that occurred in the eighth century. One of the finest early examples (FIG. 4-20) comes from Mount Sinai. The medium is encaustic on wood, continuing a tradition of panel painting in Egypt that, like so much else in the Byzantine world, dates to the Roman Empire (FIGS. 3-42 and 3-43). The icon depicts the enthroned Theotokos and Child with Saints Theodore and George. The two guardian saints intercede with the Virgin on the worshiper's behalf. Behind them, two angels gaze upward at a shaft of light where the hand of God appears. The foreground figures are strictly frontal and have a

solemn demeanor. Background details are few. The shallow forward plane of the picture dominates. Traces of Greco-Roman illusionism remain in the Virgin's rather personalized features, in her sideways glance, and in the posing of the angels' heads. But the painter rendered the saints' bodies in the new Byzantine manner.

ICONOCLASM The preservation of Early Byzantine icons at the Mount Sinai monastery is surprising because in the seventh century, a series of calamities erupted in Egypt and Syria that indirectly caused the imperial ban on images. The Sasanians, chronically at war with Rome, swept into the Eastern provinces, and between 611 and 617 they captured the great cities of Antioch, Jerusalem, and

Middle Byzantine churches typically are small and high-shouldered, with a central dome on a drum, and exterior wall surfaces with decorative patterns, probably reflecting Islamic architecture.

Alexandria. The Byzantine emperor Heraclius (r. 610–641) had hardly defeated them in 627 when a new and overwhelming power appeared unexpectedly on the stage of history. The Arabs, under the banner of the new Islamic religion, conquered not only Byzantium's eastern provinces but also Persia itself, replacing the Sasanians in the age-old balance of power with the Christian West (see page 30). In a few years the Arabs were launching attacks on Constantinople, and Byzantium was fighting for its life.

These were catastrophic years for the Eastern Roman Empire. They terminated once and for all the long story of imperial Rome, closed the Early Byzantine period, and inaugurated the medieval era of Byzantine history. The Byzantine Empire lost almost two-thirds of its territory—many cities and much of its population, wealth, and material resources. The shock of these events persuaded Emperor Leo III (r. 717–741) that God was punishing Byzantium for its idolatrous worship of icons by setting upon it the merciless armies of the infidel—an enemy that, moreover, shunned the representation not only of God but of all living things in holy places (see page 152). In 726, he formally prohibited the use of images, and for more than a century, Byzantine artists produced little new religious figurative art.

Middle Byzantine Art

In the late eighth and ninth centuries, a powerful reaction against iconoclasm set in. Two empresses in particular led the movement to restore image-making in the Byzantine Empire: Irene in 780 and Theodora in 843. The destruction of images was condemned as a heresy, and under a new line of *iconophile* ("image-loving") Byzantine rulers, known as the Macedonian dynasty, lavish commissions of religious art resumed. Basil I (r. 867–886), founder of the new dynasty, regarded himself as the restorer of the Roman Empire. He denounced as usurpers the Carolingian monarchs of the West who, since 800, had claimed the title "Roman Empire" for their realm (see page 161). Basil bluntly reminded their emissary that the only true emperor of Rome reigned in Constantinople. They were not Roman emperors but merely "kings of the Germans."

HOSIOS LOUKAS Although the Macedonian emperors did not wait long to redecorate the churches of their predecessors, they undertook little new church construction in the decades after the renunciation of iconoclasm. But in the 10th century and through the 12th, a number of monastic churches arose that are the flowers of Middle Byzantine architecture. They feature a brilliant series of variations on the domed central plan. From the exterior, the typical later Byzantine church building is a domed cube, with the dome rising above the square on a cylindrical drum. The churches are small, vertical, and high shouldered, and, unlike earlier Byzantine buildings, they have exterior wall surfaces decorated with vivid patterns, probably reflecting Islamic architecture.

The *katholikon* (FIG. 4-21), the main church in the monastery at Hosios Loukas (Saint Luke) in Greece, dates to the early 11th century and exemplifies church design during this second golden age of Byzantine art and architecture. Light stones framed by dark red

4-22 Interior of the Church of the Dormition (looking into the dome with mosaic of Christ as Pantokrator), Daphni, Greece, ca. 1090–1100.

The Daphni dome rests on an octagon formed by squinches. In the dome, the fearsome image of Christ as Pantokrator (ruler of all) is like a gigantic icon hovering above the awestruck worshiper below.

bricks make up the walls. The interplay of arcuated windows, projecting apses, and varying rooflines further enhances this surface dynamism. The plan is in the form of a domed cross in square with four equal-length, vaulted cross arms (the *Greek cross*).

DAPHNI Mosaics covered the walls, vaults, and domes of Middle Byzantine churches. Some of the best-preserved examples are in the monastic church of the Dormition (from the Latin for "sleep," referring to Christ's receiving the soul of the Virgin Mary at the moment of her death), at Daphni, near Athens. The church has a typical Middle Byzantine plan with a dome supported by a drum resting on squinches (FIG. 4-22). The main elements of the late-11th-century pictorial program are intact, although the mosaics underwent restoration in the 19th century. Gazing down from on high is the fearsome image of Christ as *Pantokrator* (literally "ruler of all" in Greek, but usually applied to Christ in his role as last judge of humankind). The dome mosaic is the climax of an elaborate hierarchical mosaic program including several New Testament episodes below. The Daphni Pantokrator is like a gigantic icon hovering dramatically in

4-23 *Crucifixion,* mosaic in the north arm of the east wall of the Church of the Dormition, Daphni, Greece, ca. 1090–1100.

The Daphni *Crucifixion* is a subtle blend of classical naturalism and the more abstract Byzantine style. The Virgin Mary and Saint John point to Christ on the cross as if to a devotional object.

space. The image serves to connect the awestruck worshiper in the church below with Heaven through Christ.

Below the dome, on the wall beneath the barrel vault of one arm of the Greek cross, is a mosaic (FIG. 4-23) depicting Christ's death on the cross. Like the dome mosaic, the Daphni *Crucifixion* is a subtle blend of the painterly, naturalistic style of classical and Early Christian art and the later, more abstract and formalistic Byzantine style. The Byzantine artist fully assimilated classicism's simplicity, dignity, and grace into a perfect synthesis with Byzantine piety and pathos. The figures have regained classical organic structure to a surprising degree, particularly compared to figures from the Justinianic period (compare FIGS. 4-17 and 4-18). The style is a masterful adaptation of classical statuesque qualities to the linear Byzantine manner.

In quiet sorrow and resignation, the Virgin and Saint John flank the crucified Christ. A skull at the foot of the cross indicates Golgotha, the Place of the Skull. The artist needed nothing else to set the scene. The picture is not a narrative of the historical event of Jesus's execution, although it contains anecdotal details. Christ has a tilted head and sagging body, and although the Savior is not overtly in pain, blood spurts from the wound that Longinus inflicted on him. The Virgin and John point to the figure on the cross as if to

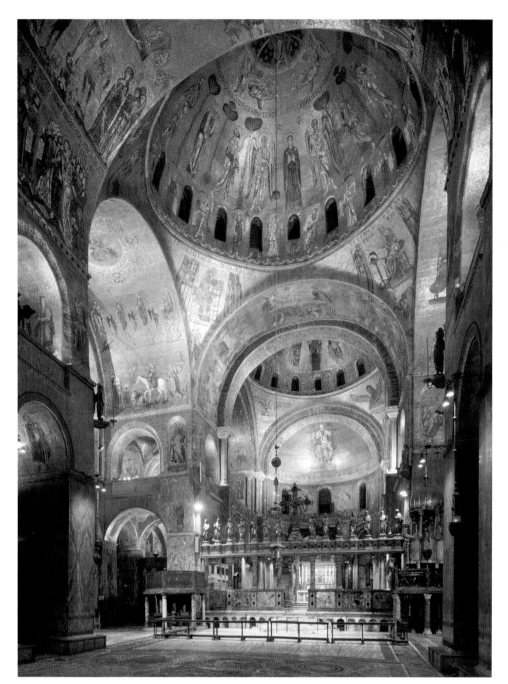

4-24 **Interior of Saint Mark's (looking east), Venice, Italy, begun 1063.**

Modeled on a church in Constantinople, Saint Mark's has a dome over the crossing, four other domes over the arms of the Greek cross, and 40,000 square feet of Byzantine-style mosaics.

a devotional object. They act as intercessors between the viewer below and Christ, who, in the dome, appears as the last judge of all humans.

SAINT MARK'S, VENICE The revival on a grand scale of church building and of figural mosaics extended beyond the Greek-speaking Byzantine East in the 10th to 12th centuries, especially in areas of the former Western Roman Empire where the ties with Constantinople were the strongest. In the Early Byzantine period, Venice, about 80 miles north of Ravenna on the eastern coast of Italy, was a dependency of that Byzantine stronghold. In 751, Ravenna fell to the Lombards, who wrested control of most of northern Italy from Constantinople. Venice, however, became an independent power. Its *doges* (dukes) enriched themselves and the city through seaborne commerce, serving as the crucial link between Byzantium and the West.

Venice had obtained the relics of Saint Mark from Alexandria in Egypt in 829, and shortly thereafter, the doges constructed the first Venetian shrine dedicated to the saint. In 1063, Doge Domenico Contarini (r. 1043–1071) began construction of the present Saint Mark's, modeled on the Church of the Holy Apostles at Constantinople, built in Justinian's time. That shrine no longer exists, but its key elements were a *cruciform* (cross-shaped) plan with a central dome over the crossing and four other domes over the four equal arms of the Greek cross, as at Saint Mark's.

The interior (FIG. 4-24) of Saint Mark's is, like its plan, Byzantine in effect. Light enters through a row of windows at the bases of all five domes, vividly illuminating a rich cycle of mosaics. Both Byzantine and local artists worked on the project over the course of several centuries. Most of the mosaics date to the 12th and 13th centuries. Cleaning and restoration have returned the mosaics to their original splendor, enabling visitors to experience the full radiance of 40,000 square feet of mosaics covering all the walls, arches, vaults, and domes, like a gold-brocaded and figured fabric.

In the vast central dome, 80 feet above the floor and 42 feet in diameter, Christ ascends to Heaven in the presence of the Virgin Mary and the 12 apostles. In the great arch framing the crossing

Byzantium **137**

4-25 Christ enthroned with saints (*Harbaville Triptych*), ca. 950. Ivory, central panel 9½″ × 5½″. Musée du Louvre, Paris.

This small three-part shrine with hinged wings was used for private devotion. The ivory carver depicted the figures with classical stances, in contrast to the frontal poses of most Byzantine figures.

are the *Crucifixion* and *Resurrection* and the liberating from death of Adam and Eve, John the Baptist, and other biblical figures by Christ. The mosaics have explanatory labels in both Latin and Greek, reflecting Venice's position as the key link between Eastern and Western Christendom in the later Middle Ages. The insubstantial figures on the walls, vaults, and domes appear weightless, and they project no farther from their flat field than the elegant Latin and Greek letters above them. As in other Byzantine mosaics, nothing here reflects on the world of matter, of solids, of light and shade, or of space.

HARBAVILLE TRIPTYCH Middle Byzantine artists also excelled in the production of costly small-scale artworks, including bejeweled icons, illuminated manuscripts, and carved ivories. A masterpiece of ivory carving is the *Harbaville Triptych* (FIG. 4-25), a portable shrine with two hinged wings used for private devotion. Ivory *triptychs* were very popular—among those who could afford such luxurious items—and they often replaced icons for use in personal prayer. Carved on the wings of the *Harbaville Triptych,* both inside and out, are four pairs of full-length figures and two pairs of medallions depicting saints. A cross dominates the central panel on the back of the triptych (not illustrated). On the inside is a scene of *Deësis* (supplication). John the Baptist and the Theotokos appear as intercessors, praying to the enthroned Savior on behalf of the viewer. Below them are five apostles.

The formality and solemnity usually associated with Byzantine art yielded here to a softer, more fluid style. The figures may lack

true classical contrapposto, but the looser stances (most stand on bases, like freestanding statues) and three-quarter views of many of the heads relieve the hard austerity of the customary frontal pose. This more natural, classical spirit was a second, equally important stylistic current of the Middle Byzantine period.

NEREZI When the emperors lifted the ban against religious images and again encouraged religious painting at Constantinople, the impact was felt far and wide. The style varied from region to region, but a renewed enthusiasm for picturing the key New Testament figures and events was universal. In 1164, at Nerezi in Macedonia, a member of the Comnenian imperial family sponsored the construction of the church of Saint Pantaleimon. Byzantine painters, possibly brought from Constantinople, embellished the church with murals of great emotional power. One of these, *Lamentation* (FIG. 4-26), is an image of passionate grief over the dead Christ. The artist captured Christ's followers in attitudes, expressions, and gestures of quite human bereavement. Joseph of Arimathea and the disciple Nicodemus kneel at his feet. Mary presses her cheek against her dead son's face. Saint John clings to Christ's left hand. In the Gospels, neither Mary nor John was present at the entombment of Christ. Their inclusion here, as elsewhere in Middle Byzantine art, intensified for the viewer the emotional impact of Christ's death.

The setting for this lamentation is a hilly landscape below a blue sky—a striking contrast to the abstract golden world of the mosaics

4-26 *Lamentation,* wall painting, Saint Pantaleimon, Nerezi, Macedonia, 1164.

Working in an alternate Byzantine mode, this Middle Byzantine painter staged the emotional lamentation over the dead Christ in a hilly landscape below a blue sky and peopled it with fully modeled figures.

1 in.

favored for church walls throughout the Byzantine Empire. In order to make utterly convincing an emotionally charged realization of the theme, this artist instead staged the mourning scene in a more natural setting and peopled it with fully modeled actors. This alternate representational mode is no less Byzantine than the frontal, flatter figures more commonly associated with Byzantine art. In time, artists in Italy (FIG. 7-32) would emulate this more naturalistic style, giving birth to Renaissance art.

PARIS PSALTER Another example of this classical-revival style is the so-called *Paris Psalter.* (A *psalter* is a book containing King David's Psalms; see "Medieval Books" ⬀). Art historians believe that the manuscript dates from the mid-10th century—the Macedonian Renaissance, a time of humanistic reverence for the classical past and of enthusiastic and careful study of the language and literature of ancient Greece. In the illustrated page (FIG. 4-27), David, surrounded by sheep, goats, and his faithful dog, plays his harp in a rocky landscape with a town in the background. Similar settings are common in Pompeian murals. Also present are several allegorical figures. Melody looks over David's shoulder, while Echo peers from behind a column. A reclining male figure points to a Greek inscription identifying him as representing the mountain of Bethlehem. These personifications do not appear in the Bible. They are

4-27 *David Composing the Psalms,* folio 1 verso of the *Paris Psalter,* ca. 950–970. Tempera on vellum, 1' 2$\frac{1}{8}$" × 10$\frac{1}{4}$". Bibliothèque Nationale, Paris.

During the Macedonian Renaissance, Byzantine artists revived the classical style. This painter portrayed David as if he were a Greek hero, accompanied by personifications of Melody, Echo, and Bethlehem.

the stock population of Greco-Roman painting. Apparently, the artist translated a classical model into a Byzantine pictorial idiom. In works such as this, Byzantine artists kept the classical style alive in the Middle Ages.

VLADIMIR VIRGIN Nothing in Middle Byzantine art better demonstrates the rejection of the iconoclastic viewpoint than the painted icon's return to prominence. After the restoration of images, icons multiplied by the thousands to meet public and private demand. In the 11th century, the clergy began to display icons in hierarchical order (Christ, the Theotokos, John the Baptist, and then other saints, as on the *Harbaville Triptych*) in tiers on the *templon,* the columnar screen separating the sanctuary from the main body of a Byzantine church.

One example is the renowned *Vladimir Virgin* (FIG. 4-28). Descended from works such as the Mount Sinai icon (FIG. 4-20), the Russian icon clearly reveals the stylized abstraction resulting from centuries of working and reworking the conventional image. Probably the work of a Constantinopolitan painter, the *Vladimir Virgin* displays all the characteristic traits of Byzantine Virgin and Child icons: the Virgin's long, straight nose and small mouth; the golden rays in the infant's drapery; the sweep of the unbroken contour that encloses the two figures; and the flat silhouette against the golden ground. But this is a much more tender and personalized image of the Virgin than that in the Mount Sinai icon. Here, Mary is the Virgin of Compassion, who presses her cheek against her son's in an intimate portrayal of mother and child. A deep pathos infuses the image as Mary contemplates the future sacrifice of her son. (The back of the icon bears images of the instruments of Christ's passion.)

The Vladimir icon has seen hard service. Placed before or above altars in churches or private chapels, it became blackened by the incense and the smoke from candles that burned before or below it. It was taken to Kiev (Ukraine) in 1131, then to Vladimir (Russia) in 1155 (hence its name), and in 1395, as a wonder-working image, to Moscow to protect that city from the Mongols. The Russians believed that the sacred picture saved the city of Kazan from later Tartar invasions and all of Russia from the Poles in the 17th century. The *Vladimir Virgin* is a historical symbol of Byzantium's religious and cultural mission to the Slavic world.

Byzantium after 1204

When rule passed from the Macedonian to the Comnenian dynasty in the later 11th and the 12th centuries, three events of fateful significance changed Byzantium's fortunes for the worse. The Seljuk Turks conquered most of Anatolia. The Byzantine Orthodox Church broke finally from the Church of Rome. And the Crusades brought the Latins (a generic term for the peoples of the West) into Byzantine lands on their way to fight for the Christian cross against the Saracens (Muslims) in the Holy Land (see "The Crusades ⏎").

Crusaders had passed through Constantinople many times en route to "smite the infidel" and had marveled at its wealth and magnificence. Envy, greed, religious fanaticism (the Latins called the Greeks "heretics"), and even ethnic enmity motivated the Crusaders when, during the Fourth Crusade in 1203 and 1204, the Venetians persuaded them to divert their expedition against the Muslims in Palestine and to attack Constantinople instead. They took the city and sacked it.

The Latins set up kingdoms within Byzantium, notably in Constantinople itself. What remained of Byzantium split into three

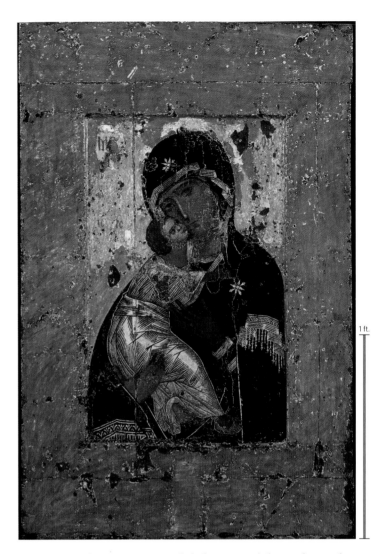

4-28 Virgin of Compassion icon (*Vladimir Virgin*), late 11th or early 12th century, with later repainting. Tempera on wood, 2' 6½" × 1' 9". Tretyakov Gallery, Moscow.

In this Middle Byzantine icon, the painter depicted Mary as the Virgin of Compassion, who presses her cheek against her son's as she contemplates his future. The reverse side shows the instruments of Christ's passion.

small states. The Palaeologans ruled one of these, the kingdom of Nicaea. In 1261, Michael VIII Palaeologus (r. 1259–1282) succeeded in recapturing Constantinople. But his empire was no more than a fragment, and even that disintegrated during the next two centuries. Isolated from the Christian West by Muslim conquests in the Balkans and besieged by Muslim Turks to the east, Byzantium sought help from the West. It was not forthcoming. In 1453, the Ottoman Turks, then a formidable power, took Constantinople and brought to an end the long history of Byzantium.

Explore the era further in MindTap with videos of major artworks and buildings, Google Earth™ coordinates, and essays by the author on the following additional subjects:

- Good Shepherd statuette (FIG. 4-2A)
- Santa Sabina, Rome (FIGS. 4-4A and 4-4B)
- ▌ART AND SOCIETY: Medieval Books
- *Ascension of Christ, Rabbula Gospels* (FIG. 4-18A)

EARLY CHRISTIANITY AND BYZANTIUM

Early Christianity

- Very little Christian art or architecture survives from the first centuries of Christianity. "Early Christian art" means the earliest art having Christian subjects, not the art of Christians at the time of Jesus. The major surviving examples are frescoes in the catacombs of Rome and marble sarcophagi depicting Old and New Testament stories.

- Constantine (r. 306–337) issued the Edict of Milan in 313, granting Christianity legal status equal or superior to the traditional Roman cults. The emperor was the first great patron of Christian art and built the first churches in Rome, including Old Saint Peter's. In 330, he moved the capital of the Roman Empire to Constantinople (Greek Byzantium).

- The emperor Theodosius I (r. 379–395) proclaimed Christianity the official religion of the Roman Empire in 380 and banned worship of the old Roman gods in 391. Honorius (r. 395–423) moved the capital of his Western Roman Empire to Ravenna in 404. Rome fell to the Visigoth king Alaric in 410.

- Mosaics became a major vehicle for the depiction of Christian themes in the naves and apses of churches, which closely resembled Roman basilicas in both plan and elevation.

Catacomb of Saints Peter and Marcellinus, Rome, early fourth century

Old Saint Peter's, Rome, begun ca. 319

Byzantium

- The reign of Justinian (r. 527–565) opened the first golden age of Byzantine art (527–726). Justinian was a great patron of the arts, and in Constantinople alone he built or restored more than 30 churches, including Hagia Sophia. A brilliant fusion of central and longitudinal plans, the church featured a 180-foot-high dome resting on pendentives, rivaling the architectural wonders of Rome.

- The seat of Byzantine power in Italy was Ravenna, which also prospered under Justinian. San Vitale is Ravenna's greatest church. Its mosaics, with their weightless, hovering, frontal figures against a gold background, reveal the new Byzantine aesthetic.

- Justinian also rebuilt the monastery at Mount Sinai in Egypt, which boasts the finest surviving Early Byzantine icons. The first manuscripts with biblical illustrations also date to the early sixth century. In 726, however, Leo III (r. 717–741) enacted a ban against picturing the divine, initiating the era of iconoclasm (726–843).

- Middle Byzantine (843–1204) churches, such as those at Hosios Loukas and Daphni, have highly decorative exterior walls, and feature domes resting on drums above the center of a Greek cross. The climax of the interior mosaic programs was often an image of Christ as Pantokrator in the dome. Middle Byzantine artists also excelled in ivory carving and manuscript illumination. The *Paris Psalter* is noteworthy for its revival of classical naturalism.

- In 1204, Latin Crusaders sacked Constantinople, bringing to an end the second golden age of Byzantine art. In 1261, Michael VIII Palaeologus (r. 1259–1282) succeeded in recapturing the city. Constantinople remained in Byzantine hands until it was taken in 1453 by the Ottoman Turks.

Hagia Sophia, Constantinople, 532–537

San Vitale, Ravenna, ca. 547

Church of the Dormition, Daphni, ca. 1090–1100

▲ **5-1a** Islamic architecture draws on diverse sources. The horseshoe arches of the Córdoba mosque's prayer hall may derive from Visigothic architecture. The Arabs overthrew that Christian kingdom in 711.

▲ **5-1b** In the 10th century, al-Hakam II added a maqsura to the Córdoba mosque. The hall highlights Muslim architects' bold experimentation with curvilinear shapes and different kinds of arches.

5-1 Aerial view of the Great Mosque (looking east), Córdoba, Spain, 8th to 10th centuries; rededicated as the Cathedral of Saint Mary, 1236.

▶ **5-1c** Byzantine artists installed the mosaics in the dome of the Córdoba mosque's mihrab, but the decorative patterns formed by the crisscrossing ribs and the multilobed arches are distinctly Islamic.

The Islamic World

THE RISE AND SPREAD OF ISLAM

At the time of Muhammad's birth around 570, the Arabian peninsula was peripheral to the Byzantine and Sasanian Empires. The Arabs, nomadic herders and caravan merchants who worshiped many gods, resisted the Prophet's teachings of Islam, an Arabic word meaning "submission to the one God (Allah in Arabic)." Within a decade of Mohammad's death in 632, however, Muslims ("those who submit") ruled Arabia, Palestine, Syria, Iraq, and northern Egypt. From there, the new religion spread rapidly both eastward and westward.

With the rise of Islam also came the birth of a compelling new worldwide tradition of art and architecture. In the Middle East and North Africa, Islamic art largely replaced Late Roman, Early Christian, and Byzantine art. In India, the establishment of Muslim rule at Delhi in the early 13th century brought Islamic art and architecture to South Asia (see page 473). In fact, perhaps the most famous building in Asia, the Taj Mahal (FIG. 17-19) at Agra, is an Islamic mausoleum. At the opposite end of the then-known world, in Spain, Abd al-Rahman I (r. 756–788) founded a Muslim dynasty at Córdoba, which became the center of a brilliant court culture that profoundly influenced medieval Europe.

The jewel of the capital at Córdoba was its Great Mosque (FIG. 5-1), begun in 784 and enlarged several times during the 9th and 10th centuries until it eventually became one of the largest *mosques* in the Islamic West (see "The Mosque," page 147). In 1236, the Christians converted the shrine into a church (the tallest part of the complex, at the center of the aerial view) after they captured the city from the Muslims.

A visual feast greets all visitors to the remodeled mosque of al-Hakam II (r. 961–976), whose designers used horseshoe-shaped arches (which became synonymous with Islamic architecture in Europe) to crown the more than 500 columns in the mosque's huge prayer hall. Even more elaborate multilobed arches on slender columns form dazzling frames for other areas of the mosque, especially in the *maqsura,* the hall reserved for the ruler, which at Córdoba connects the mosque to the palace. Crisscrossing ribs form intricate decorative patterns in the complex's largest dome.

The Córdoba *mezquita* (Spanish, "mosque") typifies Islamic architecture both in its conformity to the basic principles of mosque design and in its incorporation of distinctive regional forms.

MUHAMMAD AND ISLAM

The religion of Islam arose in Arabia early in the seventh century (see "Muhammad and Islam," page 145). At that time, the Arabs were not major players on the world stage. Yet within little more than a century, Muslim armies had subdued the Middle East, and the followers of Muhammad controlled much of the Mediterranean (MAP 5-1). The swiftness of the Islamic advance is among the wonders of history. By 640, Muslims ruled Syria, Palestine, and Iraq. In 642, the Byzantine army abandoned Alexandria, marking the Muslim conquest of northern Egypt. In 651, Islamic forces ended more than 400 years of Sasanian rule in Iran. All of North Africa was under Muslim control by 710. A victory in southern Spain in 711 seemed to open all of western Europe to the Muslims. By 732, they had advanced north to Poitiers in France. There, however, the Franks turned them back. In Spain, in contrast, the Muslim rulers of Córdoba (FIG. 5-1) flourished until 1031, and not until 1492 did Islamic influence and power end in Iberia. In the East, the Muslims reached the Indus River by 751. In Anatolia, relentless Muslim pressure against the shrinking Byzantine Empire eventually caused its collapse in 1453.

ARCHITECTURE

During the early centuries of Islamic history, the Muslim world's political and cultural center was the Fertile Crescent of ancient Mesopotamia (see page 22). The caliphs of Damascus (capital of modern Syria) and Baghdad (capital of Iraq) appointed provincial governors to rule the vast territories they controlled. These governors eventually gained relative independence by setting up dynasties in various territories and provinces, most notably the Umayyads in Syria and in Spain and the Abbasids in Iraq (see "Major Muslim Dynasties"). Like other potentates before and after, the Muslim caliphs were builders on a grand scale.

DOME OF THE ROCK The Muslims captured Jerusalem from the Byzantines in 638, and the first great Islamic building—the Dome of the Rock (FIG. 5-2)—was erected there between 687 and 692 by the Umayyad caliph Abd al-Malik (r. 685–705). The monumental shrine is not a mosque, as popularly thought, but an architectural tribute to the triumph of Islam. The Dome of the Rock marked the coming of the new religion to the city that had been, and still is, sacred to both Jews and Christians. It stands on the spot where the

MAP 5-1 The Islamic World around 1500.

THE ISLAMIC WORLD

622-756
- Muhammad abandons Mecca for Medina in 722.
- The Umayyads, the first Islamic dynasty, build the Dome of the Rock to celebrate the triumph of Islam in Jerusalem.

756-1453
- The Abbasids produce the earliest Korans with Kufic calligraphy.
- The Spanish Umayyad dynasty builds the Great Mosque in their capital at Córdoba.
- The Nasrids construct magnificent palaces in the Alhambra.
- In Egypt, the Mamluks are great patrons of art and architecture.

1453-1924
- Manuscript painting flourishes at the Timurid and Safavid courts.
- The Ottomans capture Byzantine Constantinople in 1453.

RELIGION AND MYTHOLOGY
Muhammad and Islam

Muhammad, revered by Muslims as the Final Prophet in the line including Abraham, Moses, and Jesus, was a native of Mecca on the west coast of Arabia. Born around 570 into a family of merchants, Muhammad was critical of the polytheistic religion of his fellow Arabs. In 610, he began to receive the revelations of God through the archangel Gabriel. Opposition to Muhammad's message among the Arabs was strong, and in 622, the Prophet and his followers abandoned Mecca for a desert oasis eventually called Medina ("City of the Prophet"). Islam dates its beginning from this flight—known as the *Hijra* (Arabic, "emigration"). Barely eight years later, in 630, Muhammad returned to Mecca with 10,000 soldiers. He took control of the city, converted the population to Islam, and destroyed all the idols. But he preserved as the Islamic world's symbolic center the small cubical building that had housed the idols, the *Kaaba* (from the Arabic for "cube"). The Arabs associated the Kaaba with the era of Abraham and Ishmael, the common ancestors of Jews and Arabs. Muhammad died in Medina in 632.

The essential tenet of Islam is acceptance of and submission to God's will. Muslims must live according to the rules laid down in the collected revelations communicated through Muhammad during his lifetime and recorded in the Koran, Islam's sacred book. The word *Koran* means "recitations"—a reference to Gabriel's instructions to Muhammad in 610 to "recite in the name of God."

The profession of faith in the one God is the first of the Five Pillars binding all Muslims. In addition, the faithful must worship five times daily facing Mecca, give alms to the poor, fast during the month of Ramadan, and once in a lifetime—if possible—make a pilgrimage to Mecca. The revelations in the Koran are not the only guide for Muslims. Muhammad's words and exemplary ways and customs, the *Hadith*, recorded in the *Sunnah*, offer models to all Muslims on ethical problems of everyday life. The reward for the faithful is Paradise.

Islam has much in common with Judaism and Christianity. Muslims think of their religion as a continuation, completion, and in some sense a reformation of those other great monotheisms. Islam, for example, incorporates many Hebrew biblical teachings, with their sober ethical standards and rejection of idol worship. But, unlike Jesus, Muhammad did not claim to be divine. Rather, he was God's messenger, the Final Prophet, who purified and perfected the common faith of Jews, Christians, and Muslims in one God. Islam also differs from Judaism and Christianity in its simpler organization. Muslims worship God directly, without a hierarchy of rabbis, priests, or saints acting as intermediaries.

In Islam, as Muhammad defined it in the seventh century, the union of religious and secular authority was even more complete than in Byzantium. Muhammad established a new social order and took complete charge of his community's temporal as well as spiritual affairs. After Muhammad's death, the *caliphs* (from the Arabic for "successor") continued this practice of uniting religious and political leadership in one ruler.

5-2 Dome of the Rock (looking east), Jerusalem, 687–692.

Abd al-Malik erected the Dome of the Rock to mark the triumph of Islam in Jerusalem on a site sacred to Muslims, Christians, and Jews. The shrine takes the form of an octagon with a towering dome.

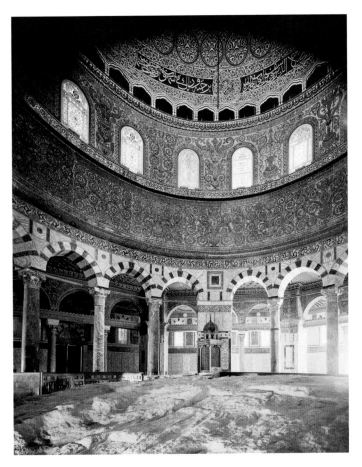

5-3 Interior of the Dome of the Rock, Jerusalem, 687–692.

The Dome of the Rock is a domed central-plan rotunda. At the center of the rotunda, below the dome, is the rocky outcropping later associated with Adam, Abraham, and Muhammad.

in its basic design. A neighboring Christian monument, Constantine's Church of the Holy Sepulchre, seems to have been the immediate model. That fourth-century domed *rotunda* bore a family resemblance to the roughly contemporaneous Santa Costanza (FIG. 4-5) in Rome. Crowning the Islamic shrine is a 75-foot-tall double-shelled wood dome, which so dominates the elevation as to reduce the octagon to functioning visually merely as its base. This soaring, majestic unit creates a decidedly more commanding effect than that of similar Late Roman and Byzantine domical structures (for example, FIG. 4-10). The silhouettes of those domes are comparatively insignificant when seen from the outside.

The Dome of the Rock's exterior has been much restored. Tiling from the 16th century and later has replaced the original mosaic. Yet the vivid, colorful patterning wrapping the walls like a textile is typical of Islamic ornamentation. It contrasts markedly with Byzantine brickwork and Greco-Roman sculptured decoration. The rich mosaic ornamentation ringing the base of the dome (FIG. 5-4) is largely intact and suggests the original appearance of the exterior walls. Against a lush vegetal background, Abd al-Malik's mosaicists depicted crowns, jewels, chalices, and other royal motifs—probably a reference to the triumph of Islam over the Byzantine and Persian Empires. Inscriptions, mostly from the Koran, underscore Islam as the superior new monotheism, superseding both Judaism and Christianity in Jerusalem.

KAIROUAN The Dome of the Rock is a unique monument. Throughout the Islamic world, the most important buildings were mosques (see "The Mosque," page 147). Of all the variations, the *hypostyle mosque* most closely reflects the mosque's supposed precursor, Muhammad's house in Medina. One of the oldest well-preserved hypostyle mosques is the mid-eighth-century Great Mosque (FIG. 5-5) at Kairouan in Tunisia. Like the Dome of the

Hebrews built the Temple of Solomon, which the Roman emperor Titus destroyed in the year 70 (see page 102). Eventually, the site acquired additional significance as the reputed location of Adam's grave and the spot where Abraham prepared to sacrifice Isaac. It houses the rock (FIG. 5-3) that later came to be identified with the place where Muhammad began his miraculous journey to Heaven (the *Miraj*) and then, in the same night, returned to his home in Mecca.

In its form, construction, and decoration, the Dome of the Rock is firmly in the Late Roman/Byzantine tradition. It is a domed octagon resembling San Vitale (FIG. 4-14) in Ravenna

5-4 View into the dome of the Dome of the Rock, Jerusalem, 687–692.

The mosaics ringing the base of the dome inside the Dome of the Rock are largely intact and suggest the original appearance of the exterior walls, today covered with 16th-century ceramic tiles.

ARCHITECTURAL BASICS
The Mosque

Islamic religious architecture is closely related to Muslim prayer. In Islam, worshiping can be a private act and requires neither prescribed ceremony nor a special locale. Only the *qibla*—the direction (toward Mecca) that Muslims face while praying—is important. But worship also became a communal act when the first Muslim community established a simple ritual for it. To celebrate the Muslim sabbath, which occurs on Friday, the community convened each Friday at noon, probably in the Prophet's house in Medina. The main feature of Muhammad's house was a large, square court with rows of palm trunks supporting thatched roofs along the north and south sides. The southern side, which faced Mecca, was wider and had a double row of trunks. The *imam*, or leader of collective worship, stood on a stepped pulpit, or *minbar*, set up in front of the southern (qibla) wall.

These features became standard in the Islamic house of worship, the *mosque* (from Arabic *masjid*, "a place of prostration"), where the faithful gather for the five daily prayers. The *congregational mosque* (also called the *Friday mosque* or *great mosque*) was ideally large enough to accommodate a community's entire population for the Friday noon prayer. An important feature both of ordinary and of congregational mosques is the *mihrab* (FIGS. 5-5, no. 2, and 5-12), a semicircular niche set into the qibla wall. Often a dome over the bay in front of the mihrab marked its position (FIGS. 5-5, no. 3, and 5-8). The niche—a common feature in Roman buildings, generally enclosing a statue—may honor the place where the Prophet stood in his house at Medina when he led communal worship.

In some mosques, a *maqsura* precedes the mihrab. The maqsura is the area reserved for the ruler or his representative. Mosques may also have one or more *minarets* (FIGS. 5-5, no. 8, and 5-6), towers used to call Muslims to worship. Early mosques were generally hypostyle halls, communal worship halls with roofs held up by a multitude of columns (FIGS. 5-5, no. 4, and 5-7). An important later variation is the mosque with four *iwans* (vaulted rectangular recesses), one on each side of a courtyard (FIG. 5-11).

Today, despite many variations in design and detail and the employment of building techniques and materials unknown in Muhammad's day, the mosque's essential features remain unchanged. The orientation of all mosques everywhere, whatever their plan, is Mecca, and the faithful worship facing the qibla wall.

5-5 Aerial view (looking north; *left*) and plan (*right*) of the Great Mosque, Kairouan, Tunisia, ca. 836–875.

Kairouan's Great Mosque is an early hypostyle mosque with forecourt and columnar prayer hall (with two domes). The plan most closely resembles the layout of Muhammad's house in Medina.

1. Qibla wall	5. Nave
2. Mihrab	6. Entrance dome
3. Mihrab dome	7. Forecourt
4. Hypostyle prayer hall	8. Minaret

Rock, the Kairouan mosque owes much to Greco-Roman and Early Christian architecture. The huge precinct is some 450 by 260 feet. Lateral entrances on the east and west lead to an arcaded forecourt (FIG. 5-5, no. 7) resembling a Roman forum (FIG. 3-35) or the atrium of an Early Christian basilica (FIGS. 4-3 and 4-4). The courtyard is oriented north-south on axis with the mosque's *minaret* (no. 8) and the two domes (nos. 3 and 6) of the hypostyle prayer hall (no. 4). The first dome (no. 6) is over the entrance bay, the second (no. 3) over the bay that fronts the *mihrab* (no. 2) set into the *qibla* wall (no. 1). A raised nave (no. 5) connects the domed spaces and prolongs the north-south axis of the minaret and courtyard. Eight columned aisles flank the nave on either side, providing space for a large congregation. The hypostyle mosque synthesizes elements received from other cultures into a novel architectural unity.

SAMARRA The three-story minaret of the Kairouan mosque is square in plan and believed to be a near copy of a Roman lighthouse. Minarets can take a variety of forms, however. Perhaps

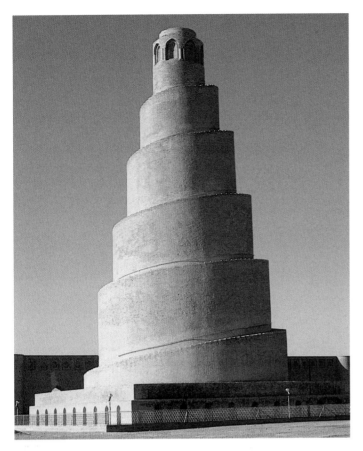

5-6 Malwiya Minaret (looking southwest), Great Mosque, Samarra, Iraq, 848–852.

The unique spiral Malwiya (snail shell) Minaret of Samarra's Great Mosque is more than 165 feet tall and can be seen from afar. It served to announce the presence of Islam in the Tigris Valley.

the minaret to the mosque. The distinguishing feature of the brick tower is its stepped spiral ramp, which increases in slope from bottom to top in order to keep each stage the same height. Because the Malwiya Minaret is too tall to have been used to call Muslims to prayer, the Abbasids probably intended the tower, which is visible from a considerable distance in the flat plain around Samarra, to announce the presence of Islam in the Tigris Valley.

CÓRDOBA At the time that the Umayyads built the Kairouan mosque (FIG. 5-5), the Abbasids ruled much of North Africa. In 750, they had overthrown the Umayyad caliphs and moved the capital from Damascus to Baghdad. Abd-al-Rahman I (r. 756–788), the only Umayyad notable to escape the Abbasid massacre of his clan in Syria, fled to Spain in 750, where the Arabs had overthrown the Christian kingdom of the Visigoths in 711. The Arabs accepted the fugitive as their overlord, and he founded the Spanish Umayyad dynasty. Their capital was Córdoba, which became the center of a brilliant culture rivaling that of the Abbasids at Baghdad and exerting major influence on the civilization of the Christian West.

The centerpiece of Umayyad Córdoba was its Mezquita—Great Mosque (FIG. 5-1)—begun in 784 by Abd al-Rahman I. The hypostyle prayer hall (FIG. 5-7), remodeled several times, has 36 piers and 514 columns topped by a unique system of double-tiered arches that originally supported a timber roof (later replaced by vaults). The two-story system was the builders' response to the need to raise the roof to an acceptable height using short columns that had been employed earlier in other structures, both *Visigothic* and Roman. The lower arches are horseshoe shaped, a form perhaps adapted from earlier Mesopotamian architecture or of Visigothic origin. In the West, the horseshoe-shaped arch quickly became closely associated with Muslim architecture. Visually, these arches seem to billow out like windblown sails, and they contribute greatly to the light and airy effect of the Córdoba mosque's interior.

the most striking and novel is the spiral minaret of the Great Mosque at Samarra, Iraq, the capital of the Abbasid caliph al-Mutawakkil (r. 847–861), who built the mosque between 848 and 852. At the time of its construction, the Samarra mosque, which covers an area of more than 45,000 square yards, was the largest in the world. Known as the *Malwiya* ("snail shell" in Arabic) Minaret (FIG. 5-6), the tower is more than 165 feet tall. Although it now stands alone, originally a bridge linked

5-7 Prayer hall of the Mezquita (Great Mosque), Córdoba, Spain, 8th to 10th centuries.

Córdoba was the capital of the Spanish Umayyad dynasty. In the Great Mosque's hypostyle prayer hall, 36 piers and 514 columns support a unique series of double-tiered horseshoe-shaped arches.

5-8 Dome in front of the mihrab of the Mezquita (Great Mosque), Córdoba, Spain, 961–965.

The dome in front of the Córdoba mihrab rests on an octagonal base of arcuated squinches. The crisscrossing ribs and multilobed arches exemplify Islamic experimentation with abstract patterning.

In 961, al-Hakam II (r. 961–976) became caliph and immediately undertook major renovations to Córdoba's Mezquita, including the addition of a series of domes in the prayer hall to emphasize the axis leading to the mihrab. The dome (FIG. 5-8) covering the area in front of the mihrab rests on an octagonal base crisscrossed by ribs that form an intricate pattern centered on two squares set at 45-degree angles to each other. It is a prime example of Islamic experimentation with highly decorative multilobed arches. The Muslim builders created rich and varied abstract patterns and further enhanced the magnificent effect of the complex arches by sheathing the surfaces with mosaics. Al-Hakam II brought the mosaicists and even the tesserae to Spain from Constantinople.

ALHAMBRA In the early years of the 11th century, the Umayyad caliphs' power in Spain unraveled, and their palaces fell prey to Berber soldiers from North Africa. The Berbers ruled southern Spain for several generations, but could not resist the pressure of Christian forces from the north. Córdoba fell to the Christians in 1236. From then until the final Christian triumph in 1492, the Nasrids, an Arab dynasty that had established its capital at Granada in 1232, ruled the remaining Muslim territories in Spain. On a rocky spur at Granada, the Nasrids constructed a huge palace-fortress called the Alhambra ("the Red" in Arabic), named for the rose color of the stone used for its walls and 23 towers. By the end of the 14th century, the complex was home to 40,000 and included at least a half dozen royal residences.

The Palace of the Lions takes its name from its courtyard (FIG. 5-9), which contains a fountain with 12 marble lions carrying

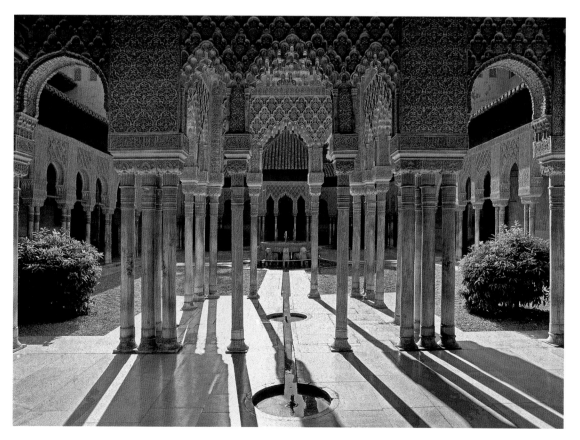

5-9 Court of the Lions (looking east), Palace of the Lions, Alhambra, Granada, Spain, 1354–1391.

The Nasrid Palace of the Lions takes its name from the fountain in this courtyard, a rare Islamic example of stone sculpture. Interwoven abstract ornamentation and Arabic calligraphy cover the stucco walls.

5-10 Muqarnas dome, Hall of the
Abencerrajes, Palace of the Lions,
Alhambra, Granada, Spain, 1354–1391.

The structure of this dome on an octagonal
drum is difficult to discern because of the intricately carved stucco muqarnas. The prismatic
forms reflect sunlight, creating the effect of a
starry sky.

a water basin on their backs. The Alhambra's lion fountain is an unusual instance
of freestanding stone sculpture in the
Islamic world, unthinkable in a sacred
setting. But the design of the courtyard
is distinctly Islamic and features many
multilobed *pointed arches* and carved
stucco walls with interwoven abstract
motifs and Arabic *calligraphy* (ornamental writing). The palace was the residence
of Muhammad V (r. 1354–1391), and its
courtyards, lush gardens, and luxurious
carpets and other furnishings served to
conjure the image of Paradise.

The Palace of the Lions is noteworthy also for its elaborate stucco ceilings.
A spectacular example is the dome (FIG.
5-10) of the so-called Hall of the Aben-
cerrajes (a leading Spanish family). The dome rests on an octagonal
drum supported by squinches (FIG. 4-13, *right*) and pierced by eight
pairs of windows, but its structure is difficult to discern because of
the intricate carved stucco decoration. Some 5,000 *muqarnas*—tier

after tier of stalactite-like prismatic forms that seem aimed at denying the structure's solidity—cover the ceiling. The muqarnas catch
and reflect sunlight as well as form beautiful abstract patterns. The
lofty vault in this hall and others in the palace symbolize the dome

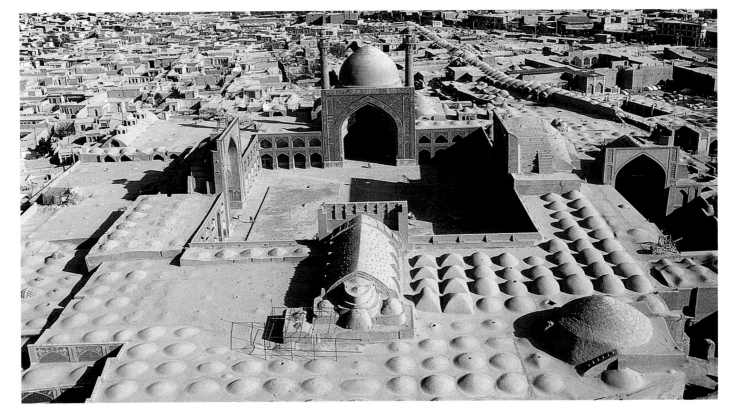

5-11 Aerial view of the Friday Mosque (looking southwest), Isfahan, Iran, 11th to 17th centuries.

Mosques take a variety of forms. In Iran, the standard type of mosque has four vaulted iwans opening onto a courtyard. The largest (qibla)
iwan leads into a dome-covered maqsura in front of the mihrab.

of Heaven. The flickering light and shadows create the effect of a starry sky as the sun's rays glide from window to window during the day. To underscore the symbolism, the palace walls were inscribed with verses by the court poet Ibn Zamrak (1333–1393), who compared the Alhambra's lacelike muqarnas ceilings to "the heavenly spheres whose orbits revolve."

ISFAHAN In the Middle Eastern core of the Islamic world, in Iran, successive dynasties erected a series of mosques at Isfahan. The first and largest is the Friday Mosque (FIG. 5-11), constructed by the Abbasids during the eighth century. In the late 11th century, the Seljuk *sultan* (ruler) Malik Shah I (r. 1072–1092) transformed the Abbasid hypostyle structure into a distinctly Iranian mosque with a large courtyard bordered by an arcade on each side. Four vaulted iwans open onto the courtyard, one at the center of each side. The southwestern iwan leads into a dome-covered room in front of the mihrab that functioned as a maqsura reserved for the sultan and his attendants. It is uncertain whether Isfahan's Friday Mosque is the earliest example of a four-iwan mosque, but that plan became standard in Iranian religious architecture. In this type of mosque, the qibla iwan is always the largest. Its size (and the dome that often accompanied it) immediately indicated to worshipers the proper direction for prayer.

MADRASA IMAMI The iwans of the Isfahan mosque feature soaring pointed arches framing tile-sheathed muqarnas vaults. The muqarnas ceilings probably date to the 14th century. The ceramic-tile revetment on the walls and vaults is the work of the 17th-century Safavid dynasty (r. 1501–1732) of Iran. The use of glazed tiles has a long history in Mesopotamia (FIG. 1-20) and Persia. The golden age of Islamic ceramic tilework was the 16th and 17th centuries in Iran and Turkey. Employed as a veneer over a brick core, tiles could sheathe entire buildings (FIG. 5-2), including domes and minarets.

One of the masterworks of Iranian tilework is the 14th-century mihrab (FIG. 5-12) from the Madrasa Imami in Isfahan. (A *madrasa* is an Islamic theological college, often incorporating a mosque.) It is also a splendid example of Arabic calligraphy. The Islamic world held the art of calligraphy in high esteem, and the walls of buildings often displayed the sacred words of the Koran. Quotations from the Koran appear, for example, in a mosaic band above the outer ring of columns inside the Dome of the Rock (FIG. 5-4). The Isfahan mihrab exemplifies the perfect aesthetic union between calligraphy and abstract ornamentation. The pointed arch framing the mihrab niche bears an inscription from the Koran in an early stately rectilinear script called *Kufic*, after the city of Kufah, one of the renowned centers of Arabic calligraphy. A cursive style, *Muhaqqaq*, fills the mihrab's outer rectangular frame. The tile decoration on the curving surface of the niche and the area above the pointed arch consists of tighter and looser networks of geometric and abstract floral motifs. The tilework technique used here is the most difficult of all the varieties Islamic artisans practiced: *mosaic tilework*. Every piece had to be cut to fit its specific place in the mihrab—even the tile inscriptions. The ceramist smoothly integrated the subtly varied decorative patterns with the framed inscription in the center of the niche proclaiming that the mosque is the domicile of the pious believer. The mihrab's outermost inscription—detailing the Five Pillars of Islamic faith—serves as a fringelike extension, as well as a boundary, for the entire design. The unification of calligraphic and geometric elements is so complete that only the practiced eye can distinguish them.

5-12 Mihrab, from the Madrasa Imami, Isfahan, Iran, ca. 1354. Glazed mosaic tilework, 11' 3" × 7' 6". Metropolitan Museum of Art, New York.

This Iranian mihrab is a masterpiece of Iranian tilework, but it is also a splendid example of Arabic calligraphy. In the Islamic world, the walls of buildings often displayed the sacred words of the Koran.

LUXURY ARTS

In the smaller-scale, and often private, realm of the luxury arts, often referred to as *minor arts*, Muslim artists also excelled. In the Islamic world, the term *minor arts* is especially inappropriate. Although of modest size, the manuscripts, ivories, textiles, colored glass, and metalwork that Muslim artists produced in great quantities are among the finest works of any age. From the vast array of Islamic luxury arts, a selection of several masterpieces may serve to suggest both the range and quality of small-scale Islamic art.

KORANS The earliest preserved Korans date to the ninth century, and the finest of them are masterpieces of Arabic calligraphy. Muslim scribes wanted to reproduce the Koran's sacred words in a script as beautiful as human hands could contrive. Koran pages were either bound into books or stored as loose sheets in boxes. Most of the early examples feature the angular Kufic script used in the central panel of the Madrasa Imami mihrab (FIG. 5-12). Arabic is written from right to left, with certain characters connected by a baseline. In Kufic script, the uprights usually form right angles with

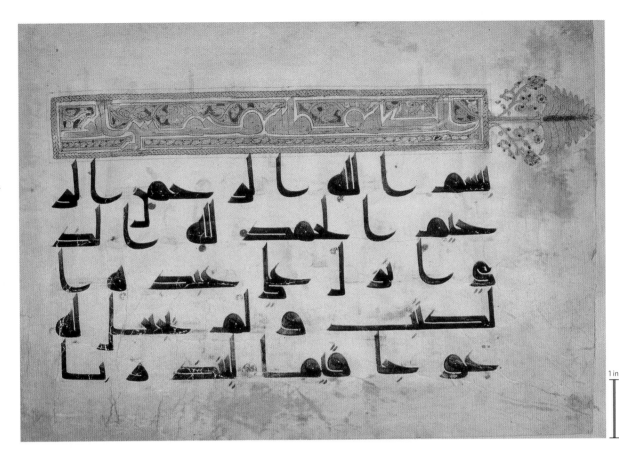

5-13 Koran page with beginning of surah 18, 9th or early 10th century. Ink and gold on vellum, $7\frac{1}{4}$" × $10\frac{1}{4}$". Chester Beatty Library and Oriental Art Gallery, Dublin.

The script used in the oldest-known Korans is the stately rectilinear Kufic. This page has five text lines and a palm-tree finial, but characteristically does not include depictions of animals or humans.

1 in.

the baseline. As with Hebrew and other Semitic languages, the usual practice was to write in consonants only. But to facilitate recitation of the Koran, scribes often indicated vowels by red or yellow symbols above or below the line.

All of these features are present in a 9th- or early 10th-century Koran page (FIG. 5-13) now in Dublin, which carries the heading and opening five text lines of *surah* (chapter) 18. The text lines are in black ink with red vowels, below a decorative band incorporating the chapter title in gold and ending in a palm-tree *finial* (a crowning ornament). This approach to page design has parallels in the early medieval manuscripts of Britain and Ireland, where text and ornamentation were similarly united (FIG. 6-4). But the stylized human and animal forms that populate those Christian books never appear in Korans. Islamic tradition shuns the representation of fauna of any kind in sacred contexts. This also explains the total absence of figural ornament in mosques, setting the Islamic world sharply apart from both the classical world and Christian Europe and Byzantium.

IVORY CARVING The centers of production for objects fashioned from more costly materials, such as ivory (FIG. 5-14) or brass inlaid with gold and silver (FIG. 5-14A ⊿), were usually the courts of the Muslim caliphs and sultans. One was Córdoba (FIGS. 5-1, 5-7, and 5-8). Abd al-Rahman III (r. 912–961), a descendant of the founder of the Umayyad dynasty in Spain, became *emir* (ruler) when he was 22. In 929, he declared himself caliph, a title previously restricted to the Muslim rulers who controlled the holy cities of Mecca and Medina. During his nearly 50-year reign, he constructed a lavish new palace for himself and his successors at Medina al-Zahra, about five miles from Córdoba. The palace complex housed royal

workshops for the production of luxury items for the caliph's family and for use as diplomatic gifts, including richly carved ivory boxes. Befitting their prospective owners, Spanish Umayyad ivory *pyxides* (singular, *pyxis*; a cylindrical box with a hemispherical lid) usually featured motifs symbolic of royal power and privilege, including hunting scenes and musical entertainments.

The pyxis shown here (FIG. 5-14) belonged to al-Mughira, the younger son of Abd al-Rahman III. The inscription carved at the base of the lid is a prayer for the 18-year-old prince's well-being: "God's blessing, favors, and happiness to al-Mughira, son of the commander of the faithful [the standard epithet for caliphs], may God have mercy upon him, in the year 357 [968 CE]." The anonymous ivory carver decorated the pyxis with a rich array of animals and hunters amid lush vine scrolls surrounding four eight-lobed figural medallions. In one medallion, lions attack bulls. In another (not visible in FIG. 5-14), the prince himself appears, serenaded by a lutenist.

ARDABIL CARPETS Because wood is scarce in most of the Islamic world, the kinds of furniture used in the West—beds, tables, and chairs—are rare in Muslim buildings. A room's function (eating or sleeping, for example) can change simply by rearranging the carpets and cushions. Textiles are among the glories of Islamic art. Unfortunately, because of their fragile nature and the heavy wear that carpets endure, only a few fragmentary early Islamic textiles have been preserved. Perhaps the best later example of the weaver's art is a pair of carpets from the funerary mosque in Ardabil, Iran, of Shaykh Safi al-Din (1252–1334), the founder of the Safavid line. The carpets date to 1540, however—two centuries after the construction of the mosque, during the reign of Shah Tahmasp (r. 1524–1576).

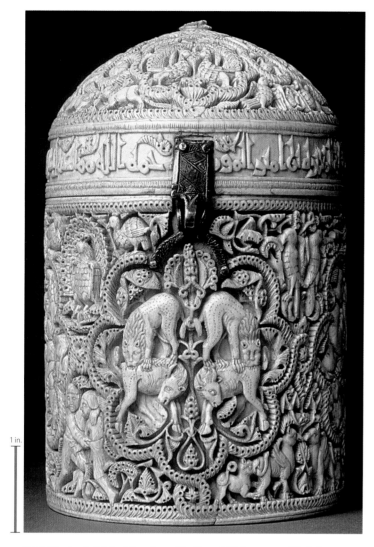

5-14 Pyxis of al-Mughira, from Medina al-Zahra, near Córdoba, Spain, 968. Ivory, $5\frac{7}{8}$" high. Musée du Louvre, Paris.

The royal workshops of Abd al-Rahman III produced luxurious objects such as this ivory pyxis decorated with hunting motifs and vine scrolls. It belonged to al-Mughira, the caliph's younger son.

5-15 MAQSUD OF KASHAN, carpet from the funerary mosque of Shaykh Safi al-Din, Ardabil, Iran, 1540. Knotted pile of wool and silk, 34' 6" × 17' 7". Victoria & Albert Museum, London.

Textiles are among the glories of Islamic art. This carpet required roughly 25 million knots. It presents the illusion of a heavenly dome with mosque lamps reflected in a lotus-blossom-filled pool of water.

Tahmasp elevated carpet weaving to a national industry and set up royal factories at Isfahan, Kashan, Kirman, and Tabriz. The name of MAQSUD OF KASHAN appears as part of the design of the Ardabil carpet illustrated here (FIG. 5-15). Maqsud must have been the artist who supplied the master pattern to two teams of royal weavers (one for each of the two carpets). The almost 35-by-18-foot carpet consists of roughly 25 million knots, some 340 to the square inch. (Its twin has even more knots.)

The design consists of a central sunburst medallion, representing the inside of a dome, surrounded by 16 pendants. Mosque lamps (compare FIG. 5-15A ⧉)—appropriate motifs for the Ardabil funerary mosque—hang from two pendants on the long axis of the carpet. The lamps are of different sizes. This may be an optical device to make the two appear equal in size when viewed from the end of the carpet at the room's threshold (the bottom end in FIG. 5-15). Covering the rich blue background are leaves and flowers attached to delicate stems that spread over the whole field. The entire composition presents the illusion of a heavenly dome with lamps reflected in a pool of water full of floating lotus blossoms.

TIMURIDS In the late 14th century, a new Islamic empire arose in Central Asia under the leadership of Timur (r. 1370–1405), known in the Western world as Tamerlane. Timur, a successor of the Mongol conqueror Genghis Khan (see page 495), quickly extended his dominions to include Iran and parts of Anatolia. The Timurids, who ruled until 1501, were great patrons of art and architecture in Herat, Bukhara, Samarqand, and other cities. Herat in particular became a leading center for the production of luxurious books under the patronage of the Timurid sultan Husayn Mayqara (r. 1470–1506).

5-16 SULTAN-MUHAMMAD, *Court of Gayumars,* folio 20 verso of the *Shahnama* of Shah Tahmasp, from Tabriz, Iran, ca. 1525–1535. Ink, watercolor, and gold on paper, 1' 1" × 9". Prince Sadruddin Aga Khan Collection, Geneva.

Sultan-Muhammad painted the legend of King Gayumars for the Safavid ruler Shah Tahmasp. The off-center placement on the page enhances the sense of lightness permeating the painting.

In contrast to Korans (FIG. 5-13), Timurid secular books—for example, the *Bustan* (FIG. 5-15B ⏺), with paintings by BIHZAD—often featured full-page narrative paintings with human and animal figures.

SAFAVID *SHAHNAMA* The successors of the Timurids in Iran were the Safavids. Shah Tahmasp, the Safavid ruler who commissioned the Ardabil carpets (FIG. 5-15), was also a great patron of books. Around 1525, he commissioned an ambitious decade-long project to produce an illustrated 742-page copy of the *Shahnama* (*Book of Kings*). The *Shahnama*, the Persian national epic poem by Firdawsi (940–1025), recounts the history of Iran from creation until the Muslim conquest. Tahmasp's *Shahnama* contains 258 illustrations by many artists, including some of the most admired painters of the day.

The page reproduced here (FIG. 5-16) is the work of SULTAN-MUHAMMAD and depicts Gayumars, the legendary first king of Iran, and his court. According to tradition, Gayumars ruled from a mountaintop when humans first learned to cook food and clothe themselves in leopard skins. In Sultan-Muhammad's representation of the story, Gayumars presides over his court from his mountain throne. The king is surrounded by light amid a golden sky. His son and grandson perch on multicolored rocky outcroppings to the viewer's left and right, respectively. The court encircles the ruler and his heirs. All of the figures wear leopard skins. Dozens of human faces appear among the rocks, and many species of animals populate the lush landscape. According to the *Shahnama*, wild beasts became instantly tame in the presence of Gayumars. Sultan-Muhammad rendered the figures, animals, trees, rocks, and sky with an extraordinarily delicate touch. The sense of lightness and airiness permeating the painting is enhanced by its placement on the page—floating, off center, on a speckled background of gold leaf. The painter gave his royal patron a singular vision of Iran's fabled past.

ISLAM IN ASIA Islamic artists and architects also brought their distinctive style to South Asia, where a Muslim sultanate was established at Delhi in India in the early 13th century. These important Islamic works are an integral part of the history of Asian art and are treated in Chapter 17.

⏺ Explore the era further in MindTap with videos of major artworks and buildings, Google Earth™ coordinates, and essays by the author on the following additional subjects:

▌ ART AND SOCIETY: Major Muslim Dynasties
* *Baptistère de Saint Louis* (FIG. 5-14A)
* Mosque lamp of Sayf al-Din Tuquztimur (FIG. 5-15A)
* Bihzad, *Seduction of Yusuf* (FIG. 5-15B)

1 in.

THE ISLAMIC WORLD

Architecture

- The Umayyads (r. 661–750) were the first Islamic dynasty. They ruled from their capital at Damascus (Syria) until the Abbasids (r. 750–1258) overthrew them and established a new capital at Baghdad (Iraq).

- The first great Islamic building was the Dome of the Rock, a domed octagon commemorating the triumph of Islam in Jerusalem, which the Muslims captured from the Byzantines in 638. It was intended to rival and surpass the Christian Church of the Holy Sepulchre.

- The earliest mosques—for example, the Great Mosque that the Abbasids erected at Kairouan (Tunisia) in the mid-9th century—were of the hypostyle-hall type and incorporated arcaded courtyards and minarets. Inside mosques, Muslims pray facing Mecca.

- The Umayyad capital in Spain was at Córdoba, where the caliphs (r. 756–1031) constructed and expanded the Great Mosque between the 8th and 10th centuries. The mosque features horseshoe and multilobed arches and mosaic-covered domes resting on arcuated squinches.

- The last Spanish Muslim dynasty was the Nasrid (r. 1230–1492), whose capital was at Granada. The Alhambra is the best surviving example of Islamic palace architecture. It is famous for its carved stucco walls, muqarnas decoration on vaults and domes, and the Court of the Lions and its fountain, which is a rare example of Islamic stone sculpture.

- The Timurid (r. 1370–1501) and Safavid (r. 1501–1732) dynasties ruled Iran and Central Asia for almost four centuries and were great patrons of art and architecture. The art of tilework reached its peak under the patronage of the Safavid dynasty. Builders of the time frequently used mosaic tiles to cover the walls and vaults of mosques and madrasas.

Dome of the Rock, Jerusalem, 687–692

Great Mosque, Córdoba, 8th to 10th centuries

Palace of the Lions, Granada, 1354–1391

Luxury Arts

- The earliest preserved Korans date to the ninth century and feature Kufic calligraphy and decorative motifs but no figural illustrations. Islamic tradition shuns the representation of fauna of any kind in sacred contexts.

- Muslim artists excelled in the art of enamel-decorated glass lamps, which illuminated mosque interiors; carved ivory pyxides; and textiles. In secular contexts, figural decoration was permitted. The ivory pyxis of al-Mughira produced at the Córdoba court features animals and hunters. Some carpets—for example, the pair designed by Maqsud of Kashan for a 16th-century funerary mosque at Ardabil (Iran)—were woven with at least 25 million knots each.

- The Timurid court at Herat (Afghanistan) and the Safavid rulers of Iran employed the most skilled painters of the day, who specialized in illustrating secular books with narrative scenes incorporating people and animals. Among the most famous manuscript painters were Bihzad, who illustrated books for Sultan Husayn Mayqara (r. 1470–1506), and Sultan-Muhammad, who worked for Shah Tahmasp (r. 1524–1576).

Koran page, 9th or early 10th century

Maqsud of Kashan, Ardabil carpet, 1540

▲ **6-1a** A vision of the second coming of Christ on judgment day greets worshipers entering Saint-Pierre at Moissac. The sculptural program reflects the belief that Christ is the door to salvation.

▶ **6-1b** The figures of crowned musicians in the grand relief above the portal are the 24 elders who accompany Christ as the kings of this world and make music in his praise. Each turns to face the enthroned judge.

6-1　**South portal of Saint-Pierre, Moissac, France, ca. 1115–1135.**

▲ **6-1c** On the front of the trumeau, six roaring lions greet worshipers as they enter the church. Lions were the church's ideal protectors. In the Middle Ages, people believed that lions slept with their eyes open.

Early Medieval and Romanesque Europe

THE DOOR TO SALVATION

The church of Saint-Pierre (Saint Peter) at Moissac in southwestern France boasts the most extensive preserved ensemble of 12th-century sculpture in Europe. An important stop along the pilgrimage route to the tomb of Saint James at Santiago de Compostela in northwestern Spain (see "Pilgrimages," page 170, and MAP 6-1), the Moissac abbey had joined the Cluniac order in 1047. Enriched by the gifts of pilgrims and noble benefactors, the monks adorned their church with an elaborate series of relief sculptures, both in the cloister (FIG. 6-20) and especially in the richly decorated south portal (FIG. 6-1) facing the town square.

The jambs and central post (*trumeau*) of the Moissac portal have scalloped contours, a borrowing from Spanish Islamic architecture (FIG. 5-7). Six roaring interlaced lions on the front of the trumeau greet worshipers as they enter the church. The notion of placing fearsome images at the gateways to important places is of very ancient origin (compare FIGS. 1-18, 2-10, 2-23, and 3-7). In the Middle Ages, lions were the church's ideal protectors because people believed that lions slept with their eyes open.

The grand stone relief in the *tympanum* above the portal depicts the second coming of Christ as king and judge of the world in its last days. As befits his majesty, the enthroned Christ is at the center, reflecting a compositional rule followed since Early Christian times. Flanking him are the signs of the four Gospel authors and attendant angels holding scrolls to record human deeds for judgment. Completing the design are 24 figures of crowned musicians. They are the 24 elders who accompany Christ as the kings of this world and make music in his praise. Each turns to face the enthroned judge, much as would the courtiers of a medieval monarch in attendance on their lord. Two courses of wavy lines symbolizing the clouds of Heaven divide the elders into three tiers.

The inclusion of a larger-than-life image of Christ as the central motif of the Moissac tympanum is a common feature of many church portals of this era. These entryways reflect the belief, dating to Early Christian times, that Christ is the door to salvation ("I am the door; who enters through me will be saved"—John 10:9). An inscription on the tympanum of the late-11th-century monastic church of Santa Cruz de la Serós in Spain made this message explicit: "I am the eternal door. Pass through me faithful. I am the source of life."[1]

Moissac's south portal is an early example of the rebirth of the art of large-scale sculpture in the Middle Ages, one hallmark of the age that art historians have dubbed *Romanesque* (Roman-like) because of the extensive use of stone sculpture and stone vaulting in 11th- and 12th-century churches.

EARLY MEDIEVAL EUROPE

Historians once referred to the thousand years (roughly 400 to 1400) between the dying Roman Empire's official adoption of Christianity and the rebirth (*Renaissance*) of interest in classical art as the Dark Ages. They viewed this period as a blank between classical antiquity and the beginning of modern Europe. This negative assessment, a legacy of the humanist scholars of Renaissance Italy, persists today in the retention of the noun *Middle Ages* and the adjective *medieval* to describe this "era in between" and its art. Modern scholars, however, long ago ceased to regard the art of medieval Europe as unsophisticated or inferior. On the contrary, medieval artists produced some of the world's innovative and beautiful artworks.

Early medieval (ca. 500–1000) art in western Europe was a unique fusion of the classical heritage of Rome's northwestern provinces, the cultures of the non-Roman peoples north of the Alps, and Christianity. Over the centuries, the various population groups merged, and a new order gradually replaced what had been the Roman Empire, resulting eventually in today's European nations.

Merovingians and Anglo-Saxons

Art historians do not know the full range of art and architecture that these non-Roman cultures produced. What has survived is probably not fully representative and consists almost exclusively of small "status symbols"—weapons and items of personal adornment such as bracelets, pendants, belt buckles, and *fibulae*—for example, the pair (FIG. 6-1A) discovered in a Merovingian grave. Earlier scholars, who viewed medieval art through a Renaissance lens, ignored these "minor arts" because of their small scale, seeming utilitarian nature, and abstract ornamentation, and because their makers rejected the classical idea that naturalistic representation should be the focus of

MAP 6-1 Western Europe around 1100.

6-2 Purse cover, from the Sutton Hoo ship burial in Suffolk, England, ca. 625. Gold, glass, and enamel cloisonné with garnets and emeralds, $7\frac{1}{2}$" long. British Museum, London (gift of Mrs. E. M. Pretty).

This purse cover with cloisonné ornamentation comes from a treasure-laden royal burial ship. The combination of abstract interlace with animal figures is the hallmark of early medieval art in western Europe.

artistic endeavor. In the early Middle Ages, people regarded these objects as treasures. The miniature artworks enhanced their owners' prestige and testified to the stature of those buried with them. In the great Anglo-Saxon epic *Beowulf,* after Beowulf dies, his comrades cremate the hero and place his ashes in a huge burial mound overlooking the sea. As an everlasting tribute, they "buried rings and brooches in the barrow, all those adornments that brave men had brought out from the hoard after Beowulf died. They bequeathed the gleaming gold, treasure of men, to the earth."[2]

SUTTON HOO SHIP BURIAL The *Beowulf* saga also recounts the funeral of the warrior lord Scyld, whom his companions laid to rest in a ship overflowing with arms and armor and costly adornments, which they set adrift in the North Sea. In 1939, archaeologists uncovered a treasure-laden ship in a burial mound at Sutton Hoo, England. Among the many precious finds in the Sutton Hoo ship were a gold belt buckle, 10 silver bowls, 40 gold coins, and 2 silver spoons inscribed "Saulos" and "Paulos" (Saint Paul's names in Greek before and after his baptism). The spoons may allude to a conversion to Christianity. Some historians have associated the ship with the East Anglian king Raedwald (r. 599?–625), who was baptized a Christian before his death in 625.

The most extraordinary Sutton Hoo find was a purse cover (FIG. 6-2) decorated with seven *cloisonné* plaques. Early medieval metalworkers produced cloisonné jewelry by soldering small metal strips, or *cloisons* (French, "partitions"), edge-up, to a metal background, and then filling the compartments with semiprecious stones, pieces of colored glass, or glass paste fired to resemble sparkling jewels. On the Sutton Hoo purse cover, four symmetrically arranged groups of cloisonné figures make up the lower row. The end groups consist of a man standing between two beasts. The trio is a pictorial parallel to the epic sagas of the era in which heroes such as Beowulf battle and conquer horrific monsters. The two center groups represent eagles attacking ducks. The convex beaks of the eagles (compare FIG. 6-1A ⟳) fit against the concave beaks of the ducks. The two figures fit together so snugly that they seem at first to be a single dense abstract design. This is true also of the man-and-animals motif.

Above these figures are three geometric designs. The outer ones are purely linear. The central design is an interlace pattern in which the interlacements evolve into writhing animal figures. Elaborate intertwining linear patterns are characteristic of many times and places, but the combination of interlace with animal figures was uncommon outside the realm of the early medieval warlords. In fact, metalcraft with interlace patterns and other motifs beautifully integrated with animal forms was, without doubt, the premier art of the early Middle Ages in northwestern Europe.

Hiberno-Saxon Art

The Christianization of the British Isles, which began in the fifth century, accelerated in the sixth. In 563, for example, Saint Columba (521–597) founded an important monastery on the Scottish island of Iona, where he successfully converted the native Picts to Christianity. Iona monks in turn established the monastery at Lindisfarne off the northern coast of Britain in 635. Art historians call the art produced in these and other early medieval monasteries in Ireland and Britain *Hiberno-Saxon* (Hibernia was the Roman name of Ireland).

MANUSCRIPT ILLUMINATION The most distinctive products of these monasteries were illuminated Christian books, which brought the word of God to a predominantly illiterate population, who regarded the monks' sumptuous volumes with awe. Books were scarce and jealously guarded treasures of monastic libraries and *scriptoria* (writing studios). One of the most characteristic features of Hiberno-Saxon book illumination is the inclusion of full pages devoted neither to text nor to illustration but to pure embellishment. Interspersed between the text pages are so-called *carpet pages* resembling textiles (FIG. 6-3), made up of decorative panels of abstract and animal forms. Many books also contain pages (for example, FIG. 6-4) on which the illuminator enormously enlarged the initial letters of an important passage of sacred text and transformed those letters into elaborate decorative patterns. Such manuscript pages have no precedents in Greco-Roman books. They reveal the striking independence of Hiberno-Saxon artists from the classical tradition.

6-3 Cross-inscribed carpet page, folio 26 verso of the *Lindisfarne Gospels,* from Northumbria, England, ca. 698–721. Tempera on vellum, 1' 1½" × 9¼". British Library, London.

The cross-inscribed carpet page of the *Lindisfarne Gospels* exemplifies the way Hiberno-Saxon illuminators married Christian imagery and the animal-and-interlace style of the early medieval warlords.

1 in.

LINDISFARNE GOSPELS The marriage between Christian imagery and the animal-and-interlace style of the Anglo-Saxon warlords is evident in the cross-inscribed carpet page (FIG. **6-3**) of the *Lindisfarne Gospels.* The Gospels (see "Medieval Books" ↗) tell the story of the life of Christ, but the painter of the *Lindisfarne Gospels* had little interest in narrative. On the page illustrated here, serpentine interlacements of fantastic animals devour one another, curling over and returning on their writhing, elastic shapes. The rhythm of expanding and contracting forms produces a vivid effect of motion and change, but the painter held it in check by the regularity of the design and by the dominating motif of the inscribed cross. The cross—the all-important symbol of the imported religion—stabilizes the rhythms of the serpentines and, perhaps by contrast with its heavy immobility, seems to heighten the effect of motion. The illuminator placed the motifs in detailed symmetries, with inversions, reversals, and repetitions that the viewer must study closely in order to appreciate not only their variety but also their mazelike complexity. The animal forms intermingle with clusters and knots of line, and the whole design vibrates with energy. The color is rich yet cool. The painter skillfully adjusted shape and color to achieve a smooth and perfectly even surface.

BOOK OF KELLS Surpassing the *Lindisfarne Gospels* in richness is the *Book of Kells,* which boasts an unprecedented number of full-page illuminations, including carpet pages, symbols of the four Gospel authors, portrayals of the Virgin Mary and of Christ, New Testament narrative scenes, canon tables, and several instances of enlarged and embellished words from the Bible (see "Beautifying God's Words," page 161, and FIG. **6-4**).

PROBLEMS AND SOLUTIONS
Beautifying God's Words

The greatest extant Hiberno-Saxon book is the *Book of Kells,* which one commentator described in the *Annals of Ulster* for 1003 as "the chief relic of the western world." The manuscript (named after the abbey in central Ireland that once owned it) was probably the work of scribes and illuminators at the monastery at Iona. The monks kept the *Book of Kells* in an elaborate metalwork box, as befitted a greatly revered "relic," and they most likely displayed it on the church altar (see "Pilgrimages and the Veneration of Relics," page 170).

Impressing the new and largely illiterate Irish Christians with the beauty of God's words was no doubt one of the goals of the monks who were entrusted with illuminating the *Book of Kells.* They achieved that goal by literally making the words beautiful. The page reproduced here (FIG. 6-4) is the first folio of the account of the nativity of Jesus in the Gospel of Saint Matthew. The initial letters of Christ in Greek (⳩, *chi-rho-iota*) occupy nearly the entire page, although two words—*autem* (abbreviated simply as *h*) and *generatio*—appear at the lower right. Together they read: "Now this is how the birth of Christ came about." The illuminator transformed the holy words into extraordinarily intricate, abstract designs recalling metalwork (FIG. 6-2), but the page is not purely embellished script and abstract pattern. The letter *rho,* for example, ends in a male head, and animals are at the base of *rho* to the left of *h generatio.* Half-figures of winged angels appear to the left of *chi.* Close observation reveals many other figures, human and animal.

When the priest Giraldus Cambrensis visited Ireland in 1185, he described a manuscript he saw that, if not the *Book of Kells* itself, must have been very much like it:

Fine craftsmanship is all about you, but you might not notice it. Look more keenly at it and you . . . will make out intricacies, so delicate and subtle, so exact and compact, so full of knots and links, with colors so fresh and vivid, that you might say that all this was the work of an angel, and not of a man. For my part, the oftener I see the book, the more carefully I study it, the more I am lost in ever fresh amazement, and I see more and more wonders in the book.*

*Translated by Françoise Henry, *The Book of Kells* (New York: Alfred A. Knopf, 1974), 165.

1 in.

6-4 *Chi-rho-iota* (⳩) **page, folio 34 recto of the *Book of Kells,* probably from Iona, Scotland, late eighth or early ninth century. Tempera on vellum, 1' 1" × 9$\frac{1}{2}$". Trinity College Library, Dublin.**

In this opening page to the Gospel of Saint Matthew, the painter transformed the biblical text into abstract pattern, literally making God's words beautiful. The intricate design recalls early medieval metalwork.

Carolingian Art

On Christmas Day of the year 800 in Saint Peter's basilica (FIG. 4-3) in Rome, Pope Leo III (r. 795–816) crowned Charles the Great (Charlemagne), king of the Franks since 768, as emperor of Rome (r. 800–814). In time, Charlemagne came to be seen as the first Holy (that is, Christian) Roman Emperor, a title that his successors in the West did not formally adopt until the 12th century. Born in 742, when northern Europe was still in chaos, Charlemagne consolidated the Frankish kingdom that his father and grandfather bequeathed

Early Medieval Europe **161**

6-5 Saint Matthew, folio 15 recto of the *Coronation Gospels* (*Gospel Book of Charlemagne*), from Aachen, Germany, ca. 800–810. Ink and tempera on vellum, 1' $\frac{3}{4}$" × 10". Schatzkammer, Kunsthistorisches Museum, Vienna.

The books produced for Charlemagne's court reveal the legacy of classical art. The Carolingian painter used light, shade, and perspective to create the illusion of three-dimensional form.

6-6 Saint Matthew, folio 18 verso of the *Ebbo Gospels* (*Gospel Book of Archbishop Ebbo of Reims*), from the abbey of Saint Peter, Hautvillers, France, ca. 816–835. Ink and tempera on vellum, $10\frac{1}{4}$" × $8\frac{3}{4}$". Bibliothèque municipale, Épernay.

Saint Matthew writes frantically, and the folds of his drapery writhe and vibrate. Even the landscape rears up alive. This painter merged classical illusionism with the northern European linear tradition.

him, and defeated the Lombards in Italy. He thus united Europe and laid claim to reviving the glory of the Roman Empire. (His official seal bore the words *renovatio imperii Romani*—"renewal of the Roman Empire.") Charlemagne gave his name (*Carolus Magnus* in Latin) to an entire era, the *Carolingian* period.

Charlemagne was a sincere admirer of learning, the arts, and classical culture. He could read and speak Latin fluently, in addition to Frankish, his native tongue. Charlemagne also could understand Greek, and placed high value on books, both sacred and secular, importing many and sponsoring the production of far more. He invited to his court at Aachen, Germany, the best minds of his age, among them Alcuin (d. 804), master of the *cathedral* (bishop's church, from *cathedra*—Latin, "throne" or "seat") school at York, the center of Northumbrian learning. One of Charlemagne's dearest projects was the recovery of the true text of the Bible, which, through centuries of errors in copying, had become quite corrupted. Alcuin of York's revision of the Bible became the most widely used.

CORONATION GOSPELS The most famous of Charlemagne's books is the *Coronation Gospels*. The text is in handsome gold letters on purple vellum. The major full-page illuminations show the four Gospel authors at work—Saints Matthew, Mark, Luke, and John, the four *evangelists* (from the Greek word for "one who announces good

news"). The page (FIG. 6-5) depicting Saint Matthew follows the venerable tradition of author portraits, which were familiar features of Greek and Latin books. Similar representations of seated philosophers or poets writing or reading (FIG. 3-49) abound in ancient art. The Matthew of the *Coronation Gospels* also reveals the legacy of classical style. The Carolingian painter used color and modulation of light and shade to create the illusion of massive drapery folds wrapped around the evangelist's body. The cross-legged chair, the lectern, and the saint's toga are familiar Roman accessories, and the placement of the book and lectern top at an angle suggests a Mediterranean model employing classical perspective. Even the frame consists of the kind of acanthus leaves commonly found in Roman art. Almost nothing is known in the Hiberno-Saxon or Frankish world that could have prepared the way for this portrayal of Saint Matthew. If a Frankish, rather than an Italian or a Byzantine, artist painted the evangelist portraits of the *Coronation Gospels*, the Carolingian artist had fully absorbed the classical manner. Classical painting style was one of the many components of Charlemagne's program to establish Aachen as the capital of a renewed Christian Roman Empire.

1 in.

6-7 *Crucifixion,* front cover of the *Lindau Gospels,* from Saint Gall, Switzerland, ca. 870. Gold, precious stones, and pearls, 1' 1$\frac{3}{8}$" × 10$\frac{3}{8}$". Pierpont Morgan Library, New York.

Sacred books with covers of gold and jewels were among the most costly and revered early medieval art objects. This Carolingian cover revives the Early Christian imagery of the youthful Jesus.

of the most opulent Carolingian book covers (FIG. 6-7) is the one later added to the *Lindau Gospels.* The gold cover, fashioned in one of the royal workshops of Charlemagne's grandson, Charles the Bald (r. 840–875), presents a youthful Christ in the Early Christian tradition, nailed to the cross but oblivious to pain. Surrounding Christ are pearls and jewels (raised on golden claw feet so that they can catch and reflect the light even more brilliantly and protect the delicate metal relief from denting). The statuesque open-eyed figure, rendered in *repoussé* (hammered relief), is classical both in conception and in execution. In contrast, the four angels and the personifications of the Moon and the Sun above and the crouching figures of the Virgin Mary and Saint John (and two other figures of uncertain identity) in the quadrants below display the vivacity and nervous energy of the *Ebbo Gospels* Saint Matthew (FIG. 6-6). The *Lindau Gospels* cover highlights the stylistic diversity of early medieval art in Europe. Here, however, the translated figural style of the Mediterranean prevailed, in keeping with the classical tastes and imperial aspirations of the Frankish emperors of Rome.

EBBO GOSPELS Another Saint Matthew (FIG. 6-6), in a Gospel book made for Archbishop Ebbo of Reims, France, may be an interpretation of an author portrait very similar to the one that the *Coronation Gospels* master used as a model. The *Ebbo Gospels* illuminator, however, replaced the classical calm and solidity of the *Coronation Gospels* evangelist with an energy approaching frenzy. Matthew writes in frantic haste. His hair stands on end, his eyes open wide, the folds of his drapery writhe and vibrate, and the landscape behind him rears up alive. The painter even set the page's leaf border in motion. The *Ebbo Gospels* painter translated a classical prototype into a new Carolingian style, merging classical illusionism and the northern linear tradition.

LINDAU GOSPELS The taste for luxurious portable objects, the hallmark of the art of the early medieval warlords, persisted under Charlemagne and his successors. The Carolingians commissioned numerous works employing costly materials, including book covers made of gold and jewels and sometimes also ivory or pearls. One

AACHEN In his eagerness to reestablish the imperial past, Charlemagne looked to Rome and Ravenna for architectural models. One was the former heart of the Roman Empire, which he wanted to renew. The other was the western outpost of Byzantine might and splendor, which he wanted to emulate at Aachen. Charlemagne often visited Ravenna, and once brought from there porphyry

6-8 West facade of the Palatine Chapel of Charlemagne, Aachen, Germany, 792–805.

The innovative design of Charlemagne's palace chapel features two cylindrical towers with spiral staircases flanking the entrance portal, foreshadowing later medieval dual-tower church facades.

6-9 Restored cutaway view of the Palatine Chapel of Charlemagne, Aachen, Germany, 792–805 (John Burge).

Charlemagne's chapel is the first vaulted medieval structure north of the Alps. The architect transformed the complexity of San Vitale's interior (FIG. 4-16) into simple, massive geometric form.

(purple marble, the royal color) columns to adorn his Palatine (palace) Chapel (FIGS. 6-8 and 6-9). The plan of the Aachen chapel resembles that of Ravenna's San Vitale (FIGS. 4-14, 4-15, and 4-16), and a direct relationship very likely exists between the two.

A comparison between the Carolingian chapel, the first vaulted structure of the Middle Ages north of the Alps, and its southern counterpart is instructive. The Aachen plan is simpler. The architect omitted San Vitale's apselike extensions reaching from the central octagon into the ambulatory. At Aachen, the two main units stand in greater independence of each other. This solution may lack the subtle sophistication of the Byzantine building, but the Palatine Chapel gains geometric clarity. A restored view of its interior (FIG. 6-9) shows that Charlemagne's builders converted the lightness and complexity of San Vitale's interior (FIG. 4-16) into massive geometric form.

On the exterior (FIG. 6-8), two cylindrical towers with spiral staircases flank the entrance portal. This was a first step toward the great dual-tower facades of western European churches from the 10th century to the present. Above the portal, Charlemagne could appear in a large framing arch and be seen by those gathered in the atrium in front of the chapel. Directly behind the arch was Charlemagne's marble throne. From there he could peer down at the altar in the apse. The Palatine Chapel's second-story gallery followed the model of the imperial gallery at Hagia Sophia (FIGS. 4-11 and 4-12) in Constantinople, even if the design of the facade broke sharply from Byzantine tradition.

SAINT GALL A major initiative of the Carolingian period was the construction and expansion of monasteries. Around 819, Haito, the abbot of Reichenau and bishop of Basel from 806 to 823, commissioned a schematic plan (FIG. 6-10) for a Benedictine monastic community (see "Medieval Monasteries and Benedictine Rule," page 165) and sent it to Abbot Gozbertus as a guide for rebuilding his monastery at Saint Gall. The design's fundamental purpose was to separate the monks from the laity (nonclergy) who also inhabited the community. The plan provides precious information about Carolingian monasteries. Variations of the scheme may be seen in later monasteries all across western Europe.

Near the center, dominating the complex, was the *oratory* (monastic church) with its *cloister,* a colonnaded courtyard (compare FIG. 6-20) not unlike the Early Christian atrium (FIG. 4-3) but situated to the side of the church instead of in front of its main portal. Reserved for monks, the cloister was a kind of earthly paradise removed from the world at large. Clustered around the cloister were the most essential buildings: the dormitory, *refectory* (dining hall), kitchen, and storage rooms. Other structures, including an infirmary, school, guesthouse, bakery, brewery, and workshops, filled the areas around this central core of church and cloister.

Haito invited the abbot of Saint Gall to adapt the plan as he saw fit, and indeed, the Saint Gall builders did not follow the Reichenau model precisely. Nonetheless, had the abbot wished, Haito's plan could have served as a practical guide for the Saint Gall masons because it was laid out using a *module* (standard unit) of 2.5 feet.

RELIGION AND MYTHOLOGY
Medieval Monasteries and Benedictine Rule

Since Early Christian times, monks who established monasteries also made the rules governing communal life. The most significant of these monks was Benedict of Nursia (Saint Benedict, ca. 480–547), who founded the Benedictine Order in 529. By the ninth century, the "Rule" Benedict wrote (*Regula Sancti Benedicti*) had become standard for all western European monastic communities, in part because Charlemagne had encouraged its adoption throughout the Frankish territories.

Saint Benedict believed that the corruption of the clergy that accompanied the increasing worldliness of the Church had its roots in the lack of firm organization and regulation. As he saw it, idleness and selfishness had led to neglect of the commandments of God and of the Church. The cure for this was communal association in an *abbey* under the absolute rule of an *abbot* whom the monks elected (or an *abbess* chosen by the nuns), who would ensure that the clergy spent each hour of the day in useful work and in sacred reading. The emphasis on work and study and not on meditation and austerity is of great historical significance. Since antiquity, manual labor had been considered unseemly, the business of the lowborn or of slaves. Benedict raised it to the dignity of religion. By thus exalting the virtue of manual labor, Benedict not only rescued it from its age-old association with slavery but also recognized it as the way to self-sufficiency for the entire religious community.

Whereas some of Saint Benedict's followers emphasized spiritual "work" over manual labor, others, most notably the Cistercians (see page 173), put Benedict's teachings about the value of physical work into practice. These monks reached into their surroundings and helped reduce the vast areas of daunting wilderness of early medieval Europe. They cleared dense forest teeming with wolves, bear, and wild boar; drained swamps; cultivated wastelands; and built roads, bridges, and dams as well as monastic churches and their associated living and service quarters.

The ideal monastery (FIG. 6-10) provided all the facilities necessary for the conduct of daily life as well as "the Work of God"—a mill, bakery, infirmary, vegetable garden, and even a brewery—so that the monks felt no need to wander outside its protective walls. Monks were also often scribes and scholars and had a monopoly on the skills of reading and writing in an age of almost universal illiteracy. Consequently, medieval monasteries were centrally important to the revival of learning. The libraries and scriptoria, where the monks and nuns read, copied, illuminated, and bound books with ornamented covers,

6-10 Schematic plan for a monastery, from Saint Gall, Switzerland, ca. 819. Red ink on parchment, 2' 4" × 3' 8$\frac{1}{8}$". Stiftsbibliothek, Saint Gall.

The purpose of this plan for an ideal, self-sufficient Benedictine monastery was to separate the monks from the laity. Near the center is the church with its cloister, the monks' earthly paradise.

became centers of study. Monasteries were almost the sole repositories of what remained of the literary culture of the Greco-Roman world and early Christianity. Saint Benedict's requirements of manual labor and sacred reading came to include writing and copying books, studying music for chanting daily prayers, and—of great significance—teaching. The monasteries were the schools of the early Middle Ages.

The designer consistently employed that module, or multiples or fractions of it, for all elements of the plan. For example, the nave's width, indicated on the plan as 40 feet, is equal to 16 modules. Each monk's bed is 2.5 modules long.

The prototypes carrying the greatest authority for Charlemagne and his builders were those from the time of Constantine. The widespread adoption of the Early Christian basilica, at Saint Gall and elsewhere, rather than the domed central plan of Byzantine churches, was crucial to the subsequent development of western European

church architecture. Unfortunately, no Carolingian basilica has survived in its original form. Nevertheless, it is possible to reconstruct the appearance of some of them with fair accuracy. The oratory at Saint Gall, for example, was essentially a traditional basilica, but it had features not found in any Early Christian church. Most obvious is the addition of a second apse on the west end of the building.

Not quite as evident but much more important to the subsequent development of church architecture in northern Europe was the presence of a *transept* at Saint Gall, a rare feature, but one that characterized the two greatest Early Christian basilicas in Rome, Saint Peter's (FIG. 4-3) and Saint Paul's. The Saint Gall transept is as wide as the nave on the plan and was probably the same height. Early Christian builders had not been concerned with proportional relationships. On the Saint Gall plan, however, the various parts of the building relate to one another by a geometric scheme that ties them together into a tight and cohesive unit. Equalizing the widths of nave and transept automatically makes the area where they cross (the *crossing*) a square. Most Carolingian churches shared this feature. But Haito's planner also used the *crossing square* as the unit of measurement for the remainder of the church plan. The transept arms are equal to one crossing square, the distance between transept and apse is one crossing square, and the nave is 4.5 crossing squares long. In addition, the two aisles are half as wide as the nave, integrating all parts of the church in a rational and orderly plan.

The Saint Gall plan also reveals another important feature of many Carolingian basilicas: towers framing the end(s) of the church. Haito's plan shows only two towers, both cylindrical and on the west side of the church, as at Charlemagne's Palatine Chapel (FIG. 6-8), but they stand apart from the church facade. If a tower existed above the crossing, the silhouette of Saint Gall would have shown three towers, altering the horizontal profile of the traditional basilica and identifying the church even from afar.

CORVEY Other Carolingian basilicas had towers incorporated in the fabric of the west end of the building, thereby creating a grandiose unified facade greeting all those who entered the church. Architectural historians call this feature of Carolingian and some later churches the *westwork* (from the German *Westwerk*, "western entrance structure"). Early medieval writers referred to it as a *castellum* (Latin, "castle" or "fortress") or *turris* ("tower"). The major surviving example is the westwork (FIG. 6-11) of the abbey church at Corvey. The uppermost parts are 12th-century additions (easily distinguishable from the original westwork by the differing masonry technique). Stairs in each tower provided access to the upper stories. On the second floor is a two-story chapel with an aisle and a gallery on three sides. As at Aachen, the chapel opens onto the nave, and from it the visiting emperor and his entourage could watch and participate in the service below. Not all Carolingian westworks, however, served as seats reserved for the emperor. They also functioned as churches within churches, housing a second altar for special celebrations on major feast days. Boys' choirs stationed in the westwork chapel participated from above in the services conducted in the church's nave.

Ottonian Art

Charlemagne was buried in the Palatine Chapel at Aachen. His empire survived him by fewer than 30 years. When his son Louis the Pious (r. 814–840) died, Louis's sons—Charles the Bald, Lothair, and Louis the German—divided the Carolingian Empire among themselves. In 843, after bloody conflicts, the brothers signed a treaty partitioning the Frankish lands into western, central, and eastern areas, very roughly foreshadowing the later nations of France and Germany and a third realm corresponding to a long strip of land stretching from the Netherlands and Belgium to Rome. In the mid-10th century, the eastern part of the former empire consolidated under the rule of a new Saxon line of German emperors called, after the names of the three most illustrious family members, the

6-11 Westwork of the abbey church, Corvey, Germany, 873–885.

An important new feature of Carolingian church architecture was the westwork, a monumental western facade incorporating two towers. The sole surviving example is the abbey church at Corvey.

Ottonians. In Rome in 962, the pope crowned the first Otto, king of the Germans since 936, as emperor, the title he held until his death in 973. The Ottonians not only preserved but enriched the culture and tradition of the Carolingian period.

HILDESHEIM A great nonimperial patron of Ottonian art and architecture was Bishop Bernward (r. 993–1022) of Hildesheim,

6-12 Saint Michael's (looking northwest), Hildesheim, Germany, 1001–1031.

Built by Bishop Bernward, a great art patron, Saint Michael's is a masterpiece of Ottonian basilica design. The church's two apses, two transepts, and multiple towers give it a distinctive profile.

6-13 Plan of the abbey church of Saint Michael's, Hildesheim, Germany, 1001–1031.

Saint Michael's entrances are on the side. Alternating piers and columns divide the space in the nave into vertical units. These features transformed the tunnel-like horizontality of Early Christian basilicas.

Germany. Bernward was an expert craftsman and bronze-caster as well as the scholar who made the Hildesheim abbey an important center of learning. He also served as the tutor of Otto III (r. 983–1002; FIG. 6-11A ⬈), and in 1001 traveled with the emperor to Rome, where he was able to study at first hand the ancient monuments revered by the Carolingian and Ottonian emperors.

Bernward's major building project as abbot was the construction of the church of Saint Michael (FIGS. 6-12 and 6-13). The work was carried out between 1001 and 1031. The abbey church, which was rebuilt after a bombing raid during World War II, is a characteristic example of Ottonian basilica design. The church features a double-transept plan, two apses, six towers, and a westwork. The two transepts create eastern and western centers of gravity. The nave merely seems to be a hall connecting them. Lateral entrances leading into the aisles from the north and south additionally make for an almost complete loss of the traditional basilican orientation toward the east. Some ancient Roman basilicas, such as the Basilica Ulpia (FIG. 3-35, no. 4) in the Forum of Trajan, also had two apses and

entrances on the side, and Bernward probably was familiar with this variant basilican plan.

At Hildesheim, as in the Saint Gall monastery plan (FIG. 6-10), the builders adopted a modular approach. The crossing squares, for example, are the basis for the nave's dimensions—three crossing squares long and one square wide. The placement of heavy piers at the corners of each square gives visual emphasis to the three units. These piers alternate with pairs of columns to form what architectural historians call the *alternate-support system*. The alternating piers and columns divide the nave into vertical units, breaking the smooth rhythm of the all-column arcade of Early Christian (FIG. 4-4A ⬈) and Carolingian basilicas and leading the eye upward.

BERNWARD'S DOORS In 1001, when Bishop Bernward was in Rome, he resided in Otto III's palace on the Aventine hill near Santa Sabina (FIGS. 4-4A and 4-4B ⬈), a fifth-century church renowned for its carved wood doors. Those doors, decorated with episodes from both the Old and New Testaments, may have inspired the

6-14 Doors with relief panels (Genesis, left door; life of Christ, right door), commissioned by Bishop Bernward for Saint Michael's, Hildesheim, Germany, 1015. Bronze, 15' 5$\frac{3}{4}$" high. Römer- und Pelizaeus-Museum, Hildesheim.

Bernward's doors tell the story of original sin and redemption, and draw parallels between the Old and New Testaments, as in the expulsion from Paradise and the infancy and suffering of Christ.

remarkable 15-foot-tall bronze doors (FIG. 6-14) that the bishop had cast for Saint Michael's. They are technological marvels because the Ottonian metalworkers cast each door in a single piece with the figural sculpture. Carolingian sculpture, like most sculpture since the fall of Rome, consisted primarily of small-scale art executed in ivory and precious metals, often for book covers (FIG. 6-7). The Hildesheim doors are huge in comparison, but the 16 individual panels stem from this tradition.

The panels of the left door illustrate highlights from Genesis, beginning with the *Creation of Eve* (at the top) and ending with the *Murder of Abel,* Adam and Eve's son, by his brother Cain (at the bottom). The right door recounts the life of Jesus (reading from the bottom up), starting with the *Annunciation* and terminating with *Noli Me Tangere* (see "The Life of Jesus," pages 120–121). Together, the doors tell the story of original sin and ultimate redemption, showing the expulsion from the Garden of Eden and the path back to Paradise through the Church. As in Early Christian times, the Ottonian clergy interpreted Hebrew scripture as prefiguring the New Testament (see "Jewish Subjects," page 119). For example, the *Fall of Adam and Eve* panel is juxtaposed with the *Crucifixion.* Eve nursing the infant Cain is opposite Mary with the Christ Child in her lap.

The Hildesheim figures show a vivid animation that recalls the *Ebbo Gospels* Saint Matthew (FIG. 6-6), but the narrative compositions also reveal the Ottonian artist's genius for anecdotal detail. For example, in the fourth panel from the top on the left door, God, portrayed as a man, accuses Adam and Eve after their fall from grace. He jabs his finger at them with the force of his whole body. The frightened pair crouch, not only to hide their shame but also to escape the lightning bolt of divine wrath. Each passes the blame—Adam pointing backward to Eve, and Eve pointing downward to the deceitful serpent. Adam and Eve both struggle to point with one arm while attempting to shield their bodies from view with the other. With an instinct for expressive pose and gesture, the artist brilliantly communicated their newfound embarrassment at their nakedness and their unconvincing denials of wrongdoing.

1 ft.

6-15 Crucifix commissioned by Archbishop Gero (*Gero Crucifix*) for Cologne Cathedral, Germany, ca. 970. Painted wood, height of figure, 6' 2". Cathedral, Cologne.

In this early example of the revival of large-scale sculpture in the Middle Ages, an Ottonian sculptor depicted with unprecedented emotional power the intense agony of Christ's ordeal on the cross.

ROMANESQUE EUROPE

The Romanesque era is the first since Archaic and Classical Greece to take its name from an artistic style rather than from politics or geography. Unlike Carolingian and Ottonian art, named for emperors, or Hiberno-Saxon art, a regional term, *Romanesque* is a title that art historians invented to describe medieval art and architecture that appeared "Roman-like." Architectural historians first employed the adjective in the early 19th century to describe European architecture of the 11th and 12th centuries. They noted that certain architectural elements of this period, principally barrel and groin vaults based on the round arch, resembled those of ancient Roman architecture. Thus the word distinguished most Romanesque buildings from earlier medieval timber-roofed structures, as well as from later Gothic churches with vaults resting on *pointed arches* (see "The Gothic Rib Vault," page 190). Scholars in other fields quickly borrowed the term. Today, "Romanesque" broadly designates the history and culture of western Europe between about 1050 and 1200.

During the 11th and 12th centuries, thousands of churches and monasteries were remodeled or newly constructed. This immense building enterprise was in part a natural by-product of the rise of independent towns and the prosperity they enjoyed. But it also was an expression of the widely felt relief and thanksgiving that the conclusion of the first Christian millennium in the year 1000 had not brought an end to the world, as many had feared. In the Romanesque age, the construction of churches became almost an obsession. As the monk Raoul Glaber (ca. 985–ca. 1046) observed in 1003, "It was as if the whole earth . . . were clothing itself everywhere in the white robe of the church."[3]

GERO CRUCIFIX The Ottonian period also witnessed a revival of interest in freestanding statuary. The outstanding example is the *crucifix* (FIG. 6-15) that Archbishop Gero (r. 969–976) commissioned in 970 for display in Cologne Cathedral. Carved in oak, then painted and gilded, the 6-foot-tall image of Christ nailed to the cross presents a conception of the Savior dramatically different from that seen on the *Lindau Gospels* cover (FIG. 6-7), with its Early Christian imagery of the youthful Christ triumphant over death. The bearded Christ of the Cologne crucifix is more akin to Byzantine representations (FIG. 4-23) of the suffering Jesus, but the emotional power of the Ottonian work is greater still. The sculptor depicted Christ as an all-too-human martyr. Blood streaks down his forehead from the (missing) crown of thorns. His eyelids are closed, his face is contorted in pain, and his body sags under its weight. The muscles stretch to their limit—those of his right shoulder and chest seem almost to rip apart. The halo behind Christ's head may foretell his subsequent resurrection, but the worshiper can sense only his pain. The *Gero Crucifix* is the most powerful characterization of intense agony of the early Middle Ages.

PILGRIMS AND RELICS The enormous investment in churches and their furnishings also reflected a significant increase in pilgrimage traffic in Romanesque Europe (see "Pilgrimage and the Veneration of Relics," page 170, and MAP 6-1). Pilgrims were important sources of funding for those monasteries that possessed the *relics* of revered saints. The monks of Sainte-Foy (FIG. 6-15A ⬈) at Conques, for example, used pilgrims' donations to pay for a magnificent cameo-and-jewel-encrusted gold-and-silver *reliquary* (FIG. 6-16) to house the skull of Saint Faith. In fact, the clergy of the various monasteries vied with one another to provide the most magnificent settings for the display of their unique relics. They found justification for their lavish expenditures on buildings and furnishings in the Bible

Pilgrimages and the Veneration of Relics

The veneration of *relics* was not new in the Romanesque era. For centuries, Christians had traveled to sacred shrines housing the body parts of, or objects associated with, the holy family or the saints. The faithful had long believed that bones, clothing, instruments of martyrdom, and the like had the power to heal body and soul. The veneration of relics, however, reached a high point in the 11th and 12th centuries.

The case of the relics of Saint Faith (Sainte Foy, in French), an early-fourth-century child martyr who refused to pay homage to the Roman gods, is a telling example. A monk from the abbey church at Conques (FIG. 6-15A ◿) stole the saint's skull from the nearby abbey of Agen around 880. The monks justified the act as *furta sacra* ("holy theft"), claiming that Saint Faith herself wished to move. The reliquary (FIG. 6-16) they provided to house the saint's remains is one of the most lavish ever produced (compare the reliquary of Saint Alexander, FIG. 6-16A ◿). It takes the form of an enthroned statuette of the martyr. Fashioned of gold leaf and silver gilt over a wood core, the reliquary prominently features inset jewels and cameos of various dates—the accumulated donations of pilgrims and church patrons over many years. The saint's oversize head is a reworked ancient Roman *parade helmet*—a masklike helmet worn by soldiers on special ceremonial occasions and not part of standard battle dress. The monks added a martyr's crown to the ancient helmet. The rear of the throne bears an image engraved in rock crystal of Christ on the cross, establishing a parallel between Christ's martyrdom and Saint Faith's.

In the Romanesque era, pilgrimage was the most conspicuous feature of public religious devotion, proclaiming pilgrims' faith in the power of saints and hope for their special favor. The major shrines—Saint Peter's and Saint Paul's in Rome and the Church of the Holy Sepulchre in Jerusalem—drew pilgrims from throughout Europe. Christians braved bad roads and hostile wildernesses infested with robbers who preyed on innocent travelers—all for the sake of salvation. The journeys could take more than a year to complete—when they were successful. People often undertook pilgrimage as an act of repentance or as a last resort in their search for a cure for some physical disability. Hardship and austerity were means of increasing pilgrims' chances for the remission of sin or of disease. The distance and peril of the pilgrimage were measures of pilgrims' sincerity of repentance, or of the reward they sought.

For those with insufficient time or money to make a pilgrimage to Rome or Jerusalem, holy destinations could be found closer to home. In France, for example, the church at Vézelay (FIG. 6-23A ◿) housed the bones of Mary Magdalene. Pilgrims could also view Saint Lazarus's

remains at Autun (FIG. 6-23) and Saint Saturninus's at Toulouse (FIG. 6-17). Each of these great shrines was also an important way station en route to the most venerated Christian shrine in western Europe, the tomb of Saint James at Santiago de Compostela in northwestern Spain (MAP 6-1).

Large crowds of pilgrims paying homage to saints placed a great burden on the churches housing their relics, but they also provided significant revenues, making possible the construction of ever grander and more luxuriously appointed shrines. The popularity of pilgrimages led to changes in church design, principally longer and wider naves and aisles, transepts and ambulatories with additional chapels (FIG. 6-18), and second-story galleries (FIG. 6-19).

6-16 Reliquary statue of Sainte Foy (Saint Faith), late 10th to early 11th century with later additions. Gold, silver gilt, jewels, and cameos over a wood core, 2' 9½" high. Treasury, Sainte-Foy, Conques.

This enthroned image containing the skull of Saint Faith is one of the most lavish Romanesque reliquaries. The head is an ancient Roman helmet, and the cameos are donations from pilgrims.

itself—for example, in Psalm 26:8, "Lord, I have loved the beauty of your house, and the place where your glory dwells." Pilgrimages were a major economic as well as conceptual catalyst for the art and architecture of the Romanesque period.

France

Although art historians use the adjective "Romanesque" to describe 11th- and 12th-century art and architecture throughout Europe, pronounced regional differences exist. To a certain extent, Romanesque art and architecture can be compared to European Romance languages, which vary regionally but have a common core in Latin, the language of the Romans. Some of the most innovative developments in Romanesque architecture and architectural sculpture occurred in France.

TOULOUSE Around 1070, construction of a great new church began in honor of Toulouse's first bishop, Saint Saturninus (Saint Sernin in French). Large congregations gathered at the southwestern French shrines along the pilgrimage routes to Santiago de Compostela, and the unknown architect designed Saint-Sernin to accommodate them. The grand scale of the building is apparent in the aerial view (FIG. 6-17), which includes automobiles, trucks, and nearly invisible pedestrians. The church's 12th-century exterior is still largely intact, although the two towers of the west facade (at the

6-17 Aerial view of Saint-Sernin (looking northwest), Toulouse, France, ca. 1070–1120.

Pilgrimages were a major economic catalyst for Romanesque art and architecture. Many churches capable of housing large congregations were constructed along the major routes to the shrine of Saint James.

left in FIG. 6-17) were never completed, and the prominent *crossing tower* dates to the Gothic and later periods.

Saint-Sernin's plan (FIG. 6-18) is extremely regular and geometrically precise. The crossing square, flanked by massive piers

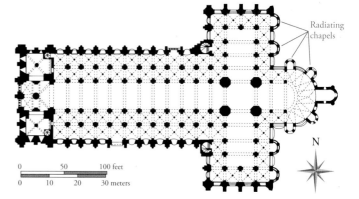

6-18 Plan of Saint-Sernin, Toulouse, France, ca. 1070–1120.

Increased traffic led to changes in church design. "Pilgrimage churches" have longer and wider naves and aisles, as well as transepts and ambulatories with radiating chapels for viewing relics.

and marked off by heavy arches, served as the module for the entire church. Each nave *bay,* for example, measures exactly one-half of the crossing square, and each aisle bay measures exactly one-quarter. The Toulouse design is a highly refined realization of the planning scheme first seen at Saint Gall (FIG. 6-10). But the Toulouse plan differs in significant ways from those of earlier monastic churches. It exemplifies what has come to be called the "pilgrimage church" type. At Toulouse, the builders provided additional space for curious pilgrims, worshipers, and liturgical processions by increasing the length of the nave, doubling the side aisles, and adding a transept and *ambulatory* with *radiating chapels* housing the church's relics so that the faithful could view them without having to enter the choir where the main altar stood.

Saint-Sernin also has upper galleries, or *tribunes,* over the inner aisles opening onto the nave (FIG. 6-19). These tribunes, which

6-19 Interior of Saint-Sernin (looking east), Toulouse, France, ca. 1070–1120.

Saint-Sernin's groin-vaulted tribune galleries housed overflow crowds and buttressed the nave's stone barrel vault, whose transverse arches continue the lines of the compound piers.

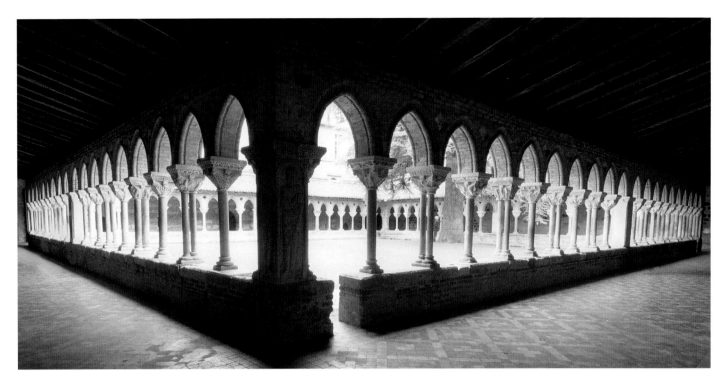

6-20 General view (*top*; looking southeast) and historiated capital (*bottom*) of the cloister of Saint-Pierre, Moissac, France, ca. 1100–1115.

The revived tradition of stonecarving probably began with historiated capitals. The most extensive preserved ensemble of sculptured early Romanesque capitals is in the cloister of the Moissac abbey.

housed overflow crowds on special occasions, played an important role in buttressing the continuous semicircular cut-stone *barrel vault* that covers Saint-Sernin's nave. *Groin vaults* (indicated by Xs on the plan, FIG. 6-18; compare FIG. 3-15*b*) in the tribunes as well as in the ground-floor aisles absorbed the pressure (*thrust*) exerted by the barrel vault along the entire length of the nave and transferred the main thrust to the thick outer walls.

The builders of Saint-Sernin were not content merely to buttress the massive nave vault. They also carefully coordinated the vault's design with that of the nave arcade below and with the modular plan of the building as a whole. The nave elevation, which features *engaged columns* embellishing the piers marking the corners of the bays, fully reflects the church's geometric floor plan (FIG. 6-18). Architectural historians refer to piers with columns or *pilasters* attached to their rectangular cores as *compound piers*. At Saint-Sernin, the engaged columns rise from the bottom of the compound piers to the vault's *springing* (the lowest stone of an arch) and continue across the nave as *transverse arches*. As a result, the Saint-Sernin nave gives the impression of being numerous identical vertical volumes of space placed one behind the other, marching down the building's length in orderly procession. Saint-Sernin's spatial organization corresponds to and renders visually the plan's geometric organization. This rationally integrated scheme, with repeated units decorated and separated by moldings, would have a long future in later European church architecture.

Saint-Sernin's stone vaults provided protection from the devastating conflagrations that regularly destroyed traditional timber-roofed basilicas (see "The Burning of Canterbury Cathedral" ☒). But although fireproofing was no doubt one of the attractions of vaulted naves and

aisles in an age when candles and lamps provided interior illumination, other factors probably played a greater role in the decision to make the enormous investment of time and funds required. The rapid spread of stone vaulting throughout Romanesque Europe was most likely the result of a desire to provide a suitably majestic setting for the display of relics as well as enhanced acoustics for the Christian liturgy and the music accompanying it. Some contemporaneous texts, in fact, comment on the "wondrous" visual impact of costly stone vaults.

MOISSAC Saint-Sernin also features a group of seven marble slabs representing angels, apostles, and Christ. Dated to the year 1096, they are among the earliest known examples of large-scale Romanesque sculpture. Stone sculpture had almost disappeared from the art of western Europe during the early Middle Ages. The revival of stone carving is a hallmark of the Romanesque age—and one of the reasons the period is aptly named. The revived tradition of stone carving seems to have begun with decorating column and pier capitals with reliefs. The most extensive preserved ensemble of

ARCHITECTURAL BASICS

The Romanesque Church Portal

Sculpture in a variety of materials adorned different areas of Romanesque churches, but the primary location was the grand stone portal through which the faithful had to pass (see "The Door to Salvation," page 157). Sculpture had appeared in church doorways before. For example, Ottonian bronze doors (FIG. 6-14) featuring Old and New Testament scenes marked the entrance from the cloister to Saint Michael's at Hildesheim. But Hildesheim was exceptional, and in the Romanesque era (and during the Gothic period that followed), sculpture usually appeared in the area *around,* rather than *on,* the doors.

Shown in FIG. 6-21 are the parts of church portals that Romanesque sculptors regularly decorated with figural reliefs:

■ **Tympanum** (FIGS. 6-1a, 6-23, and 6-23A ⬦), the prominent semicircular *lunette* above the doorway proper, comparable in importance to the triangular *pediment* of a Greco-Roman temple (see FIG. 2-20)

■ **Voussoirs** (FIG. 6-23A ⬦), the wedge-shaped blocks that together form the *archivolts* of the arch framing the tympanum

■ **Lintel** (FIGS. 6-23 and 6-23A ⬦), the horizontal beam above the doorway

■ **Trumeau** (FIGS. 6-1c and 6-22), the center post supporting the lintel in the middle of the doorway

■ **Jambs** (FIG. 6-1), the side posts of the doorway

6-21 The Romanesque church portal (John Burge).

The clergy considered the church doorway the beginning of the path to salvation through Christ. The entrance portals of many Romanesque churches feature sculptural reliefs emphasizing that theme.

---

sculptured early Romanesque capitals is in the cloister (FIG. 6-20) of Saint-Pierre at Moissac (FIG. 6-1) in southwestern France. The monks of the Moissac abbey joined the Cluniac order in 1047, and Moissac quickly became an important stop along the pilgrimage route to Santiago de Compostela.

At Moissac, as elsewhere, the cloister and its garden provided the monks (and nuns) with a foretaste of Paradise. In the cloister, they could read their devotions, pray, meditate, and carry on other activities secluded from the outside world. Moissac's cloister sculpture program consists of large figural reliefs on the piers as well as *historiated capitals* (capitals ornamented with carved figures) on the columns. The pier reliefs portray the 12 apostles and the monastery's first Cluniac abbot, Durandus (r. 1047–1072), whom the monks buried in the cloister. The 76 capitals alternately crown single and paired column shafts. They are variously decorated, some with abstract patterns, many with biblical scenes or the lives of saints, others with fantastic monsters of all sorts (FIG. 6-20, *bottom*). *Bestiaries*—collections of illustrations of real and imaginary animals—became very popular in the Romanesque age. The monstrous forms were reminders of the chaos and deformity of a world without God's order. Medieval artists delighted in inventing composite multiheaded beasts and other fantastic creations.

BERNARD OF CLAIRVAUX Historiated capitals were common in Cluniac monasteries. Many medieval monks, especially those of the Cluniac order, equated piety with the construction of beautiful churches with elegant carvings. But one of the founding principles

of monasticism was the rejection of worldly pleasures in favor of the *vita contemplativa* ("contemplative life"), as opposed to the *vita activa* ("active life") of the lay population. Some monks were appalled by lavish churches and their costly furnishings. One group of Benedictine monks founded a new order at Cîteaux in eastern France in 1098. The Cistercians (from the Latin name for Cîteaux) split from the Cluniac order to return to the strict observance of the Rule of Saint Benedict. The Cistercian movement expanded with astonishing rapidity. Within a half century, more than 500 Cistercian monasteries had been established. The Cistercians rejected figural sculpture as a distraction from their devotions. The most outspoken Cistercian critic was Abbot Bernard of Clairvaux (1090–1153), a fervent supporter of *Crusades* to wrest the Holy Land from Muslim control (see "The Crusades" ⬦), who complained bitterly about the rich outfitting of non-Cistercian churches (see "Bernard of Clairvaux on Cloister Sculpture" ⬦).

During the Romanesque period, stone sculpture also spread to other areas of the church, both inside and out. The proliferation of sculpture reflects the changing role of many churches in western Europe. In the early Middle Ages, most churches served small monastic communities, and the worshipers were primarily or exclusively clergy. With the rise of towns in the Romanesque period, churches, especially those on the major pilgrimage routes, increasingly served the lay public. To reach this new, largely illiterate audience and to draw a wider population into their places of worship, the clergy decided to display Christian symbols and stories throughout their churches, especially in the portals (see "The Romanesque Church Portal," above, and FIG. 6-21) facing onto the town squares. Stone, rather than painting or mosaic, was the most suitable durable medium for exterior decorative programs.

The focus of the sculptural program of the Moissac portal is the *Second Coming of Christ* in the tympanum (FIG. 6-1), a subject chosen to underscore the role of the church as the path to Heaven (see "The Door to Salvation," page 157). Variations on this theme adorn the tympana of many Romanesque churches, but the style of these sculptures is quite diverse. The extremely elongated bodies of the angels recording each soul's fate, the cross-legged dancing pose of Saint Matthew's angel, the jerky movement of the elders' heads, the zigzag and dovetail lines of the draperies, the bandlike folds of the torsos, and the bending back of the hands against the body are all characteristic of the anonymous Moissac master's distinctive style. The animation of the individual figures, however, contrasts with the stately monumentality of the composition as a whole, producing a dynamic tension in the tympanum.

Below the tympanum is a richly decorated trumeau with scalloped contours (FIG. 6-1c). On the front are the church's guardian lions. On the trumeau's right face is a prophet (FIG. 6-22) displaying the scroll bearing his prophetic vision. The prophet is tall and thin, and he executes a cross-legged step. The animation of the body reveals the passionate nature of the soul within. The long, serpentine locks of hair and beard frame an arresting image of the dreaming mystic. The prophet seems entranced by his vision of what is to come.

AUTUN In 1132, the Cluniac bishop Étienne de Bage consecrated the Burgundian cathedral of Saint-Lazare (Saint Lazarus) at Autun. The sculptor he entrusted with carving figural reliefs for the church was GISLEBERTUS, who placed his name beneath his dramatic vision of the Last Judgment (FIG. 6-23), the subject of the most important element of the sculptural program. No doubt the bishop permitted Gislebertus to sign his work because the sculptor had so successfully fulfilled his patron's wishes (see "Terrifying the Faithful at Autun," page 175).

MORGAN MADONNA Despite the use of stone relief sculptures to adorn church portals at Moissac (FIG. 6-1), Autun (FIG. 6-23), Vézelay (FIG. 6-23A ⬈), and many other Romanesque sites, resistance to the creation of statues in the round continued in the Romanesque period. The avoidance of anything that might be construed as an idol was still the rule, in keeping with the Second Commandment. (The *Gero Crucifix* [FIG. 6-15] is an exception.) The veneration of relics, however, brought with it a demand for small-scale images of the holy family and saints to be placed on the chapel altars of the churches along the pilgrimage roads. Reliquaries in the form of saints or parts of saints (FIG. 6-16 and 6-16A ⬈), tabletop crucifixes, and wood devotional figurines began to be produced in great numbers.

6-22 Old Testament prophet (Jeremiah or Isaiah?), right side of the trumeau (FIG. 6-1c) of the south portal of Saint-Pierre, Moissac, France, ca. 1115–1130.

On the trumeau of Moissac's south portal, this Old Testament prophet displays the scroll recounting his vision. The prophet's figure is tall, thin, and animated, like the angels in the tympanum.

THE PATRON'S VOICE
Terrifying the Faithful at Autun

In the medieval world, as in antiquity, patrons, not artists, chose the subjects to be represented on the monuments they commissioned. In the case of churches, the clergy were responsible for determining the themes of mosaics, frescoes, relief sculptures, and statues. The artists may have had considerable leeway in *how* to depict the subjects, but not in *what* to represent. Nonetheless, only in exceptional cases did the church officials append to the representations explanations of their intent. The tympanum (FIG. 6-23) of the Cathedral of Saint-Lazare at Autun is one of those exceptions. There, the clergy asked the sculptor Gislebertus to carve a relief of the Last Judgment that would encourage Christians to seek salvation through the Church by terrifying them with a graphic depiction of the horrors of Hell.

In Gislebertus's vision of the Last Judgment, four trumpet-blowing angels announce the second coming of Christ, who appears at the tympanum's center, far larger than any other figure, enthroned in a *mandorla*. He dispassionately presides over the separation of the blessed from the damned. At the left, an obliging angel boosts one of the blessed into the heavenly city. Below, the souls of the dead line up to await their fate. Two of the men near the center of the lintel carry bags emblazoned with a cross and a shell. These are the symbols of pilgrims to Jerusalem and Santiago de Compostela, respectively. Those who had made the difficult journey would be judged favorably. To their right, three small figures beg an angel to intercede on their behalf. The angel responds by pointing to the judge above.

On the right side are those who will be condemned to Hell. Giant hands pluck one poor soul from the earth. Directly above is one of the most unforgettable renditions of the weighing of souls in the history of art. Angels and the Devil's agents try to manipulate the balance for or against a soul. Hideous demons guffaw and roar. Their gaunt, lined bodies, with legs ending in sharp claws, writhe and bend like long, loathsome insects. A devilish creature, leaning from the dragon mouth of Hell, drags souls in, while, above him, a howling demon crams souls headfirst into a furnace.

The purpose of the Autun tympanum was to inspire terror in the believers who passed beneath it as they entered the cathedral. Even those who could not read could, in the words of Bernard of Clairvaux, "read in the marble." For the literate, the Autun clergy composed explicit written warnings to reinforce the pictorial message and had the words engraved in Latin on the rim of Christ's mandorla and on the upper edge of the lintel:

> I alone arrange all things and crown the deserving. Punishment, with me as judge, holds in check those whom vice stimulates. Whoever is not seduced by an impious life will rise again in this way, and the light of day will shine on him forever. May this terror terrify those whom earthly error binds, for the horror of these images here in this manner truly depicts what will be.*

*Translated by Calvin B. Kendall, *The Allegory of the Church: Romanesque Portals and Their Verse Inscriptions* (Toronto: University of Toronto Press, 1998), 207.

6-23 GISLEBERTUS, *Last Judgment*, west tympanum of Saint-Lazare, Autun, France, ca. 1120–1135. Marble, 21' wide at base.

The enthroned Christ presides over the separation of the blessed from the damned in Gislebertus's dramatic vision of the Last Judgment, designed to terrify those guilty of sin and beckon them into the church.

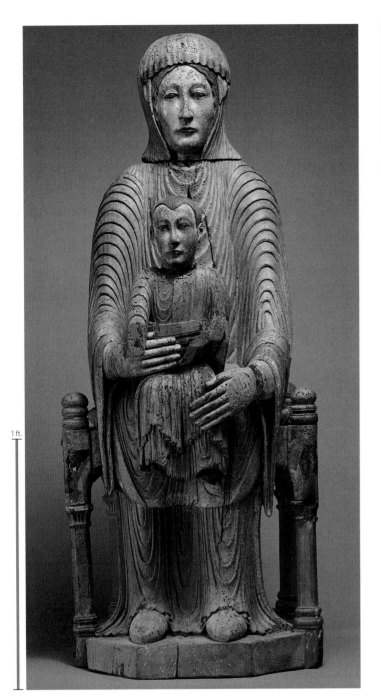

6-24 Virgin and Child (*Morgan Madonna*), from Auvergne, France, second half of 12th century. Painted wood, 2′ 7″ high. Metropolitan Museum of Art, New York (gift of J. Pierpont Morgan, 1916).

The veneration of relics created a demand for small-scale images of the holy family and saints to be placed on chapel altars. This painted wood statuette depicts the Virgin as the "throne of wisdom."

One popular type, a specialty of the workshops of Auvergne, France, was a wood statuette depicting the Virgin Mary with the Christ Child in her lap. The *Morgan Madonna* (FIG. **6-24**), so named because it once belonged to the American financier and collector J. Pierpont Morgan, is one example. The type, known as the *sedes sapientiae* (Latin, "throne of wisdom"), is a western European freestanding version of the Theotokos theme popular in Byzantine icons (FIG. 4-20) and mosaics. Christ, the embodiment of divine wisdom, holds a Bible in his left hand and raises his right arm in blessing

6-25 Initial *R* with knight fighting a dragon, folio 4 verso of the *Moralia in Job,* from Cîteaux, France, ca. 1115–1125. Ink and tempera on vellum, 1′ 1¾″ × 9¼″. Bibliothèque municipale, Dijon.

Ornamented initials date to the Hiberno-Saxon era (FIG. 6-4), but this artist translated the theme into Romanesque terms. The duel between knight and dragons symbolized a monk's spiritual struggle.

(both hands are broken off). His seated mother is in turn the throne of wisdom because her lap is the Christ Child's throne. As in Byzantine art, both Madonna and Child sit rigidly upright and are strictly frontal, emotionless figures. But the intimate scale, the gesture of benediction, the once-bright coloring of the garments, and the soft modeling of the Virgin's face make the mother-and-son pair seem much less remote than its Byzantine counterparts.

MORALIA IN JOB Unlike stone sculpture, the art of painting needed no "revival" in the Romanesque period. Monasteries had been producing large numbers of illuminated manuscripts for centuries. One of the major Romanesque scriptoria was at the abbey of Cîteaux, mother church of the Cistercian order. Just before Bernard of Clairvaux joined the monastery in 1112, the monks completed work on an illuminated copy of Saint Gregory's (Pope Gregory the Great, r. 590–604) *Moralia in Job.* It is an example of Cistercian illumination that predates Bernard's passionate opposition to monastic figural art, which in 1134 resulted in a Cistercian ban on elaborate paintings in manuscripts as well as sculptural ornamentation in monasteries (see "Bernard of Clairvaux" ⧉). After 1134, the Cistercian order prohibited full-page illustrations, and even initial letters had to be nonfigurative and of a single color. The *historiated* initial reproduced here (FIG. **6-25**) clearly would have been in violation

Hildegard of Bingen was one of the great religious figures of the Middle Ages. Here, she experiences a divine vision, shown as five tongues of fire emanating from above and entering her brain.

flourish to the swordsman's gesture. The knight, handsomely garbed, cavalierly wears no armor and calmly aims a single stroke, unmoved by the ferocious dragons lunging at him.

Holy Roman Empire and Italy

The Romanesque successors of the Ottonians were the Salians (r. 1027–1125), a dynasty of Franks. They ruled an empire corresponding roughly to present-day Germany and the Lombard region of northern Italy (MAP 6-1). Like their predecessors, the Salian emperors were important patrons of art and architecture, although, as elsewhere in Romanesque Europe, the monasteries remained great centers of artistic production.

HILDEGARD OF BINGEN The most prominent nun of the 12th century and one of the greatest religious figures of the Middle Ages was Hildegard of Bingen (1098–1179). Born into an aristocratic family that owned large estates in the German Rhineland, Hildegard began to have visions at a very early age, and her parents had her study to become a nun. In 1141, God instructed Hildegard to disclose her visions to the world. Bernard of Clairvaux certified in 1147 that those visions were authentic. Archbishop Heinrich of Mainz joined in the endorsement, and in 1148, the Cistercian pope Eugenius III (r. 1145–1153) formally authorized Hildegard "in the name of Christ and Saint Peter to publish all that she had learned from the Holy Spirit." At this time, Hildegard became the abbess of a new convent built for her near Bingen. As reports of Hildegard's visions spread, kings, popes, barons, and prelates sought her counsel.

of Bernard's ban if it had not been painted before his prohibitions took effect. A knight, his squire, and two roaring dragons form an intricate letter *R,* the initial letter of the salutation *Reverentissimo.* This page is the opening of Gregory's letter to "the most revered" Leander, bishop of Seville, Spain. The knight is a slender, regal figure who raises his shield and sword against the dragons while the squire, crouching beneath him, runs a lance through one of the monsters. The duel between knight and dragons symbolized the spiritual struggle of monks against the Devil for the salvation of souls.

Ornamented initials date to the Hiberno-Saxon period (FIG. 6-4), but in the *Moralia in Job,* the artist translated the theme into Romanesque terms. The Leander page may be a reliable picture of a medieval baron's costume. The typically French Romanesque banding of the torso and partitioning of the folds are evident, but the master painter deftly avoided stiffness and angularity. The partitioning here accentuates the knight's verticality and elegance and the thrusting action of his servant. The flowing sleeves add a spirited

Among the most interesting Romanesque books is Hildegard's *Scivias* (*Know the Ways* [*Scite vias*] *of God*). On the opening page (FIG. **6-26**), Hildegard sits within a monastery experiencing her divine vision. Five long tongues of fire emanating from above enter her brain, just as she describes the experience in the accompanying text. Using a wax tablet resting on her left knee, Hildegard immediately sets down what has been revealed to her. Nearby, the monk Volmar, Hildegard's confessor, copies into a book everything she wrote. Here, in a singularly dramatic context, is a picture of the essential nature of ancient and medieval book manufacture—individual scribes copying and recopying texts by hand.

6-27 Interior of Sant'Ambrogio (looking east), Milan, Italy, late 11th to early 12th century.

The architect of this Milanese church was one of the first to use groin vaults in the nave. Each nave bay corresponds to two aisle bays. The alternate-support system complements this modular plan.

MILAN Nowhere is the regional diversity of Romanesque art and architecture more readily apparent than in Italy. Developments in Lombardy parallel those elsewhere in the Holy Roman Empire, but in central Italy, the Early Christian tradition remained very strong. The Lombard church of Sant'Ambrogio (FIG. 6-27), erected in Milan in the late 11th or early 12th century in honor of Saint Ambrose, the city's first bishop (d. 397), is an example of the experimentation with different kinds of vaulting that characterizes Romanesque architecture north of the Alps. Sant'Ambrogio has a nave and two aisles, but no transept. Above each inner aisle is a tribune gallery.

6-28 Cathedral complex (looking northeast), Pisa, Italy; cathedral begun 1063; baptistery begun 1153; campanile begun 1174.

Pisa's cathedral more closely resembles Early Christian basilicas than structurally more experimental French and Lombard Romanesque churches. Separate bell towers and baptisteries are Italian features.

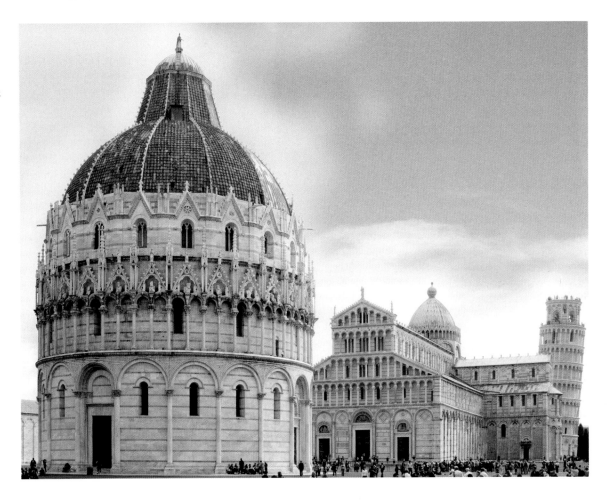

Each nave bay consists of a full square flanked by two small squares in each aisle, all covered with groin vaults. The technical problems of building groin vaults of cut stone (as opposed to concrete, knowledge of which did not survive the fall of Rome) at first limited their use to the covering of small areas, such as the individual bays of the aisles of Saint-Sernin (FIGS. 6-18 and 6-19) at Toulouse. In Sant'Ambrogio, the nave vaults are slightly domical, rising higher than the transverse arches. The windows in the octagonal dome over the last bay provide the major light source for the otherwise rather dark interior. (The building lacks a clerestory.) The emphatic alternate-support system perfectly reflects the geometric regularity of the plan. The lighter pier moldings stop at the gallery level, and the heavier ones rise to support the nave vaults. The compound piers even continue into the ponderous vaults, which have supporting arches, or *ribs,* along their groins. This is one of the first instances of *rib vaulting,* a key characteristic of mature Romanesque and later Gothic architecture (see "The Gothic Rib Vault," page 190).

PISA Although the widespread use of stone vaults in 11th- and 12th-century churches inspired the term *Romanesque,* Italian Romanesque churches outside Lombardy usually retained the timber roofs of their Early Christian predecessors. The cathedral complex (FIG. 6-28) at Pisa dramatically testifies to the regional diversity of Romanesque architecture. The cathedral, its freestanding *campanile* (bell tower), and the baptistery, where infants and converts were initiated into the Christian community, present a rare opportunity to study a coherent group of three Romanesque buildings. Save for the upper portion of the baptistery, with its remodeled Gothic exterior, the three structures are stylistically homogeneous.

Construction of Pisa Cathedral began first—in 1063, the same year work began on Saint Mark's (FIG. 4-24) in Venice, another prosperous maritime city. The spoils of a naval victory over the Muslims off Palermo in Sicily in 1062 funded the Pisan project. Pisa Cathedral is large, with a nave and four aisles, and is one of the most impressive and majestic Romanesque churches. At first glance, the cathedral resembles an Early Christian basilica, but the broadly projecting transept with apses, crossing dome, and multiple arcaded galleries on the facade distinguish it as Romanesque. So too does the rich marble *incrustation* (wall decoration consisting of bright panels of different colors, as in the Pantheon's interior; FIG. 3-40). The cathedral's campanile, detached in the standard Italian fashion, is Pisa's famous Leaning Tower (FIG. 6-28, *right*). Graceful arcaded galleries mark the tower's stages and repeat the cathedral's facade motif, effectively relating the round campanile to its mother building. The tilted vertical axis of the tower is the result of a settling foundation. The tower began to "lean" even while under construction, and now inclines some 5.5 degrees out of plumb at the top.

Normandy and England

After their conversion to Christianity in the early 10th century, the Vikings—Scandinavian traders and pirates named after the *viks* ("coves" or "trading places" of the Norwegian coastline)—settled on the northern French coast in present-day Normandy, the home of the Norsemen, or Normans. The Normans quickly developed a distinctive Romanesque architectural style that became the major source of French Gothic architecture.

CAEN Most critics consider the abbey church of Saint-Étienne at Caen the masterpiece of Norman Romanesque architecture. Begun by William of Normandy (William the Conqueror; see page 183) in 1067, work must have advanced rapidly because the Normans buried the duke in the church in 1087. Saint-Étienne's west facade (FIG. 6-29) is a striking design rooted in the tradition of Carolingian and Ottonian westworks, but it reveals a new unified organizational scheme. Four large buttresses divide the facade into three bays that correspond to the nave and aisles. Above the buttresses, the towers also display a triple division and a progressively greater piercing of the walls from lower to upper stages. (The culminating spires are a Gothic addition.) The three-part composition extends throughout the facade, both vertically and horizontally, consistent with the careful and methodical planning of the entire structure.

6-29 West facade of Saint-Étienne, Caen, France, begun 1067.

The division of Saint-Étienne's facade into three parts corresponding to the nave and aisles reflects the methodical planning of the entire structure. The towers also have three sections.

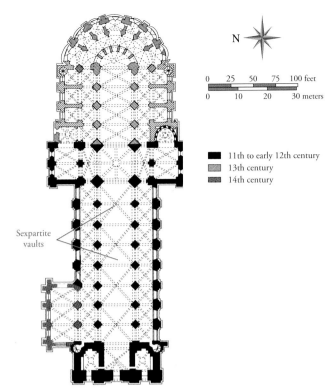

Sexpartite
vaults

11th to early 12th century
13th century
14th century

6-30 Interior (*left*; looking east) and plan (*right*) of Saint-Étienne, Caen, France, vaulted ca. 1115–1120.

The six-part groin vaults of Saint-Étienne make clerestory windows possible. The three-story elevation with its large arched openings provides ample light and makes the nave appear taller than it is.

The original design of Saint-Étienne called for a timber roof, but the Caen nave (FIG. 6-30) had compound piers with simple engaged half columns alternating with piers with half columns attached to pilasters. When the Normans decided to install groin vaults around 1115, the existing alternating compound piers proved a good match. Those piers soar all the way to the vaults' springing. Their branching ribs divide the large square-vault compartments into six sections—a *sexpartite vault*. The vaults rise high enough to provide room for clerestory windows. The resulting three-story elevation, with its large arched openings, allows ample light to reach the interior. It also makes the nave appear taller than it is. As in Sant'Ambrogio (FIG. 6-27), the Norman building has rib vaults. The diagonal and transverse ribs form a structural skeleton that partially supports the still fairly massive paneling between them. But despite the heavy masonry, Saint-Étienne's large windows and reduced interior wall surface give the nave a light and airy quality unusual in the Romanesque period.

DURHAM William of Normandy's conquest of Anglo-Saxon England in 1066 began a new epoch in English history. In architecture, it signaled the importation of Norman Romanesque building and design methods. Construction of Durham Cathedral (FIG. 6-31), on the Scottish frontier of northern England, began around 1093—before the remodeling of Saint-Étienne. Unlike the Caen church, Durham Cathedral was a vaulted structure from the outset. Consequently, the pattern of the ribs of the nave's groin vaults corresponds

perfectly to the design of the arcade below. Each seven-part nave vault covers two bays (FIG. 6-32, *left*). Large, simple pillars ornamented with abstract designs (diamond, chevron, and cable patterns, all originally painted) alternate with compound piers that carry the transverse arches of the vaults. The pier-vault relationship scarcely could be more visible or the building's structural rationale better expressed.

The bold surface patterning of the pillars in the Durham nave is a reminder that the raising of imposing stone buildings such as the Romanesque churches of England and Normandy required more than just the talents of master designers. A corps of expert masons had to transform rough stone blocks into the precise shapes necessary for their specific place in the church's fabric. Although thousands of simple quadrangular blocks make up the great walls of these buildings, the stonecutters also had to produce large numbers of blocks of far more complex shapes. To cover the nave and aisles, the masons had to carve blocks with concave faces to conform to the curve of the vault. Also required were blocks with projecting moldings for the ribs, blocks with convex surfaces for the pillars or with multiple profiles for the compound piers, and so forth. It was an immense undertaking, and it is no wonder that medieval building campaigns often lasted for decades.

Durham's builders employed the earliest known example of a rib groin vault placed over a three-story nave. In the nave's western parts, completed before 1130, the rib vaults have pointed arches, bringing together for the first time two key elements that

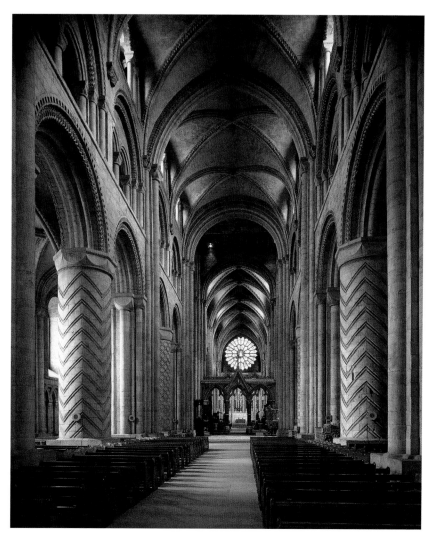

6-31 Interior of Durham Cathedral (looking east), Durham, England, begun ca. 1093.

Durham Cathedral boasts the first examples of rib groin vaults placed over a three-story nave. The builders replaced groin vaults in the tribune with quadrant arches as buttresses of the nave vaults.

determined the structural evolution of Gothic architecture (see "The Gothic Rib Vault," page 190). Also of great significance is the way the English builders buttressed the nave vaults. The lateral section (FIG. 6-32, *right*) exposes the simple *quadrant arches* (arches whose curve extends for one-quarter of a circle's circumference) that take the place of groin vaults in the Durham tribune. The structural descendants of these quadrant arches are the *flying buttresses* that are another hallmark of the mature Gothic solution to church construction (see "Building a High Gothic Cathedral," page 193).

BURY BIBLE Many of the finest illustrated manuscripts of the Romanesque age were the work of monks in English scriptoria, following in the tradition of Hiberno-Saxon books. The *Bury Bible,* produced at the Bury Saint Edmunds abbey in England around 1135, exemplifies the luxurious illumination common to the large Bibles used in wealthy Romanesque abbeys not subject to the Cistercian restrictions

Addition

Seven-part vaults

N

Quadrant arch

0   50   100 feet
0 10 20 30 meters

6-32 Plan (*left*) and lateral section (*right*) of Durham Cathedral, Durham, England, begun ca. 1093.

Durham Cathedral is typically English in its long, slender proportions. In the nave, simple pillars alternate with compound piers that support the transverse arches of the seven-part groin vaults.

on painted manuscripts. One page (FIG. 6-33) shows two scenes from Deuteronomy framed by symmetrical leaf motifs in softly glowing harmonized colors. At the top, Moses expounds the law; below, he points out the clean and unclean beasts. In both panels, the prophet has horns, consistent with Saint Jerome's translation of the Hebrew word that also means "rays." The gestures are slow and the figures possess a quiet dignity. Moses and Aaron seem to glide. This presentation is quite different from the abrupt emphasis and spastic movement of contemporaneous Romanesque relief sculptures. Yet patterning remains in the multiple divisions of the draped limbs, the lightly shaded volumes connected with sinuous lines and ladderlike folds.

The artist responsible for the *Bury Bible* is known: MASTER HUGO, who was also a sculptor and metalworker. With Gislebertus (FIG. 6-23), Hugo was one of the small but growing number of Romanesque artists who signed their works or whose names were recorded. In the 12th century, artists increasingly began to identify themselves. Although most medieval artists remained anonymous, the contrast of the Romanesque period with the early Middle Ages is striking. Hugo apparently was a secular artist, a member of the emerging class of professional artists and artisans who depended for their livelihood on commissions from well-endowed monasteries. These artists resided in towns rather than within secluded abbey walls, and they traveled frequently to find work. They were the exception, however, and most Romanesque scribes and illuminators continued to be monks and nuns working anonymously in the service of God.

EADWINE PSALTER Named for the English monk EADWINE THE SCRIBE, the *Eadwine Psalter* contains 165 biblical illustrations. The last page (FIG. 6-34), however, presents a rare picture of a Romanesque artist at work. The style of the Eadwine portrait resembles that of the *Bury Bible,* but although the patterning is still firm (notably in the cowl and the thigh), the drapery falls more softly and follows the movements of the body beneath it. Here, the abstract patterning typical of many Romanesque painted and sculpted garments

6-33 MASTER HUGO, *Moses Expounding the Law,* folio 94 recto of the *Bury Bible,* from Bury Saint Edmunds, England, ca. 1135. Ink and tempera on vellum, 1' 8" × 1' 2". Corpus Christi College, Cambridge.

Master Hugo was a rare Romanesque lay artist, one of the emerging class of professional artists and artisans who depended for their livelihood on commissions from wealthy monasteries.

6-34 EADWINE THE SCRIBE, Eadwine the scribe at work, folio 283 verso of the *Eadwine Psalter,* ca. 1160–1170. Ink and tempera on vellum, 1' 3$\frac{1}{2}$" × 11$\frac{5}{8}$". Trinity College, Cambridge.

Although he humbly offered his book as a gift to God, the English monk Eadwine added an inscription to his portrait declaring himself "the prince of scribes" whose fame would endure forever.

yielded slightly, but clearly, to the requirements of more naturalistic representation. The Romanesque artist's instinct for decorating the surface remained, as is apparent in the gown's whorls and spirals. Significantly, however, the artist painted those interior lines very lightly so that they would not conflict with the functional lines containing them.

The "portrait" of Eadwine—it is probably a generic type and not a specific likeness—is in the long tradition of author portraits in ancient and medieval manuscripts, although the true author of the *Eadwine Psalter* is King David. Eadwine exaggerated his importance by likening himself to an evangelist writing his Gospel (FIGS. 6-5 and 6-6) and by including an inscription within the inner frame giving his name and proclaiming that he is "the prince of scribes." He declares that the excellence of his work will cause his fame to endure forever, and consequently he can offer his book as an acceptable gift to God. Eadwine, like other Romanesque sculptors and painters who signed their works, may have been concerned for his fame, but these artists, whether clergy or laity, were as yet unaware of the concepts of "fine art" and "fine artist." To them, their work existed not for its own sake but for God's. Nonetheless, works such as Eadwine's portrait are an early sign of a new attitude toward the role of the artist in society that presages the reemergence in the Renaissance of the classical notion of individual artistic genius.

BAYEUX TAPESTRY The most famous work of English Romanesque art is neither a book nor Christian in subject. The so-called *Bayeux Tapestry* (FIGS. 6-35 and 6-36) is unique in medieval art. It is not a woven *tapestry* but rather an *embroidery* made of eight colors of wool yarn sewn on linen—two varieties of blue; three shades of green; yellow; buff; and terracotta red. Closely related to

Romanesque manuscript illumination, the *Bayeux Tapestry*'s borders contain the kinds of real and imaginary animals found in contemporaneous books, and an explanatory Latin text sewn in thread accompanies many of the pictures. Some 20 inches high and about 230 feet long, the embroidery is a continuous, friezelike, pictorial narrative of the Norman defeat of the Anglo-Saxons at Hastings in 1066, and of the events leading up to that crucial battle in the history of England. The Norman victory at Hastings united all of England and much of France under one rule. The dukes of Normandy became the kings of England. Commissioned by Bishop Odo, the half brother of the conquering Duke William, the embroidery may have been sewn by women at the Norman court. Many art historians, however, believe that it was the work of English stitchers in Kent, where Odo was earl after the Norman conquest. Odo donated the work to Bayeux Cathedral (hence its nickname), but it is uncertain whether it was originally intended for display in the church's nave, where the theme would have been a curious choice.

The events that precipitated the Norman invasion of England are well documented. In 1066, Edward the Confessor (r. 1042–1066), the Anglo-Saxon king of England, died. The Normans believed that Edward had recognized William of Normandy as his rightful heir. But the crown went to Harold, earl of Wessex, the king's Anglo-Saxon brother-in-law, who had sworn an oath of allegiance to William. The betrayed Normans, descendants of the seafaring Vikings, boarded their ships, crossed the English Channel, and crushed Harold's forces.

Illustrated here are two episodes of the epic tale as represented in the *Bayeux Tapestry*. The first detail (FIG. 6-35) depicts King Edward's funeral procession. The hand of God points the way to the church in London where he was buried—Westminster

6-35 Funeral procession to Westminster Abbey, detail of the *Bayeux Tapestry*, from Bayeux Cathedral, Bayeux, France, ca. 1070–1080. Embroidered wool on linen, 1' 8" high (entire length of fabric, 229' 8" long). Centre Guillaume le Conquérant, Bayeux.

The *Bayeux Tapestry* is not a tapestry but rather an embroidery. The women needleworkers employed eight colors of dyed wool yarn and sewed the threads onto the linen fabric.

6-36 Battle of Hastings, detail of the *Bayeux Tapestry,* from Bayeux Cathedral, Bayeux, France, ca. 1070–1080. Embroidered wool on linen, 1' 8" high (entire length of fabric, 229' 8" long). Centre Guillaume le Conquérant, Bayeux.

The *Bayeux Tapestry* is unique in medieval art. Like the scroll-like frieze of Trajan's Column (FIG. 3-36) and other historical narratives in Roman art, it depicts contemporaneous events in full detail.

Abbey, consecrated on December 28, 1065, just a few days before Edward's death. The church was one of the first Romanesque buildings erected in England, and the embroiderers took pains to record its main features, including the lofty crossing tower and the long nave with tribunes. There, William was crowned king of England on Christmas Day, 1066. The second detail (FIG. 6-36) shows the Battle of Hastings in progress. The Norman cavalry cuts down the English defenders. Filling the lower border are the dead and wounded, although the upper register continues the animal motifs of the rest of the embroidery. The Romanesque artist co-opted some of the characteristic motifs of Greco-Roman battle scenes—for example, the horses with twisted necks and contorted bodies (compare FIG. 2-50)—but rendered the figures in the Romanesque manner. Linear patterning and flat color replace classical three-dimensional volume and modeling in light and dark hues.

The *Bayeux Tapestry* stands apart from all other Romanesque artworks in depicting in full detail an event at a time shortly after it occurred, recalling the historical narratives of ancient Roman art. Art historians have often likened the Norman embroidery to the scroll-like frieze of the Column of Trajan (FIGS. 3-36, 3-36A, 3-36B, and 3-36C). Like the Roman account, the story told on the textile is the conqueror's version of history, a proclamation of national pride. As in the ancient frieze, the narrative is not confined to battlefield successes. It is a complete chronicle of events. Included are the preparations for war, with scenes depicting the felling and splitting of trees for ship construction, the loading of equipment onto the vessels, the cooking and serving of meals, and so forth. In this respect, the *Bayeux Tapestry* is the most *Roman*-esque work of Romanesque art.

 Explore the era further in MindTap with videos of major artworks and buildings, Google Earth™ coordinates, and essays by the author on the following additional subjects:

- Merovingian looped fibulae (FIG. 6-1A)
- *Gospel Book of Otto III* (FIG. 6-11A)
- Sainte-Foy, Conques (FIG. 6-15A)
- Head reliquary of Saint Alexander (FIG. 6-16A)
- ▌WRITTEN SOURCES: The Burning of Canterbury Cathedral
- ▌WRITTEN SOURCES: Bernard of Clairvaux on Cloister Sculpture
- *Mission of the Apostles,* Vézelay (FIG. 6-23A)
- ▌RELIGION AND MYTHOLOGY: The Crusades

EARLY MEDIEVAL AND ROMANESQUE EUROPE

Early Medieval Art

- The surviving artworks of the period following the fall of Rome in 410 are almost exclusively small-scale status symbols, especially items of personal adornment featuring cloisonné decoration consisting of abstract intertwined animal-and-interlace patterns.

- Art historians call the Christian art of early medieval Ireland and Britain *Hiberno-Saxon*. The most important extant artworks are the illuminated manuscripts produced in monastic scriptoria. Among the distinctive features of these books are "carpet pages" devoted neither to text nor to illustration but to pure embellishment, as in the *Lindisfarne Gospels,* and text pages with the initial letters of important passages enlarged and transformed into elaborate decorative patterns.

- In 800, Pope Leo III crowned Charlemagne, king of the Franks since 768, emperor of Rome (r. 800–814). Charlemagne reunited much of western Europe and initiated a conscious revival of the art and culture of Early Christian Rome during the Carolingian period (768–877). Carolingian artists merged the illusionism of classical painting with the northern linear tradition and revived the Early Christian practice of depicting Christ as a statuesque youth. Carolingian architects looked to Ravenna and Early Christian Rome for models, but transformed their sources—introducing the twin-tower west facade (westwork) for basilicas—for example, the abbey church at Corvey—and employing strict modular plans for entire monasteries—for example, Saint Gall—as well as for individual buildings.

- In the 10th century, a new line of emperors, the Ottonians (r. 919–1024), consolidated the eastern part of Charlemagne's former empire and sought to preserve and enrich the culture and tradition of the Carolingian period. Ottonian architects built basilican churches incorporating the towers and westworks of their Carolingian models, but introduced the alternate-support system into the nave. Ottonian sculptors revived the art of large-scale sculpture in works such as the *Gero Crucifix* and the colossal bronze doors of Saint Michael's at Hildesheim.

Lindisfarne Gospels, ca. 698–721

Abbey church, Corvey, 873–885

Gero Crucifix, ca. 970

Romanesque Art

- *Romanesque* takes its name from the Roman-like barrel and groin vaults based on round arches employed in many European churches built between 1050 and 1200. Romanesque vaults, however, are made of stone, not concrete. Numerous churches sprang up along the French pilgrimage roads leading to the shrine of Saint James at Santiago de Compostela in northwestern Spain. These churches were spacious enough to accommodate large crowds of pilgrims who came to view the relics displayed in radiating chapels off the ambulatory and transept. Elsewhere, especially in the Holy Roman Empire and in Normandy (Saint-Étienne, Caen) and England, innovative architects began to use groin vaults in naves and introduced the three-story elevation of nave arcade, tribune, and clerestory.

- The Romanesque period also brought the revival of large-scale stone relief sculpture in cloisters and especially in church portals—for example, Saint-Pierre, Moissac—where scenes of Christ as last judge often greeted the faithful as they entered the doorway to the road to salvation. The sculptor Gislebertus, who worked at the Cathedral of Saint Lazarus at Autun, was one of a growing number of Romanesque artists who signed their works. The names of some Romanesque manuscript painters are also known, including the Englishman Master Hugo, a rare instance of a professional lay artist during the early Middle Ages.

Saint-Étienne, Caen, ca. 1115–1120

Second Coming of Christ, Moissac, ca. 1115–1135

7-1a A primary element of the opus modernum of High Gothic France is the extensive use of stained-glass windows, such as the huge rose window and lancets of the west facade of Reims Cathedral.

▲ 7-1b The jamb statues of Reims Cathedral are almost fully detached from the walls. They stand in contrapposto poses, turn toward one another, and act out biblical dramas using gestures.

7-1 JEAN D'ORBAIS, JEAN LE LOUP, GAUCHER DE REIMS, and BERNARD DE SOISSONS, west facade of Reims Cathedral, Reims, France, ca. 1211–1290.

▲ 7-1c Reims Cathedral's facade reveals High Gothic architects' desire to replace heavy masonry with intricately framed voids. Stained-glass windows, not stone reliefs, fill the three tympana.

Gothic and Late Medieval Europe

"MODERN ARCHITECTURE" IN THE GOTHIC AGE

Although the names of very few medieval architects are known today, the identities of quite a few builders of the Gothic age have been recorded for posterity, including JEAN D'ORBAIS, JEAN LE LOUP, GAUCHER DE REIMS, and BERNARD DE SOISSONS, all of whom worked at Reims Cathedral (FIG. 7-1) during its multigeneration construction campaign. The survival of the names of these and other Gothic architects no doubt reflects the enormous prestige that accrued to all associated with the great cathedrals of the Gothic age. Gothic architecture is one of the towering achievements in the history of world architecture, the unique product of an era of peace and widespread economic prosperity, deep spirituality, and extraordinary technological innovation. Born in the region around Paris called the Île-de-France, the Gothic style quickly came to be called *opus francigenum* ("French work") or, more simply, *opus modernum* ("modern work"). Admired throughout Europe, Gothic cathedrals were regarded as stone and glass images of the City of God, the Heavenly Jerusalem.

One of the prime examples of the "modern" Gothic style of architecture is the cathedral dedicated to the Virgin Mary at Reims in the heart of France's Champagne wine district. Reims Cathedral occupies a special place in the history of France as well as in the history of architecture. Since 496 it has been the site of all French kings' coronations. The present church, begun in 1211 and completed in 1290, features a grandiose facade "punctured" with tall and narrow pointed-arch *lancets,* a huge *stained-glass* circular *rose window* above the central portal, and smaller windows in the three tympana where Romanesque designers had placed stone reliefs. Inside, mystical light streaming through tall stained-glass windows illuminates the church. The nave has three stories, including a new Gothic feature called a *triforium* below the clerestory, and huge rib vaults resting on pointed arches. The thin, window-filled walls at Reims and elsewhere are invisibly held in place by external *flying buttresses* (see "Building a High Gothic Cathedral," page 193).

Reims Cathedral is also noteworthy for its sculpture. In contrast to Romanesque churches, whose facades are adorned with reliefs, Reims and similar French Gothic cathedrals have statues that are almost fully detached from the walls. The figures, such as the Virgin Mary and Saint Elizabeth, stand in contrapposto poses, act out biblical dramas (in this instance, the Visitation), and turn toward one another and converse through gestures.

The High Gothic cathedral and the Gothic architectural style in general live on in countless chapels, academic buildings, and dormitories on college campuses throughout the world.

"GOTHIC" EUROPE

In 1550, Giorgio Vasari (1511–1574; see *"Giorgio Vasari's Lives"* 🔗) first used *Gothic* as a term of ridicule to describe late medieval art and architecture, which he attributed to the Goths and regarded as "monstrous and barbarous."[1] With the publication that year of his influential *Introduction to the Three Arts of Design*, Vasari codified for all time the notion that the early Renaissance artist Lorenzo Ghiberti (1378–1455) had already advanced in his *Commentarii*, namely that the Middle Ages was a period of decline. The Italian humanists, who regarded Greco-Roman art as the standard of excellence, believed that the uncouth Goths were responsible both for the downfall of Rome and for the decline of the classical style in art and architecture. They regarded "Gothic" art with contempt and considered it ugly and crude. "Gothic," like "medieval," is an unfortunate if unavoidable label completely out of sync with both the late medieval and the modern view of the Gothic era as one of the high points in the history of Western art and architecture.

The 12th through 14th centuries were a time of profound change in European society. The focus of both intellectual and religious life shifted definitively from monasteries in the countryside and pilgrimage churches to rapidly expanding cities with enormous cathedrals like that at Reims (FIG. 7-1) reaching to the sky. In these new urban centers, prosperous merchants made their homes and formed *guilds* (professional associations), and scholars founded the first universities. Although the papacy was at the height of its power, and Christian knights still waged Crusades against the Muslims, the independent secular nations of modern Europe were beginning to take shape (MAP 7-1). In fact, many regional variants existed within European Gothic art and architecture, just as distinct regional styles characterized the Romanesque period. Therefore, this chapter deals with contemporaneous developments in the four major regions—France, England, the Holy Roman Empire, and Italy—in separate sections. The Gothic style spread beyond these areas, however, reaching, for example, Eastern Europe and Scandinavia.

MAP 7-1 **Europe around 1200.**

GOTHIC AND LATE MEDIEVAL EUROPE

1140–1194
Early Gothic

- Abbot Suger begins rebuilding the French royal abbey church at Saint-Denis with stained-glass windows and rib vaults on pointed arches.
- Introduced at Saint-Denis, sculpted jamb figures also adorn all three portals of the west facade of Chartres Cathedral.

1194–1300
High Gothic

- The rebuilt Chartres Cathedral sets the pattern for High Gothic churches: four-part nave vaults braced by external flying buttresses, three-story elevation (arcade, triforium, clerestory), and stained-glass windows in place of heavy masonry.
- At Chartres and Reims in France, at Naumburg in Germany, and elsewhere, statues become more independent of their architectural setting.
- Manuscript illumination moves from monastic scriptoria to urban lay workshops.

1300–1400
Late Gothic

- The Perpendicular style in England emphasizes surface embellishment over structural clarity.
- Giotto, considered the first Renaissance artist, pioneers a naturalistic approach to painting based on observation.
- Duccio softens the Byzantine-inspired maniera greca and humanizes religious subject matter.
- Secular themes emerge as important subjects in civic commissions, as in the frescoes of Siena's Palazzo Pubblico.

FRANCE

About 1130, King Louis VI (r. 1108–1137) moved his official residence to Paris, spurring much commercial activity and a great building boom. Paris soon became the most important city in France, indeed in northern Europe (see "Paris, the New Center of Medieval Learning" ⏎), and the Île-de-France the leading center of Gothic art and architecture.

Architecture and Architectural Decoration

Architectural historians generally agree that the birthplace of Gothic architecture was the abbey of Saint-Denis, a few miles north of Paris. Dionysius (*Denis* in French) was the legendary saint who brought Christianity to Roman Gaul in the third century.

SUGER AND SAINT-DENIS On June 11, 1144, King Louis VII of France (r. 1137–1180), Queen Eleanor of Aquitaine, and an entourage of court members, together with five French archbishops and

other distinguished clergy, converged on the Benedictine abbey church of Saint-Denis for the dedication of its new east end. The original Carolingian basilica housed the tomb of Saint Dionysius and those of nearly all the French kings. The basilica was France's royal church, the very symbol of the monarchy. By the early 12th century, however, the church was in disrepair and had become too small to accommodate the growing number of pilgrims. Its abbot, Suger (ca. 1081–1151), also believed that the Carolingian shrine was of insufficient grandeur to serve as the official church of the French kings. In 1135, he began to rebuild Saint-Denis by erecting a new west facade with sculptured portals (see "Abbot Suger and the Rebuilding of Saint-Denis" ⏎). Work began on the east end (FIGS. **7-2** and **7-3**) in 1140. Suger died before he could remodel the nave, but he attended the 1144 dedication of the new choir, ambulatory, and radiating chapels.

The remodeled portion of Saint-Denis represented a sharp departure from past practice. Innovative rib vaults resting on pointed, or *ogival,* arches (see "The Gothic Rib Vault," page 190, and FIG. 7-4) cover the ambulatory and chapels (FIG. 7-2). These pioneering, exceptionally lightweight vaults spring from slender columns in the ambulatory and from the thin masonry walls framing the chapels. The lightness of the vaults enabled the builders to eliminate the walls between the chapels and open up the outer walls and fill them with stained-glass windows (see "Stained-Glass Windows," page 195). Suger and his contemporaries marveled at the "wonderful and uninterrupted light" that poured in through these "most luminous windows." The abbot called the colored light *lux nova,* "new light." Saint-Denis's pointed-arch vaulting and stained-glass windows became hallmarks of French Gothic architecture.

ROYAL PORTAL, CHARTRES Saint-Denis is also the key monument of Early Gothic (ca. 1140–1194) sculpture. Little of the sculpture that Suger commissioned for the west facade of the abbey church survived the French Revolution of the late 18th century, but originally, statues of Old Testament kings, queens, and prophets

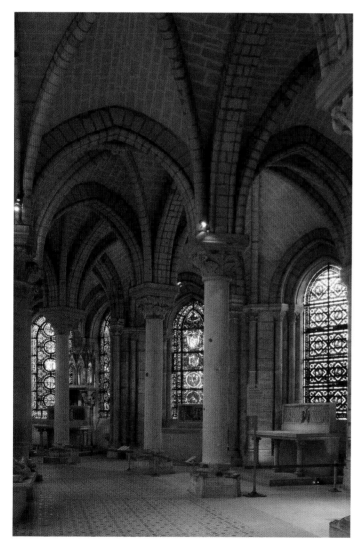

7-2 Ambulatory and radiating chapels (looking northeast), abbey church, Saint-Denis, France, 1140–1144.

Abbot Suger's remodeling of Saint-Denis marked the beginning of Gothic architecture. Rib vaults with pointed arches spring from slender columns. The radiating chapels have stained-glass windows.

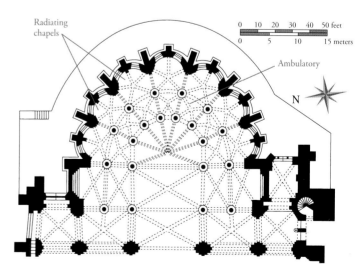

7-3 Plan of the east end, abbey church, Saint-Denis, France, 1140–1144 (after Sumner Crosby).

The innovative plan of the east end of Saint-Denis dates to Abbot Suger's lifetime. By using very light rib vaults, the builders were able to eliminate the walls between the radiating chapels.

ARCHITECTURAL BASICS
The Gothic Rib Vault

The ancestors of the Gothic *rib vault* are the Romanesque vaults found at Caen (FIG. 6-30), Durham (FIG. 6-31), and elsewhere. The rib vault's distinguishing features are the crossed, or diagonal, arches under its groins. The ribs form the *armature,* or skeletal framework, for constructing the vault. Gothic vaults generally have more thinly vaulted *webs* (the masonry between the ribs) than found in Romanesque vaults. But the chief difference between the two types of rib vaults is the *pointed arch,* an integral part of the Gothic skeletal armature. French Romanesque architects (FIG. 6-1) borrowed the form from Muslim Spain and passed it to their Gothic successors. Pointed arches enabled Gothic builders to make the crowns of all the vaults approximately the same level, regardless of the space to be vaulted. The Romanesque architects could not achieve this with their semicircular arches.

The drawings in FIG. 7-4 illustrate this key difference. In FIG. 7-4a, the rectangle *ABCD* is an oblong nave bay to be vaulted. *AC* and *DB* are the diagonal ribs; *AB* and *DC,* the transverse arches; and *AD* and *BC,* the nave arcade's arches. If the architect uses semicircular arches (*AFB, BJC,* and *DHC*), their radii and, therefore, their heights (*EF, IJ,* and *GH*) will be different because the width of a semicircular arch determines its height. The result will be a vault (FIG. 7-4b) with higher transverse arches (*DHC*) than the arcade's arches (*CJB*). The vault's crown (*F*) will be still higher. If the builder uses pointed arches (FIG. 7-4c), the transverse (*DLC*) and arcade (*BKC*) arches can have the same heights (*GL* and *IK* in FIG. 7-4a). The result will be a Gothic rib vault where the points of the arches (*L* and *K*) are at the same level as the vault's crown (*F*).

A major advantage of the Gothic vault is its flexibility, which enables the vaulting of compartments of varying shapes, as at Saint-Denis (FIGS. 7-2 and 7-3). Pointed arches also channel the weight of the vaults more directly downward than do semicircular arches. The vaults therefore require less buttressing to hold them in place, in turn making it possible to open up the walls and place large windows beneath the arches. Because pointed arches also lead the eye upward, they make the vaults appear taller than they are. In FIG. 7-4, the crown (*F*) of both the Romanesque (*b*) and Gothic (*c*) vaults is the same height from the pavement, but the Gothic vault seems taller. Both the physical and visual properties of rib vaults with pointed arches aided Gothic builders in their quest for soaring height in church interiors (FIG. 7-13).

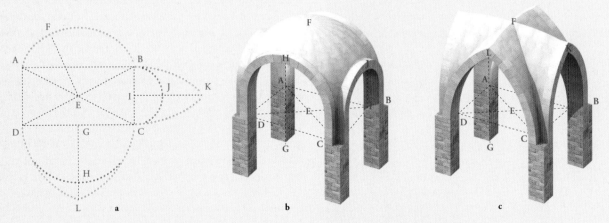

7-4 Diagram (*a*) and drawings of rib vaults with semicircular (*b*) and pointed (*c*) arches (John Burge).

Pointed arches channel the weight of the rib vaults more directly downward than do semicircular arches, requiring less buttressing. Pointed arches also make the vaults appear taller than they are.

attached to columns adorned the jambs of all three doorways. This innovative design appeared immediately afterward in the Royal Portal (FIG. 7-5) of the west facade of Chartres Cathedral, the church dedicated to Our Lady (Notre Dame), the Virgin Mary, and that housed her mantle, a precious relic. The iconographic program of the Royal Portal—named for the jamb statues of kings and queens—proclaims the majesty and power of Christ. Christ's ascension appears in the tympanum of the left doorway. The second coming is the subject of the center tympanum, as at Moissac (FIG. 6-1). In the tympanum of the right portal, the infant Jesus sits in the lap of the Virgin Mary. Mary's prominence on the Chartres facade has no parallel in the sculptural programs of Romanesque church portals. At Chartres, the Virgin assumed a central role, a position she maintained throughout the Gothic period. As the mother of the Savior, Mary stood compassionately between the last judge and the horrors

of Hell, interceding for all her faithful. Worshipers in the later 12th and 13th centuries sang hymns to the Virgin and dedicated great cathedrals to her. Soldiers carried her image into battle on banners, and Mary's name joined Saint Denis's as part of the French king's battle cry. The Virgin became the spiritual lady of chivalry, and the Christian knight dedicated his life to her. The severity of Romanesque themes stressing the last judgment yielded to the gentleness of Gothic art, in which Mary is the kindly queen of Heaven.

Statues of Old Testament kings and queens (FIG. 7-6) occupy the jambs flanking each doorway of the Royal Portal. They are the royal ancestors of Christ and, both figuratively and literally, support the New Testament figures above the doorways. They wear 12th-century clothes, and medieval observers may have regarded them as images of the kings and queens of France. (This was the motivation for vandalizing the comparable figures at Saint-Denis during

7-5 Royal Portal, west facade, Chartres Cathedral, Chartres, France, ca. 1145–1155.

The sculptures of the Royal Portal proclaim the majesty and power of Christ. The tympana depict, from left to right, Christ's ascension, the second coming, and the infant Jesus in the lap of the Virgin Mary.

the French Revolution.) The figures stand rigidly upright with their elbows held close against their hips. The linear folds of their garments—inherited from the Romanesque style, along with the elongated proportions—generally echo the vertical lines of the columns behind them. In this respect, Gothic *jamb statues* differ significantly from classical *caryatids* (FIG. 2-42). The Gothic figures are *attached* to columns. The classical statues *replaced* the columns. The Chartres jamb statues are therefore technically high reliefs. Nonetheless, the statues of kings and queens stand out from the plane of the wall and display signs of a new interest in naturalism on the part of medieval sculptors, noticeable particularly in the heads, where kindly human faces replace the masklike features of most Romanesque figures. The Royal Portal figures initiate an era of artistic concern with personality and individuality.

7-6 Old Testament kings and queen, jamb statues on the right side of the central doorway of the Royal Portal (FIG. 7-5), Chartres Cathedral, Chartres, France, ca. 1145–1155.

The biblical kings and queens of the Royal Portal are the royal ancestors of Christ. These Early Gothic jamb figures display the first signs of a new naturalism in European sculpture.

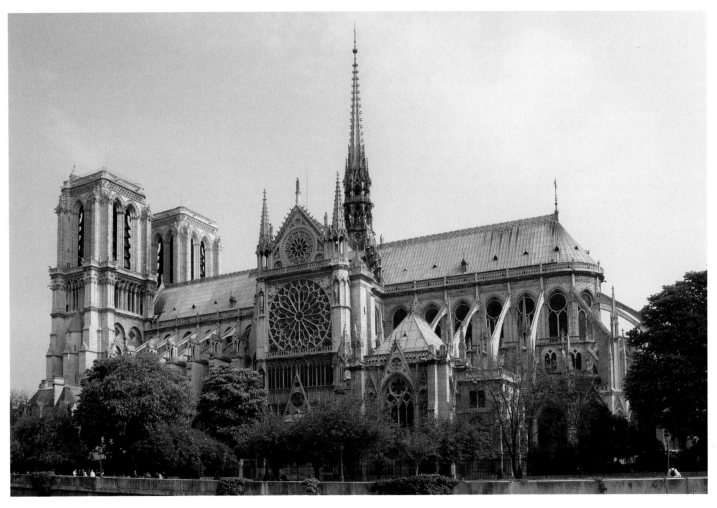

7-7 Notre-Dame (looking northwest), Paris, France, begun 1163; nave and flying buttresses, ca. 1180–1200; remodeled after 1225.

Architects first used flying buttresses on a grand scale at the Cathedral of Notre-Dame in Paris. The buttresses countered the outward thrust of the nave vaults and held up the towering nave walls.

NOTRE-DAME, PARIS Because of the rapid urbanization of Paris under Louis VI and his successors and the accompanying population boom, a new cathedral became a necessity. Notre-Dame (FIG. 7-7) occupies a picturesque site on an island in the Seine River called the Île-de-la-Cité. The Gothic church, which replaced a large Merovingian basilica, has a complicated building history. The choir and transept were in place by 1182, the nave by about 1225, and the facade not until about 1250 to 1260. The original nave elevation had four stories, with a stained-glass *oculus* (small round window) inserted between the vaulted tribune and clerestory typical of Norman Romanesque churches, such as Saint-Étienne (FIG. 6-30) at Caen. As a result, windows filled two of the four stories, further reducing the masonry area.

To hold the much thinner—and taller—walls of Notre-Dame in place, the unknown architect introduced *flying buttresses,* external arches that spring from the lower roofs over the aisles and ambulatory (FIG. 7-7) and counter the outward thrust of the nave vaults. Gothic builders had introduced flying buttresses as early as 1150 in a few smaller churches, but at Notre-Dame in Paris, they circle a great urban cathedral. The internal quadrant arches (FIG. 6-32, *right*) beneath the aisle roofs at Durham Cathedral perform a similar function and may be regarded as precedents for exposed Gothic flying buttresses. The combination of precisely positioned flying buttresses and rib vaults with pointed arches was the ideal solution to the problem of constructing lofty naves with huge windows (see "Building a High Gothic Cathedral," page 193, and FIG. 7-8).

CHARTRES AFTER 1194 Churches burned frequently in the Middle Ages (see "The Burning of Canterbury Cathedral" ☑), and the clergy often had to raise money unexpectedly for new building campaigns. In contrast to monastic churches, which usually were small and often could be completed quickly, urban cathedrals had construction histories that frequently extended over decades and sometimes centuries. The rebuilding of Chartres Cathedral following a devastating fire in 1194 that destroyed all but the lower parts of its west facade took a relatively short 27 years. Architectural historians generally consider the post-1194 Chartres Cathedral the first High Gothic building. At Chartres (FIGS. 7-9 and 7-10), rectangular nave bays with four-part vaults replaced the square bays with six-part vaults and the alternate-support system used at Saint-Étienne (FIG. 6-30) at Caen and in Early Gothic churches. The new system, in which a single square in each aisle (rather than two, as before) flanks a single rectangular unit in the nave (FIG. 7-10, *left*), became the norm. The High Gothic four-part nave vault covered only one bay and therefore could be braced more easily than its Early Gothic predecessor, making taller naves more practical to build.

ARCHITECTURAL BASICS
Building a High Gothic Cathedral

Most of the architectural components of Gothic cathedrals appeared in earlier structures, but Gothic architects combined the elements in new ways. The essential ingredients of their formula for constructing churches in the *opus modernum* style were rib vaults with pointed arches, flying buttresses, and huge colored-glass windows. The cutaway view of a typical Gothic cathedral in FIG. 7-8 illustrates how these and other important Gothic architectural devices worked together.

- **Pinnacle** (FIG. 7-8, no. 1) A sharply pointed ornament capping the piers or flying buttresses; also used on cathedral facades.
- **Flying buttresses** (2) Masonry struts that transfer the thrust of the nave vaults across the roofs of the side aisles and ambulatory to a tall pier rising above the church's exterior wall.
- **Vaulting web** (3) The masonry blocks that fill the area between the ribs of a groin vault.
- **Diagonal rib** (4) In plan, one of the ribs forming the X of a groin vault. In FIG. 7-4, the diagonal ribs are the lines *AC* and *DB*.
- **Transverse rib** (5) A rib crossing the nave or aisle at a 90-degree angle (lines *AB* and *DC* in FIG. 7-4).
- **Springing** (6) The lowest stone of an arch; in Gothic vaulting, the lowest stone of a diagonal or transverse rib.
- **Clerestory** (7) The windows below the vaults in the nave elevation's uppermost level. By using flying buttresses and rib vaults with pointed arches, Gothic architects could build huge clerestory windows and fill them with stained glass held in place by ornamental stonework called *tracery*.

- **Oculus** (8) A small, round window.
- **Lancet** (9) A tall, narrow window crowned by a pointed arch.
- **Triforium** (10) The story in the nave elevation consisting of arcades, usually *blind arcades* but occasionally filled with stained glass.
- **Nave arcade** (11) The series of arches supported by piers separating the nave from the side aisles.
- **Compound pier (cluster pier) with shafts (responds)** (12) A pier with a group, or cluster, of attached shafts, or responds, extending to the springing of the vaults.

7-8 Cutaway view of a typical French Gothic cathedral (John Burge).

The major elements of the Gothic formula for constructing a church in the opus modernum style were rib vaults with pointed arches, flying buttresses, and stained-glass windows.

The 1194 Chartres Cathedral was also the first church planned from its inception to have flying buttresses, another key High Gothic feature. The flying buttresses enabled the builders to eliminate the tribune above the aisle, which had partially braced Romanesque and Early Gothic naves. Taking its place was the *triforium*, the band of arcades between the clerestory and the nave arcade. The triforium occupies the space corresponding to the exterior strip of wall covered by the sloping timber roof above the galleries. The new

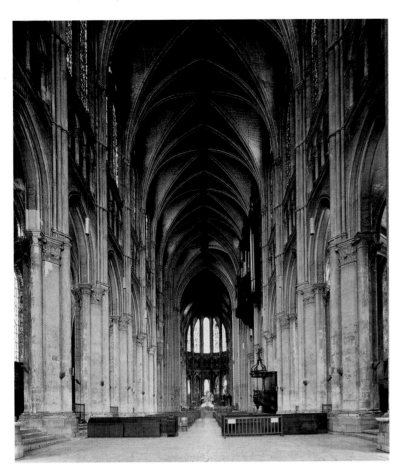

7-9 Interior of Chartres Cathedral (looking east), Chartres, France, begun 1194.

Chartres Cathedral established the High Gothic model with its four-part nave vaults and three-story elevation consisting of nave arcade, triforium, and clerestory with tall stained-glass windows.

High Gothic three-story nave elevation consisted of arcade, triforium, and clerestory with greatly enlarged windows (FIG. 7-10, *right*). The Chartres windows are almost as tall as the main arcade and consist of double lancets with a single crowning oculus. The strategic placement of flying buttresses made possible the construction of nave walls with so many voids that heavy masonry played merely a minor role.

CHARTRES STAINED GLASS Despite the vastly increased size of its clerestory windows, the Chartres nave (FIG. 7-9) is relatively dark. This seeming contradiction is the result of using colored instead of clear glass for the windows. The purpose of the Chartres windows was not to illuminate the interior with bright sunlight but to transform natural light into Suger's mystical *lux nova* (see "Stained-Glass Windows," page 195). Chartres Cathedral retains almost the full complement of its original stained glass. Although the tinted windows have a dimming effect, they transform the character of the church's interior in dramatic fashion. The immense rose window (approximately 43 feet in diameter) and tall lancets (FIG. 7-11) of the north transept were the gift of Queen Blanche

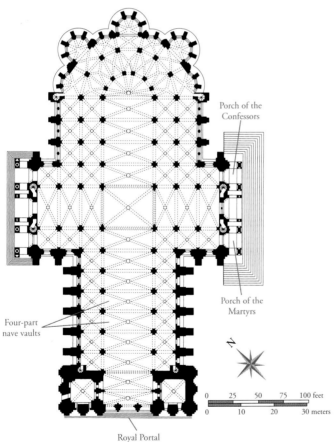

Porch of the Confessors

Porch of the Martyrs

Four-part nave vaults

Royal Portal

0   25   50   75   100 feet
0   10   20   30 meters

7-10 Plan (*left*; after Paul Frankl) and elevation (*right*; John Burge) of Chartres Cathedral, Chartres, France, as rebuilt after the 1194 fire.

The Chartres plan—with one bay in each aisle flanking a four-part vaulted bay in the nave—became the norm for High Gothic architecture. The clerestory windows are almost as tall as the nave arcade.

MATERIALS AND TECHNIQUES
Stained-Glass Windows

Stained-glass windows, although not a Gothic invention, are almost synonymous with Gothic architecture. They differ from the mural paintings and mosaics that adorned earlier churches in one all-important respect. They do not conceal walls. They replace them. Moreover, they transmit rather than reflect light, filtering and transforming the natural sunlight. Abbot Suger called this colored light *lux nova*. Suger's contemporary, Hugh of Saint-Victor (1096–1142), a prominent Parisian theologian, believed that "stained-glass windows are the Holy Scriptures . . . and since their brilliance lets the splendor of the True Light pass into the church, they enlighten those inside.* William Durandus (ca. 1237–1296), bishop of Mende, expressed a similar sentiment at the end of the 13th century: "The glass windows in a church are Holy Scriptures, which expel the wind and the rain, that is, all things hurtful, but transmit the light of the True sun, that is, God, into the hearts of the faithful."[†]

The manufacture of stained-glass windows was costly and labor-intensive. A German monk named Theophilus recorded the full process around 1100. First, the master designer drew the exact composition of the planned window on a wood panel, indicating all the linear details and noting the colors for each section. Glassblowers provided flat sheets of glass of different colors to *glaziers* (glassworkers), who cut the windowpanes to the required size and shape with special iron shears. Glaziers produced an even greater range of colors by *flashing* (fusing one layer of colored glass to another). Next, painters added details such as faces, hands, hair, and clothing in enamel by tracing the master design on the wood panel through the colored glass. Then they heated the painted glass to fuse the enamel to the surface. At that point, the glaziers "leaded" the various fragments of glass—that is, they joined them by strips of lead called *cames*. The *leading* not only held the pieces together but also separated the colors to heighten the effect of the design as a whole. The distinctive character of Gothic stained-glass windows is largely the result of this combination of fine linear details with broad, flat expanses of color framed by black lead. Finally, the glassworkers strengthened the completed window with an armature of iron bands (FIG. 7-11).

The form of the stone frames for the stained-glass windows also evolved. Early rose windows have stained glass held in place by *plate tracery*. The glass fills only the "punched holes" in the heavy ornamental stonework. *Bar tracery* (FIG. 7-11), a later development, used first at Reims (FIG. 7-1a), is much more slender. The stained-glass windows fill almost the entire opening, and the stonework is unobtrusive, resembling delicate leading more than masonry wall.

7-11 Rose window and lancets, north transept, Chartres Cathedral, Chartres, France, ca. 1220. Stained glass, rose window 43' in diameter.

Stained-glass windows transformed natural light into Suger's lux nova. This huge rose window with tall lancets fills almost the entire facade wall of the High Gothic north transept of Chartres Cathedral.

*Hugh of Saint-Victor, *Speculum de mysteriis ecclesiae*, sermon 2.
[†]William Durandus, *Rationale divinorum officiorum*, 1.1.24. Translated by John Mason Neale and Benjamin Webb, *The Symbolism of Churches and Church Ornaments* (Leeds: Green, 1843), 28.

of Castile (see page 199) around 1220. Yellow castles on a red ground and yellow *fleurs-de-lis* (three-petaled iris flowers; the French monarchy's floral emblem) on a blue ground fill the eight narrow windows in the rose's lower *spandrels*. The iconography is also fitting for a queen. The enthroned Virgin and Child appear in the *roundel* at the center of the rose, which resembles a gem-studded book cover or cloisonné brooch. Around her are four doves of the Holy Spirit and eight angels. Twelve square panels contain images of Old Testament kings, including David and Solomon (at the 12 and 1 o'clock positions respectively). These are the royal ancestors of Christ. Isaiah (11:1–3) had prophesized that the Messiah would come from the family of the patriarch Jesse, father of David. The genealogical "tree of Jesse" is a familiar motif in medieval art. Below, in the central lancet, are Saint Anne and the baby Virgin. Flanking them are four of Christ's Old Testament ancestors—Melchizedek, David, Solomon, and Aaron—echoing the royal genealogy of the rose, but at a larger scale.

Almost the entire mass of wall opens up into stained glass, held in place by an intricate stone armature of *bar tracery* and filling the church with lux nova that changes in hue and intensity with the hours. Here, the Gothic passion for luminous colored light led to a most daring and successful attempt to subtract all superfluous material bulk just short of destabilizing the structure. That this vast, complex fabric of stone-set glass has maintained its structural integrity for almost 800 years attests to the Gothic builders' engineering genius.

CHARTRES SOUTH TRANSEPT The sculptures adorning the portals of the two Chartres transepts erected after the 1194 fire are also prime examples of the new High Gothic spirit. The statues of saints on the transept portal jambs are more independent from the architectural framework than their Early Gothic predecessors. The Saint Theodore statue (FIG. 7-12), placed in the Porch of the Martyrs in the south transept around 1230, embodies the great changes that French sculpture had undergone since the Royal Portal jamb figures (FIG. 7-6) of the mid-12th century. The High Gothic sculptor portrayed Theodore as the ideal Christian knight, clothing him in the cloak and chain-mail armor of 13th-century Crusaders. The handsome, long-haired youth holds his spear firmly in his right hand and rests his left hand on his shield. He turns his head to the left and swings out his hip to the right. The body's resulting torsion and pronounced sway recall ancient Greek statuary, especially the contrapposto stance of Polykleitos's *Spear Bearer* (FIG. 2-35). The changes that occurred in 13th-century Gothic sculpture echo the revolutionary developments in Greek sculpture during the transition from the Archaic to the Classical style (see page 63) and could appropriately be described as a second "Classical revolution."

7-12 **Saint Theodore, jamb statue in the left portal of the Porch of the Martyrs, south transept, Chartres Cathedral, Chartres, France, ca. 1230.**

Although the statue of Theodore is still attached to a column, the setting no longer determines its pose. The High Gothic sculptor portrayed the saint in a contrapposto stance, as in classical statuary.

AMIENS CATHEDRAL The builders of Chartres Cathedral set a pattern that many other Gothic architects followed, even if they refined the details. Construction of Amiens Cathedral began in 1220, while work was still in progress at Chartres. The architects were ROBERT DE LUZARCHES, THOMAS DE CORMONT, and RENAUD DE CORMONT. The nave (FIG. 7-13) was ready by 1236 and the radiating chapels by 1247, but work on the choir continued until almost 1270. The Amiens elevation (FIG. 7-14) derived from the High Gothic formula of Chartres (FIG. 7-10, *right*), but Amiens Cathedral's proportions are more slender, and the number and complexity of the lancet windows in both its clerestory and triforium are greater. The whole design reflects the Amiens builders' confident use of the complete High Gothic structural vocabulary: the rectangular-bay system, the four-part rib vault, and an external buttressing system that made possible the almost complete elimination of heavy masses and thick weight-bearing walls. At Amiens, the concept of a self-sustaining skeletal architecture reached full maturity.

The nave vaults of Chartres Cathedral rise to a height of 120 feet. Those at Amiens are 144 feet above the floor, reflecting the French Gothic obsession with constructing ever taller cathedrals. At Amiens, the vault ribs converge to the colonnettes and speed down the walls to the compound piers. Almost every part of the superstructure has its corresponding element below. The overall effect is of effortless strength, of a buoyant lightness not normally associated with stone architecture. The light flooding in from the clerestory—and, in the choir, also from the triforium—makes the vaults seem even more insubstantial. The effect recalls another great building, one utterly different from Amiens but where light also plays a defining role: Hagia Sophia (FIG. 4-12) in Constantinople. The designers of Amiens Cathedral, too, reduced the building's physical mass through structural ingenuity and daring, but in the High Gothic basilica, unlike the domed Byzantine church, light further dematerializes what remains.

REIMS CATHEDRAL Construction of Reims Cathedral began only a few years after work commenced at Amiens. Gaucher de Reims and Bernard de Soissons, who were primarily responsible for the west facade (FIG. 7-1), carried the High Gothic style of Amiens still further, both architecturally and sculpturally. Especially striking, as noted in the chapter-opening essay, is the treatment of the tympana over the doorways, where stained-glass windows replaced the stone relief sculpture of earlier facades. The jamb statues that flank the Reims west portals are also more advanced than the comparable figures at Amiens or Chartres (FIG. 7-12). The subjects of the four most prominent statues (FIG. 7-15) are the Annunciation and Visitation—further testimony to the Virgin's central role in Gothic iconography. The statues appear completely detached from their architectural background because the sculptors shrank the supporting columns into insignificance. The columns in no way restrict the free and easy movements of the full-bodied figures.

The Reims statues also vividly illustrate how long it frequently took to complete the sculptured ornamentation of a large Gothic cathedral. Sculptural projects of this magnitude normally required decades to complete and entailed hiring many sculptors, often working in diverse styles. Art historians believe that three different sculptors carved the four statues in FIG. 7-15 at different times during the quarter century from 1230 to 1255. The *Visitation* figures (FIG. 7-15, *right*) are the work of an artist who must have studied classical statuary. Reims was an ancient Roman city. The heads of both Mary and Elizabeth resemble Roman portraits, and the rich folds of the garments also recall ancient statuary. The Gothic statues closely approximate the classical naturalistic style and feature contrapposto postures in which the swaying of the hips is much more pronounced than in

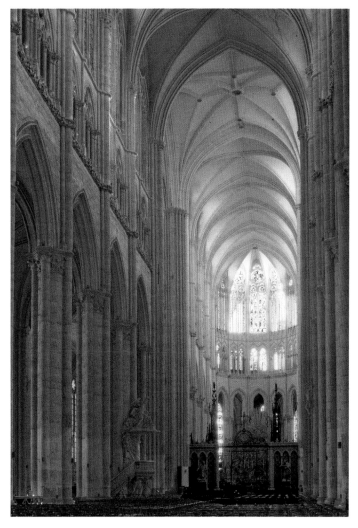

7-13 Robert de Luzarches, Thomas de Cormont, and Renaud de Cormont, interior of Amiens Cathedral (looking east), Amiens, France, begun 1220.

The concept of a self-sustaining skeletal architecture reached full maturity at Amiens Cathedral. The light entering from the clerestory and triforium creates a buoyant lightness rare in stone architecture.

7-14 Robert de Luzarches, Thomas de Cormont, and Renaud de Cormont, nave elevation of Amiens Cathedral, Amiens, France, begun 1220 (John Burge).

Amiens Cathedral's four-part vaults on pointed arches rise an astounding 144 feet, three times the width of the nave floor. The Chartres vaults (FIG. 7-10, *right*) are 120 feet tall and 2.64 times the nave width.

7-15 *Annunciation* and *Visitation*, jamb statues on the right side of the central doorway of the west facade, Reims Cathedral (FIG. 7-1), Reims, France, ca. 1230–1255.

Several sculptors working in diverse styles carved the Reims jamb statues, but all the figures resemble freestanding statues, with bodies and arms in motion. The biblical figures speak using gestures.

the Chartres Saint Theodore (FIG. 7-12). (It is even more exaggerated in the elegant elongated body of the angel Gabriel of the *Annunciation* [FIG. 7-15, *left*].) The right legs of the *Visitation* figures bend, and the knees press through the rippling folds of the garments. The sculptor also set the figures' arms in motion. Mary and Elizabeth look at each other and speak using gestures. In the Reims *Visitation,* the formerly isolated Gothic jamb statues became actors in a biblical narrative.

SAINTE-CHAPELLE, PARIS The stained-glass windows inserted into the portal tympana of Reims Cathedral (FIG. 7-1c) exemplify the wall-dissolving High Gothic architectural style. The architect of Sainte-Chapelle (FIG. 7-16) in Paris extended this approach to an entire building. Louis IX (Saint Louis, r. 1226–1270) built Sainte-Chapelle near Notre-Dame as a repository for the crown of thorns and other relics of Christ's passion that he had purchased in 1239. The chapel is a masterpiece of the so-called *Rayonnant* ("radiant") style of the High Gothic age, which was the preferred style of the royal Parisian court of Saint Louis. In Sainte-Chapelle, 6,450 square feet of stained glass make up more than three-quarters of the structure. The supporting elements are hardly more than large *mullions* (vertical stone bars). The emphasis is on the extreme slenderness of the architectural forms and on linearity in general. Sainte-Chapelle's enormous windows filter the light and fill the interior with an unearthly rose-violet atmosphere. Approximately 49 feet high and 15 feet wide, they were the largest stained-glass windows up to their time.

GUILD HALL, BRUGES One of the many signs of the growing urbanization of life in the late Middle Ages was the erection of large meeting halls and warehouses for the increasing number of craft guilds being formed throughout Europe. An early example is the imposing market and guild hall (FIG. 7-17) of the clothmakers of Bruges, Belgium, begun in 1230. Situated in the city's major square, the hall testifies to the important role of artisans and merchants in Gothic Europe. The design combines features of military construction (the corner watchtowers with their *crenellations*) and sacred architecture (lancet windows with crowning oculi). The uppermost, octagonal portion of the tower with its flying buttresses and pinnacles dates to the 15th century, but even the original two-story tower is taller than the rest of the building. Lofty towers, a common feature of late medieval guild and town halls, were designed to compete for attention and prestige with the towers of city cathedrals.

7-16 Interior of the upper chapel (looking northeast), Sainte-Chapelle, Paris, France, 1243–1248.

At Louis IX's Sainte-Chapelle, the architect succeeded in dissolving the walls to such an extent that 6,450 square feet of stained glass account for more than three-quarters of the Rayonnant Gothic structure.

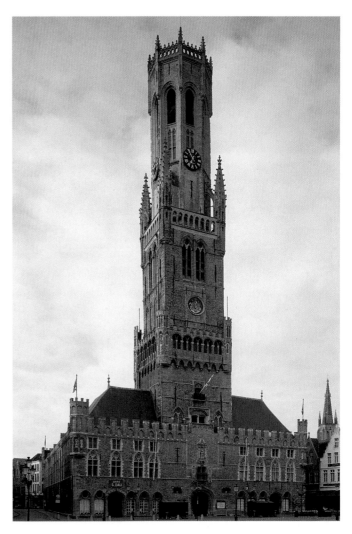

7-17 Hall of the cloth guild (looking south), Bruges, Belgium, begun 1230.

The Bruges cloth guild's meeting hall is an early example of a new type of secular architecture in the late Middle Ages. Its lofty tower competed for attention with the towers of the cathedral.

Gothic Book Production

The famous Florentine poet Dante Alighieri (1265–1321) referred to Paris in his *Divine Comedy* (ca. 1310–1320) as the city famed for the art of illumination.* During the Gothic period, book production shifted from monastic scriptoria shut off from the world to urban workshops of professional artists—and Paris boasted the most and best workshops. The owners of these new for-profit secular businesses sold their products to the royal family, scholars, and prosperous merchants. The Parisian shops were the forerunners of modern publishing houses.

Not surprisingly, some of the finest extant Gothic books belonged to the French monarchy, including a moralized Bible now in the Pierpont Morgan Library. *Moralized Bibles* are heavily illustrated, each page pairing paintings of Old and New Testament episodes with explanations of their moral significance. Blanche of Castile (1188–1252), granddaughter of Eleanor of Aquitaine (queen of France, 1137–1152, and of England, 1152–1189), ordered the Morgan Bible during her regency (1226–1234) for her teenage son, Louis IX, who inherited the throne when he was only 12 years old. The dedication page (FIG. 7-18) has a costly gold background and depicts Blanche and Louis enthroned beneath triple-lobed arches and miniature cityscapes. The latter are comparable to the architectural canopies above the heads of contemporaneous French and German statues (FIG. 7-26). Below Blanche and Louis are a monk and a professional lay scribe. The older clergyman instructs the scribe, who already has divided his page into two columns of four roundels each, a format often used for the paired illustrations of moralized Bibles. The inspirations for such pages were probably the roundels of stained-glass windows such as those of Louis's own later Sainte-Chapelle (FIG. 7-16).

The picture of Gothic book production on the dedication page of Blanche of Castile's Bible is a very abbreviated one. Book manufacture involved many steps and required numerous specialized artists, scribes, and assistants of varying skill levels. The Benedictine abbot Johannes Trithemius (1462–1516) described the way books were still made in his day in his treatise *In Praise of Scribes*:

> If you do not know how to write, you still can assist the scribes in various ways. One of you can correct what another has written. Another can add the rubrics [headings] to the corrected text. A third can add initials and signs of division. Still another can arrange the leaves and attach the binding. Another of you can prepare the covers, the leather, the buckles and clasps. All sorts of assistance can be offered the scribe to help him pursue his work without interruption. He needs many things which can be prepared by others: parchment cut, flattened and ruled for script, ready ink and pens. You will always find something with which to help the scribe.[†]

Preparation of the illuminated pages also involved several hands. Some artists, for example, specialized in painting borders or initials.

1 in.

7-18 Blanche of Castile, Louis IX, a monk, and a scribe, dedication page (folio 8 recto) of a moralized Bible, from Paris, France, 1226–1234. Ink, tempera, and gold leaf on vellum, 1' 3" × 10½". Pierpont Morgan Library, New York.

The dedication page of this royal book depicts Saint Louis, his mother and French regent Blanche of Castile, a monk, and a lay scribe at work on the paired illustrations of a moralized Bible.

Only the workshop head or one of the most advanced assistants would paint the main figural scenes. Given this division of labor and the assembly-line nature of Gothic book production, it is astonishing how uniform the style is on a single page, as well as from page to page, in most illuminated manuscripts.

Inscriptions in some Gothic books state the production costs—the prices paid for materials, especially gold, and for the execution of initials, figures, flowery script, and other embellishments. By this time, however, although the cost of materials was still the major factor determining a book's price, individual skill and "brand name" played a significant role. In the Gothic age, urban workshops of professional scribes and painters ended the centuries-old monopoly of the Church in book production.

*Dante, *Divine Comedy*, Purgatory, 11.81.
†Translated by Roland Behrendt, *Johannes Trithemius, In Praise of Scribes: De laude scriptorum* (Lawrence, Kansas: Coronado Press, 1974), 71.

Book Illumination and Luxury Arts

Paris's claim as the intellectual center of Gothic Europe (see "Paris" ⟨↗⟩) did not rest solely on the stature of its university faculty and the reputation of its architects, masons, sculptors, and stained-glass makers. The city was also a renowned center for the production of fine books, such as the Bible (FIG. 7-18) that once belonged to Blanche of Castille (see "Gothic Book Production," above).

GOD AS CREATOR Another moralized Bible produced in Paris during the 1220s features a magnificent frontispiece, *God as Creator*

1 in.

7-19 *God as Creator of the World,* folio 1 verso of a moralized Bible, from Paris, France, ca. 1220–1230. Ink, tempera, and gold leaf on vellum, 1' 1$\frac{1}{2}$" × 8$\frac{1}{4}$". Österreichische Nationalbibliothek, Vienna.

Paris boasted renowned workshops for the production of illuminated manuscripts. In this book, the artist portrayed God in the process of creating the universe using a Gothic builder's compass.

1 in.

7-20 *Virgin of Jeanne d'Evreux,* from the abbey church, Saint-Denis, France, 1339. Silver gilt and enamel, 2' 3$\frac{1}{2}$" high. Musée du Louvre, Paris.

Queen Jeanne d'Evreux donated this reliquary-statuette to the royal abbey of Saint-Denis. It exemplifies French Late Gothic style in its swaying pose and the intimate human portrayal of Mary and Jesus.

of the World (FIG. 7-19). Above the illustration, the scribe wrote (in French rather than Latin): "Here God creates heaven and earth, the sun and moon, and all the elements." The painter depicted God in the process of creating the world, shaping the universe with the aid of a compass. Within the perfect circle already created are the spherical sun and moon and the unformed matter that will become the earth once God applies the same geometric principles to it. In contrast to the biblical account of creation, in which God created the sun, moon, and stars after the earth had been formed, and made the world by sheer force of will and a simple "Let there be" command, this Gothic Bible portrays God systematically creating the universe using geometrical principles.

VIRGIN OF JEANNE D'EVREUX The royal family also patronized goldsmiths, silversmiths, and other artists specializing in the production of luxury works in metal and enamel for churches, palaces, and private homes. Especially popular were statuettes of sacred figures, which the wealthy purchased either for private devotion or as gifts to churches. The Virgin Mary was a favored subject. Perhaps the finest of these costly statuettes is the large silver-gilt figurine known as the *Virgin of Jeanne d'Evreux* (FIG. 7-20). The French queen, wife of Charles IV (r. 1322–1328), donated this image of the Virgin and

Child to the royal abbey church of Saint-Denis (FIG. 7-2) in 1339. Mary stands on a rectangular base decorated with enamel scenes of Christ's passion. But no hint of grief appears in the beautiful young Mary's face. The Christ Child, also without a care in the world, playfully reaches for his mother. The elegant proportions of the two figures, Mary's swaying posture, the heavy drapery folds, and the intimate human characterization of mother and son are also features of the roughly contemporaneous *Virgin of Paris* (FIG. 7-20A ⬀). In both instances, Mary appears not only as Christ's mother but as queen of Heaven. The Saint-Denis Mary originally had a crown on her head, and the scepter she holds is in the form of the fleur-de-lis. The statuette also served as a reliquary. The Virgin's scepter contained hairs believed to come from Mary's head.

GOTHIC OUTSIDE FRANCE In 1269, the *prior* (deputy abbot) of the church of Saint Peter at Wimpfen-im-Tal in the German Rhineland hired "a very experienced architect who had recently come from the city of Paris" to rebuild his monastery church.[2] The architect reconstructed the church *opere francigeno* ("in the French manner")—that is, in the opus modernum style of the Île-de-France, which by the second half of the 13th century became dominant throughout Europe. European architecture did not, however, turn Gothic all at once or even uniformly. Almost everywhere, patrons and builders modified the Parisian court style according to local preferences.

ENGLAND

The influence of French style in England began with William the Conqueror and the Norman invasion of 1066 (see page 183), but just as the Romanesque architecture of Normandy and England has a distinctive character, so too do English Gothic buildings.

SALISBURY CATHEDRAL Salisbury Cathedral (FIG. 7-21) embodies the essential characteristics of English Gothic architecture. Begun in 1220, the English church is contemporaneous to the cathedrals of Amiens and Reims, and the differences between the French and English buildings are instructive. Although Salisbury's facade incorporates lancet windows and blind arcades with pointed arches as well as statuary, it presents a striking contrast to French High Gothic designs. The English facade is a squat screen in front of the nave, wider than the building behind it. The Salisbury architect did not seek to match the soaring height of the Amiens and Reims (FIGS. 7-1) facades or try to make the facade correspond to the three-part division of the interior (nave and aisles). Different, too, is the emphasis on the great crossing tower (added around 1320–1330), which dominates the church's silhouette. Salisbury's height is modest compared with that of Amiens and Reims. Because height is not a decisive factor in the English building, the architect used the flying buttress sparingly. In short, the English builders adopted some of the superficial motifs of French Gothic architecture but did not embrace its structural logic or emphasis on height.

Salisbury's interior (FIG. 7-22)—although Gothic in its three-story elevation, pointed arches, four-part rib vaults, compound piers, and triforium tracery—conspicuously departs from the French Gothic style of Amiens (FIG. 7-13). The pier colonnettes stop

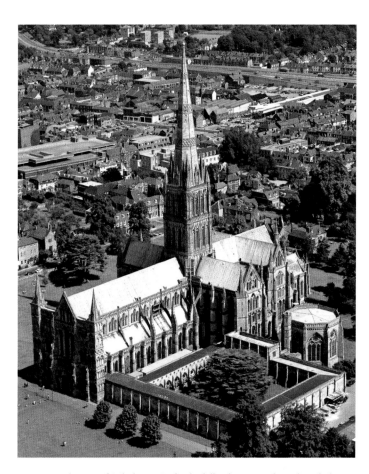

7-21 Aerial view of Salisbury Cathedral (looking northeast), Salisbury, England, 1220–1258; west facade completed 1265; spire ca. 1320–1330.

Exhibiting the distinctive regional features of English Gothic architecture, Salisbury Cathedral has a squat facade that is wider than the building behind it. The architects used flying buttresses sparingly.

7-22 Interior of Salisbury Cathedral (looking east), Salisbury, England, 1220–1258.

Salisbury Cathedral's interior also differs from contemporaneous French Gothic designs in the strong horizontal emphasis of its three-story elevation and the use of dark Purbeck marble for moldings.

7-23 ROBERT and WILLIAM VERTUE, fan vaults of the chapel of Henry VII, Westminster Abbey, London, England, 1503–1519.

Two hallmarks of the Perpendicular style of English Late Gothic architecture are the multiplication of vault ribs and the use of fan vaults with lacelike tracery pendants resembling stalactites.

at the springing of the nave arches and do not connect with the vault ribs. Instead, the vault ribs rise from *corbels* in the triforium, producing a strong horizontal emphasis. Underscoring this horizontality is the rich color contrast between the light stone of the walls and vaults and the dark marble (from the Isle of Purbeck in southeastern England) used for the triforium moldings and corbels, compound pier responds, and other details.

CHAPEL OF HENRY VII English Gothic architecture found its native language in the elaboration of architectural pattern for its own sake. The pier, wall, and vault elements, still relatively simple at Salisbury, became increasingly complex and decorative in the 14th century and later. In the early-16th-century ceiling (FIG. **7-23**) of the chapel of Henry VII adjoining Westminster Abbey in London, the so-called *Perpendicular style* of English Late Gothic is on display. The style takes its name from the pronounced verticality of its decorative details, in contrast to the horizontal emphasis of Salisbury and English Early Gothic. In Henry's chapel, ROBERT and WILLIAM VERTUE multiplied the vault ribs and pulled them into uniquely English *fan vaults* (vaults with radiating ribs forming a fanlike pattern) with large hanging *pendants* resembling stalactites. Intricate tracery recalling lace overwhelms the cones hanging from the ceiling. The chapel represents the dissolution of structural Gothic into

decorative fancy. The architects released the French Gothic style's original lines from their function and multiplied them into the uninhibited architectural virtuosity and theatrics of the English Perpendicular style.

HOLY ROMAN EMPIRE

As part of his plan to make his new church at Saint-Denis an earthly introduction to the splendors of Paradise (see "Abbot Suger" 🔗), Suger selected artists from the Meuse River region in present-day Belgium to fashion for the choir a magnificent crucifix on a base decorated with 68 enamel scenes pairing Old and New Testament episodes. The Mosan (Meuse) region long had been famous for the quality of its metalworkers and enamelers (FIG. 6-16A 🔗). Indeed, as Suger's treatises demonstrate, in the Middle Ages, the artists who worked at small scale with precious metals, ivory, and jewels produced the most admired objects in a church, far more important in the eyes of contemporaries than the jamb statues and tympanum reliefs that are the focus of modern histories of medieval art.

NICHOLAS OF VERDUN The leading Mosan artist of the late 12th and early 13th centuries was NICHOLAS OF VERDUN, who fashioned the *Shrine of the Three Kings* (FIG. **7-24**) for Cologne Cathedral (FIG. **7-24A** 🔗) around 1190. Philip von Heinsberg, archbishop of Cologne from 1167 to 1191, commissioned the huge shrine (6 feet long and almost as tall) to contain the relics of the three magi that Holy Roman Emperor Frederick Barbarossa (r. 1155–1190) acquired in the conquest of Milan in 1164. The three kings' relics, which the emperor donated to Cologne Cathedral, gave the archbishop and his successors the right to crown German kings. Nicholas's reliquary, made of silver and bronze with ornamentation in enamel and gemstones, is one of the most luxurious ever produced, especially considering its size. The shape resembles that of a basilican church. Repoussé figures of the Virgin Mary, the three magi, Old Testament prophets, and New Testament apostles fill the arcuated frames of the shrine's two stories.

The *Shrine of the Three Kings* and Suger's treatises on the furnishings of Saint-Denis are welcome reminders of how magnificently outfitted medieval church interiors were. The sumptuous small-scale objects exhibited in the choir and chapels, which also housed the church's most precious relics, played a defining role in creating a special otherworldly atmosphere for Christian ritual. These Gothic examples continued a tradition dating to the Roman emperor Constantine and the first imperial patronage of Christianity (see page 120).

STRASBOURG CATHEDRAL In 1176, work began on a new cathedral for Strasbourg in present-day France, then an important city in the German Rhineland ruled by the successors of the Ottonian dynasty. The apse, choir, and transepts were in place by around 1240. Stylistically, these sections of Strasbourg Cathedral are Romanesque. But the reliefs of the two south-transept portals are fully Gothic and reflect developments in contemporaneous French sculpture. The left tympanum (FIG. **7-25**) presents *Death of the Virgin*. A comparison of the Strasbourg Mary on her deathbed with the Mary of the Reims *Visitation* (FIG. **7-15**, *right*) shows the stylistic kinship of the Strasbourg and Reims masters. The 12 apostles gather around the Virgin, forming an arc of mourners well suited to the semicircular frame. At the center, Christ receives his mother's soul (the doll-like figure he holds in his left hand). Mary Magdalene, wringing her hands in

7-24 NICHOLAS OF VERDUN, *Shrine of the Three Kings,* begun ca. 1190. Silver, bronze, enamel, and gemstones, 5' 8" × 6' × 3' 8". Cologne Cathedral, Cologne.

This huge reliquary in the form of a basilican church is fashioned of silver and bronze with ornamentation in enamel and gemstones. It contains Cologne Cathedral's relics of the three magi.

grief, crouches beside the deathbed. The sorrowing figures express emotion in varying degrees of intensity, from serene resignation to gesturing agitation. The sculptor organized the figures both by dramatic pose and gesture and by the rippling flow of deeply incised drapery that passes among them like a rhythmic electric pulse. The

sculptor's objective was to imbue the sacred figures with human emotions and to stir emotional responses in observers. In Gothic France, as already noted, art became increasingly humanized and natural. In the Holy Roman Empire, artists carried this humanizing trend even further by emphasizing passionate drama.

7-25 *Death of the Virgin,* tympanum of the left doorway of the south transept, Strasbourg Cathedral, Strasbourg, France, ca. 1230.

Stylistically akin to the *Visitation* statues (FIG. 7-1B) of Reims Cathedral, the figures in Strasbourg's south-transept tympanum express profound sorrow through dramatic poses and gestures.

NAUMBURG CATHEDRAL During his tenure as bishop (1244–1272), Dietrich II of Wettin completed the rebuilding of the Romanesque cathedral of Naumburg in northern Germany. The most distinctive aspect of the project was the west choir, which was to be a memorial to the 12 benefactors of the original 11th-century church. Art historians call the nameless sculptor who received the commission to carve portraits of those benefactors the NAUMBURG MASTER. Two of the figures (FIG. 7-26) stand out from the group of solemn men and women because of their exceptional quality. They represent the *margrave* (German military governor) Ekkehard II of Meissen and his wife, Uta. The statues are attached to columns and stand beneath architectural canopies, following the pattern of French Gothic portal statuary, but they project from the architecture more forcefully and move more freely than contemporaneous French jamb figures. The period costumes and the individualized features and personalities of the margrave and his wife give the impression that they posed for their portraits, although the subjects lived well before the Naumburg Master's time. Ekkehard, the intense knight, contrasts with the beautiful and aloof Uta. With a

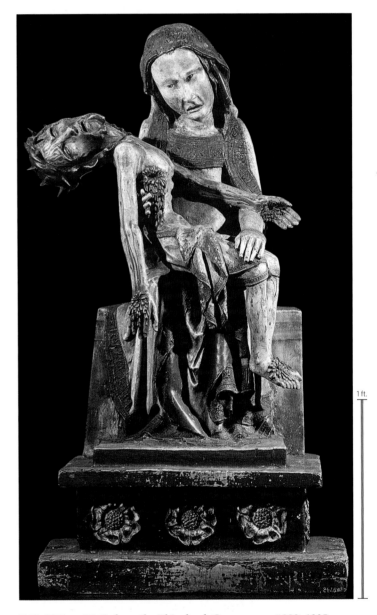

7-26 NAUMBURG MASTER, *Ekkehard and Uta*, statues in the west choir of Naumburg Cathedral, Naumburg, Germany, ca. 1249–1255. Painted limestone, Ekkehard 6' 2" high.

The period costumes and individualized features of these donor statues give the impression that Ekkehard and Uta posed for the Naumburg Master, but they lived long before the sculptor's time.

7-27 *Röttgen Pietà*, from the Rhineland, Germany, ca. 1300–1325. Painted wood, 2' 10½" high. Rheinisches Landemuseum, Bonn.

This statuette of the Virgin grieving over the distorted dead body of Christ in her lap reflects the increased interest during the 13th and 14th centuries in the Savior's suffering and the Virgin's grief.

wonderfully graceful gesture, she draws the collar of her cloak partly across her face while she gathers up a soft fold of drapery with a jeweled, delicate hand. The sculptor subtly revealed the shape of Uta's right arm beneath her cloak and rendered the fall of drapery folds with an accuracy suggesting that the Naumburg Master used a living model. The two statues are arresting images of real people, even if they bear the names of aristocrats the artist never met. In the Holy Roman Empire, life-size images of secular personages had found their way into churches by the mid-13th century.

RÖTTGEN PIETÀ The Naumburg choir statues are also noteworthy because, as indoor sculptures, they have retained their color, whereas almost all the statues on church exteriors, exposed to sun and rain for centuries, have lost their original paint. Also retaining its original appearance is a haunting 14th-century German painted wood statuette (FIG. 7-27) of the Virgin Mary holding the dead Christ in her lap. This *Pietà* (Italian, "pity" or "compassion") reflects the increased interest during the 13th and 14th centuries in humanizing biblical figures and in the suffering of Jesus and the grief of his mother and followers. This expressed emotionalism accompanied the shift toward the representation of the human body in motion. As the figures of the church portals began to twist on their columns, then move within their niches, and then stand independently, their details became more outwardly related to the human audience as indicators of recognizable human emotions.

The sculptor of the *Röttgen Pietà* (named after a collector) portrayed Christ as a stunted, distorted human wreck, stiffened in death and covered with streams of blood gushing from a huge wound. The Virgin, who cradles him as if he were a child in her lap, is the very image of maternal anguish, her oversized face twisted in an expression of unbearable grief. This statue expresses nothing of the serenity of Romanesque (FIG. 6-24) and earlier Gothic depictions of Mary (FIG. 7-5, right tympanum). Nor does it have anything in common with the aloof, iconic images of the Theotokos with the infant Jesus in her lap common in Byzantine art (FIG. 4-20). Here the artist forcibly confronts the devout with an appalling icon of agony, death, and sorrow. The work calls out to the horrified believer, "What is your suffering compared to this?"

ITALY

Nowhere is the regional diversity of late medieval art and architecture more evident than in Italy. In fact, art historians debate whether the art of Italy between 1200 and 1400 is the last phase of medieval art or the beginning of the rebirth, or *Renaissance,* of Greco-Roman naturalism, the dawn of a new artistic age when artists broke away from medieval conventions and consciously revived the classical style. Both of these characterizations have merit.

A revived interest in classical cultures—indeed, the veneration of classical antiquity as a model—was central to the notion of a renaissance in Italy. Indeed, the belief that the Renaissance represented the restoration of the glorious past of Greece and Rome gave rise to the concept of the "Middle Ages" as the era falling between antiquity and the Renaissance. This notion of artistic rebirth is the root of Vasari's condescending labeling of medieval art as "Gothic."

A significant development in 14th-century Italy was the blossoming of a vernacular literature (written in the commonly spoken language instead of Latin), which dramatically affected Italy's intellectual and cultural life. Latin remained the official language of church liturgy and state documents. However, the creation of an Italian vernacular literature was one important sign that the essentially religious view that had dominated medieval Europe was about to change dramatically. Although religion continued to occupy a primary position in the lives of Europeans, a growing concern with the natural world, the individual, and humanity's worldly existence characterized the Renaissance period—the 14th through the 16th centuries.

HUMANISM Fundamental to the development of the Italian Renaissance was *humanism.* Humanism was more a code of civil conduct, a theory of education, and a scholarly discipline than a philosophical system. The chief concerns of Italian humanists were human values and interests as distinct from—but not opposed to—religion's otherworldly values. Humanists pointed to classical cultures as particularly praiseworthy. This enthusiasm for antiquity involved study of Latin literature and a conscious emulation of what proponents believed were the Roman civic virtues. These included self-sacrificing service to the state, participation in government, defense of state institutions (especially the administration of justice), and stoic indifference to personal misfortune in the performance of duty. Classical cultures provided humanists with a model for living in this world, a model primarily of human focus derived not from an authoritative and traditional religious dogma but from reason.

Sculpture and Painting

The Renaissance humanists quickly developed a keen interest in classical art as well as literature. Although the *Visitation* statues (FIG. 7-1b) of Reims Cathedral show a familiarity with Roman statuary in 13th-century France, the emulation of Greco-Roman art was, not surprisingly, far more common in Italy, where Holy Roman Emperor Frederick II (r. 1220–1250) had been king of Sicily since 1197. Frederick's nostalgia for Rome's past grandeur fostered a revival of Roman sculpture in Sicily and southern Italy not unlike the classical *renovatio* that Charlemagne encouraged in Germany and France four centuries earlier (see page 162).

NICOLA PISANO The sculptor known as NICOLA PISANO (Nicola of Pisa, active ca. 1258–1278) received his early training in southern Italy. After Frederick's death in 1250, Nicola traveled northward and eventually settled in Pisa. Then at the height of its political and economic power, the maritime city was a magnet for artists seeking lucrative commissions. Nicola specialized in carving marble reliefs and may have been the inventor of a new kind of church furniture—the monumental *pulpit* (raised platform from which priests delivered sermons) with supports in the form of freestanding statues and featuring wraparound narrative reliefs depicting biblical themes. He made his first pulpit (FIG. 7-28) in 1260 for Pisa's baptistery (FIG. 6-28, *left*). Some elements of the pulpit's design carried on medieval traditions—for example, the *trefoil* (triple-curved) arches (compare FIG. 7-18) and the lions supporting columns—but Nicola also incorporated classical elements. The large, bushy capitals are a Gothic variation of the Corinthian capital. The arches are round, as in ancient Roman architecture, rather than pointed, as in Gothic buildings. Also, each of the large rectangular relief panels resembles the sculptured front of a Roman sarcophagus (FIGS. 3-48 and 3-49). The face types, beards, coiffures, and draperies, as well as the bulk and weight of Nicola's figures, reveal the influence of classical relief sculpture. Art historians have even been able to pinpoint the models for some of the pulpit figures on Roman sarcophagi in Pisa.

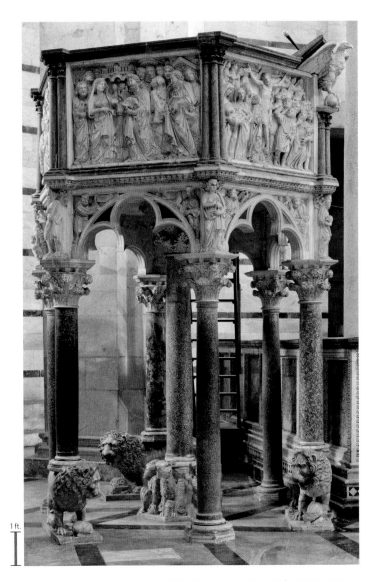

7-28 NICOLA PISANO, pulpit of the baptistery, Pisa, Italy, 1259–1260. Marble, 15' high.

The Pisa baptistery pulpit by Nicola Pisano retains many medieval features—for example, trefoil arches—but the sculptor modeled the marble figures on extant ancient Roman relief sculptures.

7-29 CIMABUE, *Madonna Enthroned with Angels and Prophets,* from Santa Trinità, Florence, Italy, ca. 1280–1290. Tempera and gold leaf on wood, 12' 7" × 7' 4". Galleria degli Uffizi, Florence.

Cimabue was one of the first artists to break away from the maniera greca. Although he relied on Byzantine models, the Italian master depicted the Madonna's massive throne as receding into space.

CIMABUE Late-13th-century Italian painting also differs sharply from the elegant court style popular north of the Alps. Byzantine style dominated Italian painting throughout the Middle Ages. The Italo-Byzantine style, or *maniera greca* ("Greek manner" or style), still characterizes the art of Cenni di Pepo, called CIMABUE (ca. 1240–1302). *Madonna Enthroned with Angels and Prophets* (FIG. 7-29) is perhaps Cimabue's finest work. In this enormous (nearly 13-foot-tall) panel painted for the church of the Holy Trinity in Florence, the heritage of Byzantine icon painting (FIGS. 4-20 and 4-27) is apparent in the careful structure and symmetry, the poses of the figures, the gold lines of Mary's garments, and the gold background. However, Cimabue constructed a deeper space for the Madonna and the surrounding figures to inhabit than was common in Byzantine painting, and he convincingly depicted the massive throne as receding into space. The overlapping bodies of the angels and the half-length prophets who look outward or upward from beneath the throne reinforce the sense of depth.

GIOTTO Critics from Giorgio Vasari to the present day have regarded GIOTTO DI BONDONE (ca. 1266–1337) as the first Renaissance painter. A pioneer in pursuing a naturalistic approach to representation based on observation, he made a much more radical break with the maniera greca than did Cimabue, whom Vasari identified as Giotto's teacher. Scholars still debate the sources of Giotto's style, although one formative influence must have been Cimabue. Mural paintings in Rome by PIETRO CAVALLINI (ca. 1240–ca. 1340; FIG. 7-29A ⟨⟩), French Gothic sculpture, and ancient Roman art must also have impressed the young Giotto. Yet no mere synthesis of these varied sources could have produced the significant shift in artistic approach that has led some scholars to describe Giotto as the father of Western pictorial art.

7-30 Giotto di Bondone, *Madonna Enthroned* (*Ognissanti Madonna*), from the Chiesa di Ognissanti (All-Saints Church), Florence, Italy, ca. 1310. Tempera and gold leaf on wood, 10′ 8″ × 6′ 8″. Galleria degli Uffizi, Florence.

Giotto displaced the Byzantine style in Italian painting and revived classical naturalism. His figures have substance, dimensionality, and bulk, and give the illusion that they could throw shadows.

MADONNA ENTHRONED On nearly the same great scale as Cimabue's enthroned Madonna (FIG. 7-29) is Giotto's *altarpiece* (FIG. 7-30) depicting the same subject. Giotto's Madonna sits on her Gothic throne with the unshakable stability of an ancient marble goddess. Giotto replaced Cimabue's slender Virgin, fragile beneath the thin ripplings of her drapery, with a weighty, queenly mother. He even showed Mary's breasts pressing through the thin fabric of her white undergarment. Gold highlights have disappeared from her heavy robe. Giotto's aim was to construct a figure with substance, dimensionality, and bulk—qualities suppressed in favor of a spiritual immateriality in Byzantine and Italo-Byzantine art. Works painted in the new style portray statuesque figures projecting into the light and giving the illusion that they could throw shadows. Giotto's *Madonna Enthroned* marks the end of medieval painting in Italy and the beginning of a new naturalism in art.

7-31 Giotto di Bondone, interior of the Arena Chapel (Cappella Scrovegni; looking west), Padua, Italy, 1305–1306.

The frescoes Giotto painted in the Arena Chapel show his art at its finest. In 38 framed panels, he presented the complete cycle of the life of Jesus, culminating in the *Last Judgment* on the entrance wall.

Giotto's restoration of the naturalistic approach to painting that the ancients developed and medieval artists largely abandoned inaugurated an age that some scholars call "early scientific." By stressing the preeminence of sight for gaining knowledge of the world, Giotto and his successors contributed to the foundation of empirical science. Praised in his own and later times for his fidelity to nature, Giotto was more than a mere imitator of it. He showed his generation a new way of seeing. With Giotto, European painters turned away from representing the spiritual world—the focus of medieval artists—and once again made recording the visible world a central, if not the sole, aim of their art.

ARENA CHAPEL Projecting onto a flat surface the illusion of solid bodies moving through space presents a double challenge. Constructing the illusion of a weighty, three-dimensional body also requires constructing the illusion of a space sufficiently ample to contain that body. In his fresco cycles (see "Fresco Painting," page 208), Giotto constantly strove to reconcile these two aspects of illusionistic painting. His murals in the Arena Chapel (Cappella Scrovegni; FIG. 7-31) at Padua show his art at its finest. A banker, Enrico Scrovegni, built the chapel on a site adjacent to his palace in the hope that the shrine would atone for the moneylender's sin of usury. Consecrated in 1305, the chapel takes its name from an adjacent ancient Roman arena (amphitheater).

MATERIALS AND TECHNIQUES
Fresco Painting

Fresco painting has a long history, particularly in the Mediterranean region, where the Minoans (FIGS. 2-5 and 2-6) used it as early as the 17th century BCE. *Fresco* (Italian for "fresh") is a mural-painting technique involving the application of permanent limeproof pigments, diluted in water, on freshly laid lime plaster. Because the surface of the wall absorbs the pigments as the plaster dries, fresco is one of the most durable painting techniques. The stable condition of the Minoan frescoes and those in the houses of Roman Pompeii (FIGS. 3-18 to 3-24) and the Arena Chapel (FIGS. 7-31 and 7-32) testify to the longevity of this painting method. The colors have remained vivid because of the chemically inert pigments the artists used.

This *buon fresco* ("good" or true fresco) process is time-consuming and demanding and requires several layers of plaster. Although buon fresco methods vary, generally the artist prepares the wall with a rough layer of lime plaster called the *arriccio* (brown coat). The artist then transfers the composition to the wall, usually by drawing directly on the arriccio with a burnt-orange pigment called *sinopia,* or by transferring a *cartoon* (a full-sized preparatory drawing). Cartoons increased in usage in the 15th and 16th centuries, largely replacing sinopia underdrawings. Finally, the painter lays the *intonaco* (painting coat) smoothly over the drawing in sections (called *giornate*—Italian for "days") only as large as the artist expects to complete in that session. (It is easy to distinguish the various giornate in Giotto's *Lamentation* [FIG. 7-32].) The buon fresco painter must apply the colors fairly quickly, because once the plaster is dry, it will no longer absorb the pigment. Any unpainted areas of the intonaco after a session must be cut away so that fresh plaster can be applied for the next giornata.

In addition to the buon fresco technique, artists used *fresco secco* ("dry" fresco). Fresco secco involves painting on dried lime plaster and

1 ft.

7-32 GIOTTO DI BONDONE, *Lamentation,* Arena Chapel (Cappella Scrovegni), Padua, Italy, ca. 1305. Fresco, 6' 6$\frac{3}{4}$" × 6' $\frac{3}{4}$".

Giotto painted *Lamentation* in several sections, each corresponding to one painting session. Artists employing the buon fresco technique must complete each section before the plaster dries.

was the norm in ancient Egypt. Although the finished product visually approximates buon fresco, the plaster wall does not absorb the pigments, which simply adhere to the surface, so fresco secco is not as permanent as buon fresco.

Some scholars have suggested that Giotto himself may have been the chapel's architect because its design so perfectly suits its interior decoration. The rectangular barrel-vaulted hall has only six windows, all in the south wall (FIG. 7-31, *left*). The other walls are well-illuminated and almost unbroken surfaces, ideal for painting. In 38 framed scenes, Giotto presented one of the most complete Christian pictorial cycles ever rendered. The narrative unfolds on the north and south walls in three zones, reading from top to bottom: at the top, incidents from the lives of the Virgin and her parents, Joachim and Anna; in the middle, the life and mission of Christ; and in the lowest zone, his passion, crucifixion, and resurrection. Below, imitation marble veneer—reminiscent of ancient Roman wall decoration (FIG. 3-40)—alternates with personified Virtues and Vices painted in *grisaille* (monochrome grays, often used for modeling in paintings) to resemble sculpture. *Last Judgment,* the climactic event of the cycle of human salvation, covers most of the west wall above the chapel's entrance.

Subtly scaled to the chapel's space, Giotto's stately and slow-moving half-life-size actors present their dramas convincingly and with great restraint. *Lamentation* (FIG. 7-32) illustrates particularly well the revolutionary nature of Giotto's art. In the presence of boldly foreshortened angels darting about in hysterical grief, a congregation mourns over the dead Savior just before his entombment. Mary cradles her son's body, while Mary Magdalene looks solemnly at the wounds in Christ's feet and John the Evangelist throws his arms back dramatically. Giotto arranged a shallow stage for the figures, bounded by a thick diagonal rock incline defining a horizontal ledge in the foreground. Though narrow, the ledge provides firm visual support for the figures, and the steep slope leads the viewer's eye toward the picture's dramatic focal point at the lower left (compare FIG. 4-26). The figures are sculpturesque, and their postures and gestures convey a broad spectrum of grief, ranging from Mary's almost fierce despair to the passionate outbursts of Mary Magdalene and John to the philosophical resignation of the two disciples at the right and the mute sorrow of the two hooded mourners in the foreground. Painters before Giotto rarely attempted, let alone achieved, this combination of naturalistic representation, compositional complexity, and emotional resonance.

The way Giotto grouped the figures within the constructed space of the *Lamentation* fresco is worth close study. Each group has its own definition, and each contributes to the rhythmic order of the composition. The strong diagonal of the rocky ledge, with its single dead tree (the tree of knowledge of good and evil, which withered after Adam and Eve's original sin), concentrates the viewer's attention on the heads of Christ and his mother, which Giotto positioned dynamically off center. The massive bulk of the seated mourner in the painting's left corner arrests and contains all movement beyond Mary and her dead son. The placement of the seated mourner at the right establishes a relation with the center figures, who, by gazes and gestures, draw the viewer's attention back to Christ's head. Figures seen from the back, which are frequent in Giotto's compositions, are the very contradiction of Byzantine frontality. They emphasize the foreground, aiding the visual placement of the intermediate figures farther back in space. This device in effect puts the viewer behind the "observer figures," who, facing the action as spectators, reinforce the sense of stagecraft as a model for painting. Markedly different too from the *maniera greca* is Giotto's habit of painting incomplete figures cut off by the composition's frame, a feature also of his *Ognissanti Madonna* (FIG. 7-30).

Giotto's innovations in depicting spatial depth and body mass could not, of course, have been possible without his management of light and shade. He shaded his figures to indicate both the direction of the light illuminating their bodies and the shadows (the diminished light), thereby giving the figures volume. In *Lamentation*, light falls on the upper surfaces of the figures (especially the two central bending figures) and passes down to dark in their garments, separating the volumes one from the other and pushing one to the fore, the other to the rear. The gradual transition from light to shade, directed by an even, neutral light from a single steady source—not shown in the picture—was the first step toward the development of *chiaroscuro* (the use of contrasts of dark and light to produce modeling) in Renaissance painting (see page 253).

Giotto's stagelike settings are pictorial counterparts to contemporaneous *mystery plays,* in which actors extended the drama of the Mass into one- and two-act performances at church portals and in city squares. The great increase in popular sermons to huge city audiences prompted a public taste for narrative, recited as dramatically as possible. The arts of illusionistic painting, of drama, and of sermon rhetoric with all their theatrical flourishes developed simultaneously and were mutually influential. Giotto's art masterfully synthesized dramatic narrative, holy lesson, and truth to human experience in a visual idiom of his own invention, accessible to all.

DUCCIO In 14th-century Italy, the Republics of Siena and Florence were the two most powerful city-states, home to wealthy bankers and merchants and well-endowed churches with ample funds for commissioning artworks (see "Artists' Guilds, Artistic Commissions, and Artists' Contracts"). The Sienese were particularly proud of their defeat of the Florentines at the battle of Monteperti in 1260 and believed that the Virgin Mary had brought them victory. To honor the Virgin, the Sienese commissioned DUCCIO DI BUONINSEGNA (active ca. 1278–1318) in 1308 to paint an immense altarpiece for Siena Cathedral—the *Maestà* (*Virgin Enthroned in Majesty*). He and his assistants completed the ambitious work in 1311. As originally executed, the altarpiece consisted of a 7-foot-high center panel (FIG. 7-33), surmounted by seven pinnacles above, and a *predella*, or raised shelf, of panels at the base, altogether some 13 feet high.

The main panel on the front of the altarpiece represents the Virgin enthroned as queen of Heaven amid choruses of angels and saints. Duccio derived the composition's formality and symmetry, along with the figures and facial types of the principal angels and saints, from Byzantine tradition. But the artist relaxed the strict frontality and rigidity of the figures, who turn to one another in quiet conversation. Further, Duccio individualized the faces of the

1 ft.

7-33 DUCCIO DI BUONINSEGNA, *Virgin and Child Enthroned with Saints,* principal panel of the front of the *Maestà* altarpiece, from Siena Cathedral, Siena, Italy, 1308–1311. Tempera and gold leaf on wood, 7' × 13'. Museo dell'Opera del Duomo, Siena.

Duccio derived the formality and symmetry of his composition from Byzantine painting, but relaxed the rigidity and frontality of the figures, softened the drapery, and individualized the faces.

7-34 DUCCIO DI BUONINSEGNA, *Life of Jesus,* 14 panels from the back of the *Maestà* altarpiece (FIG. 7-33), from Siena Cathedral, Siena, Italy, 1308–1311. Tempera and gold leaf on wood, 7' × 13'. Museo dell'Opera del Duomo, Siena.

On the back of the *Maestà* altarpiece, Duccio presented Christ's passion in 24 scenes on 14 panels, beginning with *Entry into Jerusalem,* at the lower left, through *Noli Me Tangere,* at top right.

four kneeling patron saints of Siena in the foreground, who perform their ceremonial gestures without stiffness. Similarly, he softened the usual Byzantine hard body outlines and drapery patterning. The folds of the garments, particularly those of the female saints at both ends of the panel, fall and curve loosely. This is a feature familiar in French Gothic works (FIG. 7-20) and is a mark of the artistic dialogue between Italy and northern Europe in the 14th century.

Despite these changes revealing Duccio's interest in the new naturalism, he respected the age-old requirement that as an altarpiece, his *Maestà* would be the focus of worship in Siena's largest and most important church. Duccio understood that the *Maestà* should be an object holy in itself and recognized how the function of the altarpiece limited experimentation in depicting narrative action and producing illusionistic effects (such as Giotto's) by modeling forms and adjusting their placement in pictorial space. Instead, the queen of Heaven panel is a miracle of color composition and texture manipulation, unfortunately not fully revealed in photographs. In the *Maestà,* Duccio created the glistening and shimmering effects of exotic textiles from China, Byzantium, and the Islamic world. Complementing the luxurious textiles and the (lost) gilded wood frame are the halos of the holy figures, which feature tooled decorative designs in *gold leaf* (*punchwork*).

In contrast to the main panel, the back (FIG. 7-34) of the altarpiece presents an extensive series of narrative panels of different sizes and shapes, beginning with *Annunciation* and culminating with *Resurrection.* The section reproduced here, consisting of 24 scenes in 14 panels, relates Christ's passion. In these scenes, Duccio allowed himself greater latitude for experimentation than in the *Maestà* panel. The bodies are not the flat frontal shapes of Italo-Byzantine art. Duccio imbued them with mass, modeled them with a range of tonalities from light to dark, and arranged their draperies around them convincingly. Even more novel and striking is the

way the figures seem to react to events. Through posture, gesture, and even facial expression, they display a variety of emotions. Duccio's protagonists are actors in a religious drama that the artist interpreted in terms of thoroughly human actions and reactions. In this passion cycle, Duccio took a decisive step toward the humanization of religious subject matter.

SIMONE MARTINI Duccio's successors in Siena included his pupil SIMONE MARTINI (ca. 1285–1344), who may have assisted in painting the *Maestà.* Martini worked for the French kings in Naples and Sicily and, in his last years, produced paintings for the papal court, which in the 14th century was at Avignon, where he came in contact with French painters. By adapting the luxuriant patterns of the Gothic style to Sienese art and, in turn, by acquainting French painters with the Sienese style, Martini was instrumental in creating the so-called *International Gothic* style. This new style swept Europe during the late 14th and early 15th centuries because it appealed to the aristocratic taste for brilliant colors, lavish costumes, intricate ornamentation, and themes involving splendid processions.

Martini's *Annunciation* altarpiece (FIG. 7-35), painted with his assistant LIPPO MEMMI (active ca. 1317–1350), features radiant color, fluttering lines, and weightless elongated figures in a spaceless setting—all hallmarks of the artist's style. The complex etiquette of the European chivalric courts probably inspired Martini's presentation of the theme. Gabriel has just alighted, the breeze of his passage lifting his mantle, his glittering wings still beating. His golden gown signals that he has descended from Heaven. The Virgin, putting down her book of devotions, shrinks shyly from the angel's reverent bow—an appropriate act in the presence of royalty. Mary draws about her the deep blue, golden-hemmed mantle, colors befitting the queen of Heaven. Despite Mary's modest reserve and the tremendous import of Gabriel's message, the scene subordinates

7-35 SIMONE MARTINI and LIPPO MEMMI, *Annunciation,* from the altar of Saint Ansanus, Siena Cathedral, Siena, Italy, 1333 (frame reconstructed in the 19th century). Tempera and gold leaf on wood; center panel, 10' 1" × 8' 8¼". Galleria degli Uffizi, Florence.

A pupil of Duccio's, Simone Martini was instrumental in the creation of the International Gothic style. Its hallmarks are radiant colors, fluttering lines, and weightless figures in golden, spaceless settings.

drama to court ritual, and structural experimentation to surface splendor. The intricate tracery of the richly tooled French Gothic–inspired frame and the elaborate punchwork halos enhance the tactile magnificence of the altarpiece.

AMBROGIO LORENZETTI Another of Duccio's students contributed significantly to the general experiments in pictorial realism taking place in 14th-century Italy. In a vast fresco program he executed for the Sala della Pace (FIG. 7-36) of Siena's Palazzo Pubblico, AMBROGIO LORENZETTI (active 1319–1348) elaborated in spectacular fashion the advances in illusionistic representation made by other Italian painters, while giving visual form to Sienese civic concerns in a series of allegorical paintings: *Good Government, Bad Government and the Effects of Bad Government in the City,* and *Effects of Good Government in the City and in the Country.* The turbulent politics of the Italian cities—the violent party struggles, the overthrow and reinstatement of governments—called for solemn reminders of fair and just administration, and the *palazzo pubblico* ("public palace" or city hall) was the perfect place to display murals contrasting good and bad government. Indeed, the Sienese leaders who commissioned this fresco series had undertaken the "ordering and reformation of the whole city and countryside of Siena."

7-36 AMBROGIO LORENZETTI, *Effects of Good Government in the City and in the Country,* north (*left*) and east (*right*) walls of the Sala della Pace, Palazzo Pubblico, Siena, Italy, 1338–1339. Fresco, north wall 25' 3" wide, east wall 46' wide.

In the Hall of Peace of Siena's city hall, Ambrogio Lorenzetti painted an illusionistic panorama of the bustling city. The fresco served as an allegory of good government in the Sienese republic.

Italy **211**

In *Effects of Good Government in the City and in the Country* (FIG. 7-36, *right*), Lorenzetti depicted the urban and rural effects of good government. One section of the fresco is a panoramic view of Siena, with its palaces, markets, towers, churches, streets, and walls. The city's traffic moves peacefully, guild members ply their trades and crafts, and radiant maidens, clustered hand in hand, perform a graceful circling dance. Dancers were regular features of festive springtime rituals. Here, dancing also serves as a metaphor for a peaceful commonwealth. The artist fondly observed the life of his city, and its architecture gave him an opportunity to apply Sienese artists' rapidly growing knowledge of perspective.

In the *Peaceful Country* section of the fresco, Lorenzetti presented a bird's-eye view of the undulating Tuscan terrain—its villas, castles, plowed farmlands, and peasants going about their seasonal occupations. A personification of Security hovers above the hills and fields, unfurling a scroll promising safety to all who live under the rule of law. Although the mural is an allegory, Lorenzetti's *Peaceful Country* is one of the first examples of landscape painting since antiquity.

Architecture

The picture of Siena in the Sala della Pace could not be confused with a view of a French, German, or English city of the 14th century. Italian architects stood apart from developments north of the Alps.

ORVIETO Designed in the early 14th century by the Sienese architect LORENZO MAITANI (ca. 1255–1330), Orvieto Cathedral (FIG. 7-37) is typical of late medieval architecture in Italy. The church's facade highlights the appeal of the French Gothic architectural vocabulary in Italy. Characteristically French are the pointed gables over the three doorways, the rose window and statues in niches in the upper zone, and the four large pinnacles dividing the facade into three bays. The outer pinnacles serve as miniature substitutes for the tall northern European west-front towers. Maitani's facade, however, is a Gothic overlay masking a marble-revetted basilican structure in the Tuscan Romanesque tradition, as the three-quarter view of the cathedral in FIG. 7-37 reveals. The facade

resembles a great altar screen. Its single plane is covered with Gothic carved and painted decoration, but in principle, Orvieto Cathedral belongs with Pisa Cathedral (FIG. 6-28) and other Italian buildings, rather than with French Gothic churches (FIG. 7-1). Inside, Orvieto Cathedral has a timber-roofed nave with a two-story elevation (columnar arcade with round arches and a clerestory) in the Early Christian manner.

FLORENCE In the 14th century, the historian Giovanni Villani (ca. 1270–1348) described Florence as "the daughter and the creature of Rome," suggesting a preeminence inherited from the Roman Empire. Florentines were fiercely proud of what they perceived as their economic and cultural superiority. Florence controlled the textile industry in Italy, and the republic's gold *florin* was the standard coin of exchange everywhere in Europe.

Florentines translated their pride in their predominance into landmark buildings, such as Santa Maria del Fiore (Saint Mary of

7-37 LORENZO MAITANI, Orvieto Cathedral (looking northeast), Orvieto, Italy, begun 1310.

The pointed gables over the doorways, the rose window, and the large pinnacles derive from French Gothic architecture, but the facade of Orvieto Cathedral masks a traditional timber-roofed basilica.

7-38 ARNOLFO DI CAMBIO and others, aerial view of Santa Maria del Fiore (and the Baptistery of San Giovanni; looking northeast), Florence, Italy, begun 1296. Campanile designed by GIOTTO DI BONDONE, 1334.

The Florentine Duomo's marble revetment carries on the Tuscan Romanesque architectural tradition, linking this basilican church more closely to Early Christian Italy than to Gothic France.

the Flower; FIG. 7-38). ARNOLFO DI CAMBIO (ca. 1245–1302) began work on the cathedral (*Duomo* in Italian) in 1296. Intended as the "most beautiful and honorable church in Tuscany," the Duomo reveals the competitiveness Florentines felt with such cities as Siena and Pisa (FIG. 6-28). Church authorities planned for the cathedral to hold the city's entire population, and although its capacity is only about 30,000 (Florence's population at the time was slightly less than 100,000), the building seemed so large that even the noted architect Leon Battista Alberti (see page 243) commented that it seemed to cover "all of Tuscany with its shade." The Florentine Duomo is a low, longitudinal basilican church with Tuscan-style marble-revetted walls. A vast gulf separates Santa Maria della Fiore from its towering transalpine counterparts, as is strikingly evident when comparing the Italian church with Reims Cathedral (FIG. 7-1), completed several years before work began in Florence.

Giotto di Bondone designed the Duomo's campanile in 1334. In keeping with Italian tradition (FIG. 6-28), the bell tower stands apart from the church. In fact, it is essentially self-sufficient and

could stand anywhere else in the city without looking out of place. The same cannot be said of northern European bell towers. They are essential elements of the structures behind them, and it would be unthinkable to detach one of them and place it somewhere else. In contrast, not only could Giotto's tower be removed from the building without adverse effects, but also each of the parts—cleanly separated from each other by continuous moldings—seems capable of existing independently as an object of considerable aesthetic appeal. This compartmentalization is reminiscent of the Romanesque style, but it also forecasts the ideals of Renaissance architecture.

VENICE One of the wealthiest cities of late medieval Italy—and of Europe—was Venice, renowned for its streets of water. Situated on a lagoon on the northeastern coast of Italy, Venice was secure from land attack and could rely on a powerful navy for protection against invasion from the sea. Internally, Venice was a tight corporation of powerful families that, for centuries, provided stable rule and fostered economic growth.

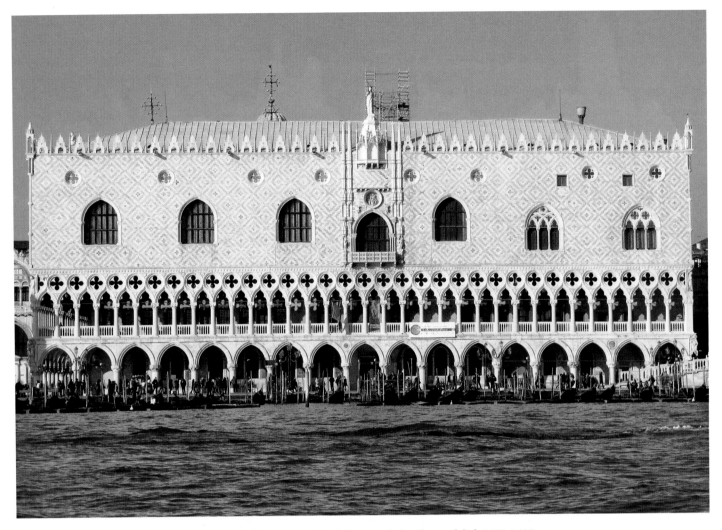

7-39 Doge's Palace (looking north), Venice, Italy, begun ca. 1340–1345; expanded and remodeled, 1424–1438.

The delicate patterning in cream- and rose-colored marbles, the pointed and ogee arches, and the quatrefoil medallions of the Doge's Palace constitute a Venetian variation of Gothic architecture.

The Venetian republic's seat of government was the Doge's (Duke's) Palace (FIG. 7-39), situated on the Grand Canal adjacent to Venice's most important church, San Marco (Saint Mark's; FIG. 4-24). Begun around 1340 to 1345 and significantly remodeled after 1424, Venice's ducal palace was the most ornate public building in medieval Italy. In a stately march, the first level's short and heavy columns support rather severe pointed arches that look strong enough to carry the weight of the upper structure. Their rhythm doubles in the upper arcades, where more slender columns carry *ogee arches* (made up of double-curving lines), which terminate in flamelike tips between medallions pierced with *quatrefoils* (four-lobed, cloverlike shapes). Each story is taller than the one beneath it, the topmost as high as the two lower arcades combined. Yet the building does not look top-heavy. This is due in part to the complete absence of articulation in the top story and in part to the walls' delicate patterning in cream- and rose-colored marbles, which makes them appear paper thin. The palace in which Venice's *doges*

conducted state business represents a delightful and charming variant of Late Gothic architecture. Colorful, decorative, light and airy in appearance, their Venetian palace is ideally suited to the unique Italian city that floats between water and air.

⏯ Explore the era further in MindTap with videos of major artworks and buildings, Google Earth™ coordinates, and essays by the author on the following additional subjects:

▌ ART AND SOCIETY: Paris, the New Center of Medieval Learning
▌ THE PATRON'S VOICE: Abbot Suger and the Rebuilding of Saint-Denis
• *Virgin of Paris* (FIG. **7-20A**)
• Cologne Cathedral (FIG. **7-24A**)
• Pietro Cavallini, *Last Judgment* (FIG. **7-29A**)
▌ THE PATRON'S VOICE: Artists' Guilds, Artistic Commissions, and Artists' Contracts

GOTHIC AND LATE MEDIEVAL EUROPE

France

- The birthplace of Gothic art and architecture was Saint-Denis, where Abbot Suger rebuilt the Carolingian royal church using rib vaults with pointed arches and stained-glass windows. The Early Gothic (1140–1194) west facade of Suger's church also introduced sculpted figures on the portal jambs, a feature that appeared shortly later on the Royal Portal of Chartres Cathedral.

- After a fire in 1194, Chartres Cathedral was rebuilt with flying buttresses, four-part nave vaults, and a three-story elevation of nave arcade, triforium, and clerestory, setting the pattern for High Gothic (1194–1300) cathedrals, including Amiens with its 144-foot-high vaults.

- Flying buttresses made possible huge stained-glass windows, which converted natural light into divine colored light (lux nova), dramatically transforming the character of church interiors.

- High Gothic jamb statues differ markedly from their Early Gothic predecessors in their contrapposto stances. The sculpted figures of Reims Cathedral not only move freely but converse with their neighbors.

- In the 13th century, professional lay artists in Parisian workshops were renowned for producing illuminated manuscripts, usurping the role of monastic scriptoria.

Royal Portal, Chartres Cathedral, ca. 1145–1155

Moralized Bible, Paris, 1226–1234

England and the Holy Roman Empire

- English Gothic churches, such as Salisbury Cathedral, differ from their French counterparts in their wider and shorter facades, and sparing use of flying buttresses. Especially characteristic of English Gothic architecture is the elaboration of architectural patterns. A prime example is the chapel of Henry VII in Westminster Abbey in London, which features Perpendicular-style fan vaults.

- In the Holy Roman Empire, architects eagerly embraced the French Gothic architectural style at Cologne Cathedral and elsewhere. German originality manifested itself most clearly in sculptures depicting emotionally charged figures in dramatic poses. The statues of secular historical figures in Naumburg Cathedral signal a revival of interest in portraiture.

Salisbury Cathedral, London, 1220–1265

Italy

- Nicola Pisano was a master sculptor from southern Italy who carved pulpits incorporating marble panels that, both stylistically and in individual motifs, derive from ancient Roman sarcophagi.

- The leading Italian painter of the late 13th century was Cimabue, who worked in the Italo-Byzantine style, or maniera greca.

- Considered the first Renaissance painter, Giotto di Bondone revived the Greco-Roman naturalistic approach to representation based on observation.

- Duccio di Buoninsegna relaxed the frontality and rigidity of the Italo-Byzantine style and took a decisive step toward humanizing religious subject matter.

- Secular themes also came to the fore in 14th-century Italy. Ambrogio Lorenzetti's frescoes for Siena's Palazzo Pubblico feature one of the first landscapes since antiquity.

- Italian 14th-century architecture underscores the regional character of late medieval art. Orvieto Cathedral's facade incorporates elements of the French Gothic vocabulary, but it is a screen masking a traditional timber-roofed basilica with round arches in the nave arcade.

Nicola Pisano, Pisa baptistery pulpit, 1259–1260

Giotto, Lamentation, ca. 1305

▶ **8-1a** Many details have symbolic meaning. The armrest depicting Adam, Eve, and the serpent reminded viewers that Mary is the new Eve and Jesus the new Adam who will redeem humanity from original sin.

1 ft.

8-1 ROGIER VAN DER WEYDEN, *Saint Luke Drawing the Virgin*, ca. 1435–1440. Oil and tempera on wood, 4' 6⅛" × 3' 7⅝". Museum of Fine Arts, Boston (gift of Mr. and Mrs. Henry Lee Higginson).

▶ **8-1b** The Virgin Mary has invited Saint Luke to paint her portrait in her elegant home—the type that wealthy 15th-century Flemish merchants owned. In the background is a view of a typical Flemish town.

▶ **8-1c** Probably commissioned by the painters' guild in Brussels, *Saint Luke* honors the first Christian artist and the profession of painting. Saint Luke may be a self-portrait of Rogier van der Weyden.

The Early Renaissance in Europe

ROGIER VAN DER WEYDEN AND SAINT LUKE

In the 15th-century, Flanders—a region corresponding to what is today Belgium, the Netherlands, Luxembourg, and part of northern France (MAP 8-1)—enjoyed widespread prosperity. Successful merchants and craft *guilds* joined the clergy and royalty in commissioning artists to produce works for both public and private display. Especially popular were paintings by artists using the recently perfected medium of oil-based pigments, which soon became the favored painting medium throughout Europe (see "Tempera and Oil Painting," page 220).

One of the early masters of oil painting was ROGIER VAN DER WEYDEN (ca. 1400–1464) of Tournai in present-day Belgium. Rogier made Brussels his home in 1435 and soon thereafter painted *Saint Luke Drawing the Virgin* (FIG. 8-1), probably for the city's artists' guild, the Guild of Saint Luke. Luke was the patron saint of artists because legend said that he had painted a portrait of the Virgin Mary (see "Early Christian Saints" ⊿). Rogier's subject was therefore perfectly suited for the headquarters of a painters' guild. It shows Luke (his identifying attribute, the ox, is at the right) at work in the kind of private residence that wealthy Flemish merchants of this era owned. Mary has miraculously appeared before Luke and invited him to paint her portrait as she nurses her son. The saint begins the process by making a preliminary drawing using a *silverpoint* (a sharp *stylus* that creates a fine line), the same instrument Rogier himself would have used when he began this commission. The painting thus not only honors Luke but also pays tribute to the profession of painting in Flanders (see "The Artist's Profession during the Renaissance" ⊿) by documenting the preparatory work required before artists can begin painting the figures and setting.

The subject also draws attention to the venerable history of portrait painting. A rare genre during the Middle Ages, portraiture became a major source of income for Flemish artists, and Rogier van der Weyden was one of the best portrait painters in Flanders. In fact, many scholars believe that Rogier's Saint Luke is a self-portrait, identifying the painter with the first Christian artist and underscoring the holy nature of painting. *Saint Luke Drawing the Virgin* is also emblematic of 15th-century Flemish painting in aiming to record every detail of a scene with loving fidelity to optical appearance, seen here in the rich fabrics, the patterned floor, and the landscape visible through the window. Also characteristic of Flemish art is the imbuing of many of the painting's details with symbolic significance. For example, the carved armrest of the Virgin's bench depicts Adam, Eve, and the serpent, reminding the viewer that Mary is the new Eve and Jesus the new Adam who will redeem humanity from Adam and Eve's original sin.

THE EARLY RENAISSANCE IN EUROPE

In the 14th and 15th centuries, Europe experienced the calamities of plague, war, and social upheaval. The Black Death that ravaged Italy in 1348, killing 50 to 60 percent of the population in the largest cities, also spread to much of the rest of Europe. Equally destabilizing—and far longer lasting—was the Hundred Years' War (1337–1453). Primarily a series of conflicts between France and England, the war also involved Flanders. Crisis in the religious realm compounded the period's political instability. In 1305, the College of Cardinals elected a French pope, Clement V (r. 1305–1314). He and the French popes who succeeded him chose to reside in Avignon. Understandably, the Italians, who saw Rome as the rightful capital of the universal Church, resented the Avignon papacy. The conflict between the French and Italians resulted in the election

in 1378 of two popes—Clement VII, who resided in Avignon, and Urban VI (r. 1378–1389), who remained in Rome. Thus began what became known as the Great Schism, which lasted until the election in 1417 of a new Roman pope, Martin V (r. 1417–1431), who was acceptable to all.

Despite the troubles of the age, a new economic system evolved—the early stage of European capitalism. In response to the financial requirements of trade, new credit and exchange systems created an economic network of enterprising European cities. Trade in money accompanied trade in commodities, and the former financed industry. Both were in the hands of international trading companies, such as that of the Medici of Florence, whose family members were among the greatest art patrons in history. North of the Alps, in 1460 Flemish entrepreneurs established the first international commercial stock exchange in Antwerp, which

MAP 8-1 France, the duchy of Burgundy, and the Holy Roman Empire in 1477.

THE EARLY RENAISSANCE IN EUROPE

1395–1425
- Claus Sluter carves life-size statues of biblical figures with portraitlike features for Philip the Bold, duke of Burgundy.
- The Limbourg brothers expand the illusionistic capabilities of manuscript illumination for Jean, duke of Berry.
- Ghiberti wins the competition to design new doors for Florence's baptistery.
- Masaccio carries Giotto's naturalism further in fresco painting.
- Brunelleschi develops linear perspective and designs the Ospedale degli Innocenti.

1425–1450
- Robert Campin, Jan van Eyck, and Rogier van der Weyden popularize the use of oil-based paints in Flanders.
- German graphic artists pioneer woodcut printing, making art affordable to the masses.
- Ghiberti installs the *Gates of Paradise* facing Florence Cathedral.
- Donatello revives freestanding nude male statuary.
- Michelozzo builds the new Medici palace in Florence.
- Alberti publishes his treatise on painting.

1450–1475
- In Germany, Johannes Gutenberg invents moveable type and prints the first Bibles on a letterpress.
- Federico da Montefeltro brings Piero della Francesca to the Urbino court.
- Alberti rebuilds Sant'Andrea and Mantegna creates illusionistic paintings for Duke Ludovico Gonzaga of Mantua.

1475–1500
- The Late Gothic style lingers in Germany in the large wood retables of Tilman Riemenschneider.
- Martin Schongauer becomes the first northern European master of engraving.
- Botticelli paints Neo-Platonic mythological allegories for the Medici.
- Alberti publishes his treatise on architecture.
- Savonarola condemns humanism, and the Medici flee Florence.
- Perugino and others decorate the Sistine Chapel in Rome.

became pivotal for Europe's integrated economic activity. Thriving commerce, industry, and finance contributed to the evolution of cities, as did the migration of a significant portion of the rural population to urban centers. With successful merchants and bankers joining kings, dukes, and popes as major patrons of painting, sculpture, and architecture, the arts also flourished throughout Europe.

BURGUNDY AND FLANDERS

In the 15th century, Duke Philip the Good (r. 1419–1467) ruled Burgundy, the fertile east-central region of France famous for its wines (MAP 8-1). In 1369, one of Philip the Good's predecessors, Philip the Bold (r. 1364–1404), married the daughter of the count of Flanders, and acquired territory in the Netherlands. Thereafter, the major source of Burgundian wealth was Bruges, the city that made Burgundy a dangerous rival of royal France. Bruges initially derived its prosperity from the wool trade, but soon expanded into banking, becoming the financial clearinghouse for all of northern Europe. Indeed, Bruges so dominated Flanders that the duke of Burgundy eventually chose to make the city his capital and moved his court there from Dijon. Due to the expanded territory and the prosperity of the duchy of Burgundy, Philip the Bold and his successors were probably the most powerful northern European rulers during the first three quarters of the 15th century. Although members of the extended French royal family, they usually supported England (on which they relied for the raw materials used in their wool industry) during the Hundred Years' War and, at times, controlled much of northern France, including Paris, the seat of the French monarchy. At the height of Burgundian power, the ducal lands stretched from the Rhône River to the North Sea.

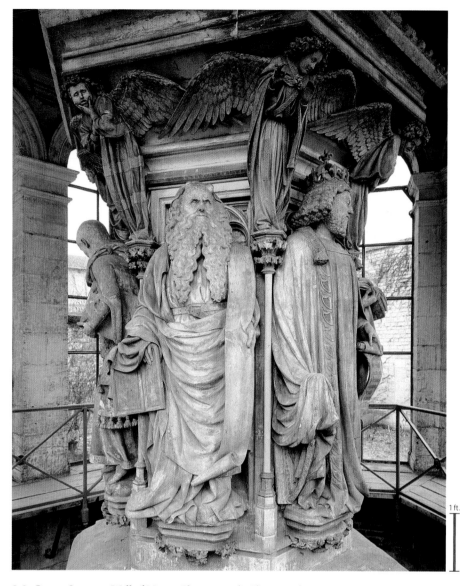

8-2 CLAUS SLUTER, *Well of Moses,* Chartreuse de Champmol, Dijon, France, 1395–1406. Limestone, painted and gilded by JEAN MALOUEL, Moses 6' high.

The *Well of Moses,* a symbolic fountain of life made for the duke of Burgundy, originally supported a sculpted crucifixion group. Sluter's figures recall French Gothic jamb statues, but are far more realistic.

CHARTREUSE DE CHAMPMOL The great wealth that the dukes of Burgundy amassed enabled them to become significant patrons of the arts. Philip the Bold's largest artistic enterprise was the Chartreuse de Champmol, near Dijon. A *chartreuse* ("charter house" in English) is a Carthusian monastery. The Carthusian order, founded by Saint Bruno (ca. 1030–1101) in the late 11th century at Chartreuse in southeastern France, consisted of monks who devoted their lives to solitary living and prayer. Inspired by Saint-Denis, the French kings' burial site (see page 189), Philip intended the Dijon chartreuse to become a ducal *mausoleum* and serve both as a means of securing salvation in perpetuity for the Burgundian dukes and as a dynastic symbol of Burgundian power.

For the Champmol cloister, Philip the Bold's head sculptor, CLAUS SLUTER (active ca. 1360–1406) of Haarlem (Netherlands), designed a large sculptural fountain located in a well that provided water for the monastery, but water probably did not spout from the fountain because the Carthusian commitment to silence and prayer would have precluded anything producing sound. Sluter's *Well of Moses* (FIG. 8-2) features statues of Moses and five other prophets (David, Daniel, Isaiah, Jeremiah, and Zachariah) surrounding a base that once supported a 25-foot-tall crucifixion group. The Carthusians called the *Well of Moses* a *fons vitae,* a fountain of everlasting life. The blood of the crucified Christ symbolically flowed down over grieving angels and the Old Testament prophets, spilling into the well below, washing over Christ's prophetic predecessors and redeeming anyone who would drink water from the well.

Although the figures recall the jamb statues (FIG. 7-15) of Gothic portals, they are much more realistically rendered. The six prophets have portraitlike features and distinct individual personalities and costumes. Sluter succeeded in sculpting realistic faces and differentiating textures from coarse drapery to smooth flesh and silky hair. Paint, much of which has flaked off, further augmented the naturalism of the figures. (The painter was JEAN MALOUEL [ca. 1365–1415], another Netherlandish master.) This fascination with the specific and tangible in the visible world became one of the chief characteristics of 15th-century Flemish art.

MATERIALS AND TECHNIQUES
Tempera and Oil Painting

The generic words *paint* and *pigment* encompass a wide range of substances that artists have used through the ages. Fresco aside (see "Fresco Painting," page 208), during the 14th century, egg *tempera* was the material of choice for most painters, both in Italy and northern Europe. Tempera consists of egg combined with a wet paste of ground pigment. Images painted with tempera have a velvety sheen. Artists usually applied tempera to the painting surface with a light touch because thick application of the pigment mixture would result in premature cracking and flaking.

Some artists used oil paints (powdered pigments mixed with linseed oil) as far back as the eighth century, but not until the early 1400s did oil painting become widespread. Flemish artists were among the first to employ oils extensively (often mixing them with tempera), and Italian painters quickly followed suit. The discovery of better drying components in the early 15th century enhanced the setting capabilities of oils. Rather than apply these oils in the light, flecked brushstrokes that the tempera technique encouraged, artists laid the oils down in

transparent layers, or *glazes*, over opaque or semiopaque underlayers. In this manner, painters could build up deep tones through repeated *glazing*. Unlike works in tempera, whose surface dries quickly due to water evaporation, oils dry more uniformly and slowly, giving the artist time to rework areas. This flexibility must have been particularly appealing to artists who worked very deliberately, such as the Flemish masters Robert Campin, Jan van Eyck, and Rogier van der Weyden, and the Italian Leonardo da Vinci. Leonardo also preferred oil paint because its gradual drying process and consistency enabled him to blend the pigments, thereby creating the impressive *sfumato* (smoky) effect that contributed to his fame (see page 255).

Both tempera and oils can be applied to various surfaces. Through the early 16th century, wood panels served as the foundation for most paintings. Linen canvas became increasingly popular in the late 16th century. Although evidence suggests that artists did not intend permanency for their early images on canvas, the material proved particularly useful in areas such as Venice where high humidity warped wood panels and made fresco unfeasible. Furthermore, until artists began to use wood bars to stretch the canvas to form a taut surface, canvas paintings could be rolled and were lighter and more easily portable than wood panels.

8-3 ROBERT CAMPIN (MASTER OF FLÉMALLE), *Mérode Altarpiece* (open), ca. 1425–1428. Oil on wood, center panel 2′ 1 3/8″ × 2′ 7/8″, each wing 2′ 1 3/8″ × 10 7/8″. Metropolitan Museum of Art, New York (The Cloisters Collection, 1956).

Campin, the leading painter of Tournai, was an early master of oil painting. In the *Mérode Altarpiece,* he used the new medium to reproduce with loving fidelity the interior of a Flemish merchant's home.

ROBERT CAMPIN One of the earliest important Flemish painters was the man known as the MASTER OF FLÉMALLE, whom many scholars identify as ROBERT CAMPIN (ca. 1378–1444) of Tournai. Campin was a highly skilled practitioner of the new medium of *oil painting* (see "Tempera and Oil Painting," above). Flemish painters built up their pictures by superimposing translucent paint layers

over a carefully planned drawing (compare FIG. 8-1) made on a panel prepared with a white ground. With the oil medium, artists could create richer colors than previously possible, giving their paintings an intense tonality, the illusion of glowing light, and glistening surfaces. These traits differed significantly from the high-keyed color, sharp light, and rather *matte* (dull) surface of *tempera*. The brilliant and versatile oil medium suited perfectly the formal intentions of 15th-century Flemish painters, who aimed for sharply focused clarity of detail in their representation of objects ranging in scale from large to almost invisible.

Campin's most famous work is the *Mérode Altarpiece* (FIG. 8-3), one of the many small altarpieces of this period produced for private patrons and intended for household prayer. Perhaps the most striking feature of these private devotional images is the integration of religious and secular concerns. For example, artists often presented biblical scenes as taking place in a house (compare FIG. 8-1). Religion was such an integral part of Flemish life that separating the sacred from the secular was almost impossible—and undesirable. Moreover, the presentation in religious art of familiar settings and objects no doubt strengthened the direct bond that the patron or viewer felt with biblical figures.

The *Mérode Altarpiece* is a small *triptych* (three-panel painting) with *Annunciation* as the center panel. Unseen by the Virgin, a tiny figure of Christ carrying the cross enters the room on a ray of light, foreshadowing his incarnation and passion (see "The Life of Jesus in Art," pages 120–121). The archangel Gabriel approaches Mary, who sits reading in a well-kept Flemish home. The view through the window in the right wing, as well as the depicted accessories, furniture, and utensils, confirm the locale as Flanders. However, the objects represented are not merely decorative. They also function as religious symbols. The book, extinguished candle, and lilies on the table; the copper basin in the corner niche; the towels, fire screen, and bench all symbolize the Virgin's purity and her divine mission.

In the right panel, Joseph, apparently unaware of Gabriel's arrival, has constructed two mousetraps, symbolic of the theological concept that Christ is bait set in the trap of the world to catch the Devil. The ax, saw, and rod that Campin painted in the foreground of Joseph's workshop not only are tools of the carpenter's trade but also are mentioned in the account of the Annunciation in Isaiah 10:15. In the left panel, the closed garden is symbolic of Mary's purity, and the flowers Campin included relate to Mary's virtues, especially humility.

The altarpiece's donor, Peter Inghelbrecht, a wealthy merchant, and his wife, Margarete Scrynmakers, kneel in the garden and witness the momentous event through an open door. *Donor portraits*—portraits of the individual(s) who commissioned (or "donated") the work—became very popular in the 15th century. In this instance, in addition to asking to be represented in their altarpiece, the Inghelbrechts probably specified the subject. Inghelbrecht means "angel bringer," a reference to Gabriel's bringing the news of Christ's birth to Mary in the central panel. Scrynmakers means "cabinet- or shrine-makers," and probably inspired the workshop scene in the right panel.

JAN VAN EYCK The first Netherlandish painter to achieve international fame was JAN VAN EYCK (ca. 1390–1441), who in 1425 became Philip the Good's court painter. In 1431, he moved his studio to Bruges, where the duke maintained his official residence. That same year, he completed the *Ghent Altarpiece* (FIGS. 8-4 and 8-5)—which his older brother, HUBERT VAN EYCK (ca. 1366–1426), had begun—for the church originally dedicated to John the Baptist (since 1540, Saint Bavo Cathedral) in Ghent. One of the most characteristic art forms in 15th-century Flanders was the monumental freestanding altarpiece, and the *Ghent Altarpiece* is one of the largest. Placed behind the altar, these imposing works served as backdrops for the Mass. Given their function, it is not surprising that many altarpieces

8-4 HUBERT and JAN VAN EYCK, *Ghent Altarpiece* (closed), Saint Bavo Cathedral, Ghent, Belgium, completed 1432. Oil on wood, 11' 5" × 7' 6".

Monumental painted altarpieces were popular in Flemish churches. Artists decorated both the interiors and exteriors of these polyptychs, which often, as here, included donor portraits.

depict scenes directly related to Christ's sacrifice. Flemish altarpieces most often took the form of *polyptychs*—hinged multipaneled paintings or relief panels. The hinges enabled the clergy to close the polyptych's side wings over the center panel(s), as in FIG. 8-4. Artists decorated both the exterior and interior of the altarpieces. This multi-panel format provided the opportunity to construct narratives through a sequence of images, somewhat as in manuscript illustration. Although concrete information is lacking about when the clergy opened and closed these altarpieces, the wings probably remained closed on regular days and open on Sundays and feast days. On this schedule, worshipers could have seen both the interior and exterior—diverse imagery at various times according to the liturgical calendar.

Jodocus Vyd, diplomat-retainer of Philip the Good, and his wife, Isabel Borluut, commissioned the *Ghent Altarpiece*. Vyd's largesse contributed to his appointment as the city's *burgomeister* (mayor) shortly after the unveiling of the work. Two of the exterior panels (FIG. 8-4) depict the donors. Husband and wife kneel with their hands clasped in prayer. They gaze piously at illusionistically rendered stone sculptures of Ghent's patron saints, John the Baptist and John the Evangelist. *Annunciation* appears on the upper register, with a careful representation of a Flemish town outside the painted

8-5 HUBERT and JAN VAN EYCK, *Ghent Altarpiece* (open), Saint Bavo Cathedral, Ghent, Belgium, completed 1432. Oil on wood, 11' 5" × 15' 1".

In this richly colored painting of salvation from the original sin of Adam and Eve (who are shown on the wings), God the Father presides in majesty between the Virgin Mary and John the Baptist.

window of the center panel. In the uppermost arched panels, Jan depicted the Old Testament prophets Zachariah and Micah, along with *sibyls*, Greco-Roman mythological female prophets whose writings the Church interpreted as prophesies of Christ.

When open (FIG. 8-5), the altarpiece reveals a richly colored painting of human redemption through Christ. In the upper register, God the Father—wearing the pope's triple tiara, with a worldly crown at his feet and resplendent in a deep-scarlet mantle—presides in majesty. To God's right is the Virgin, represented as the queen of Heaven, with a crown of 12 stars on her head. John the Baptist sits to God's left. To either side is a choir of angels, with an angel playing an organ on the right. Adam and Eve appear in the far panels, amplifying the central theme of salvation. Even though humans, symbolized by Adam and Eve, are sinful, they will be saved because God will sacrifice his own son for this purpose.

The panels of the lower register extend the symbolism of the upper. In the center panel, saints arrive from the four corners of the earth through an opulent, flower-spangled landscape. They proceed toward the altar of the lamb and the octagonal fountain of life. The lamb symbolizes the sacrificed son of God, whose heart bleeds into a chalice, while into the fountain spills the "pure river of water of

life, clear as crystal, proceeding out of the throne of God and of the Lamb" (Rev. 22:1). On the right, the 12 apostles and a group of martyrs in red robes advance. On the left appear prophets. In the right background come the virgin martyrs, and in the left background the holy confessors approach. On the lower wings, hermits, pilgrims, knights, and judges arrive from left and right. They symbolize the four cardinal virtues: Temperance, Prudence, Fortitude, and Justice, respectively. The altarpiece celebrates the whole Christian cycle from the fall to the redemption, presenting the Church triumphant in heavenly Jerusalem.

Jan used oil paints to render the entire altarpiece in shimmering oil colors that defy reproduction. No small detail escaped the painter. With pristine specificity, he revealed the beauty of the most insignificant object. He depicted the soft texture of hair, the glitter of gold in the heavy brocades, the luster of pearls, and the flashing of gems, all with loving fidelity to appearance.

GIOVANNI ARNOLFINI Both the *Mérode Altarpiece* and the *Ghent Altarpiece* include painted portraits of their donors. These paintings marked a significant revival of portraiture, a genre that had languished since antiquity. The elite wanted to memorialize themselves

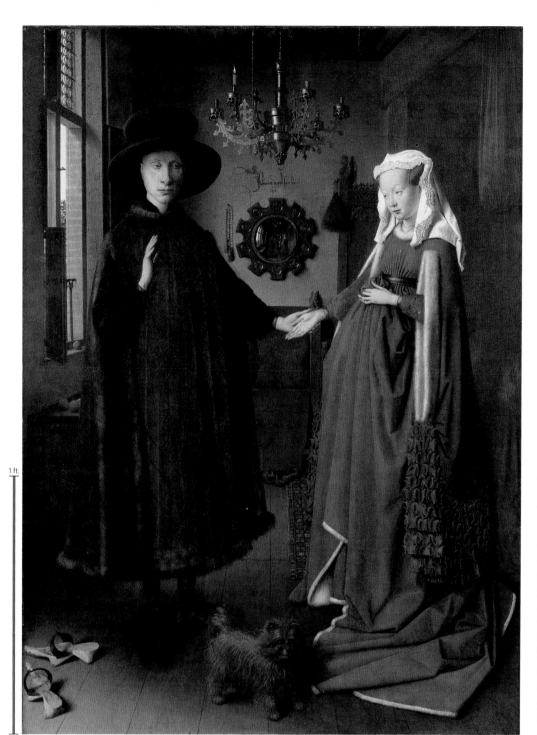

1 ft.

8-6 JAN VAN EYCK, *Giovanni Arnolfini and His Wife,* 1434. Oil on wood, 2' 9" × 1' 10½". National Gallery, London.

Jan van Eyck played a major role in establishing portraiture as an important Flemish art form. In this portrait of an Italian financier and his wife in their home, the painter depicted himself in the mirror.

the couple are taking their marriage vows. As in the *Mérode Altarpiece,* almost every object carries meaning. For example, the little dog symbolizes fidelity. The *finial* (crowning ornament) of the marriage bed is a tiny statue of Saint Margaret, patron saint of childbirth. (The bride is not yet pregnant, although the fashionable costume she wears makes her appear so.) From the finial hangs a whiskbroom, symbolic of domestic care. Indeed, even the placement of the two figures is meaningful. The woman stands near the bed and well into the room, whereas the man stands near the open window, symbolic of the outside world.

Many art historians, however, dispute this interpretation because, among other things, the room in which Arnolfini and his wife stand is a public reception area, not a bedchamber. One scholar has suggested that Arnolfini is conferring legal privileges on his wife to conduct business in his absence. In either case, the artist functions as a witness. In the background is a convex mirror, whose spatial distortion Jan brilliantly recorded. Reflected in the mirror are not only the principals, Arnolfini and his wife, but also two persons who look into the room through the door. One of these must be the artist himself, as the elegant inscription above the mirror—*Johannes de Eyck fuit hic* ("Jan van Eyck was here")—announces that he was present. The self-portrait also underscores the painter's self-consciousness as a professional artist whose role deserves to be recorded and remembered.

in their dynastic lines and to establish their identities, ranks, and stations with images far more concrete than heraldic coats of arms. Portraits also served to represent state officials at events they could not attend. Royalty, nobility, and the very rich would sometimes send artists to paint the likeness of a prospective bride or groom. For example, when young King Charles VI (r. 1380–1422) of France sought a bride, he dispatched a painter to three different royal courts to make portraits of the candidates.

Prosperous merchants also commissioned portraits for their homes. Early examples are Jan van Eyck's *Giovanni Arnolfini and His Wife* (FIG. 8-6) and the *Diptych of Martin van Nieuwenhove* (FIG. 8-6A ⏎) by HANS MEMLING (ca. 1430–1494). Jan depicted the Lucca financier (who had established himself in Bruges as an agent of the Medici family) and his second wife, whose name is not known, in their home. According to the traditional interpretation,

ROGIER VAN DER WEYDEN When Jan van Eyck began work on the *Ghent Altarpiece,* Rogier van der Weyden (FIG. 8-1) was an assistant in the workshop of Robert Campin (FIG. 8-3), but the younger Tournai painter's fame eventually rivaled Jan's. Rogier quickly became renowned for his paintings of Christian themes stressing human action and drama. He concentrated on passion episodes that elicited powerful emotions, moving observers deeply by vividly portraying the suffering of Christ.

8-7 ROGIER VAN
DER WEYDEN,
Deposition, center
panel of a triptych
from Notre-Dame
hors-les-murs,
Louvain, Belgium,
ca. 1435. Oil on wood,
7' 2⅝" × 8' 7⅛". Museo
del Prado, Madrid.

D*eposition* resembles a
carved shrine in which the
biblical figures act out a
drama of passionate sor-
row as if on a shallow theatrical stage. The painting
makes an unforgettable
emotional impact.

1 ft.

Deposition (FIG. 8-7) is the center panel of a triptych commissioned by the archers' guild of Louvain. Rogier acknowledged his
patrons by incorporating the crossbow (the guild's symbol) into the
decorative tracery in the corners. Instead of creating a deep landscape setting, as Jan van Eyck might have, Rogier compressed the
figures and action onto a shallow stage with a golden back wall.
Indeed, the painting could be a depiction of a carved shrine representing the deposition instead of the event itself. In any case, a series
of lateral undulating movements gives the group a compositional
unity, a formal cohesion that Rogier strengthened by depicting
the sorrowful anguish many of the figures share. The similar poses
of Christ and his mother reflect the belief that Mary suffered the
same pain at the crucifixion as her son. Their echoing postures also
resemble the shape of a crossbow. Few painters have equaled Rogier
in the rendering of passionate sorrow. His depiction of the agony of
loss in *Deposition* makes an unforgettable emotional impact on the
viewer.

HUGO VAN DER GOES By the mid-15th century, Flemish art had
achieved renown throughout Europe. The *Portinari Altarpiece*
(FIG. 8-8) is a large-scale Flemish triptych in a family chapel in Florence, Italy. The artist who received the commission was HUGO VAN
DER GOES (ca. 1440–1482) of Ghent. Hugo painted the altarpiece for
Tommaso Portinari, an Italian shipowner and agent in Bruges for the
Medici bank of Florence. Portinari appears on the wings of the triptych
with his family and their patron saints. The main panel, *Adoration of the
Shepherds,* based on a Swedish saint's vision, shows the Virgin, Joseph,
angels, and shepherds adoring the infant Savior, who lies on the ground
and glows with divine light. Hugo tilted the ground, a compositional
device he may have derived from the tilted stage floors of mystery plays.

The shepherds, with their lined faces, work-worn hands, and
uncouth dress and manner, are rendered far more realistically than
comparable figures in Italian art, and the *Portinari Altarpiece* created
a considerable stir among Italian artists when it was installed in the
patron's family's chapel in Sant'Egidio. Although the painting may
have seemed unstructured to the Italians and the varying scale of the
figures according to their importance perpetuated medieval conventions, Hugo's masterful technique and incredible realism in representing drapery, flowers, animals, and, above all, human character and
emotion made a deep impression on Florentine painters and the public alike.

FRANCE

In France, the anarchy of the Hundred Years' War and the weakness
of the kings gave rise to a group of powerful duchies. The strongest
and wealthiest—the duchy of Burgundy, which controlled Flanders—has already been examined. But the dukes of Berry, Bourbon,
and Nemours as well as members of the French royal court were
also important art patrons.

LIMBOURG BROTHERS During the 15th century, French artists built on the achievements of Gothic manuscript painters (see
"Gothic Book Production," page 199). Among the most significant developments was a new interest in the spatial settings of the
subjects depicted. The LIMBOURG BROTHERS (POL, HERMAN, and
JEAN)—three nephews of Jean Malouel (FIG. 8-2), the court artist
of Philip the Bold—were pioneers in expanding the illusionistic
capabilities of manuscript illumination. The Limbourgs, Netherlandish painters who moved to Paris no later than 1402, produced

8-8 Hugo van der Goes, *Adoration of the Shepherds* (*Portinari Altarpiece,* open), from Sant'Egidio, Florence, Italy, ca. 1476. Tempera and oil on wood, center panel 8' 3½" × 10', each wing 8' 3½" × 4' 7½". Galleria degli Uffizi, Florence.

This altarpiece is a rare instance of the awarding of a major commission in Italy to a Flemish painter. The Florentines admired Hugo's realistic details and brilliant portrayal of human character.

a gorgeously illustrated Book of Hours for Jean, the duke of Berry (r. 1360–1416) and brother of Philip the Bold and King Charles V (r. 1364–1380) of France. The duke was an avid art patron and focused on collecting manuscripts, jewels, and rare artifacts. The three brothers worked on *Les Très Riches Heures du Duc de Berry* (*The Very Sumptuous Hours of the Duke of Berry*) until their deaths in 1416. A *Book of Hours* was used for reciting prayers (see "Medieval Books" ✒). It contained liturgical passages to be read privately at set times during the day, as well as penitential psalms, devotional prayers, litanies to the saints, and an illustrated calendar containing local religious feast days. Books of Hours became favorite possessions of the northern European aristocracy during the 14th and 15th centuries. Illuminated prayer books eventually became available to affluent merchants and contributed to the decentralization of religious practice that was one factor in the Protestant Reformation in the early 16th century (see page 272).

The calendar pictures of *Les Très Riches Heures* represent the 12 months in terms of the associated seasonal tasks, alternating scenes of nobility and peasantry. Above each picture is a lunette depicting the zodiac signs and the chariot of the sun as it makes its yearly cycle through the heavens. Beyond its function as a religious book, *Les Très Riches Heures* also celebrates the duke and his relationship to the peasants. The illustration for October (FIG. 8-9) focuses on the peasantry. The Limbourgs depicted a sower, a man plowing on horseback, and washerwomen, along with city dwellers, who promenade in front of the Louvre (the French king's residence

8-9 Limbourg brothers (Pol, Herman, Jean), *October,* from *Les Très Riches Heures du Duc de Berry,* 1413–1416. Colors and ink on vellum, 8⅞" × 5⅜". Musée Condé, Chantilly.

The Limbourg brothers expanded the illusionistic capabilities of manuscript painting with their care in accurately rendering architectural details and their convincing depiction of cast shadows.

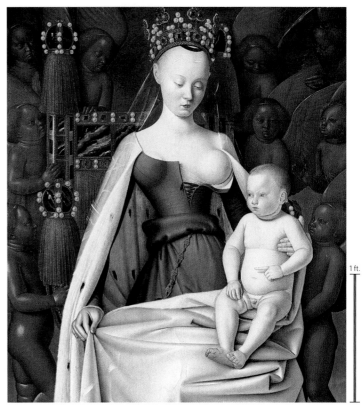

8-10 JEAN FOUQUET, *Melun Diptych*, ca. 1451. Left wing: *Étienne Chevalier and Saint Stephen*. Oil on wood, 3' $\frac{1}{2}$" × 2' 9$\frac{1}{2}$". Gemäldegalerie, Staatliche Museen zu Berlin, Berlin. Right wing: *Virgin and Child*. Oil on wood, 3' 1$\frac{1}{4}$" × 2' 9$\frac{1}{2}$". Koninklijk Museum voor Schone Kunsten, Antwerp.

Fouquet's meticulous representation of a pious kneeling donor with a standing patron saint recalls Flemish painting, as do the three-quarter-view stances and the realism of the donor's portrait head.

at the time). The peasants do not appear discontented as they go about their tasks. Surely, this imagery flattered the duke's sense of himself as a compassionate master. The growing artistic interest in naturalism is evident in the careful way the painter recorded the architectural details of the Louvre and in the convincing shadows of the people, animals, and objects (such as the archer scarecrow and the horse) in the scene.

As a whole, *Les Très Riches Heures* reinforced the image of the duke of Berry as a devout man, cultured *bibliophile* ("lover of books"), sophisticated art patron, and powerful and magnanimous leader. Further, the expanded range of subject matter, especially the prominence of *genre* subjects in a religious book, reflected the increasing integration of religious and secular concerns in both art and life at the time.

JEAN FOUQUET Images for private devotional use were popular in France, as in Flanders. Among the French artists whose paintings were in demand was JEAN FOUQUET (ca. 1420–1481), who worked for King Charles VII (r. 1422–1461) and for the duke of Nemours. Fouquet painted a *diptych* (two-panel painting; FIG. 8-10) for Étienne Chevalier, the royal treasurer of France. In the left panel, Chevalier appears with his patron saint, Saint Stephen (Étienne in French). Appropriately, Fouquet depicted Chevalier as devout— kneeling, with hands clasped in prayer. The representation of the pious donor with his standing saint recalls Flemish art, as do the three-quarter stances, the realism of Chevalier's portrait, and

the painting medium (oil-based pigment on wood). The artist portrayed Saint Stephen holding the stone of his martyrdom (death by stoning) atop a Bible. Fouquet rendered the entire image in meticulous detail and included a highly ornamented architectural setting.

The placement of the figures unites the diptych's two wings. The viewer follows the gaze of Chevalier and Saint Stephen over to the right panel, which depicts the Virgin Mary and Christ Child in a most unusual way—with marblelike flesh, surrounded by red and blue angels. A straightforward reading of the diptych is complicated, however, by the fact that Agnès Sorel (1421–1450), the mistress of Charles VII, was Fouquet's model for the Virgin Mary. The Madonna's left breast is exposed, presumably to nurse the infant Jesus, but the holy figures look neither at each other nor at the viewer. Chevalier commissioned this painting after Sorel's death, probably by poisoning while pregnant with the king's child. Thus, in addition to the religious interpretation of this diptych, there is surely a personal and political narrative here as well.

HOLY ROMAN EMPIRE

Because the Holy Roman Empire (whose core was Germany) did not participate in the drawn-out saga of the Hundred Years' War, its economy remained stable and prosperous. Without a dominant court to commission artworks, wealthy merchants and clergy became the primary German art patrons during the 15th century.

8-11 TILMAN RIEMENSCHNEIDER, *Assumption of the Virgin* (*Creglingen Altarpiece*), Herrgottskirche, Creglingen, Germany, ca. 1495–1499. Lime-wood, 30' 2" high.

Riemenschneider specialized in carving large wood retables. His works feature intricate Gothic tracery and religious figures whose bodies are almost lost within their swirling garments.

TILMAN RIEMENSCHNEIDER

Carved wood *retables* (altarpieces) were popular commissions for German churches. One prominent sculptor who specialized in producing retables was TILMAN RIEMENSCHNEIDER (ca. 1460–1531) of Würzburg. His 30-foot-tall *Creglingen Altarpiece* (FIG. 8-11) incorporates intricate Gothic forms, especially in the retable's elaborate canopy. In *Assumption of the Virgin* in the central panel, Riemenschneider succeeded in setting the whole design into fluid motion by employing an endless and restless line running through the garments of the figures. The draperies float and flow around bodies lost within them, serving not as descriptions but as design elements that tie the figures to one another and to the framework. A look of psychic strain, a facial expression common in Riemenschneider's work, heightens the spirituality of the figures.

WOODCUTS A new age blossomed with the invention by Johannes Gutenberg (ca. 1400–1468) of moveable type around 1450 and the development of the printing press. Printing had been known in China centuries before, but had never fostered, as it did in 15th-century Europe, a revolution in written communication and in the generation and management of information. Printing provided new and challenging media for artists, and the earliest form was the *woodcut* (see "Woodcuts, Engravings, and Etchings," page 228). Artists

MATERIALS AND TECHNIQUES
Woodcuts, Engravings, and Etchings

With the invention of moveable type in the 15th century and the new widespread availability of paper from commercial mills, the art of printmaking developed rapidly in Europe. A *print* is an artwork on paper, usually produced in multiple impressions. The set of prints an artist creates from a single block or plate is called an *edition*. The printmaking process involves the transfer of ink from a printing surface to paper. This can be accomplished in several ways. During the 15th and 16th centuries, artists most commonly used the *relief* and *intaglio* methods of printmaking.

Artists produce relief prints, the oldest and simplest printing method, by carving into a surface, usually wood. Relief printing requires artists to conceptualize their images in reverse—that is, they must draw a mirror image of the intended design on the wood block. They then remove the surface areas around the drawn lines using a gouging instrument. Thus when the printmaker inks the ridges, the hollow areas remain dry, and a correctly oriented image results when the artist presses the printing block against paper. Because artists produce *woodcuts* (for example, FIGS. I-7 and 8-11A ⏩) through a subtractive process (removing parts of the material), it is difficult to create very thin, fluid, and closely spaced lines.

In contrast to the production of relief prints, the intaglio method involves a positive process. The artist *incises* (cuts) the lines on a metal plate. The image can be created on the plate manually (*engraving*; for example, FIGS. 8-12 and 8-28) using a tool (a *burin* or *stylus*), or chemically (*etching*; for example FIG. 10-22). In the etching process, an acid bath eats into the exposed parts of the plate where the artist has drawn through an acid-resistant coating. When the artist inks the surface of the intaglio plate and wipes it clean, the ink is forced into the incisions. Then the printmaker runs the plate and paper through a roller press, and the paper absorbs the remaining ink, creating the print. Because the artist "draws" the image onto the plate, intaglio prints differ in character from relief prints. Engravings and etchings generally present a wider variety of linear effects. They also often reveal to a greater extent evidence of the artist's touch, the result of the hand's changing pressure and shifting directions.

The paper and inks that artists use also affect the finished look of the printed image. During the 15th and 16th centuries, European printmakers used papers produced from cotton and linen rags that papermakers mashed with water into a pulp. The papermakers then applied a thin layer of this pulp to a wire screen and allowed it to dry to create the paper. As contact with Asia increased, printmakers made greater use of what was called Japan paper (of mulberry fibers) and China paper.

1 in.

8-12 MARTIN SCHONGAUER, *Saint Anthony Tormented by Demons*, ca. 1480. Engraving, $1'\frac{1}{4}'' \times 9''$. Fondazione Magnani Rocca, Corte di Mamiano.

Schongauer was the most skilled of the early masters of metal engraving. By using a burin to incise lines in a copper plate, he was able to create a marvelous variety of tonal values and textures.

Artists, then as now, could select from a wide variety of inks. The type and proportion of the ink ingredients affect the consistency, color, and oiliness of inks, which various papers absorb differently.

Paper is lightweight, and the portability of prints has been an important factor in their appeal to artists. The opportunity to produce numerous impressions from the same print surface also made printmaking attractive to 15th- and 16th-century artists. In addition, prints can be sold at much lower prices than paintings or sculptures. Consequently, prints reached a far wider audience than did one-of-a-kind artworks. The number and quality of existing 15th- and 16th-century European prints attest to the importance of the new print medium.

produced inexpensive woodblock *prints* such as the *Buxheim Saint Christopher* (FIG. 8-11A ↗) before the development of moveable-type printing. But when the improved economy and a rise in literacy necessitated production of illustrated books on a grand scale, artists met the challenge of bringing the woodcut picture onto the same page as the letterpress.

MARTIN SCHONGAUER The woodcut medium hardly had matured when the technique of *engraving,* begun in the 1430s and well developed by 1450, proved much more flexible. Predictably, in the second half of the century, engraving began to replace the woodcut process for making both book illustrations and widely popular single prints. The most skilled and subtle early master of metal engraving in northern Europe was MARTIN SCHONGAUER (ca. 1430–1491). His *Saint Anthony Tormented by Demons* (FIG. 8-12) shows both the versatility of the medium and the artist's mastery of it. The stoic saint is caught in a revolving thornbush of spiky demons, who claw and tear at him furiously. With unsurpassed skill and subtlety, Schongauer created marvelous distinctions of tonal values and textures—from smooth skin to rough cloth, from the furry and feathery to the hairy and scaly—with *hatching.* The use of *cross-hatching* (sets of engraved lines at right angles) to describe forms, which Schongauer probably developed, became standard among German graphic artists. The Italians preferred *parallel hatching* (FIG. 8-28) and rarely adopted the other hatching method, which, in keeping with the general northern European approach to art, tends to describe the surfaces of things rather than their underlying structures.

ITALY

During the 15th century (the '400s, or *Quattrocento* in Italian), Italy (MAP 8-2) witnessed constant fluctuations in its political and economic spheres, including shifting power relations among the numerous city-states and republics and the rise of princely courts. *Condottieri* (military leaders) with large numbers of mercenary troops at their disposal played a major role in the ongoing struggle for power. Papal Rome and the courts of Urbino, Mantua, and other cities emerged as cultural and artistic centers alongside the great art centers of the 14th century, especially the Republic of Florence. The association of humanism with education and culture appealed to accomplished individuals of high status, and humanism had its greatest impact among the elite and powerful—the most influential art patrons—whether in the republics or the princely courts. As a result, humanist ideas permeate Italian Renaissance art. The intersection of art with humanist doctrines during the Quattrocento is evident in the popularity of subjects selected from classical history or mythology, in the revival of portraiture, and in the increased concern with developing perspective systems and depicting anatomy accurately.

Florence

Because high-level patronage required significant accumulated wealth, those individuals who had managed to prosper came to the fore in artistic circles. The best-known Italian Renaissance art patrons were the Medici, the leading bankers of the Republic of Florence (see page 233), yet the first important artistic commission in Quattrocento Florence was not a Medici project but rather a competition held by the Cathedral of Santa Maria del Fiore and sponsored by the city's guild of wool merchants.

BAPTISTERY COMPETITION In 1401, the Duomo's art directors held a competition to make bronze doors for the east portal of the Baptistery of San Giovanni (FIG. 7-38, *left*). The commission was prestigious because the baptistery's east entrance faced the cathedral (FIG. 7-38, *right*). The jurors required each entrant to submit a relief panel depicting the sacrifice of Isaac, a venerable biblical subject (FIG. 4-1, *top left*). From the many entries submitted, seven semifinalists were selected. Only the panels of the two finalists, FILIPPO BRUNELLESCHI (1377–1446) and LORENZO GHIBERTI (1378–1455), have survived. At 24 and 23 years old respectively, they were also the

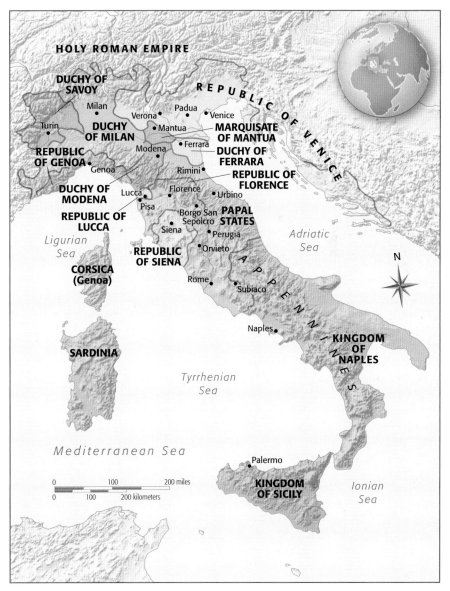

MAP 8-2 **Italy around 1400.**

8-13 **FILIPPO BRUNELLESCHI**, *Sacrifice of Isaac*, competition panel for the east doors of the Baptistery of San Giovanni (FIG. 7-38, *left*), Florence, Italy, 1401–1402. Gilded bronze, 1' 9" × 1' 5½". Museo Nazionale del Bargello, Florence.

Brunelleschi's entry in the competition to create new bronze doors for the Florentine baptistery shows a frantic angel about to halt an emotional, lunging Abraham clothed in swirling Gothic robes.

8-14 **LORENZO GHIBERTI**, *Sacrifice of Isaac*, competition panel for the east doors of the Baptistery of San Giovanni (FIG. 7-38, *left*), Florence, Italy, 1401–1402. Gilded bronze, 1' 9" × 1' 5½". Museo Nazionale del Bargello, Florence.

In contrast to Brunelleschi's panel (FIG. 8-13), Ghiberti's entry in the baptistery competition features gracefully posed figures that recall classical statuary. Even Isaac's altar has a Roman acanthus frieze.

two youngest entrants in the competition. As instructed, both artists used the same French Gothic quatrefoil frames employed earlier for the panels on the baptistery's south doors, and depicted the same moment of the narrative—the angel's halting of Abraham's sacrifice. Brunelleschi's entry (FIG. 8-13) is a vigorous interpretation of the theme and recalls the emotional agitation characteristic of Italian Gothic sculpture. Abraham seems suddenly to have summoned the dreadful courage needed to murder his son at God's command. He lunges forward, robes flying, and exposes the terrified Isaac's throat to the knife. Matching Abraham's energy, the saving angel flies in from the left, grabbing Abraham's arm to stop the killing. Brunelleschi's figures demonstrate his ability to represent faithfully and dramatically all the elements in the biblical narrative.

Whereas Brunelleschi imbued his image with violent movement and high emotion, Ghiberti emphasized grace and smoothness. In Ghiberti's panel (FIG. 8-14), Abraham appears in a typically Gothic pose with outthrust hip (compare FIG. 7-20) and seems to contemplate the act he is about to perform, even as he draws his arm back to strike. The figure of Isaac, beautifully posed and rendered, recalls Greco-Roman statuary. Unlike his medieval predecessors, Ghiberti revealed a genuine appreciation of the nude male form and a deep interest in how the muscular system and skeletal structure move the human body. Even the altar on which Isaac kneels displays Ghiberti's emulation of antique models. Decorating it are acanthus

scrolls of a type that commonly adorned Roman buildings. These classical references reflect the increasing influence of humanism. Ghiberti's *Sacrifice of Isaac* is also noteworthy for the artist's interest in spatial illusion. The rocky landscape seems to emerge from the blank panel toward the viewer, as does the strongly foreshortened angel. Brunelleschi's image, in contrast, emphasizes the planar orientation of the surface.

Ghiberti's training included both painting and metalwork. His careful treatment of the gilded bronze surfaces, with their sharply and accurately incised detail, proves his skill as a goldsmith. That Ghiberti cast his panel in only two pieces (thereby reducing the amount of bronze needed) no doubt also impressed the selection committee. Brunelleschi's panel consists of several cast pieces. Thus Ghiberti's doors, as proposed, would be both lighter and significantly less expensive. The younger artist's submission clearly had much to recommend it, both stylistically and technically, and the judges awarded the commission to him—an achievement that he noted with exceptional pride in his *Commentaries* (see "The Commentarii of Lorenzo Ghiberti" 🔗).

GATES OF PARADISE Ghiberti completed the baptistery's east doors in 1424, but church officials moved them to the north entrance so that he could execute another pair of doors for the east entrance. This second project (1425–1452) produced the famous east doors

1 ft.

8-15 **Lorenzo Ghiberti,** east doors (*Gates of Paradise*), Baptistery of San Giovanni (**fig. 7-38**, *left*), Florence, Italy, 1425–1452. Gilded bronze, 17' high. Modern replica, 1990. Original panels in Museo dell'Opera del Duomo, Florence.

In Ghiberti's later doors for the Florentine baptistery, the sculptor abandoned Gothic quatrefoil frames for the biblical scenes (compare **fig**. 8-14) and employed painterly illusionistic devices.

(**fig. 8-15**) that Michelangelo later declared were "so beautiful that they would do well for the gates of Paradise."[1] In the *Gates of Paradise,* Ghiberti abandoned the quatrefoil frames of his earlier doors and reduced the number of panels from 28 to 10. Each panel contains a relief set in a plain molding and depicts an episode from the Old Testament. The complete gilding of the reliefs creates an effect of great splendor and elegance.

The individual panels, such as *Isaac and His Sons* (**figs**. 8-15, left door, third from top, and 8-16), clearly recall painting techniques in their depiction of space as well as in their treatment of the narrative. Some exemplify more fully than painting many of the principles that the architect and theorist Leon Battista Alberti formulated in his 1435 treatise, *On Painting*. In his relief, Ghiberti created the illusion of space partly through the use of *linear perspective* and partly by sculptural means. He represented the pavement on which the figures stand according to a painter's *vanishing-point* perspective construction, but the figures themselves appear almost fully in the round. In fact, some of their heads stand completely free. As the eye progresses upward, the

PROBLEMS AND SOLUTIONS
Linear and Atmospheric Perspective

Scholars long have noted the Renaissance fascination with *perspective*. In essence, portraying perspective involves constructing a convincing illusion of space in two-dimensional imagery while unifying all objects within a single spatial system. Renaissance artists were not the first to focus on depicting illusionistic space. Both the Greeks and the Romans were well versed in perspective rendering (FIG. 3-20, *right*). However, the Renaissance rediscovery of and interest in perspective contrasted sharply with the portrayal of space during the Middle Ages, when spiritual concerns superseded the desire to depict objects illusionistically.

Renaissance knowledge of perspective included both *linear perspective* and *atmospheric perspective*.

- **Linear perspective** Developed by Filippo Brunelleschi, linear perspective enables artists to determine mathematically the relative size of rendered objects to correlate them with the visual recession into space. The artist first must identify a horizontal line that marks, in the image, the horizon in the distance (hence the term *horizon line*). The artist then selects a *vanishing point* on that horizon line (often located at the exact center of the line). By drawing *orthogonals* (diagonal lines) from the edges of the picture to the vanishing point, the artist creates a structural grid that organizes the image and determines the size of objects within the image's illusionistic space. Among the works that provide clear examples of linear perspective are Ghiberti's *Isaac and His Sons* (FIG. **8-16**), Masaccio's *Holy Trinity* (FIG. 8-22), and Perugino's *Christ Delivering the Keys of the Kingdom to Saint Peter* (FIG. 8-34).

- **Atmospheric perspective** Unlike linear perspective, which relies on a structured mathematical system, atmospheric perspective involves optical phenomena. Artists using atmospheric perspective (sometimes called *aerial perspective*) exploit the principle that the farther back the object is in space, the blurrier and less detailed it appears. Leonardo da Vinci used atmospheric perspective to great effect, as seen in such works as *Madonna of the Rocks* (FIG. 9-2) and *Mona Lisa* (FIG. 9-4).

Earlier Italian artists, such as Giotto, Duccio, and Lorenzetti, had used several devices to indicate distance, but with the development of linear perspective, Quattrocento artists acquired a way to make the illusion of distance certain and consistent. In effect, they conceived the picture plane as a transparent window through which the observer looks to see the constructed pictorial world. This discovery was

8-16 LORENZO GHIBERTI, *Isaac and His Sons* (detail of FIG. 8-15, with overlay of perspective orthogonals), east doors (*Gates of Paradise*) of the Baptistery of San Giovanni, Florence, Italy, 1425–1452. Gilded bronze, 2' 7½" × 2' 7½". Museo dell'Opera del Duomo, Florence.

All the orthogonals of the floor tiles in this early example of linear perspective converge on a vanishing point on the central axis of the composition, but the orthogonals of the architecture do not.

enormously important, for it made possible what has been called the "rationalization of sight." It brought all random and infinitely various visual sensations under a simple rule that could be expressed mathematically. Indeed, Renaissance artists' interest in linear perspective reflects the emergence at this time of modern science itself. Of course, 15th-century artists were not primarily scientists. They simply found perspective an effective way to order and clarify their compositions. Nonetheless, linear perspective, with its new mathematical certitude, conferred a kind of aesthetic legitimacy on painting and relief sculpture by making the picture measurable and exact. The projection of measurable objects on flat surfaces influenced the character of Renaissance paintings but also made possible scale drawings, maps, charts, graphs, and diagrams—means of exact representation that laid the foundation for modern science and technology.

relief increasingly flattens, concluding with the architecture in the background, which Ghiberti depicted using barely raised lines. In this manner, the artist created a sort of sculptor's *atmospheric perspective*, with forms appearing less distinct the deeper they are in space (see "Linear and Atmospheric Perspective," above).

In these panels, Ghiberti achieved a greater sense of depth than had previously seemed possible in a relief, but his principal figures do not occupy the architectural space he created for them. Rather, the artist arranged them along a parallel plane in front of the grandiose architecture. (According to Alberti in *On the Art of Building*, the grandeur of the architecture reflects the dignity of the events shown in the foreground.) Ghiberti's figure style mixes a Gothic

patterning of rhythmic line, classical poses and motifs, and a new realism in characterization, movement, and surface detail. Ghiberti retained the medieval narrative method of presenting several episodes within a single frame. In *Isaac and His Sons*, the women in the left foreground attend the birth of Esau and Jacob in the left background. In the central foreground, Isaac sends Esau and his dogs to hunt game. In the right foreground, Isaac blesses the kneeling Jacob as Rebecca looks on. Yet viewers experience little confusion because of Ghiberti's careful and subtle placement of each scene. The figures, in varying degrees of projection, gracefully twist and turn, appearing to occupy and move through a convincing stage space, which Ghiberti deepened by showing some figures from behind.

1 ft.

8-17 DONATELLO, *Saint Mark,* niche on the south side of Or San Michele, Florence, Italy, ca. 1411–1413. Marble, figure 7' 9" high. Modern replica. Original statue in the museum on the second floor of Or San Michele, Florence.

In this statue carved for the guild of linen makers and tailors, Donatello introduced classical contrapposto into Renaissance sculpture. The drapery falls naturally and moves with the body.

1 ft.

8-18 DONATELLO, *David,* from the Palazzo Medici, Florence, Italy, ca. 1440–1460. Bronze, 5' 2¼" high. Museo Nazionale del Bargello, Florence.

Donatello's *David* possesses both the relaxed contrapposto and the sensuous beauty of nude Greek gods (FIG. 2-48). The revival of classical statuary style appealed to the sculptor's patrons, the Medici.

The classicism derives from the artist's close study of ancient art. Ghiberti admired and collected classical sculpture and coins. Their influence appears throughout the panel, particularly in the figure of Rebecca, which Ghiberti based on a popular Greco-Roman statuary type. The emerging practice of collecting classical art in the 15th century had much to do with the incorporation of classical motifs and the emulation of classical style in Renaissance art.

DONATELLO A former apprentice in Ghiberti's workshop, Donato di Niccolo Bardi, called DONATELLO (ca. 1386–1466), participated along with other leading sculptors, including Ghiberti, in another major Florentine art program of the early 1400s—the decoration of Or San Michele. At various times, the building housed a church, a granary, and the headquarters of Florence's guilds. City officials had assigned each of the niches on the building's four sides to a specific guild to fill with a statue of its patron saint. Donatello carved *Saint Mark* (FIG. 8-17) for the guild of linen makers and tailors in 1413. In

this sculpture, Donatello introduced the classical principle of weight shift—*contrapposto*—into Renaissance statuary. As the saint's body moves, his garment moves with it, hanging and folding naturally from and around different body parts so that the viewer senses the figure as a nude human wearing clothing, not as a stone statue with arbitrarily composed drapery folds. Donatello's *Saint Mark* is the first Renaissance statue whose voluminous robe (the pride of the Florentine guild that paid for the statue) does not conceal but accentuates the movement of the arms, legs, shoulders, and hips. This development further contributed to the sculpted figure's independence from its architectural setting. Saint Mark's stirring limbs, shifting weight, and mobile drapery suggest impending movement out of the niche.

DAVID Donatello was one of many artists in Quattrocento Florence who enjoyed the patronage of the Medici. By the early 15th century, the banker Giovanni di Bicci de' Medici (ca. 1360–1429) had established the family fortune. His son Cosimo (1389–1464) became a great patron of art and of learning in the broadest sense. For example, he founded the first public library since antiquity. Cosimo's grandson Lorenzo (1449–1492), called "the Magnificent," a member of the Platonic Academy of Philosophy, gathered about him artists and gifted men in all fields. Together, the Medici spent lavishly on buildings, paintings, and sculptures.

Sometime between 1440 and 1460, Donatello cast the bronze statue *David* (FIG. 8-18) for display in the courtyard (FIG. 8-32B ✈)

of the Medici palace in Florence. The sculpture was the first nude statue since ancient times. During the Middle Ages, the clergy regarded nude statues as both indecent and idolatrous, and nudity in general appeared only rarely in art—and then only in biblical or moralizing contexts, such as the story of Adam and Eve or depictions of sinners in Hell. With *David*, Donatello reinvented the classical nude. His subject, however, was not a Greco-Roman god, hero, or athlete but the youthful biblical slayer of Goliath who had become the symbol of the Florentine republic. *David* possesses both the relaxed classical contrapposto stance and the proportions and sensuous beauty of Greek images of gods (FIG. 2-48), qualities absent from medieval figures. The invoking of classical poses and formats appealed to the humanist Medici, who were aware of Donatello's earlier *David* in Florence's town hall, the Palazzo della Signoria, which the artist had produced during the threat of invasion by King Ladislaus (r. 1399–1414) of Naples. David had become a symbol of Florentine strength and independence, and the Medici's selection of the same subject for their private residence suggests that the family identified themselves with Florence or, at the very least, shared Florence's ideals.

GATTAMELATA Given the increased emphasis on individual achievement and recognition that humanism fostered, it is not surprising that portraiture enjoyed a revival in 15th-century Italy. The grandest portrait of the era is the 11-foot-tall bronze equestrian statue (FIG. 8-19) that Donatello produced for the Republic of Venice. His assignment was to create a commemorative monument in honor of the recently deceased Venetian condottiere Erasmo da Narni (1370–1443), nicknamed Gattamelata ("honeyed cat," a wordplay on his mother's name, Melania Gattelli). Equestrian statues occasionally had been set up in Italy in the late Middle Ages, but Donatello's *Gattamelata* was the first to rival the grandeur of Roman imperial mounted portraits, such as that of Marcus Aurelius (FIG. 3-41), which the artist must have seen in Rome. Donatello's contemporaries, one of whom described Gattamelata as sitting on his horse "with great magnificence like a triumphant Caesar,"[2] recognized this reference to antiquity. The statue stands high on a lofty elliptical base in the square in front of the church of Sant'Antonio in Padua, the condottiere's birthplace. Massive and majestic, the great horse bears the armored general easily, for, unlike the sculptor of the Marcus Aurelius statue, Donatello did not represent the Venetian commander as superhuman and disproportionately larger than his horse. Gattamelata dominates his mighty steed by force of character rather than sheer size. The condottiere, his face set in a mask of dauntless resolution and unshakable will, is the very portrait of the Renaissance individualist. Such a man—intelligent, courageous, ambitious, and frequently of humble origin—could, by his own resourcefulness and on his own merits, rise to a commanding position in the world. Together, man and horse convey an overwhelming image of irresistible strength and unlimited power—an impression Donatello reinforced visually by placing the left forefoot of the horse on an orb, reviving a venerable ancient symbol for domination of the world. The imperial imagery is all the more remarkable because Erasmo da Narni was not an emperor, king, or duke.

GENTILE DA FABRIANO In Quattrocento Italy, humanism and the celebration of classical artistic values also largely determined the character of panel and mural painting. The new Renaissance style did not, however, immediately displace all vestiges of the Late Gothic style. In particular, the International Gothic style, the dominant mode in painting around 1400 (see page 210), persisted

1 ft.

8-19 DONATELLO, *Gattamelata* (equestrian statue of Erasmo da Narni), Piazza del Santo, Padua, Italy, ca. 1445–1453. Bronze, 12' 2" high.

Donatello based his gigantic portrait of a Venetian general on equestrian statues of ancient Roman emperors (FIG. 3-41). Together, man and horse convey an overwhelming image of irresistible strength.

well into the 15th century. The leading Quattrocento International Gothic master was GENTILE DA FABRIANO (ca. 1370–1427), who in 1423 painted *Adoration of the Magi* (FIG. 8-20) as the altarpiece for the family chapel of Palla Strozzi (1372–1462) in the church of Santa Trinità in Florence. At the beginning of the 15th century, the Strozzi family was the richest in the city. The altarpiece, with its elaborate gilded Gothic frame, is testimony to the patron's lavish tastes. So too is the painting itself, with its gorgeous surface and richly costumed kings, courtiers, captains, and retainers accompanied by a menagerie of exotic animals. Gentile portrayed all these elements in a rainbow of color with extensive use of gold. The painting presents all the pomp and ceremony of chivalric etiquette in a religious scene centered on the Madonna and Child. Although the style is fundamentally International Gothic, Gentile inserted striking naturalistic details. For example, the artist depicted animals from a variety of angles and foreshortened the forms convincingly, most notably the horse at the far right seen in a three-quarter rear view. Gentile did the same with human figures, such as the kneeling man removing the spurs from the standing *magus* in the center foreground. In the left panel of the predella, Gentile painted what may have been the first nighttime nativity scene with the central light source—the radiant Christ Child—introduced into the picture itself. Although predominantly conservative, Gentile demonstrated that he was not

8-20 GENTILE DA FABRIANO, *Adoration of the Magi,* altarpiece from the Strozzi chapel, Santa Trinità, Florence, Italy, 1423. Tempera on wood, 9' 11" × 9' 3". Galleria degli Uffizi, Florence.

Gentile was the leading Florentine painter working in the International Gothic style. He successfully blended naturalistic details with late medieval splendor in color, costume, and framing ornamentation.

oblivious to Quattrocento experimental trends and could blend naturalistic and inventive elements skillfully and subtly into a traditional composition without sacrificing Late Gothic splendor in color, costume, and framing ornamentation.

MASACCIO The artist who personifies the inventive spirit of early-15th-century Florentine painting was Tommaso di ser Giovanni di Mone Cassai, known as MASACCIO (1401–1428), whose untimely death at age 27 cut short his brilliant career. *Tribute Money* (FIG. 8-21), in the family chapel of Felice Brancacci (1382–1447) in Santa Maria del Carmine in Florence, displays Masaccio's

8-21 MASACCIO, *Tribute Money,* Brancacci chapel, Santa Maria del Carmine, Florence, Italy, ca. 1424–1427. Fresco, 8' 4 $\frac{1}{8}$" × 19' 7 $\frac{1}{8}$".

Masaccio's figures recall Giotto's in their simple grandeur, but they convey a greater psychological and physical credibility. He modeled his figures with light coming from a source outside the picture.

innovations. The fresco depicts an episode from the Gospel of Matthew (17:24–27). As the tax collector confronts Jesus at the entrance to the Roman town of Capernaum, Jesus directs Saint Peter to the shore of Lake Galilee. There, as Jesus foresaw, Peter finds the tribute coin in the mouth of a fish and returns to pay the tax. Masaccio divided the story into three parts within the fresco. In the center, Jesus, surrounded by his disciples, tells Saint Peter to retrieve the coin from the fish, while the tax collector stands in the foreground, his back to spectators and hand extended, awaiting payment. At the left, in the middle distance, Peter extracts the coin from the fish's mouth, and, at the right, he thrusts the coin into the tax collector's hand.

Masaccio's figures recall those of Giotto (FIGS. 7-30, 7-31, and 7-32) in their simple grandeur, but they convey a greater psychological and physical credibility. Masaccio created the figures' bulk through modeling not with a flat, neutral light lacking an identifiable source but with a light coming from a specific source outside the picture. Here, the light comes from the right (as if through a real window in the chapel wall) and strikes the figures at an angle, illuminating the parts of the solids that obstruct its path and leaving the rest in shadow, producing the illusion of deep sculptural relief. Between the extremes of light and dark, the light appears as a constantly active but fluctuating force highlighting the scene in varying degrees. In his frescoes, Giotto used light only to model the masses. In Masaccio's works, light has its own nature, and the masses are visible only because of the direction and intensity of the light, which plays over the forms, revealing some and concealing others, as the artist directs it. The individual figures in *Tribute Money* are solemn and weighty, but they also move freely and reveal body structure, as do Donatello's statues. Each of Masaccio's figures conveys a maximum of contained energy, suggesting the movement of bones and muscles and the pressures and tensions of joints. *Tribute Money* provides support for Giorgio Vasari's assertion that "the works made before his [Masaccio's] day can be said to be painted, while his are living, real, and natural."[3]

Masaccio's arrangement of the figures is equally inventive. They do not stand in a line in the foreground. Instead, the artist grouped them in circular depth around Jesus, and he placed the whole group in a spacious landscape, rather than in the confined stage space of Giotto's frescoes. At the right

is a building that Masaccio depicted in perspective, locating the vanishing point, where all the orthogonals converge, at Jesus's head. He also diminished the brightness of the colors as the distance increases, an aspect of atmospheric perspective, which Masaccio and his contemporaries rediscovered. As did ancient Roman painters (FIG. 3-21), they came to realize that the light and air interposed between viewers and what they see are two parts of the visual experience called "distance."

8-22 MASACCIO, *Holy Trinity*, Santa Maria Novella, Florence, Italy, ca. 1424–1427. Fresco, 21' 10$\frac{5}{8}$" × 10' 4$\frac{3}{4}$".

Masaccio's pioneering *Holy Trinity* is the premier early-15th-century example of the application of mathematics to the depiction of space according to Filippo Brunelleschi's system of perspective.

1 ft.

HOLY TRINITY Masaccio's *Holy Trinity* (FIG. 8-22) in Santa Maria Novella is the premier early-15th-century example of the application of mathematics to the depiction of space. Masaccio painted the composition on two levels of unequal height. Above, in a coffered barrel-vaulted chapel reminiscent of a Roman triumphal arch (FIG. 3-32), the Virgin Mary and Saint John appear on either side of the crucified Christ. (Mary, unlike in almost all other representations of the crucifixion, appears as an older woman, her true age at the time of her adult son's death.) God the Father emerges from behind Christ, supporting the arms of the cross and presenting his son to the worshiper as a devotional object. Christ's blood runs down the cross onto the painted ledge below—a reference to the symbolic blood of the wine of the Eucharist on the church's altar. The dove of the Holy Spirit hovers between God's head and Christ's head. Masaccio also included portraits of the donors of the painting, Lorenzo Lenzi and his wife, who kneel just in front of the pilasters framing the chapel's entrance. Below, the artist painted a tomb containing a skeleton. An inscription in Italian above the skeleton reminds the spectator, "I was once what you are, and what I am you will become."

The illusionism of *Holy Trinity* is breathtaking, a brilliant demonstration of the principles and potential of Brunelleschi's new science of perspective. Indeed, some art historians have suggested that Brunelleschi may have collaborated with Masaccio on this commission. The vanishing point of the composition is at the foot of the cross. With this point at eye level, spectators look up at the Trinity and down at the tomb. About 5 feet above the floor level, the vanishing point pulls the two views together, creating the illusion of a real structure transecting the wall's vertical plane. Whereas the tomb appears to project forward into the church, the chapel recedes visually behind the wall and appears as an extension of the church's space. This adjustment of the picture's space to the viewer's position was an important innovation in illusionistic painting that other artists of the Renaissance and the later Baroque period would develop further. Masaccio was so exact in his proportions that it is possible to calculate the dimensions of the chapel (for example, the span of the painted vault

is 7 feet, and the depth of the chapel is 9 feet). Thus he achieved not only a successful illusion but also a rational measured coherence that is responsible for the unity and harmony of the fresco.

Holy Trinity is, however, much more than an expert application of Brunelleschi's perspective system or a showpiece for the painter's ability to represent fully modeled figures bathed in light. In this painting, Masaccio also powerfully conveyed one of the central tenets of Christian faith. The ascending pyramid of figures leads viewers from the despair of death to the hope of resurrection and eternal life through Christ's crucifixion.

FRA ANGELICO As Masaccio's *Holy Trinity* clearly demonstrates, humanism and religion were not mutually exclusive, but for many Quattrocento artists, humanist concerns were not a primary consideration. The art of FRA ANGELICO (ca. 1400–1455) focused on serving the Roman Catholic Church. In the late 1430s, the abbot of the Dominican monastery of San Marco (Saint Mark) in Florence asked Fra Angelico to produce a series of frescoes for the monks' compound. The Dominicans had dedicated themselves to lives of prayer and work, and their monastery was quite spare to encourage the monks to immerse themselves in their devotional lives. *Annunciation* (FIG. 8-23) appears at the top of the stairs leading to the friars' sleeping cells. Appropriately, Fra Angelico presented the scene of the Virgin Mary and the Archangel Gabriel with simplicity and serenity. The pristinely painted figures appear in a well-lit plain *loggia* (open arcade) resembling the portico of San Marco's cloister, but they do not cast shadows. Although Fra Angelico rendered the setting according to the rules of Renaissance perspective, the unnatural lighting removes the sacred event from the everyday world. Underscoring the devotional function of the image, a small inscription at the base of the fresco reads: "As you venerate, while passing before it, this figure of the intact Virgin, beware lest you omit to say a Hail Mary." Like most of Fra Angelico's paintings, *Annunciation,* with its simplicity and directness, still has an almost universal appeal and fully reflects the artist's humble character.

8-23 FRA ANGELICO, *Annunciation,* San Marco, Florence, Italy, ca. 1438–1447. Fresco, 7' 1" × 10' 6".

Painted for the Dominican monks of San Marco, Fra Angelico's fresco is simple and direct. Its figures and architecture have a pristine clarity befitting the fresco's function as a devotional image.

1 ft.

8-24 ANDREA DEL CASTAGNO, *Last Supper,* refectory of the convent of Sant'Apollonia, Florence, Italy, 1447. Fresco, 15' 5" × 32'.

In this *Last Supper* on the wall of a nuns' dining room, Judas sits isolated. Castagno's depiction of the setting for the apostles' meal reflects his preoccupation with the new science of perspective.

ANDREA DEL CASTAGNO Fra Angelico's younger contemporary ANDREA DEL CASTAGNO (ca. 1421–1457) also accepted a commission to produce a series of frescoes for a religious establishment. Castagno's *Last Supper* (FIG. **8-24**), painted in the *refectory* (dining hall) of Sant'Apollonia in Florence, a convent for Benedictine nuns, faithfully follows the biblical narrative, although the lavish marble-revetted room that Jesus and his 12 disciples occupy has no basis in the Gospels. The setting reflects the artist's absorption with linear perspective, but closer scrutiny reveals inconsistencies. For example, in Brunelleschi's system, it is impossible to see the ceiling from inside and the roof from outside at the same time, as in Castagno's fresco. The two side walls also do not appear parallel.

Castagno chose a conventional compositional format, with the figures seated at a horizontally placed table. He derived the apparent self-absorption of most of the disciples and the menacing features of Judas (who sits alone on the outside of the table) from the Gospel of Saint John, rather than the more familiar version of the Last Supper recounted in Luke's Gospel. Castagno's dramatic and spatially convincing depiction of the event no doubt was a powerful presence for the nuns during their daily meals.

FRA FILIPPO LIPPI Another younger contemporary of Fra Angelico, FRA FILIPPO LIPPI (ca. 1406–1469), was also a friar—but there all resemblance ends. Fra Filippo was unsuited for monastic life. He indulged in misdemeanors ranging from forgery and embezzlement to the abduction of a pretty nun, Lucretia, who became his mistress. Only the intervention of the Medici on his behalf at the papal court preserved Fra Filippo from severe punishment and total disgrace.

In *Madonna and Child with Angels* (FIG. **8-25**), the errant friar interpreted his subject in a distinctly worldly manner. The Madonna is a beautiful young mother, albeit with a transparent halo, seated in an elegantly furnished Florentine home. One of the angels

8-25 FRA FILIPPO LIPPI, *Madonna and Child with Angels,* ca. 1460–1465. Tempera on wood, 2' 11½" × 2' 1". Galleria degli Uffizi, Florence.

Fra Filippo, a monk guilty of many misdemeanors, represented the Madonna and Child in a distinctly worldly manner, carrying the humanization of the holy family further than any artist before him.

holding up the Christ Child sports the mischievous, puckish grin of a boy refusing to behave for the pious occasion. Significantly, all of the figures reflect the use of live models (perhaps Lucretia for the Madonna). Fra Filippo plainly relished the charm of youth and beauty as he found it in this world. He preferred the real in landscape also. The background, seen through the window, incorporates recognizable features of the Arno River valley. Compared with the earlier Madonnas by Giotto (FIG. 7-30) and Duccio (FIG. 7-33), this work shows how far Quattrocento artists had carried the humanization of this traditional Christian theme. Whatever the ideals of spiritual perfection may have meant to artists in past centuries, Renaissance artists realized those ideals in terms of the sensuous beauty of this world.

SANDRO BOTTICELLI Many 15th-century Florentine artists also received commissions to paint secular subjects for private patrons. The greatest of these were the Medici, and the finest painter they employed was SANDRO BOTTICELLI (1444–1510). His work is a testament to the intense interest that the Medici and their circle of humanist scholars had in the art, literature, and mythology of the Greco-Roman world—often interpreted in terms of Christianity according to the philosophical tenets of *Neo-Platonism*. Botticelli painted *Primavera* (*Spring*; FIG. 8-26) for Lorenzo di Pierfrancesco

de' Medici (1463–1503), one of Lorenzo the Magnificent's cousins. The central figure in the composition is Venus, the goddess of love and beauty. Her son Cupid hovers above her head. Botticelli drew attention to Venus by opening the landscape behind her to reveal a portion of sky that forms a kind of halo around the goddess's head. At the left, seemingly the target of Cupid's arrow, are the dancing Three Graces, whom Botticelli based closely on ancient prototypes, but they are clothed, albeit in thin, transparent garments. At the right, the blue ice-cold Zephyrus, the west wind, is about to carry off and marry the nymph Chloris, whom he transforms into Flora, goddess of spring, appropriately shown wearing a rich floral gown. At the far left, Mercury turns away from all the others and reaches up with his distinctive staff, the *caduceus,* perhaps to dispel storm clouds. The sensuality of the representation, the appearance of Venus in springtime, and the abduction and marriage of Chloris all suggest that the occasion for the painting was young Lorenzo's wedding in May 1482 to Semiramide d'Appiani. But the painting also sums up the Neo-Platonists' view that earthly love is compatible with Christian theology. In their reinterpretation of classical mythology, Venus as the source of love provokes desire through Cupid. Desire can lead either to lust and violence (Zephyr) or, through reason and faith (Mercury), to the love of God. *Primavera,* read from right to left, served to urge the newlyweds to seek God through love.

8-26 SANDRO BOTTICELLI, *Primavera*, ca. 1482. Tempera on wood, 6' 8" × 10' 4". Galleria degli Uffizi, Florence.

In Botticelli's lyrical painting celebrating love in springtime, the blue, ice-cold Zephyrus, the west wind, carries off and marries the nymph Chloris, whom he transforms into Flora, goddess of spring.

8-27 SANDRO BOTTICELLI, *Birth of Venus,* ca. 1484–1486. Tempera on canvas, 5′ 9″ × 9′ 2″. Galleria degli Uffizi, Florence.

Inspired by Angelo Poliziano's poem and Greek Aphrodite statues (FIG. 2-47), Botticelli revived the theme of the female nude in this elegant and romantic representation of Venus born of sea foam.

BIRTH OF VENUS Painted a few years later, Botticelli's *Birth of Venus* (FIG. 8-27) is based on a poem by Angelo Poliziano (1454–1494), a leading humanist of the day. In Botticelli's lyrical representation of Poliziano's version of the Greek myth, Venus (the Greek Aphrodite, born of the sea foam—*aphros*) stands on a floating cockle-shell. Zephyrus, carrying Chloris, blows the goddess to her sacred island, Cyprus. There, the nymph Pomona runs to meet her with a brocaded mantle. Zephyrus's breath moves all the figures without effort. Draperies undulate easily in the gentle gusts, perfumed by rose petals that fall on the whitecaps. In this painting, unlike in *Primavera,* Venus is nude, as in the famous statue (FIG. 2-47) by the ancient Greek master Praxiteles. As noted earlier, the nude, especially the female nude, was exceedingly rare during the Middle Ages. Botticelli's depiction of Venus unclothed (especially on such a large scale—roughly life-size) could have drawn harsh criticism. But in the more accommodating Renaissance culture and under the protection of the powerful Medici, the painter's nude Venus went unchallenged, in part because *Birth of Venus,* like *Primavera,* is susceptible to a Neo-Platonic reading, namely that those who embrace the contemplative life of reason will immediately contemplate spiritual and divine beauty whenever they behold physical beauty.

Botticelli's paintings stand apart from those of many other Quattrocento artists who sought to comprehend humanity and the natural world through a rational, empirical order. Indeed, Botticelli's elegant and beautiful linear style seems removed from all the scientific knowledge that 15th-century artists had gained in the areas of perspective and anatomy. For example, the seascape in *Birth of Venus* is a flat backdrop devoid of atmospheric perspective. Botticelli's style paralleled the Florentine allegorical pageants that were chivalric tournaments structured around allusions to classical mythology. The same trend is evident in the poetry of the 1470s and 1480s. Artists and poets at this time did not directly imitate classical antiquity but used the myths, with delicate perception of their charm, in a way still tinged with medieval romance. Ultimately, Botticelli created a style of visual poetry parallel to the love poetry of Lorenzo de' Medici.

ANTONIO DEL POLLAIUOLO Another of the many artists who produced sculptures and paintings for the Medici was ANTONIO DEL POLLAIUOLO (ca. 1431–1498), who took delight in showing human figures in violent action. Masaccio and his contemporaries had dealt effectively with the problem of rendering human anatomy, but they usually depicted their figures at rest or in restrained motion. Pollaiuolo conceived the body as a powerful machine and liked to display its mechanisms, such as knotted muscles and taut sinews that activate the skeleton as ropes pull levers. To show this to best effect, Pollaiuolo developed a figure so lean and muscular that it appears as if it has no skin. His figures also feature strongly accentuated delineations at the wrists, elbows, shoulders, and knees. *Battle of Ten Nudes* (FIG. 8-28), an early Italian example of the new engraving medium

8-28 ANTONIO POLLAIUOLO, *Battle of Ten Nudes*, ca. 1465. Engraving, 1' 3$\frac{1}{8}$" × 1' 11$\frac{1}{4}$". Metropolitan Museum of Art, New York (bequest of Joseph Pulitzer, 1917).

Pollaiuolo was fascinated by how muscles and sinews activate the human skeleton. He delighted in showing nude figures in violent action and from numerous foreshortened viewpoints.

1 in.

that northern European artists (FIG. 8-12) had pioneered, shows this figure type in a variety of poses and from numerous viewpoints. The print has no identifiable subject, but it enabled Pollaiuolo to demonstrate his prowess in rendering the nude male figure. In this, he was a kindred spirit of late-sixth-century BCE Greek vase painters, such as Euthymides (FIG. 2-26), whose experiments with foreshortening also took precedence over narrative content. Even though the figures in *Ten Nudes* hack and slash at each other without mercy, they seem somewhat stiff and frozen because Pollaiuolo depicted *all* the muscle groups at maximum tension. Not until several decades later did an even greater anatomist, Leonardo da Vinci, observe that only some of the body's muscle groups participate in any one action, while the others remain relaxed.

OSPEDALE DEGLI INNOCENTI Filippo Brunelleschi's ability to codify a system of linear perspective derived in part from his skill as an architect. According to his biographer, Antonio Manetti (1423–1497), Brunelleschi turned to architecture out of disappointment over the loss of the commission for the baptistery doors (see page 230). Several trips to Rome (the first in 1402, probably with his friend Donatello), where the ruins of ancient Rome captivated him, heightened his fascination with architecture, a field he would soon reorient. Brunelleschi's close study of Roman monuments and his effort to make an accurate record of what he saw may have been the catalyst that led him to develop his revolutionary system of linear perspective.

Brunelleschi's first major architectural commission was to design the Ospedale degli Innocenti (Hospital of the Innocents, FIG. 8-29), a home for Florentine orphans and foundlings. Most scholars regard Brunelleschi's orphanage as the first building to embody the new Renaissance architectural style. As in earlier similar buildings, the facade is a loggia opening onto the street, a sheltered portico where, in this case, parents could anonymously deliver unwanted children to the care of the foundling hospital. Brunelleschi's arcade consists of a series of round arches on slender Corinthian columns. Each bay is a domed compartment with a pediment-capped window above. Both plan and elevation conform

to a module that embodies the rationality of classical architecture. Each column is 10 *braccia* (approximately 20 feet; 1 braccia, or arm, equals 23 inches) tall. The distance between the columns of the facade and the distance between the columns and the wall are also 10 braccia. Thus each of the bays is a cubical unit 10 braccia

8-29 FILIPPO BRUNELLESCHI, loggia of the Ospedale degli Innocenti (Foundling Hospital; looking northeast), Florence, Italy, begun 1419.

The loggia of Florence's orphanage is an early example of Brunelleschi's work as an architect and the first Renaissance building. It features a classically austere design based on a module of 10 braccia.

Filippo Brunelleschi, interior of San Lorenzo (looking east), Florence, Italy, ca. 1421–1469.

The mathematical clarity and austerity of the decor of San Lorenzo are key elements of Brunelleschi's classically inspired architectural style, which contrasts sharply with the soaring drama of Gothic churches.

wide, deep, and high. The height of the columns also equals the diameter of the arches (except in the two outermost bays, which are slightly wider and serve as framing elements in the overall design). The color scheme, which would become a Brunelleschi hallmark, is austere: white stucco walls with gray *pietra serena* ("serene stone") columns and moldings.

SAN LORENZO Begun around 1421, the church of San Lorenzo (Saint Lawrence; FIG. 8-30), financed primarily by Giovanni de' Medici, embodies the new Renaissance spirit of the Florentine orphanage loggia in its austerity and rationality. As in the earlier building, Brunelleschi adopted an all-encompassing modular design for the church that extended even to the diameter of the shafts of the nave columns and the dimensions of their Corinthian capitals. The nave has a simple two-story elevation (nave arcade and clerestory) with a flat, coffered timber roof. The columns support *impost blocks* from which round arches spring. Ample light enters through the arcuated clerestory windows and through *oculi* in the aisle walls, one over each chapel opening onto the domed aisle bays. The calculated logic of the design echoes that of ancient Roman buildings, but contrasts sharply with the soaring drama and spirituality of the nave arcades and vaults of Gothic churches (for example, FIG. 7-13). San Lorenzo fully expresses the new Renaissance spirit that placed its faith in reason rather than in the emotions.

PAZZI CHAPEL Shortly after Brunelleschi began work on San Lorenzo, the Pazzi family commissioned him to design the chapel (FIGS. 8-31 and 8-32) they intended to donate to the Franciscan church of Santa Croce in Florence. The project was not completed, however, until the 1460s, long after Brunelleschi's death, and the exterior probably does not reflect his original design. The loggia, admirable as it is, likely was added as an afterthought, perhaps by the sculptor-architect Giuliano da Maiano (1432–1490). The Pazzi Chapel served as the *chapter house* (meeting hall) of the local chapter

8-31 **Filippo Brunelleschi,** west facade of the Pazzi Chapel, Santa Croce, Florence, Italy, begun 1433.

The Pazzi family erected this chapel as a gift to the Franciscan church of Santa Croce. It served as the monks' chapter house and is one of the first independent Renaissance central-plan buildings.

of Franciscan monks. Historians have suggested that the monks needed the expansion to accommodate more of their brethren.

Behind the loggia stands one of the first independent Renaissance buildings conceived basically as a central-plan structure (compare FIGS. 4-5 and 4-6), so called because the various aspects of the interior resemble one another, no matter where an observer stands, in contrast to the longitudinal plan of basilican churches. Although the Pazzi Chapel's plan is rectangular, rather than square or round, Brunelleschi placed all emphasis on the central dome-covered space. The short barrel-vaulted sections bracing the dome on two sides appear to be incidental appendages.

Circular medallions (*tondi* or *roundels*) in the dome's pendentives (see "Placing a Dome over a Square," page 128) consist of terracotta reliefs representing the four evangelists. The technique for manufacturing these baked clay reliefs was of recent invention. Around 1430, LUCA DELLA ROBBIA (1400–1482) perfected the application of vitrified (heat-fused) colored potters' glazes to sculpture. Inexpensive, durable, and decorative, these ceramic sculptures became extremely popular and provided the basis for a lucrative family business. Luca's nephew Andrea della Robbia (1435–1525)

produced roundels of babies in swaddling clothes for Brunelleschi's loggia of the Ospedale degli Innocenti (FIG. 8-29) in 1487 (the only indication on the building's facade of its charitable function), and Andrea's sons, Giovanni della Robbia (1469–1529) and Girolamo della Robbia (1488–1566), carried on this tradition well into the 16th century. Most of the tondi in the Pazzi Chapel are the work of Luca della Robbia himself. Together with the images of the 12 apostles on the pilaster-framed wall panels, they add striking color accents to the tranquil interior.

LEON BATTISTA ALBERTI It seems curious that Brunelleschi, the most renowned architect of his time, did not participate in the upsurge of palace building that Florence experienced in the 1430s and 1440s. The Medici rejected his proposal to build a new palace for them, awarding the commission instead to MICHELOZZO DI BARTOLOMMEO (1396–1472). After the Palazzo Medici (FIGS. 8-32A and 8-32B ⧉), the most important residential commission in mid-15th-century Florence was the Palazzo Rucellai (FIG. 8-33), designed by LEON BATTISTA ALBERTI (1404–1472) and constructed by his pupil and collaborator, BERNARDO ROSSELLINO (1409–1464) using Alberti's plans and sketches. Alberti entered the profession of architecture rather late in life, but made a major contribution to architectural design (see "Leon Battista Alberti's *On the Art of Building*" ⧉). Alberti's architectural style represents a scholarly application of classical elements to Renaissance buildings. In the

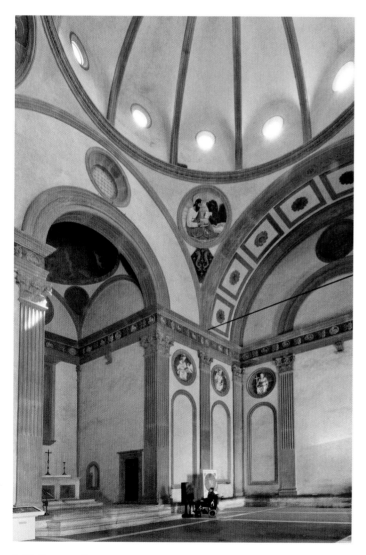

8-32 FILIPPO BRUNELLESCHI, interior of the Pazzi Chapel (looking southeast), Santa Croce, Florence, Italy, begun 1433.

Although the Pazzi Chapel is rectangular, rather than square or round, Brunelleschi created a central plan by placing all emphasis on the dome-covered space at the heart of the building.

8-33 LEON BATTISTA ALBERTI and BERNARDO ROSSELLINO, Palazzo Rucellai (looking northwest), Florence, Italy, ca. 1452–1470.

Alberti was an ardent student of classical architecture. By adapting the Roman use of different orders for each story, he created the illusion that the Palazzo Rucellai becomes lighter toward its top.

Palazzo Rucellai, pilasters define each story of the facade, and a classical cornice crowns the whole. Between the smooth pilasters are subdued and uniform wall surfaces. Alberti created the sense that the structure becomes lighter in weight toward its top by adapting the ancient Roman manner of using different capitals for the pilasters of each story. He chose the severe capitals of ancient Tuscan columns (the Etruscan variant of the Greek Doric order [FIG. 2-20, *left*], used also by the Romans) for the ground floor, capitals of his own invention with acanthus leaves and *palmettes* (palm leaves) for the second story, and Corinthian capitals for the third floor. Alberti modeled his facade on the Colosseum (FIG. 3-30), but he was no slavish copyist. On the ancient amphitheater's facade, the capitals employed are, from the bottom up, Tuscan, Ionic, and Corinthian. Moreover, Alberti adapted the Colosseum's varied surface to a flat facade, which does not allow the deep penetration of the building's mass that is so effective in the Roman structure. By converting his ancient model's engaged columns into shallow pilasters that barely project from the wall, Alberti created a large-meshed linear net. Stretched tightly across the front of his building, it not only unifies the three levels but also emphasizes the wall's flat, two-dimensional qualities.

GIROLAMO SAVONAROLA In the 1490s, Florence underwent a political, cultural, and religious upheaval. Florentine artists and their fellow citizens responded then not only to humanist ideas but also to the incursion of French armies and especially to the preaching of the Dominican monk Girolamo Savonarola (1452–1498), the reforming priest-dictator who denounced the humanistic secularism of the Medici and their artists, philosophers, and poets. Savonarola appealed to the people of Florence to repent their sins, and when

Lorenzo de' Medici died in 1492, the priest prophesied the downfall of the city and of Italy and assumed absolute control of the state. Like a large number of his fellow citizens, Savonarola believed that the Medici family's political, social, and religious power had corrupted Florence and invited the scourge of foreign invasion. Savonarola urged Florentines to burn their classical texts, scientific treatises, and philosophical publications. Scholars still debate the significance of Savonarola's brief span of power. Apologists for the undoubtedly sincere monk deny that his actions played a role in the decline of Florentine culture at the end of the 15th century. But the puritanical spirit that moved Savonarola must have dampened Florentine enthusiasm for classical antiquity. Certainly, Savonarola's condemnation of humanism as heretical nonsense, and his banishing of the Medici and other wealthy families from Florence, deprived local artists of some of their major patrons, at least in the short term. There were, however, commissions aplenty for artists elsewhere in Italy.

The Princely Courts

Although Florentine artists led the way in creating the Renaissance in art and architecture, the arts flourished throughout Italy in the 15th century. The papacy in Rome and the princely courts in Urbino, Mantua, and elsewhere also deserve credit for nurturing Renaissance art.

PERUGINO Between 1481 and 1483, Pope Sixtus IV (r. 1414–1484) summoned a group of artists to Rome, including Sandro Botticelli and Pietro Vannucci of Perugia, known as PERUGINO (ca. 1450–1523), to adorn the walls of the newly completed Sistine Chapel. Perugino's contribution to the fresco cycle was *Christ Delivering the Keys of*

8-34 PERUGINO, *Christ Delivering the Keys of the Kingdom to Saint Peter*, Sistine Chapel, Vatican City, Rome, Italy, 1481–1483. Fresco, 11' 5½" × 18' 8½".

Painted for the Vatican, this fresco depicts the event on which the papacy bases its authority. The converging lines of the pavement connect the action in the foreground with the background.

the Kingdom to Saint Peter (FIG. 8-34). The papacy had, from the beginning, based its claim to infallible and total authority over the Roman Catholic Church on this biblical event. In Perugino's fresco, Christ hands the keys to Saint Peter, who stands amid an imaginary gathering of the 12 apostles and Renaissance contemporaries. These figures occupy the apron of a great stage space that extends into the distance to a point of convergence in the doorway of a central-plan temple. (Perugino used parallel and converging lines in the pavement to mark off the intervening space; compare FIG. 8-16.) The smaller figures in the middle distance enhance the sense of depth and also act out important New Testament stories—for example (at the left), the episode of Jesus, Peter, and the tribute money (compare FIG. 8-21). At the corners of the great plaza, duplicate triumphal arches serve as the base angles of a distant compositional triangle whose apex is in the central building. Perugino modeled the arches very closely on the Arch of Constantine (FIG. 3-53) in Rome. Although they are anachronisms in a painting depicting a scene from Jesus's life, the arches served to underscore the close ties between Saint Peter and Constantine, the first Christian emperor of Rome and builder of the great basilica (FIG. 4-3) over Saint Peter's tomb. Christ and Peter flank the triangle's central axis, which runs through the temple's doorway, the vanishing point of Perugino's perspective scheme. Thus the composition interlocks both two-dimensional and three-dimensional space, and the placement of the central actors emphasizes the axial center.

URBINO Under the patronage of Federico da Montefeltro (1422–1482), Urbino, southeast of Florence across the Apennines (MAP 8-2), became an important center of Renaissance art and culture. In fact, the humanist writer Paolo Cortese (1465–1540) described Federico as one of the two greatest artistic patrons of the 15th century (the other was Cosimo de' Medici). Federico was so renowned for his military expertise that he was in demand by popes and kings, and soldiers came from across Europe to study under his direction.

One of the artists who received several commissions from Federico was PIERO DELLA FRANCESCA (ca. 1420–1492), who had already established a major reputation in his native Tuscany with works such as *Resurrection* (FIG. 8-34A ↗), a life-size fresco he painted in the town hall of his birthplace, Borgo San Sepolcro. At the Urbino court, Piero produced both religious works and official portraits for Federico, among them a double portrait (FIG. 8-35) of the count and his second wife, Battista Sforza (1446–1472), whom he married in 1460 when she was 14 years old. The daughter of Alessandro Sforza (1409–1473), lord of Pesaro and brother of the duke of Milan, Battista was a well-educated humanist who proved to be an excellent administrator of Federico's territories during his frequent military campaigns. She gave birth to eight daughters in 11 years and finally, on January 25, 1472, to the male heir for which the couple had prayed. When the countess died of pneumonia five months later at age 26, Federico went into mourning for virtually the rest of his life. He never remarried.

Federico commissioned Piero to paint their double portrait shortly after Battista's death to pay tribute to her and to have a memento of their marriage. The present frame is a 19th-century addition. Originally, the two portraits formed a hinged diptych. The format—two bust-length portraits with a landscape background—followed Flemish models (FIG. 8-6A ↗), as did Piero's use of oil-based pigment. But the Italian artist depicted the Urbino count and countess in profile, in part to emulate the profile portraits on Roman coins, which Renaissance humanists avidly collected, and in part to conceal the disfigured right side of Federico's face. (He lost his right eye and part of the bridge of his nose in a tournament in 1450.) Piero probably based Battista's portrait on her death mask, and the pallor of her skin may be a reference to her death. The backs of the panels also bear paintings. They represent Federico and Battista in triumphal chariots accompanied by personifications of their respective virtues, including Justice, Prudence, and Fortitude (Federico) and Faith, Charity, and Chastity (Battista). The placement of scenes of triumph on the reverse of profile portraits also emulates ancient Roman coinage.

8-35 PIERO DELLA FRANCESCA, *Battista Sforza and Federico da Montefeltro*, ca. 1472–1474. Oil and tempera on wood in modern frame, each panel 1' 6$\frac{1}{2}$" × 1' 1". Galleria degli Uffizi, Florence.

Piero's portraits of Federico da Montefeltro and his recently deceased wife, Battista Sforza, combine the profile views on Roman coins with the landscape backgrounds of Flemish portraiture (FIG. 8-6A ↗).

1 in.

8-36 LEON BATTISTA ALBERTI, west facade of Sant'Andrea, Mantua, Italy, designed 1470, begun 1472.

Alberti's design for Sant'Andrea reflects his study of ancient Roman architecture. Employing the colossal order, the architect combined a triumphal arch and a Roman temple front with pediment.

8-37 LEON BATTISTA ALBERTI, interior of Sant'Andrea (looking east), Mantua, Italy, designed 1470, begun 1472.

For the nave of Sant'Andrea, Alberti abandoned the traditional columnar arcade. The tremendous vaults suggest that Constantine's Basilica Nova (FIG. 3-52) in Rome may have served as a prototype.

MANTUA Marquis Ludovico Gonzaga (1412–1478) ruled Mantua in northeastern Italy (MAP 8-2) during the mid-15th century. A famed condottiere like Federico da Montefeltro, Gonzaga established his reputation as a fierce military leader while general of the Milanese armies. The visit of Pope Pius II (r. 1458–1464) to Mantua in 1459 stimulated the marquis's determination to transform his city into one that all Italy would envy.

One of the major projects Gonzaga instituted was the rebuilding of Sant'Andrea, an 11th-century church. Gonzaga turned to Leon Battista Alberti for this important commission. The facade (FIG. 8-36) that Alberti designed incorporated two major ancient Roman architectural motifs—the temple front and the triumphal arch. The combination was already a feature of Roman buildings still standing in Italy. For example, many Roman triumphal arches incorporated a pediment over the arcuated passageway and engaged columns, but there is no close parallel in antiquity for Alberti's eclectic and ingenious design. The Renaissance architect's concern for proportion led him to equalize the vertical and horizontal dimensions of the facade, which left it considerably shorter than the church behind it. Because of the primary importance of visual appeal, many Renaissance architects made this concession not only to the demands of a purely visual proportionality in the facade but also to the facade's relation to the small square in front of it, even at the expense of continuity with the body of the building. Yet structural correspondences to the building do exist in Sant'Andrea's facade. The pilasters are the same height as those on the nave's interior walls, and the large barrel vault over the central portal, with smaller barrel vaults branching off at right angles, introduces on a smaller scale the arrangement of the church's nave and aisles. The facade pilasters, as part of the wall, run uninterrupted through three stories in an early application of the *colossal* or *giant order* that became a favorite motif of Michelangelo (FIG. 9-14).

Inside (FIG. 8-37), Alberti abandoned the medieval columned arcade that Brunelleschi still used in San Lorenzo (FIG. 8-30). Thick walls alternating with vaulted chapels, interrupted by a massive dome over the crossing, support the huge coffered barrel vault. The vaulted interior calls to mind the vast spaces and dense enclosing masses of Roman architecture, especially Constantine's Basilica Nova (FIG. 3-52), which may have served as a prototype for Alberti's design because at that time it was erroneously thought to be a Roman temple. In *On the Art of Building*, Alberti criticized the traditional basilican plan (with continuous aisles flanking the central nave) as impractical because the colonnades conceal the ceremonies from the faithful in the aisles. For this reason, he designed a single huge hall with independent chapels branching off at right angles. This break with a Christian building tradition that had endured for a thousand years was extremely influential in later Renaissance and Baroque church planning.

ANDREA MANTEGNA Like other princes, Ludovico Gonzaga believed that an impressive palace was an important visual expression of his authority. One of the most spectacular rooms in the Palazzo Ducale (Ducal Palace) in Mantua is the so-called Camera

8-38 ANDREA MANTEGNA, interior of the Camera Picta, Palazzo Ducale, Mantua, Italy, 1465–1474. Fresco.

Working for Ludovico Gonzaga, who established Mantua as a great art city, Mantegna produced for the duke's palace the first completely consistent illusionistic decoration of an entire room.

degli Sposi (Room of the Newlyweds), originally the Camera Picta (Painted Room; FIGS. 8-38 and 8-39). ANDREA MANTEGNA (ca. 1431–1506) of Padua took almost nine years to complete the room's extensive fresco program, which celebrates Ludovico Gonzaga and his family. Any viewer standing in the Camera Picta, surrounded by the spectacle and majesty of courtly life, cannot help but be thoroughly impressed by both the commanding presence and elevated status of the patron and the dazzling artistic skills of Mantegna.

In the Camera Picta, Mantegna performed a triumphant feat by producing the first completely consistent illusionistic decoration of an entire room. By integrating real and painted architectural elements, Mantegna illusionistically dissolved the room's walls in a manner foretelling 17th-century Baroque decoration (see page 295). The Camera Picta recalls the efforts more than 15 centuries earlier by Italian painters on the Bay of Naples to integrate mural painting and architecture in frescoes of the Second Style of Roman painting (FIG. 3-20). Mantegna's *trompe l'oeil* (French, "deceives the eye") design, however, went far beyond anything preserved from ancient Italy. The Renaissance painter's daring experimentalism led him to complete the room's decoration with the first perspective of a ceiling

8-39 ANDREA MANTEGNA, ceiling of the Camera Picta, Palazzo Ducale, Mantua, Italy, 1465–1474. Fresco, 8' 9" in diameter.

Inside the Camera Picta, the viewer becomes the viewed as figures gaze into the room from a painted oculus opening onto a blue sky. This is the first perspective view of a ceiling from below.

1 ft.

8-40 ANDREA MANTEGNA, *Foreshortened Christ*, ca. 1500. Tempera on canvas, 2' 2¾" × 2' 7⅞". Pinacoteca di Brera, Milan.

In this work of overwhelming emotional power, Mantegna presented both a harrowing study of a strongly foreshortened cadaver and an intensely poignant depiction of a biblical tragedy.

(FIG. 8-39) seen from below (called, in Italian, *di sotto in sù*, "from below upward"). Baroque ceiling decorators later broadly developed this technique. Inside the Camera Picta, the viewer becomes the viewed as figures look down into the room from the painted oculus. Seen against the convincing illusion of a cloud-filled blue sky, several *putti* (cupids), strongly foreshortened, set the amorous mood of the Room of the Newlyweds, as the painted smiling spectators look into the room. The prominent peacock is an attribute of Juno, Jupiter's bride, who oversees lawful marriages. This brilliant feat of illusionism is the climax of decades of experimentation with perspective.

FORESHORTENED CHRIST One of Mantegna's later paintings, *Foreshortened Christ* (FIG. 8-40), is a work of overwhelming emotional power as well as another example of the artist's mastery of perspective. At first glance, this painting seems to be a strikingly realistic study in foreshortening. However, Mantegna reduced the size of Christ's feet, which, as the painter surely knew, would cover much of the Savior's body if properly represented according to Renaissance perspective rules. Thus, tempering naturalism with artistic license, Mantegna presented both a harrowing study of a strongly foreshortened cadaver and an intensely poignant depiction of a biblical tragedy. Remarkably, in the supremely gifted hands of Mantegna, all of Quattrocento science here served the purpose of devotion.

MILAN The leading city of northwestern Italy at this time was Milan, ruled by the powerful Sforza family, which also sought to lure the best artists to its court. In 1481, Ludovico Sforza (1451–1508) accepted a proposal from Leonardo da Vinci that the famed artist leave Florence for Milan to work for the Milanese court as military engineer, architect, sculptor, and painter. Several of Leonardo's early masterworks, including his world-famous *Last Supper* (FIG. 9-3), date to the closing years of the 15th century when he was in Milan. A discussion of Leonardo's Milanese career opens the examination of High Renaissance art in the next chapter.

Explore the era further in MindTap with videos of major artworks and buildings, Google Earth™ coordinates, and essays by the author on the following additional subjects:

❚ ART AND SOCIETY: The Artist's Profession during the Renaissance
• Hans Memling, *Diptych of Martin van Nieuwenhove* (FIG. 8-6A)
• *Buxheim Saint Christopher* (FIG. 8-11A)
❚ WRITTEN SOURCES: The *Commentarii* of Lorenzo Ghiberti
• Michelozzo di Bartolommeo, Palazzo Medici-Riccardi (FIGS. 8-32A and 8-32B)
❚ ARTISTS ON ART: Leon Battista Alberti's *On the Art of Building*
• Piero della Francesca, *Resurrection* (FIG. 8-34A)

THE EARLY RENAISSANCE IN EUROPE

Burgundy and Flanders

- The most powerful rulers north of the Alps during the first three-quarters of the 15th century were the dukes of Burgundy. Philip the Bold's greatest artistic project was the Chartreuse de Champmol. The head sculptor was Claus Sluter of Haarlem, who carved portraitlike statues of biblical figures.

- Flemish artists popularized the use of oil paints on wood panels. By superimposing translucent glazes, painters could create richer colors than possible using tempera or fresco. An early example is Robert Campin's *Mérode Altarpiece,* in which the everyday objects depicted have symbolic significance.

- Jan van Eyck, Rogier van der Weyden, and Hans Memling established portraiture, a rare genre during the Middle Ages, as an important art form in 15th-century Flanders.

Sluter, *Well of Moses*, 1395–1406

France and the Holy Roman Empire

- The Limbourg brothers expanded the illusionistic capabilities of manuscript illumination with full-page calendar pictures depicting naturalistic settings in the Book of Hours of Jean, duke of Berry.

- The major German innovation of the 15th century was the development of the printing press, which printers soon used to produce books with woodcut illustrations. Woodcuts are relief prints in which the artist carves out the areas around the lines to be printed. German artists, such as Martin Schongauer, were also the earliest masters of engraving. This intaglio technique enables a wider variety of linear effects because the artist incises the image directly onto a metal plate.

Limbourg brothers, *Les Très Riches Heures du Duc de Berry*, 1413–1416

Italy

- The fortunate congruence of artistic genius, the spread of humanism, and economic prosperity nourished the flowering of the artistic culture that historians call the Renaissance—the rebirth of classical values in art and life. The greatest center of Quattrocento Renaissance art was Florence, home of the powerful Medici, who were among the most ambitious art patrons in history.

- Some of the earliest examples of the new Renaissance style in sculpture are by Donatello: *Saint Mark,* which introduced the classical concept of contrapposto into Renaissance statuary; *David,* the first nude male statue since antiquity; and *Gattamelata,* modeled on imperial Roman equestrian portraits.

Donatello, *Gattamelata*, ca. 1445–1453

- Masaccio's figures recall Giotto's, but have a greater psychological and physical credibility, and the light shining on them comes from a source outside the picture. His *Holy Trinity* owes its convincing illusionism to Filippo Brunelleschi's new science of linear perspective. The humanist love of Greco-Roman themes comes to the fore in the paintings of Sandro Botticelli.

- Italian architects also revived the classical style. Brunelleschi's San Lorenzo conforms to a strict modular scheme and showcases the Roman-inspired rationality of Quattrocento Florentine architecture.

Botticelli, *Birth of Venus*, ca. 1484–1486

- Although Florentine artists led the way in creating the Renaissance in art and architecture, the papacy in Rome and the princely courts in Urbino and Mantua also were major art patrons. Among the important papal commissions of the 15th century was the decoration of the walls of the Sistine Chapel with frescoes, including Perugino's *Christ Delivering the Keys of the Kingdom to Saint Peter,* a prime example of the application of linear perspective.

- Mantua became an important art center under Marquis Ludovico Gonzaga, who brought leading artists, such as Piero della Francesca, to his court. Gonzaga also commissioned Leon Battista Alberti to rebuild Sant'Andrea, in which the architect applied the principles he developed in his influential 1450 treatise *On the Art of Building* and freely adapted forms from ancient Roman religious, triumphal, and civic architecture.

Alberti, Sant'Andrea, Mantua, 1470

◀ **9-1a** Michelangelo, the Renaissance genius who was primarily a sculptor, reluctantly spent almost four years painting the ceiling of the Sistine Chapel under commission from Pope Julius II.

▶ **9-1b** The fresco cycle illustrates the creation and fall of humankind as related in Genesis. Michelangelo always painted with a sculptor's eye. His heroic figures resemble painted statues.

9-1 **Interior of the Sistine Chapel (looking west), Vatican City, Rome, Italy, built 1473; ceiling and altar wall frescoes by MICHELANGELO BUONARROTI, 1508–1512 and 1536–1541, respectively.**

▲ **9-1c** Michelangelo completed his fresco cycle in the Sistine Chapel for another pope—Paul III—with this terrifying vision of the fate awaiting sinners. The *Last Judgment* includes his self-portrait.

High Renaissance and Mannerism in Europe

MICHELANGELO IN THE SERVICE OF JULIUS II

The first artist in history whose exceptional talent and brooding personality matched today's image of the temperamental artistic genius was MICHELANGELO BUONARROTI (1475–1564). The Florentine artist's self-imposed isolation, creative furies, proud independence, and daring innovations led Italians of his era to speak of the charismatic personality of the man and the expressive character of his works in one word—*terribilità,* "the sublime shadowed by the fearful." Yet, unlike most modern artists, who create works in their studios and offer them for sale later, Michelangelo and his contemporaries produced most of their paintings and sculptures under contract for wealthy patrons who dictated the content—and sometimes the form—of their artworks.

In Italy in the 1500s—the *Cinquecento*—the greatest art patron was the Catholic Church, headed by the pope in Rome. Michelangelo's most famous work today—the ceiling of the Sistine Chapel (FIG. 9-1) in the Vatican—was, in fact, a commission he did not want. His patron was Julius II (r. 1503–1513), an immensely ambitious man who sought to extend his spiritual authority into the temporal realm, as other medieval and Renaissance popes had done. Julius selected his name to associate himself with Julius Caesar, and found inspiration in ancient Rome. His enthusiasm for engaging in battle earned Julius the designation "warrior-pope," but his 10-year papacy was most notable for his patronage of the arts. Julius fully appreciated the propagandistic value of visual imagery and, upon his election, immediately commissioned artworks that would present an authoritative image of his rule and reinforce the primacy of the Catholic Church.

When Julius asked Michelangelo to take on the challenge of providing frescoes for the ceiling of the Sistine Chapel, the artist insisted that painting was not his profession—a protest that rings hollow after the fact, but Michelangelo's major works until then had been in sculpture. The artist had no choice, however, but to accept the pope's assignment.

In the Sistine Chapel frescoes, as in his sculptures, Michelangelo relentlessly concentrated his expressive purpose on the human figure. To him, the body was beautiful not only in its natural form but also in its spiritual and philosophical significance. The body was the manifestation of the character of the soul. In the *Creation of Adam* (FIG. 9-1a), *Fall of Man* (FIG. 9-1b), and *Last Judgment* (FIG. 9-1c) frescoes, Michelangelo represented the body in its most elemental aspect—in the nude or simply draped, with almost no background and no ornamental embellishment. He always painted with a sculptor's eye for how light and shadow reveal volume and surface. It is no coincidence that many of the figures in the Sistine Chapel seem to be painted statues.

ITALY

The art and architecture of 16th-century Italy (MAP 9-1) built on the foundation of the Early Renaissance of the 15th century, but no single artistic style characterized Cinquecento art. Regional differences abounded, especially between central Italy (Florence and Rome) and Venice. The period opened with the brief era that art historians call the High Renaissance—the quarter century between 1495 and the deaths of Leonardo da Vinci in 1519 and Raphael in 1520. The Renaissance style and the interest in classical culture, perspective, proportion, and human anatomy dominated the remainder of the 16th century (the Late Renaissance), but a new style, called *Mannerism,* challenged Renaissance naturalism almost as soon as Raphael had been laid to rest (inside the ancient Roman Pantheon, FIG. 3-40). The one constant in 16th-century Italy is the astounding quality, both technical and aesthetic, of the art and architecture produced. Indeed, the modern notion of the "fine arts" and the celebration of artistic genius originated in Renaissance Italy. During the High Renaissance, artists became international celebrities for the first time. None achieved greater fame than Leonardo da Vinci, Raphael, and Michelangelo, although even they could not create artworks freely, but had to satisfy the demands of their patrons (see "Michelangelo in the Service of Julius II," page 251).

Leonardo da Vinci

Born in the small town of Vinci, near Florence, LEONARDO DA VINCI (1452–1519) was the quintessential "Renaissance man." Art was but one of Leonardo's innumerable interests. His unquenchable curiosity is evident in the voluminous notes he interspersed with sketches in his notebooks dealing with botany, geology, geography, mapmaking, zoology, military engineering, hydraulics, and anatomy (FIG. 9-1A ⤴). Leonardo believed that his scientific investigations made him a better painter. For example, his in-depth exploration

MAP 9-1 Europe in the early 16th century.

HIGH RENAISSANCE AND MANNERISM IN EUROPE

1495–1520
- The leading artists of the High Renaissance in Florence and Rome are Leonardo da Vinci, Raphael, and Michelangelo.
- In Rome, Bramante champions the classical style in architecture.
- In northern Europe, consistent with Protestant values, art patrons prefer secular to religious themes.
- Albrecht Dürer, master printmaker, becomes the first international art celebrity outside Italy.

1520–1550
- In Venice, Giorgione and Titian pioneer colorito and poesia in oil painting.
- Mannerism emerges as an alternative to the High Renaissance style in painting and architecture in the work of Pontormo, Parmigianino, Bronzino, and Giulio Romano.
- Netherlandish painters inject moralizing religious messages into paintings of everyday life.

1550–1575
- The Council of Trent defends religious art as part of the Catholic Church's Counter-Reformation.
- Andrea Palladio becomes chief architect of the Venetian Republic.
- Giorgio Vasari publishes *Lives of the Most Eminent Painters, Sculptors, and Architects.*
- Pieter Bruegel the Elder produces masterful landscapes that nonetheless focus on human activities.

1575–1600
- Tintoretto is the leading Venetian Mannerist painter.
- Giambologna uses spiral compositions for Mannerist statuary groups.
- Greek-born El Greco settles in Toledo and creates paintings that are a uniquely personal mix of Byzantine and Italian Mannerist elements. His hybrid style captures the fervor of Spanish Catholicism.

1 ft.

9-2 LEONARDO DA VINCI, *Madonna of the Rocks,* from San Francesco Grande, Milan, Italy, 1483–1490. Oil on wood (transferred to canvas), 6' 6½" × 4'. Musée du Louvre, Paris.

Leonardo used gestures and a pyramidal composition to unite the Virgin, John the Baptist, the Christ Child, and an angel. The figures share the same light-infused environment.

Around 1481, Leonardo left Florence after offering his services to Ludovico Sforza (1451–1508), the son and heir apparent of the ruler of Milan. The political situation in Florence was uncertain, and Leonardo must have felt that his particular skills would be in greater demand at the court of Milan, where he hoped to achieve financial security. The letter that Leonardo wrote to Ludovico seeking employment is revealing. The artist focused on his qualifications as a military engineer, mentioning only at the end his abilities as a painter and sculptor:

And in short, according to the variety of cases, I can contrive various and endless means of offence and defence. . . . In time of peace I believe I can give perfect satisfaction and to the equal of any other in architecture and the composition of buildings, public and private; and in guiding water from one place to another. . . . I can carry out sculpture in marble, bronze, or clay, and also I can do in painting whatever may be done, as well as any other, be he whom he may.[1]

Ludovico agreed to hire Leonardo, although he did not offer him a salaried position until several years later.

MADONNA OF THE ROCKS Shortly after settling in Milan, Leonardo painted *Madonna of the Rocks* (FIG. 9-2) as the center panel of an altarpiece in San Francesco Grande. Leonardo presented the Madonna, Christ Child, infant John the Baptist, and angel in a pyramidal grouping. The four figures pray, point, and bless, and these acts and gestures, although their meanings are uncertain, visually unite the individuals portrayed. The angel points to the infant John and, through his outward glance, involves the viewer in the scene. John prays to the Christ Child, who blesses him in return. The Virgin herself completes the series of interlocking gestures, her left hand reaching toward her son and her right hand resting protectively on John's shoulder. A tender mood suffuses the entire composition. Nonetheless, Leonardo's most notable achievement in *Madonna of the Rocks* was to paint the figures sharing the same light-infused environment, made possible by his deep understanding of *chiaroscuro*. The biblical figures emerge through nuances of light and shade from the half-light of the mysterious cavernous landscape.

of optics provided him with an understanding of perspective, light, and color. Indeed, Leonardo's scientific drawings (see "Renaissance Drawings" ⓐ) are themselves artworks.

Leonardo's great ambition in both his scientific endeavors and his art was to discover the laws underlying the processes and flux of nature. With this end in mind, he also studied the human body and contributed immeasurably to knowledge of physiology and psychology. Leonardo believed that reality in an absolute sense is inaccessible and that humans can know it only through its changing images. He considered the eyes the most vital organs and sight the most essential function (see "Leonardo and Michelangelo on Painting versus Sculpture" ⓐ).

LAST SUPPER For Ludovico Sforza, Leonardo painted *Last Supper* (FIG. 9-3) in the refectory of Santa Maria delle Grazie in Milan. The mural—Leonardo's most impressive work, both formally and emotionally—is unfortunately in a poor state, in part because, in a bold experiment, instead of using fresco, which has a matte finish, Leonardo mixed oil and tempera, and he applied the colors *a secco* (to dried, rather than wet, plaster). Consequently, the paint quickly began to flake. The humidity of Milan further accelerated the deterioration.

Jesus and his 12 disciples sit at a long table placed parallel to the picture plane in a simple, spacious room. The austere setting amplifies the painting's highly dramatic action. Jesus, with outstretched hands, has just said, "One of you is about to betray me" (Matt. 26:21). A wave of intense excitement passes through the group as each disciple asks himself and, in some cases, his neighbor, "Is it I?" (Matt. 26:22). Leonardo linked Jesus's dramatic statement about betrayal with the initiation of the ancient liturgical ceremony of the Eucharist, when Jesus, blessing bread and wine, said, "This is my body, which is given for you. Do this for a commemoration of me. . . . This is the chalice, the new testament in my blood, which shall be shed for you" (Luke 22:19–20).

In the center, Jesus appears isolated from the disciples and in perfect repose, the calm eye of the swirling emotion around him. The central window at the back, whose curved pediment arches above his head, frames his figure. The pediment is the only curve in the architectural framework, and it serves here, along with the diffused light, as a halo. Jesus's head is the focal point of all converging perspective lines in the composition. Thus the still, psychological focus and cause of the action is also the perspective focus, as well as the center of the two-dimensional surface. The two-dimensional, the three-dimensional, and the psychodimensional focuses are the same.

Leonardo presented the agitated disciples in four groups of three, united among and within themselves by the figures' gestures and postures. The artist sacrificed traditional iconography to pictorial and dramatic consistency by placing Judas on the same side of the table as Jesus and the other disciples (compare FIG. 8-24). The light source in the painting corresponds to the windows in the refectory. Judas's face is in shadow, and he clutches a money bag in his right hand as he reaches his left forward to fulfill Jesus's declaration: "But yet behold, the hand of him that betrayeth me is with me on the table" (Luke 22:21). The two disciples at the table ends are quieter than the others, as if to bracket the energy of the composition, which is more intense closer to Jesus, whose serenity both halts and intensifies it. The disciples register a broad range of emotional responses, including fear, doubt, protestation, rage, and love. Leonardo's numerous preparatory studies—using live models—suggest that he thought of each figure as carrying a particular charge and type of emotion. Like a stage director, he read the Gospel story carefully, and scrupulously cast his actors as the Bible described their roles. In this work, as in his other religious paintings, Leonardo

1 ft.

9-3 LEONARDO DA VINCI, *Last Supper*, ca. 1495–1498. Oil and tempera on plaster, 13' 9" × 29' 10". Refectory, Santa Maria delle Grazie, Milan.

Jesus has just announced that one of his disciples will betray him, and each one reacts. He is both the psychological focus of Leonardo's fresco and the focal point of all the converging perspective lines.

revealed his extraordinary ability to apply his voluminous knowledge about the observable world to the pictorial representation of a religious scene, resulting in a psychologically complex and compelling painting.

MONA LISA Leonardo's *Mona Lisa* (FIG. 9-4) is probably the world's most famous portrait. In his biography of Leonardo, Giorgio Vasari (see "Giorgio Vasari's *Lives*" 🔊) identified the woman portrayed as Lisa di Antonio Maria Gherardini, the wife of Francesco del Giocondo, a wealthy Florentine—hence, "Mona (an Italian contraction of *ma donna,* "my lady") Lisa." Unlike earlier portraits, Leonardo's representation of Gherardini does not serve solely as an icon of status but is a convincing likeness of a specific individual. Indeed,

9-4 **LEONARDO DA VINCI,** *Mona Lisa,* ca. 1503–1505. Oil on wood, 2' 6$\frac{1}{4}$" × 1' 9". Musée du Louvre, Paris.

Leonardo's skill with chiaroscuro and atmospheric perspective is on display in this new kind of portrait depicting the sitter as an individual personality who engages the viewer psychologically.

Mona Lisa wears no jewelry and holds no attribute associated with wealth. She sits quietly, her hands folded, her mouth forming a gentle smile, and her gaze directed at the viewer. Renaissance etiquette dictated that a woman should not look directly into a man's eyes. Leonardo's portrayal of this self-assured young woman without the trappings of power but engaging the audience psychologically was unprecedented.

The enduring appeal of *Mona Lisa* also derives in large part from Leonardo's decision to set his subject against the backdrop of a mysterious uninhabited landscape. This setting, with roads and bridges seemingly leading nowhere, recalls that of his *Madonna of the Rocks* (FIG. 9-2). The composition also resembles Fra Filippo Lippi's *Madonna and Child with Angels* (FIG. 8-25) with figures seated in front of a window through which the viewer glimpses a distant landscape. Originally, the artist represented Gherardini in a loggia. A later owner trimmed the painting, eliminating the columns, but partial column bases remain to the left and right of Mona Lisa's shoulders. The painting is darker today than it was 500 years ago, and the colors are less vivid, but *Mona Lisa* still reveals Leonardo's fascination and skill with chiaroscuro and atmospheric perspective. The portrait is a prime example of Leonardo's famous smoky *sfumato* (misty haziness)—his subtle adjustment of light and blurring of precise planes.

ARCHITECTURE AND SCULPTURE Leonardo also won renown in his time as both architect and sculptor, although no extant building or sculpture can be definitively attributed to him. From his many drawings of central-plan structures, it is evident that he shared the interest of other Renaissance architects in this building type. As for Leonardo's sculptures, numerous drawings of equestrian statues survive, and he made a full-scale model for a monument to Francesco Sforza (1401–1466), Ludovico's father. The French used the statue as a target and shot it to pieces when they occupied Milan in 1499. Leonardo left Milan at that time and served for a while as a military engineer for Cesare Borgia (1476–1507), who, with the support of his father, Pope Alexander VI (r. 1492–1503), tried to conquer the cities of the Romagna region in north-central Italy and create a Borgia duchy. Leonardo eventually returned to Milan in the service of the French. At the invitation of King Francis I (see page 277), he then went to France, where he died at Cloux in 1519.

Raphael

Alexander VI's successor was Julius II (see page 251). In 1508, the new pope called Raffaello Santi (or Sanzio), known as RAPHAEL (1483–1520) in English, to the Vatican, which would soon displace Florence, Urbino, Mantua, and Milan as the leading center of Renaissance art. Born in a small town in Umbria, Raphael probably learned the basics of his art from his father, Giovanni Santi (d. 1494), before entering the studio of Perugino (FIG. 8-34). Although strongly influenced by Perugino and Leonardo, Raphael developed an individual style that embodied the ideals of High Renaissance art.

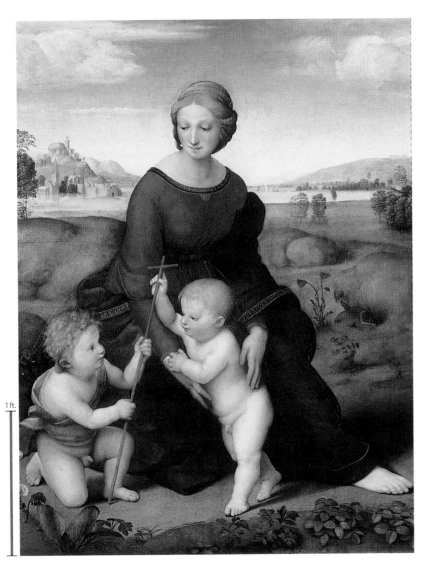

1 ft.

9-5 RAPHAEL, *Madonna in the Meadow*, 1505–1506. Oil on wood, 3' 8½" × 2' 10¼". Kunsthistorisches Museum, Vienna.

Emulating Leonardo's pyramidal composition (FIG. 9-2) but rejecting his dusky modeling and mystery, Raphael set his Madonna in a well-lit landscape and imbued her with grace, dignity, and beauty.

MADONNA IN THE MEADOW Raphael worked in Florence from 1504 to 1508, where he painted *Madonna in the Meadow* (FIG. 9-5), in which he adopted Leonardo's pyramidal composition and modeling of faces and figures in subtle chiaroscuro. But Raphael retained Perugino's lighter tonalities and blue skies, preferring clarity to obscurity, not fascinated, as Leonardo was, with mystery. Raphael quickly achieved fame for his Madonnas, which depict Mary as a beautiful young mother tenderly interacting with her young son. In *Madonna in the Meadow,* Mary almost wistfully watches Jesus play with John the Baptist's cross-shaped staff, as if she has a premonition of how her son will die.

SCHOOL OF ATHENS In 1508, Julius II awarded the 25-year-old Raphael with a prestigious commission—the decoration of the papal apartments. Of the suite's several rooms (*stanze*), Raphael painted two himself, including the Stanza della Segnatura (Room of the Signature—Julius's library, where later popes signed official documents). Pupils completed the others, following Raphael's sketches. On the four walls of the library, Raphael presented images symbolizing the four branches of human knowledge and wisdom

under the headings *Theology, Law (Justice), Poetry,* and *Philosophy*—the learning required of a Renaissance pope. Given Julius II's desire for recognition as both a spiritual and temporal leader, it is appropriate that the *Theology* and *Philosophy* frescoes face each other. The two images present a balanced picture of the pope—as a cultured, knowledgeable individual and as a wise, divinely ordained religious authority.

In Raphael's *Philosophy* mural (commonly called *School of Athens,* FIG. 9-6), the setting is not a "school" but a congregation of the great philosophers and scientists of the ancient world. Raphael depicted these famous wise men, revered by Renaissance humanists, conversing and explaining their various theories and ideas. The setting is a vast hall covered by massive vaults that recall ancient Roman architecture, especially the coffered barrel vaults of the Basilica Nova (FIG. 3-52). Colossal statues of Apollo and Athena, patron deities of the arts and of wisdom, oversee the interactions. Plato and Aristotle are the central figures around whom Raphael carefully arranged the others. Plato holds his book *Timaeus* and points to Heaven, the source of his inspiration, while Aristotle carries his book *Nichomachean Ethics* and gestures toward the earth, from which his observations of reality sprang. Appropriately, ancient philosophers, men concerned with the ultimate mysteries that transcend this world, stand on Plato's side. On Aristotle's side are the philosophers and scientists concerned with practical matters, such as mathematics. At the lower left, Pythagoras writes as a servant holds up the harmonic scale. In the foreground, Heraclitus (probably a portrait of Michelangelo) broods alone. Diogenes sprawls on the steps. At the right, students surround Euclid, who demonstrates a theorem. Euclid may be a portrait of the architect Bramante (FIG. 9-12). At the extreme right, just to the right of the astronomers Zoroaster and Ptolemy, both holding globes, Raphael included his self-portrait.

The groups appear to move easily and clearly, with eloquent poses and gestures that symbolize their doctrines and present an engaging variety of figural positions. The self-assurance and natural dignity of the figures convey calm reason, balance, and measure—the qualities that Renaissance thinkers admired as the heart of philosophy. Significantly, Raphael placed himself among the mathematicians and scientists in *School of Athens.* Certainly, the evolution of pictorial science approached perfection in this fresco in which Raphael convincingly depicted a vast space on a two-dimensional surface.

School of Athens also reveals Raphael's psychological insight along with his mastery of the problems of physical representation. As in Leonardo's *Last Supper* (FIG. 9-3), all the characters communicate moods that reflect their beliefs, and the artist's placement of each figure tied these moods together. From the center, where Plato and Aristotle stand, Raphael arranged the groups of figures in an ellipse with a wide opening in the foreground. Moving along the floor's perspective pattern, the viewer's eye penetrates the assembly of philosophers and continues, by way of the reclining Diogenes, up to the here-reconciled leaders of the two great opposing camps of Renaissance philosophy. The vanishing point falls on Plato's left hand, drawing attention to *Timaeus.* In the Stanza della Segnatura, Raphael reconciled and harmonized not only the Platonists and Aristotelians but also classical humanism and Christianity.

9-6 RAPHAEL, *Philosophy* (*School of Athens*), Stanza della Segnatura, Apostolic Palace, Vatican City, Rome, Italy, 1509–1511. Fresco, 19' × 27'.

Raphael included himself in this gathering of great philosophers and scientists whose self-assurance conveys calm reason. The setting recalls the massive vaults of the ancient Basilica Nova (FIG. 3-52).

Michelangelo

Although Michelangelo is most famous today as the painter of the Sistine Chapel (FIG. 9-1), he was also an architect, engineer, poet, and, first and foremost, a sculptor. Michelangelo considered sculpture superior to painting because the sculptor shares in the divine power to "make man" (see "Leonardo and Michelangelo on Painting versus Sculpture" ⟨⟩). Drawing a conceptual parallel to Plato's ideas, Michelangelo believed that the image which the artist's hand produces must come from the idea in the artist's mind. The idea, then, is the reality that the artist's genius has to bring forth. But artists are not the creators of the ideas they conceive. Rather, they find their ideas in the natural world, reflecting the absolute idea, which, for the artist, is beauty. One of Michelangelo's best-known observations about sculpture is that the artist must proceed by finding the idea—the image—locked in the stone. By removing the excess stone, the sculptor releases the idea from the block (FIG. I-14). The artist, Michelangelo felt, works many years at this unceasing process of revelation and "arrives late at novel and lofty things."[2]

Michelangelo did indeed arrive at "novel and lofty things," for he broke sharply from his predecessors and contemporaries in one important respect: he mistrusted the application of mathematical methods as guarantees of beauty in proportion. Measure and proportion, he believed, should be "kept in the eyes." Vasari quoted Michelangelo as declaring that "it was necessary to have the compasses in the eyes and not in the hand, because the hands work and the eye judges."[3] Thus Michelangelo set aside Polykleitos, Vitruvius, Alberti, Leonardo, and others who tirelessly sought the perfect measure, and insisted that the artist's inspired judgment could identify pleasing proportions. In addition, Michelangelo argued that the artist must not be bound, except by the demands made by realizing the idea. This assertion of the artist's authority was typical of Michelangelo and anticipated the modern concept of the right to a self-expression of talent limited only by the artist's own judgment. The artistic license to aspire far beyond the "rules" was, in part, a manifestation of the pursuit of fame and success that humanism fostered. In this context, Michelangelo created works in architecture, sculpture, and painting that departed from High Renaissance regularity. He put in its stead a style of vast, expressive strength conveyed through complex, eccentric, and often titanic forms that loom before the viewer in tragic grandeur.

PIETÀ Michelangelo began his career in Florence, but when the Medici fell in 1494 (see page 244), he fled to Bologna and then moved to Rome. There, still in his early 20s, he produced his first

9-7 MICHELANGELO BUONARROTI, *Pietà*, ca. 1498–1500. Marble, 5' 8½" high. Saint Peter's, Vatican City, Rome.

Michelangelo's representation of Mary cradling Christ's corpse captures the sadness and beauty of the young Virgin, but was controversial because the Madonna seems younger than her son.

1 ft.

masterpiece—a *Pietà* (FIG. 9-7)—for Jean de Bilhères Lagraulas (1439–1499), Cardinal of Saint-Denis and the French king's envoy to the Vatican. The cardinal commissioned the statue to be placed in the rotunda attached to the south transept of Old Saint Peter's (not shown in FIG. 4-3) in which he was to be buried. (The work is now on view in the new church [FIG. 10-3] that replaced the fourth-century basilica.) The theme—Mary cradling the dead body of Christ in her lap—was a staple in the repertoire of French and German artists (FIG. 7-27), and Michelangelo's French patron doubtless chose the subject. The Italian sculptor, however, rendered the northern European theme in an unforgettable manner. Michelangelo transformed marble into flesh, hair, and fabric with a sensitivity for texture almost without parallel. The polish and luminosity of the exquisite marble surface can be fully appreciated only in the presence of the original. Also breathtaking is the tender sadness of the beautiful and youthful Mary as she mourns the death of her son. In fact, her age—seemingly less than that of Christ—was a subject of controversy from the moment the statue was unveiled. Michelangelo explained Mary's ageless beauty as an integral part of her purity and virginity. Beautiful, too, is the son whom she holds. Christ seems less to have died a martyr's crucifixion than to have drifted off into peaceful sleep in Mary's maternal arms. His wounds are barely visible.

DAVID Michelangelo returned to Florence in 1501. In 1495, during the Medici exile, the Florentine Republic had ordered the transfer of Donatello's *David* (FIG. 8-18) from the Medici residence to the Palazzo della Signoria, the seat of the Florentine government. The importance of David as a civic symbol led the Florence Cathedral building committee to invite Michelangelo to fashion another *David* (FIG. 9-8) for the Signoria from a great block of marble left over from an earlier aborted commission. The colossal statue—Florentines referred to it as "the Giant"—that Michelangelo created from that block assured forever his reputation as an extraordinary talent. Vasari, for example, extolled the work, claiming "without any doubt the figure has put in the shade every other statue, ancient or modern, Greek or Roman."[4]

Despite the traditional association of David with heroic triumph, Michelangelo chose to represent the young biblical warrior not after his victory, with Goliath's head at his feet, but before the encounter, with David sternly watching his approaching foe. *David* exhibits the characteristic representation of energy in reserve that imbues Michelangelo's figures with the tension of a coiled spring. The anatomy of David's body plays an important part in this prelude to action. His rugged torso, sturdy limbs, and large hands and feet alert viewers to the triumph to come. Each swelling vein and tightening sinew amplifies the psychological energy of David's pose.

Michelangelo doubtless had the classical nude in mind. Like many of his colleagues, he greatly admired Greco-Roman statues, in particular the skillful and precise rendering of heroic physique. Without strictly imitating the antique style, the Renaissance sculptor captured in his *David* the tension of Lysippan athletes (FIG. 2-49) and the psychological insight and emotionalism of Hellenistic statuary. His *David* differs from Donatello's in much the same way that Hellenistic statues departed from their Classical predecessors (see Chapter 2). Michelangelo abandoned the self-contained composition of the Quattrocento statue by abruptly turning the hero's head toward his gigantic adversary. This *David* is compositionally and emotionally connected to an unseen presence beyond the statue, a feature also of Hellenistic sculpture (FIG. 2-57A ⏎). As early as 1501 then, Michelangelo invested his efforts in presenting towering, pent-up emotion rather than calm, ideal beauty.

SISTINE CHAPEL In 1508, the same year that Julius II asked Raphael to decorate the papal apartments, the pope convinced a reluctant Michelangelo to paint the ceiling (FIGs. 9-1 and 9-9) of the Sistine Chapel (see "Michelangelo in the Service of Julius II," page 251). Michelangelo faced enormous difficulties in completing this assignment: the ceiling's dimensions (some 5,800 square feet), its height above the pavement (almost 70 feet), and the complicated perspective problems that the vault's height and curve presented—in addition to his inexperience in the fresco technique. Yet, in fewer than four years, the Florentine sculptor produced an extraordinary series of frescoes incorporating his patron's agenda, Church doctrine, and his own interests. In depicting the most august and solemn themes of all—the creation, fall, and redemption of humankind—Michelangelo succeeded in weaving together more than 300 figures in a grand drama of the human race.

Nine narrative panels describing the creation, as recorded in Genesis, run along the crown of the vault, from *God's Separation of Light and Darkness* (above the altar) to *Drunkenness of Noah* (nearest the entrance to the chapel). Thus as viewers enter the chapel, look up, and walk toward the altar, they review, in reverse order, the history of the fall of humankind. The Hebrew prophets and ancient *sibyls* who foretold the coming of Christ appear seated in large thrones on both sides of the central row of scenes from Genesis, where the vault curves down. In the four corner pendentives, Michelangelo placed four Old Testament scenes with David, Judith, Haman, and Moses and the Brazen Serpent. Scores of lesser figures also appear. The ancestors of Christ fill the triangular compartments above the windows, nude youths punctuate the corners of the central panels, and small pairs of putti painted in *grisaille* (to imitate sculpture) support the painted cornice surrounding the entire central corridor. The overall conceptualization of the ceiling's design and narrative structure not only presents a sweeping chronology of Christianity but also is in keeping with Renaissance ideas

1 ft.

9-8 MICHELANGELO BUONARROTI, *David,* from Piazza della Signoria, Florence, Italy, 1501–1504. Marble, 17' high. Galleria dell'Accademia, Florence.

In this colossal statue, Michelangelo represented David turning his head toward the unseen Goliath, capturing the tension of Lysippos's athletes and the emotionalism of Hellenistic statuary.

10 ft.

9-9 MICHELANGELO BUONARROTI, ceiling of the Sistine Chapel, Vatican City, Rome, Italy, 1508–1512. Fresco, 128' × 45'.

Michelangelo labored almost four years for Pope Julius II on the frescoes for the ceiling of the Sistine Chapel. He painted more than 300 figures illustrating the creation and fall of humankind.

9-10 MICHELANGELO BUONARROTI, *Creation of Adam,* detail of the ceiling of the Sistine Chapel (FIG. 9-9), Vatican City, Rome, Italy, 1511–1512. Fresco, 9' 2" × 18' 8".

Life leaps to Adam like a spark from the extended hand of God in this fresco, which recalls the communication between gods and heroes in the classical myths that Renaissance humanists admired.

about Christian history. These ideas included interest in the conflict between good and evil and between the energy of youth and the wisdom of age. The conception of the entire ceiling was astounding in itself, and the articulation of it in its thousands of details was a superhuman achievement.

CREATION OF ADAM Unlike Andrea Mantegna's decoration of the Camera Picta (FIGS. 8-38 and 8-39) in Mantua, the strongly marked unifying architectural framework in the Sistine Chapel does not produce "picture windows" framing illusions within them. Rather, the viewer focuses on figure after figure, each sharply outlined against the neutral tone of the architectural setting or the plain background of the panels. The two central scenes are *Creation of Adam* (FIG. 9-10) and *Fall of Man* (FIG. 9-10A ⏎). In both cases, Michelangelo rejected traditional iconographical convention in favor of bold new interpretations of these momentous events. In *Creation of Adam,* God and the first man confront each other in a primordial unformed landscape of which Adam is still a material part, heavy as earth. The Lord transcends the earth, wrapped in a billowing cloud of drapery and borne up by his powers. Life leaps to Adam like a spark from the extended mighty hand of God. The communication between gods and heroes, so familiar in classical myth, is here concrete. This blunt depiction of the Lord as ruler of Heaven in the Olympian sense indicates how easily High Renaissance thought joined classical and Christian traditions. Yet the classical trappings do not obscure the essential Christian message.

Beneath the Lord's sheltering left arm is a woman, apprehensively curious but as yet uncreated. Scholars traditionally believed that she is Eve, but many now think she is the Virgin Mary (with the Christ Child at her knee). If the second identification is correct, it suggests that Michelangelo incorporated into his fresco one of the essential tenets of Christian faith—the belief that Adam's original

sin eventually led to the sacrifice of Christ, which in turn made possible the redemption of all humankind. As God reaches out to Adam, the viewer's eye follows the motion from right to left, but Adam's extended left arm leads the eye back to the right, along the Lord's right arm, shoulders, and left arm to his left forefinger, which points to the Christ Child's face. The focal point of this right-to-left-to-right movement—the fingertips of Adam and the Lord—is dramatically off-center. Michelangelo replaced the straight architectural axes found in Leonardo's compositions with curves and diagonals. For example, the bodies of the two great figures are complementary—the concave body of Adam fitting the convex body and billowing "cloak" of God. Thus motion directs not only the figures but also the whole composition. The reclining positions of the figures, the heavy musculature, and the twisting poses are all intrinsic parts of Michelangelo's style.

COUNTER-REFORMATION Paul III (r. 1534–1549) became pope at a time of widespread dissatisfaction with the leadership and policies of the Roman Catholic Church. Disgruntled Catholics voiced concerns about the sale of pardons for sins, favoritism in church appointments, and high Church officials pursuing personal wealth. This Reformation movement, based in the Holy Roman Empire, resulted in the establishment of Protestantism, discussed in detail later (see page 272). The Catholic Church, in response, mounted a full-fledged campaign—the Counter-Reformation—to counteract the defection of its members to Protestantism. The religious schism also had important consequences for artistic patronage (see "The Council of Trent" ⏎). Many papal art commissions should be viewed as an integral part of the Counter-Reformation effort. Church officials long had been aware of the power of visual imagery to construct and reinforce ideological claims, and the 16th-century popes exploited this capability.

10 ft.

9-11 MICHELANGELO
BUONARROTI, *Last Judg-
ment,* altar wall of the
Sistine Chapel (FIG. 9-1),
Vatican City, Rome, Italy,
1534–1541. Fresco,
48' × 44'.

The final component of Michelangelo's fresco cycle in the
Sistine Chapel is this terrifying
vision of judgment day. The
artist placed his own portrait
on the flayed skin that Saint
Bartholomew holds.

LAST JUDGMENT Among Paul III's first papal commissions was *Last Judgment* (FIG. 9-11), an enormous (48-foot-tall) fresco for the altar wall of the Sistine Chapel (FIG. 9-1). Here, Michelangelo depicted Christ as the stern judge of the world, but—in vivid contrast to medieval traditions—as a twisting, almost nude giant who raises his mighty right arm in a gesture of damnation so broad and universal as to suggest that he will destroy all creation. The choirs of Heaven surrounding the youthful judge pulse with anxiety and awe. Crowded into the spaces below are trumpeting angels, the ascending figures of the saved, and the downward-hurtling figures of the damned. The Virgin is already in Heaven, on Christ's right side, the side of the blessed. On the opposite side, demons, whose gargoyle masks and burning eyes revive the demons of Romanesque tympana (FIG. 6-23), torment the damned.

Michelangelo's terrifying vision of the fate awaiting sinners goes far beyond any previous rendition. Martyrs who suffered especially agonizing deaths crouch below the judge. One of them, Saint Bartholomew, who was skinned alive, holds the flaying knife and the skin, its face a grotesque self-portrait of Michelangelo. The figures are huge and violently twisted, with small heads and contorted features. Yet while this frightening fresco impresses on viewers Christ's

wrath on judgment day, it also holds out hope. A group of saved souls crowds around Christ, and on the far right appears a figure with a cross, most likely the Good Thief (crucified with Christ) or a saint martyred by crucifixion, such as Saint Andrew.

Architecture

During the High Renaissance, consistent with the humanist interest in classical antiquity, architects and patrons alike turned to the buildings of ancient Rome for inspiration. There, they discovered the perfect prototypes for the domed architecture that became the hallmark of the 16th century.

BRAMANTE The leading early Cinquecento proponent of this classical-revival style was DONATO D'ANGELO BRAMANTE (1444–1514). Born in Urbino and trained as a painter (perhaps by Piero della Francesca), Bramante went to Milan in 1481 and, as Leonardo did, stayed there until the French captured the city in 1499. In Milan, Bramante abandoned painting, and under the influence of Brunelleschi, Alberti, and perhaps Leonardo, developed the High Renaissance form of the central-plan church.

Contemporaries celebrated Bramante as the first to revive the classical style in architecture. Roman round temples inspired his "little temple," but Bramante combined the classical parts in new ways.

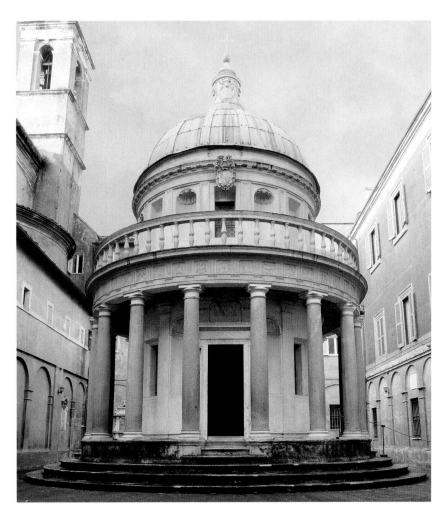

Bramante's first major project was the architectural gem in Rome known as the Tempietto (FIG. 9-12), so named because, to contemporaries, it had the look of a small ancient temple. In fact, the round temples of Roman Italy provided the direct models for the lower story of Bramante's "little temple." Standing inside the cloister of San Pietro in Montorio on the Janiculum hill overlooking the Vatican, the Tempietto marked the presumed location of Saint Peter's crucifixion. Bramante planned, though never built, a circular colonnaded courtyard to frame the "temple." His intent was to coordinate the Tempietto and its surrounding portico by aligning the columns of the two structures.

The Tempietto design is severely rational and features a stately circular *stylobate* (stepped temple platform) and austere Tuscan columns. Bramante achieved a wonderful balance and harmony in the relationship of the parts (dome, drum, and base) to one another and to the whole. Conceived as a tall domed cylinder projecting from the lower, wider cylinder of its colonnade, the "temple" is in some respects more a monument than a building. Bramante's sculptural eye is most evident in the rhythmic play of light and shadow around the columns and balustrade and across the deep-set rectangular windows, alternating with shallow shell-capped niches in the walls and drum. Although the Tempietto, superficially at least, may resemble a Greco-Roman *tholos* (circular shrine), and although antique models provided the inspiration for all its details, the combination of parts and details was new and original. (Classical tholoi, for instance, were never two-story structures and had neither a drum nor a balustrade.)

One of the main differences between the Early and High Renaissance styles of architecture is the former's emphasis on adorning flat wall surfaces versus the latter's sculptural handling of architectural masses. Bramante's Tempietto initiated the High Renaissance era in architecture. Andrea Palladio, a brilliant theorist as well as a major later Cinquecento architect (FIG. 9-16), included the Tempietto in his survey of ancient temples because Bramante was "the first to bring back to light the good and beautiful architecture that from antiquity to that time had been hidden."[5] Round in plan and elevated on a base that isolates it from its surroundings, the Tempietto conforms to Alberti's and Palladio's strictest demands for an ideal church.

NEW SAINT PETER'S One of the most important artistic projects that Julius II initiated was the replacement of the crumbling basilica of Old Saint Peter's (FIG. 4-3) with a grandiose new church that suited the ambitious pope's vision of the Renaissance papacy. Julius dreamed of gaining control over all Italy and making the Rome of

0   50   100 feet
0   15   30 meters   **D** = dome   **A** = apse   **P** = portico

N

9-13 MICHELANGELO BUONARROTI, plan for Saint Peter's, Vatican City, Rome, Italy, 1546.

Michelangelo's plan for the new Saint Peter's was radically different than that of the original basilica (FIG. 4-3). His central plan called for a domed Greek cross inscribed in a square and fronted by columns.

9-14 MICHELANGELO BUONARROTI, Saint Peter's (looking northeast), Vatican City, Rome, Italy, 1546–1564. Dome completed by GIACOMO DELLA PORTA, 1590.

The west end of Saint Peter's offers the best view of Michelangelo's intentions. The giant pilasters of his colossal order march around the undulating wall surfaces of the domed central-plan church.

on Saint Peter's became a long-term show of dedication, thankless and without pay. Among Michelangelo's difficulties was his struggle to preserve Bramante's central-plan design, which he praised. Michelangelo carried his obsession with human form over to architecture and reasoned that buildings should follow the form of the human body. This meant organizing their units symmetrically around a central axis, as the arms relate to the body or the eyes to the nose. "For it is an established fact," he once wrote, "that the members of architecture resemble the members of man. Whoever neither has been nor is a master at figures, and especially at anatomy, cannot really understand architecture."[6]

In his modification of Bramante's plan, Michelangelo replaced the complex interlocking crosses with a compact domed Greek cross inscribed in a square and fronted with a double-columned portico (FIG. 9-13). His treatment of the building's exterior further reveals his interest in creating a unified design. Because of later changes to the front of the church (FIG. 10-3), the west (apse) end (FIG. 9-14) offers the best view of Michelangelo's style and intention. His design incorporated the colossal order, the two-story pilasters first used by Alberti at Sant'Andrea (FIG. 8-36) in Mantua. The giant pilasters seem to march around the undulating wall surfaces, confining the movement without interrupting it. The architectural sculpturing here extends up from the ground through the attic stories and into the drum and the dome, unifying the whole building from base to summit.

The domed west end—as majestic as it is today and as influential as it has been on architecture throughout the centuries—is not quite as Michelangelo intended it. Originally, he had planned a dome with an *ogival* section, like the one Brunelleschi had designed for Florence's Duomo (FIG. 7-38). But in his final version, he decided on a hemispherical dome to temper the verticality of the design of the lower stories and to establish a balance between dynamic and static elements. However, when GIACOMO DELLA PORTA (ca. 1533–1602) executed the dome after Michelangelo's death, he restored the earlier high design, ignoring Michelangelo's later version. Giacomo probably believed that an ogival dome would provide greater stability and be easier to construct. The result is that the dome seems to rise from its base, rather than rest firmly on it—an effect Michelangelo might not have approved.

the popes the equal of (if not more splendid than) the Rome of the caesars (see page 251). Like its Constantinian predecessor, the new building was to serve as a *martyrium* to mark the apostle's grave, but Julius also hoped to install his own tomb (designed by Michelangelo) in it. The pope chose Bramante as the architect of the new Saint Peter's.

Bramante's ambitious design consisted of a *Greek cross* with arms of equal length, each terminating in an apse. A large dome would have covered the crossing, and smaller domes over subsidiary chapels would have covered the diagonal axes of the roughly square plan. Bramante's design also called for a boldly sculptural treatment of the walls and piers under the dome. The organization of the interior space was complex in the extreme: nine interlocking crosses, five of them supporting domes. The scale was titanic. The architect boasted that he would place the dome of the Pantheon (FIGS. 3-38, 3-39, and 3-40) over the Basilica Nova (FIG. 3-52).

During Bramante's lifetime, construction of the new Saint Peter's did not advance beyond the erection of the crossing piers and the lower choir walls. After his death, the work passed from one architect to another and, in 1546, to Michelangelo, whose work

PROBLEMS AND SOLUTIONS
Rethinking the Basilican Church

As a major participant in the Counter-Reformation, the Jesuit order needed a church appropriate to its new prominence. In 1568, with the financial backing of Cardinal Alessandro Farnese (1520–1589), the order turned to GIACOMO DA VIGNOLA (1507–1573), who designed Il Gesù's plan (FIG. 9-15, *right*), and Giacomo della Porta, who was responsible for the facade (FIG. 9-15, *left*)—and who later designed the dome of Saint Peter's (FIG. 9-14).

The plan of the Church of Jesus in Rome is a monumental expansion of Alberti's scheme for Sant'Andrea (FIG. 8-37) in Mantua. In Il Gesù, the nave takes over the main volume of space, making the structure a great hall with side chapels. The transept is no wider than the nave and chapels, and Vignola also eliminated the normal deep choir in front of the altar. Consequently, all worshipers have a clear view of the celebration of the Eucharist. The wide acceptance of Vignola's plan in the Catholic world, even in modern times, speaks to its suitability for the performance of Catholic rituals. The opening of the church building into a single great hall provides an almost theatrical setting for large promenades and processions (which combined social with priestly functions). Above all, the ample space could accommodate the great crowds that gathered to hear the eloquent preaching of the Jesuits.

The facade of Il Gesù (FIG. 9-15, *left*) was also not entirely original, but it too had an enormous influence on later church design. The union of the lower and upper stories, achieved by scroll buttresses, harks back to another Alberti design, the Florentine church of Santa Maria Novella (not illustrated). Its classical pediment is also familiar in Alberti's work (FIG. 8-36). The paired pilasters appear in Michelangelo's design for Saint Peter's (FIG. 9-14). Della Porta skillfully synthesized these existing motifs and unified the two stories. The horizontal march of the pilasters and columns builds to a dramatic climax at the central bay, and the bays of the facade snugly fit the nave-chapel system behind them. Many Roman church facades of the 17th century are architectural variations on della Porta's design. Chronologically and stylistically, Il Gesù belongs to the Late Renaissance, but its enormous influence on later basilican churches marks it as one of the most significant monuments for the development of Italian Baroque religious architecture.

N = naive
D = dome
C = chapel

9-15 Il Gesù, Rome, Italy. *Left:* GIACOMO DELLA PORTA, west facade, begun 1568. *Right:* GIACOMO DA VIGNOLA, plan, 1568.

In this Jesuit church's innovative facade, the march of pilasters and columns builds to a climax at the central bay. The wide nave with side chapels instead of aisles won wide acceptance in the Catholic world.

IL GESÙ The activity of the Society of Jesus, known as the Jesuits, was an important component of the Counter-Reformation. Ignatius of Loyola (1491–1556), a Spanish nobleman who dedicated his life to the service of God, founded the Jesuits in 1534 with preaching and missionary work as the key components of their spiritual assignment. In 1540, Paul III formally recognized the Jesuits as a religious order. They soon became the papacy's invaluable allies in the Vatican's quest to reassert the supremacy of the Catholic Church. Particularly successful in the field of education, the Jesuit order established numerous schools. In addition, its members were effective missionaries and carried the message of Catholicism to the Americas, Asia, and Africa.

The Jesuits also made their mark in the history of architecture with the construction of Il Gesù, or Church of Jesus (FIG. 9-15), in Rome. The mother church of the Jesuit order was the most important architectural project of the later 16th century and had an enormous influence on church design in the succeeding Baroque era (see "Rethinking the Basilican Church," page 264).

ANDREA PALLADIO The classical-revival style of High Renaissance architecture in Rome spread far and wide. One of its most accomplished practitioners was ANDREA PALLADIO (1508–1580), the chief architect of the Venetian Republic from 1570 until his death. In order to study the ancient buildings firsthand, Palladio made several trips to Rome. In 1556, he illustrated Daniel Barbaro's edition of Vitruvius's *De architectura* and later wrote his own treatise on architecture, *I quattro libri dell'architettura* (*The Four Books of Architecture*). Originally published in 1570, Palladio's treatise had a wide-ranging influence on succeeding generations of architects throughout Europe, most significantly in England and in colonial America.

Palladio gained his significant reputation from his many designs for *villas,* built on the Venetian mainland, of which 19 still stand. The same spirit that prompted the ancient Romans to build homes in the countryside motivated a similar villa-building boom in 16th-century Venice, which, with its very limited space, was highly congested.

But a longing for a rural setting was not the only motive. Declining fortunes prompted the Venetians to develop their mainland possessions with new land investment and reclamation projects. Citizens who could afford to do so set themselves up as aristocratic farmers and developed swamps into productive agricultural land. The villas were thus aristocratic farms (like the much later American plantations, which frequently emulated Palladio's architectural style). Palladio generally arranged the outbuildings in long, low wings branching out from the main building and enclosing a large rectangular court area.

Palladio's most famous villa, Villa Rotonda (FIG. 9-16), near Vicenza, is exceptional because the architect did not build it for an aspiring gentleman farmer but for a retired monsignor in the papal court in Rome. Paolo Almerico (1514–1589) wanted a villa for social events. Palladio planned and designed Villa Rotonda, located on a hilltop, as a kind of *belvedere* (literally, "beautiful view"; in architecture, a structure with a view of the countryside or the sea), without the usual wings of secondary buildings. It has a central plan featuring four identical facades with projecting porches, each of which resembles a Roman Ionic temple and serves as a platform for enjoying a different view of the surrounding landscape. In placing a traditional temple porch in front of a dome-covered interior, Palladio doubtless had the Pantheon (FIG. 3-38) in his mind as a model.

9-16 ANDREA PALLADIO, Villa Rotonda (looking southwest), near Vicenza, Italy, ca. 1550–1570.

Palladio's Villa Rotonda has four identical facades, each one resembling a Roman temple with a columnar porch. In the center is a great dome-covered rotunda modeled on the Pantheon (FIG. 3-38).

Venetian Painting

In addition to Palladio, Cinquecento Venice boasted some of the most renowned painters of the era, who developed a distinctive Venetian Renaissance style. The Venetians' instrument was color, that of the Florentines and Romans sculpturesque form. Scholars often distill the contrast between these two approaches down to *colorito* (colored or painted) versus *disegno* (drawing and design). Whereas most central Italian artists emphasized careful design preparation based on preliminary drawing, Venetian artists focused on color and the process of paint application.

GIORGIONE Giorgio Vasari (see "Vasari's Lives" ⤢), who held the artists of his native Florence in greater esteem than Venice's, disapprovingly drew attention to the different working methods of the Venetians and attributed them largely to the short-lived GIORGIONE DA CASTELFRANCO (ca. 1477–1510):

> Giorgione of Castelfranco . . . made use of live and natural objects and copied them as best he knew how with colors, tinting them with the crude and soft colors that Nature displays, without making preliminary drawings since he was firmly convinced that painting alone with its colors, and without any other preliminary study of designs on paper, was the truest and best method of working.[7]

Art historians frequently describe Venetian painting in general, and the work of Giorgione in particular, as "poetic"—a characterization particularly appropriate given the development of *poesia,* or painting meant to operate in a manner similar to poetry. Both classical and Renaissance poetry inspired Venetian artists, and their paintings focused on the lyrical and sensual. Thus, in many Venetian artworks, discerning concrete narratives or subjects is virtually impossible.

1 ft.

9-17 GIORGIONE DA CASTELFRANCO, *The Tempest,* ca. 1509–1510. Oil on canvas, 2' 8¼" × 2' 4¾". Galleria dell'Accademia, Venice.

The subject of Giorgione's painting featuring a nude woman in a lush landscape beneath a stormy sky is uncertain, contributing, perhaps intentionally, to the painting's intriguing air of mystery.

9-18 TITIAN, *Pastoral Symphony,* ca. 1508–1511. Oil on canvas, 3' 7¼" × 4' 6¼". Musée du Louvre, Paris.

Venetian art conjures poetry. In this painting, Titian so eloquently evoked the pastoral mood that the inability to decipher the picture's meaning is not distressing. The mood and rich color are enough.

1 ft.

That is certainly the case with Giorgione's greatest work, *The Tempest* (FIG. 9-17), a painting that continues to defy interpretation. A lush landscape fills most of Giorgione's composition, but stormy skies and lightning in the middle background threaten the tranquility of the pastoral setting. Pushed off to both sides are the few human figures depicted—a young woman nursing a baby in the right foreground and, on the left, a man with a staff. Much scholarly debate has centered on the painting's subject, fueled by X-rays of the canvas, which revealed that Giorgione altered many of the details as work progressed. Most notably, a seated nude woman originally occupied the position where Giorgione subsequently placed the standing man, whose elegant garb is out of place in this rustic setting. The changes that the painter made have led many art historians to believe that Giorgione did not intend the painting to have a definitive narrative, which is appropriate for a Venetian poetic rendering. Other scholars have suggested various mythological and biblical narratives. The uncertainty about the subject contributes to the painting's intriguing air.

TITIAN Giorgione's masterful handling of light and color and his interest in landscape, poetry, and music—Vasari reported that he was an accomplished lutenist and singer—influenced his younger contemporary Tiziano Vecelli, called TITIAN (ca. 1490–1576) in English. Indeed, a masterpiece long attributed to Giorgione—*Pastoral Symphony* (FIG. 9-18)—is now widely believed to be an early work of Titian. Out of dense shadow emerge the soft forms of figures and landscape. Titian, a supreme colorist and master of the oil medium, cast a mood of tranquil reverie and dreaminess over the entire scene, evoking the landscape of a lost but never forgotten paradise. As in Giorgione's *Tempest,* the theme is as enigmatic as the lighting. Two nude women are in the foreground, accompanied by two clothed young men—the lutenist wearing elegant clothes, the other dressed like a shepherd. The four figures occupy a bountiful landscape. In the middle ground is a shepherd and his sheep. In the distance, a villa crowns a hill.

Titian so eloquently evoked the pastoral mood that the viewer does not find the uncertainty about the picture's precise meaning distressing. The mood is enough. The musician symbolizes the poet. The pipes and lute symbolize his poetry. The two women may be thought of as the young men's invisible inspiration, their muses. One turns to lift water from the sacred well of poetic inspiration. Smoky shadow softly models the voluptuous bodies of the women. The fullness of their figures became standard in Venetian art and contributes to their effect as poetic personifications of nature's abundance.

ASSUMPTION OF THE VIRGIN In 1516, Titian became the official painter of the Republic of Venice. Shortly thereafter, he received the commission to paint *Assumption of the Virgin* (FIG. 9-19) for the main altar of Santa Maria Gloriosa dei Frari. The gigantic altarpiece (nearly 23 feet tall) depicts the ascent of the Virgin to Heaven on a great white cloud borne aloft by putti. Above, golden clouds, so luminous that they seem to glow and radiate light into the church, envelop the Virgin. God the Father appears above, awaiting Mary with open arms. Below, apostles gesticulate wildly as they witness the glorious event. Through vibrant color, Titian infused the image with an intensity that amplifies the drama.

9-19 TITIAN, *Assumption of the Virgin*, 1515–1518. Oil on wood, 22' 7½" × 11' 10". Santa Maria Gloriosa dei Frari, Venice.

Titian won renown for his skill in conveying light through color. In this dramatic depiction of the Virgin Mary's ascent to Heaven, the golden clouds seem to glow and radiate light into the church.

9-20 TITIAN, *Venus of Urbino,* 1536–1538. Oil on canvas, 3' 11" × 5' 5". Galleria degli Uffizi, Florence.

Titian established oil-based pigment on canvas as the preferred painting medium in Western art. Here, he also set the standard for representations of the reclining female nude, whether divine or mortal.

1 ft.

VENUS OF URBINO In 1538, at the height of his powers, Titian painted the so-called *Venus of Urbino* (FIG. 9-20) for Guidobaldo II, who became the duke of Urbino (r. 1539–1574) the following year. The title (given to the painting later) elevates to the status of classical mythology what is probably a representation of a sensual Italian woman in her bedchamber. Whether the subject is divine or mortal, Titian based his version on an earlier (and pioneering) painting of Venus (not illustrated) by Giorgione. Here, Titian established the compositional elements and the standard for paintings of the reclining female nude, regardless of the many ensuing variations. This "Venus" reclines on the gentle slope of her luxurious pillowed couch. Her softly rounded body contrasts with the sharp vertical edge of the curtain behind her, which serves to direct the viewer's attention to her left hand and pelvis as well as to divide the foreground from the background. At the woman's feet is a slumbering lapdog—where Cupid would be if this were Venus. In the right background, two servants bend over a chest, apparently searching for garments to clothe their nude mistress. Beyond them, a window opens onto a landscape. Titian masterfully constructed the view backward into the room and the division of the space into progressively smaller units.

As in other Venetian paintings, color plays a prominent role in *Venus of Urbino.* The red tones of the matron's skirt and the muted reds of the tapestries against the neutral whites of the matron's sleeves and of the kneeling girl's gown echo the deep Venetian reds set off against the pale neutral whites of the linen and the warm ivory gold of the flesh. The viewer must study the picture carefully to realize the subtlety of color planning. For instance, the two deep reds (in the foreground cushions and in the background skirt) play a critical role in the composition as a gauge of distance and as indicators of an implied diagonal opposed to the real one of the reclining figure. Here, Titian used color not simply to record surface appearance but also to organize his placement of forms.

Mannerism

Mannerism emerged in the 1520s in Italy as a distinctive artistic style in reaction to the High Renaissance style of Florence, Rome, and Venice. The term derives from the Italian word *maniera,* meaning "style" or "manner." Art historians usually define *style* as a characteristic or representative mode, especially of an artist or period (see page 3), but the term can also refer to an absolute quality of fashion (someone has "style"). Mannerism's style (or representative mode) is characterized by style (being stylish, cultured, elegant).

Among the features most closely associated with Mannerism is artifice. Of course, all art involves artifice, in the sense that art is not "natural"—it is something fashioned by human hands. But many artists, including High Renaissance painters such as Leonardo and Raphael, chose to conceal that artifice by using devices such as perspective and shading to make their representations of the world look natural. In contrast, Mannerist painters consciously revealed the constructed nature of their art. In other words, Renaissance artists generally strove to create art that appeared natural, whereas Mannerist artists were less inclined to disguise the contrived nature of art production. This is why artifice is a central feature of discussions about Mannerism, and why Mannerist works can seem, appropriately, "mannered." The conscious display of artifice in Mannerism often reveals itself in imbalanced compositions and unusual complexities, both visual and conceptual. Ambiguous space, departures from expected conventions, and unique presentations of traditional themes also surface frequently in Mannerist art.

PONTORMO *Entombment of Christ* (FIG. 9-21) by the Florentine painter JACOPO DA PONTORMO (1494–1557) exhibits almost all the stylistic features characteristic of Mannerism's early phase. Painters had frequently depicted this subject, and Pontormo exploited the familiarity that 16th-century viewers would have had by playing off their expectations. For example, he omitted from the painting both the cross and Christ's tomb, and instead of presenting the action as taking place across the perpendicular picture plane, as artists such as Rogier van der Weyden did (FIG. 8-7), Pontormo rotated the conventional figural groups along a vertical axis. Several of the figures seem to float in the air. Those that touch the ground do so on tiptoes, enhancing the sense of weightlessness. Unlike High Renaissance artists, who concentrated their masses in the center of the painting, Pontormo left a void. This emptiness accentuates the grouping of hands filling that hole, calling attention to the void—symbolic of loss and grief. The artist enhanced the painting's ambiguity with the curiously anxious glances that the figures cast in all directions. (The bearded young man at the upper right is probably a self-portrait.) Many of the figures have elastically elongated limbs and undersized heads, and move unnaturally. The contrasting colors, primarily light blues and pinks, add to the dynamism and complexity of the work.

The painting represents a pronounced departure from the balanced, harmoniously structured compositions of the High Renaissance.

PARMIGIANINO The best-known work of Girolamo Francesco Maria Mazzola, known as PARMIGIANINO (1503–1540), is *Madonna with the Long Neck* (FIG. 9-22), which exemplifies the elegant stylishness that was a principal aim of Mannerism. In Parmigianino's hands, this traditional, usually sedate subject became a picture of exquisite grace and precious sweetness. The Madonna's small oval head, her long and slender neck, the otherworldly attenuation and delicacy of her hand, and the sinuous, swaying elongation of her frame—all are marks of the sophisticated courtly taste of Mannerist artists and patrons alike. Parmigianino amplified this elegance by expanding the Madonna's form as viewed from head to toe. On the left stands a bevy of angelic creatures, exuding emotions as soft and smooth as their limbs. On the right, the artist included a line

9-21 JACOPO DA PONTORMO, *Entombment of Christ,* Capponi chapel, Santa Felicità, Florence, Italy, 1525–1528. Oil on wood, 10' 3" × 6' 4".

Mannerist paintings such as this one represent a departure from the compositions of the earlier Renaissance. Instead of concentrating masses in the center of the painting, Pontormo left a void.

9-22 PARMIGIANINO, *Madonna with the Long Neck,* from the Baiardi chapel, Santa Maria dei Servi, Parma, Italy, 1534–1540. Oil on wood, 7' 1" × 4' 4". Galleria degli Uffizi, Florence.

Parmigianino's Madonna displays the stylish elegance that was a principal aim of Mannerism. Mary has a small oval head, a long slender neck, attenuated hands, and a sinuous body.

of columns without capitals and a mysterious figure with a scroll, whose distance from the foreground is immeasurable and ambiguous—the antithesis of rational Renaissance perspective diminution of size with distance.

Although the elegance and beauty of the painting are due in large part to the Madonna's attenuated neck and arms, that exaggeration is not solely decorative in purpose. *Madonna with the Long Neck* takes its subject from a simile in medieval hymns comparing the Virgin's neck with a great ivory tower or column, such as the one Parmigianino inserted to the right of the Madonna.

BRONZINO Pontormo's pupil Agnolo di Cosimo, called BRONZINO (1503–1572), painted *Venus, Cupid, Folly, and Time* (FIG. 9-23) for the first grand duke of Tuscany, Cosimo I de' Medici (r. 1537–1534), as a gift for King Francis I of France (see page 277). In this painting, Bronzino demonstrated the Mannerists' fondness for learned allegories that often had erotic undertones, a shift from the simple and monumental statements and forms of the High Renaissance. Bronzino depicted Cupid—here not an infant but an adolescent who has reached puberty—fondling his mother, Venus, while Folly prepares to shower them with rose petals. Time, who appears in the upper right corner, draws back the curtain to reveal the playful incest in progress. Other figures in the painting represent other human qualities and emotions, including Envy. The masks, a favorite device of the Mannerists, symbolize deceit. The picture seems to suggest that love—accompanied by envy and plagued by inconstancy—is foolish and that lovers will discover its folly in time. But, as in many Mannerist paintings, the meaning here is ambiguous, and interpretations of the painting vary. Compositionally, Bronzino placed the figures around the front plane, and they almost entirely block the space. The contours are strong and sculptural, the surfaces of enamel smoothness. Of special interest are the heads, hands, and feet, for the Mannerists considered the extremities to be carriers of grace, and the clever depiction of them evidence of artistic skill.

TINTORETTO Jacopo Robusti, known as TINTORETTO (1518–1594), claimed to be a student of Titian and aspired to combine Titian's color with Michelangelo's drawing, but he also adopted many Mannerist pictorial devices, which he employed to produce works imbued with dramatic power, depth of spiritual vision, and glowing Venetian color schemes. Toward the end of Tintoretto's life, his art became spiritual, even visionary, as solid forms dissolved into swirling clouds of dark shot through with fitful light. In *Last Supper* (FIG. 9-24), the figures—many with shimmering halos—appear in a dark interior illuminated by a single light in the upper left of the image. The huge canvas features

1 ft.

9-23 BRONZINO, *Venus, Cupid, Folly, and Time*, ca. 1546. Oil on wood, 5' 1" × 4' 8¼". National Gallery, London.

In this painting of Cupid fondling his mother, Venus, Bronzino demonstrated a fondness for learned allegories with erotic undertones. As in many Mannerist paintings, the meaning is ambiguous.

a typically Mannerist imbalanced composition and visual complexity. In terms of design, the contrast with Leonardo's *Last Supper* (FIG. 9-3) is both extreme and instructive. Leonardo's composition, balanced and symmetrical, parallels the picture plane in a

1 ft.

9-24 TINTORETTO, *Last Supper*, 1594. Oil on canvas, 12' × 18' 8". San Giorgio Maggiore, Venice.

Tintoretto adopted many Mannerist pictorial devices to produce oil paintings imbued with emotional power, depth of spiritual vision, glowing Venetian color schemes, and dramatic lighting.

geometrically organized and closed space. The figure of Jesus is the tranquil center of the drama and the perspective focus. In Tintoretto's painting, Jesus is above and beyond the converging perspective lines racing diagonally away from the picture surface, creating disturbing effects of limitless depth and motion. The viewer locates Tintoretto's Jesus via the light flaring, beaconlike, out of darkness. The contrast of the two pictures reflects the direction Renaissance painting took in the 16th century, as it moved away from architectonic clarity of space and neutral lighting toward the dynamic perspectives and dramatic chiaroscuro of the coming Baroque.

GIAMBOLOGNA Mannerism extended beyond painting. Artists translated its principles into sculpture and architecture as well. The lure of Italy drew a brilliant young Flemish sculptor, Jean de Boulogne, to Florence, where he practiced his art under the equivalent Italian name of Giovanni da Bologna or, in its more common contracted form, GIAMBOLOGNA (1529–1608). His *Abduction of the Sabine Women* (FIG. 9-25) exemplifies Mannerist principles of figure composition in sculpture. Drawn from the legendary history of Rome, the group received its present title—relating how the early Romans abducted wives for themselves from the neighboring Sabines—only after its exhibition. In fact, the sculptor did not intend to depict any particular subject. His goal was to achieve a dynamic spiral figural composition involving an old man, a young man, and a woman, all nude in the tradition of ancient statues portraying mythological figures. *Abduction of the Sabine Women* includes references to *Laocoön* (FIG. 2-59) in the crouching old man and in the woman's up-flung arm. The three bodies interlock on a vertical axis, creating an ascending spiral movement.

To appreciate the sculpture fully, the viewer must walk around it because the work changes radically according to the vantage point. One factor contributing to the shifting imagery is the prominence of open spaces passing through the masses (for example, the space between an arm and a body), which have as great an effect as the solids. This sculpture was the first large-scale group since classical antiquity designed to be seen from multiple viewpoints, although the figures do not break out of the spiral vortex but remain as if contained within a cylinder.

GIULIO ROMANO Mannerist architects used classical architectural elements in a highly personal and unorthodox manner, rejecting the balance, order, and stability that were the hallmarks of the High Renaissance style, and aiming instead to reveal the contrived nature

9-25
GIAMBOLOGNA, *Abduction of the Sabine Women,* Loggia dei Lanzi, Piazza della Signoria, Florence, Italy, 1579–1583. Marble, 13' 5½" high.

This sculpture was the first large-scale group since classical antiquity designed to be seen from multiple viewpoints. The three bodies interlock to create a vertical spiral movement.

of architectural design. Applying that approach was the goal of GIULIO ROMANO (ca. 1499–1546) when he designed the Palazzo del Tè (FIG. 9-26) in Mantua for Duke Federigo Gonzaga (r. 1530–1540) and also provided frescoes for the building's interior (FIG. 9-26A ⟋). In the facades facing the palace's courtyard, the divergences from architectural convention are pronounced. Indeed, the Palazzo del Tè

9-26 GIULIO ROMANO, courtyard of the Palazzo del Tè (looking southeast), Mantua, Italy, 1525–1535.

The Mannerist divergences from architectural convention—for example, the slipping triglyphs—are so pronounced in the Palazzo del Tè that they constitute a parody of Bramante's classical style.

constitutes an enormous parody of Bramante's classical style, a veritable Mannerist manifesto announcing the artifice of architectural design. In a building laden with structural surprises and contradictions, the courtyard is the most unconventional of all. The *keystones* (central *voussoirs*), for example, either have not fully settled or seem to be slipping from the arches—and, even more eccentrically, Giulio placed voussoirs in the pediments over the rectangular niches, where no arches exist. The massive Tuscan columns flanking these niches carry incongruously narrow *architraves*. That these architraves break midway between the columns stresses their apparent structural insufficiency, and they seem unable to support the weight of the *triglyphs* of the Doric frieze above (see "Doric and Ionic Temples," page 57, and FIG. 2-20, *left*), which threaten to crash down on the head of anyone foolish enough to stand below them. To be sure, only a highly sophisticated observer can appreciate Giulio's witticism. Recognizing such quite subtle departures from the norm presupposes a thorough familiarity with the established rules of classical architecture. That the duke delighted in Giulio's mannered architectural inventiveness speaks to his cultivated taste.

HOLY ROMAN EMPIRE

The extraordinary flowering of art and architecture in Cinquecento Italy unfolded against the tumultuous backdrop of the split in Christendom between Catholicism and Protestantism. Prominent theologians, most notably Martin Luther (1483–1546) and John Calvin (1509–1564) in the Holy Roman Empire, directly challenged papal authority. Their major concerns were the sale of *indulgences* (pardons for sins, reducing the time a soul spent in Purgatory—equated with buying one's way into Heaven) and about *nepotism* (the appointment of relatives to important positions). Particularly damaging was the perception that the Roman popes concerned themselves more with temporal power and material wealth than with the salvation of the faithful. The fact that many 15th-century popes and cardinals came from wealthy families, such as the Medici, intensified this perception.

PROTESTANTISM Central to both Lutheranism and Calvinism, the two major Protestant sects, was a belief in personal faith rather than adherence to decreed Church practices and doctrines. Because Protestants believed that the only true religious relationship was the personal relationship between individuals and God, they were, in essence, eliminating the need for Church intercession, which is central to Catholicism.

On October 31, 1517, in Wittenberg, Luther posted for discussion his *Ninety-five Theses,* in which he enumerated his objections to Church practices. Luther's goal was significant reform and clarification of major spiritual issues, but his ideas ultimately led to a hundred years of civil war between Protestants and Catholics. According to Luther, the Catholic Church's extensive structure needed casting out, for it had no basis in the Bible, which alone could serve as the foundation for Christianity. Luther called the pope the Antichrist (for which Pope Leo X excommunicated him in 1520), and described the Church as the "whore of Babylon." He denounced ordained priests and also rejected most of Catholicism's sacraments other than baptism and communion, decrying them as obstacles to salvation (see "Catholic versus Protestant Views of Salvation" and FIG. 9-26B ⬦). Luther maintained that for Christianity to be restored to its original purity, the Catholic Church needed cleansing of all the doctrinal impurities that had collected through the ages. Only the Bible was the word of God—the sole source of all religious truth. The Church's councils, laws, and rituals carried no weight. Luther facilitated the lay public's access to biblical truths by producing the first translation of the Bible in a vernacular language (German).

ART AND THE REFORMATION In addition to doctrinal differences, Catholics and Protestants took divergent stances on the role of visual imagery in religion. Catholics embraced images of holy figures as an aid to communicating with God (see "The Council of Trent" ⬦). In contrast, Protestants believed that representations of Christ, the Virgin, and saints could lead to idolatry. Furthermore, images distracted viewers from focusing on the real reason for their presence in church—to pray. Because of this belief, Protestant churches were relatively bare. The Protestant concern over the role of religious imagery escalated at times to outright *iconoclasm*—the destruction of religious artworks. Violent waves of iconoclastic fervor swept Basel, Zurich, Strasbourg, and Wittenberg in the 1520s. In an episode known as the Great Iconoclasm, bands of Calvinists visited Catholic churches in the Netherlands in 1566, shattering stained-glass windows, smashing statues, and destroying paintings and other artworks that they perceived as idolatrous. These strong reactions dramatically demonstrate the power of art and underscore the important role that art plays in society.

MATTHIAS GRÜNEWALD At the opening of the 16th century, however, Luther had not yet posted his *Ninety-five Theses,* and the Catholic Church was still an important art patron in the Holy Roman Empire. Around 1510, Matthias Neithardt, known conventionally as MATTHIAS GRÜNEWALD (ca. 1480–1528), began work on the *Isenheim Altarpiece* (FIG. 9-27), a complex and fascinating polyptych reflecting Catholic beliefs and incorporating several references to Catholic doctrines, such as the lamb (symbol of the son of God), whose wound spurts blood into a chalice in the crucifixion scene. Created for the monastic hospital order of Saint Anthony of Isenheim, the altarpiece takes the form of a carved wood shrine (not illustrated) by Nikolaus Hagenauer (active 1493–1538) featuring large painted and gilded statues of Saints Anthony Abbot, Augustine, and Jerome. To Hagenauer's centerpiece, Grünewald added two pairs of painted moveable wings that open at the center. Hinged at the sides, one pair stands directly behind the other. Grünewald's exterior panels (visible when the altarpiece is closed, as in FIG. 9-27) present four subjects: *Crucifixion* in the center, *Saint Sebastian* on the left, *Saint Anthony Abbot* on the right, and *Lamentation* in the predella. When these exterior wings are open, four additional scenes—*Annunciation, Angelic Concert, Madonna and Child,* and *Resurrection*—appear. Opening this second pair of wings exposes Hagenauer's interior shrine, flanked by Grünewald's *Meeting of Saints Anthony and Paul* and *Temptation of Saint Anthony.*

The placement of this altarpiece in the choir of a church adjacent to the monastery's hospital dictated much of the imagery. Saints associated with the plague and other diseases and with miraculous cures, such as Saints Anthony and Sebastian, appear prominently in the *Isenheim Altarpiece.* Grünewald's panels specifically address the themes of dire illness and miraculous healing and accordingly emphasize the suffering of the order's patron saint, Anthony Abbot. The painted images served as warnings, encouraging increased devotion from monks and hospital patients. They also functioned therapeutically by offering some hope to the afflicted. Indeed, Saint

9-27 MATTHIAS GRÜNEWALD, *Isenheim Altarpiece* (closed), from the chapel of the Hospital of Saint Anthony, Isenheim, Germany, ca. 1510–1515. Oil on wood, center panel 9' 9½" × 10' 9", each wing 8' 2½" × 3' ½", predella 2' 5½" × 11' 2". Musée d'Unterlinden, Colmar.

Befitting its setting in a monastic hospital, Matthias Grünewald's *Isenheim Altarpiece* includes painted panels depicting suffering and disease but also miraculous healing, hope, and salvation.

Anthony's legend emphasized his dual role as vengeful dispenser of justice (by inflicting disease) and benevolent healer.

In the *Temptation of Saint Anthony* panel, Grünewald painted a grotesque image of a man whose oozing boils, withered arm, and distended stomach all suggest a horrible disease. Medical experts have connected these symptoms with ergotism (a disease caused by ergot, a fungus that grows especially on rye). Doctors did not discover the cause of ergotism until about 1600. People lived in fear of its recognizable symptoms (convulsions and gangrene) and called the illness "Saint Anthony's Fire." Ergotism was one of the major diseases treated at the Isenheim hospital. Indeed, Grünewald depicted Christ's skin covered with sores. Furthermore, ergotism often compelled amputation. The two moveable halves of the altarpiece's predella, if slid apart, make it appear as if Christ's legs have been amputated. The same observation applies to the two main exterior panels. Due to the off-center placement of the cross, opening the left panel "severs" one arm from the crucified figure.

Thus Grünewald carefully selected and presented his altarpiece's iconography to be particularly meaningful for patients at this hospital. In the interior shrine, the artist balanced the horrors of the disease and the punishments that awaited those who did not repent with scenes such as *Meeting of Saints Anthony and Paul*, depicting the two saints, healthy and aged, conversing peacefully. Even the exterior panels (the closed altarpiece; FIG. 9-27) convey these same concerns. *Crucifixion* emphasizes Christ's pain and suffering, but the knowledge that this act redeemed humanity tempers the misery. In addition, Saint Anthony appears in the right wing as a devout follower of Christ who, like Christ, endured intense suffering for his faith. Saint Anthony's appearance on the exterior thus reinforces the themes that Grünewald intertwined throughout this entire work—themes of pain, illness, and death, as well as those of hope, comfort, and salvation. Grünewald also brilliantly used color to enhance the impact of the imagery. He intensified the contrast of horror and hope by playing subtle tones and soft harmonies against shocking dissonances of color.

ALBRECHT DÜRER The dominant artist of the early 16th century in the Holy Roman Empire was ALBRECHT DÜRER (1471–1528) of Nuremberg. Dürer was the first artist outside Italy to become an international celebrity. He traveled extensively, visiting and studying in Colmar, Basel, Strasbourg, Venice, Antwerp, and Brussels, among other locales, and became personally acquainted with many of the leading humanists and artists of his time. Dürer achieved his lofty reputation primarily on the quality of his engravings and woodcuts. Indeed, few artists have ever rivaled the body of graphic work he produced. Dürer displayed exceptional business acumen in the marketing of his prints and became a wealthy man from the sale of his work. The lawsuit he brought in 1506 against an Italian artist for copying his prints is thought to be the first in history over intellectual property copyright.

Fascinated with the classical ideas of the Italian Renaissance, Dürer was among the first Northern Renaissance artists to travel to Italy expressly to study Italian art and its underlying theories at their source. After his first journey in 1494–1495 (the second was in 1505–1506), he incorporated many Italian Renaissance developments into his art. Art historians have acclaimed Dürer as the first artist north of the Alps to understand fully the basic aims of the Renaissance in Italy. Like Leonardo da Vinci, he wrote theoretical treatises on a variety of subjects, such as perspective, fortification, and the ideal in human proportions.

FALL OF MAN One of Dürer's early masterpieces, *Fall of Man* (*Adam and Eve*; FIG. 9-28), represents the first distillation of his studies of the Vitruvian theory of human proportions, a theory based on arithmetic ratios. Clearly outlined against the dark background of a northern European forest, the two idealized figures of Adam and Eve stand in poses derived from specific classical statues of Apollo and Venus. Preceded by numerous geometric drawings in which the artist attempted to systematize sets of ideal human proportions in balanced contrapposto poses, the final engraving presents Dürer's concept of the "perfect" male and female

figures. Yet he tempered this idealization with naturalism. The gnarled bark of the trees and the feathery leaves authenticate the scene, as do the various creatures skulking underfoot. The animals populating the print are symbolic. The choleric cat, the melancholic elk, the sanguine rabbit, and the phlegmatic ox represent humanity's temperaments based on the "four humors," fluids that were the basis of theories of the body's function developed by the ancient Greek physician Hippocrates and practiced in medieval physiology. The tension between the cat and the mouse in the foreground symbolizes the relation between Adam and Eve at the crucial moment before they commit original sin.

MELENCOLIA I Dürer took up the theme of the four humors, specifically melancholy, in one of his most famous engravings, *Melencolia I* (FIG. 9-29), which many scholars regard as a kind of self-portrait of Dürer's artistic psyche as well as a masterful example of the artist's ability to produce a wide range of tonal values and textures. (The renowned humanist Erasmus of Rotterdam [1466–1536] praised Dürer as "the Apelles [the most renowned ancient Greek painter] of black lines."[8]

9-28 ALBRECHT DÜRER, *Fall of Man* (*Adam and Eve*), 1504. Engraving, $9\frac{7}{8}"\times 7\frac{5}{8}"$. Museum of Fine Arts, Boston (centennial gift of Landon T. Clay).

Dürer was the first Northern Renaissance artist to achieve international celebrity. *Fall of Man,* with two figures based on ancient statues, reflects his studies of the Vitruvian theory of human proportions.

1 in.

9-29 ALBRECHT DÜRER, *Melencolia I,* 1514. Engraving, $9\frac{3}{8}" \times 7\frac{1}{2}"$. Victoria & Albert Museum, London.

In this "self-portrait" of his artistic personality, Dürer represented Melancholy as a brooding winged woman surrounded by artists' and builders' tools. A melancholic artist cannot use them, however.

The Italian humanist Marsilio Ficino (1433–1499) had written an influential treatise (*De vita triplici,* 1482–1489) in which he asserted that artists were distinct from the population at large because they were born under the sign of the planet Saturn, named for the ancient Roman god. They shared that deity's melancholic temperament because they had an excess of black bile, one of the four body humors, in their systems. Artists therefore were "saturnine"—eccentric and capable of both inspired artistic frenzy and melancholic depression. Raphael had depicted Michelangelo in the guise of the brooding Heraclitus in his *School of Athens* (FIG. 9-6), and Dürer used a similarly posed female figure for his winged personification of Melancholy in *Melencolia I.*

In 1510, in *De occulta philosophia,* Heinrich Cornelius Agrippa of Nettesheim (1486–1535) identified three levels of melancholy. The first was artistic melancholy, which explains the Roman numeral on the banner carried by the bat—a creature of the dark—in Dürer's engraving. Above the brooding figure of Melancholy is an hourglass with the sands of time running out. All around her are the tools of the artist and builder (compare FIG. 7-19)—compass, hammer, nails, and saw among them. However, those tools are useless to the frustrated artist while suffering from melancholy. Melancholy's face is obscured by shadow, underscoring her state of mind. But Dürer also included a burst of light on the far horizon behind the bat, an

optimistic note suggesting that artists can overcome their depression and produce works of genius—such as this engraving.

FOUR APOSTLES Dürer's impressive technical facility with different media extended also to painting. *Four Apostles* (FIG. 9-30) is a two-panel oil painting he produced without commission and presented to the city fathers of Nuremberg in 1526 to be hung in the city hall. Saints John and Peter appear on the left panel, Mark and Paul on the right. In addition to showcasing Dürer's mastery of the oil technique, his brilliant use of color and light and shade, and his ability to imbue the four saints with individual personalities and portraitlike features, *Four Apostles* documents the artist's support for Martin Luther by his positioning of the figures. Dürer relegated Saint Peter (as representative of the pope in Rome) to a secondary role by placing him behind John the Evangelist. John assumed particular prominence for Luther because of the evangelist's focus on Jesus as a person in his Gospel. In addition, Peter and John both read from the Bible, the single authoritative source of religious truth, according to Luther. At the bottom of the panels, Dürer included quotations from the four apostles' books, using Luther's German translation of the New Testament. The excerpts

9-30 ALBRECHT DÜRER, *Four Apostles,* from the city hall, Nuremberg, Germany, 1526. Oil on wood, each panel 7' 1" × 2' 6". Alte Pinakothek, Munich.

Dürer's support for Lutheranism surfaces in these portraitlike depictions of four saints on two painted panels. Peter, representative of the pope in Rome, plays a secondary role behind John the Evangelist.

9-31 HANS HOLBEIN THE YOUNGER, *The French Ambassadors*, 1533. Oil and tempera on wood, 6' 8" × 6' 9½". National Gallery, London.

In this double portrait, Holbein depicted two humanists with a collection of objects reflective of their worldliness and learning, but he also included an anamorphic skull, a reminder of death.

warn against the coming of perilous times and the preaching of false prophets who will distort God's word.

HANS HOLBEIN The leading artist of the Holy Roman Empire in the generation after Dürer was HANS HOLBEIN THE YOUNGER (ca. 1497–1543), who excelled as a portraitist. The surfaces of Holbein's paintings are as lustrous as enamel, and the details are exact and exquisitely drawn, consistent with the tradition of 15th-century Flemish art. Yet he also incorporated Italian ideas about monumental composition and sculptural form.

Holbein began his artistic career in Basel, but because of the immediate threat of a religious civil war, he left for England, where, with Erasmus's recommendation, he became painter to the court of King Henry VIII and produced a double portrait of the French ambassadors to England, Jean de Dinteville (1504–1557) and Georges de Selve (1509–1542). *The French Ambassadors* (FIG. 9-31) exhibits Holbein's considerable talents—his strong sense of composition, gift for recording likenesses, marvelous sensitivity to color, and faultless technique. The two men, both ardent humanists, stand at opposite ends of a side table covered with an oriental rug and a collection of objects reflective of their worldliness and their interest in learning and the arts. These include mathematical and astronomical models and implements, a lute with a broken string, compasses,

a sundial, flutes, globes, and an open hymnbook with Luther's translation of *Veni, Creator Spiritus* and of the Ten Commandments.

Of particular interest is the long gray shape that slashes diagonally across the picture plane and interrupts the stable, balanced, and serene composition. This form is an *anamorphic image*, a distorted image recognizable only when viewed with a special device, such as a cylindrical mirror, or by looking at the painting at an acute angle. In this case, if the viewer stands off to the right, the distorted image becomes a skull. Artists commonly incorporated skulls into paintings as reminders of mortality. Indeed, Holbein depicted a skull on the metal medallion on Jean de Dinteville's hat. Holbein may have intended the skulls, in conjunction with the crucifix that appears half hidden behind the curtain in the upper left corner, to encourage viewers to ponder death and resurrection.

The French Ambassadors may also allude to the growing tension between secular and religious authorities. Jean de Dinteville was a titled landowner, Georges de Selve a bishop. The inclusion of Luther's translations next to the lute with the broken string (a symbol of discord) may also subtly refer to religious strife. In any case, the painting is a supreme artistic achievement. Holbein rendered the still-life objects with the same meticulous care as the men themselves, the woven design of the deep emerald curtain behind them, and the Italian marble-inlay floor, drawn in perfect perspective.

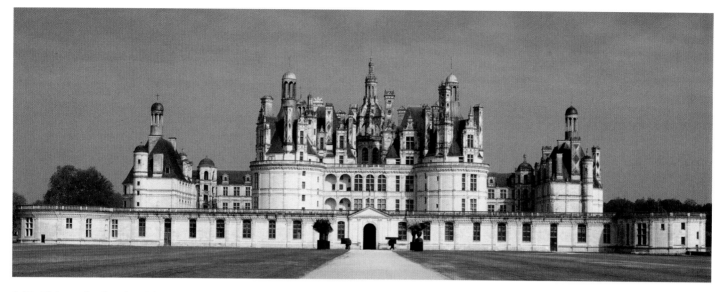

9-32 Château de Chambord (looking northwest), Chambord, France, begun 1519.

French Renaissance châteaux, which developed from medieval castles, served as country houses for royalty. King Francis I's Château de Chambord reflects Italian palazzo design, but it has a Gothic roof.

FRANCE

As *The French Ambassadors* illustrates, France in the early 16th century continued its efforts to secure widespread recognition as a political power and cultural force. Under Francis I (r. 1515–1547), the French established a firm foothold in Milan and its environs. Francis waged a campaign (known as the Habsburg-Valois Wars) against Charles V, king of Spain and Holy Roman Emperor (r. 1516–1558). These wars, which occupied Francis for most of his reign, involved disputed territories—southern France, the Netherlands, the Rhineland, northern Spain, and Italy—and reflect France's central role in the shifting geopolitical landscape. Francis also endeavored to elevate his country's cultural profile. To that end, he invited several esteemed Italian artists to his court, Leonardo da Vinci among them. Under Francis, the Church, the primary patron of art and architecture in medieval France, yielded that position to the French monarchy. Francis's art collection became the core of Paris's Musée du Louvre, one of the world's greatest museums.

CHÂTEAU DE CHAMBORD Francis I indulged his passion for building by commissioning several large *châteaux,* among them the Château de Chambord (FIG. 9-32). These châteaux developed from medieval fortified castles, but, reflecting more peaceful times, served as country houses for royalty, who usually built them near forests for use as hunting lodges. Construction of the Chambord château began in 1519, but Francis never saw its completion. The plan includes a central square block with four corridors in the shape of a cross, and a broad, central staircase that gives access to groups of rooms—ancestors of the modern suite of rooms or apartments. At each of the four corners, a round tower punctuates the square plan, and a moat surrounds the whole. From the exterior, Chambord presents a carefully contrived horizontal accent on three levels, with continuous moldings separating its floors. Windows align precisely, one exactly over another. The Italian Renaissance palazzo (FIG. 8-32A ⬀ and 8-33) served as the model for this matching of horizontal and vertical features, but above the third level, the structure's lines break chaotically into a jumble of high *dormers* (projecting gable-capped windows), chimneys, and turrets that are the heritage of French Gothic architecture.

THE NETHERLANDS

With the demise of the duchy of Burgundy in 1477 and the division of that territory between France and the Holy Roman Empire (MAP 9-1), the Netherlands at the beginning of the 16th century consisted of 17 provinces (corresponding to modern Holland, Belgium, and Luxembourg). The Netherlands was among the most commercially advanced and prosperous countries in Europe. Its extensive network of rivers and easy access to the Atlantic Ocean provided a setting that encouraged overseas trade, and shipbuilding was one of the Netherlands' most profitable enterprises. The region's commercial center shifted toward the end of the 15th century, partly because of buildup of silt in the Bruges estuary. Traffic relocated to Antwerp, which became the hub of economic activity in the Netherlands after 1510. As many as 500 ships a day passed through Antwerp's harbor, and large trading companies from Germany, Italy, Spain, Portugal, and England established themselves in the city.

During the second half of the 16th century, Philip II of Spain (r. 1556–1598) controlled the Netherlands, which he inherited from his father, Charles V. Philip sought to force the entire population to become Catholic. His heavy-handed tactics and repressive measures led in 1579 to revolt and the formation of two federations: the Union of Arras, a Catholic union of southern Netherlandish provinces, which remained under Spanish dominion, and the Union of Utrecht, a Protestant union of northern provinces, which became the Dutch Republic.

Netherlandish artists continued to receive commissions for large-scale altarpieces and other religious works from Catholic churches, but with the rise of Protestantism, most artists in the Netherlands focused on secular subjects. Netherlandish art of this period provides a wonderful glimpse into the lives of various levels of society, from nobility to peasantry, capturing their activities, environment, and values.

1 ft.

9-33 HIERONYMUS BOSCH, *Garden of Earthly Delights*, 1505–1510. Oil on wood, center panel 7' 2⅝" × 6' 4¾", each wing 7' 2⅝" × 3' 2¼". Museo del Prado, Madrid.

In the fantastic sunlit landscape that is Bosch's Paradise, scores of nude people in the prime of life blithely cavort. The horrors of Hell include sinners enduring tortures tailored to their conduct while alive.

HIERONYMUS BOSCH The leading Netherlandish painter of the early 16th century was HIERONYMUS BOSCH (ca. 1450–1516), one of the most fascinating artistic personalities in history. Bosch's most famous painting, *Garden of Earthly Delights* (FIG. 9-33), is also his most puzzling, and no interpretation has ever won universal acceptance. Although the work is a large triptych, which would suggest a religious function as an altarpiece, *Garden of Earthly Delights* was on display in the palace of Count Henry III of Nassau-Breda (r. 1516–1538) no later than seven years after its completion. This suggests that the triptych was a secular commission, and some scholars have proposed that given the work's central themes of sex and procreation, the painting may commemorate a wedding. Marriage was a familiar theme in Netherlandish painting. Among the many 15th-century examples is Jan van Eyck's *Giovanni Arnolfini and His Wife* (FIG. 8-6). Any similarity to earlier paintings ends there, however. Whereas Jan and other painters grounded their depictions of married couples in contemporary Netherlandish life and custom, Bosch's image portrays a visionary world of fantasy and intrigue—a painted world without close parallel until the advent of Surrealism more than 400 years later (see page 394).

In the left panel, God (in the form of Christ) presents Eve to Adam in a landscape, presumably the Garden of Eden. Bosch's wildly imaginative setting includes an odd pink fountainlike structure in a body of water and an array of fanciful and unusual animals, including a giraffe, an elephant, and winged fish. The central panel is a continuation of Paradise, a sunlit landscape filled with nude people, including exotic figures of African descent, who frequently appear in Renaissance paintings (for example, FIG. 8-39), both north and south of the Alps. All those in Paradise are in the prime of youth. They blithely cavort amid bizarre creatures and unidentifiable objects. Some of the youths exuberantly stand on their hands

or turn somersaults. The numerous fruits and birds in the scene are fertility symbols and suggest procreation. Indeed, many of the figures pair off as couples.

In contrast to the orgiastic overtones of the central panel is the terrifying image of Hell in the right wing, where viewers must search through the inky darkness to find all of the fascinating though repulsive details that Bosch recorded. Beastly creatures devour people, while other condemned souls endure tortures tailored to their conduct while alive. A glutton must vomit eternally. A miser squeezes gold coins from his bowels. A spidery monster fondles a promiscuous woman while toads bite her. Scholars have traditionally interpreted Bosch's triptych as a warning about the fate awaiting the sinful, decadent, and immoral, but as a secular work, *Garden of Earthly Delights* may have been intended for a learned audience fascinated by *alchemy*—the medieval study of seemingly magical chemical changes. Details throughout the triptych are based on chemical apparatus of the day, which Bosch knew well because his in-laws were pharmacists.

QUINTEN MASSYS Antwerp's growth and prosperity, along with its wealthy merchants' desire to accumulate artworks among other worldly goods, attracted artists to the city. Among them was QUINTEN MASSYS (ca. 1466–1530) of Louvain, who became Antwerp's leading master after 1510. In *Money-Changer and His Wife* (FIG. 9-34), Massys presented a professional man transacting business. He holds scales, checking the weight of coins on the table. The artist's detailed rendering of the figures, setting, and objects suggests a fidelity to observable fact. But the painting is also a commentary on Netherlandish values and mores. *Money-Changer and His Wife* highlights the financial transactions that were an increasingly prominent part of secular life in the Netherlands and that distracted Christians from

9-34 QUINTEN MASSYS, *Money-Changer and His Wife*, 1514. Oil on wood, 2′ 3¾″ × 2′ 2⅜″. Musée du Louvre, Paris.

Massys's depiction of a secular financial transaction is also a commentary on Netherlandish values. The banker's wife shows more interest in the money-weighing than in her prayer book.

their religious duties. The banker's wife, for example, shows more interest in watching her husband weigh money than in reading her prayer book. Massys incorporated into his painting numerous references to the importance of a moral, righteous, and spiritual life, including a candlestick and a carafe with water, traditional religious symbols. The couple ignores them, focusing solely on money. On the right, seen through a window, an old man talks with another man,

a reference to idleness and gossip. The reflected image in the convex mirror on the counter offsets this image of sloth and foolish chatter. There, a man reads what is most likely a Bible or prayer book. Behind him is a church steeple. An inscription on the original frame (now lost) read, "Let the balance be just and the weights equal" (Lev. 19:36), an admonition that applies both to the money-changer's professional conduct and eventually to judgment day. Nonetheless, the couple in this painting has tipped the balance in favor of the pursuit of wealth.

PIETER AERTSEN This tendency to inject reminders about spiritual well-being into paintings of everyday life emerges again in *Butcher's Stall* (FIG. 9-35) by PIETER AERTSEN (ca. 1507–1575), who worked in Antwerp for more than three decades. At first glance, this painting appears to be a descriptive *genre* scene (one from everyday life). On display is an array of meat products—a side of a hog, chickens, sausages, a stuffed intestine, pig's feet, meat pies, a cow's head, a hog's head, and hanging entrails. Also visible are fish, pretzels, cheese, and butter. But, like Massys, Aertsen embedded strategically placed religious images in his painting. In the background, Joseph leads a donkey carrying Mary and the Christ Child. The holy family stops to offer alms to a beggar and his son, while the people behind the holy family wend their way toward a church. Furthermore, the crossed fishes on the platter and the pretzels and wine in the rafters on the upper left all refer to "spiritual food" (pretzels were often served as bread during Lent). Aertsen accentuated these allusions to salvation through Christ by contrasting them to their opposite—a life of gluttony, lust, and sloth. He represented this degeneracy with the oyster and mussel shells (which Netherlanders believed possessed aphrodisiacal properties) scattered on the ground on the painting's right side, along with the people seen eating and carousing nearby under the roof. Underscoring the general theme is the placard at the right advertising land for sale—Aertsen's moralistic reference to a recent scandal involving the transfer of land from an Antwerp charitable institution to a land speculator.

9-35 PIETER AERTSEN, *Butcher's Stall*, 1551. Oil on wood, 4′ ⅜″ × 6′ 5¾″. Uppsala University Art Collection, Uppsala.

Butcher's Stall appears to be a genre painting, but in the background, Joseph leads a donkey carrying Mary and the Christ Child. Aertsen balanced images of gluttony with allusions to salvation.

CATERINA VAN HEMESSEN With the accumulation of wealth in the Netherlands, private portraits increased in popularity. The example illustrated here (FIG. 9-36), by CATERINA VAN HEMESSEN (1528–1587), is of special interest because it is the first known northern European self-portrait by a woman. The artist signed the work "Caterina van Hemessen painted me / 1548 / her age 20" and confidently presented herself as a painter who interrupts her work to look toward the viewer. She holds brushes, a palette, and a *maulstick* (a stick used to steady the hand while painting) in her left hand, and delicately applies pigment to the canvas with her right hand. Professional women artists remained unusual in the 16th century in large part because of the difficulty in obtaining formal training (see "The Artist's Profession" ◢). Caterina was typical in having been trained by her father, the painter Jan Sanders van Hemessen (ca. 1500–1556).

PIETER BRUEGEL THE ELDER The greatest Netherlandish painter of the mid-16th century was PIETER BRUEGEL THE ELDER (ca. 1528–1569). Like many of his contemporaries, Bruegel traveled to Italy, where between 1551 and 1554 he went as far south as Sicily. However, unlike other artists who visited the ruins of ancient Rome, Bruegel chose not to incorporate classical elements into his paintings. Landscapes were among his favorite subjects, but no matter how huge a slice of the world Bruegel depicted, human activities remain the dominant theme.

The setting of *Netherlandish Proverbs* (FIG. 9-37) is a village populated by a wide range of people, encompassing nobility, peasants, and clerics. Seen from a bird's-eye view is a mesmerizing array of activities reminiscent of the topsy-turvy scenes of Hieronymus Bosch (FIG. 9-33), but the purpose and meaning of Bruegel's anecdotal details are clear. By illustrating more than a hundred proverbs in this one painting, Bruegel indulged his Netherlandish audience's obsession with proverbs, passion for detailed and clever imagery, and interest in human folly—the subject of Erasmus's most famous work, *In Praise of Folly*. As the viewer scrutinizes the myriad vignettes within the painting, Bruegel's close observation and deep understanding of human nature become apparent. The proverbs depicted include, on the far left, a man in blue gnawing on a pillar. ("He who bites a church pillar" is a religious zealot engaged in folly.) To his right, a man "beats his head against a wall" (a frustrated idiot who has attempted something impossible). On the roof a man "shoots one arrow

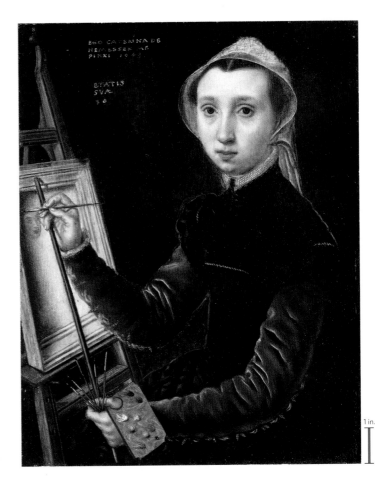

9-36 CATERINA VAN HEMESSEN, *Self-Portrait*, 1548. Oil on wood, 1'$\frac{3}{4}$" × 9$\frac{7}{8}$". Kunstmuseum Basel, Basel.

In this first known northern European self-portrait by a woman, Caterina van Hemessen represented herself as a confident artist momentarily interrupting her work to look out at the viewer.

9-37 PIETER BRUEGEL THE ELDER, *Netherlandish Proverbs*, 1559. Oil on wood, 3' 10" × 5' 4$\frac{1}{8}$". Gemäldegalerie, Staatliche Museen zu Berlin, Berlin.

In this painting of a Netherlandish village, Bruegel indulged his audience's obsession with proverbs and passion for clever imagery, and demonstrated his deep understanding of human nature.

1 ft.

9-38 PIETER BRUEGEL THE ELDER, *Hunters in the Snow*, 1565. Oil on wood, 3' 10" × 5' 3¾". Kunsthistorisches Museum, Vienna.

In *Hunters in the Snow*, one of a series of paintings illustrating different seasons, Bruegel draws the viewer diagonally deep into the landscape by his mastery of line, shape, and composition.

after the other, but hits nothing" (a fool who throws good money after bad). In the far distance, the "blind lead the blind."

Hunters in the Snow (FIG. 9-38), one of six paintings illustrating seasonal changes, is very different in character and illustrates the dynamic variety of Bruegel's work. The series was a private commission for an Antwerp merchant's home and grew out of the tradition of depicting months and peasants in Books of Hours (FIG. 8-9). The painting shows human figures and landscape locked in winter cold. The weary hunters return with their hounds, women build fires, skaters skim the frozen pond, and the town and its church huddle in their mantle of snow. Bruegel rendered the landscape in an optically accurate manner. It develops smoothly from foreground to background and draws the viewer diagonally into its depths. The painter's supreme skill in using line and shape and his subtlety in tonal harmony make this one of the great landscape paintings in Western art.

SPAIN

Spain emerged as the dominant European power at the end of the 16th century. Under the Habsburg ruler Charles V and his son, Philip II, the Spanish Empire encompassed a territory greater in extent than any ever known—a large part of Europe, the western Mediterranean, a strip of North Africa, and vast expanses in the New World. Spain acquired many of its New World colonies through aggressive overseas exploration. Among the most notable conquistadors sailing under the Spanish flag were Christopher Columbus (1451–1506), Vasco Nuñez de Balboa (ca. 1475–1517), Ferdinand Magellan (1480–1521), Hernán Cortés (1485–1547), and Francisco Pizarro (ca. 1470–1541). The Habsburg Empire, enriched by New World plunder, supported the most powerful military force in Europe. Spain defended and then promoted the interests of the Catholic Church in its battle against the inroads of the Protestant Reformation. In fact, Philip II earned the title "Most Catholic King." Spain's crusading spirit, nourished by centuries of war with Islam (see page 149), prepared the country to assume the role of the most Catholic civilization of Europe and the Americas. In the 16th century, for good or for ill, Spain left the mark of its power, religion, language, and culture on two hemispheres.

EL ESCORIAL Philip II's major building project was El Escorial (FIG. 9-39), designed by JUAN DE HERRERA (ca. 1530–1597) and JUAN BAUTISTA DE TOLEDO (d. 1567), principally the former. In his will, Charles V stipulated that a "dynastic pantheon" be built to house the remains of past and future Spanish monarchs. Philip II chose a site some 30 miles northwest of Madrid for the enormous (625-foot-wide and 520-foot-deep) complex, which is not only a royal mausoleum but also a church, a monastery, and a palace. Legend has it that El Escorial's gridlike plan symbolized the gridiron on which Saint Lawrence suffered his martyrdom. The vast structure is in keeping with Philip's austere character, his passionate Catholic

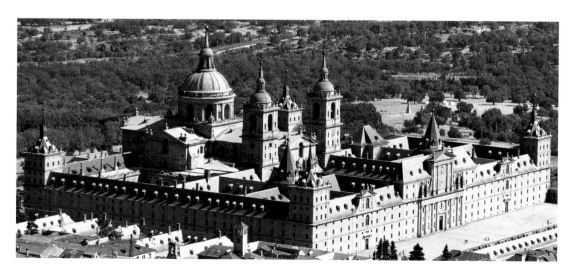

9-39 JUAN DE HERRERA and JUAN BAUTISTA DE TOLEDO, El Escorial (looking southeast), near Madrid, Spain, 1563–1584.

Conceived by Charles V and built by Philip II, El Escorial is a royal mausoleum, church, monastery, and palace in one. The complex is classical in style, with severely plain walls and massive towers.

religiosity, his proud reverence for his dynasty, and his stern determination to impose his will worldwide. He insisted that in designing El Escorial, the architects focus on simplicity of form, severity in the whole, nobility without arrogance, and majesty without ostentation. The result is a classicism of Doric severity, ultimately derived from Italian architecture, but without close parallel elsewhere in Europe.

Only the three entrances, with the dominant central portal framed by superimposed orders and topped by a pediment in the Italian fashion, break the long sweep of the structure's severely plain walls. Massive square towers punctuate the four corners. Within, the church's imposing granite facade produces an effect of overwhelming strength and weight. El Escorial stands as the overpowering architectural expression of Spain's spirit in its heroic epoch and of the character of Philip II, the extraordinary ruler who directed it.

EL GRECO Reflecting the increasingly international character of European art as well as the mobility of artists, the greatest Spanish painter of the era was not a Spaniard. Born on Crete, Domenikos Theotokopoulos, called EL GRECO (ca. 1547–1614), emigrated to Italy as a young man. In his youth, he absorbed the traditions of Late Byzantine frescoes and mosaics. While still young, El Greco went to Venice, where he worked in Titian's studio, although Tintoretto's paintings (FIG. 9-24) seem to have made a stronger impression on him. A brief trip to Rome explains the influences of Roman and Florentine Mannerism on his work. By 1577, he had left for Spain to spend the rest of his life in Toledo. El Greco's art is a strong personal blending of Byzantine and Mannerist elements. The intense emotionalism of his paintings, which naturally appealed to Spanish piety, and a great reliance on and mastery of color bound him to 16th-century Venetian art and to Mannerism. El Greco's art was not strictly Spanish, for it had no Spanish antecedents and little effect on later Spanish painters. Nevertheless, El Greco's hybrid style captured the fervor of Spanish Catholicism.

Burial of Count Orgaz (FIG. 9-40), painted in 1586 for Santo Tomé in Toledo, vividly expresses that fervor. El Greco based the painting on the legend of the count of Orgaz, who had died some three centuries before and who had been a great benefactor of Santo Tomé. According to the legend, Saints Stephen and Augustine miraculously descended from Heaven to lower the count's body into its sepulcher in the church. The radiant Heaven above illuminates the earthly scene below. The painter represented the terrestrial realm with a firm realism, whereas he depicted the celestial, in his quite personal manner, with elongated undulating figures, fluttering draperies, and a visionary swirling cloud. Below, the two saints lovingly lower the count's armor-clad body, the armor and heavy robes painted with all the rich sensuousness of the Venetian school. A solemn chorus of personages (including Philip II) dressed in black fills the background. In the carefully individualized features of these figures, El Greco demonstrated that he was also a great portraitist.

The upward glances of some of the figures below and the flight of an angel above link the painting's lower and upper spheres. The action of the angel, who carries the count's soul in his arms as Saint John and the Virgin intercede for it before the throne of Christ, reinforces this connection. El Greco's deliberate change in style to distinguish between the two levels of reality gives the viewer an opportunity to see the artist's early and late manners in the same work, one below the other. His relatively realistic presentation of the earthly sphere is still strongly rooted in Venetian art, but the abstractions and distortions that El Greco used to show the immaterial nature of the heavenly realm characterize his later style. His elongated figures existing in undefined spaces, bathed in a cool light

9-40 EL GRECO, *Burial of Count Orgaz*, 1586. Oil on canvas, 16' × 12'. Santo Tomé, Toledo.

El Greco's art is a blend of Byzantine and Italian Mannerist elements. His intense emotional content captured the fervor of Spanish Catholicism, and his dramatic use of light foreshadowed the Baroque style.

of uncertain origin, explain El Greco's usual classification as a Mannerist, but his art is difficult to classify using conventional labels. Although El Greco used Mannerist formal devices, his primary concerns were conveying emotion and religious fervor and arousing those passions in viewers. The forcefulness of his paintings is the result of his unique, highly developed expressive style, which foreshadowed developments of the Baroque era, examined next in Chapter 10.

Explore the era further in MindTap with videos of major artworks and buildings, Google Earth™ coordinates, and essays by the author on the following additional subjects:

- Leonardo da Vinci, *The Fetus and Lining of the Uterus* (FIG. 9-1A)
- MATERIALS AND TECHNIQUES: Renaissance Drawings
- ARTISTS ON ART: Leonardo and Michelangelo on Painting versus Sculpture
- WRITTEN SOURCES: Giorgio Vasari's *Lives*
- Michelangelo, *Fall of Man* (FIG. 9-10A)
- THE PATRON'S VOICE: The Council of Trent
- Giulio Romano, *Fall of the Giants from Mount Olympus* (FIG. 9-26A)
- RELIGION AND MYTHOLOGY: Catholic versus Protestant Views of Salvation
- Cranach the Elder, *Law and Gospel* (FIG. 9-26B)

HIGH RENAISSANCE AND MANNERISM IN EUROPE

Italy

- During the High (1500–1520) and Late (1520–1600) Renaissance, the major Italian artistic centers were Florence, Rome, and Venice. Whereas most Florentine and Roman artists emphasized careful design preparation based on preliminary drawing (disegno), Venetian artists focused on color and the process of paint application (colorito), and took a poetic approach to painting (poesia).

- Leonardo da Vinci was a master of chiaroscuro and atmospheric perspective. He was famous for his sfumato (misty haziness) and for his psychological insight in depicting biblical narrative.

- Raphael favored lighter tonalities than Leonardo, and clarity over obscurity. His sculpturesque figures appear in landscapes under blue skies or in grandiose architectural settings rendered in perfect perspective.

- In both sculpture and painting, Michelangelo won renown for his emotionally charged figures with heroic physiques. He preferred pent-up energy to Raphael's calm, ideal beauty.

- The leading early Cinquecento Italian architect was Bramante, who championed the classical style of the ancients and favored the central plan for churches. In Il Gesù, Giacomo della Porta introduced a widely influential plan for basilican churches: a broad nave and side chapels instead of aisles.

- The two greatest masters of the Venetian painting school were Giorgione, a pioneer of poetical painting, and Titian, famed for his rich surface textures and dazzling display of color in all its nuances.

- Mannerism (1520–1600) was a reaction against the High Renaissance style. Mannerist paintings by Pontormo and Parmigianino feature elongated figures, ambiguous space, and intentional departures from expected conventions. The leading Mannerist architect was Giulio Romano, whose designs represent a parody of Bramante's classical style.

Raphael, *Madonna in the Meadow*, 1505–1506

Bramante, Tempietto, Rome, begun 1502

Pontormo, *Entombment of Christ*, 1525–1528

Northern Europe and Spain

- Dissatisfaction with the Church in Rome led to the Protestant Reformation, which began in the Holy Roman Empire. Protestants objected to the sale of indulgences and rejected most of the sacraments of Catholicism. They also condemned ostentatious church decoration as a form of idolatry. Art, however, especially prints, still played a role in Protestantism. Albrecht Dürer's engravings rival paintings in tonal quality.

- The Netherlands was one of the most prosperous countries in 16th-century Europe. Netherlandish art provides a picture of contemporary life and values. Pieter Aertsen's *Butcher's Stall,* for example, seems to be a straightforward genre scene, but includes the holy family offering alms to a beggar, providing a stark contrast between gluttony and religious piety.

- Landscapes were the specialty of Pieter Bruegel the Elder. His *Hunters in the Snow* is one of a series of paintings depicting seasonal changes and the activities associated with them.

- The leading painter of 16th-century Spain was Greek-born El Greco, whose art combined Byzantine style, Italian Mannerism, and the religious fervor of Catholic Spain.

Dürer, *Fall of Man*, 1504

Aertsen, *Butcher's Stall*, 1551

▲ **10-1a** As water flows from a travertine grotto supporting an ancient Egyptian obelisk, Bernini's marble personifications of major rivers of four continents twist and gesticulate emphatically.

▲ **10-1b** Each of the four rivers has an identifying attribute. The Ganges (Asia) most closely resembles a Greco-Roman river god. Bernini's personification of that easily navigable river holds an oar.

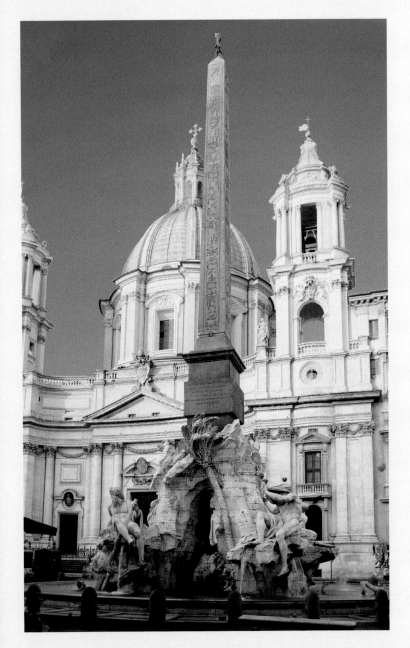

10-1 **GIANLORENZO BERNINI, Fountain of the Four Rivers (looking southwest with Sant'Agnese in Agone, by FRANCESCO BORROMINI, in the background), Piazza Navona, Rome, Italy, 1648–1651.**

▲ **10-1c** Crowning the grotto is Pope Innocent X's coat of arms, with the Pamphili family's dove symbolizing the Holy Spirit and the triumph of the Catholic Church in all regions of the world.

Baroque Europe

BAROQUE ART AND SPECTACLE

One of the most popular tourist attractions in Rome is the Fountain of the Four Rivers (FIG. 10-1) in Piazza Navona, by GIANLORENZO BERNINI (1598–1680). Architect, painter, sculptor, playwright, and stage designer, Bernini was one of the most important and imaginative artists of the Baroque era in Italy and its most characteristic and sustaining spirit. Nonetheless, the fountain's patron, Pope Innocent X (r. 1644–1655), did not want Bernini to win this commission. Bernini had been the favorite sculptor of the Pamphili pope's predecessor, Urban VIII (r. 1623–1644), who spent so extravagantly on art and on himself and his family that he nearly bankrupted the Vatican treasury. Innocent emphatically opposed the excesses of the Barberini pope and shunned Bernini, awarding new papal commissions to other sculptors and architects. Bernini was also in disgrace at the time because of his failed attempt to erect bell towers for the new facade of Saint Peter's (FIG. 10-2). When Innocent announced a competition for a fountain in Piazza Navona, site of the Pamphili family's palace and parish church, Sant'Agnese in Agone (FIG. 10-1, *rear*), he pointedly did not invite Bernini to submit a design. However, the renowned sculptor succeeded in having a model of his proposed fountain placed where the pope would see it. When Innocent examined it, he was so captivated that he declared that the only way anyone could avoid employing Bernini was not to look at his work.

Bernini's bold design, executed in large part by his assistants, called for a sculptured travertine grotto supporting an ancient *obelisk* that Innocent had transferred to Piazza Navona from the *circus* (chariot racecourse) of the Roman emperor Maxentius (r. 305–312) on the Via Appia. Piazza Navona was once the site of the *stadium* of Domitian (r. 81–96), a long and narrow theater-like structure for foot races, which explains the piazza's unusual shape and the church's name (*agone* means "foot race" in Italian). Water rushes from the artificial grotto into a basin filled with marble statues personifying major rivers on four continents—the Danube (Europe), Nile (Africa), Ganges (Asia), and Plata (Americas). The reclining figures twist and gesticulate, consistent with the contemporary taste for movement and drama. The Nile covers his face—Bernini's way of acknowledging that the Nile's source was unknown at the time. The Rio de la Plata has a hoard of coins, signifying the wealth of the New World. The Ganges, easily navigable, holds an oar. The Danube, awestruck, reaches up to the papal coat of arms. A second reference to Innocent X is at the apex of the obelisk, where the Pamphili dove also symbolizes the Holy Spirit and the triumph of Christianity in every region of the world. The scenic effect of the cascading water would have been heightened whenever Piazza Navona was flooded for festival pageants. Bernini's fountain exemplifies the Baroque era's love for uniting art and spectacle.

EUROPE IN THE 17TH CENTURY

During the 17th century, numerous geopolitical shifts occurred in Europe as the fortunes of individual countries rose and fell. Pronounced political and religious friction resulted in widespread unrest and warfare. Indeed, between 1562 and 1721, all of Europe was at peace for a mere four years. The major conflict of this period was the Thirty Years' War (1618–1648), which ensnared Spain, France, Sweden, Denmark, the Netherlands, Germany, Austria, Poland, the Ottoman Empire, and the Holy Roman Empire. Although the outbreak of this war had its roots in the conflict between militant Catholics and militant Protestants, the driving force quickly shifted to secular, dynastic, and nationalistic concerns. Among the major political entities vying for expanded power and authority in Europe were the Bourbon dynasty of France and the Habsburg dynasties of Spain and the Holy Roman Empire. The war, which concluded with the Treaty of Westphalia in 1648, was largely responsible for the political restructuring of Europe (MAP 10-1). As a result, the United Provinces of the Netherlands (the Dutch Republic), Sweden, and France expanded their authority. Spanish and Danish power diminished. In addition to reconfiguring territorial boundaries, the Treaty of Westphalia in essence granted freedom of religious choice throughout Europe. This treaty thus marked the abandonment of the idea of a united Christian Europe and accepted the practical realities of secular political systems. The building of today's nation-states was emphatically under way.

The 17th century also brought heightened economic competition to Europe. Much of the foundation for worldwide mercantilism—extensive voyaging and geographic exploration, improved mapmaking, and advances in shipbuilding—had been laid in the previous century. In the 17th century, however, changes in financial systems, lifestyles, and trading patterns, along with expanding colonialism,

MAP 10-1 Europe in 1648 after the Treaty of Westphalia.

BAROQUE EUROPE

1600–1625
- Carracci introduces quadro riportato fresco painting.
- Caravaggio pioneers tenebrism in oil painting.
- Bernini incorporates drama and movement in marble statuary.
- Rubens is the leading painter in Catholic Flanders.
- In the northern Netherlands, Calvinist patrons favor genre scenes, portraits, and still lifes.

1625–1650
- Borromini designs San Carlo alle Quattro Fontane.
- Gentileschi is the leading woman artist in Europe.
- Zurbarán paints scenes of martyrdom in Catholic Spain.
- Hals achieves renown for his group portraits.
- Rembrandt is the foremost Dutch Baroque painter and printmaker.

1650–1675
- Bernini designs the colonnaded oval piazza in front of Saint Peter's.
- Velázquez, the chief court painter of Philip IV of Spain, paints Las Meninas.
- Vermeer uses a camera obscura as an aid in painting domestic interiors.
- Poussin champions "grand manner" painting.

1675–1700
- Pozzo paints illusionistic ceiling frescoes in Sant'Ignazio.
- Louis XIV, the "Sun King," builds the palace at Versailles with vast landscaped gardens.
- Christopher Wren designs Saint Paul's Cathedral in London based in part on French and Italian models.

fueled the creation of a worldwide marketplace. The Dutch founded the Bank of Amsterdam in 1609, which eventually became the center of European transfer banking. By establishing a system in which merchant firms held money on account, the bank relieved traders of having to transport precious metals as payment. Trading practices became more complex. Rather than simple reciprocal trading, triangular trade (trade among three parties) facilitated access to a larger pool of desirable goods. Exposure to an ever-growing array of goods affected European diets and lifestyles. Tea (from China) and, later, coffee (from island colonies) became popular beverages over the course of the 17th century. Equally explosive was the growth of sugar use. Sugar, tobacco, and rice were slave crops, and the slave trade expanded to meet the demand for these goods. The resulting worldwide mercantile system permanently changed the face of Europe. The prosperity generated by international trade affected social and political relationships, necessitating new rules of etiquette and careful diplomacy. With increased disposable income, more of the newly wealthy spent money on art, significantly expanding the market for artworks, especially small-scale paintings for private homes.

"BAROQUE" ART Art historians traditionally describe 17th-century European art as *Baroque,* but the term is problematic because the period encompasses a broad range of styles and genres. Although its origin is unclear, "Baroque" may have come from the Portuguese word *barroco,* meaning an irregularly shaped pearl. Use of the term can be traced to the late 18th century, when critics belittled the Baroque period's artistic production, in large part because of perceived deficiencies in comparison to the art of the Italian Renaissance. Over time, this negative connotation faded, but the term stuck. "Baroque" remains useful to describe the distinctive new style that emerged during the early 1600s—a style of complexity and drama seen especially in Italian art of this period. Whereas Renaissance artists embraced the precise, orderly rationality of classical models, Baroque artists reveled in dynamism, theatricality, and elaborate ornamentation, often on a grandiose scale, as in Bernini's Four Rivers Fountain (FIG. 10-1).

ITALY

Although the Protestant Reformation brought with it fundamental changes in artistic patronage in many northern European countries, in Italy the Catholic Church remained the leading source of artistic commissions. The aim of much of Italian Baroque art was to restore Roman Catholicism's predominance and centrality.

Architecture and Sculpture

Baroque art and architecture in Italy, especially in Rome, embodied the renewed energy of the Counter-Reformation (see "The Council of Trent" ⬀). At the end of the 16th century, Pope Sixtus V (r. 1585–1590) had augmented the papal treasury and intended to rebuild Rome as an even more magnificent showcase of Church power. Between 1606 and 1667, several strong and ambitious popes—Paul V, Urban VIII, Innocent X, and Alexander VII—made many of Sixtus V's dreams a reality. Rome still bears the marks of their patronage everywhere.

BERNINI'S BALDACCHINO A quarter century before Gianlorenzo Bernini designed the Four Rivers Fountain (FIG. 10-1) for Innocent X, Urban VIII had awarded him the commission to erect a gigantic bronze *baldacchino* (FIG. 10-2) in Saint Peter's directly beneath Giacomo della Porta's dome (FIG. 9-14). Completed between 1624 and 1633, the canopy-like structure (*baldacco* is Italian

10-2 GIANLORENZO BERNINI, baldacchino (looking west), Saint Peter's, Vatican City, Rome, Italy, 1624–1633.

Bernini's baldacchino serves both functional and symbolic purposes. It marks Saint Peter's tomb and the high altar, and it visually bridges the marble floor and the lofty vaults and dome above.

for "silk from Baghdad," such as for a cloth canopy) stands almost 100 feet high and serves both functional and symbolic purposes. It marks the high altar and the tomb of Saint Peter beneath the basilica, and provides a dramatic presence at the crossing, visually bridging the marble floor to the lofty vaults and dome above. Its columns also serve as a visual frame for the elaborate sculpture representing the throne of Saint Peter (the Cathedra Petri) at the far end of the nave (FIG. 10-2, *rear*). On a symbolic level, the baldacchino's decorative elements speak to the power of the Catholic Church. Partially fluted and wreathed with vines, the structure's four spiral columns are Baroque versions of those of the ancient baldacchino over the same spot in Old Saint Peter's, thereby invoking the past to reinforce the primacy of the Church of Rome in the 17th century. At the top of the columns, four colossal angels stand guard at the upper corners of the canopy. Forming the canopy's apex are four serpentine brackets that elevate the orb and the cross. Since the time of the emperor Constantine, builder of the original Saint Peter's basilica (FIGS. 4-3 and 4-4), the orb and the cross had served as symbols of the Church's triumph. The baldacchino also features numerous bees, symbols of Urban VIII's family, the Barberini. Bernini's design

PROBLEMS AND SOLUTIONS
Completing Saint Peter's

Old Saint Peter's had a large forecourt, or *atrium* (FIGS. 4-3 and 4-4), in front of the church proper, and in the mid-17th century, Gianlorenzo Bernini (FIG. 10-1) received the prestigious commission to construct a grand colonnade-framed piazza (FIG. 10-3) in front of Maderno's facade. Bernini's design had to incorporate two preexisting structures on the site—an obelisk that the ancient Romans had brought from Egypt (which Pope Sixtus V had moved to its present location in 1585 as part of his vision of Christian triumph in Rome) and a fountain that Maderno had constructed in front of the church. Bernini's solution was to co-opt these features to define the long axis of a vast oval embraced by two colonnades joined to Maderno's facade. Four rows of huge Tuscan columns make up the two colonnades, which terminate in classical temple fronts. The colonnades extend a dramatic gesture of embrace to all who enter the piazza, symbolizing the welcome that the Roman Catholic Church gave its members during the Counter-Reformation. Bernini himself referred to his colonnades as the welcoming arms of Saint Peter's.

Beyond their symbolic resonance, the colonnades served visually to counteract the natural perspective and bring the facade closer to the viewer. Emphasizing the facade's height in this manner, Bernini subtly and effectively compensated for its extensive width. Thus a Baroque transformation expanded the compact central designs of Bramante and Michelangelo into a dynamic complex of axially ordered elements that reach out and enclose spaces of vast dimension. By its sheer scale and theatricality, the completed Saint Peter's fulfilled the desire of the Counter-Reformation Church to present an awe-inspiring and authoritative vision of itself.

10-3 Aerial view of Saint Peter's (looking northwest), Vatican City, Rome, Italy. Facade by CARLO MADERNO, 1606–1612. Piazza by GIANLORENZO BERNINI, 1656–1667.

The dramatic gesture of embrace that Bernini's colonnade makes as worshipers enter Saint Peter's piazza symbolizes the welcome the Catholic Church wished to extend during the Counter-Reformation.

thus effectively gives visual form to the triumph of Christianity and to the papal claim to supremacy in formulating Church doctrine.

MADERNO'S SAINT PETER'S The installation of Bernini's baldacchino was the last major transformation of the interior of Saint Peter's after CARLO MADERNO (1556–1629) completed the century-long project to rebuild the Constantinian basilica. Pope Paul V (r. 1605–1621) had asked Maderno to design a new facade (FIG. 10-3, *left*) for Michelangelo's incomplete building (FIGS. 9-13 and 9-14). Although Maderno did not have the luxury of formulating a totally new concept for Saint Peter's, his facade nonetheless embodies the design principles of early Italian Baroque architecture. The rhythm of vigorously projecting columns and pilasters mounts dramatically toward the emphatically stressed pediment-capped central section. The recessed niches, which contain statues and create pockets of shadow, heighten the sculptural effect. The two outer bays with bell towers were not part of Maderno's original design, however. Had the facade been constructed according to the architect's concept, it would have exhibited greater verticality and visual coherence.

Behind the facade, Maderno's Saint Peter's also departed from the 16th-century plans of Bramante and Michelangelo. At the pope's request, Maderno added three nave bays to the earlier nucleus because Paul V considered the central plan too closely associated with ancient temples, such as the Pantheon (FIG. 3-38). Further, the traditional longitudinal basilica plan reinforced the symbolic distinction between clergy and laity and also was much better suited for large congregations and religious processions. Lengthening the nave, however, pushed the dome farther back from the facade and all but destroyed the effect Michelangelo had planned—a structure pulled together and dominated by its dome (FIG. 9-14). When viewed at close range, the dome barely emerges above the facade's soaring frontal plane. Seen from the great piazza (FIG. 10-3) erected later by Bernini (see "Completing Saint Peter's," page 288), Maderno's dome appears to have no drum. Visitors must move back quite a distance from the front (or fly over the church) to see the dome and drum together.

DAVID Although Bernini won fame as an architect, his international reputation rested primarily on his sculpture. The biographer Filippo Baldinucci (1625–1696) observed: "[No sculptor] manipulated marble with more facility and boldness. He gave his works a marvelous softness . . . making the marble, so to say, flexible."[1] Bernini's sculpture is expansive and theatrical, and the element of time usually plays an important role in it, as in the pronounced movement of the personified rivers—and the cascading water—in his Piazza Navona fountain (FIG. 10-1).

An earlier masterwork is Bernini's *David* (FIG. 10-4), which fundamentally differs from the Renaissance portrayals of the same subject by Donatello (FIG. 8-18) and Michelangelo (FIG. 9-8). Michelangelo portrayed David before his encounter with Goliath. Donatello depicted David after his triumph over the giant. Bernini chose to represent the combat itself and aimed to capture the split-second of maximum action. Bernini's hero, his muscular legs widely and firmly planted, begins the violent, pivoting motion that will launch the stone from his sling. Unlike Myron, the fifth-century BCE Greek sculptor who froze his *Discus Thrower* (FIG. 2-32) at a fleeting moment of inaction, Bernini selected the most dramatic of an implied sequence of poses, requiring the viewer to think simultaneously of the continuum and of this tiny fraction of it. The suggested

10-4 GIANLORENZO BERNINI, *David,* from the Villa Borghese, Rome, 1623. Marble, 5' 7" high. Galleria Borghese, Rome.

Bernini's sculptures are expansive and theatrical, and the element of time plays an important role in them. His emotion-packed *David* seems to be moving through both time and space.

continuum imparts a dynamic burst of energy. The Baroque statue seems to be moving through time and through space. This kind of sculpture cannot be inscribed in a cylinder or confined in a niche. Its unrestrained action demands space around it. Nor is it self-sufficient in the Renaissance sense, as its pose and attitude direct attention beyond it to the unseen Goliath. Bernini's *David* moves out into the space surrounding it, as do Apollo and Daphne in the marble group (FIG. 10-4A ⬚) that he carved for the same patron, Cardinal Scipione Borghese (1576–1633). Further, the expression of intense concentration on David's face contrasts vividly with the classically placid visage of Donatello's biblical hero and is more emotionally charged even than Michelangelo's. The tension in David's face augments the dramatic impact of Bernini's sculpture.

1 ft.

10-5 GIANLORENZO BERNINI, Cornaro chapel, Santa Maria della Vittoria, Rome, Italy, 1645–1652. *Left:* general view. *Right: Ecstasy of Saint Teresa.* Marble, 11′ 6″ high.

In the Cornaro chapel, Bernini marshaled the full capabilities of architecture, sculpture, and painting to re-create a spiritual experience for worshipers, consistent with the ideas of Ignatius Loyola.

ECSTASY OF SAINT TERESA Another work displaying the motion and emotion that are hallmarks of Italian Baroque art is Bernini's *Ecstasy of Saint Teresa* in the Cornaro chapel (FIG. 10-5, *left*) of Santa Maria della Vittoria. The work exemplifies Bernini's refusal to limit his statues to firmly defined spatial settings. For this commission, the Baroque master, drawing on the considerable knowledge of the theater that he derived from writing plays and producing stage designs, marshaled the full capabilities of architecture, sculpture, and painting to charge the entire chapel with palpable tension. The marble sculpture (FIG. 10-5, *right*) that serves as the chapel's focus depicts Saint Teresa of Avila (1515–1582), one of the great mystical saints of the Spanish Counter-Reformation. Her conversion occurred after the death of her father, when she fell into a series of trances, saw visions, and heard voices. Feeling a persistent pain, she attributed it to the fire-tipped arrow of divine love that an angel had thrust repeatedly into her heart. In her writings, Saint Teresa described this experience as making her swoon in delightful anguish. In Bernini's hands, the entire Cornaro chapel became a theater for the production of this mystical drama. The niche in which it takes place appears as a shallow *proscenium* (the part of the stage in front of the curtain) crowned with a broken pediment and ornamented with polychrome marble. On either side of the chapel, sculpted relief portraits of Cardinal Federico Cornaro (1579–1673) and his family watch the heavenly drama unfold from choice balcony seats. Bernini depicted the saint in ecstasy, unmistakably a mingling of spiritual and physical passion, swooning back on a cloud, while the smiling angel aims his arrow. The sculptor's supreme technical virtuosity is evident in

the visual differentiation in texture among the clouds, rough cloth and gauzy material, smooth flesh, and feathery wings—all carved from the same white marble. Light from a hidden window of yellow glass pours down in golden rays suggesting the radiance of Heaven, whose painted representation covers the vault.

The passionate drama of Bernini's *Ecstasy of Saint Teresa* correlated with the ideas disseminated earlier by Ignatius Loyola (1491–1556), who founded the Jesuit order in 1534 (see page 265) and whom the Catholic Church canonized as Saint Ignatius in 1622. In his book *Spiritual Exercises,* Ignatius argued that the re-creation of spiritual experiences in artworks would do much to increase devotion and piety. Thus theatricality and sensory impact were useful vehicles for achieving Counter-Reformation goals (see "The Council of Trent" ☑). Bernini was a devout Catholic, which undoubtedly contributed to his understanding of those goals. His inventiveness, technical skill, sensitivity to his patrons' needs, and energy made him the quintessential Italian Baroque artist.

FRANCESCO BORROMINI As gifted as Bernini was as an architect, FRANCESCO BORROMINI (1599–1667) took Italian Baroque architecture to even greater dramatic heights. In San Carlo alle Quattro Fontane (Saint Charles at the Four Fountains; FIG. 10-6), Borromini went much further than any of his predecessors or contemporaries in emphasizing a building's sculptural qualities (see "Rethinking the Church Facade," page 291). Inside, San Carlo is a hybrid of a Greek cross and an oval, with a long axis between entrance and apse. The side walls move in an undulating flow that reverses the facade's

PROBLEMS AND SOLUTIONS
Rethinking the Church Facade

Although Carlo Maderno incorporated sculptural elements in his facade of Saint Peter's (FIG. 10-3), the church fronts he designed still develop along relatively lateral planes, the traditional approach to facade design. In contrast, Francesco Borromini rethought the very nature of a church facade. In his design for San Carlo alle Quattro Fontane (FIG. 10-6) in Rome, Borromini set the building's front in undulating motion, creating a dynamic counterpoint of concave and convex elements on two levels (for example, the sway of the cornices). He enhanced the three-dimensional effect with deeply recessed niches. Borromini's facade therefore stands in sharp opposition to the idea, which has its roots in antiquity, that a facade should be a flat frontispiece that defines a building's outer limits. In Borromini's hands, the church facade became a pulsating, engaging screen inserted between interior and exterior space, designed not to separate but to provide a fluid transition between the two.

In fact, San Carlo has not one but two facades, underscoring the functional interrelation of the building and its environment. The second facade, a narrow bay crowned with its own small tower, turns away from the main facade and, following the curve of the street, faces an intersection.

10-6 FRANCESCO BORROMINI, San Carlo alle Quattro Fontane (looking south), Rome, Italy, 1638–1641.

Borromini rejected the notion that a church should have a flat frontispiece. He set San Carlo's facade in undulating motion, creating a dynamic counterpoint of concave and convex elements.

motion. Vigorously projecting columns define the space into which they protrude just as much as they accent the walls to which they are attached. Capping this molded interior space is a deeply coffered oval dome (FIG. 10-7) that seems to float on the light entering through windows hidden in its base. Rich variations on the basic theme of the oval—dynamic relative to the static circle—create an interior that flows from entrance to altar, unimpeded by the segmentation so characteristic of Renaissance buildings.

10-7 FRANCESCO BORROMINI, view into the dome of San Carlo alle Quattro Fontane, Rome, Italy, 1638–1641.

Instead of using a traditional round dome, Borromini capped the interior of San Carlo with a deeply coffered oval dome that seems to float on the light entering through windows hidden in its base.

Painting

Although architecture and sculpture provided the most obvious vehicles for manipulating space and creating theatrical effects, painting continued to be an important art form in 17th-century Italy.

ANNIBALE CARRACCI One of the most renowned Italian Baroque painters was ANNIBALE CARRACCI (1560–1609), who received much of his training at an art academy in his native Bologna founded by his extended family, among them his cousin Ludovico Carracci (1555–1619) and brother Agostino Carracci (1557–1602). The Bolognese academy was the first significant institution of its kind in the history of Western art. The Carracci established it on the premises that art can be taught—the basis of any academic philosophy of art—and that art instruction must include the classical and Renaissance traditions in addition to the study of anatomy and life drawing.

Annibale Carracci's most notable works are his frescoes (FIG. 10-8) in the Palazzo Farnese in Rome. Cardinal Odoardo Farnese (1573–1626), a wealthy descendant of Pope Paul III, who built the palace, commissioned Carracci to decorate the ceiling of the palace's gallery to celebrate the wedding of the cardinal's brother. Appropriately, the title of the fresco's iconographic program is *Loves of the Gods*—interpretations of the varieties of earthly and divine love in classical mythology.

Carracci arranged the scenes in a format resembling framed easel paintings on a wall, but in the Farnese gallery, the paintings cover a shallow curved vault. The term for this type of simulation of easel painting for ceiling design is *quadro riportato* ("transferred framed panel").

Carracci made the quadro riportato format fashionable in Italy for more than a century. Flanking the framed pictures are polychrome seated nude youths, who turn their heads to gaze at the scenes around them, and standing Atlas figures painted to resemble marble statues. Carracci derived these motifs from the Sistine Chapel ceiling (FIG. 9-9), but he did not copy Michelangelo's figures. Notably, the chiaroscuro of the Farnese frescoes differs for the pictures and the figures surrounding them. Carracci modeled the figures inside the panels in an even light. In contrast, light from beneath illuminates the outside figures, as if they were tangible three-dimensional beings or statues illuminated by torches in the gallery below. In the crown of the vault, the long panel, *Triumph of Bacchus,* is an ingenious mixture of Raphael's drawing style and lighting and Titian's more sensuous and animated figures. Carracci succeeded in adjusting their authoritative styles to create something of his own—no easy achievement.

10-8 ANNIBALE CARRACCI, *Loves of the Gods,* ceiling frescoes in the gallery, Palazzo Farnese, Rome, Italy, 1597–1601.

On the shallow curved vault of this large gallery in the Palazzo Farnese, Carracci arranged the mythological scenes in a quadro riportato format resembling easel paintings on a wall.

CARAVAGGIO Michelangelo Merisi, known as CARAVAGGIO (1573–1610) after his northern Italian birthplace, developed a distinctive personal style that had tremendous influence throughout Europe. His outspoken disdain for the classical masters (probably more rhetorical than real) drew bitter criticism from many painters, one of whom denounced him as the "anti-Christ of painting." Giovanni Pietro Bellori (1613–1696), the most influential critic of the age and an admirer of Annibale Carracci, believed that Caravaggio's refusal to emulate the models of his distinguished predecessors threatened the whole classical tradition of Italian painting that had reached its zenith in Raphael's work (see "Giovanni Pietro Bellori on Annibale Carracci and Caravaggio" ⬀). Yet despite this criticism and the problems in Caravaggio's troubled life (police records are an important source of information about the artist), Caravaggio received many commissions, both public and private, and numerous painters paid him the supreme compliment of borrowing from his innovations. His influence on later artists, as much outside Italy as within, was immense. In his art, Caravaggio injected naturalism into the representation of sacred subjects, reducing them to human dramas played out in the harsh and dingy settings of his time and place by unidealized figures that he selected from the fields and the streets.

The setting of Caravaggio's early masterpiece, *Calling of Saint Matthew* (FIG. 10-9), is a modest tavern with unadorned walls. Into this mundane environment, cloaked in mysterious shadow and almost unseen, Christ, identifiable initially only by his indistinct halo, enters from the right. With a commanding gesture, he summons Levi, the Roman tax collector, to a higher calling. The astonished Levi—his face illuminated by the beam of light emanating from an unspecified source above Christ's head and outside the picture—points to himself in disbelief. Although Christ's extended arm is reminiscent of the Lord's in *Creation of Adam* (FIG. 9-10), the position of his hand and wrist is similar to that of Adam's. This reference was highly appropriate because the Church considered Christ the second Adam. Whereas Adam was responsible for the fall of humankind, Christ is the vehicle of its redemption. The conversion of Levi (who became Matthew) brought his salvation.

In *Calling of Saint Matthew* and Caravaggio's other religious paintings—for example, *Conversion of Saint Paul* (FIG. 10-9A ⬀)—the figures are still heroic, with powerful bodies and clearly delineated contours in the Renaissance tradition, but the stark and dramatic contrast of light and dark, which at first shocked and then fascinated his contemporaries, obscures the more traditional aspects of his style. Art historians call Caravaggio's use of dark settings that envelop their occupants *tenebrism,* from the Italian word *tenebroso,* or "shadowy" manner. In Caravaggio's work, tenebrism also contributed greatly to the essential meaning of his pictures. For example, in *Calling of Saint Matthew,* the beam of light directing the viewer's attention to the seated tax collector is the divine light beckoning him to join the Son of God in his earthly mission.

1 ft.

10-9 CARAVAGGIO, *Calling of Saint Matthew,* ca. 1597–1601. Oil on canvas, 11' 1" × 11' 5". Contarelli chapel, San Luigi dei Francesi, Rome.

The stark contrast of light and dark is a key feature of Caravaggio's style. Here, Christ, cloaked in mysterious shadow, summons Levi the tax collector (Saint Matthew) to a higher calling.

ARTISTS ON ART
The Letters of Artemisia Gentileschi

Artemisia Gentileschi (FIGS. 10-10 and 10-10A ⏺) was the most renowned woman painter in Europe during the first half of the 17th century and the first woman ever admitted to membership in Florence's Accademia del Disegno. In addition to scores of paintings created for wealthy patrons, among them the king of England and the grand duke of Tuscany, Gentileschi left behind 28 letters, some of which reveal that she believed that patrons treated her differently because of her gender. Two 1649 letters written in Naples to Don Antonio Ruffo (1610–1678) in Messina make her feelings explicit.

> I fear that before you saw the painting you must have thought me arrogant and presumptuous. . . . [I]f it were not for Your Most Illustrious Lordship . . . I would not have been induced to give it for one hundred and sixty, because everywhere else I have been I was paid one hundred scudi per figure. . . . You think me pitiful, because a woman's name raises doubts until her work is seen.*

> As for my doing a drawing and sending it, [tell the gentleman who wishes to know the price for a painting that] I have made a solemn vow never to send my drawings because people have cheated me. In particular, just today I found myself [in the situation] that, having done a drawing of souls in Purgatory for the Bishop of St. Gata, he, in order to spend less, commissioned another painter to do the painting using my work. If I were a man, I can't imagine it would have turned out this way, because when the concept has been realized and defined with lights and darks, and established by means of planes, the rest is a trifle.†

*Letter dated January 30, 1649. Translated by Mary D. Garrard, *Artemisia Gentileschi: The Image of the Female Hero in Italian Baroque Art* (Princeton, N.J.: Princeton University Press, 1989), 390.

†Letter dated November 13, 1649. Ibid., 397–398.

1 ft.

10-10 ARTEMISIA GENTILESCHI, *Judith Slaying Holofernes*, ca. 1614–1620. Oil on canvas, 6' 6⅓" × 5' 4". Galleria degli Uffizi, Florence.

Narratives involving heroic women were a favorite theme of Gentileschi. In *Judith Slaying Holofernes*, the dramatic lighting of the action in the foreground emulates Caravaggio's tenebrism.

ARTEMISIA GENTILESCHI Caravaggio's combination of naturalism and drama appealed both to patrons and to artists, and he had many followers. Among them was the most celebrated woman artist of the era, ARTEMISIA GENTILESCHI (ca. 1593–1653; FIGS. 10-10 and 10-10A ⏺), whose father, Orazio (1563–1639), her teacher, was himself strongly influenced by Caravaggio. The daughter's successful career, pursued in Florence, Venice, Naples, and Rome (see "The Letters of Artemisia Gentileschi," above), helped disseminate Caravaggio's style throughout the peninsula.

In *Judith Slaying Holofernes* (FIG. 10-10), Gentileschi adopted the tenebrism and what might be called the "dark" subject matter Caravaggio favored. Significantly, she chose a narrative involving a heroic woman, a favorite theme of hers. The story, from the book of Judith, relates the delivery of Israel from the Assyrians. Having succumbed to Judith's charms, the Assyrian general Holofernes invited her to his tent for the night. When he fell asleep, Judith cut off his head. In this version of the scene (Gentileschi produced more than one painting of the subject), Judith and her maidservant behead Holofernes. Blood spurts everywhere as the two women summon all their strength to wield the heavy sword. The tension and strain are palpable. The controlled highlights on the action in the foreground recall Caravaggio's work and heighten the drama here as well.

FRA ANDREA POZZO With the Sistine Chapel (FIG. 9-9) and Farnese Palace (FIG. 10-8) as prestigious models, many Italian Baroque painters created ceiling frescoes for both churches and palaces. One late-17th-century master of ceiling decoration was FRA ANDREA POZZO (1642–1709), a lay brother of the Jesuit order and a master of perspective, on which he wrote an influential treatise. Pozzo designed and executed the huge painting *Glorification of Saint Ignatius* (FIG. 10-11) for the nave of the church of Sant'Ignazio in Rome (see "How to Make a Ceiling Disappear," page 295). Like Il Gesù, which also boasts a vast fresco—*Triumph of the Name of Jesus* (FIG. 10-11A ⏺) by GIOVANNI BATTISTA GAULLI (1639–1709)—on its nave vault, Sant'Ignazio was a prominent Counter-Reformation church because of its dedication to the founder of the Jesuit order. The Jesuits played a major role in Catholic education and sent legions of missionaries to the New World and Asia.

How to Make a Ceiling Disappear

The effectiveness of Italian Baroque religious art depended on the drama and theatricality of individual images, as well as on the interaction and fusion of architecture, sculpture, and painting. Sound enhanced this experience. Architects designed churches with acoustical effects in mind, and in an Italian Baroque church filled with music, the power of both image and sound must have been very moving. Through simultaneous stimulation of the senses of both sight and hearing, the faithful might well have been transported into a trancelike state that would, indeed, as the great English poet John Milton (1608–1674) eloquently stated in *Il Penseroso* (1631), "bring all Heaven before [their] eyes."*

Seventeenth-century church officials keenly realized that spectacular paintings high above the ground offered perfect opportunities to impress on worshipers the glory and power of the Catholic Church. Looking up at a painting is different from viewing a painting hanging on a wall, even in the case of quadro riportato ceiling designs. The considerable height and expansive scale of most ceiling frescoes induce a feeling of awe. In conjunction with the theatricality of Italian Baroque architecture and sculpture, grandiose frescoes on church ceilings contributed to creating transcendent spiritual environments well suited to the needs of the Catholic Church in Counter-Reformation Rome.

In his fresco (FIG. 10-11) for the ceiling of the nave of the Roman church honoring Saint Ignatius, Fra Andrea Pozzo created the illusion of Heaven opening up above the congregation. To accomplish this, the artist painted an extension of the church's architecture into the vault so that the roof seems to be lifted off. As Heaven and earth commingle, Christ receives Saint Ignatius in the presence of figures personifying the four corners of the world. A disk in the nave floor marks the spot where the viewer should stand to gain the whole perspective illusion. For worshipers looking up from this point, the vision is complete. They find themselves in the presence of the heavenly and spiritual, the ultimate goal of Italian Baroque church art and architecture.

*John Milton, *Il Penseroso* (1631, published 1645), 166.

10-11 FRA ANDREA POZZO, *Glorification of Saint Ignatius*, ceiling fresco in the nave of Sant'Ignazio, Rome, Italy, 1691–1694.

By merging real and painted architecture, Pozzo created the illusion that the vaulted ceiling of Sant'Ignazio has been lifted off and the nave opens to Heaven above the worshipers' heads.

SPAIN

During the 16th century, Spain had established itself as an international power. The Habsburg kings had built a dynastic state encompassing Portugal, part of Italy, the Netherlands, and extensive areas of the New World (see page 527). By the beginning of the 17th century, however, the Habsburg Empire was in decline, and although

Spain mounted an aggressive effort during the Thirty Years' War, by 1660 the imperial age of the Spanish Habsburgs was over. In part, the demise of the Habsburg Empire was due to economic woes. The military campaigns of Philip III (r. 1598–1621) and his son Philip IV (r. 1621–1665) waged during the Thirty Years' War were costly and led to higher taxes. The increasing tax burden placed on Spanish subjects in turn incited revolts and civil war in Catalonia and Portugal in the 1640s, further straining an already fragile economy. Nevertheless, both Philip III and Philip IV continued to spend lavishly on art.

In a country passionately committed to Catholic orthodoxy, Spanish Baroque artists, like their counterparts in Counter-Reformation Italy, sought ways to move viewers and to encourage greater devotion and piety. Scenes of death and suffering had great appeal in Spain. They provided artists with opportunities both to depict extreme emotion and to elicit passionate feelings. Spain prided itself on its saints—Saint Teresa of Avila (FIG. 10-5) and Saint Ignatius Loyola (FIG. 10-11) were both Spanish-born—and martyrdom scenes were staples of Spanish Baroque art.

FRANCISCO DE ZURBARÁN One prominent Spanish Baroque painter of religious works was FRANCISCO DE ZURBARÁN (1598–1664), whose primary patrons were rich monastic orders. Many of his paintings are quiet and contemplative, appropriate for prayer. Zurbarán painted *Saint Serapion* (FIG. 10-12) as a devotional image for the funerary chapel of the monastic Order of Mercy in Seville, which was founded to aid Christians who had been taken prisoner by the Moors. The saint, who participated in the Third Crusade of 1196, suffered martyrdom while preaching the Gospel to Muslims. According to one account, the monk's captors tied him to a tree and then tortured and decapitated him. The Order of Mercy dedicated itself to self-sacrifice, and Serapion's membership in this order amplified the resonance of Zurbarán's painting. In *Saint Serapion,* the monk emerges from a dark background and fills the foreground. The bright light shining on him calls attention to the saint's tragic death and increases the dramatic

impact of the image. In the background are two barely visible tree branches. A small note next to the saint identifies him. The coarse features of the Spanish monk label him as common (Serapion had not yet been declared a saint at the time Zurbarán portrayed him), no doubt evoking empathy from a wide audience.

DIEGO VELÁZQUEZ The foremost Spanish painter of the Baroque age—and the greatest beneficiary of royal patronage—was DIEGO VELÁZQUEZ (1599–1660). Trained in Seville, Velázquez was quite young when he came to the attention of Philip IV, who, struck by the artist's immense talent, named him chief court painter and palace chamberlain. With the exception of two extended trips to Italy and a few excursions, Velázquez remained in Madrid for the rest of his life. His close relationship with Philip IV and his high office as chamberlain gave him prestige and a rare guaranteed income, although, like Michelangelo in the service of Julius II (see page 251), Velázquez had little opportunity to choose his own subjects.

An early work, *Water Carrier of Seville* (FIG. 10-13), reveals Velázquez's impressive command of the painter's craft when he was only about 20 years old. In this genre scene that seems to carry a deeper significance, Velázquez rendered the figures with clarity and dignity, and his careful depiction of the water jugs in the foreground, complete with droplets of water, adds to the scene's credibility. As in Zurbarán's *Saint Serapion* (FIG. 10-12), the commonplace characters

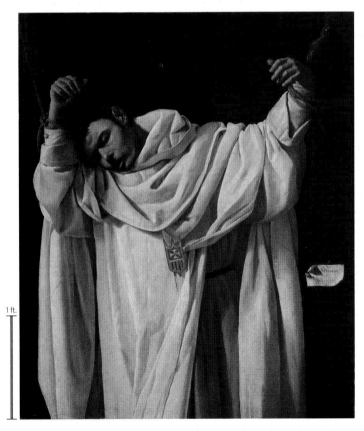

10-12 FRANCISCO DE ZURBARÁN, *Saint Serapion,* 1628. Oil on canvas, 3' 11½" × 3' 4¾". Wadsworth Atheneum Museum of Art, Hartford (Ella Gallup Sumner and Mary Catlin Sumner Collection Fund).

The light shining on Serapion calls attention to his tragic death and increases the painting's dramatic impact. The monk's coarse features label him as common, evoking empathy from a wide audience.

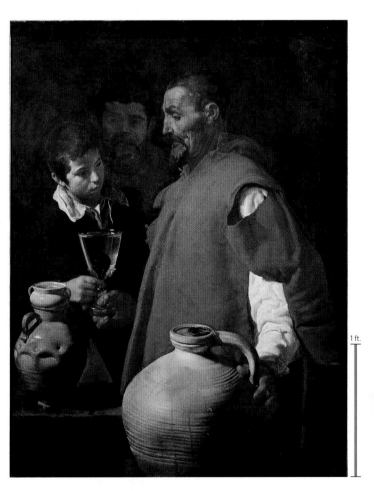

10-13 DIEGO VELÁZQUEZ, *Water Carrier of Seville,* ca. 1619. Oil on canvas, 3' 5½" × 2' 7½". Victoria & Albert Museum, London.

In this early work—a genre scene that seems to convey a deeper significance—the contrast of darks and lights and the commonplace characters reveal Velázquez's indebtedness to Caravaggio.

and the contrast of darks and lights reveal the influence of Caravaggio, whose work Velázquez had studied.

LAS MENINAS After an extended visit to Rome from 1648 to 1651, Velázquez returned to Spain and, in 1656, painted his greatest work, *Las Meninas* (*The Maids of Honor*; FIG. 10-14). The setting is the artist's studio in the Alcázar, the royal residence in Madrid. The young Infanta (Princess) Margarita appears in the foreground with her two maids-in-waiting, her favorite dwarfs, and a large dog. In the middle ground are a woman in widow's attire and a male escort. In the background, a chamberlain stands in a brightly lit open doorway. Scholars have been able to identify everyone in the room, including the two meninas and the dwarfs.

Las Meninas is noteworthy for its visual and narrative complexity. Indeed, art historians have yet to agree on any particular reading or interpretation. A central issue has been what, exactly, is taking place in *Las Meninas*. What is Velázquez depicting on the huge canvas in front of him? He may be painting this very picture—an informal image of the infanta and her entourage. Alternately, Velázquez may be painting a portrait of King Philip IV and Queen Mariana, whose reflections appear in the mirror on the far wall. If so, that would suggest the presence of the king and queen in the viewer's space, outside the confines of the picture. Other scholars have proposed that the mirror image is not a reflection of the royal couple standing in Velázquez's studio but a reflection of the portrait the artist is in the process of painting on the canvas before him.

More generally, *Las Meninas* is Velázquez's attempt to elevate both himself and his profession. Throughout his career, Velázquez hoped to be ennobled by royal appointment to membership in the ancient and illustrious Order of Santiago (Saint James). Because he lacked a sufficiently noble lineage, he gained entrance only with difficulty at the very end of his life, and then only through the pope's dispensation. In the painting, Velázquez wears the order's red cross on his doublet. In the artist's mind, *Las Meninas* might have embodied the idea of the great king visiting his studio, as Alexander the Great visited the studio of the painter Apelles. The figures in the painting all appear to acknowledge the royal presence. Placed among them in equal dignity is Velázquez, face-to-face with his sovereign.

The location of the completed painting reinforced this act of looking—of seeing and being seen. *Las Meninas* hung in Philip IV's personal office. Thus, although occasional visitors admitted to the king's private quarters may have seen this painting, Philip was the primary audience. Each time he stood before the canvas, he again participated in the work as the probable subject of Velázquez's painting within the painting and as the object of the figures' gazes. In *Las Meninas,* Velázquez elevated the art of painting, in the person of the painter, to the highest status. The king's presence enhanced this status—either in person as the viewer of *Las Meninas* or as a reflected image in the painting itself. The paintings that appear in *Las Meninas* further reinforce this celebration of the painter's craft. On the wall above the doorway and mirror, two canvases depict the immortal gods as the source of art.

Las Meninas is extraordinarily complex visually. Velázquez's optical report of the event, authentic in every detail, pictorially summarizes the various kinds of images in their different levels and degrees of reality. He portrayed the realities of image on canvas, of mirror image, of optical image, and of the two painted images. This work—with its cunning contrasts of real spaces, mirrored spaces, picture spaces, and pictures within pictures—itself appears to have been taken from a large mirror reflecting the entire scene. This would mean that the artist did not paint the princess and her suite as the main subjects of *Las Meninas* but himself in the process of painting them. *Las Meninas* is a pictorial summary and a commentary on the essential mystery of the visual world, as well as on the ambiguity that results when different states or levels interact or are juxtaposed.

Velázquez employed several devices in order to achieve these results. For example, the extension of the composition's pictorial depth in both directions is noteworthy. The open doorway and its ascending staircase lead the eye beyond the artist's studio, and the mirror and the outward glances of several of the figures incorporate the viewer's space into the picture as well. (Compare how the mirror in Jan van Eyck's *Giovanni Arnolfini and His Wife* [FIG. 8-6] similarly incorporates the area in front of the canvas into the picture, although less obviously and without a comparable extension of space beyond the rear wall of the room.) Velázquez also masterfully

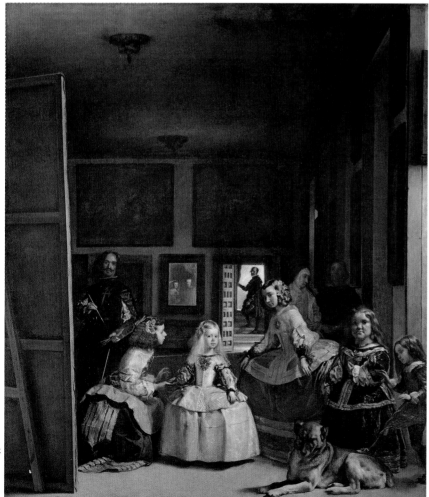

1 ft.

10-14 DIEGO VELAZQUEZ, *Las Meninas* (*The Maids of Honor*), 1656. Oil on canvas, 10' 5" × 9". Museo del Prado, Madrid.

Velázquez intended this huge and complex work, with its cunning contrasts of real, mirrored, and picture spaces, to elevate both himself and the profession of painting in the eyes of Philip IV.

observed and represented form and shadow. Instead of putting lights abruptly beside darks, following Caravaggio, Velázquez allowed a great number of intermediate values of gray to come between the two extremes. His matching of tonal gradations approached effects that were later discovered in the age of photography.

FLANDERS

In the 16th century, the Netherlands had come under the crown of Habsburg Spain when Emperor Charles V retired, leaving the Spanish kingdoms, their Italian and American possessions, and the Netherlandish provinces to his only legitimate son, Philip II (r. 1556–1598). (Charles bestowed his imperial title and German lands to his brother.) Philip's repressive measures against Protestants led the northern provinces to break from Spain and establish the Dutch Republic. The southern provinces remained under Spanish control, and they retained Catholicism as their official religion. The political distinction between modern Holland and Belgium more or less reflects this original separation, which in the 17th century signaled not only religious but also artistic differences. The Baroque art of Flanders (the Spanish Netherlands) retained close connections to the Baroque art of Catholic Europe, whereas the Dutch schools of painting developed their own subjects and styles.

PETER PAUL RUBENS The greatest 17th-century Flemish painter was PETER PAUL RUBENS (1577–1640), who built on the innovations of the Italian Renaissance and Baroque masters to formulate the first truly pan-European painting style. Rubens's art is an original and powerful synthesis of the manners of many painters, especially Michelangelo, Titian, Carracci, and Caravaggio. His style had wide appeal, and his influence was international. Among the most learned individuals of his time, Rubens possessed an aristocratic education and a courtier's manner, diplomacy, and tact, which, with his facility for language, made him the associate of princes and scholars.

He became court painter to the dukes of Mantua, friend of King Philip IV (r. 1621–1665) of Spain and his adviser on collecting art, painter to Charles I (r. 1625–1649) of England and Marie de' Medici (1573–1642) of France, and permanent court painter to the Spanish governors of Flanders. Rubens also won the confidence of his royal patrons in matters of state, and they often entrusted him with diplomatic missions of the highest importance. To produce a steady stream of paintings for an international clientele, Rubens employed scores of assistants. He also became a highly successful art dealer, buying and selling contemporary artworks and classical antiquities. Rubens's many enterprises made him a rich man, able to afford a magnificent townhouse in Antwerp and a castle in the countryside.

ELEVATION OF THE CROSS When he was 23 years old, Rubens departed Flanders for Italy and remained there from 1600 until 1608. During these years, he laid the foundations of his mature style. Shortly after returning home, he painted *Elevation of the Cross* (FIG. 10-15) for Saint Walburga in Antwerp. The triptych reveals his careful study in Italy of the works of Michelangelo and Caravaggio, as well as ancient statuary. In a treatise he wrote in Latin—*De imitatione statuarum* (*On the Imitation of Statues*)—Rubens stated: "I am convinced that in order to achieve the highest perfection one needs a full understanding of the [ancient] statues, indeed a complete absorption in them; but one must make judicious use of them and before all avoid the effect of stone."[2]

Elevation of the Cross provided Rubens with the opportunity to depict heavily muscled men in unusual poses straining to lift the heavy cross with Christ's body nailed to it. Here, as in his *Lion Hunt* (FIG. I-11), Rubens, deeply impressed by Michelangelo's twisting sculpted and painted figures (FIGS. I-14, 9-10, 9-10A, and 9-11), showed his prowess in representing foreshortened anatomy and the contortions of violent action. Rubens placed the body of Christ on the cross as a diagonal that cuts dynamically across the picture while inclining back into it. The whole composition seethes with a power

10-15 PETER PAUL RUBENS, *Elevation of the Cross*, from Saint Walburga, Antwerp, 1610. Oil on wood, center panel 15' 1⅞" × 11' 1½", each wing 15' 1⅞" × 4' 11". Antwerp Cathedral, Antwerp.

In this triptych, Rubens explored foreshortened anatomy and violent action. The whole composition seethes with a power that comes from heroic exertion. The tension is emotional as well as physical.

that comes from strenuous exertion, from elastic human sinew taut with effort. The tension is emotional as well as physical, as reflected not only in Christ's face but also in the features of his followers. Bright highlights and areas of deep shadow inspired by Caravaggio's tenebrism, hallmarks of Rubens's work at this stage of his career, enhance the drama. He later developed a much subtler coloristic style.

MARIE DE' MEDICI Rubens's interaction with royalty and aristocracy provided him with an understanding of the ostentation and spectacle of Baroque (particularly Italian) art that appealed to the wealthy and privileged. Rubens, the born courtier, reveled in the pomp and majesty of royalty. Likewise, those in power embraced the lavish spectacle that served the Catholic Church so well in Italy. The magnificence and splendor of Baroque imagery reinforced the authority and right to rule of the highborn. Among Rubens's royal patrons was Marie de' Medici, a member of the famous Florentine banking family and widow of Henry IV (r. 1589–1610), the first Bourbon king of France. She commissioned Rubens to paint a series of huge canvases memorializing and glorifying her career. Between 1622 and 1626, Rubens, working with amazing creative energy, produced 21 huge historical-allegorical pictures designed to hang in the queen's new palace, the Luxembourg, in Paris.

In *Arrival of Marie de' Medici at Marseilles* (FIG. 10-16), Marie disembarks after the sea voyage from Italy. A personification of France, draped in a cloak decorated with the royal *fleur-de-lis* (compare FIG. 10-30), welcomes her. The sea and sky rejoice at the queen's safe arrival. Neptune and the Nereids (daughters of the sea god Nereus) salute her, and the winged and trumpeting personified Fame swoops overhead. Conspicuous in the galley's opulently carved stern-castle, under the Medici coat of arms, stands the commander of the vessel, the only immobile figure in the composition. In black and silver, this figure makes a sharp accent amid the swirling tonality of ivory, gold, and red brushstrokes. Rubens enriched the surfaces with a decorative splendor that pulls the whole composition together. The vigorous motion that customarily enlivens the artist's figures, beginning with the monumental, twisting sea creatures, vibrates through the entire design.

ANTHONY VAN DYCK The most famous of Rubens's Flemish successors was ANTHONY VAN DYCK (1599–1641), who was an assistant in the master's studio. Early on, the younger man, unwilling to be overshadowed by Rubens's undisputed stature, left his native Antwerp for Genoa and then London, where he became court portraitist to Charles I. Although Van Dyck created dramatic compositions of high quality, his specialty became the portrait. In one of his finest works, *Charles I at the Hunt* (FIG. 10-17), the ill-fated English king stands on a hillock with the Thames River in the background. The portrait is a stylish image of relaxed authority, as if the king is out for a casual ride in his park, but no one can mistake the regal poise

10-16 PETER PAUL RUBENS, *Arrival of Marie de' Medici at Marseilles,* from the Luxembourg Palace, Paris, France, 1622–1625. Oil on canvas, 12' 11½" × 9' 7". Musée du Louvre, Paris.

Rubens painted 21 large canvases glorifying Marie de' Medici's career. In this historical-allegorical picture of robust figures in an opulent setting, the sea and sky rejoice at the queen's arrival in France.

10-17 ANTHONY VAN DYCK, *Charles I at the Hunt,* ca. 1635. Oil on canvas, 8' 11" × 6' 11½". Musée du Louvre, Paris.

Van Dyck specialized in court portraiture. In this painting, he depicted the absolutist monarch Charles I at a sharp angle so that the king, a short man, appears to be looking down at the viewer.

and the air of absolute authority that Charles's Parliament resented and was soon to rise against. Van Dyck's placement of the monarch is exceedingly artful. He stands off center but, as the sole figure seen against the sky and with the tree branches pointing to him, he is the focus of the viewer's attention, whose gaze the king returns. Van Dyck also managed to make Charles I, who was of short stature, seem taller than his attendants and even his horse. The painter also portrayed the king turning his back on his attendants and looking down on the observer, befitting his exalted position.

DUTCH REPUBLIC

With the founding of the Bank of Amsterdam in 1609, Amsterdam emerged as the financial center of the Continent. The Dutch economy also benefited enormously from the country's expertise on the open seas, which facilitated establishing lucrative trade routes as far away as Japan, Africa, and South America. Due to this prosperity and in the absence of an absolute ruler, political power increasingly passed into the hands of a class of wealthy merchants and

PROBLEMS AND SOLUTIONS
Frans Hals's Group Portraits

Portrait artists traditionally relied heavily on convention—for example, specific poses, settings, attire, and furnishings—to convey a sense of the sitter. Because the subject was usually someone of status or note, such as a pope, king, duchess, condottiere, or wealthy banker, the artist's goal was to produce an image appropriate to the subject's station in life. With the increasing number of Dutch middle-class patrons, portrait painting became more challenging. The Calvinists shunned ostentation, instead wearing subdued and dark clothing with little variation or decoration, and the traditional conventions became inappropriate and thus unusable. Despite these difficulties, or perhaps because of them, Frans Hals produced lively portraits that seem far more relaxed than traditional formulaic portraiture. He injected an engaging spontaneity into his images and conveyed the individuality of his sitters as well. His manner of execution, using light and rapid brushstrokes, intensified the casualness, immediacy, and intimacy in his paintings. The poses of his figures, the highlights on their clothing, and their facial expression all seem instantaneously created.

Hals's most ambitious portraits reflect the widespread popularity in the Dutch Republic of very large canvases commemorating the participation of Dutch citizens in civic organizations. These commissions presented greater difficulties to the painter than requests to depict a single sitter. Hals rose to the challenge and achieved great success with this new portrait genre. His *Archers of Saint Hadrian* (FIG. 10-18) is typical in that the subject is one of the many Dutch civic militia groups that claimed credit for liberating the Dutch Republic

from Spain. As did other companies, each year the Archers met in dress uniform for a grand banquet on their saint's feast day. The celebrations sometimes lasted an entire week, prompting an ordinance limiting them to three or four days. These events often included sitting for a group portrait.

In *Archers of Saint Hadrian,* Hals attacked the problem of how to represent each militia member satisfactorily yet retain action and variety in the composition. Whereas earlier group portraits in the Netherlands were rather ordered and regimented images, Hals sought to enliven the depictions. In his portrait of the Saint Hadrian militiamen, each member is both part of the troop and an individual with unique features. The sitters' movements and moods vary markedly. Some engage the viewer directly. Others look away or at a companion. Some are stern, others animated. Each archer is equally visible and clearly recognizable. The uniformity of attire—black military dress, white ruffs, and sashes—did not deter Hals from injecting spontaneity into the work. Indeed, he used those elements to create a lively rhythm extending throughout the composition and energizing the portrait. The impromptu effect—the preservation of every detail and fleeting facial expression—is, of course, the result of careful planning. Yet Hals's energetic brush appears to have moved instinctively, directed by a plan in his mind but not traceable in any preparatory scheme on the canvas. The result is a portrait that is less a record of "sitters posing for the painter" than it is a snapshot of a social gathering.

10-18 FRANS HALS, *Archers of Saint Hadrian,* ca. 1633. Oil on canvas, 6' 9" × 11'. Frans Halsmuseum, Haarlem.

In this brilliant composition, Hals succeeded in solving the problem of portraying each individual in a group portrait while retaining action and variety in the painting as a whole.

1 ft.

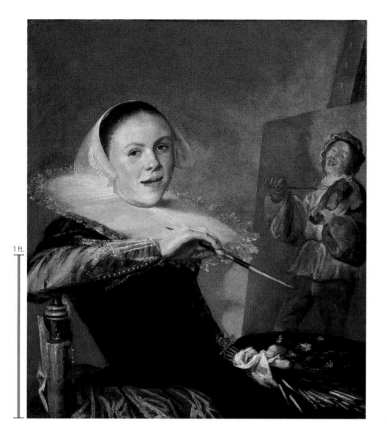

10-19 JUDITH LEYSTER, *Self-Portrait,* ca. 1630. Oil on canvas, 2' 5$\frac{3}{8}$" × 2' 1$\frac{5}{8}$". National Gallery of Art, Washington, D.C. (gift of Mr. and Mrs. Robert Woods Bliss).

Although presenting herself as an artist specializing in genre scenes, Leyster wears elegant attire instead of a painter's smock, placing her socially as a member of a well-to-do family.

individual patrons, groups of Dutch citizens often asked Hals to paint portraits of them. Representing the members of a group, such as the Saint Hadrian militia (FIG. 10-18), rather than separate individuals, presented a special problem for the painter, but Hals quickly became a master of the new genre of group portraiture (see "Frans Hals's Group Portraits," page 300).

JUDITH LEYSTER Some of Hals's followers developed thriving careers of their own as portraitists. One was JUDITH LEYSTER (1609–1660), whose *Self-Portrait* (FIG. 10-19) is detailed, precise, and accurate, but also exhibits the spontaneity found in Hals's works. In her portrait, Leyster succeeded at communicating a great deal about herself. She depicted herself as an artist, seated in front of a painting resting on an easel. The palette in her left hand and brush in her right announce the painting as her creation. She thus invites the viewer to evaluate her skill, which both the fiddler on the canvas and the image of herself demonstrate as considerable. Although she produced a wide range of paintings, including still lifes and floral pieces, her specialty was genre scenes such as the comic image seen on the easel. Leyster's quick smile and relaxed pose as she stops her work to meet the viewer's gaze reveal her self-assurance. Although presenting herself as an artist, Leyster did not paint herself wearing the traditional artist's smock (compare FIG. 10-21). Her elegant attire distinguishes her socially as a member of a well-to-do family, another important aspect of Leyster's identity.

manufacturers, especially in cities such as Amsterdam, Haarlem, and Delft. They in turn emerged as the most important sources of art commissions. As a result of this shift in patronage, and consistent with the Calvinist rejection of most religious art, 17th-century Dutch art centered on genre scenes, landscapes, portraits of middle-class men and women, and still lifes.

FRANS HALS The leading painter in Haarlem was FRANS HALS (ca. 1581–1666), who made portraits his specialty. In addition to

REMBRANDT VAN RIJN The foremost Dutch artist of the 17th century was REMBRANDT VAN RIJN (1606–1669), an undisputed genius and one of the greatest painters and printmakers who ever lived. Born in Leiden, Rembrandt moved to Amsterdam around 1631, where he could attract a more extensive clientele. He quickly gained renown for his portraits, which delve deeply into the psyche and personality of his sitters. Like Hals, Rembrandt also produced memorable group portraits. The most famous is *The Company of Captain Frans Banning Cocq* (FIG. 10-20), better known as *Night Watch.* This more commonly used title is a misnomer, however. The painting is not a nocturnal scene, nor are the figures portrayed posted on a watch in defense of their city. The painting features

10-20 REMBRANDT VAN RIJN, *The Company of Captain Frans Banning Cocq* (*Night Watch*), from the Musketeers Hall, Amsterdam, Netherlands, 1642. Oil on canvas, 11' 11" × 14' 4" (trimmed from original size). Rijksmuseum, Amsterdam.

Rembrandt's dramatic use of light contributes to the animation of this militia group portrait in which the artist showed the company rushing to organize themselves for a parade.

dramatic lighting, but its tonality today is the result of the varnish the artist used, which darkened considerably over time.

Night Watch was one of six paintings by different artists commissioned by various groups around 1640 for the assembly and banquet hall of Amsterdam's new Musketeers' Hall. From the limited information available about the commission, it appears that Captain Frans Banning Cocq and Lieutenant Willem van Ruytenburch, along with 16 members of their militia, contributed to Rembrandt's fee. Unfortunately, in 1715, when city officials moved Rembrandt's painting to the town hall, they trimmed it on all sides (by as much as 2 feet). Even in its truncated form, *Night Watch* succeeds in capturing the excitement and frenetic activity of men preparing for a parade. Comparing this militia group portrait with Hals's *Archers of Saint Hadrian* (FIG. 10-18) reveals Rembrandt's inventiveness in enlivening what was, by then, becoming a conventional format for Dutch group portraits. Rather than present assembled men posed in orderly fashion, the younger artist chose to portray the company rushing about in the act of organizing themselves, thereby animating the image considerably. At the same time, Rembrandt managed to record the three most important stages of using a musket—loading, firing, and readying the weapon for reloading—details that must have pleased his 18 patrons.

Night Watch is also noteworthy for Rembrandt's masterful use of light and shade. His pictorial method involved refining light and dark into finer and finer nuances until they blended with one another. Earlier painters' use of abrupt lights and darks gave way, in the work of artists such as Rembrandt and Velázquez, to gradation. Although both masters sacrificed some of the dramatic effects of sharp chiaroscuro, a greater fidelity to appearances more than offsets those sacrifices. In fact, the recording of light in small gradations is closer to reality because the eye perceives light and dark not as static but as always subtly changing. In general, Renaissance artists represented forms in a flat, neutral modeling light (even Leonardo's shading is of a standard kind). They represented the *idea* of light, rather than showed how humans perceive light. Artists such as Rembrandt discovered gradations of light and dark as well as degrees of differences in pose, in the movements of facial features, and in psychic states. They arrived at these differences optically, not conceptually or in terms of some ideal. Rembrandt found that by manipulating the direction, intensity, and distance of light and shadow, and by varying the surface texture with tactile brushstrokes, he could render subtle nuances of character and mood, both in individuals and whole scenes. He discovered for the modern world that variation of light and shade, subtly modulated, can be read as emotional differences. In the visible world, light, dark, and the wide spectrum of values between the two are charged with meanings and feelings that sometimes are independent of the shapes and figures they modify.

SELF-PORTRAITS Rembrandt's portraits reveal his complete understanding of what could be called the "psychology of light." Light and dark are not in conflict in his portraits. They are reconciled, merging softly and subtly to produce the visual equivalent of quietness. Their prevailing mood is one of tranquil meditation, of philosophical resignation, of musing recollection—indeed, a whole cluster of emotional tones heard only in silence. In the self-portrait reproduced here (FIG. 10-21), the light source outside the upper left of the painting bathes the artist's face in soft highlights, leaving the lower part of his body in shadow. Rembrandt depicted himself here as possessing dignity and strength, and the portrait serves as a summary of the many stylistic and professional concerns that occupied him throughout his career. Rembrandt's distinctive use of light is

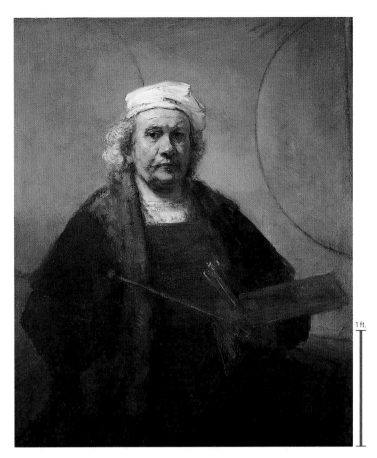

1 ft.

10-21 REMBRANDT VAN RIJN, *Self-Portrait,* ca. 1659–1660. Oil on canvas, 3' 8¾" × 3' 1". Kenwood House, London (Iveagh Bequest).

In this self-portrait, Rembrandt's interest in revealing the soul is evident in the attention given to his expressive face. The controlled use of light and the nonspecific setting contribute to this focus.

evident, as is the assertive brushwork suggesting his self-assurance. He presented himself as a working artist holding his brushes, palette, and maulstick (compare FIG. 9-36) and wearing his studio garb—a smock and painter's turban. The circles on the wall behind him may allude to a legendary sign of artistic virtuosity—the ability to draw a perfect circle freehand. Rembrandt's abiding interest in revealing the human soul emerges here in his careful focus on his expressive visage. His controlled use of light and the nonspecific setting contribute to drawing the viewer's attention to his face. This is a portrait not just of the artist but of the man as well.

HUNDRED-GUILDER PRINT Rembrandt's virtuosity also extended to the graphic arts, especially etching. Many printmakers adopted etching after its perfection early in the 17th century, because the technique affords greater freedom in drawing the design than engraving does (see "Woodcuts, Engravings, and Etchings," page 228). The etcher covers a copper plate with a layer of wax or varnish, and then incises the design into this surface with a pointed tool, exposing the metal below but not cutting into its surface. Next, the artist immerses the plate in acid, which etches, or eats away, the exposed parts of the metal, acting in the same way the burin does in engraving. The wax's softness gives etchers greater carving freedom than woodcutters and engravers have working directly in more resistant wood and metal. If Rembrandt had never painted, he still would be acclaimed, as he principally was in his lifetime, for his prints. Prints were a major source of income for Rembrandt, as they were

1 in.

10-22 REMBRANDT VAN RIJN, *Christ with the Sick around Him, Receiving the Children* (*Hundred-Guilder Print*), ca. 1649. Etching, 11" × 1' 3¼". Pierpont Morgan Library, New York.

Rembrandt's mastery of the newly perfected medium of etching is evident in his expert use of light and dark to draw attention to Christ as he preaches compassionately to the blind and lame.

for Albrecht Dürer (see page 274), and he often reworked the plates so that they could be used to produce a new edition.

Christ with the Sick around Him, Receiving the Children (FIG. 10-22) is one of Rembrandt's most celebrated prints. Indeed, the title by which this work has been known since the early 18th century—*Hundred-Guilder Print*—refers to the high sale price it brought during the artist's lifetime. Rembrandt produced the print using both etching and engraving techniques. As in his other religious works, he suffused *Christ with the Sick* with a deep and abiding piety, presenting the viewer not the celestial triumph of the Catholic Church but the humanity and humility of Jesus. Christ appears in the center

preaching compassionately to, and simultaneously blessing, the blind, the lame, and the young, who are spread throughout the composition in a dazzling array of standing, kneeling, and lying positions. Also present is a young man in elegant garments with his head in his hand, lamenting Christ's insistence that the wealthy need to give their possessions to the poor in order to gain entrance to Heaven. The tonal range of the print is remarkable. At the right, the figures near the city gate are in deep shadow. At the left, the figures, some rendered almost exclusively in outline, are in bright light—not the light of day but the illumination radiating from Christ himself. A second, unseen source of light comes from the right and casts the shadow of the praying man's arms and head onto Christ's tunic. Technically and in terms of its humanity, Rembrandt's *Hundred-Guilder Print* is his supreme achievement as a printmaker.

JACOB VAN RUISDAEL In addition to portraiture, the Dutch avidly collected landscapes, interior scenes, and still lifes. Each of these painting genres dealt directly with the daily lives of the urban mercantile public, accounting for their appeal. Landscape scenes abound in 17th-century Dutch art. Due to topography and politics, the Dutch had a unique relationship to the land, one that differed from attitudes of people living in other European countries. After gaining independence from Spain, the Dutch undertook an extensive reclamation project lasting almost a century. Dikes and drainage systems cropped up across the countryside, and most Dutch families owned and worked their own farms, cultivating a feeling of closeness to the land.

JACOB VAN RUISDAEL (ca. 1628–1682) became famous for his precise and sensitive depictions of the Dutch landscape. In *View of Haarlem from the Dunes at Overveen* (FIG. 10-23), Ruisdael provided an overarching view of this major Dutch city. The specificity of the artist's image—the Saint Bavo church in the background, the numerous

10-23 JACOB VAN RUISDAEL, *View of Haarlem from the Dunes at Overveen,* ca. 1670. Oil on canvas, 1' 10" × 2' 1". Mauritshuis, The Hague.

In this painting, Ruisdael succeeded in capturing a realistic view of Haarlem, its windmills, and Saint Bavo church, but he also imbued the landscape with a quiet serenity approaching the spiritual.

1 in.

windmills that were part of the land reclamation efforts, and the figures in the foreground stretching linen to be bleached (a major industry in Haarlem)—reflects the pride that Dutch painters took in recording their homeland and the activities of their fellow citizens. Nonetheless, in this painting the inhabitants and dwellings are so small that they blend into the land itself. Moreover, the horizon line is low, so the sky fills almost three-quarters of the picture space, and the sun illuminates the landscape only in patches, where it has broken through the clouds above. In *View of Haarlem,* Ruisdael not only captured the appearance of a specific locale but also succeeded in imbuing the work with a quiet serenity that becomes almost spiritual.

JAN VERMEER Although he also painted landscapes, Jan Vermeer (1632–1675) of Delft made his reputation as a painter of interior scenes, another popular subject among Dutch middle-class patrons. These paintings offer the viewer glimpses into the private lives of prosperous, responsible, and cultured citizens of the United Provinces. Despite his fame as a painter today, Vermeer derived much of his income from his work as an innkeeper and art dealer, and he completed no more than 35 paintings that can be definitively attributed to him. He began his career as a painter of biblical and historical themes, but soon abandoned those traditional subjects in favor of domestic scenes. Flemish artists of the 15th century also had painted domestic interiors, but sacred personages often occupied those scenes (for example, FIGS. 8-1 and 8-3). In contrast, Vermeer and his contemporaries composed neat, quietly opulent interiors of Dutch homes featuring women especially but also men and occasionally children engaging in household tasks or at leisure.

WOMAN HOLDING A BALANCE One of Vermeer's finest domestic scenes, *Woman Holding a Balance* (FIG. 10-24), is a highly idealized depiction of the social values of Dutch citizens of his day. A beautiful young woman wearing a veil and a fur-trimmed jacket stands in a room in her home. Light coming from a window illuminates the scene. The woman stands before a table on which are spread her most precious possessions—pearl necklaces, gold chains, and gold coins, which reflect the sunlight that also shines on the woman's face and the fingers of her right hand. In fact, the perspective orthogonals direct the viewer's attention neither to the woman's head nor to her treasures but to the hand in which she holds a balance for weighing gold. The scales, however, are empty—in perfect balance, the way Ignatius of Loyola advised Catholics (Vermeer was a Catholic convert in the Protestant Dutch Republic) to lead a temperate, self-aware life and to balance one's sins with virtuous behavior. The mirror on the wall may refer to self-knowledge, but it may also symbolize, as do the pearls and gold, the sin of vanity. Bolstering that interpretation is the large framed *Last Judgment* painting on the back wall in which Christ, weigher of souls, appears in a golden aureole directly above the young woman's head. Therefore, this serene domestic scene is pregnant with hidden meaning. The woman holds the scales in balance and contemplates the kind of life (one free from the temptations of worldly riches) that she must lead in order to be judged favorably on judgment day.

THE ART OF PAINTING In Vermeer's most complex and intriguing painting, *Allegory of the Art of Painting* (FIG. 10-25), the artist himself appears with his back to the viewer and dressed in clothing of an earlier era. He is hard at work on a painting of the model standing before him. She wears a laurel wreath and holds a trumpet and book, traditional attributes of Clio, the muse of history. The map of the provinces (an increasingly common feature of Dutch homes)

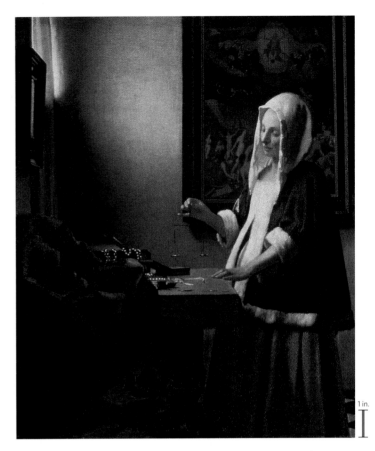

1 in.

10-24 Jan Vermeer, *Woman Holding a Balance,* ca. 1664. Oil on canvas, 1' 3 $\frac{7}{8}$" × 1' 2". National Gallery of Art, Washington, D.C. (Widener Collection).

Vermeer's woman holding empty scales in perfect balance, ignoring pearls and gold on the table, is probably an allegory of the temperate life. On the wall behind her is a depiction of the Last Judgment.

on the back wall serves as yet another reference to history. As in *Woman Holding a Balance,* the viewer is outside the space of the action, looking through the drawn curtain, which also separates the artist in his studio from the rest of the house. Some art historians have suggested that the light radiating from an unseen window on the left, illuminating both the model and the canvas being painted, alludes to the light of artistic inspiration. Accordingly, many scholars have interpreted this painting as an allegory—a reference to painting inspired by history. Vermeer's mother-in-law confirmed this allegorical reading in 1677 when, after the artist's death, 26 of his works were scheduled to be sold to pay his widow's debts. In her written claim to retain the painting for herself, she described the work as "the piece . . . wherein the Art of Painting is portrayed."[3]

Vermeer, like Rembrandt, was a master of pictorial light and used it with immense virtuosity. He could render space so convincingly through his depiction of light that in his works, the picture surface functions as an invisible glass pane through which the viewer looks into the constructed illusion. Art historians believe that Vermeer used as tools both mirrors and the *camera obscura,* an ancestor of the modern camera based on passing light through a tiny pinhole or lens to project an image on a screen or the wall of a room. (In later versions, artists projected the image on a ground-glass wall of a box whose opposite wall contained the pinhole or lens.) Vermeer did not simply copy the camera's image, however. Instead, the camera obscura and the mirrors helped him obtain results that he reworked compositionally, enabling him to achieve,

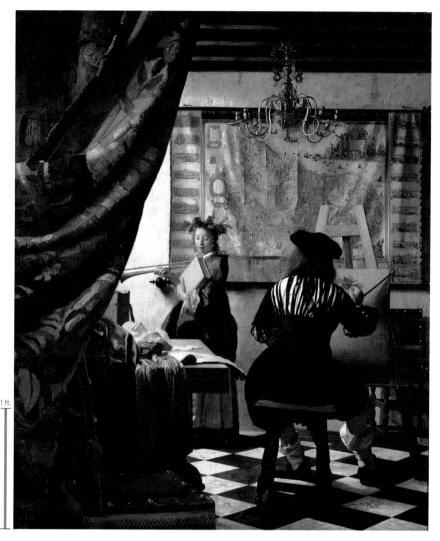

10-25 Jan Vermeer, *Allegory of the Art of Painting,* 1670–1675. Oil on canvas, 4' 4" × 3' 8". Kunsthistorisches Museum, Vienna.

Usually interpreted as an allegory of the art of painting inspired by history, this "domestic scene" shows Vermeer at work depicting a model holding the attributes of Clio, the muse of history.

for example, a beautiful stability of rectilinear shapes by carefully positioning the figures and furniture in a room. Vermeer's compositions evoke a matchless classical serenity.

Enhancing this quality are colors so true to the optical facts and so subtly modulated that they suggest that Vermeer was far ahead of his time in color science. For example, Vermeer realized that shadows are not colorless and dark, that adjoining colors affect each other, and that light is composed of colors (see page 7). Thus he painted reflections off of surfaces in colors modified by others nearby. Some scholars have suggested that Vermeer also perceived the phenomenon that modern photographers call "circles of confusion," which appear on out-of-focus negatives. Vermeer could have seen them in images projected by the camera obscura's primitive lenses. He approximated these effects with light dabs that, in close view, give the impression of an image slightly "out of focus." When the observer draws back a step, however, as if adjusting the lens, the color spots cohere, giving an astonishingly accurate illusion of the third dimension.

PIETER CLAESZ The prosperous Dutch were justifiably proud of their accomplishments, and the popularity of still-life paintings—particularly images of accumulated goods—reflected this pride. These paintings, like Vermeer's interior scenes, are meticulously crafted images both scientific in their optical accuracy and poetic in their beauty and lyricism. One of the best Dutch paintings of this genre is *Vanitas Still Life* (FIG. 10-26) by PIETER CLAESZ (1597–1660), in which the painter presented the material possessions of a prosperous household strewn across a tabletop or dresser. The ever-present morality and humility central to the Calvinist faith tempered Dutch pride in worldly goods, however. Thus, although Claesz fostered the appreciation and enjoyment of the beauty

10-26 PIETER CLAESZ, *Vanitas Still Life,* 1630s. Oil on panel, 1' 2" × 1' 11½". Germanisches National-museum, Nuremberg.

Calvinist morality tempered Dutch citizens' delight in worldly possessions and accumulated wealth. In this vanitas still life, the skull and timepiece are memento mori, reminders of life's transience.

and value of the objects he depicted, he also reminded the viewer of life's transience by incorporating references to death. Art historians call works of this type *vanitas* ("vanity") paintings, and each features a *memento mori* ("reminder of death"). In *Vanitas Still Life,* references to mortality include the skull, timepiece, tipped glass, and cracked walnut. All suggest the passage of time or someone who was here but has departed. Claesz emphasized this element of time (and demonstrated his skill as a painter) by including a self-portrait, reflected in the glass ball on the left side of the table. He appears to be painting this still life. But in an apparent challenge to the message of inevitable mortality that vanitas paintings convey, the portrait serves to immortalize the artist.

RACHEL RUYSCH As living objects that soon die, flowers, particularly cut blossoms, appeared frequently in vanitas paintings. However, floral painting as a distinct genre also enjoyed great popularity in the Dutch Republic because the Dutch were the leading growers and exporters of flowers in 17th-century Europe. One of the major practitioners of flower painting was RACHEL RUYSCH (1663–1750). Ruysch's father was a professor of botany and anatomy, which may account for her interest in and knowledge of plants and insects. She acquired an international reputation for lush paintings, such as *Flower Still Life* (FIG. 10-27). In this canvas, the floral arrangement is so full that many of the blossoms seem to be spilling out of the vase. However, Ruysch's floral still lifes are not pictures of real floral

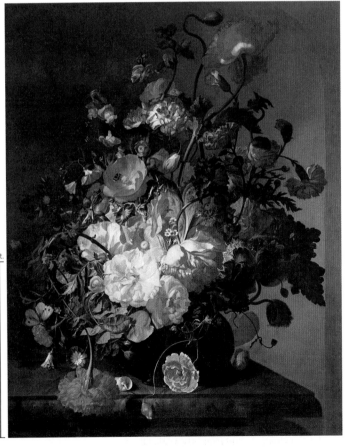

1 ft.

10-27 RACHEL RUYSCH, *Flower Still Life,* after 1700. Oil on canvas, 2' 5¾" × 1' 11⅞". Toledo Museum of Art, Toledo (purchased with funds from the Libbey Endowment, gift of Edward Drummond Libbey).

Flower paintings were very popular in the Dutch Republic. Ruysch achieved international renown for her lush paintings of floral arrangements, noted also for their careful compositions.

arrangements, but idealized groupings of individually studied flowers, often involving perfect specimens of flowers that bloomed at different times of the year and could never be placed on a table at the same time. Her careful composition of the individual elements in the illustrated example is evident in her arrangement of the flowers to create a diagonal running from the lower left to the upper right corner of the canvas, offsetting the opposing diagonal of the table edge.

FRANCE

In France, monarchical authority had been increasing for centuries, culminating in the reign of Louis XIV (r. 1661–1715), who sought to determine the direction of French society and culture. Although its economy was not as expansive as the Dutch Republic's, France became Europe's largest and most powerful nation in the 17th century. Against this backdrop, the arts of painting, sculpture, and architecture all flourished.

NICOLAS POUSSIN Rome's ancient and Renaissance monuments enticed many French artists to study there. For example, NICOLAS POUSSIN (1594–1665) of Normandy spent most of his life in Rome, where he produced grandly severe paintings modeled on those of Titian and Raphael. He also carefully formulated a theoretical explanation of his method and was ultimately responsible for establishing classical painting as an important ingredient of 17th-century French art (see "Poussin's Notes for a Treatise on Painting," page 307). Poussin's classical style presents a striking contrast to the contemporaneous Baroque style of his Italian counterparts in Rome, underscoring the multifaceted character of European art of this era.

Poussin's *Et in Arcadia Ego* (*Even in Arcadia, I* [am present]; FIG. 10-28) exemplifies the "grand manner" of painting that the artist advocated. It features a lofty subject rooted in the classical world and figures based on antique statuary. Rather than depicting dynamic movement and intense emotions, as his Italian contemporaries in Rome did, Poussin emulated the rational order and stability of Raphael's paintings. Dominating the foreground are three shepherds living in the idyllic land of Arcadia. They study an inscription on a tomb as a statuesque female figure quietly places her hand on the shoulder of one of them. She may be the spirit of death, reminding these mortals, as does the inscription, that death is found even in Arcadia, supposedly a spot of paradisiacal bliss. The countless draped female statues surviving in Italy from Roman times supplied the models for this figure, and the posture of the youth with one foot resting on a boulder derives from Greco-Roman statues of Neptune, the sea god, leaning on his trident. The classically compact and balanced grouping of the figures, the even light, and the thoughtful and reserved mood complement Poussin's classical figure types.

CLAUDE LORRAIN Claude Gellée, called CLAUDE LORRAIN (1600–1682) after his birthplace in the duchy of Lorraine, rivaled Poussin in fame. Claude modulated in a softer style Poussin's disciplined rational art, with its sophisticated revelation of the geometry of landscape. Unlike the figures in Poussin's pictures, those in Claude's landscapes tell no dramatic story, point out no moral, and praise no hero. Indeed, they often appear to be added as mere excuses for the radiant landscape itself. For Claude, painting involved essentially one theme—the beauty of a broad sky suffused with the golden light of dawn or sunset glowing through a hazy atmosphere and reflecting brilliantly off rippling water.

In *Landscape with Cattle and Peasants* (FIG. 10-29), the figures in the right foreground chat in animated fashion. In the left foreground, cattle relax contentedly. In the middle ground, cattle amble

ARTISTS ON ART
Poussin's Notes for a Treatise on Painting

As the leading champion of classical painting in 17th-century Rome, Nicolas Poussin outlined the principles of classicism in notes for an intended treatise on painting, left incomplete at his death. In those notes, Poussin described the essential ingredients necessary to produce a beautiful painting in "the grand manner":

The grand manner consists of four things: subject-matter or theme, thought, structure, and style. The first thing that, as the foundation of all others, is required, is that the subject-matter shall be grand, as are battles, heroic actions, and divine things. But assuming that the subject on which the painter is laboring is grand, his next consideration is to keep away from minutiae . . . [and paint only] things magnificent and grand . . . Those who elect mean subjects take refuge in them because of the weakness of their talents.*

The idea of beauty does not descend into matter unless this is prepared as carefully as possible. This preparation consists of three things: arrangement, measure, and aspect or form. Arrangement means the relative position of the parts; measure refers to their size; and form consists of lines and colors. Arrangement and relative position of the parts and making every limb of the body hold its natural place are not sufficient unless measure is added, which gives to each limb its correct size, proportionate to that of the whole body [compare "Polykleitos's Prescription for the Perfect Statue," page 65], and unless form joins in, so that the lines will be drawn with grace and with a harmonious juxtaposition of light and shadow.†

Poussin applied these principles in paintings such as *Et in Arcadia Ego* (FIG. 10-28), a work peopled with perfectly proportioned statuesque figures attired in antique garb.

*Translated by Robert Goldwater and Marco Treves, eds., *Artists on Art,* 3rd ed. (New York: Pantheon Books, 1958), 155.
†Ibid., 156.

1 ft.

10-28 NICOLAS POUSSIN, *Et in Arcadia Ego,* ca. 1655. Oil on canvas, 2' 10" × 4'. Musée du Louvre, Paris.

Poussin was the leading champion of classicism in 17th-century Rome. His "grand manner" paintings are models of "arrangement and measure" and incorporate figures inspired by ancient statuary.

1 ft.

slowly away. The well-defined foreground, distinct middle ground, and dim background recede in serene orderliness, until all form dissolves in a luminous mist. Atmospheric and linear perspective reinforce each other to turn a vista into a typical Claudian vision, an ideal classical world bathed in sunlight in infinite space (compare FIG. I-1). Claude's formalizing of nature with balanced groups of architectural masses, screens of trees, and sheets of water followed the great tradition of classical landscape.

10-29 CLAUDE LORRAIN, *Landscape with Cattle and Peasants,* 1629. Oil on canvas, 3' 6" × 4' 10$\frac{1}{2}$". Philadelphia Museum of Art, Philadelphia (George W. Elkins Collection).

Claude used atmospheric and linear perspective to transform the rustic Roman countryside filled with peasants and animals into an ideal classical landscape bathed in sunlight in infinite space.

It began with the backgrounds of Venetian painting (FIGS. 9-17 and 9-18) and continued in the art of Poussin (FIG. 10-28). Yet Claude, like the Dutch painters, studied the light and the atmospheric nuances of nature, making an important contribution. He recorded carefully in hundreds of sketches the look of the Roman countryside, its gentle terrain accented by stone-pines, cypresses, and poplars and by the ever-present ruins of ancient aqueducts, tombs, and towers. Claude achieved his marvelous effects of light by painstakingly placing tiny value gradations, which imitated, though on a very small scale, the range of values of outdoor light and shade. Avoiding the problem of high-noon sunlight overhead, Claude preferred, and convincingly represented, the sun's rays as they gradually illuminated the morning sky or, with their dying glow, set the pensive mood of evening. Thus he infused nature with human feeling. His landscapes owe their timeless appeal to the combination of the natural beauty of the outskirts of Rome and the mystique of the past.

LOUIS XIV The preeminent French art patron of the 17th century was King Louis XIV. Determined to consolidate and expand his power, Louis was a master of political strategy and propaganda. He established a carefully crafted and nuanced relationship with the nobility, granting them sufficient benefits to keep them pacified

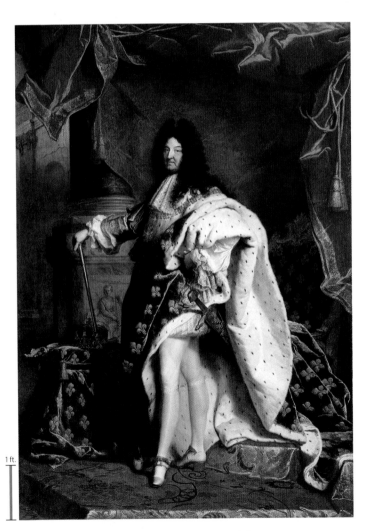

10-30 HYACINTHE RIGAUD, *Louis XIV,* 1701. Oil on canvas, 9' 2" × 6' 3". Musée du Louvre, Paris.

In this portrait set against a stately backdrop, Rigaud portrayed the 5' 4" Sun King wearing red high-heeled shoes and with his ermine-lined coronation robes thrown over his left shoulder.

but simultaneously maintaining rigorous control to avoid rebellion. He also ensured subservience by anchoring his rule in *divine right* (belief in a king's absolute power as God's will) and adopting the title "the Sun King." Like the sun, Louis was the center of the universe.

Louis's desire for control extended to all realms of French life, including art. The king and his principal adviser, Jean-Baptiste Colbert (1619–1683), strove to organize art and architecture in the service of the state. They understood well the power of art as propaganda and the value of visual imagery for cultivating a public persona, and they spared no pains to raise monuments to the Sun King's absolute power. Louis and Colbert sought to regularize taste and establish the classical style as the preferred French manner. The founding of the Royal Academy of Painting and Sculpture in 1648 served to advance this goal.

Louis XIV (FIG. 10-30) by HYACINTHE RIGAUD (1659–1743) successfully conveys the image of an absolute monarch. The king, age 63 when he commissioned this portrait, stands with his left hand on his hip and gazes directly at the viewer. His elegant ermine-lined fleur-de-lis coronation robes (compare FIG. 10-16) hang loosely from his left shoulder, suggesting an air of haughtiness. Louis also draws his garment back to expose his legs. (The king was a ballet dancer in his youth and was proud of his well-toned legs.) The portrait's majesty derives in large part from the composition. The Sun King is the unmistakable focal point, and Rigaud placed him so that he seems to look down on the viewer. (Louis XIV was only 5 feet 4 inches tall—a fact that drove him to invent the red-heeled shoes he wears in this painting.) The carefully detailed environment in which the king stands also contributes to the portrait's stateliness and grandiosity, as does the painting's sheer size (more than 9 feet tall).

VERSAILLES Louis XIV was also a builder on a grand scale. One of his projects was to convert a royal hunting lodge at Versailles, south of Paris, into a great palace. He assembled a veritable army of architects, decorators, sculptors, painters, and landscape architects under the general management of CHARLES LE BRUN (1619–1690). In their hands, the conversion of a simple lodge into the palace of Versailles (FIG. 10-31) became the greatest architectural project of the age—a defining statement of French Baroque style and a grandiose symbol of Louis XIV's power and ambition. Planned on a gigantic scale, the project called not only for a large palace flanking a vast park but also for the construction of a satellite city to house court and government officials, military and guard detachments, courtiers, and servants (thereby keeping them all under the king's close supervision). Le Brun laid out this town to the east of the palace along three radial avenues that converge on the palace. Their axes, in a symbolic assertion of the ruler's absolute power over his domains, intersected in the king's spacious bedroom, which also served as an official audience chamber. The palace itself, more than a quarter mile long, is perpendicular to the dominant east-west axis running through the associated city and park.

Every detail of the extremely rich decoration of the palace's interior received careful attention. The architects and decorators designed everything from wall paintings to doorknobs in order to reinforce the splendor of Versailles and to exhibit the very finest sense of artisanship. Of the literally hundreds of rooms within the palace, the most famous is the Galerie des Glaces, or Hall of Mirrors (FIG. 10-32), designed by JULES HARDOUIN-MANSART (1646–1708) and Le Brun. This hall overlooks the park from the second floor and extends along most of the width of the central block. Although deprived of its original furniture, which included gold and silver chairs and bejeweled trees, the 240-foot-long hall retains much of

10-31 JULES HARDOUIN-
MANSART, CHARLES LE
BRUN, and ANDRÉ LE
NÔTRE, aerial view of the
palace and gardens (look-
ing northwest), Versailles,
France, begun 1669.

Louis XIV ordered his
architects to convert a royal
hunting lodge at Versailles
into a gigantic palace and
park with a satellite city with
three radial avenues whose
axes intersect in the king's
bedroom.

central axis and across
terraces, lawns, pools, and
lakes toward the horizon.
Designed by ANDRÉ LE
NÔTRE (1613–1700), the
park of Versailles must
rank among the world's

its splendor today. Hundreds of mirrors, set into the wall opposite the windows, alleviate the gallery's tunnel-like quality and illusionistically extend its width. The mirror, that ultimate source of illusion, was a favorite element of Baroque interior design. Here, it also enhanced the dazzling extravagance of the great festivals that Louis XIV was so fond of hosting.

The enormous palace might appear unbearably ostentatious were it not for its extraordinary setting in a vast park, which makes the palace seem almost an adjunct. From the Galerie des Glaces, the king and his guests could enjoy a sweeping vista down the park's tree-lined

greatest artworks in both size and concept. Here, the French architect transformed an entire forest into a park. Although its geometric plan may appear stiff and formal, the park in fact offers an almost unlimited assortment of vistas, as Le Nôtre used not only the multiplicity of natural forms but also the terrain's slightly rolling contours with stunning effectiveness.

The formal gardens near the palace provide a rational transition from the frozen architectural forms to the natural living ones. Here, the elegant shapes of trimmed shrubs and hedges define the tightly designed geometric units. Each unit differs from its neighbor

and has a focal point in the form of a sculptured group (for example, *Apollo Attended by the Nymphs of Thetis* [FIG. 10-32A ↗]), a pavilion, a reflecting pool, or a fountain. Farther away from the palace, the design loosens as trees, in shadowy masses, screen or frame views of open countryside. Le Nôtre carefully composed all vistas for maximum effect. Light and shadow, formal and informal, dense growth and open meadows—all play against one another in unending combinations and variations. No photograph or series of photographs can reveal the design's full richness. The park unfolds itself only to those walking through it.

10-32 JULES HARDOUIN-MANSART and
CHARLES LE BRUN, Galerie des Glaces
(Hall of Mirrors), palace of Versailles,
Versailles, France, ca. 1680.

In this grandiose hall overlooking the park of the Sun King's palace at Versailles, hundreds of mirrors illusionistically extend the room's width and once reflected gilded and jeweled furnishings.

10-33 SIR CHRISTOPHER WREN, west facade of Saint Paul's Cathedral, London, England, 1675–1710.

Wren's cathedral replaced an old Gothic church. The facade design owes much to the Italian architects Andrea Palladio and Francesco Borromini. The great dome recalls Saint Peter's in Rome.

ENGLAND

In England, in sharp distinction to France, the common law and the Parliament kept royal power in check. England also differed from France (and Europe in general) in other significant ways. Although an important part of English life, religion was not the contentious issue it was on the Continent. The religious affiliations of the English included Catholicism, Anglicanism, Protestantism, and Puritanism (the English version of Calvinism). In the economic realm, England was the one country (other than the Dutch Republic) to take advantage of the opportunities that overseas trade offered. England, like the Dutch Republic, possessed a large and powerful navy, as well as excellent maritime capabilities.

In the realm of art, the most important English contributions were in the field of architecture, much of it, as in France, incorporating classical elements.

CHRISTOPHER WREN London's majestic Saint Paul's Cathedral (FIG. 10-33) is the work of England's most renowned architect, CHRISTOPHER WREN (1632–1723). A mathematical genius and skilled engineer whose work won Isaac Newton's praise, Wren became professor of astronomy in London at age 25. Mathematics led to architecture, and Charles II (r. 1660–1685) asked Wren to prepare a plan for restoring the old Gothic church dedicated to Saint Paul. Wren proposed remodeling the building based on Roman structures. Within a few months, the Great Fire of London, which destroyed the old structure and many churches in the city in 1666, gave Wren his opportunity. The architect had traveled in France, where the splendid palaces and state buildings being created in and around Paris must have impressed him. Wren also closely studied prints illustrating Baroque architecture in Italy. In Saint Paul's, he harmonized Palladian, French, and Italian Baroque features.

In view of its size, the cathedral was built with remarkable speed—in little more than 30 years—and Wren lived to see it completed. The building's form underwent constant refinement during construction, and Wren did not determine the final appearance of the towers until after 1700. In the splendid skyline composition, two foreground towers act effectively as foils to the great dome. Wren must have known similar schemes that Italian architects devised

for Saint Peter's (FIG. 10-2) in Rome to solve the problem of the relationship between the facade and dome. The influence of Borromini (FIGS. 10-1, *rear,* and 10-6) is evident in the upper levels and lanterns of the towers. The lower levels owe a debt to Palladio, and the superposed paired columnar porticos have parallels in contemporaneous French architecture. Wren's skillful eclecticism brought all these foreign features into a grand and unified design.

Wren received commissions for many other churches after the Great Fire. Even today, Wren's towers and domes punctuate the London skyline. Saint Paul's dome is the tallest of all. Wren's legacy was significant and long-lasting, both in England and in colonial America, examined in the next chapter.

⊿ Explore the era further in MindTap with videos of major artworks and buildings, Google Earth™ coordinates, and essays by the author on the following additional subjects:

- Gianlorenzo Bernini, *Apollo and Daphne* (FIG. 10-4A)
- ▌ WRITTEN SOURCES: Giovanni Pietro Bellori on Annibale Carracci and Caravaggio
- Caravaggio, *Conversion of Saint Paul* (FIG. 10-9A)
- Artemisia Gentileschi, *Self-Portrait as the Allegory of Painting* (FIG. 10-10A)
- Giovanni Battista Gaulli, *Triumph of the Name of Jesus* (FIG. 10-11A)
- François Girardon and Thomas Regnaudin, *Apollo Attended by the Nymphs of Thetis* (FIG. 10-32A)

BAROQUE EUROPE

Italy and Spain

- In contrast to classical Renaissance architecture, Italian Baroque architecture is dynamic, theatrical, and highly ornate. The facades of Francesco Borromini's churches—for example, San Carlo alle Quattro Fontane—are not flat frontispieces but undulating surfaces that provide a fluid transition from exterior to interior space. The interiors of his buildings pulsate with energy and feature complex domes that grow organically from curving walls.

- The greatest Italian Baroque sculptor was Gianlorenzo Bernini, who was also an important architect. In *Ecstasy of Saint Teresa,* he marshaled the full capabilities of architecture, sculpture, and painting to create an intensely emotional experience for worshipers, consistent with the Counter-Reformation principle of using artworks to inspire devotion and piety.

- In painting, Caravaggio broke new ground by employing stark and dramatic contrasts of light and dark (tenebrism) and by setting religious scenes, such as *Calling of Saint Matthew,* in everyday locales filled with rough-looking common people.

- The greatest Spanish Baroque painter was Diego Velázquez, court painter to Philip IV (r. 1621–1665). His masterwork, *Las Meninas,* is extraordinarily complex and mixes real spaces, mirrored spaces, picture spaces, and pictures within pictures. It is a celebration of the art of painting itself.

Bernini, *Ecstasy of Saint Teresa,* 1645–1652

Caravaggio, *Calling of Saint Matthew,* ca. 1597–1601

Flanders and the Dutch Republic

- In the 17th century, Flanders remained Catholic and under Spanish control. Flemish Baroque art is more closely tied to the Baroque art of Italy than is the art of much of the rest of northern Europe. The leading Flemish painter of this era was Peter Paul Rubens, whose works feature robust and foreshortened figures in swirling motion.

- The Dutch Republic received official recognition of its independence from Spain in the Treaty of Westphalia of 1648. Worldwide trade and banking brought prosperity to its predominantly Protestant citizenry, which largely rejected church art in favor of private commissions of portraits, genre scenes, landscapes, and still lifes.

- Frans Hals produced innovative portraits of middle-class patrons in which a lively informality replaced the formulaic patterns of traditional portraiture. Jacob van Ruisdael specialized in landscapes depicting specific places, not idealized Renaissance settings. Peter Claesz painted vanitas still lifes featuring meticulous depictions of worldly goods and reminders of death. Jan Vermeer specialized in painting Dutch families in serenely opulent homes. Vermeer's convincing representation of interior spaces depended in part on his use of the camera obscura.

- Rembrandt van Rijn was the greatest Dutch artist of the age. His oil paintings are notable for their dramatic impact and subtle gradations of light and shade as well as the artist's ability to convey human emotions. Rembrandt was also a master printmaker renowned for his etchings, such as *Christ with the Sick,* known as the *Hundred-Guilder Print.*

Rubens, *Elevation of the Cross,* 1610

Vermeer, *Woman Holding a Balance,* ca. 1664

France and England

- The major art patron in 17th-century France was Louis XIV, the "Sun King," who built a gigantic palace-and-garden complex at Versailles featuring opulent furnishings and sweeping vistas. Among the architects Louis employed were Charles Le Brun and Jules Hardouin-Mansart, who succeeded in marrying Italian Baroque and French classical styles. The leading French champion of classical painting was Nicolas Poussin, who spent most of his life in Rome and promoted the "grand manner" of painting. This style called for heroic or divine subjects and classical compositions with figures often modeled on ancient statues, as in *Et in Arcadia Ego.*

- In England, architecture was the most important art form. Christopher Wren harmonized the architectural principles of Palladio with the Italian Baroque and French classical styles.

Galerie des Glaces, Versailles, ca. 1680

◄ **11-1a** The Enlightenment fascination with classical antiquity gave rise to the art movement called Neoclassicism. In this painting, Kauffman chose a classical subject and clothed her figures in Roman garb.

◄ **11-1b** Kauffman's heroine is Cornelia, mother of Tiberius and Gaius Gracchus, political reformers during the Roman Republic. The portraits of the mother and her sons are based on ancient statuary.

1 ft.

11-1 **ANGELICA KAUFFMANN**, *Cornelia Presenting Her Children as Her Treasures*, or *Mother of the Gracchi*, ca. 1785. Oil on canvas, 3' 4" × 4' 2". Virginia Museum of Fine Arts, Richmond (Adolph D. and Wilkins C. Williams Fund).

◄ **11-1c** The painting is an Enlightenment exemplum virtutis ("example of virtue"). When a visitor shows Cornelia her jewelry and asks to see Cornelia's, the mother of the Gracchi presents her children as her jewels.

Rococo to Neoclassicism in Europe and America

THE ENLIGHTENMENT, ANGELICA KAUFFMAN, AND NEOCLASSICISM

The dawn of the *Enlightenment* in the 18th century brought a new way of thinking critically about the world and about men and women, independently of religion, myth, or tradition. Enlightenment thinkers rejected unfounded beliefs in favor of empirical evidence and promoted the questioning of all assertions. This new worldview was a major factor in the revolutionary political, social, and economic changes that swept Europe and America in the mid- to late 1700s. Among these were the wars for independence in America and France, the Industrial Revolution in England, and a renewed admiration in both Europe and America for the art and architecture of classical antiquity. The Enlightenment's emphasis on rationality in part explains this classical focus, because the geometric harmony of classical art and architecture embodied Enlightenment ideals. Moreover, Greece and Rome represented the pinnacle of civilized society—paragons of enlightened political organization. With their traditions of liberty, civic virtue, morality, and sacrifice, these cultures were ideal models during a period of political upheaval.

The Enlightenment interest in classical antiquity in turn gave rise to the artistic movement known as *Neoclassicism,* which incorporated the subjects and styles of Greek and Roman art. One of the pioneers of Neoclassical painting was Angelica Kauffman (1741–1807). Born in Switzerland and trained in Italy, Kauffman spent many of her productive years in England. In an era when nearly all successful artists were men, Kauffman enjoyed an enviable reputation and was a founding member of the British Royal Academy of Arts.

Cornelia Presenting Her Children as Her Treasures, or *Mother of the Gracchi* (FIG. 11-1), is perhaps Kauffman's best-known work. The theme of the painting is the virtue of Cornelia, mother of the future political leaders Tiberius and Gaius Gracchus, who, in the second century BCE, attempted to reform the Roman Republic. Cornelia reveals her character in this scene, which takes place after a visitor has shown off her fine jewelry and then haughtily insists that Cornelia show hers. Instead of taking out her own precious adornments, Cornelia brings her sons forward, presenting them as her jewels. *Mother of the Gracchi* is a characteristic example of the Enlightenment embrace of the values of the classical world, an *exemplum virtutis* ("example of virtue") drawn from Greek and Roman history and literature.

To give her retelling of the story an authentic air, Kauffman studied ancient statuary and then clothed her actors in ancient Roman garb and posed them in statuesque attitudes within Roman interiors. The architectural setting is severe, and the composition and drawing have the simplicity and firmness of low-relief carving, qualities that became hallmarks of the Neoclassical style.

A CENTURY OF REVOLUTIONS

In 1700, Louis XIV still ruled France as the Sun King (see page 308), presiding over his realm and French culture from his palatial residence at Versailles (FIGS. 10-31 and 10-32). By 1800, revolutions had overthrown the monarchy in France and achieved independence for the British colonies in America. The 18th century also gave birth to a revolution of a different kind—the Industrial Revolution, which began in England and soon transformed the economies of continental Europe and North America. Against this backdrop of revolutionary change—social as well as political, economic, and technological—came major transformations in the arts.

ROCOCO

The death of Louis XIV in 1715 brought many changes in French high society. The grandiose palace-based culture of Baroque France gave way to a much more intimate and decentralized culture based in the *hôtels* (private townhouses) of Paris. These opulent homes of the French elite became the centers of a new style called *Rococo*, which was primarily a style of interior design. The term derived from the French word *rocaille* ("pebble"), but it referred especially to the small stones and shells used to decorate grotto interiors. Shells or forms resembling shells were the principal motifs in Rococo ornamentation.

In the early 1700s, Paris was the social capital of Europe, and the Rococo salon was the center of Parisian society. Wealthy, ambitious, and clever society hostesses competed to attract the most famous and the most accomplished people to their salons (see "Femmes Savantes and Rococo Salon Culture" ⊿). Social gatherings centered on conversation spiced with wit, repartee as quick and deft as a fencing match. Artifice reigned supreme, and participants considered enthusiasm or sincerity in bad taste. French Rococo salons were lively total works of art. Exquisitely wrought furniture, ornamented mirror frames, delightful ceramics and silver, decorative tapestries, small paintings, and enchanting statuettes—for example, *Nymph and Satyr Carousing* (FIG. 11-1A ⊿) by CLODION (1738–1814)—complemented the architecture and mural paintings.

SALON DE LA PRINCESSE A typical French Rococo room is the Salon de la Princesse (FIG. 11-2) in the Hôtel de Soubise in Paris, designed by GERMAIN BOFFRAND (1667–1754) in collaboration with the painter CHARLES-JOSEPH NATOIRE (1700–1777) and the sculptor JEAN-BAPTISTE LEMOYNE (1704–1778). A comparison between the Salon de la Princesse and the Galerie des Glaces (FIG. 10-32) in the Sun King's palace at Versailles reveals how Boffrand softened the strong architectural lines and panels of the French Baroque style into flexible, sinuous curves. The walls melt into the vault. Irregular painted shapes, topped by sculpture and

11-2 GERMAIN BOFFRAND, Salon de la Princesse, with paintings by CHARLES-JOSEPH NATOIRE and sculptures by JEAN-BAPTISTE LEMOYNE, Hôtel de Soubise, Paris, France, 1737–1740.

Rococo rooms such as this one, featuring sinuous curves, gilded moldings and mirrors, small sculptures and paintings, and floral ornamentation, were the center of Parisian social and intellectual life.

separated by rocaille shells, replace the hall's cornices. Painting, architecture, and sculpture combine to form a single ensemble. The profusion of curving tendrils and sprays of foliage blend with the shell forms to give an effect of freely growing nature, suggesting that the designer permanently decked the Rococo room for a festival.

ANTOINE WATTEAU The painter most closely associated with French Rococo is Antoine Watteau (1684–1721). He was largely responsible for creating a specific type of Rococo painting genre called a *fête galante* ("amorous festival"). Fête galante paintings depicted the outdoor amusements of French high society. The premier example is Watteau's masterpiece, *Pilgrimage to Cythera* (FIG. 11-3). The painting was the artist's entry for admission to the French Royal Academy of Painting and Sculpture. In 1717, the fête galante was not an acceptable category for submission, but rather than reject Watteau's candidacy, the jurors created a new category to accommodate his entry.

At the turn of the 18th century, two competing doctrines sharply divided the membership of the French Royal Academy. Many members followed Nicolas Poussin (FIG. 10-28) in teaching that form was the most important element in painting, whereas "colors in painting are as allurements for persuading the eyes."[1] Colors, argued Poussin's admirers, were additions for effect and not really essential. The other group took Peter Paul Rubens (FIGS. 10-15 and 10-16) as its model and proclaimed the supremacy of color. Depending on which doctrine they supported, members of the French Academy were either *Poussinistes* or *Rubénistes*. Watteau was Flemish, and Rubens's coloristic style heavily influenced his work. With Watteau in their ranks, the Rubénistes carried the day, establishing Rococo painting as the preferred style in early-18th-century France.

Pilgrimage to Cythera presents luxuriously costumed lovers who have made a "pilgrimage" to Cythera, the island of eternal youth and love, sacred to Aphrodite. The elegant figures move gracefully from the protective shade of a woodland park filled with playful cupids and voluptuous statuary. Watteau's figural poses blend elegance and sweetness. He prepared his generally quite small paintings using albums of drawings in which he sought to capture slow movement from difficult and unusual angles, searching for the smoothest, most poised, and most refined attitudes. Watteau also strove for the most exquisite shades of color difference, defining in a single stroke the shimmer of silk at a bent knee or the shine appearing on a glossy surface as it emerges from shadow. The haze of color, the subtly modeled shapes, the gliding motion, and the air of suave gentility appealed greatly to Watteau's wealthy patrons.

11-3 Antoine Watteau, *Pilgrimage to Cythera,* 1717. Oil on canvas, 4' 3" × 6' 4½". Musée du Louvre, Paris.

Watteau's fête galante paintings depict the outdoor amusements of French high society and feature the Rococo taste for hazy color, subtly modeled shapes, gliding motion, and an air of suave gentility.

1 ft.

11-4 JEAN-HONORÉ FRAGONARD, *The Swing*, 1766. Oil on canvas, 2' 8⅝" × 2' 2". Wallace Collection, London.

Fragonard's *Swing* exemplifies Rococo style. Pastel colors and soft light complement a scene in which a young lady flirtatiously kicks off her shoe at a statue of Cupid while her lover gazes at her.

JEAN-HONORÉ FRAGONARD Watteau died from tuberculosis when he was only 37 years old, but JEAN-HONORÉ FRAGONARD (1732–1806) and others carried on the Rococo painting manner that Watteau pioneered. In *The Swing* (FIG. 11-4), a young gentleman has convinced an unsuspecting old bishop to swing the young man's pretty sweetheart higher and higher, while her lover (and the work's patron), in the lower left-hand corner, stretches out to admire her from a strategic position on the ground. The young lady flirtatiously kicks off her shoe toward the little statue of Cupid. The infant love god holds his finger to his lips. The landscape emulates Watteau's— a luxuriant perfumed bower in a park that very much resembles a stage scene for comic opera. The glowing pastel colors and soft light convey, almost by themselves, the theme's sensuality.

THE ENLIGHTENMENT

In the course of the 18th century, the feudal system that served as the foundation of social and economic life in Europe dissolved, and the rigid social hierarchies that provided the basis for Rococo art and patronage relaxed. A major factor in these societal changes was the Enlightenment (see "The Enlightenment," page 313). Enlightenment thinkers championed an approach to the acquisition of knowledge based on empirical observation and scientific experimentation. Enlightenment-era science had roots in the work of René Descartes, Blaise Pascal, Isaac Newton, and Gottfried Wilhelm von Leibniz in

the 17th century. England and France were the principal centers of the Enlightenment, though its maxims influenced the thinking of intellectuals throughout Europe and in the American colonies. Benjamin Franklin, Thomas Jefferson, and other American notables embraced its principles.

NEWTON AND LOCKE Of particular importance for Enlightenment thought was the work of Isaac Newton (1642–1727) and John Locke (1632–1704) in England. In his scientific studies, Newton insisted on empirical proof of his theories and encouraged others to avoid metaphysics and the supernatural—realms that extended beyond the natural physical world. This emphasis on both tangible data and concrete experience became a cornerstone of Enlightenment thought. Locke, whose works acquired the status of Enlightenment gospel, developed these ideas further. According to Locke's "doctrine of empiricism," knowledge comes through sensory perception of the material world. From these perceptions alone, people form ideas. Locke asserted that human beings are born good, not cursed by original sin. The laws of nature grant them the natural rights of life, liberty, and property, as well as the right to freedom of conscience. Government is by contract, and its purpose is to protect these rights. If and when government abuses these rights, the citizenry has the further natural right of revolution.

PHILOSOPHES The work of Newton and Locke also inspired many French intellectuals, or *philosophes*. These thinkers conceived of individuals and societies as parts of physical nature. They shared the conviction that the ills of humanity could be remedied by applying reason and common sense to human problems. They criticized the powers of Church and State as irrational limits placed on political and intellectual freedom. They believed that by accumulating and propagating knowledge, humanity could advance by degrees to a happier state than it had ever known. This conviction matured into the "doctrine of progress" and its corollary doctrine, the "perfectibility of humankind."

Animated by their belief in human progress and perfectibility, the philosophes took on the task of gathering knowledge and making it accessible to all who could read. Their program was, in effect, the democratization of knowledge. Denis Diderot (1713–1784) became editor of the groundbreaking 35-volume *Encyclopédie*, a compilation of articles written by more than a hundred contributors, including all the leading philosophes. The *Encyclopédie* was truly comprehensive (its formal title was *Systematic Dictionary of the Sciences, Arts, and Crafts*) and included all available knowledge—historical, scientific, and technical, as well as religious and moral—and political theory.

François Marie Arouet, better known as Voltaire (1694–1778), was the most representative figure—almost the personification—of the Enlightenment spirit. Voltaire was instrumental in introducing Newton and Locke to the French intelligentsia. He hated, and attacked through his writings, the arbitrary despotic rule of kings, the selfish privileges of the nobility and the Church, religious intolerance, and, above all, the injustice of the *ancien regime* (the "old order"). Voltaire persuaded a whole generation that fundamental changes were necessary, paving the way for revolutions in France and America at the end of the century.

INDUSTRIAL REVOLUTION The Enlightenment emphasis on scientific investigation and technological invention opened up new possibilities for human understanding of the world and for control of its material forces. Research into the phenomena of electricity

Joseph Wright of Derby and the Industrial Revolution

The scientific advances of the Enlightenment era affected the lives of everyone, and most people responded enthusiastically to the wonders of the Industrial Revolution such as the steam engine, which gave birth to the modern manufacturing economy and the prospect of a seemingly limitless supply of goods and services.

The fascination that science held for ordinary people as well as for the learned was a favorite subject of the English painter Joseph Wright of Derby. Wright studied painting near Birmingham, the center of the Industrial Revolution, and specialized in dramatically lit scenes showcasing modern scientific instruments and experiments. A characteristic example of Wright's work is *A Philosopher Giving a Lecture on the Orrery* (FIG. 11-5). In this painting, a scholar demonstrates a mechanical model of the solar system called an *orrery*, in which each planet (represented by a metal orb) revolves around the sun (a lamp) at the correct relative velocity. Light from the lamp pours forth from in front of the

boy silhouetted in the foreground to create shadows that heighten the drama of the scene. Curious children crowd close to the tiny orbs representing the planets within the curving bands symbolizing their orbits. An earnest listener makes notes, while the lone woman seated at the left and the two gentlemen at the right pay rapt attention. Scientific knowledge mesmerizes everyone in Wright's painting. The artist visually reinforced the fascination with the orrery by composing his image in a circular fashion, echoing the device's orbital design. The postures and gazes of all the participants and observers focus attention on the cosmic model. Wright scrupulously and accurately rendered every detail of the figures, the mechanisms of the orrery, and even the books and curtain in the shadowy background.

Wright's choice of subjects and realism in depicting them appealed to the great industrialists of his day, including Josiah Wedgwood (1730–1795), who pioneered many techniques of mass-produced pottery, and Sir Richard Arkwright (1732–1792), whose spinning frame revolutionized the textile industry. Both men often purchased paintings by Wright featuring scientific advances. To them, the Derby artist's elevation of the theories and inventions of the Industrial Revolution to the plane of history painting was exciting and appropriately in tune with the new era of Enlightenment.

1 ft.

11-5 Joseph Wright of Derby, *A Philosopher Giving a Lecture on the Orrery*, ca. 1763–1765. Oil on canvas, 4' 10" × 6' 8". Derby Museums and Art Gallery, Derby.

Wright specialized in dramatically lit paintings celebrating the modern scientific instruments of the Industrial Revolution. Here, a scholar demonstrates an orrery, a revolving model of the solar system.

and combustion, along with the discovery of oxygen and the power of steam, had enormous consequences. Steam power as an adjunct to, or replacement for, human labor initiated a new era in world history. These and other technological advances—admiringly recorded in the paintings of Joseph Wright of Derby (1734–1797; see "Joseph Wright of Derby and the Industrial Revolution," above, and FIG. 11-5)—exemplified the Enlightenment notion of progress and gave birth to the Industrial Revolution. Most scholars mark the dawn of that technological revolution in the 1740s with the invention in England of steam engines for industrial production.

ROUSSEAU The second key figure of the French Enlightenment, who was also instrumental in preparing the way ideologically for the French Revolution, was Jean-Jacques Rousseau (1712–1778). Voltaire believed that the salvation of humanity lay in the advancement of science and in the rational improvement of society. In contrast, Rousseau argued that the arts, sciences, society, and civilization in general had corrupted "natural man." According to Rousseau, "Man by nature is good . . . he is depraved and perverted by society." He rejected the idea of progress, insisting that "our minds have been corrupted in proportion as the arts and sciences have improved."[2]

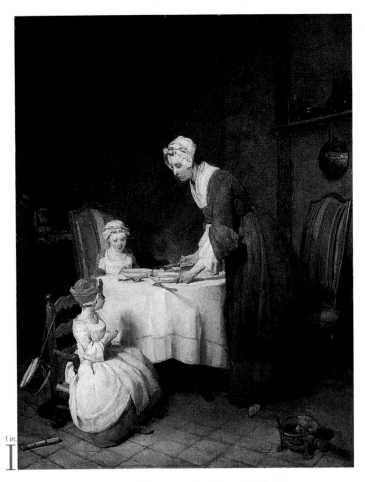

1 in.

11-6 JEAN-BAPTISTE-SIMÉON CHARDIN, *Grace,* 1740. Oil on canvas, 1' 7" × 1' 3". Musée du Louvre, Paris.

Consistent with the ideas of Rousseau, Chardin celebrated the simple goodness of ordinary people, especially mothers and children, who lived in a world far from the frivolous Rococo salons of Paris.

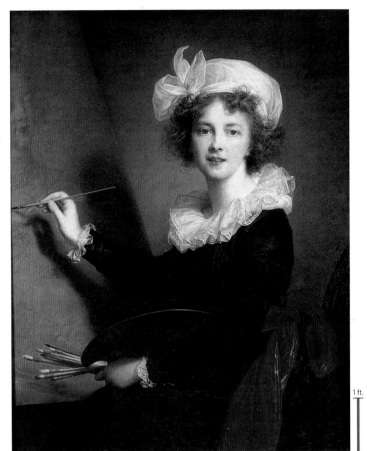

1 ft.

11-7 ÉLISABETH LOUISE VIGÉE-LEBRUN, *Self-Portrait,* 1790. Oil on canvas, 8' 4" × 6' 9". Galleria degli Uffizi, Florence.

Vigée-Lebrun was one of the few women admitted to France's Royal Academy of Painting and Sculpture. In this self-portrait, she depicted herself confidently painting the likeness of Queen Marie Antoinette.

Rousseau's elevation of feelings above reason as the most "natural" human expression led him to exalt as the ideal the peasant's simple life, with its honest and unsullied emotions.

CHARDIN Rousseau, popular and widely read, was largely responsible for the turning away from the Rococo sensibility in the arts and the formation of a taste for the "natural," as opposed to the artificial and frivolous. Reflecting Rousseau's views, JEAN-BAPTISTE-SIMÉON CHARDIN (1699–1779) painted quiet scenes of domestic life in praise of the simple goodness of ordinary people, especially mothers and young children, who in spirit, occupation, and environment lived far from corrupt society. In *Grace* (FIG. 11-6), Chardin ushers the viewer into a modest room where a mother and her daughters are about to dine. The mood of quiet attention is at one with the hushed lighting and mellow color and with the closely studied still-life accessories whose worn surfaces tell their own humble history. The viewer witnesses a moment of social instruction, when mother and older sister supervise the younger sister in the simple, pious ritual of giving thanks to God before a meal. The simplicity of the composition reinforces the subdued charm of this scene, with the three figures highlighted against the dark background. Chardin was the Enlightenment's poet of the commonplace and master of its nuances. A gentle sentiment prevails in all his pictures, an emotion

not contrived and artificial but born of the painter's honesty, insight, and sympathy. Chardin's paintings had wide appeal, even in unexpected places. Louis XV (r. 1723–1774), the royal personification of the Rococo in his life and tastes, once owned *Grace.*

VIGÉE-LEBRUN Another manifestation of the "naturalistic" impulse in 18th-century French art was the emergence of a new more personal and less pretentious mode of portraiture, exemplified by the self-portrait (FIG. 11-7) of ÉLISABETH LOUISE VIGÉE-LEBRUN (1755–1842). The painter looks directly at viewers and pauses in her work to return their gaze. Although her mood is lighthearted and her costume's details echo the serpentine curve that Rococo artists and wealthy patrons loved, nothing about Vigée-Lebrun's pose appears contrived. Hers is the self-confident, natural stance of a woman whose art has won her an independent role in society. She portrayed herself in a close-up, intimate view at work on one of the many portraits she painted of her most important patron, Queen Marie Antoinette (1755–1793). Vigée-Lebrun was famous for the force and grace of her portraits and, with ADÉLAÏDE LABILLE-GUIARD (1749–1803; FIG. 11-7A ▢), was one of the few women admitted to the Royal Academy of Painting and Sculpture (see "Vigée-Lebrun, Labille-Guiard, and the French Royal Academy" ▢).

11-8 WILLIAM HOGARTH, *The Tête à Tête,* from *Marriage à la Mode,* ca. 1745. Oil on canvas, 2' 4" × 3'. National Gallery, London.

Hogarth won fame for his paintings and prints satirizing English life with comic zest. This is one of a series of six paintings in which he chronicled the marital immoralities of the moneyed class.

WILLIAM HOGARTH Across the Channel, a truly English style of painting emerged with WILLIAM HOGARTH (1697–1764), who satirized with comic zest the lifestyle of the newly prosperous middle class. Traditionally, the British imported painters from the Continent—Holbein, Rubens, and Van Dyck among them. Throughout his career, Hogarth waged a lively campaign against the English feeling of dependence on, and inferiority to, these artists. Although Hogarth would have been the last to admit it, his own painting owed much to the work of his contemporaries in France, the Rococo artists. Yet his subject matter, frequently moral in tone, was distinctively English. This was the great age of English satirical writing, and Hogarth saw himself as translating satire into the visual arts.

Hogarth's favorite device was to make a series of narrative paintings and prints, in a sequence similar to chapters in a book or scenes in a play, following a character or group of characters in their encounters with some social evil. *The Tête à Tête* (FIG. 11-8), from *Marriage à la Mode,* is one of six paintings satirizing the marital immoralities of the moneyed classes in England. In it, a marriage is just beginning to founder. The husband and wife are tired after a long night spent in separate pursuits. While the wife stayed at home for an evening of cards and music-making, her young husband had been out on the town with another woman. He thrusts his hands deep into the empty money-pockets of his breeches, while his wife's small dog sniffs inquiringly at a woman's lacy cap protruding from his coat pocket. A steward, his hands full of unpaid bills, raises his eyes in despair at the actions of his noble master and mistress. The couple's home is luxurious, but Hogarth filled it with witty clues to the dubious taste of its occupants. For example, the row of pious religious paintings on the upper wall of the distant room concludes with a curtained canvas undoubtedly depicting an erotic subject. According to the custom of the day, ladies could not view this discretely hidden painting, but at the pull of a cord, the master and his male guests could enjoy a tableau of cavorting figures. In *The Tête à Tête,* as in all his work, Hogarth proceeded as a novelist might, elaborating on his subject with carefully chosen detail, the discovery of which heightens the comedy.

PROBLEMS AND SOLUTIONS
Grand Manner Portraiture

The Enlightenment concept of "nobility," especially in the view of Rousseau (page 317), referred to character, not to aristocratic birth. In an era of revolutions, the virtues of courage and resolution, patriotism, and self-sacrifice assumed greater importance. Having risen from humble origins, the modern military hero joined the well-born aristocrat as a major patron of portrait painting.

Sir Joshua Reynolds was one of those who often received commissions to paint likenesses of key participants in the great events of the latter part of the 18th century. Indeed, he soon specialized in what became known as *Grand Manner portraiture*, echoing the term that Nicolas Poussin used in the previous century to describe his paintings of "grand subjects" such as "battles, heroic actions, and divine things" (see "Poussin's Notes for a Treatise on Painting," page 307). Although clearly depicting specific individuals, Grand Manner portraits elevated the sitters by conveying refinement and elegance. Reynolds and other painters communicated a person's grace and class through certain standardized conventions, such as the large scale of the figure relative to the canvas, the controlled pose, the landscape setting, and the low horizon line.

Reynolds painted *Lord Heathfield* (FIG. 11-9) in 1787. The sitter was a perfect subject for a Grand Manner portrait—a burly, ruddy English officer, the commandant of the fortress at Gibraltar. Heathfield had doggedly defended the British stronghold against the Spanish and French, and later received the honorary title Baron Heathfield of Gibraltar. Here, he holds the huge key to the fortress, the symbol of his victory. He stands in front of a curtain of dark smoke rising from the battleground, flanked by one cannon pointing ineffectively downward and another whose tilted barrel indicates that it lies uselessly on its back. Reynolds portrayed the features of the general's heavy, honest face and his uniform with unidealized realism. But Lord Heathfield's posture and the setting dramatically suggest the heroic themes of battle, courage, and patriotism.

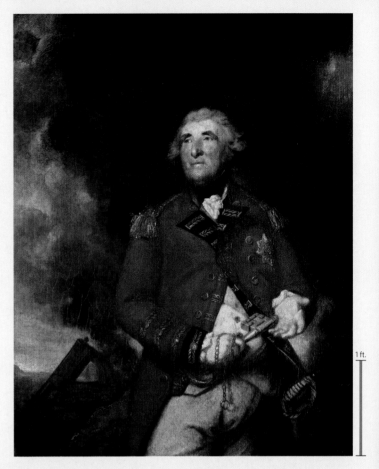

11-9 SIR JOSHUA REYNOLDS, *Lord Heathfield*, 1787. Oil on canvas, 4' 8" × 3' 9". National Gallery, London.

In this Grand Manner portrait, Reynolds depicted the English commander who defended Gibraltar. Heathfield stands in a dramatic pose, and his figure takes up most of the canvas.

SIR JOSHUA REYNOLDS Quite different in both style and subject is the work of England's greatest painter of the Enlightenment era, SIR JOSHUA REYNOLDS (1723–1792), who achieved renown for his portraits (see "Grand Manner Portraiture," above, and FIG. 11-9).

BENJAMIN WEST Some American artists also became well known in England. BENJAMIN WEST (1738–1820), born in Pennsylvania on what was then the colonial frontier, traveled on the Continent early in life to study art and then went to England, where he met with almost immediate success. One of the 36 founding members of the Royal Academy of Arts, West succeeded Reynolds as its president. He became official painter to King George III (r. 1760–1801) and retained that position during the strained period of the American Revolution. In *Death of General Wolfe* (FIG. 11-10), West depicted the mortally wounded young English commander just after his defeat of the French in the decisive battle of Quebec in 1759, which gave Canada to Great Britain. Because his subject was a recent event, West clothed his characters in contemporary costumes and included a rare glimpse for his English audience of a Native American warrior, depicted as an exemplary "noble savage." However, West blended this realism of detail with the grand tradition of history painting by arranging his figures in a complex, theatrically ordered composition. His modern hero dies among grieving officers on the field of victorious battle in a way that suggests the death of a saint. (The composition, in fact, derives from paintings of the lamentation over the dead Christ; compare FIG. 8-7.) West wanted to present this hero's death in the service of the state as a martyrdom charged with religious emotions. His innovative combination of the conventions of traditional heroic painting with a look of modern realism influenced history painting well into the 19th century.

JOHN SINGLETON COPLEY American artist JOHN SINGLETON COPLEY (1738–1815) matured as a painter in the Massachusetts Bay Colony. Like West, Copley later settled in England, where he absorbed the fashionable English portrait style. But unlike Grand Manner portraits, Copley's *Paul Revere* (FIG. 11-11), painted before the artist left Boston, conveys a sense of directness and faithfulness to visual fact that marked the taste for honesty and plainness noted by many late-18th- and early-19th-century visitors to America. When Copley painted his portrait, Revere was not yet the familiar hero of the American Revolution. In this picture, he is a working professional silversmith. The setting is plain, the lighting clear and revealing. Revere sits in his shirtsleeves, bent over a teapot in progress. He pauses and turns his head to look the observer straight in

11-10 Benjamin West, *Death of General Wolfe,* 1771. Oil on canvas. 4' 11½" × 7'. National Gallery of Canada, Ottawa (gift of the Duke of Westminster, 1918).

West's great innovation was to blend contemporary subject matter and costumes with the grand tradition of history painting. Here, the painter likened General Wolfe's death to that of a martyred saint.

the eyes. The painter treated the reflections in the polished wood of the tabletop with as much care as he did Revere's figure, his tools, and the teapot resting on its leather graver's pillow. The informality and the sense of the moment link this painting to contemporaneous English and Continental portraits. But the spare style and the emphasis on the sitter's down-to-earth character differentiate this American work from its European counterparts.

THE GRAND TOUR The 18th-century public also sought "naturalness" in artists' depictions of landscapes. Documentation of specific places became popular, in part due to growing travel opportunities and expanding colonialism. These depictions of geographic settings also served the needs of the many scientific expeditions mounted during the century and satisfied the desires of genteel tourists for mementos of their journeys. By this time, a "Grand Tour" of the major sites of Europe was an essential part of every well-bred person's education (see "The Grand Tour and Veduta Painting," page 322). Those who embarked on a tour of the Continent wished to return with souvenirs to help them remember their experiences and

11-11 John Singleton Copley, *Paul Revere,* ca. 1768–1770. Oil on canvas, 2' 11⅛" × 2' 4". Museum of Fine Arts, Boston (gift of Joseph W., William B., and Edward H. R. Revere).

In contrast to Grand Manner portraits, Copley's *Paul Revere* emphasizes the subject's down-to-earth character, differentiating this American work from its European counterparts.

ART AND SOCIETY
The Grand Tour and Veduta Painting

Although travel throughout Europe was commonplace in the 18th century, Italy became an especially popular destination. This "pilgrimage" of the wealthy from France, England, Germany, and even the British colonies in America came to be known as the Grand Tour. The Grand Tour was not simply leisure travel. The education available in Italy to the inquisitive mind made the trip an indispensable experience for anyone who wished to make a mark in society. The Enlightenment had made knowledge of ancient Rome imperative, and a steady stream of Europeans and Americans traveled to Italy in the late 18th and early 19th centuries. These tourists aimed to increase their knowledge of literature, the visual arts, architecture, theater, music, and history. Given this extensive agenda, it is not surprising that a Grand Tour could take a number of years to complete.

The British were the most avid travelers, and they conceived the initial "tour code," including required itineraries and important destinations. Although they designated Rome early on as the primary destination in Italy, visitors traveled as far north as Venice and as far south as Naples and even Sicily. Many returned home from their Grand Tour with a painting by Antonio Canaletto, the leading painter of scenic views (*vedute*) of Venice. It must have been very cheering on a gray winter afternoon in England to look up and see a sunny, panoramic view such as that in Canaletto's *Riva degli Schiavoni, Venice* (FIG. 11-12), with its cloud-studded sky, picturesque water traffic, and well-known Venetian landmarks, such as the Doge's Palace (FIG. 7-39), painted in scrupulous perspective and minute detail. Canaletto usually made drawings "on location" to take back to his studio and use as sources for paintings. To help make the on-site drawings true to life, he often used a camera obscura, as Vermeer (FIGS. 10-24 and 10-25) did before him, enabling Canaletto to create convincing representations incorporating the variable focus of objects at different distances. Canaletto's paintings give the impression of capturing every detail, with no "editing." In fact, he presented each site within Renaissance perspective conventions and exercised great selectivity about which details to include and which to omit to make a coherent and engagingly attractive veduta.

11-12 ANTONIO CANALETTO, *Riva degli Schiavoni, Venice*, ca. 1735–1740. Oil on canvas, 1' 6$\frac{1}{2}$" × 2' $\frac{7}{8}$". Toledo Museum of Art, Toledo.

Canaletto was the leading painter of Venetian vedute, which were treasured souvenirs for 18th-century travelers visiting Italy on the Grand Tour. He used a camera obscura for his on-site drawings.

impress those at home with the wonders they had seen. The English were especially eager collectors of travel pictures. Venetian artists in particular found it profitable to produce paintings of the most characteristic *vedute* ("scenic views") of their city to sell to British visitors. Chief among those artists was ANTONIO CANALETTO (1697–1768), whose works—for example, *Riva degli Schiavoni, Venice* (FIG. 11-12)—English tourists avidly acquired as evidence of their visit to Italy's magical city of water.

Prosperous visitors to Rome on the Grand Tour frequently commissioned Batoni to paint their portraits. Here, an English gentleman poses with items attesting to his learning and passion for antiquity.

NEOCLASSICISM

As Batoni's *Charles John Crowle* vividly illustrates, the popularity of the Grand Tour among the cultural elite of Europe both reflected and contributed to the heightened interest in classical antiquity during the Enlightenment. Exposure to the art treasures of Italy was also a major factor in the rise of Neoclassicism as the leading art movement of the late 18th century (see "The Enlightenment, Angelica Kauffman, and Neoclassicism," page 313) as well as to intensified study of the ancient world in academic circles.

WINCKELMANN In 1755, Johann Joachim Winckelmann (1717–1768), widely recognized as the first modern art historian, published *Reflections on the Imitation of Greek Works in Painting and Sculpture,* in which the German scholar unequivocally designated Greek art as the most perfect to come from human hands. For Winckelmann, classical art was far superior to the "natural" art of his day.

[An enlightened person] will find beauties hitherto seldom revealed when he compares the total structure of Greek figures with most modern ones, especially those modelled more on nature than on Greek taste.[3]

In his later *History of Ancient Art* (1764), Winckelmann carefully described major works of classical art and positioned each one within a huge inventory organized by subject matter, style, and period. Before Winckelmann, art historians had focused on biography, as did Giorgio Vasari and Giovanni Pietro Bellori in the 16th and 17th centuries (see "Vasari" and "Bellori" ⏎). Winckelmann thus initiated one modern art historical method thoroughly in accord with Enlightenment ideas of ordering knowledge—a system of description and classification that provided a pioneering model for the understanding of stylistic evolution.

JACQUES-LOUIS DAVID One of the pioneers of Neoclassical painting was the Swiss artist Angelica Kauffman (FIG. 11-1), but Frenchman JACQUES-LOUIS DAVID (1748–1825) is generally considered the greatest Neoclassical master. Although his early paintings were in the Rococo manner, a period of study in Rome of the works of ancient and Renaissance artists converted David to Neoclassicism. He rebelled against the Rococo style as an "artificial taste" and exalted the "perfect form" of Greek art (see "Jacques-Louis David on Greek Style and Public Art," page 324). David, who became the Neoclassical painter-ideologist of the French Revolution, concurred with the Enlightenment idea that the subject of an artwork should have a moral. He believed that paintings representing noble deeds in the past could inspire virtue in the present.

POMPEO BATONI Some of those who embarked on the Grand Tour sought to obtain a more personalized memento of their cultural journey than a portrait of Venice: a portrait of themselves by the leading Italian portrait painter of the day, POMPEO BATONI (1708–1787). Born in Lucca and trained in Rome, where he eventually became curator of the papal art collection, Batoni received commissions for "Grand Tour portraits" from prosperous visitors of various nationalities, but especially from Englishmen. Batoni's portrait (FIG. 11-13) of Charles John Crowle (1738–1811) is a characteristic example. Crowle, a second-generation member of the British Parliament from Yorkshire, stands in a palatial columnar study with a view of the Roman countryside behind him. Attended by his faithful dog, Crowle is surrounded by abundant evidence of his learning and passion for antiquity. Most prominent are copies of reduced size of the much-admired *Farnese Hercules* in Naples and of a statue of the sleeping Ariadne in the Vatican. On the elegant table on which Crowle leans is an astronomical model (compare FIG. 11-5) and an unrolled plan of Saint Peter's (FIG. 10-2). In 1764, after returning from Rome, Crowle was elected a member of the Society of Dilettanti, a prestigious group of British connoisseur-admirers of Greco-Roman art.

Jacques-Louis David on Greek Style and Public Art

Jacques-Louis David was the leading Neoclassical painter in France at the end of the 18th century. He championed a return to Greek style and the painting of inspiring heroic and patriotic subjects. In 1796, he made the following statement to his pupils:

> I want to work in a pure Greek style. I feed my eyes on antique statues, I even have the intention of imitating some of them. The Greeks had no scruples about copying a composition, a gesture, a type that had already been accepted and used. They put all their attention and all their art on perfecting an idea that had been already conceived. They thought, and they were right, that in the arts the way in which an idea is rendered, and the manner in which it is expressed, is much more important than the idea itself. To give a body and a perfect form to one's thought, this—and only this—is to be an artist.*

David also strongly believed that paintings depicting noble events in ancient history, such as his *Oath of the Horatii* (FIG. 11-14), would serve to instill patriotism and civic virtue in the public at large in post-revolutionary France. In November 1793, he wrote:

> [The arts] should help to spread the progress of the human spirit, and to propagate and transmit to posterity the striking examples of the efforts of a tremendous people who, guided by reason and philosophy, are bringing back to earth the reign of liberty, equality, and law. The arts must therefore contribute forcefully to the education of the public. . . . The arts are the imitation of nature in her most beautiful and perfect form. . . . [T]hose marks of heroism and civic virtue offered the eyes of the people [will] electrify the soul, and plant the seeds of glory and devotion to the fatherland.†

*Translated by Robert Goldwater and Marco Treves, eds., *Artists on Art,* 3d ed. (New York: Pantheon Books, 1958), 206.
†Ibid., 205.

11-14 Jacques-Louis David, *Oath of the Horatii,* 1784. Oil on canvas, 10' 10" × 13' 11". Musée du Louvre, Paris.

David was the Neoclassical painter-ideologist of the French Revolution. This huge canvas celebrating ancient Roman patriotism and sacrifice features statuesque figures and classical architecture.

A milestone painting in David's career, *Oath of the Horatii* (FIG. 11-14), depicts a story from pre-Republican Rome, the heroic phase of Roman history. The topic was not too obscure for David's audience. Pierre Corneille (1606–1684) had retold this story of conflict between love and patriotism, first recounted by the ancient Roman historian Livy, in a play performed in Paris several years earlier. The leaders of the warring cities of Rome and Alba Longa decided to resolve their conflicts in a series of encounters waged by three representatives from each side. The Romans chose as their champions the three Horatius brothers, who had to face the three sons of the Curatius family from Alba Longa. A sister of the Horatii, Camilla, was the bride-to-be of one of the Curatius sons, and the wife of the youngest Horatius was the sister of the Curatii. David's painting shows the Horatii as they swear on their swords, held high by their father, to win or die for Rome, oblivious to the anguish and sorrow of the Horatius women.

Oath of the Horatii exemplifies the Neoclassical style. The subject is a narrative of patriotism and sacrifice excerpted from Roman history. The action unfolds in a shallow space much like a stage setting, defined by a severely simple architectural framework. David deployed his statuesque and carefully modeled figures across the space, close to the foreground, in a manner recalling ancient relief sculpture. The rigid, angular, and virile forms of the men on the left effectively contrast with the soft curvilinear shapes of the distraught women on the right. This juxtaposition visually pits virtues that Enlightenment thinkers ascribed to men (such as courage, patriotism, and unwavering loyalty to a cause) against the emotions of love, sorrow, and despair expressed by the women in the painting. The French viewing audience perceived such emotionalism as characteristic of the female nature. The message was clear and of a type readily identifiable to the prerevolutionary French public. The picture created a sensation at its first exhibition in Paris in 1785. Although David had painted it under royal patronage and did not intend the painting as a revolutionary statement, *Oath of the Horatii* aroused his audiences to patriotic zeal. The Neoclassical style soon became the semiofficial voice of the French Revolution.

DEATH OF MARAT When the revolution broke out in 1789, David threw in his lot with the Jacobins, the radical and militant revolutionary faction. He accepted the role of de facto minister of propaganda, organizing political pageants and ceremonies requiring floats, costumes, and sculptural props. David believed that art could play an important role in educating the public and that dramatic paintings emphasizing patriotism and civic virtue would prove effective as rallying calls. However, rather than continuing to create artworks focused on scenes from antiquity, David began to portray events from the French Revolution itself. He intended *Death of Marat* (FIG. 11-15) not only to serve as a record of an important episode in the struggle to overthrow the monarchy but also to provide inspiration and encouragement to the revolutionary forces. The painting commemorates the assassination of Jean-Paul Marat (1743–1793), an influential writer who was David's friend. The artist depicted the martyred revolutionary in his medicinal bath after Charlotte Corday (1768–1793), a member of a rival political faction, stabbed him to death. (Marat suffered from a painful skin disease.) The cold neutral space above Marat's figure slumped at his "desk" in the tub produces a chilling oppressiveness. Indeed, the writing stand, which bears the words "To Marat, David" resembles a tombstone, and David vividly placed all narrative details in the foreground—the knife, the wound, the blood, the letter with which Corday gained entrance—to sharpen the sense of pain and outrage. He masterfully composed the painting to present Marat as a tragic martyr who died in the service of the revolution. David based Marat's figure on Christ in Michelangelo's *Pietà* (FIG. 9-7). The reference

1 ft.

11-15 JACQUES-LOUIS DAVID, *Death of Marat*, 1793. Oil on canvas, 5' 5" × 4' 2½". Musées royaux des Beaux-Arts de Belgique, Brussels.

David depicted the revolutionary Marat as a tragic martyr, stabbed to death in his bath. Although the painting displays severe Neoclassical spareness, its convincing realism conveys pain and outrage.

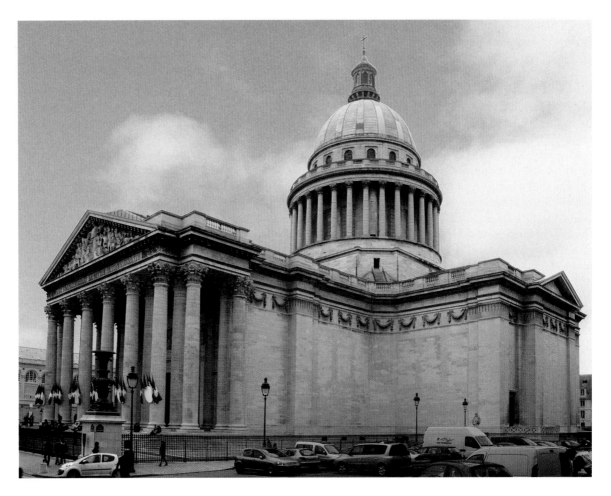

11-16 JACQUES-GERMAIN SOUFFLOT, Panthéon (Sainte-Geneviève; looking northeast), Paris, France, 1755–1792.

Soufflot's Panthéon is a testament to the Enlightenment admiration for Greece and Rome. It combines a portico based on an ancient Roman temple with a colonnaded dome and a Greek-cross plan.

to Christ's martyrdom made the painting a kind of "altarpiece" for the new civic "religion," inspiring the French people with the saintly dedication of their slain leader.

PANTHÉON, PARIS Architects in the Enlightenment era also admired and emulated Greco-Roman style. Early in the 18th century, they began to turn away from the theatricality and ostentation of Baroque and Rococo design and embraced a more streamlined antique look. Sainte-Geneviève, the Parisian Panthéon (FIG. 11-16), by JACQUES-GERMAIN SOUFFLOT (1713–1780) stands as testament to the revived interest in classical architecture. The columns, based on those of a Roman temple in Lebanon (reproduced with studied archaeological precision), stand out from walls that are severely blank, except for a repeated garland motif near the top. The colonnaded dome, a Neoclassical version of the domes of Saint Peter's (FIGS. 9-14 and 10-2) in Rome and Saint Paul's (FIG. 10-33) in London, rises above a Greek-cross plan. Both the dome and the vaults rest on an interior grid of splendid freestanding Corinthian columns, as if the portico's colonnade continued within. Although the whole effect, inside and out, is Roman, the structural principles employed were essentially Gothic. Soufflot was one of the first 18th-century builders to apply the logical engineering of Gothic cathedrals (see "Building a High Gothic Cathedral," page 193) to modern buildings.

CHISWICK HOUSE The appeal of classical architecture extended well beyond French borders. The popularity of Greek and Roman cultures was due not only to their association with morality, rationality, and integrity but also to their connection to political systems

ranging from Athenian democracy to Roman imperial rule. Thus parliamentary England joined revolutionary France in embracing Neoclassicism. In England, Neoclassicism's appeal also was due to its clarity and simplicity. These characteristics provided a stark contrast to the complexity and opulence of Baroque art, then associated with the flamboyant rule of absolute monarchy. In English architecture, the preference for a simple and rational style derived indirectly from the authority of the ancient Roman architect Vitruvius (see "Vitruvius's *Ten Books on Architecture*" ↗) and more directly from the Renaissance and Baroque architects who revived the classical style in the 15th, 16th, and the 17th centuries, especially Andrea Palladio.

RICHARD BOYLE (1695–1753) strongly restated the Palladian style in the new Neoclassical idiom in Chiswick House (FIG. 11-17), which he built on London's outskirts with the help of WILLIAM KENT (ca. 1686–1748). Paving the way for this shift in style was, among other things, the publication of Colin Campbell's *Vitruvius Britannicus* (1715), three volumes of engravings of ancient buildings, prefaced by a denunciation of the Italian Baroque style and high praise for Palladio. Chiswick House is a free variation on the theme of Palladio's Villa Rotonda (FIG. 9-16). The exterior design provided a clear alternative to the colorful splendor of Versailles (FIGS. 10-31 and 10-32). In its simple symmetry, unadorned planes, right angles, and precise proportions, Chiswick House looks very classical and rational.

THOMAS JEFFERSON Because the appeal of Neoclassicism was due in part to the values with which it was associated—morality, idealism, patriotism, and civic virtue—it is not surprising that in the new American republic, THOMAS JEFFERSON (1743–1826) spearheaded a movement to adopt Neoclassicism as the national

11-17 Richard Boyle and William Kent, Chiswick House (looking northwest), near London, England, begun 1725.

For this English villa, Boyle and Kent emulated the simple symmetry and unadorned planes of the Palladian architectural style. Chiswick House is a free variation on the Villa Rotonda (FIG. 9-16).

architectural style. Jefferson—economist, educational theorist, and gifted amateur architect, as well as statesman (see "Thomas Jefferson, Patron and Practitioner" ⟨⟩)—admired Palladio immensely and read carefully the Italian architect's *Four Books of Architecture.* Later, while minister to France, he studied 18th-century French classical architecture and visited the Maison Carrée (FIG. 3-28A ⟨⟩),

an ancient Roman temple at Nîmes, which inspired his design for the State House in Richmond, Virginia. Equally influential was the Pantheon (FIG. 3-38) in Rome, which served as the model for the centerpiece of Jefferson's University of Virginia campus (FIG. 11-17A ⟨⟩). After his European sojourn, Jefferson decided to completely remodel Monticello (FIG. 11-18), his home near Charlottesville, Virginia,

11-18 Thomas Jefferson, Monticello, Charlottesville, Virginia, 1770–1806.

Jefferson led the movement to adopt Neoclassicism as the architectural style of the United States. Although built of local materials, his Palladian Virginia home recalls Chiswick House (FIG. 11-17).

11-19 Jean-Antoine Houdon, *George Washington*, 1788–1792. Marble, 6' 2" high. State Capitol, Richmond.

Houdon portrayed Washington in contemporary garb, but he incorporated the Roman fasces and Cincinnatus's plow in the statue because Washington similarly had returned to his farm after his war service.

1 ft.

which he originally had designed in a different style. The final version of Monticello is somewhat reminiscent of Palladio's Villa Rotonda (FIG. 9-16) and of Chiswick House (FIG. 11-17), but its materials are the local wood and brick used in Virginia. The single-story home has an octagonal dome set above the central drawing room behind a pediment-capped columnar porch. It sits on a wooded plot of land with mountain vistas all around. (*Monticello* means "hillock" or "little mountain" in Italian.) The setting fulfilled another of Jefferson's goals—to build for himself a country villa inspired by the ones described by the first-century Roman author Pliny.

JEAN-ANTOINE HOUDON Neoclassicism also became the preferred style for public sculpture in the newly independent United States. When the members of the Virginia legislature wanted to erect a life-size marble statue of Virginia-born George Washington (1732–1799), they awarded the commission to the leading French Neoclassical sculptor of the late 18th century, JEAN-ANTOINE HOUDON (1741–1828). Houdon had already carved a bust portrait of Benjamin Franklin (1706–1790) when he was America's ambassador to France. Houdon's portrait of Washington (FIG. 11-19) is the sculptural equivalent of a Grand Manner portrait (FIG. 11-9). But although the first American president wears contemporary garb, the statue makes an overt reference to the Roman Republic. The "column" on which Washington leans is a bundle of rods with an ax attached—the ancient Roman *fasces,* an emblem of authority. The 13 rods symbolize the 13 original states. The plow behind Washington and the fasces alludes to Cincinnatus, a patrician of the early Roman Republic who was elected dictator during a time of war and resigned his position as soon as victory had been achieved in order to return to his farm. Washington wears the badge of the Society of the Cincinnati (visible beneath the bottom of his waistcoat), an association founded in 1783 for officers in the revolutionary army who had resumed their peacetime roles. Tellingly, Washington no longer holds his sword in Houdon's statue.

The Neoclassical style, so closely associated with democracy in the late 18th century, ironically also became the ideal vehicle for promoting the empire of Napoleon Bonaparte in the opening decade of the 19th century. Napoleonic art and the revolutionary new styles that eventually displaced Neoclassicism are the subjects of Chapter 12.

🖝 Explore the era further in MindTap with videos of major artworks and buildings, Google Earth™ coordinates, and essays by the author on the following additional subjects:

▌WRITTEN SOURCES: Femmes Savantes and Rococo Salon Culture

• Clodion, *Nymph and Satyr Carousing* (FIG. 11-1A)

▌ART AND SOCIETY: Vigée-Lebrun, Labille-Guiard, and the French Royal Academy

• Adélaïde Labille-Guiard, *Self-Portrait with Two Pupils* (FIG. 11-7A)

▌THE PATRON'S VOICE: Thomas Jefferson, Patron and Practitioner

• Thomas Jefferson, University of Virginia (FIG. 11-17A)

ROCOCO TO NEOCLASSICISM IN EUROPE AND AMERICA

Rococo

- In the early 18th century, the centralized and grandiose palace-based culture of Baroque France gave way to the much more intimate Rococo culture based in the townhouses of Paris. There, aristocrats and intellectuals gathered for witty conversation in salons featuring delicate colors, sinuous lines, gilded mirrors, elegant furniture, and small paintings and sculptures.

- The leading Rococo painter was Antoine Watteau, whose usually small canvases feature light colors and elegant figures in ornate costumes moving gracefully through lush landscapes. Jean-Honoré Fragonard carried on the Rococo style late into the 18th century.

Watteau, *Pilgrimage to Cythera*, 1717

The Enlightenment

- By the end of the 18th century, revolutions had overthrown the monarchy in France and achieved independence for the British colonies in America. A major factor was the Enlightenment, a new way of thinking critically about the world independently of religion and tradition that also helped foster the Industrial Revolution, which began in England in the 1740s. The paintings of Joseph Wright of Derby celebrated the scientific inventions of the Enlightenment era.

- The Enlightenment also made knowledge of ancient Rome essential for the cultured elite, and Europeans and Americans in large numbers undertook a Grand Tour of Italy. Among the most popular souvenirs of the Grand Tour were Antonio Canaletto's cityscapes of Venice. Other travelers returned with a portrait by Pompeo Batoni of themselves posing with classical antiquities.

Batoni, *Charles John Crowle*, ca. 1761–1762

- Rejecting the idea of progress, Jean-Jacques Rousseau, one of the leading French intellectuals, argued for a return to natural values and exalted the simple life of peasants. His ideas influenced artists such as Jean-Baptiste-Siméon Chardin, who painted sentimental narratives about rural families.

- The taste for naturalism also led to a reawakening of an interest in realism. Benjamin West represented the protagonists in his history paintings wearing contemporary costumes.

West, *Death of General Wolfe*, 1771

Neoclassicism

- The Enlightenment revival of interest in Greece and Rome also gave rise in the late 18th century to the artistic movement known as Neoclassicism, which incorporated the subjects and styles of ancient art.

- A pioneer of the new style was Angelica Kauffman, who often chose subjects drawn from Roman history. Jacques-Louis David, who exalted classical art as "the imitation of nature in her most beautiful and perfect form," also favored Roman themes. Painted on the eve of the French Revolution, *Oath of the Horatii*, set in a severe classical hall, served as an example of patriotism and sacrifice.

David, *Oath of the Horatii*, 1784

- Neoclassicism also became the dominant style in 18th-century architecture. Ancient Roman and Italian Renaissance structures inspired Jacques-Germain Soufflot's Panthéon in Paris. In the United States, Thomas Jefferson championed Neoclassicism as the official architectural style of the new American republic. It represented for him idealism, patriotism, and civic virtue.

Jefferson, Monticello, 1770–1806

◄ **12-1a** In this gigantic painting, Géricault rejected Neoclassical compositional principles and, in the Romantic spirit, presented a jumble of writhing bodies in every attitude of suffering, despair, and death.

▶ **12-1b** At the apex of a diagonal axis stretching from the lower left, a seminude black man, one of the few survivors, waves a tattered garment in the hope of attracting the attention of the rescue ship.

12-1 THÉODORE GÉRICAULT, *Raft of the Medusa*, 1818–1819. Oil on canvas, 16' 1" × 23' 6". Musée du Louvre, Paris.

▶ **12-1c** Barely visible in the distance is the ship *Argus,* which would eventually rescue the *Medusa*'s 15 survivors, who told Géricault the story of the captain's incompetence and described the horrors of the raft.

Romanticism, Realism, and Photography, 1800 to 1870

THE HORROR—AND ROMANCE—OF DEATH AT SEA

At the close of the 18th century, Neoclassicism was the dominant artistic style in Europe, but it soon gave way to a movement that historians of art, music, and literature call *Romanticism*. In France, one of the pioneering Romantic painters was THÉODORE GÉRICAULT (1791–1824). Although Géricault retained an interest in the heroic and the epic, and studied drawing in the studio of Neoclassical painter Pierre-Narcisse Guérin (1774–1833), he chafed at the rigidity of the Neoclassical style, instead producing works that captivate viewers with their drama, visual complexity, and emotional force.

Géricault's most ambitious project was *Raft of the Medusa* (FIG. 12-1), an immense (23-foot-wide) canvas with figures larger than life. The painting immortalized the July 2, 1816, shipwreck off the Mauritanian coast of the French frigate *Medusa,* which ran aground on a reef due to the incompetence of its inexperienced captain, a political appointee. The captain and his officers safely abandoned the ship. In an attempt to survive, 147 passengers built a makeshift raft from pieces of the disintegrating frigate. The raft drifted for 13 days, and the starving survivors dwindled to 15, in part because of cannibalism. Finally, the ship *Argus* spotted the raft and rescued those still alive. This horrendous event was political dynamite once it became public knowledge.

In *Raft of the Medusa,* Géricault chose to represent the moment when some of those still alive summon what little strength they have left to flag down the *Argus* far on the horizon, not knowing if the ship's crew could see their raft. Géricault sought to capture accurately the horror, chaos, and emotion of the tragedy yet invoke the grandeur and impact of Neoclassical history painting. He visited hospitals and morgues to study the bodies of the dying and dead, interviewed survivors, and had a model of the raft constructed in his studio. The legacy of Neoclassicism is still evident in the incongruously muscular bodies of the starving. But Géricault rejected Neoclassical composition principles and instead presented a jumble of writhing bodies. He arranged the survivors and several corpses in a powerful X-shaped composition, and piled one body on another in every attitude of suffering, despair, and death. One light-filled diagonal axis stretches from the bodies at the lower left up to the black man raised on his comrades' shoulders and waving a tattered garment toward the horizon. Yet the man, seen from the back and faceless, is an anonymous antihero, in striking contrast to the protagonists of the historical and mythological works then in vogue. The cross axis descends from the dark, billowing sail at the upper left to the shadowed upper torso of the body trailing in the open sea. Géricault's bold decision to place the raft at a diagonal so that a corner juts outward makes it seem as though some of the corpses are sliding off the raft into the viewer's space. *Raft of the Medusa,* like the event itself, caused a sensation. It established Géricault's reputation and reoriented the history of painting.

ART UNDER NAPOLEON

The revolution of 1789 initiated a new era in France, but the overthrow of the monarchy also opened the door for Napoleon Bonaparte (1769–1821) to exploit the resulting disarray and establish a different kind of monarchy with himself at its head. In 1800, after serving in various French army commands, Napoleon assumed a newly created position—First Consul of the French Republic, a title with clear and intentional links to the ancient Roman Republic (see page 88). During the next 15 years, the ambitious general gained control of almost all of continental Europe in name or through alliances, and in 1804 the pope journeyed to Paris for Napoleon's coronation as Emperor of the French.

In 1812, however, Napoleon launched a disastrous invasion of Russia that ended in retreat, and in 1815 the emperor suffered a devastating defeat at the hands of the British at Waterloo in present-day Belgium. Forced to abdicate the imperial throne, Napoleon went into exile on the island of Saint Helena in the South Atlantic, where he died six years later.

After Napoleon's death, the political geography of Europe changed dramatically (MAP 12-1), but in many ways, the more significant changes during the first half of the 19th century were technological and economic. The Industrial Revolution caused a population boom in European cities, and railroads spread to many parts of the Continent, facilitating the transportation of both goods and people.

Transformation also occurred in the art world. The century opened with Neoclassicism still supreme, but by 1870, Romanticism and Realism in turn had captured the imagination of artists and public alike. New construction techniques had a major impact on architectural design, and the invention of photography revolutionized picture making of all kinds.

MAP 12-1 **Europe around 1850.**

ROMANTICISM, REALISM, AND PHOTOGRAPHY, 1800 TO 1870

1800–1815
- Napoleon appoints David as First Painter of the Empire and brings Canova from Rome to Paris.
- Vignon models La Madeleine, Napoleon's Neoclassical "temple of glory," on ancient Roman temples.
- David's students Gros and Ingres form a bridge between Neoclassicism and Romanticism.

1815–1840
- Romanticism is the leading European art movement. Delacroix and other painters favor exotic subjects featuring unleashed emotion, vibrant color, and bold brushstrokes.
- Friedrich, Turner, Cole, and other Romantic artists specialize in painting transcendental landscapes.
- Gothic style enjoys a revival in architecture.
- Daguerre and Talbot invent photography.

1840–1870
- Courbet and other Realist painters in Europe and America insist that people and events of their own time are the only valid subjects for art.
- Manet's paintings get a hostile reception because of their shocking subject matter and nonillusionistic style.
- Paxton pioneers prefabricated glass-and-iron construction in the Crystal Palace.
- O'Sullivan makes on-the-spot photographs of the Civil War.

12-2 ANTONIO CANOVA, *Pauline Borghese as Venus Victorious,* from the Villa Borghese, Rome, Italy, 1808. Marble, 6' 7" long. Galleria Borghese, Rome.

Canova was Napoleon Bonaparte's favorite sculptor. Here, the artist depicted the emperor's sister—at her insistence—as the nude Roman goddess of love in a marble statue inspired by classical models.

Napoleon's sister Pauline Borghese (1780–1825) in the guise of Venus Victorious (FIG. 12-2). Initially, Canova had suggested depicting Pauline as Diana, goddess of the hunt. She demanded, however, that she be portrayed as Venus, the goddess of love. Thus Pauline appears, seminude and reclining on a divan, gracefully holding the golden apple, the symbol of the goddess's triumph in the judgment of Paris. Canova clearly based his work on Greek statuary and on the reclining figures on Roman sarcophagus lids. The French public never got to admire Canova's portrait, however. Napoleon had arranged the marriage of his sister to an heir of the noble Roman Borghese family. Once Pauline was in Rome, she took several lovers, and the public gossiped extensively about her affairs. Pauline's insistence on being represented as the goddess of love reflected her self-perception. Because of his wife's notoriety, Prince Camillo Borghese (1775–1832), the work's official patron, kept the sculpture hidden in his palatial villa in Rome and allowed relatively few people to see the portrait.

ANTONIO CANOVA Not surprisingly, Napoleon, who aspired to rule an empire that might one day rival ancient Rome's, embraced Neoclassicism as the ideal stylistic vehicle for linking his rule with the classical past and for expressing his imperial authority. He appointed Jacques-Louis David First Painter of the Empire and commissioned PIERRE-ALEXANDRE BARTHÉLÉMY VIGNON (1763–1828; FIG. 12-1A ⬈) and other architects to design buildings and monuments based on ancient Roman models. Napoleon's favorite sculptor was ANTONIO CANOVA (1757–1822), who somewhat reluctantly left his native Italy to settle in Paris and serve the emperor. Canova had gained renown for his sculptures of classical gods and heroes. In Paris, he made numerous portraits of the emperor and his family in the Neoclassical style. The most famous is the marble statue of

ANTOINE-JEAN GROS David was not the only Neoclassical painter in Napoleon's employ. One of David's best students, ANTOINE-JEAN GROS (1771–1835), also produced paintings that contributed to the emperor's growing mythic status. In *Napoleon Visiting the Plague-Stricken in Jaffa* (FIG. 12-3), Gros recorded an incident during an outbreak of the bubonic plague in the course of Napoleon's Syrian campaign of 1799. This fearsome disease struck Muslim and French forces alike, and to quell the growing panic and hysteria, on March 11, 1799, Napoleon himself visited the mosque at Jaffa that had been converted into a hospital for those who had contracted the dreaded disease. Gros depicted Napoleon's staff officers covering their noses against the stench of the place,

12-3 ANTOINE-JEAN GROS, *Napoleon Visiting the Plague-Stricken in Jaffa,* 1804. Oil on canvas, 17' 5" × 23' 7". Musée du Louvre, Paris.

In his depiction of Napoleon as a Christlike healer, Gros foreshadowed Romanticism by recording the exotic people, costumes, and architecture of Jaffa, including the striped horseshoe arches of the mosque-hospital.

12-4 Jean-Auguste-Dominique Ingres, *Grande Odalisque*, 1814. Oil on canvas, 2' 11$\frac{7}{8}$" × 5' 4". Musée du Louvre, Paris.

The reclining female nude was a Greco-Roman subject, but Ingres converted his Neoclassical figure into an odalisque in a Turkish harem, consistent with the new Romantic taste for the exotic.

1 ft.

whereas Napoleon, amid the dead and dying, is fearless and in control. He comforts those still alive, who are clearly awed by his presence and authority. Indeed, by depicting the French leader as having removed his glove to touch the sores of a French plague victim, Gros implied that Napoleon possessed the miraculous power to heal. The composition recalls scenes of the doubting Thomas touching Christ's wound. Here, however, Napoleon is not Saint Thomas but a Christlike figure tending to the sick, as in Rembrandt's *Hundred-Guilder Print* (FIG. 10-22), which Gros certainly knew. The French painter also based the despairing seated Arab figure at the lower left on the comparable figure (one of the damned) in Michelangelo's *Last Judgment* (FIG. 9-11). The kneeling nude Frenchman with extended arm at the right recalls the dead Christ in another Michelangelo work, the *Pietà* he carved toward the end of his life for his own tomb (not illustrated).

The action in *Napoleon in Jaffa* unfolds against the exotic backdrop of the horseshoe arches and Moorish arcades of the mosque-hospital's courtyard (compare FIG. 5-7). On the left are Muslim doctors distributing bread and ministering to plague-stricken Arabs in the shadows. On the right, in radiant light, are Napoleon and his soldiers in their splendid tailored uniforms. David had used this polarized compositional scheme and an arcaded backdrop to great effect in his *Oath of the Horatii* (FIG. 11-14), and Gros emulated these features in this painting, but employed brighter colors and looser brushstrokes. The younger artist's fascination with the exoticism of the Muslim world, as is evident in his attention to the details of architecture and costume, also represented a departure from his teacher's Neoclassicism and reflects a growing interest among the French in the Middle East and North Africa, spurred in large measure by Napoleon's eastern campaigns. Historians and art historians alike refer to this European curiosity about the decidedly non-Western culture of the East as *Orientalism*. The setting of *Napoleon in Jaffa*, along with Gros's emphasis on death, suffering, and an emotional rendering of the scene, also foreshadowed core elements of the artistic movement that would soon displace Neoclassicism—Romanticism.

INGRES David's greatest pupil was JEAN-AUGUSTE-DOMINIQUE INGRES (1780–1867), but his study in David's studio was short-lived.

Ingres soon broke with his teacher on matters of style and adopted what he believed to be a truer and purer Greek style than David's Neoclassical manner. The younger artist employed linear forms approximating those found in Greek vase painting (for example, FIGS. 2-25 and 2-26), and often placed the main figures in the foreground of his composition, emulating classical low-relief sculpture. In *Grande Odalisque* (FIG. **12-4**), painted for Napoleon's sister Caroline Murat (1782–1839), queen of Naples, Ingres's subject—the reclining nude female figure—followed the grand tradition of classical antiquity and the Renaissance (FIG. 9-20), as did Canova's *Pauline Borghese* (FIG. 12-2). The work also shows Ingres's admiration for Raphael in his borrowing of that master's type of female head (FIG. 9-5). The figure's languid pose and elongated limbs and torso reveal the French painter's debt to Parmigianino (FIG. 9-22) and Giambologna (FIG. 9-25). However, by converting the figure to an *odalisque* (woman in a Turkish harem), Ingres, unlike Canova (FIG. 12-2), made a strong concession to the burgeoning Romantic taste for Orientalist subjects.

ROMANTICISM

Whereas Neoclassicism's rationality reinforced Enlightenment thought, particularly Voltaire's views (see page 316), Romanticism owed much to the ideas of Jean-Jacques Rousseau (see page 317). Rousseau's exclamation, "Man is born free, but is everywhere in chains!"—the opening line of his *Social Contract* (1762)—summarizes a fundamental Romantic premise. Romanticism emerged from a desire for freedom—not only political freedom but also freedom of thought, feeling, action, worship, speech, and taste. Romantics asserted that freedom was the right and property of all. They believed that the path to freedom was through imagination and feeling rather than reason. Romanticism as a phenomenon began around 1750 and ended about 1850, but most art historians use the term more narrowly to denote an art movement that flourished from about 1800 to 1840, between Neoclassicism and Realism.

The transition from Neoclassicism to Romanticism represented a shift in emphasis from calculation to intuition, from objective nature to subjective emotion. Among the leading manifestations of

ART AND SOCIETY

The Romantic Spirit in Art, Music, and Literature

The appeal of Romanticism, with its emphasis on freedom and emotions unrestrained by rational thought (FIG. 12-5), extended well beyond the realm of the visual arts. In European music, literature, and poetry, the Romantic spirit dominated the late 18th and early 19th centuries. Composers and authors as well as painters rejected classicism's structured order in favor of the emotive and expressive. In music, the compositions of Franz Schubert (1797-1828), Franz Liszt (1811-1886), Frédéric Chopin (1810-1849), and Johannes Brahms (1833-1897) emphasized the melodic or lyrical. For these composers, music had the power to express what cannot be expressed with words and to communicate the subtlest and most powerful human emotions.

In literature, Romantic poets such as John Keats (1795-1821), William Wordsworth (1770-1850), and Samuel Taylor Coleridge (1772-1834) published volumes of poetry manifesting the Romantic interest in lyrical drama. *Ozymandias,* by Percy Bysshe Shelley (1792-1822), transported readers to faraway, exotic locales. The setting of *Sardanapalus* (1821) by Lord Byron (1788-1824) is the ancient Assyrian Empire (see page 27). Byron's poem conjures images of eroticism and fury unleashed—images Eugène Delacroix made concrete in his painting *Death of Sardanapalus* (FIG. 12-7).

One of the best examples of the Romantic spirit is the engrossing novel *Frankenstein,* written in 1818 by Shelley's wife, Mary Wollstonecraft Shelley (1797-1851). This fantastic tale of a monstrous creature run amok not only embraced emotionalism but also rejected the rationalism underlying Enlightenment thought. Dr. Frankenstein's monster was a product of science, and the novel is an indictment of the deep belief in science that Voltaire and other Enlightenment thinkers promoted. *Frankenstein* served as a cautionary tale of the havoc that could result from unrestrained scientific experimentation and from the arrogance of scientists.

12-5 FRANCISCO GOYA, *The Sleep of Reason Produces Monsters,* no. 43 from *Los Caprichos,* ca. 1798. Etching and aquatint, $8\frac{7}{16}$" × $5\frac{7}{8}$". Metropolitan Museum of Art, New York (gift of M. Knoedler & Co., 1918).

In this print, Goya depicted himself asleep while threatening creatures converge on him, revealing his embrace of the Romantic spirit—the unleashing of imagination, emotions, and nightmares.

Romanticism was heightened interest in the medieval period and in the sublime. For people living in the 18th century, the Middle Ages were the "dark ages," a time of barbarism, superstition, mystery, and miracle. The Romantic imagination stretched its perception of the Middle Ages into all the worlds of fantasy open to it, including the ghoulish, infernal, terrible, nightmarish, grotesque, sadistic—all the imagery that comes from the chamber of horrors when reason sleeps (FIG. 12-5).

Related to the imaginative sensibility was the period's notion of the sublime. Among the individuals most involved in studying the sublime was the British politician and philosopher Edmund Burke (1729-1797). In *A Philosophical Enquiry into the Origins of Our Ideas of the Sublime and Beautiful* (1757), Burke articulated his definition of the sublime—feelings of awe mixed with terror. Burke observed that pain or fear evoked the most intense human emotions and that these emotions can also be thrilling. Thus raging rivers and great storms at sea could be sublime to their viewers. Accompanying this taste for the sublime was the taste for the fantastic, occult, and macabre—for the adventures of the soul voyaging into the dangerous reaches of the imagination.

FRANCISCO GOYA Although FRANCISCO JOSE DE GOYA LUCIENTES (1746–1828) was Jacques-Louis David's contemporary, their work has little in common. Both, however, rose to prominence as official court artists. In 1786, Goya entered the employ of Charles IV (r. 1788–1808) of Spain, and in 1799, the king promoted him to First Court Painter. At about that time, Goya produced perhaps his most famous print, *The Sleep of Reason Produces Monsters* (FIG. 12-5), from the series titled *Los Caprichos* (*The Caprices*). *Sleep of Reason* exemplifies Romantic artists' rejection of the Neoclassical penchant for rationality and order.

In the etching, Goya depicted an artist, probably himself, asleep, slumped onto a desk, while threatening creatures converge on him, at least in his dream. Seemingly poised to attack the artist are owls (symbols of folly) and bats (symbols of ignorance). The viewer might read this as a portrayal of what emerges when reason is suppressed and, therefore, as advocating Enlightenment ideals. However, the print should be interpreted as Goya's commitment to the creative process and the Romantic spirit—the unleashing of imagination, emotions, and even nightmares (see "The Romantic Spirit in Art, Music, and Literature," above).

12-6 Francisco Goya, *Third of May, 1808,* 1814–1815. Oil on canvas, 8' 9" × 13' 4". Museo del Prado, Madrid.

Goya encouraged empathy for the Spanish peasants massacred on May 3, 1808, by portraying horrified expressions on their faces, endowing them with a humanity lacking in the French firing squad.

1 ft.

THIRD OF MAY, 1808 Much of Goya's multifaceted work deals not with Romantic fantasies but with contemporary events. Dissatisfaction with the rule of Charles IV increased dramatically during Goya's tenure at the court, and the Spanish people eventually threw their support behind the king's son, Ferdinand VII, in the hope that he would initiate reform. To overthrow his father, Ferdinand enlisted the aid of Napoleon Bonaparte. Because he had designs on Spain, Napoleon readily agreed to send French troops to Spain. Not surprisingly, as soon as he ousted Charles IV, Napoleon installed his brother Joseph Bonaparte (r. 1808–1813) on the Spanish throne as his surrogate.

The Spanish people, finally recognizing the French as invaders, sought a way to expel the foreign troops. On May 2, 1808, Spaniards attacked Napoleon's soldiers in a chaotic and violent clash. In retaliation and as a show of force, the French responded the next day by rounding up and executing Spanish citizens. This tragic event is the subject of Goya's most famous painting, *Third of May, 1808* (FIG. 12-6). In emotional fashion, Goya depicted the anonymous murderous wall of Napoleonic soldiers ruthlessly executing the unarmed and terrified Spanish peasants. The artist encouraged empathy for the Spaniards by portraying horrified expressions and anguish on their faces, endowing them with a humanity lacking in the faceless French firing squad. Moreover, the peasant about to be shot throws his arms out in a cruciform gesture reminiscent of Christ's position on the cross. Goya enhanced the emotional drama of the massacre by starkly contrasting darks and lights and by extending the time frame depicted. Although Goya captured the specific moment when one man is about to be executed, he also recorded the bloody bodies of others lying dead on the ground. Still others have been herded together and will be shot in a few moments.

EUGÈNE DELACROIX In France, Théodore Géricault (FIG. 12-1) was instrumental in the launching of Romanticism as a major art movement, but the leading French Romantic painter was EUGÈNE DELACROIX (1798–1863). Art historians often present the history of painting during the first half of the 19th century as a contest between Delacroix, the Romantic colorist, and Ingres, the Neoclassical draftsman. Their dialogue recalls the quarrel at the end of the 17th century and the beginning of the 18th between the Poussinistes and the Rubénistes (see page 315). No other painter of the time explored the domain of Romantic subject and mood as thoroughly and definitively as Delacroix. His technique was impetuous, improvisational, and instinctive, in contrast to the deliberate, studious, and cold method of the Neoclassicists (see "Delacroix on David and Neoclassicism," page 337). His work exemplified Romantic colorist painting, catching the impression quickly and developing it in the execution process. Delacroix's contemporaries commented on how furiously he worked once he had an idea, keeping the whole painting progressing at once. The fury of his attack matched the fury of his imagination and his subjects.

DEATH OF SARDANAPALUS Delacroix's richly colored and emotionally charged *Death of Sardanapalus* (FIG. 12-7) is perhaps the grandest Romantic pictorial drama ever painted. Although inspired by Lord Byron's 1821 poem *Sardanapalus* (see "The Romantic Spirit," page 335), the painting does not illustrate that text faithfully. Delacroix depicted the last hour of the Assyrian king Ashurbanipal (r. 668–627 BCE), whom the Greeks called Sardanapalus. The king has just received news of his army's defeat and the enemy's entry into his city. The setting is much more tempestuous and crowded than Byron described, and orgiastic destruction has replaced the

ARTISTS ON ART
Delacroix on David and Neoclassicism

Eugène Delacroix (FIGS. 12-7 and 12-8), the leading French Romantic painter of the 19th century, expressed his contempt for the Neoclassical style of Jacques-Louis David (FIGS. 11-14 and 11-15) and others in a series of letters he wrote in 1832 from Morocco. Romantic artists often depicted exotic faraway places they had never seen, but Delacroix journeyed to northern Africa in search of fresh inspiration for his paintings. He discovered in the sun-drenched Moroccan landscape—and in the hardy and colorful Moroccans dressed in robes reminiscent of the Roman toga—new insights into a culture that he believed was more classical than anything European Neoclassicism could conceive. In a letter to his friend Fréderic Villot dated February 29, 1832, he wrote:

> This place is made for painters.... [B]eauty abounds here; not the over-praised beauty of fashionable paintings. The heroes of David

and Co. with their rose-pink limbs would cut a sorry figure beside these children of the sun, who moreover wear the dress of classical antiquity with a nobler air, I dare assert.*

In a second letter, written June 4, 1832, he reported to Auguste Jal:

> I have Romans and Greeks on my doorstep: it makes me laugh heartily at David's Greeks, ... I know now what they were really like; ... If painting schools persist in [depicting classical subjects], I am convinced, and you will agree with me, that they would gain far more from being shipped off as cabin boys on the first boat bound for the Barbary coast than from spending any more time wearing out the classical soil of Rome. Rome is no longer to be found in Rome.[†]

*Translated by Jean Stewart, in Charles Harrison, Paul Wood, and Jason Gaiger, eds., *Art in Theory 1815–1900: An Anthology of Changing Ideas* (Oxford: Blackwell, 1998), 87.
[†]Ibid., 88.

1 ft.

12-7 EUGÈNE DELACROIX, *Death of Sardanapalus*, 1827. Oil on canvas, 12' 1$\frac{1}{2}$" × 16' 2$\frac{7}{8}$". Musée du Louvre, Paris.

Inspired by Lord Byron's 1821 poem, Delacroix painted the Romantic spectacle of an Assyrian king on his funeral pyre. The richly colored and emotionally charged canvas is filled with exotic figures.

sacrificial suicide of the poem. Sardanapalus reclines on his funeral pyre, soon to be set alight, and gloomily watches the destruction of all his most precious possessions—his women, slaves, horses, and treasure. The king's favorite concubine throws herself on the bed, determined to go up in flames with her master. The Assyrian presides like a genius of evil over the tragic scene. Most conspicuous are the tortured and dying bodies of the harem women. In

the foreground, a muscular slave plunges his knife into the neck of one woman.

Delacroix filled this awful spectacle of suffering and death with the most daringly difficult and tortuous poses, and chose the richest intensities of hue. With its exotic and erotic overtones and violent Orientalist subject, *Death of Sardanapalus* tapped into the Romantic fantasies of 19th-century viewers.

12-8 Eugène Delacroix, *Liberty Leading the People*, 1830. Oil on canvas, 8' 6" × 10' 8". Musée du Louvre, Paris.

In a balanced mix of history and poetic allegory, Delacroix captured the passion and energy of the 1830 revolution in this painting of Liberty leading the Parisian uprising against Charles X.

1 ft.

LIBERTY LEADING THE PEOPLE Although *Death of Sardanapalus* is a seventh-century BCE drama, Delacroix, like Géricault, also turned to current events, particularly tragic or sensational ones, for his subject matter. In *Liberty Leading the People* (FIG. 12-8), Delacroix captured the passion and the energy of the July 27–29, 1830, Parisian uprising against Charles X (r. 1824–1830). The painting is at once a historical record and a Romantic allegory. Dominating the composition is the bare-breasted personification of Liberty defiantly thrusting forth France's tricolor banner as she urges the masses to fight on. She wears a scarlet Phrygian cap (the symbol of a freed slave in antiquity), reinforcing the urgency of this struggle. Arrayed around Liberty are bold Parisian types—the street boy brandishing his pistols, the menacing worker with a cutlass, and the intellectual dandy in top hat armed with a musket. As in Géricault's *Raft of the Medusa* (FIG. 12-1), dead bodies lie all around. In the background, the Gothic towers of Notre-Dame (FIG. 7-7) rise through the smoke and haze. The painter's inclusion of this recognizable Parisian landmark specifies the locale and event, balancing historical fact with poetic allegory.

CASPAR DAVID FRIEDRICH Landscape painting came into its own in the 19th century as a fully independent and respected genre. Briefly eclipsed at the century's beginning by the taste for ideal form, which favored figural composition and history, landscape painting expressed the Romantic view (first extolled by Rousseau) of nature as a "being" that included the totality of existence in organic unity and harmony. In nature—"the living garment of God," as German poet and dramatist Johann Wolfgang von Goethe (1749–1832) called it—artists found an ideal subject to express the Romantic theme of the soul unified with the natural world. As all nature was

mysteriously permeated by "being," landscape artists had the task of interpreting the signs, symbols, and emblems of universal spirit disguised within visible material things. Artists no longer merely beheld a landscape but rather participated in its spirit, becoming translators of nature's transcendent meanings.

Among the artists best known for their Romantic transcendental landscape paintings is CASPAR DAVID FRIEDRICH (1774–1840). For Friedrich, the personal experience of nature led to a deeper understanding of God, nature's creator. The reverential mood of his works demands from the viewer the silence appropriate to sacred places filled with a divine presence. "The artist," Friedrich wrote, "should not only paint what he sees before him, but also what he sees within him."[1] In many of Friedrich's landscapes, the human figure plays an insignificant role. Indeed, the human actors are often difficult even to discern. But in other paintings, one or more figures seen from behind gazing at the natural vista dominate the canvas. In *Wanderer above a Sea of Mist* (FIG. 12-9), a solitary man dressed in attire suggestive of a bygone era stands on a rocky promontory and leans on his cane. He surveys a vast panorama of clouds, mountains, and thick mist. Because Friedrich chose a point of view on the level of the man's head, the viewer has the sensation of hovering in space behind him—an impossible position that enhances the aura of mystery that the scene conveys. Art historians dispute whether Friedrich intended the viewer to identify with the man seen from behind or if he wanted the viewer to contemplate the man gazing at the misty landscape. In either case, the painter communicated an almost religious awe at the beauty and vastness of the natural world. *Wanderer above a Sea of Mist* perfectly expresses the Romantic notion of the sublime in nature.

12-9 CASPAR DAVID FRIEDRICH, *Wanderer above a Sea of Mist,* 1817–1818. Oil on canvas, 3' 1¾" × 2' 5⅜". Hamburger Kunsthalle, Hamburg.

Friedrich's painting of a solitary man on a rocky promontory gazing at a vast panorama of clouds, mountains, and thick mist perfectly expresses the Romantic notion of the sublime in nature.

JOHN CONSTABLE In England, one of the most momentous developments in history—the Industrial Revolution—had a profound impact on the evolution of Romantic landscape painting. Although discussion of the Industrial Revolution invariably focuses on technological advances, factory development, and growth of urban centers, industrialization had no less pronounced an effect on the countryside and the land itself. The detrimental economic effect that the Industrial Revolution had on prices for agrarian products created significant unrest in the English countryside. In particular, increasing numbers of farmers could no longer afford to farm their small plots and had to abandon their land. JOHN CONSTABLE (1776–1837) addressed this agrarian situation in his landscape paintings. He made countless sketches from nature for each of his canvases, studying nature as a meteorologist. His special gift was for capturing the texture that climate and weather give to landscape. Constable's use of tiny dabs of local color, stippled with white, created a sparkling shimmer of light and hue across the canvas surface—the vibration itself suggestive of movement and process.

The Hay Wain (FIG. 12-10) is a serenely pastoral scene of the countryside. A small cottage is on the left, and in the center foreground, a man leads a horse and a hay-filled wagon (a *hay wain*) across the Stour River. Billowy clouds float lazily across the sky. The muted greens and golds and the delicacy of Constable's brushstrokes complement the scene's tranquility. The artist portrayed the oneness with nature that the Romantic poets sought. The relaxed figures are not observers but participants in the landscape's "being." *The Hay Wain* is also significant for precisely what it does not show—the civil unrest of the agrarian working class and the resulting outbreaks of violence and arson. The people inhabiting Constable's landscapes blend into the scenes and become one with nature. Rarely does the viewer see workers engaged in tedious labor. Indeed, this painting has a wistful air to it and reflects Constable's memories of a disappearing rural pastoralism. This nostalgia, presented in such naturalistic terms, renders Constable's works Romantic in tone, although they are not sublime. That the painter felt a kindred spirit with the Romantic artists is revealed by his comment, "Painting is with me but another word for feeling."[2]

12-10 JOHN CONSTABLE, *The Hay Wain,* 1821. Oil on canvas, 4' 3¼" × 6' 1". National Gallery, London.

The Hay Wain is a nostalgic view of the disappearing English countryside during the Industrial Revolution. Constable had a special gift for capturing the texture that climate and weather give to landscape.

PROBLEMS AND SOLUTIONS
Unleashing the Emotive Power of Color

The passion and energy of Turner's landscapes and seascapes reveal the sensibility that was the foundation for much of the art of the Romantic era, but Turner discovered a new means of capturing in painting Edmund Burke's concept of the sublime—awe mixed with terror.

Turner's *The Slave Ship* (FIG. 12-11), although strikingly different in form from Géricault's *Raft of the Medusa* (FIG. 12-1), also has as its subject a politically explosive disaster at sea. *The Slave Ship* depicts a 1781 incident reported in the widely read *History of the Abolition of the Slave Trade* by Thomas Clarkson (1760–1846). Clarkson's account, reprinted in 1839, undoubtedly was the reason Turner chose this subject for this 1840 painting. The incident involved the slave ship *Zong,* en route from Africa to Liverpool. The ship's captain, on realizing that his insurance would reimburse him only for slaves lost at sea but not for those who died en route, ordered more than 50 sick and dying slaves to be thrown overboard. Appropriately, the painting's subtitle is *Slavers Throwing Overboard the Dead and Dying, Typhoon Coming On.*

Turner's frenzied emotional depiction of the dumping of the sick slaves into the sea matches its barbaric nature. The artist transformed the sun into an incandescent comet amid flying scarlet clouds. The slave ship moves into the distance, leaving in its wake a turbulent sea choked with the bodies of slaves sinking to their deaths. The relative scale of the minuscule human forms compared with the vast sea and overarching sky reinforces the sense of the sublime, especially the immense power of nature over humans. *The Slave Ship* is the polar opposite of *Raft of the Medusa,* in which heroic, over-life-size bodies fill the canvas and block out most of the ocean. Almost lost in the boiling colors of Turner's painting are the event's particulars, but on close inspection, the viewer can discern the iron shackles and manacles around the wrists and ankles of the drowning slaves, cruelly denying them any chance of saving themselves from the predatory fish circling about them.

A key ingredient of Turner's highly personal style is the emotive power of pure color. The haziness of the painter's forms and the indistinctness of his compositions intensify the colors and energetic brushstrokes. Turner's innovation in works such as *The Slave Ship* was to release color from any defining outlines so as to express both the forces of nature and the painter's emotional response to them. In his paintings, the reality of color is at one with the reality of feeling.

Turner's methods had a profound effect on the later development of painting. His discovery of the aesthetic and emotive power of pure color and his pushing of the medium's fluidity to a point where the paint itself is almost the subject were important steps toward 20th-century Abstract Expressionist art, which dispensed with identifiable forms altogether (see page 413).

1 ft.

12-11 JOSEPH MALLORD WILLIAM TURNER, *The Slave Ship (Slavers Throwing Overboard the Dead and Dying, Typhoon Coming On),* 1840. Oil on canvas, 2' 11¼" × 4'. Museum of Fine Arts, Boston (Henry Lillie Pierce Fund).

The essence of Turner's innovative style is the emotive power of color. He released color from any defining outlines to express both the forces of nature and the painter's emotional response to them.

12-12 THOMAS COLE, *The Oxbow* (*View from Mount Holyoke, Northampton, Massachusetts, after a Thunderstorm*), 1836. Oil on canvas, 4' 3½" × 6' 4". Metropolitan Museum of Art, New York (gift of Mrs. Russell Sage, 1908).

Cole championed the idea of America having a landscape distinct from Europe's. Here, he contrasted dark wilderness on the left and sunlit civilization on the right, with a minuscule painter at the bottom center.

J.M.W. TURNER Constable's great contemporary in the English school of landscape painting was JOSEPH MALLORD WILLIAM TURNER (1775–1851). Both artists tirelessly sought to raise the prestige of landscape painting in the Royal Academy. However, whereas Constable's canvases are serene and precisely painted, and have as their exclusive subject the rural countryside of his birthplace, Turner's paintings have a much wider range of themes and, as in *The Slave Ship* (FIG. 12-11), feature turbulent swirls of frothy pigment (see "Unleashing the Emotive Power of Color," page 340).

THOMAS COLE In America, landscape painting was the specialty of a group of artists known as the Hudson River School, so named because its members drew their subjects primarily from the uncultivated regions of New York's Hudson River Valley, although many of these painters depicted scenes from across the country. As did the early-19th-century landscape painters in Germany and England, the artists of the Hudson River School not only presented Romantic panoramic landscape views but also participated in the ongoing exploration of the individual's and the country's relationship to the land. American landscape painters frequently focused on identifying qualities that made America unique. THOMAS COLE (1801–1848), often referred to as the leader of the Hudson River School, best articulated this idea (see "Thomas Cole on the American Landscape" ▲).

Another issue that surfaced frequently in Hudson River School paintings was the moral question of America's direction as a civilization. Cole addressed this question in *The Oxbow* (FIG. 12-12).

A splendid scene opens before the viewer, dominated by the lazy oxbow-shaped curve of the Connecticut River near Northampton, Massachusetts. Cole divided the composition in two, with the dark, stormy wilderness on the left and the more developed civilization on the right. The minuscule artist wearing a top hat in the bottom center of the painting, dwarfed by the landscape's scale, turns to the viewer as if to ask for input in deciding the country's future course. Cole's depiction of expansive wilderness incorporated reflections and moods romantically appealing to the public.

REALISM

Advances in industrial technology during the early 19th century reinforced Enlightenment faith in the connection between science and progress. Both intellectuals and the general public increasingly embraced *empiricism* and *positivism*. To empiricists, the basis of knowledge is observation and direct experience. Positivists ascribed to the philosophical model developed by Auguste Comte (1798–1857), who believed that scientific laws governed the environment and human activity and could be revealed through careful recording and analysis of observable data. Comte's followers promoted science as the mind's highest achievement and advocated a purely empirical approach to nature and society.

Realism was a movement that developed in France around midcentury against this backdrop of an increasing emphasis on science. Consistent with the philosophical tenets of the empiricists

ARTISTS ON ART
Gustave Courbet on Realism

The academic jury selecting work for the 1855 Salon (part of the Exposition Universelle in Paris that year) rejected 3 of the 14 paintings that Gustave Courbet (FIGS. 12-13 and 12-14) submitted, declaring that their subjects and figures were too coarse and too large. In response, Courbet withdrew all of his works and set up his own exhibition outside the grounds, calling it the Pavilion of Realism, featuring not 14 but 40 of his paintings. Courbet was the first artist ever known to have staged a private exhibition of his own work. His pavilion and the statement he issued to explain the paintings shown there amounted to the Realist movement's manifestos.

> The title of "realist" has been imposed upon me.... Titles have never given a just idea of things; were it otherwise, the work would be superfluous.... I have studied the art of the ancients and the moderns, avoiding any preconceived system and without prejudice. I have no more wanted to imitate the former than to copy the latter; nor have I thought of achieving the idle aim of "art for art's sake." No! I have simply wanted to draw from a thorough knowledge of tradition the reasoned and free sense of my own individuality.... To be able to translate the customs, ideas, and appearances of my time as I see them—in a word, to create a living art—this has been my aim.*

Six years later, on Christmas Day, 1861, Courbet wrote an open letter, published a few days later in the *Courier du dimanche*, addressed to prospective students.

> [An artist must apply] his personal faculties to the ideas and the events of the times in which he lives. . . . [A]rt in painting should consist only of the representation of things that are visible and tangible to the artist. Every age should be represented only by its own artists, that is to say, by the artists who have lived in it. I also maintain that painting is an essentially concrete art form and can consist only of the representation of both real and existing things . . . . An abstract object, not visible, nonexistent, is not within the domain of painting.†

Courbet's most famous statement, however, is his blunt dismissal of academic painting, in which he concisely summed up the core principle of Realist painting:

> I have never seen an angel. Show me an angel, and I'll paint one.‡

*Translated by Robert Goldwater and Marco Treves, eds., *Artists on Art from the XIV to the XX Century* (New York: Pantheon, 1958), 295.
†Translated by Petra ten-Doesschate Chu, *Letters of Gustave Courbet* (Chicago: University of Chicago Press, 1992), 203–204.
‡Quoted by Vincent van Gogh in a July 1885 letter to his brother Theo. Ronald de Leeuw, *The Letters of Vincent van Gogh* (New York: Penguin, 1996), 302.

12-13 GUSTAVE COURBET, *The Stone Breakers*, 1849. Oil on canvas, 5' 3" × 8' 6". Formerly Gemäldegalerie, Dresden (destroyed in 1945).

Courbet was the leading figure in the Realist movement. Using a palette of dirty browns and grays, he conveyed the dreary and dismal nature of menial labor in mid-19th-century France.

1 ft.

and positivists, Realist artists argued that only the contemporary world—what people could see—was "real." Accordingly, Realists focused their attention on the people and events of their own time and disapproved of historical and fictional subjects on the grounds that they were neither visible nor present and therefore were not real.

GUSTAVE COURBET The leading figure of the Realist movement was GUSTAVE COURBET (1819–1877). In fact, even though he shunned labels, Courbet used the term "Realism" when exhibiting his own works (see "Gustave Courbet on Realism," above). The Realists' sincerity about scrutinizing their environment led them to paint mundane subjects that artists had traditionally deemed

1 ft.

12-14 GUSTAVE COURBET, *Burial at Ornans*, 1849. Oil on canvas, 10' 3½" × 21' 9½". Musée d'Orsay, Paris.

Although as monumental in scale as a traditional history painting, *Burial at Ornans* horrified critics because of the ordinary nature of the subject and Courbet's starkly antiheroic composition.

unworthy of depiction—for example, working-class laborers and peasants. Moreover, the Realists depicted these scenes on a scale and with a seriousness that implied parity between contemporary subject matter and historical, mythological, and religious painting.

THE STONE BREAKERS In *The Stone Breakers* (FIG. 12-13), Courbet represented in a straightforward manner, and nearly at life size, two men—one about 70, the other quite young—in the decidedly nonheroic act of breaking stones to provide paving for roads, traditionally the lot of the lowest members of French society. By juxtaposing youth and age, Courbet suggested that those born to poverty will remain poor their entire lives. The artist neither romanticized nor idealized the men's menial labor but depicted their thankless toil with directness and accuracy. Courbet's palette of dirty browns and grays further conveys the dreary and dismal nature of the task, and the angular positioning of the older stone breaker's limbs suggests a mechanical monotony.

Courbet's portrayal of the working poor had a special resonance for his mid-19th-century French audience. In 1848, laborers rebelled against the bourgeois leaders of the newly formed Second Republic and against the rest of the nation, demanding better working conditions and a redistribution of property. The army quelled the uprising in three days, but not without long-lasting trauma and significant loss of life. The 1848 revolution raised the issue of labor as a national concern. Courbet's depiction of stone breakers in 1849 was thus both timely and populist.

BURIAL AT ORNANS Many art historians regard Courbet's *Burial at Ornans* (FIG. 12-14) as his masterpiece. The huge (10-by-22-foot) canvas depicts a funeral set in a bleak provincial landscape outside the artist's hometown. Attending the funeral are the types of common people that Honoré de Balzac (1799–1850) and Gustave Flaubert (1821–1880) presented in their novels. Although the painting

has the imposing scale of a traditional history painting, the subject's ordinariness and the starkly antiheroic composition horrified critics. (Courbet had the audacity to submit *Burial at Ornans* to the 1851 Salon in the category of history painting.) Arranged in a wavering line extending across the breadth of the canvas are three groups—the somberly clad women at the back right, a semicircle of similarly clad men by the open grave, and assorted churchmen at the left. The seemingly equal stature of all at the funeral also offended the hierarchical social sensibility of the Salon jurors. This wall of figures blocks any view into deep space. Behind and above the figures are bands of overcast sky and barren cliffs. The dark pit of the grave opens into the viewer's space in the center foreground. In place of the heroic, the sublime, and the dramatic, Courbet aggressively presented the viewer with mundane realities. Unlike the theatricality of Romanticism, Realism captured the ordinary rhythms of daily life.

Of great importance for the later history of art, Realism also involved a reconsideration of the painter's primary goals and departed from the established emphasis on illusionism. Accordingly, Realists called attention to painting as a pictorial construction by the ways they applied pigment or manipulated composition. Courbet's intentionally simple and direct methods of expression in composition and technique seemed unbearably crude to many of his more traditional contemporaries, who called him a primitive. Although his bold, somber palette was essentially traditional, Courbet often used the *palette knife* to quickly place and unify large daubs of paint, producing a roughly wrought surface. The public accused him of carelessness, and critics wrote of his "brutalities."

JEAN-FRANÇOIS MILLET Like Courbet, JEAN-FRANÇOIS MILLET (1814–1878) found his subjects in the people and occupations of the everyday world. Millet was the most prominent member of the group of French painters of country life who, to be close to their

12-15 Jean-François Millet, *The Gleaners*, 1857. Oil on canvas, 2′ 9″ × 3′ 8″. Musée d'Orsay, Paris.

Millet and the Barbizon School painters specialized in depictions of French country life. Here, Millet portrayed three impoverished women gathering the scraps left in the field after a harvest.

1 ft.

rural subjects, settled near the village of Barbizon. This Barbizon School specialized in detailed pictures of forest and countryside. In *The Gleaners* (FIG. **12-15**), Millet depicted three impoverished women—members of the lowest level of peasant society—performing the back-breaking task of *gleaning*. Landowning nobles traditionally permitted peasants to glean, or collect, the wheat scraps left in the field after the harvest. Millet characteristically placed his large figures in the foreground, against a broad sky. Although the field stretches back to a rim of haystacks, cottages, trees, and distant workers and a flat horizon, the gleaners quietly doing their tedious and time-consuming work dominate the canvas. It is hard to imagine a sharper contrast with the almost invisible agricultural workers in Constable's *Hay Wain* (FIG. 12-10).

Although Millet's paintings evoke a sentimentality absent from Courbet's, the French public still reacted to his work with disdain and suspicion. In the aftermath of the 1848 revolution, Millet's investiture of the poor with solemn grandeur did not meet with approval from the prosperous class. Further, the middle class linked the poor with the dangerous, newly defined working class, which was finding outspoken champions in men such as Karl Marx (1818–1883), Friedrich Engels (1820–1895), and the novelists Émile Zola (1840–1902) and Charles Dickens (1812–1870). Socialism was a growing movement, and both its views on property and its call for social justice, even economic equality, threatened the bourgeoisie. Millet's sympathetic portrayal of the poor seemed to much of the public to be a political manifesto.

HONORÉ DAUMIER Because people widely recognized the power of art to serve political ends, the political and social agitation accompanying the violent revolutions in France and the rest of Europe in the later 18th and early 19th centuries prompted the French people to suspect artists of subversive intention. Realist artist HONORÉ DAUMIER (1808–1879) was a defender of the urban working class, and in his art he boldly confronted authority with social criticism and political protest. In response, the authorities imprisoned him. A painter, sculptor, and one of history's great printmakers, Daumier produced *lithographs* (see "Lithography," page 345) that enabled him to create an exceptionally large number of prints. Daumier also contributed satirical lithographs to the widely read, liberal French Republican journal *Caricature,* in which he mercilessly lampooned the foibles and misbehavior of politicians, lawyers, doctors, and the rich bourgeoisie in general.

Daumier's lithograph *Rue Transnonain* (FIG. **12-16**) depicts the atrocity that unfolded on that Parisian street in April 1834 after an unknown sniper killed a civil guard, part of a government force trying to repress a worker demonstration. Because the fatal shot had come from a workers' housing block, the remaining guards immediately stormed the building and massacred all of its inhabitants. With the power Goya displayed in *Third of May, 1808* (FIG. 12-6), Daumier created a view of the slaughter from a sharp angle of vision. But unlike Goya, he depicted not the dramatic moment of execution but the terrible, quiet aftermath. The limp bodies of the workers—and of a child crushed beneath his father's corpse—lie amid violent disorder. Daumier's pictorial manner is rough and spontaneous, and that approach to representation, which is a central characteristic of Realist art, accounts in large measure for its remarkable force.

ÉDOUARD MANET Like Gustave Courbet, ÉDOUARD MANET (1832–1883) was a pivotal figure in 19th-century European art. His work too was influential in articulating Realist principles, but the younger artist also played an important role in the development of Impressionism in the 1870s (see page 357). Manet's *Le Déjeuner sur l'Herbe* (*Luncheon on the Grass*; FIG. **12-17**), widely recognized only later as a seminal work in the history of art, depicts two clothed men and one nude and one clothed woman at a picnic. Consistent with Realist principles, Manet based all four figures on real people, including Manet's favorite model at the time and his brother. The two men wear fashionable Parisian attire of the 1860s. The nude woman—her discarded clothes are on the grass—is a distressingly unidealized figure who also seems completely unfazed by her nakedness. She gazes directly at the viewer without shame or flirtatiousness. Neither she nor her companion pays any attention to what the second man is saying to them. The second woman appears to be looking for something in a pool of water. This is no luncheon on the grass, although it may be the aftermath of a meal. Nor is this truly Realism, because the subject is incomprehensible—as Manet wished it to be. In this work, he sought to reassess the nature of painting. The composition contains sophisticated references and allusions to many painting genres—history painting, portraiture, pastoral scenes, nudes, and even religious scenes. *Le Déjeuner sur*

MATERIALS AND TECHNIQUES
Lithography

In 1798, the German printmaker Alois Senefelder (1771–1834) created the first prints using stone instead of metal plates or wood blocks. In contrast to earlier printing techniques (see "Woodcuts, Engravings, and Etchings," page 228), in which the artist applied ink either to a raised or incised surface, in *lithography* (Greek, "stone writing or drawing") the printing and nonprinting areas of the plate are on the same plane.

The chemical phenomenon fundamental to lithography is the repellence of oil and water. The lithographer uses a greasy, oil-based crayon to draw directly on a stone plate, and then wipes water onto the stone, which clings only to the areas the drawing does not cover. Next, the artist rolls oil-based ink onto the stone, which adheres to the drawing but is repelled by the water. When the artist presses the stone against paper, only the inked areas—the drawing—transfer to the paper. Color lithography requires multiple plates, one for each color, and the printmaker must take special care to make sure that each impression lines up perfectly with the previous one so that each color prints in its proper place.

12-16 HONORÉ DAUMIER, *Rue Transnonain, April 15, 1834,* 1834. Lithograph, 1' 1$\frac{3}{8}$" × 1' 6$\frac{1}{4}$". Yale University Art Gallery, New Haven (Everett V. Meeks, B.A. 1901, Fund).

Daumier used the recent invention of lithography to reach a wide audience for his social criticism and political protest. This print records the horrific 1834 massacre in a workers' housing block in Paris.

One of the earliest masters of this new printmaking process was Honoré Daumier, whose lithographs (FIGS. 12-16 and 12-24A ⬈) in leading French journals reached an audience of unprecedented size.

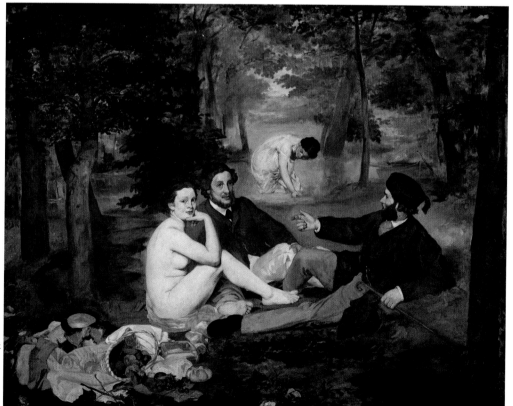

l'Herbe is Manet's synthesis and critique of the history of painting.

This audacious painting outraged the French public. Rather than depicting a traditional pastoral scene (compare FIG. 9-18), *Le Déjeuner* features ordinary men and promiscuous women in a Parisian park. The negative response to Manet's painting on the part of public and critics alike extended beyond subject matter, however. The painter's technique also elicited severe criticism. Manet rendered the men and women in soft focus

12-17 ÉDOUARD MANET, *Le Déjeuner sur l'Herbe* (*Luncheon on the Grass*), 1863. Oil on canvas, 7' × 8' 8". Musée d'Orsay, Paris.

Manet shocked his contemporaries with both his subject matter and manner of painting. Moving away from illusionism, he used colors to flatten form and to draw attention to the painting surface.

12-18 ÉDOUARD MANET, *Olympia*, 1863. Oil on canvas, 4' 3" × 6' 2¼". Musée d'Orsay, Paris.

Manet's painting of a nude prostitute and her black maid carrying a bouquet from a client scandalized the public. Critics also faulted his rough brushstrokes and abruptly shifting tonalities.

and broadly painted the landscape. The loose manner of painting contrasts with the clear forms of the harshly lit foreground trio as well as the pile of clothes and picnic foods at the lower left. The lighting creates strong contrasts between dark and highlighted areas. In the main figures, many values are summed up in one or two lights or darks. The effect is both to flatten the forms and set them off sharply from the setting. Manet aimed to move away from illusionism toward an open acknowledgment of painting's properties, such as the flatness of the painting surface, which would become a core principle of many later 19th-century painters and their successors to the present day.

OLYMPIA Even more scandalous to the French viewing public was Manet's *Olympia* (FIG. 12-18). This work depicts a young white prostitute (Olympia was a common "professional" name for prostitutes) reclining on a bed. Nude except for a thin black ribbon tied around her neck, a bracelet on her arm, an orchid in her hair, and fashionable slippers on her feet, Olympia meets the viewer's eye with a look of cool indifference. The only other figure in the painting is a black maid, who presents Olympia with a bouquet of flowers from a client.

Olympia horrified the public and critics alike. Although images of prostitutes were not unheard of during this period, the shamelessness of Olympia and her look verging on defiance shocked viewers. The depiction of a black woman was also

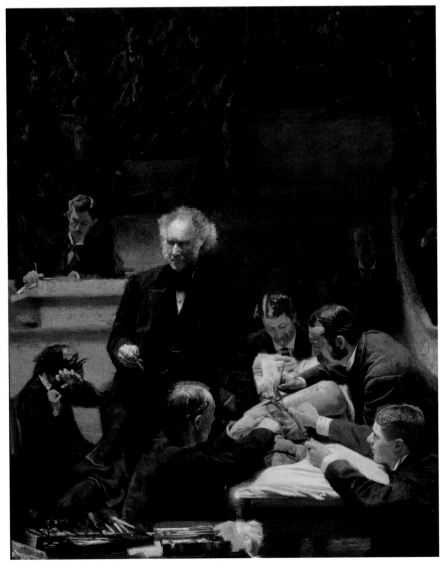

12-19 THOMAS EAKINS, *The Gross Clinic*, from Jefferson Medical College, Philadelphia, Pennsylvania, 1875. Oil on canvas, 8' × 6' 6". Philadelphia Museum of Art, Philadelphia.

The too-brutal realism of Eakins's depiction of a medical college operating amphitheater caused this painting's rejection from the Philadelphia exhibition celebrating America's centennial.

Edmonia Lewis, an African American Sculptor in Rome

Sculptor Edmonia Lewis, whose works are stylistically indebted to Neoclassicism but depict contemporary Realist themes, stands apart from all other important 19th-century artists by virtue of the circumstances of her birth. The daughter of a Chippewa mother and African American father in upstate New York, she was given the name Wildfire. Lewis became an orphan when she was four years old and was raised by the Chippewa. She adopted the name Edmonia Lewis in 1859 when she was admitted to Oberlin College (the first American college to grant degrees to women and among the first to admit African Americans). After Oberlin, Lewis became an apprentice in a sculpture studio in Boston. She financed her 1865 trip to Rome, which became her permanent home, with the sale of portrait medallions and marble busts, mostly representing abolitionist leaders. Lewis's success in a field dominated by white European and American men is a testament to both her artistic skill and her determination, but also speaks to the increasing access to training available to women during the 19th century.

Forever Free (FIG. 12-20) is a marble statue that Lewis carved while living in Rome, surrounded by examples of both classical and Renaissance art. It represents two freed African American slaves immediately after President Lincoln's issuance of the Emancipation Proclamation. The man stands triumphantly in a contrapposto stance reminiscent of classical statues. His right hand rests on the shoulder of the kneeling woman with her hands clasped in thankful prayer. The man holds aloft in his left hand a broken manacle and chain as literal and symbolic references to his former servitude. Produced four years after Lincoln's proclamation, *Forever Free* (originally titled *The Morning of Liberty*) was widely perceived as an abolitionist statement. ("Forever free" is a phrase that Lincoln used in both his preliminary September 1862 and final January 1863 emancipation proclamations.) Although emancipated, the former slaves still have shackles attached, in contrast to those born free. However, other factors caution against an overly

12-20 EDMONIA LEWIS, *Forever Free*, 1867. Marble, 3' 5¼" high. James A. Porter Gallery of Afro-American Art, Howard University, Washington, D.C.

African American–Chippewa Lewis's sculptures owe a stylistic debt to Neoclassicism but depict contemporary Realist themes. She carved *Forever Free* four years after Lincoln's Emancipation Proclamation.

1 ft.

simplistic reading. For example, scholars have debated the degree to which the sculptor attempted to inject a statement about gender relationships into this statue and whether the kneeling position of the woman is a reference to female subordination in the African American community.

---

not new to painting, but the French public perceived Manet's inclusion of both a black maid and a nude prostitute as evoking moral depravity, inferiority, and animalistic sexuality. The contrast of the black servant with the fair-skinned courtesan also conjured racial divisions. One critic described Olympia as "a courtesan with dirty hands and wrinkled feet . . . her body has the livid tint of a cadaver displayed in the morgue; her outlines are drawn in charcoal and her greenish, bloodshot eyes appear to be provoking the public, protected all the while by a hideous Negress."[3] From this and similar reviews, it is clear that critics were responding not solely to the subject matter but to Manet's artistic style as well. The painter's brushstrokes are much rougher and the shifts in tonality far more abrupt than those found in traditional painting. This departure from accepted practice compounded the audacity of the subject matter.

THOMAS EAKINS Although French artists took the lead in promoting the depiction of the realities of modern life, the Realist movement was neither exclusively French nor confined to Europe. Two of the leading American Realist painters were WINSLOW HOMER (1836–1910; FIG. 12-18A ⊡) of Boston and THOMAS EAKINS (1844–1916) of Philadelphia. The too-brutal Realism of

Eakins's early masterpiece, *The Gross Clinic* (FIG. 12-19), prompted the art jury to reject it for the Philadelphia exhibition celebrating the American independence centennial in 1876. The painting portrays the renowned surgeon Samuel D. Gross (1805–1884) in the operating amphitheater of the Jefferson Medical College in Philadelphia. Dr. Gross, with bloody fingers and scalpel, lectures about his surgery on a young man's leg. Watching the surgeon are several colleagues—all of whom historians have identified—and the patient's mother, who covers her face. The painting is an unsparing description of an unfolding event, with a good deal more reality than many viewers could endure. "It is a picture," one critic said, "that even strong men find difficult to look at long, if they can look at it at all."[4]

JOHN EVERETT MILLAIS Realism also appealed to sculptors, most notably American EDMONIA LEWIS (ca. 1844–ca. 1911; see "Edmonia Lewis, an African American Sculptor in Rome," above, and FIG. 12-20), but other artists rejected many of the basic premises of Realism. In England, a group of painters who called themselves the *Pre-Raphaelite Brotherhood* refused to be limited to the contemporary scenes that strict Realists portrayed. These artists chose instead to represent fictional and historical subjects, but with

12-21 JOHN EVERETT
MILLAIS, *Ophelia*, 1852.
Oil on canvas, 2' 6" × 3' 8".
Tate Britain, London.

Millet was a founder of the
Pre-Raphaelite Brotherhood,
whose members refused to be
limited to the contemporary
scenes that strict Realists portrayed. The drowning of Ophelia
is a Shakespearean subject.

1 ft.

a significant degree of convincing illusion. Organized in 1848, the Pre-Raphaelites wished to create fresh and sincere art, free from what they considered the tired and artificial manner promoted in the national painting academies by the successors of Raphael. Influenced by the critic, artist, and writer John Ruskin (1819–1900), the Pre-Raphaelites shared his distaste for the materialism and ugliness of the contemporary industrializing world. The Pre-Raphaelites also appreciated the spirituality and idealism (as well as the art and artisanship) of past times, especially the Early Renaissance.

One of the founders of the Pre-Raphaelite Brotherhood was JOHN EVERETT MILLAIS (1829–1896). Millais's painstaking observation of nature is evident in *Ophelia* (FIG. 12-21), which he exhibited in the Universal Exposition in Paris in 1855—the exhibition at which Courbet set up his Pavilion of Realism. The subject, from Shakespeare's *Hamlet* (4.7.176–179), is the drowning of Ophelia. To make the pathos of the scene visible, Millais became a faithful and feeling witness of its every detail, reconstructing it with a lyricism worthy of the original poetry. Although the scene is fictitious, Millais worked diligently to present it with unswerving fidelity to visual fact. He painted the background at a spot along the Hogsmill River in Surrey. For the figure of Ophelia, Millais had a friend lie in a heated bathtub full of water for hours at a time.

ARCHITECTURE

The buildings constructed during the 19th century are among the most stylistically diverse in history, ranging from the Neoclassical architecture of the Napoleonic Empire to the Neo-Gothic. At the same time, architects were exploring the expressive possibilities that new construction technologies had made possible.

HOUSES OF PARLIAMENT The revival of historical styles often was a reflection of nationalistic pride. England, for example, celebrated its medieval heritage with *Neo-Gothic* buildings. In London, when the old Houses of Parliament burned in 1834, CHARLES

BARRY (1795–1860), with the assistance of AUGUSTUS WELBY NORTHMORE PUGIN (1812–1852), submitted the winning design (FIG. 12-22) for the new government complex. Barry had traveled widely in Europe, Greece, Turkey, Egypt, and Palestine, studying the architecture of each place. He preferred the classical Renaissance styles, but he had designed some earlier Neo-Gothic buildings, and Pugin successfully influenced him in the direction of English Late Gothic. Pugin was one of a group of English artists and critics who saw moral purity and spiritual authenticity in the religious architecture of the Middle Ages and revered the careful medieval artisans who built the great cathedrals. The Industrial Revolution was flooding the market with cheaply made and ill-designed commodities. Machine work was replacing handicraft. Many, Pugin included, believed in the necessity of restoring the old artisanship, which they felt embodied honesty as well as quality. The design of the Houses of Parliament, however, is not genuinely Gothic, despite its picturesque tower groupings (the Clock Tower, housing Big Ben, at the north end, and the Victoria Tower at the south). The building has a formal axial plan and a kind of Palladian regularity beneath its Neo-Gothic detail. Pugin himself said of it, "All Grecian, Sir. Tudor [late English Gothic] details on a classical body."[5]

ROYAL PAVILION Although the Neoclassical and Neo-Gothic styles dominated early-19th-century architecture, exotic new approaches of all manner soon began to appear, due in part to European imperialism and in part to the Romantic spirit permeating all the arts. Great Britain's forays throughout the world, particularly India, had exposed English culture to a broad range of artistic traditions. The Royal Pavilion (FIG. 12-23), designed by JOHN NASH (1752–1835), is an eclectic mix of architectural styles. Nash was an established architect, known for Neoclassical buildings in London, when the prince regent (later King George IV) asked him to design a royal pleasure palace in the seaside resort of Brighton. The architecture of Greece, Egypt, and China influenced the interior décor of the Royal Pavilion, but the fantastic exterior is a conglomeration of Islamic domes, minarets, and

12-22 CHARLES BARRY and AUGUSTUS WELBY NORTHMORE PUGIN, Houses of Parliament (aerial view looking southwest), London, England, designed 1835.

During the 19th century, architects revived many historical styles, often reflecting nationalistic pride. The Houses of Parliament have an exterior veneer and towers that recall English Late Gothic style.

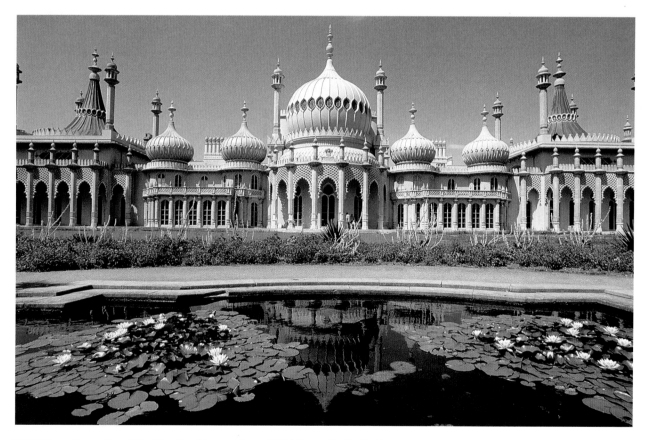

12-23 JOHN NASH, Royal Pavilion (looking northwest), Brighton, England, 1815–1818.

British territorial expansion brought a familiarity with many exotic styles. This palatial "Indian Gothic" seaside pavilion is a conglomeration of Islamic domes, minarets, and screens.

PROBLEMS AND SOLUTIONS
Prefabricated Architecture

Completely "undraped" construction—that is, the erection of buildings that did not conceal their cast-iron structural skeletons—first became popular in the conservatories (greenhouses) of English country estates. Joseph Paxton built several of these structures for his patron, the duke of Devonshire. In the largest—300 feet long—he used an experimental system of glass-and-metal roof construction. Encouraged by the success of this system, Paxton submitted a winning glass-and-iron building design in the competition for the hall to house the 1851 Great Exhibition of the Works of Industry of All Nations in London.

As innovative as Paxton's use of modern materials in place of stone was his adoption of a new cost-effective way to erect his exhibition building, the Crystal Palace (FIG. 12-24). Paxton was the champion of *prefabricated architecture*—the use of structural elements manufactured in advance and transported to the construction site ready for assembly. In traditional stone architecture, masons carved the column capitals, moldings, and the like on site to ensure that these delicate features would not be damaged during transport. This slowed down construction considerably. Paxton's use of prefabricated parts—primarily glass panes in wood frames and cast-iron pillars and beams—for the Crystal Palace enabled workers to build the vast (18-acre) structure in the then unheard-of time of six months and to dismantle it quickly at the exhibition's closing to avoid permanent obstruction of the park. The building was the perfect expression of the new industrial age that the Great Exhibition celebrated.

Paxton's design, nonetheless, borrowed much from traditional architecture, especially Roman and Christian basilicas. The Crystal Palace had a central flat-roofed "nave" and a barrel-vaulted crossing "transept," providing ample interior space to contain displays of huge machines as well as to accommodate decorative touches in the form of large working fountains and giant trees. The public admired the Crystal Palace so much that the workers who dismantled it put up an enlarged version of the glass-and-iron exhibition hall at a new location on the outskirts of London at Sydenham, where it remained until fire destroyed it in 1936. Fortunately, a few old black-and-white photographs and several color lithographs (FIG. 12-24) preserve a record of the Crystal Palace's appearance.

12-24 JOSEPH PAXTON, Crystal Palace, London, England, 1850–1851; enlarged and relocated at Sydenham, England, 1852–1854. Detail of a color lithograph by ACHILLE-LOUIS MARTINET, ca. 1862. Private collection.

The tensile strength of iron enabled Paxton to experiment with a new system of glass-and-metal roof construction. Constructed of prefabricated parts, the vast Crystal Palace required only six months to build.

screens that some architectural historians describe as "Indian Gothic." Underlying the exotic facade is a cast-iron skeleton, an early (if hidden) use of this material in noncommercial construction. Nash also put this metal to fanciful use, creating life-size palm-tree columns in cast iron to support the Royal Pavilion's kitchen ceiling.

CRYSTAL PALACE Other architects abandoned sentimental and Romantic designs from the past. Most utilitarian structures—factories, warehouses, dockyard structures, mills, bridges, and the like—long had been built simply and without historical ornamentation, often, as in the Royal Pavilion, using cast iron because of its tensile strength and resistance to fire. After 1860, steel became available, enabling architects to create new designs involving vast enclosed spaces, as in the great train sheds of railroad stations (FIG. 13-3) and in exposition halls. JOSEPH PAXTON (1801–1865) was the leading proponent of what became known as "undraped" architecture as well as a pioneer in the rapid construction of buildings using parts prepared in advance off-site (see "Prefabricated Architecture," page 350, and FIG. 12-24).

PHOTOGRAPHY

A technological device of immense consequence for the modern experience was invented shortly before the mid-19th century: the camera, with its attendant art of photography. From the time that Frenchman LOUIS-JACQUES-MANDÉ DAGUERRE (1789–1851) and Briton William Henry Fox Talbot (1800–1877) announced the first practical photographic processes in 1839, people have celebrated photography's ability to make convincing pictures of humans, animals, places, and things. The relative ease of the process, even in its earliest and most primitive form, seemed a dream come true for 19th-century scientists and artists, who for centuries had grappled with less satisfying methods for capturing accurate images of their subjects. Photography also perfectly suited an age that saw the emergence of Realism as an art movement and a pronounced shift of artistic patronage away from the elite few toward a broader base of support. The growing and increasingly powerful middle class embraced both the comprehensible images of the new medium and their lower cost.

For the traditional artist, photography suggested new answers to the great debate about what is real and how to represent the real in art. Because photography easily and accurately made possible the representation of three-dimensional objects on a two-dimensional surface, the new medium also challenged the place of traditional modes of pictorial representation originating in the Renaissance. Artists as diverse as Ingres, Delacroix, and Courbet welcomed photography as a helpful auxiliary to painting. Other artists, however, feared that the camera was a mechanism that would displace the painstaking work of skilled painters. From the moment of its invention, photography threatened to expropriate the realistic image, until then the exclusive property of painting. But just as some painters looked to the new medium of photography for answers on how best to render an image in paint, so some photographers looked to painting for suggestions about ways to enhance the photographic image with qualities beyond simple reproduction. Indeed, the first subjects that photographers chose to record were traditional painting themes—for example, still lifes and portraits—in part to establish photography as a legitimate artistic medium on a par with painting. A debate immediately began over whether the photograph was an art form or whether the camera was merely a scientific instrument. An 1862 court case provided the answer: photography was an art, and photographs were entitled to copyright protection, a legal ruling immediately celebrated by Daumier in a memorable lithograph (FIG. 12-24A ⬀).

Artists themselves were instrumental in the development of the new photographic technology. The camera obscura was familiar to 17th- and 18th-century artists (see pages 304 and 322). In 1807, the invention of the *camera lucida* ("lighted room") replaced the enclosed chamber of the camera obscura. Now the photographer aimed a small prism lens, hung on a stand, downward at an object. The lens projected the image of the object onto a sheet of paper. Artists using either of these devices found this process long and arduous, no matter how accurate the resulting work. All yearned for a more direct way to capture a subject's image. Two very different scientific inventions that accomplished this—the *daguerreotype* and the *calotype* (see "Daguerreotypes, Calotypes, and Wet-Plate Photography," page 352)—appeared almost simultaneously in France and England in 1839.

DAGUERREOTYPES The French government presented the new daguerreotype process at the Academy of Science in Paris on January 7, 1839, with the understanding that its details would be made available to all interested parties without charge (although the inventor received a large annuity in appreciation). Soon, people worldwide began making daguerreotype pictures in a process almost immediately christened "photography," from the Greek *photos* ("light") and *graphos* ("writing or drawing"). Each daguerreotype was a unique work. *Still Life in Studio* (FIG. 12-25) is one of the first successful plates

1 in.

12-25 LOUIS-JACQUES-MANDÉ DAGUERRE, *Still Life in Studio*, 1837. Daguerreotype, $6\frac{1}{4}" \times 8\frac{1}{4}"$. Collection Société Française de Photographie, Paris.

One of the first plates Daguerre produced after perfecting his new photographic process was this still life, in which he was able to capture amazing detail and finely graduated tones of light and shadow.

MATERIALS AND TECHNIQUES
Daguerreotypes, Calotypes, and Wet-Plate Photography

The earliest photographic processes were the *daguerreotype* (FIG. 12-25), named after L.J.M. Daguerre, and the *calotype*. Daguerre was an architect and theatrical set painter and designer who used a camera obscura in his work. Through a mutual acquaintance, he met Joseph Nicéphore Niépce (1765–1833), who in 1826 had successfully made a permanent picture of the cityscape outside his upper-story window by exposing, in a camera obscura, a metal plate covered with a light-sensitive coating. Niépce's process, however, had the significant drawback that it required an eight-hour exposure time. After Niépce died in 1833, Daguerre continued his work, making two important discoveries. Latent development—that is, bringing out the image through treatment in chemical solutions—considerably shortened the length of time needed for exposure. Daguerre also discovered a better way to "fix" the image by chemically stopping the action of light on the photographic plate, which otherwise would continue to darken until the image turned solid black.

The daguerreotype reigned supreme in photography until the 1850s, but the second major photographic invention, the ancestor of the modern negative-print system, eventually replaced it. On January 31, 1839, less than three weeks after Daguerre unveiled his method in Paris, William Henry Fox Talbot presented a paper on his "photogenic drawings" to the Royal Institution in London. As early as 1835, Talbot made "negative" images by placing objects on sensitized paper and exposing the arrangement to light. This created a design of light-colored silhouettes recording the places where opaque or translucent objects had blocked light from darkening the paper's emulsion. In his experiments, Talbot next exposed sensitized papers inside simple cameras and, with a second sheet, created "positive" images. He further improved the process with more light-sensitive chemicals and a chemical development of the negative image. Thus this technique could produce multiple prints. However, in Talbot's process, which he named the calotype (from the Greek word *kalos*, "beautiful"), the photographic images incorporated the texture of the paper. This produced a slightly blurred, grainy effect very different from the crisp detail and wide tonal range available with the daguerreotype. Also discouraging widespread adoption of the calotype were the stiff licensing and equipment fees charged for many years after Talbot patented his new process in 1841.

One of the earliest masters of an improved kind of calotype photography was the multitalented Frenchman known as Nadar (FIGS. 12-24A ↗ and 12-26). He used glass negatives and albumen (prepared with egg white) printing paper, which could record finer

12-26 NADAR, *Eugène Delacroix*, ca. 1855. Modern print, $8\frac{1}{2}'' \times 6\frac{2}{3}''$, from the original negative. Bibliothèque nationale, Paris.

Nadar was one of the earliest portrait photographers. His photographs of the leading artists of the day, such as this one of Eugène Delacroix, reveal the sitters' personalities as well as record their features.

detail and a wider range of light and shadow than Talbot's calotype process. The new "wet-plate" technology (so named because the photographic plate was exposed, developed, and fixed while wet) almost at once became the universal way of making negatives until 1880. However, *wet-plate photography* (FIG. 12-27) had drawbacks. The plates had to be prepared and processed on the spot. Working outdoors meant taking along a portable darkroom—a wagon, tent, or box with light-tight sleeves for the photographer's arms.

Daguerre produced after perfecting his method. The process captured every detail—the subtle forms, the varied textures, the finely graduated tones of light and shadow—in Daguerre's carefully constructed tableau. The three-dimensional forms of the sculptures, the basket, and the bits of cloth spring into high relief. The inspiration for the composition came from 17th-century Dutch *vanitas* still lifes, such as those of Pieter Claesz (FIG. 10-26). Like Claesz, Daguerre arranged his objects to reveal their textures and shapes clearly. Unlike a painter, Daguerre could not alter anything within

his arrangement to create a stronger image. However, he could suggest a symbolic meaning through his choice of objects. Like the skull and timepiece in Claesz's painting, Daguerre's sculptural and architectural fragments and the framed print of a couple embracing suggest that even art is vanitas and will not endure forever.

NADAR Making portraits was an important economic opportunity for most photographers, and portraiture quickly became one of the most popular early photographic genres. The greatest of the early portrait photographers was French novelist, journalist, and caricaturist Gaspar-Félix Tournachon, known simply as NADAR (1828–1910). Photographic studies for his caricatures led Nadar to open a portrait studio. So talented was he at capturing the essence of his subjects that the most important people in France, including Delacroix, Daumier, Courbet, and Manet, flocked to his studio to have their calotype portraits made. Nadar said he sought in his work "that instant of understanding that puts you in touch with the model—helps you sum him up, guides you to his habits, his ideas, and character and enables you to produce . . . a really convincing and sympathetic likeness, an intimate portrait."[6] Nadar's *Eugène Delacroix* (FIG. 12-26) shows the painter at the height of his career. Even in half-length, the painter's gesture and expression create a mood that seems to reveal much about him. Perhaps Delacroix responded to Nadar's famous gift for putting his clients at ease by assuming the pose that best expressed his personality.

TIMOTHY O'SULLIVAN Photographers were quick to realize the documentary power of their new medium. Thus began the story of photography's influence on modern life and of the immense changes it brought to communication and information management. His-

torical events could be recorded in permanent form on the spot for the first time. The photographs taken of the American Civil War by Mathew B. Brady (1823–1896), ALEXANDER GARDNER (1821–1882), and TIMOTHY O'SULLIVAN (1840–1882) remain unsurpassed as incisive accounts of military life, unsparing in their truthful detail and poignant as expressions of human experience. The most moving are the inhumanly objective records of combat deaths. Perhaps the most reproduced of these is Gardner's print of O'Sullivan's *A Harvest of Death, Gettysburg, Pennsylvania* (FIG. 12-27). Although viewers could regard this image as simple news reportage, it also functions to impress on people the high price of war. Corpses litter the battlefield as far as the eye can see. As the photograph modulates from the precise clarity of the bodies of Union soldiers in the foreground, boots stolen and pockets picked, to the indistinct corpses in the distance, the suggestion of innumerable other dead soldiers is unavoidable. This "harvest" is far more sobering and depressing than that in Winslow Homer's Civil War painting, *Veteran in a New Field* (FIG. 12-18A ☑). Though it was years before photolithography could reproduce photographs such as this in newspapers, photographers exhibited them publicly. They made an impression that newsprint engravings never could.

Negative by T. H. O'SULLIVAN.   Entered according to act of Congress, in the year 1865, by A. Gardner, in the Clerk's Office of the District Court of the District of Columbia.   Positive by A. GARDNER, 511 7th St., Washington.

A HARVEST OF DEATH, GETTYSBURG, PENNSYLVANIA.

12-27 TIMOTHY O'SULLIVAN, *A Harvest of Death, Gettysburg, Pennsylvania,* 1863. Negative by Timothy O'Sullivan. Albumen print by ALEXANDER GARDNER, $6\frac{3}{4}"\times 8\frac{3}{4}"$. New York Public Library (Astor, Lenox, and Tilden Foundations, Rare Books and Manuscript Division), New York.

Wet-plate technology enabled photographers to record historical events on the spot—and to comment on the high price of war, as in this photograph of dead Union soldiers at Gettysburg in July 1863.

12-28 EADWEARD MUYBRIDGE, *Horse Galloping*, 1878. Calotype print, 9" × 12". George Eastman House International Museum of Photography and Film, Rochester.

Muybridge specialized in photographic studies of the successive stages in human and animal motion—details too quick for the human eye to capture. Modern cinema owes a great deal to his work.

EADWEARD MUYBRIDGE The Realist photographer and scientist EADWEARD MUYBRIDGE (1830–1904) came to the United States from England in the 1850s and settled in San Francisco, where he established a prominent international reputation for his photographs of the western United States. In 1872, the governor of California, Leland Stanford (1824–1893), sought Muybridge's assistance in settling a bet about whether, at any point in a stride, all four feet of a horse galloping at top speed are off the ground. Through his sequential photography, as seen in *Horse Galloping* (FIG. 12-28), Muybridge proved that racing horses did in fact at times have all four feet in midair. This experience was the beginning of Muybridge's photographic studies of the successive stages in human and animal motion—details too quick for the human eye to capture. These investigations culminated in 1885 at the University of Pennsylvania with a series of multiple-camera motion studies that produced separate photographs of progressive moments in a single action. Muybridge's discoveries received extensive publicity through the book *Animal Locomotion* (1887), and his motion photographs earned him a place in the history of science, as well as art. These sequential motion studies influenced many other artists, including his contemporary, the painter and sculptor Edgar Degas (FIG. 13-5), and 20th-century artists such as Marcel Duchamp (FIG. 14-18).

Muybridge presented his work to scientists and general audiences with a device called the *zoopraxiscope,* which he invented to project his sequences of images (mounted on special glass plates) onto a screen. The result was so lifelike that one viewer said it "threw upon the screen apparently the living, moving animals. Nothing was wanting but the clatter of hoofs upon the turf."[7] The illusion of motion in Muybridge's photographic exhibits was the result of a physical fact of human eyesight called "persistence of vision." Stated simply, it means that the brain retains whatever the eye sees for a fraction of a second after the eye stops seeing it. Thus viewers saw a rapid succession of different images merging one into the next, producing the illusion of continuous change. This illusion lies at the heart of the motion-picture industry that debuted in the 20th century. Thus, with Muybridge's innovations in photography, yet another new art form was born—cinema.

Explore the era further in MindTap with videos of major artworks and buildings, Google Earth™ coordinates, and essays by the author on the following additional subjects:

- Pierre-Alexandre Barthélémy Vignon, La Madeleine, Paris (FIG. 12-1A)
- ARTISTS ON ART: Thomas Cole on the American Landscape
- Winslow Homer, *Veteran in a New Field* (FIG. 12-18A)
- Honoré Daumier, *Nadar Raising Photography to the Height of Art* (FIG. 12-24A)

ROMANTICISM, REALISM, AND PHOTOGRAPHY, 1800 TO 1870

Art under Napoleon

- As Emperor of the French from 1804 to 1815, Napoleon embraced the Neoclassical style in order to associate his regime with the empire of ancient Rome. Napoleon chose Jacques-Louis David as First Painter of the Empire. Napoleon's favorite sculptor was Antonio Canova, who carved marble Neoclassical portraits of the imperial family. Antoine-Jean Gros painted a propagandistic portrayal of the emperor seemingly healing the plague-stricken at Jaffa.

Gros, *Napoleon Visiting the Plague-Stricken in Jaffa*, 1804

Romanticism

- The term *Romanticism* denotes the artistic movement that flourished from 1800 to 1840. Romantic artists gave precedence to feeling and imagination over Enlightenment reason, and explored the exotic, erotic, and fantastic. The leading Romantic artist in Spain was Francisco Goya, whose *Sleep of Reason* celebrates the unleashing of imagination, emotions, and even nightmares. In France, Eugène Delacroix led the way in depicting Romantic narratives set in faraway places and distant times—for example, *Death of Sardanapalus*. Romantic painters often chose landscapes as an ideal subject to express the theme of the soul unified with the natural world. Masters of the transcendental landscape include Friedrich in Germany, Constable and Turner in England, and Cole in the United States.

Goya, *The Sleep of Reason Produces Monsters*, ca. 1798

Realism

- Realism developed as an artistic movement in mid-19th-century France. Its leading proponent was Gustave Courbet, whose paintings of ordinary people and everyday events exemplify his belief that painters should depict only their own time and place. Honoré Daumier boldly confronted authority with his satirical lithographs commenting on the plight of the urban working class. Édouard Manet shocked the public with his paintings' subjects—for example, promiscuous women—and his rough brushstrokes, which emphasized the flatness of the painting surface, paving the way for modern abstract art. Among the leading American Realists were Winslow Homer and Thomas Eakins.

Manet, *Olympia*, 1863

Architecture

- Territorial expansion, the Romantic interest in exotic locales and earlier eras, and nationalistic pride led to the revival in the 19th century of older architectural styles, especially the Gothic, exemplified by London's Houses of Parliament. By the middle of the century, many architects had already abandoned sentimental and Romantic designs from the past in favor of exploring the possibilities of cast-iron construction, as in Joseph Paxton's Crystal Palace in London.

Paxton, Crystal Palace, London, 1850–1851

Photography

- In 1839, Daguerre in Paris and Talbot in London invented the first practical photographic processes. Many of the earliest photographers, chief among them Nadar in France, specialized in portrait photography, but others, including O'Sullivan in the United States, quickly realized the documentary power of the new medium.

O'Sullivan, *Harvest of Death, Gettysburg*, 1863

13-1a The Folies-Bergère was a popular café and music hall where Parisians enjoyed their leisure—a characteristic Impressionist subject that broke sharply with tradition, as did Manet's sketchy application of paint.

▲ **13-1b** The central figure in *A Bar at the Folies-Bergère* is a young barmaid who looks out from the canvas but seems detached both from the viewer and the gentleman in a top hat who may be propositioning her.

1 ft.

13-1   ÉDOUARD MANET, *A Bar at the Folies-Bergère*, 1882. Oil on canvas, 3' 1" × 4' 3". Courtauld Gallery, London.

▶ **13-1c** In accord with modernist principles, Manet called attention to the canvas surface by creating spatial inconsistencies, such as the relationship between the barmaid and her apparent reflection in the mirror.

Impressionism, Post-Impressionism, and Symbolism, 1870 to 1900

MODERNISM AT THE FOLIES-BERGÈRE

Between 1800 and 1900, the population of Europe's major cities exploded. In Paris, for example, the number of residents expanded from 500,000 to 2,700,000. It was there that the art movement called *Impressionism* was born, an aesthetic by-product of the sometimes brutal and chaotic transformation of French life, which made the world seem unstable and insubstantial. As the poet and critic Charles Baudelaire (1821–1867) observed in his 1860 essay *The Painter of Modern Life*: "[Modernity is] the ephemeral, the fugitive, the contingent, the half of art whose other half is the eternal and the immutable."[1] Accordingly, Impressionist painters built on the innovations of the Realists in turning away from traditional mythological and religious themes in favor of the daily life of the newly industrialized French capital and its suburbs along the Seine. But, in contrast to the Realists, the Impressionists sought to convey the elusiveness and impermanence of the subjects they portrayed.

One of the most popular Impressionist subjects was Paris's vibrant nightlife. The immensely versatile Édouard Manet (FIGS. 12-17 and 12-18), whose career bridged Realism and Impressionism, painted his last great work—*A Bar at the Folies-Bergère* (FIG. 13-1)—under the influence of the younger Impressionists. The Folies-Bergère was a popular café with music-hall performances, one of Paris's most fashionable gathering places. At the center of Manet's *Folies-Bergère* is a barmaid, who looks out from the canvas but seems disinterested or lost in thought, divorced from her patrons as well as from the viewer. In front of her, Manet painted a marvelous still life of bottles, flowers, and fruit—all for sale to the bar's customers. In the mirror is the reflection of a gentleman wearing a dapper top hat and carrying an elegant walking stick. He has approached the barmaid, perhaps to order a drink, but more likely to ask the price of her company after the bar closes. Also visible in the mirror, at the upper left corner of the canvas, are the lower legs of a trapeze artist and a woman in the nightclub's balcony watching some other performance through opera glasses.

What seems at first to be a straightforward representation of the bar, barmaid, and customers quickly fades as visual discrepancies immediately emerge. For example, is the reflection of the woman on the right the barmaid's? If both figures are the same person, it is impossible to reconcile the spatial relationship between the gentleman, the bar, the barmaid, and her seemingly displaced reflection. These visual contradictions complement Manet's blurred brushstrokes and rough application of paint. Together, they draw attention to the tactile surface of the canvas, consistent with late-19th-century artists' emerging insistence on underscoring the artifice of the act of painting, one of the central principles of *modernist* art.

MARXISM, DARWINISM, MODERNISM

The Industrial Revolution, born in England, spread so rapidly to France (MAP 13-1), the rest of Europe, and the United States that historians often refer to the scientific advances that occurred during the third quarter of the 19th century as the second Industrial Revolution. Whereas the first Industrial Revolution centered on textiles, steam, and iron, the second focused on steel, electricity, chemicals, and oil. The discoveries in these fields provided the foundation for developments in plastics, machinery, building construction, and automobile manufacturing, and paved the way for the invention of the radio, telephone, electric lightbulb, and electric streetcar.

Expanding industrialization was closely tied to rapid urbanization. The number and size of European cities grew dramatically during the latter part of the 19th century, mainly due to migration from the countryside. Farmers in large numbers relocated to urban centers because expanded agricultural enterprises squeezed smaller property owners from their land. The widely available work opportunities in the cities, especially in the factories, were also a major factor in this population shift. Improving health and living conditions in the cities further contributed to their explosive growth.

MARXISM AND DARWINISM The rise of the urban working class was fundamental to the ideas of German political and social theorist Karl Marx (1818–1883), whose *Communist Manifesto* (1848), written with Friedrich Engels (1820–1895), called for workers to overthrow the capitalist system. Marx believed that those who controlled the means of production conflicted with those whose labor they exploited for their own enrichment. Marx advocated the creation of a socialist state in which the working class seized power and destroyed capitalism. Marxism held great appeal for the working poor as well as for many intellectuals.

Equally influential was the English naturalist Charles Darwin (1809–1882), who postulated the theory of natural selection. Darwin argued that evolution was the natural result of a competitive system in which only the fittest survived. Darwin's controversial ideas, as presented in *On the Origin of Species by Means of Natural Selection* (1859), contradicted the biblical narrative of creation and were greeted with hostility by many people.

MODERNISM Marx's emphasis on social conflict and Darwin's ideas about evolution were consistent with the growing sense of the world's impermanence and of a constantly shifting reality, which Baudelaire insisted was the essential characteristic of the modern world and the proper subject of a modernist painter (see page 357). *Modernism* in art, however, transcends the simple depiction of the contemporary world—the goal of Realism. Modernist artists also critically examine the premises of art itself, as Manet did in his groundbreaking 1863 painting *Le Déjeuner sur l'Herbe* (FIG. 12-17) and carried further in his 1882 *A Bar at the Folies-Bergère* (FIG. 13-1). Modernism thus implies certain concerns about art and aesthetics internal to art production, regardless of whether the artist is portraying modern life.

Clement Greenberg (1909–1994), an influential American art critic, explained:

> The essence of Modernism lies . . . in the use of the characteristic methods of a discipline to criticize the discipline itself. . . . Realistic, illusionist art had dissembled the medium, using art to conceal art. Modernism used art to call attention to art. The limitations that constitute the

MAP 13-1 **France around 1870 with towns along the Seine.**

IMPRESSIONISM, POST-IMPRESSIONISM, AND SYMBOLISM, 1870 TO 1900

1870–1880
- The Impressionists paint subjects that capture the transitory nature of modern life in urbanized Paris and its suburbs on the Seine, and mount their first independent exhibition.
- European artists collect Japanese prints and incorporate elements of Japanese style and composition in their paintings.

1880–1890
- Georges Seurat develops pointillism.
- Vincent van Gogh explores the expressive power of color.
- Auguste Rodin receives the commission for *The Gates of Hell.*
- Alexandre-Gustave Eiffel builds the Eiffel Tower in Paris.

1890–1900
- Paul Cézanne seeks "to do Poussin over entirely from nature."
- The Art Nouveau movement emerges in architecture and the decorative arts.
- Gustav Klimt's paintings reflect fin-de-siècle culture in Austria.
- Louis Sullivan builds steel, glass, and stone skyscrapers in America.

PROBLEMS AND SOLUTIONS
Painting Impressions of Light and Color

Claude Monet often set up his easel on the banks of the Seine (FIG. 13-2) or in a boat on the river (FIG. 13-2A ☑). Painting *en plein air* was how the pioneering Impressionist painter was able to meet his goal of capturing an instantaneous representation of atmosphere and climate. Of course, landscape painters had always drawn and made preliminary color studies outdoors and then used those sketches to produce formal paintings in their studios. Finishing as well as beginning his landscapes—for example, *Impression: Sunrise* (FIG. 13-2)—outdoors sharpened Monet's focus on the roles that light and color play in the way nature appears to the eye. The systematic investigation of light and color and the elimination of the traditional distinction between a sketch and a formal painting enabled Monet to paint images that truly conveyed a sense of the momentary and transitory. Lilla Cabot Perry (1848–1933), a student of Monet's late in his career, gave this description of Monet's approach:

> I remember his once saying to me: "When you go out to paint, try to forget what objects you have before you—a tree, a house, a field, or whatever. Merely think, here is a little square of blue, here an oblong of pink, here a streak of yellow, and paint it just as it looks to you, the exact color and shape, until it gives your own naïve impression of the scene before you."*

Another factor encouraging Monet and some of his contemporaries to paint outdoors was the introduction of premixed pigments conveniently sold in easily portable tubes. These readily available oil paints gave artists new colors for their work and heightened their sensitivity to the multiplicity of colors in nature. After scrutinizing the effects of light and color on forms, many late-19th-century painters concluded that *local color*—an object's color in white light—becomes modified by the quality of the light shining on it, by reflections from other objects, and by the effects that juxtaposed colors produce. Shadows do not appear gray or black, as many earlier painters thought, but seem to be composed of colors modified by reflections or other conditions. If artists use complementary colors side by side over large enough areas, the colors intensify each other, unlike the effect of small quantities of adjoining mixed pigments, which blend into neutral tones. Furthermore, the "mixing" of colors by juxtaposing them directly on a white canvas without any preliminary sketch—also a sharp break from traditional painting practice—produces a more intense hue than the same colors mixed on the palette. Monet achieved remarkably brilliant effects with his characteristically short, choppy brushstrokes, which so accurately catch the vibrating quality of light. The reason for much of the early adverse criticism leveled at Monet's paintings was that they lacked the polished surfaces and sharp contours of academic painting. In Monet's canvases, the forms take on clarity only when the eye fuses the brushstrokes at a certain distance.

*Quoted in Linda Nochlin, *Impressionism and Post-Impressionism 1874–1904: Sources and Documents* (Englewood Cliffs, N.J.: Prentice Hall, 1966), 35.

13-2 CLAUDE MONET, *Impression: Sunrise*, 1872. Oil on canvas, 1' 7½" × 2' 1½". Musée Marmottan, Paris.

Fascinated by reflected sunlight on water, Monet broke with traditional studio practice and painted his "impression" en plein air, using short brushstrokes of pure color on canvas without any preliminary sketch.

medium of painting—the flat surface, the shape of the support, the properties of pigment—were treated by the Old Masters as negative factors that could be acknowledged only implicitly or indirectly. Modernist painting has come to regard these same limitations as positive factors that are to be acknowledged openly. Manet's paintings became the first Modernist ones by virtue of the frankness with which they declared the surfaces on which they were painted. The Impressionists, in Manet's wake, abjured underpainting and glazing, to leave the eye under no doubt as to the fact that the colors used were made of real paint that came from pots or tubes.[2]

Although the work of Gustave Courbet and the Realists already expressed this modernist viewpoint, modernism emerged even more forcefully in the late-19th-century movements that art historians call Impressionism, Post-Impressionism, and Symbolism.

IMPRESSIONISM

A hostile critic applied the term *Impressionism* in response to *Impression: Sunrise* (FIG. 13-2), one of the paintings exhibited in the first Impressionist show in 1874 (see "Academic Salons and Independent Art Exhibitions" ⊡). Although the critic intended the label to be derogatory, by the third Impressionist show in 1878, the artists had embraced it and were calling themselves Impressionists. Both artists and critics had used the term before, but only in relation to sketches. Impressionist paintings do incorporate the qualities of sketches—abbreviation, speed, and spontaneity—but the artists considered their sketchlike works to be finished paintings, a radically modernist idea at the time.

CLAUDE MONET The painter of *Impression: Sunrise* was CLAUDE MONET (1840–1926), who grew up on the Normandy coast of France at Le Havre, the great seaport at the mouth of the Seine (MAP 13-1). *Impression: Sunrise* is a view of that harbor, in which Monet, breaking sharply from traditional landscape painting, made no attempt to disguise the brushstrokes or blend the pigment to create smooth tonal gradations and an optically accurate scene. The "impressionistic" application of paint is, however, only one aspect of Impressionism. Beyond its affinity with sketches, Impressionism operated at the intersection of what the artists saw and what they felt. In other words, the "impressions" these artists recorded in their paintings were neither purely objective descriptions of the exterior world nor solely subjective responses, but the interaction between the two. They were sensations, the Impressionists' subjective and personal responses to nature, formed and recorded *en plein air*—that is, outdoors (see "Painting Impressions of Light and Color," page 359).

SAINT-LAZARE Most of the Impressionists painted scenes in and around Paris, the heart of modern life in France. Monet's *Saint-Lazare Train Station* (FIG. 13-3) depicts a characteristic aspect of the contemporary urban scene. The expanding railway network had made travel more convenient, bringing large numbers of people into Paris and enabling city dwellers to reach suburban areas, such as Argenteuil (MAP 13-1; FIG. 13-2A ⊡), quickly. In his "impression" of the Saint-Lazare railway terminal, Monet captured the energy and vitality of Paris's modern transportation hub. The train, emerging from the steam and smoke it emits, rumbles into the station. In the background haze are the tall buildings that were becoming a major component of the Parisian landscape. Monet's agitated

13-3 CLAUDE MONET, *Saint-Lazare Train Station*, 1877. Oil on canvas, 2' 5 3/4" × 3' 5". Musée d'Orsay, Paris.

The Impressionists often painted scenes of the new urbanized Paris, the heart of modern life in France. Monet's agitated application of paint contributes to the sense of energy in this railway terminal.

1 ft.

13-4 Pierre-Auguste Renoir, *Le Moulin de la Galette,* 1876. Oil on canvas, 4' 3" × 5' 8". Musée d'Orsay, Paris.

Renoir's painting of this popular Parisian dance hall is dappled by sunlight and shade, artfully blurred into the figures to produce the effect of floating and fleeting light that many Impressionists cultivated.

paint application contributes to the sense of energy and conveys the atmosphere of urban life.

Georges Rivière (1855–1943), a rare art critic who admired the Impressionists, recorded the essence of what Monet had tried to achieve:

> Like a fiery steed, stimulated rather than exhausted by the long trek that it has only just finished, [the locomotive] tosses its mane of smoke, which lashes the glass roof of the main hall. . . . We see the vast and manic movements at the station where the ground shakes with every turn of the wheel. The platforms are sticky with soot, and the air is full of that bitter scent exuded by burning coal. As we look at this magnificent picture, we are overcome by the same feelings as if we were really there, and these feelings are perhaps even more powerful, because in the picture the artist has conveyed his own feelings as well.[3]

PIERRE-AUGUSTE RENOIR Modern industrialized Paris provided ample time for leisure activities, and scenes of dining, dancing, café-concerts, opera, and ballet became mainstays of Impressionism (see "The Folies-Bergère," page 357). *Le Moulin de la Galette* (FIG. 13-4) by Pierre-Auguste Renoir (1841–1919) depicts a Parisian dance hall that was popular with ordinary working-class people. Some crowd

the tables and chatter, while others dance energetically. So lively is the atmosphere that the viewer can virtually hear the sounds of music, laughter, and tinkling glasses. The painter dappled the whole scene with sunlight and shade, artfully blurred into the figures to produce precisely the effect of floating and fleeting light that many Impressionists cultivated. The casual poses and asymmetrical placement of the figures and the suggested continuity of space, spreading in all directions and only accidentally limited by the frame, position the viewer as a participant rather than as an outsider. Whereas artists favored by the French Academy sought to express universal and timeless qualities, the Impressionists attempted to depict just the opposite—the incidental and the momentary.

EDGAR DEGAS Dancing of a very different kind—ballet—was one of the favorite subjects of Edgar Degas (1834–1917). Although also a "painter of modern life," Degas, unlike Monet and Renoir, was not concerned with light and atmosphere. Indeed, he specialized in indoor subjects and made many preliminary studies for his finished paintings. Degas's interests were primarily with recording body movement and exploring unusual angles of viewing. He was fascinated by the formalized patterns of motion of the performers at the Paris Opéra and its ballet school. In his 1874 canvas—

13-5 EDGAR DEGAS, *The Rehearsal,* 1874. Oil on canvas, 1' 11" × 2' 9". Glasgow Art Galleries and Museum, Glasgow (Burrell Collection).

Degas favored subjects, such as the Paris ballet, that gave him the opportunity to study the human body in motion. The high viewpoint and off-center placement of figures are characteristic aspects of his work.

1 ft.

The Rehearsal (FIG. 13-5)—most of the ballerinas are paradoxically hidden from the viewer by other figures or by the spiral stairway. The painting is the antithesis of a classically balanced composition. The center is empty, and the floor takes up most of the canvas surface. At the margins, Degas arranged the figures in a seemingly random manner. The cutting off of the dancers at the left and right enhances the sense that the viewer is witnessing a fleeting moment.

Because of his interest in patterns of movement, Degas became fascinated by photography and often used a camera to make preliminary studies for his works. Japanese prints, which often depicted figures and places from sharply oblique angles, were another inspirational source for Degas's paintings (see "Japanese Woodblock Prints," page 522). Japanese artists used diverging lines not only to organize the flat shapes of figures but also to direct the viewer's attention into the picture space (compare FIG. 19-1). The Impressionists, acquainted with these prints as early as the 1860s, greatly admired their spatial organization, familiar and intimate themes, and flat, unmodeled color areas.

CASSATT AND MORISOT The Impressionists were a diverse group of artists, women as well as men, from disparate economic, social, national, and religious backgrounds, united by a shared interest in the modern world that they experienced daily and a distaste for the stylistic constraints and restricted themes of academic art. The two most accomplished Impressionist women were MARY CASSATT (1844–1926), an American, and BERTHE MORISOT (1841–1895), a

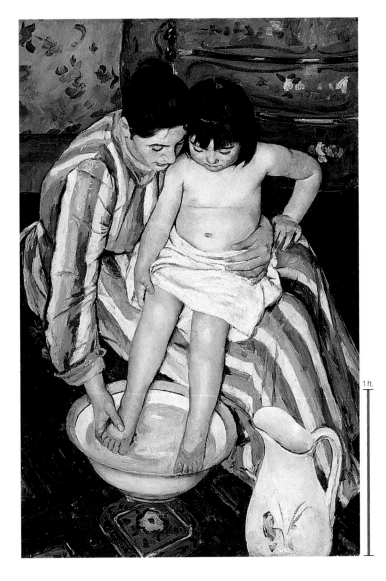

1 ft.

13-6 MARY CASSATT, *The Child's Bath,* 1893. Oil on canvas, 3' 3" × 2' 2". Art Institute of Chicago, Chicago (Robert A. Walker Fund).

Cassatt's compositions owe much to Degas and Japanese prints, but her subjects differ from those of most Impressionists, in part because, as a woman, she could not frequent cafés with her male friends.

ART AND SOCIETY
Women Impressionists

Two of the best-known Impressionists were women. Although they came from very different backgrounds and their paintings could never be confused, both Mary Cassatt and Berthe Morisot brought a distinctively feminine viewpoint to their work, especially with regard to the subjects they chose and the way they portrayed women.

Cassatt, the daughter of a wealthy Philadelphia banker, was fortunate to live at a time when formerly all-male American colleges and art academies were opening their doors to women. She trained at the Pennsylvania Academy of the Fine Arts and then moved to Europe to study masterworks in France and Italy. Cassatt came to the attention of Degas when he saw a painting of hers in the Salon of 1874. Thereafter, she exhibited regularly with the Impressionists, but as a woman, she could not easily frequent the cafés with her male artist friends. She also had the responsibility of caring for her aging parents, who had moved to Paris to join her. Because of these restrictions, Cassatt's subjects were principally women and children, whom she presented with a combination of objectivity and genuine sentiment.

Cassatt's *The Child's Bath* (FIG. 13-6) owes much to the compositional devices of Degas (FIG. 13-5) as well as to Degas's sources—Japanese prints. But whereas Degas's favorite subjects were professional ballerinas, Cassatt's canvas celebrates the tender relationship between a mother and her child, both of whom gaze at their joint reflection in the tub of water.

In contrast to the expatriate American Cassatt, Morisot was raised in an upper-middle-class home in Paris, and she could not study painting at the École des Beaux-Arts because the European academies were still closed to women. Instead, she and her sister Edma took lessons from a private tutor. Berthe enjoyed some early success exhibiting in the official salons, but after meeting Édouard Manet in late 1867 or 1868 (she married his brother, Eugène, in 1874), she came in contact with the Impressionists and submitted many paintings to their exhibitions.

Morisot's subject matter—the leisure activities of Parisians at resorts along the Seine or in Paris's great park called the Bois de Boulogne—typifies the interests of many of the Impressionists. But the people who inhabit her canvases are almost exclusively women and their children, always well dressed and thoughtful, never frivolous or objects of male desire. *Summer's Day* (FIG. 13-7) depicts two women in a boat on the Bois de Boulogne lake. It is similar in spirit to some of Claude Monet's paintings of the Seine, but Morisot's focus is the women, not the setting. Morisot herself is in the same boat, unseen, and she represented the women at a sharp angle, with parts of their bodies and most of the boat cut off by the frame, using the compositional format pioneered by Edgar Degas (FIG. 13-5) and adopted also by Cassatt. In *Summer's Day*, Morisot rejected contour lines in favor of patches of color that define the shapes of her figures. The sketchy brushstrokes used to paint the women merge with those of the water, unifying figure and ground in a striking two-dimensional composition that also captures all the freshness of a brightly lit summer day en plein air.

13-7 BERTHE MORISOT, *Summer's Day*, 1879. Oil on canvas, $1' 5\frac{3}{4}'' \times 2' 5\frac{3}{8}''$. National Gallery, London (Lane Bequest, 1917).

Morisot's subject (Parisians at leisure), bright palette, and sketchy brushstrokes typify Impressionism, but the people who inhabit her paintings are almost exclusively well-dressed, thoughtful women.

1 in.

Frenchwoman, who painted *The Child's Bath* (FIG. 13-6) and *Summer's Day* (FIG. 13-7), respectively. Their works, while having much in common with those of their male colleagues, differed from the paintings of Monet, Renoir, Degas, and the other Impressionists in important ways (see "Women Impressionists," above).

JAMES WHISTLER Like Cassatt, JAMES ABBOTT MCNEILL WHISTLER (1834–1903) was an American expatriate artist in Europe. He spent time in Paris, but eventually settled in London. While in Paris, Whistler met many of the Impressionists, and his art incorporates some of their concerns and his own. Whistler shared the

13-8 JAMES ABBOTT McNEILL WHISTLER, *Nocturne in Black and Gold* (*The Falling Rocket*), ca. 1875. Oil on panel, 1' 11⅝" × 1' 6½". Detroit Institute of the Arts, Detroit (gift of Dexter M. Ferry Jr.).

In this painting, Whistler displayed an Impressionist's interest in conveying atmospheric effects of fireworks at night, but he also emphasized the abstract arrangement of shapes and colors.

Impressionists' fondness for recording contemporary life and the sensations that color produces on the eye. To these interests he added a desire to create harmonies paralleling those achieved in music. To underscore his artistic intentions, Whistler began calling his paintings "arrangements" or "nocturnes." *Nocturne in Black and Gold*, or *The Falling Rocket* (FIG. 13-8), is a daring painting with gold flecks and splatters representing an exploded firework punctuating the darkness of the night sky. More interested in conveying the atmospheric effects than in providing details of the scene, Whistler emphasized creating a harmonious arrangement of shapes and colors on the rectangle of his panel, an approach that many 20th-century painters adopted. Whistler's works angered many 19th-century viewers, however. The British critic John Ruskin (see page 348) responded to this painting by writing a scathing review accusing Whistler of "flinging a pot of paint in the public's face."[4] In reply, Whistler sued Ruskin for libel. Although Whistler won the case, his victory had sadly ironic consequences for him. The judge, showing where his—and the public's—sympathies lay, awarded the artist only one farthing (less than a penny) in damages and required Whistler to pay all of the court costs, which ruined him financially.

POST-IMPRESSIONISM

By the mid-1880s, just as the Impressionists' sketchlike paintings of contemporary life were gaining wider acceptance, a group of younger artists came to feel that in attempting to capture momentary sensations of light and color on canvas, too many important elements of traditional painting were being sacrificed. These artists were much more interested in systematically examining the properties and expressive qualities of line, pattern, form, and color. Because their art had its roots in Impressionism, but was not stylistically homogeneous, these artists became known as the *Post-Impressionists*.

HENRI DE TOULOUSE-LAUTREC Closest to the Impressionists in many ways was the French artist HENRI DE TOULOUSE-LAUTREC (1864–1901). His work, however, has an added satirical edge to it and often borders on caricature. Genetic defects had stunted Toulouse-Lautrec's growth and partially crippled him, leading to his self-exile from the high society that his ancient aristocratic name entitled him to enter. He became a citizen of the night world of Paris, consorting with the underclass of entertainers, prostitutes, and other social outcasts. *At the Moulin Rouge* (FIG. 13-9) reveals the influences of Degas, of Japanese prints, and of photography in the oblique and asymmetrical composition, the spatial diagonals, and the strong line patterns with added dissonant colors. But Toulouse-Lautrec so emphasized or exaggerated each element that the tone is new. Compare, for instance, the mood of *Moulin Rouge* with the relaxed and casual atmosphere of Renoir's *Le Moulin de la Galette* (FIG. 13-4). Toulouse-Lautrec's scene is decadent nightlife, with its glaring artificial light, brassy music, and assortment of corrupt, cruel, and masklike faces. (He included himself in the background—the short man wearing a derby hat accompanying the very tall man, his cousin.) Such distortions by simplification of the figures and faces anticipated Expressionism (see page 380), when artists' use of formal elements—for example, brighter colors and bolder lines than ever before—increased the effect of the images on observers.

GEORGES SEURAT The themes that GEORGES SEURAT (1859–1891) addressed in his paintings were also Impressionist subjects, but he depicted modern life in a strictly intellectual way. Seurat devised a disciplined and painstaking system of painting focused on color analysis. He was less concerned with the recording of immediate color sensations than with their careful and systematic organization into a new kind of pictorial order. Seurat disciplined the free and fluent play of color characterizing Impressionism into a calculated arrangement based on scientific color theory. Seurat's system—*pointillism*—involves carefully observing color and separating it into its component parts (see "Pointillism and 19th-Century Color Theory"). The artist then applies these pure component colors to the canvas in tiny dots (points) or daubs. Thus the shapes, figures, and spaces in the image become comprehensible only from a distance, when the viewer's eye blends the many pigment dots.

Seurat introduced pointillism to the French public at the eighth and last Impressionist exhibition in 1886, where he displayed *A Sunday on La Grande Jatte* (FIGS. 13-10 and 13-10A), a huge canvas in the tradition of the official Salon. The subject of the painting—Parisians at leisure on an island in the Seine near Asnières—is consistent with Impressionist recreational themes, but Seurat's figures are rigid and remote, unlike the spontaneous representations of Impressionism. He played on repeated motifs both to create flat patterns and to suggest spatial depth. Reiterating the profile of the women and

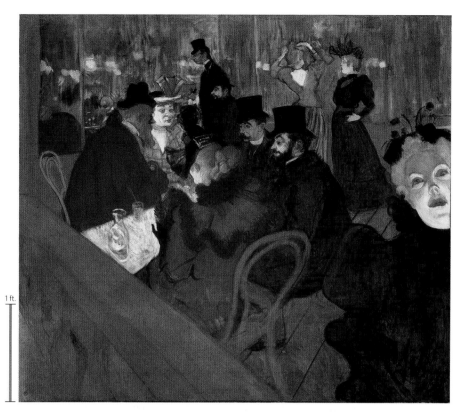

13-9 Henri de Toulouse-Lautrec, *At the Moulin Rouge,* 1892–1895. Oil on canvas, 4' × 4' 7". Art Institute of Chicago, Chicago (Helen Birch Bartlett Memorial Collection).

Toulouse-Lautrec devoted his brief career to depicting the bohemian lifestyle of Paris at night. The oblique composition, glaring lighting, masklike faces, and dissonant colors of *Moulin Rouge* typify his work.

1 ft.

1 ft.

13-10 Georges Seurat, *A Sunday on La Grande Jatte,* 1884–1886. Oil on canvas, 6' 9" × 10'. Art Institute of Chicago, Chicago (Helen Birch Bartlett Memorial Collection).

Seurat's color system—pointillism—involved dividing colors into their component parts and applying those colors to the canvas in tiny dots. The forms become comprehensible only from a distance.

The Letters of Vincent van Gogh

Throughout his life, Vincent van Gogh wrote letters to his brother Theo van Gogh (1857–1891), a Parisian art dealer, on matters both mundane and philosophical. The letters are precious documents of the ups and downs of the painter's life and reveal his emotional anguish. In many of the letters, van Gogh also forcefully stated his views about art, including his admiration for Japanese prints, which he collected and in some cases copied.

In one letter, Vincent told Theo: "In both my life and in my painting, I can very well do without God but I cannot, ill as I am, do without something which is greater than I, . . . the power to create."* For van Gogh, the power to create involved the expressive use of color. "Instead of trying to reproduce exactly what I have before my eyes, I use color more arbitrarily so as to express myself forcibly."† Color in painting, he argued, is "not locally true from the point of view of the delusive realist, but color suggesting some emotion of an ardent temperament."‡

Some of van Gogh's letters contain vivid descriptions of his paintings. For example, about *Night Café* (FIG. 13-11), he wrote:

I have tried to express the terrible passions of humanity by means of red and green. The room is blood red and dark yellow with a green billiard table in the middle; there are four citron-yellow lamps with a glow of orange and green. Everywhere there is a clash and contrast of the most disparate reds and greens in the figures of little sleeping hooligans, in the empty, dreary room, in violet and blue. The blood-red and the yellow-green of the billiard table, for instance, contrast with the soft, tender Louis XV green of the counter, on which there is a pink nosegay. The white coat of the landlord, awake in a corner of that furnace, turns citron-yellow, or pale luminous green.§

*Vincent van Gogh to Theo van Gogh, September 3, 1888, in W. H. Auden, ed., *Van Gogh: A Self-Portrait. Letters Revealing His Life as a Painter* (New York: Dutton, 1963), 319.
†August 11, 1888. Ibid., 313.
‡September 8, 1888. Ibid., 321.
§September 8, 1888. Ibid., 320.

13-11 VINCENT VAN GOGH, *Night Café,* 1888. Oil on canvas, 2' 4$\frac{1}{2}$" × 3'. Yale University Art Gallery, New Haven (bequest of Stephen Carlton Clark).

In *Night Café,* van Gogh explored ways that colors and distorted forms can express emotions. The thickness, shape, and direction of his brushstrokes create a tactile counterpart to the intense colors.

1 ft.

parasols, Seurat placed each form in space to set up a rhythmic movement in depth as well as from side to side. Sunshine fills the picture, but the painter did not break the light into transient patches of color. Light, air, people, and landscape are formal elements in an abstract design in which line, color, value, and shape cohere in a precise and tightly controlled organization.

VINCENT VAN GOGH In marked contrast to Seurat, VINCENT VAN GOGH (1853–1890) explored the capabilities of colors and distorted forms to express his emotions. The son of a Dutch Protestant pastor, van Gogh believed he had a religious calling and did missionary work in the coal-mining area of Belgium. Repeated professional and personal failures brought him close to despair. Only after he turned to painting did he find a way to communicate his experiences. When van Gogh died of a self-inflicted gunshot wound at age 37, he considered himself an outcast from society and a failure as an artist. But his work profoundly influenced later artists, especially the Fauves and German Expressionists (see pages 378–382), who built on van Gogh's innovative use of color.

Van Gogh moved to Paris in 1886, and then, in 1888, to Arles in southern France, where he painted *Night Café* (FIG. 13-11). Although the subject is apparently benign, van Gogh invested it with a charged energy. As he stated in a letter to his brother Theo (see "The Letters of Vincent van Gogh," page 366), he wanted the painting to convey an oppressive atmosphere—"a place where one can ruin oneself, go mad, or commit a crime."[5] The room is seen from above, and the floor takes up a large portion of the canvas, as in the paintings of Degas (FIG. 13-5). The ghostly proprietor stands at the edge of the café's billiard table, which the painter depicted in such a steeply tilted perspective that it threatens to slide out of the painting into the viewer's space. Van Gogh communicated the "madness" of the place by selecting vivid hues whose juxtaposition augmented their intensity. His insistence on the expressive values of color led him to develop a corresponding expressiveness in his paint application. The thickness, shape, and direction of his brushstrokes created a tactile counterpart to his intense color schemes. He moved the brush vehemently back and forth or at right angles, giving a textilelike effect, or squeezed dots or streaks onto the canvas directly from his paint tubes. This bold, almost slapdash attack enhanced the intensity of his colors.

STARRY NIGHT Similarly illustrative of van Gogh's "expressionist" method is *Starry Night* (FIG. 13-12), which the artist painted in 1889, the year before his death. At this time, van Gogh was living in an asylum in Saint-Rémy, where he had committed himself. In *Starry Night*, the artist did not represent the sky's appearance. Rather, he communicated his feelings about the electrifying vastness of the universe, filled with whirling and exploding stars, with the earth and humanity huddling beneath it. Given van Gogh's determination to "use color . . . to express [him]self forcibly," the dark, deep blue suffusing the entire painting cannot be overlooked. Together with the turbulent brushstrokes, the color suggests a quiet but pervasive depression. A letter Vincent wrote to his brother reveals his contemplative state of mind at this time:

> [L]ooking at the stars always makes me dream, . . . Why, I ask myself, shouldn't the shining dots of the sky be as accessible as the black dots on the map of France? Just as we take the train to get to Tarascon or Rouen, we take death to reach a star.[6]

PAUL GAUGUIN Like van Gogh, with whom he painted in Arles in 1888, PAUL GAUGUIN (1848–1903) rejected objective representation in favor of subjective expression. For Gauguin, the artist's power to determine the colors in a painting was a central element of creativity. However, whereas van Gogh's heavy, thick brushstrokes were an important component of his expressive style, Gauguin's color areas appear flatter, often visually dissolving into abstract patches or patterns.

In 1883, after losing his job as a Parisian stockbroker in the crash of 1882, Gauguin tried to make a living as an artist. Three years later, attracted by Brittany's unspoiled culture, Gauguin moved from Paris to Pont-Aven. Although in the 1870s and 1880s Brittany had been transformed into a profitable market economy focused on tourism, Gauguin still viewed the Bretons as "natural" men and women at ease in their "unspoiled" environment. At Pont-Aven, he painted *Vision after the Sermon*, also called *Jacob Wrestling*

1 ft.

13-12 VINCENT VAN GOGH, *Starry Night*, 1889. Oil on canvas, 2' 5" × 3' $\frac{1}{4}$". Museum of Modern Art, New York (acquired through the Lillie P. Bliss Bequest).

In this late work, van Gogh painted the vast night sky filled with whirling and exploding stars, the earth huddled beneath it. The painting is an almost abstract pattern of expressive line, shape, and color.

13-13 PAUL GAUGUIN, *Vision after the Sermon (Jacob Wrestling with the Angel)*, 1888. Oil on canvas, 2' 4¾" × 3' ½". National Gallery of Scotland, Edinburgh.

Gauguin admired Japanese prints, cloisonné enamels, and stained glass. Their influences are evident in this painting of Breton women, in which firm outlines enclose large areas of unmodulated color.

with the Angel (FIG. **13-13**). The painting shows Breton women, wearing their starched white Sunday caps and black dresses, visualizing the sermon they have just heard at church on Jacob's encounter with the Holy Spirit (Gen. 32:24–30). At the far right is a monk who has Gauguin's features. The women and the monk pray devoutly before the apparition. Gauguin departed from optical realism and composed the picture elements to focus the viewer's attention on the idea and intensify its message. The images are not what the Impressionist eye would have seen and replicated but what Gauguin's memory recalled and his imagination modified. Thus the artist twisted the perspective and allotted most of the space to emphasize the innocent faith of the unquestioning women, and he shrank Jacob and the angel, wrestling in a ring enclosed by a Breton stone fence. Wrestling matches were regular features of the entertainment held after high mass, so Gauguin's women are spectators at a contest that was, for them, a familiar part of their culture.

Gauguin did not unify the picture with a horizon perspective, light and shade, or naturalistic use of color. Instead, he abstracted the scene into a pattern, with the diagonal tree limb symbolically dividing the spiritual from the earthly realm. Pure unmodulated color fills flat planes and shapes bounded by firm lines: white caps, black dresses, and the red field of combat. Gauguin admired Japanese prints and medieval cloisonné metalwork (FIG. 6-2) and stained glass (FIG. 7-11). These art forms contributed to his daring experiment to transform traditional painting and Impressionism into abstract, expressive patterns of line, shape, and pure color.

WHERE DO WE COME FROM? In 1888, Gauguin settled in Tahiti because he believed that it offered him a life far removed from materialistic Europe as well as an opportunity to reconnect with nature. On his arrival, he discovered that the South Pacific island, under French control since 1842, had been extensively colonized. Disappointed, Gauguin tried to maintain his vision of an untamed paradise by moving to the Tahitian countryside, where he expressed his fascination with primitive life in a series of canvases in which he often based the design on native motifs. The tropical flora of the island inspired the harmonies of lilac, pink, and lemon in his paintings.

13-14 PAUL GAUGUIN, *Where Do We Come From? What Are We? Where Are We Going?* 1897. Oil on canvas, 4' 6¾" × 12' 3". Museum of Fine Arts, Boston (Tompkins Collection).

In search of a place far removed from European materialism, Gauguin moved to Tahiti, where he used native women and tropical colors to present a pessimistic view of the inevitability of the life cycle.

PROBLEMS AND SOLUTIONS
Making Impressionism Solid and Enduring

Paul Cézanne's desire to "make of Impressionism something solid and enduring" led him to formulate a new approach to the art of painting, whether his subject was landscape (FIG. 13-15), still life (FIG. 13-15A ⬈), or the human figure. Cézanne's distinctive way of studying nature is evident in *Mont Sainte-Victoire* (FIG. 13-15), one of many views that he painted of this mountain near his home in Aix-en-Provence. His aim was not truth in appearance, especially not photographic truth, nor was it the "truth" of Impressionism. Cézanne, like Seurat, developed a more analytical style. His goal was to order the lines, planes, and colors of nature, "[to do] Poussin over entirely from nature . . . in the open air, with color and light, instead of one of those works imagined in a studio, where everything has the brown coloring of feeble daylight without reflections from the sky and sun."* He sought to achieve Poussin's effects of distance, depth, structure, and solidity, not by using traditional perspective and chiaroscuro, but rather by recording the color patterns that he deduced from an optical analysis of nature.

Cézanne set out to explore the properties and interrelationships of line, plane, and color. He studied the intrinsic qualities of color and the capacity of lines and planes to create the sensation of depth, as well as the power of colors to modify the direction and depth of lines and planes. To create the illusion of three-dimensional form and space, Cézanne focused on carefully selecting colors. He understood that cool colors tend to recede, whereas warm ones advance. By applying to the canvas small patches of juxtaposed colors, some advancing and some receding, Cézanne created volume and depth in his works. On occasion, the artist depicted objects chiefly in one hue and achieved convincing solidity by modulating the intensity (or saturation). At other times, he juxtaposed contrasting colors—for example, green, yellow, and red—of similar saturation.

In *Mont Sainte-Victoire,* Cézanne replaced the transitory visual effects of changing atmospheric conditions, effects that preoccupied Monet, with a more concentrated, lengthier analysis of the colors in large lighted spaces. The main space stretches out behind and beyond the canvas plane and includes numerous small elements, such as roads, fields, houses, and the viaduct at the far right, each seen from a slightly different viewpoint. Above this shifting, receding perspective—so different from traditional Renaissance perspective—the largest mass of all, the mountain, seems simultaneously to be both near and far away, an effect achieved by equally stressing background and foreground contours. Cézanne's rendition of nature approximates the experience that a person has when viewing the forms of nature piecemeal. The relative proportions of objects vary, rather than being fixed by strict linear perspective. Cézanne immobilized the shifting colors of Impressionism into an array of clearly defined planes composing the objects and spaces in his scene. He described his method in a letter to a fellow painter:

> [T]reat nature by the cylinder, the sphere, the cone, everything in proper perspective so that each side of an object or a plane is directed towards a central point. Lines parallel to the horizon give breadth . . . Lines perpendicular to this horizon give depth. But nature for us men is more depth than surface, whence the need of introducing into our light vibrations, represented by reds and yellows, a sufficient amount of blue to give the impression of air.†

*Cézanne to Émile Bernard, March 1904. Quoted in Robert Goldwater and Mario Treves, eds., *Artists on Art, from the XIV to the XX Century* (New York: Pantheon, 1945), 363.
†Cézanne to Émile Bernard, April 15, 1904. Ibid., 363.

1 ft.

13-15 PAUL CÉZANNE, *Mont Sainte-Victoire,* 1902–1904. Oil on canvas, 2' 3$\frac{1}{2}$" × 2' 11$\frac{1}{4}$". Philadelphia Museum of Art, Philadelphia (George W. Elkins Collection).

In his landscapes, Cézanne replaced the transitory visual effects of changing atmospheric conditions—the Impressionists' focus—with careful analysis of the lines, planes, and colors of nature.

In 1897, worn down by failing health and the hostile reception of his work, Gauguin tried unsuccessfully to take his own life, but not before painting *Where Do We Come From? What Are We? Where Are We Going?* (FIG. 13-14). Gauguin judged this to be his most important painting. It can be read as a summary of his art and his views on life. The scene is a tropical landscape, populated with native women and children. Gauguin described the huge canvas in a letter to a friend:

> Where are we going? Near to death an old woman. . . . What are we? Day to day existence. . . . Where do we come from? Source. Child. Life begins. . . . Behind a tree two sinister figures, cloaked in garments

of somber color, introduce, near the tree of knowledge, their note of anguish caused by that very knowledge in contrast to some simple beings in a virgin nature, which might be paradise as conceived by humanity, who give themselves up to the happiness of living.[7]

Where Do We Come From? is a sobering, pessimistic image of the inevitability of the life cycle. At the center is a Polynesian Eve in the prime of youth. At the left is a crouching old woman contemplating death. Gauguin died a few years later in the Marquesas Islands, his artistic genius still unrecognized.

PAUL CÉZANNE Trained as a painter in his native Aix-en-Provence in southern France, Paul Cézanne (1839–1906) allied himself early in his career with the Impressionists, accepting their color theories and their faith in subjects chosen from everyday life. But Cézanne's studies of traditional works of Western art in the Louvre persuaded him that Impressionism lacked form and structure. Cézanne declared that he wanted to "make of Impressionism something solid and enduring like the art in the museums."[8] In works such as *Mont Sainte-Victoire* (FIG. 13-15), he achieved that goal (see "Making Impressionism Solid and Enduring," page 369).

SYMBOLISM

The Impressionists and Post-Impressionists believed that their emotions and sensations were important elements for interpreting the world around them, but the depiction of what they could see remained their primary focus, as it had been for the Realists before them. By the end of the 19th century, many artists turned their attention away from the real world to the imaginary. These artists rejected the optical world of daily life in favor of a fantasy world, of forms they conjured in their free imagination. Color, line, and shape, divorced from conformity to the optical image, became symbols of personal emotions in response to the world. Many of the artists following this path adopted an approach to subject and form that associated them with a general European movement called *Symbolism*. Symbolists, whether painters or writers, disdained Realism as trivial. The task of Symbolist artists was to see through things to a significance and reality far deeper than what superficial

appearance revealed. Symbolists cultivated all the resources of imagination, and their subjects became exotic, mysterious, visionary, dreamlike, and fantastic. Perhaps not coincidentally, at about this time Sigmund Freud (1856–1939), the founder of psychoanalysis, published *Interpretations of Dreams* (1900), an introduction to the concept and the world of unconscious experience.

HENRI ROUSSEAU Paul Gauguin had journeyed to the South Seas in search of primitive innocence. Henri Rousseau (1844–1910) was a "primitive" without leaving Paris—a self-taught amateur painter. Derided by the critics, Rousseau compensated for his apparent visual, conceptual, and technical naïveté with a natural talent for design and an imagination teeming with exotic images of mysterious tropical landscapes. In *Sleeping Gypsy* (FIG. 13-16), the recumbent figure occupies a desert world, silent and secret, and dreams beneath a pale, perfectly round moon. In the foreground, a lion resembling a stuffed, but somehow menacing, animal doll sniffs at the gypsy. The imagery suggests the kind of uneasy encounter a person's vulnerable subconscious self might experience during sleep (the focus of Freud's research). Rousseau's art of drama and fantasy has its own sophistication and, after the artist's death, influenced the development of Surrealism (see page 394).

EDVARD MUNCH Linked in spirit to the Symbolists was the Norwegian artist Edvard Munch (1863–1944). Munch felt deeply the pain of human life and believed that humans were powerless before the great natural forces of death and love. The emotions associated with them—jealousy, loneliness, fear, desire, despair—became the theme of most of his art. Because Munch's goal was, in his own words, to describe the conditions of "modern psychic life," Realist and Impressionist techniques were inappropriate, focusing as they did on the tangible world. Instead, in the spirit of Symbolism, Munch used color, line, and figural distortion for expressive ends.

The Scream (FIG. 13-17) exemplifies Munch's style. The image— a man standing on a bridge—belongs to the real world, but Munch's depiction of the scene departs significantly from visual reality. *The Scream* evokes a powerful emotional response from the viewer because of the painter's dramatic presentation. The man in the foreground, simplified to almost skeletal form, emits a primal scream.

13-16 Henri Rousseau, *Sleeping Gypsy,* 1897. Oil on canvas, 4' 3" × 6' 7". Museum of Modern Art, New York (gift of Mrs. Simon Guggenheim).

In *Sleeping Gypsy,* Rousseau depicted a doll-like but menacing lion sniffing at a recumbent dreaming figure in a mysterious landscape. The painting suggests the vulnerable subconscious during sleep.

1 ft.

1 ft.

13-17 EDVARD MUNCH, *The Scream*, 1893. Tempera and pastels on cardboard, 2' 11¾" × 2' 5". National Gallery, Oslo.

Although grounded in the real world, *The Scream* departs significantly from visual reality. Munch used color, line, and figural distortion to evoke a strong emotional response from the viewer.

The landscape's sweeping curvilinear lines reiterate the shapes of the man's mouth and head, almost like an echo, as the cry seems to reverberate through the setting. The fiery red and yellow stripes that give the sky an eerie glow also contribute to this work's resonance. Munch wrote a revealing epigraph to accompany the painting:

> I was walking along the road with two friends. The sun was setting. I felt a breath of melancholy—Suddenly the sky turned blood-red. I stopped, and leaned against the railing, deathly tired—looking out across the flaming clouds that hung like blood and a sword over the blue-black fjord and town. My friends walked on—I stood there, trembling with fear. And I sensed a great, infinite scream pass through nature.[9]

Appropriately, the original title of this work was *Despair*.

FIN-DE-SIÈCLE Historians have adopted the term *fin-de-siècle* (French, "end of the century") to describe European culture of the late 1800s. This designation is not merely chronological but also refers to a certain sensibility. At that time, the increasingly large and prosperous middle classes were aspiring to gain the advantages that the aristocracy traditionally enjoyed. The masses, striving to live "the good life," embraced a culture of decadence and indulgence. Characteristic of the fin-de-siècle period was an intense preoccupation with sexual drives, powers, and perversions. People at the end of the century also immersed themselves in an exploration of the unconscious. This culture was unrestrained and freewheeling, but the determination to enjoy life masked an anxiety prompted by significant political upheaval and an uncertain future. The country most closely associated with fin-de-siècle culture was Austria.

GUSTAV KLIMT The Viennese artist GUSTAV KLIMT (1863–1918) captured this period's flamboyance in his work, but tempered it with unsettling undertones. In *The Kiss* (FIG. 13-18), Klimt depicted a kneeling couple locked in an embrace. The setting is ambiguous, perhaps a flower garden, and all the viewer sees of the man and woman is a small segment of each body—and virtually nothing of the man's face. The rest of the

1 ft.

13-18 GUSTAV KLIMT, *The Kiss*, 1907–1908. Oil on canvas, 5' 10¾" × 5' 10¾". Österreichische Galerie Belvedere, Vienna.

Klimt's paintings exemplify the Viennese fin-de-siècle spirit. In *The Kiss*, he revealed only a small segment of each lover's body. The rest of the painting dissolves into shimmering, extravagant flat patterning.

canvas dissolves into shimmering, extravagant flat patterning, evoking the tension between two- and three-dimensionality intrinsic to the work of many other modernists. In *The Kiss*, however, those patterns also signify gender contrasts—rectangles for the man's garment, circles for the woman's. Yet the patterning also unites the two lovers into a single formal entity, underscoring their erotic union.

SCULPTURE

The names of the sculptors of the late 19th century are not as familiar as those of the painters of the same era, in part because their work was less revolutionary in nature, in part because their biographies are not as colorful.

AUGUSTE RODIN The leading French sculptor of the era was AUGUSTE RODIN (1840–1917), who conceived and executed his sculptures with a Realist sensibility. Rodin was also well aware of the Impressionists' innovations. Although color was not a significant factor in his work, the influence of Impressionism is evident in Rodin's abiding concern for the effect of light on sculpted surfaces. When focusing on the human form, he joined his profound knowledge of anatomy and movement with special attention to the body's exterior, saying, "The sculptor must learn to reproduce the surface, which means all that vibrates on the surface, soul, love, passion, life. . . . Sculpture is thus the art of hollows and mounds, not of smoothness, or even polished planes."[10] Primarily a modeler of pliable material rather than a stone-carver, Rodin worked his surfaces with fingers sensitive to the subtlest variations of texture, catching the fugitive play of constantly shifting light on cast bronze. In his studio, he often would have a model move around in front of him while he created preliminary versions of his sculptures with coils of clay.

THE GATES OF HELL Rodin's most ambitious work, the nearly 21-foot-tall *Gates of Hell* (FIG. 13-19), occupied him for two decades, during which he also produced what is perhaps his best-known sculptural group, *Burghers of Calais* (FIG. 13-19A ⬈). On August 16, 1880, Rodin received the commission to design a pair of doors for a planned Museum of Decorative Arts in Paris. The museum was never built, however, and it was not until after the sculptor's death that others cast his still-unfinished doors in bronze. Rodin derived the theme of his doors from Dante's *Inferno* and Baudelaire's *Flowers of Evil*. Originally inspired by Lorenzo Ghiberti's *Gates of Paradise* (FIG. 8-15), Rodin quickly abandoned the idea of a series of framed narrative panels and decided instead to cover each of the doors with a continuous writhing mass of tormented men and women, sinners condemned to Dante's second circle of Hell for their lust. Because of the varying height of the relief, the complex poses, and the effect of light on the highly textured surfaces, the figures seem to be in flux, moving in and out of an undefined space in a reflection of their psychic turmoil. The dreamlike (or rather, the nightmarish) vision connects Rodin with the Symbolists, and the pessimistic

mood and sensuality embody the fin-de-siècle spirit. The swirling composition and emotionalism recall Delacroix's *Death of Sardanapalus* (FIG. 12-7) and Michelangelo's *Last Judgment* (FIG. 9-11). But Rodin's work defies easy stylistic classification.

The nearly 200 figures of *The Gates of Hell* spill over onto the jambs and the lintel. Rodin also included freestanding figures, which, cast separately in multiple versions, are among his best-known works. Above the doors, *The Three Shades* is a trio of twisted nude male figures, essentially the same figure with elongated arms in three different positions. *The Thinker*, Rodin's famous seated nude man with a powerful body who rests his chin on his clenched right hand, ponders the fate of the tormented souls on the doors below.

13-19 AUGUSTE RODIN, *The Gates of Hell*, 1880–1900 (cast in 1917). Bronze, 20′ 10″ × 13′ 1″. Musée Rodin, Paris.

Rodin's most ambitious work, inspired by Dante's *Inferno* and Ghiberti's *Gates of Paradise* (FIG. 8-15), presents nearly 200 tormented sinners in relief below *The Three Shades* and *The Thinker*.

The Art Nouveau movement was an attempt to create art and architecture based on natural forms. Here, every detail conforms to the theme of the twining plant and functions as part of a living whole.

ARCHITECTURE

In the later 19th century, new technologies, the availability of steel, and the changing needs of urbanized, industrialized society affected architecture throughout the Western world. The Realist impulse also encouraged architectural designs that honestly expressed a building's purpose rather than elaborately disguised a building's function. But the taste for elaborate ornamentation also remained strong in an era characterized by stylistic diversity.

ART NOUVEAU An important international architectural and design movement that developed in the closing decades of the 19th century was *Art Nouveau* (New Art), which took its name from a shop in Paris called L'Art Nouveau. Proponents of this movement tried to synthesize all the arts in a determined attempt to create art based on natural forms that could be mass-produced for a large audience. The Art Nouveau style adapted the twining-plant form to the needs of architecture, painting, sculpture, and the decorative arts.

The mature Art Nouveau style is on display in the staircase (FIG. 13-20) of the Van Eetvelde House in Brussels, designed by the Belgian architect VICTOR HORTA (1861–1947). Every detail of the Van Eetvelde interior functions as part of a living whole. Furniture, drapery folds, veining in the lavish stone paneling, and the patterning of the door moldings join with real plants to provide graceful counterpoints for the twining-plant theme. Metallic tendrils curl around the railings and posts, delicate metal tracery fills the glass dome, and floral and leaf motifs spread across the fabric panels of the screen.

Art Nouveau was not solely a French/Belgian phenomenon. The style was also popular in Holland, England, and the United States and, under different names, in Austria and Germany (*Jugendstil*), Italy (*Stile Floreale*), and Spain (*Modernismo*), where ANTONIO GAUDI (1852–1926; FIG. 13-20A ⬈) was its leading proponent.

ALEXANDRE-GUSTAVE EIFFEL The French engineer-architect who is best known for exploiting new technologies to create larger, stronger, and more fire-resistant structures free of superfluous ornamentation was ALEXANDRE-GUSTAVE EIFFEL (1832–1923). Eiffel created the interior armature for France's anniversary gift to the United States—the *Statue of Liberty*—but he designed his signature work, the Eiffel Tower (FIG. 13-21), for an

13-21 ALEXANDRE-GUSTAVE EIFFEL, Eiffel Tower (looking southeast), Paris, France, 1889.

New materials and technologies and the modernist aesthetic fueled radically new architectural designs in the late 19th century. Eiffel jolted the world with the exposed iron skeleton of his tower.

exhibition in Paris in 1889. Although the tower pays tribute to traditional architectural forms, such as the Roman arch and the Gothic spire, it immediately became the symbol of modern Paris. The elegant iron tower thrusts its needle shaft 984 feet above the city, making it at the time of its construction the world's tallest structure. The tower rests on four giant supports connected by gracefully arching open-frame skirts that provide a pleasing mask for the heavy horizontal girders needed to strengthen the legs. The transparency of the structure blurs the distinction between interior and exterior to an extent never before achieved or even attempted. Eiffel jolted the architectural profession into a realization that modern materials and processes made possible a radically innovative approach to architectural design.

LOUIS HENRY SULLIVAN The desire for greater speed and economy in building, as well as for a reduction in fire hazards, prompted the use of cast and wrought iron for many building programs, especially commercial ones. Architects in the United States enthusiastically developed cast-iron architecture until a series of disastrous fires in the early 1870s in New York, Boston, and Chicago demonstrated that cast iron by itself was far from impervious to fire. This discovery led to encasing the metal in masonry, combining the first material's strength with the second's fire resistance. In cities, convenience required closely grouped buildings, and increased property values forced architects literally to raise the roof. The new construction materials, which could support structures of unprecedented height, gave birth to the American skyscraper.

As skyscrapers proliferated, in large part because of the introduction of elevators beginning in 1868, architects refined the visual vocabulary of these buildings. Louis Henry Sullivan (1856–1924) arrived at a synthesis of industrial structure and ornamentation that perfectly expressed the spirit of late-19th-century commerce. To achieve this, he used the latest technological developments to create light-filled, well-ventilated office buildings and adorned both exteriors and interiors with ornate embellishments. Such decoration served to connect commerce and culture, and imbued these white-collar workspaces with a sense of refinement and taste. These characteristics are evident in Sullivan's Sullivan Center (FIG. 13-22) in Chicago. Built between 1899 and 1904, this department store required broad, open, well-illuminated display spaces. Sullivan designed the building as a minimal structural steel skeleton with a stone overlay and gave over the lowest two levels to an ornament in cast iron (of his invention) made of wildly fantastic motifs. The architect regarded the display windows as pictures, which merited elaborate frames. In this early skyscraper, Sullivan revealed his profound understanding of the maturing consumer economy and tailored the department store's design to meet the functional and symbolic needs of its users. The Sullivan Center illustrates Sullivan's famous dictum that "form follows function," which became the slogan of many early-20th-century architects.

13-22 **Louis Henry Sullivan**, Sullivan Center (formerly Carson, Pirie, Scott Building; looking southeast), Chicago, 1899–1904.

Sullivan's motto was "form follows function." This Chicago department store required broad, open, well-illuminated display spaces. It has a minimal structural steel skeleton with a glass and stone skin.

Thus in architecture as well as in the pictorial arts, the late 19th century was a period during which artists challenged traditional modes of expression, often emphatically rejecting the past. Architects and painters as different as Sullivan, Monet, van Gogh, and Cézanne, each in his own way, contributed significantly to the entrenchment of modernism as the new cultural orthodoxy of the early 20th century.

Explore the era further in MindTap with videos of major artworks and buildings, Google Earth™ coordinates, and essays by the author on the following additional subjects:

▌ ART AND SOCIETY: Academic Salons and Independent Art Exhibitions
• Édouard Manet, *Claude Monet in His Studio Boat* (FIG. 13-2A)
• George Seurat, detail of *La Grande Jatte* (FIG. 13-10A)
▌ MATERIALS AND TECHNIQUES: Pointillism and 19th-Century Color Theory
• Paul Cézanne, *Basket of Apples* (FIG. 13-15A)
• Auguste Rodin, *Burghers of Calais* (FIG. 13-19A)
• Antonio Gaudi, Casa Milá, Barcelona (FIG. 13-20A)

IMPRESSIONISM, POST-IMPRESSIONISM, AND SYMBOLISM, 1870 TO 1900

Impressionism

- A hostile critic applied the term *Impressionism* to the paintings of Claude Monet because of their sketchy quality. The Impressionists—Monet, Pierre-Auguste Renoir, Edgar Degas, and others—were a diverse group. Some strove to capture fleeting moments and transient effects of light and climate on canvas. Others focused on recording the contemporary urban scene in Paris, frequently painting in bars, dance halls, and railroad stations. Many Impressionist compositions feature figures seen at sharply oblique angles and arbitrarily cut off by the frame, reflecting the influence of Japanese prints.

Degas, *The Rehearsal*, 1874

Post-Impressionism

- Post-Impressionism is not a unified style. The term refers to the group of late-19th-century artists who followed the Impressionists and took painting in new directions.
- Georges Seurat refined the Impressionist approach to color and light into pointillism—the disciplined application of pure color in tiny daubs.
- Vincent van Gogh explored the capabilities of colors and distorted forms to express emotions, as in his dramatic depiction of a billiard parlor in *Night Café*.
- Paul Gauguin moved away from Impressionism in favor of large areas of flat color bounded by firm lines.
- Paul Cézanne replaced the transitory visual effects of the Impressionists with a rigorous analysis of the lines, planes, and colors that make up landscapes and still lifes.

Van Gogh, *Night Café*, 1888

Gauguin, *Where Do We Come From?* 1897

Symbolism

- Henri Rousseau and the Symbolists disdained Realism as trivial and sought to depict a reality beyond that of the everyday world, rejecting materialism and celebrating fantasy and imagination. The subjects of their paintings were often mysterious, exotic, and sensuous, sometimes alluding to the world of the subconscious during sleep.
- The leading sculptor at the end of the 19th century was Auguste Rodin, who explored Realist themes and the representation of movement. His vision of tormented, writhing figures in Hell connects his work with the Symbolists.

Rodin, *Gates of Hell*, 1880–1900

Architecture

- New technologies and the changing needs of urbanized, industrialized society transformed architecture in the late 19th century. The exposed iron skeleton of the Eiffel Tower, which blurs the distinction between interior and exterior, jolted architects into a realization of how modern materials and processes could revolutionize architectural design. In the United States, Louis Sullivan was a pioneer in designing the first metal, stone, and glass skyscrapers.

Sullivan, Sullivan Center, Chicago, 1899–1904

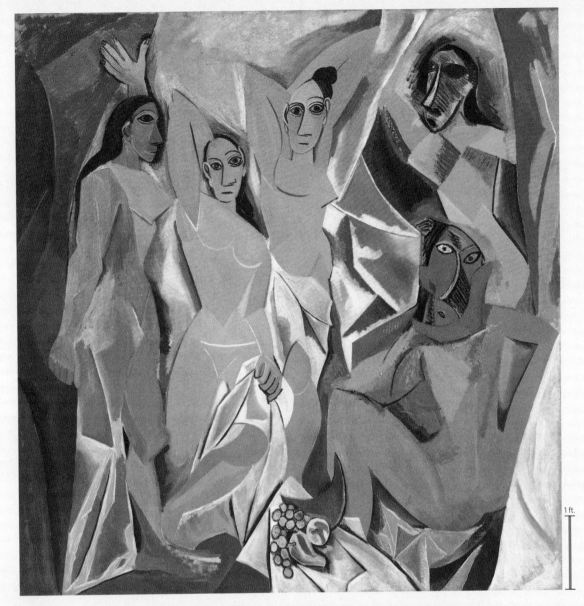

14-1 **PABLO PICASSO**, *Les Demoiselles d'Avignon*, 1907. Oil on canvas, 8' × 7' 8".
Museum of Modern Art, New York (acquired through the Lillie P. Bliss Bequest).

1 ft.

▲ **14-1a** "Primitive" art helped inspire Picasso's radical break with traditional Western norms of pictorial representation. Ancient Iberian sculptures were the sources of the features of the three young women at the left.

▲ **14-1b** The striated features of the distorted heads of the two young Avignon Street prostitutes at the right grew directly from Picasso's increasing fascination with African artworks, which he studied and collected.

▲ **14-1c** By breaking the figures of the demoiselles into ambiguous planes, as if the viewer were seeing them from more than one place in space at once, Picasso disrupted the standards of Western art since the Renaissance.

Modernism in Europe and America, 1900 to 1945

PICASSO DISRUPTS THE WESTERN PICTORIAL TRADITION

An artist whose importance to the history of art is uncontested, PABLO PICASSO (1881–1973) was blessed with boundless talent and an inquisitive intellect that led him to make groundbreaking contributions to Western pictorial art. In 1907, with *Les Demoiselles d'Avignon* (*The Young Ladies of Avignon*; FIG. 14-1), he opened the door to a radically new method of representing forms in space. Picasso began the work as a symbolic picture to be titled *Philosophical Bordello,* portraying two male clients (who, based on surviving drawings, had features resembling Picasso's) intermingling with women in the reception room of a brothel on Avignon Street in Barcelona. One was a sailor. The other carried a skull, an obvious reference to death. By the time the artist finished, he had eliminated both men and simplified the room's details to a suggestion of drapery and a schematic foreground still life. Picasso had become wholly absorbed in the problem of finding a new way to represent the five women in their interior space. Instead of depicting the figures as continuous volumes, he fractured their shapes and interwove them with the equally jagged planes representing drapery and empty space. Indeed, the space, so entwined with the bodies, is virtually illegible. The tension between Picasso's representation of three-dimensional space and his modernist conviction that a painting is a two-dimensional design on the surface of a stretched canvas is a tension between representation and abstraction.

Picasso extended the radical nature of *Les Demoiselles d'Avignon* even further by depicting the figures inconsistently. Ancient Iberian sculptures inspired the calm, ideal features of the three prostitutes at the left. The energetic, violently striated features of the heads of the two women at the right emerged late in Picasso's production of the work and grew directly from his increasing fascination with African sculpture. Perhaps responding to the energy of these two new heads, Picasso also revised the women's bodies. He broke them into more ambiguous planes suggesting a combination of views, as if the observer sees the figures from more than one place in space at once. The woman seated at the lower right shows these multiple angles most clearly, seeming to present the observer simultaneously with a three-quarter back view from the left, another from the right, and a front view of the head that suggests seeing the figure frontally as well. Gone is the traditional Renaissance concept of an orderly, constructed, and unified pictorial space mirroring the world. In its place are the rudimentary beginnings of a new approach to representing the world—as a dynamic interplay of time and space. Picasso's *Les Demoiselles d'Avignon* was nothing less than a dramatic departure from and disruption of the Western pictorial tradition. It set the stage for many other artistic revolutions in the 20th century.

GLOBAL UPHEAVAL AND ARTISTIC REVOLUTION

The first half of the 20th century was a period of significant upheaval worldwide. Between 1900 and 1945, the major industrial powers fought two global wars, witnessed the rise of Communism, Fascism, and Nazism, and suffered the Great Depression. These decades were also a time of radical change in the arts when painters and sculptors challenged some of the most basic assumptions about the purpose of art and what form an artwork should take. Throughout history, artistic revolution has often accompanied political, social, and economic upheaval, but never before had the new directions that artists explored been as pronounced or as long-lasting as those born during the first half of the last century.

AVANT-GARDE Like other members of society, artists deeply felt the effects of the political and economic disruptions of the early 20th century. As the old social orders collapsed and new ones, from Communism to corporate capitalism, took their places, artists searched for new definitions of and uses for art in a changed world.

Beginning in the 19th century, each successive modernist movement had challenged artistic conventions with ever-greater intensity. This relentless questioning of the status quo gave rise to the notion of an artistic *avant-garde*. The term, which means "front guard," refers to the French troops that bravely scouted behind enemy lines. Avant-garde artists were likewise trailblazers. They questioned the premises and formal conventions of Western art and explored new avenues of expression in all artistic media.

EUROPE, 1900 TO 1920

Avant-garde artists in all their diversity became a major force in Europe (MAP 14-1; page 380) during the opening decades of the 20th century, beginning with the artistic movement known as *Fauvism*.

Fauvism

In 1905, a group of young French painters exhibited canvases so simplified in design and so shockingly bright in color that a startled critic, Louis Vauxcelles (1870–1943), described the artists as *fauves* ("wild beasts"). Driving the Fauve movement was a desire to develop an art having the directness of Impressionism but employing intense color juxtapositions for expressive ends. Building on the legacy of artists such as Vincent van Gogh and Paul Gauguin (see pages 366–370), the Fauves went even further in liberating color from its descriptive function and exploring the effects that different colors have on emotions.

14-2 HENRI MATISSE, *Woman with the Hat*, 1905. Oil on canvas, 2' 7¾" × 1' 11½". San Francisco Museum of Modern Art, San Francisco (bequest of Elise S. Haas).

Matisse's portrayal of his wife, Amélie, features patches and splotches of seemingly arbitrary colors. He and the other Fauve painters used color not to imitate nature but to produce a reaction in the viewer.

HENRI MATISSE The dominant figure of the Fauve group was HENRI MATISSE (1869–1954), who believed that color could play a primary role in conveying meaning, and consequently focused his efforts on developing this notion (see "Henri Matisse on Color," page 379). In *Woman with the Hat* (FIG. 14-2), Matisse depicted his wife, Amélie, in a rather conventional manner compositionally, but the seemingly arbitrary colors startle the viewer. The entire image—the woman's face, clothes, hat, and background—consists of patches and splotches of color juxtaposed in ways that sometimes produce

MODERNISM IN EUROPE AND AMERICA, 1900 TO 1945

1900–1910
- Matisse and the Fauves free color from its descriptive function.
- German Expressionist groups—Die Brücke and Der Blaue Reiter—produce paintings featuring bold colors and distorted forms.
- "Primitive" art inspires Picasso to reject traditional Western modes of representation.

1910–1920
- Picasso and Braque invent Cubism.
- Italian Futurists celebrate dynamic motion and modern technology.
- Kandinsky produces completely abstract paintings.
- The Dadaists explore the role of chance in irreverent artworks.
- The Armory Show introduces America to European modernism.

1920–1930
- Neue Sachlichkeit painters depict the horrors of war.
- The Surrealists represent the world of the unconscious.
- De Stijl artists create "pure plastic art" using geometric forms and primary colors.
- Brancusi and Hepworth promote abstract sculpture.
- The Bauhaus advocates the integration of all the arts.

1930–1945
- Douglas and Lawrence's paintings celebrate African American culture.
- Calder creates abstract sculptures with moving parts.
- The Regionalists celebrate life in rural America.
- Orozco and Rivera paint mural cycles of Mexican history.
- Lange and Bourke-White achieve fame for their documentary photographs.

ARTISTS ON ART
Henri Matisse on Color

In an essay titled "Notes of a Painter," published in the Parisian journal *La Grande Revue* on Christmas Day 1908, Henri Matisse responded to his critics and set forth his principles and goals as a painter. The following excerpts help explain what Matisse was trying to achieve in paintings such as *Red Room* (FIG. 14-3).

What I am after, above all, is expression.... Expression, for me, does not reside in passions glowing in a human face or manifested by violent movement. The entire arrangement of my picture is expressive: the place occupied by the figures, the empty spaces around them, the proportions, everything has its share. Composition is the art of arranging in a decorative manner the diverse elements at the painter's command to express his feelings....

Both harmonies and dissonances of color can produce agreeable effects.... Suppose I have to paint an interior: I have before me a cupboard; it gives me a sensation of vivid red, and I put down a red which satisfies me. A relation is established between this red and the white of the canvas. Let me put a green near the red, and make the floor yellow; and again there will be relationships between the green or yellow and the white of the canvas which will satisfy me.... A new combination of colors will succeed the first.... From the relationship I have found in all the tones there must result a living harmony of colors, a harmony analogous to that of a musical composition....

The chief function of color should be to serve expression as well as possible.... I simply try to put down colors which render my sensation. There is an impelling proportion of tones that may lead me to change the shape of a figure or to transform my composition. Until I have achieved this proportion in all parts of the composition I strive towards it and keep on working. Then a moment comes when all the parts have found their definite relationships, and from then on it would be impossible for me to add a stroke to my picture without having to repaint it entirely.*

*Translated by Jack D. Flam, *Matisse on Art* (London: Phaidon, 1973), 32–40.

1 ft.

14-3 HENRI MATISSE, *Red Room* (*Harmony in Red*), 1908–1909. Oil on canvas, 5' 11" × 8' 1". State Hermitage Museum, Saint Petersburg.

Matisse believed that painters should choose compositions and colors that express their feelings. Here, the table and the wall seem to merge because they are the same color and have identical patterning.

jarring contrasts. Matisse explained his approach: "What characterized Fauvism was that we rejected imitative colors, and that with pure colors we obtained stronger reactions."[1]

Matisse's exploration of the expressive power of color reached maturity in *Red Room* (*Harmony in Red*; FIG. 14-3). The subject is the interior of a comfortable, prosperous household with a maid placing fruit and wine on the table, but Matisse's canvas is radically different from traditional paintings of domestic interiors (compare FIG. 10-24). The Fauve painter depicted objects in simplified and schematized fashion and flattened out the forms. For example, Matisse eliminated the front edge of the table, rendering the table, with its identical patterning, as flat as the wall behind it. The window at the upper left could also be a painting on the wall, further flattening the space. Everywhere, the colors contrast richly and intensely. Initially, this work was predominantly green. Matisse repainted it blue, but blue also did not seem appropriate to him. Not until he repainted the canvas red did Matisse feel that he had found the right color for the "harmony" he wished to compose.

German Expressionism

The immediacy and boldness of the canvases of Matisse, ANDRÉ DERAIN (1880–1954; FIG. 14-3A ⟋), and the other Fauves appealed to many artists, especially the German Expressionists. However, although color plays a prominent role in German *Expressionism,* the "expressiveness" of many of the images is due as much to wrenching distortions of form, ragged outlines, and agitated brushstrokes.

ERNST LUDWIG KIRCHNER The first group of German Expressionists—*Die Brücke* (The Bridge)—gathered in Dresden (MAP 14-1) in 1905 under the leadership of ERNST LUDWIG KIRCHNER (1880–1938). The group members thought of themselves as paving the way for a more perfect age by bridging the old age and the new, hence their name. The Bridge artists lamented the state of German society at the opening of the 20th century. Kirchner, in particular, focused much of his attention on the detrimental effects of industrialization, such as the alienation of individuals in cities, which he felt fostered a mechanized and impersonal society. His *Street, Dresden* (FIG. 14-4) provides a glimpse into the frenzied urban activity of a bustling German city of that time. Rather than offering the distant, panoramic urban view of the Impressionists, Kirchner's street scene is jarring and dissonant in both composition and color. The women in the foreground loom large, approaching somewhat menacingly. The steep perspective of the street, which threatens to push the women into the viewer's space, increases their confrontational nature. Harshly rendered, the women's features make them appear ghoulish, and the garish, clashing colors—juxtapositions of bright orange, emerald green, chartreuse, and pink—add to the expressive impact of the image. Kirchner's perspective distortions, disquieting figures, and color choices reflect the influence of the work of Edvard Munch, who made similar expressive use of formal elements in *The Scream* (FIG. 13-17).

VASSILY KANDINSKY The second major German Expressionist group, *Der Blaue Reiter* (The Blue Rider), formed in Munich in 1911. The two founding members, Vassily Kandinsky and Franz Marc, whimsically selected this name because of their mutual interest in the color blue and in horses. Like Die Brücke, this group produced paintings that captured the artists' feelings in visual form while also eliciting intense emotional responses from viewers.

Born in Russia, VASSILY KANDINSKY (1866–1944) moved to Munich in 1896 and soon developed a spontaneous expressive style. Indeed, Kandinsky was one of the first artists to explore complete abstraction, as in *Improvisation 28* (FIG. 14-5). A true intellectual, Kandinsky was one of the few artists to read with some comprehension the new scientific theories of the era (see "Science and Art in the Early 20th Century" ⟋), which convinced him that material objects had no real substance, thereby shattering his belief in a world of tangible things. He articulated his ideas in an influential treatise, *Concerning the Spiritual in Art,* published in 1912, the same year that he painted *Improvisation 28.* Artists, Kandinsky believed, must express their innermost feelings by orchestrating color, form, line, and space, much like composers create music out of notes, which do not

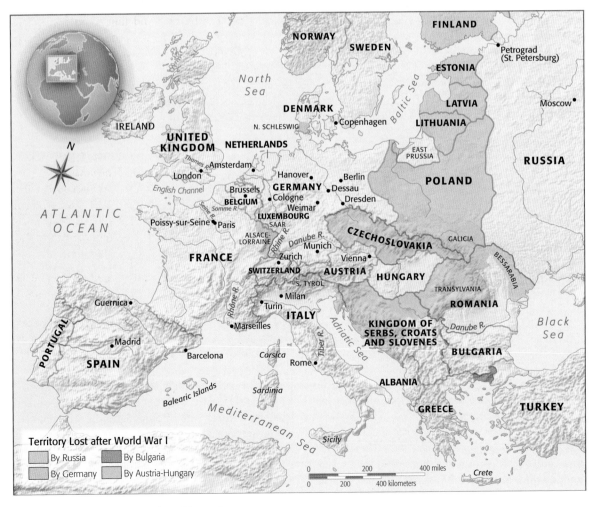

MAP 14-1 **Europe at the end of World War I.**

1 ft.

14-4 ERNST LUDWIG KIRCHNER, *Street, Dresden*, 1908 (dated 1907). Oil on canvas, 4' 11¼" × 6' 6⅞". Museum of Modern Art, New York.

Kirchner's perspective distortions, disquieting figures, and color choices reflect the influence of the Fauves and of Edvard Munch (FIG. 13-17), who made similar expressive use of formal elements.

mimic the sounds of nature. In his *Improvisation* series, Kandinsky sought to convey feelings solely by color juxtapositions, intersecting lines, and implied spatial relationships. Ultimately, Kandinsky saw these abstractions as evolving blueprints for a more enlightened and liberated society emphasizing spirituality.

FRANZ MARC Like many of the other German Expressionists, FRANZ MARC (1880–1916) grew increasingly pessimistic about the state of humanity, especially as World War I loomed on the horizon.

His perception of human beings as deeply flawed prompted him to turn to the animal world for his subjects. Animals, he believed, were more pure than humans and thus more appropriate vehicles for expressing an inner truth. In his quest to imbue his paintings with greater emotional intensity, Marc focused on color and developed a system of correspondences between specific colors and feelings or ideas. According to Marc, "Blue is the *male* principle, severe and spiritual. Yellow is the *female* principle, gentle, happy and sensual. Red is *matter*, brutal and heavy."[2]

1 ft.

14-5 VASSILY KANDINSKY, *Improvisation 28* (second version), 1912. Oil on canvas, 3' 7⅞" × 5' 3⅞". Solomon R. Guggenheim Museum, New York (gift of Solomon R. Guggenheim, 1937).

Kandinsky believed that artists must express their innermost feelings by orchestrating color, form, line, and space. He was one of the first artists to explore complete abstraction in paintings called *Improvisations*.

14-6 FRANZ MARC, *Fate of the Animals*, 1913. Oil on canvas, 6' 4¼" × 8' 9½". Kunstmuseum Basel, Basel.

Marc developed a system of correspondences between specific colors and feelings or ideas. In this apocalyptic scene of animals trapped in a forest, the colors of severity and brutality dominate.

1 ft.

Fate of the Animals (FIG. 14-6) represents the culmination of Marc's efforts to create, in a sense, an iconography of color. Painted in 1913, when the horrific tension of impending warfare had pervaded society, the animals appear trapped in a forest amid falling trees, some apocalyptic event destroying both the forest and the animals inhabiting it. The painter distorted the entire scene and shattered it into fragments. Significantly, the lighter and brighter colors—the passive, gentle, and cheerful ones—are absent, and the colors of severity and brutality dominate the work. Marc discovered just how well his painting portended war's anguish and tragedy when he ended up at the front the following year. His experiences in battle prompted him to tell his wife in a letter: "[*Fate of the Animals*] is like a premonition of this war—horrible and shattering. I can hardly conceive that I painted it."[3] Marc's contempt for people's inhumanity and his attempt to express that through his art ended, with tragic irony, in his death in action in World War I in 1916.

KÄTHE KOLLWITZ The emotional power of postwar German Expressionism is also evident in the graphic work of KÄTHE KOLLWITZ (1867–1945), although she had no formal association with any Expressionist group. Kollwitz explored a range of issues from the overtly political to the deeply personal. One subject that she treated repeatedly was that of a mother with her dead child. Although she initially derived the theme from the Christian Pietà, Kollwitz transformed it into a universal statement of maternal loss and grief. In *Woman with Dead Child* (FIG. 14-7), she replaced the reverence and grace pervading most depictions of Mary holding the dead Christ (FIG. 9-7) with an animalistic passion. The grieving mother ferociously grips the body of her dead child. The primal nature of the undeniably powerful image is in keeping with the aims of the Expressionists. Not since the Gothic age in Germany (FIG. 7-27) had any artist produced a mother-and-son group with a comparable emotional impact. Because Kollwitz used her son Peter as the model for the dead child, the image was no doubt all the more personal to her. The print stands as a poignant premonition. Peter died fighting in World War I at age 21.

1 in.

14-7 KÄTHE KOLLWITZ, *Woman with Dead Child*, 1903. Etching overprinted lithographically with a gold-tone plate, 1' 4⅝" × 1' 7⅛". British Museum, London.

The theme of the mother mourning over her dead child derives from images of the Pietà in Christian art, but Kollwitz transformed it into a powerful universal statement of maternal loss and grief.

Cubism and Purism

At the same time that the Fauves and German Expressionists were taking painting in new directions, Pablo Picasso was disrupting the history of art in other ways with his revolutionary 1907 *Les Demoiselles d'Avignon* (FIG. 14-1). Although the painting incorporates references to the Western pictorial tradition—for example, a variation on an Archaic Greek *kouros* statue (FIG. 2-17) for the standing woman at the left and a doubtless intentional tribute to Manet's *Déjeuner sur l'Herbe* (FIG. 12-17) for the seated woman at the right—it stands apart from that tradition not only in formal terms but in the representation of nude women as threatening rather than as passive figures on display for the pleasure of male viewers. Picasso's rethinking of the premises of Western art was largely inspired by his fascination with "primitive" art, which he had studied in Paris's Trocadéro ethnography museum and collected and kept in his Paris studio (see "Primitivism and Colonialism" ⬀).

ANALYTIC CUBISM For many years, Picasso showed *Les Demoiselles d'Avignon* only to other painters. One of the first to see it was Georges Braque (1882–1963), a Fauve painter who found it so challenging that he began to rethink his own painting style. Using the painting's revolutionary elements as a point of departure, together Braque and Picasso formulated *Cubism* around 1908 in the belief that the art of painting had to move far beyond the description of visual reality. Cubism represented a radical turning point in the history of art, nothing less than a dismissal of the pictorial illusionism that had dominated Western art since the Renaissance. The Cubists rejected naturalistic depictions, preferring compositions of shapes and forms abstracted from the conventionally perceived world. As Picasso once explained: "I paint forms as I think them, not as I see them."[4] Together, Picasso and Braque pursued the analysis of form central to Cézanne's artistic explorations (see "Making Impressionism Solid and Enduring," page 369) by dissecting everything around them into their many constituent features, which they then recomposed, by a new logic of design, into a coherent, independent aesthetic picture.

The new style received its name after Matisse described some of Braque's work to the critic Louis Vauxcelles as having been painted "with little cubes." In his review, Vauxcelles described the new paintings as "cubic oddities."[5] The French writer and theorist Guillaume Apollinaire (1880–1918) summarized well the central concepts of Cubism in 1913:

> Authentic cubism [is] the art of depicting new wholes with formal elements borrowed not from the reality of vision, but from that of conception. This tendency leads to a poetic kind of painting which stands outside the world of observation; for, even in a simple cubism, the geometrical surfaces of an object must be opened out in order to give a complete representation of it. . . . Everyone must agree that a chair, from whichever side it is viewed, never ceases to have four legs, a seat and back, and that if it is robbed of one of these elements, it is robbed of an important part.[6]

Most art historians refer to the first phase of Cubism, developed jointly by Picasso and Braque, as *Analytic Cubism*. Because Cubists could not achieve the kind of total view Apollinaire described by the traditional method of drawing or painting objects and people from one position, they began to dissect the forms of their subjects and to present their analysis of form across the canvas surface.

1 ft.

14-8 Georges Braque, *The Portuguese,* 1911. Oil on canvas, 3' 10⅛" × 2' 8". Kunstmuseum Basel, Basel (gift of Raoul La Roche, 1952).

The Cubists rejected the pictorial illusionism that had dominated Western art for centuries. Here, Braque concentrated on dissecting form and placing it in dynamic interaction with space.

Georges Braque's *The Portuguese* (FIG. 14-8) is a characteristic Analytic Cubist painting. The subject is a Portuguese musician whom the artist recalled seeing years earlier in a bar in Marseilles. Braque dissected the man and his instrument and placed the resulting forms in dynamic interaction with the space around them. Unlike the Fauves and German Expressionists, who used vibrant colors, the Cubists chose subdued hues—here solely brown tones—in order to focus attention on form. In *The Portuguese,* Braque carried his analysis so far that the viewer must work diligently to discover clues to the subject. The construction of large intersecting planes suggests the forms of a man and a guitar. Smaller shapes interpenetrate and hover in the large planes. The way that Braque treated light and shadow reveals his departure from conventional artistic practice. Light and dark passages suggest both chiaroscuro modeling and transparent planes that enable the viewer to see through one level to another. Solid forms emerge only to be canceled almost immediately by a different reading of the subject.

The stenciled letters and numbers add to the painting's complexity. Letters and numbers are flat shapes, but as elements of a Cubist painting such as *The Portuguese,* they enable the painter to

14-9 PABLO PICASSO, *Still Life with Chair-Caning*, 1912. Oil, oilcloth, and rope on canvas, $10\frac{5}{8}$" × 1' $1\frac{3}{4}$". Musée Picasso, Paris.

This painting includes a piece of oilcloth and brushstrokes on top of a photolithograph of a cane chair seat. Framed with a piece of rope, the still life challenges the viewer's understanding of reality.

14-9 PABLO PICASSO, *Still Life with Chair-Caning*, 1912. Oil, oilcloth, and rope on canvas, $10\frac{5}{8}$" × 1' $1\frac{3}{4}$". Musée Picasso, Paris.

This painting includes a piece of oilcloth and brushstrokes on top of a photolithograph of a cane chair seat. Framed with a piece of rope, the still life challenges the viewer's understanding of reality.

play with the viewer's perception of two- and three-dimensional space. The letters and numbers lie flat on the painted canvas surface, yet the shading and shapes of other forms flow behind and underneath them, pushing the letters and numbers forward into the viewing space. Occasionally, they seem attached to the surface of some object within the painting. Ultimately, the constantly shifting imagery makes it impossible to arrive at any definitive reading of the image. Analytical Cubist paintings radically disrupt expectations about the representation of forms, space, and time.

SYNTHETIC CUBISM In 1912, Cubism entered a new phase called *Synthetic Cubism,* in which, instead of dissecting forms, artists constructed paintings and drawings from objects and shapes cut from paper or other materials. The point of departure for this new style was Picasso's *Still Life with Chair-Caning* (FIG. **14-9**), a mixed-media work in which the artist placed a piece of oilcloth and brushstrokes on top of a photolithograph of a cane chair pasted to the canvas. Framed with rope, this work challenges the viewer's understanding of reality. The photographically replicated chair caning seems so "real" that one expects the holes to break any brushstrokes laid on it. But the chair caning, although optically suggestive of the real, is only an illusion or representation of an object. In contrast, the painted abstract areas do not refer to tangible objects in the real world. Yet the fact that they

do not imitate anything makes them more "real" than the chair caning. No pretense exists. Picasso extended the visual play by making the letter *U* escape from the space of the accompanying *J* and *O* and partially covering it with a cylindrical shape that pushes across its left side. The letters *JOU,* which appear in many Cubist paintings, formed part of the masthead of the daily French newspapers (*journaux*) often found among the objects represented. Picasso and Braque especially delighted in the punning references to *jouer* and *jouir*—the French verbs meaning "to play" and "to enjoy."

After *Still Life with Chair-Caning,* both Picasso and Braque continued to explore the medium of *collage* introduced into the realm of

14-10 PABLO PICASSO, *Guernica*, 1937. Oil on canvas, 11' $5\frac{1}{2}$" × 25' $5\frac{3}{4}$". Museo Nacional Centro de Arte Reina Sofia, Madrid.

Picasso used Cubist techniques, especially the fragmentation of objects and dislocation of anatomical features, to expressive effect in this condemnation of the Nazi bombing of the Basque capital.

"high art" (as opposed to unself-conscious "folk art") in that work. From the French verb *coller* ("to stick"), a collage is a composition of bits of objects, such as newspaper or cloth, glued to a surface.

Although most discussions of Cubism and collage focus on the innovations in artistic form they represented, it is important to note that contemporary critics also viewed the revolutionary nature of Cubism in sociopolitical terms. Many considered Cubism's challenge to artistic convention and tradition a subversive attack on 20th-century society. In fact, many modernist artists and writers of the period did ally themselves with various anarchist groups whose social critiques and utopian visions appealed to progressive thinkers. The French press consistently equated Cubism's disdain for tradition with anarchism and revolution.

GUERNICA Picasso continued to experiment with different artistic styles and media right up until his death in 1973. Celebrated primarily for his brilliant formal innovations, in the late 1930s Picasso became openly involved in political issues as he watched his homeland descend into civil war. He declared: "[P]ainting is not made to decorate apartments. It is an instrument for offensive and defensive war against the enemy."[7] In January 1937, the Spanish Republican government-in-exile in Paris asked Picasso to produce a major work for the Spanish Pavilion at the Paris International Exposition that summer. He did not formally accept the invitation, however, until he received word that Guernica, capital of the Basque region in southern France and northern Spain, had been almost totally destroyed in an air raid on April 26. Nazi pilots acting on behalf of the rebel general Francisco Franco (1892–1975) bombed the city at the busiest hour of a market day, killing or wounding many of Guernica's 7,000 citizens. The event jolted Picasso into action. By the end of June, he had completed *Guernica* (FIG. 14-10), a mural-sized canvas of immense power.

Despite the painting's title, Picasso made no specific reference to the event in *Guernica*. The imagery includes no bombs and no German planes. It is a universal outcry of human grief. In the center, along the lower edge of the painting, lies a slain warrior clutching a broken and useless sword. A gored horse tramples him and rears back in fright as it dies. On the left, a shrieking woman cradles her dead child (compare FIG. 14-7). On the far right, a woman on fire runs screaming from a burning building, while another woman flees mindlessly. In the upper right corner, a woman, represented by only a head, emerges from the burning building, thrusting forth a light to illuminate the horror. Overlooking the destruction is a bull, which, according to the artist, represents "brutality and darkness."[8]

In *Guernica,* Picasso brilliantly used aspects of his earlier Cubist discoveries to expressive effect, particularly the fragmentation of objects and the dislocation of anatomical features. The dissections and contortions of the human form in Picasso's painting paralleled what happened to the Basque people during the aerial bombardment. To emphasize the scene's severity and starkness, Picasso reduced his palette to black, white, and shades of gray, suppressing color once again, as he had in his Analytic Cubist works.

FERNAND LÉGER AND PURISM Best known today as one of the most important modernist architects, Le Corbusier (FIG. 14-42) was also a painter. In 1918, he founded a movement called *Purism,* which opposed Synthetic Cubism on the grounds that it was becoming merely an esoteric, decorative art out of touch with the machine age. Purists maintained that machinery's clean functional lines and the pure forms of its parts should direct artists' experiments in design, whether in painting, architecture, or industrially produced objects. This "machine aesthetic" inspired FERNAND LÉGER (1881–1955), a French artist who had painted with the Cubists. In his works—for example, *The City* (FIG. 14-11)—Léger brought together meticulous Cubist analysis of form with Purism's broad simplification and machinelike finish of the design components. He retained from his Cubist practice a preference for cylindrical and tube-shaped motifs, suggestive of machined parts such as pistons and cylinders.

Léger's paintings have the sharp precision of the machine, whose beauty and quality he was one of the first artists to appreciate. For example, in his film *Ballet Mécanique* (*Mechanical Ballet*; 1924), Léger contrasted inanimate objects such as functioning machines with humans in dancelike variations. In *The City,* he incorporated the massive effects of modern posters and billboard advertisements, the harsh flashing of electric lights, and the noise of traffic. In a definitive way, Léger depicted the mechanical commotion of urban life.

1 ft.

14-11 FERNAND LÉGER, *The City,* 1919. Oil on canvas, 7' 7" × 9' 9½". Philadelphia Museum of Art, Philadelphia (A. E. Gallatin Collection).

Léger championed the "machine aesthetic." In *The City,* he captured the mechanical commotion of urban life, incorporating the effects of billboard ads, flashing lights, and noisy traffic.

Futurism

Artists associated with another early-20th-century movement, *Futurism,* pursued many of the ideas that the Cubists and Purists explored. Equally important to the Futurists, however, was their well-defined sociopolitical agenda. Inaugurated and named by the charismatic Italian poet and playwright Filippo Tommaso Marinetti (1876–1944) in 1909, Futurism began as a literary movement but soon encompassed the visual arts, cinema, theater, music, and architecture. Indignant over the political and cultural decline of Italy, the Futurists published numerous manifestos in which they aggressively advocated revolution, both in society and in art (see "Futurist Manifestos," page 387). In their quest to launch Italian society toward a glorious future, the Futurists championed war as a means of washing away the stagnant past, and agitated for the destruction of museums, libraries, and similar repositories of accumulated culture, which they described as mausoleums. They also called for radical innovation in the arts. Of particular interest to the Futurists were the speed and dynamism of modern technology. Marinetti insisted that a racing "automobile adorned with great pipes like serpents with explosive breath . . . is more beautiful than the *Victory of Samothrace*"[9] (FIG. 2-55), which in the early 20th century exemplified classicism and the glories of past civilizations. Appropriately, Futurist art often focused on motion in time and space.

14-12 GIACOMO BALLA, *Dynamism of a Dog on a Leash,* 1912. Oil on canvas, 2' 11$\frac{3}{8}$" × 3' 7$\frac{1}{4}$". Albright-Knox Art Gallery, Buffalo (bequest of A. Conger Goodyear, gift of George F. Goodyear, 1964).

The Futurists' interest in motion and in the Cubist dissection of form is evident in Balla's painting of a passing dog and its owner. Simultaneity of views was central to the Futurist program.

GIACOMO BALLA The Futurists' interest in motion and in the Cubist dissection of form is evident in *Dynamism of a Dog on a Leash* (FIG. 14-12), in which GIACOMO BALLA (1871–1958) represented a passing dog and its owner, whose skirts are just within visual range. Balla achieved the effect of motion by repeating shapes—for example, the dog's legs and tail and the swinging line of the leash. Simultaneity of views was central to the Futurist program, as it was to Cubism.

UMBERTO BOCCIONI The definitive work of Futurist sculpture is *Unique Forms of Continuity in Space* (FIG. 14-13). In this bronze statue, UMBERTO BOCCIONI (1882–1916) highlighted the formal and spatial effects of motion rather than their source, the striding human figure. The figure is so expanded, interrupted, and broken in plane and contour that it almost disappears behind the blur of its movement—just as people, buildings, and stationary objects become blurred when seen from an automobile traveling at great speed on a highway. Although Boccioni's figure bears a curious resemblance to the *Nike of Samothrace* (FIG. 2-55), the ancient sculptor suggested motion only through posture and agitated drapery, not through distortion and fragmentation of the human body.

This Futurist representation of motion in sculpture has its limitations, however. The eventual development of the motion picture, based on the rapid sequential projection of fixed images (compare FIG. 12-28), produced more convincing illusions of movement. And several decades later, Alexander Calder (FIG. 14-32) pioneered the development of *kinetic sculpture*—sculptures with parts that really move. But in the early 20th century, Boccioni was unsurpassed for his ability to capture the sensation of motion in statuary.

Dada

Although the Futurists celebrated World War I and the changes they hoped it would effect, the mass destruction and chaos that the conflict unleashed horrified other artists. Humanity had never before witnessed such wholesale slaughter on so grand a scale over such an extended period. The new technology of armaments, bred of the age of steel, changed the nature of combat. In the face of massed artillery hurling millions of tons of high explosives and gas shells and in the sheets of fire from thousands of machine guns, attack was suicidal, and warfare became a frustrating stalemate of soldiers holed up in trenches. The mud, filth, and blood of the trenches; the pounding and shattering of incessant shell fire; and the terrible deaths and mutilations were psychologically devastating for a generation brought up with the doctrine of progress and a belief in the fundamental values of civilization.

One major consequence in the art world was the emergence of a movement known as *Dada.* The Dadaists believed that Enlightenment reasoning had been responsible for the insane spectacle of collective homicide and global destruction that was the "Great War," and they concluded that the only route to salvation was through political anarchy, the irrational, and the intuitive. Although Dada began independently in New York and Zurich, it also took root in Paris, Berlin, and Cologne, among other cities. Dada was

ARTISTS ON ART
Futurist Manifestos

On April 11, 1910, a group of young Italian artists published *Futurist Painting: Technical Manifesto* in Milan in an attempt to apply the writer Filippo Tommaso Marinetti's views on literature to the visual arts. Signed jointly by Giacomo Balla, Umberto Boccioni, and three other artists, the manifesto states in part:

> On account of the persistency of an image on the retina, moving objects constantly multiply themselves [and] their form changes. . . . Thus a running horse has not four legs, but twenty. . . .
>
> What was true for the painters of yesterday is but a falsehood today. . . . To paint a human figure you must not paint it; you must render the whole of its surrounding atmosphere. . . . The shadows which we shall paint shall be more luminous than the highlights of our predecessors, and our pictures, next to those of the museums, will shine like blinding daylight compared with deepest night. . . .
>
> We declare . . . that all forms of imitation must be despised, all forms of originality glorified . . . that all subjects previously used must be swept aside in order to express our whirling life of steel, of pride, of fever and of speed . . . that movement and light destroy the materiality of bodies.*

Two years later, Boccioni published *Technical Manifesto of Futurist Sculpture,* in which he argued that traditional sculpture was "a monstrous anachronism" and that modern sculpture should be

> a translation, in plaster, bronze, glass, wood or any other material, of those atmospheric planes which bind and intersect things. . . . Let's . . . proclaim the absolute and complete abolition of finite lines and the contained statue. Let's split open our figures and place the environment inside them. We declare that the environment must form part of the plastic whole.†

The paintings of Balla (FIG. 14-12) and the sculptures of Boccioni (FIG. 14-13) are the perfect expressions of these Futurist principles and goals.

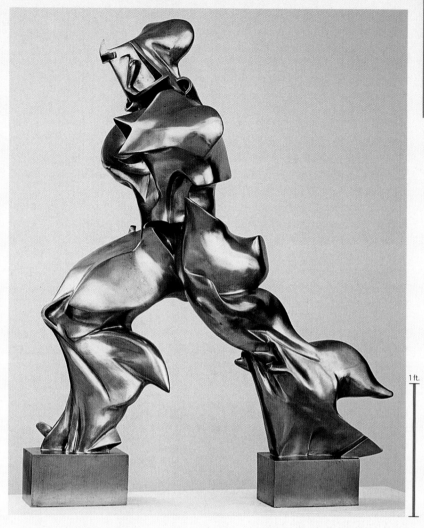

1 ft.

14-13 UMBERTO BOCCIONI, *Unique Forms of Continuity in Space,* 1913 (cast 1931). Bronze, 3' 7⅞" high. Museum of Modern Art, New York (acquired through the Lillie P. Bliss Bequest).

Boccioni's Futurist manifesto for sculpture advocated abolishing the enclosed statue. This running figure's body is so expanded that it almost disappears behind the blur of its movement.

Futurist Painting: Technical Manifesto (*Poesia,* April 11, 1910). Translated by Filippo Tommaso Marinetti, in Umbro Apollonio, ed., *Futurist Manifestos* (Boston: Museum of Fine Arts, 1970), 27–31.
†Translated by Robert Brain, in Apollonio, 51–65.

more a mind-set or attitude than a single identifiable style. The Dadaists turned away from logic in favor of the irrational. Thus an element of absurdity is a cornerstone of Dada—reflected in the movement's very name. According to an oft-repeated anecdote, the Dadaists chose "Dada" at random by sticking a knife into a French-German dictionary. Dada is French for a child's hobby horse. The word satisfied the Dadaists' desire for something irrational and nonsensical.

A central goal of the Dadaists was to undermine cherished notions about art. By attacking convention and logic, they unlocked new avenues for creative invention, thereby fostering a more serious examination of the basic premises of art. But the Dadaists could also be lighthearted in their subversion. Although horror and disgust about the war initially prompted Dada, an undercurrent of humor and whimsy runs through much of the art. In its emphasis on the spontaneous and intuitive, Dada paralleled the views of Sigmund

Freud (see page 370). In *The Interpretation of Dreams,* Freud argued that unconscious and inner drives control human behavior. The Dadaists were particularly interested in exploring the unconscious. They believed that art was a powerfully practical means of self-revelation and healing, and that the images arising out of the subconscious mind had a truth of their own, independent of conventional vision.

JEAN ARP The Zurich-based Dadaist JEAN (HANS) ARP (1887–1966) pioneered the use of chance in composing his images. Tiring of the look of some Cubist-related collages he was making, he tore several sheets of paper into roughly shaped squares, haphazardly dropped them onto a sheet of paper on the floor, and glued them into the resulting arrangement. The rectilinearity of the shapes guaranteed a somewhat regular design, but chance had introduced an imbalance that seemed to Arp to restore to his work a special mysterious vitality that he wanted to preserve. *Collage Arranged According to the Laws of Chance* (FIG. 14-14) is one of the works that Arp created by this method. As the Dada filmmaker Hans Richter (1888–1976)

stated, "For us chance was the 'unconscious mind' that Freud had discovered in 1900. . . . Adoption of chance had another purpose, a secret one. This was to restore to the work of art its primeval magic power and to find a way back to the immediacy it had lost through contact with . . . classicism."[10] Arp's renunciation of artistic control and reliance on chance in creating his compositions reinforced the anarchy and subversion inherent in Dada.

MARCEL DUCHAMP Perhaps the most influential Dadaist was MARCEL DUCHAMP (1887–1968), a Frenchman who became the central artist of New York Dada. In 1913, he exhibited his first "readymade" sculptures, which were mass-produced common objects that the artist selected and sometimes "rectified" by modifying their substance or combining them with another object. The creation of readymades, Duchamp insisted, was free from any consideration of either good or bad taste, qualities shaped by a society that he and other Dada artists found aesthetically bankrupt. Perhaps his most outrageous readymade was *Fountain* (FIG. 14-15), a porcelain urinal presented on its back, signed "R. Mutt," and dated (1917). The "artist's signature" was, in fact, a witty pseudonym derived from the Mott plumbing company's name and that of the taller man of the then-popular comic-strip duo Mutt and Jeff. The "art" of this "artwork" lay in the artist's choice of object, which had the effect of conferring the status of art on it and forcing the viewer to see the object in a new light.

HANNAH HÖCH In Berlin, Dada took on an activist political edge. The Berlin Dadaists pioneered a variation of collage that they called

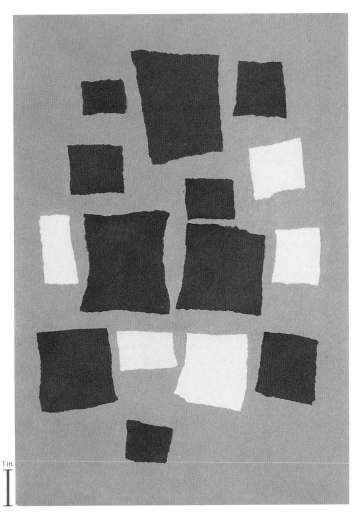

1 in.

14-14 JEAN (HANS) ARP, *Collage Arranged According to the Laws of Chance,* 1916–1917. Torn and pasted paper, 1' 1⅞" × 1' 1⅝". Museum of Modern Art, New York.

In this collage, Arp dropped torn paper squares onto a sheet of paper and then glued them where they fell. His reliance on chance in composing images reinforced the anarchy inherent in Dada.

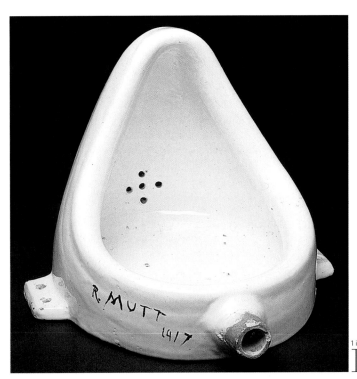

1 in.

14-15 MARCEL DUCHAMP, *Fountain* (second version), 1950 (original version produced 1917). Glazed sanitary china with black paint, 1' high. Philadelphia Museum of Art, Philadelphia.

Duchamp's "readymade" sculptures were mass-produced objects that the Dada artist modified. In *Fountain,* he conferred the status of art on a urinal and forced people to see the object in a new light.

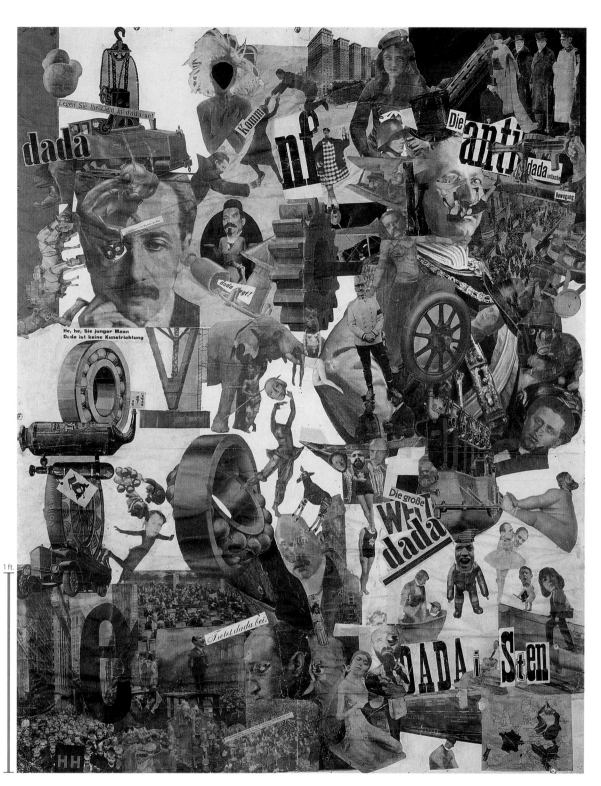

1 ft.

14-16 **HANNAH HÖCH**, *Cut with the Kitchen Knife Dada through the Last Weimar Beer Belly Cultural Epoch of Germany,* 1919–1920. Photomontage, 3' 9" × 2' 11½". Neue Nationalgalerie, Staatliche Museen zu Berlin, Berlin.

Photographs of some of Höch's fellow Dadaists appear among images of Marx and Lenin, and the artist juxtaposed herself with a map of Europe showing the progress of women's right to vote.

photomontage because their assemblages consisted almost entirely of pieces of magazine photographs, usually combined into deliberately antilogical compositions. Collage lent itself well to the Dada desire to use chance when creating art—and antiart. One of the Berlin Dadaists who perfected the photomontage technique was HANNAH HÖCH (1889–1978). Höch's photomontages advanced the absurd illogic of Dada by creating chaotic, contradictory, and satiric compositions. They also provided scathing and insightful commentary on two of the most dramatic developments during the Weimar Republic (1918–1933) in Germany—the redefinition of women's social roles and the explosive growth of mass print media.

Höch, a passionate early feminist, revealed these combined themes in *Cut with the Kitchen Knife Dada through the Last Weimar Beer Belly Cultural Epoch of Germany* (FIG. 14-16). In this work, whose title refers to the story that the name "Dada" resulted from thrusting a knife into a dictionary, Höch arranged an eclectic mixture of cutout photos in seemingly haphazard fashion. Closer inspection, however, reveals the artist's careful selection and placement of the photographs. For example, the key figures in the Weimar Republic are together at the upper right (identified as the "anti-Dada movement"). Some of Höch's fellow Dadaists appear among images of Karl Marx and Vladimir Lenin, aligning Dada with other revolutionary forces in what she prominently labeled with cutout lettering *Die grosse Welt dada* ("the great Dada world"). Certainly, juxtaposing the heads of German military leaders with exotic dancers' bodies provided the wickedly humorous critique central to much of Dada. Höch also positioned herself in the topsy-turvy Dada world that she created. A photograph of her head appears in the lower right corner, juxtaposed with a map of Europe showing which countries had granted women the right to vote—a commentary on the power that both women and Dada had to destabilize society.

Suprematism

Dada was a movement born of pessimism and cynicism. However, not all early-20th-century artists reacted to the profound turmoil of the times by retreating from society. Some promoted utopian ideals, believing staunchly in art's ability to contribute to improving society. These efforts often surfaced in the face of significant political upheaval, as was the case with Suprematism in Russia.

KAZIMIR MALEVICH Russian artist KAZIMIR MALEVICH (1878–1935) developed an abstract style to convey his belief that the supreme reality in the world is "pure feeling," which attaches to no object. Thus this belief called for new, nonobjective forms in

art—shapes not related to objects in the visible world. Malevich christened his new artistic approach *Suprematism,* explaining:

> Under Suprematism I understand the supremacy of pure feeling in creative art. To the Suprematist, the visual phenomena of the objective world are, in themselves, meaningless; the significant thing is feeling, as such, quite apart from the environment in which it is called forth.[11]

The basic form of Malevich's new Suprematist nonobjective art was the square. Combined with its relatives, the straight line and the rectangle, the square soon filled his paintings, such as *Suprematist Composition: Airplane Flying* (FIG. 14-17). In this work, the brightly colored shapes float against and within a white space, and the artist placed them in dynamic relationship to one another. Malevich believed that all peoples would easily understand his new art because of the universality of its symbols. It used the pure language of shape and color, to which everyone could respond intuitively.

UNITED STATES, 1900 TO 1930

Avant-garde experiments in the arts were not limited to Europe. Increasingly common transatlantic travel resulted in a lively exchange of artistic ideas between European and American artists, such as Cassatt (FIG. 13-6), Whistler (FIG. 13-8), and ARTHUR DOVE (1880–1946; FIG. **14-17A** ⟋), generally considered America's first abstract painter. However, after 1913, American artists did not have to travel to Europe to become exposed to modernist art.

ARMORY SHOW The relative isolation of American artists from developments across the Atlantic came to an abrupt end on February 17, 1913, when the Armory Show opened in New York City (see "The Armory Show," page 391). Although later recognized as the foundational event in the development of American modernist art, the exhibition received a hostile response from the press. The work that the journalists most maligned was Marcel Duchamp's *Nude Descending a Staircase, No. 2* (FIG. **14-18**). The painting represents a single figure moving in a time continuum and suggests the effect of a sequence of overlaid film stills. Unlike Duchamp's Dadaist work (FIG. 14-15), *Nude Descending a Staircase* shares many characteristics with the work of the Cubists and the Futurists. The monochromatic palette is reminiscent of Analytic Cubism, as is Duchamp's faceted presentation of the human form. The artist's interest in depicting the figure in motion reveals an affinity to the Futurists' ideas. One critic described this work as "an explosion in a shingle factory,"[12] and newspaper cartoonists delighted in lampooning the painting.

AARON DOUGLAS The impact of European modernist art in America is evident in the work of African American artist AARON DOUGLAS (1898–1979), who adapted Synthetic Cubism to represent symbolically the historical and cultural memories of African Americans. Born in Kansas, Douglas spent time in Paris before settling in New York City, where he became a key figure in the Harlem Renaissance. The artists and writers who spearheaded this movement aimed to cultivate pride among fellow African Americans by creating art that celebrated the cultural history of their race. Douglas responded by incorporating motifs from African sculpture, broadly defined to include ancient Egyptian statues and reliefs,

1 in.

14-17 KAZIMIR MALEVICH, *Suprematist Composition: Airplane Flying,* 1915 (dated 1914). Oil on canvas, 1' 10$\frac{7}{8}$" × 1' 7". Museum of Modern Art, New York.

Malevich developed an abstract style that he called Suprematism to convey that the supreme reality in the world is pure feeling. Here, the brightly colored rectilinear shapes float against white space.

ART AND SOCIETY
The Armory Show

From February 17 to March 15, 1913, the American public flocked in large numbers to view the International Exhibition of Modern Art at the 69th Regiment Armory in New York City. The "Armory Show," as it universally came to be called, was an ambitious endeavor organized primarily by two artists, Walt Kuhn (1877–1949) and Arthur B. Davies (1862–1928). The show included more than 1,600 artworks by American and European artists. Among the European artists represented were Matisse, Derain, Kirchner, Kandinsky, Picasso, Braque, and Duchamp (FIG. 14-18). In addition to exposing American artists and the public to the latest European artistic developments, the Armory Show also provided American artists with a prime showcase for their work. The foreword to the exhibition catalogue spelled out the goals of the organizers:

> The American artists exhibiting here consider
> the exhibition of equal importance for them-
> selves as for the public. The less they find their
> work showing signs of the developments indi-
> cated in the Europeans, the more reason they
> will have to consider whether or not painters or
> sculptors here have fallen behind . . . the forces
> that have manifested themselves on the other
> side of the Atlantic.*

On its opening, this provocative exhibition served as a lightning rod for commentary, immediately attracting heated controversy. The *New York Times* described the show as "pathological" and called the modernist artists "cousins to the anarchists," while the magazine *Art and Progress* compared them to "bomb throwers, lunatics, depravers."[†] Other critics demanded that the exhibition be closed as a menace to public morality. The *New York Herald,* for example, asserted: "The United States is invaded by aliens, thousands of whom constitute so many perils to the health of the body politic. Modernism is of precisely the same hetero-geneous alien origin and is imperiling the republic of art in the same way."[‡]

Nonetheless, the exhibition was an important milestone in the history of art in the United States. The Armory Show traveled to Chicago and Boston after it closed in New York and was a significant catalyst for the reevaluation of the nature and purpose of American art.

1 ft.

14-18 MARCEL DUCHAMP, *Nude Descending a Staircase, No. 2,* 1912. Oil on canvas, 4' 10" × 2' 11". Philadelphia Museum of Art, Philadelphia (Louise and Walter Arensberg Collection).

The Armory Show introduced European modernist art to America. Duchamp's figure moving in a time continuum owes a debt to Cubism and Futurism. The press gave his painting a hostile reception.

*Quoted in Herschel B. Chipp, *Theories of Modern Art: A Source Book by Artists and Critics* (Berkeley and Los Angeles: University of California Press, 1968), 503.

[†]Quoted in Sam Hunter, John Jacobus, and Daniel Wheeler, *Modern Art,* rev. 3d. ed. (Upper Saddle River, N.J.: Prentice Hall, 2005), 250.

[‡]Quoted in Francis K. Pohl, *Framing America: A Social History of American Art,* 2d ed. (New York: Thames & Hudson, 2002), 341.

In *Noah's Ark* and other paintings of the cultural history of African Americans, Douglas incorporated motifs from African sculpture and the transparent angular planes characteristic of Synthetic Cubism.

into compositions painted in a version of Synthetic Cubism stressing transparent angular planes. *Noah's Ark* (FIG. 14-19) is one of seven paintings that Douglas based on a book of poems by James Weldon Johnson (1871–1938) called *God's Trombones: Seven Negro Sermons in Verse.* In *Noah's Ark,* Douglas used flat planes to evoke a sense of mystical space and miraculous happenings. Lightning strikes and rays of light crisscross the pairs of animals entering the ark, while men load supplies in preparation for departure. Douglas suggested deep space by differentiating the size of the large human head and shoulders of the worker at the bottom and the small person at work on the far deck of the ship. Yet the composition's unmodulated color shapes create a pattern that cancels any illusion of three-dimensional depth. Here, Douglas used Cubism's formal language to express a powerful religious vision.

GEORGIA O'KEEFFE In 1918, Wisconsin-born GEORGIA O'KEEFFE (1887–1986) moved from the tiny town of Canyon, Texas, to New York City, where she met Alfred Stieglitz (FIG. 14-20), who played a major role in promoting the avant-garde in the United States through "291," his gallery at 291 Fifth Avenue. (Also significant in championing modernist art in America was a remarkable group of wealthy women; see "Art 'Matronage' in the United States" 🔲.) Stieglitz had seen and exhibited some of O'Keeffe's work, and he drew her into his circle of avant-garde painters and photographers. He became one of O'Keeffe's staunchest supporters and, eventually, her husband. O'Keeffe is best known for her paintings of cow skulls and of flowers—for example, *Jack-in-the-Pulpit No. 4* (FIG. I-5), which reveals her interest in stripping subjects to their purest forms and colors to heighten their expressive power. In this work, O'Keeffe reduced the curved planes and contours of the flower to a symphony of basic colors, shapes, textures, and vital rhythms, simplifying the forms almost to the point of complete abstraction. The fluid planes unfold like undulant petals from a subtly placed axis—the white jetlike streak—in a vision of the slow, controlled motion of growing life. O'Keeffe's painting, in its graceful, quiet poetry, reveals the organic reality of the object by strengthening its characteristic features.

ALFRED STIEGLITZ As an artist, ALFRED STIEGLITZ (1864–1946) is best known for his photographs. Taking his camera everywhere he went, Stieglitz photographed whatever he saw around him, from the bustling streets of New York City to cloudscapes in upstate New York to the faces of friends and relatives. He believed in making only "straight, unmanipulated" photographs. Thus he exposed and printed them using basic photographic processes, without resorting to techniques such as double-exposure or double-printing that

14-20 ALFRED STIEGLITZ, *The Steerage,* 1907 (print 1915). Photogravure (on tissue), 1' $\frac{3}{8}$" × 10$\frac{1}{8}$". Amon Carter Museum, Fort Worth.

Stieglitz waged a lifelong campaign to win a place for photography among the fine arts. This 1907 image taken on an ocean liner captures human activity in terms of arrangements of lines and forms.

would add information absent in the subject when he released the shutter. Stieglitz said that he wanted the photographs he made with this direct technique "to hold a moment, to record something so completely that those who see it would relive an equivalent of what has been expressed."[13]

Stieglitz conducted a lifelong campaign to win a place for photography among the fine arts. He founded the Photo-Secession group, which mounted traveling exhibitions in the United States and sent loan collections abroad, and he also published an influential journal titled *Camera Work*. Stieglitz's own work is noteworthy for his insistence on seeing his subjects in terms of arrangements of lines and shapes and of the "colors" of his black-and-white materials. His aesthetic approach crystallized in *The Steerage* (FIG. 14-20), a photograph he took during a voyage to Europe with his first wife and daughter in 1907. Traveling first class, Stieglitz rapidly grew bored with the company of prosperous passengers. From his section of the ship, he could see the lower deck reserved for the steerage passengers whom the government sent back to Europe after refusing them entrance into the United States. Stieglitz described what he saw:

> The scene fascinated me: A round hat; the funnel leaning left, the stairway leaning right; the white drawbridge, its railing made of chain; white

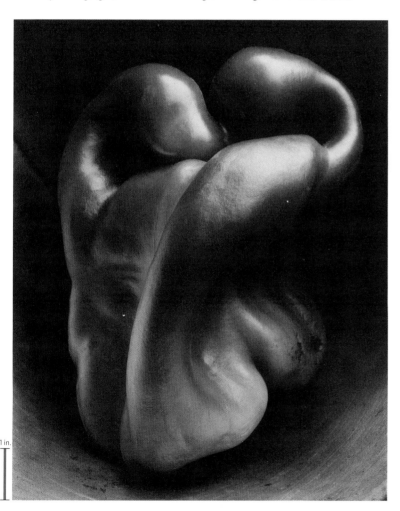

1 in.

14-21 EDWARD WESTON, *Pepper No. 30,* 1930. Gelatin silver print, $9\frac{1}{2}" \times 7\frac{1}{2}"$. Center for Creative Photography, University of Arizona, Tucson.

Weston "previsualized" his still lifes, choosing the exact angle, lighting, and framing that he desired. His vegetables often resemble human bodies, in this case a seated nude seen from behind.

suspenders crossed on the back of a man below; circular iron machinery; a mast that cut into the sky, completing a triangle. I stood spellbound. I saw shapes related to one another—a picture of shapes, and underlying it, a new vision that held me: simple people; the feeling of ship, ocean, sky; a sense of release that I was away from the mob called rich. . . . I had only one plate holder with one unexposed plate. Could I catch what I saw and felt? I released the shutter. If I had captured what I wanted, the photograph would go far beyond any of my previous prints. It would be a picture based on related shapes and deepest human feeling—a step in my own evolution, a spontaneous discovery.[14]

EDWARD WESTON Like Alfred Stieglitz, EDWARD WESTON (1886–1958) played a major role in establishing photography as an important artistic medium. But unlike Stieglitz, who worked outdoors and sought to capture transitory moments in his photographs, Weston meticulously composed his subjects in a controlled studio setting, whether he was doing still lifes of peppers, shells, and other natural forms of irregular shape, or figure studies. In the 1930 photograph of a pepper illustrated here (FIG. 14-21), the artificial lighting accentuates the undulating surfaces and crevices of the vegetable. Weston left nothing to chance, choosing the exact angle and play of light over the object, "previsualizing" the final photographic print before snapping the camera's shutter. Weston frequently chose peppers whose shapes reminded him of human bodies. *Pepper No. 30* looks like a seated nude figure seen from behind with raised arms emerging from broad shoulders. Viewers can read the vertical crease down the center of the vegetable as the spinal column leading to the buttocks. Although highly successful as a purely abstract composition of shapes and of light and dark, Weston's still life also conveys mystery and sensuality through its dramatic lighting and rich texture.

EUROPE, 1920 TO 1945

Because World War I was fought entirely in Europe, European artists experienced its devastating effects to a much greater degree than did American artists. The war had a profound impact on Europe's geopolitical terrain (MAP 14-1), on individual and national psyches, and on the art of the 1920s and 1930s.

Neue Sachlichkeit

In Germany, World War I gave rise to an artistic movement called *Neue Sachlichkeit* (New Objectivity). All of the artists associated with Neue Sachlichkeit served, at some point, in the German army. Their military experiences deeply influenced their worldviews and informed their art, which aimed to present an objective image of the world, especially the Great War and its effects.

MAX BECKMANN Because he believed that a better society would emerge from the war, MAX BECKMANN (1884–1950) enlisted in the German army, but over time the massive loss of life and widespread destruction disillusioned him. Soon his work began to emphasize the horrors of war and of a society that he regarded as descending into madness. Beckmann's disturbing view of wartime Germany is evident in

14-22 MAX BECKMANN, *Night*, 1918–1919. Oil on canvas, 4' 4 3/8" × 5' 1 1/4". Kunstsammlung Nordrhein-Westfalen, Düsseldorf.

Beckmann's treatment of forms and space in *Night* matched his view of the brutality of early-20th-century society. Objects seem dislocated and contorted, and the space appears buckled and illogical.

Night (FIG. **14-22**), which depicts a cramped room invaded by three intruders. A bound woman, apparently raped, is splayed across the foreground of the painting. At the left, one of the intruders hangs her husband, while another one twists his left arm out of its socket. An unidentified woman cowers in the background. On the far right, the third intruder prepares to flee with the child.

Although this image does not depict a war scene, the wrenching brutality pervading the home is a searing comment on society's condition. Beckmann also injected a personal reference by using himself, his wife, and his son as the models for the three family members. The stilted angularity of the figures and the roughness of the paint surface contribute to the image's savageness. In addition, the artist's treatment of forms and space reflects the world's violence. Objects are dislocated and contorted, and the space is buckled and illogical. For example, the woman's hands are bound to the window opening from the room's back wall, but her body appears to hang vertically, rather than lying across the plane of the intervening table.

Surrealism

The exuberantly aggressive momentum of the Dada movement that emerged during World War I lasted for only a short time. By 1924, with the publication in France of the *First Surrealist Manifesto*, most of the artists associated with Dada had joined the *Surrealism* movement, which had begun as a literary movement (see "André Breton's *First Surrealist Manifesto*," page 395). The Surrealists were determined to explore ways to express in art the world of dreams and the unconscious. Not surprisingly, the Surrealists incorporated many of the Dadaists' improvisational techniques. They believed that these methods were important for engaging the elements of fantasy and activating the unconscious forces deep within every human being. The Surrealists' dominant motivation was to bring the aspects of outer and inner "reality" together into a single position, in much the same way that life's seemingly unrelated fragments combine in the vivid world of dreams. Surrealism developed along two lines. In *Naturalistic Surrealism*, artists present recognizable scenes that seem to have metamorphosed into a dream or nightmare image. In *Biomorphic Surrealism*, artists produce largely abstract compositions, although the imagery sometimes suggests organisms or natural forms.

GIORGIO DE CHIRICO The widely recognized precursor of Surrealism was the Italian *Pittura Metafisica*, or Metaphysical Painting, movement led by GIORGIO DE CHIRICO (1888–1978). Returning to Italy after studying in Munich, de Chirico found hidden reality

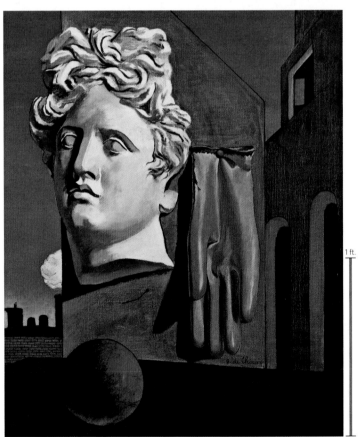

14-23 GIORGIO DE CHIRICO, *The Song of Love*, 1914. Oil on canvas, 2' 4 3/4" × 1' 11 3/8". Museum of Modern Art, New York (Nelson A. Rockefeller bequest).

De Chirico's Metaphysical Painting movement was a precursor of Surrealism. In this dreamlike scene set in a deserted square, a classical head of Apollo floats mysteriously next to a gigantic red glove.

WRITTEN SOURCES
André Breton's *First Surrealist Manifesto*

A poet, novelist, and critic rather than a visual artist, André Breton (1896–1966) nonetheless played a leading role in the formation of two of the 20th century's most important art movements: Dada and Surrealism. Although it was Guillaume Apollinaire who first proposed the term "Surrealism," the movement did not begin to take firm shape until 1924, when Breton published the *First Surrealist Manifesto* in the inaugural issue of *La revolution surréaliste*.

Some excerpts:

The mere word "freedom" is the only one that still excites me. . . . We are still living under the reign of logic . . . The absolute rationalism that is still in vogue allows us to consider only facts relating directly to our experience. . . . Under the pretense of civilization and progress, we have managed to banish from the mind everything that may rightly or wrongly be termed superstition, or fancy; forbidden is any kind of search for truth which is not in conformance with accepted practices. . . . [T]hanks to the discoveries of Sigmund Freud . . . [t]he imagination is perhaps on the point of reasserting itself, of reclaiming its rights. . . . Freud very rightly brought his critical faculties to bear upon the dream. . . . I have always been amazed at the way an ordinary observer lends so much more credence and attaches so much more importance to waking events than to those occurring in dreams. . . . I believe in the future resolution of these two states, dream and reality, which are seemingly so contradictory, into a kind of absolute reality, a "surreality," if one may so speak. It is in quest of this surreality that I am going. . . .

Surrealism . . . is [p]sychic automatism in its pure state, by which one proposes to express—verbally . . . or in any other manner—the actual function of thought. . . . Surrealism is based on the belief in the superior reality of certain forms of previously neglected associations, in the omnipotence of dream, in the disinterested play of thought. It tends to ruin once and for all all other psychic mechanisms and to substitute itself for them in solving all the principal problems of life.*

*Translated by Richard Seaver and Helen R. Lane, *André Breton: Manifestoes of Surrealism* (Ann Arbor: University of Michigan Press, 1969), 3–47.

1 in.

14-24 Salvador Dalí, *The Persistence of Memory*, 1931. Oil on canvas, $9\frac{1}{2}$" × 1' 1". Museum of Modern Art, New York.

Dalí painted "images of concrete irrationality." In this realistically rendered Surrealist landscape featuring three "decaying" watches, he created a haunting allegory of empty space where time has ended.

revealed through strange juxtapositions, such as those seen on late autumn afternoons in the city of Turin, when the long shadows of the setting sun transformed vast open squares and silent public monuments into what the painter called "metaphysical towns." De Chirico translated this vision into paint in works such as *The Song of Love* (FIG. 14-23), a dreamlike scene set in the deserted piazza of an Italian town. A huge marble head—a fragment of the famous *Apollo Belvedere* in the Vatican (not illustrated)—is suspended in midair above a green ball. To the right is a gigantic red glove nailed to a wall. The buildings and the three over-life-size objects cast shadows that direct the viewer's eye to the left and to a locomotive puffing smoke—a favorite Futurist motif, here shown in slow motion and incongruously placed near the central square. The choice of the term *metaphysical* to describe de Chirico's paintings suggests that these images transcend their physical appearances. *The Song of Love*, for all its clarity and simplicity, takes on a rather sinister air. The sense of strangeness that de Chirico could conjure with familiar objects and scenes recalls the observation of philosopher Friedrich Nietzsche (1844–1900) that "underneath this reality in which we live and have our being, another and altogether different reality lies concealed."[15]

SALVADOR DALÍ Spaniard Salvador Dalí (1904–1989) was the most famous Naturalistic Surrealist painter. As he described it, in his painting he aimed "to materialize the images of concrete irrationality with the most imperialistic fury of precision . . . in order that the world of imagination and of concrete irrationality may be as objectively evident . . . as that of the exterior world of phenomenal reality."[16] In *The Persistence of Memory* (FIG. 14-24), Dalí created a haunting allegory of empty space where time has ended. An eerie, never-setting sun illuminates the barren landscape. An amorphous creature draped with a limp pocket watch sleeps in the foreground. Another watch hangs from the branch of a dead tree springing unexpectedly from a blocky architectural form. A third watch hangs half

14-25 René Magritte, *The Treachery (or Perfidy) of Images*, 1928–1929. Oil on canvas, 1' 11⅝" × 3' 1". Los Angeles County Museum of Art, Los Angeles (purchased with funds provided by the Mr. and Mrs. William Preston Harrison Collection).

The discrepancy between Magritte's meticulously painted briar pipe and his caption, "This is not a pipe," challenges the viewer's reliance on the conscious and the rational in the reading of visual art.

over the edge of the rectangular form, beside a small timepiece resting dial-down on the block's surface. Ants swarm mysteriously over the small watch, while a fly walks along the face of its large neighbor, almost as if this assembly of watches were decaying organic life—soft and sticky. Dalí rendered every detail of this dreamscape with precise control, striving to make the world of his paintings convincingly real—in his words, to make the irrational concrete.

RENÉ MAGRITTE The Belgian painter René Magritte (1898–1967) moved to Paris in 1927 and joined the intellectual circle of André Breton. In 1929, Magritte published an important essay in the Surrealist journal *La revolution surréaliste* in which he discussed the disjunction between objects, pictures of objects, and names of objects and pictures. The essay explains the intellectual basis for *The Treachery (or Perfidy) of Images* (FIG. **14-25**), in which Magritte presented a meticulously rendered depiction of a briar pipe. The caption beneath the image, however, contradicts what seems obvious: "Ceci n'est pas une pipe" ("This is not a pipe"). The discrepancy between image and caption clearly challenges the assumptions underlying the reading of visual art. As is true of the other Surrealists' work, this painting wreaks havoc on the viewer's reliance on the conscious and the rational.

MERET OPPENHEIM Sculpture especially appealed to the Surrealists because its concrete tangibility made their art all the more disquieting. *Object* (FIG. **14-26**), also called *Le Déjeuner en Fourrure*

14-26 Meret Oppenheim, *Object* (*Le Déjeuner en Fourrure*), 1936. Fur-covered cup 4⅜" diameter, saucer 9⅜" diameter, spoon 8" long. Museum of Modern Art, New York.

The Surrealists loved the concrete tangibility of sculpture, which made their art even more disquieting. Oppenheim's fur-covered manufactured object captures the Surrealist flair for magical transformation.

(*Luncheon in Fur*), by Swiss artist Meret Oppenheim (1913–1985) captures the incongruity, humor, visual appeal, and, often, eroticism characterizing Surrealism. The artist presented a fur-lined teacup inspired by a conversation with Picasso. After admiring a bracelet that Oppenheim had made from a piece of brass covered with fur, Picasso noted that anything might be covered with fur. When her tea grew cold, Oppenheim responded to Picasso's comment by ordering "un peu plus de fourrure" (a little more fur), and the sculpture had its genesis. *Object* takes on an anthropomorphic quality, animated by the quirky combination of the animal fur with a manufactured object. Further, the sculpture captures the Surrealist flair for alchemical, seemingly magical or mystical, transformation. It incorporates a sensuality and eroticism (seen here in the seductively soft, tactile fur lining the concave form) that are also components of much of Surrealist art.

JOAN MIRÓ Like the Dadaists, the Surrealists used many methods to free the creative process from reliance on the kind of conscious control that they believed society had shaped too much. The Spanish artist Joan Miró (1893–1983) used *automatism*—the creation of art without conscious control—and various types of planned "accidents" to provoke reactions closely related to subconscious experience. Although Miró resisted formal association with any movement or group, including the Surrealists, Breton identified him as "the most Surrealist of us all."[17] From the beginning, Miró's work contained an element of fantasy and hallucination. After Surrealist poets in Paris introduced him to the use of chance in the creation of art, Miró devised a new painting method that enabled him to create works such as *Painting* (FIG. **14-27**). He began *Painting* by making random doodles. The abstract curvilinear forms became motifs that the artist freely reshaped on the canvas to create black silhouettes—solid or in outline, with dramatic accents of white and vermilion. They suggest a host of amoebic organisms or constellations in outer space floating in an immaterial background space filled with soft reds, blues, and greens.

Miró described his creative process as a switching back and forth between unconscious and conscious image-making: "Rather than setting out to paint something, I begin painting and as I paint the picture begins to assert itself, or suggest itself under my brush. The form becomes a sign for a woman or a bird as I work. . . . The first

14-27 JOAN MIRÓ, *Painting*, 1933. 5' 8" × 6' 5". Museum of Modern Art, New York (Loula D. Lasker Bequest by exchange).

Miró promoted automatism, the creation of art without conscious control. He began this painting with random doodles and completed the composition with forms suggesting floating amoebic organisms.

stage is free, unconscious. . . . The second stage is carefully calculated."[18] Even the artist could not always explain the meanings of pictures such as *Painting*. They are, in the truest sense, spontaneous and intuitive expressions of the little-understood, submerged unconscious part of life.

WIFREDO LAM Loosely associated with the Surrealists was WIFREDO LAM (1902–1982), an artist whose work is as distinctive as his background. Cuban by birth, Lam was the son of a Chinese immigrant father and a mother of Cuban-African descent. He studied painting in Havana and later in Madrid, where he fought alongside the Republicans in the Spanish Civil War. That endeared Lam to Picasso, whom he met in Paris in 1938. Picasso introduced Lam to Braque and Breton and many other avant-garde artists and critics, and Lam's mature work, although the distinctive by-product of his Caribbean-African heritage, shows the influence of both Cubism and Surrealism.

The Jungle (FIG. 14-28) is generally considered Lam's greatest work. The complex, crowded composition indeed suggests a dense jungle, populated by Surrealistic creatures whose fragmented forms recall Cubism. Inspired also by Santería, the Cuban religion that is a blend of African ritual and European Catholicism, *The Jungle* depicts four hybrid figures with long legs, prominent buttocks, and heads resembling African masks in a tropical jungle of sugarcane and tobacco plants. Two of Lam's composite figures have a horse's tail. The figure at the right holds a scissors—as if she, not the artist, is the one responsible for dismembering

14-28 WIFREDO LAM, *The Jungle*, 1943. Gouache on paper mounted on canvas, 7' 10¼" × 7' 6½". Museum of Modern Art, New York (Inter-American Fund).

In Lam's tropical jungle stand four composite creatures with long legs, prominent buttocks, and faces resembling African masks. The painting draws on Cubism, Surrealism, and Cuban religious ritual.

herself and her companions. In many ways, *The Jungle* is a bridge between Cubism, Surrealism, and the nonrepresentational canvases of the New York School Abstract Expressionists of the 1940s and 1950s (see pages 413–416).

De Stijl

The utopian spirit and ideals of the Suprematists (FIG. 14-17) in Russia were shared by a group of young Dutch artists. They formed a new movement in 1917 called *De Stijl* (The Style). The name reflected confidence that this style—*the* style—revealed the underlying eternal structure of existence. Accordingly, De Stijl artists reduced their formal vocabulary to simple geometric elements.

PIET MONDRIAN The cofounders of De Stijl were the painters Piet Mondrian (FIG. 14-29) and Theo van Doesburg (1883–1931). Their goal, according to van Doesburg and architect Cor van Eesteren (1897–1988), was a total integration of art and life:

> We must realize that life and art are no longer separate domains. That is why the "idea" of "art" as an illusion separate from real life must disappear. The word "Art" no longer means anything to us. In its place we demand the construction of our environment in accordance with creative laws based upon a fixed principle. These laws, following those of economics, mathematics, technique, sanitation, etc., are leading to a new, plastic unity.[19]

14-29 PIET MONDRIAN, *Composition with Red, Blue, and Yellow,* 1930. Oil on canvas, 1' 6⅛" × 1' 6⅛". Kunsthaus, Zurich. © Mondrian/ Holtzman Trust c/o HCR International USA.

Mondrian's "pure plastic" paintings consist of primary colors locked into a grid of intersecting vertical and horizontal lines. By altering the grid patterns, he created a "dynamic equilibrium."

Time spent in Paris before World War I introduced Mondrian to Cubism. However, as his attraction to contemporary theological writings grew, Mondrian sought to purge his art of every overt reference to individual objects in the external world. He formulated a conception of nonobjective design—"pure plastic art"—that he believed expressed universal reality:

> Art is higher than reality and has no direct relation to reality. . . . To approach the spiritual in art, one will make as little use as possible of reality, because reality is opposed to the spiritual. . . . [W]e find ourselves in the presence of an abstract art. Art should be above reality, otherwise it would have no value for man.[20]

To achieve "pure plastic art," or *Neoplasticism,* as Mondrian called it, he eventually limited his formal vocabulary to the three primary colors (red, blue, and yellow), the three primary values (black, white, and gray), and the two primary directions (horizontal and vertical). He believed that primary colors and values were the purest colors and therefore the perfect tools to help an artist construct a harmonious composition. Mondrian created numerous paintings locking color planes into a grid of intersecting vertical and horizontal lines, as in *Composition with Red, Blue, and Yellow* (FIG. 14-29). In each of these paintings, he altered the grid patterns and the size and placement of the color planes to create an internal cohesion and harmony. This did not mean inertia. Rather, Mondrian worked to maintain what he called a "dynamic equilibrium" in his paintings through the size and position of lines, shapes, and colors.

Sculpture

During the second quarter of the 20th century, European sculptors also explored avant-garde ideas in their work, especially abstraction.

CONSTANTIN BRANCUSI In his sculptures, Romanian artist CONSTANTIN BRANCUSI (1876–1957) sought to move beyond surface appearances to capture the essence or spirit of the object depicted. He asserted: "What is real is not the external form but the essence of things. Starting from this truth it is impossible for anyone to express anything essentially real by imitating its exterior surface."[21] Brancusi's ability to design rhythmic, elegant sculptures conveying the essence of his subjects is evident in *Bird in Space* (FIG. 14-30). Clearly not a literal depiction of a bird, the abstract form of the work is the final result of a long process. Brancusi started with the image of a bird at rest with its wings folded at its sides, and ended with a gently curving columnar form sharply tapered at each end. Despite the abstraction, the sculpture retains the suggestion of a bird about to soar in free flight through the heavens. The highly reflective surface of the polished bronze does not allow the viewer's eye to linger on the sculpture itself. Instead, the eye follows the gleaming reflection along the delicate curves right off the tip of the work, thereby inducing a feeling of flight.

The British sculptor HENRY MOORE (1898–1986; FIG. 14-30A ⬈) summed up Brancusi's contribution to the history of sculpture as follows: "Since the Gothic, European sculpture had become overgrown with moss, weeds—all sorts of surface excrescences which completely concealed shape. It has been Brancusi's special mission to get rid of this overgrowth, and to make us once more shape-conscious. To do this he has had to concentrate on very simple direct shapes. . . . Abstract qualities of design are essential to the value of a work."[22]

14-30 Constantin Brancusi, *Bird in Space,* 1924. Bronze, 4' 2 $\frac{5}{16}$" high. Philadelphia Museum of Art, Philadelphia (Louise and Walter Arensberg Collection, 1950).

Although not a literal depiction of a bird, Brancusi's softly curving, light-reflecting abstract sculpture in polished bronze suggests a bird about to soar in free flight through the heavens.

1 ft.

1 in.

14-31 Barbara Hepworth, *Oval Sculpture* (*No. 2*), 1943. Plaster cast, 11 $\frac{1}{4}$" × 1' 4 $\frac{1}{4}$" × 10". Tate, London.

Hepworth's major contribution to the history of sculpture was the introduction of the hole, or void, as an abstract element that is as integral and important to the sculpture as its mass.

in four places, the work is as much defined by the smooth, curving holes as by the volume of white plaster. Like the forms in all of Hepworth's mature works, those in *Oval Sculpture* are basic and universal, expressing a sense of timelessness.

UNITED STATES AND MEXICO, 1930 TO 1945

In the years leading up to and during World War II, many European artists emigrated to the United States. Their collective presence in America was critical for the development of American art in the decades following the 1913 Armory Show. Yet few of the leading American artists of this period pursued abstraction, either in painting or sculpture.

Sculpture and Photography

ALEXANDER CALDER One exception was Alexander Calder (1898–1976), who rose to international prominence because of his contributions to the development of abstract art. The son and grandson of sculptors, Calder initially studied mechanical engineering. Fascinated all his life by motion, he explored movement in relationship to three-dimensional form in much of his work. As a young artist in Paris in the late 1920s, Calder invented a circus full of wire-based miniature performers that mimicked the motion of their real-life counterparts. After a visit to Piet Mondrian's studio in the early 1930s, Calder set out to put the Dutch painter's brightly colored rectangular shapes (FIG. 14-29) into motion. (Marcel Duchamp, intrigued by Calder's early motorized and hand-cranked examples of moving abstract pieces, named them *mobiles*.) Calder soon used his engineering skills to fashion a series of balanced structures hanging from rods, wires, and colored, organically shaped plates. This new kind of sculpture, which combined nonobjective organic

BARBARA HEPWORTH Another leading British artist of this era was Barbara Hepworth (1903–1975), who developed her personal kind of essential sculptural form, combining pristine shape with a sense of organic vitality. She sought a sculptural idiom that would express her sense both of nature and the landscape and of the person who is in and observes nature. By 1929, Hepworth arrived at a breakthrough that evolved into an enduring and commanding element in her work from that point on. It represents her major contribution to the history of sculpture: the use of the hole, or void. In Hepworth's sculptures, holes are abstract elements. They do not represent anything specific, but they are as integral and important as the masses. *Oval Sculpture* (*No. 2*) is a plaster cast (FIG. 14-31) of an earlier wood sculpture that Hepworth carved in 1943. Pierced

14-32 ALEXANDER CALDER, *Lobster Trap and Fish Tail*, 1939. Painted sheet aluminum and steel wire, 8' 6" × 9' 6". Museum of Modern Art, New York.

Using his thorough knowledge of engineering to combine nonobjective organic forms and motion, Calder created a new kind of sculpture—the mobile—that expressed reality's innate dynamism.

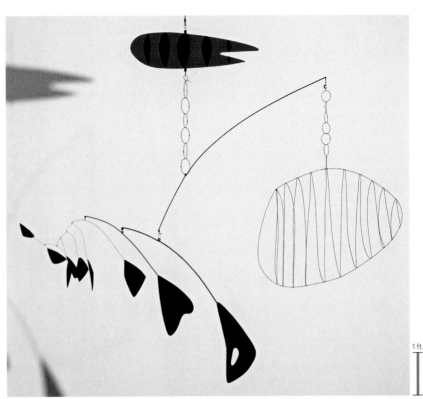

forms and motion, succeeded in expressing the innate dynamism of the natural world.

An early Calder mobile is *Lobster Trap and Fish Tail* (FIG. 14-32). The artist carefully planned each mobile so that any air current would set the parts moving to create a constantly shifting dance in space. Mondrian's work may have provided the initial inspiration for the mobiles, but their organic shapes resemble those in Joan Miró's Surrealist paintings (FIG. 14-27). Indeed, viewers can read Calder's forms as either geometric or organic. Geometrically, the lines suggest circuitry and rigging, and the shapes derive from circles and ovoid forms. Organically, the lines suggest nerve axons, and the shapes resemble cells, leaves, fins, wings, and other bioforms.

GREAT DEPRESSION The catastrophic stock market crash of October 1929 marked the onset of the Great Depression, which dramatically changed the nation, and artists were among the millions of economic victims. The limited art market virtually disappeared, and museums curtailed both their purchases and exhibition schedules. Many artists sought financial support from the federal government, which established numerous programs to provide relief, assist recovery, and promote reform. Among the programs supporting artists were the Treasury Relief Art Project, founded in 1934 to commission art for federal buildings, and the Works Progress Administration (WPA), founded in 1935 to relieve widespread unemployment. Under the WPA, the government paid artists, writers, and theater people a regular wage in exchange for work in their professions. Another important program was the Resettlement Administration (RA), which oversaw emergency aid programs for farm families.

DOROTHEA LANGE The RA hired American photographer DOROTHEA LANGE (1895–1965) in 1935 and dispatched her to document the deplorable living conditions of the rural poor. At the end of an assignment photographing migratory pea pickers in California, Lange stopped at a camp in Nipomo and found the workers there starving because the crops had frozen in the fields. Among the pictures Lange made on this occasion was *Migrant Mother, Nipomo Valley* (FIG. 14-33), in which she captured the mixture of strength and worry in the raised hand and careworn face of a mother, who holds a baby on her lap. Two older children cling to their mother trustfully while turning their faces away from the camera. Within days after Lange's moving photograph appeared in a San Francisco newspaper, people rushed food to Nipomo to feed the hungry workers.

MARGARET BOURKE-WHITE Almost 10 years younger than Dorothea Lange, MARGARET BOURKE-WHITE (1904–1971) also made her reputation as a photojournalist in Depression-era America. She was the first staff photographer that Henry Luce (1898–1967) hired to furnish illustrations for the magazines in his publishing empire. Beginning in 1929, Bourke-White worked for *Fortune*, then for *Life*

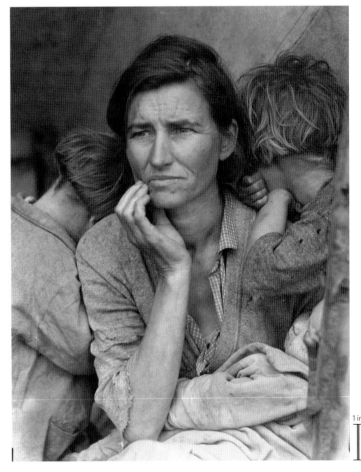

14-33 DOROTHEA LANGE, *Migrant Mother, Nipomo Valley*, 1935. Gelatin silver print, 1' 1" × 9". Oakland Museum of California, Oakland (gift of Paul S. Taylor).

While documenting the lives of migratory farm workers during the Depression, Lange made this unforgettable photograph of a mother in which she captured the woman's strength and worry.

14-34 MARGARET BOURKE-WHITE, *Fort Peck Dam, Montana,* 1936. Gelatin silver print, 1' 1" × 10½". Metropolitan Museum of Art, New York (gift of Ford Motor Company and John C. Waddell, 1987).

Bourke-White's dramatic photograph of Fort Peck Dam graced the cover of the first issue of *Life* magazine and celebrated the achievements of American engineering during the depths of the Great Depression.

when Luce launched the famous newsweekly in 1936. Her most memorable photographs for Luce were not of people or events but of the triumphs of 20th-century engineering, which instilled pride in an American public severely lacking in confidence during the

Depression. For example, Bourke-White photographed the Chrysler Building (FIG. 14-41A ▣) while it was under construction in New York, attracting media attention for her daring balancing act on steel girders high above the pavement. Her photograph *Fort Peck Dam, Montana* (FIG. 14-34) appeared on the cover of the first issue of *Life* (November 23, 1936). Fort Peck Dam was at the time the largest earth-filled dam in the world. Bourke-White photographed the still unfinished dam before the installation of the elevated highway at its summit. (The supports of that highway fortuitously conjure the image of a crenellated medieval fortress.) She chose a sharp angle from below to communicate the dam's soaring height, underscoring the immense scale by including two dwarfed figures of men in the foreground. The tight framing, which shuts out all of the landscape and much of the sky, transforms the dam into an almost abstract composition, a kind of still life, like Edward Weston's peppers (FIG. 14-21).

Painting

Although many European modernist artists emigrated to the United States during the 1930s and 1940s, the leading American painters of this period were figural artists with little interest in abstraction.

EDWARD HOPPER Trained as a commercial artist, EDWARD HOPPER (1882–1967) studied painting and printmaking in New York and then in Paris. When he returned to the United States, he concentrated on scenes of contemporary American life. His paintings depict buildings, streets, and landscapes that are curiously muted, still, and filled with empty spaces, evoking the national mindset during the Depression era. Hopper did not paint historically specific scenes. He took as his subject the more generalized theme of the overwhelming loneliness and echoing isolation of modern life in the United States. In his paintings, motion is stopped and time suspended.

From the darkened streets outside a restaurant in Hopper's *Nighthawks* (FIG. 14-35), the viewer glimpses the lighted interior through huge windows, which lend the inner space the paradoxical sense of being both a safe refuge and a vulnerable place for the three

14-35 EDWARD HOPPER, *Nighthawks,* 1942. Oil on canvas, 2' 6" × 4' 8¾". Art Institute of Chicago, Chicago (Friends of American Art Collection).

The seeming indifference of Hopper's characters to one another, and the echoing spaces that surround them, evoke the overwhelming loneliness and isolation of Depression-era life in the United States.

Jacob Lawrence's
Migration of the Negro

Disillusioned with their lives in the South, hundreds of thousands of African Americans migrated north in the years following World War I, seeking improved economic opportunities and a more hospitable political and social environment. But the conditions that African Americans encountered both during their migration and in the North were often as difficult and discriminatory as those they had left behind in the South, as the artist Jacob Lawrence knew from his own experience.

> I was part of the migration, as was my family, my mother, my sister, and my brother. . . . I grew up hearing tales about people "coming up," another family arriving. . . . I didn't realize what was happening until about the middle of the 1930s, and that's when the *Migration* series began to take form in my mind.*

Lawrence sought funding for his project from the Julius Rosenwald Fund. In his successful fellowship application, Lawrence argued that his proposal was of high educational value. He stated:

> It is important as a part of the evolution of America, since this Migration has affected the whole of America mentally, economically and socially. Since it has had this effect, I feel that my project would lay before the Negroes themselves a little of what part they have played in the History of the United States. In addition the whole of America might learn some of the history of this particular minority group, of which they know very little.†

His plan was to depict the history of the great African American migration northward in eight sections: Causes of the Migration; Stimulation of the Migration; The Spread of the Migration; The Efforts to Check the Migration; Public Opinion Regarding the Migration; The Effects of the Migration on the South; The Effects of the Migration on Various Parts of the North; and The Effects of the Migration on the Negro. The resulting series consists of 60 panels, all with explanatory captions—for example, "They did not always leave because they were promised work in the North. Many of them left because of Southern conditions, one of them being great floods that ruined the crops, and therefore they were unable to make a living where they were" (*No. 8*) and "They also found discrimination in the North although it was much different from that which they had known in the South" (*No. 49*; FIG. 14-36).

14-36 JACOB LAWRENCE, *No. 49 from The Migration of the Negro*, 1940–1941. Tempera on Masonite, 1' 6" × 1'. Phillips Collection, Washington, D.C.

The 49th in a series of 60 paintings documenting African American life in the North, Lawrence's depiction of a segregated dining room underscored that the migrants had not left discrimination behind.

*Quoted in Henry Louis Gates Jr., "New Negroes, Migration, and Cultural Exchange," in Elizabeth Hutton Turner, ed., *Jacob Lawrence: The Migration Series* (Washington, D.C.: Phillips Collection, 1993), 20.
†Quoted in Patricia Hills, *Painting Harlem Modern: The Art of Jacob Lawrence* (Berkeley and Los Angeles: University of California Press, 2009), 98.

customers and the man behind the counter. The seeming indifference of Hopper's characters to one another as well as the echoing spaces surrounding them evoke the pervasive loneliness of modern humans. *Nighthawks* recalls the work of 19th-century Realist painters, but in keeping with more recent trends in painting, Hopper simplified the shapes in a move toward abstraction.

JACOB LAWRENCE African American artist Jacob Lawrence (1917–2000) moved to Harlem, New York, in 1927 while still a boy. There, he came under the spell of the African art and the African American history he found in lectures and exhibitions and in the special programs sponsored by the 135th Street branch of the New York Public Library. The everyday life of Harlem and African American history became the subjects of Lawrence's paintings. In 1941, he began a series titled *The Migration of the Negro,* in which he defined his vision of the continuing African American struggle against discrimination (see "Jacob Lawrence's *Migration of the Negro,*" page 402).

Lawrence's *Migration* paintings provide numerous vignettes capturing the experiences of the African Americans who had moved to the North. Often, a sense of the bleakness and degradation of their new life dominates the images. In *No. 49* (FIG. **14-36**), which tells of the unexpected and different kind of discrimination that African Americans encountered in the North, Lawrence depicted a blatantly segregated dining room with a barrier running down the room's center separating the whites on the left from the African Americans on the right. To ensure a continuity and visual integrity among all 60 paintings, Lawrence interpreted his themes systematically in rhythmic arrangements of bold, flat, and strongly colored shapes. His style drew equally from his interest in the push-pull effects of Cubist space and his memories of the patterns made by the colored scatter rugs brightening the floors of his childhood homes. He unified the narrative with a consistent palette of bluish green, orange, yellow, and grayish brown throughout the entire series.

GRANT WOOD A very different picture of life in America appears in the paintings of Grant Wood (1891–1942), the leading figure in a Midwestern art movement known as *Regionalism,* which focused on American subjects, in opposition to the modernist abstraction of Europe and New York. The Regionalists chronicled rural life, which they believed was America's cultural backbone. Wood's paintings focus on the people of Iowa, where he was born and raised. The work that catapulted Wood to national prominence was *American Gothic* (FIG. **14-37**). The artist depicted his dentist and his sister posing as a farmer and his spinster daughter standing in front of a neat house with a small lancet window, a motif associated with Gothic churches and religious piety. The man and woman wear traditional attire. He appears in worn overalls and she in an apron trimmed with rickrack. The dour expression on both faces gives the

painting a severe quality, which Wood enhanced with his meticulous brushwork. The public immediately embraced *American Gothic* as embodying qualities that represented the true spirit of America, and the painting became an American icon.

DIEGO RIVERA During the period between the two world wars, several Mexican painters achieved international renown for their work both in Mexico and the United States. The eldest was José Clemente Orozco (1883–1949; FIG. **14-37A** ⏎), but the most famous is Diego Rivera (1886–1957). Orozco and Rivera were determined to base their art on the culture of their homeland. The movement that these artists formed was part of the idealistic rethinking of society that occurred in conjunction with the Mexican Revolution (1910–1920) and the lingering political turmoil of the 1920s. Among the projects these politically motivated artists undertook were vast mural cycles placed in public buildings to dramatize and validate the history of Mexico's native peoples. A staunch Marxist, Rivera strove to develop an art that served his people's needs. Toward that end, he sought to create a national Mexican style incorporating a popular, generally accessible aesthetic in keeping with the socialist spirit of the Mexican Revolution.

Perhaps Rivera's finest mural cycle is the one lining the staircase of the National Palace in Mexico City. In these images, painted

14-37 Grant Wood, *American Gothic,* 1930. Oil on beaverboard, 2' 5 $\frac{7}{8}$" × 2' $\frac{7}{8}$". Art Institute of Chicago, Chicago (Friends of American Art Collection).

In reaction to modernist abstract painting, the Midwestern Regionalism movement focused on American subjects. Wood's painting of an Iowa farmer and his daughter became an American icon.

1 ft.

14-38 DIEGO RIVERA, *Ancient Mexico,* detail of *History of Mexico,* fresco in the Palacio Nacional, Mexico City, 1929–1935.

A staunch Marxist, Rivera painted vast mural cycles in public buildings to dramatize the history of his native land. This fresco depicts the conflicts between indigenous Mexicans and Spanish colonizers.

between 1929 and 1935, he depicted scenes from Mexico's history, of which *Ancient Mexico* (FIG. 14-38) is one. This section of the mural represents the conflicts between the indigenous people and the Spanish colonizers. Rivera included portraits of important figures in Mexican history, especially those involved in the struggle for Mexican independence. Although the composition is complex, the simple monumental shapes and areas of bold color make the story easy to read.

FRIDA KAHLO Born to a Mexican mother and German father, the painter FRIDA KAHLO (1907–1954), who married Diego Rivera, used the details of her life as powerful symbols for the psychological pain of human existence. Art historians often consider Kahlo a Surrealist due to the psychic, autobiographical issues she dealt with in her art. Indeed, André Breton described her as a Naturalistic Surrealist. Kahlo herself, however, rejected any association with the Surrealists. She began painting seriously as a young student, during convalescence from an accident that tragically left her in constant

pain. Her life became a heroic and tumultuous battle for survival against illness and stormy personal relationships.

Typical of her long series of unflinching self-portraits is *The Two Fridas* (FIG. 14-39). The twin figures sit side by side on a low bench in a barren landscape under a stormy sky. The figures suggest different sides of the artist's personality, inextricably linked by the clasped hands and by the thin artery stretching between them, joining their exposed hearts. The artery ends on one side in surgical forceps and on the other in a miniature portrait of her husband as a child. Kahlo's deeply personal paintings touch sensual and psychological memories in her audience.

To read Kahlo's paintings solely as autobiographical overlooks the powerful political dimension of her art. Kahlo was deeply nationalistic and committed to her Mexican heritage. Politically active, she joined the Communist Party in 1920 and participated in public political protests. *The Two Fridas* incorporates Kahlo's commentary on the struggle facing Mexicans in the early 20th century in defining their national cultural identity. The Frida on the right

14-39 FRIDA KAHLO, *The Two Fridas,* 1939. Oil on canvas, 5' 7" × 5' 7". Museo de Arte Moderno, Mexico City.

Kahlo's deeply personal paintings touch sensual and psychological memories in her audience. Here, twin self-portraits linked by clasped hands and a common artery suggest two sides of her personality.

(representing indigenous culture) appears in a Tehuana dress, the traditional costume of Zapotec women from the Isthmus of Tehuantepec, whereas the Frida on the left (representing imperialist forces) wears a European-style white lace dress. The heart, depicted here in such dramatic fashion, was an important symbol in the art of the Aztecs, whom Mexican nationalists idealized as the last independent rulers of their land. Thus *The Two Fridas* represents both Kahlo's personal struggles and the struggles of her homeland.

ARCHITECTURE

The first half of the 20th century was a time of great innovation in architecture too. As in painting, sculpture, and photography, new ideas came from both sides of the Atlantic.

WALTER GROPIUS The De Stijl group developed an appealing simplified geometric style in architecture as well as painting, and promoted the notion that art should be thoroughly incorporated into living environments. In Germany, WALTER GROPIUS (1883–1969) developed the concept of "total architecture" at a school called the *Bauhaus.* In 1919, he became the director of the Weimar School

of Arts and Crafts, founded in 1906. Under Gropius, the school assumed a new name—Das Staatliche Bauhaus (State School of Building). Gropius's goal was to train artists, architects, and designers to accept and anticipate 20th-century needs. He staunchly advocated the importance of strong basic design and craftsmanship as fundamental to good art and architecture, and promoted the unity of art, architecture, and design. Further, Gropius emphasized the need for thorough knowledge of machine-age technologies and materials. To encourage the elimination of the boundaries that traditionally separated art from architecture and art from craft, Gropius developed a curriculum for the Bauhaus that included courses in a wide range of artistic disciplines: weaving, pottery, bookbinding, carpentry, metalwork, stained glass, mural painting, stage design, advertising, and typography, in addition to architecture, painting, and sculpture. Ultimately, Gropius hoped to achieve a marriage between art and industry—a synthesis of design and production. Like the De Stijl movement, the Bauhaus philosophy had its roots in utopian principles. Gropius declared: "Let us collectively desire, conceive, and create the new building of the future, which will be everything in one structure: architecture and sculpture and painting, which, from the million hands of draftsmen, will one day

Gropius constructed this Bauhaus building by sheathing a reinforced concrete skeleton in glass. The design followed his dictum that architecture should avoid "all romantic embellishment and whimsy."

rise towards heaven as the crystalline symbol of a new and coming faith."[23] In its reference to a unity of workers, this statement also reveals the undercurrent of socialism in Germany at the time.

BAUHAUS IN DESSAU After encountering increasing hostility from a new government elected in 1924, the Bauhaus moved north to Dessau in early 1925. By this time, the Bauhaus program had matured. In a statement, Gropius listed the school's goals:

- A decidedly positive attitude to the living environment of vehicles and machines.
- The organic shaping of things in accordance with their own current laws, avoiding all romantic embellishment and whimsy.
- Restriction of basic forms and colors to what is typical and universally intelligible.
- Simplicity in complexity, economy in the use of space, materials, time, and money.[24]

The building that Gropius designed for the Dessau Bauhaus was the school's architectural manifesto. The Dessau complex consisted of workshop and class areas, a dining room, a theater, a gymnasium, a wing with studio apartments, and an enclosed two-story bridge housing administrative offices. Of the major wings, the most dramatic was the Shop Block (FIG. 14-40). Three stories tall, the Shop Block housed a printing shop and dye works facility, in addition to other work areas. The builders constructed the skeleton of reinforced concrete but set these supports well back, sheathing the entire structure in glass, creating a streamlined and light effect. This design's simplicity followed Gropius's dictum that architecture should avoid "all romantic embellishment and whimsy." Further, he realized his principle of "economy in the use of space" in his interior layout of the Shop Block, which consisted of large areas of free-flowing undivided space. Gropius believed that this kind of spatial organization encouraged interaction and the sharing of ideas.

LUDWIG MIES VAN DER ROHE In 1928, Gropius left the Bauhaus, and LUDWIG MIES VAN DER ROHE (1886–1969) eventually took over the directorship, moving the school to Berlin in 1932. Taking as his motto "less is more" and calling his architecture "skin and bones," the new Bauhaus director had already fully formed his aesthetic when he conceived the model (FIG. 14-41) for a glass skyscraper building in 1921. Three irregularly shaped towers flow outward from a central court designed to hold a lobby, a porter's room, and a community center. Two cylindrical entrance shafts rise at the ends of the court, each containing elevators, stairways, and toilets. Wholly transparent, the perimeter walls reveal the regular horizontal patterning of the cantilevered floor planes and their thin vertical supporting elements. The bold use of glass sheathing and inset supports was, at the time, technically and aesthetically adventurous. The weblike delicacy of the lines of the model, as well as the illusion of movement created by reflection and by light changes seen through the glass, prefigured the design of many of the glass-and-steel skyscrapers found in major cities throughout the world today.

END OF THE BAUHAUS One of the first actions that Adolf Hitler (1889–1945) took after coming to power was to close the Bauhaus in 1933. The Nazis suspected that the school housed a press that printed antigovernment brochures. During its 14-year existence, the Bauhaus graduated fewer than 500 students, yet it achieved legendary status. Its phenomenal influence extended beyond architecture, painting, and sculpture to interior design, graphic design, and advertising. Moreover, art schools everywhere began to structure their curricula in line with the program that the Bauhaus pioneered.

14-41 LUDWIG MIES VAN DER ROHE, model for a glass skyscraper, Berlin, Germany, 1922 (no longer extant).

In this technically and aesthetically adventurous design, the architect whose motto was "less is more" proposed a transparent building that revealed its cantilevered floor planes and thin supports.

The numerous Bauhaus instructors who fled Nazi Germany spread the school's philosophy and aesthetic widely. Many, including Gropius and Mies van der Rohe, settled in the United States.

LE CORBUSIER The simple geometric aesthetic developed by Gropius and Mies van der Rohe became known as the *International Style* because of its widespread popularity, although a highly decorative style, *Art Deco,* also had many proponents, both in Europe and America—for example, WILLIAM VAN ALEN (1882–1954), who designed the Chrysler Building (FIG. 14-41A ⬈) in New York City. The first and purest champion of the International Style was the Swiss architect Charles-Edouard Jeanneret, who took the name LE CORBUSIER (1887–1965). An influential theorist (see page 385) as well as practitioner, Le Corbusier sought to design a functional living space, which he described as a "machine for living."

Le Corbusier's Villa Savoye (FIG. 14-42) at Poissy-sur-Seine near Paris is a cube of lightly enclosed and deeply penetrated space with only a partially confined ground floor (containing a three-car garage, bedrooms, a bathroom, and utility rooms). Much of the house's interior is open space, with thin columns supporting the main living floor and roof garden area. The major living rooms in the Villa Savoye are on the second floor, wrapping around an open central court. Strip windows running along the membranelike exterior walls provide illumination to the rooms as well as views out to nature. From the second-floor court, a ramp leads up to the roof-terrace and an interior garden protected by a curving windbreak along the north side. The building has no traditional facade. The ostensible approach to the house does not define an entrance. Visitors must walk around and through the house to comprehend its layout, which incorporates spiral staircases and several changes of

14-42 LE CORBUSIER, Villa Savoye (looking southeast), Poissy-sur-Seine, France, 1929.

Steel and ferroconcrete made it possible for Le Corbusier to invert the traditional practice of placing light architectural elements above heavy ones and to eliminate weight-bearing walls on the ground story.

14-43 FRANK LLOYD WRIGHT, Kaufmann House (Fallingwater; looking northeast), Bear Run, Pennsylvania, 1936–1939.

Perched on a rocky hillside over a waterfall, Wright's Fallingwater has long, sweeping lines, unconfined by abrupt wall limits, that reach out and capture the expansiveness of the natural environment.

direction. Spaces and masses interpenetrate so fluidly that inside and outside space intermingle. In the Villa Savoye, Le Corbusier inverted traditional design practice by placing heavy elements above and light ones below, and by refusing to enclose the ground story of the Villa Savoye with masonry walls. This openness, made possible by the use of steel and *ferroconcrete* (concrete strengthened by a skeleton of iron bars), makes the "load" of the Villa Savoye's upper stories appear to hover lightly on the slender column supports.

FRANK LLOYD WRIGHT Perhaps America's greatest architect, Wisconsin-born FRANK LLOYD WRIGHT (1867–1959) moved to Chicago, where he eventually joined the firm headed by Louis Sullivan (FIG. 13-22). Wright believed in "natural" or "organic" architecture—that is, buildings designed to serve free individuals who have the right to move within a "free" space, which he envisioned as a nonsymmetrical design interacting spatially with its natural surroundings. He sought to develop an organic unity of planning, structure, materials, and site.

Wright's universally acclaimed masterpiece is the house nicknamed "Fallingwater" (FIG. 14-43), which he designed as a weekend retreat at Bear Run, Pennsylvania, for the Pittsburgh department store magnate Edgar Kaufmann Sr. Perched on a rocky hillside over a small waterfall, the Kaufmann House has long, sweeping lines, unconfined by abrupt wall limits, that reach out toward and capture the expansiveness of the natural environment. Rather than build the house overlooking or next to the waterfall, Wright decided to build it over the waterfall because he believed that the Kaufmanns would become desensitized to the waterfall's presence and power if they merely overlooked it. To take advantage of the location, Wright designed a series of terraces that extend on three levels from a central core structure. Abandoning all symmetry, he

eliminated a facade, extended the roofs far beyond the walls, and all but concealed the entrance. The contrast in texture among concrete, painted metal, and natural stones in the house's terraces and walls enlivens its shapes, as does Wright's use of full-length strip windows to create a stunning interweaving of interior and exterior space. The key element of Wright's new architecture was space, not mass—a space designed to fit the patron's life and enclosed and divided as required.

Frank Lloyd Wright achieved international fame. As early as 1940, Mies van der Rohe wrote that the "dynamic impulse from [Wright's] work invigorated a whole generation."[25] Wright's influence in Europe was exceptional for any American artist before World War II. However, in the decades following that new global conflict, American painters, sculptors, and architects often took the lead in establishing innovative styles that artists elsewhere quickly emulated. This new preeminence of the United States in the arts is the subject of Chapter 15.

⏹ Explore the era further in MindTap with videos of major artworks and buildings, Google Earth™ coordinates, and essays by the author on the following additional subjects:

- André Derain, *The Dance* (FIG. 14-3A)
- ▮ ART AND SOCIETY: Science and Art in the Early 20th Century
- ▮ ART AND SOCIETY: Primitivism and Colonialism
- Arthur Dove, *Nature Symbolized No. 2* (FIG. 14-17A)
- ▮ ART AND SOCIETY: Art "Matronage" in the United States
- Henry Moore, *Reclining Figure* (FIG. 14-30A)
- José Clemente Orozco, *Epic of American Civilization: Hispano-America* (FIG. 14-37A)
- William van Alen, Chrysler Building, New York (FIG. 14-41A)

MODERNISM IN EUROPE AND AMERICA, 1900 TO 1945

Europe, 1900 to 1920

- In the early 1900s, avant-garde artists searched for new definitions of art in a changed world. The Fauves used bold colors as the primary means of conveying feeling. German Expressionist paintings feature clashing colors, disquieting figures, and perspective distortions.

- Picasso and Braque radically challenged prevailing artistic conventions with Cubism. The Cubists dissected forms and placed them in interaction with the space around them.

- The Futurists focused on motion in time and space to create paintings and sculptures capturing the dynamic quality of modern life. The Dadaists celebrated the spontaneous and intuitive, often incorporating found objects in their artworks.

Boccioni, *Unique Forms of Continuity in Space*, 1913

United States, 1900 to 1930

- The Armory Show of 1913 introduced European avant-garde art to American artists.

- The Harlem Renaissance brought African American artists, such as Douglas, to the forefront.

- Photography emerged as an important American art form in the work of Stieglitz, who promoted "straight photography," and Weston, who emphasized the careful arrangement of forms and patterns of light and dark.

Douglas, *Noah's Ark*, ca. 1927

Europe, 1920 to 1945

- World War I gave rise to the Neue Sachlichkeit movement in Germany. "New Objectivity" artists focused on depicting the horrors of war.

- The Surrealists investigated ways to express in art the world of dreams and the unconscious. Naturalistic Surrealists aimed for "concrete irrationality" in their naturalistic paintings of dreamlike scenes. Biomorphic Surrealists experimented with automatism and employed abstract imagery.

- Many European modernists pursued utopian ideals. The Suprematists developed an abstract style to express pure feeling. De Stijl artists employed simple geometric forms in their "pure plastic art." Brancusi and Hepworth also turned to abstraction in their sculptures.

Dalí, *The Persistence of Memory*, 1931

United States and Mexico, 1930 to 1945

- Although Calder created abstract works between the wars, other American artists favored figural art. Hopper explored the loneliness of life in the Depression era. Lawrence recorded the struggle of African Americans. Wood depicted life in rural Iowa.

- Mexican artists Orozco and Rivera painted epic mural cycles of the history of Mexico. Kahlo's powerful paintings explore the human psyche.

Hopper, *Nighthawks*, 1942

Architecture

- The Bauhaus in Germany promoted "total architecture"—the integration of all the arts in constructing modern living environments. In France, Le Corbusier used modern construction materials in his "machines for living"—simple houses with open plans and unadorned surfaces.

- The leading American architect of the first half of the 20th century was Wright. Fallingwater is a bold asymmetrical design integrating a private home with nature.

Gropius, Bauhaus, Dessau, 1925–1926

◄ **15-1a** Moore's circular postmodern Italian plaza incorporates elements drawn from classical architecture, including a portico inspired by ancient Roman fora and an exedra loosely based on a triumphal arch.

◄ **15-1b** Postmodernist architects frequently incorporate references to historical styles in their designs. In addition to motifs based on Roman buildings, Moore included modern versions of medieval flying buttresses.

15-1   **CHARLES MOORE, Piazza d'Italia (looking northeast), New Orleans, 1976–1980.**

▶ **15-1c** Many of Moore's historical motifs are rendered in high-tech materials unavailable to earlier architects—for example, stainless-steel columns and capitals and neon lighting for multicolored nighttime illumination.

Modernism and Postmodernism in Europe and America, 1945 to 1980

AFTER MODERNISM: POSTMODERNIST ARCHITECTURE

One of the most significant developments in later-20th-century architecture was *postmodernism.* Postmodernist architects rejected the severity and simplicity of the modernist idiom pioneered by Gropius (FIG. 14-40), Mies van der Rohe (FIG. 14-41), Le Corbusier (FIG. 14-42), and their postwar successors. Instead, they celebrated complexity and incorporated historical references in their designs, often rendered in high-tech materials unavailable to earlier architects.

An outstanding example of a postmodernist design that creates a dialogue between the past and the present is Piazza d'Italia (Plaza of Italy; FIG. 15-1) in New Orleans, designed by CHARLES MOORE (1925–1993), dean of the Yale School of Architecture from 1965 to 1970. Erected in the late 1970s and restored after sustaining serious damage in the wake of Hurricane Katrina in 2005, Piazza d'Italia is dedicated to the city's Italian American community. Appropriately, Moore selected elements relating specifically to Italian history, all the way back to ancient Roman culture.

Piazza d'Italia is an open circular area partially formed by short segments of colonnades arranged in staggered concentric arcs, which direct the eye to the focal point of the composition—an *exedra.* This recessed area on a raised platform serves as a *rostrum* (speaker's platform) during the annual festivities of Saint Joseph's Day. Moore inlaid the piazza's pavement with a map of Italy centered on Sicily, from which the majority of the city's Italian families originated. From there, the map's Italian "boot" stretches to the steps, which correspond to the Alps, and ascends the rostrum.

The piazza's most immediate historical references are to the porticos of an ancient Roman forum (FIGS. 3-12 and 3-35) and to triumphal arches (FIG. 3-32), but the irregular placement of the concentrically arranged colonnade fragments inserts a note of instability into the design reminiscent of Mannerism (FIG. 9-26). Illusionistic devices, such as the continuation of the piazza's pavement design (apparently through a building and out into the street), are Baroque in character (FIG. 10-2). Moore incorporated all the classical orders—most with whimsical modifications, such as the stainless-steel columns and capitals, neon collars around the column necks, and neon lights framing various parts of the exedra and porticos for dramatic multicolored nighttime illumination. He even made references to medieval architecture by including modern versions of *flying buttresses,* and alternating white and gray-green stones in emulation of the revetment of medieval Italian buildings (FIGS. 7-37 and 7-38). This kind of eclecticism, especially rich in Piazza d'Italia, is a key ingredient of postmodernist architectural design.

THE AFTERMATH OF WORLD WAR II

World War II, with the global devastation it unleashed, set the stage for further conflict and upheaval during the second half of the 20th century. In 1947, the British left India, dividing the subcontinent into two hostile nations, India and Pakistan. After a bloody civil war, Communists came to power in China in 1949. North Korea invaded South Korea in 1950 and fought a grim war with the United States and its allies. The Soviets brutally suppressed uprisings in East Germany, Poland, Hungary, and Czechoslovakia. The United States intervened in disputes in Central and South America. Almost as soon as many African nations—Kenya, Uganda, Nigeria, Angola, Mozambique, Sudan, Congo, and Rwanda—won their independence from colonial powers, civil wars devastated them. Civil war also broke out in Indonesia, leaving more than 100,000 dead. Algeria expelled France in 1962 after the French waged a prolonged war with Algeria's Muslim natives. After 15 years of bitter fighting in Southeast Asia, the United States suffered defeat in Vietnam.

The period from 1945 to 1980 also brought upheaval in the cultural sphere. In the United States, for example, the struggles for civil rights for African Americans, for free speech on university campuses, and for disengagement from the Vietnam War led to a rebellion of the young. A new system of values emerged—a "youth culture," expressed in the radical rejection not only of national policies but often also of the society generating them. Young Americans mocked their elders' lifestyles and adopted unconventional dress, manners, habits, and morals deliberately subversive of mainstream social standards. The postwar youth era witnessed the sexual revolution, the widespread use and abuse of drugs, and the development of rock music. Young people "dropped out" of regulated society, embraced alternative belief systems, and rejected Western university curricula as irrelevant.

The civil rights movement of the 1960s and the women's liberation movement of the 1970s reflected this spirit of rebellion, coupled with the rejection of racism and sexism. African Americans fought discrimination and sought equal rights. Women systematically began to challenge the male-dominated culture, which they perceived as having limited their political and economic opportunities for centuries. Gays and lesbians and various ethnic groups also mounted challenges to discriminatory policies and attitudes.

The impact of these developments was immediate and profound in the artworld. Painters, sculptors, and photographers fully participated in these challenges to the established institutions of Western society, producing compelling artworks addressing the pressing social and political issues of the day.

PAINTING, SCULPTURE, AND PHOTOGRAPHY

The end of World War II in 1945 left devastated cities, ruptured economies, and governments in chaos throughout Europe. These factors, coupled with the massive loss of life and the horrors of the bombing of Hiroshima and Nagasaki and of the Holocaust, resulted in a pervasive sense of despair, disillusionment, and skepticism. Although many people (for example, the Futurists in Italy; see page 386) had tried to find redemptive value in World War I, it was nearly impossible to do the same with World War II, coming as it did so soon after the "war to end all wars." Further, World War I was largely a European conflict that left roughly 10 million people dead, whereas World War II was a truly global catastrophe, claiming 35 million lives.

Postwar Expressionism in Europe

The cynicism pervading Europe in the 1940s found voice in *existentialism,* a philosophy asserting the absurdity of human existence and the impossibility of achieving certitude. Many existentialists also promoted atheism. The writings of French author Jean-Paul Sartre (1905–1980) most clearly captured the existentialist spirit. According to Sartre, if God does not exist, then individuals must constantly struggle in isolation with the anguish of making decisions in a world without absolutes or traditional values. This spirit of pessimism and despair emerged frequently in European art of the immediate postwar period. A brutality or roughness appropriately expressing both the artist's state of mind and the larger cultural sensibility characterized the work of many European sculptors and painters.

ALBERTO GIACOMETTI The sculptures of Swiss artist ALBERTO GIACOMETTI (1901–1966) perhaps best express the existentialist spirit. Although Giacometti never claimed that he pursued existentialist ideas in his art, his works capture the spirit of that philosophy. Indeed, Sartre, Giacometti's friend, saw the artist's sculptured figures as the personification of existentialist humanity—alienated, solitary, and lost in the world's immensity. Giacometti's sculptures of the 1940s, such as *Man Pointing No. 5* (FIG. 15-2), are thin, nearly featureless figures with rough, agitated surfaces. Rather than conveying the solidity and mass of conventional bronze sculpture, these thin and elongated figures seem swallowed up by the space surrounding them, imparting a sense of isolation and fragility. Giacometti's evocative sculptures spoke to the pervasive despair that emerged in the aftermath of world war.

MODERNISM AND POSTMODERNISM IN EUROPE AND AMERICA, 1945 TO 1980

1945-1960
- European Expressionists capture in paintings and sculptures the revulsion and cynicism that emerged in the wake of World War II.
- New York School painters develop Abstract Expressionism, emphasizing form and raw energy over subject matter.
- Sleek, geometrically rigid modernist skyscrapers become familiar sights in cities throughout the world.

1960-1970
- Post-Painterly Abstractionists reject the passion and texture of action painting and celebrate the flatness of pigment on canvas.
- Op artists produce the illusion of motion and depth using only geometric forms.
- Minimalists reduce sculpture to basic shapes and emphasize their works' "objecthood."
- Pop artists find inspiration in popular culture and commercial products.
- Superrealists strive for scrupulous fidelity to optical reality.
- Performance artists replace traditional artworks with temporal actions.

1970-1980
- Artists play a leading role in the feminist movement by promoting women's themes and employing materials traditionally associated with women.
- Postmodern architects erect complex and eclectic buildings that often incorporate references to historical styles.
- Environmental artists redefine what constitutes "art" by creating earthworks composed of natural materials.
- Artists embrace new media—video recorders, computers—as tools for creating art.

15-2 ALBERTO GIACOMETTI, *Man Pointing No. 5*, 1947. Bronze, 5' 10" high. Des Moines Art Center, Des Moines (Nathan Emory Coffin Collection).

The writer Jean-Paul Sartre saw Giacometti's thin and virtually featureless sculpted figures as the personification of existentialist humanity—alienated, solitary, and lost in the world's immensity.

15-3 FRANCIS BACON, *Painting*, 1946. Oil and pastel on linen, 6' 5 $\frac{7}{8}$" × 4' 4". Museum of Modern Art, New York.

Painted in the aftermath of World War II, this intentionally repulsive image of a powerful figure presiding over a slaughter is a reflection of war's butchery. It is Bacon's indictment of humanity.

FRANCIS BACON Created in the year after World War II ended, *Painting* (FIG. 15-3) by British artist FRANCIS BACON (1910–1992) is a reflection of war's butchery and an indictment of humanity. Bacon presented a repulsive image of a powerful, stocky man with a gaping mouth and a vivid red stain on his upper lip, as if he were a carnivore devouring the raw meat sitting on the railing surrounding him. Bacon may have based his depiction of this central figure on news photos of similarly dressed European and American officials. The umbrella in particular recalls images of Neville Chamberlain (1869–1940), the wartime British prime minister who frequently appeared in photographs with an umbrella. The artist added to the gut-wrenching impact of the painting by depicting the flayed carcass hanging behind the central figure like a crucified human form. *Painting* is unmistakably "an attempt to remake the violence of reality itself," as Bacon often described his art based on what he referred to as "the brutality of fact."[1]

Abstract Expressionism

The devastation that World War II had inflicted across Europe resulted in an influx of artists escaping to the United States. In the 1950s, the center of the Western art world shifted from Paris to New York. It was there that the first major American avant-garde art movement—*Abstract Expressionism*—emerged. The most important forerunner of the Abstract Expressionists, however, was an Armenian.

ARSHILE GORKY Born a Christian in Islamic Turkish Armenia, ARSHILE GORKY (1904–1948) was four years old when his father escaped being drafted into the Turkish army by fleeing the country. His mother died of starvation in her 15-year-old son's arms in a refugee camp for victims of the Turkish campaign of genocide against the Christian minority. Penniless, Gorky managed in 1920 to make his way to America, settling in New York City four years later.

In a career lasting only two decades, Gorky contributed significantly to the artistic revolution born in New York. His work is the bridge between the Biomorphic Surrealism of Joan Miró (FIG. 14-27) and the totally abstract canvases of Jackson Pollock (FIG. 15-5).

1 ft.

15-4 Arshile Gorky, *Garden in Sochi*, ca. 1943. Oil on canvas, 2' 7" × 3' 3". Museum of Modern Art, New York (acquired through the Lillie P. Bliss Bequest).

Gorky's paintings of the 1940s, which still incorporate recognizable forms, are the bridge between the Biomorphic Surrealist canvases of Miró and the Abstract Expressionist paintings of Pollock.

Garden in Sochi (FIG. 15-4), painted in 1943 and named after a Black Sea resort, was inspired by Gorky's childhood memories of the Garden of Wish Fulfillment in his birthplace. The women of the Armenian village of Khorkom believed that their wishes would be granted if they rubbed their bare breasts against a rock in that garden beneath a tree to which they tied torn strips of their clothing. The brightly colored and thinly outlined forms in *Garden in Sochi,* which initially appear to be purely abstract biomorphic shapes, are loose sketches representing, at the left, a bare-breasted woman, and, at the center, a tree trunk with fluttering fabric. At the bottom are two oversized shoes—the Armenian slippers that Gorky's father gave his son shortly before abandoning the family.

CLEMENT GREENBERG The few traces of representational art in Gorky's work disappeared in Abstract Expressionism. As the name suggests, the artists associated with the New York School of Abstract Expressionism produced paintings that are, for the most part, abstract but express the artist's state of mind, with the goal also of striking emotional chords in the viewer. The most important champion of this strict *formalism*—an emphasis on an artwork's visual elements rather than its subject—was the American art critic Clement Greenberg (see page 358), who wielded considerable influence from the 1940s through the 1970s. Greenberg helped redefine the parameters of modernism by advocating the rejection of illusionism and the exploration of the properties of each artistic medium. So dominant was Greenberg that scholars often refer to the general modernist tenets during this period as Greenbergian formalism. Greenberg championed abstraction because he believed that it represented purity in art. He thought that artists should strive for a

more explicit focus on the properties exclusive to each medium—for example, flatness in painting and three-dimensionality in sculpture. Greenberg argued that

> a modernist work of art must try, in principle, to avoid communication with any order of experience not inherent in the most literally and essentially construed nature of its medium. Among other things, this means renouncing illusion and explicit subject matter. The arts are to achieve concreteness, "purity," by dealing solely with their respective selves—that is, by becoming "abstract" or nonfigurative.[2]

The Abstract Expressionist movement developed along two lines—*gestural abstraction* and *chromatic abstraction*. The gestural abstractionists relied on the expressiveness of energetically applied pigment. In contrast, the chromatic abstractionists focused on color's emotional resonance.

JACKSON POLLOCK The artist whose work best exemplifies gestural abstraction is JACKSON POLLOCK (1912–1956), who developed his signature style in the mid-1940s. By 1950, Pollock had refined his technique and was producing large-scale abstract paintings, such as *Number 1, 1950* (*Lavender Mist*; FIG. 15-5), which consist of rhythmic drips, splatters, and dribbles of paint. The mural-sized fields of energetic skeins of pigment envelop viewers, drawing them into a lacy spider web. Using sticks or brushes, Pollock flung, poured, and dripped paint (not only traditional oil paints but aluminum paints and household enamels as well) onto a section of canvas that he simply unrolled across his studio floor. This working method earned Pollock the derisive nickname "Jack

ARTISTS ON ART
Jackson Pollock on Action Painting

The kind of vigorous physical interaction between the painter and the canvas that Jackson Pollock championed led the critic Harold Rosenberg (1896–1989) to label Pollock's work (FIG. 15-5) *action painting.* In an influential 1952 article, Rosenberg described the attempts of Pollock and other Abstract Expressionists to get "in the painting":

> At a certain moment the canvas began to appear to one American painter after another as an arena in which to act—rather than as a space in which to reproduce, redesign, analyze or "express" an object, actual or imagined. What was to go on the canvas was not a picture but an event. The painter no longer approached his easel with an image in his mind; he went up to it with material in his hand to do something to that other piece of material in front of him. The image would be the result of this encounter.*

In an essay he published in 1947, Pollock explained the motivations for his action painting and described the tools he used and the way he produced his room-size canvases.

> My painting does not come from the easel. I hardly ever stretch my canvas before painting. I prefer to tack the unstretched canvas to the hard wall or the floor. I need the resistance of a hard surface. On the floor I am more at ease. I feel nearer, more a part of the painting, since this way I can walk around it, work from the four sides and literally be *in* the painting. . . . I continue to get further away from the usual painter's tools such as easel, palette, brushes, etc. I prefer sticks, trowels, knives and dripping fluid paint or a heavy impasto with sand, broken glass and other foreign matter added. When I am *in* my painting, I'm not aware of what I'm doing. . . . [T]he painting has a life of its own. I try to let it come through. . . . The source of my painting is the unconscious.†

*Harold Rosenberg, "The American Action Painters," *Art News* 51 (December 1952): 22–29.
†Quoted in Francis V. O'Connor, *Jackson Pollock* (New York: Museum of Modern Art, 1967), 39–40.

1 ft.

15-5 JACKSON POLLOCK, *Number 1, 1950 (Lavender Mist),* 1950. Oil, enamel, and aluminum paint on canvas, 7' 3" × 9' 10". National Gallery of Art, Washington, D.C. (Ailsa Mellon Bruce Fund).

Pollock's "action paintings" emphasize the creative process. His mural-size canvases consist of rhythmic drips, splatters, and dribbles of paint that envelop viewers, drawing them into a lacy spider web.

the Dripper." Responding to the image as it developed, he created art that was spontaneous yet choreographed. Pollock's painting technique highlights the most significant aspect of gestural abstraction—its emphasis on the creative process. Indeed, Pollock literally immersed himself in the painting during its creation (see "Jackson Pollock on Action Painting," above). Art historians have linked his ideas about improvisation in the creative process to his interest in what Swiss psychiatrist Carl Jung (1875–1961) called the collective unconscious. Pollock's reliance on improvisation and the subconscious has parallels in Surrealism and the work of Vassily Kandinsky (FIG. 14-5), whom critics described as an Abstract Expressionist as early as 1919.

LEE KRASNER A towering figure in 20th-century art, Pollock tragically died in a car accident at age 44, cutting short the development of his innovative artistic vision. Surviving him was his wife, LEE KRASNER (1908–1984), whom art historians recognize as a major Abstract Expressionist painter, although overshadowed by Pollock during her lifetime. *The Seasons* (FIG. 15-5A ⬈) is one of her finest works.

WILLEM DE KOONING Despite the public's skepticism about Pollock's art, other artists enthusiastically pursued similar avenues of expression. Dutch-born WILLEM DE KOONING (1904–1997) also developed a gestural abstractionist style. Even his images rooted in figuration, such as

15-6 WILLEM DE KOONING, *Woman I*, 1950–1952. Oil on canvas, 6' 3$\frac{7}{8}$" × 4' 10". Museum of Modern Art, New York.

Although rooted in figuration, including pictures of female models on advertising billboards, de Kooning's *Woman I* displays the energetic application of pigment typical of gestural abstraction.

15-7 MARK ROTHKO, *No. 14*, 1960. Oil on canvas, 9' 6" × 8' 9". San Francisco Museum of Modern Art, San Francisco (Helen Crocker Russell Fund Purchase).

Rothko's chromatic abstractionist paintings—consisting of hazy rectangles of pure color hovering in front of a colored background—are compositionally simple but compelling visual experiences.

Woman I (FIG. 15-6), display the sweeping gestural brushstrokes and energetic application of pigment typical of gestural abstraction. Out of the jumbled array of slashing lines and agitated patches of color appears a ferocious-looking woman with staring eyes and ponderous breasts. Her toothy smile, inspired by an ad for Camel cigarettes, seems to devolve into a grimace. Female models on advertising billboards partly inspired *Woman I* and de Kooning's other paintings of women, which he considered generic fertility goddesses or a satiric inversion of the traditional image of Venus, goddess of love.

Process was important to de Kooning, as it was for Pollock. Continually working on *Woman I* for almost two years, de Kooning painted an image and then scraped it away the next day and began anew. His wife, Elaine, also an accomplished painter, estimated that he painted approximately 200 scraped-away images of women on this canvas before settling on the final one.

MARK ROTHKO In contrast to the aggressively energetic images of the gestural abstractionists, the work of the chromatic abstractionists exudes a quieter aesthetic, exemplified by the work of Russian-born MARK ROTHKO (1903–1970). Rothko believed that references to anything specific in the physical world conflicted with the sublime idea of the universal, supernatural "spirit of myth," which he saw as the core of meaning in art. Rothko's paintings are compositionally simple, with color serving as the primary conveyor of meaning. In

works such as *No. 14* (FIG. 15-7), Rothko created compelling visual experiences by confining his compositions to two or three large rectangles of pure color with hazy edges. The forms are shimmering veils of intensely luminous colors that appear to be suspended in front of the colored backgrounds of his canvases. Although the color juxtapositions are visually captivating, Rothko intended them as more than decorative. He saw color as a doorway to another reality, and insisted that color could express "basic human emotions—tragedy, ecstasy, doom. . . . The people who weep before my pictures are having the same religious experience I had when I painted them."[3] Like the other Abstract Expressionists, Rothko produced highly evocative paintings reliant on formal elements rather than on specific representational content to elicit emotional responses in viewers.

Post-Painterly Abstraction

Post-Painterly Abstraction, a term that Clement Greenberg coined, was another postwar American art movement. It developed out of Abstract Expressionism, but manifests a radically different sensibility. Whereas Abstract Expressionism conveys a feeling of intense passion, Post-Painterly Abstraction is characterized by detached rationality emphasizing tighter pictorial control. Greenberg saw this art as contrasting with "painterly" art, which emphasized loose, visible pigment application. Evidence of the artist's hand, so prominent in gestural abstraction, is conspicuously absent in Post-Painterly Abstraction. Greenberg championed this art form because it embodied his idea of purity in art.

FRANK STELLA Attempting to arrive at pure painting, the Post-Painterly Abstractionists distilled painting down to its essential elements, producing spare, elemental images. One variant of Post-Painterly Abstraction was *hard-edge painting.* Its leading exponent was FRANK STELLA (b. 1936). In works such as *Mas o Menos* (*More or Less*; FIG. 15-8), Stella eliminated many of the variables associated with painting. His simplified compositions of thin, evenly spaced pinstripes on colored grounds have no central focus, no painterly or expressive elements, only limited surface modulation, and no tactile quality. Stella's systematic method of painting illustrates Greenberg's insistence on purity in art. The artist's own famous comment on his work, "What you see is what you see," reinforces the notions that painters interested in producing advanced art must reduce their work to its essential elements and that the viewer must acknowledge that a painting is simply pigment on a flat surface.

HELEN FRANKENTHALER *Color-field painting,* another variant of Post-Painterly Abstraction, also emphasized painting's basic properties. However, rather than produce sharp, unmodulated shapes as the hard-edge artists had done, the color-field painters poured diluted paint onto unprimed canvas and allowed the pigments to soak in. No other painting method results in such literal flatness. The images created, such as *The Bay* (FIG. 15-9) by HELEN FRANKENTHALER (1928–2011), appear spontaneous and almost accidental (see "Helen Frankenthaler on Color-Field Painting," below).

15-8 FRANK STELLA, *Mas o Menos* (*More or Less*), 1964. Metallic powder in acrylic emulsion on canvas, 9' 10" × 13' 8$\frac{1}{2}$". Musée national d'art moderne, Centre Georges Pompidou, Paris (purchase 1983 with participation of Scaler Foundation).

In his hard-edge paintings, Stella tried to achieve purity using evenly spaced pinstripes on colored grounds. His canvases have no central focus, no painterly or expressive elements, and no tactile quality.

ARTISTS ON ART
Helen Frankenthaler on Color-Field Painting

In 1965, the art critic Henry Geldzahler (1935–1994) interviewed Helen Frankenthaler about her work as a color-field painter. In the following excerpt, Frankenthaler described her approach to placing color on canvas in works such as *The Bay* (FIG. 15-9), and compared her method with the way earlier modernist artists used color in their paintings.

> I will sometimes start a picture feeling "What will happen if I work with three blues and another color, and maybe more or less of the other color than the combined blues?" And very often midway through the picture I have to change the basis of the experience. Or I add and add to the canvas. And if it's over-worked and beyond help I throw it away. I used to try to work from a given, made shape. But I'm less involved now with the shape as such. . . . When you first saw a Cubist or Impressionist picture there was a whole way of instructing the eye or the subconscious. Dabs of color had to stand for real things; it was an abstraction of a guitar or a hillside. The opposite is going on now. If you have bands of blue, green, and pink, the mind doesn't think sky, grass, and flesh. These are colors and the question is what are they doing with themselves and with each other. Sentiment and nuance are being squeezed out.[*]

Frankenthaler's "unsentimental" abstract canvases are very different from Matisse's emotive Fauve representations of recognizable figures, objects, and places, but her comments on a painter's struggle to find the right combination of colors without regard to colors in nature echo those of Matisse almost 60 years before (see "Henri Matisse on Color," page 379).

[*]Henry Geldzahler, "Interview with Helen Frankenthaler," *Artforum* 4, no. 2 (October 1965): 37–38.

15-9 HELEN FRANKENTHALER, *The Bay,* 1963. Acrylic on canvas, 6' 8$\frac{7}{8}$" × 6' 9$\frac{7}{8}$". Detroit Institute of Arts, Detroit.

Frankenthaler and other color-field painters poured paint onto plain canvas, allowing the pigments to soak into the fabric. Her works underscore that a painting is simply pigment on a flat surface.

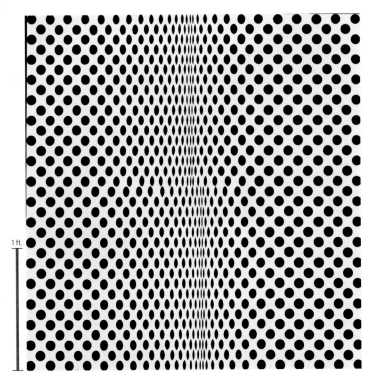

15-10 BRIDGET RILEY, *Fission*, 1963. Tempera on composition board, 2' 11" × 2' 10". Museum of Modern Art, New York (gift of Philip Johnson).

Op Art paintings create the illusion of motion and depth using only geometric forms. The effect can be disorienting. The pattern of black dots in Riley's *Fission* appears to cave in at the center.

Op Art

A major artistic movement of the 1960s was *Op Art* (short for Optical Art), in which painters sought to produce optical illusions of motion and depth using only geometric forms on flat surfaces.

BRIDGET RILEY The artist whose name is synonymous with Op Art is the British painter BRIDGET RILEY (b. 1931), who developed her signature black-and-white Op Art style in the early 1960s. Her paintings—for example, *Fission* (FIG. 15-10)—came to the public's attention after being featured in the December 1964 issue of *Life* magazine. The publicity unleashed a craze for Op Art designs in clothing. In 1965, the exhibition *The Responsive Eye* at the Museum of Modern Art bestowed an official stamp of approval on the movement. In *Fission,* Riley filled the canvas with black dots of varied sizes and shapes, creating the illusion of a pulsating surface that caves in at the center (hence the painting's title). The effect on the viewer of Op Art paintings such as this one is disorienting and sometimes disturbing, and some works can even induce motion sickness. Thoroughly modernist is the Op artist's insistence that a painting is a two-dimensional surface covered with pigment and not a representation of any person, object, or place. Nonetheless, the Op Art movement embraced the Renaissance notion that the painter can create the illusion of depth through perspective.

Abstraction in Sculpture

Painters were not the only artists interested in Clement Greenberg's formalist ideas. American sculptors also strove for purity in their medium. While painters worked to emphasize flatness, sculptors,

understandably, chose to focus on three-dimensionality as the essential characteristic and inherent limitation of the sculptural medium.

DAVID SMITH Sculptor DAVID SMITH (1906–1965) produced metal sculptures that have affinities with the Abstract Expressionist movement in painting. In the 1960s, he created a series of large-scale works called *Cubi* that he intended to be seen in the open air (see "David Smith on Outdoor Sculpture" ⬈). *Cubi XII* (FIG. 15-11), a characteristic example, consists of simple geometric forms—cubes and rectangular bars. Made of stainless-steel sections piled on top of one another, often at unstable angles, and then welded together, the *Cubi* sculptures make a striking visual statement.

DONALD JUDD A predominantly sculptural movement that emerged in the 1960s among artists seeking Greenbergian purity of form was *Minimalism.* Minimalist artworks generally lack identifiable subjects, colors, surface textures, and narrative elements. By rejecting illusionism and reducing sculpture to basic geometric forms, Minimalists emphasized their art's "objecthood" and concrete tangibility. In so doing, they reduced experience to its most fundamental level. Two of the leading Minimalist sculptors were ISAMU NOGUCHI (1904–1988; FIG. 15-11A ⬈) and Missouri native

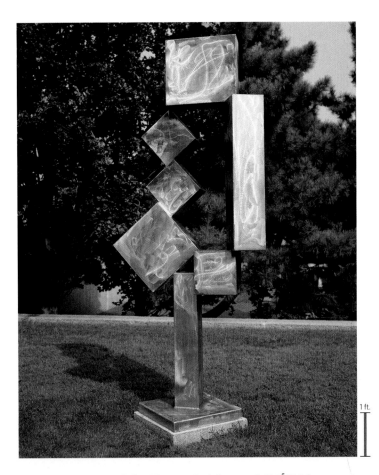

15-11 DAVID SMITH, *Cubi XII*, 1963. Stainless steel, 9' 1⅝" high. Hirshhorn Museum and Sculpture Garden, Smithsonian Institution, Washington, D.C. (gift of the Joseph H. Hirshhorn Foundation, 1972). © Estate of David Smith/Licensed by VAGA, New York, NY.

David Smith designed his abstract metal sculptures of simple geometric forms to reflect the natural light and color of their outdoor settings, not the sterile illumination of a museum gallery.

15-12 DONALD JUDD, *Untitled,* 1969. Brass and colored fluorescent Plexiglas on steel brackets, 10 units $6\frac{1}{8}$" × 2' × 2' 3" each, with 6" intervals. Hirshhorn Museum and Sculpture Garden, Smithsonian Institution, Washington, D.C. (gift of Joseph H. Hirshhorn, 1972). © Donald Judd Estate/ Licensed by VAGA, New York, NY.

By rejecting illusionism and symbolism and reducing sculpture to basic geometric forms, Donald Judd and other Minimalist artists emphasized the "objecthood" and concrete tangibility of their works.

1 ft.

DONALD JUDD (1928–1994), who produced most of his major works in New York City. Judd's determination to arrive at a visual vocabulary devoid of deception or ambiguity propelled him away from representation and toward precise and simple sculpture. For Judd, a work's power derived from its character as a whole and from the specificity of its materials.

Untitled (FIG. 15-12) presents basic geometric boxes constructed of brass and red Plexiglas, undisguised by paint or other materials. The artist did not intend the work to be metaphorical or symbolic. It is a straightforward declaration of sculpture's objecthood. Judd used Plexiglas because its translucency enables the viewer access to the interior, thereby rendering the sculpture both open and enclosed. This aspect of the design reflects Judd's desire to banish ambiguity or falseness from his works.

LOUISE NEVELSON Although Minimalism was a dominant sculptural trend in the 1960s, many sculptors pursued other styles. Russian-born LOUISE NEVELSON (1899–1988) created sculpture combining a sense of the architectural fragment with the power of Dada and Surrealist found objects to express her personal sense of life's underlying significance. Beginning in the late 1950s, Nevelson assembled sculptures of wood objects and forms. She enclosed small sculptural compositions in boxes of varied sizes, and joined the boxes to one another to form "walls." She then painted the forms in a single hue—usually black, white, or gold. This monochromatic color scheme unifies the diverse parts of pieces such as *Tropical Garden II* (FIG. 15-13) and creates a mysterious field of shapes and shadows. The structures suggest magical environments resembling the treasured secret hideaways dimly remembered from childhood. Yet the boxy frames and the precision of the manufactured found objects create a rough geometric structure that the eye roams over freely, lingering on some details. The effect is rather like viewing the side of an apartment building from a moving elevated train.

1 ft.

15-13 LOUISE NEVELSON, *Tropical Garden II,* 1957–1959. Wood painted black, 5' $11\frac{1}{2}$" × 10' $11\frac{3}{4}$" × 1'. Musée national d'art moderne, Centre Georges Pompidou, Paris.

The monochromatic color scheme unifies the diverse sculpted forms and found objects in Nevelson's "walls" and creates a mysterious field of shapes and shadows suggesting magical environments.

15-14 LOUISE BOURGEOIS, *Cumul I*, 1969. Marble, 1' 10$\frac{3}{8}$" × 4' 2" × 4'. Musée national d'art moderne, Centre Georges Pompidou, Paris. © Louise Bourgeois/ Licensed by VAGA, New York, NY.

Bourgeois's sculptures consist of sensuous organic forms that recall the Biomorphic Surrealist forms of Miró (FIG. 14-27). Although the shapes remain abstract, they refer strongly to human figures.

1 in.

LOUISE BOURGEOIS In contrast to the architectural nature of Nevelson's work, a sensuous organic quality recalling the evocative Biomorphic Surrealist forms of Joan Miró (FIG. 14-27) pervades the work of French-American artist LOUISE BOURGEOIS (1911–2010). *Cumul I* (FIG. 15-14) is a collection of round-headed units huddled, with their heads protruding, within a collective cloak dotted with holes. The units differ in size, and their position within the group lends a distinctive personality to each. Although the shapes remain abstract, they refer strongly to human figures. Bourgeois used a wide variety of materials in her works, including wood, plaster, latex, and plastics, in addition to alabaster, marble, and bronze. She exploited each material's qualities to suit the expressiveness of the piece. In *Cumul I,* the alternating high gloss and matte finish of the marble increases the sensuous distinction between the group of swelling forms and the soft folds swaddling them.

Bourgeois connected her sculpture with the body's multiple relationships to landscape: "[My pieces] are anthropomorphic and they are landscape also, since our body could be considered from a topographical point of view, as a land with mounds and valleys and caves and holes."[4] Sculptures such as *Cumul I* are openly sexual: "There has always been sexual suggestiveness in my work. Sometimes I am totally concerned with female shapes—characters of breasts like clouds—but often I merge the activity—phallic breasts, male and female, active and passive."[5]

Pop Art

Despite their differences, the Abstract Expressionists, Post-Painterly Abstractionists, Op Art painters, and Minimalist sculptors all adopted an artistic vocabulary of pure abstraction. Other artists, however, observing that the insular and introspective attitude of the avant-garde had alienated the public, sought to harness the communicative power of art to reach a wide audience. Thus was born the art movement that came to be known as Pop. Art historians trace the roots of *Pop Art* to the young British artists, architects, and writers who formed the Independent Group at the Institute of Contemporary Art in London in 1952. They sought to initiate fresh thinking in art, in part by sharing their fascination with the aesthetics and content of such facets of popular culture as advertising, comic books, and movies (see "Pop Art and Consumer Culture," page 421).

RICHARD HAMILTON In 1956, an Independent Group member, RICHARD HAMILTON (1922–2011), made a small collage, *Just What Is It That Makes Today's Homes So Different, So Appealing?* (FIG. 15-15), which exemplifies British Pop Art. Trained as an engineering draftsman, exhibition designer, and painter, Hamilton studied the way that advertising shapes public attitudes. Long intrigued by Marcel Duchamp's ideas (see page 388), Hamilton consistently combined elements of popular art and fine art, seeing both as belonging to the whole world of visual communication. He created *Just What Is It?* for the poster and catalog of one section of an exhibition titled *This Is Tomorrow,* which included images from Hollywood cinema, science fiction, and the mass media.

JASPER JOHNS Although Pop Art originated in England, the movement found its greatest success in the United States, in large part because the more fully matured American consumer culture provided a fertile environment for the movement. Indeed, Independent Group members claimed that their inspiration came from Hollywood, Detroit, and New York's Madison Avenue, paying homage to America's predominance in the realms of mass media, mass production, and advertising. One of the artists pivotal to the early development of American Pop Art was JASPER JOHNS (b. 1930), who

ART AND SOCIETY
Pop Art and Consumer Culture

Although the acceptance of pure abstraction as an artistic mode had gained significant momentum in the decades after the end of World War II, many artists, as well as the general public, reacted against pure formalism in painting and sculpture. In the 1950s and 1960s, the artists of the Pop Art movement reintroduced all the devices that the postwar abstractionists had purged from their artworks. Pop artists revived the tools traditionally used to convey meaning in art, such as signs, symbols, metaphors, allusions, illusions, and figural imagery. They not only embraced representation but also firmly grounded their art in the consumer culture and mass media of the postwar period, thereby making it much more accessible and understandable to the average person. Indeed, the name "Pop Art"—credited to the British art critic Lawrence Alloway (1926–1990)—is short for "popular art" and referred to the popular mass culture and familiar imagery of the contemporary urban environment, such as the collection of everyday objects, advertisements, and celebrity photographs featured in Richard Hamilton's collage *Just What Is It That Makes Today's Homes So Different, So Appealing?* (FIG. 15-15).

The fantasy interior in Hamilton's collage reflects the values of mid-20th-century consumer culture through figures and objects cut from glossy magazines. *Just What Is It?* includes references to mass media (the television, the theater marquee outside the window, the newspaper), to advertising (Hoover vacuum cleaners, Ford cars, Armour hams, Tootsie Pops), and to popular culture (the "girlie magazine," the body builder Charles Atlas, romance comic books). Artworks of this sort stimulated viewers' wide-ranging speculation about society's values. This kind of intellectual toying with mass-media meaning and imagery typified Pop Art both in Europe and America.

Alloway eloquently described the intellectual basis of Pop Art in a 1958 essay:

> The definition of culture is changing as the result of the pressure of the great audience . . . [I]t is no longer sufficient to define culture solely as something that a minority guards for the few and the future . . . Our definition of culture is being stretched beyond the fine art limits imposed on it by Renaissance theory, and refers now, increasingly, to the whole complex of human activities. Within this definition, rejection of the mass produced arts is not, as critics think, a defense of culture but an attack on it.*

*Lawrence Alloway, "The Arts and the Mass Media," *Architectural Design* (February 1958): 34–35.

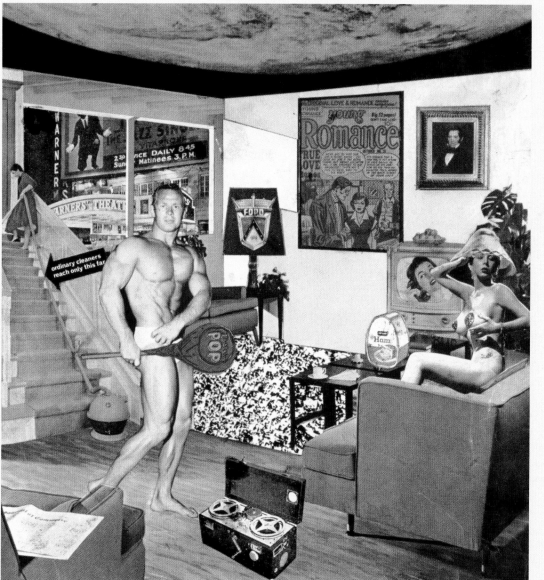

15-15 Richard Hamilton, *Just What Is It That Makes Today's Homes So Different, So Appealing?* 1956. Collage, $10\frac{1}{4}$" × $9\frac{3}{4}$". Kunsthalle Tübingen, Tübingen.

The fantasy interior in Hamilton's collage of figures and objects cut from glossy magazines reflects the values of modern consumer culture. Toying with mass-media imagery typifies British Pop Art.

1 in.

15-16 Jasper Johns, *Three Flags*, 1958. Encaustic on canvas, 2' 6⅞" × 3' 9½". Whitney Museum of American Art, New York (50th Anniversary Gift of the Gilman Foundation, the Lauder Foundation, and A. Alfred Taubman). © Jasper Johns/Licensed by VAGA, New York, NY.

American Pop artist Jasper Johns wanted to draw attention to common objects that people view frequently but rarely scrutinize. He made many paintings of targets, flags, numbers, and alphabets.

moved to New York City in 1952. Johns sought to draw attention to common objects in the world—what he called things "seen but not looked at."[6] To this end, he did several series of paintings of numbers, letters, flags, and maps of the United States.

In *Three Flags* (FIG. 15-16), Johns painted a trio of overlapping American banners of decreasing size, reversing traditional perspective. By reducing the American flag to a repetitive pattern, Johns drained meaning from the patriotic emblem. This is not the flag itself but three pictures of a flag in one. Nonetheless, the heritage of Abstract Expressionism is still apparent in Johns's choice of medium—*encaustic,* an ancient method of painting with liquid wax and dissolved pigment (FIG. 3-42), here mixed with newsprint. Thus the flags, painted on three overlapping canvases, have a pronounced surface texture, emphasizing that the viewer is looking at a handmade painting, not a machine-made fabric.

ROBERT RAUSCHENBERG A close friend of Johns's, Robert Rauschenberg (1925–2008) began using mass-media images in his work in the 1950s. Rauschenberg set out to create works that would be open and indeterminate, and he began making multimedia works that he called *combines,* which intersperse painted passages with sculptural elements. Some Rauschenberg combines seem to be sculptures with painting incorporated into certain sections. Others are paintings with three-dimensional objects attached to the surface.

Canyon (FIG. 15-17) is typical of his combines. Pieces of printed paper and photographs cover parts of the canvas. Much of the unevenly painted surface consists of pigment roughly applied in a manner reminiscent of de Kooning's work (FIG. 15-6). A stuffed bald eagle attached to the lower part of the combine spreads its wings as if lifting off in flight toward the viewer. Completing the combine, a pillow dangles from a string attached to a wood stick below the eagle. Rauschenberg tilted or turned some of the images sideways, and each overlays part of another image. The compositional confusion may resemble that of a Dada collage, but the combine's parts maintain their individuality. The various recognizable images and objects seem unrelated and defy a consistent reading, although Rauschenberg chose all the elements of his combines with specific

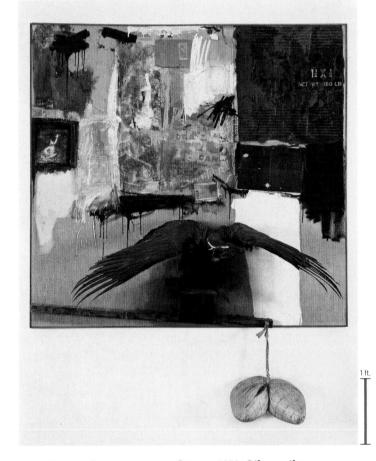

15-17 Robert Rauschenberg, *Canyon*, 1959. Oil, pencil, paper, fabric, metal, cardboard box, printed paper, printed reproductions, photograph, wood, paint tube, and mirror on canvas, with oil on bald eagle, string, and pillow, 6' 9¾" × 5' 10" × 2'. Sonnabend Collection, New York. © Estate of Robert Rauschenberg/Licensed by VAGA, New York, NY.

Rauschenberg's "combines" intersperse painted passages with sculptural elements. *Canyon* incorporates pigment on canvas with pieces of printed paper, photographs, a pillow, and a stuffed eagle.

1 ft.

15-18 ROY LICHTENSTEIN, *Hopeless,* 1963. Oil and synthetic polymer paint on canvas, 3' 8" × 3' 8". Kunstmuseum Basel, Basel. © Estate of Roy Lichtenstein.

Comic books appealed to Lichtenstein because they were a mainstay of popular culture, meant to be read and discarded. The Pop artist immortalized their images on large canvases.

meanings in mind. For example, he based *Canyon* on a Rembrandt painting of Jupiter in the form of an eagle carrying the boy Ganymede heavenward. The photo in the combine is a reference to the Greek boy, and the hanging pillow is a visual pun on his buttocks.

ROY LICHTENSTEIN As the Pop Art movement matured, the images became more concrete and tightly controlled. In the late 1950s, ROY LICHTENSTEIN (1923–1997), who was born in Manhattan not far from Madison Avenue, the center of the American advertising industry, turned his attention to commercial art and especially to the comic book as a mainstay of American popular culture (see "Roy Lichtenstein on Pop Art and Comic Books" ⏎). In paintings such as *Hopeless* (FIG. 15-18), Lichtenstein excerpted an image from a comic book, a form of entertainment meant to be read and discarded, and immortalized the image on a large canvas.

ANDY WARHOL The quintessential American Pop artist was ANDY WARHOL (1928–1987). An early successful career as a commercial artist and illustrator grounded Warhol in the sensibility and visual rhetoric of advertising and the mass media. This knowledge proved useful for his Pop artworks, which often depicted icons of mass-produced consumer culture, such as Coca Cola bottles (FIG. 15-19), and Hollywood celebrities, such as Marilyn Monroe (1926–1962; FIG. 15-19A ⏎). Warhol favored reassuringly familiar objects and people. He explained his attraction to the omnipresent curved Coke bottle:

What's great about this country is that America started the tradition where the richest consumers buy essentially the same things as the poorest. You can be watching TV and see Coca-Cola, and you can know that the President drinks Coke, Liz Taylor drinks Coke, and just think, you can drink Coke, too. A Coke is a Coke and no amount of money can get you a better Coke.[7]

Like other Pop artists, Warhol used a visual vocabulary and a printing method that reinforced the image's connections to consumer culture. The *silk-screen printing* technique enabled Warhol to reproduce the image endlessly (although in *Green Coca Cola Bottles* he varied each bottle slightly). The repetition and redundancy of the Coke bottle reflect the saturation of this product in American society.

1 ft.

15-19 ANDY WARHOL, *Green Coca-Cola Bottles,* 1962. Oil on canvas, 6' 10 $\frac{1}{2}$" × 4' 9". Whitney Museum of American Art, New York.

Warhol was the quintessential American Pop artist. Here, he selected an icon of mass-produced consumer culture and then multiplied it, reflecting Coke's omnipresence in American society.

Painting, Sculpture, and Photography   **423**

Warhol's ascendance to the rank of celebrity artist underscored his remarkable and astute understanding of the dynamics and visual language of mass culture. He predicted that the age of mass media would enable everyone to become famous for 15 minutes. His own fame has lasted much longer.

CLAES OLDENBURG In the 1960s, CLAES OLDENBURG (b. 1929) also produced Pop artworks that incisively commented on American consumer culture, but his medium was sculpture. Born in Sweden, Oldenburg graduated from Yale University in 1950. He is best known for his mammoth outdoor sculptures—for example, *Lipstick* (*Ascending*) *on Caterpillar Tracks* (FIG. 15-20), which, at the request of a group of graduate students at the Yale School of Architecture, he created (in secret and without a fee) as a gift to his alma mater. He installed the 21-foot-tall sculpture on Ascension Day, May 15, 1969, on Beinecke Plaza across from the office of the university's president, the site of many raucous protests against the Vietnam War. Oldenburg's characteristic humor emerges unmistakably in the combination of phallic and militaristic imagery, especially in the double irony of the "phallus" being a woman's cosmetic item, and the Caterpillar-type endless-loop metal tracks suggesting not

a tractor-earthmover for construction work but a military tank designed for destruction in warfare. *Lipstick* was to be a speaker's platform for protesters, and originally the lipstick tip was a drooping red vinyl balloon that the speaker had to inflate, underscoring the sexual innuendo. Vandalism and exposure to the elements (the original tractor was plywood) caused so much damage to *Lipstick* that it had to be removed. Oldenburg reconstructed it in metal and fiberglass.

Superrealism and Photography

Like the Pop artists, the artists associated with *Superrealism* sought a form of artistic communication that was more accessible to the public than the remote, unfamiliar visual language of the postwar abstractionists. The Superrealists expanded Pop's iconography in both painting and sculpture by making images in the late 1960s and 1970s involving scrupulous fidelity to optical fact. Because many Superrealists used photographs as sources for their imagery, art historians also refer to this movement as *Photorealism.*

AUDREY FLACK One of Superrealism's pioneers was AUDREY FLACK (b. 1931), who was intrigued by both the formal and technical qualities of photography. For paintings such as *Marilyn* (FIG. 15-21), Flack first projected a photograph onto the canvas. By next using an *airbrush* (a device originally designed as a photo-retouching tool that sprays paint with compressed air), she could duplicate the smooth gradations of tone and color found in photographs. Most of her paintings are still lifes that present the viewer with a collection of familiar objects painted with great optical

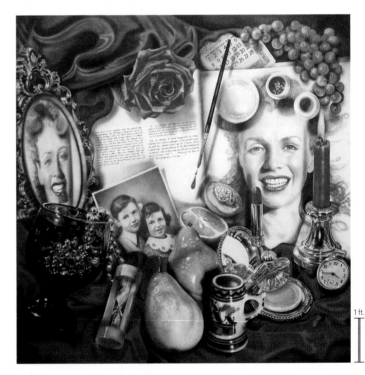

15-20 CLAES OLDENBURG, *Lipstick* (*Ascending*) *on Caterpillar Tracks*, 1969; reworked, 1974. Painted steel, aluminum, and fiberglass, 21' high. Morse College, Yale University, New Haven (gift of Colossal Keepsake Corporation).

Designed as a speaker's platform for antiwar protesters, *Lipstick* humorously combines phallic and militaristic imagery. Originally, the lipstick tip was soft red vinyl and had to be inflated.

15-21 AUDREY FLACK, *Marilyn,* 1977. Oil over acrylic on canvas, 8' × 8'. University of Arizona Museum, Tucson (museum purchase with funds provided by the Edward J. Gallagher Jr. Memorial Fund).

Flack's pioneering Photorealist still lifes record objects with great optical fidelity. *Marilyn* alludes to Dutch vanitas paintings (FIG. 10-26) and incorporates multiple references to the transience of life.

1 ft.

15-22 CHUCK CLOSE, *Big Self-Portrait*, 1967–1968. Acrylic on canvas, 8' 11" × 6' 11". Walker Art Center, Minneapolis (Art Center Acquisition Fund, 1969).

Close's goal was to translate photographic information into painted information. In his portraits, he deliberately avoided creative compositions, flattering lighting effects, and revealing facial expressions.

1 ft.

15-23 DUANE HANSON, *Supermarket Shopper*, 1970. Polyester resin and fiberglass polychromed in oil, with clothing, steel cart, and groceries, life-size. Nachfolgeinstitut, Neue Galerie, Sammlung Ludwig, Aachen. © Estate of Duane Hanson/Licensed by VAGA, New York, NY.

Hanson used molds from live models to create his Superrealist life-size painted plaster sculptures. His aim was to capture the emptiness and loneliness of average Americans in familiar settings.

fidelity. *Marilyn* is a still life incorporating photographs of the face of Hollywood actress Marilyn Monroe (1926–1962). It is a poignant commentary on Monroe's tragic life and differs markedly from Warhol's *Marilyn Diptych* (FIG. 15-19A ⬈), which celebrates celebrity and makes no allusion to the death of the glamorous star. Flack's still life includes multiple references to death and alludes to Dutch *vanitas* paintings (FIG. 10-26). The fresh fruit, hourglass, burning candle, watch, and calendar all refer to the passage of time and the transience of life.

CHUCK CLOSE Also usually considered a Superrealist is Seattle-born CHUCK CLOSE (b. 1940), best known for his large-scale portraits, such as *Big Self-Portrait* (FIG. 15-22). However, Close felt that his connection to the Photorealists was tenuous, because for him, realism was not an end in itself but rather the result of an intellectually rigorous, systematic approach to painting (see "Chuck Close on Photorealist Portrait Painting" ⬈).

LUCIAN FREUD Born in Berlin in 1922, LUCIAN FREUD (1922–2011) moved to London with his family in 1933 when Adolph Hitler became German chancellor. The grandson of Sigmund Freud, the painter is best known for his unflattering close-up views

of faces in which the sitter seems almost unaware of the painter's presence, and for his portrayals of female and male nudes in foreshortened and often contorted poses—for example, *Naked Portrait* (FIG. 15-22A ⬈).

DUANE HANSON Not surprisingly, many sculptors also were Superrealists, including DUANE HANSON (1925–1996), who perfected a casting technique that enabled him to create life-size sculptures that many viewers mistake at first for real people. Hanson began by making plaster molds from live models and then filled the molds with polyester resin. After the resin hardened, he removed the outer molds and cleaned and painted the sculptures with an airbrush, and added wigs, clothes, and other accessories. These works, such as *Supermarket Shopper* (FIG. 15-23), depict stereotypical average Americans, striking chords with the public precisely because of their familiarity. Hanson explained:

> The subject matter that I like best deals with the familiar lower and middle-class American types of today. To me, the resignation, emptiness and loneliness of their existence captures the true reality of life for these people. . . . I want to achieve a certain tough realism which speaks of the fascinating idiosyncrasies of our time.[8]

MINOR WHITE, *Moencopi Strata, Capitol Reef, Utah,* 1962. Gelatin silver print, $1'\frac{1}{8}" \times 9\frac{1}{4}"$. Museum of Modern Art, New York. © The Minor White Archive, Princeton University.

White's "straight photograph" of a natural rock formation is also an abstract composition of jagged shapes and contrasts of light and dark reminiscent of Abstract Expressionist paintings.

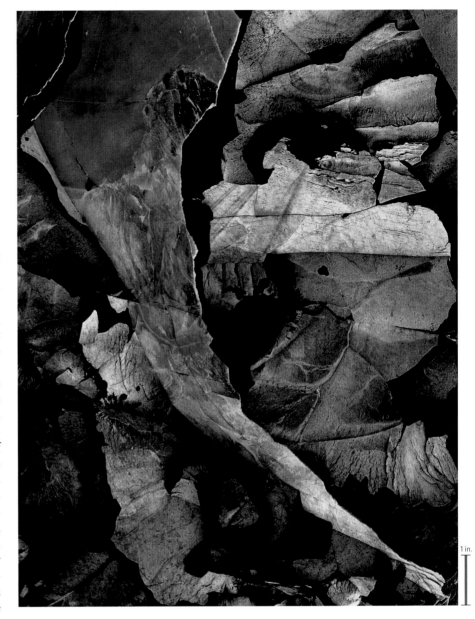

1 in.

MINOR WHITE Although Superrealist artists admired the ability of photography to reproduce faithfully the appearance of people, objects, and places, photographers themselves used their medium to pursue varied ends, including abstraction. In 1938, MINOR WHITE (1908–1976) became a photographer for the Works Progress Administration (see page 400), and, after serving in the United States Army in World War II, settled in New York City, where he met Alfred Stieglitz, whose photographs of clouds he greatly admired. Deeply influenced by Zen Buddhism (see "Zen Buddhism," page 515), White sought to incorporate a mystical element in his own work. His 1962 photograph (FIG. 15-24) of a rock formation in Utah is a characteristic example. A "straight photograph" in the tradition of Stieglitz and Weston (see page 392), it is also an abstract composition of jagged shapes and contrasts of light and dark. Viewers of *Moencopi Strata* may recognize White's nominal subject as a detail of a landscape, but in his hands, nature becomes the springboard for meditation. As one of the founders and the longtime editor (1952–1975) of *Aperture,* the leading art photography magazine of the time, White had a profound influence on the development of the medium in the postwar period.

Feminist Art

With the renewed interest in representation that the Pop artists and Superrealists introduced in the 1960s and 1970s, painters and sculptors once again began to embrace the persuasive powers of art to communicate with a wide audience. In the 1970s, many artists began to investigate the social dynamics of power and privilege, especially in relation to gender, although racial, ethnic, and sexual orientation issues have also figured prominently in the art of recent decades (see Chapter 16).

JUDY CHICAGO Women artists played a significant role in the feminist movement, which sought equal rights for women and focused attention on the subservient place of women in societies throughout history. Chicago native JUDY CHICAGO (Judy Cohen, b. 1939), a cofounder of the Feminist Art Program in California, was a leader of that movement. In the early 1970s, she began planning an ambitious piece, *The Dinner Party* (FIG. 15-25), using craft techniques (such as china painting and needlework) traditionally practiced by women, to celebrate the achievements and contributions that women had made throughout history (see "Judy Chicago

on *The Dinner Party,*" page 427). She originally conceived the work as a feminist *Last Supper* for 13 "honored guests," as in the biblical account of Christ's passion, but at Chicago's table the guests are women instead of men. A witches' coven also comprises 13 women, and Chicago's *Dinner Party* additionally refers to witchcraft and the worship of the Mother Goddess. But because Chicago had uncovered so many worthy women in the course of her research, she tripled the number of guests and placed table settings for 39 women around a triangular table 48 feet long on each side. The triangular form refers to the ancient symbol for both woman and the Goddess. The notion of a dinner party also alludes to women's traditional role as homemakers.

CINDY SHERMAN The primary means of expression for CINDY SHERMAN (b. 1954) is photography. Sherman addresses in her work how Western artists have traditionally presented female beauty for the enjoyment of the "male gaze," a primary focus of contemporary feminist theory, which explores gender as a socially constructed concept. Beginning in 1977, she produced more than 80 black-and-white photographs called *Untitled Film Stills.* She got the idea for the series after examining soft-core pornography magazines and noting

ARTISTS ON ART
Judy Chicago on *The Dinner Party*

One of the acknowledged masterpieces of feminist art is Judy Chicago's *The Dinner Party* (FIG. 15-25), which required a team of nearly 400 to create and assemble. In 1979, Chicago published a book explaining the genesis and symbolism of the work.

[By 1974] I had discarded [my original] idea of painting a hundred abstract portraits on plates, each paying tribute to a different historic female figure. . . . In my research I realized over and over again that women's achievements had been left out of history. . . . My new idea was to try to symbolize this. . . . [I thought] about putting the plates on a table with silver, glasses, napkins, and tablecloths, and over the next year and a half the concept of *The Dinner Party* slowly evolved. I began to think about the piece as a reinterpretation of the Last Supper from the point of view of women, who, throughout history, had prepared the meals and set the table. In my "Last Supper," however, the women would be the honored guests. Their representation in the form of plates set on the table would express the way women had been confined, and the piece would thus reflect both women's achievements and their oppression. . . . My goal with *The Dinner Party* was . . . to forge a new kind of art expressing women's experience. . . . [It] seemed appropriate to relate our history through art, particularly through techniques traditionally associated with women—china-painting and needlework.*

The Dinner Party rests on a triangular white tile floor inscribed with the names of 999 additional women of achievement to signify that the accomplishments of the 39 honored guests rest on a foundation that other women had laid. Among those with place settings at the table are the Egyptian pharaoh Hatshepsut (FIG. 1-31), the Minoan snake goddess (FIG. 2-8), the Byzantine empress Theodora (FIG. 4-18), the medieval nun Hildegard of Bingen (FIG. 6-26), and the painters Artemisia Gentileschi (FIG. 10-10 and 10-10A ⬀) and Georgia O'Keeffe (FIG. I-5). Other woman artists among the 999 names include Élisabeth-Louise Vigée-Lebrun (FIG. 11-7), Adélaïde Labille-Guiard (FIG. 11-7A ⬀), Angelica Kauffman (FIG. 11-1), Mary Cassatt (FIG. 13-6), Berthe Morisot (FIG. 13-7), Käthe Kollwitz (FIG. 14-7), Barbara Hepworth (FIG. 14-31), Dorothea Lange (FIG. 14-33), and Louise Nevelson (FIG. 15-13).

Each woman's place has identical eating utensils and a goblet, but features a unique oversized porcelain plate and a long place mat or table runner covered with imagery reflecting significant facts about that woman's life and culture. The plates range from simple concave shapes with china-painted imagery to dishes whose sculptured three-dimensional designs almost seem to struggle to free themselves. The designs on each plate incorporate both butterfly and vulval motifs—the butterfly as the ancient symbol of liberation and the vulva as the symbol of female sexuality. Each table runner combines traditional needlework techniques, including needlepoint, embroidery, crochet, beading, patchwork, and appliqué.

The Dinner Party is more than the sum of its parts, however. Of monumental size, as so many great works of public art have been throughout the ages, Chicago's 1979 masterwork provides viewers with a powerful launching point for considering broad feminist concerns.

*Judy Chicago, *"The Dinner Party": A Symbol of Our Heritage* (Garden City, N.Y.: Anchor Press, 1979), 11–12.

10 ft.

15-25 JUDY CHICAGO, *The Dinner Party,* 1979. Multimedia, including ceramics and stitchery, 48' × 48' × 48'. The Brooklyn Museum, Brooklyn.

Chicago's *Dinner Party* honors 39 women from antiquity to the 20th century. The triangular form and the materials—painted china and fabric—are traditionally associated with women.

15-26 CINDY SHERMAN, *Untitled Film Still #35,* 1979. Gelatin silverprint, 10" × 8". Private collection.

Sherman here assumed a role for one of a series of 80 photographs resembling film stills in which she addressed the way women have been presented in Western art for the enjoyment of the "male gaze."

the stereotypical ways that they depicted women. She decided to produce photographs showing herself designing, acting in, directing, and photographing the works. In so doing, Sherman took control of her own image and constructed her own identity, a primary feminist concern. In *Untitled Film Still #35* (FIG. 15-26), for example, Sherman appears in costume and wig in a photograph that seems to be a film still. Most of the images in this series recall popular film genres but are sufficiently generic that the viewer cannot relate them to specific movies. Sherman often reveals the constructed nature of these images by holding in her hand the shutter release cable used to take the pictures. (The cord runs across the floor in *#35.*) Although the artist is still the object of the viewer's gaze in these photographs, the identity is one she alone chose to assume.

MAGDALENA ABAKANOWICZ Not strictly feminist in subject, but created using materials traditionally associated with women, are the sculptures of Polish fiber artist MAGDALENA ABAKANOWICZ (b. 1930). A leader in the exploration of the expressive powers of weaving techniques in large-scale artworks, Abakanowicz gained fame with experimental freestanding figural works expressing the

15-27 MAGDALENA ABAKANOWICZ, *80 Backs,* 1976–1980. Burlap and resin, each 2' 3" high. Museum of Modern Art, Dallas.

Polish fiber artist Abakanowicz explored the stoic, everyday toughness of the human spirit in this group of nearly identical sculptures that serve as symbols of distinctive individuals lost in the crowd.

stoic, everyday toughness of the human spirit. For Abakanowicz, fiber materials are deeply symbolic:

> I see fiber as the basic element constructing the organic world on our planet, as the greatest mystery of our environment. It is from fiber that all living organisms are built—the tissues of plants and ourselves. . . . Fabric is our covering and our attire. Made with our hands, it is a record of our souls.[9]

Abakanowicz's sculptures are to a great degree reflections of her early life experiences as a member of an aristocratic family disturbed by the dislocations of World War II and its aftermath. Best known for her works based on human forms, she multiplies each form for exhibition in groups as symbols for the individual in society, lost in the crowd yet retaining some distinctiveness. This impression is especially powerful in *80 Backs* (FIG. 15-27). Abakanowicz made each piece by pressing layers of natural organic fibers into a plaster mold. Every sculpture depicts the slumping shoulders, back, and arms of a figure of indeterminate sex and rests legless directly on the floor. The repeated pose of the figures in *80 Backs* suggests meditation, submission, and anticipation. Although made from a single mold, the figures achieve a touching sense of individuality because each assumed a slightly different posture as the material dried and because the artist imprinted a different pattern of fiber texture on each.

ARCHITECTURE AND SITE-SPECIFIC ART

Some of the most innovative architects of the first half of the 20th century, most notably Frank Lloyd Wright (FIG. 14-43), Le Corbusier (FIG. 14-42), and Ludwig Mies van der Rohe (FIG. 14-41), concluded their long and productive careers in the postwar period. At the same time, younger architects rose to international prominence, some working in the modernist idiom, others taking architectural design in new, postmodern directions (see "After Modernism: Postmodernist Architecture," page 411).

Modernism

In parallel with the progressive postwar movement toward formal abstraction in painting and sculpture, modernist architects stressed formalist simplicity in buildings adhering to a rigid geometry as well as buildings featuring organic sculptural qualities.

FRANK LLOYD WRIGHT The last great building Frank Lloyd Wright designed was the Solomon R. Guggenheim Museum (FIG. 15-28) in New York City. Using reinforced concrete almost as a sculptor might use resilient clay, Wright, who often described his architecture as "organic," designed a structure inspired by the spiral of a snail's shell. The shape of the shell expands toward the top, and a winding interior ramp (FIG. 16-28) spirals to connect the gallery bays. A skylight strip embedded in the museum's outer wall provides illumination to the ramp, which visitors can stroll up or down, viewing the artworks displayed along the gently sloping pathway. Thick walls and the solid organic shape give the building, outside and inside, the sense of turning in on itself, and the long interior viewing area opening onto a 90-foot central well of space creates a sheltered environment, secure from the bustling city outside.

LE CORBUSIER Compared with his pristine geometric design for Villa Savoye (FIG. 14-42), the organic forms of Le Corbusier's Notre-Dame-du-Haut (FIG. 15-29) come as a startling surprise. Completed in 1955 at Ronchamp, France, the chapel attests to the boundless

15-28 FRANK LLOYD WRIGHT, Solomon R. Guggenheim Museum (looking southeast), New York, 1943–1959.

Using reinforced concrete almost as a sculptor might use resilient clay, Wright designed a snail shell–shaped museum with a winding, gently inclined interior ramp (FIG. 16-28) for the display of artworks.

15-29 LE CORBUSIER, exterior of Notre-Dame-du-Haut (looking northwest), Ronchamp, France, 1950–1955.

The organic forms of Le Corbusier's mountaintop chapel present a fusion of architecture and sculpture. The architect based the shapes on praying hands, a dove's wings, and a ship's prow.

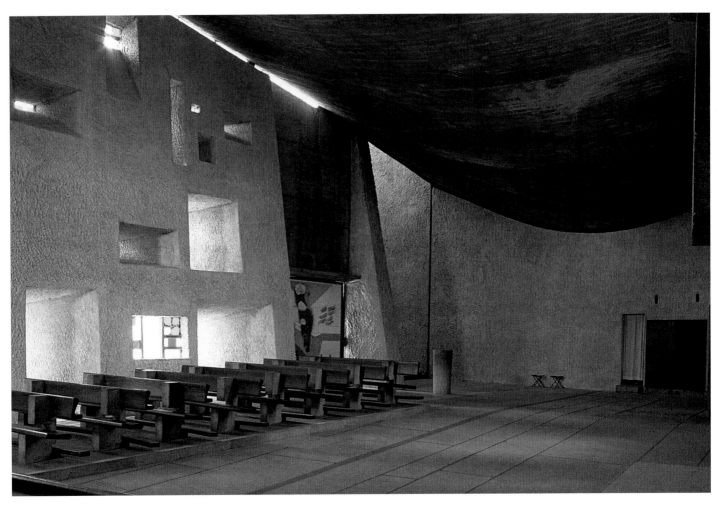

15-30 LE CORBUSIER, interior of Notre-Dame-du-Haut (looking southwest), Ronchamp, France, 1950–1955.

Constructed of concrete sprayed on a frame of steel and metal mesh, the heavy walls of the Ronchamp chapel enclose an intimate and mysteriously lit interior that has the aura of a sacred cave.

creativity of this great architect. A fusion of architecture and sculpture, the small chapel occupies a pilgrimage site in the Vosges Mountains. The monumental impression of Notre-Dame-du-Haut seen from afar is deceptive. Although one massive exterior wall (FIG. 15-29, *right*) contains a pulpit resembling a balcony that faces a spacious outdoor area for large-scale open-air services on holy days, the interior (FIG. 15-30) holds at most 200 people. The intimate scale, stark and heavy walls, and mysterious illumination (jewel tones cast from the deeply recessed stained-glass windows) give this space an aura reminiscent of a sacred cave or a medieval monastery.

Notre-Dame-du-Haut's structure may look free-form to the untrained eye, but Le Corbusier, like the designers of late medieval cathedrals, based it on an underlying mathematical system. The church has a frame of steel and metal mesh, which the builders sprayed with concrete and painted white, except for two interior private chapel niches with colored walls and the roof, which Le Corbusier wished to have darken naturally with the passage of time. The roof appears to float freely above the worshipers in their pews (FIG. 15-30), intensifying the quality of mystery in the interior space. In reality, a series of nearly invisible blocks holds up the roof. The mystery of the roof's means of support recalls the reaction to Hagia Sophia's miraculously floating dome (FIG. 4-12) a millennium and a half before in Byzantium.

Le Corbusier's preliminary sketches for the building indicate that he linked the design with the shape of praying hands, with the

wings of a dove (representing both peace and the Holy Spirit), and with the prow of a ship (a reminder that the term for the central aisle in a traditional basilican church is *nave*—Latin for "ship"). The architect hoped that in the mystical interior he created and in the rolling hills around the church, worshipers would reflect on the sacred and the natural. No one who has visited Notre-Dame-du-Haut, whether on a bright sunlit day or in a thundering storm, has come away unmoved.

MIES VAN DER ROHE In contrast to the sculpturesque postwar idiom of Wright and Le Corbusier, other modernist architects created massive, sleek, and geometrically rigid buildings, following Bauhaus architect Ludwig Mies van der Rohe's contention that "less is more" (see page 406). Many of these more Minimalist designs are heroic presences in the urban landscape, effectively symbolizing the giant corporations that often were the skyscrapers' primary tenants.

The purest example of these corporate towers is the rectilinear glass-and-bronze Seagram Building (FIG. 15-31) in Manhattan, designed by Mies van der Rohe and American architect PHILIP JOHNSON (1906–2005). By the mid-1950s, the steel-and-glass skyscrapers pioneered by Louis Sullivan (FIG. 13-22) and carried further by Mies van der Rohe himself (FIG. 14-41) had become a familiar sight in cities throughout the world. Appealing in its structural logic and clarity, the style, easily imitated, quickly became the norm for postwar commercial high-rise buildings. The architects of the Seagram

Postmodernism

Within a few years of the completion of the Seagram Building (FIG. 15-31), some architects were already questioning the validity of the modernist approach to architectural design. Thus was born the diverse and complex style called *postmodernism* (see page 411). Among the first to explore this new direction in architecture were Jane Jacobs (1916–2006) and Robert Venturi (b. 1925). In their influential books *The Death and Life of Great American Cities* (Jacobs, 1961) and *Complexity and Contradiction in Architecture* (Venturi, 1966), Jacobs and Venturi argued that the uniformity and anonymity of modernist architecture (in particular, the corporate skyscrapers dominating many urban skylines) were unsuited to human social interaction and that diversity is the great advantage of urban life. Postmodern architects accepted, indeed embraced, the messy and chaotic nature of big-city life. When designing these varied buildings, many postmodern architects consciously selected past architectural elements or references and juxtaposed them with contemporary elements or fashioned them of high-tech materials, thereby creating a dialogue between past and present, as Charles Moore did in Piazza d'Italia (FIG. 15-1). Postmodern architecture incorporates references not only to traditional architecture but also to mass culture and popular imagery.

MICHAEL GRAVES The Portland Building (FIG. 15-32), designed by MICHAEL GRAVES (1934–2015), reasserts the wall's horizontality against the verticality of modernist skyscrapers. Graves favored

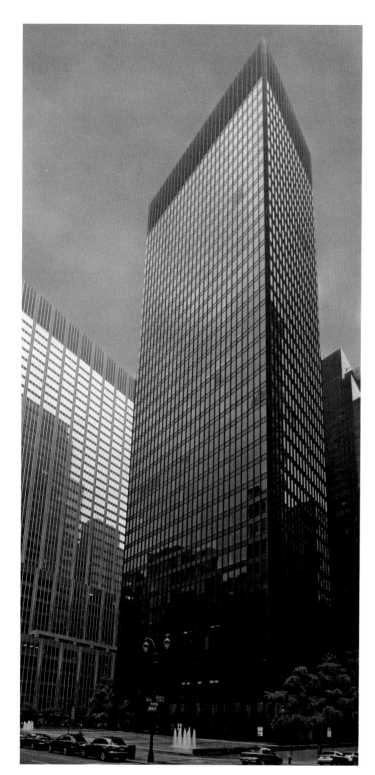

15-31 LUDWIG MIES VAN DER ROHE and PHILIP JOHNSON, Seagram Building (looking northeast), New York, 1956–1958.

Massive, sleek, and geometrically rigid, this modernist skyscraper has a bronze and glass skin that masks its concrete-and-steel frame. The giant corporate tower appears to rise from the pavement on stilts.

15-32 MICHAEL GRAVES, Portland Building (looking northeast), Portland, Oregon, 1980.

In this early example of postmodern architecture, Graves reasserted the horizontality and solidity of the wall. He drew attention to the mural surfaces through polychromy and ornamental motifs.

Building deliberately designed it as a thin shaft, leaving the front quarter of its midtown site as an open pedestrian plaza. The tower appears to rise from the pavement on stilts. Glass walls even surround the recessed lobby. The building's recessed structural elements make it appear to have a glass skin, interrupted only by the thin strips of bronze anchoring the windows. The bronze strips and the amber glass windows give the tower a richness found in few of its neighbors.

15-33 RICHARD ROGERS and RENZO PIANO, Centre Georges Pompidou (the "Beaubourg," looking northeast), Paris, France, 1977.

The architects fully exposed the anatomy of this six-level building, as in the century-earlier Crystal Palace (FIG. 12-24), and color-coded the internal parts according to function, as in a factory.

the square's solidity and stability, making it the main body of his composition (echoed in the windows), which rests on a wider base and carries a set-back penthouse crown. Narrow vertical windows tying together seven stories open two paired facades. These support capital-like large hoods on one pair of opposite facades and a frieze of stylized Baroque roundels tied by bands on the other pair. A huge painted keystone motif joins five upper levels on one facade pair, and painted surfaces further define the building's base, body, and penthouse levels. The modernist purist surely would not welcome the ornamental wall, color painting, or symbolic references. These features, taken together, raised a storm of criticism. Various critics denounced Graves's Portland Building as "an enlarged jukebox" and an "oversized Christmas package," but others approvingly noted its classical references as constituting a "symbolic temple" and praised the building as a courageous architectural adventure. Whatever history's verdict will be, the Portland Building is an early marker of postmodernist innovation that borrowed from the lively, garish language of pop culture.

ROGERS AND PIANO During their short-lived partnership, British architect RICHARD ROGERS (b. 1933) and Italian architect RENZO PIANO (b. 1937) used motifs and techniques from ordinary industrial buildings in their design for the Georges Pompidou National Center of Art and Culture (FIG. 15-33) in Paris. The architects fully

exposed the anatomy of this six-level building, which is a kind of updated version of the Crystal Palace (FIG. 12-24), and made its "metabolism" visible. They color-coded pipes, ducts, tubes, and corridors according to function (red for the movement of people, green for water, blue for air-conditioning, and yellow for electricity), much as in a sophisticated factory. Critics who deplore the building's industrial qualities disparagingly refer to the complex as a "cultural supermarket" and point out that its exposed entrails require excessive maintenance to protect them from the elements. Nevertheless, the Pompidou Center has been popular with visitors since it opened. The flexible interior spaces and the colorful structural body provide a festive environment for the crowds flowing through the building enjoying its art galleries, industrial design center, library, science and music centers, conference rooms, research and archival facilities, movie theaters, rest areas, and restaurant (which looks down and inside the building), as well as dramatic panoramas of Paris from its terrace.

Environmental and Site-Specific Art

One of the most exciting developments in postwar art and architecture has been *Environmental Art*, sometimes called *earthworks*. Environmental Art stands at the intersection of architecture and sculpture. It emerged in the 1960s and includes a wide range of artworks, most of which are *site-specific* (created for a unique location) and in the open air. Many artists associated with the movement also use natural or organic materials, including the land itself. It is no coincidence that this art form developed during a period of increased concern for the environment. The ecology movement of the 1960s and 1970s aimed to publicize and combat escalating pollution, depletion of natural resources, and the dangers of toxic waste. The problems of public aesthetics (for example, litter, urban sprawl, and compromised scenic areas) were also at issue. Widespread concern in the United States about the environment led to the passage of the National Environmental Policy Act in 1969 and the creation of the federal Environmental Protection Agency. Environmental artists use their art to call attention to the landscape and, in so doing, are an important part of this national dialogue.

As an innovative art form challenging traditional assumptions about art making, Environmental Art clearly has an avant-garde, progressive dimension. But as Pop artists did, Environmental artists insist on moving art out of the rarefied atmosphere of museums and galleries and into the public sphere. Most encourage spectator interaction with their works. Ironically, the remote locations of many earthworks have limited public access.

ROBERT SMITHSON One of the pioneering Environmental artists was ROBERT SMITHSON (1938–1973), who used industrial construction equipment to manipulate vast quantities of earth and rock on isolated sites. Smithson's best-known project is *Spiral Jetty* (FIG. 15-34), a mammoth 1,500-foot-long coil of black basalt, limestone rocks, and earth extending out into Utah's Great Salt Lake. As he was driving by the lake one day, Smithson came across some abandoned mining equipment, left there by a company that had tried and failed to extract oil from the site. Smithson saw this as a testament to the enduring power of nature and to the inability of humans to conquer it. He decided to create an artwork in the lake that ultimately became a mammoth coil curving out from the shoreline into the water. Smithson insisted on designing his work in response to the location itself. He wanted to avoid the arrogance of an artist merely imposing an unrelated concept on the site. The spiral idea grew from Smithson's first impression of the location. Then, while researching Great Salt Lake, Smithson discovered that the molecular structure of the salt crystals coating the rocks at the water's edge is spiral in form.

As I looked at the site, it reverberated out to the horizons only to suggest an immobile cyclone while flickering light made the entire

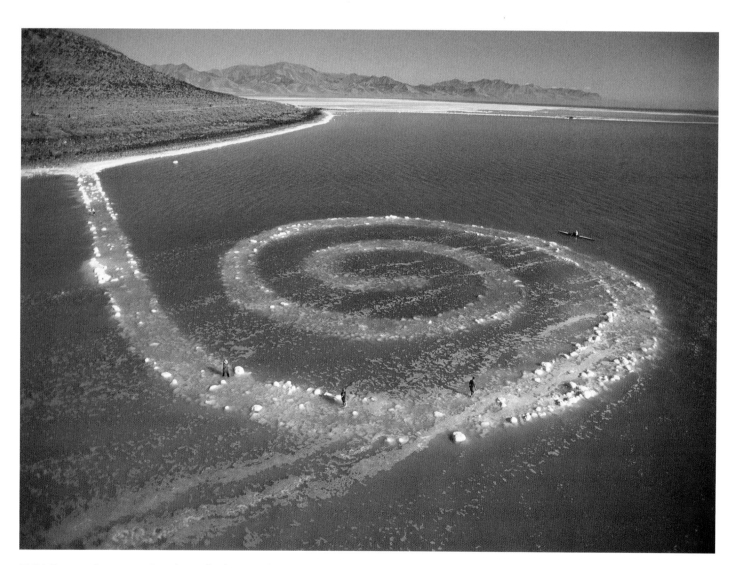

15-34 ROBERT SMITHSON, *Spiral Jetty* (looking northeast), Great Salt Lake, Utah, 1970. © Estate of Robert Smithson/Licensed by VAGA, New York, NY.

Smithson used industrial equipment to create Environmental artworks by manipulating earth and rock. *Spiral Jetty* is a mammoth coil of black basalt, limestone, and earth extending into Great Salt Lake.

landscape appear to quake. A dormant earthquake spread into the fluttering stillness, into a spinning sensation without movement. The site was a rotary that enclosed itself in an immense roundness. From that gyrating space emerged the possibility of the Spiral Jetty.[10]

PERFORMANCE AND CONCEPTUAL ART AND NEW MEDIA

Environmental art, although a singular artistic phenomenon, typifies postwar developments in the art world in redefining the nature of an "artwork" and expanding the range of works that artists and the general public consider "art." Some of the new types of artworks are the result of the invention of new media, such as computers and video cameras. But the new art forms also reflect avant-garde artists' continued questioning of the status quo.

Performance Art

One of the new artistic genres is *Performance Art*. Performance artists replace traditional stationary artworks with movements, gestures, and sounds performed before an audience, whose members sometimes participate in the performance. The informal and spontaneous events staged by early Performance artists anticipated the rebellion and youthful exuberance of the 1960s and at first pushed art outside the confines of mainstream art institutions—museums and galleries. Performance Art also served as an antidote to the pretentiousness of most traditional art objects and challenged art's function as a commodity.

Beginning in the later 1960s, however, museums commissioned artists to create and stage performances with increasing frequency, thereby neutralizing much of the subversiveness characteristic of this new art form.

CAROLEE SCHNEEMANN One of the pioneering Performance artists of the 1960s was CAROLEE SCHNEEMANN (b. 1939). In notes she wrote in 1962–1963, Schneemann reflected on the nature of art production and contrasted her kinetic works with more traditional art forms.

> Environments, happenings—concretions—are an extension of my painting-constructions which often have moving (motorized) sections. . . . [But the] steady exploration and repeated viewing which the eye is required to make with my painting-constructions is reversed in the performance situation where the spectator is overwhelmed with changing recognitions, carried emotionally by a flux of evocative actions and led or held by the specified time sequence which marks the duration of a performance. In this way the audience is actually *visually* more *passive* than when confronting a . . . "still" work . . . With paintings, constructions and sculptures the viewers are able to carry out repeated examinations of the work, to select and vary viewing positions (to walk with the eye), to touch surfaces and to freely indulge responses to areas of color and texture at their chosen speed.[11]

Schneemann's self-described "kinetic theater" radically transformed the nature of Performance art by introducing a feminist dimension through the use of her body (often nude) to challenge gender stereotypes. In her 1964 performance, *Meat Joy* (FIG. 15-35), which was intended to be both erotic and repulsive, Schneemann cavorted with male performers and reveled in the taste, smell, and feel of raw sausages, chickens, and fish.

15-35 CAROLEE SCHNEEMANN, *Meat Joy* (performance at Judson Church, New York City), 1964.

In her performances, Schneemann transformed the nature of Performance Art by introducing a feminist dimension through the use of her body (often nude) to challenge traditional gender roles.

Conceptual Art

The relentless challenges to artistic convention fundamental to the historical avant-garde reached a logical conclusion with *Conceptual Art* in the late 1960s. Conceptual artists maintain that the "artfulness" of art lies in the artist's idea, rather than in its final expression. These artists regard the idea, or concept, as the defining component of the artwork. Indeed, some Conceptual artists eliminate the object altogether.

JOSEPH KOSUTH Among the earliest proponents of Conceptual Art was JOSEPH KOSUTH (b. 1945), whose work operates at the intersection of language and vision, and deals with the relationship between the abstract and the concrete. For example, in *One and Three Chairs* (FIG. 15-36), Kosuth juxtaposed a real chair, a full-scale photograph of the same chair, and an enlarged reproduction of a dictionary definition of the word "chair." By so doing, the Conceptual artist asked viewers to ponder the notion of what constitutes "chairness."

15-36 JOSEPH KOSUTH, *One and Three Chairs,* 1965. Wood folding chair, photographic copy of a chair, and photographic enlargement of a dictionary definition of "chair"; chair 2' 8 $\frac{3}{8}$" × 1' 2 $\frac{7}{8}$" × 1' 8 $\frac{7}{8}$"; photo panel 3' × 2' $\frac{1}{8}$"; text panel 2' × 2' $\frac{1}{8}$". Museum of Modern Art, New York (Larry Aldrich Foundation Fund).

Conceptual artists regard the concept as an artwork's defining component. To portray "chairness," Kosuth juxtaposed a chair, a photograph of the chair, and a dictionary definition of "chair."

He explained:

> Like everyone else I inherited the idea of art as a set of *formal* problems. . . . [T]he radical shift was in changing the idea of art itself. . . . It meant you could have an art work which was that *idea* of an art work, and its formal components weren't important. I felt I had found a way to make art without formal components being confused for an expressionist composition. The expression was in the idea, not the form—the forms were only a device in the service of the idea.[12]

Conceptual artists such as Kosuth challenge the very premises of artistic production, pushing art's boundaries to a point where no concrete definition of "art" is possible.

New Media

During the 1960s and 1970s, in their attempt to find new avenues of artistic expression, many avant-garde artists eagerly embraced technologies previously unavailable. Among the most popular new media were video recording and computer graphics. Initially, only commercial television studios possessed video equipment, but in the 1960s, with the development of relatively inexpensive portable video recorders and of electronic devices allowing manipulation of recorded video material, artists began to explore in earnest the expressive possibilities of this new technology. In its basic form, video recording involves a special motion-picture camera that captures visible images and translates them into electronic data for display on a video monitor or television screen. Video pictures resemble photographs in the amount of detail they contain, but a video image consists of a series of points of light on a grid. Viewers looking at television or video art are not aware of the monitor's surface. Instead, fulfilling the ideal of Renaissance artists, they concentrate on the image and look through the glass surface, as through a window, into the "space" beyond. Video images combine the optical realism of photography with the sense that the subjects move in real time in a deep space "inside" the monitor.

NAM JUNE PAIK When video introduced the possibility of manipulating subjects in real time, artists such as NAM JUNE PAIK (1932–2006) were eager to work with the medium. After studying music performance, art history, and Eastern philosophy in Korea and Japan, Paik worked with electronic music in Germany in the late 1950s. In 1965, after relocating to New York City, Paik acquired the first inexpensive video recorder (the Sony Porta-Pak). Experience acquired as artist-in-residence at television stations WGBH in Boston and WNET in New York enabled him to experiment with the most advanced broadcast video technology.

Paik collaborated with the gifted Japanese engineer-inventor Shuya Abe (b. 1932) in developing a video synthesizer. This instrument enables artists to manipulate and change electronic video information in various ways, causing images or parts of images to stretch, shrink, change color, or break up. With the synthesizer, artists can also layer images, inset one image into another, or merge images from various cameras with those from video recorders to make a single visual kaleidoscopic "time-collage." This kind of compositional freedom enabled Paik to combine his interests in

15-37 NAM JUNE PAIK, video still from *Global Groove*, 1973. $\frac{3}{4}$" color videotape, sound, 30 minutes. Collection of the artist.

Korean-born video artist Paik's best-known work is a cascade of fragmented sequences of performances and commercials intended as a sample of the rich worldwide television menu of the future.

painting, music, Eastern philosophy, global politics for survival, humanized technology, and cybernetics. Paik called his video works "physical music" and said his musical background enabled him to understand time better than could video artists trained only in painting or sculpture.

Paik's best-known video work, *Global Groove* (FIG. 15-37), combines in quick succession fragmented sequences of female tap dancers, poet Allen Ginsberg (1926–1997) reading his work, a performance by cellist Charlotte Moorman (1933–1991) using a man's back as her instrument, Pepsi commercials from Japanese television, Korean drummers, and a shot of the Living Theatre group performing a controversial piece called *Paradise Now*. The cascade of imagery in *Global Groove* gives viewers a glimpse of the rich worldwide television menu that Paik predicted would be available in the future—a prediction that has been fulfilled with the advent of affordable cable and satellite television service.

AFTER 1980 The decades following the conclusion of World War II were unparalleled in the history of art for innovation in form and content and for the development of new media. Those exciting trends have continued unabated since 1980—and with an increasingly international dimension that will be explored in Chapter 16.

⏎ Explore the era further in MindTap with videos of major artworks and buildings, Google Earth™ coordinates, and essays by the author on the following additional subjects:

- Lee Krasner, *The Seasons* (FIG. 15-5A)
- ▌ARTISTS ON ART: David Smith on Outdoor Sculpture
- Isamu Noguchi, *Shodo Shima Stone Study* (FIG. 15-11A)
- ▌ARTISTS ON ART: Roy Lichtenstein on Pop Art and Comic Books
- Andy Warhol, *Marilyn Diptych* (FIG. 15-19A)
- ▌ARTISTS ON ART: Chuck Close on Photorealist Portrait Painting
- Lucian Freud, *Naked Portrait* (FIG. 15-22A)

MODERNISM AND POSTMODERNISM IN EUROPE AND AMERICA, 1945 TO 1980

Painting, Sculpture, and Photography

- The art of the decades following World War II reflects cultural upheaval—the rejection of traditional values, the civil rights and feminist movements, and the new consumer society.

- The first major postwar avant-garde art movement was Abstract Expressionism, which championed an artwork's formal elements rather than its subject. Gestural abstractionists, such as Pollock and de Kooning, sought expressiveness through energetically applied pigment. Chromatic abstractionists, such as Rothko, struck emotional chords through large areas of pure color.

- Post-Painterly Abstraction promoted a cool rationality in contrast to Abstract Expressionism's passion. Both hard-edge painters, such as Stella, and color-field painters, such as Frankenthaler, pursued purity in art by emphasizing the flatness of pigment on canvas.

- Pop artists, such as Johns, Lichtenstein, and Warhol, turned away from abstraction to represent subjects grounded in popular culture—flags, comic strips, Coca-Cola bottles—sometimes employing commercial printing techniques.

- Riley and other Op artists sought to produce optical illusions of motion and depth using only geometric forms on two-dimensional surfaces.

- Superrealists, such as Flack, Close, and Hanson—kindred spirits to Pop artists in many ways—created paintings and sculptures featuring scrupulous fidelity to optical fact.

- The leading sculptural movement of this period was Minimalism. Judd created artworks consisting of simple unadorned geometric shapes to underscore the "objecthood" of his sculptures.

- Many artists pursued social agendas in their work. Postwar feminist artists include Chicago, whose *Dinner Party* honors women throughout history, and Sherman, who explored the "male gaze" in her photographs resembling film stills.

Frankenthaler, *The Bay*, 1963

Lichtenstein, *Hopeless*, 1963

Sherman, *Untitled Film Still #35*, 1979

Architecture and Site-Specific Art

- Some of the leading early-20th-century modernist architects remained active after 1945. Wright built the snail-shell Guggenheim Museum, Le Corbusier the sculpturesque Notre-Dame-du-Haut, and Mies van der Rohe the Minimalist Seagram skyscraper.

- In contrast to modernist architecture, postmodern architecture is complex and eclectic and often incorporates references to historical styles. Two pioneering postmodern projects are Graves's Portland Building and Moore's Piazza d'Italia.

- Site-specific art stands at the intersection of architecture and sculpture. Smithson's *Spiral Jetty* is a mammoth coil of natural materials in Utah's Great Salt Lake.

Moore, Piazza d'Italia, New Orleans, 1976–1980

Performance and Conceptual Art and New Media

- Among the most significant developments in the art world after World War II has been the expansion of the range of works considered "art."

- Performance artists, such as Schneemann, replace traditional stationary artworks with movements and sounds performed before an audience.

- Conceptual artists, such as Kosuth, believe that the "artfulness" of art is in the artist's idea, not the work resulting from the idea.

- Paik and others have embraced video recording technology to produce artworks combining images and sounds.

Schneemann, *Meat Joy*, 1964

▲ **16-1a** Smith's *Trade* celebrates her Native American identity. The cheap trinkets she offers in return for confiscated land include sports team memorabilia with offensive names, such as Braves and Redskins.

▲ **16-1b** Newspaper clippings chronicle the conquest of Native America by Europeans and include references to the problems facing those living on reservations today—poverty, alcoholism, and disease.

1 ft.

16-1 **JAUNE QUICK-TO-SEE SMITH,** *Trade (Gifts for Trading Land with White People),* **1992. Oil and mixed media on canvas, 5' × 14' 2". Chrysler Museum of Art, Norfolk.**

▶ **16-1c** Overlapping the collage and the central motif of the canoe in Smith's anti-Columbus Quincentenary Celebration is dripping red paint, symbolic of the shedding of Native American blood.

Contemporary Art Worldwide

ART AS SOCIOPOLITICAL MESSAGE

Although televisions, smartphones, and the Internet have brought people all over the world closer together than ever before, national, ethnic, religious, and racial conflicts are also an unfortunate and pervasive characteristic of contemporary life. Some of the most eloquent voices raised in protest about the major political and social issues of the day have been those of painters and sculptors, who can harness the power of art to amplify the power of the written and spoken word.

Jaune Quick-to-See Smith (b. 1940) is a Native American artist descended from the Shoshone, Salish, and Cree peoples. Raised on the Flatrock Reservation in Montana, she is steeped in the traditional culture of her ancestors, but she trained as an artist in the European American tradition at Framingham State University in Massachusetts and at the University of New Mexico. Smith's ethnic heritage has always informed her art, however, and her concern about the invisibility of Native American artists has led her to organize exhibitions of their art. Her self-identity has also been the central theme of her mature work as an artist.

In 1992, Smith created what many critics consider her masterpiece: *Trade* (FIG. 16-1), subtitled *Gifts for Trading Land with White People*. A complex multimedia work of imposing size, *Trade* is Smith's response to what she called "the Quincentenary Non-Celebration"—that is, white America's celebration of the 500th anniversary of Christopher Columbus's arrival in what Europeans called the New World. *Trade* incorporates collage elements and attached objects, reminiscent of a Rauschenberg combine (FIG. 15-17), with energetic brushwork recalling Willem de Kooning's Abstract Expressionist canvases (FIG. 15-6). Among the items in *Trade*'s collage are clippings from Native American newspapers featuring images chronicling the conquest of North America by Europeans and references to the problems facing those living on reservations today—poverty, alcoholism, and disease. The dripping red paint overlaying the collage with the central motif of the canoe is symbolic of the shedding of Native American blood.

Above the painting, as if hung from a clothesline, is an array of objects. These include Native American artifacts, such as beaded belts and feather headdresses; plastic tomahawks; "Indian princess" dolls; and contemporary sports memorabilia from teams with American Indian–derived names: the Cleveland Indians, Atlanta Braves, and Washington Redskins. The inclusion of these objects reminds viewers of the vocal opposition to the use of these and similar names for high school and college as well as professional sports teams. All the cheap artifacts together also have a deeper significance. As the title indicates and Smith explained: "Why won't you consider trading the land we handed over to you for these silly trinkets that so honor us? Sound like a bad deal? Well, that's the deal you gave us."[1]

ART TODAY

This is an "incomplete" chapter, because the story of the art of the present generation—that is, the history of the art and architecture of the past 35 to 40 years—is still unfolding, and the body of material to be surveyed is increasing literally daily. It is both impractical and unwise to try to impose a strict chronological development scheme on the extraordinarily diverse range of works produced worldwide since 1980. Instead, this survey of contemporary art is organized thematically and stylistically and, to a lesser degree, by medium, under the following headings: Personal and Group Identity; Political and Social Commentary; Representation and Abstraction; Architecture and Site-Specific Art; and New Media. Most contemporary artworks fall into more than one of these categories, however. For example, a painting that explores personal and group identity, such as Jaune Quick-to-See Smith's *Trade* (FIG. 16-1), can also be a work of social commentary and combine representation and abstraction and several different media. Nevertheless, these six categories constitute a useful way to approach the complex phenomenon of contemporary art and architecture.

PERSONAL AND GROUP IDENTITY

Trade is the unique product of Smith's heritage as a Native American who has sought to bridge native and European artistic traditions, but her work parallels that of many other innovative artists of the decades since 1980 in addressing contemporary social and political issues. This focus on the content and meaning of art represents, as did the earlier work of the Pop artists and Superrealists (see pages 420–425), a rejection of modernist formalist doctrine and a desire on the part of artists once again to embrace the persuasive powers of art to communicate with a wide audience—an audience that, thanks to 21st-century technological breakthroughs, is now instantly international in character.

The multicultural diversity of the world today has made almost everybody keenly aware of her or his distinct national, ethnic, racial, and religious identity. Not surprisingly, many contemporary artists have made their personal and group identity the focus of their work.

African American Art

Prominent among those for whom race has been a key element of their art are African Americans. This is a very significant development in the history of art because outside Africa, Africans and people of African descent have rarely been the subject of artworks produced by European and American artists except in marginal and

16-2 JEAN-MICHEL BASQUIAT, *Horn Players*, 1983. Acrylic and oil paintstick on three canvas panels, 8' × 6' 3". Broad Art Foundation, Santa Monica.

In this tribute to two legendary African American musicians, Basquiat combined bold colors, fractured figures, and graffiti to capture the dynamic rhythms of jazz and the excitement of New York.

often demeaning roles. Black artists have also been omitted from most histories of Western art until recently.

JEAN-MICHEL BASQUIAT One artist whose work focused on the experiences of American men of African descent was JEAN-MICHEL BASQUIAT (1960–1988). Born in Brooklyn, the son of an accountant from Haiti and a black Puerto Rican mother, Basquiat rebelled against middle-class values, dropped out of school at 17, and took to the streets. He first drew attention as an artist in 1980 when he

1980-1990
- Social and political issues—gender and sexuality; ethnic, religious, and national identity—figure prominently in the art of Basquiat, Ringgold, Kruger, Mapplethorpe, and many others.
- Site-specific artworks by Lin and Serra and exhibitions of the work of Mapplethorpe and Ofili become lightning rods for debate over the public financing of art.

1990-2000
- Artworks addressing pressing political and social issues continue to be produced in great numbers by, among others, Quick-to-See Smith, Sikander, Neshat, Bester, and Zhang.
- Realistic figure painting and sculpture (Saville, Kiki Smith) as well as abstraction (Schnabel, Murray) remain vital components of the contemporary art scene.
- Deconstructivist (Gehry, Hadid) and Hi-Tech and Green architecture (Piano, Foster) emerge as major movements.

2000-
- Modern, postmodern, and traditional art forms coexist today in the increasingly interconnected worldwide art scene as artists on all continents work with age-old materials and also experiment with the new media of digital photography, computer graphics, and video.

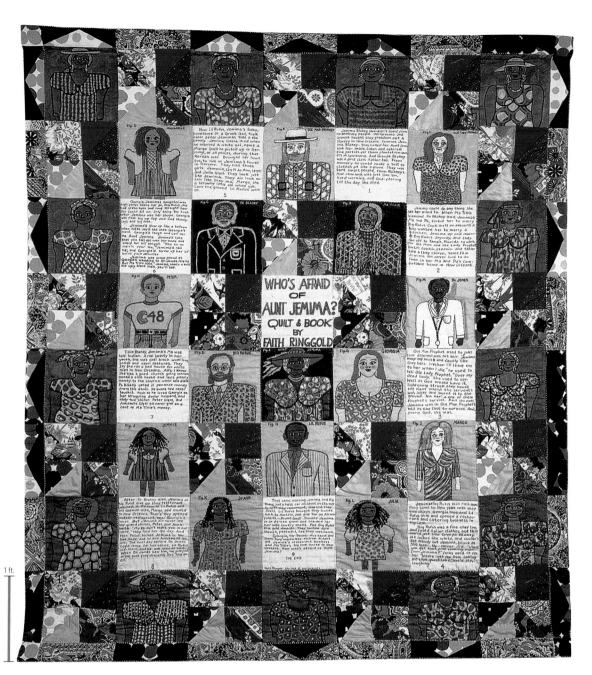

16-3 FAITH RINGGOLD, *Who's Afraid of Aunt Jemima?* 1983. Acrylic on canvas with fabric borders, quilted, 7' 6" × 6' 8". Private collection.

In this quilt, a medium associated with women, Ringgold presented a tribute to her mother that also addresses African American culture and the struggles of women to overcome oppression.

participated in a group show—the "Times Square Show"—in an abandoned 42nd Street building. Eight years later, after a meteoric rise to fame, he died of a heroin overdose at age 27. Basquiat was self-taught, both as an artist and about the history of art, but he was not a "primitive." His sophisticated style owes a debt to diverse sources, including the late paintings of Pablo Picasso, Abstract Expressionism, and urban graffiti. Many of Basquiat's paintings celebrate black heroes—for example, the legendary jazz musicians Charlie "Bird" Parker and Dizzy Gillespie, whom he memorialized in *Horn Players* (FIG. 16-2). The fractured figures, the bold colors against a black background, and the deliberately scrawled, crossed-out, and misspelled graffiti ("ornithology"—the study of birds—is a pun on Parker's nickname and also the title of one of Parker's musical compositions) create a dynamic composition suggesting the rhythms of jazz music and the excitement of the streets of New York.

FAITH RINGGOLD One of the leading artists addressing issues associated with African American women is Harlem native FAITH

RINGGOLD (b. 1930). In the 1960s, Ringgold produced numerous works that provided incisive commentary on the realities of racial prejudice. She increasingly incorporated references to gender as well and, in the 1970s, turned to fabric as the predominant material in her art. Using fabric enabled Ringgold to make more pointed reference to the domestic sphere, traditionally associated with women, and to collaborate with her mother, Willi Posey, a fashion designer. After her mother's death, Ringgold created *Who's Afraid of Aunt Jemima?* (FIG. 16-3), a quilt composed of dyed, painted, and pieced fabric. A moving tribute to her mother, this "story quilt"—Ringgold's signature art form—merges the personal and the political. The quilt tells the witty story of the family of the stereotypical black "mammy" in the mind of the public, but here Aunt Jemima is a successful African American businesswoman. Ringgold narrates the story using black dialect interspersed with embroidered portraits and traditional patterned squares. *Aunt Jemima,* while resonating with autobiographical references, also speaks to the larger issues of the history of African American culture and the struggles of women to overcome oppression.

Gender and Sexuality

The interest in feminist issues among African American women artists is but one aspect of a more general concern among contemporary artists of all races and nationalities with gender and sexuality as core elements of their personal identity. Feminism and homosexuality are the central themes explored by a diverse group of artists, including Barbara Kruger and Robert Mapplethorpe in America and the Pakistani artist Shahzia Sikander.

BARBARA KRUGER In the 1970s, some feminist artists, chief among them Cindy Sherman (FIG. 15-26), explored the "male gaze" and the culturally constructed notion of gender in their art. BARBARA KRUGER (b. 1945) examines similar issues in her photographs. The strategies and techniques of contemporary mass media fascinate Kruger, who was the art director of *Mademoiselle* magazine in the late 1960s. In *Untitled* (*Your Gaze Hits the Side of My Face*; FIG. **16-4**), Kruger incorporated the layout techniques that magazines and billboards use to sell consumer goods. Although she chose the reassuringly familiar format and look of advertising, Kruger's goal was to subvert the typical use of advertising imagery. She aimed to expose the deceptiveness of the media messages that viewers complacently absorb. Kruger wants to undermine the myths—particularly those about women—that the media constantly reinforce. Her word-and-photograph collages challenge the cultural attitudes embedded in commercial advertising. In *Your Gaze,* Kruger overlaid a photograph of a classically beautiful sculpted head of a woman with a vertical row of text composed of eight words. The words cannot be taken in with a single glance. Reading them is a staccato exercise, with a cumulative quality that delays understanding and intensifies the meaning (rather like a series of words painted on the pavement to be read by a driver in a moving car). Kruger's use of text in her work is significant. Many cultural theorists have asserted that language is one of the most powerful vehicles for internalizing stereotypes and conditioned roles.

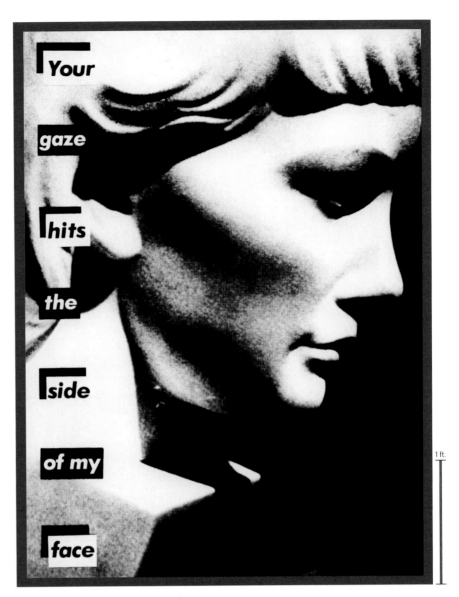

1 ft.

16-4 BARBARA KRUGER, *Untitled* (*Your Gaze Hits the Side of My Face*), 1981. Photograph, paper letters, red painted frame, 4' 7" × 3' 5". © Barbara Kruger/Courtesy Mary Boone Gallery, New York.

Kruger has explored the "male gaze" in her art. Using the layout techniques of mass media, she constructed this word-and-photograph collage to challenge culturally constructed notions of gender.

ROBERT MAPPLETHORPE For many artists, their homosexuality is as important an element of their personal identity as their gender, ethnicity, or race—often more important. One brilliant gay artist who became the central figure in a heated debate in the halls of the U.S. Congress as well as among the public at large was ROBERT MAPPLETHORPE (1946–1989). His *Perfect Moment* traveling exhibition, funded in part by the National Endowment for the Arts, featured an extensive series of photographs, including many nudes, some depicting children, some homoerotic and sadomasochistic in nature. The show led to a landmark court case on freedom of expression for artists and prompted new legislation establishing restrictions on government funding of the arts (see "Public Funding of Controversial Art," page 443).

Never at issue was Mapplethorpe's technical mastery of the photographic medium. His gelatin silver prints have glowing textures with rich tonal gradations of black, gray, and white. In many ways, Mapplethorpe was the heir of Edward Weston, whose innovative compositions of still lifes (FIG. 14-21) and nudes helped establish photography as an art form on a par with painting and sculpture. What shocked the public was not nudity per se—a traditional subject with roots in antiquity—but the openly gay character of many of Mapplethorpe's images. *The Perfect Moment* photographs included, in addition to some very graphic images of homosexual men, a series of self-portraits documenting Mapplethorpe's changing appearance (from having contracted AIDS) almost up until he died only months after the show opened in Philadelphia in December 1988. The self-portrait reproduced here (FIG. 16-5) presents Mapplethorpe as an androgynous young man with long hair and makeup, confronting the viewer with a steady gaze. Mapplethorpe's photographs, like the work of other gay and lesbian artists of the time, are inextricably bound up with the social upheavals in American society and the struggle for equal rights for women, homosexuals, minorities, and the disabled during the second half of the 20th century.

ART AND SOCIETY
Public Funding of Controversial Art

Although art can be beautiful and uplifting, throughout history art has also challenged and offended. Since the early 1980s, a number of heated controversies about art have surfaced in the United States. There have been many calls to remove "offensive" works from public view (see "Richard Serra's *Tilted Arc*," page 455) and, in reaction, accusations of censorship. The central questions in all cases have been whether there are limits to what art can appropriately be exhibited and whether governmental authorities have the right to monitor and pass judgment on creative endeavors. A related question is whether the acceptability of a work should be a criterion in determining the public funding of art.

Two exhibits in 1989 placed the National Endowment for the Arts (NEA), a U.S. government agency charged with distributing federal funds to support the arts, squarely in the middle of this debate. One of the exhibitions, devoted to recipients of the Awards for the Visual Arts (AVA), took place at the Southeastern Center for Contemporary Art in North Carolina. Among the award winners was Andres Serrano (b. 1950), whose *Piss Christ,* a photograph of a crucifix submerged in urine, sparked an uproar. Responding to this artwork, Donald Wildmon, an evangelical minister from Mississippi and head of the American Family Association, expressed outrage that this kind of work was in an exhibition funded by the NEA and the Equitable Life Assurance Society (a sponsor of the AVA). He demanded that *Piss Christ* be removed and launched a letter-writing campaign that caused Equitable Life to cancel its sponsorship of the awards. To staunch conservatives, this exhibition, along with *Robert Mapplethorpe: The Perfect Moment,* which included erotic homosexual images of the artist (FIG. 16-5) and others, served as evidence of cultural depravity and immorality. These critics insisted that art of an offensive character should not receive public funding. As a result of media furor over *The Perfect Moment,* the director of the Corcoran Museum of Art canceled the scheduled exhibition of this traveling show. But Dennis Barrie, director of the Contemporary Arts Center in Cincinnati, did mount the show, resulting in his indictment on charges of obscenity, but a jury acquitted him six months later.

These controversies intensified public criticism of the NEA and its funding practices. The next year, the head of the NEA, John Frohnmayer, vetoed grants for four lesbian, gay, or feminist performance artists, who became known as the "NEA Four." Infuriated by what they perceived as overt censorship, the artists filed suit, eventually settling the case and winning reinstatement of their grants. Congress responded by dramatically reducing the NEA's budget, and the agency no longer awards grants or fellowships to individual artists.

Controversies have also erupted on the municipal level. In 1999, Rudolph Giuliani, then mayor of New York, joined the protest over the inclusion of several artworks in the exhibition *Sensation: Young British Artists from the Saatchi Collection* at the Brooklyn Museum. Chris Ofili's *The Holy Virgin Mary* (FIG. 16-7) became the flashpoint for public furor. Denouncing the show as "sick stuff," the mayor threatened to cut off all city subsidies to the museum.

Art that seeks to unsettle and challenge is critical to the cultural, political, and psychological life of a society. The regularity with which unconventional art raises controversy suggests that it operates at the intersection of two competing principles: free speech and artistic expression on the one hand, and a reluctance to impose images on an audience that finds them repugnant or offensive on the other. What these controversies do demonstrate, beyond doubt, is the enduring power of art—and artists.

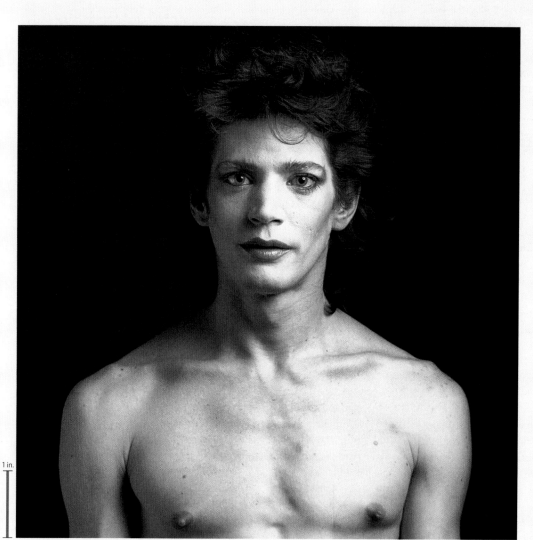

1 in.

16-5 ROBERT MAPPLETHORPE, *Self-Portrait,* **1980. Gelatin silver print, $7\frac{3}{4}$" × $7\frac{3}{4}$". Robert Mapplethorpe Foundation, New York.**

Mapplethorpe's *Perfect Moment* show led to a landmark court case on freedom of expression for artists. In this self-portrait, an androgynous Mapplethorpe confronts the viewer with a steady gaze.

16-6 SHAHZIA SIKANDER, *Perilous Order,* 1994–1997. Vegetable color, dry pigment, watercolor, and tea on Wasli paper, $10\frac{1}{2}$" × 8". Whitney Museum of American Art, New York (purchase, with funds from the Drawing Committee).

Imbuing miniature painting with a contemporary message about hypocrisy and intolerance, Sikander portrayed a gay friend as a homosexual Mughal emperor who enforced Muslim orthodoxy.

16-7 CHRIS OFILI, *The Holy Virgin Mary,* 1996. Paper collage, oil paint, glitter, polyester resin, map pins, elephant dung on linen, 7' 11" × 5' $11\frac{5}{16}$". Museum of Old and New Art, Hobart.

Ofili, a British-born Catholic of Nigerian descent, represented the Virgin Mary with African elephant dung as a breast and with genitalia and buttocks surrounding her. The painting produced a public outcry.

SHAHZIA SIKANDER The struggle for recognition and equal rights has never been confined to the United States. In the Muslim world, women and homosexuals face especially difficult challenges, which Pakistani artist SHAHZIA SIKANDER (b. 1969) brilliantly addresses in her work. Sikander, who now lives in New York City, has revived the demanding South Asian/Persian art of miniature painting (see page 474), but imbued this traditional art form with contemporary meaning. In *Perilous Order* (FIG. 16-6), she addresses homosexuality, intolerance, and hypocrisy by portraying a gay friend in the guise of the Mughal emperor Aurangzeb (r. 1658–1707), who was a strict enforcer of Islamic orthodoxy although reputed to be a homosexual. Sikander depicted him framed against a magnificent marbleized background ringed by voluptuous nude Hindu nymphs and behind the shadow of a veiled Hindu goddess. *Perilous Order* thus also incorporates a reference to the tensions between the Muslim and Hindu populations of Pakistan and India today.

National Identity

As in the case of Shahzia Sikander, a person's birthplace is often a central component of personal identity, even if the artist has migrated to another country. National identity looms large in the work of many contemporary artists.

CHRIS OFILI A British-born Catholic of Nigerian descent, CHRIS OFILI (b. 1968) is one of the leading European artists whose familial homeland figures prominently in his art. One of the major themes Ofili has addressed is religion, as interpreted through the eyes of an artist with his racial and national background. His *Holy Virgin Mary* (FIG. 16-7) depicts Mary in a manner that departs radically from conventional Renaissance representations. Ofili's work presents the Virgin in simplified form, and she appears to float in an indeterminate space. The artist employed brightly colored pigments applied to the canvas in multiple layers of beadlike dots (inspired by images from ancient caves in Zimbabwe). Surrounding the Virgin, whose face is that of an African woman, are tiny images of genitalia and buttocks cut out from pornographic magazines, which, to the artist, parallel the putti often surrounding Mary in Renaissance paintings. Another reference to Ofili's African heritage surfaces in the clumps of elephant dung—one forming the Virgin's breast, and two more serving as supports for the canvas. The dung enabled Ofili to incorporate Africa into his work in a literal way. Still, he wants the viewer to move beyond the cultural associations of the materials and see them in new ways. Not surprisingly, *The Holy Virgin Mary* elicited strong reactions, as Ofili clearly intended it to do when he decided to merge the sacred and the vile (see "Public Funding of Controversial Art," page 443).

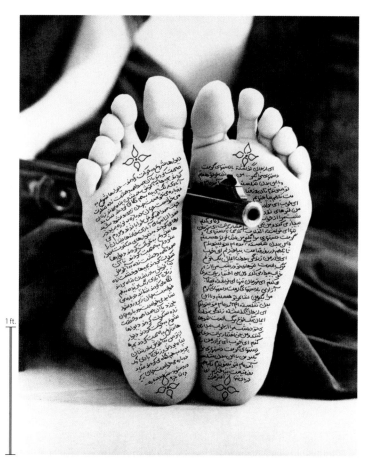

16-8 SHIRIN NESHAT, *Allegiance and Wakefulness,* 1994. Offset print with ink calligraphy, 3' 5¼" × 2' 9". Israel Museum, Jerusalem (anonymous gift, New York, to American Friends of the Israel Museum).

Neshat's photographs address the repression of women in postrevolutionary Iran. She poses in traditional veiled garb but wields a rifle and displays militant Farsi poetry on her exposed body parts.

SHIRIN NESHAT Political and social oppression also plays a significant role in the art of SHIRIN NESHAT (b. 1957), who grew up in a Westernized Iranian home and attended a Catholic boarding school in Tehran before leaving her homeland for the United States. Neshat produces films, video, and photographs critical of the fundamentalist Islamic regime in Iran, especially its treatment of women (see *"Shirin Neshat on Iran after the Revolution"* ⬈). She often poses for her photographs wearing a veil—which is for her a symbol both of ethnic pride and of the repression of Muslim women—and with her face and exposed parts of her body covered with Farsi (Persian) messages. Unlike the words in Kruger's photographs (FIG. 16-4), which evoke commercial typography, Neshat's handwritten additions to her photographs remind the viewer of the long tradition of calligraphy in Persian art (see page 151). A rifle also often figures prominently in Neshat's photographs as an emblem of militant feminism, a notion foreign to the Muslim faith. In *Allegiance and Wakefulness* (FIG. 16-8) from her *Women of Allah* series, Neshat omitted her face and most of her body, and focused on her feet covered with verses of militant Farsi poetry and on the barrel of a rifle she points menacingly toward the viewer.

POLITICAL AND SOCIAL COMMENTARY

Although almost all of the works discussed thus far are commentaries on contemporary society (seen through the lens of the artists' personal experiences), they do not incorporate references to specific events, nor do they address conditions affecting all people regardless of their race, national origin, gender, or sexual orientation—for example, homelessness, industrial pollution, and street violence. Other artists, including Canadian photographer EDWARD BURTYNSKY (b. 1955; FIG. 16-8A ⬈), have confronted precisely those aspects of late 20th- and early 21st-century life in their work.

MARTHA ROSLER Violence and armed combat are themes that have been explored by MARTHA ROSLER (b. 1943), who has produced a diverse body of artistic work, including photography, videos, and performance art. Throughout her career, Rosler has focused on social and political commentary, primarily issues concerning women, housing and homelessness, and war and its depiction in the media. *Gladiators* (FIG. 16-9) is one of the recent additions to Rosler's *Bringing the War Home: House Beautiful* photomontage series. Originally created between 1967 and 1972 as a critical commentary on the Vietnam War, Rosler expanded *House Beautiful* in 2004 in reaction to the war in Iraq. Like the other photomontages in the series, *Gladiators* brings disturbing images of combat into the domestic sphere by inserting armed soldiers (modern "gladiators") into the tranquil living rooms of upscale houses, literally "bringing the war home" to those whose sons and daughters, unlike those of working-class families, rarely enlist in the armed forces and fight for their country.

16-9 MARTHA ROSLER, *Gladiators,* 2004, from *Bringing the War Home: House Beautiful.* Photomontage, 1' 8" × 2'. Mitchell-Innes & Nash Gallery, New York.

Rosler's *House Beautiful* photomontages disturbingly insert images of armed soldiers (modern "gladiators") into the tranquil living rooms of upscale houses, literally "bringing the war home."

16-10 FERNANDO BOTERO, *Abu Ghraib 46*, 2005. Oil on canvas, 4' 9½" × 5' 9⅝". Berkeley Art Museum, Berkeley (gift of the artist).

Botero's *Abu Ghraib* series is a condemnation of the humiliation and torture of Iraqi prisoners by American military personnel. Critics have compared the paintings to scenes of martyrdom.

1 ft.

FERNANDO BOTERO Perhaps the most emotionally wrenching recent artworks to express outrage against war in general and specifically the inhumane treatment of prisoners is the large series of paintings and drawings by Colombian artist FERNANDO BOTERO (b. 1932). Still active in his 80s, Botero reacted with horror to the news reports and photographs of the humiliation and torture of Iraqi prisoners at the hands of American military personnel at Abu Ghraib prison. The paintings—for example, *Abu Ghraib 46* (FIG. 16-10)—are peopled by Botero's trademark larger-than-life inflated bodies, but they differ markedly from his usually tranquil domestic subjects. As in the published photographs from Abu Ghraib, the men in Botero's paintings are stripped of their clothes, blindfolded, bound, beaten, and bloodied, and are often threatened by ferocious dogs or forced to wear women's underwear. Critics have compared these graphic depictions of physical and mental torture to the passion of Christ and the martyrdom of saints. Botero has insisted that the paintings are not intended as anti-American but as a broad condemnation of cruelty in violation of the Geneva Convention. He has refused to profit from sales of the Abu Ghraib paintings and has donated them to museums on the condition that they forever remain on display.

WILLIE BESTER Political oppression in South Africa figures prominently in the paintings of WILLIE BESTER (b. 1956), one of many South African artists who were vocal critics of apartheid (government-sponsored racial separation). Bester's 1992 *Homage to Steve Biko* (FIG. 16-11) is a tribute to the gentle and heroic leader of the South African Black Consciousness Movement whom the authorities killed while he was in detention. The exoneration of the two white doctors in charge of him sparked protests around the world. Bester packed his picture with references to death and injustice. Biko's portrait, at the center, is near another of the police minister, James Kruger, who had him transported 1,100 kilometers (almost 700 miles) to Pretoria in the yellow Land Rover ambulance seen left of center and again beneath Biko's portrait. Bester portrayed Biko with his chained fists raised in the classic worldwide protest gesture. This portrait memorializes both Biko and the many other antiapartheid activists, as indicated by the white graveyard crosses above a blue sea of skulls beside Biko's head. The crosses stand out against a red background, recalling the inferno of burned townships. The stop sign (lower left) seems to mean "stop Kruger," or perhaps "stop apartheid." The tagged foot, as if in a morgue, above the ambulance (to the left) also refers to Biko's death. The red crosses on this vehicle's door and on Kruger's reflective dark glasses repeat, with sad irony, the graveyard crosses.

Blood-red and ambulance-yellow are in fact unifying colors dripped or painted on many parts of the canvas. Writing and numbers, found fragments, and stenciled and painted signs—favorite Cubist motifs (FIGS. 14-8 and 14-9)—also appear throughout the composition. Numbers refer to the dehumanized life of blacks under apartheid. Found objects—wire, sticks, cardboard, sheet metal, cans, and other discards—from which the poor construct fragile, impermanent township dwellings—remind viewers of the degraded lives of most South African people of color. The oilcan guitar (bottom center), another recurrent Bester symbol, refers both to the social harmony and joy provided by music and to the control imposed by apartheid policies. The whole composition is rich in texture and dense in its collage combinations of objects, photographs, signs, symbols, and pigment. *Homage to Steve Biko* is a powerful critique of an oppressive sociopolitical system, and it exemplifies the extent to which art can be invoked in the political process.

ZHANG XIAOGANG Political and social commentary is also the principal interest of Chinese painter ZHANG XIAOGANG (b. 1958). Zhang is best known for his *Bloodline* portraits—for example, *Big Family No. 2* (FIG. 16-12). Based on the black-and-white photographs of Chinese families popular during the Cultural Revolution of 1966 to 1976 under Mao Tse-tung (1893–1976), the *Bloodline* paintings are not really portraits. Instead, they depict generic, personality-less fathers, mothers, and children wearing the approved plain clothes of the Mao era in China. Ironically titled *Big Family*, these somber three-figure groups are also commentaries on the long-standing, though recently eased, government policy of restricting most married couples to having only a single child, a policy that has led many families to seek abortions, often in order to raise a boy instead of a girl. The *Bloodline* series takes its name from the faint red lines connecting the figures—a device used earlier by Frida Kahlo (FIG. 14-39). The red bloodlines are the only touches of color in Zhang's otherwise intentionally subdued palette, save for, in the illustrated example, the yellow that draws attention to the highly desirable male child.

1 ft.

16-11 WILLIE BESTER, *Homage to Steve Biko,* 1992. Mixed media, 3' 7$\frac{5}{6}$" × 3' 7$\frac{5}{6}$". Collection of the artist.

Homage to Steve Biko is a tribute to a leader of the Black Consciousness Movement, which protested apartheid in South Africa. References to the injustice of Biko's death fill this complex painting.

1 ft.

16-12 ZHANG XIAOGANG, *Bloodline: Big Family No. 2,* 1995. Oil on canvas, 5' 11" × 7' 6$\frac{5}{8}$". Private collection.

Ironically titled *Big Family* in reaction to the government's one-child policy, Zhang's generic, personality-less portraits intentionally recall black-and-white family photographs of the Mao era in China.

Political and Social Commentary **447**

16-13 Xu Bing, *A Book from the Sky*, 1987. Installation of woodblock-printed books at the Elvehjem
(now Chazen) Museum of Art, University of Wisconsin, Madison, 1991.

Xu trained as a printmaker in Beijing. *A Book from the Sky*,
with its invented Chinese woodblock characters, may be a
stinging critique of the meaninglessness of contemporary
political language.

XU BING A different kind of commentary on Chinese culture has been the hallmark of the work of
Xu Bing (b. 1955), a Chongqing native who was
forced to work in the countryside with peasants
during the Cultural Revolution. In 1987, Xu exhibited his most famous work, a large *installation* (an
assemblage that creates an artistic environment in
a room) called *A Book from the Sky* (FIG. 16-13), at
the University of Wisconsin. The work presents
an enormous number of woodblock-printed texts
in characters evocative of Chinese writing but
invented by the artist. Producing them required
both an intimate knowledge of genuine Chinese
characters and extensive training in woodblock
carving. *A Book from the Sky,* however, is no hymn
to tradition. Critics have interpreted it both as a
stinging critique of the meaninglessness of contemporary political language and as a commentary on
the illegibility of the past. Indeed, Xu intended *A
Book from the Sky* to be read on many levels.

REPRESENTATION AND ABSTRACTION

Despite the high visibility of contemporary artists whose work deals
with the pressing social and political issues of the world, some critically acclaimed living artists have produced innovative modernist
art during the postmodern era. Abstraction remains a valid and
compelling approach to painting and sculpture in the 21st century,
as does more traditional figural art.

Figural Painting and Sculpture

Recent decades have brought a revival of interest in figural art, both
in painting and sculpture, a trend best exemplified in the earlier
postwar period by Lucian Freud (FIG. 15-22A ⬀), who remained an
active and influential painter until his death in July 2011.

JENNY SAVILLE Fellow Briton Jenny Saville (b. 1970) is the leading figure painter in the Freud mold of the younger generation of
European and American artists. She is best known for her over-life-
size self-portraits in which she exaggerates the girth of her body
and delights in depicting heavy folds of flesh with visible veins in
minute detail and from a sharply foreshortened angle, which further distorts the body's proportions. Saville's nude self-portraits are
a commentary on the contemporary obsession with the lithe bodies of fashion models. In *Branded* (FIG. 16-14), she highlights the
dichotomy between the popular notion of a beautiful body and the
imperfect bodies of most people by "branding" her body with words
inscribed in her flesh—"delicate," "decorative," "petite." Art critic
Michelle Meagher has described Saville's paintings as embodying a
"feminist aesthetics of disgust."[2]

1 ft.

16-14 Jenny Saville, *Branded*, 1992. Oil on canvas, 7' × 6'. Saatchi
Gallery, London.

Saville's unflattering foreshortened self-portrait "branded" with words such as
"delicate" and "petite" underscores the dichotomy between the perfect bodies
of fashion models and those of most people.

KIKI SMITH A distinctly unflattering approach to the representation of the human body is also the hallmark of the sculptures of KIKI SMITH (b. 1954). In her work, Smith has explored the question of who controls the human body, an interest that grew out of her training as an emergency medical service technician. Smith, however, also wants to reveal the socially constructed nature of the body, and she encourages the viewer to consider how external forces shape people's perceptions of their bodies. In works such as *Untitled* (FIG. 16-15), the artist dramatically departed from conventional representations of the body, both in art and in the media. She suspended two life-size wax figures, one male and one female, both nude, from metal stands. Smith marked each of the sculptures with long white drips—body fluids running from the woman's breasts and down the man's leg. She commented:

> Most of the functions of the body are hidden . . . from society. . . . [W]e separate our bodies from our lives. But, when people are dying, they are losing control of their bodies. That loss of function can seem

humiliating and frightening. But, on the other hand, you can look at it as a kind of liberation of the body. It seems like a nice metaphor—a way to think about the social—that people lose control despite the many agendas of different ideologies in society, which are trying to control the body(ies) . . . medicine, religion, law, etc. Just thinking about control—who has control of the body? . . . Does the mind have control of the body? Does the social?[3]

JEFF KOONS The sculptures of JEFF KOONS (b. 1955) form a striking counterpoint to the figural art of Kiki Smith. Koons first became prominent in the art world for a series of works in the early 1980s involving the exhibition of everyday commercial products such as vacuum cleaners. Clearly following in the footsteps of Marcel Duchamp (FIG. 14-15), Koons made no attempt to manipulate or alter the machine-made objects. More recently, he turned to ceramic sculpture. In *Pink Panther* (FIG. 16-16), Koons intertwined a pin-up nude with a famous cartoon character. He reinforced the trite and kitschy nature of this imagery by titling the exhibition of which this sculpture was a part *The Banality Show*. Koons intends his work to

1 ft.

16-15 KIKI SMITH, *Untitled,* 1990. Beeswax and microcrystalline wax figures on metal stands, female figure installed height 6' 1½", male figure installed height 6' 4¹⁵⁄₁₆". Whitney Museum of American Art, New York (purchased with funds from the Painting and Sculpture Committee).

Asking "Who controls the body?" Kiki Smith sculpted two life-size wax figures of a nude man and woman with body fluids running from the woman's breasts and down the man's leg.

1 ft.

16-16 JEFF KOONS, *Pink Panther,* 1988. Porcelain, 3' 5" high. Museum of Contemporary Art, Chicago (Gerald S. Elliot Collection).

Koons creates sculptures highlighting everything he considers wrong with contemporary American consumer culture. In this work, he intertwined a centerfold nude and a cartoon character.

PROBLEMS AND SOLUTIONS
Rethinking the Shape of Painting

Since antiquity, rectangular frames for paintings have been the norm worldwide for wood panels, frescoed walls, oil paintings on canvas, manuscript illustrations, and silk scrolls alike. Even during the past century, when artists have rethought almost every traditional tenet of the art of painting, the vertically or horizontally oriented rectilinear painting surface has with few exceptions (for example, FIG. 15-8) reigned supreme, even among artists who have abandoned easel painting in favor of applying pigment to unstretched canvas spread out on the floor (FIG. 15-5). Recently, however, some artists have experimented not merely with other geometric shapes but with highly irregular formats.

Chief among them is Elizabeth Murray. Born in Chicago, Murray moved to New York City in 1967 and painted there until her death in 2007, the year after a major retrospective exhibition of her work was mounted at the Museum of Modern Art—a rare honor accorded to few women before her.

Can You Hear Me? (FIG. 16-17) is typical of Murray's innovative approach to abstract painting. It is an irregularly shaped composite of several small canvas-on-wood panels that bear comparison not only to Abstract Expressionist works but to the Biomorphic Surrealist paintings of Joan Miró (FIG. 14-27) and also to cartoon art. The central—although almost unnoticed at first—motif of *Can You Hear Me?* is a face with a wide-open mouth out of which emerges a shape resembling an elongated comic-strip balloon (compare FIG. 15-18) but without words—the reason the viewer cannot hear what the face is saying. Murray has acknowledged that Edvard Munch's *Scream* (FIG. 13-17) was the source of inspiration for her painting, but in *Can You Hear Me?* emotional frenzy is expressed by purely abstract means, most notably through the centrifugal force of the propeller-like shape of the painting itself.

16-17 ELIZABETH MURRAY, *Can You Hear Me?* 1984. Oil on canvas on wood, 8' 10" × 13' 3" × 1'. Dallas Museum of Art, Dallas (Foundation for the Arts Collection).

Elizabeth Murray's abstract compositions are of unusual format. She rejected the traditional rectilinear format for painting in favor of a multilayered composite of canvas-on-wood panels.

1 ft.

draw attention to everything that he believes is wrong with contemporary American society. His prominence in the art world is based on his acute understanding of the dynamics of consumer culture.

Abstract Painting and Sculpture

Today, many artists continue to explore abstraction as a compelling means of expression in pictorial art, among them JULIAN SCHNABEL (b. 1951; FIG. 16-16A ⟋) and Elizabeth Murray (FIG. 16-17) in the United States, SONG SU-NAM (b. 1938; FIG. 16-16B ⟋) in Korea, and El Anatsui (FIG. 16-18) in Ghana.

ELIZABETH MURRAY One of the few things that paintings as diverse as those examined so far have in common is that they share the standard rectilinear format that has characterized paintings on wood, canvas, or silk from antiquity to the present day. A leading contemporary artist who experimented with alternate shapes was ELIZABETH MURRAY (1940–2007; see "Rethinking the Shape of Painting," above, and FIG. 16-17).

EL ANATSUI Probably the most unusual abstract artworks being created today are those of EL ANATSUI (b. 1944) of Ghana, who, unique among African artists, established his international reputation without moving his studio to Europe or America. Anatsui has spent his entire adult life in Nigeria and, even more remarkably, did not begin producing the art that has made him famous until his 60s. *Bleeding Takari II* (FIG. 16-18) is a characteristic example of the artistic genre that Anatsui invented, a kind of artwork that is so different from all others that art historians have yet to agree on a label for it. A cross between sculpture and textile design, Anatsui's "metal

16-18 EL ANATSUI, *Bleeding Takari II*, 2007. Aluminum bottle tops and copper wire, 12' 11" × 18' 11". Museum of Modern Art, New York (gift of Donald L. Bryant Jr. and Jerry Speyer, 2008).

Anatsui's unique "metal hangings" are a cross between abstract sculptures and textiles. They are assemblages of thousands of crushed and pierced bottle caps and aluminum cans stitched together with copper wire.

hangings" (as they are often called) are labor-intensive constructions of crushed bottle caps and lids of aluminum cans pierced and stitched together using copper wire. The colors (primarily red, gold, and black) that Anatsui uses have close parallels in Asante *kente* cloth, and his works can be rolled and folded like fabric. When displayed on museum walls or hanging from a ceiling—or even draped on a building's facade—the metal sheets undulate with any breeze. Anatsui's artworks-in-motion deserve comparison with Alexander Calder's pioneering mobiles (FIG. 14-32). They are, however, thoroughly in tune with 21st-century concerns in being assembled (by a large team of assistants) almost entirely from recycled materials.

ARCHITECTURE AND SITE-SPECIFIC ART

The work of architects and Environmental artists today is as varied as that of contemporary painters and sculptors, but the common denominator in the diversity of contemporary architectural design and site-specific projects is the breaking down of national boundaries.

Architecture

In the late 20th and early 21st centuries, one of the by-products of the globalization of the world's economy has been that leading architects have received commissions to design buildings far from their home bases. In the rapidly developing emerging markets of

Asia, the Middle East, Africa, Latin America, and elsewhere, virtually every architect with an international reputation can list on his or her résumé a recent building in a bustling new urban center.

DECONSTRUCTIVISM Perhaps the most radical development in architectural design during the closing decades of the 20th century was *Deconstructivism*. Deconstructivist architects attempt to disrupt the conventional categories of architecture and to rupture the viewer's expectations based on them. Disorder, dissonance, imbalance, asymmetry, irregularity, and confusion replace their opposites— order, harmony, balance, symmetry, regularity, and clarity. The seemingly haphazardly presented volumes, masses, planes, borders, lighting, locations, directions, and spatial relations, as well as the disguised structural facts of Deconstructivist design, challenge the viewer's assumptions about architectural form as it relates to function. According to Deconstructivist principles, the very absence of the stability of traditional categories of architecture in a structure announces a "deconstructed" building.

FRANK GEHRY One of the first practitioners of this audacious architectural mode was German architect GÜNTER BEHNISCH (1922–2010); FIG. 16-18A ☑). The architect most closely identified with Deconstructivist architecture, however, is Canadian FRANK GEHRY (b. 1929). Gehry works up his designs by constructing models and then cutting them up and arranging the parts until he has a satisfying composition. Among Gehry's most notable projects is

Gehry's limestone-and-titanium Bilbao museum is an immensely dramatic building. Its disorder and seeming randomness of design exemplify Deconstructivist architectural principles.

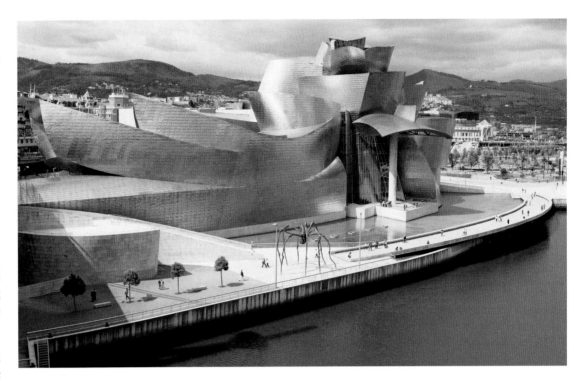

the Guggenheim Museum (FIG. 16-19) in Bilbao, Spain, which appears to be a collapsed or collapsing aggregate of units. Visitors approaching the building see a mass of irregular asymmetrical and imbalanced forms whose profiles change dramatically with every shift of the viewer's position. The limestone- and titanium-clad exterior lends a space-age character to the structure and highlights further the unique cluster effect of the many forms. A group of organic forms that Gehry refers to as a "metallic flower" tops the museum. In the center of the building, an enormous glass-walled atrium soars 165 feet above the ground, serving as the focal point for the three levels of galleries radiating from it. The seemingly weightless screens, vaults, and volumes of the interior float and flow into one another, guided only by light and dark cues. The Guggenheim Museum in Bilbao is a profoundly compelling structure. Its disorder, its deceptive randomness of design, and the disequilibrium it prompts in viewers epitomize Deconstructivist principles, as do the designs of London-based Iraqi Zaha Hadid (b. 1950; FIG. 16-19A ⬈).

NORMAN FOSTER British architect Norman Foster (b. 1935) met Richard Rogers (FIG. 15-33) at the Yale School of Architecture, and they opened a joint architectural firm when they returned to London in 1962, although they established separate practices several years later. Foster and Rogers are the leading proponents of what critics call *High-Tech architecture,* the roots of which can be traced to Joseph Paxton's mid-19th-century Crystal Palace (FIG. 12-24) in London. High-Tech architects design buildings incorporating the latest innovations in engineering and technology and exposing the structures' component parts. High-Tech architecture is distinct from other postmodern architectural movements in dispensing with all historical references.

Foster's design for the headquarters (FIG. 16-20) of the Hong Kong and Shanghai Bank Corporation (HSBC), which cost $1 billion to build, exemplifies the High-Tech approach to architecture. The 47-story skyscraper has an exposed steel skeleton with the elevators and other service elements located in giant piers at the short ends of the building, a design that provides uninterrupted communal working spaces on each cantilevered floor. Foster divided the HSBC tower into five horizontal units of six to nine floors each that he calls "villages," suspended from steel girders resembling bridges. At the base of the building is a plaza opening onto the neighboring

16-20 Norman Foster, Hong Kong and Shanghai Bank (looking southwest), Hong Kong, China, 1979–1986.

Foster's High-Tech tower has an exposed steel skeleton featuring floors with uninterrupted working spaces. At the base is a 10-story atrium illuminated by computerized mirrors that reflect sunlight.

16-21 RENZO PIANO, Tjibaou Cultural Centre (looking southeast), Noumea, New Caledonia, 1998.

A pioneering example of Green architecture, Piano's complex of 10 bamboo units, based on traditional New Caledonian village huts, has adjustable skylights in the roofs for natural climate control.

streets. Visitors ascend on escalators from the plaza to a spectacular 10-story, 170-foot-tall atrium bordered by balconies with additional workspaces. What Foster calls "sun scoops"—computerized mirrors on the south side of the building—track the movement of the sun across the Hong Kong sky and reflect the sunlight into the atrium and plaza, flooding the dramatic spaces with light at all hours of the day. Not surprisingly, the roof of this High-Tech skyscraper serves as a landing pad for corporate helicopters.

GREEN ARCHITECTURE The harnessing of solar energy as a power source is one of the key features of what critics commonly refer to as *Green architecture*—ecologically friendly buildings that use "clean energy" and sustain the natural environment. Green architecture is the most important trend in architectural design in the early 21st century. A pioneer in this field is Renzo Piano, the codesigner with

Richard Rogers of the Pompidou Center (FIG. 15-33) in Paris. Piano won an international competition to design the Tjibaou Cultural Centre (FIG. 16-21) in Noumea. Rooted in the village architecture of the Kanak people of New Caledonia, the center consists of 10 beehive-shaped bamboo "huts" nestled in pine trees on a narrow island peninsula in the Pacific Ocean. Each unit has an adjustable skylight as a roof to provide natural—sustainable—climate control. The curved profile of the Tjibaou pavilions also helps the structures withstand the pressure of the hurricane-force winds common in the South Pacific.

Environmental and Site-Specific Art

When Robert Smithson created *Spiral Jetty* (FIG. 15-34) in Utah's Great Salt Lake in 1970, he was a trailblazer in the new genre of Environmental Art, or earthworks. In recent decades, earthworks and other site-specific artworks that bridge the gap between architecture and sculpture have become an established mode of artistic expression. As is true of all other media in the postmodern era, these artworks take a dazzling variety of forms.

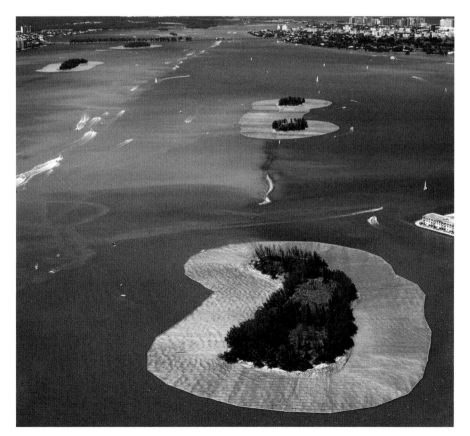

CHRISTO AND JEANNE-CLAUDE The most famous Environmental artists of the past few decades are CHRISTO (b. 1935) and JEANNE-CLAUDE (1935–2009). In their works, the couple sought to intensify the viewer's awareness of the space and features of rural and urban sites. However, rather than physically alter the land itself, as Smithson often did, Christo and Jeanne-Claude prompted this awareness by temporarily modifying the landscape with cloth. Their projects required years of preparation and research, and scores of meetings with local authorities and interested groups of citizens. These temporary artworks were usually on view for only a few weeks.

Surrounded Islands (FIG. 16-22), created in Biscayne Bay in Miami, Florida, for two weeks in May 1983, typifies Christo and Jeanne-Claude's work. For this project, they surrounded 11 small

16-22 CHRISTO and JEANNE-CLAUDE, *Surrounded Islands, Biscayne Bay, Miami, Florida, 1980–1983.*

Christo and Jeanne-Claude created this Environmental artwork by surrounding 11 small islands with 6.5 million square feet of pink fabric. Characteristically, the work existed for only two weeks.

ART AND SOCIETY
Maya Lin's Vietnam Veterans Memorial

Maya Lin's Vietnam Veterans Memorial (FIG. 16-23) is, like Minimalist sculptures (FIG. 15-12), an unadorned geometric form. Yet the monument, despite its serene simplicity, actively engages viewers in a psychological dialogue, giving visitors the opportunity to explore their feelings about the Vietnam War. The history of the memorial provides dramatic testimony to this monument's power. In 1981, a jury of architects, sculptors, and landscape architects selected Lin's design from among 1,400 entries in a blind competition. Conceivably, the jurors not only found her design compelling but also thought that its simplicity would be the least likely to provoke controversy. But when the jury made its selection public, heated debate ensued. Even the wall's color came under attack. One veteran charged that black is "the universal color of shame, sorrow and degradation in all races, all societies worldwide."* But the sharpest protests concerned the form and siting of the monument. Because of the stark contrast between the massive white memorials (the Washington Monument and the Lincoln Memorial) bracketing Lin's sunken wall, some people interpreted her Minimalist design as minimizing the Vietnam War and, by extension, Vietnam veterans. Lin herself, however, described the wall as follows:

> The Vietnam Veterans Memorial is not an object inserted into the earth but a work formed from the act of cutting open the earth and polishing the earth's surface—dematerializing the stone to pure surface, creating an interface between the world of the light and the quieter world beyond the names.[†]

Because of the vocal opposition, a compromise was necessary to ensure the memorial's completion. In 1983,

the Commission of Fine Arts, the federal group overseeing the project, commissioned a larger-than-life-size realistic bronze sculpture by artist Frederick Hart (1943–1999) of three soldiers, armed and uniformed, which stands approximately 120 feet from Lin's wall. Several years later, a group of nurses won approval for a sculpture honoring women's service in the Vietnam War. The 7-foot-tall bronze statue by Glenna Goodacre (b. 1939) depicts three female figures, one cradling a wounded soldier in her arms. Unveiled in 1993, the work occupies a site about 300 feet south of the Lin memorial.

Commonly, visitors react very emotionally to Lin's Vietnam Veterans Memorial, even those who know none of the soldiers named on the monument. The polished granite surface prompts individual soul-searching—viewers see themselves reflected among the names. Many leave mementos at the foot of the wall in memory of loved ones they lost in the Vietnam War or make rubbings from the incised names. It can be argued that much of this memorial's power derives from its Minimalist simplicity. It does not dictate response and therefore successfully encourages personal exploration.

*Elizabeth Hess, "A Tale of Two Memorials," *Art in America* 71, no. 4 (April 1983): 122.
[†]Excerpt from an unpublished 1995 lecture, quoted in Kristine Stiles and Peter Selz, *Theories and Documents of Contemporary Art: A Sourcebook of Artists' Writings* (Berkeley and Los Angeles: University of California Press, 1996), 525.

16-23 MAYA YING LIN, Vietnam Veterans Memorial (looking north), Washington, D.C., 1981–1983.

Like Minimalist sculpture, Lin's memorial to veterans of the Vietnam War is a simple geometric form. Its inscribed polished walls actively engage viewers in a psychological dialogue about the war.

artificial islands in the bay (created from a dredging project) with 6.5 million square feet of specially fabricated pink polypropylene floating fabric. This Environmental artwork required three years of preparation to obtain the required permits, assemble the labor force, and obtain the $3.2 million needed to complete the project. The artists raised the money by selling preparatory drawings, collages, and models of works they created in the 1950s and 1960s. Huge crowds watched as crews removed accumulated trash from the 11 islands (to assure maximum contrast between their dark colors, the pink of the cloth, and the blue of the bay) and then unfurled the fabric "cocoons" to form magical floating "skirts" around each tiny bit of land.

MAYA YING LIN Often classified as either a work of Minimalist sculpture or as an architectural monument, the Vietnam Veterans Memorial (FIG. 16-23) in Washington, D.C., is perhaps best considered under the heading of site-specific art. The now-acclaimed war memorial was designed in 1981 by MAYA YING LIN (b. 1959) when she was a 21-year-old student at the Yale School of Architecture. Austere and simple, the Vietnam memorial takes the form of a V-shaped wall constructed of polished black granite panels. The two 246-foot-long wings of the wall begin at ground level at each end and gradually ascend to a height of 10 feet at the center of the V. Lin set the memorial into the landscape, enhancing visitors' awareness of descent as they walk along the wall toward the center. The

ART AND SOCIETY

Richard Serra's *Tilted Arc*

When Richard Serra installed *Tilted Arc* (FIG. 16-24) in the plaza in front of the Javits Federal Building in New York City in 1981, much of the public immediately responded with hostile criticism. Prompting the chorus of complaints was the uncompromising presence of a Minimalist sculpture bisecting the plaza. Many argued that *Tilted Arc* was ugly, attracted graffiti, interfered with the view across the plaza, and prevented use of the plaza for performances or concerts. Because of the sustained barrage of protests and petitions demanding the removal of *Tilted Arc,* the General Services Administration, which had commissioned the sculpture, held a series of public hearings. Afterward, the agency decided to remove Serra's sculpture despite its prior approval of the artist's model. Understandably, this infuriated Serra, who had a legally binding contract acknowledging the site-specific nature of *Tilted Arc.* "To remove the work is to destroy the work," the artist stated.*

This episode raised intriguing issues about the nature of public art, including the public reception of experimental art, the artist's responsibilities and rights when executing public commissions, censorship in the arts, and the purpose of public art. If an artwork is on display in a public space outside the relatively private confines of a museum or gallery, do different guidelines apply? As one participant in the *Tilted Arc* saga asked, "Should an artist have the right to impose his values and taste on a public that now rejects his taste and values?"† Historically, one of the express functions of the artistic avant-garde was to challenge convention by rejecting tradition and disrupting the complacency of the viewer. Will placing experimental art in a public place always cause controversy? From Serra's statements, it is clear that he intended the sculpture to challenge the public.

Another issue that *Tilted Arc* presented involved the rights of the artist, who in this case accused the GSA of censorship. Serra filed a lawsuit against the federal government for infringement of his First Amendment rights and insisted that "the artist's work must be uncensored, respected, and tolerated, although deemed abhorrent, or perceived as challenging, or experienced as threatening."‡ Did removal of the work constitute censorship? A U.S. district court held that it did not.

Ultimately, who should decide what artworks are appropriate for the public arena? One artist argued, "We cannot have public art by plebiscite [popular vote]."§ But to avoid recurrences of the *Tilted Arc* controversy, the GSA changed its procedures and now solicits input from a wide range of civic and neighborhood groups before commissioning public artworks. Despite the removal of *Tilted Arc* (now languishing in storage), the sculpture maintains a powerful presence in all discussions of the aesthetics, politics, and dynamics of public art.

*Grace Glueck, "What Part Should the Public Play in Choosing Public Art?" *New York Times,* February 3, 1985, 27.
†Calvin Tomkins, "The Art World: Tilted Arc," *New Yorker,* May 20, 1985, 98.
‡Ibid., 98–99.
§Ibid., 98.

16-24 RICHARD SERRA, *Tilted Arc,* as installed before its removal from Jacob K. Javits Federal Plaza (looking southwest), New York City, 1981.

Serra intended his Minimalist *Tilted Arc* to alter the character of an existing public space. He succeeded, but unleashed a storm of protest that caused the government to remove the work.

---

names of the Vietnam War's 57,939 American casualties (and those missing in action) incised on the wings (in the order of their deaths) contribute to the memorial's dramatic effect.

When Lin designed this pristinely simple monument, she gave a great deal of thought to the purpose of war memorials. She was determined to create a memorial that would

> be honest about the reality of war and be for the people who gave their lives. . . . [I] didn't want a static object that people would just look at, but something they could relate to as on a journey, or passage, that would bring each to his own conclusions. . . . I wanted to work with the land and not dominate it. I had an impulse to cut open the earth . . . an initial violence that in time would heal. The grass would grow back, but the cut would remain.⁴

In light of the tragedy of the war, this unpretentious memorial's allusion to a wound and a "long-lasting scar" contributes to its visual and psychological impact (see "Maya Lin's Vietnam Veterans Memorial," page 454). In 2000, a long-lasting scar of a different kind—the Holocaust of World War II—was brilliantly memorialized by British sculptor RACHEL WHITEREAD (b. 1963) in the former Jewish Ghetto of Vienna (FIG. 16-23A ⬀).

RICHARD SERRA Also unleashing a heated public debate, but for different reasons and with a decidedly different outcome, was *Tilted Arc* (FIG. 16-24) by RICHARD SERRA (b. 1939), who as a young man worked in steel mills in California. In 1979, he received a commission from the U.S. General Services Administration (GSA) to install a 120-foot-long, 12-foot-high curved wall of Cor-Ten steel in the

16-25 Anish Kapoor, *Cloud Gate*, 2004. Stainless steel, 33' × 66' × 42'. Millennium Park, Chicago.

Kapoor's enormous polished stainless steel sculpture has delighted visitors to Chicago's Millennium Park, who enjoy seeing distorted views of themselves and the city's skyline in *Cloud Gate's* curving mirrored surface.

10 ft

plaza in front of the Jacob K. Javits Federal Building in lower Manhattan. He completed the project in 1981. Serra wished *Tilted Arc* to "dislocate or alter the decorative function of the plaza and actively bring people into the sculpture's context."[5] In pursuit of that goal, Serra situated the sculpture so that it bisected and consequently significantly altered the space of the open plaza and interrupted the traffic flow across the square. By creating such an intrusive presence in this large public space, Serra forced viewers to reconsider the plaza's physical space as a sculptural form—but only temporarily, because the public succeeded in having the sculpture removed (see "Richard Serra's *Tilted Arc*," page 455).

ANISH KAPOOR The public reacted very differently to the installation in 2004 in Chicago's Millennium Park of *Cloud Gate* (FIG. **16-25**), a 33-foot-tall and 66-foot-long polished stainless steel abstract sculpture by the recently knighted Mumbai-born British sculptor Anish Kapoor (b. 1954). Affectionately known to Chicagoans as the Bean, Kapoor's gigantic, gently curving sculpture is large enough that people can walk under its swelling arched form, hence its title *Cloud Gate*. Rather than disrupting activity in the park, as Serra's *Tilted Arc* did in Manhattan, Kapoor's *Cloud Gate* encourages viewers to interact with it. Indeed, most people delight in seeing their reflection (with the backdrop of the panorama of Chicago's skyline) in the mirrorlike surface. On many days, *Cloud Gate* also reflects clouds of similar bean shape. However, the reflections of people, buildings, and clouds are distorted by the Bean's curved surface, as Kapoor intended them to be, adding another dimension to the pleasure of looking at the work.

Among the many other contemporary artists creating exciting site-specific artworks today is Korean Do-Ho Suh (b. 1962), whose installations—for example, *Bridging Home* (FIG. **16-25A** ⬈)—have been exhibited worldwide, underscoring the truly international nature of artistic production today.

NEW MEDIA

In addition to taking the ancient arts of painting, sculpture, and architecture in new directions, contemporary artists have continued to explore the expressive possibilities of the various new media developed in the postwar period, especially digital photography, computer graphics, and video.

ANDREAS GURSKY Since the mid-1990s, German photographer Andreas Gursky (b. 1955) has used computer and digital technology to produce gigantic color prints in which he combines and manipulates photographs taken with a wide-angle lens, usually from a high vantage point. The size of his photographs, sometimes almost a dozen feet wide, intentionally rivals 19th-century history paintings. But as was true of Gustave Courbet (FIGS. 12-13 and 12-14) in his day, Gursky's subjects come from everyday life. He records the mundane world of the modern global economy—vast industrial plants, major department stores, hotel lobbies, and stock and commodity exchanges—and, like Edward Burtynsky (FIG. 16-8A ⬈), transforms the commonplace into striking, almost abstract compositions.

Gursky's enormous 1999 print (FIG. **16-26**) documenting the frenzied activity on the main floor of the Chicago Board of Trade is a characteristic example of his work. He took a series of photographs from a gallery, creating a panoramic view of the traders in their brightly colored jackets. He then combined several digital images using commercial photo-editing software to produce a blurred tableau of bodies, desks, computer terminals, and strewn paper in which both mass and color are so evenly distributed as to negate the traditional Renaissance notion of perspective. In using the computer to modify the "objective truth" and spatial recession of "straight photography," Gursky blurs the distinction between painting and photography.

16-26 ANDREAS GURSKY, *Chicago Board of Trade II*, 1999. C-print, 6' 9 $\frac{1}{2}$" × 11' 5 $\frac{5}{8}$". Matthew Marks Gallery, New York.

Gursky manipulates digital photographs to produce vast tableaus depicting places that are characteristic of the modern global economy. The size of his prints rivals that of 19th-century history paintings.

BILL VIOLA For much of his artistic career, BILL VIOLA (b. 1951) has also explored the capabilities of digitized imagery, producing many video installations and single-channel works. Often focusing on sensory perception, the pieces not only heighten viewer awareness of the senses but also suggest an exploration into the spiritual realm. Viola spent years seriously studying Buddhist, Christian, Sufi, and Zen mysticism. Because he fervently believes in art's transformative power and in a spiritual view of human nature, Viola designs works encouraging spectator introspection. His video projects have involved using techniques such as extreme slow motion, contrasts in scale, shifts in focus, mirrored reflections, staccato editing, and multiple or layered screens to achieve dramatic effects.

The power of Viola's work is evident in *The Crossing* (FIG. 16-27), an installation piece involving two color video channels projected on 16-foot-high screens. The artist either shows the two projections on the front and back of the same screen or on two separate screens in the same installation. In these two companion videos, shown simultaneously on the two screens, a man surrounded in darkness appears, moving closer until he fills the screen. On one screen, drops of water fall from above onto the man's head, while on the other screen, a small fire breaks out at the man's feet. Over the next few

16-27 BILL VIOLA, *The Crossing*, 1996. Video/sound installation with two channels of color video projection onto screens 16' high.

Viola's video projects use extreme slow motion, contrasts in scale, shifts in focus, mirrored reflections, and staccato editing to create dramatic sensory experiences rooted in tangible reality.

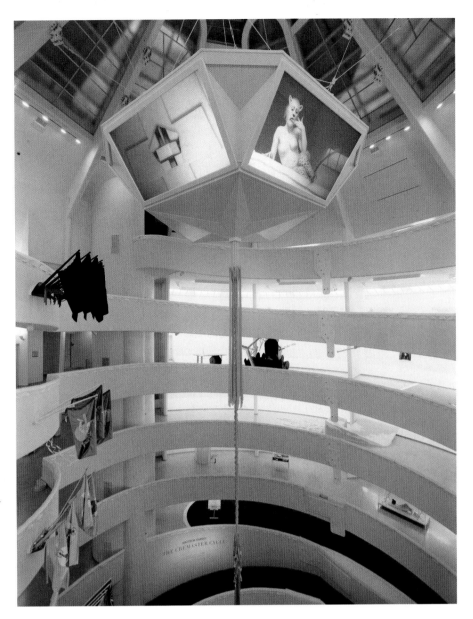

16-28 MATTHEW BARNEY, *Cremaster* cycle, installation at the Solomon R. Guggenheim Museum, New York, 2003.

Barney's vast multimedia installations of drawings, photographs, sculptures, and videos typify the relaxation at the opening of the 21st century of the traditional boundaries among artistic media.

minutes, the water and fire increase in intensity until the man disappears in a torrent of water on one screen (FIG. 16-27) and flames consume the man on the other screen. The deafening roar of a raging fire and a torrential downpour accompany these visual images. Eventually, everything subsides and fades into darkness. This installation's elemental nature and its presentation in a dark space immerse viewers in a pure sensory experience very much rooted in tangible reality.

MATTHEW BARNEY A major trend in the art world today is the relaxation of the traditional boundaries between artistic media. In fact, many contemporary artists are creating vast and complex multimedia installations combining new and traditional media. One of these artists is MATTHEW BARNEY (b. 1967), whose 2003 installation (FIG. 16-28) of his epic *Cremaster* cycle (1994–2002) at the Guggenheim Museum in New York typifies the expansive scale of many contemporary works. A multimedia extravaganza involving drawings, photographs, sculptures, videos, films, and performances (presented in videos), the *Cremaster* cycle is a lengthy narrative set in a self-enclosed universe that Barney created. The title of the work refers to the cremaster muscle, which controls testicular contractions in response to external stimuli. Barney uses the development of this muscle in the embryonic process of sexual differentiation as the conceptual springboard for the entire *Cremaster* project, in which he explores the notion of creation in expansive and complicated ways.

The cycle's narrative, revealed in the five feature-length films and the artworks, makes reference to, among other things, a musical revue in Boise, Idaho (where Barney grew up), the life cycle of bees, the execution of convicted murderer Gary Gilmore, the construction of the Chrysler Building (FIG. 14-41A ⏺), Celtic mythology, Masonic rituals, a motorcycle race, and a lyric opera set in late-19th-century Budapest. In the installation, Barney tied the artworks together conceptually by a five-channel video piece projected on screens hanging in the Guggenheim's rotunda. Immersion in Barney's constructed world is disorienting and overwhelming and has a force that competes with the immense scale and often frenzied pace of contemporary life.

WHAT NEXT? No one knows what the next years and decades will bring, but given the expansive scope of contemporary art and architecture, it is certain that no single approach to or style of art will dominate. New technologies will undoubtedly continue to redefine what constitutes a "work of art." The universally expanding presence of computers, digital technology, and the Internet may well erode what few conceptual and geographical boundaries remain, and make art and information about art available to virtually everyone, thereby creating a truly global artistic community. As this chapter has revealed, substantial progress has already been made in that direction.

⏺ Explore the era further in MindTap with videos of major artworks and buildings, Google Earth™ coordinates, and essays by the author on the following additional subjects:

▌ ARTISTS ON ART: Shirin Neshat on Iran after the Revolution
- Edward Burtynsky, *Densified Scrap Metal #3A, Toronto, Ontario* (FIG. 16-8A)
- Julian Schnabel, *The Walk Home* (FIG. 16-16A)
- Song Su-nam, *Summer Trees* (FIG. 16-16B)
- Günter Behnisch, Hysolar Institute, Stuttgart (FIG. 16-18A)
- Zaha Hadid, proposal for Signature Towers, Dubai, United Arab Emirates (FIG. 16-19A)
- Rachel Whiteread, Holocaust Memorial, Vienna (FIG. 16-23A)
- Do-Ho Suh, *Bridging Home* (FIG. 16-25A)

CONTEMPORARY ART WORLDWIDE

Personal and Group Identity

■ The innumerable artworks created since 1980 worldwide are extraordinarily diverse in style, format, content, and technique, but can be classified under a few major themes, including personal and group identity. Many artists of African descent, including Jean-Michel Basquiat and Faith Ringgold, have produced important works addressing issues of concern to black Americans. Jaune Quick-to-See Smith has focused on her Native American heritage. Gender and sexuality are central themes in the work of Barbara Kruger, Robert Mapplethorpe, and Shahzia Sikander. National identity looms large in the art created by Shirin Neshat (Iran) and Chris Ofili (Nigeria).

Ringgold, *Who's Afraid of Aunt Jemima?* 1983

Political and Social Commentary

■ Rather than addressing the concerns of individuals and groups, other contemporary artists have treated political and economic issues that affect society at large.

■ Edward Burtynsky's photographs of "manufactured landscapes" highlight the destructive effects of industrial pollution.

■ The violence of contemporary life has been addressed by Martha Rosler (the effects of war on the home front) and Fernando Botero (torture at Abu Ghraib).

■ Willie Bester has protested apartheid in South Africa, and Zhang Xiaogang has produced biting commentaries on the Cultural Revolution in China.

■ Xu Bing is best known for his stinging critiques of the meaninglessness of contemporary political language.

Rosler, *Gladiators*, 2004

Zhang, *Big Family No. 2*, 1995

Representation and Abstraction

■ Among today's best-known figural painters and sculptors are Jenny Saville and Kiki Smith, who have revived the tradition of brutal realism.

■ Leading abstract painters and sculptors include Julian Schnabel and Elizabeth Murray in the United States, Song Su-nam in Korea, and El Anatsui in Nigeria.

Anatsui, *Bleeding Takari II*, 2007

Architecture, Site-Specific Art, and New Media

■ Contemporary architecture is as diverse as painting and sculpture. Among the major champions of Deconstructivism are Otto Behnisch, Frank Gehry, and Zaha Hadid. Leading Hi-Tech and Green architects include Norman Foster and Renzo Piano.

■ The site-specific works of Maya Lin, Rachel Whiteread, Richard Serra, Anish Kapoor, and Do-Ho Suh bridge the gap between architecture and sculpture.

■ Many contemporary artists have harnessed new technologies for their art: Andreas Gursky (digital photography), Bill Viola (video), and Matthew Barney (multimedia installations).

Piano, Tjibaou Cultural Centre, Noumea, 1998

Notes

INTRODUCTION

1. Quoted in George Heard Hamilton, *Painting and Sculpture in Europe, 1880–1940,* 6th ed. (New Haven, Conn.: Yale University Press, 1993), 345.
2. Quoted in *Josef Albers: Homage to the Square* (New York: Museum of Modern Art, 1964), n.p.

CHAPTER 1

1. The chronology adopted in this chapter is that of John Baines and Jaromír Malék, *Atlas of Ancient Egypt* (Oxford: Oxford University Press, 1980), 36–37. The division of kingdoms is that of, among others, Mark Lehner, *The Complete Pyramids* (New York: Thames & Hudson, 1997), 89, and David P. Silverman, ed., *Ancient Egypt* (New York: Oxford University Press, 1997), 20–39.

CHAPTER 2

1. Pliny, *Natural History*, 36.20.
2. Lucian, *Amores*, 13–14; *Imagines*, 6.
3. Pliny, 35.110.

CHAPTER 3

1. Livy, *History of Rome*, 25.40.1–3.
2. Pliny the Elder, *Natural History*, 35.133.
3. Bernard Berenson, *The Arch of Constantine: or, The Decline of Form* (London: Chapman & Hall, 1954).

CHAPTER 4

1. Procopius, *De aedificiis*, 1.1.23ff. Translated by Cyril Mango, *The Art of the Byzantine Empire, 312–1453: Sources and Documents* (reprint of 1972 ed., Toronto: University of Toronto Press, 1986), 74.
2. Paulus Silentiarius, *Descriptio Sanctae Sophiae*, 489, 668. Translated by Mango, 83, 86.
3. Procopius, 1.1.23ff. Translated by Mango, 75.
4. *Libri Carolini*, 4.2. Translated by Herbert L. Kessler, *Spiritual Seeing: Picturing God's Invisibility in Medieval Art* (Philadelphia: University of Pennsylvania Press, 2000), 119.

CHAPTER 6

1. Translated by Giovanna De Appolonia, Boston University.
2. *Beowulf*, 3162–3164. Translated by Kevin Crossley-Holland (New York: Farrar, Straus & Giroux, 1968), 119.
3. Translated by Charles P. Parkhurst Jr., in Elizabeth G. Holt, *A Documentary History of Art*, 2d ed. (Princeton, N.J.: Princeton University Press, 1981), 1:18.

CHAPTER 7

1. Paul Frankl, *The Gothic: Literary Sources and Interpretation through Eight Centuries* (Princeton, N.J.: Princeton University Press, 1960), 55.

CHAPTER 8

1. Giorgio Vasari, "Life of Lorenzo Ghiberti." Translated by Gaston du C. de Vere, ed., *Giorgio Vasari, Lives of the Painters, Sculptors and Architects* (New York: Knopf, 1996), 1:304.
2. Quoted in H. W. Janson, *The Sculpture of Donatello* (Princeton, N.J.: Princeton University Press, 1965), 154.
3. Vasari, "Life of Masaccio." Translated by Gaston du C. de Vere, 1:318.

CHAPTER 9

1. Leonardo da Vinci to Ludovico Sforza, ca. 1480–1481. Elizabeth Gilmore Holt, ed., *A Documentary History of Art* (Princeton: Princeton University Press, 1981), 1:274–275.
2. Quoted in James M. Saslow, *The Poetry of Michelangelo: An Annotated Translation* (New Haven, Conn.: Yale University Press, 1991), 407.
3. Giorgio Vasari, *Lives of the Painters, Sculptors and Architects.* Translated by Gaston du C. de Vere (New York: Knopf, 1996), 2:736.
4. Quoted in A. Richard Turner, *Renaissance Florence: The Invention of a New Art* (New York: Abrams, 1997), 163.
5. Quoted in Bruce Boucher, *Andrea Palladio: The Architect in His Time* (New York: Abbeville Press, 1998), 229.
6. Quoted in Robert J. Clements, *Michelangelo's Theory of Art* (New York: New York University Press, 1961), 320.
7. *Giorgio Vasari: The Lives of the Artists.* Translated by Julia Conaway Bondanella and Peter Bondanella (New York: Oxford University Press, 1991), 489.
8. Translated by Erwin Panofsky, in Wolfgang Stechow, *Northern Renaissance Art 1400–1600: Sources and Documents* (Evanston, Ill.: Northwestern University Press, 1989), 123.

CHAPTER 10

1. Filippo Baldinucci, *Vita del Cavaliere Giovanni Lorenzo Bernini* (1681). Translated by Robert Enggass, in Robert Enggass and Jonathan Brown, *Italian and Spanish Art 1600–1750: Sources and Documents* (Evanston, Ill.: Northwestern University Press, 1992), 116.
2. Translated by Kristin Lohse Belkin, *Rubens* (London: Phaidon, 1998), 47.
3. Albert Blankert, *Johannes Vermeer van Delft 1632–1675* (Utrecht: Spectrum, 1975), 133, no. 51. Translated by Bob Haak, *The Golden Age: Dutch Painters of the Seventeenth Century* (New York: Abrams, 1984), 450.

CHAPTER 11

1. Translated by Robert Goldwater and Marco Treves , eds., *Artists on Art*, 3d ed. (New York: Pantheon Books, 1958), 157.
2. Quoted in Thomas A. Bailey, *The American Pageant: A History of the Republic*, 2d ed. (Boston: Heath, 1961), 280.
3. Translated by Elfriede Heyer and Roger C. Norton in Charles Harrison, Paul Wood, and Jason Gaiger, eds., *Art in Theory 1648–1815: An Anthology of Changing Ideas* (Oxford: Blackwell, 2000), 453.

CHAPTER 12

1. Helmut Bösch-Supan, *Caspar David Friedrich* (New York: Braziller, 1974), 7–8.
2. Quoted in Charles Harrison, Paul Wood, and Jason Gaiger, eds., *Art in Theory 1815–1900: An Anthology of Changing Ideas* (Oxford: Blackwell, 1998), 119.
3. Quoted in Harrison, Wood, and Gaiger, 518.
4. Quoted in Lloyd Goodrich, *Thomas Eakins, His Life and Work* (New York: Whitney Museum of American Art, 1933), 51–52.
5. Quoted in Nicholas Pevsner, *An Outline of European Architecture* (Baltimore: Penguin, 1960), 627.
6. Quoted in Naomi Rosenblum, *A World History of Photography*, 4th ed. (New York: Abbeville Press, 2007), 69.
7. Quoted in Kenneth MacGowan, *Behind the Screen* (New York: Delta, 1965), 49.

CHAPTER 13

1. Charles Baudelaire, *Le peintre de la vie moderne* (1863). Translated by Jonathan Mayne, *The Painter of Modern Life and Other Essays by Charles Baudelaire,* 2d ed. (New York: Phaidon, 1995), 12.

2. Clement Greenberg, "Modernist Painting," *Art and Literature,* no. 4 (Spring 1965): 193–194.

3. Translated by Carola Hicks, in Charles Harrison, Paul Wood, and Jason Gaiger, *Art in Theory 1815–1900: An Anthology of Changing Ideas* (Oxford: Blackwell, 1998), 595.

4. Quoted in John McCoubrey, *American Art 1700–1960: Sources and Documents* (Englewood Cliffs, N.J.: Prentice Hall, 1965), 184.

5. Vincent van Gogh to Theo van Gogh, September 1888, in J. van Gogh-Bonger and V. W. van Gogh, eds., *The Complete Letters of Vincent van Gogh* (Greenwich, Conn.: New York Graphic Society, 1979), 3:534.

6. Vincent van Gogh to Theo van Gogh, July 16, 1888, in W. H. Auden, ed., *Van Gogh: A Self-Portrait. Letters Revealing His Life as a Painter* (New York: Dutton, 1963), 299.

7. Letter to Charles Morice, March 1898. Translated by Belinda Thompson, *Gauguin by Himself* (Boston: Little, Brown, 1993), 270–271.

8. Reported by Joachim Gasquet (1873–1921). Quoted in Michael Doran, ed., *Conversations with Cézanne* (Berkeley: University of California Press, 2000), 122.

9. Quoted in Petra ten-Doesschate Chu, *Nineteenth-Century European Art,* 3d ed. (Upper Saddle River, N.J.: Pearson, 2011), 515.

10. Quoted in V. Frisch and J. T. Shipley, *Auguste Rodin* (New York: Stokes, 1939), 203.

CHAPTER 14

1. Quoted in John Elderfield, *The "Wild Beasts": Fauvism and Its Affinities* (New York: Museum of Modern Art, 1976), 29.

2. Quoted in Frederick S. Levine, *The Apocalyptic Vision: The Art of Franz Marc as German Expressionism* (New York: Harper & Row, 1979), 57.

3. Quoted in Sam Hunter, John Jacobus, and Daniel Wheeler, *Modern Art,* rev. 3d. ed. (Upper Saddle Hill, N.J.: Prentice Hall, 2004), 121.

4. Quoted in George Heard Hamilton, *Painting and Sculpture in Europe, 1880–1940,* 6th ed. (New Haven: Yale University Press, 1993), 246.

5. Ibid., 238.

6. Quoted in Edward Fry, ed., *Cubism* (London: Thames & Hudson, 1966), 112–113.

7. Pablo Picasso, "Statement to Simone Téry," in Charles Harrison and Paul Wood, eds., *Art in Theory 1900–2000: An Anthology of Changing Ideas* (Oxford: Blackwell, 2003), 649.

8. Quoted in Roland Penrose, *Picasso: His Life and Work,* rev. ed. (New York: Harper & Row, 1971), 311.

9. Filippo Tommaso Marinetti, *The Foundation and Manifesto of Futurism* (*Le Figaro,* February 20, 1909). Translated by Joshua C. Taylor, in Herschel B. Chipp, *Theories of Modern Art: A Source Book by Artists and Critics* (Berkeley and Los Angeles: University of California Press, 1968), 286.

10. Hans Richter, *Dada: Art and Anti-Art* (London: Thames & Hudson, 1961), 57.

11. Translated by Howard Dearstyne, in Robert L. Herbert, *Modern Artists on Art,* 2nd ed. (Mineola, N.Y.: Dover, 2000), 117.

12. Charles C. Eldredge, "The Arrival of European Modernism," *Art in America* 61 (July–August 1973): 35.

13. Dorothy Norman, *Alfred Stieglitz: An American Seer* (Millerton, N.Y.: Aperture, 1973), 9–10.

14. Ibid., 161.

15. Quoted in Hamilton, 392.

16. Quoted in William S. Rubin, *Dada, Surrealism, and Their Heritage* (New York: Museum of Modern Art, 1968), 64.

17. Quoted in Hunter, Jacobus, and Wheeler, 179.

18. Quoted in William S. Rubin, *Miró in the Collection of the Museum of Modern Art* (New York: Museum of Modern Art, 1973), 32.

19. Quoted in Kenneth Frampton, *Modern Architecture: A Critical History,* 4th ed. (New York: Thames & Hudson, 2007), 147.

20. Quoted in Michel Seuphor, *Piet Mondrian: Life and Work* (New York: Abrams, 1956), 117.

21. Quoted in Hamilton, 426.

22. Quoted in Herbert, 173–179.

23. Translated by Charles Haxthausen, in Barry Bergdoll, ed., *Bauhaus 1919–1933* (New York: Museum of Modern Art, 2009), 64.

24. Quoted in John Willett, *Art and Politics in the Weimar Period: The New Sobriety, 1917–1933* (New York: Da Capo Press, 1978), 119.

25. Quoted in Philip Johnson, *Mies van der Rohe,* rev. ed. (New York: Museum of Modern Art, 1954), 200–201.

CHAPTER 15

1. Dawn Ades and Andrew Forge, *Francis Bacon* (London: Thames & Hudson, 1985), 8; and David Sylvester, *The Brutality of Fact: Interviews with Francis Bacon,* 3d ed. (London: Thames & Hudson, 1987), 182.

2. Clement Greenberg, "Modernist Painting," *Art & Literature* 4 (Spring 1965): 195.

3. Quoted in Selden Rodman, *Conversations with Artists* (New York: Devin-Adair, 1957), 93–94.

4. Quoted in Deborah Wye, *Louise Bourgeois* (New York: Museum of Modern Art, 1982), 22.

5. Ibid., 25.

6. Quoted in Richard Francis, *Jasper Johns* (New York: Abbeville Press, 1984), 21.

7. Andy Warhol, *The Philosophy of Andy Warhol* (New York: Harcourt Brace Jovanovich, 1975), 100.

8. Quoted in Christine Lindey, *Superrealist Painting and Sculpture* (London: Orbis, 1980), 130.

9. Quoted in Mary Jane Jacob, *Magdalena Abakanowicz* (New York: Abbeville, 1982), 94.

10. Quoted in Nancy Holt, ed., *The Writings of Robert Smithson* (New York: New York University Press, 1975), 111.

11. Quoted in Bruce McPherson, ed., *More Than Meat Joy: Complete Performance Works and Selected Writings* (New Paltz, N.Y.: Documentext, 1979), 52.

12. Quoted in "Joseph Kosuth: Art as Idea as Idea," in Jeanne Siegel, ed., *Artwords: Discourse on the 60s and 70s* (Ann Arbor, Mich.: UMI Research Press, 1985), 221, 225.

CHAPTER 16

1. Quoted in Arlene Hirschfelder, *Artists and Craftspeople* (New York: Facts on File, 1994), 115.

2. Michelle Meagher, "Jenny Saville and a Feminist Aesthetics of Disgust," *Hypatia* 18, no. 4 (2003): 23–41.

3. Quoted in Donald Hall, *Corporal Politics* (Cambridge: MIT List Visual Arts Center, 1993), 46.

4. Quoted in "Vietnam Memorial: America Remembers," *National Geographic* 167, no. 5 (May 1985): 557.

5. Quoted in Calvin Tomkins, "The Art World: Tilted Arc," *New Yorker,* May 20, 1985, 100.

Glossary

a secco—Italian, "dry." See *fresco*.

abacus—The uppermost portion of the *capital* of a *column*, usually a thin slab.

abbess—See *abbey*.

abbey—A religious community under the direction of an abbot (for monks) or an abbess (for nuns).

abbot—See *abbey*.

abrasion—The rubbing or grinding of stone or another material to produce a smooth finish.

abstract—Nonrepresentational; forms and colors arranged without reference to the depiction of an object.

Abstract Expressionism—The first major American avant-garde movement, Abstract Expressionism emerged in New York City in the 1940s. The artists produced *abstract* paintings that expressed their state of mind and that they hoped would strike emotional chords in viewers. The movement developed along two lines: *gestural abstraction* and *chromatic abstraction*.

acropolis—Greek, "high city." In ancient Greece, usually the site of the city's most important temple(s).

action painting—Also called *gestural abstraction*. The kind of *Abstract Expressionism* practiced by Jackson Pollock, in which the emphasis was on the creation process, the artist's gesture in making art. Pollock poured liquid paint in linear webs on his canvases, which he laid out on the floor, thereby physically surrounding himself in the painting during its creation.

ad catacumbas—Latin, "in the hollows." See *catacombs*.

additive light—Natural light, or sunlight, the sum of all the wavelengths of the visible *spectrum*. See also *subtractive light*.

additive sculpture—A kind of sculpture *technique* in which materials (for example, clay) are built up or "added" to create form.

aerial perspective—See *perspective*.

agone—Italian, "foot race."

agora—An open square or space used for public meetings or business in ancient Greek cities.

aisle—The portion of a *basilica* flanking the *nave* and separated from it by a row of *columns* or *piers*.

ala (pl. **alae**)—One of a pair of rectangular recesses at the back of the *atrium* of a Roman *domus*.

alchemy—The study of seemingly magical changes, especially chemical changes.

altar frontal—A decorative panel on the front of a *church* altar.

altarpiece—A panel, painted or sculpted, situated above and behind an altar. See also *retable*.

alternate-support system—In *church* architecture, the use of alternating wall supports in the *nave*, usually *piers* and *columns* or *compound piers* of alternating form.

Amazonomachy—In Greek mythology, the battle between the Greeks and Amazons.

ambulatory—A covered walkway, outdoors (as in a *church cloister*) or indoors; especially the passageway around the *apse* and the *choir* of a *church*.

amphiprostyle—A *classical* temple *plan* in which the *columns* are placed across both the front and back but not along the sides.

amphitheater—Greek, "double theater." A Roman building type resembling two Greek theaters put together. The Roman amphitheater featured a continuous elliptical *cavea* around a central *arena*.

amphora—An ancient Greek two-handled jar used for general storage purposes, usually to hold wine or oil.

amulet—An object worn to ward off evil or to aid the wearer.

Analytic Cubism—The first phase of *Cubism*, developed jointly by Pablo Picasso and Georges Braque, in which the artists analyzed form from every possible vantage point to combine the various views into one pictorial whole.

anamorphic image—A distorted image that must be viewed by some special means (such as a mirror) to be recognized.

ancien régime—French, "old order." The term used to describe the political, social, and religious order in France before the Revolution at the end of the 18th century.

antae—The molded projecting ends of the walls forming the *pronaos* or *opisthodomos* of an ancient Greek temple.

apadana—The great audience hall in ancient Persian palaces.

aphros—Greek, "foam."

apostle—Greek, "messenger." One of the 12 disciples of Jesus.

apotheosis—Elevated to the rank of gods, or the ascent to Heaven.

apoxyomenos—Greek, "athlete scraping oil from his body."

apse—A recess, usually semicircular, in the wall of a building, commonly found at the east end of a *church*.

apsidal—Rounded; *apse*-shaped.

aqueduct—A channel for carrying water, often elevated on *arches*.

arcade—A series of *arches* supported by *piers* or *columns*.

arch—A curved structural member that spans an opening and is generally composed of wedge-shaped blocks (*voussoirs*) that transmit the downward pressure laterally. See also *thrust*.

Archaic—The artistic style of 600–480 BCE in Greece, characterized in part by the use of the *composite view* for painted and *relief* figures and of Egyptian stances for *statues*.

Archaic smile—The smile that appears on all *Archaic* Greek *statues* from about 570 to 480 BCE. The smile is the Archaic sculptor's way of indicating that the person portrayed is alive.

architrave—The *lintel* or lowest division of the *entablature*; also called the epistyle.

archivolt—The continuous molding framing an *arch*. In *Romanesque* and *Gothic* architecture, one of the series of concentric bands framing the *tympanum*.

arcuated—*Arch*-shaped.

arena—In a Roman *amphitheater*, the central area where bloody *gladiator* combats and other boisterous events took place.

armature—The crossed, or diagonal, *arches* that form the skeletal framework of a *Gothic rib vault*. In sculpture, the framework for a clay form.

arriccio—In *fresco* painting, the first layer of rough lime plaster applied to the wall.

arringatore—Italian, "orator."

Art Deco—Descended from *Art Nouveau*, this movement of the 1920s and 1930s sought to upgrade industrial design as a "fine art" and to work new materials into decorative patterns that could be either machined or handcrafted. Characterized by streamlined, elongated, and symmetrical design.

Art Nouveau—French, "new art." A late-19th- and *early*-20th-century art movement whose proponents tried to synthesize all the arts in an effort to create art based on natural forms that could be mass produced by technologies of the industrial age. The movement had other names in other countries: Jugendstil in Austria and Germany, Modernismo in Spain, and Stile Floreale in Italy.

ascetic—One who follows a path of self-denial.

ashlar masonry—Carefully cut and regularly shaped blocks of stone used in construction, fitted together without mortar.

atlantid—A male figure that functions as a supporting *column* or *pier*. See also *caryatid*.

atmospheric perspective—See *perspective*.

atrium (pl. **atria**)—The central reception room of a Roman *domus* that is partly open to the sky. Also, the open, *colonnaded* court in front of and attached to a Christian *basilica*.

attic—The uppermost story of a building, *triumphal arch*, city gate, or *aqueduct*.

attribute—(n.) The distinctive identifying aspect of **a person**—for example, an object held, an associated animal, or a mark on the body. (v.) To make an *attribution*.

attribution—Assignment of a work to a maker or makers.

augustus—Latin, "majestic" or "exalted."

autem generatio—Latin, "now this is how the birth of Christ came about."

automatism—In painting, the process of yielding oneself to instinctive motions of the hands after establishing a set of conditions (such as size of paper or *medium*) within which a work is to be created.

avant-garde—French, "advance guard" (in a platoon). Late-19th- and 20th-century artists who emphasized innovation and challenged established convention in their work. Also used as an adjective.

axial plan—See *plan*.

baldacchino—A canopy on *columns*, frequently built over an altar. The term derives from *baldacco*.

baldacco—Italian, "silk from Baghdad." See *baldacchino*.

baldric—A sashlike belt worn over one shoulder and across the chest to support a sword.

baptism—The Christian bathing ceremony in which an infant or a convert becomes a member of the Christian community.

baptistery—In Christian architecture, the building used for *baptism*, usually situated next to a *church*. Also, the designated area or hall within a *church* for baptismal rites.

bar tracery—See *tracery*.

Baroque/baroque—The traditional blanket designation for European art from 1600 to 1750. Uppercase *Baroque* refers to the art of this period, which features dramatic theatricality and elaborate ornamentation in contrast to the simplicity and orderly rationality of *Renaissance* art, and is most appropriately applied to Italian art. Lowercase *baroque* describes similar stylistic features found in the art of other periods—for example, the *Hellenistic* period in ancient Greece. The term derives from *barroco*.

barrel vault—See *vault*.

barroco—Portuguese, "irregularly shaped pearl." See *Baroque*.

base—In ancient Greek architecture, the molded projecting lowest part of *Ionic* and *Corinthian columns*. (*Doric* columns do not have bases.)

basilica (adj. **basilican**)—In Roman architecture, a public building for legal and other civic proceedings, rectangular in plan, with an entrance usually on a long side. In Christian architecture, a *church* somewhat resembling the Roman basilica, usually entered from one end and with an *apse* at the other.

Bauhaus—A *school* of architecture in Germany in the 1920s under the aegis of Walter Gropius, who emphasized the unity of art, architecture, and design.

bay—The space between two *columns*, or one unit in the *nave arcade* of a *church*; also, the passageway in an *arcuated* gate.

belvedere—Italian, "beautiful view." A building or other structure with a view of a *landscape* or seascape.

ben-ben—A pyramidal stone; an emblem of the Egyptian god Re.

benday dots—Named after the newspaper printer Benjamin Day, the benday dot system involves the modulation of *colors* through the placement and size of colored dots.

benedictional—A Christian religious book containing bishops' blessings.

bestiary—A collection of illustrations of real and imaginary animals.

bibliophile—Lover of books.

bilateral symmetry—Having the same *forms* on either side of a central axis.

Biomorphic Surrealism—See *Surrealism*.

black-figure painting—In early Greek pottery, the silhouetting of dark figures against a light background of natural, reddish clay, with linear details *incised* through the silhouettes.

blind arcade—An *arcade* having no true openings, applied as decoration to a wall surface.

Book of Hours—A Christian religious book for private devotion containing prayers to be read at specified times of the day.

braccia—Italian, "arm." A unit of measurement; 1 braccia equals 23 inches.

breviary—A Christian religious book of selected daily prayers and Psalms.

buon fresco—See *fresco*.

burgher—A middle-class citizen.

burgomeister—Chief magistrate (mayor) of a Flemish city.

burin—A pointed tool used for *engraving* or *incising*.

bust—A freestanding sculpture of the head, shoulders, and chest of a person.

buttress—An exterior masonry structure that opposes the lateral *thrust* of an *arch* or a *vault*. A pier buttress is a solid mass of masonry. A flying buttress consists typically of an inclined member carried on an arch or a series of arches and a solid buttress to which it transmits lateral thrust.

Byzantine—The art, territory, history, and culture of the Eastern Christian Empire and its capital of Constantinople (ancient Byzantium).

caduceus—In ancient Greek mythology, a serpent-entwined herald's rod (Latin, *caduceus*), the attribute of Hermes (Roman Mercury), the messenger of the gods.

caementa—Latin, "small stones." A key ingredient of Roman *concrete*.

caldarium—The hot-bath section of a Roman bathing establishment.

caliph(s)—Islamic rulers, regarded as successors of Muhammad.

calligraphy—Greek, "beautiful writing." Handwriting or penmanship, especially elegant writing as a decorative art.

calotype—From the Greek *kalos*, "beautiful." A photographic process in which a positive image is made by shining light through a negative image onto a sheet of sensitized paper.

came—A lead strip in a *stained-glass* window that joins separate pieces of colored glass.

camera lucida—Latin, "lighted room." A device in which a small lens projects the image of an object downward onto a sheet of paper.

camera obscura—Latin, "dark room." An ancestor of the modern camera in which a tiny pinhole, acting as a lens, projects an image on a screen, the wall of a room, or the ground-glass wall of a box; used by artists in the 17th, 18th, and early 19th centuries as an aid in drawing from nature.

campanile—A bell tower of a *church*, usually, but not always, freestanding.

canon—A rule (for example, of proportion). The ancient Greeks considered beauty to be a matter of "correct" proportion and sought a canon of proportion, for the human figure and for buildings. The fifth-century BCE sculptor Polykleitos wrote the *Canon*, a treatise incorporating his formula for the perfectly proportioned *statue*. Also, a *church* official who preaches, teaches, administers sacraments, and tends to pilgrims and the sick.

canon table—A concordance, or matching, of the corresponding passages of the four *Gospels* as compiled by Eusebius of Caesarea in the fourth century.

capital—The uppermost member of a *column*, serving as a transition from the *shaft* to the *lintel*. In *classical* architecture, the form of the capital varies with the *order*.

Capitolium—An ancient Roman temple dedicated to the gods Jupiter, Juno, and Minerva.

capriccio—Italian, "originality." One of several terms used in Italian *Renaissance* literature to praise the originality and talent of artists.

caput mundi—Latin, "head (capital) of the world."

Carolingian—Pertaining to the empire of Charlemagne (Latin, "Carolus Magnus") and his successors.

carpet page—In early medieval manuscripts, a decorative page resembling a textile.

cartoon—In painting, a full-size preliminary drawing from which a painting is made.

carving—A sculptural *technique* in which the artist cuts away material (for example, from a stone block) in order to create a *statue* or a *relief*.

caryatid—A female figure that functions as a supporting *column*. See also *atlantid*.

castellum—See *westwork*.

casting—A sculptural *technique* in which the artist pours liquid metal, plaster, clay, or another material into a *mold*. When the material dries, the sculptor removes the cast piece from the mold.

catacombs—Subterranean networks of rock-cut galleries and chambers designed as cemeteries for the burial of the dead.

cathedra—Latin, "seat." See *cathedral*.

cathedral—A bishop's *church*. The word derives from *cathedra*, referring to the bishop's chair.

causeway—A raised roadway.

cavea—Latin, "hollow place or cavity." The seating area in ancient Greek and Roman theaters and *amphitheaters*.

cella—The chamber at the center of an ancient temple; in a *classical* temple, the room (Greek, *naos*) in which the *cult statue* usually stood.

centaur—In ancient Greek mythology, a creature with the front or top half of a human and the back or bottom half of a horse.

centauromachy—In ancient Greek mythology, a battle between the Greeks and *centaurs*.

central plan—See *plan*.

chancel arch—The arch separating the chancel (the *apse* or *choir*) or the *transept* from the *nave* of a basilica or *church*.

chaplet—A metal pin used in hollow-casting to connect the *investment* with the clay core.

chapter house—The meeting hall in a *monastery*.

characters—In Chinese writing, signs that record spoken words.

chartreuse—A Carthusian *monastery*.

château (pl. **châteaux**)—French, "castle." A luxurious country residence for French royalty, developed from medieval castles.

chiaroscuro—In drawing or painting, the treatment and use of light and dark, especially the gradations of light that produce the effect of modeling.

chisel—A tool with a straight blade at one end for cutting and shaping stone or wood.

chiton—A Greek tunic, the essential (and often only) garment of both men and women, the other being the *himation*, or mantle.

choir—The space reserved for the clergy and singers in the *church*, usually east of the *transept* but, in some instances, extending into the *nave*.

Christ—Savior. From Latin *Christus* and Greek *Christos*, "the anointed one."

Christogram—The monogram comprising the three initial letters (chi-rho-iota) of Christ's name in Greek.

Christophoros—Greek, "he who carries Christ"—that is, Saint Christopher.

chromatic abstraction—A kind of *Abstract Expressionism* that focuses on the emotional resonance of color, as exemplified by the work of Barnett Newman and Mark Rothko.

chronology—In art history, the dating of art objects and buildings.

chryselephantine—Fashioned of gold and ivory.

church—Christian house of worship.

Cinquecento—Italian, "500"—that is, the 16th century (the 1500s) in Italy.

circus—An ancient Roman chariot racecourse.

cire perdue—See *lost-wax process*.

cista (pl. **cistae**)—An Etruscan cylindrical container made of sheet bronze with cast handles and feet, often with elaborately engraved bodies, used for women's toiletry articles.

city-state—An independent, self-governing city.

Classical/classical—The art and culture of ancient Greece between 480 and 323 BCE. Lowercase *classical* refers more generally to Greco-Roman art and culture.

clerestory—The *fenestrated* part of a building that rises above the roofs of the other parts. The oldest known clerestories are Egyptian. In Roman *basilicas* and medieval *churches*, clerestories are the windows that form the *nave's* uppermost level below the timber ceiling or the *vaults*.

cloison—French, "partition." A cell made of metal wire or a narrow metal strip soldered edge-up to a metal base to hold *enamel*, semi-precious stones, pieces of colored glass, or glass paste fired to resemble sparkling jewels.

cloisonné—A decorative metalwork *technique* employing *cloisons*; also, decorative brickwork in later Byzantine architecture.

cloister—A *monastery* courtyard, usually with covered walks or *ambulatories* along its sides.

cluster pier—See *compound pier*.

codex (pl. **codices**)—Separate pages of *vellum* or *parchment* bound together at one side; the predecessor of the modern book. The codex superseded the *rotulus*. In *Mesoamerica*, a painted and inscribed book on long sheets of bark paper or deerskin coated with fine white plaster and folded into accordion-like pleats.

coffer—A sunken panel, often ornamental, in a *vault* or a ceiling.

collage—A composition made by combining on a flat surface various materials, such as newspaper, wallpaper, printed text and illustrations, photographs, and cloth.

coller—French, "to stick."

colonnade—A series or row of *columns*, usually spanned by *lintels*.

colonnette—A thin *column*.

color—The value, or tonality, of a color is the degree of its lightness or darkness. The intensity, or saturation, of a color is its purity, its brightness or dullness. See also *primary colors, secondary colors,* and *complementary colors*.

color-field painting—A variant of *Post-Painterly Abstraction* in which artists sought to reduce painting to its physical essence by pouring diluted paint onto unprimed canvas and letting these pigments soak into the fabric, as exemplified by the work of Helen Frankenthaler and Morris Louis.

colorito—Italian, "colored" or "painted." A term used to describe the application of paint. Characteristic of the work of 16th-century Venetian artists who emphasized the application of paint as an important element of the creative process. Central Italian artists, in contrast, largely emphasized *disegno*—careful design preparation based on preliminary drawing.

colossal order—An architectural design in which the *columns* or *pilasters* are two or more stories tall. Also called a giant order.

column—A vertical, weight-carrying architectural member, circular in cross-*section* and consisting of a *base* (sometimes omitted), a *shaft*, and a *capital*.

combines—The name that American artist Robert Rauschenberg gave to his assemblages of painted passages and sculptural elements.

complementary colors—Those pairs of *colors,* such as red and green, that together embrace the entire *spectrum.* The complement of one of the three *primary colors* is a mixture of the other two.

compose—See *composition.*

composite view—A convention of representation in which part of a figure is shown in profile and another part of the same figure is shown frontally; also called twisted perspective.

composition—The way in which an artist organizes *forms* in an artwork, either by placing shapes on a flat surface or arranging forms in space.

compound pier—A *pier* with a group, or cluster, of attached *shafts,* or *responds,* especially characteristic of *Gothic* architecture.

Conceptual Art—An American *avant-garde* art movement of the 1960s whose premise was that the "artfulness" of art lay in the artist's idea rather than its final expression.

conceptual representation—The representation of the fundamental distinguishing properties of a person or object, not the way a figure or object appears in space and light at a specific moment. See also *composite view.*

concrete—A building material invented by the Romans and consisting of various proportions of lime mortar, volcanic sand, water, and small stones.

condottiere (pl. **condottieri**)—An Italian mercenary general.

congregational mosque—A city's main *mosque,* designed to accommodate the entire *Muslim* population for the Friday noon prayer. Also called the great mosque or Friday mosque.

connoisseur—An expert in *attributing* artworks to one artist rather than another. More generally, an expert on artistic *style.*

consuls—In the Roman Republic, the two chief magistrates.

contour line—In art, a continuous *line* defining the outer shape of an object.

contrapposto—The disposition of the human figure in which one part is turned in opposition to another part (usually hips and legs one way, shoulders and chest another), creating a counterpositioning of the body about its central axis. Sometimes called "weight shift" because the weight of the body tends to be thrown to one foot, creating tension on one side and relaxation on the other.

corbel—A projecting wall member used as a support for some element in the superstructure. Also, *courses* of stone or brick in which each course projects beyond the one beneath it. Two such walls, meeting at the topmost course, create a *corbeled arch.*

corbeled arch—An *arch* formed by the piling of stone blocks in horizontal *courses,* cantilevered inward until the blocks meet at a *keystone.*

corbeled dome—A *dome* formed by the piling of stone blocks in successive circles of horizontal *courses,* cantilevered inward to form a conical dome.

Corinthian capital—A more ornate form than *Doric* or *Ionic;* it consists of a double row of acanthus leaves from which tendrils and flowers grow, wrapped around a bell-shaped *echinus.* Although this *capital* is often cited as the distinguishing feature of the Corinthian *order,* in strict terms no such order exists. The Corinthian capital is a substitute for the standard capital used in the Ionic order.

cornice—The projecting, crowning member of the *entablature* framing the *pediment;* also, any crowning projection.

corona civica—Latin, "civic crown." A Roman honorary wreath worn on the head.

course—In masonry construction, a horizontal row of stone blocks.

crenellation—Alternating solid merlons and open crenels in the notched tops of walls, as in battlements.

cross vault—See *vault.*

crossing—The space in a *cruciform church* formed by the intersection of the *nave* and the *transept.*

crossing tower—The tower over the *crossing* of a *church.*

crucifix—A freestanding sculptural representation of Christ on the cross.

cruciform—Cross-shaped.

Crusades—In medieval Europe, armed pilgrimages aimed at recapturing the Holy Land from the *Muslims.*

cubiculum (pl. **cubicula**)—A small cubicle or bedroom that opened onto the *atrium* of a Roman *domus.* Also, a chamber in an Early Christian *catacomb* that served as a mortuary chapel.

Cubism—An early-20th-century art movement that rejected *naturalistic* depictions, preferring *compositions* of shapes and *forms abstracted* from the conventionally perceived world. See also *Analytic Cubism* and *Synthetic Cubism.*

cuirass—A military leather breastplate.

cult statue—The *statue* of the deity that stood in the *cella* of an ancient temple.

cuneiform—Latin, "wedge-shaped." A system of writing used in ancient Mesopotamia, in which wedge-shaped characters were produced by pressing a *stylus* into a soft clay tablet, which was then baked or otherwise allowed to harden.

cura animarum—Latin, "care of souls," the duty of a Catholic priest.

cutaway—An architectural drawing that combines an exterior view with an interior view of part of a building.

Cycladic—The prehistoric art of the Aegean Islands around Delos, excluding Crete.

Cyclopean masonry—A method of stone construction, named after the mythical *Cyclopes,* using massive, irregular blocks without mortar, characteristic of the Bronze Age fortifications of Tiryns and other *Mycenaean* sites.

Cyclops (pl. **Cyclopes**)—A mythical Greek one-eyed giant.

Dada—An early-20th-century art movement prompted by a revulsion against the horror of World War I. Dada embraced political anarchy, the irrational, and the intuitive. A disdain for convention, often enlivened by humor or whimsy, is characteristic of the art the Dadaists produced.

Daedalic—The Greek *Orientalizing* sculptural style of the seventh century BCE named after the legendary artist Daedalus.

daguerreotype—A photograph made by an early method on a plate of chemically treated metal; developed by Louis J. M. Daguerre.

damnatio memoriae—The Roman decree condemning those who ran afoul of the Senate. Those who suffered damnatio memoriae had their memorials demolished and their names erased from public inscriptions.

De Stijl—Dutch, "the style." An early-20th-century art movement (and magazine), founded by Piet Mondrian and Theo van Doesburg, whose members promoted utopian ideals and developed a simplified geometric style.

Deconstructivism—A late-20th-century architectural *style.* Deconstructivist architects attempt to disorient the observer by disrupting the conventional categories of architecture. The haphazard presentation of *masses, planes,* lighting, and so forth challenges the viewer's assumptions about *form* as it relates to function.

Deësis—Greek, "supplication." An image of Christ flanked by the figures of the Virgin Mary and John the Baptist, who intercede on behalf of humankind.

demos—Greek, "the people," from which the word *democracy* derives.

Der Blaue Reiter—German, "the blue rider." An early-20th-century *German Expressionist* art movement founded by Vassily Kandinsky and Franz Marc. The artists selected the whimsical name because of their mutual interest in the color blue and horses.

di sotto in sù—Italian, "from below upward." A *perspective* view seen from below.

diagonal rib—See *rib.*

dictator—In the Roman Republic, the supreme magistrate with extraordinary powers, appointed during a crisis for a specified period. Julius Caesar eventually became *dictator perpetuo, or* "dictator for life."

Die Brücke—German, "the bridge." An early-20th-century *German Expressionist* art movement under the leadership of Ernst Ludwig Kirchner. The group thought of itself as the bridge between the old age and the new.

diptych—A two-paneled painting or *altarpiece*; also, an ancient Roman, Early Christian, or Byzantine hinged writing tablet, often of ivory and carved on the external sides.

disegno—Italian, "drawing" and "design." *Renaissance* artists considered drawing to be the external physical manifestation (*disegno esterno*) of an internal intellectual idea of design (*disegno interno*).

diskobolos—Greek, "discus thrower."

disputatio—Latin, "logical argument." The philosophical methodology used in *Scholasticism*.

divine right—The belief in a king's absolute power as God's will.

documentary evidence—In art history, the examination of written sources in order to determine the date of an artwork, the circumstances of its creation, or the identity of the artist(s) who made it.

doge—Italian (Venetian dialect), "duke."

dome—A hemispherical *vault*; theoretically, an *arch* rotated on its vertical axis. In *Mycenaean* architecture, domes are beehive-shaped.

domus—A Roman private house.

donor portrait—A portrait of the individual(s) who commissioned (donated) a religious work (for example, an *altarpiece*) as evidence of devotion.

Doric—One of the two systems (or *orders*) invented in ancient Greece for articulating the three units of the *elevation* of a *classical* building—the platform, the *colonnade,* and the superstructure (*entablature*). The Doric order is characterized by, among other features, *capitals* with funnel-shaped *echinuses, columns* without *bases,* and a *frieze* of *triglyphs* and *metopes*. See also *Ionic*.

dormer—A projecting gable-capped window.

doryphoros—Greek, "spear bearer."

dressed masonry—Stone blocks shaped to the exact dimensions required, with smooth faces for a perfect fit.

drum—One of the stacked cylindrical stones that form the *shaft* of a *column*. Also, the cylindrical wall that supports a *dome*.

duomo—Italian, "cathedral."

earthworks—See *Environmental Art*.

echinus—The convex element of a *capital* directly below the *abacus*.

edition—A set of impressions taken from a single *incised* metal plate or carved woodblock.

elevation—In architecture, a head-on view of an external or internal wall, showing its features and often other elements that would be visible beyond or before the wall.

embroidery—The *technique* of sewing threads onto a finished ground to form contrasting designs. Stem stitching employs short overlapping strands of thread to form jagged lines. Laid-and-couched work creates solid blocks of color.

emir—A Muslim ruler.

empiricism—The search for knowledge based on observation and direct experience.

en plein air—See *plein air*.

enamel—A decorative coating, usually colored, fused onto the surface of metal, glass, or ceramics.

encaustic—A painting *technique* in which pigment is mixed with melted wax and applied to the surface while the mixture is hot.

engaged column—A half-round *column* attached to a wall. See also *pilaster*.

engraving—The process of *incising* a design in hard material, often a metal plate (usually copper); also, the *print* or impression made from such a plate.

Enlightenment—The 18th-century Western philosophy based on empirical evidence. The Enlightenment was a new way of thinking critically about the world and about humankind, independently of religion, myth, or tradition.

entablature—The part of a building above the *columns* and below the roof. The entablature has three parts: *architrave, frieze,* and *pediment*.

entasis—The convex profile (an apparent swelling) in the *shaft* of a *column*.

Environmental Art—An American art form that emerged in the 1960s. Often using the land itself as their material, Environmental artists construct monuments of great scale and minimal form. Permanent or impermanent, these works transform some section of the environment, calling attention both to the land itself and to the hand of the artist. Sometimes referred to as earthworks.

etching—A kind of *engraving* in which the design is *incised* in a layer of wax or varnish on a metal plate. The parts of the plate left exposed are then etched (slightly eaten away) by the acid in which the plate is immersed after incising. See also *drypoint, intaglio*.

Eucharist—In Christianity, the partaking of the bread and wine, which believers hold to be either Christ himself or symbolic of him.

eunuch—A castrated male.

evangelist—One of the four authors (Matthew, Mark, Luke, John) of the New Testament *Gospels*.

exedra—Recessed area, usually semicircular.

exemplum virtutis—Latin, "example or model of virtue."

existentialism—A philosophy asserting the absurdity of human existence and the improbability of achieving certitude.

Expressionism—Twentieth-century art that is the result of the artist's unique inner or personal vision and that often has an emotional dimension. Expressionism contrasts with art focused on visually describing the empirical world.

facade—Usually, the front of a building; also, the other sides when they are emphasized architecturally.

faience—A low-fired opaque glasslike silicate.

fan vault—See *vault*.

fantasia—Italian, "imagination." One of several terms used in Italian *Renaissance* literature to praise the originality and talent of artists.

fasces—A bundle of rods with an ax attached, an emblem of authority in ancient Rome.

fauces—Latin, "jaws." In a Roman *domus,* the narrow foyer leading to the *atrium*.

Fauves—French, "wild beasts." See *Fauvism*.

Fauvism—An early-20th-century art movement led by Henri Matisse. For the Fauves, *color* became the formal element most responsible for pictorial coherence and the primary conveyor of meaning.

femme savante—French, "learned woman." The term used to describe the cultured hostesses of *Rococo* salons.

fenestrated—Having windows.

ferroconcrete—*Concrete* strengthened by a skeleton of iron bars; also called reinforced concrete.

fête galante—French, "amorous festival." A type of *Rococo* painting depicting the outdoor amusements of French upper-class society.

fibula (pl. **fibulae**)—A decorative pin, usually used to fasten garments.

fin-de-siècle—French, "end of the century." A period in Western cultural history from the end of the 19th century until just before World War I, when decadence and indulgence masked anxiety about an uncertain future.

findspot—Place where an artifact was found; *provenance*.

finial—A crowning ornament.

First Style mural—The earliest style of Roman *mural* painting. The aim of the artist was to imitate, using painted *stucco relief,* the appearance of costly marble panels.

flagellate—To whip.

flashing—In making *stained-glass* windows, fusing one layer of colored glass to another to produce a greater range of *colors*.

fleur-de-lis—A three-petaled iris flower; the royal flower of France.

florin—The denomination of gold coin of *Renaissance* Florence that became an international currency for trade.

flute or fluting—Vertical channeling, roughly semicircular in cross-*section* and used principally on *columns* and *pilasters*.

flying buttress—See *buttress*.

folio—A page of a manuscript or book.

fons vitae—Latin, "fountain of life." A symbolic fountain of everlasting life.

foreshortening (adj. **foreshortened**)—The use of *perspective* to represent in art the apparent visual contraction of an object that extends back in space at an angle to the perpendicular plane of sight.

form—In art, an object's shape and structure, either in two dimensions (for example, a figure painted on a surface) or in three dimensions (such as a *statue*).

formal analysis—The visual analysis of artistic *form*.

forum (pl. **fora**)—The public square of an ancient Roman city.

Fourth Style mural—In Roman *mural* painting, the Fourth Style marks a return to architectural *illusionism,* but the architectural vistas of the Fourth Style are irrational fantasies.

freestanding sculpture—See *sculpture in the round*.

fresco—Painting on lime plaster, either dry (dry fresco, or fresco secco) or wet (true, or buon, fresco). In the latter method, the pigments are mixed with water and become chemically bound to the freshly laid lime plaster. Also, a painting executed in either method.

fresco secco—See *fresco*.

Friday mosque—See *congregational mosque*.

frieze—The part of the *entablature* between the *architrave* and the *cornice*; also, any sculptured or painted band. See *register*.

frigidarium—The cold-bath section of a Roman bathing establishment.

furta sacra—Latin, "holy theft."

Futurism—An early-20th-century Italian art movement that championed war as a cleansing agent and that celebrated the speed and dynamism of modern technology.

genre—A *style* or category of art; also, a kind of painting that realistically depicts scenes from everyday life.

Geometric—The *style* of Greek art during the ninth and eighth centuries BCE, characterized by *abstract* geometric ornament and schematic figures.

German Expressionism—An early-20th-century regional *Expressionist* movement.

gesso—Plaster mixed with a binding material, used as the base coat for paintings on wood panels.

gestural abstraction—Also known as *action painting*. A kind of *abstract* painting in which the gesture, or act of painting, is seen as the subject of art. Its most renowned proponent was Jackson Pollock. See also *Abstract Expressionism*.

giant order—See *colossal order*.

gigantomachy—In ancient Greek mythology, the battle between gods and giants.

giornata (pl. **giornate**)—Italian, "day." The section of plaster that a *fresco* painter expects to complete in one session.

gladiator—An ancient Roman professional fighter, usually a slave, who competed in an *amphitheater*.

glaze—A vitreous coating applied to pottery to seal and decorate the surface; it may be colored, transparent, or opaque, and glossy or *matte*. In *oil painting*, a thin, transparent, or semitransparent layer applied over a *color* to alter it slightly.

glazier—A glassworker.

glazing—The application of successive layers of *glaze* in *oil painting*.

gleaning—The collection by peasants of wheat scraps left in the field after a harvest.

gold leaf—Gold beaten into tissue-paper-thin sheets that then can be applied to surfaces.

gorgon—In ancient Greek mythology, a hideous female demon with snake hair. Medusa, the most famous gorgon, was capable of turning anyone who gazed at her into stone.

Gospels—The four New Testament books that relate the life and teachings of Jesus.

Gothic—Originally a derogatory term named after the Goths, used to describe the history, culture, and art of western Europe in the 12th to 14th centuries. Typically divided into periods designated Early (1140–1194), High (1194–1300), and Late (1300–1500).

Grand Manner portraiture—A type of 18th-century portrait painting designed to communicate a person's grace and class through certain standardized conventions, such as the large scale of the figure relative to the canvas, the controlled pose, the *landscape* setting, and the low *horizon line*.

graver—An *engraving* tool. See also *burin*.

great mosque—See *congregational mosque*.

Greek cross—A cross with four arms of equal length.

green architecture—Ecologically friendly architectural design using clean energy to sustain the natural environment.

grisaille—A *monochrome* painting done mainly in neutral grays to simulate sculpture.

groin—The edge formed by the intersection of two barrel *vaults*.

groin vault—See *vault*.

ground line—In paintings and *reliefs*, a painted or carved baseline on which figures appear to stand.

guild—An association of merchants, craftspersons, or scholars in medieval and *Renaissance* Europe.

Hadith—The words and exemplary deeds of the Prophet Muhammad.

halo—An aureole appearing around the head of a holy figure to signify divinity. See also *nimbus*.

hard-edge painting—A variant of *Post-Painterly Abstraction* that rigidly excluded all reference to gesture and incorporated smooth knife-edge geometric forms to express the notion that painting should be reduced to its visual components.

hatching—A series of closely spaced drawn or *engraved* parallel *lines*. Cross-hatching employs sets of lines placed at right angles.

hay wain—A hay-filled wagon.

Hellas—The ancient name of Greece.

Hellenes (adj. **Hellenic**)—The name the ancient Greeks called themselves as the people of *Hellas*.

Hellenistic—The term given to the art and culture of the roughly three centuries between the death of Alexander the Great in 323 BCE and the death of Queen Cleopatra in 30 BCE, when Egypt became a Roman province.

henge—An arrangement of *megalithic* stones in a circle, often surrounded by a ditch.

Hiberno-Saxon—An art *style* that flourished in the *monasteries* of the British Isles in the early Middle Ages. Also called Insular.

hierarchy of scale—An artistic convention in which greater size indicates greater importance.

hieroglyph—A *symbol* or picture used to confer meaning in *hieroglyphic* writing.

high relief—See *relief*.

High-Tech—A contemporary architectural *style* calling for buildings that incorporate the latest innovations in engineering and technology and expose the structures' component parts.

Hijra—The flight of Muhammad from Mecca to Medina in 622, the year from which Islam dates its beginnings.

himation—An ancient Greek mantle worn by men and women over the *chiton* and draped in various ways.

historiated—Ornamented with representations, such as plants, animals, or human figures, that have a narrative—as distinct from a purely decorative—function.

historiated capital—A *capital* with a carved figural ornament.

horizon line—See *perspective*.

hôtel—French, "town house."

hubris—Greek, "arrogant pride."

hue—The name of a *color*. See also *primary colors, secondary colors,* and *complementary colors*.

humanism—In the *Renaissance,* an emphasis on education and on expanding knowledge (especially of *classical* antiquity), the exploration of individual potential and a desire to excel, and a commitment to civic responsibility and moral duty.

hydria—An ancient Greek three-handled water pitcher.

hypostyle hall—A hall with a roof supported by *columns*.

icon—A portrait or image; especially in *Byzantine churches*, a panel with a painting of sacred personages that are objects of veneration. In the visual arts, a painting, a piece of sculpture, or even a building regarded as an object of veneration.

iconoclasm—The destruction of religious or sacred images. In Byzantium, the period from 726 to 843 when there was an imperial ban on such images. The destroyers of images were known as iconoclasts. Those who opposed such a ban were known as iconophiles.

iconoclast—See *iconoclasm*.

iconography—Greek, the "writing of images." The term refers both to the content, or subject, of an artwork and to the study of content in art. It also includes the study of the symbolic, often religious, meaning of objects, persons, or events depicted in works of art.

iconophile—See *iconoclasm*.

illuminated manuscript—A luxurious handmade book with painted illustrations and decorations.

illusionism (adj. **illusionistic**)—The representation of the three-dimensional world on a two-dimensional surface in a manner that creates the illusion that the person, object, or place represented is three-dimensional. See also *perspective*.

imagines—In ancient Rome, wax portraits of ancestors displayed in the *atrium* of a *domus*.

imam—In Islam, the leader of collective worship.

imperator—Latin, "commander in chief," from which the word *emperor* derives.

impluvium—In a Roman *domus*, the basin located in the *atrium* that collected rainwater.

impost block—The uppermost block of a wall or *pier* beneath the *springing* of an *arch*.

Impressionism—A late-19th-century art movement that sought to capture a fleeting moment, thereby conveying the elusiveness and impermanence of images and conditions.

in antis—In ancient Greek architecture, the area between the *antae*.

incise—To cut into a surface with a sharp instrument, especially to decorate metal and pottery.

incrustation—Wall decoration consisting of bright panels of different *colors*.

indulgence—A religious pardon for a sin committed.

ingegno—Italian, "innate talent." One of several terms used in Italian *Renaissance* literature to praise the originality and talent of artists.

installation—An artwork that creates an artistic environment in a room or gallery.

intaglio—A graphic *technique* in which the design is *incised*, or scratched, on a metal plate, either manually (*engraving*) or chemically (*etching*). The incised lines of the design take the ink, making this the reverse of the *woodcut technique*.

intercolumniation—See *interaxial*.

internal evidence—In art history, the examination of what an artwork represents (people, clothing, hairstyles, and so on) in order to determine its date. Also, the examination of the *style* of an artwork to identify the artist who created it.

International Gothic—A *style* of 14th- and 15th-century painting begun by Simone Martini, who fused the French *Gothic* manner with Sienese art. This style appealed to the aristocracy because of its brilliant *color*, lavish costumes, intricate ornamentation, and themes involving splendid processions of knights and ladies.

International style—A *style* of 20th-century architecture associated with Le Corbusier, whose elegance of design came to influence the look of modern office buildings and skyscrapers.

intonaco—In *fresco* painting, the last layer of smooth lime plaster applied to the wall; the painting layer.

invenzione—Italian, "invention." One of several terms used in Italian *Renaissance* literature to praise the originality and talent of artists.

investment—In hollow-casting, the final clay *mold* applied to the exterior of the wax model.

Ionic—One of the two systems (or *orders*) invented in ancient Greece for articulating the three units of the *elevation* of a *classical* building: the platform, the *colonnade*, and the superstructure (*entablature*). The Ionic order is characterized by, among other features, *volutes, capitals, columns* with *bases,* and an uninterrupted *frieze*.

iwan—In Islamic architecture, a *vaulted* rectangular recess opening onto a courtyard.

jamb statue—A *statue*, usually attached to a *column*, set against the *jamb* of a *Gothic church* portal.

jambs—In architecture, the side posts of a doorway.

jouer—French, "to play."

jouir—French, "to enjoy."

journaux—French, "newspapers."

Jugendstil—See *Art Nouveau*.

ka—In ancient Egypt, the immortal human life force.

Kaaba—Arabic, "cube." A small cubical building in Mecca, the symbolic center of the Islamic world.

katholikon—The main *church* in a Greek Orthodox *monastery*.

kente—Brightly colored patterned cloth woven by Asante men on horizontal looms in long, narrow strips sewn together to form *toga*-like robes.

keystone—See *voussoir*.

kinetic sculpture—Sculpture with parts that move.

Koran—Islam's sacred book, composed of *surahs* (chapters) divided into verses.

kore (pl. **korai**)—Greek, "young woman." An *Archaic* Greek *statue* of a young woman.

kouros (pl. **kouroi**)—Greek, "young man." An *Archaic* Greek *statue* of a young man.

krater—An ancient Greek wide-mouthed bowl for mixing wine and water.

Kufic—An early form of Arabic script, characterized by angularity, with the uprights forming almost right angles with the baseline. Named after the city of Kufa.

labyrinth—Maze. The English word derives from the mazelike plan of the *Minoan* palace at Knossos.

lamassu—Assyrian guardian in the form of a man-headed winged bull or lion.

lancet—In *Gothic* architecture, a tall narrow window ending in a *pointed arch*.

landscape—A picture showing natural scenery, without narrative content.

Late Antique—The non-*naturalistic* artistic *style* of the Late Roman Empire.

lateral section—See *section*.

leading—In the manufacture of *stained-glass* windows, the joining of colored glass pieces using lead *cames*.

lectionary—A book containing passages from the *Gospels,* arranged in the sequence that they are to be read during the celebration of religious services, including the *Mass,* throughout the year.

lekythos (pl. **lekythoi**)—A flask containing perfumed oil; lekythoi were often placed in Greek graves as offerings to the deceased.

libation—The pouring of liquid as part of a religious ritual.

line—The extension of a point along a path, made concrete in art by drawing on or chiseling into a *plane*.

linear perspective—See *perspective*.

lintel—A horizontal *beam* used to span an opening.

lithograph—See *lithography*.

lithography—A printmaking *technique* in which the artist uses an oil-based crayon to draw directly on a stone plate and then wipes water onto the stone. When ink is rolled onto the plate, it adheres only to the drawing. The *print* produced by this method is a lithograph.

liturgy (adj. **liturgical**)—The official ritual of public worship.

local color—An object's true *color* in white light.

loggia—A gallery with an open *arcade* or a *colonnade* on one or both sides.

longitudinal plan—See *plan*.

longitudinal section—See *section*.

lost-wax process—A bronze-*casting* method in which a figure is modeled in wax and covered with clay; the whole is fired, melting away the wax (French, *cire perdue*) and hardening the clay, which then becomes a *mold* for molten metal. Also called the cire perdue process.

low relief—See *relief*.

lunette—A semicircular area (with the flat side down) in a wall over a door, niche, or window; also, a painting or *relief* with a semicircular frame.

lux nova—Latin, "new light." Abbot Suger's term for the light that enters a *Gothic church* through *stained-glass* windows.

magus (pl. **magi**)—One of the three wise men from the East who presented gifts to the infant Jesus.

malwiya—Arabic, "snail shell."

mandorla—An almond-shaped *nimbus* surrounding the figure of Christ or other sacred figure. In Buddhist Japan, a lotus-petal-shaped nimbus.

maniera—Italian, "style" or "manner." See *Mannerism*.

maniera greca—Italian, "Greek manner." The Italo-*Byzantine* painting *style* of the 13th century.

Mannerism—A *style* of later *Renaissance* art that emphasized "artifice," often involving contrived imagery not derived directly from nature. Such artworks showed a self-conscious stylization involving complexity, caprice, fantasy, and polish. Mannerist architecture tended to flout the *classical* rules of order, stability, and symmetry, sometimes to the point of parody.

manu scriptus—Latin, "manuscript."

manuscript—A handwritten book; see *manu scriptus*.

maqsura—In some *mosques*, a screened area in front of the *mihrab* reserved for a ruler.

margrave—Military governor of the Holy Roman Empire.

martyr—A person who chooses to die rather than deny his or her religious belief. See also *saint*.

martyrium (pl. **martyria**)—A shrine to a Christian *martyr*.

mass—The bulk, density, and weight of matter in *space*.

Mass—The Catholic and Orthodox ritual in which believers understand that Christ's redeeming sacrifice on the cross is repeated when the priest consecrates the bread and wine in the *Eucharist*.

mastaba—Arabic, "bench." An ancient Egyptian rectangular brick or stone structure with sloping sides erected over a subterranean tomb chamber connected with the outside by a shaft.

matte—In painting, pottery, and photography, a dull finish.

maulstick—A stick used to steady the hand while painting.

mausoleum (pl. **mausolea**)—A monumental tomb. The name derives from the mid-fourth-century BCE tomb of Mausolos at Halikarnassos, one of the Seven Wonders of the ancient world.

meander—An ornament, usually in bands but also covering broad surfaces, consisting of interlocking geometric motifs. An ornamental pattern of contiguous straight lines joined usually at right angles.

medium (pl. **media**)—The material (for example, marble, bronze, clay, *fresco*) in which an artist works; also, in painting, the vehicle (usually liquid) that carries the pigment.

megalith (adj. **megalithic**)—Greek, "great stone." A large, roughly hewn stone used in the construction of monumental prehistoric structures.

memento mori—Latin, "reminder of death." In painting, a reminder of human mortality, usually represented by a skull.

Mesolithic—The "middle" Stone Age, between the *Paleolithic* and the *Neolithic* ages.

Messiah—The savior of the Jews prophesied in Hebrew scripture. Christians believe that Jesus of Nazareth was the Messiah.

metope—The square panel between the *triglyphs* in a *Doric frieze*, often sculpted in *relief*.

mezquita—Spanish, "mosque."

mihrab—A semicircular niche set into the *qibla* wall of a *mosque*.

mina—A unit of ancient Mesopotamian currency.

minaret—A distinctive feature of *mosque* architecture, a tower from which the faithful are called to worship.

minbar—In a *mosque*, the *pulpit* on which the *imam* stands.

Minimalism—A predominantly sculptural American trend of the 1960s characterized by works featuring a severe reduction of *form*, often to single, homogeneous units.

Minoan—The prehistoric art of Crete, named after the legendary King Minos of Knossos.

Minotaur—The mythical beast, half man and half bull, that inhabited the *labyrinth* of the *Minoan* palace at Knossos.

Miraj—The ascension of the Prophet Muhammad to Heaven.

mobile—A kind of sculpture, invented by Alexander Calder, combining nonobjective organic forms and motion in balanced structures hanging from rods, wires, and colored, organically shaped plates.

modernism—A movement in Western art that developed in the second half of the 19th century and sought to capture the images and sensibilities of the age. Modernist art goes beyond simply dealing with the present and involves the artist's critical examination of the premises of art itself.

Modernismo—See *Art Nouveau*.

module (adj. **modular**)—A basic unit of which the dimensions of the major parts of a work are multiples. The principle is used in sculpture and other art forms, but it is most often employed in architecture, where the module may be the dimensions of an important part of a building, such as the diameter of a *column*.

mold—A hollow form for *casting*.

monastery—A group of buildings in which monks live together, set apart from the secular community of a town.

monasticism—The religious practice in which monks live together in a *monastery* set apart from the secular community of a town.

monochrome (adj. **monochromatic**)—One *color*.

monolith (adj. **monolithic**)—A stone *column shaft* that is all in one piece (not composed of *drums*); a large, single block or piece of stone used in *megalithic* structures. Also, a colossal *statue* carved from a single piece of stone.

monotheism—The worship of one all-powerful god.

moralized Bible—A heavily illustrated Bible, each page pairing paintings of Old and New Testament episodes with explanations of their moral significance.

mortuary temple—In Egyptian architecture, a temple erected for the worship of a deceased *pharaoh*.

mosaic—Patterns or pictures made by embedding small pieces (*tesserae*) of stone or glass in cement on surfaces such as walls and floors; also, the *technique* of making such works.

mosaic tilework—An Islamic decorative *technique* in which large ceramic panels are fired, cut into smaller pieces, and set in plaster.

moschophoros—Greek, "calf bearer."

mosque—The Islamic building for collective worship. From the Arabic word *masjid*, meaning a "place for bowing down."

Muhaqqaq—A cursive *style* of Islamic *calligraphy*.

mullion—A vertical member that divides a window or that separates one window from another.

mummification—A *technique* used by ancient Egyptians to preserve human bodies so that they may serve as the eternal home of the immortal *ka*.

mummy—An embalmed Egyptian corpse; see *mummification*.

muqarnas—Stucco decorations of Islamic buildings in which stalactite-like forms break a structure's solidity.

mural—A wall painting.

Muslim—A believer in Islam.

Mycenaean—The prehistoric art of the Late *Helladic* period in Greece, named after the citadel of Mycenae.

mystery play—A dramatic enactment of the holy mysteries of the Christian faith, performed at *church* portals and in city squares.

naos—See *cella*.

narthex—A porch or vestibule of a *church*, generally *colonnaded* or *arcaded* and preceding the *nave*.

natatio—The swimming pool in a Roman bathing establishment.

naturalism (adj. **naturalistic**)—The *style* of painted or sculpted representation based on close observation of the natural world that was at the core of the *classical* tradition.

Naturalistic Surrealism—See *Surrealism*.

nave—The central area of an ancient Roman *basilica* or of a *church*, demarcated from *aisles* by *piers* or *columns*.

nave arcade—In *basilica* architecture, the series of *arches* supported by *piers* or *columns* separating the *nave* from the *aisles*.

necropolis—Greek, "city of the dead." A large burial area or cemetery.

nemes—In ancient Egypt, the linen headdress worn by the *pharaoh*, with the *uraeus* cobra of kingship on the front.

Neoclassicism—A *style* of art and architecture that emerged in the late 18th century as part of a general revival of interest in *classical* cultures. Neoclassical artists adopted themes and *styles* from ancient Greece and Rome.

Neo-Expressionism—An art movement that emerged in the 1970s and that reflects artists' interest in the expressive capability of art, seen earlier in *German Expressionism* and *Abstract Expressionism*.

Neo-Gothic—The revival of the *Gothic style* in architecture, especially in the 19th century.

Neolithic—The "new" Stone Age.

Neoplasticism—The Dutch artist Piet Mondrian's theory of "pure plastic art," an ideal balance between the universal and the individual using an *abstract* formal vocabulary.

Neo-Platonism—An ancient school of philosophy based on the ideas of Plato, revived during the *Renaissance* and modified by the teachings of Christianity.

nepotism—The appointment of relatives to important positions.

Neue Sachlichkeit—German, "new objectivity." An art movement that grew directly out of the World War I experiences of a group of German artists who sought to show the horrors of the war and its effects.

nimbus—A *halo* or aureole appearing around the head of a holy figure to signify divinity.

nymphs—In *classical* mythology, female divinities of springs, caves, and woods.

obelisk—A tall four-sided *monolithic pillar* with a pyramidal top—symbolic of the Egyptian sun god Re.

oculus (pl. **oculi**)—Latin, "eye." The round central opening of a *dome*. Also, a small round window in a *Gothic cathedral*.

odalisque—A woman in a Turkish harem.

ogee arch—An *arch* composed of two double-curving lines meeting at a point.

ogive (adj. **ogival**)—The diagonal *rib* of a *Gothic vault*; a pointed, or Gothic, *arch*.

oil painting—A painting *technique* using oil-based pigments that rose to prominence in northern Europe in the 15th century and is now the standard medium for painting on canvas.

Op Art—An artistic movement of the 1960s in which painters sought to produce optical illusions of motion and depth using only geometric forms on two-dimensional surfaces.

opere francigeno—See *opus francigenum*.

opisthodomos—In ancient Greek architecture, a porch at the rear of a temple, set against the blank back wall of the *cella*.

optical mixture—The visual effect of juxtaposed *complementary colors*.

optical representation—The representation of people and objects seen from a fixed viewpoint.

opus francigenum—Latin, "French work." Architecture in the *style* of *Gothic* France; *opere francigeno* (adj.), "in the French manner."

opus modernum—Latin, "modern work." The late medieval term for *Gothic* art and architecture. Also called *opus francigenum*.

orant—In Early Christian art, a figure with both arms raised in the ancient gesture of prayer.

oratory—The *church* of a Christian *monastery*.

orchestra—Greek, "dancing place." In ancient Greek theaters, the circular piece of earth with a hard and level surface on which the performance took place.

order—In *classical* architecture, a *style* represented by a characteristic design of the *columns* and *entablature*. See also *superimposed orders*.

Orientalism—The fascination on the part of Westerners with Oriental cultures, especially characteristic of the *Romanticism* movement in 19th-century European painting.

orrery—A mechanical model of the solar system demonstrating how the planets revolve around the sun.

orthogonal—A line imagined to be behind and perpendicular to the picture *plane*; the orthogonals in a painting appear to recede toward a *vanishing point* on the horizon.

Ottonian (adj.)—Pertaining to the empire of Otto I and his successors.

palaestra—An ancient Greek and Roman exercise area, usually framed by a *colonnade*. In Greece, the palaestra was an independent building; in Rome, palaestras were also frequently incorporated into a bathing complex.

palazzo pubblico—Italian, "public palace." City hall.

Paleolithic—The "old" Stone Age, during which humankind produced the first sculptures and paintings.

palette—A thin board with a thumb hole at one end on which an artist lays and mixes *colors*; any surface so used. Also, the colors or kinds of colors characteristically used by an artist. In ancient Egypt, a slate slab used for preparing makeup.

palette knife—A flat tool used to scrape paint off the *palette*. Artists sometimes also use the palette knife in place of a brush to apply paint directly to the canvas.

palmette—A *classical* decorative motif in the form of stylized palm leaves.

Pantokrator—Greek, "ruler of all." Christ as ruler and judge.

papyrus—A plant native to Egypt and adjacent lands used to make paperlike writing material; also, the material or any writing on it.

parade helmet—A masklike helmet worn by Roman soldiers on special ceremonial occasions.

parallel hatching—See *hatching*.

parapet—A low, protective wall along the edge of a balcony, roof, or bastion.

parchment—Lambskin prepared as a surface for painting or writing.

parthenos—Greek, "virgin." The epithet of Athena, the virgin goddess.

passio—Latin, "suffering."

Passover—The annual feast celebrating the release of the Jews from bondage to the *pharaohs* of Egypt.

paten—A large shallow bowl or plate for the bread used in the *Eucharist*.

patrician—A Roman freeborn landowner.

patron—The person or entity that pays an artist to produce individual artworks or employs an artist on a continuing basis.

pebble mosaic—A *mosaic* made of irregularly shaped stones of various *colors*.

pediment—In *classical* architecture, the triangular space (gable) at the end of a building, formed by the ends of the sloping roof above the *colonnade*; also, an ornamental feature having this shape.

pendant—The large hanging terminal element of a *Gothic* fan *vault*.

pendentive—A concave, triangular section of a hemisphere, four of which provide the transition from a square area to the circular base of a covering *dome*. Although pendentives appear to be hanging (pendant) from the dome, they in fact support it.

Pentateuch—The first five books of the Old Testament.

peplos (pl. **peploi**)—A simple, long, belted garment of wool worn by women in ancient Greece.

Performance Art—An American *avant-garde* art trend of the 1960s that made time an integral element of art. It produced works in which movements, gestures, and sounds of persons communicating with an audience replace physical objects. Documentary photographs are generally the only evidence remaining after these events. See also *Happenings*.

period style—See *style*.

peripteral—See *peristyle*.

peristyle—In *classical* architecture, a *colonnade* all around the *cella* and its porch(es). A peripteral colonnade consists of a single row of *columns* on all sides; a dipteral colonnade has a double row all around.

Perpendicular—An English Late *Gothic style* of architecture distinguished by the pronounced verticality of its decorative details.

personal style—See *style*.

personification—An *abstract* idea represented in bodily form.

perspective—A method of presenting an illusion of the three-dimensional world on a two-dimensional surface. In linear perspective, the most common type, all parallel lines or surface edges converge on one, two, or three vanishing points located with reference to the eye level of the viewer (the horizon line of the picture), and associated objects are rendered smaller the farther from the viewer they are intended to seem. Atmospheric, or aerial, perspective creates the illusion of distance by the greater diminution of *color* intensity, the shift in color toward an almost neutral blue, and the blurring of contours as the intended distance between eye and object increases.

pharaoh (adj. **pharaonic**)—An ancient Egyptian king.

philosophe—French, "thinker, philosopher." The term applied to French intellectuals of the *Enlightenment*.

Phoibos—Greek, "radiant." The epithet of the Greek god Apollo.

photomontage—A *composition* made by pasting together pictures or parts of pictures, especially photographs. See also *collage*.

Photorealism—See *Superrealism*.

physical evidence—In art history, the examination of the materials used to produce an artwork in order to determine its date.

pictograph—A picture, usually stylized, that represents an idea; also, writing using such means; also, painting on rock. See also *hieroglyphic*.

pier—A vertical, freestanding masonry support.

Pietà—A painted or sculpted representation of the Virgin Mary mourning over the body of the dead Christ.

pilaster—A flat, rectangular, vertical member projecting from a wall of which it forms a part. It usually has a *base* and a *capital* and is often *fluted*.

pillar—Usually a weight-carrying member, such as a *pier* or a *column*; sometimes an isolated, freestanding structure used for commemorative purposes.

pinnacle—In *Gothic churches*, a sharply pointed ornament capping the *piers* or flying *buttresses*; also used on *church facades*.

pittura—Italian, "painting.

Pittura Metafisica—Italian, "metaphysical painting." An early-20th-century Italian art movement led by Giorgio de Chirico, whose work conveys an eerie mood and visionary quality.

plan—The horizontal arrangement of the parts of a building or of the buildings and streets of a city or town, or a drawing or diagram showing such an arrangement. In an axial plan, the parts of a building are organized longitudinally, or along a given axis; in a central plan, the parts of the structure are of equal or almost equal dimensions around the center.

plane—A flat surface.

plate tracery—See *tracery*.

poesia—A term describing "poetic" art, notably Venetian *Renaissance* painting, which emphasizes the lyrical and sensual.

pointed arch—A narrow *arch* of pointed profile, in contrast to a semicircular arch.

pointillism—A system of painting devised by the 19th-century French painter Georges Seurat. The artist separates *color* into its component parts and then applies the component colors to the canvas in tiny dots (points). The image becomes comprehensible only from a distance, when the viewer's eyes optically blend the pigment dots.

polyptych—An *altarpiece* composed of more than three sections.

polytheism—The belief in multiple gods.

pontifex maximus—Latin, "chief priest." The high priest of the Roman state religion, often the emperor himself.

Pop Art—A term coined by British art critic Lawrence Alloway to refer to art, first appearing in the 1950s, that incorporated elements from consumer culture, the mass media, and popular culture, such as images from motion pictures and advertising.

portico—A roofed *colonnade*; also an entrance porch.

positivism—A Western philosophical model that promoted science as the mind's highest achievement.

post-and-lintel system—A system of construction in which two posts support a *lintel*.

Post-Impressionism—The term used to describe the stylistically heterogeneous work of the group of late-19th-century painters in France, including van Gogh, Gauguin, Seurat, and Cézanne, who more systematically examined the properties and expressive qualities of *line*, pattern, *form*, and *color* than the *Impressionists* did.

postmodernism—A reaction against *modernist formalism*, which was seen as elitist. Far more encompassing and accepting than the more rigid confines of modernist practice, postmodernism offers something for everyone by accommodating a wide range of *styles*, subjects, and formats, from traditional easel painting to *installation* and from *abstraction* to *illusionistic* scenes. Postmodern art often includes irony or reveals a self-conscious awareness on the position of the artist in the history of art.

Post-Painterly Abstraction—An American art movement that emerged in the 1960s and was characterized by a cool, detached rationality emphasizing tighter pictorial control. See also *color-field painting* and *hard-edge painting*.

Poussiniste—A member of the French Royal Academy of Painting and Sculpture during the early 18th century who followed Nicolas Poussin in insisting that *form* was the most important element of painting. See also *Rubéniste*.

predella—The narrow ledge on which an *altarpiece* rests on an altar.

prefabricated architecture—Construction using structural elements manufactured in advance and transported to the building site ready for assembly.

prefiguration—In Early Christian art, the depiction of Old Testament persons and events as prophetic forerunners of Christ and New Testament events.

Pre-Raphaelite art—A 19th-century English art movement whose members wished to create art free from what they considered the artificial manner propagated in the academies by the successors of Raphael.

primary colors—Red, yellow, and blue—the *colors* from which all other colors may be derived.

primitivism—The incorporation in early-20th-century Western art of stylistic elements from the artifacts of Africa, Oceania, and the native peoples of the Americas.

princeps—Latin, "first citizen." The title Augustus and his successors as Roman emperor used to distinguish themselves from Hellenistic monarchs.

print—An artwork on paper, usually produced in multiple impressions.

pronaos—The space, or porch, in front of the *cella*, or naos, of an ancient Greek temple.

proportion—The relationship in size of the parts of persons, buildings, or objects, often based on a *module*.

proscenium—The part of a theatrical stage in front of the curtain.

prostyle—A *classical* temple *plan* in which the *columns* are only in front of the *cella* and not on the sides or back.

provenance—Origin or source; *findspot*.

psalter—A book containing the Psalms.

pseudoperipteral—In Roman architecture, a pseudoperipteral temple has a series of *engaged columns* all around the sides and back of the *cella* to give the appearance of a *peripteral colonnade.*

pulpit—A raised platform in a *church* or *mosque* on which a priest or *imam* stands while leading the religious service.

punchwork—Tooled decorative work in *gold leaf.*

Purism—An early-20th-century art movement that embraced the "machine aesthetic" and sought purity of *form* in the clean functional lines of industrial machinery.

putto (pl. **putti**)—A cherubic young boy.

pylon—The wide entrance gateway of an Egyptian temple, characterized by its sloping walls.

pyxis (pl. **pyxides**)—A cylindrical container with a hemispherical lid.

qibla—The direction (toward Mecca) that Muslims face when praying.

quadrant arch—An *arch* whose curve extends for one-quarter of a circle's circumference.

quadro riportato—A ceiling design in which painted scenes are arranged in panels that resemble framed pictures transferred to the surface of a shallow, curved *vault.*

quatrefoil—A shape or *plan* in which the parts assume the form of a cloverleaf.

Quattrocento—Italian, "400"—that is, the 15th century (the 1400s) in Italy.

radiating chapels—In medieval *churches*, chapels for the display of *relics* that opened directly onto the *ambulatory* and the *transept.*

raking cornice—The *cornice* on the sloping sides of a *pediment.*

Rayonnant—The "radiant" style of *Gothic* architecture, dominant in the second half of the 13th century and associated with the French royal court of Louis IX at Paris.

Realism (adj. **Realist**)—A movement that emerged in mid-19th-century France. Realist artists represented the subject matter of everyday life (especially subjects that previously had been considered inappropriate for depiction) in a relatively *naturalistic* mode.

recto—The front side of a manuscript *folio.*

red-figure painting—In later Greek pottery, the silhouetting of red figures against a black background, with painted linear details; the reverse of *black-figure painting.*

refectory—The dining hall of a Christian *monastery.*

regional style—See *style.*

Regionalism—A 20th-century American art movement that portrayed American rural life in a clearly readable, *Realist* style. Major Regionalists include Grant Wood and Thomas Hart Benton.

register—One of a series of superimposed bands or *friezes* in a pictorial narrative, or the particular levels on which motifs are placed.

relics—The body parts, clothing, or objects associated with a holy figure, such as the Buddha or Christ or a Christian *saint.* Also, in Africa, the bones of ancestors.

relief—In sculpture, figures projecting from a background of which they are part. The degree of relief is designated high, low (bas), or sunken. In the last, the artist cuts the design into the surface so that the highest projecting parts of the image are no higher than the surface itself. See also *repoussé.*

relief sculpture—See *relief.*

relieving triangle—In *Mycenaean* architecture, the triangular opening above the *lintel* that serves to lighten the weight to be carried by the lintel itself.

reliquary—A container for holding *relics.*

Renaissance—French, "rebirth." The term used to describe the history, culture, and art of 14th- through 16th-century western Europe during which artists consciously revived the *classical* style.

renovatio—Latin, "renewal." During the *Carolingian* period, Charlemagne sought to revive the culture of ancient Rome (*renovatio imperii Romani*).

renovatio imperii Romani—See *renovatio.*

repoussé—Formed in *relief* by beating a metal plate from the back, leaving the impression on the face. The metal sheet is hammered into a hollow *mold* of wood or some other pliable material and finished with a *graver.* See also *relief.*

respond—An engaged *column, pilaster,* or similar element that either projects from a *compound pier* or some other supporting device or is bonded to a wall and carries one end of an *arch.*

retable—An architectural screen or wall above and behind an altar, usually containing painting, sculpture, or other decorations. See also *altarpiece.*

reverentissimo—Latin, "most revered."

revetment—In architecture, a wall covering or facing.

rib—A relatively slender, molded masonry *arch* that projects from a surface. In *Gothic* architecture, the ribs form the framework of the *vaulting.* A diagonal rib is one of the ribs that form the X of a *groin vault.* A transverse rib crosses the *nave* or *aisle* at a 90-degree angle.

rib vault—A *vault* in which the diagonal and transverse *ribs* compose a structural skeleton that partially supports the masonry *web* between them.

ridgepole—The *beam* running the length of a building below the peak of the gabled roof.

rocaille—See *Rococo.*

Rococo—A style, primarily of interior design, that appeared in France around 1700. Rococo interiors featured lavish decoration, including small sculptures, ornamental mirrors, easel paintings, *tapestries, reliefs,* wall paintings, and elegant furniture. The term *Rococo* derived from the French word *rocaille* (pebble) and referred to the small stones and shells used to decorate grotto interiors.

Romanesque—"Roman-like." A term used to describe the history, culture, and art of medieval western Europe from ca. 1050 to ca. 1200.

Romanticism—A Western cultural phenomenon, beginning around 1750 and ending about 1850, that gave precedence to feeling and imagination over reason and thought. More narrowly, the art movement that flourished from about 1800 to 1840.

rose window—A circular *stained-glass* window.

rostrum—A speaker's platform.

rotulus (pl. **rotuli**)—The manuscript scroll used by Egyptians, Greeks, Etruscans, and Romans; predecessor of the *codex.*

rotunda—The circular area under a *dome*; also, a domed round building.

roundel—See *tondo.*

Rubéniste—A member of the French Royal Academy of Painting and Sculpture during the early 18th century who followed Peter Paul Rubens in insisting that *color* was the most important element of painting. See also *Poussiniste.*

rustication (adj. **rusticated**)—To give a rustic appearance by roughening the surfaces and beveling the edges of stone blocks to emphasize the joints between them. Rustication is a *technique* employed in ancient Roman architecture and was also popular during the *Renaissance,* especially for stone *courses* at the ground-floor level.

sacramentary—A Christian religious book incorporating the prayers that priests recite during *Mass.*

saint—From the Latin word *sanctus,* meaning "made holy by God." Applied to persons who suffered and died for their Christian faith or who merited reverence for their Christian devotion while alive. In the Roman Catholic Church, a worthy deceased Catholic who is canonized by the pope.

sarcophagus (pl. **sarcophagi**)—Greek, "consumer of flesh." A coffin, usually of stone.

saturation—See *color.*

satyr—A Greek mythological follower of Dionysos having a man's upper body, a goat's hindquarters and horns, and a horse's ears and tail.

scarification—Decorative markings on the human body made by cutting or piercing the flesh to create scars.

Scholasticism—The *Gothic* school of philosophy in which scholars applied Aristotle's system of rational inquiry to the interpretation of religious belief.

school—A chronological and stylistic classification of works of art with a stipulation of place.

scriptorium (pl. **scriptoria**)—The writing studio of a *monastery*.

sculpture in the round—Freestanding figures, *carved* or *modeled* in three dimensions.

Second Style mural—The *style* of Roman *mural* painting in which the aim was to dissolve the confining walls of a room and replace them with the illusion of a three-dimensional world constructed in the artist's imagination.

secondary colors—Orange, green, and purple, obtained by mixing pairs of *primary colors* (red, yellow, blue).

section—In architecture, a diagram or representation of a part of a structure or building along an imaginary *plane* that passes through it vertically. Drawings showing a theoretical slice across a structure's width are lateral sections. Those cutting through a building's length are longitudinal sections. See also *elevation* and *cutaway*.

sedes sapientiae—Latin, "throne of wisdom." A *Romanesque* sculptural type depicting the Virgin Mary with the Christ Child in her lap.

senate—Latin *senatus*, "council of elders." The Senate was the main legislative body in Roman constitutional government.

serdab—A small concealed chamber in an Egyptian *mastaba* for the *statue* of the deceased.

sexpartite vault—See *vault*.

sfumato—Italian, "smoky." A smokelike haziness that subtly softens outlines in painting; particularly applied to the paintings of Leonardo da Vinci and Correggio.

shaft—The tall, cylindrical part of a *column* between the *capital* and the *base*.

shekel—A unit of ancient Mesopotamian currency.

sibyl—A Greco-Roman mythological prophetess.

signoria—Italian, "lordship." The governing body of medieval and *Renaissance* Florence.

silentiary—An usher responsible for maintaining silence in the *Byzantine* imperial palace in Constantinople.

silk-screen printing—An industrial printing *technique* that creates a sharp-edged image by pressing ink through a design on silk or a similar tightly woven porous fabric stretched tight on a frame.

silverpoint—A *stylus* made of silver, used in drawing in the 14th and 15th centuries because of the fine *line* it produced and the sharp point it maintained.

simultaneous contrasts—The phenomenon of juxtaposed *colors* affecting the eye's reception of each, as when a painter places dark green next to light green, making the former appear even darker and the latter even lighter. See also *successive contrasts*.

sinopia—A burnt-orange pigment used in *fresco* painting to transfer a *cartoon* to the *arriccio* before the artist paints the plaster.

site-specific art—Art created for a specific location. See also *Environmental Art*.

skene—Greek, "stage." The stage of a *classical* theater.

skenographia—Greek, "scene painting"; the Greek term for *perspective* painting.

slip—A mixture of fine clay and water used in ceramic decoration.

solidus (pl. **solidi**)—A *Byzantine* gold coin.

space—In art history, both the actual area that an object occupies or a building encloses and the *illusionistic* representation of space in painting and sculpture.

spandrel—The roughly triangular space enclosed by the curves of adjacent *arches* and a horizontal member connecting their vertexes; also, the space enclosed by the curve of an *arch* and an enclosing right angle. The area between the arch proper and the framing *columns* and *entablature*.

spectrum—The range or band of visible *colors* in natural light.

sphinx—A mythical Egyptian beast with the body of a lion and the head of a human.

springing—The lowest stone of an *arch*, resting on the *impost block*. In *Gothic vaulting*, the lowest stone of a diagonal or transverse *rib*.

squinch—An architectural device used as a transition from a square to a polygonal or circular base for a *dome*. It may be composed of *lintels*, *corbels*, or *arches*.

stadium—An ancient Roman long and narrow theater-like structure for footraces and other athletic contests.

stained glass—In *Gothic* architecture, the colored glass used for windows.

stanza (pl. **stanze**)—Italian, "room."

statue—A three-dimensional sculpture.

stele (pl. **stelae**)—A *carved* stone slab used to mark graves or to commemorate historical events.

Stile Floreale—See *Art Nouveau*.

still life—A picture depicting an arrangement of inanimate objects.

strigil—A tool ancient Greek athletes used to scrape oil from their bodies after exercising.

stucco—A type of plaster used as a coating on exterior and interior walls. Also used as a sculptural *medium*.

style—A distinctive artistic manner. Period style is the characteristic style of a specific time. Regional style is the style of a particular geographical area. Personal style is an individual artist's unique manner.

stylistic evidence—In art history, the examination of the *style* of an artwork in order to determine its date or the identity of the artist.

stylobate—The uppermost course of the platform of a *classical* Greek temple, which supports the *columns*.

stylus—A needlelike tool used in *engraving* and *incising*; also, an ancient writing instrument used to inscribe clay or wax tablets.

subtractive light—The painter's light in art; the light reflected from pigments and objects. See also *additive light*.

subtractive sculpture—A kind of sculpture *technique* in which materials are taken away from the original mass; *carving*.

successive contrasts—The phenomenon of colored afterimages. When a person looks intently at a *color* (green, for example) and then shifts to a white area, the fatigued eye momentarily perceives the *complementary color* (red). See also *simultaneous contrasts*.

sultan—A *Muslim* ruler.

Sunnah—The collection of the Prophet Muhammad's moral sayings and descriptions of his deeds.

Superrealism—A painting and sculpture movement of the 1960s and 1970s that emphasized producing artworks based on scrupulous fidelity to optical fact. The Superrealist painters were also called Photorealists because many used photographs as sources for their imagery.

Suprematism—A type of art formulated by Kazimir Malevich to convey his belief that the supreme reality in the world is pure feeling, which attaches to no object and thus calls for new, nonobjective *forms* in art—shapes not related to objects in the visible world.

surah—A chapter of the *Koran*, divided into verses.

Surrealism—A successor to *Dada*, Surrealism incorporated the improvisational nature of its predecessor into its exploration of the ways to express in art the world of dreams and the unconscious. Biomorphic Surrealists, such as Joan Miró, produced largely *abstract compositions*. Naturalistic Surrealists, notably Salvador Dalí, presented recognizable scenes transformed into a dream or nightmare image.

symbol—An image that stands for another image or encapsulates an idea.

Symbolism—A late-19th-century movement based on the idea that the artist was not an imitator of nature but a creator who transformed the facts of nature into a *symbol* of the inner experience of that fact.

Synthetic Cubism—A later phase of *Cubism,* in which paintings and drawings were constructed from objects and shapes cut from paper or other materials to represent parts of a subject, in order to engage the viewer with pictorial issues, such as figuration, realism, and abstraction.

taberna—In Roman architecture, a single-room shop usually covered by a *barrel vault.*

tablinum—The study or office in a Roman *domus.*

tapestry—A weaving *technique* in which the horizontal threads are packed densely over the vertical threads so that the designs are woven directly into the fabric.

tattoo—A permanent design on the skin produced using indelible dyes. The term derives from the Tahitian, Samoan, and Tongan word *tatau* or *tatu.*

technique—The processes artists employ to create *form,* as well as the distinctive, personal ways in which they handle their materials and tools.

tempera—A *technique* of painting using pigment mixed with egg yolk, glue, or casein; also, the *medium* itself.

templon—The columnar screen separating the sanctuary from the main body of a *Byzantine church.*

tenebrism—Painting in the "shadowy manner," using violent contrasts of light and dark, as in the work of Caravaggio. The term derives from *tenebroso.*

tenebroso—Italian, "shadowy." See *tenebrism.*

tepidarium—The warm-bath section of a Roman bathing establishment.

terminus ante quem—Latin, "point [date] before which."

terminus post quem—Latin, "point [date] after which."

terracotta—Hard-baked clay, used for sculpture and as a building material. It may be *glazed* or painted.

terribilità—Italian, "the sublime shadowed by the fearful." A term used to describe Michelangelo Buonarroti.

tessera (pl. tesserae)—Greek, "cube." A tiny stone or piece of glass cut to the desired shape and size for use in forming a *mosaic.*

tetrarch—One of four corulers.

tetrarchy—Greek, "rule by four." A type of Roman government established in the late third century CE by Diocletian in an attempt to foster order by sharing power with potential rivals.

texture—The quality of a surface (rough, smooth, hard, soft, shiny, dull) as revealed by light. In represented texture, a painter depicts an object as having a certain texture even though the pigment is the real texture.

theatron—Greek, "place for seeing." In ancient Greek theaters, the slope overlooking the *orchestra* on which the spectators sat.

Theotokos—Greek, "she who bore God." The Virgin Mary, the mother of Jesus.

Third Style mural—In Roman *mural* painting, the *style* in which delicate linear fantasies were sketched on predominantly *monochromatic* backgrounds.

tholos (pl. tholoi)—A temple with a circular plan. Also, the burial chamber of a *tholos tomb.*

tholos tomb—In *Mycenaean* architecture, a beehive-shaped tomb with a circular plan.

thrust—The outward force exerted by an *arch* or a *vault* that must be counterbalanced by a *buttress.*

toga—The garment worn by an ancient Roman male citizen.

tonality—See *color.*

tondo (pl. tondi)—A circular painting or *relief* sculpture.

Torah—The Hebrew religious scroll containing the *Pentateuch.*

torque—The distinctive necklace worn by the Gauls.

tracery—Ornamental stonework for holding *stained glass* in place, characteristic of *Gothic cathedrals.* In plate tracery, the glass fills only the "punched holes" in the heavy ornamental stonework. In bar tracery, the stained-glass windows fill almost the entire opening, and the stonework is unobtrusive.

transept—The part of a *church* with an axis that crosses the *nave* at a right angle.

transverse arch—An *arch* separating one *vaulted bay* from the next.

transverse rib—See *rib.*

treasury—In ancient Greece, a small building set up for the safe storage of *votive offerings.*

Trecento—Italian, "300"—that is, the 14th century (the 1300s) in Italy.

trefoil—A cloverlike ornament or symbol with stylized leaves in groups of three.

trefoil arch—A triple-lobed arch.

tria—Greek, "three."

tribune—In *church* architecture, a gallery over the inner *aisle* flanking the *nave.*

triclinium (pl. triclinia)—The dining room of a Roman *domus.*

trident—The three-pronged pitchfork associated with the ancient Greek sea god Poseidon (Roman Neptune).

triforium—In a *Gothic cathedral,* the *blind arcaded* gallery below the *clerestory;* occasionally, the *arcades* are filled with *stained glass.*

triglyph—A triple projecting, grooved member of a *Doric frieze* that alternates with *metopes.*

trilithon—A pair of *monoliths* topped with a *lintel;* found in *megalithic* structures.

Trinity—In Christianity, God the Father, his son Jesus Christ, and the Holy Spirit.

triptych—A three-paneled painting, ivory plaque, or *altarpiece.* Also, a small, portable shrine with hinged wings used for private devotion.

triumphal arch—In Roman architecture, a freestanding *arch* commemorating an important event, such as a military victory or the opening of a new road.

trompe l'oeil—French, "fools the eye." A form of *illusionistic* painting that aims to deceive viewers into believing that they are seeing real objects rather than a representation of those objects.

trumeau—In *church* architecture, the *pillar* or center post supporting the *lintel* in the middle of the doorway.

tubicen—Latin, "trumpet player."

tumulus (pl. tumuli)—Latin, "burial mound." In Etruscan architecture, tumuli cover one or more subterranean multichambered tombs cut out of the local tufa (limestone). Tumuli are also characteristic of the Japanese Kofun period of the third and fourth centuries CE.

tunnel vault—See *vault.*

turris—See *westwork.*

Tuscan column—The standard type of Etruscan *column.* It resembles ancient Greek *Doric* columns but is made of wood, is un*fluted,* and has a *base.* Also a popular motif in *Renaissance* and *Baroque* architecture.

twisted perspective—See *composite view.*

tympanum (pl. tympana)—The space enclosed by a *lintel* and an *arch* over a doorway.

uraeus—An Egyptian cobra; one of the emblems of *pharaonic* kingship.

ushabti—In ancient Egypt, a figurine placed in a tomb to act as a servant to the deceased in the afterlife.

valley temple—The temple closest to the Nile River, associated with each of the Old Kingdom pyramids at Gizeh in ancient Egypt.

value—See *color.*

vanishing point—See *perspective.*

vanitas—Latin, "vanity." A term describing paintings (particularly 17th-century Dutch *still lifes*) that include references to death.

vault (adj. vaulted)—A masonry roof or ceiling constructed on the *arch* principle, or a concrete roof of the same shape. A barrel (or tunnel) vault, semicylindrical in cross-*section,* is in effect a deep arch or an uninterrupted series of arches, one behind the other, over an oblong space. A quadrant vault is a half-barrel vault. A groin (or cross) vault is formed at the point at which two barrel vaults intersect at right angles. In a ribbed vault, there is a framework of *ribs* or arches under the intersections of the vaulting sections. A sexpartite vault is one whose ribs divide the vault into six compartments. A fan vault is a vault characteristic of English *Perpendicular Gothic* architecture, in which radiating ribs form a fanlike pattern.

vaulting web—See *web*.

veduta (pl. **vedute**)—Italian, "scenic view."

velarium—In a Roman *amphitheater,* the cloth awning that could be rolled down from the top of the *cavea* to shield spectators from sun or rain.

vellum—Calfskin prepared as a surface for writing or painting.

venationes—Ancient Roman wild animal hunts staged in an *amphitheater.*

veristic—True to natural appearance; super-realistic.

verso—The back side of a manuscript *folio.*

vik—Old Norse, "cove."

vita—Italian, "life." Also, the title of a biography.

vita contemplativa—Latin, "contemplative life." The secluded spiritual life of monks and nuns.

volute—A spiral, scroll-like form characteristic of the ancient Greek Ionic capital.

votive offering—A gift of gratitude to a deity.

voussoir—A wedge-shaped stone block used in the construction of a true *arch.* The central voussoir, which sets the arch, is called the *keystone.*

Vulgate—Common tongue; spoken medieval Latin.

web—The masonry blocks that fill the area between the *ribs* of a *groin vault.* Also called vaulting web.

weld—To join metal parts by heating, as in assembling the separate parts of a *statue* made by *casting.*

Westwerk—German, "western entrance structure."

westwork—The *facade* and towers at the western end (*Westwerk*) of a medieval *church,* principally in Germany. In contemporaneous documents, the westwork is called a castellum (Latin, "castle" or "fortress") or turris ("tower").

wet-plate photography—An early photographic process in which the photographic plate is exposed, developed, and fixed while wet.

white-ground painting—An ancient Greek vase-painting *technique* in which the pot was first covered with a *slip* of very fine white clay, over which black *glaze* was used to outline figures, and diluted brown, purple, red, and white were used to color them.

woodcut—A wood block on the surface of which those parts not intended to *print* are cut away to a slight depth, leaving the design raised; also, the printed impression made with such a block.

ziggurat—In ancient Mesopotamian architecture, a tiered platform for a temple.

zoopraxiscope—A device invented by Eadweard Muybridge in the 19th century to project sequences of still photographic images; a predecessor of the modern motion-picture projector.

Bibliography

This list of books is very selective, but comprehensive enough to satisfy the reading interests of the beginning art history student and general reader. The resources listed range from works that are valuable primarily for their reproductions to those that are scholarly surveys of schools and periods or monographs on individual artists. The emphasis is on recent in-print books and on books likely to be found in college and municipal libraries. No entries for periodical articles appear, but the bibliography begins with a list of some the major journals that publish art historical scholarship in English.

Selected Periodicals

African Arts
American Art
American Indian Art
American Journal of Archaeology
Antiquity
Archaeology
Archives of American Art
Archives of Asian Art
Ars Orientalis
Art Bulletin
Art History
Art in America
Art Journal
Artforum International
Artnews
Burlington Magazine
Gesta
History of Photography
Journal of Egyptian Archaeology
Journal of Roman Archaeology
Journal of the Society of Architectural Historians
Journal of the Warburg and Courtauld Institutes
Latin American Antiquity
October
Oxford Art Journal
Women's Art Journal

General Studies

Baxandall, Michael. *Patterns of Intention: On the Historical Explanation of Pictures.* New Haven, Conn.: Yale University Press, 1985.
Boström, Antonia. *The Encyclopedia of Sculpture.* 3 vols. London: Rout-ledge, 2003.
Broude, Norma, and Mary D. Garrard, eds. *The Expanding Discourse: Feminism and Art History.* New York: HarperCollins, 1992.
Bryson, Norman, Michael Ann Holly, and Keith Moxey. *Visual Theory: Painting and Interpretation.* New York: Cambridge University Press, 1991.
Burden, Ernst. *Illustrated Dictionary of Architecture.* 2d ed. New York: McGraw-Hill, 2002.
Büttner, Nils. *Landscape Painting: A History.* New York: Abbeville, 2006.
Carrier, David. *A World Art History and Its Objects.* University Park: Pennsylvania State University Press, 2009.
Chadwick, Whitney. *Women, Art, and Society.* 5th ed. New York: Thames & Hudson, 2012.
Cheetham, Mark A., Michael Ann Holly, and Keith Moxey, eds. *The Subjects of Art History: Historical Objects in Contemporary Perspective.* New York: Cambridge University Press, 1998.

Chilvers, Ian, and Harold Osborne, eds. *The Oxford Dictionary of Art.* 3d ed. New York: Oxford University Press, 2004.
Crouch, Dora P., and June G. Johnson. *Traditions in Architecture: Africa, America, Asia, and Oceania.* New York: Oxford University Press, 2000.
Curl, James Stevens. *Oxford Dictionary of Architecture and Landscape Architecture.* 2d ed. New York: Oxford University Press, 2006.
Davis, Whitney. *A General Theory of Visual Culture.* Princeton, N.J.: Princeton University Press, 2011.
Encyclopedia of World Art. 17 vols. New York: McGraw-Hill, 1959–1987.
Evers, Bernd, and Christof Thoenes. *Architectural Theory from the Renaissance to the Present.* Cologne: Taschen, 2011.
Fine, Sylvia Honig. *Women and Art: A History of Women Painters and Sculptors from the Renaissance to the 20th Century.* Montclair: Alanheld & Schram, 1978.
Fleming, John, Hugh Honour, and Nikolaus Pevsner. *The Penguin Dictionary of Architecture and Landscape Architecture.* 5th ed. New York: Penguin, 2000.
Freedberg, David. *The Power of Images: Studies in the History and Theory of Response.* Chicago: University of Chicago Press, 1989.
Gaze, Delia, ed. *Dictionary of Women Artists.* 2 vols. London: Routledge, 1997.
Hall, James. *Illustrated Dictionary of Subjects and Symbols in Eastern and Western Art.* 2d ed. Boulder, Colo.: Westview, 2008.
Harris, Anne Sutherland, and Linda Nochlin. *Women Artists: 1550– 1950.* Los Angeles: Los Angeles County Museum of Art, 1977.
Ingersoll, Richard, and Spiro Kostof. *World Architecture: A Cross-Cultural History.* New York: Oxford University Press, 2012.
Kemp, Martin. *The Science of Art: Optical Themes in Western Art from Brunelleschi to Seurat.* New Haven, Conn.: Yale University Press, 1990.
Kultermann, Udo. *The History of Art History.* New York: Abaris, 1993.
Lucie-Smith, Edward. *The Thames & Hudson Dictionary of Art Terms.* 2d ed. New York: Thames & Hudson, 2004.
Moffett, Marian, Michael Fazio, and Lawrence Wadehouse. *A World History of Architecture.* Boston: McGraw-Hill, 2004.
Nelson, Robert S., and Richard Shiff, eds. *Critical Terms for Art History.* Chicago: University of Chicago Press, 1996.
Pazanelli, Roberta, ed. *The Color of Life: Polychromy in Sculpture from Antiquity to the Present.* Los Angeles: J. Paul Getty Museum, 2008.
Penny, Nicholas. *The Materials of Sculpture.* New Haven, Conn.: Yale University Press, 1993.
Pevsner, Nikolaus. *A History of Building Types.* London: Thames & Hudson, 1987. Reprint of 1979 ed.
———. *An Outline of European Architecture.* 8th ed. Baltimore: Penguin, 1974.
Pierce, James Smith. *From Abacus to Zeus: A Handbook of Art History.* 7th ed. Upper Saddle River, N.J.: Pearson Prentice Hall, 2003.
Placzek, Adolf K., ed. *Macmillan Encyclopedia of Architects.* 4 vols. New York: Macmillan, 1982.
Podro, Michael. *The Critical Historians of Art.* New Haven, Conn.: Yale University Press, 1982.
Pollock, Griselda. *Vision and Difference: Femininity, Feminism and Histories of Art.* London: Routledge, 1988.
Preziosi, Donald, ed. *The Art of Art History: A Critical Anthology.* New York: Oxford University Press, 1998.
Reid, Jane D. *The Oxford Guide to Classical Mythology in the Arts 1300–1990s.* 2 vols. New York: Oxford University Press, 1993.
Roth, Leland M. *Understanding Architecture: Its Elements, History, and Meaning.* 2d ed. Boulder, Colo.: Westview, 2006.
Schama, Simon. *The Power of Art.* New York: Ecco, 2006.
Slatkin, Wendy. *Women Artists in History: From Antiquity to the 20th Century.* 4th ed. Upper Saddle River, N.J.: Prentice Hall, 2000.
Steer, John, and Antony White. *Atlas of Western Art History: Artists, Sites and Monuments from Ancient Greece to the Modern Age.* New York: Facts on File, 1994.

Stratton, Arthur. *The Orders of Architecture: Greek, Roman and Renaissance.* London: Studio, 1986.

Sutton, Ian. *Western Architecture: From Ancient Greece to the Present.* New York: Thames & Hudson, 1999.

Trachtenberg, Marvin, and Isabelle Hyman. *Architecture: From Prehistory to Post-Modernism.* 2d ed. Upper Saddle River, N.J.: Prentice Hall, 2003.

Turner, Jane, ed. *The Dictionary of Art.* 34 vols. New ed. New York: Oxford University Press, 2003.

Watkin, David. *A History of Western Architecture.* 5th ed. London: Laurence King, 2011.

West, Shearer. *Portraiture.* New York: Oxford University Press, 2004.

Wittkower, Rudolf. *Sculpture Processes and Principles.* New York: Harper & Row, 1977.

Ancient Art, General

Boardman, John. *The World of Ancient Art.* London: Thames & Hudson, 2006.

———, ed. *The Oxford History of Classical Art.* New York: Oxford University Press, 1997.

Chitham, Robert. *The Classical Orders of Architecture.* 2d ed. Boston: Architectural Press, 2005.

Gates, Charles. *Ancient Cities: The Archaeology of Urban Life in the Ancient Near East and Egypt, Greece, and Rome.* 2d ed. London: Routledge, 2011.

Grossman, Janet Burnett. *Looking at Greek and Roman Sculpture in Stone: A Guide to Terms, Styles, and Techniques.* Los Angeles: J. Paul Getty Museum, 2003.

Malacrino, Carmelo. *Constructing the Ancient World: Architectural Techniques of the Greeks and Romans.* Los Angeles: J. Paul Getty Museum, 2010.

Oleson, John Peter, ed. *The Oxford Handbook of Engineering and Technology in the Classical World.* New York: Oxford University Press, 2008.

Renfrew, Colin, and Paul G. Bahn. *Archaeology: Theories, Methods, and Practices.* London: Thames & Hudson, 1991.

Trigger, Bruce. *Understanding Early Civilizations: A Comparative Study.* New York: Cambridge University Press, 2003.

CHAPTER 1
Prehistory and the First Civilizations

Prehistory

Aujoulat, Norbert. *Lascaux: Movement, Space, and Time.* New York: Abrams, 2005.

Bahn, Paul G. *The Cambridge Illustrated History of Prehistoric Art.* New York: Cambridge University Press, 1998.

———. *Cave Art: A Guide to the Decorated Ice Age Caves of Europe.* London: Frances Lincoln, 2007.

Bahn, Paul G., and Jean Vertut. *Journey through the Ice Age.* Berkeley: University of California Press, 1997.

Clottes, Jean. *Cave Art.* London: Phaidon, 2008.

Cunliffe, Barry, ed. *The Oxford Illustrated Prehistory of Europe.* New York: Oxford University Press, 1994.

Guthrie, R. Dale. *The Nature of Paleolithic Art.* Chicago: University of Chicago Press, 2005.

Scarre, Chris. *Exploring Prehistoric Europe.* New York: Oxford University Press, 1998.

White, Randall. *Prehistoric Art: The Symbolic Journey of Humankind.* New York: Abrams, 2003.

Ancient Near East

Allen, Lindsay. *The Persian Empire.* Chicago: University of Chicago Press, 2005.

Amiet, Pierre. *Art of the Ancient Near East.* New York: Abrams, 1980.

Ascalone, Enrico. *Mesopotamia: Assyrians, Sumerians, Babylonians.* Berkeley and Los Angeles: University of California Press, 2007.

Bahrani, Zainab. *The Graven Image: Representation in Babylonia and Assyria.* Philadelphia: University of Pennsylvania Press, 2003.

Collins, Paul. *Assyrian Palace Sculptures.* Austin: University of Texas Press, 2008.

Collon, Dominique. *Ancient Near Eastern Art.* Berkeley: University of California Press, 1995.

Crawford, Harriet, ed. *The Sumerian World.* London: Routledge, 2013.

Curatola, Giovanni, ed. *The Art and Architecture of Mesopotamia.* New York: Abbeville, 2007.

Curtis, John E., and Nigel Tallis. *Forgotten Empire: The World of Ancient Persia.* Berkeley: University of California Press, 2005.

Finkel, Irving L., and Michael J. Seymour, eds. *Babylon.* New York: Oxford University Press, 2008.

Foster, Benjamin R., and Karen Polinger Foster. *Civilizations of Ancient Iraq.* Princeton, N.J.: Princeton University Press, 2009.

Frankfort, Henri. *The Art and Architecture of the Ancient Orient.* 5th ed. New Haven, Conn.: Yale University Press, 1996.

Meyers, Eric M., ed. *The Oxford Encyclopedia of Archaeology in the Near East.* 5 vols. New York: Oxford University Press, 1997.

Moortgat, Anton. *The Art of Ancient Mesopotamia.* New York: Phaidon, 1969.

Parrot, André. *The Arts of Assyria.* New York: Golden Press, 1961.

———. *Sumer: The Dawn of Art.* New York: Golden Press, 1961.

Reade, Julian E. *Assyrian Sculpture.* Cambridge, Mass.: Harvard University Press, 1999.

———. *Mesopotamia.* Cambridge, Mass.: Harvard University Press, 1991.

Roaf, Michael. *Cultural Atlas of Mesopotamia and the Ancient Near East.* New York: Facts on File, 1990.

Sasson, Jack M., ed. *Civilizations of the Ancient Near East.* 4 vols. New York: Scribner, 1995.

Strommenger, Eva, and Max Hirmer. *5,000 Years of the Art of Mesopotamia.* New York: Abrams, 1964.

Egypt

Arnold, Dieter. *Building in Egypt: Pharaonic Stone Masonry.* New York: Oxford University Press, 1991.

Arnold, Dorothea. *When the Pyramids Were Built: Egyptian Art of the Old Kingdom.* New York: Rizzoli, 1999.

Baines, John, and Jaromír Málek. *Atlas of Ancient Egypt.* New York: Facts on File, 1980.

Bard, Kathryn A. *An Introduction to the Archaeology of Ancient Egypt.* Oxford: Blackwell, 2007.

———, ed. *Encyclopedia of the Archaeology of Ancient Egypt.* London: Routledge, 1999.

Davis, Whitney. *The Canonical Tradition in Ancient Egyptian Art.* New York: Cambridge University Press, 1989.

Dodson, Aidam, and Salima Ikram. *The Tomb in Ancient Egypt.* New York: Thames & Hudson, 2008.

Ikram, Salima, and Aidan Dodson. *The Mummy in Ancient Egypt: Equipping the Dead for Eternity.* New York: Thames & Hudson, 1998.

Kemp, Barry J. *Ancient Egypt: Anatomy of a Civilization.* 2d ed. New York: Routledge, 2006.

Lehner, Mark. *The Complete Pyramids: Solving the Ancient Mysteries.* New York: Thames & Hudson, 1997.

Málek, Jaromír. *Egypt: 4,000 Years of Art.* New York: Phaidon, 2003.

———. *Egyptian Art.* London: Phaidon, 1999.

O'Neill, John P. *Egyptian Art in the Age of the Pyramids.* New York: Abrams, 1999.

Redford, Donald B., ed. *The Oxford Encyclopedia of Ancient Egypt.* 3 vols. New York: Oxford University Press, 2001.

Robins, Gay. *The Art of Ancient Egypt.* Rev. ed. Cambridge, Mass.: Harvard University Press, 2008.

Schulz, Regina, and Matthias Seidel, eds. *Egypt: The World of the Pharaohs.* Cologne: Känemann, 1999.

Shafer, Byron E., ed. *Temples of Ancient Egypt.* Ithaca, N.Y.: Cornell University Press, 1997.

Shaw, Ian, and Paul Nicholson. *The Dictionary of Ancient Egypt.* London: British Museum, 1995.

Silverman, David P., ed. *Ancient Egypt.* New York: Oxford University Press, 1997.

Smith, William Stevenson, and William Kelly Simpson. *The Art and Architecture of Ancient Egypt.* Rev. ed. New Haven, Conn.: Yale University Press, 1998.

Snape, Steven. *Ancient Egyptian Tombs: The Culture of Life and Death.* Oxford: Wiley-Blackwell, 2011.

Taylor, John H. *Journey through the Afterlife: The Ancient Egyptian Book of the Dead.* Cambridge, Mass.: Harvard University Press, 2010.

Weeks, Kent R., ed. *Valley of the Kings.* Vercelli: White Star, 2001.

Wilkinson, Toby. *The Egyptian World.* London: Routledge, 2009.

CHAPTER 2
Ancient Greece

Prehistoric Aegean

Betancourt, Philip P. *Introduction to Aegean Art.* New York: Institute for Aegean Prehistory, 2007.

Castleden, Rodney. *Mycenaeans.* London: Routledge, 2005.

Cline, Eric H., ed. *The Oxford Handbook of the Bronze Age Aegean*. New York: Oxford University Press, 2010.

Cullen, Tracey, ed. *Aegean Prehistory: A Review*. Boston: Archaeological Institute of America, 2001.

Dickinson, Oliver P.T.K. *The Aegean Bronze Age*. New York: Cambridge University Press, 1994.

Doumas, Christos. *The Wall-Paintings of Thera*. Athens: Thera Foundation, 1992.

Fitton, J. Lesley. *Cycladic Art*. 2d ed. Cambridge, Mass.: Harvard University Press, 1999.

———. *The Discovery of the Greek Bronze Age*. London: British Museum, 1995.

Forsyth, Phyllis Young. *Thera in the Bronze Age*. New York: Peter Lang, 1997.

Graham, James W. *The Palaces of Crete*. Princeton, N.J.: Princeton University Press, 1987.

Hood, Sinclair. *The Arts in Prehistoric Greece*. New Haven, Conn.: Yale University Press, 1992.

Immerwahr, Sarah A. *Aegean Painting in the Bronze Age*. University Park: Pennsylvania State University Press, 1990.

McEnroe, John. *Architecture of Minoan Crete: Constructing Identity in the Aegean Bronze Age*. Austin: University of Texas Press, 2010.

Preziosi, Donald, and Louise A. Hitchcock. *Aegean Art and Architecture*. New York: Oxford University Press, 1999.

Schofield, Louise. *The Mycenaeans*. London: British Museum, 2007.

Shelmerdine, Cynthia W., ed. *The Cambridge Companion to the Aegean Bronze Age*. New York: Cambridge University Press, 2008.

Warren, Peter. *The Aegean Civilizations: The Making of the Past*. New York: Peter Bedrick, 1989.

Greece

Boardman, John. *Athenian Black Figure Vases*. Rev. ed. New York: Thames & Hudson, 1985.

———. *Athenian Red Figure Vases: The Archaic Period*. New York: Thames & Hudson, 1988.

———. *Athenian Red Figure Vases: The Classical Period*. New York: Thames & Hudson, 1989.

———. *Greek Sculpture: The Archaic Period*. Rev. ed. New York: Thames & Hudson, 1985.

———. *Greek Sculpture: The Classical Period*. New York: Thames & Hudson, 1987.

———. *Greek Sculpture: The Late Classical Period and Sculpture in Colonies and Overseas*. New York: Thames & Hudson, 1995.

Camp, John M. *The Archaeology of Athens*. New Haven, Conn.: Yale University Press, 2001.

Clark, Andrew J., Maya Elston, and Mary Louise Hart. *Understanding Greek Vases: A Guide to Terms, Styles, and Techniques*. Los Angeles: J. Paul Getty Museum, 2002.

Coldstream, J. Nicholas. *Geometric Greece: 900–700 BC*. 2d ed. London: Routledge, 2003.

Fullerton, Mark D. *Greek Art*. New York: Cambridge University Press, 2000.

Gunter, Ann C. *Greek Art and the Orient*. New York: Cambridge University Press, 2009.

Haynes, Denys E. L. *The Technique of Greek Bronze Statuary*. Mainz: von Zabern, 1992.

Hurwit, Jeffrey M. *The Art and Culture of Early Greece, 1100–480 B.C.* Ithaca, N.Y.: Cornell University Press, 1985.

———. *The Athenian Acropolis: History, Mythology, and Archaeology from the Neolithic Era to the Present*. New York: Cambridge University Press, 1999.

Jenkins, Ian. *Greek Architecture and Its Sculpture*. Cambridge, Mass.: Harvard University Press, 2006.

Junker, Klaus. *Interpreting the Images of Greek Myths: An Introduction*. New York: Cambridge University Press, 2012.

Keesling, Catherine M. *The Votive Statues of the Athenian Acropolis*. New York: Cambridge University Press, 2008.

Lawrence, Arnold W., and R. A. Tomlinson. *Greek Architecture*. Rev. ed. New Haven, Conn.: Yale University Press, 1996.

Mattusch, Carol C. *Classical Bronzes: The Art and Craft of Greek and Roman Statuary*. Ithaca, N.Y.: Cornell University Press, 1996.

Mee, Christopher. *Greek Archaeology*. Hoboken, N.J.: Wiley-Blackwell, 2011.

Mee, Christopher, and Tony Spawforth. *Greece: An Oxford Archaeological Guide*. New York: Oxford University Press, 2001.

Morris, Sarah P. *Daidalos and the Origins of Greek Art*. Princeton, N.J.: Princeton University Press, 1992.

Neer, Richard T. *The Emergence of the Classical Style in Greek Sculpture*. Chicago: University of Chicago Press, 2010.

———. *Greek Art and Archaeology: A New History, c. 2500–c. 150 BCE*. New York: Thames & Hudson, 2011.

Osborne, Robin. *Archaic and Classical Greek Art*. New York: Oxford University Press, 1998.

Palagia, Olga, ed. *Greek Sculpture. Functions, Materials, and Techniques in the Archaic and Classical Periods*. New York: Cambridge University Press, 2006.

Pedley, John Griffiths. *Greek Art and Archaeology*. 5th ed. Upper Saddle River, N.J.: Prentice Hall, 2007.

Pollitt, Jerome J. *Art in the Hellenistic Age*. New York: Cambridge University Press, 2011.

———. *The Art of Ancient Greece: Sources and Documents*. 2d ed. New York: Cambridge University Press, 1990.

Rhodes, Robin F. *Architecture and Meaning on the Athenian Acropolis*. New York: Cambridge University Press, 1995.

Ridgway, Brunilde S. *The Archaic Style in Greek Sculpture*. 2d ed. Chicago: Ares, 1993.

———. *Fifth Century Styles in Greek Sculpture*. Princeton, N.J.: Princeton University Press, 1981.

———. *Fourth-Century Styles in Greek Sculpture*. Madison: University of Wisconsin Press, 1997.

———. *Hellenistic Sculpture I: The Styles of ca. 331–200 B.C.* Madison: University of Wisconsin Press, 1990.

———. *Hellenistic Sculpture II: The Styles of ca. 200–100 B.C.* Madison: University of Wisconsin Press, 2000.

———. *Prayers in Stone: Greek Architectural Sculpture*. Berkeley: University of California Press, 1999.

Robertson, Martin. *A History of Greek Art*. Rev. ed. 2 vols. New York: Cambridge University Press, 1986.

Smith, R.R.R. *Hellenistic Sculpture*. New York: Thames & Hudson, 1991.

Spawforth, Tony. *The Complete Greek Temples*. London: Thames & Hudson, 2006.

Spivey, Nigel. *Greek Art*. London: Phaidon, 1997.

Stansbury-O'Donnell, Mark D. *Looking at Greek Art*. New York: Cambridge University Press, 2011.

———. *Pictorial Narrative in Ancient Greek Art*. New York: Cambridge University Press, 1999.

Stewart, Andrew. *Classical Greece and the Birth of Western Art*. New York: Cambridge University Press, 2008.

———. *Greek Sculpture: An Exploration*. 2 vols. New Haven, Conn.: Yale University Press, 1990.

CHAPTER 3
The Roman Empire

Etruria

Barker, Graeme, and Tom Rasmussen. *The Etruscans*. Oxford: Blackwell, 1998.

Bonfante, Larissa, ed. *Etruscan Life and Afterlife: A Handbook of Etruscan Studies*. Detroit: Wayne State University Press, 1986.

Brendel, Otto J. *Etruscan Art*. 2d ed. New Haven, Conn.: Yale University Press, 1995.

Haynes, Sybille. *Etruscan Civilization: A Cultural History*. Los Angeles: J. Paul Getty Museum, 2000.

Spivey, Nigel. *Etruscan Art*. New York: Thames & Hudson, 1997.

Sprenger, Maja, Gilda Bartoloni, and Max Hirmer. *The Etruscans: Their History, Art, and Architecture*. New York: Abrams, 1983.

Steingräber, Stephan. *Abundance of Life: Etruscan Wall Painting*. Los Angeles: J. Paul Getty Museum, 2006.

Torelli, Mario, ed. *The Etruscans*. New York: Rizzoli, 2001.

Turfa, Jean Macintosh, ed. *The Etruscan World*. London: Routledge, 2013.

Rome

Anderson, James C., Jr. *Roman Architecture and Society*. Baltimore: Johns Hopkins University Press, 1997.

Barton, Ian M., ed. *Roman Domestic Buildings*. Exeter: University of Exeter Press, 1996.

———. *Roman Public Buildings*. 2d ed. Exeter: University of Exeter Press, 1995.

Claridge, Amanda. *Rome: An Oxford Archaeological Guide*. 2d ed. New York: Oxford University Press, 2010.

Clarke, John R. *The Houses of Roman Italy, 100 B.C.–A.D. 250*. Berkeley and Los Angeles: University of California Press, 1991.

Coarelli, Filippo. *Rome and Environs: An Archaeological Guide*. Berkeley and Los Angeles: University of California Press, 2007.

D'Ambra, Eve. *Roman Art*. New York: Cambridge University Press, 1998.

Dobbins, John J., and Pedar W. Foss, eds. *The World of Pompeii*. London: Routledge, 2007.

Dyson, Stephen L. *Rome: A Living Portrait of an Ancient City*. Baltimore: Johns Hopkins University Press, 2010.

Hannestad, Niels. *Roman Art and Imperial Policy*. Aarhus: Aarhus University Press, 1986.

Kleiner, Diana E. E. *Roman Sculpture*. New Haven, Conn.: Yale University Press, 1992.

Kleiner, Fred S. *A History of Roman Art*. Enhanced ed. Belmont, Calif.: Wadsworth, 2010.

Kraus, Theodor. *Pompeii and Herculaneum: The Living Cities of the Dead*. New York: Abrams, 1975.

Lancaster, Lynne. *Concrete Vaulted Construction in Imperial Rome*. New York: Cambridge University Press, 2006.

Ling, Roger. *Roman Painting*. New York: Cambridge University Press, 1991.

MacDonald, William L. *The Architecture of the Roman Empire I: An Introductory Study*. Rev. ed. New Haven, Conn.: Yale University Press, 1982.

Mattusch, Carol C., ed. *Pompeii and the Roman Villa: Art and Culture around the Bay of Naples*. New York: Thames & Hudson, 2008.

Mazzoleni, Donatella. *Domus: Wall Painting in the Roman House*. Los Angeles: J. Paul Getty Museum, 2004.

Pollitt, Jerome J. *The Art of Rome, 753 B.C.–A.D. 337: Sources and Documents*. Rev. ed. New York: Cambridge University Press, 1983.

Potter, T. W. *Roman Italy*. Berkeley and Los Angeles: University of California Press, 1990.

Richardson, Lawrence, Jr. *A New Topographical Dictionary of Ancient Rome*. Baltimore: Johns Hopkins University Press, 1992.

———. *Pompeii: An Architectural History*. Baltimore: Johns Hopkins University Press, 1988.

Stewart, Peter. *The Social History of Roman Art*. New York: Cambridge University Press, 2008.

Taylor, Rabun. *Roman Builders*. New York: Cambridge University Press, 2003.

Toynbee, Jocelyn M. C. *Death and Burial in the Roman World*. London: Thames & Hudson, 1971.

Wallace-Hadrill, Andrew. *Houses and Society in Pompeii and Herculaneum*. Princeton, N.J.: Princeton University Press, 1994.

Ward-Perkins, John B. *Roman Imperial Architecture*. 2d ed. New Haven, Conn.: Yale University Press, 1981.

Wilson-Jones, Mark. *Principles of Roman Architecture*. New Haven, Conn.: Yale University Press, 2000.

Zanker, Paul. *The Power of Images in the Age of Augustus*. Ann Arbor: University of Michigan Press, 1988.

———. *Roman Art*. Los Angeles: J. Paul Getty Museum, 2010.

Medieval Art, General

Alexander, Jonathan J. G. *Medieval Illuminators and Their Methods of Work*. New Haven, Conn.: Yale University Press, 1992.

Calkins, Robert G. *Medieval Architecture in Western Europe: From A.D. 300 to 1500*. New York: Oxford University Press, 1998.

Coldstream, Nicola. *Medieval Architecture*. New York: Oxford University Press, 2002.

Cross, Frank L., and Elizabeth A. Livingstone, eds. *The Oxford Dictionary of the Christian Church*. 3d ed. New York: Oxford University Press, 1997.

De Hamel, Christopher. *A History of Illuminated Manuscripts*. Oxford: Phaidon, 1986.

Hourihane, Colum, ed. *The Grove Encyclopedia of Medieval Art and Architecture*. New York: Oxford University Press, 2012.

Kessler, Herbert L. *Seeing Medieval Art*. Toronto: Broadview Press, 2004.

Murray, Peter, and Linda Murray. *The Oxford Companion to Christian Art and Architecture*. New York: Oxford University Press, 1996.

Ross, Leslie. *Medieval Art: A Topical Dictionary*. Westport, Conn.: Greenwood, 1996.

Sekules, Veronica. *Medieval Art*. New York: Oxford University Press, 2001.

Snyder, James, Henry Luttikhuizen, and Dorothy Verkerk. *Art of the Middle Ages*. 2d ed. Upper Saddle River, N.J.: Prentice Hall, 2006.

Stokstad, Marilyn. *Medieval Art*. 2d ed. Boulder, Colo.: Westview, 2004.

CHAPTER 4
Early Christianity and Byzantium

Cioffarelli, Ada. *Guide to the Catacombs of Rome and Its Surroundings*. Rome: Bonsignori, 2000.

Cormack, Robin. *Byzantine Art*. New York: Oxford University Press, 2000.

———. *Icons*. Cambridge, Mass.: Harvard University Press, 2007.

Cormack, Robin, and Maria Vassiliki. *Byzantium, 330–1453*. London: Royal Academy of Arts, 2008.

Deliyannis, Deborah Mauskopf. *Ravenna in Late Antiquity*. New York: Cambridge University Press, 2010.

Elsner, Jás. *Art and the Roman Viewer: The Transformation of Art from the Pagan World to Christianity*. New York: Cambridge University Press, 1995.

———. *Imperial Rome and Christian Triumph*. New York: Oxford University Press, 1998.

Freely, John. *Byzantine Monuments of Istanbul*. New York: Cambridge University Press, 2004.

Grabar, André. *The Beginnings of Christian Art, 200–395*. London: Thames & Hudson, 1967.

———. *Christian Iconography*. Princeton, N.J.: Princeton University Press, 1980.

———. *The Golden Age of Justinian: From the Death of Theodosius to the Rise of Islam*. New York: Odyssey Press, 1967.

Jensen, Robin Margaret. *Understanding Early Christian Art*. New York: Routledge, 2000.

Kleinbauer, W. Eugene. *Hagia Sophia*. London: Scala, 2004.

Koch, Guntram. *Early Christian Art and Architecture*. London: SCM Press, 1996.

Krautheimer, Richard, and Slobodan Ćurčić. *Early Christian and Byzantine Architecture*. 4th ed. New Haven, Conn.: Yale University Press, 1986.

Lowden, John. *Early Christian and Byzantine Art*. London: Phaidon, 1997.
Mango, Cyril. *Art of the Byzantine Empire, 312–1453: Sources and Documents*. Toronto: University of Toronto Press, 1986. Reprint of 1972 ed.

———. *Byzantine Architecture*. New York: Electa/Rizzoli, 1985.

Mathews, Thomas F. *Byzantium: From Antiquity to the Renaissance*. New York: Abrams, 1998.

———. *The Clash of Gods: A Reinterpretation of Early Christian Art*. Rev. ed. Princeton, N.J.: Princeton University Press, 1999.

Ousterhout, Robert. *Master Builders of Byzantium*. Princeton, N.J.: Princeton University Press, 2000.

Pelikan, Jaroslav. *Imago Dei: The Byzantine Apologia for Icons*. Princeton, N.J.: Princeton University Press, 1990.

Poeschke, Joachim. *Italian Mosaics, 300–1300*. New York: Abbeville, 2010.

Rodley, Lyn. *Byzantine Art and Architecture: An Introduction*. New York: Cambridge University Press, 1994.

Spier, Jeffrey, ed. *Picturing the Bible: The Earliest Christian Art*. New Haven, Conn.: Yale University Press, 2007.

Webster, Leslie, and Michelle Brown, eds. *The Transformation of the Roman World, A.D. 400–900*. Berkeley: University of California Press, 1997.

CHAPTER 5
The Islamic World

Baker, Patricia L. *Islam and the Religious Arts*. London: Continuum, 2004.

Blair, Sheila S. *Islamic Calligraphy*. Edinburgh: Edinburgh University Press, 2008.

Blair, Sheila S., and Jonathan Bloom. *The Art and Architecture of Islam 1250–1800*. New Haven, Conn.: Yale University Press, 1994.

Bloom, Jonathan, and Sheila S. Blair. *The Grove Encyclopedia of Islamic Art and Architecture*. New York: Oxford University Press, 2009.

———. *Islamic Arts*. London: Phaidon, 1997.

Brend, Barbara. *Islamic Art*. Cambridge, Mass.: Harvard University Press, 1991.

Ettinghausen, Richard, Oleg Grabar, and Marilyn Jenkins-Madina. *The Art and Architecture of Islam, 650–1250*. Rev. ed. New Haven, Conn.: Yale University Press, 2001.

Frishman, Martin, and Hasan-Uddin Khan. *The Mosque: History, Architectural Development and Regional Diversity*. New York: Thames & Hudson, 1994.

Grabar, Oleg. *The Formation of Islamic Art*. Rev. ed. New Haven, Conn.: Yale University Press, 1987.

———. *Islamic Visual Culture, 1100–1800*. New York: Ashgate, 2006.

Grube, Ernst J. *Architecture of the Islamic World: Its History and Social Meaning*. 2d ed. New York: Thames & Hudson, 1984.

Hattstein, Markus, and Peter Delius, eds. *Islam: Art and Architecture*. Cologne: Känemann, 2000.

Hillenbrand, Robert. *Islamic Architecture: Form, Function, Meaning*. Edinburgh: Edinburgh University Press, 1994.

———. *Islamic Art and Architecture*. New York: Thames & Hudson, 1999.

Irwin, Robert. *The Alhambra*. Cambridge, Mass.: Harvard University Press, 2004.

———. *Islamic Art in Context: Art, Architecture, and the Literary World*. New York: Abrams, 1997.

Mozzati, Luca. *Islamic Art: Architecture, Painting, Calligraphy, Ceramics, Glass, Carpets*. New York: Prestel, 2010.

Ruggles, D. Fairchild, ed. *Islamic Art & Visual Culture: An Anthology of Sources*. Malden, Mass.: Wiley-Blackwell, 2011.

Schimmel, Annemarie. *Calligraphy and Islamic Culture*. New York: New York University Press, 1984.

Tadgell, Christopher. *Four Caliphates: The Formation and Development of the Islamic Tradition*. London: Ellipsis, 1998.

CHAPTER 6
Early Medieval and Romanesque Europe

Ashley, Kathleen, and Marilyn Deegan. *Being a Pilgrim: Art and Ritual on the Medieval Routes to Santiago*. Burlington, Vt.: Lund Humphries, 2009.

Bagnoli, Martina, Holger A. Kleiner, C. Griffith Mann, and James Robinson, eds. *Treasures of Heaven: Saints, Relics, and Devotion in Medieval Europe*. New Haven, Conn.: Yale University Press, 2010.

Cahn, Walter. *Romanesque Manuscripts: The Twelfth Century*. 2 vols. London: Miller, 1998.

Conant, Kenneth J. *Carolingian and Romanesque Architecture, 800–1200*. 4th ed. New Haven, Conn.: Yale University Press, 1992.

Davis-Weyer, Caecilia. *Early Medieval Art, 300–1150: Sources and Documents*. Toronto: University of Toronto Press, 1986. Reprint of 1971 ed.

Diebold, William J. *Word and Image: An Introduction to Early Medieval Art*. Boulder, Colo.: Westview Press, 2000.

Dodwell, Charles R. *The Pictorial Arts of the West, 800–1200*. New Haven, Conn.: Yale University Press, 1993.

Fernie, Eric. *Romanesque Architecture*. New Haven, Conn.: Yale University Press, 2014.

Harbison, Peter. *The Golden Age of Irish Art: The Medieval Achievement 600–1200*. New York: Thames & Hudson, 1999.

Hearn, Millard F. *Romanesque Sculpture: The Revival of Monumental Stone Sculpture in the Eleventh and Twelfth Centuries*. Ithaca, N.Y.: Cornell University Press, 1981.

Henderson, George. *From Durrow to Kells: The Insular Gospel-Books, 650–800*. London: Thames & Hudson, 1987.

Hubert, Jean, Jean Porcher, and Wolfgang Fritz Volbach. *The Carolingian Renaissance*. New York: Braziller, 1970.

Lasko, Peter. *Ars Sacra, 800–1200*. 2d ed. New Haven, Conn.: Yale University Press, 1994.

McClendon, Charles. *The Origins of Medieval Architecture: Building in Europe, A.D. 600–900*. New Haven, Conn.: Yale University Press, 2005.

Meehan, Bernard. *The Book of Kells*. London: Tate, 2002.

Minne-Sève, Viviane, and Hervé Kergall. *Romanesque and Gothic France: Architecture and Sculpture*. New York: Abrams, 2000.

Nees, Lawrence J. *Early Medieval Art*. New York: Oxford University Press, 2002.

Petzold, Andreas. *Romanesque Art*. New York: Abrams, 1995.

Stalley, Roger. *Early Medieval Architecture*. New York: Oxford University Press, 1999.

Toman, Rolf, ed. *Romanesque: Architecture, Sculpture, Painting*. Cologne: Känemann, 1997.

Webster, Leslie. *Anglo-Saxon Art*. Ithaca: Cornell University Press, 2012.

CHAPTER 7
Gothic and Late Medieval Europe

Bony, Jean. *French Gothic Architecture of the Twelfth and Thirteenth Centuries*. Berkeley: University of California Press, 1983.

Branner, Robert. *Manuscript Painting in Paris during the Reign of St. Louis*. Berkeley: University of California Press, 1977.

———. *St. Louis and the Court Style in Gothic Architecture*. London: Zwemmer, 1965.

Camille, Michael. *Gothic Art: Glorious Visions*. New York: Abrams, 1996.

Cole, Bruce. *Sienese Painting: From Its Origins to the Fifteenth Century*. New York: HarperCollins, 1987.

Courtenay, Lynn T., ed. *The Engineering of Medieval Cathedrals*. Alder-shot: Scolar, 1997.

Derbes, Anne, and Mark Sandona, eds. *The Cambridge Companion to Giotto*. New York: Cambridge University Press, 2004.

Erlande-Brandenburg, Alain. *The Cathedral: The Social and Architectural Dynamics of Construction*. New York: Cambridge University Press, 1994.

Flores d'Arcais, Francesca. *Giotto*. 2d ed. New York: Abbeville, 2012.

Frankl, Paul, and Paul Crossley. *Gothic Architecture*. New Haven, Conn.: Yale University Press, 2000.

Frisch, Teresa G. *Gothic Art 1140–c. 1450: Sources and Documents*. Toronto: University of Toronto Press, 1987. Reprint of 1971 ed.

Grodecki, Louis. *Gothic Architecture*. New York: Electa/Rizzoli, 1985.

Grodecki, Louis, and Catherine Brisac. *Gothic Stained Glass, 1200–1300*. Ithaca, N.Y.: Cornell University Press, 1985.

Maginnis, Hayden B. J. *The World of the Early Sienese Painter*. University Park: Pennsylvania State University Press, 2001.

Minne-Sève, Viviane, and Hervé Kergall. *Romanesque and Gothic France: Architecture and Sculpture*. New York: Abrams, 2000.

Moskowitz, Anita Fiderer. *Italian Gothic Sculpture: c. 1250–c. 1400*. New York: Cambridge University Press, 2001.

Murray, Stephen. Notre Dame, *Cathedral of Amiens: The Power of Change in Gothic*. New York: Cambridge University Press, 1996.

Norman, Diana, ed. *Siena, Florence, and Padua: Art, Society, and Religion 1280–1400*. New Haven, Conn.: Yale University Press, 1995.

Panofsky, Erwin. *Abbot Suger on the Abbey Church of Saint-Denis and Its Art Treasures*. 2d ed. Princeton: Princeton University Press, 1979.

Poeschke, Joachim. *Italian Frescoes: The Age of Giotto, 1280–1400*. New York: Abbeville, 2005.

Raguin, Virginia Chieffo. *Stained Glass from its Origins to the Present*. New York: Abrams, 2003.

Rudolph, Conrad. *Artistic Change at St-Denis: Abbot Suger's Program and the Early Twelfth-Century Controversy over Art*. Princeton, N.J.: Princeton University Press, 1990.

Sauerländer, Willibald, and Max Hirmer. *Gothic Sculpture in France, 1140–1270*. New York: Abrams, 1973.

Stubblebine, James H. *Duccio di Buoninsegna and His School*. Princeton, N.J.: Princeton University Press, 1979.

Toman, Rolf, ed. *The Art of Gothic: Architecture, Sculpture, Painting*. Cologne: Känemann, 1999.

White, John. *Art and Architecture in Italy: 1250–1400*. 3d ed. New Haven, Conn.: Yale University Press, 1993.

Williamson, Paul. *Gothic Sculpture, 1140–1300*. New Haven, Conn.: Yale University Press, 1995.

Wilson, Christopher. *The Gothic Cathedral: The Architecture of the Great Church, 1130–1530*. London: Thames & Hudson, 1990.

Renaissance Art, General

Ames-Lewis, Francis, ed. *Florence*. (*Artistic Centers of the Italian Renaissance*.) New York: Cambridge University Press, 2011.

Anderson, Christy. *Renaissance Architecture*. New York: Oxford University Press, 2013.

Andrés, Glenn M., John M. Hunisak, and Richard Turner. *The Art of Florence*. 2 vols. New York: Abbeville Press, 1988.

Campbell, Gordon, ed. *The Grove Encyclopedia of Northern Renaissance Art*. New York: Oxford University Press, 2009.

Campbell, Stephen J., and Michael W. Cole. *Italian Renaissance Art*. New York: Thames & Hudson, 2011.

Christian, Kathleen, and David J. Drogin, eds. *Patronage and Italian Renaissance Sculpture*. Burlington, Vt.: Ashgate, 2010.

Cole, Bruce. *Italian Art, 1250–1550: The Relation of Renaissance Art to Life and Society*. New York: Harper & Row, 1987.

———. *The Renaissance Artist at Work: From Pisano to Titian*. New York: HarperCollins, 1983.

Freedman, Luba. *The Revival of the Olympian Gods in Renaissance Art*. New York: Cambridge University Press, 2003.

Frommel, Christoph Luitpold. *The Architecture of the Italian Renaissance*. London: Thames & Hudson, 2007.

Hall, Marcia B, ed. *Rome*. (*Artistic Centers of the Italian Renaissance*.) New York: Cambridge University Press, 2005.

Hartt, Frederick, and David G. Wilkins. *History of Italian Renaissance Art*. 7th ed. Upper Saddle River, N.J.: Prentice Hall, 2010.

Humfrey, Peter, ed. *Venice and the Veneto*. (*Artistic Centers of the Italian Renaissance*.) New York: Cambridge University Press, 2008.

Levey, Michael. *Florence: A Portrait*. Cambridge, Mass.: Harvard University Press, 1998.

Paoletti, John T., and Gary M. Radke. *Art, Power, and Patronage in Renaissance Italy*. Upper Saddle River, N.J.: Prentice Hall, 2005.

Partridge, Loren. *Art of Renaissance Florence, 1400–1600*. Berkeley and Los Angeles: University of California Press, 2009.

Richardson, Carol M., Kim W. Woods, and Michael W. Franklin. *Renaissance Art Reconsidered: An Anthology of Primary Sources*. Oxford: Blackwell, 2007.

Romanelli, Giandomencio, ed., *Venice: Art & Architecture*. Cologne: Käne-mann, 2005.

Rosenberg, Charles M., ed. *The Court Cities of Northern Italy: Milan, Parma, Piacenza, Mantua, Ferrara, Bologna, Urbino, Pesaro, and Rimini*. (*Artistic Centers of the Italian Renaissance*.) New York: Cambridge University Press, 2010.

Smith, Jeffrey Chipps. *The Northern Renaissance.* New York: Phaidon, 2004.

Snyder, James, Larry Silver, and Henry Luttikhuizen. *Northern Renaissance Art: Painting, Sculpture, the Graphic Arts from 1350 to 1575.* 2d ed. Upper Saddle River, N.J.: Prentice Hall, 2005.

Thomson, David. *Renaissance Architecture: Critics, Patrons, and Luxury.* Manchester: Manchester University Press, 1993.

Tingali, Paola. *Women in Italian Renaissance Art: Gender, Representation, Identity.* Manchester: Manchester University Press, 1997.

Woods, Kim W. *Making Renaissance Art.* New Haven, Conn.: Yale University Press, 2007.

———. *Viewing Renaissance Art.* New Haven, Conn.: Yale University Press, 2007.

CHAPTER 8
The Early Renaissance in Europe

Ahl, Diane Cole. *Fra Angelico.* New York: Phaidon, 2008.

Baxandall, Michael. *Painting and Experience in Fifteenth Century Italy: A Primer in the Social History of Pictorial Style.* 2d ed. New York: Oxford University Press, 1988.

Campbell, Lorne. *The Fifteenth Century Netherlandish Schools.* London: National Gallery Publications, 1998.

Chapuis, Julien, ed. *Tilman Riemenschneider, c. 1460–1531.* Washington, D.C.: National Gallery of Art, 2004.

Cole, Alison. *Virtue and Magnificence: Art of the Italian Renaissance Courts.* New York: Abrams, 1995.

Cole, Bruce. *Masaccio and the Art of Early Renaissance Florence.* Bloomington: Indiana University Press, 1980.

Edgerton, Samuel Y., Jr. *The Heritage of Giotto's Geometry: Art and Science on the Eve of the Scientific Revolution.* Ithaca, N.Y.: Cornell University Press, 1991.

Gilbert, Creighton, ed. *Italian Art 1400–1500: Sources and Documents.* Evanston, Ill.: Northwestern University Press, 1992.

Grafton, Antonhy. *Leon Battista Alberti: Master Builder of the Italian Renaissance.* Cambridge, Mass.: Harvard University Press, 2002.

Harbison, Craig. *The Mirror of the Artist: Northern Renaissance Art in Its Historical Context.* New York: Abrams, 1995.

Heydenreich, Ludwig H. *Architecture in Italy, 1400–1500.* 2d ed. New Haven, Conn.: Yale University Press, 1996.

Hollingsworth, Mary. *Patronage in Renaissance Italy: From 1400 to the Early Sixteenth Century.* Baltimore: Johns Hopkins University Press, 1994.

Kemperdick, Stephan, and Jochen Sander, eds. *The Master of Flémalle and Rogier van der Weyden.* Ostfildern: Hatje Cantz, 2009.

Kempers, Bram. *Painting, Power, and Patronage: The Rise of the Professional Artist in the Italian Renaissance.* London: Penguin, 1992.

Kent, Dale. *Cosimo de' Medici and the Florentine Renaissance: The Patron's Oeuvre.* New Haven, Conn.: Yale University Press, 2000.

Lane, Barbara G. *The Altar and the Altarpiece: Sacramental Themes in Early Netherlandish Painting.* New York: Harper & Row, 1984.

Manca, Joseph. *Andrea Mantegna and the Italian Renaissance.* New York: Parkstone, 2006.

Michels, Alfred. *Hans Memling.* London: Parkstone, 2008.

Morand, Kathleen. *Claus Sluter: Artist at the Court of Burgundy.* Austin: University of Texas Press, 1991.

Müller, Theodor. *Sculpture in the Netherlands, Germany, France and Spain: 1400–1500.* New Haven, Conn.: Yale University Press, 1986.

Nash, Susie. *Northern Renaissance Art.* New York: Oxford University Press, 2008.

Olson, Roberta J. M. *Italian Renaissance Sculpture.* London: Thames & Hudson, 1992.

Pächt, Otto. *Early Netherlandish Painting from Rogier van der Weyden to Gerard David.* New York: Harvey Miller, 1997.

Parshall, Peter, and Rainer Schoch. *Origins of European Printmaking: Fifteenth-Century Woodcuts and Their Public.* New Haven, Conn.: Yale University Press, 2005.

Poeschke, Joachim. *Donatello and His World: Sculpture of the Italian Renaissance.* New York: Abrams, 1993.

Seymour, Charles. *Sculpture in Italy: 1400–1500.* New Haven, Conn.: Yale University Press, 1992.

Smith, Jeffrey Chipps. *The Northern Renaissance.* New York: Phaidon, 2004.

Tavernor, Robert. *On Alberti and the Art of Building.* New Haven, Conn.: Yale University Press, 1999.

Tomlinson, Amanda. *Van Eyck.* London: Chaucer, 2007.

Turner, A. Richard. *Renaissance Florence: The Invention of a New Art.* New York: Abrams, 1997.

Welch, Evelyn. *Art and Society in Italy 1350–1500.* Oxford: Oxford University Press, 1997.

White, John. *The Birth and Rebirth of Pictorial Space.* 3d ed. Boston: Faber & Faber, 1987.

CHAPTER 9
High Renaissance and Mannerism in Europe

Bartrum, Giulia, ed. *Albrecht Dürer and His Legacy: The Graphic Work of a Renaissance Artist.* Princeton, N.J.: Princeton University Press, 2003.

Bazzotti, Ugo. *Palazzo Tè: Giulio Romano's Masterwork.* London: Thames & Hudson, 2012.

Blunt, Anthony. *Art and Architecture in France, 1500–1700.* Rev. ed. New Haven, Conn.: Yale University Press, 1999.

Brock, Maurice. *Bronzino.* Paris: Flammarion, 2002.

Brown, David Alan, and Sylvia Ferino-Pagden. *Bellini, Giorgione, Titian and the Renaissance of Venetian Painting.* New Haven, Conn.: Yale University Press, 2006.

Brown, Patricia Fortini. *Art and Life in Renaissance Venice.* New York: Abrams, 1997.

Cole, Bruce. *Titian and Venetian Painting, 1450–1590.* Boulder, Colo.: Westview, 2000.

Dal Pozzolo, Enrico. *Giorgione.* Milan: Motta, 2010.

Ekserdjian, David. *Parmigianino.* New Haven, Conn.: Yale University Press, 2006.

Franklin, David. *Painting in Renaissance Florence, 1500–1550.* New Haven, Conn.: Yale University Press, 2001.

Freedberg, Sydney J. *Painting in Italy: 1500–1600.* 3d ed. New Haven, Conn.: Yale University Press, 1993.

Goffen, Rona. *Renaissance Rivals. Michelangelo, Leonardo, Raphael, Titian.* New Haven, Conn.: Yale University Press, 2002.

Hall, Marcia B. *After Raphael: Painting in Central Italy in the Sixteenth Century.* New York: Cambridge University Press, 1999.

Humfry, Peter. *Painting in Renaissance Venice.* New Haven, Conn.: Yale University Press, 1995.

———. *Titian.* London: Phaidon, 2007.

Huse, Norbert, and Wolfgang Wolters. *The Art of Renaissance Venice: Architecture, Sculpture, and Painting.* Chicago: University of Chicago Press, 1990.

Kliemann, Julian-Matthias, and Michael Rohlmann. *Italian Frescoes: High Renaissance and Mannerism, 1510–1600.* New York: Abbeville, 2004.

Koerner, Joseph Leo. *The Reformation of the Image.* Chicago: University of Chicago Press, 2004.

Landau, David, and Peter Parshall. *The Renaissance Print: 1470–1550.* New Haven, Conn.: Yale University Press, 1994.

Lotz, Wolfgang. *Architecture in Italy, 1500–1600.* 2d ed. New Haven, Conn.: Yale University Press, 1995.

Marías, Fernando. *El Greco: Life and Work—A New History.* London: Thames & Hudson, 2013.

Partridge, Loren. *The Art of Renaissance Rome.* New York: Abrams, 1996.

Rowe, Colin, and Leon Satkowski. *Italian Architecture of the 16th Century.* New York: Princeton Architectural Press, 2002.

Rubin, Patricia Lee. *Giorgio Vasari: Art and History.* New Haven, Conn.: Yale University Press, 1995.

Shearman, John K. G. *Mannerism.* Baltimore: Penguin, 1978.

Silver, Larry. *Hieronymous Bosch.* New York: Abbeville, 2006.

———. *Pieter Bruegel.* New York: Abbeville, 2011.

Smith, Jeffrey Chipps. *Dürer.* London: Phaidon: 2012.

———. *German Sculpture of the Later Renaissance, c. 1520–1580: Art in an Age of Uncertainty.* Princeton, N.J.: Princeton University Press, 1993.

Stechow, Wolfgang. *Northern Renaissance Art, 1400–1600: Sources and Documents.* Upper Saddle River, N.J.: Prentice Hall, 1966.

Summers, David. *Michelangelo and the Language of Art.* Princeton, N.J.: Princeton University Press, 1981.

Talvacchia, Bette. *Raphael.* London: Phaidon, 2007.

Tronzo, William, ed. *St. Peter's in the Vatican.* New York: Cambridge University Press, 2005.

Wallace, William. *Michelangelo: The Artist, the Man, and His Times.* New York: Cambridge University Press, 2009.

Wolf, Norbert. *Albrecht Dürer.* New York: Prestel, 2010.

Zerner, Henri. *Renaissance Art in France: The Invention of Classicism.* Paris: Flammarion, 2003.

Zöllner, Frank. *Leonardo da Vinci: The Complete Paintings and Drawings.* Cologne: Taschen, 2007.

CHAPTER 10
Baroque Europe

Alpers, Svetlana. *The Art of Describing: Dutch Art in the Seventeenth Century.* Chicago: University of Chicago Press, 1984.

Bailey, Gauvin Alexander. *Baroque & Rococo.* London: Phaidon, 2012.

Bajou, Valérie. *Versailles.* New York: Abrams, 2012.

Belkin, Kristin Lohse. *Rubens.* London: Phaidon, 1998.

Bissel, R. Ward. *Artemisia Gentileschi and the Authority of Art.* University Park: Pennsylvania State University Press, 1999.

Blunt, Anthony. *Art and Architecture in France, 1500–1700.* Rev. ed. New Haven, Conn.: Yale University Press, 1999.

Brown, Jonathan. *The Golden Age of Painting in Spain.* New Haven, Conn.: Yale University Press, 1991.

Carr, Dawson W., ed. *Velázquez.* London: National Gallery, 2006.

Enggass, Robert, and Jonathan Brown. *Italy and Spain, 1600–1750: Sources and Documents.* Upper Saddle River, N.J.: Prentice Hall, 1970. Franits, Wayne. *Dutch Seventeenth-Century Genre Painting: Its Stylistic and Thematic Evolution.* New Haven, Conn.: Yale University Press, 2008.

Haak, Bob. *The Golden Age: Dutch Painters of the Seventeenth Century.* New York: Abrams, 1984.

Harris, Ann Sutherland. *Seventeenth-Century Art & Architecture.* 2d ed. Upper Saddle River, N.J.: Prentice Hall, 2008.

Harrison, Charles, Paul Wood, and Jason Gaiger, eds. *Art in Theory 1648–1815: An Anthology of Changing Ideas.* Oxford: Blackwell, 2000.

Held, Julius, and Donald Posner. *17th and 18th Century Art: Baroque Painting, Sculpture, Architecture.* New York: Abrams, 1971.

Keazor, Henry. *Nicholas Poussin, 1594–1665.* Cologne: Taschen, 2007.

Lagerläf, Margaretha R. *Ideal Landscape: Annibale Carracci, Nicolas Poussin and Claude Lorrain.* New Haven, Conn.: Yale University Press, 1990.

Lemerle, Frédérique, and Yves Pauwels. *Baroque Architecture, 1600–1750.* Paris: Flammarion, 2008.

Liedtke, Walter. *Vermeer: The Complete Paintings.* Antwerp: Ludion, 2008.

Mérot, Alain. *French Painting in the Seventeenth Century.* New Haven, Conn.: Yale University Press, 1995.

Norberg-Schulz, Christian. *Baroque Architecture.* New York: Rizzoli, 1986.

North, Michael. *Art and Commerce in the Dutch Golden Age.* New Haven, Conn.: Yale University Press, 1997.

Puglisi, Catherine. *Caravaggio.* London: Phaidon, 2000.

Rosenberg, Jakob, Seymour Slive, and E. H. ter Kuile. *Dutch Art and Architecture, 1600–1800.* New Haven, Conn.: Yale University Press, 1979.

Schama, Simon. *The Embarrassment of Riches: An Interpretation of Dutch Culture in the Golden Age.* Berkeley: University of California Press, 1988.

Slive, Seymour. *Frans Hals.* New York: Phaidon, 2014.

Strinati, Claudio, and Jordana Pomeroy. *Italian Women Artists from Renaissance to Baroque.* Milan: Skira, 2007.

Toman, Rolf. *Baroque: Architecture, Sculpture, Painting.* Cologne: Känemann, 1998.

Varriano, John. *Italian Baroque and Rococo Architecture.* New York: Oxford University Press, 1986.

Vlieghe, Hans. *Flemish Art and Architecture, 1585–1700.* New Haven, Conn.: Yale University Press, 1998.

Westermann, Mariët. *Rembrandt.* London: Phaidon, 2000.

———. *A Worldly Art: The Dutch Republic 1585–1718.* New Haven, Conn.: Yale University Press, 1996.

Wittkower, Rudolf. *Art and Architecture in Italy 1600–1750.* 3 vols. 6th ed., revised by Joseph Connors and Jennifer Montagu. New Haven, Conn.: Yale University Press, 1999.

CHAPTER 11
Rococo to Neoclassicism in Europe and America

Boime, Albert. *Art in the Age of Revolution, 1750–1800.* Chicago: University of Chicago Press, 1987.

Craske, Matthew. *Art in Europe, 1700–1830: A History of the Visual Arts in an Era of Unprecedented Urban Economic Growth.* New York: Oxford University Press, 1997.

Gaunt, W. *The Great Century of British Painting: Hogarth to Turner.* New York: Phaidon, 1971.

Goodman, Elise, ed. *Art and Culture in the Eighteenth Century: New Dimensions and Multiple Perspectives.* Newark: University of Delaware Press, 2001.

Herrmann, Luke. *British Landscape Painting of the Eighteenth Century.* New York: Oxford University Press, 1974.

Irwin, David. *Neoclassicism.* London: Phaidon, 1997.

Jarrassé, Dominique. *18th-Century French Painting.* Paris: Terrail, 1999.

Lee, Simon. *David.* London: Phaidon, 1999.

Plax, Julie-Ann. *Watteau and the Cultural Politics of Eighteenth-Century France.* New York: Cambridge University Press, 2000.

Roworth, Wendy Wassyng. *Angelica Kauffman: A Continental Artist in Georgian England.* London: Reaktion, 1992.

Sheriff, Mary D. *The Exceptional Woman: Elisabeth Vigée-Lebrun and the Cultural Politics of Art.* Chicago: University of Chicago Press, 1996.

Waterhouse, Ellis Kirkham. *Painting in Britain: 1530–1790.* 4th ed. New Haven, Conn.: Yale University Press, 1979.

19th and 20th Centuries, General

Arnason, H. H., and Elizabeth C. Mansfield. *History of Modern Art: Painting, Sculpture, Architecture, Photography.* 6th ed. Upper Saddle River, N.J.: Prentice Hall, 2009.

Ashton, Dore. *Twentieth-Century Artists on Art.* New York: Pantheon Books, 1985.

Butler, Cornelia, and Alexandra Schwartz, eds. *Modern Women: Women Artists at the Museum of Modern Art.* New York: Museum of Modern Art, 2010.

Chipp, Herschel B. *Theories of Modern Art.* Berkeley: University of California Press, 1968.

Chu, Petra ten-Doesschate. *Nineteenth-Century European Art.* 3d ed. Upper Saddle River, N.J.: Prentice Hall, 2011.

Colquhoun, Alan. *Modern Architecture.* New York: Oxford University Press, 2002.

Craven, Wayne. *American Art: History and Culture.* Rev. ed. New York: McGraw-Hill, 2002.

Doss, Erika. *Twentieth-Century American Art.* New York: Oxford University Press, 2002.

Eisenman, Stephen F., ed. *Nineteenth Century Art: A Critical History.* 4th ed. New York: Thames & Hudson, 2011.

Foster, Hal, Rosalind Krauss, Yve-Alain Bois, and Benjamin H. D. Buchloh. *Art since 1900: Modernism, Antimodernism, Postmodernism.* 2d ed. New York: Thames & Hudson, 2011.

Frampton, Kenneth. *Modern Architecture: A Critical History.* 4th ed. New York: Thames & Hudson, 2007.

Hamilton, George H. *Painting and Sculpture in Europe, 1880–1940.* 6th ed. New Haven, Conn.: Yale University Press, 1993.

Harrison, Charles, and Paul Wood. *Art in Theory 1900–2000: An Anthology of Changing Ideas.* Oxford: Blackwell, 2003.

Herbert, Robert L., ed. *Modern Artists on Art.* Upper Saddle River, N.J.: Prentice Hall, 1971.

Hertz, Richard, and Norman M. Klein, eds. *Twentieth-Century Art Theory: Urbanism, Politics, and Mass Culture.* Englewood Cliffs: Prentice-Hall, 1990.

Heyer, Paul. *Architects on Architecture: New Directions in America.* New York: Van Nostrand Reinhold, 1993.

Hills, Patricia. *Modern Art in the USA: Issues and Controversies of the 20th Century.* Upper Saddle River, N.J.: Prentice Hall, 2000.

Hunter, Sam, John Jacobus, and Daniel Wheeler. *Modern Art: Painting, Sculpture, Architecture, Photography.* Rev. 3d ed. Upper Saddle River, N.J.: Prentice Hall, 2004.

Lewis, Samella S. *African American Art and Artists.* Rev. ed. Berkeley and Los Angeles: University of California Press, 1994.

Marien, Mary Warner. *Photography: A Cultural History.* 3d ed. Upper Saddle River, N.J.: Prentice Hall, 2011.

Pohl, Frances K. *Framing America: A Social History of American Art.* 3d ed. New York: Thames & Hudson, 2012.

Rosenblum, Naomi. *A World History of Photography.* 4th ed. New York: Abbeville, 2007.

Rosenblum, Robert, and Horst W. Janson. *19th-Century Art.* Rev. ed. Upper Saddle River, N.J.: Prentice Hall, 2005.

Upton, Dell. *Architecture in the United States.* Oxford: Oxford University Press, 1998.

CHAPTER 12
Romanticism, Realism, and Photography, 1800 to 1870

Amic, Sylvain, et al. *Gustave Courbet.* Ostfildern: Hatje Cantz, 2008.

Athanassaglou-Kallmyer, Nina. *Théodore Géricault.* London: Phaidon, 2008.

Bergdoll, Barry. *European Architecture 1750–1890.* New York: Oxford University Press, 2000.

Boime, Albert. *The Academy and French Painting in the 19th Century.* London: Phaidon, 1971.

———. *Art in the Age of Bonapartism, 1800–1815.* Chicago: University of Chicago Press, 1990.

Bordes, Philippe. *Jacques-Louis David: Empire to Exile.* New Haven, Conn.: Yale University Press, 2007.

Brown, David Blayney. *Romanticism.* London: Phaidon, 2001.

Bryson, Norman. *Tradition and Desire: From David to Delacroix.* New York: Cambridge University Press, 1984.

Clark, T. J. *The Painting of Modern Life: Paris in the Art of Manet and His Followers.* Princeton, N.J.: Princeton University Press, 1984.

Eitner, Lorenz. *Neoclassicism and Romanticism, 1750–1850: An Anthology of Sources and Documents.* New York: Harper & Row, 1989.

Fried, Michael. *Manet's Modernism, or, The Face of Painting in the 1860s.* Chicago: University of Chicago Press, 1996.

Grave, Johannes. *Caspar David Friedrich.* New York: Prestel, 2012.

Hofmann, Werner. *Goya.* New York: Thames & Hudson, 2003.

Holt, Elizabeth Gilmore, ed. *From the Classicists to the Impressionists: A Documentary History of Art and Architecture in the Nineteenth Century.* Garden City, N.J.: Anchor Books/Doubleday, 1966.

Krell, Alain. *Manet and the Painters of Contemporary Life.* London: Thames & Hudson, 1996.

Kroeber, Karl. *British Romantic Art.* Berkeley: University of California Press, 1986.

Lampert, Catherine, ed. *Daumier: Visions of Paris.* London: Royal Academy of Arts, 2013.

Le Men, Ségolène. *Courbet.* New York: Abbeville, 2008.

Licht, Fred. *Goya.* New York: Abbeville, 2001.

Middleton, Robin. *Architecture of the Nineteenth Century.* London: Phaidon, 2003.

Nochlin, Linda. *Realism and Tradition in Art, 1848–1900: Sources and Documents.* Upper Saddle River, N.J.: Prentice Hall, 1966.

Novotny, Fritz. *Painting and Sculpture in Europe, 1780–1880.* 3d ed. New Haven, Conn.: Yale University Press, 1988.

Porterfield, Todd. *The Allure of Empire: Art in the Service of French Imperialism 1798–1836.* Princeton, N.J.: Princeton University Press, 1998.

Porterfield, Todd, and Susan L. Siegfried. *Staging Empire: Napoleon, Ingres, and David.* University Park, Pa.: Pennsylvania State University Press, 2006.

Rubin, James Henry. *Manet: Initial M, Hand and Eye.* Paris: Flammarion, 2010.

Shelton, Andrew Carrington. *Ingres.* London: Phaidon, 2008.

Toman, Rolf, ed. *Neoclassicism and Romanticism: Architecture, Sculpture, Painting, Drawings, 1750–1848.* Cologne: Känemann, 2006.

CHAPTER 13

Impressionism, Post-Impressionism, and Symbolism, 1870 to 1900

Breuer, Karin. *Japanesque: The Japanese Print in the Era of Impressionism.* New York: Prestel, 2010.

Broude, Norma. *Impressionism: A Feminist Reading.* New York: Rizzoli, 1991.

Cogeval, Guy, ed. *Claude Monet, 1840–1926.* Paris: Réunion des Musées Nationaux, 2010.

Distel, Anne. *Renoir.* New York: Abbeville, 2010.

Escritt, Stephen. *Art Nouveau.* London: Phaidon, 2000.

Herbert, Robert L. *Impressionism: Art, Leisure, and Parisian Society.* New Haven, Conn.: Yale University Press, 1988.

Lewis, Mary Tompkins. *Cézanne.* London: Phaidon, 2000.

Loyette, Henri, Sebastien Allard, and Laurence Des Cars. *Nineteenth Century French Art: From Romanticism to Impressionism, Post-Impressionism, and Art Nouveau.* Paris: Flammarion, 2007.

Masson, Raphaël, and Véronique Mattiussi. *Rodin.* Paris: Flammarion, 2004.

Nochlin, Linda. *Impressionism and Post-Impressionism, 1874–1904: Sources and Documents.* Upper Saddle River, N.J.: Prentice Hall, 1966.

Pfeiffer, Ingrid, et al. *Women Impressionists.* Ostfildern: Hatje Cantz, 2008.

Rachman, Carla. *Monet.* London: Phaidon, 1997.

Rey, Jean-Dominique. *Berthe Morisot.* Paris: Flammarion, 2011.

Rubin, James H. *Impressionism.* London: Phaidon, 1999.

Smith, Paul. *Impressionism: Beneath the Surface.* New York: Abrams, 1995.

Sund, Judy. *Van Gogh.* London: Phaidon, 2002.

Thomson, Belinda, ed. *Gauguin: Maker of Myth.* London: Tate, 2010.

CHAPTER 14

Modernism in Europe and America, 1900 to 1945

Antliff, Mark, and Patricia Leighten. *Cubism and Culture.* New York: Thames & Hudson, 2001.

Bearden, Romare, and Harry Henderson. *A History of African-American Artists from 1792 to the Present.* New York: Pantheon Books, 1993.

Bergdoll, Barry. *Bauhaus 1919–1933.* New York: Museum of Modern Art, 2009.

Bouvet, Vincent, and Gérard Durozoi. *Paris between the Wars 1919–1939: Art, Life & Culture.* New York: Vendome, 2010.

Breton, André. *Surrealism and Painting.* New York: Harper & Row, 1972.

Clark, T.J. *Picasso and Truth: From Cubism to Guernica.* Princeton, N.J.: Princeton University Press, 2013.

Cowling, Elizabeth, ed. *Picasso: Challenging the Past.* London: National Gallery, 2011.

Cox, Neil. *Cubism.* London: Phaidon: 2000.

Curtis, Penelope. *Sculpture 1900–1945.* New York: Oxford University Press, 1999.

Curtis, William J. R. *Modern Architecture since 1900.* Upper Saddle River, N.J.: Prentice Hall, 1996.

D'Alessandro, Stephanie, ed. *Magritte: The Mystery of the Ordinary, 1926–1938.* New York: Museum of Modern Art, 2013.

Davidson, Abraham A. *Early American Modernist Painting, 1910–1935.* New York: Harper & Row, 1981.

Dickerman, Leah, ed. *Inventing Abstraction, 1910–1925.* New York: Museum of Modern Art, 2013.

Dietrich, Dorothea, ed. *Dada: Zurich, Berlin, Hannover, Cologne, New York, Paris.* Washington, D.C.: National Gallery, 2008.

Gale, Matthew. *Dada and Surrealism.* London: Phaidon, 1997.

Harrison, Charles, Francis Frascina, and Gil Perry. *Primitivism, Cubism, Abstraction: The Early Twentieth Century.* New Haven, Conn.: Yale University Press, 1993.

Herbert, James D. *Fauve Painting: The Making of Cultural Politics.* New Haven, Conn.: Yale University Press, 1992.

Hurlburt, Laurance P. *The Mexican Muralists in the United States.* Albuquerque: University of New Mexico Press, 1989.

Kushner, Marilyn Satin, Kimberly Orcutt, and Casey Nelson Blake, eds. *The Armory Show at 100: Modernism and Revolution.* New York: New York Historical Society, 2013.

Lloyd, Jill. *German Expressionism: Primitivism and Modernity.* New Haven, Conn.: Yale University Press, 1991.

Motherwell, Robert, ed. *The Dada Painters and Poets: An Anthology.* 2d ed. Boston: Hall, 1981.

Poggi, Christine. *Inventing Futurism: The Art and Politics of Artificial Optimism.* Princeton, N.J.: Princeton University Press, 2009.

Rhodes, Colin. *Primitivism and Modern Art.* New York: Thames & Hudson, 1994.

Rubin, William S. *Dada and Surrealist Art.* New York: Abrams, 1968.

———, ed. *Pablo Picasso: A Retrospective.* New York: Museum of Modern Art; Boston: New York Graphic Society, 1980.

———, ed. *"Primitivism" in 20th-Century Art: Affinity of the Tribal and the Modern.* 2 vols. New York: Museum of Modern Art, 1984.

Taylor, Michael R., ed. *Arshile Gorky: A Retrospective.* New Haven, Conn.: Yale University Press, 2009.

Terraroli, Valerio, ed. *Art of the Twentieth Century, 1900–1919: The Avant-Garde Movements.* Milan: Skira, 2006.

———. *Art of the Twentieth Century, 1920–1945: The Artistic Culture between the Wars.* Milan: Skira, 2006.

Tisdall, Caroline, and Angelo Bozzolla. *Futurism.* New York: Oxford University Press, 1978.

CHAPTER 15

Modernism and Postmodernism in Europe and America, 1945 to 1980

Anfam, David. *Abstract Expressionism.* New York: Thames & Hudson, 1990.

Anreus, Alejandro, Robin Adèle Greeley, and Leonard Folgarait, eds. *Mexican Muralism: A Critical History.* Berkeley and Los Angeles: University of California Press, 2012.

Archer, Michael. *Art since 1960.* New ed. New York: Thames & Hudson, 2002.

Ashton, Dore. *American Art since 1945.* New York: Oxford University Press, 1983.

Beardsley, Richard. *Earthworks and Beyond: Contemporary Art in the Landscape.* New York: Abbeville Press, 1984.

Broude, Norma, and Mary D. Garrard. *The Power of Feminist Art: The American Movement of the 1970s, History and Impact.* New York: Abrams, 1994.

Butler, Cornelia H., ed. *WACK! Art and the Feminist Revolution.* Cambridge, Mass.: MIT Press, 2007.

Causey, Andrew. *Sculpture since 1945.* New York: Oxford University Press, 1998.

Celant, Germano, ed. *Louise Nevelson.* Turin: Skira, 2012.

Collins, Bradford R. *Pop Art.* London: Phaidon, 2012.

Crow, Thomas. *The Rise of the Sixties: American and European Art in the Era of Dissent.* New Haven, Conn.: Yale University Press, 2005.

Fineberg, Jonathan. *Art since 1940: Strategies of Being.* 3d ed. Upper Saddle River, N.J.: Prentice Hall, 2010.

Foster, Hal. *The First Pop Age: Painting and Subjectivity in the Art of Hamilton, Lichtenstein, Warhol, Richter, and Ruscha.* Princeton, N.J.: Princeton University Press, 2011.

Godfrey, Tony. *Conceptual Art.* London: Phaidon, 1998.

Goodman, Cynthia. *Digital Visions: Computers and Art.* New York: Abrams, 1987.

Grundberg, Andy. *Photography and Art: Interactions since 1945.* New York: Abbeville, 1987.

Hopkins, David. *After Modern Art, 1945–2000.* New York: Oxford University Press, 2000.

Jacobus, John. *Twentieth-Century Architecture: The Middle Years, 1940–1964.* New York: Praeger, 1966.

Jencks, Charles. *The Language of Post-Modern Architecture.* 6th ed. New York: Rizzoli, 1991.

———. *What Is Post-Modernism?* 3d rev. ed. London: Academy Editions, 1989.

Joselit, David. *American Art since 1945.* New York: Thames & Hudson, 2003.

Lovejoy, Margot. *Postmodern Currents: Art and Artists in the Age of the Electronic Media.* Ann Arbor, Mich.: UMI Research Press, 1989.

Lucie-Smith, Edward. *Movements in Art since 1945.* New ed. New York: Thames & Hudson, 2001.

Mamiya, Christin J. *Pop Art and Consumer Culture: American Super Market.* Austin: University of Texas Press, 1992.

Rondeau, James, and Sheena Wagstaff, eds. *Roy Lichtenstein: A Retrospective.* Chicago: Art Institute of Chicago, 2012.

Rosen, Randy, and Catherine C. Brawer, eds. *Making Their Mark: Women Artists Move into the Mainstream, 1970–1985.* New York: Abbeville, 1989.

Rush, Michael. *New Media in Art.* 2d ed., New York: Thames & Hudson, 2005.

Sackler, Elizabeth A., ed. *Judy Chicago.* New York: Watson-Guptill, 2002.

Shapiro, David, and Cecile Shapiro. *Abstract Expressionism: A Critical Record.* New York: Cambridge University Press, 1990.

Siegel, Katy. *Since '45: America and the Making of Contemporary Art.* London: Reaktion, 2011.

———, ed. *Abstract Expressionism.* New York: Phaidon, 2011.

Stiles, Kristine, and Peter Selz. *Theories and Documents of Contemporary Art: A Sourcebook of Artists' Writings.* Berkeley and Los Angeles: University of California Press, 1996.

Taylor, Brendon. *Contemporary Art: Art since 1970.* Upper Saddle River, N.J.: Prentice Hall, 2005.

Terraroli, Valerio, ed. *Art of the Twentieth Century, 1946–1968: The Birth of Contemporary Art.* Milan: Skira, 2007.

Theriault, Kim S. *Rethinking Arshile Gorky.* University Park: Pennsylvania State University Press, 2009.

Varnedoe, Kirk. *Pictures of Nothing: Abstract Art since Pollock.* Princeton, N.J.: Princeton University Press, 2006.

Waldman, Diane. *Collage, Assemblage, and the Found Object.* New York: Abrams, 1992.

Wheeler, Daniel. *Art since Mid-Century: 1945 to the Present.* Upper Saddle River, N.J.: Prentice Hall, 1991.

Wood, Paul. *Modernism in Dispute: Art since the Forties.* New Haven, Conn.: Yale University Press, 1993.

CHAPTER 16
Contemporary Art Worldwide

Andrews, Julia F., and Kuiyi Shen. *The Art of Modern China.* Berkeley and Los Angeles: University of California Press, 2012.

Anfam, David, ed. *Anish Kapoor.* New York: Phaidon, 2009.

Chilwers, Ian, and John Glaves-Smith. *Oxford Dictionary of Modern and Contemporary Art.* 2d ed. New York: Oxford University Press, 2009.

Danto, Arthur C., and Marina Abramovic. *Shirin Neshat.* New York: Rizzoli, 2010.

Enwezor, Okwui, and Chika Okeke-Agulu. *Contemporary African Art since 1980.* Bologna: Damiani, 2009.

Heartney, Eleanor. *Art & Today.* New York: Phaidon, 2008.

Heartney, Eleanor, Helaine Posner, Nancy Princenthal, and Sue Scott. *After the Revolution: Women Who Transformed Contemporary Art.* New York: Prestel, 2007.

Jencks, Charles. *The New Paradigm in Architecture: The Language of Post-Modernism.* New Haven, Conn.: Yale University Press, 2002.

Joselit, David. *After Art.* Princeton, N.J.: Princeton University Press, 2013.

Moszynska, Anna. *Sculpture Now.* New York: Thames & Hudson, 2013.

Mullins, Charlotte. *Painting People: Figure Painting Today.* New York: Thames & Hudson, 2008.

O'Brien, Elaine, Everlyn Nicodemus, Melissa Chiu, Benjamin Genocchio, Mary K. Coffey, and Roberto Tejada, eds. *Modern Art in Africa, Asia, and Latin America: An Introduction to Global Modernisms.* Malden, Mass.: Wiley-Blackwell, 2013.

Paul, Christiane. *Digital Art.* 2d ed. New York: Thames & Hudson, 2008.

Perry, Gill, and Paul Wood. *Themes in Contemporary Art.* New Haven, Conn.: Yale University Press, 2004.

Risatti, Howard, ed. *Postmodern Perspectives: Issues in Contemporary Art.* Upper Saddle River, N.J.: Prentice Hall, 1990.

Sandler, Irving. *Art of the Postmodern Era.* New York: HarperCollins, 1996.

Smith, Terry. *Contemporary Art: World Currents.* Upper Saddle River, N.J.: Prentice Hall, 2011.

———. *What Is Contemporary Art?* Chicago: University of Chicago Press, 2009.

Sollins, Susan, ed. *Art:21 (Art in the Twenty-first Century).* 5 vols. New York: Abrams, 2001–2009.

Stiles, Kristine, and Peter Selz. *Theories and Documents of Contemporary Art: A Sourcebook of Artists' Writings.* 2d ed. Berkeley and Los Angeles: University of California Press, 2012.

Storr, Robert. *Elizabeth Murray.* New York: Museum of Modern Art, 2005.

Vogel, Susan Mullin. *El Anatsui: Art and Life.* New York: Prestel, 2012.

Wands, Bruce. *Art of the Digital Age.* New York: Thames & Hudson, 2007.

Wines, James. *Green Architecture.* Cologne: Taschen, 2008.

Credits

The authors and publisher are grateful to the proprietors and custodians of various works of art for photographs of these works and permission to reproduce them in this book. Sources not included in the captions are listed here.

NOTE: *All references in the following credits are to figure numbers unless otherwise indicated.*

Introduction—I-1 (all): National Gallery, London/Art Resource, NY; **I-2:** Hirshhorn Museum and Culture Garden, Smithsonian Institution, Washington, DC, Joseph H. Hirshhorn Purchase Fund, 1992 © City and county of Denver, courtesy the Clyfford Still Museum. Photo: akg images; **I-3:** Interior view of the choir, begun after 1284 (photo), French School, (13th century)/Beauvais Cathedral, Beauvais, France/© Paul Maeyaert/The Bridgeman Art Library; **I-4:** akg-images/Rabatti-Domingie; **I-5:** National Gallery of Art, Alfred Stieglitz Collection, Bequest of Georgia O'Keeffe 1987.58.3; **I-6:** Art © Estate of Ben Shahn/Licensed by VAGA, New York, NY. Photo: Whitney Museum of American Art, New York (gift of Edith and Milton Lowenthal in memory of Juliana Force); **I-7:** The Metropolitan Museum of Art/Art Resource, NY; **I-8:** Courtesy Saskia Ltd., © Dr. Ron Wiedenhoeft; **I-9:** © 2011 The Josef and Anni Albers Foundation/Artists Rights Society (ARS), New York. Photo: © Whitney Museum of American Art; **I-10:** Photograph © 2011 Museum of Fine Arts, Boston. 11.4584; **I-11:** bpk, Berlin/Staatsgemaeldesammlungen, Munich, Germany/Art Resource, NY; **I-12:** Jürgen Liepe, Berlin; **I-13:** The Trustees of the British Museum/Art Resource, NY; **I-14:** Nimatallah/Art Resource, NY; **I-15:** Scala/Art Resource, NY; **1-16:** Cengage Learning; **I-17 left:** Portrait of Te Pehi Kupe wearing European clothes, c. 1826 (w/c), Sylvester, John (fl. 1826)/© National Library of Australia, Canberra, Australia/The Bridgeman Art Library; **I-17 right:** Public Domain.

Chapter 1—1-1 (all): Erich Lessing/Art Resource, NY; **1-2:** Erich Lessing/Art Resource, NY; **1-3:** Jean Vertut; **1-4:** Jean Vertut; **1-5:** Jean Vertut; **1-6:** Jean Vertut; **1-7s:** Gianni Dagli Orti/Fine Art/Corbis; **1-8:** Erich Lessing/Art Resource, NY; **1-9:** F1 ONLINE/SuperStock; **1-10:** Richard Ashworth/Robert Harding; **1-11:** Silvio Fiore/SuperStock; **1-12:** Erich Lessing/Art Resource, NY; **1-13:** The Trustees of the British Museum/Art Resource, NY; **1-14:** © The Trustees of The British Museum/Art Resource, NY; **1-15:** Iraq Museum/akg-images; **1-16:** RMN-Grand Palais/Art Resource, NY; **1-17:** Rmn-Grand Palais/Art Resource, NY; **1-18:** © The Bridgeman Art Library Ltd./Alamy; **1-19:** The Trustees of The British Museum/Art Resource, NY; **1-20:** Bildarchiv Preussischer Kulturbesitz/Art Resource, NY; **1-21:** The Art Archive/Alfredo Dagli Orti/Picture Desk; **1-22:** Werner Forman/Art Resource, NY; **1-23:** Werner Forman/Art Resource, NY; **1-24:** Cengage Learning; **1-25:** akg-images; **1-26:** Courtesy of the Semitic Museum, Harvard University; **1-27:** © Jon Arnold Images Ltd/Alamy; **1-28:** Araldo de Luca; **1-29:** Photograph © 2011 Museum of Fine Arts, Boston. 11.1738; **1-30:** Jean Vertut; **1-31:** De Agostini/SuperStock; **1-32:** akg-images/Robert O'Dea; **1-33:** Yann Arthus-Bertrand/Corbis; **1-35:** Araldo de Luca; **1-36:** Sean Gallup/Getty Images; **1-37:** Egyptian Museum and Papyrus Collection Berlin; **1-38:** Robert Harding World Imagery/Getty Images.

Chapter 2—2-1: Carolyn Clarke/Alamy; **2-1a:** © Fred S. Kleiner 2012; **2-1b:** A Centaur triumphing over a Lapith, metope XXVIII from the south side of the Parthenon, 447–432 BC (marble), Greek, (5th century BC)/British Museum, London, UK/The Bridgeman Art Library; **2-1c:** Royal Ontario Museum; **2-2:** Erich Lessing/Art Resource, NY; **2-3:** John Burge; **2-4:** Roger Wood/Fine Art/Corbis; **2-5:** The Art Archive/Heraklion Museum/Gianni Dagli Orti/Picture Desk; **2-6:** Nimatallah/Art Resource, NY; **2-7:** Scala/Art Resource, NY; **2-8:** The Art Archive/Heraklion Museum/Gianni Dagli Orti/Picture Desk; **2-9:** STUDIO KONTOS/PHOTOSTOCK; **2-10:** © Bildarchiv Monheim GmbH/Alamy; **2-11:** © Fred S. Kleiner 2012; **2-12:** © Vanni Archive/CORBIS; **2-13:** Joe Vogan/SuperStock; **2-14:** The Metropolitan Museum of Art/Art Resource, NY; **2-15:** RMN-Grand Palais/Art Resource, NY; **2-16:** The Metropolitan Museum of Art/Art Resource, NY; **2-17:** Gianni Dagli Orti/Fine Art/Corbis; **2-18:** Nimatallah/Art Resource, NY; **2-19:** Cengage Learning, 2014; **2-20:** John Burge/Cengage Learning; **2-21:** © 2008 Fred S. Kleiner; **2-22:** Cengage Learning; **2-23:** Vanni/Art Resource, NY; **2-24:** Scala/Art Resource, NY; **2-25:** Bridgeman-Giraudon/Art Resource, NY; **2-26:** Courtesy Saskia Ltd., © Dr. Ron Wiedenhoeft; **2-27:** Courtesy Saskia Ltd., © Dr. Ron Wiedenhoeft and Cengage Learning; **2-28:** Gianni Dagli Orti/Fine Art/Corbis; **2-29:** Saskia Ltd., © Dr. Ron Wiedenhoeft; **2-30:** SASKIA Ltd. Cultural Documentation. © Dr. Ron Wiedenhoeft; **2-31:** Marie Mauzy/Art Resource, NY;

2-32: Scala/Art Resource, NY; **2-33:** Cengage Learning, 2014; **2-34:** Erich Lessing/Art Resource, NY; **2-35:** Scala/Ministero per i Beni e le Attività culturali/Art Resource, NY; **2-36:** Cengage Learning; **2-37:** Cengage Learning, 2014; **2-38:** A Centaur triumphing over a Lapith, metope XXVIII from the south side of the Parthenon, 447–432 BC (marble), Greek, (5th century BC)/British Museum, London, UK/The Bridgeman Art Library; **2-39:** STUDIO KONTOS/PHOTOSTOCK; **2-40:** R Sheridan/Ancient Art & Architecture Collection Ltd.; **2-41:** © Ancient Art and Architecture Collection Ltd. (bottom) STUDIO KONTOS/PHOTOSTOCK (middle) © Chao-Yang Chan/Alamy (top); **2-42:** © Fred S. Kleiner 2012; **2-43:** © Fred S. Kleiner 2012; **2-44:** Marie Mauzy/Art Resource, NY; **2-45:** Nimatallah/Art Resource, NY; **2-46:** Scala/Art Resource, NY; **2-47:** Scala/Art Resource, NY; **2-48:** Statue of Hermes and the Infant Dionysus, c. 330 BC (parian marble), Praxiteles (c. 400–c. 330 BC)/Archaeological Museum, Olympia, Archaia, Greece/The Bridgeman Art Library; **2-49:** Canali Photobank; **2-50:** Canali Photobank; **2-51:** © Duby Tal/Albatross/Alamy; **2-52:** Antikensammlung, Staatliche Museen, Berlin, Germany/Jürgen Liepe/Art Resource, NY; **2-53:** bpk, Berlin/Antikensammlung, Staatliche Museen, Berlin, Germany/Johannes Laurentius/Art Resource, NY; **2-54:** Dying Gaul/Fine Art/Corbis; **2-55:** The Victory of Samothrace (Parian marble) (see also 92583 & 94601-03 & 154093), Greek, (2nd century BC)/Louvre, Paris, France/Giraudon/The Bridgeman Art Library; **2-56:** RMN-Grand Palais/Art Resource, NY; **2-57:** Saskia Ltd.; **2-58:** © The Metropolitan Museum of Art/Art Resource, NY; **2-59:** Araldo de Luca/Fine Art Premium/Corbis.

Chapter 3—3-1: Scala/Art Resource, NY; **3-1a:** © Fred S. Kleiner 2010; **3-1b:** Scala/Art Resource, NY; **3-1c:** © Fred S. Kleiner 2010; **3-2:** Model of an Etruscan temple, reconstruction, 4th–5th century BC (plastic)/Institute of Etruscology, University of Rome, Italy/The Bridgeman Art Library; **3-3:** Araldo de Luca/Corbis Art/Corbis; **3-5:** © 2006 Fred S. Kleiner; **3-6:** Leemage/Getty Images; **3-8:** Scala/Art Resource, NY; **3-7:** Charles Bowman/Getty Images; **3-9:** Charles & Josette Lenars/Encyclopedia/Corbis; **3-10:** © Fred S. Kleiner 2013; **3-12:** Alinari/Art Resource, NY; **3-13:** © Guido Alberto Rossi/AGE Fotostock; **3-14:** Erich Lessing/Art Resource, NY; **3-15:** John Burge; **3-16:** John Burge/Cengage Learning; **3-17:** Copyright: Photo Henri Stierlin, Geneve; **3-18:** Wayne Howes/Photographer's Direct; **3-19:** Scala/Art Resource, NY; **3-20 left:** © The Metropolitan Museum of Art/Art Resource, NY; **3-20 right:** The Metropolitan Museum of Art/Art Resource, NY; **3-21:** Luciano Romano; **3-22:** © The Metropolitan Museum of Art/Art Resource, NY; **3-24:** Canali Photobank; **3-25:** Scala/Art Resource, NY; **3-26:** Ny Carlsberg Glyptotek; **3-27:** Brenda Kean/Alamy; **3-28:** SASKIA Ltd. Cultural Documentation; **3-29:** © Jonathan Poore/Cengage Learning; **3-30:** © Jonathan Poore/Cengage Learning; **3-31:** Araldo de Luca/Corbis art/Corbis; **3-32:** © Jonathan Poore/Cengage Learning; **3-33:** © Jonathan Poore/Cengage Learning; **3-34:** © Jonathan Poore/Cengage Learning; **3-35:** John Burge and James Packer/Cengage Learning; **3-36:** © Jonathan Poore/Cengage Learning; **3-37:** © Fred S. Kleiner 2011; **3-38:** © Jonathan Poore/Cengage Learning; **3-39:** John Burge/Cengage Learning; **3-40:** Copyright: Photo Henri Stierlin, Geneve; **3-41:** © 2006 Fred S. Kleiner; **3-42:** The Trustees of The British Museum; **3-43:** Bildarchiv Preussischer Kulturbesitz/Art Resource, NY; **3-44:** Bildarchiv Preussischer Kulturbesitz/Art Resource, NY; **3-45:** Cengage Learning; **3-46:** Scala/Art Resource, NY; **3-47:** Araldo de Luca; **3-48:** Araldo de Luca/CORBIS; **3-49:** Scala/Art Resource, NY; **3-50:** © Fred S. Kleiner 2010; **3-51:** © Jonathan Poore/Cengage Learning; **3-52:** John Burge/Cengage Learning, Originally published in A History of Roman Art by © Fred S. Kleiner (Belmont, Calif.: Thomson Wadsworth, 2007); **3-53:** © Jonathan Poore/Cengage Learning; **3-54:** © Jonathan Poore/Cengage Learning.

Chapter 4—4-1 (all): Scala/Art Resource, NY; **4-2:** foto Pontificia Commissione per l'Archeologia Sacra; **4-3:** John Burge/Cengage Learning; **4-4:** Cengage Learning; **4-5:** © Jonathan Poore/Cengage Learning; **4-6:** Cengage Learning; **4-7:** Scala/Art Resource, NY; **4-8:** Scala/Art Resource, NY; **4-9:** Images & Stories/Alamy; **4-10:** John Burge/Cengage Learning; **4-11:** John Burge/Cengage Learning; **4-12:** david pearson/Alamy; **4-13:** Cengage Learning; **4-14:** Archivio e Studio Folco Quilici; **4-15:** Cengage Learning; **4-16:** Canali Photobank, Italy; **4-17:** Canali Photobank, Italy; **4-18:** Canali Photobank, Italy; **4-19:** Österreichische Nationalbibliothek, Vienna, Bildarchiv, folio 7 recto of the Vienna Genesis; **4-20:** Ronald Sheraton/Ancient Art and Architecture Collection Ltd.; **4-21:** © Fred S. Kleiner 2012; **4-22:** Vanni/Art Resource, NY; **4-23:** STUDIO KONTOS/PHOTOSTOCK; **4-24:** Alinari/Art Resource, NY; **4-25:** Réunion des Musées Nationaux/Art Resource, NY; **4-26:** © Josephine Powell; **4-27:** Snark/Art Resource, NY; **4-28:** Scala/Art Resource, NY.

Chapter 5—5-1: Album/Oronoz/Album/SuperStock; **5-1a:** © BednorzImages; **5-1b:** © Bednorz-Images; **5-1c:** Adam Woolfit/Robert Harding Picture Library;

5-2: Hanan Isachar/SuperStock; 5-3: Erich Lessing/Art Resource, NY; 5-4: © Richard T. Nowitz/CORBIS; 5-5 left: Guido Alberto Rossi/Tips Images/Tips Italia Srl a socio unico/Alamy; 5-5 right: Copyright: Cengage Learning; 5-6: Copyright: Photo Henri Stierlin, Geneve; 5-7: © Bednorz-Images; 5-8: Adam Woolfit/Robert Harding Picture Library; 5-9: Mauritius/SuperStock; 5-10: Toyohiro Yamada/Taxi/Getty Images; 5-11: Copyright: Photo Henri Stierlin, Geneve; 5-12: © The Metropolitan Museum of Art/Art Resource, NY; 5-13: The Trustees of the Chester Beatty Library, Dublin; 5-14: Réunion des Musées Nationaux/Art Resource, NY; 5-15: Victoria & Albert Museum, London/Art Resource, NY; 5-16: The Court of Gayumars (2005.1.165 M200) © Aga Khan Trust for Culture Geneva.

Chapter 6—6-1 (all): © Jonathan Poore/Cengage Learning; 6-2: © The Trustees of the British Museum/Art Resource, NY; 6-3: Erich Lessing/Art Resource, NY; 6-4: Album/Art Resource, NY; 6-5: Kunsthistorisches Museums, Wien; 6-6: © Gianni Dagli Orti/Corbis; 6-7: Front cover of the Lindau Gospels. Court School of Charles the Bald, France. Ca. 880 CE. Repousse gold and jewels. M.1, front cover. The Pierpont Morgan Library, New York, NY, USA. Photo Credit: The Pierpont Morgan Library/Art Resource, NY; 6-8: © Jonathan Poore/Cengage Learning; 6-9: Cengage Learning, 2016; 6-10: akg-images; 6-11: © Jonathan Poore/Cengage Learning; 6-12: © Bednorz-Images; 6-13: Cengage Learning, 2016; 6-14: Dom-Museum, Hildesheim; 6-15: Photo: © Rheinisches Bildarchiv Köln, rba_c000008; 6-16: The Art Archive/Abbaye de Saint Foy Conques/Gianni Dagli Orti/Picture Desk; 6-17: Jean Dieuzaide; 6-18: Cengage Learning, 2016; 6-19: © Jonathan Poore/Cengage Learning; 6-20: © Fred S. Kleiner 2010; 6-21: John Burge/Cengage Learning; 6-22: © Jonathan Poore/Cengage Learning; 6-23: © Jonathan Poore/Cengage Learning; 6-24: © The Metropolitan Museum of Art/Art Resource, NY; 6-25: Erich Lessing/Art Resource, NY; 6-26: Abtei St. Hildegard; 6-27: Canali Photobank, Italy; 6-28: © Jonathan Poore/Cengage Learning; 6-29: © Jonathan Poore/Cengage Learning; 6-30 left: © Jonathan Poore/Cengage Learning; 6-30 right: Cengage Learning, 2016; 6-31: Angelo Hornak/Corbis; 6-32: Cengage Learning, 2016; 6-33: The Master and Fellows of Corpus Christi College, Cambridge; 6-34: The Bridgeman Art Library; 6-35: By special permission of the City of Bayeux; 6-36: By special permission of the City of Bayeux.

Chapter 7—7-1: Bertl123/Shutterstock.com; 7-1a–c: © Jonathan Poore/Cengage Learning; 7-2: © Jonathan Poore/Cengage Learning; 7-3: Cengage Learning, 2016; 7-4: Cengage Learning, 2016; 7-5: © Jonathan Poore/Cengage Learning; 7-6: © Jonathan Poore/Cengage Learning; 7-7: © Jonathan Poore/Cengage Learning; 7-8: John Burge/Cengage Learning; 7-9: View of the nave, begun 1194 (photo), French School, (12th century)/Chartres Cathedral, Chartres, France/© Paul Maeyaert/The Bridgeman Art Library; 7-10: Cengage Learning, 2016; 7-11: © Jonathan Poore/Cengage Learning; 7-12: Four martyr saints, column figures from the west door of the south portal, c. 1220 (stone)/Chartres Cathedral, Chartres, France/Peter Willi/The Bridgeman Art Library; 7-13: © Jonathan Poore/Cengage Learning; 7-14: Cengage Learning, 2016; 7-15: © Jonathan Poore/Cengage Learning; 7-16: Bridgeman-Giraudon/Art Resource, NY; 7-17: © Bednorz-Images; 7-18: The Pierpont Morgan Library/Art Resource, NY; 7-19: Österreichische Nationalbibliothek, Vienna; 7-20: Réunion des Musées Nationaux/Art Resource, NY; 7-21: Edmund Nagele PCL/SuperStock; 7-22: Sites & Photos/Art Resource, NY; 7-23: Werner Forman/Corbis Art/Corbis; 7-24: Erich Lessing/Art Resource, NY; 7-25: © Jonathan Poore/Cengage Learning; 7-26: © Jonathan Poore/Cengage Learning; 7-27: Erich Lessing/Art Resource, NY; 7-28: © Jonathan Poore/Cengage Learning; 7-29: Scala/Ministero per i Beni e le Attività culturali/Art Resource, NY; 7-30: Summerfield Press/Corbis Art/Corbis; 7-31: Scala/Art Resource, NY; 7-32: Scala/Art Resource, NY; 7-33: Scala/Art Resource, NY; 7-34: Scala/Art Resource, NY; 7-35: Canali Photobank; 7-36: Scala/Art Resource, NY; 7-37: © Jonathan Poore/Cengage Learning; 7-38: Alinari/Art Resource, NY; 7-39: © Fred S. Kleiner, 2012.

Chapter 8—8-1 (all): Photograph © 2011 Museum of Fine Arts, Boston. 93.153; 8-2: Erich Lessing/Art Resource, NY; 8-3: Image copyright © The Metropolitan Museum of Art. Image source: Art Resource, NY; 8-4: Scala/Art Resource, NY; 8-5: Erich Lessing/Art Resource, NY; 8-6: Erich Lessing/Art Resource, NY; 8-7: Erich Lessing/Art Resource, NY; 8-8: Scala/Art Resource, NY; 8-9: Musée Condé/Grand Palais/Art Resource, NY; 8-10: bpk, Berlin/Gemaeldegalerie, Staatliche Museen/Art Resource, NY; 8-11: AKG Images; 8-12: Scala/Art Resource, NY; 8-13: Erich Lessing/Art Resource, NY; 8-14: Erich Lessing/Art Resource, NY; 8-15: Scala/Art Resource, NY; 8-16: © Jonathan Poore/Cengage Learning; 8-17: © Jonathan Poore/Cengage Learning; 8-18: Erich Lessing/Art Resource; 8-19: © 2013 Fred S. Kleiner; 8-20: Erich Lessing/Art Resource, NY; 8-21: Scala/Art Resource, NY; 8-22: Erich Lessing/Art Resource, NY; 8-23: Canali Photobank, Italy; 8-24: Scala/Art Resource, NY; 8-25: Canali Photobank, Italy; 8-26: Scala/Art Resource, NY; 8-27: Summerfield Press Ltd.; 8-28: Image copyright © The Metropolitan Museum of Art/Art Resource, NY; 8-29: © Jonathan Poore/Cengage Learning; 8-30: View of the Nave, 1425–46 (photo), Brunelleschi, Filippo (1377–1446)/San Lorenzo, Florence, Italy/The Bridgeman Art Library; 8-31: © Jonathan Poore/Cengage Learning; 8-32: © Jonathan Poore/Cengage Learning; 8-33: © Jonathan Poore/Cengage Learning; 8-34: Scala/Art Resource, Inc.; 8-35: Scala/Ministero per i Beni e le Attività culturali/Art Resource, NY; 8-36: Alinari/Art Resource, NY; 8-37: Canali Photobank, Italy; 8-38: Scala/Art Resource, NY; 8-39: Scala/Art Resource, NY; 8-40: Erich Lessing/Art Resource, NY.

Chapter 9—9-1: Canali Photobank; 9-1a: © Bracchietti-Zigrosi/Vatican Museums; 9-1b: Vatican Museums and Galleries, Vatican City, Italy/The Bridgeman Art Library International; 9-1c: akg-images/Electa; 9-2: Erich Lessing/Art Resource, NY; 9-3: Alinari/Art Resource, NY; 9-4: RMN-Grand Palais/Art Resource, NY; 9-5: Erich Lessing/Art Resource, NY; 9-6: M. Sarri 1983/Photo Vatican Museums; 9-7: Araldo de Luca/CORBIS; 9-8: Arte & Immagini srl/CORBIS; 9-9: Photo Vatican Museums; 9-10: © BracchiettiZigrosi/Vatican Museums; 9-11:

akgimages/Electa; 9-12: © Jonathan Poore/Cengage Learning; 9-13: Cengage Learning; 9-14: Tips Images/SuperStock; 9-15 left: © Jonathan Poore/Cengage Learning; 9-15 right: Cengage Learning; 9-16: Marka/SuperStock; 9-17: Camera-photo Arte, Venice/Art Resource, NY; 9-18: Erich Lessing/Art Resource, NY; 9-19: Scala/Art Resource, NY; 9-20: Scala/Ministero per i Beni e le Attività culturali/Art Resource, NY; 9-21: Scala/Art Resource, NY; 9-22: Scala/Ministero per i Beni e le Attività culturali/Art Resource, NY; 9-23: National Gallery, London/Art Resource, NY; 9-24: Scala/Art Resource, NY; 9-25: © 2006 Fred S. Kleiner; 9-26: SuperStock/SuperStock; 9-27: O. Zimmermann/Musée d'Unterlinden, Colmar; 9-28: Photograph © 2011 Museum of Fine Arts, Boston. 68.187; 9-29: V&A Images, London/Art Resource, NY; 9-30: Bildarchiv Preussischer Kulturbesitz/Art Resource, NY; 9-31: Heritage Image Partnership Ltd/Alamy; 9-32: © Jonathan Poore/Cengage Learning; 9-33: The Garden of Earthly Delights, c. 1500 (oil on panel), Bosch, Hieronymus (c. 1450–1516)/Prado, Madrid, Spain/The Bridgeman Art Library; 9-34: RMN-Grand Palais/Art Resource, NY; 9-35: Uppsala University Art Collection; 9-36: Oeffentliche Kunstsammlung Basel, photo Martin Bühler; 9-37: bpk, Berlin/Gemaeldegalerie, Staatliche Museen/Joerg P. Anders/Art Resource, NY; 9-38: Kunsthistorisches Museum, Vienna; 9-39: Adam Woolfitt/Robert Harding/Getty Images; 9-40: Scala/Art Resource, NY.

Chapter 10—10-1 (all): Jonathan Poore/Cengage Learning; 10-2: akg-images/Joseph Martin; 10-3: Alinari Archives/Corbis; 10-4: Scala/Art Resource, NY; 10-5: akg-images/Pirozzi; 10-5: Araldo de Luca; 10-6: © Jonathan Poore/Cengage Learning; 10-7: © Jonathan Poore/Cengage Learning; 10-8: Scala/Art Resource, NY; 10-9: Scala/Art Resource, NY; 10-10: Alinari/Art Resource, NY; 10-11: © Jonathan Poore/Cengage Learning; 10-12: Wadsworth Atheneum Museum of Art/Art Resource, NY; 10-13: Erich Lessing/Art Resource, NY; 10-14: Erich Lessing/Art Resource, NY; 10-15: IRPA-KIK, Brussels, www.kikirpa.be; 10-16: Erich Lessing/Art Resource, NY; 10-17: RMN-Grand Palais/Art Resource, NY; 10-18: age fotostock/Alamy; 10-19: National Gallery of Art; 10-20: The Nightwatch, c. 1642 (oil on canvas), Rembrandt Harmenszoon van Rijn (1606–69)/Rijksmuseum, Amsterdam, The Netherlands/Artothek/The Bridgeman Art Library; 10-21: © English Heritage Photo Library/The Bridgeman Art Library International; 10-22: The Pierpont Morgan Library/Art Resource, NY; 10-23: Mauritshuis, The Hague; 10-24: National Gallery of Art/Art Resource, NY; 10-25: Erich Lessing/Art Resource, NY; 10-26: akg-images; 10-27: The Toledo Museum of Art, OH. Purchased with funds from the Libbey Endowment, Gift of Edward Drummond Libbey, 1956.57; 10-28: Erich Lessing/Art Resource, NY; 10-29: Photo copyright © Philadelphia Museum of Art, E1950-2-1; 10-30: © RMN-Grand Palais/Art Resource, NY; 10-31: © Yann Arthus-Bertrand/Altitude; 10-32: Massimo Listri/Corbis; 10-33: Angelo Hornak/Corbis.

Chapter 11—11-1 (all): Photo: Katherine Wetzel © Virginia Museum of Fine Arts; 11-2: Bildarchiv Monheim/akg-images; 11-3: Scala/Art Resource, NY; 11-4: © Wallace Collection, London, UK/The Bridgeman Art Library; 11-5: Bridgeman-Giraudon/Art Resource, NY; 11-6: Réunion des Musées Nationaux/Art Resource, NY; 11-7: Summerfield Press, Ltd.; 11-8: National Gallery, London//Art Resource, NY; 11-9: National Gallery, London, UK/The Bridgeman Art Library; 11-10: National Gallery of Canada; 11-11: Photograph © 2011 Museum of Fine Arts, Boston, 30.781; 11-12: Scala/Art Resource, NY; 11-13: Portrait of Charles John Crowle (1738–1811) of Crowle Park, c. 1761–62 (oil on canvas), Batoni, Pompeo Girolamo (1708–87)/Louvre, Paris, France/Giraudon/The Bridgeman Art Library; 11-14: Réunion des Musées Nationaux/Art Resource, Inc.; 11-15: Scala/Art Resource, NY; 11-16: © Jonathan Poore/Cengage Learning; 11-17: © Eric Crichton/Encyclopedia/Corbis; 11-18: Thomas Jefferson Foundation; 11-19: Photo © The Library of Virginia.

Chapter 12—12-1 (all): Erich Lessing/Art Resource, NY; 12-2: Scala/Ministero per i Beni e le Attività culturali/Art Resource, NY; 12-3: RMN-Grand Palais/Art Resource, NY; 12-4: Réunion des Musées Nationaux/Art Resource, NY; 12-5: The Metropolitan Museum of Art/Art Resource, NY; 12-6: The Art Archive/Museo del Prado Madrid/Gianni Dagli Orti; 12-7: RMN-Grand Palais/Art Resource, NY; 12-8: RMN-Grand Palais/Art Resource, NY; 12-9: Friedrich, Caspar David (1774–1840), Der Wanderer über dem Nebelmeer, ca. 1817. Oil on canvas. Bildarchiv Preussischer Kulturbesitz/Art Resource, NY; 12-10: National Gallery, London/Art Resource, NY; 12-11: Photography © 2011 Museum of Fine Arts, Boston, 99.22; 12-12: The Metropolitan Museum of Art/Art Resource, NY; 12-13: The Stone Breakers, 1849 (oil on canvas) (destroyed in 1945), Courbet, Gustave (1819–77)/Galerie Neue Meister, Dresden, Germany/© Staatliche Kunstsammlungen Dresden/The Bridgeman Art Library; 12-14: Erich Lessing/Art Resource, NY; 12-15: RMN-Grand Palais/Art Resource, NY; 12-16: Yale University Art Gallery/Art Resource, NY; 12-17: Erich Lessing/Art Resource, NY; 12-18: Scala/Art Resource, NY; 12-19: The Philadelphia Museum of Art/Art Resource, NY; 12-20: The Granger Collection, NYC. All rights reserved; 12-21: Tate, London/Art Resource, NY; 12-22: Andrew Aitchison/Alamy; 12-23: Roger Antrobus/Terra/Corbis; 12-24: Crystal Palace, Sydenham, c. 1862 (colour litho), Martinet, Achille-Louis (1806–77)/Private Collection/The Stapleton Collection/The Bridgeman Art Library; 12-25: Louis Daguerre/Time & Life Pictures/Getty Images; 12-26: Nadar/Bettmann/Corbis; 12-27: New York Public Library/Art Resource, NY; 12-28: Courtesy George Eastman House.

Chapter 13—13-1 (all): A Bar at the Folies-Bergere, 1881–82 (oil on canvas), Manet, Edouard (1832–83)/© Samuel Courtauld Trust, The Courtauld Gallery, London, UK/The Bridgeman Art Library; 13-2: Erich Lessing/Art Resource, NY; 13-3: Erich Lessing/Art Resource, NY; 13-4: RMN-Grand Palais/Art Resource, NY; 13-5: © Culture and Sport Glasgow (Museums); 13-6: Photography © The Art Institute of Chicago, 1910.2; 13-7: Summer's Day, 1879 (oil on canvas), Morisot, Berthe (1841–95)/National Gallery, London, UK/The Bridgeman Art Library; 13-8: Nocturne in Black and Gold, the Falling Rocket, 1875 (oil on panel), Whistler, James Abbott McNeill

(1834–1903)/Detroit Institute of Arts, USA/Gift of Dexter M. Ferry Jr./The Bridgeman Art Library; **13-9:** Photography © The Art Institute of Chicago, 1928.610; **13-10:** Helen Birch Bartlett Memorial Collection, 1926.224, The Art Institute of Chicago. Photography © The Art Institute of Chicago; **13-11:** Yale University Art Gallery/Art Resource, NY; **13-12:** Digital Image © The Museum of Modern Art/Licensed by SCALA/Art Resource, NY; **13-13:** National Galleries of Scotland, Dist./RMN-Grand Palais/Art Resource, NY; **13-14:** Photograph © 2011 Museum of Fine Arts, Boston, 36.270; **13-15:** Photograph © Philadelphia Museum of Art, E1936-1-1; **13-16:** Digital Image © The Museum of Modern Art/Licensed by SCALA/Art Resource, NY; **13-17:** © 2011 The Munch Museum/The Munch-Ellingsen Group/Artists Rights Society (ARS), NY. Photo: © Erich Lessing/Art Resource, NY; **13-18:** Erich Lessing/Art Resource, NY; **13-19:** The Gates of Hell, 1880–90 (bronze), Rodin, Auguste (1840–1917)/Musee Rodin, Paris, France/Peter Willi/The Bridgeman Art Library; **13-20:** SOFAM; **13-21:** © Jonathan Poore/Cengage Learning; **13-22:** Hedrich Blessing Collection/Archive Photos/Chicago History Museum/Getty Images.

Chapter 14—14-1 (all): © 2014 Estate of Pablo Picasso/Artists Rights Society (ARS), New York, Digital Image © The Museum of Modern Art/Licensed by SCALA/Art Resource; **14-2:** © 2011 Succession H. Matisse, Paris/Artists Rights Society (ARS), NY. Photo © San Francisco Museum of Modern Art; **14-3:** © 2011 Succession H. Matisse, Paris/Artists Rights Society (ARS); **14-4:** Digital Image © The Museum of Modern Art/Licensed by SCALA/Art Resource, NY; **14-5:** © 2011 Artists Rights Society (ARS), New York/ADAGP, Paris. Photo: © Solomon R. Guggenheim Museum; **14-6:** Oeffentliche Kunstsammlung Basel, photo Martin Bühler; **14-7:** © 2011 Artist's Rights Society (ARS), New York/VG Bild-Kunst, Bonn. Photo: © Erich Lessing/Art Resource, NY; **14-8:** © 2011 Artists Rights Society (ARS), NY/ADAGP, Paris. Photo: © Bridgeman-Giraudon/Art Resource, NY; **14-9:** © 2011 Estate of Pablo Picasso. Licensed by Artist's Rights Society (ARS), NY. Photo: © Réunion des Musées Nationaux/Art Resource, NY; **14-10:** © 2011 Estate of Pablo Picasso/Artists Rights Society (ARS), NY. Photo: © Erich Lessing/Art Resource, NY; **14-11:** © 2011 Artists Rights Society (ARS), New York/ADAGP, Paris. Photo: © The Philadelphia Museum of Art/Art Resource, NY; **14-12:** © 2011 Artist's Rights Society (ARS), NY. © DACS/The Bridgeman Art Library; **14-13:** Digital Image © The Museum of Modern Art/Licensed by SCALA/Art Resource, NY; **14-14:** © 2011 Artists Rights Society (ARS), NY Photo Credit: Digital Image © The Museum of Modern Art/Licensed by SCALA/Art Resource, NY; **14-15:** © 2011 Artists Rights Society (ARS), New York/ADAGP, Paris/Succession Marcel Duchamp. Photo: © Philadelphia Museum of Art, 1998-74-1; **14-16:** © 2014 Artists Rights Society (ARS), New York/VG Bild-Kunst, Bonn. Digital image: bpk, Berlin/Nationalgalerie, Staatliche Museen, Berlin, Germany/Jörg P. Anders/Art Resource, NY; **14-17:** Digital Image © The Museum of Modern Art/Licensed by SCALA/Art Resource, NY; **14-18:** Photo © Philadelphia Museum of Art, 1950-134-59, © 2008 Artists Rights Society (ARS), New York/ADAGP, Paris/Succession Marcel Duchamp; **14-19:** Fisk University Galleries, University of Tennessee, Nashville; **14-20:** Digital Image © The Museum of Modern Art/Licensed by SCALA/Art Resource, NY; **14-21:** Photograph by Edward Weston. Collection Center for Creative Photography ©1981 Arizona Board of Regents; **14-22:** © 2011 Artists Rights Society (ARS), NY/VG Bild-Kunst, Bonn. Photo © Erich Lessing/Art Resource, NY; **14-23:** © 2011 Estate of Giorgio de Chirico, Licensed by Artist's Rights Society (ARS), NY. Photo: © The Museum of Modern Art/Licensed by SCALA/Art Resource, NY; **14-24:** © 2012 Salvador Dali, GalaSalvador Dali Foundation/Artists Rights Society (ARS), NY. Digital Image © The Museum of Modern Art/Licensed by Scala/Art Resource, NY, 162.1934; **14-25:** Digital Image © 2009 Museum Associates/LACMA/Art Resource, NY; **14-26:** © 2011 Artist's Right's Society (ARS), NY/ProLitteris, Zürich. Digital Image © The Museum of Modern Art/Licensed by SCALA/Art Resource, NY; **14-27:** © 2011 Successió Miró/Artists Rights Society (ARS), NY/ADAGP, Paris. Digital Image © The Museum of Modern Art/Licensed by Scala/Art Resource, NY, 229.1937; **14-28:** © 2011 Artists Rights Society (ARS), New York Photo: Digital Image © The Museum of Modern Art/Licensed by SCALA/Art Resource, NY; **14-29:** © 2011 Mondrian/Holtzman Trust c/o HCR International, VA, USA; **14-30:** © 2012 Artists Rights Society (ARS), NY/ADAGP, Paris. © Philadelphia Museum of Art/Corbis, 1950-134-14, 15; **14-31:** © Bowness, Hepworth Estate. Photo © Tate, London/Art Resource, NY; **14-32:** © 2011 Estate of Alexander Calder/Artist's Rights Society (ARS), NY. Digital Image © The Museum of Modern Art/Licensed by Scala/Art Resource, NY, 590.1939 a-d; **14-33:** Courtesy The Dorothea Lange Collection, The Oakland Museum of California; **14-34:** Margaret Bourke-White/Time & Life Pictures/Getty Images; **14-35:** Photography © The Art Institute of Chicago, 1942.51, Estate of Edward Hopper © The Whitney Museum of American Art; **14-36:** © 2011 The Jacob and Gwendolyn Lawrence Foundation, Seattle/Artists Rights Society (ARS), NY. Photo: The Phillips Collection, Washington, DC; **14-37:** Art © Figge Art Museum, successors to the Estate of Nan Wood Graham/Licensed by VAGA, New York, NY Photography © The Art Institute of Chicago,1930.934; **14-38:** © 2011 Banco de México Trust. Licensed by Artist's Rights Society (ARS), NY. Dirk Bakker, photographer for the Detroit Institute of Arts/The Bridgeman Art Library; **14-39:** © 2011 Banco de México Trust. Licensed by Artists Rights Society (ARS), NY. Photo © Schalkwijk/Art Resource, NY; **14-40:** © Jonathan Poore/Cengage Learning; **14-41:** © 2011 Artists Rights Society (ARS), NY/VG Bild-Kunst, Bonn. Digital Image © The Museum of Modern Art/Licensed by Scala/Art Resource, NY; **14-42:** © Jonathan Poore/Cengage Learning; **14-43:** Peter Cook/VIEW View Pictures/Newscom.

Chapter 15—15-1 (all): © Fred S. Kleiner; **15-2:** © 2011 Artists Rights Society (ARS), NY/ADAGP, Paris. Photo: © Des Moines Art Center; **15-3:** © The Estate of Francis Bacon. All rights reserved/DACS, London/ARS, NY 2014. Digital Image © Museum of Modern Art/Licensed by Scala/Art Resource, NY, 229.1948; **15-4:** © 2014 The Arshile Gorky Foundation/The Artists Rights Society (ARS), New York. Photograph: © The Museum of Modern Art/Licensed by SCALA/Art Resource, NY; **15-5:** © 2011 The Pollock-Krasner Foundation/Artists Rights Society (ARS), NY. Photo © National Gallery of Art, 1976.37.1; **15-6:** © 2011 The Willem de Kooning Foundation/Artists Rights Society (ARS), NY. Digital Image © The Museum of Modern Art/Licensed by Scala/Art Resource, NY, 478.1953; **15-7:** © 2011 Kate Rothko Prizel & Christopher Rothko. Licensed by Artists Rights Society (ARS), NY. Photo: © San Francisco Museum of Modern Art; **15-8:** © 2011 Frank Stella/Artists Rights Society (ARS), NY. Photo © CNAC/MNAM/Dist. Réunion des Musées Nationaux/Art Resource, NY; **15-9:** Helen Frankenthaler, The Bay, 1963 (acrylic on canvas), 205.1 × 207.7 cm, Detroit Institute of Arts, USA/© DACS/Founders Society Purchase, Dr. & Mrs. Hilbert H. DeLawter Fund/The Bridgeman Art Library International. Art © 2011 Helen Frankenthaler/Artists Rights Society (ARS), New York; **15-10:** The Museum of Modern Art/Licensed by SCALA/Art Resource, NY. © Bridget Riley 2014. All rights reserved, courtesy Karsten Schubert, London; **15-11:** Hirshhorn Museum and Sculpture Garden, Smithsonian Institution. Photo: Lee Stalsworth. Art: Estate of David Smith/Licensed by VAGA, New York, NY; **15-12:** Art © Judd Foundation/Licensed by VAGA, NY Hirshhorn Museum and Sculpture Garden, Smithsonian Institution, photo Lee Stalsworth, 72.154; **15-13:** © 2012 Estate of Louise Nevelson/Artists Rights Society (ARS), NY. Photo © CNAC/MNAM/Dist. Réunion des Musées Nationaux/Art Resource, NY; **15-14:** Art © Louise Bourgeois Trust/Licensed by VAGA, New York, NY Photo © CNAC/MNAM/Dist. Réunion des Musées Nationaux/Art Resource, NY; **15-15:** © 2011 Artists Rights Society (ARS), NY/DACS, London. Photo © The Bridgeman Art Library; **15-16:** Art © Jasper Johns/Licensed by VAGA, New York, NY Photo: Whitney Museum of American Art, New York, USA/© DACS/The Bridgeman Art Library; **15-17:** Art © Estate of Robert Rauschenberg/Licensed by VAGA, New York, NY. Digital Image © The Museum of Modern Art/Licensed by SCALA/Art Resource, NY; **15-18:** © Estate of Roy Lichtenstein; **15-19:** © The Whitney Museum of American Art, New York, Photograph by Geoffrey Clements, © 2012 The Andy Warhol Foundation for the Visual Arts, Inc./Artists Rights Society (ARS), New York; **15-20:** Art © Copyright 1969 Claes Oldenburg. Photo: © 2009 Fred S. Kleiner; **15-21:** © Audrey Flack, Collection of The University of Arizona Museum of Art & Archive of Visual Arts, Tucson Museum Purchase with Funds Provided By the Edward J. Gallagher, Jr. Memorial Fund; **15-22:** Close, Chuck Big Self Portrait 1967–68, acrylic on canvas. Collection Walker Art Center Minneapolis. Art Center Acquisition Fund, 1969; **15-23:** Art © Estate of Duane Hanson/Licensed by VAGA, New York, NY Photo by Anne Gold; **15-24:** Reproduced with permission of the Minor White Archive, Princeton University Art Museum. © Trustees of Princeton University. Digital Image © The Museum of Modern Art/Licensed by SCALA/Art Resource, NY; **15-25:** © 2011 Judy Chicago. Licensed by Artists Rights Society (ARS), NY. Photo: © The Brooklyn Museum; **15-26:** Cindy Sherman, courtesy the artist and Metro Pictures; **15-27:** Magdalena Abakanowicz, courtesy Marlborough Gallery, NY; **15-28:** © Jonathan Poore/Cengage Learning; **15-29:** © 2012 Artists Rights Society (ARS), New York/ADAGP, Paris/F.L.C./Photo by Jonathan Poore/Cengage Learning; **15-30:** © 2012 Artists Rights Society (ARS), New York/ADAGP, Paris/F.L.C. Photo: © Francis G. Mayer/CORBIS; **15-31:** © Jonathan Poore/Cengage Learning; **15-32:** dk/Alamy; **15-33:** © Jonathan Poore/Cengage Learning; **15-34:** Art © Estate of Robert Smithson/Licensed by VAGA, New York, NY//Photo © George Steinmetz/Corbis; **15-35:** © 2011 Carolee Schneemann/Artists Rights Society (ARS), NY. Photo © Al Geise, Courtesy PPOW Gallery; **15-36:** Digital Image © The Museum of Modern Art/Licensed by SCALA/Art Resource, NY; **15-37:** Courtesy Nam June Paik Studios, Inc.

Chapter 16—16-1 (all): Courtesy artist Jaune Quick-to-See Smith (Salish member of the Confederated Salish and Kootenai Nation, MT, and The Accola Griefen Gallery, New York). Digital Photo: Chrysler Museum of Art; **16-2:** The Broad Art Foundation, Santa Monica Photography credit: Douglas M. Parker Studio, Los Angeles; **16-3:** © 1983 Faith Ringgold; **16-4:** Copyright: Barbara Kruger. Courtesy: Mary Boone Gallery, New York; **16-5:** Self-Portrait, 1980 © Copyright The Robert Mapplethorpe Foundation. Courtesy Art + Commerce; **16-6:** © Shahzia Sikander. Photograph: Sheldan C. Collins, courtesy Whitney Museum of American Art; **16-7:** © Chris Ofili, courtesy Chris Ofili-Afroco and Victoria Miro Gallery, photo by Stephen White; **16-8:** Allegiance with Wakefulness, 1994 (offset print), Neshat, Shirin (b. 1957)/84 × 105 cm/The Israel Museum, Jerusalem, Israel/Anonymous gift, New York/to American Friends of the Israel Museum/The Bridgeman Art Library; **16-9:** Photograph by Martha Rosler, Represented by Mitchell-Innes & Nash, NYC; **16-10:** Marlborough Gallery in NY; **16-11:** Willie Bester; **16-12:** Bloodline: Big Family, No. 2, 1995 (oil on canvas), Zhang Xiaogang (b. 1958)/Private Collection/Photo © Christie's Images/The Bridgeman Art Library; **16-13:** Copyright © Xu Bing, courtesy Chazen Museum of Art (formerly Elvehjem Museum of Art), University of Wisconsin; **16-14 :** © Jenny Saville. Courtesy Gagosian Gallery; **16-15:** Photo © Whitney Museum of American Art, © Kiki Smith; **16-16:** Museum of Contemporary Art, Chicago © Jeff Koons; **16-17:** Dallas Museum of Art, Dallas; **16-18:** Digital Image © The Museum of Modern Art/Licensed by SCALA/Art Resource, NY; **16-19:** 2006 © Joe Sohm/The Image Works; **16-20:** Martin Jones/Ecoscene/Encyclopedia/Corbis; **16-21:** John Gollings/Arcaid/Architecture (RM)/Corbis; **16-22:** Wolfgang Volz © 1983 Christo; **16-23:** Kokyat Choong/The Image Works; **16-24:** © 2011 Richard Serra/Artists Rights Society (ARS), NY. Photo © Burt Roberts, courtesy of Harriet Senie; **16-25:** © Richard T. Nowitz/Corbis; **16-26:** © 2011 Andreas Gursky/Artists Rights Society (ARS), New York/VG Bild-Kunst, Bonn. Photo, Courtesy Sprüth Magers Berlin London; **16-27:** Bill Viola, photo: Kira Perov; **16-28:** Photograph by David Heald © The Solomon R. Guggenheim Foundation, NY.

Index

NOTE: *Italic page numbers indicate illustrations.*